The VAMPIRE Book

The Encyclopedia of the Undead

The VAMPIRE Book

The Encyclopedia of the Undead

J. GORDON MELTON

VISIBLE INK PRESS

DETROIT • WASHINGTON D.C. • LONDON

The Vampire Book:
The Encyclopedia of the Undead

Published by **Visible Ink Press**™
a division of Gale Research Inc.
835 Penobscot Bldg.
Detroit, MI 48226-4094

Visible Ink Press is a trademark of Gale Research Inc.

ISBN: 0-8103-2295-1

Cover and Page Design: Mark Howell

Frontispiece: Statue of Vlad the Impaler, Budapest

For Melanie.

CONTENTS

Illustration Credits xi

A Brief Cultural History of the Vampire by Martin C. Riccardo xiii

Preface: What Is a Vampire? xxi

Introduction xxix

Vampires: A Chronology xxxiii

A 1
Ackerman, Forrest J   Aconite
The Addams Family   Africa, Vampires in
African American Vampires   Allatius, Leo
Alnwick Castle, The Vampire of
Alternate Shadows   *Aluka*   American Vampires
Anemia   Animals
Anne Rice's Vampire Lestat Fan Club
Appearance of a Vampire   Armenia, Vampires in
Australia, Vampires in

B 25
Babylon and Assyria, Vampires in Ancient
Baker, Roy Ward   Balderston, John L.
Baltic States, Vampires in the   Baron Blood
Bathory, Elizabeth   *Bathory Palace*   Batman
Bats, Vampire   Bava, Mario   Bergstrom, Elaine
Berwick, The Vampire of
Bibliography, Vampire   Bistritz
Bite Me in the Coffin Not in the Closet Fan Club
Blacula   Blade the Vampire Slayer   Blood
Borgo Pass   The Bram Stoker Society
Bram Stoker's Dracula   Brides, Vampire

Browning, Tod   *Bruja   Bruxa*
Bulgaria, Vampires in   Bullet
Burton, Richard Francis   Byron, Lord

C 75
Calmet, Dom Augustin
The Camarilla: A Vampire Fan Association
Carfax   Carmilla   Carradine, John
Carter, Margaret   Castle Dracula
Chaney, Alonso "Lon"
Characteristics of Vampires
Cheeky Devil Vampire Research
Chetwynd-Hayes, Ronald Henry Glynn
China, Vampires in   Christianity and Vampires
Club Vampyre   Coffins
Coleridge, Samuel Taylor   Collins, Barnabas
Collinsport Players   Comic Books, The Vampire in
Coppola, Francis Ford   Corman, Roger William
Count Dracula   The Count Dracula Fan Club
The Count Dracula Society   Count Ken Fan Club
Crime, Vampiric
Croglin Grange, The Vampire of   Cross, Ben
Crucifix   Cruise, Tom   Cuntius, Johannes
Curtis, Dan   Cushing, Peter
Czech Republics and Slovakia, Vampires in the

D 149

Daniels, Leslie Noel, III
Danis the Dark Productions   *Dark Shadows*
Dark Shadows Festival
Dark Shadows Over Oklahoma
Dark Shadows Society of Milwaukee
Davanzati, Giuseppe   Deane, Hamilton
Decapitation   Destroying the Vampire
de Villenueva, Sebastian   *Dhampir*   Dracula
Dracula (1931)   *Dracula* (Spanish 1931)
Dracula (1973)   *Dracula* (1979)
Dracula and Company
Dracula (Dell Comics Superhero)
Dracula (Marvel Comics Character)
The Dracula Museum
Dracula: Senzational—Infractional
The Dracula Society   *Dracula—The Series*
Dracula: The Vampire Play in Three Acts
Drama, Vampire   Dreyer, Carl Theodor
Duckula, Count   Dumas, Alexandre   Dust
Dynamite Fan Club

E 203

El Conde Dracula   Elliott, Denholm Mitchell
Elrod, P. N.   Elvira   Eucharistic Wafer
Explanations of Vampirism

F 215

Fangs   Fingernails   Fire   Fisher, Terence
Florescu, Radu R.   Flying Vampires
Forever Knight   Forever Knight Fan Club
Fortune, Dion   France, Vampires in
Frankenstein's Monster   Frid, Jonathan
Friends of Dark Shadows

G 239

Games, Vampire   Garden, Nancy   Garlic
Gautier, Theophile   Germain, St.
Germany, Vampires in   Ghouls
Glut, Donald Frank   Goethe, Johann Wolfgang von
Good Guys Wear Fangs   Gothic
The Gothic Society   Gothic Society of Canada
Gothica   Greece, Vampires in
Gypsies, Vampires and the

H 283

Haarman, Fritz   Haigh, John George
Haining, Peter Alexander   Hammer Films
Harker, Jonathan   HarmonyRoad Press
Hartmann, Franz   Hawthorn
The Highgate Vampire   Holmwood, Arthur
Homosexuality and the Vampire
The Horror of Dracula
Houston Dark Shadows Society
Humor, Vampire   Hungary, Vampires in
Hurwood, Bernhardt J.   Hypnotic Powers

I 317

I. . .Vampire   Incubus/Succubus
India, Vampires in   *International Vampire*
Ireland, Vampires in
Italy, Vampires and Vampirism in
Ivan the Terrible

J 335

Japan, Vampires in   Java, Vampires in
Jourdan, Louis   *Journal of Vampirology*
Juvenile Literature

K...................347

Kali   Keats, John   King, Stephen   Kürten, Peter

L...................355

Lampir   Langella, Frank   *Langsuyar*
Le Fanu, Joseph Thomas Sheridan
Lee, Christopher   Lesbian Vampires
Lestat de Lioncourt   Lilith
Lilith, The Daughter of Dracula   *Lobishomen*
London After Midnight   London, Dracula's
Lone Gull Press
Long Island Dark Shadows Society   Loogaroo
Lory, Robert Edward
Loyalists of the Vampire Realm
International Vampire Association   Lugosi, Bela
Lumley, Brian

M...................389

Malaysia, Vampires in   Man-Bat
Marschner, Heinrich August
Marshall, William B.   Matheson, Richard
McNally, Raymond T.
Melrose Abbey, The Vampire of
Mexico, Vampires in   Midnight Sons
Midnight to Midnight   Mirrors
The Miss Lucy Westenra Society of the Undead
Mist   Moon   Morbius   Morris, Quincey P.
Mountain Ash   *The Munsters*
The Munsters and The Addams Family Fan Club
Murray (Harker), Mina   Music, Vampire
Myanmar, Vampires in

N...................429

Name, The Vampire's   Native Soil
Necromancy   *Nefarious*
New England Dark Shadows Society

The Night Stalker   *Nightlore*
Nodier, Jean Charles Emmanuel   Nosferatu
Nosferatu, Eine Symphonie des Garuens   *Nox*

O...................441

Old House Publishing   Oldman, Gary
Onyx: The "Literary" Vampire Magazine
Order of the Vampyre
Oregon Dark Shadows Society
Origins of the Vampire   Orlock, Graf

P...................453

Palance, Jack   Paraphernalia, Vampire
Parry, Michael   Paul (Paole), Arnold
Philippines, Vampires in the   Piérart, Z. J.
Pitt, Ingrid   Pittsburgh Dark Shadows Fan Club
Planché, James Robinson   Plogojowitz, Peter
Poe, Edgar Allan   Poetry, The Vampire in
Poland, Vampires in   Polidori, John
Political/Economic vampires   *Pontianak*
Porphyria   *Prisoners of the Night*
Protection against Vampires   Psychic Vampirism
Psychological Perspectives on Vampire
    Mythology   Pulp Magazines, Vampires in the

R...................503

Realm of the Vampire   Redcaps
Renfield, R. N.   Riccardo, Martin V.
Rice, Anne   Rollin, Jean   Romania, Vampires in
Rome, Vampires in Ancient
Ross, William Edward Daniel
Russia, Vampires in   Ruthven, Lord
Rymer, James Malcolm

S 531

Saberhagen, Frederick Thomas   St. George's Day
Sangster, Jimmy   Santo   Satan
Scandinavia, Vampires in
Science Fiction and the Vampire
The Secret Order of the Undead
The Secret Room   Seeds   Selene   Seward, John
Sexuality and the Vampire   Shadowcon
Shadowdance   Shadowgram
Shadows of the Night   Shepard, Leslie Alan
Sherlock Holmes   *Shtriga*   Sighisoara
Slavs, Vampires among the   Sleep, Vampire
Snow-Lang, Wendy   South America, Vampires in
Southern Slavs, Vampires among the
Southey, Robert   Spain, Vampires in   Spider
Stake   Steele, Barbara
Stoker, Abraham "Bram"   Strength, Physical
Suicide   *Sukuyan*   Summers, Montague
Sunlight   Szekelys

T 597

Talamaur   Television, Vampires on
Temple of the Vampire   Thailand, Vampires in
Tibet, Vampires in   Tirgoviste
Tolstoy, Alexey Konstantinovitch
The Tomb of Dracula   Transformation
Transylvania   Transylvanian Society of Dracula
Tremayne, Peter   Trevisan, Dalton

U 615

Uncle Alucard   United Kingdom, Vampires in the
Universal Pictures

V 623

Vadim, Roger   Vambéry, Arminius   The Vamp
Vampira   The Vampire   *Vampire Archives*

Vampire Bats   The Vampire Guild
Vampire Hunters
The Vampire Information Exchange
Vampire Junction   The Vampire Legion
Vampire Research Center
Vampire Research Society   Vampire Studies
Vampirella
Vampires, Werewolves, Ghosts & Other Such
    Things That Go Bump in the Night
Vampirism Research Institute   *Vampyr*
The Vampyre Society (Bohanan)
The Vampyre Society (Gittens)
Van Helsing, Abraham   *Varney the Vampyre*
Victims   Visegrad   Vision   *Vjesci*   Vlad
Vlad Dracul   Vlad the Impaler

W 673

Water   Weather   Werewolves and Vampires
Westenra, Lucy   Whitby   William of Newburgh
Williamson, J. N.   Wine
Witchcraft and Vampires   Wolf, Leonard
Women as Vampires
The World of Dark Shadows
Wyndcliffe Dark Shadows Society

Y 701

Yama   Yarbro, Chelsea Quinn   Yorga, Count
Youngson, Jeanne Keyes

APPENDICES

Resources .... .711
Vampire Filmography .... .719
Vampire Drama .... .775
Vampire Novels .... .783
Master Index .... .807

ILLUSTRATION CREDITS

Illustrations appearing in *The Vampire Book: The Encyclopedia of the Undead* were received from the following sources:

Author's Collection 7, 18, 23, 39, 63, 72, 93, 110, 183, 201, 319, 322, 332, 336, 339, 350, 374, 403, 438, 538, 585, 594, 611, 628, 655, 656, 676, 678

Forrest Ackerman 2, 20, 48, 84, 130, 180, 266, 383, 650

American International Pictures 9, 166, 704

The Bram Stoker Society 348

Carter, Margaret L. 86

Columbia Pictures Industries, Inc. 60, 443

Concorde Films 125, 217, 448

The Count Dracula Fan Club 161, 592, 706

Dan Curtis Productions, Inc. 113, 137, 143, 152, 157, 237, 432, 454, 582, 695

Eclipse Enterprises 118

P. N. Elrod 205

Donald F. Glut 260

Hammer Film Productions Limited 34, 146, 296, 304, 361, 465

Raymond T. McNally 398

Nosferatu Productions 266, 268, 270, 419

Maila Nurmi 629

Malibu Comics 121, 386

Palladium Books, Inc. 245

Queen "B" Productions 207

The Realm of the Vampire 504

Recycled Paper Greetings 309, 457

Santa Barbara Centre for Humanistic Studies Frontispiece, 88, 91, 299, 312, 376, 483, 515, 519, 605, 606, 660, 663, 667, 670

Shepard, Leslie 58

Wendy Snow-Lang 566

Tess Productions 422

Jeff Thompson 114, 523

Twentieth Century Fox 638

Vampire Information Network 640

Vampire Junction 368

Vampire Research Society 644

Vampire Studies, Chicago 44, 178, 192, 508, 509, 690

Warner Bros., Inc. 224

White Wolf Publishing 78, 243

A Brief Cultural History of the Vampire

By Martin V. Riccardo

Back in 1977, when I founded one of the first periodicals devoted to vampires, *The Journal of Vampirism,* the subject of vampires was thought to be nothing more than a rather offbeat specialty interest for a relatively small number of enthusiasts. At that time, this may have been true. Over the years, however, what had been considered just a peculiar specialty interest has grown to become a permanent fascination for millions.

Today, the popular appeal of the vampire is reflected in the more than 20 active vampire interest organizations in the United States and England with their own regular publications. This doesn't even include the fan clubs devoted to such vampire television shows as *Dark Shadows* and *Forever Knight;* nor does it include the vampire interest computer bulletin boards, clubs for vampire role-playing games, or the dozen or more publications devoted to Gothic music and lifestyle—a realm that has many affinities with the vampire image. Clearly Western culture has been increasingly drawn to the vampire.

In order to understand the current perception of the vampire, it is helpful to look at some of the primary influences on the image of the vampire as it has culturally evolved over the centuries. Belief in vampire-like creatures probably goes back in human experience long before written record. Both a respectful fear of the dead and a belief in the magical qualities of blood may be found in cultures around the world. Ancient and modern tales of supernatural night-flying bloodsuckers such as the *lamia* are features, in various forms, of many world cultures. Most of these stories, however, involve demonic beings, spirit beings, practitioners of black magic, or other supernatural creatures that were not required to die first in order to achieve their powers and behaviors.

The specific concept of the dead returning in order to attack and feed off the blood of the living found its strongest expression in Christian Europe. In the twelfth century, English historian William of Newburgh recounted several cases of the dead coming back to terrorize, attack, and kill in the night. He identified this kind of fiend with the Latin term *sanguisuga* or "bloodsucker." In most of the cases he wrote about, the only permanent solution was to unearth and burn the body of the dead accused assailant.

While no long-term belief in such creatures continued among the English, a wave of virtually identical accounts swept through vast areas of Eastern Europe from the sixteenth through the eighteenth century. A wide variety of terms developed for these beings, such as variations on the Serbian *vukodlak* (taken from the word for werewolf). Another term used in Serbia, *vampir* (of debated origin), and related words (such as the Russian *upyr*) also spread widely.

In these regions of Slavic peoples and their neighbors, the concept of vampires became ingrained into the cultural belief systems. Extensive traditions involving the causes of vampirism, the protection against, and the detection and destruction of vampires were developed with many local variations. Dying after a particularly evil life was a common cause; garlic was a common protection; unearthing a corpse that was not properly decomposing was a common method of detection; and staking or burning the body was a common method of destruction. Unexplained illnesses and deaths in a particular locality could trigger a hysteria over vampires and result in the exhumation and destruction of numerous bodies.

Over time, these reports of the vampire trickled to Western Europe, where they became the focus of intellectual discussion. On January 7, 1732, an official report was signed by Regimental Field Surgeon Johannes Fluckinger of the Austrian government (and three of his assistants) detailing their investigation of vampirism in Serbia. The report related local accounts of several deaths in the village of Meduegna five years earlier, which were blamed on a man named Arnold (Paole) Paul, who had claimed to have once been bitten by a vampire and subsequently died. Some believed he had come back from the dead and was tormenting them. When his body was disinterred, it seemed well preserved, but blood was flowing from its head, and more blood spurted out when he was staked. The field surgeon and his assistants were investigating a new wave of alleged vampiric attacks in the area and examined other suspected vampires that were unearthed. Eight that were thought to be unnaturally fresh in appearance were burned.

A short time after the report was signed, it was published in Belgrade, and within a few months versions of the Arnold Paul story were published in several European publications. It is believed the word "vampire" or "vampyre" (taken from the Serbian usage) first entered the English language when the story was printed in two English periodicals, the *London Journal* and the *Gentleman's Magazine* in 1732. The story created a sensation in the West that stimulated debate in intellectual circles, primarily in finding ways to rationally explain the phenomena in vampire reports. Even the prestigious Sorbonne in Paris put forward a position on the topic, condemning the way the dead were being violated. Dom Augustin Calmet, a French Benedictine abbot and renowned Bible scholar, published a treatise on vampires in 1746 in which he recounted the Arnold Paul story and other vampire reports. He presented the various rational explanations, but he also left open the possibility that something supernatural could be involved. His treatise enjoyed a wide circulation and provoked further controversy on the subject. By 1755 Empress Maria Theresa of Austria felt it necessary to institute laws to prevent the unearthing of suspected vampires in the Slavic areas of her realm where this had been practiced, which included areas of Serbia where the Arnold Paul case originated. When the French naturalist Georges Louis Leclerc de Buffon learned of a bat in the New World that drank blood, he classified it with the name "Vampire" in a volume of his *Histoire Naturelle,* published in 1765. Prior to this, bats had not been associated with vampires in Eastern European lore. He specifically chose to give the name "Vampire" to these nocturnal mammals because their ability to suck blood from sleeping animals and people without awakening them was reminiscent of the vampire legends of his day.

A young writer and physician in the nineteenth century who may have been familiar with Calmet's treatise on vampires was John Polidori, an Italian immigrant living in England. For a time in 1816, Polidori was the traveling companion of the acclaimed English poet and writer Lord Byron. While with Byron and a small group of people staying at the Villa Diodati outside Geneva, Polidori joined in with those who, at Byron's suggestion, created ghost stories for their mutual entertainment. Another of those present was Mary Shelly, whose story later developed into the classic horror novel *Frankenstein.* Byron's story involved a man on the verge of dying who makes his traveling companion swear an oath not to reveal the fact of his death to anyone. Years later Polidori combined Byron's basic idea with a vampire motif. Using Byron as a model, he created the vampire Lord Ruthven, a heartless world-traveling aristocrat who lures and kills innocent women in order to feed on their blood. Polidori's short story, "The Vampyre," was the first full work of fiction about a vampire written in English. First published in the April, 1819, issue of *New Monthly Magazine* (incorrectly under Lord Byron's name), it is considered by many to be the foundation of modern vampire fiction.

Polidori's story inspired a number of plays and other creative works in the nineteenth century, especially in France and England, that featured the character of the vampire Lord Ruthven. Polidori's direct influence may also be seen in the first vampire novel in English, *Varney the Vampyre* by James Malcolm Rymer, sold in "penny dreadful" installments in the 1840s in England. Rymer's vampire also seeks out innocent women to marry and destroy for his nefarious purposes. As well, Rymer adopted Polidori's notion of the power of moonlight to revive the vampire's corpse. In 1872 a more innovative approach to the vampire was provided by Irish writer Sheridan Le Fanu with the release of his short story "Carmilla," which incorporates vampire lore with a Gothic setting. The story involves a female vampire who develops a long-term attachment to a female victim. Erotic undertones in the strange, unearthly bond that develops between vampire and victim echo throughout the story. These contributions to vampire fiction notwithstanding, while the nineteenth century produced a vast amount of ghost stories, Gothic novels, penny dreadfuls, and many other stories, plays, and operas with a supernatural theme, only a minute amount of this material had a true vampire theme.

Toward the end of the nineteenth century the novel *Dracula,* by Bram Stoker, initiated the era of vampire fiction that has continued to this day. *Dracula* created the ultimate vampire villain, utilizing elements found in the works of Polidori and Le Fanu to produce a Gothic backdrop for the story of an unholy aristocratic predator from the grave who mesmerizes, defiles, and feeds from the beautiful young women he kills. Stoker revealed the full impact of the psychosexual connotations involved in the relationship between vampire and victim, showing the striking similarity between the bloodlust of the undead and the repressed carnality of mere mortals. An even deeper psychic bond is indicated when a female victim is forced to drink the blood of Dracula as a part of her transformation into a vampire.

Stoker created a set of characters and character types that were used again and again in later vampire stories. These include Dracula himself, the mysterious foreign nobleman who is eventually revealed to be a fiendish and murderous vampire; Mina, a victim of the vampire who is unnaturally torn between Dracula and the mortal man she loves; Dr. Van Helsing, the scholarly and relentless vampire hunter; and Renfield, a mentally unbalanced individual who feels compelled to serve Dracula. Stoker also created a set of vampire traits for the purposes of the novel that came from his own imagination rather than from actual vampire lore. These include the concept of a vampire needing to lie in a coffin with native soil, requiring an invitation to enter a building, having the ability to turn into a bat and other forms, casting no reflection in mirrors, etc. The archetype of the vampire that Stoker molded has become the standard against which all other fictional vampires are compared.

After Stoker's preeminent vampire novel *Dracula* came out in 1897, few vampire novels were published for more than half a century, and those were not worthy of much attention. Not until 1954 did a vampire novel again create a major literary impact. Richard Matheson's *I Am Legend* told the story of a man who finds that he is the only living human left in a world of vampires. No vampire novel, however, has ever surpassed the general popularity of *Dracula,* which has been in print continuously since it was first published.

Apart from the novel, new blood was infused into the vampire theme from other media in the first half of the twentieth century. Short stories in the horror genre continued to feature the vampire, particularly in such "pulp" magazines as *Weird Tales,* which first appeared in the 1920s. These publications were known for their sensationalistic fiction in the realms of fantasy, horror, and science fiction. Such writers as Clark Ashton Smith, Seabury Quinn, and Robert Bloch wrote a number of vampire stories for these publications. The popularity of short stories about vampires has continued to the present.

The greatest influence on public perception of the vampire, however, came from the vampire movies that reached a wide audience. A few early films did not garner much attention upon release. The 1922 German silent film *Nosferatu, Eine Symphonie des Garuens,* directed by F. W. Murnau, gave an excellent portrayal of a ghoulish-looking vampire. The film's plot was based on Stoker's *Dracula,* prompting Stoker's widow to sue for copyright infringement, which limited the film's initial release. It was rediscovered and acclaimed by film buffs in the second half of the century, and its weird atmosphere, striking shadow effects, and other unique features strongly influenced several later vampire films, including a remake of *Nosferatu* in 1979 and *Bram Stoker's Dracula* in 1992. An American silent film with a vampiric character was released as *London After Midnight* in 1927. This film featured the actor Lon Chaney, whose make-up gave him a ferocious, unearthly appearance; it was directed by Tod Browning, who later directed the 1931 version of *Dracula. London After Midnight,* however, had a minimal impact, and it was actually lost for more than sixty years. The 1931 French film *Vampyr,* directed by Carl Dreyer, presented some unusual images of dreamlike unreality, but only many years later did it find favor among a small number of film enthusiasts.

Then in 1931 Universal's *Dracula,* starring Bela Lugosi, was released and became the landmark motion picture for the vampire in films. A British play by Hamilton Deane, rewritten for the American stage by John L. Balderston, had been a hit on Broadway for several years before serving as the basis for the movie. The primary male actors who starred in both the stage and film versions included Lugosi as the count, Edward Van Sloan as Van Helsing, and Dwight Frye as Renfield. Both the play and the movie established the visual image of the male vampire that became a standard: a sinister aristocratic figure with elegant manners who has a strange foreign accent and dresses in formal evening wear with a long flowing cape. Lugosi's striking looks, distinct mannerisms, and thick Hungarian accent made his performance both frightening and memorable for that era, and for many, his persona in the role would forever cast him as either the epitome of what Dracula should be or as the ultimate caricature of the vampire stereotype. He played the role of the vampire again on stage and screen at various times, but he never matched the impact he made in *Dracula.* The quality of the movie itself is debated today, but the impression it made on the public mind regarding vampires is unquestionable. Universal made a number of movies in the 1930s and 1940s with a Dracula or Dracula-related character, such as the somber and atmospheric *Dracula's Daughter* in 1936 with Gloria Holden as the vampire.

Another powerful influence on the movie image of *Dracula* came in 1958 when the tall, distinguished actor Christopher Lee played the role for Hammer Studios in England. In this film, titled *The Horror of Dracula* in the United States and simply *Dracula* in England, Lee's solemn tones and formidable appearance contributed to a portrayal of the Count that was more violently dynamic and physically powerful. The cape and formal apparel remained, but Lee's version added a characteristic that became a standard trait for vampires in all media—elongated eye teeth, or fangs. A few previous films had experimented with variations of teeth or fangs for vampires, but Lee's Dracula established vampire fangs for all time. Peter Cushing played Dracula's determined nemesis in the film, the vampire-hunting Van Helsing. Each actor became identified with these roles, Lee playing vampires and Cushing playing vampire hunters in a number of films in the 1960s and 1970s. Hammer made quite a few vampire movies in general, and between 1965 and 1973 Lee reprised the role of Dracula for the studio in six more films. Since Lee was an expensive actor, Hammer deliberately limited the amount of Lee's screen time and lines in the films to cut costs.

While Hammer was restricting the role of England's star vampire, the opposite was happening in the United States with the highly successful daytime television soap opera *Dark Shadows.* Producer Dan Curtis came up with this revolutionary concept in daytime television, loosely basing it on the style of Gothic romance novels that were quite popular at the time. When the show first aired in 1966 on ABC, the initial plotline involved a governess named Victoria Winters who arrives at the Collinwood Manor in Collinsport, Maine, and becomes involved in various mysterious and supernatural family intrigues. The show was failing in the ratings until the vampire character Barnabas Collins, played by actor Jonathan Frid, was introduced in 1967. He became the most well-known vampire character in North America after Dracula. Like previous vampires, Barnabas was aristocratic and murderous in nature, and eventually seen with fangs; but he was one of the few male vampires in the visual media who did not wear a cape. The show rapidly became a hit, and the popularity of Barnabas required the writers to include him in the storylines as much as possible. In this highly expanded characterization, Barnabas became the first vampire to be fully portrayed as both a tragic hero seeking an escape from his undead existence and an antihero who could be both fiendish and sympathetic.

Several years after the *Dark Shadows* series ended in 1971, a novel appeared that also portrayed the vampire as both tragic hero and antihero. Anne Rice's *Interview with a Vampire,* published in 1976, gives a highly introspective look at the life of a vampire named Louis. Rice paints a macabre picture of a highly cultured and sensitive person who is unwittingly cast into the ghoulish world of vampires. Louis is forced to deal with his immortality as he seeks some sense of identity in his existence as a blood-driven murderer. While Stoker's Dracula is still the dominant vampire image for the general public, Rice's romanticized vision of the vampire was a literary watershed for millions who became enthralled with this new image of the vampire. In the 1980s, Rice returned to writing vampire novels, this time centering on the vampire Lestat, the character who had made Louis into a vampire. Her continuing series of novels, known as the "Vampire Chronicles," developed the theme of sensitive, beautiful, artistic vampires who feel rapture and intimacy when they drink blood, and who find various ways of coping with their dark world and murderous natures. The ever-mysterious vampire world Rice has created has made her the most popular vampire novelist after Bram Stoker.

Other prominent and influential vampire novels also had their debut in the 1970s, such as *The Night Stalker* by Jeff Rice in 1973 (produced as a made-for-television movie in 1972, the year before it was published), *Salem's Lot* by Stephen King in 1975 (produced as an extended made-for-television movie in 1979), and *The Space Vampires* by Colin Wilson in 1976 (produced as the movie *Lifeforce* in 1985). Several authors of vampire novels in the 1970s became a part of the emerging trend to write vampire novels in a series, most noteworthy being the writers Les Daniels, Fred Saberhagen, Peter Tremayne, and Chelsea Quinn Yarbro. Of these, Yarbro has written the most vampire novels. The adventures of her handsome and popular vampire hero, le Comte de Saint-Germain, often seemed to be more in the

,style of historical romances than standard horror novels. Vampire characters also came into their own in comic books during the 1970s, with regular figures such as Vampirella, Morbius, and the Marvel Comics version of Dracula.

In addition, a nonfiction book came out in 1972 that produced a profound effect on the image of one particular vampire. The book was *In Search of Dracula* by Raymond T. McNally and Radu Florescu, both scholars of Eastern European studies at Boston College. In this and subsequent books they presented their research showing that the character of Dracula in Bram Stoker's novel was actually based on an historical figure who used that name, a fifteenth century warlord and prince of Wallachia, a Romanian region that borders on Transylvania. Also known as Vlad Tepes (meaning "Vlad the Impaler"), he was known as a fierce warrior and sadistic ruler who ordered the deaths of thousands, often causing his victims to be impaled on long stakes. The historical findings echoed in numerous stories, novels, and films about Dracula, including the movie *Bram Stoker's Dracula*.

Vampire movies reached a pivotal point in the late 1970s with several popular movies in which a handsome actor was deliberately picked for the role of Dracula—in contrast to the previous tendency to choose actors with the most fearsome qualities. Most prominent was the Universal film *Dracula* (1979), starring Frank Langella. Like Lugosi, Langella had starred in a hit broadway play of *Dracula* prior to the movie. Other movies included the comedy *Love at First Bite* (1979) with George Hamilton, and *Count Dracula* (1978) with Louis Jordan (which was made for British television, but seen in the United States on PBS). A number of vampire films with big budgets and significant production quality followed in the 1980s and 1990s, including *The Hunger* (1983) based on the 1981 novel by Whitley Streiber, *Fright Night* (1985), *The Lost Boys* (1987), *Near Dark* (1987), *Innocent Blood* (1992), and *Bram Stoker's Dracula* (1992).

The 1990s have ushered in what seems to be an absolute explosion in vampire interest. The cable and videotape revolution has made almost all of the numerous vampire movies accessible. Some videotape rental stores devote an entire section to the *Dark Shadows* television series. These old shows are also finding new life as a regular part of the Sci-Fi Channel cable network, just as many old vampire movies find new fans on various cable channels. Several new television series with a vampire character have also aired in the 1990s. These include a new but short-lived *Dark Shadows* series on NBC, starring Ben Cross as Barnabas Collins, and *Forever Knight*, a late-night series on CBS featuring a vampire detective. In comic books, all of the major vampire characters, such as Vampirella and Morbius, have been revived, and new ones are constantly being created. An endless stream of vampire novels has been released, several every month—sometimes every week. A continuous growth of vampire novels in a series has reached numbers unprecedented for a single subject considered just a part of the horror genre. Besides the vampire novel series writers who started in the 1970s, the trend grew with novels that first appeared in the 1980s by writers such as J. N. Williamson, Brian Lumley, Nancy A. Collins, and Elaine Bergstrom. The growth has continued in the 1990s with new series of novels by writers such as P. N. Elrod, Scott Ciencin, Lori Herter, and L. J.

Smith. In many ways, the growing ranks of vampire fandom have made the subject of vampires a significant genre in its own right.

For some it even goes beyond the mere appreciation of a genre and becomes a part of a lifestyle. One example of this is in the modern Gothic music scene, in which appreciation of vampires and a stylized vampiric appearance can be quite normal. The popular vampire novel *Lost Souls* (1992) by Poppy Z. Bright incorporates some of these modern "Goths" in the story.

This brief sketch on the historical development of the vampire image for society at large barely scratches the surface of the pervasive influence it has had. The underlying question remains: What is behind this tremendous fascination with vampires? It is likely that there is no simple answer to this question, since the vampire embodies many aspects related to the human condition. These include death (and all of its psychological ramifications), immortality, forbidden sexuality, sexual power and surrender, intimacy, alienation, rebellion, and a fascination with the mysterious. J. Gordon Melton's *Vampire Book* should provide individual readers with insights on the elements they find themselves most drawn to. In my own endeavors on the subject of vampires, Gordon has often provided key support, and I appreciate the monumental effort this encyclopedia required. It provides a comprehensive examination of the subject and includes new findings that have never before appeared in print. For all vampire enthusiasts it will certainly be a standard reference. This is fitting for the subject in light of a simple motto that fans will understand: Vampires are forever!

PREFACE: WHAT IS A VAMPIRE?

While having spent the greater part of my adult life studying the many different religious groups in North America and devoting my career to research and writing about religious groups, I have also had a fascination with the vampire since my teen years. During high school, I discovered first science fiction and then horror fiction. In sampling the horror novels, I soon found that I enjoyed vampire novels by far the most. Thus for the past 30 years a measurable percentage of my recreation derived from reading vampire books and watching vampire movies.

Reading vampire novels led quite logically to the perusal of the few available nonfiction books on vampires, especially those dealing with vampire folklore and accounts of reportedly "real" vampires. Raymond T. McNally and Radu Florescu's *In Search of Dracula* had a profound effect on the image of the vampire in the 1970s. The authors claimed that the character Dracula in Bram Stoker's novel was actually based on Vlad Tepes, a fifteenth-century warlord and prince of Wallachia, a region in Romania. However, to attempt a survey of nonfiction vampire literature in any systematic fashion is to step into a morass as deep and murky as any pictured in a gothic novel. The field of vampirology has been dominated by the pioneering work of Dudley Wright and the volumes of Montague Summers. While their frequently reprinted works provided a starting point for consideration of the vampire and made available previously hard-to-obtain texts, they also introduced a number of errors into the popular literature. Many subsequent writers on the subject have relied upon them and repeated these errors in book after book.

The over-reliance on Wright and Summers, the scholarly marginalization of the study of vampire beliefs, and the enthusiasm of vampire fans for cheap novels and genre movies created a climate that did not favor the correction of common errors in vampire literature. Only with the development of a new and growing interest in vampires over the last two decades have questions of the origin of vampire lore and the historical nature and role of belief in vampires once again assumed a place on the scholarly agenda. During the last decade especially, a significant amount of scholarship has appeared on the subject of vampires, though much of it is confined to poorly circulated scholarly journals. This lack of accessible information led directly to this volume.

The Vampire Book: The Encyclopedia of the Undead was conceived as an encyclopedic compendium of vampires, vampirism, and vampire lore in modern popular culture. The literature is vast, and not since Summers has an attempt been made to gather and summarize all of the writing on vampires. To accomplish that task I relied on my personal collection, which includes more than 500 titles on vampires (primarily novels and short story collections) as well as an extensive collection of vampire comic books. In addition, the Davidson Library at the University of California at Santa Barbara houses hundreds of additional resources (in particular, books and journals of folklore, psychology, and literary and film criticism) that contain chapters and articles on vampires. Recent books on ethnic folklore have provided a particularly rich and largely untapped resource. These materials became the starting point for this volume. During the course of writing this book, I met with numerous people involved at various levels with vampirism in the popular culture and corresponded with many of the leaders of vampire organizations and publishers of vampire fanzines. Martin Riccardo of Vampire Studies in Chicago was particularly helpful in calling my attention to the location of needed material.

While assembling *The Vampire Book,* I assumed a decidedly contemporary perspective. Along with my coverage of vampire folklore and literature, I turned the contemporary organizations, movies, television shows, and fanzines into a topic of consideration. Today's heightened interest in vampires and the ideas currently dominating fiction and nonfiction oriented me whenever I got lost in the mass of data. Thus, by beginning with a popular idea about the nature of vampires, I could then check the idea against Bram Stoker's Dracula and work my way through the literature, tracing its origins and assessing its relationship to vampire folklore and history as a whole. Not the least of the important and perennial questions to which that process constantly forced me to return was the simple definitional one: "What is a vampire?"

WHAT IS A VAMPIRE?

The common dictionary definition of a vampire serves as a starting point for inquiry: A vampire is a reanimated corpse that rises from the grave to suck the blood of living people and thus retain a semblance of life. That description certainly fits Dracula, the most famous vampire, but it is only a starting point and quickly proves inadequate in approaching the realm of vampire folklore. By no means do all vampires conform to that definition.

For example, while the subject of vampires almost always leads to a discussion of death, all vampires are not resuscitated corpses. Numerous vampires are disembodied demonic spirits. In this vein are the numerous vampires and vampirelike demons of Indian mythology and the *lamiai* of Greece. Vampires can also appear as the disembodied spirit of a dead person that retains a substantial existence; like many reported ghosts, these vampires can be mistaken for a fully embodied living corpse. Likewise, in the modern secular literary context, vampires sometimes emerge as a different species of intelligent life (possibly from outer space or the product of genetic mutation) or as otherwise normal human beings who have an unusual habit (such as blood-drinking) or an odd power (such as the ability to drain people emotionally). Vampire animals, from the traditional bat to the delightful children's characters Bunnicula and Count Duckula, are by no means absent from the literature. Thus vampires exist in a number of forms, although by far the majority of them are the risen dead.

As commonly understood, the characteristic shared by all of these different vampire entities is their need for blood, which they take from living human beings and animals. A multitude of creatures from the world's mythology have been called vampires in the popular literature simply because periodic blood sucking was among their many attributes. When the entire spectrum of vampires is considered, however, that seemingly common definition falls by the wayside, or at the very least must be considerably supplemented. Some vampires do not take blood, rather they steal what is thought of as the life force from their victim. A person attacked by a traditional vampire suffers from the loss of blood, which causes a variety of symptoms: fatigue, loss of color in the face, listlessness, depleted motivation, and weakness. Various conditions that involve no loss of blood share those symptoms. For example, left unchecked, tuberculosis is a wasting disease that is similar to the traditional descriptions of the results of a vampire's attack.

Nineteenth-century romantic novelists and occultists suggested that real vampirism involved the loss of psychic energy to the vampire and wrote of vampiric relationships that had little to do with the exchange of blood. Dracula himself quoted the Bible in noting that "the blood is the life." Thus it is not necessarily the blood itself that the vampire seeks, but the psychic energy or "life force" believed to be carried by it. The metaphor of psychic vampirism can easily be extended to cover various relationships in which one party steals essential life elements from the other, such as when rulers sap the strength of the people they dominate.

On the other extreme, some modern "vampires" are simply blood drinkers. They do not attack and drain victims, but obtain blood in a variety of legal manners (such as locating a willing donor or a source at a blood bank). In such cases, the consumption of the blood has little to do with any ongoing relationship to the source of the blood. It, like food, is merely consumed. Often times, modern vampires even report getting a psychological or sexual high from drinking blood.

APPROACHING THE VAMPIRE

Once it is settled that "vampire" covers a wide variety of creatures, a second problem arises. As a whole, the vampires themselves are unavailable for direct examination. With a few minor exceptions, the subject of this volume is not vampires per se, but rather human belief in vampirism. That being the case, some methodology was needed for considering human belief in entities that objectively do not exist, indeed for understanding my own fascination with a fictional archetype. Not a new problem, the vast literature on vampirism favors one of two basic approaches. The first offers explanations in a social context. That is to say, the existence of vampires provides people with an explanation for otherwise inexplicable events (which in the modern West we tend to explain in scientific terms). The second approach is psychological and explains the vampire as existing in the inner psychic landscape of the individual. The two approaches are not necessarily exclusive of each other.

The worldwide distribution of creatures that can properly be termed "vampires" or have vampirelike characteristics suggests an approach that allows some semblance of order to emerge from the chaos of data. I began with the obvious: The very different vampirelike creatures found around the world function quite differently in their distinct cultures and environments. Thus the *camazotz* of Central America shares several characteristics with the vampire of Eastern Europe, but each plays a different role in its own culture's mythology and is encountered in different situations. While a host of statues and pictures of the *camazotz* survived in Central America, no Eastern European peasant would think of creating such a memorial to the vampire. In each culture the "vampire" takes on unique characteristics; because of this, each must be considered in its indigenous context.

Despite these cultural differences, there are common vampire types that seem to bridge cultural boundaries. For example, the *lamiai,* among the oldest of the Greek vampire creatures, seems to have arisen in response to the variety of problems surrounding childbirth. The *lamiai* attacked babies and very young children, so otherwise unexplained deaths of a mother giving birth and/or her child could be attributed to the work of vampires. This is similar to the function of the Malaysian *langsuyar* and the Jewish *Lilith.*

In like measure, vastly different cultures possessed a vampire who primarily attacked young women. Such vampires, which appeared repeatedly in the folk tales of Eastern Europe, served a vital role in the processes of social control. Stories of these young handsome male vampires warned maidens in their early post-pubescent years not to stray from the counsel of their elders and priests and to avoid glamorous visiting strangers who would only lead to disaster.

Another large group of vampires grew out of encounters with death, especially the sudden unexpected death of a loved one due to suicide, accident, or an unknown illness. People dying unexpectedly left relatives and friends behind with unfinished agendas with the dead. Strong emotional ties and uncorrected wrongs felt by the recently deceased caused them to leave their resting place and attack family members, lovers, and neighbors against whom they might have had a grievance. If unable to reach a human target, they turned on the victim's food supply (i.e., livestock). Stories of attacks by these recently deceased adult vampires on their relatives and neighbors or their livestock directly underlay the emergence of the modern literary and cinematic vampire.

Thus as the entries on different vampires and vampirelike creatures were written for this book, some attempt was made to supply background on the particular culture and larger mythological context in which the vampire entity operated. Such an approach led to the inclusion of what, strictly speaking, were nonvampire entities; these creatures were included because they filled a role in their cultures that was filled by vampires in other cultures. For example, most African tribes did not have a vampire creature in their mythology, but many of the characteristics and abilities commonly associated with vampire beings in Asia or Eastern Europe were attributed to the African witch.

THE LITERARY AND SCREEN VAMPIRE

Leaving folktales behind, the literary vampire of the nineteenth century transformed the ethnic vampire into a cosmopolitan citizen of the modern imagination. The literary vampire interacted in new ways with human society. While the early literary vampires pictured by Goethe, Coleridge, Southey, Polidori, Byron, and Nodier, were basically parasites, possessing few traits to endear them to the people they encountered, nevertheless they performed a vital function by assisting the personification of that darker side possessed by human beings. The Romantic writers of the last century assigned themselves the task of exploring that dark side of human consciousness.

In the movement to the stage and screen, the vampire was further transformed. The dramatic vampire gained some degree of human feelings and, even as a villain, projected some admirable traits that brought the likes of Bela Lugosi a large and loyal following. Lugosi brought before the public an erotic vampire who embodied the release of the sexual urges that were so suppressed by Victorian society. In the original stage and screen presentations of *Dracula,* the vampire's bite substituted for the sexual activity that could not be more directly portrayed. That inherent sexuality of the vampire's attack upon its victims became more literally portrayed in the 1960s, on the one hand through new adult-oriented pornographic vampire movies and on the other in a series of novels and movies that centered on a sensual, seductive vampire. Frank Langella's *Dracula* (1979) and Gary Oldman's *Bram Stoker's Dracula* (1992) are outstanding examples of this latter type of vampire.

THE CONTINUED POPULARITY OF VAMPIRES

The vampire's amazing adaptability accounts for much of its popularity. It served numerous vital functions for different people during previous centuries. For enthusiasts, today's vampire symbolizes important elements of their lives that they feel are being otherwise suppressed or ignored by the culture. The most obvious role thrust upon the contemporary vampire has been that of cultural rebel, a symbolic leader advocating outrageous alternative patterns of living in a culture demanding conformity. An extreme example of this is a new type of vegetarian vampire, such as Bunnicula or Count Duckula, that is introducing the vampire to children and has emerged as an effective tool in teaching children tolerance of other children who are noticeably different.

A psychological approach to the vampire supplements an understanding of its social function. Twentieth-century psychotherapists discovered that modern post-Dracula vampires and vampiric relationships actively distorted their patients' lives. Out of the experiences reported to them, particularly the classic nightmare, many psychologists called attention to the role of specific, common human psychological events in the creation and continual reinforcement of vampire beliefs. Margaret Shanahan, who wrote the entry on psychological perspective for this volume, has noted the role of the vampire as a symbol of the widespread experience of inner emptiness she and her colleagues find in their clients. Such inner emptiness leads to a longing for emotional nutrients. Such longing can lead some to become fixed on an envy of those perceived to possess an abundance of nutrients (rich in the life force) and a desire to steal that energy. In its most extreme form, such fixation can lead to various forms of blood consumption and even homicidal acts.

Such psychological approaches also explain some popular social pathologies, especially the common practice of scapegoating. Groups can be assigned characteristics of a vampire and treated accordingly with rhetoric that condemns them to the realms outside of social communion. If not checked, such rhetoric can easily lead to modern forms of staking and decapitation. Throughout the twentieth century, various social groups have been singled out and labeled as "vampires." Women became vamps and bosses became bloodsuckers. Self-declared victims have branded a wide variety of social groups, rightly or wrongly, as their vampire oppressors.

These two approaches to the vampire—which emerge at various appropriate points—through the text in this book seem to account for most of the phenomena of vampirism that I encountered. Further, it suggests that the vampire (or its structural equivalent) was a universal figure in human culture, which emerged in the natural course of life. That is to say, the vampire probably emerged independently at many points in human culture. There is little evidence to suggest that the vampire emerged at one time and place, and then diffused around the world from that primal source.

ACKNOWLEDGMENTS

The Vampire Book could not have been completed without the assistance of individuals too numerous to mention. Topping the list are the many people with whom I corresponded, who sent me information about various vampire organizations and publications, and who graciously double-checked the contents of entries for accuracy. Some of these people stand out for their service above and beyond the call of duty.

Without Martin V. Riccardo, an old friend and head of the Vampire Studies network, this encyclopedia would not and could not have been completed. We first worked together on a vampire bibliography in the early 1980s and have shared our interest in vampires for nearly a quarter of a century. While I was content to quietly read vampire books and watch vampire movies, Marty became one of the creators of the contemporary vampire subculture. Far beyond giving me free reign in his own vampire collection, he read and commented on the entire text of this volume. He also pointed me to source material I had missed and contributed the foreword.

Jeanne Youngson, through the resources of The Count Dracula Fan Club (which she founded), backed up the effort that went into this work and supplied me with a set of the club's publications and numerous specialized resources from the club's files.

Bernard Davies, chairman of The Dracula Society based in London, offered his most welcomed expertise in vampire folklore and read a number of entries on Eastern Europe, *Dracula,* and the vampire in the United Kingdom. I am most thankful to him for pointing out errors I'd missed in the vampire literature I had compiled.

Several people agreed to write entries for *The Vampire Book* in areas that required some special expertise. Their talents have greatly added to the production of this volume. Dr. Margaret Shanahan, who wrote the entry on Psychology and the Vampire, is a clinical psychologist in private practice in Chicago and an instructor at the Jung Institute. Susan Kagan, a computer technician, is a self-made expert on vampire music. Isotta Poggi, a staff member of the Santa Barbara Centre for Humanistic Studies and with whom I have worked on a number of previous projects, contributed the article on the vampires in her native Italy.

Closer to my home in Santa Barbara, I am in debt to "Guy Guden's Space Pirate Radio," whose host is a lifelong vampire fan and who has numerous ties into the motion picture world and popular culture. He supplied a steady stream of additional resources, kept me informed of happenings in the motion picture world, and passed along tidbits of interesting and important information that have found their way into the text. As I began writing this volume, I visited the two Santa Barbara comic book stores, Comics on Parade and Metro Comics, and made almost weekly visits to harass the employees about the latest vampire comics, game material, and trading cards. The owner and employees at each were always patient and good humored with me, and I am grateful for their assistance.

Marcy Robin and Jim Pierson worked with me on *Dark Shadows* resources, and both read and checked the accuracy of all of the *Dark Shadows* entries. Jeff Thompson provided additional valuable assistance in the several areas of *Dark Shadows* in which he is especially versed.

For editorial expertise, I wish to thank Bradley J. Morgan and Diane M. Sawinski.

Other names that come to the fore who assisted in various ways include Margaret Carter, Candy Cosner, Mike Homer, Masimo Introvigne, Lee Scott, and Vlad.

Last, but by no means the least, my wife Suzie assisted with the otherwise unrewarding proofreading and indexing process.

J. Gordon Melton

INTRODUCTION

Our continuing interest in the nightblooming, bloodsucking ladies and gentlemen of the night is obvious. No other creature in the world of horror has caused more fear, more dread, yet more fascination than the vampire. The single work of fiction most frequently brought to the movie screen is not one of the great works of literature but the nineteenth-century gothic novel *Dracula*. The novel has been made into a movie more than a dozen times and, encouraged by the technological improvement in special effects, *Dracula* has inspired more than 200 additional movies in which Count Dracula is the central character. In fact, the count is second only to Sherlock Holmes in frequency of appearance on the silver screen. Since the publication of *Dracula* in 1897, the book has remained continually in print in numerous editions and versions, and it has inspired hundreds of novels and short stories. While it may seem that writers have exhausted the theme, the number of new vampire novels has surprisingly continued to grow. As of 1992, an average of two additional Dracula or vampire novels appear every month.

VAMPIROLOGY: THIRSTING FOR THE ORIGIN OF THE VAMPIRE

Despite the humorous element and even the touch of the absurd in the contemporary appearance of the vampire, it is the subject of serious consideration. Vampirology, the name given the field of study of the vampire and the myth it has spawned, has at least three significant components. The prime concern of vampirology is the investigation of reports of encounters with a vampire—these reports date to ancient Greece and Rome and are just as numerous today—and the subsequent development of theories concerning the nature of vampires. Such theories fall roughly into two categories: those that suppose the actual existence of vampires and those that relegate it to the realm of superstition or various psychological causes. In modern times, the search for real vampires has been promoted by the development of the modern discipline of parapsychology.

A second aspect of vampirology, which arose in the early nineteenth century, is the vampire as the subject of popular imaginative fiction writing. Beginning with the single most successful vampire novel, *Dracula* (1897), literally hundreds of novels, short stories, and comic books have developed the vampire concept. In the twentieth century, vampires were quickly adopted by the burgeoning movie industry and have provided mass culture with a popular theme.

Third, popular interest in vampires has produced two very different reactions. On the one hand, it has prompted devoted fans to organize a number of movie fan clubs and vampire interest and study groups. Realizing the depth and scope of popular interest, the market responded by providing numerous vampire collectibles, from trading cards to board games to tee-shirts and dolls. On the other hand, serious scholars, attracted to the presence of the vampire myth, have attempted to make sense of its popular appeal. Psychologists, sociologists, folklorists, and literary movie critics in turn have utilized their analytic skills to explain why a horrific mythical creature could so enthrall and entrance the public and even lead individuals to identify themselves as vampires. Historians have taken pains to track down the real individuals (primarily Vlad Tepes and Elizabeth Bathory) who have been accused of being the original source of vampire legends.

An exploration of vampire myth and reality created for both the casual vampire fan and the dedicated vampire scholar, *The Vampire Book: The Encyclopedia of the Undead* is a comprehensive work that explores, in an encyclopedic fashion, the entire realm of the vampire phenomenon. *The Vampire Book* highlights accounts of the famous real vampires and presents the various theories that explain the claims that vampires exist. It surveys the vampire myth as it has appeared around the world, and it explores the development of the vampire theme in modern novels, short stories, comic books, the stage, opera, and movies. Entries cite the rise of fan clubs and special interest groups and summarize the serious scholarship.

The Vampire Book contains more than 375 descriptive entries arranged in a single alphabetic sequence. Some are brief (100 to 300 words) and cover either definitions of terms associated with the vampire or offer brief descriptions of places—such as Borgo Pass or the fictional Carfax—that are associated with Dracula and other vampires. A number of medium-length entries (500 to 1,000 words) present biographies of vampires (such as Count Yorga and Morbius); major figures associated with vampires, from actors who have played Dracula (like Bela Lugosi, Frank Langella, and John Carradine) to the authors of vampire writings (notably Bram Stoker and Anne Rice); and vampire organizations (such as the Vampire Research Center and the Count Dracula Society). Longer entries (up to 5,000 words) explore major topics associated with vampires (vampire bats and sexuality, for two), the appearance of the vampire in different cultures (like Romania or China), vampiric creatures and deities in different cultures, and the life of the vampire in the differing media (from the stage to movies and comic books).

Within the text of each entry, those entities that have their own entry appear in boldface. Also, there is a variety of topics under which some entries could have been placed (such as destroying the vampire or killing a vampire). Where one subject could have easily been treated under a different heading, an entry cross-heading has been added that provides the location of the discussion of the subject.

For example:

Alien Vampires *See:* Science Fiction and the Vampire.

SPECIAL FEATURES

The Vampire Book: The Encyclopedia of the Undead also contains a number of helpful special features. The first, following this introduction, is a chronology of the vampire, which provides a handy summary of the major events in the development of the vampire myth from early history to the present. It notes such key events as the birth of Vlad Tepes in 1428 to the enactment of the Comics Code in 1954 (which banished vampires from comic books) to the release of the movie *Bram Stoker's Dracula* in 1992.

Four appendices provide lists of some of the more interesting vampire items. First, the "Resources" section lists vampire organizations and independent vampire fanzines and periodicals. Attached is a set of addresses of some selected publishers and supply houses from whom vampire books, dramas, and the more obscure films can be located.

Next, the "Vampire Filmography" contains the most complete list ever assembled of professional feature films about vampires and vampirism—more than 650 in number. The filmography is limited to those movies that either focus on vampires or have a prominent vampire character that is integral to the plot of the film. It excludes films that treat the vamp (including many silent films with the word vampire in their titles), films in which a vampire makes only a cameo appearance, amateur productions that were never released to the public, and films about other closely related monsters such as werewolves, ghouls, and zombies. A list of books on vampire films follows the filmography.

A section covering vampire drama, opera, and ballet productions follows the filmography. Again, the great majority of these works have appeared in the last generation.

The fourth appendix lists vampire novels that have appeared in the last century, beginning with *Dracula* (1897). It is divided into three sections: vampire novels to 1970, vampire novels from 1970 to the present, and *Dark Shadows* novels (a special category of vampire-related literature). It should be noted that more that 60 percent of all vampire novels written have appeared in the last 30 years. The interested reader should also consult the entry on vampire bibliography in the main body of the text.

The Vampire Book's extensive subject and proper name index provides readers ready access to any topic, organization, person, literary work, or production. Both boldface and lightface entry numbers may appear after a citation. A boldface number indicates the principal listing for the entry cited; lightface numbers refer to references to that entity made within the text of other entries. The index also contains cross-references that direct users to related topics and inversions on significant words appearing in proper names.

J. Gordon Melton

VAMPIRES: A CHRONOLOGY

Prehistory: Vampire beliefs and myths emerge in cultures around the world.

1047   First appearance in written form of the word *upir* (an early form of the word later to become "vampire") in a document referring to a Russian prince as *"Upir Lichy,"* or wicked vampire.

1190   Walter Map's *De Nagis Curialium* includes accounts of vampire-like beings in England.

1196   William of Newburgh's *Chronicles* records several stories of vampire-like revenants in England.

1428/29   Vlad Tepes, the son of Vlad Dracul, is born.

1436   Vlad Tepes becomes Prince of Wallachia and moves to Tirgoviste.

1442   Vlad Tepes is imprisoned with his father by the Turks.

1443   Vlad Tepes becomes a hostage of the Turks.

1447   Vlad Dracul is beheaded.

1448   Vlad briefly attains the Wallachian throne. Dethroned, he goes to Moldavia and he friends Prince Stefan.

1451   Vlad and Stefan flee to Transylvania.

1455   Constantinople falls.

1456   John Hunyadi assists Vlad Tepes to attain Wallachian throne. Vladislav Dan is executed.

1458   Matthias Corvinus succeeds John Hunyadi as King of Hungary.

1459   Easter massacre of boyers and rebuilding of Dracula's castle. Bucharest is established as the second governmental center.

1460	Attack upon Brasov, Romania.
1461	Successful campaign against Turkish settlements along the Danube. Summer retreat to Tirgoviste.
1462	Following the battle at Dracula's castle, Vlad flees to Transylvania. Vlad begins 13 years of imprisonment.
1475	Summer wars in Serbia against Turks take place. November: Vlad resumes throne of Wallachia.
1476/77	Vlad is assassinated.
1560	Elizabeth Bathory is born.
1610	Bathory is arrested for killing several hundred people and bathing in their blood. Tried and convicted, she is sentenced to life imprisonment.
1614	Elizabeth Bathory dies.
1645	Leo Allatius finishes writing the first modern treatment of vampires, *De Graecorum hodie quirundam opinationabus.*
1657	Fr. Francoise Richard's *Relation de ce qui s'est passé á Sant-Erini Isle de l'Archipel* links vampirism and witchcraft.
1672	Wave of vampire hysteria sweeps through Istra.
1679	A German vampire text, *De Masticatione Mortuorum,* by Philip Rohr is written.
1710	Vampire hysteria sweeps through East Prussia.
1725	Vampire hysteria returns to East Prussia.
1725–30	Vampire hysteria lingers in Hungary.
1725–32	The wave of vampire hysteria in Austrian Serbia produces the famous cases of Peter Plogojowitz and Arnold Paul (Paole).
1734	The word "vampyre" enters the English language in translations of German accounts of the European waves of vampire hysteria.
1744	Cardinal Giuseppe Davanzati publishes his treatise, *Dissertazione sopre I Vampiri.*
1746	Dom Augustin Calmet publishes his treatise on vampires, *Dissertations sur les Apparitions des Anges des Démons et des Espits, et sur les revenants, et Vampires de Hundrie, de Boheme, de Moravie, et de Silésie.*
1748	The first modern vampire poem, "Der Vampir," is published by Heinrich August Ossenfelder.
1750	Another wave of vampire hysteria occurs in East Prussia.
1756	Vampire hysteria peaks in Wallachia.

1772   Vampire hysteria occurs in Russia.

1797   Goethe's "Bride of Corinth" (a poem concerning a vampire) is published.

**1798–
1800**   Samuel Taylor Coleridge writes "Christabel," now conceded to be the first vampire poem in English.

1800   *I Vampiri,* an opera by Silvestro de Palma, opens in Milan, Italy.

1801   "Thalaba" by Robert Southey is the first poem to mention the vampire in English.

1810   Reports of sheep being killed by having their jugular veins cut and their blood drained circulate through northern England. "The Vampyre" by John Stagg, an early vampire poem, is published.

1813   Lord Byron's poem "The Giaour" includes the hero's encounter with a vampire.

1819   John Polidori's *The Vampyre,* the first vampire story in English, is published in the April issue of *New Monthly Magazine.* John Keats composes "The Lamia," a poem built on ancient Greek legends.

1820   *Lord Ruthwen ou Les Vampires* by Cyprien Berard is published anonymously in Paris. June 13: *Le Vampire,* the play by Charles Nodier, opens at the Theatre de la Porte Saint-Martin in Paris. August: *The Vampire; or, The Bride of the Isles,* a translation of Nodier's play by James R. Planché, opens in London.

1829   March: Heinrich Marschner's opera, *Der Vampyr,* based on Nodier's story, opens in Liepzig.

1841   Alexey Tolstoy publishes his short story, "Upyr," while living in Paris. It is the first modern vampire story by a Russian.

1847   Bram Stoker is born. *Varney the Vampyre* begins lengthy serialization.

1851   Alexandre Dumas's last dramatic work, *Le Vampire,* opens in Paris.

1854   The case of vampirism in the Ray family of Jewett, Connecticut, is published in local newspapers.

1872   "Carmilla" is written by Sheridan Le Fanu. In Italy, Vincenzo Verzeni is convicted of murdering two people and drinking their blood.

1874   Reports from Ceven, Ireland, tell of sheep having their throats cut and their blood drained.

1888   Emily Gerard's *Land Beyond the Forest* is published. It will become a major source of information about Transylvania for Bram Stoker's *Dracula.*

1894   H. G. Wells's short story, "The Flowering of the Strange Orchid," is a precursor to science fiction vampire stories.

1897   *Dracula* by Bram Stoker is published in England. "The Vampire" by Rudyard Kipling becomes the inspiration for the creation of the vamp as a stereotypical character on stage and screen.

1912   *The Secrets of House No. 5,* possibly the first vampire movie, is produced in Great Britain.

1913   *Dracula's Guest* by Stoker is published.

1920   *Dracula,* the first film based on the novel, is made in Russia. No copy has survived.

1921   Hungarian filmmakers produce a version of *Dracula.*

1922   *Nosferatu,* a German-made silent film produced by Prana Films, is the third attempt to film *Dracula.*

1924   Hamilton Deane's stage version of *Dracula* opens in Derby. Fritz Harmaann of Hanover, Germany, is arrested, tried, and convicted of killing more than 20 people in a vampiric crime spree. Sherlock Holmes has his only encounter with a vampire in "The Case of the Sussex Vampire."

1927   February 14: Stage version of *Dracula* debuts at the Little Theatre in London. October: American version of *Dracula,* starring Bela Lugosi, opens at Fulton Theatre in New York City. Tod Browning directs Lon Chaney in *London After Midnight,* the first full-length vampire feature film.

1928   The first edition of Montague Summers's influential work *The Vampire: His Kith and Kin* appears in England.

1929   Montague Summers's second vampire book, *The Vampire in Europe,* is published.

1931   January: Spanish film version of *Dracula* is previewed. February: American film version of *Dracula* with Bela Lugosi premieres at the Roxy Theatre in New York City. Peter Kürten of Dusseldorf, Germany, is executed after being found guilty of murdering a number of people in a vampiric killing spree.

1932   The highly acclaimed movie *Vampyr,* directed by Carl Theodor Dreyer, is released.

1936   *Dracula's Daughter* is released by Universal Pictures.

1942   A. E. Van Vogt's "Asylum" is the first story about an alien vampire.

1943   *Son of Dracula* (Universal Pictures) stars Lon Chaney, Jr., as Dracula.

1944   John Carradine plays Dracula for the first time in *Horror of Frankenstein.*

1953   Drakula Istanbula, a Turkish film adaptation of *Dracula,* is released. *Eerie* No. 8 includes the first comic book adaptation of *Dracula.*

1954   The Comics Code banishes vampires from comic books. *I Am Legend* by Richard Matheson presents vampirism as a disease that alters the body.

1956   John Carradine plays Dracula in the first television adaptation of the play for "Matinee Theater." *Kyuketsuki Ga,* the first Japanese vampire film, is released.

1957   The first Italian vampire movie, *I Vampiri*, is released. American producer Roger Corman makes the first science fiction vampire movie, *Not of This Earth*. *El Vampiro* with German Robles is the first of a new wave of Mexican vampire films.

1958   Hammer Films in Great Britain initiates a new wave of interest in vampires with the first of its *Dracula* films, released in the United States as *The Horror of Dracula*. First issue of *Famous Monsters of Filmland* signals a new interest in horror films in the United States.

1959   *Plan 9 from Outer Space* is Bela Lugosi's last film.

1961   *The Bad Flower* is the first Korean adaptation of *Dracula*.

1962   The Count Dracula Society is founded in Los Angeles by Donald Reed.

1964   *Parque de Juelos* (*Park of Games*) is the first Spanish-made vampire movie.

1964   *The Munsters* and *The Addams Family*, two horror comedies with vampire characters, open in the fall television season.

1965   Jeanne Youngson founds The Count Dracula Fan Club. *The Munsters*, based on the television show of the same name, is the first comic book series featuring a vampire character.

1966   *Dark Shadows* debuts on ABC afternoon television.

1967   April: In episode 210 of *Dark Shadows*, vampire Barnabas Collins makes his first appearance.

1969   First issue of *Vampirella*, the longest running vampire comic book to date, is released. Denholm Elliott plays the title role in a BBC television production of *Dracula*. *Does Dracula Really Suck?* (aka *Dracula and the Boys*) is released as the first gay vampire movie.

1970   Christopher Lee stars in *El Conde Dracula*, the Spanish film adaptation of *Dracula*. Sean Manchester founds The Vampire Research Society.

1971   Marvel Comics releases the first copy of a post-Comics Code vampire comic book, *The Tomb of Dracula*. Morbius, the Living Vampire, is the first new vampire character introduced after the revision of the Comics Code allowed vampires to reappear in comic books.

1972   *The Night Stalker* with Darrin McGavin becomes the most watched television movie to that point in time. *Vampire Kung-Fu* is released in Hong King as the first of a string of vampire martial arts films. *In Search of Dracula* by Raymond T. McNally and Radu Florescu introduces Vlad the Impaler, the historical Dracula, to the world of contemporary vampire fans. *A Dream of Dracula* by Leonard Wolf complements McNally's and Florescu's effort in calling attention to vampire lore. *True Vampires of History* by Donald Glut is the first attempt to assemble the stories of all of the historical vampire figures. Stephen Kaplan founds The Vampire Research Center.

1973   Dan Curtis Productions' version of *Dracula* (1973) stars Jack Palance in a made-for-television movie. Nancy Garden's *Vampires* launches a wave of juvenile literature for children and youth.

1975 Fred Saberhagen proposes viewing Dracula as a hero rather than a villain in *The Dracula Tape*. *The World of Dark Shadows* is founded as the first *Dark Shadows* fanzine.

1976 *Interview with the Vampire* by Anne Rice is published. Stephen King is nominated for the World Fantasy Award for his vampire novel, *Salem's Lot*. Shadowcon, the first national *Dark Shadows* convention, is organized by Dark Shadows fans.

1977 A new, dramatic version of *Dracula* opens on Broadway starring Frank Langella. Louis Jourdan stars in the title role in *Count Dracula,* a three-hour version of Bram Stoker's book on BBC television. Martin V. Riccardo founds the Vampire Studies Society.

1978 Chelsea Quinn Yarbro's *Hotel Transylvania* joins the volumes of Fred Saberhagen and Anne Rice as a third major effort to begin a reappraisal of the vampire myth during the decade. Eric Held and Dorothy Nixon found the Vampire Information Exchange.

1979 Based on the success of the new Broadway production, Universal Pictures remakes *Dracula* (1979), starring Frank Langella. The band Bauhaus's recording of "Bela Lugosi's Dead" becomes the first hit of the new gothic rock music movement. *Shadowgram* is founded as a *Dark Shadows* fanzine.

1980 The Bram Stoker Society is founded in Dublin, Ireland. Richard Chase, the so-called Dracula killer of Sacramento, California, commits suicide in prison. The World Federation of Dark Shadows Clubs (now the Dark Shadows Official Fan Club) is founded.

1983 In the December issue of *Dr. Strange,* Marvel Comics' ace occultist kills all the vampires in the world, thus banishing them from Marvel Comics for the next six years. Dark Shadows Festival is founded to host an annual *Dark Shadows* convention.

1985 *The Vampire Lestat* by Anne Rice is published and reaches the best seller lists.

1989 Overthrow of Romanian dictator Nikolai Ceaucescu opens Transylvania to Dracula enthusiasts. Nancy Collins wins a Bram Stoker Award for her vampire novel, *Sunglasses After Dark.*

1991 *Vampire: The Masquerade,* the most successful of the vampire role-playing games, is released by White Wolf.

1992 *Bram Stoker's Dracula* directed by Francis Ford Coppola opens. Andrei Chikatilo of Rostov, Russia, is sentenced to death after killing and vampirizing some 55 people.

1994 The film version of Anne Rice's *Interview with the Vampire* opens with Tom Cruise as the Vampire Lestat and Brad Pitt as Louis.

The Encyclopedia of the Undead

A

ACKERMAN, FORREST JAMES (1916-)

Forrest James Ackerman, science fiction and horror fiction writer and editor, was born on November 24, 1916, in Los Angeles, the son of Carroll Cridland Wyman and William Schilling Ackerman. After attending the University of California at Berkeley for a year (1934-35), Ackerman held a variety of jobs and spent three years in the U.S. Army before founding the Ackerman Science Fiction Agency in 1947. By that time, he had been a science fiction fan of many years and in 1932 had been a cofounder of *The Time Travelers,* the first science fiction fanzine. He was a charter member of the Los Angeles chapter of the Science Fiction League, an early fan club, and attended the first science fiction fan convention in 1939.

Since that time he has spent his life promoting the science fiction and horror genres in both print and film mediums. That lifetime of work has earned him a special place in the world of science fiction as a behind-the-scenes mover and shaker in the development of the field. Besides writing numerous fiction and nonfiction articles, Ackerman worked as the literary agent for a number of science fiction writers. Along the way he amassed an impressive collection of genre literature and artifacts now housed at his Hollywood home, the Ackermansion. Among his prized artifacts is **Bela Lugosi**'s Dracula cape. He also owns more than 200 editions of **Bram Stoker**'s *Dracula* novel.

Ackerman is most remembered by the general public as the editor of and main writer for *Famous Monsters of Filmland,* an important fan magazine that emerged in 1958 as monster movies were becoming recognized as a separate genre of film with their own peculiar audience. During the 20 years of its existence, the magazine filled a void for the growing legion of horror and monster movie fans. Up to this time, there were no vampire fan clubs or periodicals. Ackerman sold the idea of *Famous Monsters* to publisher James Warren. The first issue was released as a one-time

◄

FORREST ACKERMAN FENDS OFF
THE ATTACK OF VAMPIRESS NAI
BONNETT, STAR OF *NOCTURNA*.

publication, but the response was far beyond what either had imagined. It soon became a periodical. In the first article of the premier issue, ''Monsters Are Good for You,'' Dr. Acula (one of Ackerman's pseudonyms) suggested, ''A vampire a day keeps the doctor away.''

Ackerman made broad contributions to the larger science fiction and horror worlds while furthering the development of the vampire in popular culture. He regularly featured vampire movies and personalities—though they shared space with other monsters—on the pages of *Famous Monsters*. He edited and authored a number of books including an important vampire title, *London After Midnight Revisited* (1981), a volume about the famous original vampire feature directed by **Tod Browning.** More recently, he put together several retrospective volumes on *Famous Monsters of Filmland*. He appeared in a number of genre movies, mostly in cameo parts, including two vampire films, *Queen of Blood* (1966) and *Dracula vs. Frankenstein* (1971).

Possibly his most significant contribution to the vampire field was the creation of **Vampirella.** Ackerman partly developed the idea of Vampirella, a sexy young vampire from outer space, from the movie character Barbarella, who was created by

Roger Vadim and portrayed by Jane Fonda (Vadim's wife at the time). The first issue of the *Vampirella* comic book appeared in 1969 and went on to become the most successful vampire comic book ever. It ran for 112 issues and was recently revived by Harris comics.

In 1953 he was given the first Hugo Award as science fiction's number one fan personality. He was awarded the Ann Radcliffe Award from the The Count Dracula Society in 1963 and again in 1966. In 1993 *Famous Monsters of Filmland* was revived as a newsstand magazine.

Sources:

Ackerman, Forrest J. *Famous Monsters of Filmland*. Pittsburgh, PA: Imagine, Inc., 1986. 151 pp.
———, and Philip J. Riley, eds. *London After Midnight Revisited*. Metropolis Books, 1981.

ACONITE

Aconite (*aconitum napellus*) is another name for wolfsbane or monkshood. This poisonous plant was believed by the ancient Greeks to have arisen in the mouths of Cerberus (a three-headed dog that guards the entrance to Hades) while under the influence of Hecate, the goddess of magic and the underworld. It later was noted as one of the ingredients of the ointment that witches put on their body in order to fly off to their sabbats. In *Dracula* **(Spanish, 1931),** aconite was substituted for **garlic** as the primary plant used to repel the vampire.

Sources:

Emboden, William A. *Bizarre Plants: Magical, Monstrous, Mythical*. New York: Macmillan Publishing, 1974. 214 pp.

THE ADDAMS FAMILY

Originating as a cartoon series that first appeared in the *New Yorker* magazine, *The Addams Family* became one of the more notable sets of comic characters in American popular culture. The cartoons were originally the product of Charles S. Addams (1912-1988), whose work had become a regular feature of the *New Yorker* in the 1930s. His work was anthologized in a series of books beginning with *Drawn and Quartered* in 1942. *The Addams Family* was but one aspect of Addams' world which included a wide variety of the bizarre and monstrous that he tended to portray in everyday settings.

The Addams Family cartoons were transformed into a situation comedy television series for the fall 1964 season. Since Addams had never assigned names to the members of the cartoon family, they had to be created. Carolyn Jones was selected to play Morticia Addams, the vampiric family matriarch with the long black hair and revealing, skin-tight black dress. She continued the image of the **vamp** made popular earlier in the century and utilized by horror film hostesses **Vampira** and **Elvira.** John Astin portrayed her husband, Gomez, a lawyer. Their children were named Pugsley and Wednesday (Ken Weatherwax and Lisa Loring). Uncle Fester (Jackie Coogan), Grandmama (Blossom Rock), and the butler, Lurch (Ted Cassidy) rounded out the home's residents. The dynamics of the show, true to Charles Addams' world, rested on the family's turning the bizarre into the norm, and then interacting with the members of normal society.

The Addams Family first aired on ABC on September 18, 1964 and lasted for two seasons. It went up against a similar series on CBS, ***The Munsters,*** which also began in 1964 and ran for two years. *The Addams Family* was revived in 1973 as an animated children's show produced by the Hanna-Barbera Studios and aired on Saturday mornings. Hanna-Barbera also produced a comic book version of *The Addams Family,* which first appeared in October 1974, but only three issues were published before the series folded. *Halloween with the Addams Family* (first aired on October 30, 1977), a full-length feature film with the original cast, was another unsuccessful attempt to revive interest in *The Addams Family* during the 1970s.

Little was heard from the family through the 1980s, but in 1991, Angelica Huston and Raul Julia were selected to star in the full-length movie of *The Addams Family,* produced by Paramount Pictures. The highly successful movie, in turn, inspired two board **games,** The Addams Family Family Reunion Game and The Addams Family Find Uncle Fester Game, an Addams Family pinball game, a home computer game, and two separate juvenile novelizations aimed at different age groups. In 1992, a new *The Addams Family* cartoon series, also produced by Paramount, starred the voices of Nanci Linari and John Astin as Morticia and Gomez, respectively. At the end of 1993, a new movie, *Addams Family Values,* was released. A sequel to the 1991 film, it again starred Angelica Huston and Raul Julia.

Fans of the Addams Family have organized the **The Munsters** and **The Addams Family Fan Club.**

Sources:

The Addams Family—The Official Poster Book. New York: Starlog Communications International, 1992.

Anchors, William E., Jr. "The Addams Family." *Epi-log* 37 (December 1993): 44-51, 64. Calmenson, Stephanie. *The Addams Family.* New York: Scholastic, Inc., 1991. 72 pp. A novelization of the 1991 movie for children.

Faucher, Elizabeth. *The Addams Family.* New York: Scholastic, Inc., 1991. 141 pp. A novelization of the 1991 movie for teens.

Ferrante, Anthony C. "The Campaign for *Addams Family Values.*" *Fangoria* 129 (December 1993): 46-52.

Jones, Stephen. *The Illustrated Vampire Movie Guide.* London: Titan Books, 1993. 144 pp.

The Official Addams Family Magazine. New York: Starlog Communications International, 1991.

Van Hise, James. *Addams Family Revealed: An Unauthorized Look at America's Spookiest Family.* Las Vegas, NV: Pioneer Books, 1991. 157 pp.

AFRICA, VAMPIRES IN

The peoples of Africa have not been known, in spite of their elaborate mythology, to hold a prominent belief in vampires. **Montague Summers,** in his 1920's survey of vampirism around the world, could find only two examples: the *asasabonsam* and the *obayifo*. Since Summers, very little work has been done to explore vampirism in African beliefs.

The *obayifo,* unknown to Summers, was actually the Ashanti name for a West African vampire that reappeared under similar names in the mythology of most of the neighboring tribes. For example, among the Dahomeans, the vampire was known as the *asiman*. The *obayifo* was a witch living incognito in the community. The process of becoming a witch was an acquired trait—there was no genetic link. Hence, there was no way to tell who might be a witch. Secretly, the witch was able to leave its body and travel at night as a glowing ball of light. The witches attacked people—especially children—and sucked their blood. They also had the ability to suck the juice from fruits and vegetables.

The *asasabonsam* was a vampirelike monster species found in the folklore of the Ashanti people of Ghana in western Africa. In the brief description provided by R. Sutherland Rattray, the *asasabonsam* was humanoid in appearance and had a set of iron teeth. It lived deep in the forest and was rarely encountered. It sat on treetops and allowed its legs to dangle downward, using its hook-shaped feet to capture unwary passers-by.

Working among the tribes of the Niger River delta area, Arthur Glyn Leonard found a belief that witches left their homes at night to hold meetings with demons and to plot the death of neighbors. Death was accomplished by ''gradually sucking the blood of the victim through some supernatural and invisible means, the effects of which on the victim is imperceptible to others.'' Among the Ibo, it was believed that the blood-sucking process was done so skillfully that the victim felt the pain but was unable to perceive the physical cause of it, even though it would eventually prove fatal. Leonard believed that witchcraft was, in reality, a very sophisticated system of poisoning (as was a certain amount of sorcery in medieval Europe).

P. Amaury Talbot, working among the tribes in Nigeria, found witchcraft a pervasive influence, and that the most terrible power attributed to witches was the ''sucking out the heart'' of the victims without them knowing what was happening to them. The witch could sit on the roof at night and by magical powers accomplish the sucking. A person dying of tuberculosis was often thought to be the victim of such witchcraft.

Among the Yakö people of Nigeria, Daryll Forde discovered that disembodied witches were believed to attack people while they slept at night. They could suck their blood, and ulcers were believed to be a sign of their attack. They could also operate like an **incubus/succubus** and suffocate people by lying on top of them.

The question of witchcraft was evoked by anyone who suffered a hurtful condition, and anyone accused was severely dealt with by various trials by ordeal. Generally women who were barren or post-menopausal were primary subjects for accusations. It was not uncommon to sentence a convicted witch to death by fire. Melville Herskovits and his wife Frances Herskovits were able to trace a witch/ vampire, whose existence was acknowledged by most West African tribes, to similar vampire figures found in the Caribbean, the *loogaroo* of Haiti, the *asema* of Surinam, and the *sukuyan* of Trinidad. These three vampires are virtually identical, though found in colonies of the French, Dutch, and English. The vampire beliefs seem an obvious example of a common view carried from Africa by the slaves, which then persisted through the decades of slavery into the present.

More recently, John L. Vellutini, editor of the *Journal of Vampirology,* took up the challenge of exploring the whole question of vampirism in Africa. The results of his discoveries have been summarized in two lengthy articles. Like researchers before him, Vellutini found scarce literal vampirism in Africa. However, he argued that beneath the surface of African beliefs about witchcraft, much material analogous to the Eastern European or **Slavic vampire** could be found. Witches were seen as powerful figures in African culture with numerous powers, including the ability to transform into a variety of animal shapes. Using their powers, they indulged themselves in acts of cannibalism, necrophagy (i.e. feeding on corpses), and vampirism. These actions usually constituted acts of **psychic vampirism** rather than physical malevolence. For example, Thomas Winterbottom, working in Sierre Leone in the 1960s, noted:

> A person killed by witchcraft is supposed to die from the effects of a poison secretly administered or infused into his system by the witch; or the latter is supposed to assume the shape of some animal, as a cat, or a rat, which, during the night, sucks the blood from a small and imperceptible wound, by which a lingering illness and death are produced.

With similar results, the *obayifo,* an Ashanti witch, sucked the blood of children as it flew about in its spirit body at night. Among the Ga people, M. J. Field found that witches gathered around a *baisea,* a type of pot, which contained the blood of their victims—though anyone looking into it would see only water. In fact, the liquid was believed to hold the vitality they had taken from their victims.

When a person was accused of witchcraft, he or she was put through an ordeal to determine guilt, and if found guilty, executed. The methods adopted by some tribes bore a strange resemblance to the methods applied to suspected vampires in Eastern Europe. For example, one tribe began the execution by pulling the tongue out and pinning it to the chin with a thorn (thus preventing any final curses being given to the executioners). The witch was then killed by being impaled on a sharpened **stake.** On occasion, the head was severed from the body and the body burnt or left in the woods for predators.

Even more closely tied to the practices of European witchcraft were the efforts taken to ascertain if a deceased person was a witch. The corpse of the accused witch

AN AFRICAN FAMILY SHRINE BUILT TO PROTECT A FAMILY FROM WITCHCRAFT/VAMPIRISM.

would be taken from the ground and examined for signs of blood in the burial plot, incorruption, and abnormal swelling of the corpse. The grave of a true witch would be found to have a hole in the dirt that lead from the body to the surface that the witch could use to exit the ground in the form of a **bat,** rat, or other small animal. It was believed that the witch could continue to operate after his/her death, and that the body would remain as at the time of death. By destroying the body, the spirit was unable to continue its witchcraft activity.

Witches also had the power to raise the dead and to capture a departed spirit, which they turned into a ghost capable of annoying the kinsmen of the departed person. There was also widespread belief throughout West Africa, in the *isithfuntela* (known by different names among different peoples), the disinterred body of a person enslaved by a witch to do the witch's bidding. The witch reportedly cuts out the tongue and drives a peg into the brain of the creature so that it becomes zombie-like. The *isithfuntela* similarly attacked people by hypnotizing them and then driving a nail in their heads.

Vellutini concluded that Africans shared the belief with Europeans in the existence of a class of persons who could defy death and exert a malignant influence from the grave. Like the European vampires, African vampires were often people who died in defiance of the community mores or from **suicide.** Unlike the literary vampire, the African vampires were simply common people like the vampires of Eastern Europe.

Vellutini speculated that African beliefs in witches and witchcraft might have spread to the rest of the world, although anthropologists and ethnologists did not encounter these beliefs firsthand until the nineteenth century. While certainly possible, further research and comparison with evidence for alternative theories, such as that proposed by Devendra P. Varma for the Asian origin of vampire beliefs, must be completed before a consensus can be reached.

Sources:

Forde, Daryll. *Yakö Studies.* London: Oxford University Press, 1964. 288 pp. Leonard, Arthur Glyn. *The Lower Niger and Its Tribes.* London: Macmillan and Co., 1906.

Rattray, R. Sutherland. *Ashanti Proverbs.* Oxford: Claredon Press, 1916. 190 pp. Summers, Montague. *The Vampire: His Kith and Kin.* London: Routledge, Kegan Paul, Trench, Trubner, & Co., 1928. 356 pp. Reprint. New Hyde Park, NY: University Books, 1960. 356 pp.

Talbot, P. Amaury. *In the Shadow of the Bush.* London: William Heinemann, 1912. 500 pp.

Vellutini, John L. "The African Origins of Vampirism." *Journal of Vampirology* 5, 2 (1988): 2-16.

———. "The Vampire in Africa." *Journal of Vampirology* 5, 3 (1988): 2-14.

AFRICAN AMERICAN VAMPIRES

Vampire beliefs have not been prominent among African Americans, though a few have been reported. These few were seemingly derived from the mythologies of Africa, which believed in both vampires and witches who acted like vampires, and were brought to the United States either directly or by way of Haiti or the other French islands in the Caribbean. Folklorists working among African Americans in the southern United States in the late-nineteenth and early-twentieth centuries found a number of accounts of vampires. Some were more traditional bloodsuckers. One

account from Tennessee told of an old woman whose health seemed to constantly improve while the children's health declined because she sucked their blood while they slept: ''de chillun dies, an' she keeps on a-livin'.''

The most definable vampire figure reported among African Americans was the *fifollet,* or the *feu-follet,* known to the residents of Louisiana. The *fifollet,* the traditional will-o-the-wisp (light seen at night over the swamp areas), derived from the French **incubus/succubus** figure, was the soul of a dead person that had been sent back to Earth by God to do penance, but instead attacked people. Most of the attacks were mere mischief, but on occasion, the *fifollet* became a vampire who sucked the blood of people, especially children. Some believed that the *fifollet* was the soul of a child who had died before baptism.

MODERN AFRICAN AMERICAN VAMPIRES: Vampires have made only infrequent appearances in African American folklore, and, similarly, African Americans have been largely absent from modern vampire movies and novels. The few black vampire movies emerged in the era of blaxploitation movies in the early- and mid-1970s. Only one African American vampire character, Prince Mamuwalde (better known as Blacula), attained any fame beyond the fans of vampire movies. The Prince, portrayed by Shakespearean actor **William Marshall,** appeared in two movies, *Blacula* (1972) and *Scream Blacula Scream* (1973). Released the same year as *Blacula* was *Alabama's Ghost* (1972), a blaxploitation movie in which a vampire rock group battles a ghost. Another lesser-known African American vampire movie is the 1973 *Ganja and Hess* (released in video under a variety of names including *Blood Couple, Double Possession, Black Evil,* and *Black Vampire*). Like *Blacula,* the movie was set in New York. It concerned Dr. Hess Green (played by Duane Jones), who becomes a vampire after being stabbed with an ancient African dagger by his assistant. The vampire never became a prominent role for black actors, however, and with a few notable instances—Teresa Graves in *Old Dracula* (also known as *Vampira*) and Grace Jones in *Vamp* —few have appeared in leading roles.

Sources:

Brandon, Elizabeth. "Superstitions in Vermillion Parish." In Mody C. Boatright, Wilson M. Hudson, and Allen Maxwell, eds. *The Golden Log.* Dallas: Southern Methodist University, 1962, 108-18.

Gross, Edward, and Marc Shapiro. *The Vampire Interview Book: Conversations with the Undead.* East Meadow, NY: Image Publishing, 1991. 134 pp. Lavergne, Remi. *A Phonetic Transcription of the Creole Negro's Medical Treatments, Superstitions, and Folklore in the Parish of Pointe Coupée.* New Orleans, LA: Master of Arts thesis, Louisiana State University, 1930.

Murphy, Michael J. *The Celluloid Vampires: A History and Filmography, 1897-1779.* Ann Arbor, MI: Pierian Press, 1979. 351 pp.

Puckett, Newbell Niles. *Folk Beliefs of the Southern Negro.* Chapel Hill, NC: University of North Carolina Press, 1926. Rept: New York: Negro Universities Press, 1968.

Rovin, Jeff. *The Encyclopedia of Super Villains.* New York: Facts on File, 1987. 416 pp.

ALIEN VAMPIRES *See:* SCIENCE FICTION AND THE VAMPIRE

ALLATIUS, LEO (1586-1669)

Leo Allatius (also known as Leone Allacci) seventeenth-century Greek vampirologist, was possibly the first modern author to write a book on vampires. Allatius was born in 1586 on the Greek island of Chios. In 1600 he moved to Rome to attend the Greek College there. After completing his studies, he returned to Chios as the assistant to the Roman Catholic Bishop Marco Giustiniani. He later moved back to Italy to study medicine and rhetoric, and worked for many years at the Vatican library. Among his passions was the reunion of the Greek and Roman churches.

In 1645 he completed *De Graecorum hodie quirundam opinationibus,* in which he discussed many of the beliefs common to the people of **Greece.** Allatius covered the Greek vampire traditions in great detail. He described the *vrykolakas,* the undecomposed corpse that has been taken over by a demon, and noted the regulations of the Greek Church for the discernment and disposal of a *vrykolakas.* He then noted his own belief in the existence of vampires, which had occasionally been reported on Chios.

While Allatius personally accepted the reality of vampires, and his book helped to popularize the connection between Greece and vampires, he did not dwell upon the subject throughout his life. He continued to work at the Vatican library, and in 1661, was honored by being appointed its custodian. Allatius died in Rome on January 19, 1669.

Sources:

Summers, Montague. *The Vampire: His Kith and Kin.* London: Routledge, Kegan Paul, Trench, Trubner, & Co., 1928. 356 pp. Reprint. New Hyde Park, NY: University Books, 1960. 356 pp.

ALNWICK CASTLE, THE VAMPIRE OF

Among the famous case reports of real vampires were those of **William of Newburgh,** who, in the twelfth century, collected a variety of accounts of vampires in England. One incident that occurred in his lifetime concerned a man who served the Lord of Alnwick Castle. The man, who was himself known for his wicked ways, was further plagued by an unfaithful wife. Having hidden on the roof above his bed to see her actions for himself, he fell to the ground and died the next day.

Following his burial, the man was seen wandering through the town. People became afraid of encountering him and locked themselves in their houses after dark each day. During this time an epidemic of an unnamed disease broke out and a number of people died. The sickness was blamed on the ''vampire.'' Finally, on Palm Sunday, the local priest assembled a group of the more devout residents and some of the leading citizens who proceeded to the cemetery. They uncovered the body, which appeared gorged with blood that gushed forth when it was struck with a spade. Having decided that the body had fed off the blood of its many victims, it was dragged out of town and burned. Soon thereafter, the epidemic ended, and the town returned to normal.

Sources:

Glut, Donald G. *True Vampires of History.* New York: H.C. Publishers, 1971. 191 pp.

ALQUL *See:* GHOULS

ALTERNATE SHADOWS

Alternate Shadows was a *Dark Shadows* fan club headquartered in Ithaca, New York. It was founded and led by Patrick Garrison and his wife Josette Garrison, who also edited a fanzine called *Parallel Times.* The magazine contained articles and original fiction based on the *Dark Shadows* television program, poetry, cartoons, and fan news. In 1983, 1984, and 1985, the group sponsored the Manhattan Shadows convention, which included a blood donation contest with the prize being a dinner in New York City with **Jonathan Frid,** the actor who originally played vampire

Barnabas Collins in the *Dark Shadows* series. The club disbanded in 1988 and the fanzine was discontinued soon afterward.

Sources:

Dresser, Norine. *American Vampires: Fans, Victims, Practitioners.* New York: W. W. Norton & Company, 1989. 255 pp.

ALUKA

Aluka is the word for a leech (*Haemopsis sanguisuga*) in ancient Hebrew. The word appeared in the Jewish Bible in Proverbs 30:15, where it was variously translated as leech or horseleech. The word was derived from an Arabic word (*alukah*), meaning "to hang to." In Syria and Israel, there were several species of leeches, one of which would attach itself to the neck of horses as they drank from streams. Others dwelt in more stagnant waters and would cling to the legs of any who wandered their way. They were known for their tenacity in adhering to the skin, and often could only be detached by killing them.

Some have suggested that the cryptic expression in Proverbs, "The leech (*aluka*) has two daughters, Give, Give," in fact, referred not to the common leech but to a mythological vampire figure, a Syrian/Hebrew derivation of the Arabic **ghoul,** which sucked blood and dined on the flesh of the dead. During the nineteenth century, such an interpretation was offered by several Bible scholars, however, it was always a minority interpretation and is no longer regarded as a viable option by contemporary scholars.

Sources:

Gehman, Henry Snyder. *The New Westminister Dictionary of the Bible.* Philadelphia: Westminster Press, 1970. 1027 pp.

AMERICAN VAMPIRES

European settlers who came to America brought their belief in vampires with them, though most English colonists arrived before the vampire became part of the popular culture of Great Britain. Certainly, Polish settlers from the northern Kashab area of **Poland** brought and kept alive vampire beliefs in their Canadian settlements. Amid the vast mythology of the many Native American tribes there have been few vampires reported, and even passing references to American Indians are rare in vampire literature. Similarly, there have been few reports from the **African American** community, though remnants of **African** vampire mythologies have appeared in the South.

VAMPIRISM IN NEW ENGLAND: While reports of vampires in the United States have been infrequent, there were stories scattered throughout the nineteenth century of what appear, at least on cursory examination, to document a belief in vampires and action taken against them by settlers in a rather confined area in New England. The first such incident reportedly occurred during the American Revolution. A man named Stukeley, who had 14 children, began to experience the death of his brood one by one. After six had died, one of the deceased, his daughter Sarah, began to appear in dreams to his wife. The bodies were exhumed and all but that of Sarah had decomposed. Her body was remarkably preserved. From each body, they cut out the heart, which they burned before reburying the bodies. The first account of this story was not published until 1888, a century after it supposedly occurred. No contemporary accounts of this story exist.

A similar early case was reported in 1854, much closer to the time of its occurrence. It concerned the Ray family of Jewett City, Connecticut. Besides the father and mother, there were five children. Between 1845 and 1854, the father and two sons died of consumption, and a third son had taken ill. (Throughout the nineteenth century, consumption, i.e., tuberculosis, was a deadly disease with no known cause or cure. It thus became the subject of much occult speculation.) The family, believing that their deceased relatives were the cause of the problem, exhumed the bodies and burned them. How prevalent this belief was is not known, but there certainly existed a community of belief that passed from generation to generation. Henry David Thoreau recorded in his journal on September 16, 1859, ''I have just read of a family in Vermont who, several of its members having died of consumption, just burned the lungs, heart, and liver of the last deceased in order to prevent any more from having it.''

Another story was published in a Vermont paper in 1890. It concerned the Corwin family, who lived in Woodstock, Vermont. Six months after one of the Corwins had died of consumption, a brother took sick. The family disinterred the body of the first brother and burned the heart. Unfortunately, there is no contemporary account, of this incident, only a newspaper story published 60 years after the reported occurrence.

Among the widely retold accounts was that of the family of Mary E. Brown of Exeter, Rhode Island. Mary died of tuberculosis in December 1883. Six months later, her oldest daughter also died. In 1888, her son Edwin and his sister Mercy contracted the disease. Mercy died in January 1892. Edwin, though ill, clung to life. Two months later, the family, deciding that a vampire was involved, exhumed the bodies of all their dead relatives. The mother and oldest daughter were mere skeletons, but Mercy's body appeared to be healthy and full of blood, and the body was turned sideways in the coffin. They concluded that Mercy was a vampire, and therefore, her heart was cut out and burned before the body was reburied. The ashes were dissolved in medicine and given to Edwin. It did not help, however, and he died soon afterward. Mercy's body remains buried in the cemetery behind the Chestnut Hill Baptist Church in Exeter, and some local residents still think of her as the town's vampire.

George R. Stetson, the first scholar to examine the stories, noted, ''In New England the vampire superstition is unknown by its proper name. It is there believed that consumption is not a physical but a spiritual disease, obsession, or visitation; that as long as the body of a dead consumptive relative has blood in its heart it is proof that an occult influence steals from it for death and is at work draining the blood of the living into the heart of the dead and causing its rapid decline.'' John L. Vellutini, editor of the *Journal of Vampirology,* has done the most complete examination of the accounts and has made a number of pertinent observations on these cases. Like Stetson, he found that ''vampirism'' was not used in the earlier accounts to describe the actions against the corpses. The subject of vampirism was seemingly added into the accounts by later writers, especially journalists and local historians. Thus, by the time of the Mercy Brown case in 1892, vampirism was being used as a label to describe such incidents.

PSYCHIC VAMPIRISM IN NEW ENGLAND: As early as 1871, pioneer anthropologist Edward B. Tyler, in his work *Primitive Culture,* proposed a definition of vampirism, possibly with the New England cases in mind. Tyler wrote, ''Vampires are not mere creations of groundless fancy, but causes conceived in spiritual form to account for specific facts of wasting disease.'' In this interpretation, vampirism occurred when ''the soul of a deadman goes out from its buried corpse and sucks the blood of living men. The victim becomes thin, languid, bloodless, and, falling into rapid decline, dies.'' He further noted, ''The corpse thus supplied by its returning soul with blood, is imagined to remain unnaturally fresh and supple and ruddy . . . '' Tyler's definition of vampirism was close to what had become known as **psychic vampirism.** It was almost identical to the definition proposed by the French psychical researcher **Z. J. Piérart** during the 1860s that was popular in occult circles for the rest of the 1800s. It differed radically from the idea of the Eastern European vampire, which was believed to be a revived corpse that attacked living people from whom it sucked the blood.

The belief, discovered by Stetson, underlying the practice of removing and burning the heart of a deceased tubercular patient could properly be described as a form of psychic vampirism. Vellutini was also quite correct in his observation that no belief in vampires (that is, the resuscitated corpse of Eastern European vampire lore) was ever present in the belief system of New England.

The practice of attacking the corpses of dead tubercular patients disappeared in the early-twentieth century, due, no doubt, to the discovery of the cause and then the cure of tuberculosis. Periodically, accounts of the New England cases were rediscovered and published. As recently as 1993, Paul S. Sledzik of the National Museum of Health and Medicine reported on his examination of a cemetery near Griswold, Connecticut, of corpses that showed signs of tuberculosis, which had been mutilated in the nineteenth century.

Sources:

"Early New Englanders Ritually 'Killed' Corpses, Experts Say." *New York Times* (October 31, 1993): 1.
Stetson, George R. "The Animistic Vampire in New England." *The American Anthropologist* 9, 1 (January 1896): 1-13.

Tyler, Edward B. *Primitive Culture.* 2 vols. 1871. 4th ed.: London: John Murray, 1903.
Vellutini, John L. "The Myth of the New England Vampire." *Journal of Vampirology* 7, 1 (1990): 2-21.

ANEMIA

Anemia is a disease of the **blood** that has come, in some quarters, to be associated with vampirism. Anemia is caused by a reduction of either red blood cells or hemoglobin (the oxygen-carrying pigment of the cells) relative to the other ingredients in the blood. The symptoms include a pale complexion, fatigue, and in its more extreme instances, fainting spells. All are symptoms usually associated with a vampire attack. In **Bram Stoker**'s novel, *Dracula,* during the early stages of **Lucy Westenra**'s illness, Dr. **John Seward** hypothesized that possibly she was suffering from anemia. He later concluded that she was not suffering from the loss of red blood cells, but from the loss of whole blood. Dr. **Abraham Van Helsing** agreed with his friend, ''I have made careful examination, but there is no functional cause. With you I agree that there has been much blood lost; it has been, but is not. But the conditions of her are in no way anaemic.'' (Chapter 9) Thus, the association of anemia and vampirism was dismissed.

ANIMALS

The vampire's relationship to the animal kingdom is manifested in its ability to achieve **transformation** into various animal shapes; its command over the animal kingdom, especially the rat, the owl, the bat, the moth, the fox, and the wolf; and to a lesser extent its prey upon animals for food. Also, on rare occasions, animal vampires have been reported.

ANIMALS IN VAMPIRE FOLKLORE: In the older folklore, the vampire's command of animals or the ability to transform into animals was a minimal element at best. However, the vampire was often associated with other creatures, such as **werewolves,** who were defined by their ability to transform themselves. Among the vampires who did change into animals were the *chiang-shih* vampires of **China,** who could transform into wolves.

More importantly, the vampire, especially in Western Europe, saw the animal world as a food supply and would often attack the village's cattle herd and suck the animals' blood. Sudden, unexpected, and unexplained deaths of cattle would often be attributed to vampires. For example, Agnes Murgoci noted that one of the first tests in determining if a recently deceased man had become a vampire would be the sudden death of his livestock. Sir James Frazer observed that in **Bulgaria,** where the cattle suffered from frequent vampire attacks, people treated such attacks by having their herds pass between two bonfires constructed at a nearby crossroads known to be frequented by wolves. Afterward, the coals from the bonfires were used to relight the fires in the village. In **Japan** the vampire **kappa** lived at the water's edge and would attack cows and horses and try to drag them into the water.

A few animals, particularly cats and horses, were also believed to have a special relationship to vampires. It was thought in many Eastern European countries that if one allowed an animal such as a cat to jump over the corpse of a dead person prior to burial, the person would return as a vampire. (This belief emphasized the necessity of the deceased's loved ones to properly mourn, prepare, and care for the body.) The horse, on the other hand, was frequently used to locate a vampire. Brought to the graveyard, the horse would be led around various graves in the belief that it would hesitate and refuse to cross over the body of a vampire.

DRACULA'S ANIMALS: **Dracula**'s command of the animal kingdom appeared quite early in **Bram Stoker**'s novel. In the first chapter of *Dracula,* even before **Jonathan Harker** arrived at **Castle Dracula,** the carriage he was traveling in was suddenly surrounded by an intimidating ring of wolves. Just as suddenly, the driver (later shown to be Dracula in disguise) dismissed the wolves with a wave of his arm. After he arrived at the castle and began to familiarize himself with the Count, Harker noticed the howling of the wolves. Dracula then spoke one of his most memorable lines: ''Listen to them—the children of the night. What music they make.'' Later, in London, while Dracula was continuing his attack upon **Lucy Westenra,** he called Bersicker, a wolf from the local zoo, to his aid. Bersicker assisted Dracula by breaking the window at the Westenra home to give Dracula a means of entrance.

Abraham Van Helsing warned the men who would finally track Dracula and kill him that Dracula could not only alter the weather, but that he also could ''command the meaner things; the rat, and the owl, and the bat—the moth, and the fox, and the wolf.'' The men discovered the truth of his words for themselves when they broke into Dracula's residence, **Carfax,** and were suddenly set upon by thousands of rats.

TRANSFORMATION: Stoker first hinted at Dracula's ability to transform himself into animal form when the imprisoned Harker looked out of his window to see Dracula crawling down the castle wall. ''What manner of man is this, or what manner of creature is it in the semblance of man?'' Harker wondered. (Chapter 3) Dracula traveled to England aboard a ship, the *Demeter,* which he caused to be wrecked upon the shore at **Whitby.** Dracula escaped the wreckage in the form of a dog. Through the rest of the novel Dracula made few appearances, however, he constantly hovered in the background in the form of a bat. Observed outside of **R. N. Renfield**'s window at the asylum, Dr. **John Seward** noted the strange behavior of a large bat. ''Bats usually wheel and flit about, but this one seemed to go straight on, as if it knew where it was bound for or had some intention of its own.'' (Chapter 11)

Stoker's characters were, of course, familiar with the vampire **bat**s of Central and South America and understood the vampire's close association with the bat. At one point Seward examined one of the children bitten by Lucy who had been admitted to a hospital. The doctor attending the boy hypothesized that the wounds on his neck were caused by a bat. '''Out of so many harmless ones,' he said, 'there may be some wild specimen from the south of a more malignant species. Some sailor may have brought one home, and it managed to escape; or even from some Zoological Gardens a young one may have got loose, or one be bred there from a vampire.'" (Chapter 15)

ANIMALS AND THE CONTEMPORARY VAMPIRE MYTH: While there has been, as a whole, less attention paid to animals in the *Dracula* movies and stage plays, the command of animals is an essential element in the alteration of the plot in the first of the Dracula movies, *Nosferatu, Eine Symphonie des Garuens.* Building upon Dracula's command of the rats that so bedeviled Van Helsing and the men as they entered Carfax, **Graf Orlock,** the Dracula character in *Nosferatu,* commanded plague—bearing rats. He arrived at Bremen with the rats, and the pestilence that accompanied them was a sign of the vampire's presence. The death of the vampire brought an end to the plague.

The vampire's ability to transform into different forms, especially that of a bat, has remained an essential element to most modern vampire movies and novels. The improvement of special effects in movies has allowed for more life-like transformations to be depicted. Special effects in the recent *Bram Stoker's Dracula* were among the movie's more impressive features. There has been a noticeable trend, however, to strip the vampire of its less believable qualities. Both **Anne Rice** and **Chelsea Quinn Yarbro,** for example, have denied their vampires the ability to transform themselves out of human shape, though they retain other supernatural abilities.

During the last generation, as the vampire became the hero or at least the sympathetic figure with whom the reader identified, the question of the vampire feeding off of humans rose to the fore. If a vampire renounces the taking of blood from human victims, there are few nutritional options remaining: purchasing blood from various sources, finding willing donors, artificial blood substitutes, or animals. Animals were the most frequently chosen objects, and novels frequently include reflections on the adequacy of animal blood. In Rice's *Interview with the Vampire,* Louis was unable to bring himself to attack a human for the first four years of his vampiric existence and lived off the blood of rats and other animals.

ANIMAL VAMPIRES: On occasion, quite apart from stories of vampires changing into animal forms, stories of vampire animals have surfaced. As early as 1810, stories came from the borderland between England and Scotland of sheep, sometimes as many as ten a night, having their jugular vein cut and their blood drained. The best known incident of a similar occurrence, reported by Charles Fort, concerned a rash of sheep killings near Caven, **Ireland,** in 1874. Some 42 instances of sheep having their throats cut and blood drained (but no flesh consumed) had been noted. Near the dead sheep footprints of a dog-like animal were found. Finally a dog, seemingly the offending animal, was shot. At that point the affair should have ended. However, the sheep kept dying and more dogs were shot. Then reports began to come in from Limerick, more than one hundred miles away. Accounts ended in both communities without any final resolution. In 1905, a similar spat of sheep killings occurred in England near Badminton in Gloucester. Such incidents have become part of the UFO lore of the last generation in North America. Another famous event involving possible

◀
THE CAT IS AMONG THE MOST
UBIQUITOUS ANIMALS
ASSOCIATED WITH VAMPIRISM.

animal vampires was the cutting of the throat of Snippy the horse in Colorado in September 1967.

Several novels have featured animal vampires, the most famous being Ken Johnson's *Hounds of Dracula* (1977, also released as *Dracula's Dog*) that was made into the movie, *Zoltan: Hound of Dracula.* Youthful vampire readers may be familiar with the vampire rabbit Bunnicula, the subject of several books by James Howe, and the vampire duck, **Count Duckula,** star of an animated television series and a Marvel comic book. Both Bunnicula and Count Duckula were vegetarians.

Sources:

Fort, Charles. *Lo!.* London: V. Gollancz, 1931. 351 pp. Reprint. New York: Ace Books, 1931, 1941.
Keel, John A. *Strange Creatures from Time and Space.* Greenwich, CT: Fawcett Publications, 1970. 288 pp.

ANNE RICE'S VAMPIRE LESTAT FAN CLUB

Anne Rice's Vampire Lestat Fan Club was founded in 1988 as a popular response to the very successful vampire novels of **Anne Rice.** It originated at an autograph party held October 18, 1988 at de Ville Books & Prints in New Orleans. Sue Quiroz suggested the idea of starting a club to two of her friends—Susan Miller and Theresa Simmons. The three immediately began to gather the names of potential members among those at the store. They sought and received Rice's approval. She suggested the addition of a reference to **Lestat de Lioncourt** to the name of the club since most of the public response was to him. The original three founders of the club were joined by Melanie Scott, and the club was soon launched.

The first quarterly newsletter was issued in March 1989. The group sponsored its initial major event, the ''Coven Party'', a costume gala, in October 1989. The party has become an annual event complete with guest celebrities and a theme drawn from the Lestat books. At the time of the first party, the club had some 400 members. It grew slowly over the next few years until the release of the first issue of *The Vampire Companion,* an irregular publication of the Innovation Corporation. The *Companion* was intended to compliment the comic book version of Rice's books that Innovation was releasing. The *Companion* carried an article about the club and a membership form. Membership rose quickly from some 500 members to several thousand.

The Anne Rice's Vampire Lestat Fan Club may be contacted at PO Box 58277, New Orleans, LA 70158-8277. It publishes a newsletter.

Sources:

The Vampire Companion. Nos. 1-3. Wheeling, WV: Innovation Corporation, 1991-92.

APPEARANCE OF A VAMPIRE

Any discussion of the appearance of the vampire must take into account the several vampire types. The contemporary vampire of the 1980s and 1990s has shown a distinct trend toward a normal appearance that allows them to completely fit in with human society and move about undetected. Such modern vampires have almost no distinguishing characteristics with the exception of **fangs** (extended canine teeth), which may be retractable and show only when the vampire is feeding. As such, the contemporary vampire harks back to the vampire characters of the pre-Dracula literary vampires. There was little in the appearance of Geraldine, **Lord Ruthven, Varney the Vampyre,** or **Carmilla** to distinguish them from their contemporaries, not even their teeth.

However, the contemporary vampire is still largely based on the dominant figure of **Dracula** as developed for the stage by **Hamilton Deane** and especially as portrayed by **Bela Lugosi.** Hamilton Deane must be credited with the domestication of Dracula and making him an acceptable attendee at the evening activities of Victorian British society. Deane's Dracula donned evening clothes and an opera cape with a high collar.

Bela Lugosi in the movie *Dracula* **(1931)** confirmed Deane's image of the vampire in popular culture and added to it. He gave Dracula an Eastern European accent and a swept-back, slicked-down hairdo with a prominent widow's peak. In the

BELA LUGOSI SUPPLIED THE IMAGE OF THE STEREOTYPICAL VAMPIRE OFTEN SEEN AT HALLOWEEN.

Horror of Dracula (1968), **Christopher Lee** added the final prominent feature to Dracula's appearance, the fangs. Prior to Lee the vampire had no fangs, at least no visible ones. Lee, the first prominent vampire in Technicolor, also gave Dracula a set of red eyes, which to a lesser extent have become a standard (though by no means unanimous) aspect of the vampire's appearance, especially in motion pictures. Since Lee, the image of the vampire in popular culture has been set. The fangs, the cape, and to a lesser extent, the evening clothes, the red eyes, and the widow's peak now quickly convey the idea that a person is a vampire. The use of these definitive signs of a vampire's appearance is most evident on greeting cards and the artwork on the cover of vampire novels and **comic books.**

This modern image of the vampire, with the exception of the extended canine teeth, varies considerably from both that of Dracula, as presented in the original novel of **Bram Stoker,** and the vampire of folklore. The latter, at least in its Eastern European incarnation, was a corpse, but a corpse notable for several uncorpselike characteristics. Its body might be bloated and extended so that the skin was tight like a drum. It would have extended **fingernails** that had grown since its burial. It would be dressed in burial clothes. It would stink of death. The ends of its appendages might show signs of having been eaten away. In appearance the folkloric vampire was horrible, not so much because it was monstrous, but because of its disgusting semi-decayed nature.

Between the folklore vampire and the contemporary vampire of popular culture lies the Dracula of Bram Stoker's novel. He was described in some detail in the second chapter of the book—he was dressed in black clothes; his hair was profuse and his eyebrows massive and bushy; he had a heavy moustache; his skin was pale; he had hair in the palm of his hand and long extended fingernails. Most noticeable were the brilliant extended canines that protruded over his lower lips when the mouth was closed. His eyes were blue, though they flashed red when he was angry or upset. He was of mature years, though he got younger as the novel proceeded. **John Carradine**'s stage productions of *Dracula* in the 1950s were probably closest to Dracula as he appeared in the novel.

ARMENIA, VAMPIRES IN

Armenia is an ancient land situated between Turkey and **Russia.** It was the first land to make **Christianity** its state religion. The Armenian church is similar to the Eastern Orthodox churches, but did not follow the development of Orthodox theology through the fifth to seventh centuries. Late in the nineteenth century Armenia was the location of a number of massacres by occupying Turkish soldiers. Through most of the twentieth century it was a part of the Soviet Union until that country broke up in the early 1990s.

Little has been written about vampirism in Armenia. Its place in vampire history is due to an account in an 1854 text by Baron August von Haxthausen that was mentioned by **Montague Summers.** von Haxthausen visited Mount Ararat in the Caucasians. According to local legend there was a vampire, *Dakhanavar,* who protected the valleys in the area from intruders. He attacked travelers in the night and sucked the blood from people's feet. He was outwitted by two men who heard of the vampire's habits and slept with their feet under the other's head. The vampire, frustrated by encountering a creature that seemed to have two heads and no feet, ran away and was never heard of again.

Sources:

Summers, Montague. *The Vampire in Europe.* London: Routledge, Kegan Paul, Trench, Trubner & Co., 1929. 329 pp. Reprint. New Hyde Park, NY: University Press, 1961. 329 pp.
von Haxthausen, August. *Transcaucasia.* London: Chapman and Hall, 1854. 448 pp.

ASASABONSAM See: AFRICA, VAMPIRES IN

ASEMA See: SOUTH AMERICA, VAMPIRES IN

ASIMAN See: AFRICA, VAMPIRES IN

ASPEN *See:* STAKE

ASSYRIA, VAMPIRES IN *See:* BABYLON AND ASSYRIA, VAMPIRES IN ANCIENT

ASWANG See: PHILIPPINES, VAMPIRES IN THE

AUSTRALIA, VAMPIRES IN

Vampires do not play a large part in the folklore of Australia. However, in Aboriginal cultures, there existed the *yara-ma-yha-who,* a vampirelike being. It was described as a little red man, approximately four feet tall, with an exceptionally large head and mouth. It had no teeth and simply swallowed its food whole. Its most distinguishing features, however, were its hands and feet. The tips of the fingers and toes were shaped like the suckers of an octopus.

The *yara-ma-yha-who* lived in the tops of wild fig trees. It did not hunt for food, but waited until unsuspecting victims sought shelter in the tree and then dropped on them. The story of the *yara-ma-yha-who* was told to young children who might wander from the tribe, and naughty children were warned that it might come and take them away.

When a person camped under a fig tree, a *yara-ma-yha-who* might jump down and place its hands and feet on the body. It would then drain the blood from the victim to the point that the person was left weak and helpless, but rarely enough, at least initially, to cause the victim to die. The creature would later return and consume its

THE YARA-MA-YHA-WHO IS THE VAMPIRE OF AUSTRALIAN ABORIGINAL MYTHOLOGY.

meal. It then drank water and took a nap. When it awoke, the undigested portion of its meal would be regurgitated. According to the story, the person regurgitated was still

AUSTRALIA, VAMPIRES IN

alive, and children were advised to offer no resistance should it be their misfortune to meet a *yara-ma-yha-who*. Their chances of survival were better if they let the creature swallow them.

People might be captured on several occasions. Each time, they would grow a little shorter until they were the same size as the *yara-ma-yha-who*. Their skin would first become very smooth and then they would begin to grow hair all over their body. Gradually they were changed into one of the mythical little furry creatures of the forest.

Sources:

Smith, W. Ramsey. *Myths and Legends of the Australian Aboriginals.* New York: Farrar & Rinehart, n.d. 356 pp.

B

BABYLON AND ASSYRIA, VAMPIRES IN ANCIENT

During the nineteenth century, the writings of ancient Mesopotamia (the lands between the Tigris and Euphrates River Valleys, present-day Iraq) were discovered and translated. They indicated the development of an elaborate mythology and a universe inhabited by a legion of deities of greater and lesser rank. From this vast pantheon, the closest equivalent of the true vampire in ancient Mesopotamian mythology were the seven evil spirits described in a poem quoted by R. Campbell Thompson that begins with the line, ''Seven are they! Seven are they!'':

> Spirits that minish the heaven and earth,
> That minish the land
> Spirits that minish the land,
> Of giant strength,
> Of giant strength and giant tread,
> Demons (like raging bulls, great ghosts),
> Ghosts that break through all houses,
> Demons that have no shame,
> Seven are they!
> Knowing no care, they grind the land like corn;
> Knowing no mercy they rage against mankind,
> They spill their blood like rain,
> Devouring their flesh (and) sucking their veins.
>
> They are demons full of violence, ceaselessly devouring blood.

Montague Summers suggested that vampires had a prominent place in Mesopotamian mythology, beyond that suggested by the belief in the seven spirits. In particular he spoke of the *ekimmu,* the spirit of an unburied person. He based his case on an exploration of the literature concerning the Netherworld, the abode of the dead. The Netherworld was portrayed as a somewhat gloomy place. However, an individual's life there could be considerably improved if at the end of their earthly existence they received a proper, if simple, burial that included the affectionate care of the corpse. At the end of tablet 12 of the famous Gilgamesh (or Gilgamish) Epic, there was an accounting of the various degrees of comfort of the dead. It closed with several couplets concerning the state of the person who died alone and unburied, which Summers quoted as:

> The man whose corpse lieth in the desert—
> Thou and I have often seen such an one—
> His spirit resteth not in the earth;
> The spirit hath none to care for it—
> Thou and I have often seen such an one
> The dregs of the vessel—the leaving of the feast, And that which is cast into
>   the street are his food.

The key line in this passage was "His spirit resteth not in the earth," which Summers took to mean that the spirits of those who died alone (i.e., the *ekimmu*) could not even enter the Netherworld and thus were condemned to roam the earth. He then connected this passage with other passages concerning the exorcism of ghosts, and quoted at length various texts that enumerated the various ghosts that had been seen. However, the ghosts were of a wide variety, as one text stated:

> The evil spirit, the evil demon, the evil ghost, the evil devil,
> From the earth have come forth;
> From the underworld into the land of the living they have come forth;
> In heaven they are unknown
> On earth they are not understood
> They neither stand nor sit,
> Not eat nor drink.

It appeared that Summers confused the issue of revenants and the return of the dead who could become vampires with ghosts of the deceased who might simply haunt the land. The ghosts were plainly noncorporeal—they neither ate nor drank, whereas the dead in the underworld had a form of corporeal existence and enjoyed some meager pleasures. The source of this misunderstanding was an inadequate translation of the last parts of the Gilgamish Epic. The line "The spirit resteth not in the earth," was originally translated in such a way as to leave open the possibility of the dead wandering in the world of human habitation. However, more recent translations and a survey of the context of the last couplets of the Gilgamish Epic made it clear that the dead who died in the desert uncared for (the *ekimmu*) roamed restlessly not on earth but through the Netherworld. David Ferry's translation, for example, rendered the passage thusly:

And he whose corpse was thrown away unburied?
He wanders without rest through the world down there
The One who goes to the Netherworld without
leaving behind anyone to mourn for him?
Garbage is what he eats in the Netherworld.
No dog would eat the food he has to eat.

Thus while the idea of vampires did exist in Mesopotamia, it was not as prominent as Summers would indicate. Summers should not be overly chastised for his error, however, because even eminent scholar E. A. Wallis Budge made a similar mistake in his brief comments on tablet 12 in 1920:

> The last lines of the tablet seem to say that the spirit of the unburied man reposeth both in the earth, and that the spirit of the friendless man wandereth about the street eating the remains of food which are cast out of the cooking pots.

However, neither Budge nor E. Campbell Thompson, whom Summers quoted from directly, made the error of pushing these several texts in the direction of a vampirish interpretation.

Sources:

Ferry, David. *Gilgamesh: A New Rendering in English Verse.* New York: Farrar, Strauss, and Giroux, 1992. 99 pp.
Spence, Lewis. *Myths and Legends of Babylonia and Assyria.* London: G. G. Harrap, 1928. 411 pp.
Summers, Montague. *The Vampire: His Kith and Kin.* London: Routledge, Kegan Paul, Trench, Trubner, & Co., 1928. 356 pp. Reprint. New Hyde Park, NY: University Books, 1960. 356 pp.
Thompson, E. Campbell. *The Devils and Evil Spirits of Babylonia.* 2 vols. London: Luzac, 1903-04.
———. *Semitic Magic: Its Origin and Development.* London: Luzac, 1908. 286 pp.

BAKER, ROY WARD (1916-)

Roy Ward Baker, a director of vampire movies for **Hammer Films** in the 1970s, was born in London. In 1934, he joined Gainsborough Studios as an assistant director. He worked at Gainsborough through the decade, but left in 1940 to become an officer in the British army. While in the service, he directed films for the Army Kinematograph Service. After the war he returned to directing for various studios including 20th Century Fox, where he directed four films in the early 1950s.

In the late 1960s, Baker began to work for Hammer Films, where he directed *The Anniversary, Quartermass and the Pit* (1969), one of the studio's very successful Quartermass series. In 1971, he was assigned the first of several vampire movies that Hammer Films became so well-known for during the 1960s. *The Vampire Lovers* (1970) was the first of the Hammer productions based on **Sheridan Le Fanu**'s story of a female vampire, "**Carmilla.**" Starring **Ingrid Pitt,** it was one of the best of the Hammer productions. Baker was then immediately put to work on the next **Christopher Lee** Dracula movie, *The Scars of Dracula* (1970). It was an original story involving a young man who wandered into **Castle Dracula** only to meet disaster. The man was avenged by his girlfriend and brother, and Dracula was finally killed by a bolt of lightening. The film was a commercial success in both England and America and Baker continued to work on other Hammer horror movies such as *Dr. Jekyll and Sister Hyde* (1971).

Baker's last vampire film for Hammer came at a crucial point in the studio's life. The company was in financial trouble and gambled on a project in cooperation with Shaw Brothers, a film company in Hong Kong. The project was a movie that mixed the vampire horror genre with the martial arts movie. Baker was chosen to direct the film variously known as *The Legend of the Seven Golden Vampires* and *The Seven Brothers Meet Dracula*. In the story **Abraham Van Helsing** (played by **Peter Cushing**) traveled to China in search of the elusive Dracula. The crusade to destroy Dracula and his new Chinese vampire allies frequently turned into a martial arts demonstration. Even the combination of Cushing's serious performance and Baker's mature direction could not rescue the unbelievable plot. Rather than saving Hammer, the film helped seal its fate. Warner Brothers refused to release the film to its potential major market in America, and Hammer went into bankruptcy in 1975.

In his post-Hammer period, Baker was called on to direct at least one other vampire/horror movie, *The Monster Club* (1981). The movie, which starred an aging **John Carradine** as author **Ronald Chetwynd-Hayes,** featured several episodes based on Chetwynd-Hayes' short stories, including one vampire tale. Veteran actor Vincent Price helped Carradine introduce the film's distinct episodes and provided a transition between each. Price played Eramus, one of the few times he played a vampire.

Sources:

Flynn, John L. *Cinematic Vampires.* Jefferson, NC: McFarland and Company, 1992. 320 pp.
Smith, John M., and Tim Caldwell. *The World Encyclopedia of Film.* New York: Galahad Books, 1972. 444 pp.

BALDERSTON, JOHN L. (1889-1954)

John L. Balderston was the playwright of the American version of *Dracula, the Vampire Play in Three Acts.* He was born on October 22, 1889, in Philadelphia, the son of Mary Alsop and Lloyd Balderston. He attended Columbia University and began a career in journalism in 1911 as the New York correspondent of the *Philadelphia Record*. In 1915, he moved to England and worked as editor for *The Outlook*; from 1923 to 1931 he was the chief London correspondent of the *New York World*.

Balderston authored his first play, *The Genius of the Marne,* in 1919. He followed with *Morality Play for the Leisured Class* (1920), *Tongo* (1924), and *Berkeley Square* (1926). Balderston was still in England in 1927 when producer Horace Liveright attempted to purchase the American dramatic rights to *Dracula* from Bram Stoker's widow. Florence Stoker did not like Liveright, who turned to

Balderston to assist him in the negotiations. Balderston had become known to Liveright after his play, *Berkeley Square,* a ghost story, became a hit both in London and New York. Balderston secured the rights from Mrs. Stoker, and Liveright then hired him to modernize the stage version of *Dracula* by **Hamilton Deane** that had been playing in England.

Balderston's version of the play was very different from earlier ones. His major changes included combining the characters of **Lucy Westenra** and **Mina Murray** into a single character, Lucy Seward, who became the daughter of the now mature **John Seward.** Originally Seward had been Lucy's young suitor. Lucy's other suitors, **Quincey P. Morris** and **Arthur Holmwood,** completely disappeared from the play.

Published by Samuel French, Balderston's version has become the most influential of the several dramatic versions of the novel. It opened on Broadway on October 5, 1927 and, after 241 performances, went on the road to Los Angeles and San Francisco. It spawned both a midwestern and East Coast touring company. It has subsequently been the version most frequently used when the play has been revived through the years. Its most important revival began in 1977 when it opened for a new run on Broadway. Balderston's version also became the basis of two film versions of *Dracula*—the 1931 version with **Bela Lugosi** and the 1979 version with **Frank Langella.** Langella, it should be noted, starred in the 1977 stage revival.

Balderston went on to work on two more plays: *Red Planet* (1932, with J. E. Hoare), and *Frankenstein* (1932, with Peggy Webling). He also translated the Hungarian play *Farewell Performance* (1935) into English. He retired to Beverly Hills, California, where he died on March 8, 1954.

Sources:

Glut, Donald F. *The Dracula Book.* Metuchen, NJ: Scarecrow Press, 1975. 388 pp.

Skal, David J., ed. *Dracula: The Ultimate, Illustrated Edition of the World-Famous Vampire Play.* New York: St. Martin's Press, 1993. 153 pp.

———. *Hollywood Gothic: The Tangled Web of Dracula from Novel to Stage to Screen.* New York: W. W. Norton & Company, 1990. 242 pp.

Who Was Who in the Theatre: 1912-1976. London: Pitman, 1972. Reprint. Detroit, MI: Gale Research Inc., 1972.

BALTIC STATES, VAMPIRES IN THE

The Baltic States of Estonia, Latvia, and Lithuania are three small countries located on the southeastern shore of the Baltic Sea. They share a common religion, Roman Catholicism, and have a long history of withstanding the encroachments of their neighbors to the south (Poland) and east (Russia). They are not united ethnically, though they are not Slavs. The Estonians were closely related to the Finns. The Latvians descended from the Letts, an ancient Baltic tribe. The Lithuanians derived from the ancient Balts, a tribe that moved into the Niemen River valley from the West. Lithuanian is the oldest of the Baltic languages.

Both Estonia and Latvia were brought into the Roman Catholic fold in the thirteenth century by the Germanic Knights. In the fourteenth century, Lithuania grew into a large kingdom that included Byelorussia and parts of the Ukraine and Russia. During the next centuries, however, it faded in power. All of the Baltic States existed as independent nations between World Wars I and II. They were annexed by **Russia** during World War II and remained a part of the U.S.S.R. until the disintegration of the Soviet Union in the early 1990s. Historically, the Baltic States have not shown a vital vampiric tradition, although they shared a belief in revenants with their Polish and Russian neighbors.

TWENTIETH CENTURY VAMPIRES: In this century, the story of one case of vampirism in Lithuania has been frequently repeated since its inclusion by Montague Summers in his book *The Vampire in Europe*. The case referred to events in the life of a Captain Pokrovsky. In a village near his family estate, Captain Pokrovsky learned of a man who had recently remarried and was growing pale and listless. He reported that the villagers believed him under attack by a vampire. Pokrovsky sent a physician to examine the man. The doctor discovered a loss of blood and a small puncture wound on the neck. There was no other wound that could account for the blood loss. Various efforts did not prevent the wound on his neck from growing larger, and the man eventually died. Following his death, his wife felt compelled for her own safety to leave the community lest she be attacked by the villagers as the vampire who killed her husband.

Sources:

Summers, Montague. *The Vampire in Europe*. London: Routledge, Kegan Paul, Trench, Trubner, & Co., 1929. 329 pp. Reprint. New Hyde Park, NY: University Books, 1961. 329 pp.

BAOBBAN SITH See: IRELAND, VAMPIRES IN

BARON BLOOD

The vampire Baron Blood was one of a host of super villains created by Marvel Comics as worthy adversaries of its very successful super heroes. He first appeared in *The Invaders* (No. 7) in 1976, a time when Marvel was well into its creation of what came to be known as the alternative "Marvel Universe" (a world where all of their comic superheroes could exist and interact). Baron Blood was born late in the nineteenth century as John Falsworth, the younger son of Lord William Falsworth, a British nobleman. Shortly after the turn of the century, when his brother inherited control of the family fortune, the younger Falsworth went to **Romania** to search for **Dracula.** He planned to gain control of Dracula and become a powerful person, but he underestimated the Count's powers and was instead turned into a vampire. Falsworth returned to England as Dracula's servant and agent to create havoc in England. He became Dracula's instrument of revenge for the defeat described in **Bram Stoker's** novel.

Falsworth became a German agent during World War I, which is when he first assumed his identity as Baron Blood. After the war, he disappeared until he reemerged as a Hitler supporter in World War II. He returned to England, posing as his own grandson, and took up residence at Falsworth Manor. He attacked his own family, but was defeated by the Invaders, the super-team that had been assembled to defeat the Third Reich. He was killed by a stalactite threaded through with silver. He was then entombed in a chapel with a **stake** in his heart and his casket surrounded by **garlic.**

Baron Blood did not reappear until 1981, when Captain America, one of the original Invaders, was summoned to England. The now aged Lord Falsworth believed that Baron Blood was the cause of a rash of what had been defined as slasher murders. Captain America then discovered that Baron Blood was not in his tomb. He had been resurrected some years before by a Dr. Charles Cromwell, who had been sent to Blood's tomb by Dracula. After awakening, Blood killed Cromwell and assumed his identity. He lived quietly for many years taking blood from his patients. Captain America tracked him down, killed him, then decapitated him and burned his body.

Captain America had finally disposed of Baron Blood, but he was too worthy a villain to leave in the ashes. He reappeared in the form of Victor Strange, brother of Marvel's sorcerer hero Dr. Stephen Strange. Victor had died and was frozen cryogenically. When Dr. Strange tried to revive him with magical spells, one of the spells worked but turned Victor into a vampire. Therefore, when the cryogenic machine was turned off in 1989, Victor awoke as a vampire. He donned a costume similar to Baron Blood's, and was named Baron Blood by Marie Laveau, the voodoo priestess that Dr. Steven Strange was fighting at the time of Victor's resurrection. Baron Blood settled in Greenwich Village and like the vampire **Morbius** (another Marvel vampire), satisfied his craving for blood by attacking criminals. He reappeared occasionally in Dr. Strange episodes until August 1993, when he committed suicide by plunging a knife into his midsection. Dr. Strange buried the Baron, but there was no reason to believe that Baron Blood has finally been destroyed and will not be able to return again.

Sources:

Captain America. Nos. 253-354. New York: Marvel Comics, 1981.
David, Alan. "Baron Blood." *Official Handbook of the Marvel Universe* 2, 16 (June 1987).
Dr. Strange: Sorcerer Supreme. Nos. 10, 14, 16, 29, 56. New York: Marvel Comics, 1989-93.
The Invaders. Nos. 7-9. New York: Marvel Comics, 1976. Rovin, Jeff. *The Encyclopedia of Super Villains.*
    New York: Facts on File, 1987.

BATHORY, ELIZABETH (1560-1614)

Elizabeth Bathory was the countess who tortured and murdered numerous young women and, because of these acts, became known as one of the "true" vampires in history. She was born in 1560, the daughter of George and Anna Bathory. Though frequently cited as Hungarian, due in large part to the shifting borders of the Hungarian Empire, she was in fact more closely associated with what is now the

Slovak Republic. Most of her adult life was spent at Castle Cachtice, near the town of Vishine, northeast of present-day Bratislava, where Austria, Hungary, and the Slovak Republic come together. (The castle was mistakenly cited by **Raymond T. McNally** as being in Transylvania.)

Bathory grew up in an era when much of **Hungary** had been overrun by the Turkish forces of the Ottoman empire and was a battleground between Turkish and Austrian (Hapsburg) armies. The area was also split by religious differences. Her family sided with the new wave of Protestantism that opposed the traditional Roman Catholicism. She was raised on the Bathory family estate at Ecsed in **Transylvania.** As a child she was subject to seizures accompanied by intense rage and uncontrollable behavior. In 1571, her cousin Stephen became Prince of Transylvania and, later in the decade, additionally assumed the throne of Poland. He was one of the most effective rulers of his day, though his plans for uniting Europe against the Turks were somewhat foiled by having to turn his attention toward fighting **Ivan the Terrible,** who desired Stephen's territory.

In 1574, Elizabeth became pregnant as a result of a brief affair with a peasant man. When her condition became evident, she was sequestered until the baby arrived because she was engaged to marry Count Ferenc Nadasdy. The marriage took place in May 1575. Count Nadasdy was a soldier and frequently away from home for long periods. Meanwhile, Elizabeth assumed the duties of managing the affairs at Castle Sarvar, the Nadasdy family estate. It was here that her career of evil really began— with the disciplining of the large household staff, particularly the young girls.

In a time period in which cruel and arbitrary behavior by those in power toward those who were servants was common, Elizabeth's level of cruelty was noteworthy. She did not just punish infringements on her rules, but found excuses to inflict punishments and delighted in the torture and death of her victims far beyond what her contemporaries could accept. She would stick pins in various sensitive body parts, such as under the fingernails. In the winter she would execute victims by having them stripped, led out into the snow, and doused with water until they were frozen.

Elizabeth's husband joined in some of the sadistic behavior and actually taught his wife some new varieties of punishment. For example, he showed her a summertime version of her freezing exercise—he had a woman stripped, covered with honey, then left outside to be bitten by numerous insects. He died in 1604, and Elizabeth moved to Vienna soon after his burial. She also began to spend time at her estate at Beckov and at a manor house at Cachtice, both located in the present-day country of Slovakia. These were the scenes of her most famous and vicious acts.

In the years immediately after her husband's death, Elizabeth's main cohort in crime was a woman named Anna Darvulia, about whom little is known. When Darvulia's health failed in 1609, Elizabeth turned to Erzsi Majorova, the widow of a local tenant farmer. It was Majorova who seems to have been responsible for Elizabeth's eventual downfall by encouraging her to include a few women of noble birth among her victims. Because she was having trouble procuring more young servant girls as rumors of her activities spread through the countryside, Elizabeth followed Majorova's advice. At some point in 1609, she killed a young noble woman and covered it by charges of suicide.

As early as the summer of 1610, an initial inquiry had begun into Elizabeth's crimes. Underlying the inquiry, quite apart from the steadily increasing number of victims, were political concerns. The crown hoped to confiscate Elizabeth's large landholdings and escape having to pay back the extensive loan that her husband had made to the king. With these things in mind, Elizabeth was arrested on December 29, 1610.

Elizabeth was placed on trial a few days later. It was conducted by Count Thurzo as an agent of the king. As noted, the trial (rightly characterized as a show trial by Bathory's biographer Raymond T. McNally) was initiated to not only obtain a conviction, but to also confiscate her lands. A week after the first trial, a second trial was convened on January 7, 1611. At this trial, a register found in Elizabeth's living quarters was introduced as evidence. It noted the names of 650 victims, all recorded in her handwriting. Her accomplices were sentenced to be executed, the manner determined by their roles in the tortures. Elizabeth was sentenced to life imprisonment in solitary confinement. She was placed in a room in her castle at Cachtice without windows or doors and only a small opening for food and a few slits for air. There she remained for the next three years until her death on August 21, 1614. She was buried in the Bathory land at Ecsed.

Above and beyond Elizabeth's reputation as a sadistic killer with more than 600 victims, she has been accused of being both a werewolf and a vampire. During her trials, testimony was presented that on occasion, she bit the flesh of the girls while torturing them. These accusations became the basis of her connection with werewolfism. The connection between Elizabeth and vampirism is somewhat more tenuous. Of course, it was a popular belief in Slavic lands that people who were **werewolves** in life became vampires in death, but that was not the accusation leveled at Elizabeth. Rather, she was accused of draining the blood of her victims and bathing in it to retain her youthful beauty, and she was by all accounts a most attractive woman.

RECOVERING ELIZABETH'S STORY: No testimony to this activity was offered at her trial, and in fact, there was no contemporary testimony that she engaged in such a practice. Following her death, the records of the trials were sealed because the revelations of her activities were quite scandalous for the Hungarian ruling community. Hungarian King Matthias II forbade the mention of her name in polite society. It was not until 100 years later that a Jesuit priest, Laszlo Turoczy, located copies of some of the original trial documents and gathered stories circulating among the people of Cachtice, the site of Elizabeth's castle. Turoczy included an account of her life in a book he wrote on Hungarian history. His book initially suggested the possibility that she bathed in blood. Published in the 1720s, it appeared during the wave of vampirism in Eastern Europe that excited the interest of the continent. Later writers would pick up and embellish the story. Two stories illustrate the legends that had gathered around Elizabeth in the absence of the court records of her life and the attempts to remove any mention of her from Hungarian history:

INGRID PITT, AS COUNTESS BATHORY, FIGHTS OLD AGE.

It was said that one day, the aging countess was having her hair combed by a young servant girl. The girl accidently pulled her hair, and Elizabeth turned and slapped the servant. Blood was drawn, and some of it spurted onto Elizabeth's hands. As she rubbed it on her hands, they seemed to take on the girl's youthful appearance. It was from this incident that Elizabeth developed her reputation for desiring the blood of young virgins.

The second story involves Elizabeth's behavior after her husband's death, when it was said she associated herself with younger men. On one occasion when she was with one of those men, she saw an old woman. She remarked, "What would you do if you had to kiss that old hag?" He responded with expected words of distaste. The old woman, however, on hearing the exchange, accused Elizabeth of excessive vanity and noted that such an aged appearance was inescapable, even for the countess. Several historians have tied the death of Bathory's husband and this story into the hypothesized concern with her own aging, and thus, the bathing in blood.

Elizabeth has not been accused of being a traditional blood-drinking or blood-sucking vampire, though her attempts to take and use the blood to make herself more youthful would certainly qualify her as at least a vampire by metaphor. Previously a little known historical figure, she was rediscovered when interest in vampires rose sharply in the 1970s; since that time she has repeatedly been tied to vampirism in popular culture. Noticeable interest in Elizabeth was evident in the publication of a series of books in the early 1970s beginning with Valentine Penrose's *Erzsebet Bathory, La Comtesse Sanglante,* a 1962 French volume whose English translation, *The Bloody Countess,* was published in 1970. It was followed by Donald Glut's *True Vampires of History* (1971) and Gabriel Ronay's *The Truth about Dracula* (1972). Penrose's book inspired the first of the Bathory films; the movie in turn, inspired a novel based on its screenplay, *Countess Dracula* by Michael Parry. The celebration of the mythical countess in the 1970s motivated Dracula scholar Raymond McNally to produce by far the most authoritative book on Elizabeth to date—*Dracula was a Woman: In Search of the Blood Countess of Transylvania*—which appeared in 1984. Based on a new search through the original court documents, and a broad understanding of Eastern European history and folklore, McNally thoroughly demythologized the legend and explained many of the problems that had baffled previous researchers. Recently, **Elaine Bergstrom** authored a novel, *Daughter of the Night* (1992), that drew inspiration from McNally's study.

BATHORY ON FILM: The first movie inspired by the Bathory legend was the now largely forgotten *I Vampiri* (released in the United States as *The Devil's Commandment*), notable today because of the work of future director **Mario Bava** as the film's cameraman. A decade later, as part of its vampire cycle, **Hammer Films** released what is possibly the best of the several movies based on Elizabeth's life, *Countess Dracula* (1970). **Ingrid Pitt** starred in the title role. The film was built around the mythical blood baths and portrayed her as going increasingly crazy as she continued her murderous career.

Daughters of Darkness (1971), one of the most artistic of all vampire films, brought the countess into the twentieth century in a tale with strong **lesbian** overtones. In the movie, Elizabeth and her companion Iona check into an almost empty hotel where they meet a newlywed couple. When it is revealed that the husband has a violent streak, the stage is set for Elizabeth and Iona to move in and ''help'' the new bride. A series of vampiric encounters ensues, and in the end, the wife (the newest vampire) emerges as the only survivor.

Elizabeth, (or a character modeled on her) also appeared in *Legend of Blood Castle* (1972), *Curse of the Devil* (1973), and *Immoral Tales* (1974), all films of lesser note. In 1981, a full-length animated version of Elizabeth's story was released in Czechoslovakia. More recent films include *Thirst* (1980) and *The Mysterious Death of Nina Chereau* (1987).

BATHORY AND DRACULA: Bram Stoker, the author of *Dracula* (1897), read of Elizabeth in *The Book of Werewolves* by Sabine Baring-Gould (1865) where the first lengthy English-language account of Elizabeth's life appeared. McNally has suggested that the description of Elizabeth might have influenced Stoker to shift the site of his novel from Austria (Strigia), where he initially seemed to have set it, to Transylvania. In like measure, McNally noted that Dracula became younger and younger as the novel proceeded, an obvious allusion to the stories of Elizabeth bathing in blood to retain her youth. He made a strong case that the legends about her ''played a major role in the creation of the character of Count Dracula in the midst of Bram Stoker.''

Sources:

Baring-Gould, Sabine. *The Book of Werewolves*. London: Smith, Elder, 1865. Reprint. New York: Causeway Books, 1973. Glut, Donald F. *True Vampires of History*. New York: HC Publishers, 1971.

McNally, Raymond T. *Dracula was a Woman: In Search of the Blood Countess of Transylvania*. New York: McGraw-Hill, 1983. Reprint. London: Robert Hale, 1984. Reprint. London: Hamlyn, 1984.

Parry, Michel. *Countess Dracula*. London: Sphere Books, 1971. Reprint. New York: Beagle Books, 1971.

Penrose, Valentine. *Erzsebet Bathory, La Comtesse Sanglante*. Paris: Mercure du Paris, 1962. English translation as: *The Bloody Countess*. London: Calder & Boyars, 1970.

Ronay, Gabriel. *The Truth about Dracula*. London: Gallancz, 1972. Reprint. New York: Stein and Day, 1972.

BATHORY PALACE

Bathory Palace is a vampire-oriented fanzine named for the Countess **Elizabeth Bathory**; it was first issued in 1991 by founder/editor Lara A. Haynes. Haynes was a college student at the time and found herself rather isolated by her fascination with such things as **gothic** music, vampires, and obscure belief systems. She began the magazine as a way of communicating with others of like interest. The magazine has covered a broad range of topics, from H. P. Lovecraft to Eastern European vampires. It also features art, poetry, and short stories, reviews of books and gothic recordings, and news of gothic events.

Bathory Palace may be ordered from Lara Haynes, 1618 SW 3rd, Topeka, KS 66606-1215.

BATMAN

Like Superman, Batman is one of the most popular late twentieth century superheroes. Batman (a DC Comics character) created a popularized image of the bat, the development of which to some extent must be credited to *Dracula,* the 1897 book by **Bram Stoker,** and its translation in the 1920s and 1930s to the stage and motion picture screen. However, Batman was not a vampire—he was a human hero with human resources, and his enemies, while often very strange, were usually human as well.

Batman first appeared in *Detective Comics* No. 27 in 1939. Dr. Thomas Wayne and his wife were killed in a mugging. In his grief, their son Bruce Wayne, grew up with the idea of becoming a policeman. He studied criminology and developed his body to an amazing degree. As a young adult, he changed his plans and decided to become a vigilante. He settled on the Batman costume after two events—first a bat flew in the window as he was trying to find a uniform to put fear into the hearts of his criminal enemies. Later, the independently wealthy Wayne fell through the floor of his mansion and discovered a bat-infested cave—the perfect headquarters for Batman.

The clear association of Batman with Dracula must have been in the mind of his creators, because a scant four months after his initial appearance, he encountered a vampire in a two-part story in issues No. 31 and No. 32 of *Detective Comics* in September and October 1939. A vampire tried to take control of Bruce Wayne's girlfriend, unaware that Wayne was Batman. Batman tracked the Monk, as the vampire was known, to his home in **Hungary,** which was also the home of his allies, the **werewolves.** Batman eventually found the vampire and his vampire bride asleep and killed them with a silver **bullet** fired into the **coffin**s.

The full development of Batman as a definitive comic book hero in the years after World War II occurred as the debate over the effect of comic books on children proceeded. After DC Comics subscribed to the Comics Code in 1954, there was little opportunity (or reason) for Batman and his new sidekick Robin the Boy Wonder to encounter vampires and the supernatural. However, as Batman's popularity and subsequently the number of comic books carrying his stories increased, new villains were continually generated. Thus it was inevitable, after the lifting of the ban on vampires by the revised Comics Code in 1971, that Batman would come face-to-face with another bloodthirsty enemy.

Batman's next encounter with a vampire, Gustav Decobra, occured in the January 1976 *Detective Comics* (No. 455). Stranded by car trouble, Bruce Wayne and his butler Alfred entered a seemingly deserted house only to find a coffin in the center of the living room. As they searched the house, the vampire emerged from the **coffin.** After Wayne saw the vampire, he changed into Batman. In the ensuing fight, Batman rammed a **stake** into the vampire's chest. However, this did no good because Decobra had cleverly hidden his heart elsewhere. Batman then retreated from this first battle. By the time of their next confrontation, he figured out that Decobra had hidden his heart in a grandfather clock at the house. When Batman impaled the heart with an arrow, Decobra died.

Several years prior to this encounter with Decobra, Batman had begun an ongoing relationship with Kirk Langstrom. Langstrom developed a serum to turn himself into **Man-Bat.** Though not originally a vampire **bat,** Man-Bat would eventually encounter vampires and bring Batman into the realm with him. Both Man-Bat's and Batman's encounter with vampires were orchestrated by writer Gerry Conway, the first writer for Marvel's *The Tomb of Dracula,* and artist Gene Colan, who had worked through the 1970s on *The Tomb of Dracula.* Both were working for DC during the early 1980s.

In 1982, immediately after the conclusion of the first episode with Man-Bat, where he was cured of the condition that had turned him into a bat, Batman (now in the hands of writer Conway and artist Colan) squared off against vampires again. An unsuspecting Robin was captured by his girlfriend, Dala, who turned out to be a vampire. He attempted to escape, but in the process he was confronted by Dala's colleague, the resurrected Monk. Robin was bitten and then allowed to escape. Because the only way to save Robin was with a serum made from the vampire's blood, Batman went after the vampires. Unsuccessful in his first encounter, Batman was bitten and also became a vampire. He then set up a second confrontation that was successful and he was able to obtain the necessary ingredients to return himself and Robin to normalcy.

Except for his ongoing relationship with Man-Bat, Batman did not confront a vampire again until 1991. The new story was published in a comic book monograph rather than either of the Batman comic book serials. It concerned Batman's adventures in what was described in the introduction as an "alternative future" and a Batman who was "an altogether different Batman than we're used to." In *Batman and Dracula: Red Rain,* Gotham City was under attack by a group of vampires led by Dracula. Batman (without Robin) was drawn into the fray. In his effort to find what was believed to be a serial killer, he met Tanya, a "good" vampire who had previously organized opposition to Dracula. She had developed a methadone-like artificial substitute that quenched the vampire's need for blood. After they united to fight Dracula, Batman was wounded in battle and became a vampire. In his closing lines he repeated Tanya's phrase, "Vampires are real . . . but not all of them are evil." Meanwhile, the unvampirized Batman continued his adventures in *Batman* and *Detective Comics.*

Sources:

Batman. No. 348-51. New York: DC Comics, 1982.

Detective Comics. No. 455. New York: DC Comics, 1982. *The Greatest Batman Stories Ever Told.* New York: DC Comics, 1988.

Moench, Doug. *Batman & Dracula: Red Rain.* New York: DC Comics, 1991.

Rovin, Jeff. *The Encyclopedia of Superheroes.* New York: Facts on File, 1986.

BATS, VAMPIRE

Vampire bats, three species of which exist in **Mexico** and Central and **South America,** have become an integral part of the modern myth of vampires, and bat symbolism is inseparable from current iconography of the contemporary vampire. Europeans discovered and first described vampire bats in the sixteenth century. Modern biologists who specialize in the study of bats recognize as vampires only three species of the mammalian family Phyllostomatidae, subfamily Desmodontinae. The most common is *Desmodus rotundus.* Rarer are *Diaemus youngi* and *Diphylla ecaudata.*

THE NATURE OF VAMPIRE BATS: Bats are the only mammals that can fly. There are almost 1,000 species, nearly one-fourth of all the mammalian species now on

▶

GOYA'S "SLEEP OF REASON
PRODUCES MONSTERS" HELPED
TO POPULARIZED THE
ASSOCIATION OF THE BAT WITH
VAMPIRISM.

earth. The largest have a wingspan of several feet. Much of their time is spent sleeping while hanging upside down, a position from which they can drop into space and easily begin flying.

Vampire bats are characteristically distinguished from other bats by their feeding habits. Whereas most species of bats feed off fruits and other plants and/or insects, the vampires live exclusively off the blood of various vertebrates. *Diaemus* and *Diphylla* will feed on birds, but *Desmodus,* the common vampire bat, feeds exclusively on other mammals. Their teeth include razor-sharp incisors with which they cut into their prey. Rather than suck the blood, however, they allow it to flow and lap it up with their tongue, somewhat like a cat drinking milk. They also seem to have an anticoagulant substance in their saliva that helps keep the blood of their victims flowing during feeding. They are quite agile and mobile and can walk, run, and hop, unlike some species. They have a good sense of smell and large eyes that provide clear vision. The average adult vampire bat nightly consumes some 15 milliliters of blood—approximately 40 percent of their prefeeding weight. After feeding, the stomach and intestinal area appear bloated, and some of the feast will have to be digested before the bat can return home.

In real life, the vampire bat has emerged as a problem among South American farmers as a carrier of rabies, which it transmits to the cattle it feeds on. Vast eradication programs have been developed but with mixed results.

Two sixteenth-century Europeans, Dr. Oliedo y Valdez (1526) and M. Giroalme Benzoni, (1565) were the first to bring word of the vampire bat to their homelands. Benzoni, in his *History of the New World,* notes:

> There are many beasts which bite people during the night; they are found all along this coast to the Gulf of Paria and in other areas, but in no other part are they as pestiferous as in this province Nuevo Cartago, today Costa Rica; they have gotten to me at several places along this coast and especially at Nombre de Dios, where while I was sleeping they bit the toes of my feet so delicately that I felt nothing, and in the morning I found the sheets and mattresses with so much blood that it seemed that I had suffered some great injury. (Turner, 2)

A reoccurrence of this rare event (as vampire bats do not normally like human blood) was noted several centuries later by Charles Waterton, author of *Wanderings in South America,* who awakened one morning after sleeping on a hammock to find his friend complaining that vampire bats had attacked him. Waterton looked into the matter:

> On examining his foot, I found the vampire had tapped his great toe: there was a wound somewhat less than that made by a leech; the blood was still oozing from it. Whilst examining it, I think I put him in a worse mood by remarking that an European surgeon would not have been so generous as to have blooded him without making a charge. (Robertson, 71)

Waterton had a much friendlier attitude toward the vampires:

> I had often wished to have been once sucked by the vampire. . . There can be no pain in the operation, for the patient is always asleep when the vampire is sucking him; and for the loss of a few ounces of blood, that would be a triffle in the long run. Many a night have I slept with my foot out of the hammock to tempt this winged surgeon, expecting he would be there; but it was all in vain.

On his journey around the world in the 1880s, Charles Darwin observed the vampire bat feeding and wrote the first brief "scientific" account, which was published in 1890.

THE BAT IN SOUTH AMERICAN FOLKLORE: Bats in general, and the vampire bat in particular, have not gone unnoticed by the peoples of South America, who have integrated them into their mythology. E. W. Roth, an ethnologist who studied the people of Guyana (Guinea), had informally designated one of their plants "bat's bane" because its juice, when rubbed on the toes, would kill an attacking bat. The native folklore contains several tales of such bats. **Camazotz** was a significant deity among the ancient Maya of Guatemala. A god of the caves, he was seen as dwelling in the Bathouse in the Underworld, and he played a key part in the story told in the Maya's sacred book, *Popul Vuh.*

THE BAT IN WESTERN FOLKLORE: Although the bat was not tied to the vampire myth until the nineteenth century, it has appeared repeatedly since the days of Aesop and his fables. Early observers of bats commented on the likeness in features with human beings. They also observed bats suckling their young from a pair of breast nipples. Because bats are creatures of the night, in many cultures, they came to be associated, as did the owls, with the unknown, the supernatural, and more sinister aspects of life. In Greek mythology, bats were sacred to Proserpina, the wife of Pluto, god of the underworld. In the Middle Ages, bats came to be associated with the Christian Devil. They were often believed to be signs of and even agents of death.

Bats did have some positive associations. Among the **Gypsies,** for example, they were seen as bearers of good luck. Gypsies prepared small bags of dried bat parts for children to wear around their necks. In Macedonia, bat bones were kept as good luck objects. Possibly the most positive use of the bat has been in heraldry. Several families in both continental Europe and the British Isles have a bat on the family heraldic crest. The Wakefield family crest, for example, is topped by a bat with wings outspread and also has three owls, another night creature, on the shield.

The Spanish conquistadors interpreted the new variety of bats, the blood-drinking ones that they found in Mexico and South America, in light of both the prior image of bats in Western folklore and their traditional beliefs about "human" vampires. For example, they not only called them vampire bats but also described them as "blood-sucking" creatures rather than "blood-lapping" ones. Over the next centuries the association of bats and vampires gradually grew stronger. William Blake utilized a vampire bat in the artwork for his epic poem *Jerusalem* to symbolize the Spectre, the annihilating and constricting energies in the human psyche. Bats also appear in Francisco Goya's *Los Caprichos* (1796-98), where they hover above the figure of Reason in "The Sleep of Reason Produces Monsters" and behind the babies in "There is Plenty to Suck."

Although bats and vampires were often connected by the mid-nineteenth century (for example, they appear on the cover page of *Varney the Vampyre),* it was not until *Dracula* (1897) that they became inextricably associated. In *Dracula,* the bat is one of the creatures of the night that Dracula rules and into which he can transform. The bat appears early in the story and hovers outside the window of **Jonathan Harker**'s room at **Castle Dracula.** Later, Harker observes Dracula assuming batlike characteristics as he crawls down the outside wall of the castle. Once the action transfers to England, Dracula's presence is more often signaled by the bat than by his human form. Dracula's appearances in bat form are always at night, and the association of the vampire with the bat contributed substantively to the twentieth-century understanding of the vampire as an exclusively nocturnal being.

With the popularization of vampires in the post-World War II West, the bat became one of the most common images at horror movies and Halloween. Naturalists who study bats have carried on a ''public relations'' program for them because they believe bats have a bad image as a result of their popular association with Dracula.

Sources:

Allen, Glover Morrill. *Bats.* New York: Dover Publications, 1939, pp. 1-25.

Darwin, Charles. *Journal of researches into the Natural history and Geology of the Countries Visited during the Voyage of H. M. S. Beagle Round the World.* London: John Murray, 1879, p. 22.

Hill, John E., and James D. Smith. *Bats: A Natural History.* London: British Museum, 1984, pp. 158-64.
Robertson, James. *The Complete Bat.* London: Chatto & Windus, 1990, pp. 62-72.

Turner, Dennis C. *The Vampire Bat: A Field Study in Behavior and Ecology.* Baltimore, MD: Johns Hopkins University Press, 1975, pp. 1-7.

BAVA, MARIO (1914-1980)

Mario Bava was the horror film director responsible for several of the most memorable vampire films of the 1960s. He was born on July 31, 1914, in San Remo, Italy, the son of Eugenio Bava, a pioneer Italian cameraman. Bava followed his father's occupation and entered the film industry in the 1930s as World War II began. He worked as a cameraman for two decades before he became a director. The disruption of the industry through the 1940s limited the number of features he worked on; but beginning in 1950, he worked on one or more films almost every year. His first directing work was in 1956 when Riccardo Freda quit his directing position in the middle of filming *I Vampiri,* one of several movies inspired by the **Elizabeth Bathory** legend. Bava was asked to finish the film, and his directing career was born.

In 1960, Bava directed *La Maschera del Demonio,* now an important and classic vampire film. Among other things, the film lifted its female lead, **Barbara Steele,** to stardom, at least among horror movie fans. The story concerned a seventeenth century witch, Princess Ada, who was killed by having a spiked mask (hence the name of the movie) driven onto her face. She was revived by a drop of blood that fell on her tomb simultaneously with the arrival of a present-day double named Katia (also portrayed by Steele). Princess Ada, aided by Dominici, a vampire, attempted to find a new life by taking over the body of Katia.

La Maschera del Demonia (released in the United States as *Black Sunday* and in Great Britain as *Revenge of the Vampire*) was a black and white feature, but it set the stage for Bava's color productions later in the decade. While Bava often made his films on a low budget, he became known for his ability to take inexpensive sets and, through the utilization of light, convey the gothic atmosphere of the supernatural world. Bava believed in the worlds of the real and the unreal, the natural and the supernatural, and felt that he lived his life at the border between the two. At that borderland horror arose and intruded upon normal reality, and Bava assumed that each person was more or less aware of the presence of that borderland in their own life. In his films, the psychological state of his characters was more important than the plot, which led many viewers to complain about the slow movement and lack of action in Bava productions. Although his plots moved slowly at times, Bava had no problem showing explicit violence on the screen. *La Maschera del Demonio* was banned in

England for many years and faced problems with censors in both Canada and Mexico. Several of its scenes were edited before release in the United States.

Before the 1960s were over, Bava made four more movies that featured vampirism. After *Black Sunday,* Bava returned to the vampire theme in 1961 with *Ercole al Centro della Terra* (released in the United States as *Hercules in the Haunted World*). Bava brought in **Christopher Lee** from England to play Lico the vampire, Hercules opponent. He then returned to Russian literature for inspiration. (*Black Sunday* was based on a story by Nicolas Gogol). *I tre Volti della Paura* (released in the United States as *Black Sabbath,* an attempt to associate it with the very successful *Black Sunday*) consisted of three short stories brought together to create a full-length feature. The third story (in the American version) was a rather faithful adaptation of **Alexey Tolstoy**'s *The Wurdalak,* and was notable for the only appearance of horror superstar Boris Karloff as a vampire. He played a peasant who returned to his home to attack his family.

Sei Donne per l'Assassino (released in the United States as *Blood and Black Lace*) was the bloodiest of Bava's vampire movies. He took a mystery story and rewrote it as a vampire tale. In the movie, the vampire was shown as a serial killer who attacked models at a beauty salon. When found, each victim was half-naked, disfigured, and drained of blood. Blood abounded on the screen, and Bava dwelt on the gore as a means of drawing the audience into the mind of the killer.

In 1965, Bava made his last vampire movie, *Terrore nello Spazio* (released in the United States as the *Planet of the Vampires*), which turned out to be one of the pioneering **science fiction** vampire motion pictures. In the film, a space crew lands on another planet and encounters vampires. The vampires take over the ship and, as the movie ends, are preparing to invade Earth.

Bava continued to make movies regularly through the mid-1970s. He spent part of that time in the United States making some of the early ''splatter'' movies. His *Blood and Black Lace* served as somewhat of a transition film into this emerging horror genre. He directed his last movie, *La Venere dell'ille,* in 1979, the year before his death.

While Bava made more than 20 movies, his vampire movies were his most memorable. Although the vampire movies were only a small percentage of his total output, his name belongs on the short list of directors who made the most vampire movies during their careers.

Sources:

Flynn, John L. *Cinematic Vampires.* Jefferson, NC: McFarland & Company, 1992.
Guariento, Steve. "Bava Fever!" *Samhain* Part 1, 37 (March/April 1993): 22-26; Part 2, 38 (May/June 1993): 23-26; Part 3, 40 (September/October 1993): 22-26.
Parish, James Robert. *Film Directors Guide: Western Europe.* Metuchen, NJ: Scarecrow Press, 1976.
Quinlan, David. *The Illustrated Guide to Film Directors.* Totowa, NJ: Barnes & Noble Books, 1984.

Thompson, David. *A Biographical Dictionary of Film.* New York: William Morrow and Company, 1976.
Ursini, James, and Alain Silver. *The Vampire Film.* South Brunswick, NJ: A. S. Barns and Company, 1975.

BERGSTROM, ELAINE (1946-)

Elaine Bergstrom, a science fiction/horror fiction writer who has written five vampire books, was born in 1946 in Cleveland, Ohio. Bergstrom burst into the vampire scene in 1989 with the publication of *Shattered Glass,* a novel that introduced a new vampire, Stephen Austra, and his vampire family. They were an old and powerful family who quietly existed as glass workers, specifically the special leaded glass that went into the old cathedrals of Europe and their modern imitations. *Shattered Glass* brought Austra to the United States where he met artist Helen Wells, who he turned into a vampire like himself. She became a continuing part of his story. The initial conflict concerned Austra's renegade brother who forced the ''good'' Stephen into a final showdown. Included in the novel was one of the more horrific chapters in vampire literature—Austra's brother surprised the two lovers in bed in a hotel room and proceeded to vampirize them in a slow torturous act.

◀

NOVELIST ELAINE BERGSTROM

Austra and Helen Wells' story was resumed in two subsequent novels, *Blood Alone* (1990) and *Blood Rites* (1991). Bergstrom's fourth vampire novel, *Daughter of the Night* (1992), was based on the life of **Elizabeth Bathory** and was especially inspired by its treatment in **Raymond T. McNally**'s biographical study, *Dracula Was a Woman*. Bergstrom recently developed a novel around the characters of TSR, Inc.'s *Ravencroft,* one of the vampire-oriented, role-playing **games.** Called *Tapestry of Dark Souls,* the book was published in 1993. Other vampire novels have been planned.

Sources:

Bergstrom, Elaine. *Blood Alone.* New York: Jove Books, 1990.
———. *Blood Rites.* New York: Jove Books, 1991.
———. *Daughter of the Night.* New York: Jove Books, 1992.
———. *Shattered Glass.* New York: Jove Books, 1989.
———. *Tapestry of Dark Souls.* Geneva, WI: TSR, Inc., 1993.

BERWICK, THE VAMPIRE OF

Among the incidents of vampirism reported by **William of Newburgh** in his *Chronicles,* completed in 1196 A.D., was the case of the Berwick vampire. The subject of the account was a rather wealthy man who lived in the twelfth century in the town of Berwick in the northern part of England near the Scottish border. After his death, the townspeople reported seeing his body roaming through the streets at night keeping the dogs howling far into the evening. Fearful that a plague (associated with such revenants in popular lore) might attack the population, the townspeople decided to dismember the body and burn it. That action having been accomplished, the body no longer appeared in town; however, a disease did sweep through the town causing many deaths that were attributed to the after-effects of the vampire's presence.

Sources:

Glut, Donald G. *True Vampires of History.* New York: H C Publishers, 1971.

BHUTA See: INDIA, VAMPIRES IN

BIBLIOGRAPHY, VAMPIRE

Essential to the development of the modern movement of vampire enthusiasts and of scholarship on the subject has been the bibliographical work done by a small group of dedicated researchers/collectors. Besides the rather brief bibliographies in some of the more important volumes of vampire studies, an early comprehensive attempt to list vampire titles can be found in Donald Glut's *The Dracula Book* (1975). However, Glut limited himself to the single character Dracula rather than vampires in general. The first attempt to compile a comprehensive bibliography of English-language vampire literature (both fiction and nonfiction) appeared in 1983. *Vampires Un-*

earthed was compiled by **Martin V. Riccardo** and became the basis of all future vampire bibliographical work.

Literary vampires have received the most attention. Beginning in the mid-1970s, **Margaret L. Carter** began to compile a bibliography of English-language fictional works on the vampire. Her work has resulted in a series of publications combining her interests in bibliography and literary criticism. Her earlier works, *Shadow of a Shade: A Survey of Vampirism in Literature* (1975), *Specter or Delusion? The Supernatural in Gothic Fiction* (1987), and *Dracula: The Vampire and the Critics* (1988), culminated in her more comprehensive *The Vampire in Literature: A Critical Bibliography* (1989). To deal with the vast outpouring of new vampire fiction and to add references to items missed in the 1989 work, Carter produces an annual supplement. Carter's work is especially notable for her attention to the vampire in short fiction, the only such listing that has been attempted. Carter has also compiled anthologies of vampire fiction, written vampire short stories, and edited a vampire fiction magazine.

The new popularity of vampire fiction was further demonstrated by an excellent annotated bibliography of vampire literature compiled by Greg Cox. *The Transylvanian Library: A Consumer's Guide to Vampire Fiction* (1993) provides a light, but no less useful, romp through the world of the literary vampire from **John Polidori**'s original tale ''The Vampyre,'' through the novels of 1988. Cox is an assistant editor for TOR Books, which has published a number of vampire books including the novels of **Brian Lumley** and **Chelsea Quinn Yarbro.**

Of a more serious nature is Brian Frost's *Monster with a Thousand Faces* (1989), which also covers vampire fiction through the nineteenth and twentieth centuries and is notable for its discussion of many obscure works.

While most of the bibliographical work was being done in North America, at least one important effort occurred in Europe. Author and anthologist Jacques Finné, who has produced a number of titles in fantasy and horror literature, produced the *Bibliographie de Dracula* in 1986 . This book-length annotated work, which built upon Riccardo's earlier effort, is important for its inclusion of non-English titles.

Most recently, **comic books,** treated in a chapter by Riccardo, have become an important home to the vampire. An exhaustive bibliography was compiled by J. Gordon Melton and appeared in 1994 as *The Vampire in the Comic Book* by the **The Count Dracula Fan Club.**

The comprehensive efforts of Riccardo, Carter, Cox, Frost, Finné, and Melton have been most useful to scholars, but they have been supplemented by a variety of selective bibliographies which have circulated widely among enthusiasts. For example, Eric Held of the **Vampire Information Exchange** has regularly published lists of vampire literature, music, and films in the *V.I.E. Newsletter.* In 1992 he issued a 35-page *Vampire Bibliography of Fiction and Non-Fiction,* a selected listing with some brief annotations for the members of the V.I.E.

Sources:

Carter, Margaret L. *Dracula: The Vampire and the Critics.* Ann Arbor, MI: UMI Research Press, 1988.

———. *Shadow of a Shade: A Survey of Vampirism in Literature.* New York: Gordon Press, 1975.

———. *Specter or Delusion? The Supernatural in Gothic Fiction.* Ann Arbor, MI: UMI Research Press, 1987. A revision of Ph.D. dissertation at the University of California-Irvine.

———. *The Vampire in Literature: A Critical Bibliography.* Ann Arbor, MI: UMI Research Press, 1989.

Cox, Greg. *The Transylvanian Library: A Consumer's Guide to Vampire Fiction.* San Bernadino, CA: Borgo Press, 1993. Finné, Jacques. *Bibliographie de Dracula.* Lausanne, Switzerland: L'Age d'Homme, 1986.

Frost, Brian. *Monster with a Thousand Faces.* Bowling Green, OH: Bowling Green State University Press, 1989. Glut, Donald F. *The Dracula Book.* Metuchen, NJ: Scarecrow Press, 1975.

Melton, J. Gordon. *The Vampire in the Comic Book.* New York: Count Dracula Fan Club, 1994.

Riccardo, Martin V. *Vampires Unearthed: The Complete Multi-Media Vampire and Dracula Bibliography.* New York: Garland Publishing, 1983.

BISTRITZ

Bistritz (or Bistrita) is a town of some 35,000 inhabitants located in northeastern **Transylvania** in present-day **Romania.** It entered into the world of vampires as the first location visited by **Jonathan Harker,** in **Bram Stoker**'s novel, *Dracula.* It is only 50 miles from **Borgo Pass** where Harker was met by the carriage that took him to **Castle Dracula.** Bistritz was an old German settlement and the tower of the German Church found there is still the highest in all of **Romania.** Harker's account mentions a series of fires between 1836 and 1850 that destroyed much of the old town. In Stoker's day, the town had approximately 12,000 residents.

While there Harker stayed at the Golden Krone Hotel. Unlike the very real Bistritz, the Golden Krone is a complete fiction, or at least it was. In 1974, in order to take advantage of the tourists interested in Dracula, a Golden Krone Hotel was opened, and the meal Harker ate while at the hotel was placed on the menu. ''Robber steak'' consisted of bits of bacon, onion, and beef roasted on an open fire together with red pepper on a stick. It was served with Mediasch wine. Today a tourist at the Golden Krone can also dine on ''Elixir Dracula,'' (a red liquor made from plums), stuffed cabbage Birgau, Dracula cakes, and Dracula red **wine.** The hotel also sells a line of Dracula **paraphernalia** and souvenirs.

Sources:

McKenzie, Andrew. *Dracula Country.* London: Arthur Barker, 1977.

BITE ME IN THE COFFIN NOT IN THE CLOSET FAN CLUB

Bite Me in the Coffin Not in the Closet Fan Club is a vampire fan organization for gay and lesbian people who have an interest in vampires and vampirism. Founder Jeff Flaster is the editor of the club's monthly fanzine, which publishes short fiction for and about gay and lesbian vampires, contact information for members, and other items of interest.

Bite Me in the Coffin Not in the Closet may be contacted c/o Jeff Flaster, 72 Sarah Ln., Middletown, NY 10940.

BLACULA

In the late 1960s the movie industry began to generate a series of movies specifically directed toward the African American community. While the vampire was essentially a European folk character, and there have been only a few references to vampires in **Africa** or in African American lore, it was inevitable that "blaxploitation" producers would consider the possibilities of a Black vampire motion picture. In 1972 the first of the two most important **African American vampire** movies, *Blacula,* starring **William Marshall,** appeared.

Blacula told the story of Prince Mamuwalde, an African leader in 1780 who was trying to find a way to stop the slave trade which haunted Africa's west coast. He

WILLIAM MARSHALL, STAR OF *BLACULA,* ACCEPTS AN AWARD FROM THE COUNT DRACULA SOCIETY.

sought out Count Dracula (Charles Macaulay) to obtain his assistance in the endeavor. Dracula merely laughed at the Prince, who with his wife, Luva, started to leave. Before they could get away, however, they were attacked by Dracula and his vampire cohorts. Mamuwalde was vampirized and sealed in a tomb. Luva was left to die of starvation, unable to help her husband as Dracula cursed Mamuwalde to become Blacula, his African counterpart.

The story then switched to 1965 when some Americans purchased the furnishings of **Castle Dracula** and shipped them to Los Angeles, unaware that the ornate coffin they had obtained housed Blacula's body. Blacula was awakened and discovered a new love, Tina, the exact image of his Luva. As the plot progressed, she fell victim to a shooting incident, and he turned her into a vampire to save her. But then she was staked to death, and in his grief Blacula committed **suicide** by walking into the **sunlight.**

Blacula was revived by the magic of voodoo a year later in a sequel, *Scream Blacula Scream.* In collusion with the voodoo priestess Lisa, he searched for a way to rid himself of his vampirism, but was thwarted by the police. In a novel, but entirely appropriate, twist of the storyline, he was killed by a pin stuck through the heart of a voodoo doll.

Because of the large audience of vampire movie enthusiasts, the *Blacula* movies have had a heightened popularity and joined the list of those few blaxploitation films which found a broad audience beyond the African American community. *Blacula* was awarded the Ann Radcliffe Award by the **The Count Dracula Society.**

Sources:

Flynn, John L. *Cinematic Vampires.* Jefferson, NC: McFarland and Company, 1992.
Gross, Edward, and Marc Shapiro. *The Vampire Interview Book: Conversations with the Undead.* East Meadow, NY: Image Publishing, 1991.

BLADE THE VAMPIRE SLAYER

In April 1971, following the change in the Comics Code that allowed vampires to return to **comic books,** Marvel Comics introduced its new vampire comic book, ***The Tomb of Dracula.*** It brought the story of ***Dracula*** into the 1970s and brought together descendants of the characters in **Bram Stoker**'s novel to fight the revived vampire. During the course of the long running series, Marvel also introduced several new characters. Among the most enduring was Blade the Vampire Slayer. Blade, an African American, further reflected the social changes in post World War II America previously noted by readers in the appearance of a woman, Rachel Van Helsing, as a strong weapon-carrying vampire slayer who assumed the role once held by her grandfather, **Abraham Van Helsing.**

Blade was a warrior equipped with a set of teakwood knives. He initially appeared in the July 1973 (No. 10) issue of *The Tomb of Dracula* on the London docks, where he proceeded to kill several vampire members of Dracula's Legion.

Their deaths led to Blade meeting Quincy Harker and Rachel Van Helsing. After introductions, the action took Blade to the ship *Michelle* over which Dracula had assumed control. Their initial confrontation ended in a draw, but Dracula escaped and the ship was destroyed by an explosion. Blade returned two issues later to help Harker and Frank Drake (a modern descendent of Dracula) find Harker's daughter Edith who had been kidnapped by Dracula.

The story of Blade's early involvement with vampires was finally told in the October 1973 (No. 13) issue. At the time of his birth, his mother was visited by a physician, Deacon Frost who turned out to be a vampire. Frost killed his mother, and Blade dedicated his life to looking for him. That search grew into an enmity against all vampires and led him to the recently revived Dracula. He had worked primarily in America, and thus had never met Harker, Van Helsing, or Drake, but had heard about their activities.

Blade frequently reappeared through the 70 issues of *The Tomb of Dracula*. He also made a guest appearance in the Fall 1976 issue (No. 8) of *Marvel Preview*. The battle between Blade and Dracula seemed to reach a conclusion when Blade stuck one of his knives into Dracula, who apparently died. However, others stole the body, the knife was removed, and Dracula was revived. Later, Dracula seemed to win when he bit Blade. But it turned out that because of the unusual circumstances involving the vampire present at the time of Blade's birth, Blade was immune to the vampire state.

In the June 1976 issue (No. 48), Blade teamed with another new character introduced into *The Tomb of Dracula,* Hannibal King. He, too, had an encounter with Deacon Frost, the vampire that killed Blade's mother. In the February 1977 issue (No. 53) the two finally tracked Frost down and destroyed him.

Vampires were banished from Marvel Comics in 1983, and very few characters from *The Tomb of Dracula* appeared during the next six years. Blade practically disappeared, but quickly made his presence felt after the reintroduction of vampires into the Marvel Universe in issues 10 and 14 of *Dr. Strange: Sorcerer Supreme* (November 1989, February 1990). Blade next appeared in the revival by Epic Comics (a subsidiary of Marvel) of *The Tomb of Dracula* (1991-1992), which resumed the story from the end of the first series without reference to the banishment of vampires and the destruction of Dracula in 1983.

In 1992 Marvel united its older occult-oriented characters and created some new ones when it created a new realm on the edge of the Marvel Universe that would be the arena of the **Midnight Sons.** In this new storyline, vampires had been banished from the world in 1983 by a magical formula of Marvel's master of the occult arts, Dr. Strange. His magical operation created the Montesi effect. That effect was being weakened and allowed a new assault upon the world by the forces of supernatural evil. These forces were led by **Lilith** (the ancient Hebrew demoness, not Dracula's daughter).

The new evil forced the return of the old vampire fighters, including Blade, who received a new image more akin to Marvel's other super-heroes and had his weapons system upgraded. The fresh storyline was created simultaneously in five different comic book titles under the collective heading **Midnight Sons.** Blade and his old acquaintances Frank Drake and Hannibal King united as a private investigation organization, *The Nightstalkers*. The adventures of *The Nightstalkers* lasted until early in 1994 when both Drake and King were killed in the war with the supernatural forces of evil. Blade survived to continue the fight in his own new comic book series *Blade, the Vampire-Hunter*.

Sources:

The Nightstalkers. Nos. 1-18. New York: Marvel Comics, 1992-1994.
The Tomb of Dracula. 4 vols. New York: Epic Comics, 1991.
The Tomb of Dracula. 70 vols. New York: Marvel Comics, 1971-1979.

BLUATSAUGER See: GERMANY, VAMPIRES IN

BLOOD

Nothing has so defined the vampire as its relationship to blood. The vampire was essentially a bloodsucker, a creature who lived off of the blood of humans. Quite early in his visit to **Castle Dracula, Jonathan Harker** was lectured by his host on the general importance of blood. He noted that the **Szekelys,** ''we of the Dracula blood,'' helped to throw off the despised Hungarian yoke. He further noted, in a line which soon would take on a double meaning, ''Blood is too precious a thing in these days of dishonorable peace . . . '' (Chapter 3) As Harker tried to understand his desperate situation, he noted that **Dracula** had bad breath with ''a bitter offensiveness, as one smells in blood.'' He discovered the secret when he found Dracula asleep with his mouth redder than ever and ''on the lips were gouts of fresh blood, which trickled from the corners of the mouth and ran over the chin and neck. . . . It seemed as if the whole awful creature were simply gorged with blood; he lay like a filthy leech, exhausted with his repletion.'' Harker lamented his role in freeing Dracula on **London.**

THE SIGNIFICANCE OF BLOOD: Since ancient times, humans have seen the connection between blood and life. Women made the connection between birth and their menstrual flow. Hunters observed the relationship between the spilling of blood and the subsequent loss of consciousness, the ceasing of breath, and eventual death of the animals they sought. And if an animal died of some cause with no outward wound, when cut, the blood often did not flow. Blood was identified with life, and thinkers through the ages produced endless speculations about that connection. People assigned various sacred and magical qualities to blood and used it in a variety of rituals. People drank it, rubbed it on their bodies, and manipulated it in ceremonies.

Some believed that by drinking the blood of a victim the conqueror absorbed the additional strength of the conquered. By drinking the blood of an animal one took on its qualities. As late as the seventeenth century, the women of the Yorkshire area of

England were reported to believe that by drinking the blood of their enemies they could increase their fecundity.

Among blood's more noticeable qualities was its red color as it flowed out of the body, and as a result redness came to be seen as an essential characteristic of blood, the vehicle of its power. Red objects were often endowed with the same potency as blood. In particular, red wine was identified with blood, and in ancient **Greece,** for example, red wine was drunk by the devotees of the god Dionysus in a symbolic ritual drinking of his blood.

Blood was (and continues to be) seen as somehow related to the qualities possessed by an individual, and beliefs carried references to admirable people as having "good" blood or evil persons as possessing "bad" blood. The blood of the mother was passed to the child, and with it the virtues and defects of the parents were passed to any offspring. Thus blood, in a somewhat literal sense, carried the essential characteristics of the larger collectives—families, clans, national/ethnic groups, even whole races. Such beliefs underlie the modern myth which permitted the Nazi purge of Jews and other supposed lesser races and the practices in American blood banks until recent decades to separate "negro" blood from that of "white" people.

To a lesser extent, blood was identified with other body fluids, most notably semen. In the process of creating a baby, men do not supply blood, only their seed. Thus it was through the semen that male characteristics were passed to the child. In the mythology of race, each of the body fluids—semen, the blood that flowed when the hymen was broken, and menstrual blood—were associated together as part of the sexual life and ascribed magical properties. This association was quite explicit in the sexual teaching of modern ritual magic.

BLOOD IN THE BIBLICAL TRADITION: The ancient Jewish leaders made the same identification of blood and life. In the biblical book of Genesis, God tells Noah,

> But you must not eat the flesh with the life, which is the blood, still in it. And further, for your life-blood I will demand satisfaction; from every animal will I require it, and from a man also will require satisfaction for the death of his fellow-man.

> He that shed the blood of a man, for that man his blood shall be shed; for in the image of God has God made man.

Israel instituted a system of blood sacrifice in which animal blood was shed as an offering to God for the sins of the people. The book of Leviticus included detailed rules for such offerings with special attention given to the proper priestly actions to be taken with the blood. The very first chapter stated the simple rules for offering a bull. It was to be slaughtered before the Tent of the Presence, and the priest was to present the blood and then fling it against the altar. The mysterious sacredness of the blood was emphasized in that God reserved it to himself. The remaining blood was spilled before the altar, and strictures were announced against the people eating the blood. "Every person who eats the blood shall be cut off from his father's kin" (Lev.7:27).

Special rules were also established for women concerning their menstrual flow and the flow of blood that accompanied childbirth. Both made a woman ritually impure, and purification rituals had to be performed before she could again enter a sanctuary. In like measure, the discharge of semen caused a man to be ritually impure.

The most stringent rules concerning blood were in that section of Leviticus called the Holiness Code, a special set of rules stressing the role of the people, as opposed to the priest, in being holy before God. Very early in the code, the people are told:

> If any Israelite or alien settled in Israel eats blood, I will see my face against the eater; and cut him off from his people, because the life of a creature is the blood, and I appoint it to make expiation on the altar for yourselves; for the blood is the life that makes expiation. Therefore I have told the Israelites that neither you, nor any alien settled among you, shall eat blood.

Indeed, ''For the blood is the life'' has been the most quoted Biblical phrase in the vampire literature.

Christianity took Jewish belief and practice to its extreme and logical conclusion. Following his death and (as Christians believe) his resurrection, Jesus, its founder, was worshipped as an incarnation of God who died at the hands of Roman executioners. Christians depicted his death as a human sacrifice, analogous, yet far more powerful, than the Jewish animal sacrifices. As the accounts of his last days were assembled Jesus instituted the Lord's Supper during which he took a cup of wine and told his disciples, ''Drink from it, all of you. For this is my blood, the blood of the covenant, shed for many for the forgiveness of sins'' (Matthew 26: 27). Following his sentencing of Jesus, the Roman governor Pilate washed his hands and told the crowd who had demanded Jesus' death, ''My hands are clean of this man's blood.'' The crowd replied, ''His blood be upon us, and on our children'' (Matthew 27:24-26). As he hung on the cross, a soldier pierced his side with a lance, and his blood flowed from the wound.

Early Christian thought on the significance of Christ's death was clearly presented in the Apocalypse (The Book of Revelation) in which John spoke of Jesus as the one who ''freed us from our sins with his life's blood'' (Revelation 1:5). He admonished those suffering persecution by picturing their glory in heaven as the martyrs for the faith. They wore a white robe which had been washed in the blood of the Lamb.

In Christian lands, to the common wisdom concerning life and blood, theological reflection added a special importance to blood. The blood of Christ, in the form of the red **wine** of the Eucharist, became the most sacred of objects. So holy had the wine become that during the Middle Ages a great controversy arose over allowing the laity to have the cup. Because of possible carelessness with the wine, the Roman Catholic Church denied the cup, a practice which added more fuel to the fire of the Protestant Reformation of the sixteenth century.

In the light of the special sacredness of Christ's blood, the vampire, at least in its European appearances, took on added significance. The vampire drank blood in direct defiance of the biblical command. It defiled the holy and stole that which was reserved for God alone.

THE VAMPIRE AND HEMATOLOGY: The vampire myth arose, of course, prior to modern medicine. It has been of some interest that *Dracula* was written just as modern medicine was emerging, and **Bram Stoker** mixed traditional lore about blood with the new medicine. **Lucy Westenra,** even as she anticipated her marriage to **Arthur Holmwood,** lay hovering near death. Reacting quickly, Dr. **Abraham Van Helsing** gathered Holmwood and Lucy's two other suitors, **Quincey P. Morris** and Dr. **John Seward,** to apply a wholly unique scientific remedy to the vampire's attack. He had diagnosed a loss of blood, and now Van Helsing ordered a transfusion, at the time a new medical option. He and each of Lucy's suitors in turn gave her their blood. Following her death, Holmwood, in his grief and disappointment, made the observation that in the giving of blood he had in fact married Lucy and that in the sight of God they were husband and wife. Van Helsing, assuming his scientific role, countered his idea by suggesting that such an observation would make Lucy a polyandrist and the previously married Van Helsing a bigamist.

The idea of using a transfusion to counter the vampire introduced a new concern into the developing myth of the vampire through the twentieth century, especially as the supernatural elements of the myth were being discarded. If vampirism was not a supernatural state, and rather was caused ultimately by a moral or theological flaw of the original vampires, then possibly the blood thirst was the symptom of a diseased condition, caused by a germ or a chemical disorder of the blood, either of which might be passed by the vampire's bite. In the mid-1960s there was brief, yet serious, medical speculation that vampirism was the result of misdiagnosed **porphyria,** a disease that causes its victims to be sensitive to **sunlight** and which could be cured or helped. Increasingly through the century, as knowledge of the minute details concerning the function and makeup of human blood were explored by research specialists, novelists and screenwriters toyed with the idea of vampirism as a disease.

During the last years of the **pulp fiction** era, writers such as Robert Bloch, George Whitley, David H. Keller, and William Tenn suggested the diseased origin of vampirism in a series of short stories. For example, in William Tenn's 1956 short story "She Only Goes Out at Night," Tom Judd, the son of a village doctor, falls in love with a strange woman. Tom's father coincidentally discovered an epidemic in town whose victims were all anemic. The woman, who had just moved to town, was a Romanian by descent and only came out at night. Putting the sudden wave of **anemia** together with the behavior patterns of the woman, the wise old doctor suggested she was a vampire. As he explained it, the vampire condition was passed from parent to child, though usually only one child in each generation developed it. His son still wanted to marry the woman. He responded with a medical observation, "Vampirism may have been an incurable disease in the fifteenth century, but I am sure it can be handled in the twentieth." Her symptoms suggested she had an allergy to the sun, for which he prescribed sunglasses and hormone injections. He then dealt with her blood thirst by supplying her with dehydrated crystalline blood which she mixed with water and drank once a day. The vampire and Tom lived happily ever after.

Vampirism as disease came powerfully to the fore in the late 1960s television series *Dark Shadows.* Dr. Julia Hoffman was introduced into the show to treat the problems of Maggie Evans, one of the show's main characters. A short time after her initial appearance, she met **Barnabas Collins** and discovered that he was a vampire. Rather than seek to destroy him, however, she devised a plan to assist him in a cure of his vampiric condition. Collins soon grew impatient and demanded that the process be speeded up. His body did not react favorably to the increased dosages of Hoffman's medicines, and he reverted to his true age—200 years old. He was able to revive his youth by biting a young woman, and he then turned on Hoffman. Hoffman was able to thwart his efforts by threatening him with her research book, which contained all the details of her treatments and revealed Collins's true nature. Before Barnabas could locate the book, he and the storyline were transported into the past, to 1795.

Shortly after his return to the present (1968), Collins was in a car accident. Hospitalized, he received a transfusion that temporarily cured him. He was a human and for the first time in 200 years was able to walk in the sunlight. He was, however, returned to his vampiric state by the bite of his former love, Angelique Bouchard, who had died and returned as a vampire.

A character similar to Hoffman also appeared in the recent television series, *Forever Knight.* Nicolas Knight, the show's vampire, was a policeman on the Toronto police force. His friend and confidante was Dr. Natalie Lambert, a forensic pathologist. Throughout the series, she sought a means to transform Knight into a human, but with negative results to date.

In the decades since World War II, novelists have also explored the idea that a diseased condition produced vampirism. Simon Raven's *Doctors Wear Scarlet* (1960), for example, described vampirism as a form of ''sado-sexual perversion.'' The story sent the hero, Richard Fountain, to Greece to escape an oppressive personal situation in England. In Greece he met a beautiful vampiress who slowly drained his blood. He was rescued before he was killed and returned safe to his British home.

Jan Jennings' *Vampyr* (1981) brought a research scientist into a relationship with Valan Anderwalt, a vampiress. The scientist, in love with Valan, tried to find the causes of her state. He traced vampirism to ancient China and found it to be a contagious physical condition which had been brought to America by the early Dutch colonists. Unfortunately, he was not able to make any progress in curing her.

That same year Whitley Strieber introduced an interesting triangle relationship in *The Hunger.* Miriam Blaylock was an immortal alien vampire. She was on earth and could transform humans into vampires. Such human vampires, however, were not immortal and began to age and disintegrate after several centuries passed. Not wishing to lose another companion, Blaylock sought out the services of an expert in longevity, Sarah Roberts, in the hopes that she would be able to save John, her present male companion. Unfortunately, no solution presented itself before John succumbed to his deteriorating condition.

Most recently, Dan Simmons sent his leading character, Kate Neuman, a hematologist, into post-revolutionary **Romania** in *Children of the Night*. The book began with her using her knowledge of rare blood diseases to treat people in Bucharest. While there, she fell in love with a seven-month-old boy, Joshua, presumedly an orphan. He was unique in that he required biweekly transfusions to stay alive. He also had unusual blood which, she came to believe, held the clue to cures for AIDS, cancer, and other blood diseases. She arranged his adoption and brought him home with her to Colorado. Soon after, the boy was kidnapped and returned to Romania. In the exciting climax of the story, she was forced to return to Romania and to face the boy's father, **Vlad the Impaler,** the real Dracula. Dracula was dying, and his son, Joshua, was to become the leader of the family in his place.

CONCLUSION: The traditional beliefs that surrounded blood, the medical exploration of its properties, and the analogies it harbored to life itself, facilitated the adaptability of the vampire myth to a seemingly endless number of situations. Such adaptability has provided an understanding of why the vampire myth has stayed alive and has so many devotees to this day. Scientific considerations of the vital function played by blood in the human body have, if anything, given it an even more mystical place in human life and promoted its resacralization in this post-secular society.

Sources:

Cox, Greg. *The Transylvanian Library: A Consumer's Guide to Vampire Fiction.* San Bernadino, CA: Borgo Press, 1993. Scott, Kathryn Leigh, ed. *The Dark Shadows Companion: 25th Anniversary Collection.* Los Angeles: Pomegranate Press, 1990.
Simmons, Dan. *Children of the Night.* New York: G. P. Putnam's Sons, 1992.
Strieber, Whitley. *The Hunger.* New York: William Morrow, 1981.
Teem, William. "She Only Goes Out at Night." *Fantastic Universe* 6, 3 (October 1956). Rept. in: *Weird Vampire Tales.* Ed. by Robert Weinberg, Stefan R. Dziemianowicz, and Martin H. Greenberg. New York: Gramercy Press, 1992.

BLOOD DRINKING *See:* CRIME, VAMPIRIC

BORGO PASS

A mountain pass in **Transylvania** (at the time a part of **Hungary** and now located in **Romania**) made famous in the opening chapter of **Bram Stoker**'s *Dracula,* Borgo Pass (or Birgau Pass) is an oft-trod passageway through the Carpathian Mountains in Eastern Europe. *Dracula* opened with the journey of **Jonathan Harker** to **Castle Dracula.** Arriving at the city of **Bistritz,** he received a letter from Count Dracula directing him to the Borgo Pass (which begins near the town of Tihucza). The next day he took the coach from Bistritz to Bukovina and was let out at the Pass. Here he was met by a coach with a mysterious driver (later revealed to be Count Dracula himself) and taken to Castle Dracula. The scene at Borgo Pass has been most effectively used over the years in the various Dracula movies to build an initial atmosphere of foreboding.

Sources:

The Annotated Dracula. Edited by Leonard Wolf. New York: Ballantine Books, 1975.

THE BRAM STOKER CLUB *See:* THE BRAM STOKER SOCIETY

THE BRAM STOKER SOCIETY

The Bram Stoker Society was founded in 1980 to encourage the study and appreciation of the work of **Bram Stoker,** the author of *Dracula.* The society has developed a program to promote the appreciation of Stoker's work, especially as it relates to his life in Ireland, his birthplace. The society encourages research into the Irish associations of the Stoker family, promotes tourism connected with Stoker and other Irish gothic novelists (such as **Sheridan Le Fanu**), and campaigns for plaques to be placed on the Irish sites associated with the Stoker family. In 1983, partially in response to the society's efforts, a plaque was placed at No. 30 Kildare Street in Dublin, where Stoker resided in 1871. Stoker's granddaughter Ann Stoker, and his grandnephew Ivan Stoker-Dixon, attended the unveiling of the plaque, sponsored by the Irish Tourist Board.

In September 1986, the society suspended its independent existence and reorganized as The Bram Stoker Club of the Philosophical Society in Trinity College, Dublin. Stoker was at one time president of the Philosophical Society. On the occasion of the inauguration of the society, the Bram Stoker Archives were opened. The archives consisted of **Leslie Shepard**'s collection of Bram Stoker materials (first editions, autographs, and other memorabilia) on display in the Graduate Memorial Building. The exhibition was intended to be on permanent public display, but the issue of lack of proper security for the collection led Shepard to withdraw the materials from the room in May 1989.

In the wake of the disruption caused by the withdrawal of the collection, the society reorganized separately from the club and the college. The club has continued in existence as an approved independent body in Trinity College, and is affiliated with the Bram Stoker Society in Dublin. It currently sponsors the Bram Stoker International Summer School for a weekend each June (since 1991), held in Clontarf, Dublin, near where Stoker was born. It publishes a newsletter and an annual journal. It has pressed for the establishment of a permanent Bram Stoker museum in Dublin, a goal yet to be realized. Leslie Shepard, editor of *The Dracula Book of Great Vampire Stories,* is currently the chairman of the society. It may be contacted through David Lass, Hon. Secretary, The Bram Stoker Club and Society, Regent House, Trinity College, Dublin 2, Ireland.

◀

LESLIE SHEPARD, FOUNDER OF
THE BRAM STOKER SOCIETY

Sources:

Shepard, Leslie. *Encyclopedia of Occultism and Parapsychology.* 2 vols. Detroit, MI: Gale Research Inc., 3rd
 ed. 1991.

BRAM STOKER'S DRACULA

The most recent of the many attempts to bring the novel *Dracula,* by **Bram Stoker,** to
the motion picture screen appeared in 1992 from Columbia Pictures. Directed by one
of Hollywood's top directors, **Francis Ford Coppola,** it opened on Friday, November 13, and became the largest non-summer movie opening of all time.

Coppola had a goal of making a more accurate version of Stoker's original novel,
and his version relied more closely on the storyline of the book than any previous
Dracula movie. The story opened with **Jonathan Harker** (played by Keanu Reeves)
leaving his fiance, **Mina Murray** (Winona Ryder), to travel to **Castle Dracula** in
Transylvania. His first encounters with Dracula (Gary Oldman) reflected the major
incidents recorded in the book, though Dracula's colorful appearance could hardly

have been more different from his description in the novel. Their encounter as Harker was shaving produced one of the film's most memorable moments. Harker had cut himself, and Dracula took the razor from Harker and licked it to taste the drops of blood. Harker was attacked by the three female **vampire brides,** residents of the castle, and was only able to escape after Dracula left for England.

In England, the three suitors of **Lucy Westenra** (Sadie Frost)—**Quincey P. Morris** (Bill Campbell), **Arthur Holmwood** (Cary Elwes), and Dr. **John Seward** (Richard E. Grant)—rose to the occasion as Dracula launched his attack on her. Unable at first to determine the cause of her problems, Seward called in Dr. **Abraham Van Helsing** (Anthony Hopkins). Van Helsing organized the opposition that finally defeated Dracula after tracking him back to his castle.

While Coppola's version of *Dracula* is by far the most faithful to the book, it deviated at several important points. For example, as a prelude to the movie, Coppola briefly told the story of **Vlad the Impaler,** the fifteenth-century Romanian ruler who served as a historical reference for the Dracula character. This prelude indicated the influence of the books by **Raymond T. McNally** and **Radu Florescu** that created fans for Vlad, the historical Dracula. In introducing the theme of Vlad the Impaler, Coppola borrowed an idea from the **Dan Curtis/Jack Palance** version of *Dracula* **(1973).** Curtis used Vlad's story to provide the rationale for Dracula's attack upon the specific women he chose as targets in England. In *Dracula* (1974), Palance saw a picture of Mina Murray, Harker's fiance, who was the mirror image of his lost love of the fifteenth century. He traveled to England in order to recapture the love of his pre-vampire life. In *Bram Stoker's Dracula,* Winona Ryder played not only Mina Murray, but Elizabeth, Dracula's original love. To continue the storyline, Coppola allowed Dracula to walk around **London** freely in the daytime (as Dracula seemed able to do in the novel), but he now used his time in the city to establish a liaison with Mina and with his suave continental manners win her love. In the final scene, Mina went to the dying Dracula and through her love facilitated his redemption as he died.

Vlad's reaction to the death of Elizabeth (or Elisabeta), who committed **suicide** and hence could not go to heaven in Eastern Orthodox theology, provided Coppola with an explanation of the origin of Dracula's vampirism. Since she could not go to heaven, Dracula blasphemed God and symbolically attacked the cross with his sword. Blood flowed from the impaled cross, Dracula drank, and presumedly as a result was transformed into a vampire.

Coppola also enlarged upon the account of **R. N. Renfield,** another character in the original novel who was introduced as a resident of the insane asylum managed by John Seward, with no explanation as to the reason for his being there. His mental condition was explained by Coppola as due to his having traveled to **Castle Dracula** and becoming insane because of his encounters with the residents. This earlier connection with Dracula also explained why he, but none of the other inmates of the asylum, reacted to Dracula's arrival and activities in London.

Bram Stoker's Dracula was accompanied by a massive advertising campaign which included more than 100 separate pieces of **paraphernalia** and souvenir items,

GARY OLDMAN AS DRACULA AND WINONA RYDER AS MINA MURRAY IN *BRAM STOKER'S DRACULA.*

including a novelization of the script, a four-issue comic book series, two sets of trading cards, jewelry, tee shirts, posters, a board game, and several home computer

games. The TNT cable television network sponsored a sweepstakes the week of the movie's opening that offered the winner a trip to London, "one of Dracula's favorite cities!" While it opened to mixed reviews (an occupational hazard with any horror genre film), the Coppola movie shows every sign of taking its place as one of the most memorable *Dracula* adaptations of all time. It opened in Bucharest, **Romania,** in July 1993, at which time a special drink, dubbed "Dracula's Spirits" and made of vodka and red fruit juice, was issued by a Romanian distillery. In spite of the mixed reviews, the movie surprised media observers by becoming the largest box office opening ever experienced by Columbia and the largest ever for a non-summer opening. It played on almost 2,500 screens around the country and grossed more than $32 million.

Sources:

Biowrowski, Steve. "Coppola's Dracula." *Cinefantastique* 23, 4 (December 1992): 24-26, 31, 35, 39, 43, 47, 51, 55. One of a set of articles on the Coppola film in this issue of *Cinefantastique.*
Coppola, Francis Ford, and James V. Hart. *Bram Stoker's Dracula: The Film and the Legend.* New York: Newmarket Press, 1992. 172 pp. Reprint. London: Pan Books, 1992. 172 pp.
Saberhagen, Fred, and James V. Hart. *Bram Stoker's Dracula.* New York: New American Library, 1992. 301 pp.
Steranko, Jim. "Bram Stoker's Dracula." *Preview* 2, 49 (November/February 1993): 18-39, 59.
Rohrer, Trish Deitch. "Coppola's Bloody Valentine." *Entertainment Weekly* No. 145 (November 20, 1992): 22-31.

BRIDES, VAMPIRE

"Vampire Brides" is a popular term that refers to the harem-like arrangement that is believed to exist between the vampire (a male) and his **victims** (a group of young women). The idea derived entirely from **Bram Stoker**'s novel *Dracula.* During the opening chapters the title character lived in his remote castle home with three young women. They were described by a number of names including "young women," "weird sisters," and "ghostly women." At the end of the novel, **Abraham Van Helsing** entered **Castle Dracula** to kill the women, whom he simply called "sisters."

The idea of calling them "brides" possibly derived from the incident in the novel when, following the death of **Lucy Westenra,** Lucy's fiance **Arthur Holmwood** suggested that the sharing of blood created a husband-wife relationship between himself and his now dead wife-to-be. However, it received its substance from various movies which pictured a male vampire in a continuing relationship with several female vampires. Commonly in vampire novels and movies, vampires attacked a person of the opposite sex. Most vampires were male and most of their victims, with whom they developed a close relationship, were women. This relationship has often been developed, by implication if not actual reference, in a manner similar to the popular image of the Middle Eastern harem. Frequently, the women were clothed in frilly bed clothes while the man was in formal dress. This image of the vampire brides was present in the two **Count Yorga** films and in **John Carradine**'s *The Vampire Hookers* (1979).

The idea of the vampire brides emphasized the sexual nature of the vampire's relationship to his victims. The vampire attacked (raped) his victims and then tied them to him in a slavelike structure in which love played little or no part. In *Dracula,* the three women accused him of never having loved and of loving no one in the present.

BROWNING, TOD (1882-1962)

Tod Browning, a career director of horror films who brought both **Lon Chaney** and **Bela Lugosi** to the screen in their first vampire roles, is most remembered today for his work on a single film, *Dracula* **(1931).** He was born July 12, 1882, and raised in Louisville, Kentucky, but at the age of 16 ran away from home and joined a carnival. For years he made his living by assuming various "horror" persona. His carnival performances led to his becoming an actor. He appeared in his first film in 1913 and was soon working behind the camera. He assisted in directing for a couple of years and in 1917 directed his first movies, *Jim Bludso* and *Peggy, the Will o' the Wisp.* In 1919 he met Lon Chaney, who had a part in *The Wicked Darling.* They went their separate ways through the early 1920s, but were reunited at MGM in 1925 and for the next five years had one of the most fruitful collaborations Hollywood had known. Browning appreciated Chaney's ability to distort his face and apply makeup and developed scripts especially for him. Together they made *The Unholy Three* (1925), *The Blackbird* (1926), *The Road to Mandalay* (1926), *The Unknown* (1927), *London After Midnight* (1927), *West of Zanzibar* (1928), *The Big City* (1928), and *Where East Is East* (1929).

In 1927 Browning directed *London After Midnight,* the first vampire feature film, in which Chaney played both the vampire and the detective who pursued him. The film was memorable because of the extraordinary distorting makeup Chaney developed. Even he complained of its discomfort. The movie was based upon a novel, *The Hypnotist,* written by Browning, and then became the basis of a novelization by Marie Coolidge-Rask published in 1928 with stills from the movie. In Browning's plot, the vampire turned out to be an identity assumed by the detective to trap a criminal.

In 1930, as **Universal Pictures** was making its transition to talking movies, the company hired Browning to film *Dracula.* Browning immediately thought of Chaney for the starring role and approached him about the part. Unfortunately, before he could respond, Chaney died. Eventually, after a highly publicized search for an actor to play the title role, Bela Lugosi was selected.

Browning has been seen by most film critics as a mediocre and unimaginative director, especially criticized for his largely stationary camera. He was now set to do what would become his most memorable film, an adaptation of the **Hamilton Deane** play as revised by **John L. Balderston.** He is best remembered for adding the opening

► HORROR FILM DIRECTOR TOD
BROWNING.

scenes that occur in **Castle Dracula** during which Lugosi speaks his most memorable lines. The scene with Dracula standing on the stairs with a giant spider web behind him to welcome **R. N. Renfield** (who went to Transylvania instead of **Jonathan Harker** in this version) has been among the most reproduced pictures in movie history. These opening scenes lifted the movie from being merely a filmed stage play, the impression it gave once the action shifted to **London.**

Browning's *Dracula* must be seen in the context of its time. For all practical purposes it was the first *Dracula* movie, few people having seen the banned *Nosferatu* or the other even lesser-known European attempts at adaptation. It was also one of the first horror movies with sound. Given the level to which movies had progressed, the low expectations for the film's success, and the financial hardship then being experienced by Universal, the production values of *Dracula* were appropriate. Even today the opening scenes are effective, though post-**Hammer Films** audiences have been quick to note the sanitized presentation of a Dracula without visible **fangs** who never bit his victims for the audience to see. Most importantly, one cannot deny the audience response to the movie, and Universal credited it with keeping the company from bankruptcy.

Browning would go on to make several more films in the 1930s. His next film, *Freaks,* became one of the most controversial movies of the era. A pet project, the movie harked back to his carnival days and pictured the lives of various people who were born with bodies that pushed them outside of acceptable society. It was banned in 28 countries and was a commercial flop in the United States. He returned to the vampire theme in 1935 with *Mark of the Vampire,* a talkie remake of *London After Midnight.* Browning retired in 1939 following his work on *The Devil Dolls,* and lived quietly until his death on October 6, 1962.

Sources:

Coolidge-Rask, Marie. *London After Midnight.* New York: Grosset & Dunlap, 1928.

Everson, William K. *Classics of the Horror Film.* New York: Citadel Press, 1990. 247 pp.

Glut, Donald G. *The Dracula Book.* Metuchen, NJ: Scarecrow Press, 1975. 388 pp.

Quinlan, David. *The Illustrated Guide to Film Directors.* Totowa, NJ: Barnes & Noble Books, 1984.

Thompson, David. *A Biographical Dictionary of Film.* New York: William Morrow and Company, 1976. 629 pp.

BRUJA

Bruja is the Spanish name for a witch. A *bruja* was very much like the *strega* of **Italy** and *bruxa* of neighboring Portugal. The term was found throughout Latin America where it was used simultaneously with local names for witches and for witch/vampires, such as the *tlahuelpuchi,* the blood-sucking witch of **Mexico.** In both **Spain** and the Americas, the *bruja* was a living person, usually a woman, who was able to transform herself into various kinds of **animals** and attack infants.

Sources:

Nutini, Hugo G., and John M. Roberts. *Bloodsucking Witchcraft: An Epistomological Study of Anthropomorphic Supernaturalism in Rural Thaxcala.* Tucson: University of Arizona Press, 1993. 476 pp.

BRUXA

The *bruxa* (female) or *bruxo* (male) was the witch figure of Portugal, similar in many ways to the *bruja* of **Spain** and **Mexico.** The *bruxa* was a pre-Christian figure that became prominent in the Middle Ages. At that time, the Inquisition focused attention upon Pagan beliefs and demonized them as malevolent activities of Satan. In rural Portugal, belief in **witchcraft** survived into the twentieth century and the government periodically has taken measures to destroy its continuing influence.

The *bruxa* (who was generally described as a woman) entered the lists of vampire entities due to her blood-sucking attacks upon infants. She also assumed the form of various *animals,* most often a duck, rat, goose, dove, or ant. Her power was largely confined to the hours from midnight to 2:00 in the morning. The witches in a region gathered at the crossroads on Tuesdays and Fridays, and these days assumed negative connotations in Portuguese folklore. At their gatherings, the witches were believed to worship Satan, from whom they gained various evil powers, such as the evil eye.

Protection from a *bruxa* was supplied by a wide variety of magical amulets. Children were also protected by the use of iron and steel. A steel nail on the ground or a pair of scissors under their pillow would keep the witches away. There was also a belief in the spoken word, and the folklore was rich in examples of various incantations against witches. **Garlic** would be sewn into the clothes of children to protect them from being carried away by witches.

After an attack, attempts would be made to identify the malevolent witch. The mother of the deceased child could boil the child's clothes while jabbing them with a sharp instrument. The witch would supposedly feel the jabs on her own body and would be compelled to come and ask for mercy. Or the mother might take a broom and sweep the house backwards, from the door inward, while repeating an incantation to make the witch manifest. The broom, a symbol of witchcraft, was used to cause witches to relax. As recently as 1932, author Rodney Gallop reported the case of an infant in the town of Santa Leocadia de Baiao who had died of suffocation. The parents were sure that it had been "sucked by witches." The grandmother reported seeing the witch fly away disguised as a black sparrow.

Because of her ability to transform into animal forms, the *bruxa* was often associated with the *lobishomen,* the name by which **werewolves** were known in Portugal. The lobishomen was also known to change form on Tuesdays and Fridays, the same days the witches gathered.

Sources:

Gallop, Rodney. *Portugal: A Book of Folk-Ways.* Cambridge: Cambridge University Press, 1936. 291 pp.

BULGARIA, VAMPIRES IN

Bulgaria is one of the oldest areas of Slavic settlement. It is located south of **Romania** and sandwiched between the Black Sea and Macedonia. In the seventh century A.D., the Bulgar tribes arrived in the area of modern Bulgaria and established a military aristocracy over the Slavic tribes of the region. The Bulgars were only a small percentage of the population, and they eventually adopted the Slavic language.

Christianity arrived with force among the Bulgarians in the ninth century when Pope Nicholas I (858-67) claimed jurisdiction over the lands of the former Roman province of Illyricum. He sent missionaries into Bulgaria and brought it under Roman hegemony. The Bulgarian ruler, Boris-Michael, was baptized in 865, and the country officially accepted Christianity. The pope sent two bishops but would not send an archbishop or appoint a patriarch, causing Boris to switch his allegiance to the eastern church in Constantinople. A Slavic liturgy was introduced to the church and has remained its rite to the present.

Among the many side effects of Byzantine influence in Bulgaria was the growth of a new rival religious group, the Bogomils. The Bogomils grew directly out of an older group, the Paulicians, whose roots went back to the dualistic Maniceans. The Paulicians had been moved into Bulgaria from Asia Minor in order to prevent their alignment with the Muslim Arabs. The Bogomils believed that the world had been created by the rejected son of God, Satanael. While the earthly bodies of humans were created by Satanael, the soul came from God. It was seen by the church as a rebirth of the old gnostic heresy. Perkowski has argued at length that it was in the conflict of Bogomil ideas, surviving Paganism, and emerging Christianity that the mature idea of the Slavic vampire developed and evolved. However, his argument was not entirely convincing in that vampires developed in quite similar ways in countries without any Bogomilism. When the Christian Church split in 1054, the Bulgarians adhered to the orthodoxy of Constantinople.

The Bulgarians gained their independence at the end of the twelfth century, but were overrun by the Ottomans in 1396. They remained under Ottoman rule until 1878, when Turkish control was restricted by the Congress of Berlin, but did not become independent until 1908.

THE BULGARIAN VAMPIRE: The Bulgarian words for the vampire, a variety of the **Slavic vampire,** derived from the original Slavic opyri/opiri. Its modern form appears variously as *vipir, vepir,* or *vapir),* or even more commonly as *vampir,* a borrowing from Russian. The modern idea of the vampire in Bulgaria evolved over several centuries. Most commonly, the Bulgarian vampire was associated with problems of death and burial, and the emergence of vampires was embedded in the very elaborate myth and ritual surrounding death. At the heart of the myth was a belief that the spirits of the dead went on a journey immediately after death. Guided by their guardian angel, they traveled to all of the places they had visited during their earthly life. At the completion of their journey, which occurred in the 40 days after their death, the spirit then journeyed to the next life. However, if the burial routine was done improperly, the dead might find their passage to the next world blocked. Generally, in Bulgaria, the family was responsible for preparing the body for burial. There were a number of ways in which the family could err or become negligent in their preparation. Also, the body had to be guarded against a dog or cat jumping over it or a shadow falling on it prior to burial. The body had to be properly washed. Even with proper burial, a person who died a violent death might return as a vampire.

As in other Slavic countries, certain people were likely candidates to become vampires. Those who died while under excommunication from the church might become a vampire. Drunkards, thieves, murderers, and witches were also to be watched. Bulgaria was a source of tales of vampires who had returned to life, taken up residence in a town where they were not known, and lived for many years as if alive. They even married and fathered children. Such people were detected after many years because of some unusual event which occurred. Apart from their nightly journeys in search of blood, the vampire would appear normal, even eating a normal diet.

Among the Gagauz people—Bulgarians who speak their own language, Gagauzi—the vampire was called *obur,* possibly a borrowing from the Turkish word for glutton. As with other vampires among the southern Slavs, the *obur* was noted as a gluttonous blood drinker. As part of the efforts to get rid of it, it would be enticed by the offerings of rich food or excrement. The *obur* was also loud, capable of creating noises like firecrackers, and could move objects like a poltergeist.

James Frazer noted the existence of a particular Bulgarian vampire, the *ustrel.* The *ustrel* was described as the spirit of a child who had been born on a Saturday but who died before receiving baptism. On the ninth day after its burial, a *ustrel* was believed to work its way out of its grave and attack cattle or sheep by draining their blood. After feasting all night, it returned to its grave before dawn. After some 10 days of feeding, the *ustrel* was believed to be strong enough that it did not need to return to its grave. It found a place to rest during the day either between the horns of a calf or ram or between the hind legs of a milch-cow. It was able to pick out a large herd and begin to work its way through it, the fattest animals first. The animals it attacked—as many as five a night—would die the same night. If a dead animal was cut open, the signs of the wound that the vampire made would be evident.

As might be suspected, the unexplained death of cows and sheep was the primary sign that a vampire was present in the community. If a *ustrel* was believed to be present, the owner of the herd could hire a *vampirdzhija,* or **vampire hunter,** a special person who had the ability to see them, so that all doubt as to its presence was put aside. Once it was detected, the village would go through a particular ritual known throughout Europe as the lighting of a needfire. Beginning on a Saturday morning, all the fires in the village were put out. The cattle and sheep were gathered in an open space. They were then marched to a nearby crossroads where two bonfires had been constructed. The bonfires were lit by a new fire created by rubbing sticks together. The herds were guided between the fires. Those who performed this ritual believed that the vampire dropped from the animal on whose body it had made its home and remained at the crossroads where wolves devoured it. Before the bonfires burned out, someone took the flame into the village and used it to rekindle all the household fires.

Other vampires, those that originated from the corpse of an improperly buried person or a person who died a violent death, were handled with the traditional **stake.** There were also reports from Bulgaria of a unique method of dealing with the vampire: bottling. This practice required a specialist, the *djadadjii,* who had mastered the art. The *djadadjii*'s major asset was an icon, a holy picture of Jesus, Mary, or one of the Christian saints. The vampire hunter took his icon and waited where the suspected vampire was likely to appear. Once he saw the vampire, he chased it, icon in hand. The vampire was driven toward a bottle that had been stuffed with its favorite food. Once the vampire entered the bottle, it was corked and then thrown into the **fire.**

The folklore of the vampire has suffered in recent decades. The government manifested great hostility toward all it considered superstitious beliefs, which included both vampires and the church. As the church was suppressed, so was the unity of village life that provided a place for tales of vampires to exist.

Sources:

Abbott, G. F. *Macedonian Folklore.* Chicago: Argonaut, Inc., Publishers, 1986

Blum, Richard, and Eva Blum. *The Dangerous Hour: The Lore of Crisis and Mystery in Rural Greece*. London: Chatto & Windus, 1970. 410 pp.

Bratigam, Rob. "Vampires in Bulgaria." *International Vampire* 1, 2 (Winter 91): 16-17.

Frazer, James G. *The Golden Bough*. Vol. 10. *Balder the Beautiful: The Fire-Festivals of Europe and the Doctrine of the External Soul*. London: Macmillan and Co., 1930. 346 pp.

Georgieva, Ivanichka. *Bulgarian Mythology*. Sofia: Svyet, 1985.

Nicoloff, Assen. *Bulgarian Folklore*. Cleveland, OH: The Author, 1975. 133 pp.

———. *Bulgarian Folktales*. Cleveland, OH: The Author, 1979. 296 pp.

Perkowski, Jan L. *The Darkling: A Treatise on Slavic Vampirism*. Columbus, OH: Slavica Publishers, 1989. 174 pp.

St. Clair, Stanislas Graham Bower, and Charles A. Brophy. *Twelve Years Study of the Eastern Question in Bulgaria*. London: Chapman & Hall, 1877. 319 pp.

Summers, Montague. *The Vampire in Europe*. 1929. New Hyde Park, NY: University Books, 1961. 329 pp.

BULLET

According to **Abraham Van Helsing,** the vampire expert in the novel ***Dracula,*** a ''sacred bullet'' fired into a coffin containing a vampire will kill it. It was not an option that was pursued during the course of *Dracula.* Generally, however, a bullet, in this case a silver bullet, was the traditional means of killing **werewolves,** and guns have been thought to have little or no effect on vampires. Stoker derived this insight directly from Emily Gerard's *The Land Beyond the Forest,* his major source for information on **Transylvania,** who reported that a bullet fired into the coffin was a means of killing vampires among the Transylvanian peasantry.

The idea was considered by twentieth-century novels and movies, which frequently pictured the vampire's fate when confronted with modern weaponry. In those cases, however, if the vampire was hurt by the attack, the harm was very temporary, and the vampire quickly recovered to wreak vengeance upon those secularists who would put their faith in modern mechanical artifacts.

Sources:

Gerard, Emily. *The Land Beyond the Forest*. 2 vols. New York: Harper and Brothers, 1888.

BURMA, VAMPIRES IN *See:* MYANMAR, VAMPIRES IN

BURTON, RICHARD FRANCIS (1821-1890)

Richard Francis Burton, the writer and explorer who first opened the world of Asian vampires to the West, was born March 19, 1821, in Hertfordshire, England. He never participated in the school system as his parents were constantly on the move. He was educated by tutors at the different locations around the world. However, he became fluent in half a dozen languages as a youth and acquired new ones at a regular pace throughout his adult years.

In 1842 he became a cadet in the Indian army and began his adult career, which, like his childhood, was one of wandering. While in **India** he acquired several of the Indian languages and gathered a number of manuscripts of Indian works. Following his return to England in 1849, he published his first books, early studies of Indian languages, and a series of papers for the Asiatic Society. However, by this time he had his eye on what was to become his most famous venture, a pilgrimage to Mecca. Disguising himself as a Muslim he joined the Hijj in Egypt and made his way to the shrine forbidden to all non-Muslims. His three-volume account, *A Pilgrimage to El-Medinah and Meccah,* appeared in 1855.

Meanwhile he returned to India, which he used as a launching point for his explorations of Africa. In 1858 he penetrated the then unexplored territories of central Africa and discovered one of the sources of the Nile. He followed this with a trip across America to Utah and wrote a book on the Mormons. He also served as a consul in West Africa and South America. He first visited Damascus in 1869.

In the early 1860s Burton lost many of the manuscripts that he had gathered through the years in a fire at the warehouse where they were stored. One of the manuscripts that survived, however, was a collection of tales of King Vikram, a real historical figure in Indian history who had become a mythological giant, much as King Arthur had in British history. The particular set of stories translated and published by Burton were the Indian equivalent to the more famous *Arabian Nights* tales. They were of further interest, however, in that the storyteller was a vampire, in the mythology of India, the *vetala,* or *betail*. According to the story, King Vikram had been tricked by a yogi to come to the local cremation grounds and then further tricked to go a distance and bring back a body he would find. When Vikram found the body, it turned out to be the vampire.

Upon reaching the cremation ground, Vikram's final audience with the yogi revealed a considerable amount concerning the Indian attitude toward the afterlife and included a confrontation with several vampire figures. There was, for example, a Kali temple, with **Kali** in her most vampiric setting, described in some detail. *Vikram and the Vampire* was first published in 1870.

In 1872 Burton became consul in Trieste, Italy and lived there for the rest of his life. He published two more outstanding books, *The Book of the Sword,* a comprehensive history of the weapon, and 15 volumes of *The Book of a Thousand Nights and a Night*. The latter became and has remained Burton's most popular book. Its immediate sales provided him with enough money in royalties for a more than comfortable retirement.

After his death at Trieste, on October 20, 1890, Burton's wife burned a number of his writings, including his private diary and his commentary on *The Perfumed Garden,* a Persian sex manual. (He had earlier published an edition of the renowned Indian sex manual the *Kama Sutra*.) As his literary executor, she took complete control of his writings, regulated their publication, and tried to suppress knowledge of those aspects of Burton's romantic life which might have brought offense to Victorian society. In 1897 she oversaw the publication of a new edition of *Vikram and the Vampire,* for which she wrote the preface.

Sources:

Burton, Isabel. *The Life of Sir Richard Burton.* 1893. 2nd ed.: 2 vols. London: W. W. Wilkins, 1898.
Burton, Richard F. *Vikram and the Vampire.* 1870. Reprint. London: Tylston and Edwards, 1897. 243 pp. Reprint. New York: Dover Publications 1969. 243 pp.

BYRON, LORD (1788-1824)

Lord George Gordon Byron, purported author of the first modern vampire story in English, was born in 1788 in London, the son of Catherine Gordon and John Byron. After his father spent the fortune brought to the marriage by his mother, she took Byron to Aberdeen, Scotland in 1790, where he had a poor but somewhat normal childhood, disturbed only by a lame foot. His father died in 1791. Due to the untimely death of a cousin in 1794, he became the family heir, and when his great-uncle died in 1798, he became Lord Byron. Soon thereafter, he and his mother moved to the family estate in Nottinghamshire. In 1801 he entered Harrow School, and four years later went on to Trinity College at Cambridge University.

While at Cambridge Byron privately published his first poetry collection, *Fugitive Pieces* (1806). The next year another collection was published as *Hours of Idleness* (1807). He received his master's degree in 1808 and the following year took his seat in the House of Lords. He spent much of 1809 and 1810 traveling and writing Cantos I and II of *Child Harolde.* Its publication in 1812 brought him immediate fame. He also began his brief liaison with Lady Caroline Lamb.

The following year he broke off the relationship with Lamb and began his affair with his half-sister Augusta Leigh. At about the same time he was also initially exploring the subject of vampirism in his poem "The Giaour," completed and published in 1813. In the midst of the battles described in the poem, the Muslim antagonist speaks a lengthy curse against the title character, the *giaour* (an infidel, one outside the faith). Upon death, the infidel's spirit would surely be punished. However, the Muslim declared that there would be more:

> But first, on earth as Vampire sent,
> Thy corpse shall from its tomb be rent:
> Then ghastly haunt thy native place,
> And suck the blood of all thy race;
> There from thy daughter, sister, wife,
> At midnight drain the stream of life;
> Yet loathe the banquet which perforce
> Must feed thy livid living corpse.
> Thy victims are they yet expire
> Shall know the demon for their sire,

As cursing thee, thou cursing them,
Thy flowers are withered on the stem.

In "The Giaour" Byron demonstrated his familiarity with the Greek *vrykolakas,* a corpse that was animated by a devilish spirit and returned to its own family to make them its first victims. While the Greek vampire in "The Giaour" would be the only overt mention of the vampire in Byron's vast literary output, it merely set the stage for the more famous "vampiric" incident in Byron's life. Meanwhile, in January 1814, Byron married Annabelle Milbanke. Their daughter was born in December. Early in 1816, the couple separated after she and British society became aware of Byron's various sexual encounters. When both turned on him, he decided to leave the country (for good as it turned out).

In the spring of 1816, Byron left for the Continent. Accompanying him was a young physician/writer, **John Polidori.** By the end of May, they had arrived in Geneva and early in June rented the Villa Diodati, overlooking the Lake of Geneva. Joining him were Percy Shelley, Mary Godwin, and Godwin's step sister, Claire Clairmont, another of Byron's mistresses. On June 15, weather having forced them inside, Byron suggested that each person write and share a ghost story with the small group. Two evenings later the stories began. The most serious product of this adventure was, of course, *Frankenstein,* Godwin's story expanded into a full novel.

Byron's contribution to the ghostly evening was soon abandoned and never developed. It concerned two friends who, like himself and Polidori, left England to travel on the Continent, in the story's case, to **Greece.** While there, one of the friends died, but before his death obtained from the other a promise to keep secret the matter of his death. The second man returned to England only to discover that his former companion had beaten him back home and had begun an affair with the second man's sister. Polidori kept notes on Byron's story, which Byron had jotted down in his notebook.

Byron and Polidori parted company several months later. Polidori left for England and Byron continued his writing and the romantic adventures that were to fill his remaining years. The ghost story seemed a matter of no consequence. Then in May 1819, he saw an item concerning a tale, "The Vampyre," supposedly written by him and published in the *New Monthly Magazine* in England. He immediately wrote a letter denying his authorship and asking a retraction. As the story unfolded, Byron discovered that Polidori had written a short story from his notes on the tale told by Byron in 1816 in Switzerland. Polidori's story was the first piece of prose fiction to treat a literal vampire, and the publisher of the *New Monthly Magazine* took it upon himself, based upon Polidori's account of the story's origin, to put Byron's name on it. In the light of a not unexpected response, he quickly published it in a separate booklet over Byron's name, and had it translated into French and German. Both Polidori and Byron made attempts to correct the error, and before the year was out Byron had the "Fragment of a Story" published as part of his attempt to distance himself from the finished story. The problem he encountered in denying his authorship was amply demonstrated in 1830 by the inclusion of "The Vampyre" in the French edition of his

◀
LORD GEORGE GORDON BYRON

collected works. Byron must have been further irritated by Polidori's choice of a name for the vampire character in the story, **Lord Ruthven,** the same name given to the Byron-figure in Lady Caroline Lamb's fictionalized account of their liaison, *Glenarvon* (1816).

Once the Polidori incident was behind him, Byron never returned to the vampire in any of his writings. Twentieth century critics, however, have seen vampirism as a prominent metaphor in the Romantic treatment of human relations, especially destructive ones. Vampires are characters who suck the life-force from those they love, and the Romantic authors of the early nineteenth century, such as Byron, utilized **psychic vampirism** in spite of their never labeling such characters as vampires.

For example, critic James Twitchell saw the psychic vampire theme as an integral aspect of Byron's dramatic poem *Manfred,* the first acts of which were written in the summer of 1816 at the Villa Diodati. Illustrative of this "vampirism" was a scene in the first act in which the person who had just stopped Manfred from suicide offered him a glass of wine. Manfred refused comparing the wine to blood—both his and that of his half sister with whom he had an affair. Here Twitchell saw a return to the Greek vampires who first drank/attacked the blood/life of those closest to them. Manfred was an early manifestation of ''l'homme fatal,'' the man who acts upon those around him as if he were a vampire.

During a severe illness in April 1824, Byron underwent a series of bleedings that, ironically, probably caused his death. He died April 19, 1824. His body was returned to England for burial.

Sources:

Byron, Lord. *The Complete Poetic Works of Byron*. Boston: Houghton Mifflin Company, 1933. 1055 pp.

Dangerfield, Elma. *Byron and the Romantics in Switzerland, 1816*. London: Ascent Books, 1978. 93 pp.

Marchand, Leslie A. *Byron: A Biography*. 3 Vols. New York: Alfred A. Knopf, 1957.

Senf, Carol. *The Vampire in Nineteenth-Century English Literature*. Bowling Green, OH: Popular Press, 1988. 204 pp.

Trueblood, Paul G. *Lord Byron*. New York: Twauyne Publishers, 1969. 177 pp.

Twitchell, James B. *The Living Dead: A Study of the Vampire in Romantic Literature*. Durham, NC: Duke University Press, 1981. 219 pp.

C

CALLICANTZAROS *See:* GREECE, VAMPIRES IN

CALMET, DOM AUGUSTIN (1672-1757)

Dom Augustin Calmet, a French Roman Catholic biblical scholar and the most famous vampirologist of the early eighteenth century, was born February 16, 1672, at Minil-la-Horgne, Lorraine, France. He studied at the Benedictine monastery at Breuil, and entered the order in 1688. He was ordained to the priesthood in 1696. He taught philosophy and theology at the Abbey at Moyen-Moutier and during the early years of his career worked on a massive 23-volume commentary of the Bible which appeared between 1707 and 1716. His biblical writings established him as one of the church's leading scholars, and he spent many years trying to popularize the work of biblical exegesis in the church. He was offered a bishopric by Pope Benedict XIII, but Calmet turned it down. However, in spite of his learned accomplishments, Calmet is most remembered today for his single 1746 work on vampires, *Dissertations sur les Apparitions des Anges des Démons et des Espits, et sur les revenants, et Vampires de Hingrie, de Boheme, de Moravie, et de Silésie.*

Like the work of his Italian colleague, **Giuseppe Davanzati,** Calmet's study of vampirism was started by the waves of vampire reports from Germany and Eastern Europe. Vampirism, for all practical purposes, did not exist in France, and was largely unknown to the scholarly community there until the early eighteenth century. Calmet was impressed with the detail and corroborative testimonies of incidents of vampirism coming out of Eastern Europe and believed that it was unreasonable to simply dismiss them. In addition, as a theologian, he recognized that the existence and actions of such bloodsucking revenants could have an important bearing on various theological conclusions concerning the nature of the afterlife. Calmet felt it necessary to establish the veracity of such reports and to understand the phenomena in light of the church's view of the world. Calmet finished his work a short time after the Sorbonne roundly condemned the reports and especially the desecration of the bodies of the people believed to be vampires.

Calmet defined vampires as people who had been dead and buried and who then returned from their graves to disturb the living by sucking their blood and even causing death. The only remedy for vampirism was to dig up the body of the reported vampire and either sever its head and drive a stake through the chest or burn the body. Using that definition, Calmet collected as many of the accounts of vampirism as possible from official reports, newspapers, eyewitness reports, travelogues, and critical pieces from his learned colleagues. The majority of space in his published volume was taken up with the anthology of all his collected data.

Calmet then offered his reflections upon the reports. He condemned the hysteria which had followed several of the reported incidents of vampirism and seconded the Sorbonne's condemnation of the mutilation of exhumed bodies. He also considered all of the explanations that had been offered for the phenomena, including regional folklore, normal but little known body changes after death, and premature burial. He focused a critical eye upon the reports and pointed out problems and internal inconsistencies.

In the end, however, Calmet was unable to conclude that the reports supported the various natural explanations which had been offered, though he was unwilling to propose an alternative. He left the whole matter open, but seemed to favor the existence of vampires by noting, " that it seems impossible not to subscribe to the belief which prevails in these countries that these apparitions do actually come forth from the graves and that they are able to produce the terrible effects which are so widely and so positively attributed to them." He thus touched off the heated debate, which was to ensue during the 1750s. Calmet's book became a bestseller. It went through three French editions in 1746, 1747, and 1748. It appeared in a German edition in 1752 and an English edition in 1759 (reprinted in 1850 as *The Phantom World*). Calmet was immediately attacked by colleagues for taking the vampire stories seriously. While he tried to apply such critical methods as he had available to him, he never really questioned the legitimacy of the reports of vampiric manifestations.

As the controversy swelled following publication of his book, a skeptical Empress Maria Theresa stepped in. A new outbreak of vampirism had been reported in Silesia. She dispatched her personal physician to examine the case. He wrote a report denouncing the incident as supernatural quackery and condemned the mutilation of the bodies. In response, in 1755 and 1756, Maria Theresa issued laws to stop the spread of the vampire hysteria, including removing the matter of dealing with such reports from the hands of the clergy and placing it instead under civil authority. Maria Theresa's edicts came just before Calmet's death on October 25, 1757.

In the generation after his death, Calmet was treated harshly by French intellectuals, both inside and outside the church. Later in the century, Diderot condemned him. Possibly the final word on Calmet came from Voltaire, who sarcastically ridiculed him in his *Philosophical Dictionary*. Though Calmet was favorably cited by **Montague Summers,** who used him as a major source for his study of vampires, his importance lies in his reprinting and preserving some of the now obscure texts of the vampire wave of eighteenth century Europe.

Sources:

Calmet, Dom Augustine. *Dissertations sur les Apparitions des Anges des Démons et des Espits, et sur les revenants, et Vampires de Hingrie, de Boheme, de Moravie, et de Silésie.* Paris, 1746. Rept. as: *The Phantom World.* 2 vols. London: Richard Bentley, 1850.

Frayling, Christopher. *Vampyres: From Lord Byron to Count Dracula.* London: Faber and Faber, 1991. 429 pp.

Summers, Montague. *The Vampire: His Kith and Kin.* London: Routledge, Kegan Paul, Trench, Trubner & Co., 1928. 356 pp. Reprint. New York: University Books, 1960. 356 pp.

THE CAMARILLA: A VAMPIRE FAN ASSOCIATION

The Camarilla: A Vampire Fan Association is a **gothic** vampire fan club founded in the early 1990s by players of *Vampire: The Masquerade,* the most popular of the vampire-oriented "role-playing" (or story-telling) **games.** In the game, the players assume the role of a vampire who is a member of a vampire society called The Camarilla. In the myth, vampires created The Camarilla after the Inquisition in an effort to keep their race from being totally annihilated. They organized The Camarilla into clans, each of which was distinguished by a peculiar aesthetic/intellectual approach to the vampiric condition, or by a certain ethnic origin.

The Camarilla: A Vampire Fan Association focuses on the vampire as a tragic and romantic figure and tends to avoid its violent aspects. Members of the club join a clan and create a vampire persona which is lived out in club activities, such as gaming sessions. The club emphasizes member participation and encourages new members to become active in a local chapter or even begin one themselves. Chapters are often involved in raising money for local charities or hosting blood drives, etc. Community service is emphasized as much as role-playing.

The Camarilla is headed by a governing board, referred to as The Inner Circle. Each of the primary clans is represented on the board. In each city there is a city coordinator (referred to as the Prince), chapter coordinators and their assistants (Elders and Regents), and the gaming referee (the City Storyteller). This helps keep the real world and the game world separate.

Chapters must have at least five members to receive a charter, and is first termed a "coterie." After six months of activity that includes the sponsoring of gaming sessions and some additional self-chosen task (the publication of a fanzine, organization of a special event, etc.) it can be designated as a "House," an honored position in the city.

Individual members receive the membership handbook, *The Tome of the Kindred* (which explains the club's organization and assists members in developing their personae), and the club's quarterly fanzine, *Requiem,* plus a host of other

REGNANT AND THRALL ARE TYPICAL OF THE MODERN VAMPIRES WHO INHABIT THE WORLD OF THE CAMARILLA.

materials. The Camarilla may be contacted at 8314 Greenwood Ave. N., Box 2850, Seattle, WA 98103.

Sources:

Rein-Hagen, Mark. *Vampire: The Masquerade*. Stone Mountain, GA: White Wolf, 1991. 263 pp.
Wright, Jana. *The Tome of the Kindred*. Seattle, WA: The Camarilla, 1993. 44 pp.

CAMAZOTZ *See:* MEXICO, VAMPIRES IN

CARFAX

In **Bram Stoker**'s novel *Dracula,* Carfax was a residence purchased by Dracula prior to his leaving his castle. The purpose of **Jonathan Harker**'s visit to **Transylvania** at the beginning of the novel was to complete the transaction by which Dracula secured a somewhat secluded home for himself relatively close to London. (Other firms were employed to secure his London residences and carry out various business transactions. Thus, neither Harker or any other single person would know more than a small portion of what Dracula was attempting to accomplish.)

Carfax was a fictional estate of some 20 acres located by Stoker in Purfleet. While modern **London** has almost reached out to Purfleet, in the 1890s Purfleet was a secluded village some 10 miles from the edge of london's East End, on the northern side of the River Thames in Essex. Stoker described the estate as being surrounded by a high wall built of stone. It had been abandoned for some years and was in a state of decay. He continued, ''There are many trees on it, which makes it in places gloomy, and there is a deep, dark-looking pond or small lake, evidently fed by some springs . . .'' It was located adjacent to an old church on one side and a lunatic asylum (the one run by Dr. **John Seward**) on the other.

Dracula's boxes of native soil were shipped from **Whitby,** where Dracula landed in England, to London. From there they were transported to Carfax. Carfax served as Dracula's ''headquarters'' from which he launched his attacks upon **Lucy Westenra, Mina Murray,** and **R. N. Renfield,** the resident of the asylum next door. Later Dr. **Abraham Van Helsing** and the cadre of men dedicated to destroying Dracula entered Carfax and sanitized the boxes of earth with a **eucharistic wafer** thus rendering them useless.

In the rewritten script for **Universal Pictures' *Dracula* (1931)** movie with **Bela Lugosi,** Carfax and the church next door were combined and called Carfax Abbey. That change seems to have been the idea of screenwriter Louis Bloomfield, who had been hired to rework the **John L. Balderston** version of the **Hamilton Deane** play, the basis of the movie's script. Carfax ''Abbey'' initially appeared in the preliminary ''First Treatment'' submitted by Bloomfield to Carl Laemmle, Jr., at Universal, on August 7, 1930. That document was then rewritten by Bloomfield and Dudley Murphy, the first screenwriter assigned to the movie. Their work was finally revised by Garrett Fort. Bloomfield and Universal parted company, and his work was not acknowledged in the final credits for the film. However, the idea of Carfax Abbey continued through both the Murphy and Fort revisions into the final movie. From the movie, it passed into the popular culture and reappeared in later movies which relied more on Universal's production than any rereading of the book.

Carfax, like Seward's asylum, was pure fiction. As **Leonard Wolf** noted, there was a Carfax Road and a Carfax Square in London, but neither were near Purfleet. **Raymond T. McNally** and **Radu Florescu** seem to have confused Carfax estate and the later idea of Carfax Abbey and searched for a possible reference to the latter in Purfleet. Based on information supplied by Alan Davidson, they accepted the idea that Lesnes Abbey, originally founded in 1178 A.D., but on the opposite side of the Thames River from Purfleet, might have inspired Stoker's Carfax. The Abbot's House, part of the Lesnes complex later used as a manor house, still existed in the 1890s. However, if Lesnes Abbey (on the south side of the Thames) was the historical reference to Carfax, then there would be no reason for Dracula (as a bat) to fly south across the Thames (as he did in chapter 23).

Sources:

Riley, Philip J. *Dracula (The Original 1931 Shooting Script)*. Atlantic City, NJ: MagicImage Filmbooks, 1990. Unpaged.
Stoker, Bram. *The Annotated Dracula*. Ed. by Leonard Wolf. New York: Ballantine Books, 1975. 362 pp.
———. *The Essential Dracula*. Ed. by Raymond McNally and Radu Florescu. New York: Mayflower, 1979. 320 pp.

CARMILLA

Carmilla is the title character in the vampire novelette by British writer **Sheridan Le Fanu.** ''Carmilla'' was originally published as a short story in a story collection entitled *In a Glass Darkly* in 1872. The story took place in rural Styria, where Laura, the heroine and narrator, lived. Her father, a retired Austrian civil servant, had been able to purchase an abandoned castle cheaply. Carmilla first appeared in the opening scene of the story as she entered the six-year-old Laura's bed. Laura fell asleep in her arms but suddenly awakened with a sensation of two needles entering her breast. She cried out, and the person Laura described only as ''the lady'' slipped out of bed onto the floor and disappeared, possibly under the bed. Her nurse and the housekeeper came into the room in response to her cries, but found no one and no marks on her chest.

Carmilla reappeared when Laura was 19 years old. The carriage in which Carmilla was traveling had a wreck in sight of the castle. Carmilla's mother, seemingly in a hurry to reach her destination, left Carmilla at the castle to recover from the accident. When Laura finally met their new guest, she immediately recognized Carmilla as the same person who had visited her 12 years previously, and thus the vampire was loosed again to prey on Laura. Gradually her identity was uncovered. She began to visit Laura in the form of a cat and a female phantom. Laura also noticed that she looked exactly like the 1698 portrait of Countess Mircalla Karnstein. Through her mother, Laura was a descendent of the Karnsteins.

At this point, an old friend of the family, General Spielsdorf, arrived at the castle to relate the account of his daughter's death. She had been wasting away; her condition had no known natural causes. A physician deduced she was the victim of a vampire. The skeptical general waited hidden in his daughter's room and actually caught the vampire, a young woman he knew by the name of Millarca, in the act. He tried to kill her with his sword, but she easily escaped.

As he finished his account, Carmilla entered. He recognized her as Millarca, but she escaped them before they could deal with her. They all then tracked her to the Karnstein castle some three miles away where they found her resting in her grave. Her body was lifelike, and a faint heartbeat detected. The casket floated in fresh blood. They drove a **stake** through her heart in reaction to which Carmilla let out a "piercing shriek." They finished their gruesome task by severing her head, burning the body, and scattering the ashes.

One can see in Le Fanu's tale, which would later be read by **Bram Stoker,** the progress of the developing vampire myth to that point. People became vampires after committing **suicide** or following their death if they had been bitten by a vampire during their life. The latter was the cause in Carmilla's case. Le Fanu understood the vampire to be a dead person returned, not a demonic spirit. The returned vampire had a tendency to attack family and loved ones, in this case, a descendent, and was somewhat geographically confined to the area near their grave. And while somewhat pale in complexion, the vampire was quite capable of fitting into society without undue notice. The vampire had two needle-like teeth, but these were not visible at most times. Bites generally occurred on the neck or chest.

Carmilla had nocturnal habits, but was not totally confined to the darkness. She had superhuman **strength** and was able to undergo a **transformation** into various shapes, especially those of **animals.** Her favorite shape was that of a cat, rather than either a wolf or a **bat.** She slept in a **coffin,** which she could leave without disturbing any dirt covering the grave.

As would be true in *Dracula,* the mere bite of the vampire neither turned victims into vampires nor killed them. The vampire fed off the victim over a period of time while the victim slowly withered away. The victim thus fulfilled both the vampire's daily need for blood and its fascination for a particular person whom it chose as its victim.

As many have noted in discussing Carmilla, her fascination with Laura and the general's daughter, an attachment "resembling the passion of love," has more than passing **lesbian** overtones. In horror stories, in general, authors have been able to treat sexual themes in ways that would not have been available to them otherwise. Early in the story, for example, Carmilla began her attack upon Laura by placing her "pretty arms" around her neck, and with her cheek touching Laura's lips, speaking soft seductive words. While earlier writers had written about the vampirelike *lamiai* and other female vampires who attacked their male lovers, "Carmilla" introduced the female revenant vampire to **gothic** literature.

One unique element of vampire lore in "Carmilla" that was not used by later writers was Le Fanu's suggestion that the vampire was limited to choosing a **name** that was anagrammatically related to its real name. Both Carmilla and Millarca were derived from Mircalla.

"Carmilla" would directly influence Stoker's presentation of the vampire, especially his treatment of the female vampires who attack **Jonathan Harker** early in *Dracula*. The influence of "Carmilla" was even more visible in "Dracula's Guest," the deleted chapter of *Dracula* later published as a short story.

Through the twentieth century, "Carmilla" has had a vital existence on the motion picture screen. The story served loosely as inspiration for *Vampyr*, **Carl Theodor Dreyer**'s 1931 classic, though "Dracula's Guest" provided the base for Universal's first post-*Dracula* movie with a female vampire, *Dracula's Daughter* (1936). However, with the expanded exploration of the vampire theme in the movies after World War II, "Carmilla" would be rediscovered. The first movie based directly on "Carmilla" was the 1961 French *Et Mourir de Plaisir* (also called *Blood and Roses*) directed by **Roger Vadim** and starring his wife, Annette Vadim. It was followed in 1962 by *La Maldicion of the Karnsteins* (also known as *Terror in the Crypt*). Then at the beginning of the 1970s, in the wake of its other successful vampire movies, **Hammer Films** would turn to Carmilla and her family for three movies: *Lust for a Vampire* (1970), *The Vampire Lovers* (1970)—possibly the most faithful attempt to tell the Le Fanu story—and *Twins of Evil* (1971). The Hammer movies inspired other attempts on the continent to bring "Carmilla" to the screen, the first being three Spanish productions. *La Hija de Dracula* (*The Daughter of Dracula*) was released in 1972. *La Comtesse aux Seiens Nux* (1973) was released under a variety of titles, including a 1981 highly edited version, *Erotikill*. *La Novia Ensangretada* (1974) was released in the United States as *Till Death Do Us Part* and *The Blood Spattered Bride*. Over the last 20 years, "Carmilla"-inspired movies have included *The Evil of Dracula* (1975) and *Valerie* (1991). Television adaptations were made in England in 1966, Spain in 1987, and the United States in 1989.

"Carmilla" was brought to the world of **comic books** in 1968 by Warren Publishing Company's *Creepy* No. 19, one of the comic magazines which operated outside of the Comics Code that forbade the picturing of vampires in comic books. More recently, Malibu Comics released a six-part adult version of *Carmilla*. In 1972, the story was included on a record album, *Carmilla: A Vampire Tale,* released under the Vanguard label by the Etc. Company.

Sources:

Glut, Donald F. *The Dracula Book.* Metuchen, NJ: Scarecrow Press, 1975. 388 pp.

Le Fanu, Sheridan. *In a Glass Darkly*. London: P. Davies, 1929. "Carmilla" has recently been reprinted in Alan Ryan, ed. *Vampires: Two Centuries of Great Vampire Stories*. Garden City, NY: Doubleday & Company, 1987, pp. 71-137.

CARRADINE, JOHN (1905-1988)

Born Richmond Reed Carradine on February 5, 1905, in New York City, John Carradine first appeared as **Dracula** in the 1944 movie *House of Frankenstein,* and frequently recreated the part throughout the rest of his career. Carradine grew up in a educated family. His mother was a surgeon and his father a lawyer who also at times worked as a poet, artist, and Associated Press correspondent in London. Carradine originally planned to become a sculptor and to that end attended the Graphic Art School in Philadelphia. However, inspired by the Shakespearean actor Robert Mitchell, he began to train for the stage.

In 1925 he set out on his own, making a living as a sketch artist. In New Orleans that year he made his stage debut in "Camille" and then joined a touring Shakespearean company. In 1927 he moved to Hollywood and worked as an actor, in Shakespearean plays when possible. In 1930 he appeared for the first time in a movie, *Tol'able David,* using the name Peter Richmond. He appeared in his first horror movie, which was also his first motion picture for **Universal Pictures,** in 1933's *The Invisible Man.* In 1935 he signed a long-term contract with 20th Century Fox and changed his stage name to John Carradine. That same year he married Ardanelle Cosner.

Through the 1930s he appeared in a number of notable movies including *The Prisoner of Shark Island* (1936) and *Stagecoach* (1939), but is possibly most remembered for his portrayal of the drunk minister in *The Grapes of Wrath* (1939). In the 1940s he appeared in the "B" horror movies which had become a staple of Universal Studios' schedule. Then in 1944 he accepted the role of Dracula in *Horror of Frankenstein,* which he agreed to do if he could take his portrayal from Stoker's novel rather than the then more famous portrayal of **Bela Lugosi.** Carradine's performance somewhat saved the movie and its highly contrived plot and established him as one of the most popular interpreters of the Count.

Meanwhile, Carradine had formed a drama company and laid plans for a career as a Shakespearean actor. His work was greeted with rave reviews, but his plans were blocked by his first wife (whom he had divorced in 1944), who had him thrown in jail for "alimony contempt." With his new wife, Sonia Sorel, he returned to Hollywood and accepted the offer to assume his vampiric role in *House of Dracula.* Carradine's most famous scene was Dracula's attack upon the heroine as she played "Moonlight Sonata" on the piano. About to claim his victim, he was repulsed by the cross hanging around her neck.

Carradine returned to the Dracula role in the 1950s on the stage. He moved even further from the Lugosi presentation of Dracula, and referred directly to the text of the novel in creating his own make-up, which included white hair and a white mustache.

JOHN CARRADINE PORTRAYED
DRACULA IN MORE MOVIES
THAN ANYONE EXCEPT
CHRISTOPHER LEE.

He kept both the opera cape and the evening clothes. Memorable in his performance was a humorous line he added to the script at the end, "If I'm alive, what am I doing here? On the other hand, if I'm dead, why do I have to wee-wee?" In 1957 Carradine became possibly the first **television** Dracula in a program for NBC's live "Matinee Theatre." In 1957, following a divorce two years earlier, Carradine married Doris Rich.

From the 1960s until his death in the 1988, Carradine appeared in numerous "B" films, including a variety of vampire movies. The first of the new vampire movies was *Billy the Kid vs. Dracula,* an unfortunate marriage of the vampire and western genres. In 1967 Carradine traveled to Mexico for *Las Vampiros* (*The Vampires*), a film in which he had little creative input. The only English-speaking person on the set, he learned enough Spanish to deliver the famous line he had added to the play. He followed *Las Vampiros* with *The Blood of Dracula's Coffin* (1968), the first of several movies he made under the direction of Al Abramson. The next came almost immediately, *Dracula vs. Frankenstein* (also known as *The Blood of Frankenstein,* 1969). Through the 1970s he appeared in *Vampire Men of the Lost Planet* (1970), *Horror of the Blood Monsters* (1971), *House of Dracula's Daughter*

(1973), *Mary Mary Bloody Mary* (1975), *Nocturna* (1978), and *The Vampire Hookers* (1979). His final appearances in vampire movies were in *Doctor Dracula* (1980) and *The Monster Club* (1981). In most of these movies, though by no means all, Carradine played the part of the vampire.

Carradine married Emily Cisneros in 1975, four years after the death of his third wife. He continued to make movies through the 1980s and won an award at the Sitges Film Festival in 1983 as best male actor for his work in *House of Long Shadows* (1983). He died November 27, 1988, in Milan, Italy, after climbing the 328 steps of the Duomo, the famous cathedral. He collapsed and was taken to the hospital where he died of heart and kidney failure.

Known for his deep, distinctive, classically-trained baritone voice, Carradine appeared in an unknown number of films (some estimates go as high as 500). In spite of the negative reaction to his later portrayals of Dracula (and other vampires), he is remembered from his early films and stage work as one of the most important people to take up these roles. Except for **Christopher Lee,** he played Dracula more than any other actor, and appeared in a starring role in more vampire movies than any actor before or since.

Sources:

The Annual Obituary, 1988. Edited by Patricia Burgess. Chicago: St. James Press, 1989.
Carradine, John. "Introduction." *House of Dracula (The Original Shooting Script).* Edited by Philip Riley. Absecon, NJ: MagicImage Filmbooks, 1993. Unpaged.
Glut, Donald. *The Dracula Book.* Metuchen, NJ: Scarecrow Press, 1975. 388 pp.
The International Dictionary of Films and Filmmakers: Volume II, Actors and Actresses. Edited by James Vinson. Chicago: St. James Press, 1985.

CARTER, MARGARET (1948-)

Margaret Louise Carter, bibliographer, author, and editor, was born in Norfolk, Virginia. She had developed an interest in vampires after reading *Dracula* at the age of 13. In 1970, while in college, she compiled an anthology of vampire stories, *Curse of the Undead.* That same year she wrote the preface to a reprint of *Varney the Vampyre* edited by D. P. Varma. Two years later she edited a second collection of short stories, *Demon Lovers and Strange Seductions.*

In 1975 she began the work that has to date brought her the greatest degree of fame in the vampire world. *Shadow of a Shade: A Survey of Vampirism in Literature,* which won **The Count Dracula Society** award in 1976, was the first of four books on vampire and gothic horror bibliography and literary fiction. It was followed by *Specter or Delusion? The Supernatural in Gothic Fiction* (1987), *Dracula: The Vampire and the Critics* (1988), and her monumental *The Vampire in Literature: A*

▲

MARGARET L. CARTER,
BIBLIOGRAPHER OF VAMPIRE
FICTION

Critical Bibliography (1989), which included a comprehensive listing of English-language vampire fiction. Each item in the bibliography was annotated with a set of codes indicating the nature of the vampire and/or vampirism to be found in the work. It appeared amidst an unprecedented growth in interest in the literary vampire. Carter has annually issued a supplement that cites all of the year's new fiction as well as any past items she missed in the original bibliography. In her work she has placed all future writers on vampires in her debt.

Carter is also a writer of vampire fiction. Her first vampire short story, ''A Call in the Blood,'' appeared in 1987. She has continued as a productive author to the present. In 1991 she started *The Vampire's Crypt,* a journal featuring vampire-oriented short fiction.

Sources:

Carter, Margaret L. *Curse of the Undead.* Greenwich, CT: Fawcett, 1970. 223 pp.
———. *Demon Lovers and Strange Seductions.* Greenwich, CT: Fawcett, 1972. 207 pp.
———. *Dracula: The Vampire and the Critics.* Ann Arbor, MI: UMI Research Press, 1988. 274 pp.
———. *Shadow of a Shade: A Survey of Vampirism in Literature.* New York: Gordon Press, 1975. 176 pp.
———. *Specter or Delusion? The Supernatural in Gothic Fiction.* Ann Arbor, MI: UMI Research Press, 1987. 131 pp.

———. *The Vampire in Literature: A Critical Bibliography.* Ann Arbor, MI: UMI Research Press, 1989. 135 pp.

CASTLE DRACULA

The first section of **Bram Stoker**'s novel *Dracula* concerns **Jonathan Harker**'s trip to Castle Dracula and his adventures after he arrives. During the last generation, as it was discovered that Stoker's character Dracula was based, in part, upon a real person, **Vlad the Impaler,** the question was posed, ''Could Castle Dracula be a real place?'' The search for Dracula's castle began. This search took on two aspects: the search for the castle that was the home for Vlad the Impaler and the search for the castle that Bram Stoker actually used as a model for the castle described in his novel.

As described in the novel, the castle was near **Borgo Pass.** It was reached from Pasul Tihuts, a point near the summit of the crossing, on a road leading south along mountainous road into the high mountains where the castle was located. Harker's journey from the pass to the castle was at night, and he reached it by horse drawn coach with enough of the evening left to have dinner and his first visit with Dracula before dawn. Upon his arrival, he noticed a large courtyard. He was dropped in front of an old large door placed at an opening in a stone wall. Even in the dim light of the evening, the wall showed signs of age and weathering. In the light of day, he discovered that the castle sat on a great rock overlooking the surrounding forest which was sliced by several river gorges.

The castle was built so as to be nearly impregnable to attack. The large windows were placed above the level where arrows and other projectiles (at least those of premodern warfare) could reach. To the west was a large valley and a mountain range.

Entering the castle he saw a large winding staircase and a long corridor. At the end of the corridor, he entered a room where supper awaited him. The rooms in which Harker was to spend most of his time joined an octagonal room that stood between the room in which he ate and his bedroom. His bedroom overlooked the court where he had originally stepped off the coach. The door to the room opposite his bedroom was locked, but another opened to the library, which was full of materials from England.

He explored one forbidden wing of the castle in the southwest corner at a lower level. Here he found comfortable furniture, but it lay covered in the dust of abandonment. The windows were filled with diamond-shaped panes of colored glass. Here he would encounter the three **vampire brides** who resided at the castle with Dracula.

Harker climbed out a window on the south wall to make his way to the window on the east side of the castle, below his bedroom, into which he had seen Dracula go. In the first room he entered, he found a pile of gold, also covered with dust. He followed a staircase downward to a tunnel, and meandering through the tunnel he came upon the chapel that had been used as a burial place. Here he discovered the

CASTLE DRACULA, CURTEA DE ARGES, ROMANIA

boxes of earth ready to be sent to England, in one of which Dracula lay in his sleep-like state. The three women slept in the chapel. There was one large tomb, not noticed by Harker but later sanitized by **Abraham Van Helsing,** labeled with the single word DRACULA.

THE SEARCH FOR CASTLE DRACULA: In recent decades, as the fact that the title character in Stoker's novel was based on a real person, Vlad the Impaler, a ruler in what today is **Romania,** the thought was that there was possibly a real Castle Dracula. Given the accuracy of Stoker's novel in describing many aspects of the Transylvanian landscape, the first place to look for a real Castle Dracula would seem to be near Borgo Pass. And in fact there were two different castles near both **Bistritz** (also spelled Bistrita) and the Borgo Pass road. The first was built in the thirteenth century some five kilometers north of the city at Dealu Cetatii. It fell into disuse and was in a dilapidated state by the early fifteenth century at which time the townspeople took the stones and reused them in refortifying Bistritz proper.

Castle Bistrita was built in the 1440s by John Hunyadi (d. 1456), a contemporary of Vlad the Impaler. Hunyadi was the "governor" of **Hungary** whose territory covered much of **Transylvania.** The two, whose lands adjoined each other, were in frequent competition and on occasion were allied. Hunyadi died in the siege of Belgrade, though the Christian forces won the battle and turned back the Turkish attempt to take the city. While it may be that Vlad the Impaler resided at Castle Bistrita for a brief period during the last years of Hunyadi's life, it could in no sense be called Castle Dracula. Today no remains of Castle Bistrita exist. It was destroyed at the end of the fifteenth century by the largely German population of the area in an act of defiance against their former Hungarian rulers.

Hunyadi had a second and more important castle located at Hundoara some 100 miles southwest of Borgo Pass. This impressive thirteenth-century structure still exists and has been restored and opened to the public. Vlad Dracul was believed to have visited this castle on at least one occasion during his early years. In 1452, while loosely allied with Hunyadi, Dracula was greeted somewhat as a friend. A decade later, however, he returned as a prisoner of Hunyadi's son Matthias Corvinus and began 12 years of imprisonment at Pest and **Visegrad.** Despite Vlad's presence at the castle at Hundoara, it was not Castle Dracula.

Dracula was actually the prince (ruler) of Wallachia. His territory was south of Transylvania, immediately on the other side of the Carpathian Mountains. In the mountains, overlooking the Dambovita River, near the town of Campulung, and protecting Bran Pass (the road through the Bucegi Mountains), is Castle Bran. It was originally built in the thirteenth century by the knights of the Teutonic Order. In the fourteenth century, the Teutonic Oder having been expelled, the castle was taken over by the German merchants of Brasov who used it as their defense post and customs station. Brasov was located in the Transalpine area, which included the Carpathian Mountians and that area immediately to the north and south of the mountians. Though the Transalpine area was officially part of Hungarian territory, the Prince of Wallachia served as military overseer of the area in return for certain Transylvania duchies. Most of the time, neither Hungary nor Wallachia actually controlled the castle, which was in the hands of the very independent German merchants.

Castle Bran has often been touted, especially by the Romanian tourist authorities, as the real Castle Dracula. During its years under the control of the German leadership in Brasov, it is possible that Vlad Dracula visited it on occasion in the early 1850s. He was officially the Voivode of the Transalpine area. Historians **Radu Florescu** and **Raymond T. McNally** noted that it possessed the atmosphere that Stoker was attempting to evoke in his descriptions of Castle Dracula. "The analogies between Stoker's mythical Castle Dracula and the real Castle Bran are simply too close to be coincidental." It had an inner courtyard and a secret underground passageway. A steep winding staircase could take a resident to a secret escape route deep inside the mountain. Though Florescu and McNally may have somewhat overstated their case, Dracula may have drawn, in part, from his knowledge of Castle Bran when he built his own mountain retreat.

THE REAL CASTLE DRACULA?: The only castle that might be considered the actual Castle Dracula (remembering that no castle other than the one in Stoker's imagination ever had that name) was the castle built and inhabited by Vlad the Impaler during his years as Prince of Wallachia. This castle overlooks the River Arges near the town of Poenari, in the foothills of the Transylvanian Alps. It is located approximately 20 miles north of Curtea de Arges, the original capital of Wallachia, and for many years the center of the Romanian Orthodox Church. When Vlad assumed the throne in 1456, there were two fortresses about a mile from each other on opposite sides of the river. Castle Poenari, the castle on the left side of the river, seems to have been built on the site of an even older fortress on the Arges River when this land was the center of the country called Dacia. Abandoned, it was rebuilt in the thirteenth century by Romanians attempting to block the incursions by Hungarian and/or Teutonic soldiers from the north. In 1455 it was in disrepair from recent battles with various invading armies, but was still habitable.

On the right side of the river was the Castle of the Arges. It was built a century before Vlad's time, although some historians have argued that it was even earlier a Teutonic outpost tied to the castle at Fagaras, just across the mountains to the north. McNally and Florescu have argued that it was not Teutonic, but built by the early Wallachian rulers and modeled on Byzantine patterns.

At the end of the fourteenth century, Tartars invaded the area. The remnant of the Wallachian forces (and many of the country's elite) eventually took refuge in the Castle of the Arges. The Tartars lay seize to the castle and finding almost no opposition soon captured it. However, its inhabitants escaped through the secret passageway under the castle. As a consolation prize, the Tartars largely destroyed the castle.

Of the two castles that Dracula found, the Castle of Arges was in the more strategic position, possibly the major reason for his choice to rebuild it instead of settling at Poenari. It was located on a precipice overlooking the River Arges at the point where the valley of the Arges narrows and the foothills of the Carpathians turn into mountains.

The rebuilding process has become one of the more famous stories of Vlad, one of the earlier incidents confirming his nickname, ''The Impaler.'' He had discovered that the boyars, the elite families of Wallachia, had been responsible for the death of his father and the torture and murder of his older brother. He decided to gain his revenge and get his castle built at the same time. During the Easter celebration following his taking up residence in his capital at **Tirgoviste,** he arrested all of the boyars (men, women, and children). Still dressed in their finest Easter clothes, they were forced to march to Poenari and rebuild the castle. The material from Poenari was carried across the river to construct the new residence overlooking the Arges. The boyars were forced to work until the clothes fell off their backs . . . and then had to continue naked.

Vlad's Castle was quite small when compared to either Castle Bran or Hundoara. It was only some 100 feet by 120 feet. It rested on a precipice that looked out over the

INSIDE CASTLE DRACULA, CURTEA DE ARGES, ROMANIA

River Arges. To the north were the mountains dividing Transylvania and Wallachia, and to the south a commanding view of the countryside. There were three towers and walls thick enough to resist Turkish cannon fire. It seems to have been made to house about 200 people. According to legend, a secret staircase led into the mountain to a tunnel, which in turn, led to a grotto that opened on the bank of the river below the castle, though no evidence of the secret passage has been uncovered.

The Turks attacked and captured the castle in 1462. Vlad escaped north through the mountains, but his castle was severely damaged by the invaders. It was used by some of his successors as a mountain retreat. However, it was gradually abandoned and left to the ravages of time and weather. Built originally as a defensive position, it was too far outside the commercial routes that dominated the life of the region.

As late as 1912 the towers of the castle still stood. However, on January 13, 1913, an earthquake hit the area. It toppled the main tower into the river. A second earthquake in 1940 further damaged the castle. Then in the 1970s the Romanian government, responding to increased tourist interest in locations associated with Dracula, carried out a partial reconstruction and built a walkway up the mountainside to the castle's entrance. Today the mountain upon which Castle Dracula rests can be reached by car about an hour's drive north of the city of Pitesti. The walk up the mountain to the entrance takes approximately 45 minutes.

THE PROBLEM OF DRACULA'S CASTLE: The search for Dracula's Castle highlighted the problem of reconciling Stoker's fictional Dracula with historical reality, a problem created by readers' excursions into Stoker's fictional world and made possible by Stoker's attempts to create as realistic a setting as possible. His book was set in Transylvania. Vlad the Impaler was a prince of Wallachia. While born in Transylvania, he resided all of his adult life in Wallachia, except for a period of imprisonment in Hungary. The geography of the novel and of Vlad's life are impossible to reconcile, a fact clearly demonstrated in **Francis Ford Coppola**'s movie **Bram Stoker's Dracula** and its almost comical attempts to place Dracula at the Castle on the Arges and near Borgo Pass at the same time.

There was no actual structure ever called Castle Dracula, only a small castle built by Vlad the Impaler. Though Vlad the Impaler's small castle had its place of importance in Romanian history, it was not known by Stoker and did not serve as a model for his Castle Dracula. It is probable that no castle in Eastern Europe served as the model for Castle Dracula, and the search must be directed closer to home. Thus some suggested that a castle at Cruden Bay, Scotland, where Stoker stayed while writing Dracula, was the model. However, from Stoker's manuscripts it is now known that the section of the novel on the castle was written before he traveled to Cruden Bay and that that section of the book remained essentially unchanged through publication. It would appear that Stoker's castle was a matter of pure imagination, a castle constructed from images of the romantic castles of European fairy tales and folklore.

Sources:

Ambrogio, Anthony. "Dracula Schmacula! Misinformation Never Dies." *Video Watchdog* No. 19 (September/October 1993): 32-47.

Florescu, Radu, and Raymond T. McNally. *Dracula: A Biography of Vlad the Impaler, 1431-1476.* New York: Hawthorn Books, 1973. 239 pp. This volume contains pictures of the several castles associated with Vlad the Impaler.

McNally, Raymond T., and Radu Florescu. *In Search of Dracula.* Greenwich, CT: New York Graphic Society, 1972. 223 pp. Reprint. New York: Warner Books, 1973. 247 pp.

Moisescu, Nicolae. *Curtea de Arges.* Bucharest, Romania: CORESI, 1993. 76 pp.

CHANEY, ALONSO "LON"
(1893-1930)

Alonso "Lon" Chaney, the actor known for his numerous extraordinary characterizations in over a hundred silent movies during the first decades of the twentieth century, was the first actor to play a vampire in an American feature-length movie. He was born on April 1, 1893. Both of Chaney's parents were deaf, and during most of his

LON CHANEY IN *LONDON AFTER MIDNIGHT.*

early life his mother was bedridden. Chaney developed his skill as a silent movie actor by communicating to his mother through mimicry and gesture every day. He was still a boy when in 1901 he began his acting career on the stage. He played a variety of roles and became fascinated with makeup and its interaction with characterization.

Chaney's first film role was in 1913 in *Poor Jake's Demise*. Then **Universal Pictures** signed him to an exclusive contract (for $5.00 a day), and through the rest of the decade he assumed roles in over 100 films. He was first promoted as a star in 1919 when he played a fake cripple in *The Miracle Man*. He went on to his greatest successes as Quasimodo in *The Hunchback of Notre Dame* (1923) and in the title role of *The Phantom of the Opera* (1925).

Chaney worked on occasion with director **Tod Browning.** Their first collaboration was in 1921 in *Outside the Law.* Browning's alcoholism prevented their steady association. It was Chaney's second encounter with alcoholism; earlier he had divorced his wife and taken custody of their son because of her addiction to the bottle.

In 1925 Chaney signed a long-term contract with MGM. Soon afterward he again teamed with Browning to do *The Unholy Three*. He would return to Universal only once, for *The Hunchback of Notre Dame*.

In 1927 Browning and Chaney teamed for the last time in *London After Midnight*. Chaney played a double part as a vampire and a police inspector from Scotland Yard. As the police sleuth, Chaney initiated a scheme to uncover a murder. He assumed the role of a vampire in order to force the real murderer to reveal himself. Once that occurred, Chaney took off the elaborate makeup and revealed himself as the inspector.

Although *London After Midnight* turned out to be his only vampire role, this was almost not the case. In 1930 he made the transition to sound in a new version of *The Unholy Three,* directed by Jack Conway. Meanwhile Browning had moved back to Universal, which had finally attained the film rights to *Dracula.* The studio announced the reunion of Browning and Chaney for the film. Unfortunately, Chaney had developed cancer, and before he could even be signed for the part he died on August 26, 1930. In 1957 his life was brought to the screen in *Man of a Thousand Faces* with James Cagney in the title role.

Sources:

Flynn, John L. *Cinematic Vampires.* Jefferson, NC: McFarland Company, 1992. 320 pp.
Gifford, Denis. *A Pictorial History of Horror Movies.* London: Hamlyn, 1973. 216 pp.

CHARACTERISTICS OF VAMPIRES

Throughout history, vampires have been known by their defining characteristics. Vampires were known to be dead humans who returned from the grave and attacked and sucked the blood of the living as a means of sustaining themselves. The idea of the vampire came to the attention of both the scholarly community and the public in the West because of reports of such creatures in Eastern Europe in the seventeenth and eighteenth centuries. The vampire was seen as a prominent character in the folklore of people from **Greece** and Turkey in the south to **Germany** and **Russia** in the north. The descriptions of vampires in these countries set the image of vampires for the debates about their existence in the eighteenth century. The descriptions of the vampire from Greece and among the southern Slavs became the basis of the development of the literary vampire of the nineteenth century. **Bram Stoker,** the author of *Dracula* (1897), drew heavily upon earlier vampire stories and the accounts of vampires in **Transylvania** and **Romania.** By the end of the nineteenth century and through the twentieth century, using a definition of the vampire drawn from European folklore and mythology, ethnographers and anthropologists began to recognize the existence of analogous beings in the folklore and mythology of other cultures around the world. While these entities from Asian, African, and other cultures rarely conformed entirely to the Eastern European vampire, they shared significant characteristics and could rightly be termed vampires or at least vampirelike entities.

THE MODERN VAMPIRE: The vampire has become an easily recognizable character in Western popular culture. As defined by recent novels and motion pictures and as pictured in comic books and on greeting cards, vampires have several key attributes. Vampires are like "normal" human beings in most respects and are thus able to live more or less comfortably in modern society. They are different, however, in that they possess a pair of **fangs,** tend to dress in formal wear with an opera cape, have a pale complexion, sleep in **coffin**s, are associated with **bat**s, and only come out at night. Their fangs are used to bite people on the neck and suck blood, the substance from which they are nourished. Fangs have become the single most recognizable feature of a male or female vampire, immediately identifying the vampire character to a motion picture audience and signaling immediate danger to the prospective victim.

In addition, vampires are basically creatures of the night, and during the day they enter a coma-like **vampire sleep.** They have red eyes and are cold to the touch. They may not be able to enter a room until invited. In addition, vampires possess some unusual "supernatural" attributes. They have great **strength,** they can fly (or at least levitate), they possess a level of **hypnotic power** (thus forcing the compliance of victims or causing the forgetfulness of the vampire's presence), they have acute night **vision,** and they can undergo a **transformation** into a variety of **animals** (usually a bat or possibly a wolf). Vampires avoid **garlic, sunlight,** sacred symbols such as the cross (the **crucifix**) and holy **water,** and they may need to sleep on their **native soil.** They may be killed by a wooden **stake** thrust in their heart, or by **fire.**

While the stereotype has been challenged in recent decades, a disproportionate number of vampires were drawn from European nobility. They were suave and cultured and readily welcomed into almost any social context. The most recognizable vampire is, of course, **Dracula.** He was preceded by **Lord Ruthven** and Countess **Carmilla** Karnstein. More recently **Barnabas Collins** of an aristocratic American family and the **Lestat de Lioncourt** born of the French lesser nobility have reinforced popular images of the vampire.

FOLKLORIC VAMPIRES: The vampire was not always so described. Folkloric vampires appeared in numerous forms as demonic creatures. The Malaysian *penanggalan,* for example, was pictured as a severed head with entrails dangling down. The Indian goddess **Kali** had a hideous form and was often shown dancing on corpses with fangs protruding from her bloodied lips. However, most commonly the vampire appeared as the corpse of a person recently deceased. It could be recognized by its dress in burial clothes and but could be identified by someone who had known them in life and understood that they were deceased and should not be walking around the town. As often as not, the vampire would never be seen, but its presence would be detected by the effects of its action, usually the wasting away and dying of people from unknown causes or the unusual and unexpected deaths of livestock.

Vampires, if seen, generally appeared to the people closest to them. In some cases, especially among the **Gypsies** and **southern Slavs,** they would return to engage in sexual relations with a former spouse or lover; in most other cases, they would launch a personal attack on family members, friends, or local livestock. Often the vampire would assume a new existence, something that approached normal life. In Malaysia, for example, the *langsuyar* assumed the role of a wife and could bear and raise children. She would usually be detected by some chance event during the course of her life. In Eastern Europe, primarily male vampires were reported to have ventured far from home, where they were not known, and continued their life as before their death, even to the point of marrying and fathering children.

The vampire of folklore had some supernatural attributes above and beyond the mobility one generally does not expect of the dead. It could change form and appear as a host of different animals, from the wolf to the moth. Interestingly, the bat was rarely reported as a vampiric form. Some people reported vampires with **flying** ability, especially in Oriental cultures, but flying or levitation was not prominent among Eastern European vampires.

The original vampires, those described in the folklore and mythology of the world's people, exist as an evil entity within a complex understanding of the world by a particular ethnic group. Thus they would assume characteristics drawn from that group's culture and fitting that group's particular need. Given the variety of vampirelike creatures, both demons and revenants, reported from cultures around the world, almost any characteristic reported of a vampire would be true of one or more such entities.

THE LITERARY VAMPIRE: At the beginning of the nineteenth century, the vampire became the focus of attention of a set of writers, primarily in France and England. In their hands, the folkloric vampire, almost exclusively in its Eastern and Southern European form, was transformed into a gothic villain. While retaining many of the characteristics from the reports of vampires which had filtered into Western Europe in the previous century, writers were quite selective in their choice of acceptable attributes. In the process of creating a literary character, they also added attributes which had no correlate in the folklore literature. Lord Ruthven, the character of the original vampire story written by **John Polidori,** was of noble birth.

CHEDIPE See: INDIA, VAMPIRES IN

CHEEKY DEVIL VAMPIRE RESEARCH

Cheeky Devil Vampire Research was founded in 1992 by L. E. Elliott, its director. Its goal was to research the vampire mythos in all its variant forms of rumor, legend, and fact. Of particular interest were the sociological ramifications of vampire fandom, the fact that many people have embraced such a ''dark'' mythos. To that end, the organization initiated contact with a variety of vampire fans, some of whom claim either to be vampires or believe that they have encountered true vampires.

Cheeky Devil Vampire Research publishes a newsletter. For information on the organization, write Cheeky Devil Vampire Research, PO Box 7633, Abilene, TX 79608.

CHETWYND-HAYES, RONALD HENRY GLYNN (1919-)

Ronald Henry Glynn Chetwynd-Hayes, horror short story writer and anthologist, was born in Middlesex, England, the son of Rose May Cooper and Henry Chetwynd-Hayes. He grew up in England and following his service in the British Army during World War II began a career in sales. His first novel, *The Man from the Bomb,* appeared in 1959. During the 1970s he emerged as a popular writer and anthologist of horror stories. His first vampire story, ''Great Grandad Walks Again,'' appeared in 1973 in *Cold Terror,* a collection of his short stories.

Through the 1970s he edited more than 20 volumes of horror, ghost, and monster stories, as well as several collections of his own works; he was equally productive through the 1980s. Most notable among his titles was *The Monster Club* (1975), later made into a 1980 movie starring **John Carradine** and Vincent Price (who played the author). In 1980 he authored a vampire novel, *The Partaker,* and later edited two anthologies of vampire stories, *Dracula's Children* (1987) and *The House of Dracula* (1988). In 1988 Chetwynd-Hayes received the Bram Stoker Award for his achievements from the Horror Writers of America.

Sources:

Chetwynd-Hayes, Ronald, ed. *Dracula's Children.* London: William Kimber, 1987. 208 pp.
————. *The House of Dracula.* London: William Kimber, 1988. 206 pp.
————. *The Monster Club.* London: New English Library, 1975. 192 pp.
————. *The Partaker.* London: William Kimber, 1980. 224 pp.

CHIANG-SHIH See: CHINA, VAMPIRES IN

CHILDREN'S VAMPIRIC LITERATURE *See:* JUVENILE LITERATURE

CHINA, VAMPIRES IN

When Western scholars began to gather the folklore of China in the nineteenth century, they very quickly encountered tales of the *chiang-shih* (also spelled *kiang shi*), the Chinese vampire. Belief in vampires partially derived from a Chinese belief in two souls. Each person had a superior or rational soul and an inferior irrational soul. The former had the form of the body and upon separation could appear as its exact double. The superior soul could leave the sleeping body and wander about the countryside. For a short period it could possess the body of another and speak through it. If accidents befell the wandering soul, it would have negative repercussions on the body. On occasion the superior soul appeared in an animal form.

The inferior soul, called the *p'ai,* or *p'o,* was the soul that inhabited the body of a fetus during pregnancy and often lingered in the body of a deceased person leading to its unnatural preservation. When the *p'ai* left, the body disintegrated. The *p'ai,* if strong, preserved and inhabited the body for a long period and could use the body for its own ends. The body animated by the *p'ai* was called a *chiang-shih,* or vampire. The *chiang-shih* appeared normal and was not recognized as a vampire until some action gave it away. However, at other times it took on a hideous aspect and assumed a green phosphorescent glow. In this form the *chiang-shih* developed serrated teeth and long talons.

THE ORIGIN AND DESTRUCTION OF THE CHIANG-SHIH: The *chiang-shih* seems to have originated as a means of explaining problems associated with death. The *chiang-shih* arose following a violent death due to **suicide,** hanging, drowning, or smothering. It could also appear in a person who had died suddenly, or as a result of improper burial procedures. The dead were thought to become angry and restless if their burial was postponed for a long time after their death. Also **animals,** especially cats, were kept away from the unburied corpse, to prevent them from jumping over it, lest it become a vampire.

The *chiang-shih* lacked some of the powers of the **Slavic vampire.** It could not, for example, dematerialize, hence it was unable to rise from the grave, being inhibited both by **coffin**s and the soil. Thus their transformation had to take place prior to burial, an added incentive to a quick burial of the dead. The Chinese vampires were nocturnal creatures and limited in their activity to the night hours. The *chiang-shih* had trouble crossing running **water.**

The *chiang-shihs* were very strong and vicious. Reports detailed their attacks upon living people, where they ripped off the head or limbs of their victims. This homicidal viciousness was their most often reported trait. They usually had to surprise their victims because they had no particular powers to lure or entrance them. Besides their homicidal nature, the *chiang-shih* might also demonstrate a strong sexual drive that led it to attack and rape women. Over a period of time, the vampires gained **strength** and began to transform to a mobile state. They would forsake the **coffin** habitat, master the art of **flying,** and develop a covering of long white hair. They might also change into wolves.

In general, the vampire began its existence as an unburied corpse. However, on occasion there were reports of unburied body segments, especially the head, being reanimated and having an existence as a vampire. Also, reports have survived of the ever-present Chinese dragon appearing as a vampire.

People knew of several means of protection from a vampire. **Garlic,** an almost universal medicinal herb, kept vampires away. Salt was believed to have a corrosive effect on the vampire's skin. Vampires were offended by loud noises, and thunder would occasionally kill one. Brooms were handy weapons with which a brave soul could literally sweep the vampire back to its resting spot. Iron filings, rice, and red peas created barriers to the entry of the vampire and would often be placed around a vacant coffin to keep a vampire from taking it as a resting place.

If the vampire reached its transformative stage as the flying hairy creature, only thunder or a **bullet** could bring it down. In the end, the ultimate solution was cremation, the purifying **fire** being something of a universal tool of humankind.

THE *CHIANG-SHIH* IN LITERATURE: The *chiang-shih* was the subject of numerous stories and folktales. In the seventeenth century, the vampire became the subject for one of China's most famous short story writers, P'u Sung-ling, author of the 16-volume *Liao Choi*. His story "The Resuscitated Corpse," for example, concerned four merchants who stopped at an inn. They were housed for the night in the barn, where, as it happened, the body of the innkeeper's daughter-in-law lay awaiting burial. One of the four could not sleep and stayed up reading. The corpse, now bearing **fangs,** approached the three sleeping men and bit each one. The other man watched frozen in fright. He finally came to his senses and grabbing his clothes fled with the vampire hot on his trail. As she caught up to him, he stood under a willow tree. She charged with great speed and ferocity, but at the last second the man dodged, and she hit the tree with full force, her long fingernails imbedded in the tree. The man fainted from fright and exhaustion. The next day the innkeeper's staff found the three dead merchants and the body of his daughter-in-law lying in her place but covered with blood. She was as fresh as the day she died, as she still had her *p'ai,* her inferior soul. He confessed that she had died six months earlier, but he was waiting for an astrologically auspicious day for her burial.

MODERN VAMPIRES IN CHINA: The Chinese vampire was given a new lease on life by the post-World War II development of the film industry in Hong Kong and to a lesser extent in Taiwan. During the 1950s and 1960s, two Hong Kong based firms, Catay-Keris and the Shaw Brothers, began making vampire films in Malaysia using Malaysian themes, but were rather late in developing Chinese vampire movies. Among the first Chinese vampire movies was *Xi Xuefu* (*Vampire Woman*) produced by Zhong Lian in 1962. Like many first ventures into vampirism, it was ultimately a case of mistaken attribution. The story concerned a woman who, after she was found sucking the blood out of her baby, was accused of vampirism and executed by burning. Later it was discovered that the baby had been poisoned, and she was only trying to save it.

The vampire theme in Chinese movies was really launched a decade later with the first of the vampire-martial arts movies, *Vampire Kung-fu* (1972). Then two years later a combined Shaw Brothers-**Hammer Films** production, variously titled *The Legend of the Seven Golden Vampires* and *The Seven Brothers Meet Dracula,* became one of the great disasters in horror film history. *The Legend of the Seven Golden Vampires,* directed by **Roy Ward Baker** and starring **Peter Cushing,** transferred the Dracula story to China where **Abraham Van Helsing** was called to protect a village from a band of vampires who had learned martial arts skills. The film was so bad that its American distributor refused to handle it.

In the 1980s, the Hong Kong filmmakers rediscovered the vampire horror genre. Among the best known movies was the *Mr. Vampire* comedy series begun in 1985 by Golden Harvest and Paragon Films. Drawing on several aspects of Chinese folklore, the films featured what have come to be known as the hopping vampires—loose-robed vampires that hopped to move around. The first film was so popular it spawned four sequels, a **television** series in Japan, and a rival production, *Kung-fu Vampire Buster* (1985). A second very successful movie was *Haunted Cop Shop* (1984) concerning vampires who took over a meat-packing plant and were opposed by a Monster Police Squad. A sequel appeared in 1986. Other notable Hong Kong films included: *Pao Dan Fei Che (The Trail,* 1983), *Curse of the Wicked Wife* (1984), *Blue Lamp in a Winter Night* (1985), *Dragon Against Vampire* (1985), *The Close Encounter of the Vampire* (1985), *Love Me Vampire* (1986), *Vampire's Breakfast* (1986), *Vampires Live Again* (1987), *Toothless Vampires* (1987), *Hello Dracula* (1986), *Vampires Strike Back* (1988), *Spooky Family* (1989), *Crazy Safari* (1990), *First Vampire in China* (1990), *Spooky Family II* (1991), and *Robo Vampire* (1993). As might be perceived by the titles, many of these movies were comedies. Taiwanese films of the same era included *The Vampire Shows His Teeth* I, II, and III (1984-86), *New Mr. Vampire* (1985), *Elusive Song of the Vampire* (1987), and *Spirit vs. Zombi* (1989).

With the hopping or jumping vampires, a different mythology about dealing with vampires evolved. They could be subdued with magical talismans. Holding one's breath would temporarily stop them. Eating sticky rice was an antidote to a vampire bite. By creating a separate vampire myth, the Chinese movies have built a new popular image of vampire for the Orient much as the ***Dracula*** movies created one in the West.

Sources:

de Groot, J. J. M. *The Religious System of China.* 5 vols. Leyden, The Netherlands: E. J. Brill, 1892-1910.

De Visser, M. W. *The Dragon in China and Japan.* Wiesbaden, Germany: Dr. Martin Sändig, 1913, 1969. 242 pp.

Hurwood, Bernhardt J. *Passport to Supernatural: An Occult Compendium from Many Lands.* New York: Taplinger Publishing Company, 1972. 319 pp.

MacKenzie, Donald A. *Myths of China and Japan.* London: Gresham Publishing Company, 1923. 404 pp.

Vellutini, John L. "The Vampire in China." *Journal of Vampirology* 6, 1 (1989): 1-10.

Wieger, Leo. *A History of the Religious Beliefs and Philosophical Opinions in China.* 1927. Reprint. New York: Paragon Book Reprint Corp., 1969. 774 pp.

Willis, Donald C. "The Fantastic Asian Video Invasion: Hopping Vampires, Annoying Aliens, and Atomic Cats." *Midnight Marquee* 43 (Winter 1992): 4-11.

Willoughby-Meade, G. *Chinese Ghouls and Goblins.* New York: Frederick A. Stokes Co., 1926. 431 pp.

CHRISTIANITY AND VAMPIRES

The belief in vampires preceded the introduction of Christianity into southern and eastern Europe. It seems to have originated independently as a response to unexplained phenomena common to most cultures. Ancient Greek writings tell of the *lamiai,* the *mormolykiai,* and other vampirelike creatures. Independent accounts of vampires emerged and spread among the Slavic people and were passed to their non-Slavic neighbors. Possibly the **Gypsies** brought some belief in vampires from **India** that contributed to the development of the myth. As Christianity spread through the lands of the Mediterranean Basin and then northward across Europe, it encountered these vampire beliefs that had already arisen among the many Pagan peoples. However, vampirism was never high on the Christian agenda and was thus rarely mentioned. Its continued presence was indicated by occasional documents such as an eleventh-century law promulgated by Charlemagne as emperor of the new Holy Roman Empire. The law condemned anyone who promoted the belief in the witch/vampire (specifically in its form as a *strix*), and who on account of that belief caused a person thought to be a vampire to be attacked and killed.

By the end of the first Christian millennium, the Christian Church was still organizationally united and in agreement upon the basic Christian affirmation (as contained in the Nicene Creed) but had already begun to differentiate itself into its primarily Greek (Eastern Orthodox) and Latin (Roman Catholic) branches. The Church formally broke in the year 1054 with each side excommunicating the other.

During the second Christian millennium, the two churches completed their conquests through the remaining parts of Europe, especially eastern Europe. Meanwhile, quite apart from the major doctrinal issues which had separated them in the eleventh century, the theology in the two churches began to develop numerous lesser differences. These would become important especially in those areas where the boundaries of the two churches met and wars brought people of one church under the control of political leaders of the other. Such a situation arose, for example, in the twelfth century when the predominantly Roman Catholic Hungarians conquered **Transylvania,** then populated by Romanians, the majority of whom were Eastern Orthodox. Slavic but Roman Catholic **Poland** was bounded on the east by Orthodox Russian states. In the Balkans, Roman Catholic Croatia existed beside predominantly Orthodox Serbia.

One divergence between the two churches frequently noted in the vampire literature was their different understanding of the noncorruptibility of dead bodies. In the East, if the soft tissue of a body did not decay quickly once placed in the ground, it was generally considered a sign of evil. That the body refused to disintegrate meant that the earth would, for some reason, not receive it. A noncorrupting body became a candidate for vampirism. In the West, quite the opposite was true. The body of a dead saint often did not experience corruption like that of an ordinary body. Not only did it not decay, but it frequently emitted a pleasant odor. It did not stink of putrefaction. These differing understandings of incorruptibility explain in large part the demise of belief in vampires in the Catholic West, and the parallel survival of belief in Orthodox lands, even though the Greek Church officially tried to suppress the belief.

VAMPIRES AND SATAN: Admittedly, vampires were not a priority issue on the agenda of Christian theologians and thinkers of either church. However, by 1645 when **Leo Allatius** (1586-1669) wrote the first book to treat the subject of vampires systematically, it was obvious that much thought, especially at the parish level, had been devoted to the subject. The vampire had been part of the efforts of the church to eliminate Paganism by treating it as a false religion. The deities of the Pagans were considered unreal, nonexistent. In like measure, the demons of Pagan lore were unreal.

Through the thirteenth and fourteenth centuries, as the Inquisition became a force in the Roman Catholic Church, a noticeable change took place in theological perspectives. A shift occurred in viewing Paganism (or **witchcraft**). It was no longer considered merely a product of the unenlightened imagination, it was the work of the devil. Witchcraft was transformed in the popular mind into Satanism. The change of opinion on Satanism also provided a opening for a reconsideration of, for example, the **incubus/succubus** and the vampire as also somehow the work of the devil. By the time Allatius wrote his treatise on the vampire, this changing climate had overtaken the church. Allatius was Greek, but he was also a Roman Catholic rather than an Orthodox believer. He possessed a broad knowledge of both churches. In his *De Greacorum bodie quirundam opinationibus,* the vampire toward which he primarily turned his attention was the *vrykolakas,* the Greek vampire.

Allatius noted that among the Eastern Orthodox Greeks a *noncanon,* that is, an ordinance of uncertain authorship and date, was operative in the sixteenth century. It defined a *vrykolakas* as a dead man who remained whole and incorrupt, who did not follow the normal pattern of disintegration which usually occurred very quickly in a time before embalming. Occasionally, such a *vrykolakas* was found, and it was believed to be the work of the devil. When a person discovered a *vrykolakas,* the local priest was to be summoned. The priest chanted an invocation to the Mother of God and again repeated the services of the dead. The earlier noncanon, however, originated in the period when the church was attacking the belief in vampires as superstition and was designed to reverse some centuries-old beliefs about vampires. It ascribed incidents involving *vrykolakas* to someone seeing a dead person, usually at night, frequently in dreams. Such dreams were the work of the devil. The devil had not caused the dead to rise and attack its victims, but deluded the individual with a false dream.

Allatius himself promoted the belief that was gaining dominance in the West through the sixteenth century: Vampires were real and were themselves the work of the devil. Just as the Inquisition in the previous century had championed the idea that witchcraft was real and that witches actually communed with the devil, so vampires were actually walking around the towns and villages of Europe. They were not the dead returned, they were bodies reanimated by the devil and his minions. Allatius even quoted the witchfinders bible, the *Malleus Maleficarum (The Witch's Hammer),* which noted the three conditions necessary for witchcraft to exist: the devil, a witch, and the permission of God. In like measure, Allatius asserted that for vampires to exist all that was needed was the devil, a dead body, and the permission of God.

The tying of vampirism to the devil by Allatius and his colleagues brought **Satan** into the vampire equation. Vampirism became another form of Satanism and the vampire the instrument of the devil. Also, his victims were tainted by evil. Like the demons, vampires were alienated from the things of God. They could not exist in the realms of the sacred and would flee from the effective symbols of the true God, such as the **crucifix,** or from holy things, such as holy **water** and the **eucharistic wafer,** which both Orthodox and Roman Catholics believed to be the very body of Christ. In like measure, the offices of the church through the priest were an effective means of stopping the vampire. In the Eastern Orthodox church, the people always invited the priest to participate in their anti-vampire efforts. In its attempt to counter the superstitious beliefs in vampires, the Orthodox church ordered its priests not to participate in such activities, even threatening excommunication.

THE EIGHTEENTH CENTURY VAMPIRE DEBATES: During the seventeenth century, reports, not just of vampires, but of vampire epidemics, began to filter out of eastern Europe, especially Prussia and Poland. These incidents involved cases in which bodies were exhumed and mutilated. The mutilation of the bodies of people buried as Christians and presumedly awaiting the resurrection was of utmost and serious concern to Christian intellectuals and church leaders in western Europe. The majority of these reports came from Roman Catholic-dominated lands, the most important from that area of Serbia which had been taken over by Austria in the wake of a fading Ottoman Empire. The cases of **Peter Plogojowitz** and **Arnold Paul** launched a heated debate in the German (both Lutheran and Catholic) universities. In the midst of this debate, Cardinal Schtrattembach, the Roman Catholic bishop of Olmütz, Germany, turned to Rome for some advice on how to handle the vampire reports. The pope, in turn, called upon the learned archbishop of Trani, Italy, **Giuseppe Davanzati,** who spent five years studying the problem before writing his *Dissertazione sopra I Vampiri,* finally published in 1744.

Davanzati was swayed by the more skeptical arguments which had emerged as the consensus in the German debates. He advised the pope that the vampire reports were originating in human fantasies. While these fantasies might possibly be of diabolical origin, pastoral attention should be directed to the person reporting the vampire. The bodies of the suspected vampires should be left undisturbed. The church followed Davanzati's wisdom.

Meanwhile, as Davanzati was pursuing his research, so was **Dom Augustin Calmet.** Calmet, known throughout France as a Bible scholar, published his *Dissertations sur les Apparitions des Anges des Démons et des Espits, et sur les revenants, et Vampires de Hingrie, de Boheme, de Moravie, et de Silésie* two years after Davanzati. Calmet played devil's advocate to his fellow churchman. He described in some detail the reports of the eastern European vampires and called upon theologians and his scholarly colleagues to give them some serious study. He essentially argued the medieval position that the bodies of suspected vampires were animated by the devil and/or evil spirits. His colleagues in the church did not receive his report favorably. Even members of the Benedictine order, of which he was a member, chided him for giving credence to what amounted to nothing more than children's horror stories. Though finding little support among the theologians and church hierarchy, he found broad popular support. His book went through several printings in **France** and was translated and published in **Germany** and England.

The sign of the future came in 1755 and 1756 when in two actions Empress Maria Theresa took the authority of handling the vampire cases out of the hands of parish priests and local authorities and placed it in the hands of Austrian government officials. The clear intent of the law was to stop the disturbance of the graves. During the decades following Maria Theresa's action, the spokespersons of what would become known as the Enlightenment would take over the final stages of the debate and essentially end it with their consensus opinion that vampires were unreal. After a generation in which the likes of Diderot and Voltaire expressed their opinion of vampires, scholars have not found it necessary to refute a belief in the vampire. Calmet became an intellectual relic, though he provided a number of interesting stories from which a popular literary vampire could be created.

DRACULA AND THE CHURCH: Interestingly enough, the first vampire stories—from **Johann Wolfgang von Goethe**'s ''The Bride of Corinth'' to **Sheridan Le Fanu**'s ''Carmilla''—were largely secular works. Religious artifacts and religious characters were almost completely absent. At the end of ''Carmilla,'' as Laura's father began his quest to locate and destroy Carmilla, he suggested to Laura that they call upon the local priest. The priest performed certain solemn, but unnamed, rituals which allowed the troubled Laura to sleep in peace. However, he did not accompany the men to finally kill Carmilla, though two medical men were present to oversee the act. It was left to **Bram Stoker** and his novel *Dracula* to reintroduce Christianity into the vampire's life. In the very first chapter, as **Jonathan Harker** made his way to **Castle Dracula,** a woman took off a rosary, with an attached **crucifix,** and gave it to him. In spite of his anti-Roman Catholic background, Harker put the rosary around his neck and wore it. Later, an enraged Dracula lunged for Harker's neck but quickly withdrew when he touched the rosary. **Abraham Van Helsing,** the pious vampire hunter from Holland, explained that the crucifix was one of several sacred objects whose presence deprived the vampire of its power.

Besides the crucifix, Van Helsing used the **eucharistic wafer,** the bread consecrated as the body of Christ in the church's communion service (in this case the Roman Catholic mass). He placed the wafers around the openings of the tomb of **Lucy Westenra** and sanitized (destroyed the effectiveness of) the boxes of **native soil** Dracula brought from his homeland. Most importantly, the wafer burned its imprint into the forehead of the tainted **Mina Murray** after her encounter with Dracula.

In subsequent productions of *Dracula,* the eucharistic wafer largely dropped from the picture. It was used on occasion to sanitize the earth, but only in *Bram Stoker's Dracula* did the scene of Mina's being branded by the wafer become a part of a dramatic presentation. Instead, it was the crucifix that became the religious symbol most frequently used to cause the vampire to lose its **strength** or to harm the vampire.

THE VAMPIRE AND THE CHURCH SINCE STOKER: Through the twentieth century, the crucifix became a standard part of the vampire hunter's kit. Frequently he would flash it just in time to save himself. On many occasions, heroines were saved from a vampire about to pounce upon them by a shining cross hanging around their neck. At the same time, especially since midcentury, the vampire novel began to show signs of secularization. Some vampires came from outer space or arose as victims of a disease. Such vampires, lacking any negative supernatural origins, were unaffected by the holy objects.

As the century progressed, vampire writers challenged the role of Christianity in the culture. Some expressed their doubts as to its claims to exclusive truth concerning God and the world. Writer **Anne Rice,** for example, very early in her life became a skeptic of Roman Catholicism, in which she was raised. Her vampires, reflecting her nonbelief, were unaffected by Christian symbols. They walked in churches with impunity and handled crucifixes with no negative reaction. In like measure, **Chelsea Quinn Yarbro**'s hero, **St. Germain,** and other ''good guy'' vampires, were not Satanic; quite the opposite, they were moral agents. The vampires in Yarbro's books had no negative reaction to Christian objects or places.

Vampires in **science fiction** were raised in an alien culture that had never heard of Christianity. They were among the first group of vampires that had no reaction to Christian sacred symbols. The vampires of *The Hunger* by Whitley Strieber and those in **Elaine Bergstrom**'s novels, were unaffected by the cross because they were aliens. Bergstrom's vampires, the Austra family, made their living working in cathedrals repairing stained glass. Other writers affected by the religiously pluralistic culture in the West questioned the value of Christian symbols for people raised in or adhering to another faith. For example, they asked if Jewish symbols served as protection from Jewish vampires. In Roman Polanski's *The Fearless Vampire Killers,* or *Pardon Me but Your Teeth Are in My Neck* (1967), one of the more humorous moments came from a Jewish vampire attacking a young girl who tried to protect herself with a cross.

The relation to the sacred in general and Christianity in particular will continue to be a problem for vampire novelists, especially those working in the Christian West. The vampire is a supernatural gothic entity whose popular myth dictated its aversion for the crucifix. The literary vampire derives its popularity from the participation of its readers in a world of fantasy and supernatural power. At the same time, an increasing number of novelists do not have a Christian heritage and thus possess no understanding or appreciation of any power derived from Christian symbols. For the foreseeable future, new vampire fiction will be written out of the pull and tug between these traditional and contemporary perspectives.

Sources:

Frayling, Christopher. *Vampyres: Lord Byron to Count Dracula.* London: Faber and Faber, 1991. 429 pp.
Summers, Montague. *The Vampire: His Kith and Kin.* London: Routledge, Kegan Paul, Trench, Trubner, & Co., 1928. 356 pp. Reprint. New Hyde Park, NY: University Books, 1960. 356 pp.

CHUREL *See:* INDIA, VAMPIRES IN

CIHUACOATL See: MEXICO, VAMPIRES IN

CIHUATETEO See: MEXICO, VAMPIRES IN

CLUB VAMPYRE

Club Vampyre was founded in 1993 by Riyn Gray, who developed a fascination for vampires from her broad interest in horror and fantasy in general. In 1992 she read Rosemary Ellen Guiley's book, *Vampires Among Us,* from which she got the idea of starting a fan club. A member of Queens Own, the fan club for fantasy author Mercedes Lackey (who had written several novels featuring vampires), she inserted a letter in the club magazine's pen pal page inquiring if anyone would like to start a vampire fan club. Out of the response, Club Vampyre was born. The first issue of the club magazine, *Fresh Blood,* appeared in June 1993. It is co-edited by Gray and Liza Campbell.

Fresh Blood is the major means of contact between club members. It contains short stories, poetry, interviews, art, reviews, and non fiction articles. The club attempts to cover every aspect of the vampire phenomenon. It is the intention of the editors to keep Club members informed of everything in the field, including other organizations, the new underground vampire nightclubs, and various kinds of vampire merchandise, including new vampire games. The magazine includes free pen pal ads and a letters to the editor column.

Club Vampyre may be contacted at 1764 Lugonia, Ste. 104, No. 223, Redlands, CA 92374. (Please include a self-addressed stamped envelope when corresponding with the club.) The members are organizing a vampire role-playing game where members can develop and play their own vampire character.

COATLICUE See: MEXICO, VAMPIRES IN

COFFINS

In both novels and motion pictures, vampires sleep in coffins, and as they move from place to place, they transport their coffins with them. The association of vampires and coffins began with the simple fact that vampires were dead, and dead people, by the time of the development of the literary vampire in the nineteenth century, were buried in coffins. It should be noted that much vampire lore originated in an era prior to the use of coffins. Until recent centuries, the use of coffins was limited to those wealthy enough to afford them. The dead were commonly wrapped in a burial shroud and placed in a relatively shallow grave. In times of epidemics, the dead might be buried quite hastily and in very shallow graves. Such bodies were subject to predator damage, seemingly the source of northern European beliefs that vampires first devour their own extremities. To keep predators away from bodies buried without a coffin, a flat rock could be placed over part or all of the body. The problems of burial were further complicated by winter weather and frozen ground that would delay burials for weeks or months until the spring thaw, and by various beliefs in astrology that suggested that some moments were better than others for an auspicious burial.

The practice of putting a **stake** into a vampire's body may have originated as a means of fixing the vampire to the ground without a coffin, rather than attacking the vampire itself. Since keeping the corpse in the ground was one purpose of staking someone, the stake did not have to go through the heart. It could just as appropriately go through the stomach or the back. Also the material from which the stake was made was not as important as its functionality. Thus stakes were made of various kinds of wood or iron.

At the time of the great vampire epidemics in eastern Europe in the early eighteenth century, it was the common practice to bury the dead in coffins. Anti-vampire measures consisted of various actions to keep the vampire, usually designated as a recently deceased member of the community, confined to the coffin. The coffin would be opened and the body staked. In some areas the clothes would be attached to the sides of the coffin in order to hold the body in place. The appendages would be nailed to the sides of the coffin so that the vampire could not eat them. The coffin could then be returned to the grave.

Early literary vampires did not have coffins. Geraldine (from **Samuel Taylor Coleridge**'s ''Christabel''), **Lord Ruthven,** and **Varney the Vampyre** had no casket home. **Carmilla** brought no coffin with her, though she was eventually found resting in her crypt at the old chapel. Otherwise, these vampires seemed perfectly comfortable to rest wherever they happened to be.

In **Bram Stoker**'s **Dracula,** the vampire did not rest in a coffin, but he did need to rest on his **native soil.** Thus he transported large crates (not coffins) of soil with him to England, and the desecration of the soil with sacred objects led to his return to his native land. At the end of the novel, **Abraham Van Helsing** entered **Castle Dracula** to destroy the three **vampire brides** who resided at the castle. He found them in their tombs and destroyed them. He also found a large ornate tomb with the word DRACULA written on it. There he laid bits of a eucharistic wafer, thus destroying it as a resting place for a vampire.

The idea of the vampire resting in a coffin primarily derived from the *Dracula* **(1931)** movie in which the vampires were shown rising out of their coffins in the basement of the castle. In later movies, the boxes of earth that Dracula carried to England tended to be replaced by a coffin partially filled with dirt. Numerous vampire movies made use of a scene in which the vampire awakened and slowly thrust his hand out of the coffin.

While modern novels and movies tended to picture vampires sleeping in coffins, this was not a necessity. The coffin was merely one way to meet the requirement that the vampire rest on native soil. Throughout the twentieth century, the vampire increasingly lost any attachment to native soil, and the coffin was utilized more as a protective device shading the vampire from the **sunlight.** At the same time, the coffin served several additional useful purposes, especially in the movies. As a visual object immediately recognized by the audience, it helped build atmosphere. It also provided comic moments, as in George Hamilton's *Love at First Bite,* with all of the problems inherent in transporting, protecting, and explaining the presence of a coffin. The coffin also supplied a ready means of international transportation for the mobile vampire of the modern world. In the movie *Pale Blood* (1989) the vampire carried a light, unobtrusive, portable ''coffin,'' which he could set up like a tent. Finally, and probably most importantly, the coffin supplied a target for the vampire hunter that made locating the vampire during the day far easier.

In developing her modern vampire myth, **Anne Rice** altered the importance of the coffin through the several novels of the ''Vampire Chronicles.'' In *Interview with the Vampire,* the vampire **Lestat de Lioncourt** slept in a coffin, and the night he made Louis a vampire, he forgot to obtain a coffin for him. Thus Louis had to sleep with Lestat as dawn approached. Coffins were a convenience for Rice's vampires, not a necessity. Her vampires could simply return to the earth (as Lestat did for many years) or stay in a sealed chamber protected from the sunlight as the two original vampires (Akasha and Enkil) had done for centuries. Though coffins were not required, most vampires slept in them and only after some years of vampiric existence realized all they needed was a shield of protection from the sun's rays.

Sources:

Barber, Paul. *Vampires, Burial, and Death: Folklore and Reality.* New Haven, CT: Yale University Press, 1988. 236 pp.

COLERIDGE, SAMUEL TAYLOR (1772-1834)

Samuel Taylor Coleridge, a romantic poet and the first to introduce the vampire theme to British poetry, was born in Ottery St. Mary, the son of a minister in the Church of England. His father died when Coleridge was nine, and he was sent to Christ's Hospital, London, as a charity pupil. In 1790 he entered Jesus College, Cambridge. He left college briefly in 1793, but returned the following year. There he met fellow poet **Robert Southey,** who would become his lifelong friend. Through Southey he met Sara Fricker, his future wife, and got his first contract to prepare a book of poetry.

In 1797 Coleridge met William Wordsworth, who was credited with bringing Coleridge's poetic genius to the fore. The initial result of this friendship was ''The Rime of the Ancient Mariner,'' published in the celebrated *Lyrical Ballads,* which Wordsworth put together. Coleridge wrote almost all of his famous poems during the next five years of his close association with Wordsworth.

Among the poems Coleridge worked on during this creative period was ''Christabel.'' Though never mentioning vampires directly, it is now generally conceded that vampirism was the intended theme of ''Christabel,'' the substantive case having been made by Arthur H. Nethercot in the 1930s. Nethercot argued that the essential vampiric nature of the Lady Geraldine, who was "rescued" after being left in the woods by her kidnappers, was demonstrated by examining her characteristics. First, throughout the poem, Christabel was portrayed as a potential victim who needed to be shielded from the forces of evil. Geraldine, however, was pictured as a richly clad woman first seen bathing in the moonlight (the element that revived vampires in nineteenth-century vampire tales). Second, as Geraldine approached the door of the castle of Christabel's father, she fainted. After Christabel assisted her across the threshold, she quickly revived. Vampires had to be formally invited into a home the first time they entered. Third, Geraldine then walked by the dog, who let out an uncharacteristically angry moan. It was commonly believed that vampires had negative effects upon **animals.**

Coleridge dwelt upon the evening encounter of the two women. Christabel showed Geraldine to a place of rest. She opened a bottle of wine, which they shared. At Geraldine's suggestion, Christabel undressed, after which Geraldine partially disrobed, revealing her breast and half her side. What did Christabel see? In lines later deleted from the published version, Coleridge noted that Geraldine's appearance was "lean and old and foul of hue." Christabel entered a trance-like state:

> Yet Geraldine nor speaks nor stirs;
> Ah! what a stricken look was hers!
> Deep from within she seems half-way
> To lift some weight with sick assay,
> And eyes the maid and seeks delay;
> Then suddenly, as one defied,
> Collects herself in scorn and pride,
> And lay down at the Maiden's side!

In a scene with obvious **lesbian** overtones, the two women lay together for an hour and again the animals were affected:

> O Geraldine! one hour was thine—
> Thou'st had thy will! By tairn and rill,
> The night-birds all that hour were still.
> But now they are jubilant anew,
> From cliff and tower, tu-whoo! tu-whoo!

The next morning, Geraldine awoke refreshed and her lean, old, and foul body was rejuvenated, "That (so it seemed) her girded vests/Grew tight beneath her heaving breasts." Christabel, on the other hand, awoke with a sense of guilt and immediately went to prayer. She then led Geraldine to the audience with her father, the lord of the castle. Geraldine immediately attached herself to Lord Leoline while Christabel had a momentary flashback of Geraldine's body when she first disrobed. She attempted to

SAMUEL TAYLOR COLERIDGE

have her father send Geraldine away, but he was already enraptured, and in the end turned from his daughter and departed with Geraldine at his side.

"Christabel" was composed in two parts, the first being written and published in 1798. A second part was finished around 1800. "Christabel" thus preceded Southey's "Thalaba," the first English- language poem to actually mention the vampire in its text.

After 1802, Coleridge wrote little and drew his income primarily from lecturing and writing critical articles. Most of his life he was addicted to drugs, having been hooked on opium in an attempt to deal with chronic pain and later consuming vast quantities of laudanum. He received some recognition of his literary work in 1824 when he was named a "Royal Associate" of the Royal Society of Literature. He died on July 25, 1834, at the age of 61.

Sources:

Nethercot, Arthur H. *The Road to Tryermaine: A Study of the History, Background, and Purposes of Coleridge's "Christabel."* Chicago: University of Chicago Press, 1939. 230 pp. Reprint. New York: Russell & Russell, 1962. 230 pp.

Keesey, Pam, ed. *Daughters of Darkness: Lesbian Vampire Stories.* Pittsburgh/San Francisco: Cleis Press, 1993. 243 pp.

**COLLINS,
BARNABAS**

COLLECTIBLES, PARAPHERNALIA, AND SOUVENIRS *See:* PARAPHERNALIA, VAMPIRE

COLLINS, BARNABAS

Barnabas Collins was a vampire character introduced into the story line of the daytime **television** soap opera *Dark Shadows.* He went on to become the show's central character and saved it from early cancellation. *Dark Shadows,* the **gothic** tale of the Collins family, had begun in 1966 on ABC's afternoon schedule, however, by early 1967 the show was facing cancellation. Threatened with that fate, producer **Dan Curtis** began to experiment successfully with supernatural elements. Finally, he decided to add a vampire.

Barnabas, played by actor **Jonathan Frid,** made his first appearance in episode 210. Willie Loomis, looking for a hidden treasure, discovered a secret room in the nearby mausoleum which contained a coffin secured shut with a chain. Not knowing what he was doing, he released Barnabas from his prison of many decades. In the next episode, Barnabas presented himself at the door of Collinswood, the family estate, as the family's long lost English cousin. He received permission to take up residence in the Old House, the former family manor. In his search for blood, Barnabas discovered Maggie Evans (Kathryn Leigh Scott), the image of his long lost love whom Barnabas vampirized in an attempt to bring her into his world. Barnabas' attacks upon Maggie led to the introduction of Dr. Julia Hoffman (Grayson Hall), a **blood** specialist. Brought in to deal with Maggie's illness, she discovered Barnabas' nature, but rather than destroying him, she fell in love. In her infatuation, she initiated a process to cure him.

At this point, Barnabas Collins and *Dark Shadows* had become a phenomenon of daytime television. As the audience grew, the decision was made to give Barnabas a history. Through the instrument of a seance, the cast of *Dark Shadows* was thrust into the 1790s to assume the roles of their ancestors or eighteenth-century counterparts. The new story line began with episode 366. In 1795 Barnabas was the son of family patriarch Joshua Collins. As the story developed, the family became host to Andre du Prés and his daughter Josette DuPres Collins (Kathryn Leigh Scott), Barnabas' fiancée, who arrived from their plantation in Martinique for the wedding. Josette was accompanied by her maid, Angelique Bouchard (played by Lara Parker, a new addition to the cast), who was a witch. Angélique, in her desire for everything her employers possessed, moved on Barnabas but was repelled. She then turned on Josette and through her witchcraft caused Josette's to marry Barnabas's uncle Jeremiah Collins instead. Barnabas killed Jeremiah in a duel.

Eventually, Barnabas was tricked into marrying Angélique, but when he discovered her occult actions, he shot her. Believing that she was dying, Angélique cursed Barnabas with the words that set the pattern of his character for the future, ''I set a curse on you, Barnabas Collins. You will never rest. And you will never be able to love. Whoever loves you will die. That is my curse—and you will live with it through all eternity.'' As the words died out, a vampire **bat** flew into the room and headed straight for Barnabas' throat. He died from the attack only to arise a vampire. He decided that Josette should join him in his vampiric existence, and began to drain her of blood. Before he could finish the transformation, however, Angélique's spirit lured Josette to a cliff, where she fell to her death. Jeremiah Collins having learned of his son's condition, locked him in the mausoleum and chained him up to stop the plague of his vampiric attacks.

With episode 461, the story line returned to the present. Barnabas had been given a history and a complex personality. Besides his blood thirst, he had a moral sensitivity, the ability to show great passion and love, and was the victim of great suffering. In Angélique he had an enemy who returned in various guises to thwart his plans for happiness. His adventures would continue for almost 800 more *Dark Shadows* episodes. In 1970 *Dark Shadows* creator/producer Curtis borrowed the cast for a feature movie, *House of Dark Shadows,* at the close of which Barnabas was killed. Thus he did not appear in the 1971 follow-up, *Night of Dark Shadows.*

In 1990 Barnabas' story was revived when NBC began a prime time version of *Dark Shadows.* It covered the basic story line of the emergence of Barnabas Collins (portrayed by **Ben Cross**) in the present and his origin in the 1790s prior to its cancellation after only one season.

In 1966 Marilyn Ross (pseudonym of **Daniel Ross**), began what would become 33 *Dark Shadows* novels based upon the television series. Barnabas appeared first in the sixth volume and his name and image dominated it for the remaining titles. The first issue of the comic book *Dark Shadows* (from Gold Key), which included a picture of Barnabas on the cover of most issues, appeared in March 1969. The series continued through 1976. In 1992 a new *Dark Shadows* comic based on the NBC series was initiated by Innovation Comics. In spite of the television series being canceled, Innovation's comic book continued beyond the television story with a fresh story line until Innovation's demise in 1994.

By 1968, Barnabas' image began to appear on a wide variety of products, among the first being the *''Dark Shadows'' Game* from gum card, Whitman, and a Halloween costume. Through 1969, the variety of **paraphernalia** included another set of trading cards, two jig-saw puzzles, pillows, a poster, and several model kits. Other items appeared over the years, and a new set of memorabilia was generated in response to the 1991 television series.

Collins was only the second vampire of modern history to gain a wide public following. Though there is little likelihood that a new *Dark Shadows* series will come to television, the continuation of *Dark Shadows* conventions, the return of the series to

BARNABAS COLLINS WAS MOST RECENTLY PORTRAYED BY BEN CROSS, HERE PICTURED WITH OTHERS FROM THE *DARK SHADOWS* (1990) CAST.

cable television on the Sci-Fi Channel, and the numerous new *Dark Shadows* writings, ensure that Barnabas will have high visibility for some years to come.

Sources:

Scott, Kathryn Leigh. *The Dark Shadows Companion: 25th Anniversary Collection.* New York: Pomegranate Press, 1990. 208 pp.

Stockel, Shirley, and Victoria Weidner. *A Guide to Collecting "Dark Shadows" Memorabilia.* Florissant, MO: Collinwood Chronicle, 1992. 107 pp.

COLLINSPORT PLAYERS

The Collinsport Players is a fan-led *Dark Shadows* dramatic group founded at the **Dark Shadows Festival** in Newark, New Jersey, in 1984 by Jeff Thompson and Dr. Laura Brodian, hosts of the festival. Both were already in costume and decided to

COLLINSPORT PLAYERS (WITH JEFF THOMPSON AS BARNABAS) LIVE IT UP AT THE ANNUAL DARK SHADOWS FESTIVAL.

enliven their hosting chores with a set of improvisational sketches. The positive reaction of the audience led to a formalizing of their activities as the Collinsport Players (named for the town in which the Collins family resided in the television show). Improvisation dominated the 1985 performance of a skit entitled *Julia's Trump.* From that point, scripts were written and the cast size increased. *Spelling Bee,* presented in 1985, involved five actors. In 1986, the twentieth anniversary of the premiere of *Dark Shadows,* the group performed *The More Things Change: The Official Twentieth Anniversary Skit,* a major step forward into a full one-act play with some two dozen actors participating.

The Collinsport Players now regularly perform at the annual national Dark Shadows Festival. It draws its cast from fans around the country. The new scripts each year are sent to the players six weeks ahead of time. They memorize their parts and gather upon their arrival at the festival site for two rehearsals before their performances. The plays have been comedies full of inside jokes. Many have spoofed actual episodes of the television series while others have moved in more speculative directions, taking the characters into hypothesized situations. Among the Collinsport Players' most successful comedies, complete with costumes, sound effects, and music, have been *Quiet on the Set, The Times They Change, The Loco-Motion, Double Play,* and *A Julia Carol.* In 1993 the first of two volumes of the Players' skits was published by **HarmonyRoad Press.** Connie Jonas, the press' founder, is a member of the group.

Jeff Thompson, co-founder of the players and its current producer-director, has been a *Dark Shadows* fan for many years, and has written widely for several of the fanzines. He wrote most of the plays for the players, one fan-press book on *The Dark Shadows Comic Books,* and in 1990 completed his master's degree program with a thesis on the historical novels of **Daniel Ross,** who wrote 33 *Dark Shadows* novels under the pseudonym Marilyn Ross. Thompson completed his thesis at Tennessee State University, where he teaches English.

The Collinsport Players may be contacted c/o Jeff Thompson, 6807 Pennywell Dr., Nashville, TN 37205-3011.

Sources:

Thompson, Jeff. *The Dark Shadows Comic Books.* Los Angeles: Joseph Collins Publications, 1984, Rev. ed. 1988. 115 pp.
———. *The Effective Use of Actual Persons and Events in the Historical Novels of Dan Ross.* Nashville, M.A. thesis, Tennessee State University, 1991. 207 pp.
———, and Connie Jonas, eds. *The Collinsport Players Companion.* 2 vols. Portland, OR: HarmonyRoad Press, 1993-94.

COMIC BOOKS, THE VAMPIRE IN

Comic books emerged as a distinct form of popular literature in the 1930s, arising from the comic strips that had become a standard item in newspapers. The first vampire seems to have appeared in an early comic book title, *More Fun.* Each issue of *More Fun* carried the continuing stories of Dr. Occult, a ghost detective who fought various supernatural villains. In issue No. 6, Dr. Occult's first major case pitted him against a creature called the "Vampire Master". His undead evil was stopped by a knife plunged into his heart. Before the end of the decade, in the fall of 1939, **Batman** would encounter a vampire in issues 31 and 32 of *Detective Comics.* As more horror stories appeared in the 1940s adventure and crime comics, response suggested that there was an audience for an all-horror comic book. In 1948 the American Comics Group issued the first and one of the most successful horror comics, *Adventures into the Unknown.* Very quickly vampires found their way onto its pages, and through the early 1950s each issue commonly had at least one vampire story. *Adventures into the Unknown* soon spawned imitators. In 1950 William Grimes and artist Al Feldman of EC Comics began *Crypt of Terror* (later *Tales from the Crypt*) which was quickly joined by the *Vault of Horror* and *Haunt of Fear.* During the next four years, over 100 horror comic book titles joined the pioneering efforts.

Among the horror comics of the 1950s were a variety of titles by Atlas Comics (later Marvel Comics) such as *Suspense Comics* (1950-1953), *Mystic* (1951-57), and *Journey into the Unknown* (1951-57), each of which carried vampire stories. Avon's *Eerie* No. 8 (August 1953) became the first of many to adapt **Bram Stoker**'s novel *Dracula* to comic book format.

VAMPIRES UNDER ATTACK: The boom in horror comics did not go unnoticed by the larger society, and attacks upon them began to mount. Psychology spokespersons such as Frederic Wertham decried the violence and sex he found in some comic books as a direct source of the growing phenomenon of juvenile delinquency and began to demand their suppression. Feeling the intensity of the attack, a number of the comic book publishing firms found it in their best interest to create the Comic Magazine Association of America (CMAA). The CMAA quickly concluded that some form of self-regulation was necessary to prevent government intervention in its business. In 1954 the CMAA issued a Comics Code, which went into effect in October of that year. The code dealt with some broad issues such as glamorizing crime and the graphic portrayal of death and responded to the criticisms of horror comics directly. At the same time that controversy raged in America, a similar controversy developed in England. In 1955 the Children and Young Persons (Harmful Publications) Act was passed, which led to the disappearance of horror comics from the stores. The bill was renewed in 1965 and is still on the books, one reason that so few horror/vampire comics have originated in the United Kingdom.

The Comics Code called for the discontinuance of the words ''horror'' or ''terror'' in the title of comic books and forbad the picturing of, among other things, scenes of depravity, sadism, or excessive gruesomeness. One paragraph dealt forcefully with the major characters associated with the horror story:

> Scenes dealing with, or instruments associated with walking dead, torture, vampires and vampirism, ghouls, cannibalism, and werewolfism are prohibited.

Thus, in October 1954, Dracula and his kin were banished from the pages of the comic book. The only major appearance of a vampire following the implementation of the code was by Dell Comics, a company that did not formally subscribe to the code, though in large part tried to adhere to it. A single October/December issue of a new title, *Dracula,* appeared in 1962. The story, set in the present time, centered upon an encounter between several Americans and Count Dracula in **Transylvania.** However promising the first issue might have been, the second never appeared. Meanwhile, Dracula and his cohorts were discovering a new format by which they could sneak back into the comic book world.

In 1958, four years after the implementation of the Comics Code, a new type of magazine, the horror movie fan magazine, arrived on the newsstands. The first, *Famous Monsters of Filmland,* was developed by James Warren and **Forrest J. Ackerman** and published by the Warren Publishing Company. Projected as a movie fanzine, it was not subject to the regulations of the Comics Code, even though it began to include black and white horror comics interspersed with movie stills and feature stories. In 1964 Warren risked the publication of a black and white horror comic, featuring the very characters and scenes specifically banned by the Comics Code, in a new full size (8 1/2'' x 11'') magazine format. Technically, *Creepy* was not a comic book, but it reached the same youthful audience. It was so successful that in 1965 it was joined by *Eerie,* which followed a similar format. That same year, vampires crept back into comic books through *The Munsters,* a comic book based upon the popular television series which featured two vampires, Lily and Grandpa (really Count Dracula), in a comedy format with no visible bloodsucking.

Finally in 1966, Dell decided to release a second issue of *Dracula.* While continuing the numbering of the original issue of 1962, the new issue carried a completely new story line and an entirely new ''Dracula'' recast in the image of a superhero. The new Dracula character, according to the plot a descendent of the original Count, had been experimenting with a new serum made from the brains of bats. After he accidentally consumed some of the potion, he discovered that he had the ability to transform into a bat. In two subsequent issues he moved to the United States, donned a superhero costume, and launched a war on the forces of evil.

In 1969, with rising pressure to revamp the Comics Code and provide some liberalization in its enforcement, Gold Key issued the first new comic books to feature a vampire as the leading figure. Like *The Munsters,* also by Gold Key, *Dark Shadows* was based on a popular television series. It featured the adventures of vampire **Barnabas Collins.** *Dark Shadows* was joined in September by Warren Publishing Company's *Vampirella.* The latter, featuring a sexy female vampire from outer space in stories combining humor, horror, and romance, became the most popular and long-lived vampire comic book in the history of the medium.

THE VAMPIRE'S RETURN: Finally, bowing to the needs of companies eager to compete with the black and white comic books, CMAA formally revised the Comics Code, effective January 1, 1971. The change also reflected both an awareness of changing times and the inability of the critics of comic book art to produce the evidence to back up the charges leveled at them in the 1950s. The code still discouraged the portrayal of situations that involved, for example, excessive gore, torture, or sadism. However, the important sentence concerning vampires was rewritten to read:

> Vampires, ghouls, and werewolves shall be permitted to be used when handled in the classic tradition such as Frankenstein, Dracula, and other high calibre literary works written by Edgar Allan Poe, Saki (H. H. Munro), Conan Doyle, and other respected authors whose works are read in schools throughout the world.

Marvel Comics responded immediately to the new situation. It launched a line of new horror titles and in 1972 led in the return of the vampire. Joining Warren's *Vampirella* was *The Tomb of Dracula,* which provided a new set of imaginative adventures for Dracula in the modern world. It lasted for 70 issues, had two revivals, and undergirded the 1990s adventures of the **Midnight Sons,** who united a variety of forces to fight

SEDUCTION OF THE INNOCENT! PLAYED AN IMPORTANT ROLE IN THE BANNING OF VAMPIRES FROM COMIC BOOKS IN THE 1950s.

malevolent occultism. That same year, Marvel introduced a new vampire, **Morbius.** After several appearances as a guest villain in other Marvel magazines, Morbius became part of the regular cast appearing in *Vampire Tales* (beginning in 1973), was the leading figure in *Fear* (beginning in February 1974), and more recently was an integral part of the Midnight Sons.

The rapidly rising sales in horror comics during the early 1970s slowly leveled off and during the later part of the decade began to decline. While *Vampirella* survived the decade, few others did. The enthusiasm for horror comics had been overwhelmed by the proliferating number of super heroes. As horror comics in general slumped, the vampire comics all but died. *The Tomb of Dracula* was discontinued in 1979, to be followed by six issues of a black and white full-sized comic magazine, which died in 1980. *Vampirella* was issued for the last time in 1981. With two exceptions, no comic book in which a vampire was the leading character was issued through the early and mid-1980s.

In 1981 DC Comics, by no means a major voice in the horror comics field, introduced a new vampire character, Andrew Bennett, in its long-standing horror comic book *The House of Mystery.* His life and adventures were told in a series of episodes under the title **"I . . . Vampire"**. Bennett was, according to the story, 400 years old. Four centuries ago he bit his fiance, Mary, who, of course, also became a vampire. She resented what had happened to her, and as a result spent the rest of her existence trying to get even with Bennett and with the world. *"I . . . Vampire"* dominated most (but not all) issues of *House of Mystery* from March 1981 (No. 290) through August 1983 (No. 319). DC had also introduced another vampirelike character, **Man-Bat** appeared periodically throughout the decade, usually in association with Batman. In 1975-76, DC tried to establish Man-Bat in a comic book of his own, but it lasted for only two issues. A second attempt at a Man-Bat comic was discontinued after only one issue in December 1984.

Following the demise of the *Tomb of Dracula* in 1979 and its sequel in 1980, Dracula made a number of appearances as a guest villain in various Marvel comics. A definitive encounter occurred in *Doctor Strange* (No. 62, December 1983). In a face off with Dracula, the occultist Dr. Stephen Strange performed a magical ritual, the Montesi Formula, which demolished Dracula and supposedly killed all of the vampires in the world. By this act, Marvel banished the vampire from the Marvel Universe.

THE VAMPIRE REVIVAL: After this low point of interest in vampirism following Marvel's new banishment, the vampire slowly made a comeback. Examining the events of a decade, one can now trace the annual increase of the number of vampire movies, the production of which hit bottom in 1984 when only one, *The Keep,* was released. At the same time the number of new vampire novels dropped to nine in 1983, half the number of 1977.

Meanwhile, radical changes had occurred in the world of comic books. First, and most noticeably, the technology of producing comic books measurably improved. A higher quality paper allowed a more brilliant eye-catching color. Meanwhile, as comic book illustrations were recognized as an art form, artists demanded and got more freedom, most obvious in the disappearance of the box into which cartoon art had traditionally fit. Second, the comic book market had shifted to accommodate a new adult readership. No longer were comic books just for children and youth; numerous new titles were developed exclusively for that ever-expanding adult audience that had grown up with comics. Third, the x-rated comic had emerged as part of the new specialty line for the adult reader. Fourth, a significant portion of the new adult-oriented comics were designed to last, for a predetermined number of issues, most frequently four. Fifth, to accommodate the new market, a host of new companies, collectively called "the independents," came into existence.

Thus, when the vampire comic began to make its comeback in the 1990s, it did so in a radically new context. The first issue of *Blood of the Innocent,* the first of the new vampire comics, was released at the beginning of 1986 by WarP Comics. It ran four issues and was followed by *Blood of Dracula* from Apple Comics. Rick Shanklin was the writer of both projects. Marvel, the giant of the comic book industry, entered the picture with its very unconventional vampire title *Blood* (four issues, 1987-88), a good example of the new artistic and technological advances that were setting the standards of the industry. In 1989 Eternity Comics (an imprint of Malibu Graphics) released the first of two four-issue titles, *Dracula* and *Scarlet in Gaslight.* Then in 1990, Innovation (another of the new companies) launched a 12-issue adaptation of **Anne Rice**'s best selling novel *The Vampire Lestat.* These six titles heralded the spectacular expansion of vampire comic book publishing, which became evident in 1991. The 10 new vampire titles which appeared in 1990 became 23 titles in 1991. In 1992 no fewer than 34 new titles were published, followed by a similar number in 1993.

In 1983 Marvel had killed off all of the vampires and for six years none appeared. At the end of 1989, Morbius reappeared in issue No. 10 (November 1989) of *Dr. Strange: Sorcerer Supreme.* It seemed that he had survived when the other vampires had been killed. He had been returned to his human state before Dr. Strange worked his magic and for a number of years lived a somewhat normal life. On a vacation in New Orleans at the end of the decade, he encountered the witch Marie Leveau, who changed him back into a vampire. The cover of *Dr. Strange: Sorcerer Supreme* No. 14 (February 1990) announced the return of the vampires to the Marvel Universe. Morbius, after several appearances with Dr. Strange, got his own comic in September 1992.

Innovation's *The Vampire Lestat* featured some of the best art work in the field, and its success justified the equally well-done series adapting Rice's other vampire novels, *Interview with a Vampire* and *The Queen of the Damned.* Following Innovation's lead were *Big Bad Blood of Dracula* (Apple), *Blood Junkies on Capitol Hill* (Eternity), the adult adaptation of **"Carmilla"** (Aircel), *Death Dreams of Dracula* (Apple), *Dracula the Impaler* (Comax), *Dracula's Daughter* (Eros), *Ghosts of Dracula* (Eternity), **Richard Matheson**'s *I Am Legend* (Eclipse), *Night's Children* (Fanta Co), *Nosferatu* (Tome), and ***The Tomb of Dracula*** (Epic). In 1991 Harris

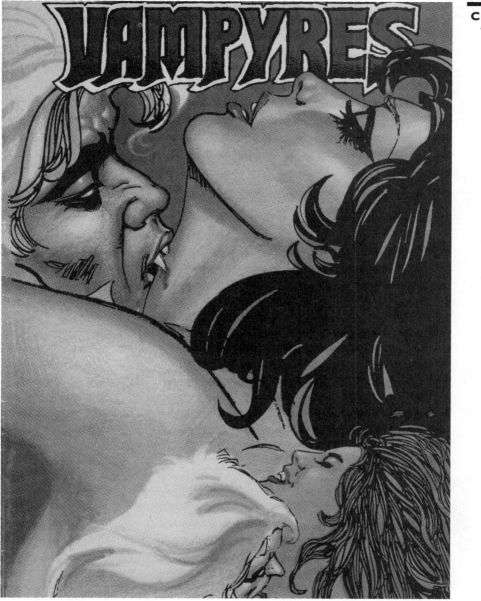

COVER OF THE *VAMPYRE* COMIC BOOK.

Comics acquired the rights to *Vampirella* and revived it with a new storyline that picked up the title character 10 years after the last episode in the original series. The response led to a new full-color *Vampirella* and a set of reprints from the original series.

1992 proved an equally expansive year for vampire comics, with a 50 percent growth in new titles from the previous year. Innovation continued its leadership with its adaptation of the briefly revived television series *Dark Shadows*. Its art work was rivaled by the equally spectacular Topps Comics production of *Bram Stoker's Dracula* based on the **Francis Ford Coppola** movie. Other new titles included *Blood Is the Harvest* (Eclipse), *Children of the Night* (Night Wynd Enterprises), *Cristian Dark* (Darque Studios), *Dracula in Hell* (Apple), *Dracula, the Suicide Club* (Adventure), *Little Dracula* (Harvey), and *Vampire's Kiss* (Friendly).

By 1992 Marvel Comics was fully involved in the vampire revival. It issued several reprints of its 1970s success *The Tomb of Dracula* under new titles: *Requiem for Dracula, The Savage Return of Dracula,* and *The Wedding of Dracula.* More importantly, it began several entirely new comics that featured vampires. *Team Titans,* a spin-off of the superhero *New Titans,* included the vampire Night Rider. *The Nightstalkers* was built around vampire hunters **Blade, the Vampire Slayer,** Frank Drake, and Hannibal King, all characters from *The Tomb of Dracula* who had disappeared in 1983. Morbius finally got is own series. These titles were then integrated through crossover stories with several other horror (but not vampiric) series, including *Ghost Rider, Darkhold,* and *Spirits of Vengeance.* The response was significant enough for Marvel to begin talking about a separate area of the Marvel Universe which dealt with occult issues. In late 1993 Marvel announced its new Universe structure by briefly setting apart these five titles, plus a new title, *Midnight Sons Unlimited,* and the older *Dr. Strange: Sorcerer Supreme* under a distinct Marvel imprint, Midnight Sons, which appeared in the October, November, and December issues of its occult titles.

THE FUTURE: It is difficult to predict how long the boom in vampire comics that started in the late 1980s will last and what its permanent effect will be. However, the industry has discovered that the vampire, far more than any of the other standard horror creatures, has a large audience of both adults and youth, who will respond to a steady diet of fresh vampire stories. There is every reason to believe that the vampire will be a significant aspect of comic art for the foreseeable future.

Sources:

Barker, Martin. *A Haunt of Fears: The Strange History of the British Horror Comics Campaign.* London: Pluto Press, 1984. 227 pp.

Benton, Mike. *Horror Comics: The Illustrated History.* Dallas, TX: Taylor Publishing, 1991. 144 pp.

Glut, Donald R. *The Dracula Book.* Metuchen, NJ: Scarecrow Press, 1975. 388 pp.

Goulart, Ron. *The Encyclopedia of American Comics.* New York: Facts on File, 1990. 408 pp.

Horn, Maurice, ed. *The World Encyclopedia of Comics.* New York: Chelsea House Publishers, 1976. 785 pp.

Melton, J. Gordon. *The Vampire in the Comic Book.* New York: Count Dracula Fan Club, 1993. 36 pp.

Thompson, Jeff. *The Dark Shadows Comic Books.* Los Angeles, CA: Joseph Collins Publications, 1984, 1988. 115 pp.

COPPOLA, FRANCIS FORD (1939-)

Francis Ford Coppola, Oscar-winning director of the 1992 motion picture *Bram Stoker's Dracula,* was born on April 7, 1939, in Detroit, Michigan. In 1962, three years after completing his degree at Hofstra University (B.A., 1959), he went to work for **Roger Corman** at American International Pictures. He served as co-director and co- screenwriter for *The Playgirls and the Bellboy* before directing his first horror films *The Terror* and *Dementia 13* in 1963. That same year he married Eleanor Neil. In 1964 he became the director at Seven Arts and while there also completed a Masters of Fine Arts degree at UCLA (1967). His film *You're a Big Boy Now* was accepted by the school as his master's thesis. He would become the first major American film director to come out of one of the several university film programs that had arisen in post-World War II America. Three years after his graduation he won his first Oscar for his screenplay for *Patton.*

In 1972, he founded the Directors Company with Peter Bogdanovich and William Franklin. That same year he had his first major motion picture, *The Godfather.* Which he won an Oscar for best screenplay (with Mario Puzo). He also won an Oscar for the screen play (again with Puzo) for *The Godfather, Part II.* His 1979 production *Apocalypse Now* was the first major picture about the Vietnam War. It won the Palme d'Or and the Fipresci Prize from the Cannes Festival. He moved on to do a number of notable films, including *Peggy Sue Got Married* (1986), *Tucker: The Man and His Dream* (1988), and *The Godfather, Part III.*

Coppola thus emerged in the early 1990s as the most acclaimed director ever to turn his attention to the Dracula theme. The production began with a screenplay by Jim Hart and with Winona Ryder (who gave Coppola the screenplay) as **Mina Murray,** the female lead. There were budget limitations, and a decision was reached to film the picture entirely at Columbia's studios in Los Angeles. It took 68 days. A basically youthful cast was selected along with Anthony Hopkins, fresh from his notable success in *Silence of the Lambs,* as **Abraham Van Helsing.** His goal was to take the old theme, return to the novel for fresh direct inspiration, and produce a new movie which would stand out from the prior *Dracula* versions.

The screenplay, by Jim Hart, not only relied upon the Bram Stoker novel, but the extensive research on the historical Dracula, the fifteenth-century Romanian prince **Vlad the Impaler** by historians **Raymond T. McNally** and **Radu Florescu.** In order to integrate that new historical material, a rationale for the actions of Dracula (based in part upon unresolved personal issues from the fifteenth century) was injected into the story line from the novel. The movie was also helped by changing guidelines concerning what could be shown on the screen. For example, It was not until 1979 in the **Frank Langella** *Dracula* that the vital scene from the novel in which Dracula and Mina shared blood was incorporated into a film.

Though Coppola had available to him the high-tech special effects developed in the decade since the previous *Dracula* **(1979),** he chose not to use them. Instead, he returned to some older tricks of cinematic illusions. Elaborate use of double exposures was employed and miniatures were used instead of matte paintings to provide more depth.

The finished product quickly took its place among the best of the *Dracula* films, though Dracula aficionados were divided on it. The initial response to its opening surprised many, grossing double the original expectations for its first week when it played on almost 2,500 screens. The movie provided Columbia Pictures with its largest opening ever, surpassing *Ghostbusters 2* (1989). It has proved equally popular on video. A sequel, *Van Helsing's Chronicles,* will continue the story of the vampire hunter starring Anthony Hopkins.

Sources:

Biodrowski, Steve. "Coppola's Dracula: Directing the Horror Classic." *Cinefantastique* 23, 4 (December 1992): 32- 34. One of a set of articles on Coppola in the same issue.

Goodwin, Michael, and Naomi Wise. *On the Edge: The Life and Times of Francis Coppola.* New York: William Morrow, 1989. 512 pp.

Johnson, Robert. *Francis Ford Coppola.* Boston: Twayne Publishers, 1977. 199 pp.

Thomas, Nicolas, ed. *International Dictionary of Films and Filmmakers II, Directors.* Chicago: St. James Press, 1991.

Zuker, Joel Stewart. *Francis Ford Coppola: A Guide to References and Resources.* Boston: G. K. Hall, 1984. 241 pp.

CORMAN, ROGER WILLIAM (1926-)

Roger William Corman, independent film director and producer, was born April 5, 1926, in Detroit, Michigan. Following his service in the U.S. Navy during World War II, he earned an engineering degree at Stanford University. His career in motion pictures began as a messenger boy at 20th Century-Fox in the early 1950s. He worked his way up from scriptwriter to director and producer. His first directing job was on *Guns West,* a western for American International Pictures, for whom he would direct and produce for almost two decades. Over the next four decades Corman would direct and/or produce over 100 films. He left AIP to found his own New World Pictures in 1970. At New World Pictures he developed specialized sub-genre films that were distinctive for their formulaic amount of violence, nudity, humor, and social commentary incorporated into each plot. In 1985 Corman established a new distribution company, Concorde Pictures. He currently heads Concorde and New Horizons Home Video.

Corman's films seem to have treated every subject imaginable. They have become known for their quick production on a low budget. At the same time Corman is applauded for the opportunity he gave many young actors and the relative freedom to experiment he gave new directors. Such diverse people as Jack Nicholson and **Francis Ford Coppola** started with Corman. As might be expected, among his more

ROGER CORMAN DIRECTING.

that 100 movies, Corman produced his share of vampire movies, including some of the more important films of the genre.

Corman's first vampire film, which he both directed and produced, was also possibly the first **science fiction** vampire movie. *Not of this Earth* (1957) had humanoid aliens checking out earthlings as possible sources for blood for their race. In *Little Shop of Horrors* (1960), later a broadway musical and a 1980s movie from Warner Brothers, the plant in the quaint florist shop was the vampire.

In 1966 Corman acquired footage from a Russian film, *Niebo Zowiet,* around which Curtis Harrington wrote a script. A week of shooting and a new sci-fi vampire, the *Queen of Blood,* emerged. Still an interesting picture, it featured **Forrest J. Ackerman** in a brief role and started assistant director Stephanie Rothman on her directing career. Rothman then directed Corman's next vampire production, *The Velvet Vampire* (1971), which featured a female vampire wreaking damage on the unsuspecting until she encounters a groups of savvy hippies.

Through the remainder of the decade at New World, Corman did not pursue the vampire, there being plenty of other interesting themes to explore. However, through the 1980s New World and its successor Concorde/New Horizons were responsible for a series of vampire movies, including: *Saturday the 14th* (1981), *Hysterical* (1982), *Transylvania 6-5000* (1985), *Vamp* (1986), *Saturday the 14th Strikes Back* (1987), *Not of This Earth* (1987), and *Transylvania Twist* (1989).

Then in 1988, with the noticeable increase in interest in vampires, Corman's Concorde initiated a new effort titled *Dance of the Damned.* The story centered on a stripper with a suicidal impulse who unknowingly took a vampire home. He wanted to know about the experiences he had been denied. The idea worked well enough that it was remade in 1992 as *To Sleep with a Vampire.* The relative success of these two movies led immediately to a third film that combined the Dracula myth with the new contemporary vampire popularized by the **Anne Rice** novels. The result, *Dracula Rising,* had a young female art historian encountering Dracula while working in **Transylvania.** Picking up the suggestion from **Dan Curtis**'s *Dracula* (1973), Dracula saw her as the image of his lost love of four centuries earlier. Dracula had originally become a vampire when his love had been executed as a witch. When he finally found her again, his vampiric condition kept him from her.

In 1990 Corman authored his autobiography, which he appropriately titled *How I Made a Hundred Movies in Hollywood and Never Lost a Dime.* After 40 years he continues to make movies and given the perspective of four decades, his accomplishments are bringing him some of the recognition he had been denied through most of his career. In 1992 he was awarded the 30th Annual Career Award by **The Count Dracula Society.**

Sources:

Corman, Roger, with Jim Jerome. *How I Made a Hundred Movies in Hollywood and Never Lost a Dime.* New York: Random House, 1990. 237 pp.

McGee, Mark Thomas. *Roger Corman: The Best of the Cheap Acts.* Jefferson, NC: McFarland, 1988. 247 pp.

Morris, Gary. *Roger Corman.* Boston: Twayne Publishers, 1985. 165 pp.

Naha, Ed. *The Films of Roger Corman.* New York: Arco Press, 1982. 209 pp.

Shairo, Marc. "*Dracula Rising*: Corman's Count." In *Dracula the Complete Vampire.* New York: Starlog Communications International, 1992, pp. 66-71.

Will, David, et al. *Roger Corman: The Millenic Vision.* Edinburgh: Edinburgh Film Festival, 1970. 102 pp.

COUNT DRACULA

Count Dracula (1977) was a made for television co-production of the British Broadcasting Company and American Public Television. It consisted of three 45 minutes segments, and thus was the screen adaptation of *Dracula* with the longest running time.

Count Dracula began with **Jonathan Harker** saying goodbye to **Mina Murray** (now **Lucy Westenra**'s sister), Lucy, and their mother. He traveled to **Castle Dracula** where he had his initial confrontation with Dracula (**Louis Jourdan**) and the three female vampire residents. He eventually escaped and returned to England. Lucy was engaged to **Quincey P. Morris,** now transformed from a Texan into a staff person at the American embassy in London. Once Dracula began his attack on Lucy, Dr. **John Seward** called **Abraham Van Helsing** to his assistance. Van Helsing arrived, as in the novel, as an elderly foreign expert. He taught the men that supernatural evil existed and that they must unite to fight it.

Lucy finally died, and her post death activity convinced the men that Van Helsing was correct. They proceeded to Lucy's tomb to finally kill her in one of the most graphic vampire death scenes to that point in time. With Harker back in England and married to Mina, Van Helsing built a united front to kill Dracula. Meanwhile Dracula attacked Mina and forced her to drink his blood. The attack made her a full partner in the final drive to kill the vampire.

In the final scenes, Van Helsing and Mina arrived at **Castle Dracula** only to confront the three women who call to Mina as their new sister. Van Helsing protected her before going into the castle to kill the women. The **Gypsies** who brought Dracula's sleeping body back to the castle were fought off in a Western-style gunfight. The last Gypsy got the box to the entrance of the castle where he was stopped. In the end, it was Van Helsing, not the younger men, who pried open the lid of the box and killed Dracula with a **stake.**

Count Dracula, even more than *El Conde Dracula,* relied on the story of **Bram Stoker**'s novel. Only the more recent *Bram Stoker's Dracula* (1992) would, for example, return all of the major characters in the novel to the movie storyline. *Count Dracula* also raised the level of realism in the depiction of the vampire's attack and the scenes of the vampire women attacking the baby in the early segment of the movie (which was cut from the American version). *Count Dracula* returned the essential scene in the novel, in which Dracula forced Mina to drink his blood, and the subsequent events in which she was branded with a **eucharistic wafer.**

Louis Jourdan assumed the role of Dracula in this version. He brought to the part a suave, continental manner. He was an aristocratic lover, but a man used to getting what he wanted. He seduced women and took them away from the mundane gentlemen with whom they had been paired. Jourdan thus anticipated the sensual Dracula so effectively portrayed by **Frank Langella** in *Dracula* (1979).

Sources:

Waller, Gregory A. *The Living and the Undead: From Stoker's Dracula to Romero's Dawn of the Dead.* Urbana, IL: University of Illinois Press, 1986. 376 pp.

THE COUNT DRACULA FAN CLUB

The Count Dracula Fan Club was founded in 1965 by Dr. **Jeanne Keyes Youngson,** then a successful animation filmmaker, to promote and encourage the study of **Bram Stoker, Dracula,** and vampirism in general. She had been introduced to Dracula and to **Vlad the Impaler,** the fourteenth-century prince of Wallachia, who was one source of Bram Stoker's literary figure, while at Maryville College in Tennessee. The occasion for the founding of the Club, however, was her trip to Romania, which brought together her fascination with Dracula and new knowledge concerning Prince Vlad. While in Romania she made the decision to found a Dracula society, and The Count Dracula Fan Club was formally constituted soon after her return.

The club developed two headquarters—one in New York and one in London—and Youngson began to establish its various specialized divisions. The first, The Count Dracula Fan Club Research Library, was opened in 1970. It now has over 25,000 volumes that include special collections on Dracula, Bram Stoker, vampirism, and *The Shadow* and other adventure/mystery series. It is assisted by the Friends of the Library and the related Bram Stoker Memorial Collection of Rare Books. In 1978 the London center closed and was moved to a second location in New York. By this time the club had developed a large membership. The current divisions of the club founded over the last two decades include:

The Special Research Division, which assists authors who are working on books on vampirism.

The Research Referral Centre, which assists researchers in locating information on particular questions on Dracula, vampires, and vampirism.

Dracula Press publishes a variety of vampire monographs, poetry, fiction, the Club's periodicals *The Dracula News-Journal* and *Letterzine.*

The associated Vampire Bookshop is the book service for the club and serves as the exclusive distributor of Dracula Press publications.

The club also operates Booksearch, which attempts to locate out- of-print titles for members.

The Moldavian Marketplace carries various items of special interest from stationary, toys, and photographs to t- shirts, records, and jewelry.

Founded in 1990, **The Dracula Museum** houses a broad collection of Dracula, Bram Stoker, and vampire-related memorabilia.

The Bram Stoker Memorial Association preserves a collection of approximately 500 books and other documents associated with Bram Stoker.

The related Bram Stoker Picture File is a collection of photographs relating to Bram Stoker, *Dracula,* and the annual Bram Stoker Summer School in **Ireland.**

Dracula World Enterprises keeps an up-to-date list of vampires organizations worldwide. It also serves as a clearinghouse for vampire penpals and, to that end, possesses a master list of vampire fans internationally.

The Vampire Institute is dedicated to the study of vampirism and has been designed to relate to individuals who wish to participate in the critical analysis, examination, and appreciation of the vampire and correspond with others of like mind.

Members of the Institute, the club's most scholarly structure, are automatically enrolled in the Vampire Pen Friends Network.

Vampires Are Us is the junior division for members of the club aged 16 and under.

In 1993 the club had more than 5,000 members. It publishes four periodicals, *The Dracula News-Journal*, *Bites & Pieces*, *Letterzine*, and *Undead Undulations*. The high point of the year for the club is in the Christmas season when a special issue of the *News-Journal* is produced and a two-week open house of the museum is held for members in the New York City area.

The club can be contacted at Penthouse N., 29 Washington Sq. W., New York, NY 10011. It is headed by Dr. Youngson, its founder/president; Carole Lambert, acting president; and two associate directors, Thomas A. Peck and Mary Jane Oz.

Some members of the club are also interested in related fields. The Club's Special Interest Division serves members interested in science fiction and other genres. It also has a special collection of werewolf material, The Werewolf in Fact, Fiction, and Fantasy. In 1992 it was decided to change the status of the International Frankenstein Society from that of an independent organization to a division of the Count Dracula Fan Club.

Sources:

The Count Dracula Fan Club Handbook. New York: Count Dracula Fan Club, 1992. 20 pp.
Moore, Steven, ed. *The Vampire in Verse: An Anthology*. New York: Dracula Press, 1985. 196 pp.
Oz, Jane. *So You Want to be a Vampire*. New York: Dracula Press, 1989. 12 pp.
Perkowski, Jan. *Daemon Contamination in Balkan Vampire Lore*. New York: Dracula Press, 1992. 15 pp.
———. *The Vampire as Remnant*. New York: Vampire Press, 1992. 6 pp.
Polidori, et al. *The Count Dracula Fan Club Book of Vampire Stories*. Chicago: Adams Press, 1980. 91 pp.
Sanders, Lewis, ed. *Vampire Haiku*. New York: Dracula Press, 1990. 28 pp.
Youngson, Jeanne, ed. *A Child's Garden of Vampires*. Chicago: Adams Press, 1980. 60 pp.
———. *The Count Dracula Chicken Cookbook*. Chicago: Adams Press, 1979. 60 pp.

THE COUNT DRACULA SOCIETY

The Count Dracula Society was founded in 1962 by Dr. Donald A. Reed, a law librarian, who continues to serve as its president. It is devoted to the serious study of horror films and gothic literature. Its members gather periodically for screenings of new vampire and horror films, but the highlight of the society's program is the annual awards gathering at which the Ann Radcliffe Award is announced.

Closely associated with The Count Dracula Society (and also founded by Reed) is the Academy of Science Fiction, Fantasy and Horror Films, dedicated to honoring films and filmmakers in the several horror genres. Like The Count Dracula Society, the academy hosts regular screenings of films (approximately 100 annually) and sponsors an annual awards ceremony at which the Saturn Trophy is presented to winners in a variety of categories, including the best film in each of the three areas of prime concern (science fiction, fantasy, and horror), and an annual lifetime achievement award.

For membership information contact Dr. Reed at The Count Dracula Society, 334 W. 54th St., Los Angeles, CA 90037. *The Count Dracula Society Quarterly* (also

FOUNDER DONALD REED WELCOMES FORREST ACKERMAN TO AWARD NIGHT AT THE COUNT DRACULA SOCIETY.

known at various times as *The Castle Dracula Quarterly* and *The Gothick Gathway*), formerly published by the society, has been discontinued.

Sources:

The Castle Dracula Quarterly. 1, 1 (1978). Special Bela Lugosi issue.
Reed, Donald. *The Vampire on the Screen.* Inglewood, CA: Wagon & Star Publishers, 1965. Unpaged
The World Almanac Book of Buffs, Masters, Mavens and Uncommon Experts. New York: World Almanac Publications, 1980. 342 pp.

COUNT KEN FAN CLUB

The Count Ken Fan Club was founded April 24, 1984, by Ken Gilbert (b. October 31, 1950). Its members are dedicated to the celebration of the fantasy world of the cinematic and literary vampire. According to the biography circulated by Gilbert, his father was a Transylvanian nobleman, and he was raised by his aunt and uncle rather than his unwed mother. As a youth he became interested in horror films. In 1976 he attended a vampire convention in Hollywood where he met Veronica, a vampire, whom he dated for awhile. Subsequently he dated Donna, who was a friend of Veronica and also a vampire.

According to Gilbert, he was bitten three times by Donna, and thus became a vampire and began to call himself Count Ken. Meanwhile Jonathan Price, a vampire hunter, entered the scene. He killed Donna, after which Gilbert and Veronica moved to Salem, Massachusetts. In 1983 Price tracked them to Salem and, with the help of a Professor Frank Rodgers, confronted the pair of vampires. Gilbert says that he killed both Price and Rodgers. To date no action has been taken on these reported homicides.

The following year Gilbert founded the club and initially advertised in *Fangoria* magazine. He publishes a monthly newsletter that includes art, poetry, and fiction by club members; film reviews; and an occasional reprinted newspaper article. The club remains small, with fewer than a hundred members. It may be contacted c/o Ken Gilbert, 12 Palmer Street, Salem, MA 01970.

Sources:

Kelly, Nancy. "Dracula Is Spinning in His Graveyard." *The Times* (Beverly, Massachusetts) (May 27, 1986).

CRIME, VAMPIRIC

The great majority of people labeled as "real" vampires during the last two centuries manifested symptoms of what psychologists call hematomania, a blood fetish (Sexual pleasure and other psychological needs of persons with this condition are met by the regular consumption of human blood, occasionally in conjunction with the eating of human flesh.) Presumably most of those who regularly drank blood located legal means of obtaining it, usually from a willing donor. Some, however, turned to crime, and a few joined the list of the West's most notorious serial killers. The modern stream of vampiric crime related to hematomania had its precedent in the career of Countess **Elizabeth Bathory** (1560-1614), who allegedly killed more than 600 people for their blood.

The Marquis de Sade and Gilles de Rais are frequently listed among the modern vampiric criminals, but the list of crimes attributed to neither included the drinking of the blood they might have shed. There is a distinction between those who draw pleasure from killing people or from the drawing of blood (Jack the Ripper?) and those vampiric types who derive pleasure from its consumption. Likewise there is a distinction between people who drink blood for the overpowering pleasure it brings and those who occasionally sip blood (usually of an animal) as part of a religious ritual and believe they draw some supernatural power from the otherwise repulsive act.

Several vampiric killers emerged in the nineteenth century. The earliest reported case was that of a man named Sorgel, a German who killed a man in the forest and drank his blood in an attempt to cure himself of epilepsy. His actions led to his arrest and confinement in an asylum. That same year Antoine Léger killed a 12-year-old girl, drank her blood, and ate her heart. After his execution, Sorgel's brain was examined by pathologists.

A more famous incident involved Sergeant Francoise Bertrand (1924-1949), who was arrested in 1849 in Paris for opening the graves of the dead and eating flesh from the corpses. While termed a vampire by some, he engaged in much more ghoul-like behavior, and went on to become the model of one of the more successful novels about **werewolves,** including *The Werewolf of London.* A generation later, in 1886, Henri Blot was arrested for a similar crime. He was caught because he fell into a sleeplike hypnotic trance after completing his work. He was apprehended quickly; he had violated only two bodies.

The United States has been home to one vampire killer, seaman James Brown. In 1967 Brown was discovered on board his ship, a fishing boat on its way to Labrador, sucking the blood from the body of a crewman he had murdered. He had already killed and drained another sailor. He was arrested and returned to Boston. Brown was sentenced to life in prison, where he killed at least two more people and drank their blood. Following the second killing, he was sent to the National Asylum in Washington, D.C., where he remained confined in a padded cell until he died.

Fritz Haarman (1879-1924) is another famous vampiric killer. By the time of his arrest and execution in 1924 in Germany, he had killed and cannibalized more than 20 people. However, during the last several years, he also began to bite and suck the blood of his victims. Contemporary with Haarman was **Peter Kürten** (1883-1931), also from Germany. Kürten killed first as a nine-year-old boy. He killed again in 1913. Then in 1929 he began a series of ghoulish crimes in which he stabbed and then mutilated his victims. At the height of his crime spree in August of that year, he killed nine people, mostly young women. His initial excitement at killing someone gave way to a fixation on blood. He began to drink the blood of his victims, continuing even after the blood he consumed made him sick. In one case he bit and drank from the wound. Finally arrested in 1930, he was executed the following year.

Through the twentieth century a number of reports of vampirelike criminals have surfaced. A few, such as **John George Haigh** (1910-1949) and Richard Chase, became famous. Others received no more than passing notice. During the 1940s, Haigh operated out of a home in London. There he killed his victims, drained their blood, and then disposed of the bodies in a vat of sulfuric acid. Richard Chase (1950-1980) began his crime spree in Sacramento, California, in December 1977, when he shot and killed a man. The following month, he killed again, and this time he drank his victim's blood. He continued this practice in a string of killings in January, until his arrest at the end of the month. It turned out that as early as 1974, he had killed a cat and drunk its blood. In the following years he killed a number of animals and drank their blood in hopes that it would improve his physical health. After his arrest he moved through a complex legal process, including scrutiny of his sanity. Tried and convicted of multiple murders, he was sentenced to death, but cheated the executioner by committing suicide.

Lesser known vampiric crimes included:

1861—Martin Dumollard of Montluel, France, was convicted of murdering several young girls whose blood he drank. He was executed.

1872—Vincenzo Verzeni of Bottanaucco, Italy, was sentenced to life imprisonment in two cases of murder and four of attempted murder. He confessed that drinking the blood of his victims gave him immense satisfaction.

1897—Joseph Vacher of Bourg, France, while on a walking tour through the country, killed at least a dozen people and drank their blood from bites in their neck. He was finally captured, convicted, and executed.

1916?—Following a notice that Bela Kiss, of Czinkota, Hungary, had been killed in World War I, neighbors searched her property and found the bodies of 31 individuals, all of whom had been strangled. Each corpse possessed puncture wounds in the neck and had been drained of blood.

1920—Baron Roman von Sternberg-Ungern, a nobleman in postrevolutionary Russia, drank human blood on occasion, seemingly in connection with a belief that he was a reincarnation of Genghis Khan. For his habits (and other reasons), he came into conflict with the new government and was executed.

1947—Elizabeth Short of Hollywood, California, was murdered and her body dismembered. Later examination discovered that her body had been drained of its blood.

1952—Estelita Forencio of Passi, Iloilo Province, the Philippines, bit a number of people and then sucked the blood from the wounds. She was arrested for attempted murder. She said that she had acquired the urge from her husband and that it came on her at regular intervals.

1959—Salvatore Agron, a 16-year-old resident of New York City, was convicted of several murders that he carried out at night while dressed as a **Bela Lugosi**-style vampire. In court he claimed to be a vampire. He was executed for his crimes.

1960—Florencio Roque Fernandez of Manteros, Argentina, was arrested after more than 15 women said someone had entered their bedroom, bit them, and drank their blood.

1963—Alfred Käser of Munich, Germany, was tried for killing a 10-year-old boy. He drank blood from the boy's neck after stabbing him.

1969—Stanislav Modzieliewski of Lodz, Poland, was convicted of seven murders and six attempted murders. One witness against him was a young woman he attacked, who pretended to be dead while he drank blood from her. Modzieliewski confessed to thinking that blood was delicious.

1971—Wayne Boden was arrested for a series of murders that began in 1968. In each case he had handcuffed the victim, raped her, and then bitten her and sucked blood from her breast.

1973—Kuno Hoffman of Nürnberg, Germany, confessed to murdering two people and drinking their blood and to digging up and drinking the blood of several corpses. He was sentenced to life imprisonment.

1979—Richard Cottingham was arrested for raping, slashing, and drinking the blood of a young prostitute. It was later discovered that he had killed a number of women, and in most cases had bitten them and lapped up their flowing blood.

1980—James P. Riva shot his grandmother and drank the blood coming from the wound. He later said that several years earlier he had begun to hear the voices of a vampire, who eventually had told him what to do and promised him eternal life.

1982—Julian Koltun of Warsaw, Poland, was sentenced to death for raping seven women and drinking their blood. He killed two of the women.

1984—Renato Antonio Cirillo was tried for the rape and vampire-style biting of more than 40 women.

1985—John Crutchley was arrested for raping a woman. He held her prisoner and drank much of her blood. It was later discovered that he had been drinking the blood of more willing donors for many years.

1987—A jogger in a San Francisco park was kidnapped and held for an hour in a van while a man drank his blood.

1988—An unknown woman picked up at least six men over the summer in the Soho section of London. After she returned home with a victim, she slipped drugs into his drink. While he was unconscious, she cut his wrist and sucked his blood. She was never arrested.

1991—Marcelo da Andrade of Rio de Janeiro killed 14 young boys, after which he drank their blood and ate some of their flesh.

1991—Tracy Wigginton of Brisbane, Australia, was convicted of the vampire murder of Clyde Blaylock. She stabbed him and then drank his blood. A **lesbian,** Wigginton claimed to be a vampire and regularly drank blood from her friends.

1992—Andrei Chikatilo of Rostov, Russia, was sentenced to death after confessing to killing some 55 people whom he vampirized and cannibalized.

1992—Deborah Joan Finch was tried for the murder of a neighbor. She stabbed the victim 27 times and then drank the flowing blood.

Sources:

Biondi, Ray, and Walt Hecox. *The Dracula Killer.* New York: Pocket Books, 1992. 212 pp.
Brautigam, Rob. "Some Blood Drinkers." *For the Blood Is the Life* 2, 9 (Summer 1991): 12-14.
"Human Vampire." *Fate* 6, 5 (May 1953): 46.
Monaco, Richard, with Bill Burt. *The Dracula Syndrome.* New York: Avon, 1993. 167 pp.
Shay, V. B. "James Brown, Vampire." *Fate* 2, 4 (November 1949): 59.

"Vampire Arrested in Argentina." *Fate* 13, 10 (October 1960): 45.
Volta, Ornella. *The Vampire.* New York: Award Books, 1962. 153 pp.

CROGLIN GRANGE, THE VAMPIRE OF

Among frequently cited incidents involving "real" vampirism, the story of the vampire of Croglin Grange, an old house located in Cumberland, England, has proved most intriguing. An account of the vampire originally appeared in the *Story of My Life* by August Hare, written during the last years of the 1890s. According to Hare, the various episodes occurred around 1875-76. Owned at the time by a family named Fisher, the house was rented to a woman and her two brothers: Amelia, Edward, and Michael Cranswell. During one summer, the district experienced a hot spell, so when the three retired for the night, the woman slept near the window. She shut the window but did not close the shutters. Unable to go to sleep, she spotted something approaching that eventually reached the window and began to scratch and then to pick at it, removing a pane. A creature then reached in and unlocked the window. The terrified woman, frozen in fear, waited as a brown face with flaming eyes came to her, grabbed her, and bit her throat.

She screamed, and when her brothers rushed to her rescue, the creature hurriedly left. One brother tended his sister and the other pursued the creature, which disappeared over a wall by a nearby church. The doctor who later treated the woman suggested a change of scenery, and the brothers took her to Switzerland for an extended visit. The three eventually returned to Croglin Grange. The following spring the creature appeared again. One brother chased it, shot it in the leg, and traced it to a vault in the local cemetery. The next day, accompanied by some townspeople, the brothers entered the vault, which was in complete disarray except for one coffin. When they opened the coffin, they found a body with a fresh gunshot wound in the leg. A bullet was extracted, and they burned the corpse.

In 1924, Charles G. Harper, basing his assertions on a visit to the area, challenged the Hare book. Harper could find no place named Croglin Grange. Though there were two other buildings, Croglin High Hall and Croglin Low Hall, neither fit the description of Croglin Grange. There was no church, the closest one being over a mile away, and no vault corresponding to the description of the one opened by the brothers and their neighbors. Harper's own account was challenged at a later date, when F. Clive-Ross visited the area. In interviews with the local residents, he determined that Low Croglin Hall was the house referred to in Hare's story and that a chapel had existed near it for many years, its foundation stones still visible into the 1930s. Clive-Ross seemed to have answered all of Harper's objections.

The Croglin Grange story continued when, in 1968, psychic researcher Scott Rogo offered a new challenge. He noted the likeness of the story of the vampire at Croglin Grange to the first chapter of **Varney the Vampyre,** the popular vampire story originally published in 1847. The accounts, both of which were published in 1929 by **Montague Summers,** are very similar, and it is likely that one is based on the other, according to Rogo. He suggested that the entire Croglin Grange story could be dismissed as a simple hoax.

A final footnote to the controversy: Clive-Ross, later discussed the case again with residents of the area, and was told that there was a significant mistake in Hare's original account: the story took place not in the 1870s, but in the 1680s, almost two centuries earlier. While this fact would definitely place the events prior to the publication of *Varney the Vampyre,* it also pushes the story far enough into the past as to turn it into an unverifiable legend.

Sources:

Dyall, Valentine. "Vampire of Croglin Grange." *Fate* (April 1954): 96-104.
Glut, Donald F. *True Vampires of History.* Secaucus, NJ: Castle Books, 1971. 191 pp.
Hare, Augustine. *Story of My Life.* 6 vols. London: George Allen, 1896-1900.
Harper, Charles C. *Haunted Houses.* Detroit: Tower Books, 1971. 288 pp..
Rogo, Scott. "Second Thoughts on the Vampire of Croglin Grange." *Fate* 21, 6 (June 1968): 44-48.
Summers, Montague. *The Vampire in Europe.* London: Routledge, Kegan Paul, Trench, Trubner, & Co. 1929. 329 pp. Reprint. New Hyde Park, NY: University Books, 1962. 329 pp.

CROSS, BEN (1947-)

Ben Cross, the actor who portrayed **Barnabas Collins** in the 1991 revival of the *Dark Shadows* television series, was born Bernard Cross on December 16, 1947, in London, England. He attended the Royal Academy of Dramatic Art and began his career in the theater as a stagehand, carpenter, and set builder. He made his stage acting debut in 1972 in *The Importance of Being Earnest* and the following year appeared in a made-for-television movie, *Melancholy Hussar of the German Legion,* a BBC special. He appeared in his first motion picture, *A Bridge Too Far,* in 1977. His most acclaimed role, for which he received an Academy Award nomination, was in *Chariots of Fire* (1981). Cross played his first vampire role in 1989 in *Nightlife,* a made-for-TV comedy in which Maryam D'Obo portrayed a female vampire being chased by her former lover Vlad (Cross) around Mexico City.

In 1990, NBC announced that it had asked **Dan Curtis,** the creator of *Dark Shadows,* to put together a new cast for a prime-time version of the old soap opera. Ben Cross was chosen to play the vampire Barnabas Collins. He accepted in part because he had never worked in the American television industry. His role was strongly reminiscent of **Jonathan Frid,** the original Barnabas Collins. In spite of his moments of genuine anger and vicious attacks on individuals, Cross's Barnabas was a sensitive, reluctant vampire who allowed hematologist Julia Hoffman to try to cure his vampiric condition.

Even though *Dark Shadows* fans gave the new series strong support, it was cancelled after only 12 episodes (13 hours of programming) during the second half of the 1990-1991 season. The programs have been released on video, and Cross's likeness has been captured for the *Dark Shadows* comic book that Innovation Publishing began issuing in April 1992. Cross has moved on to other roles, including

BEN CROSS AS BARNABAS COLLINS.

parts in several made-for-TV movies: *Diamond Fleece* (1992), *Live Wire* (1992), and *Deep Trouble* (1993).

Sources:

Gross, Edward, and Marc Shapiro. *The Vampire Interview Book: Conversations with the Undead.* East Meadow, NY: Image Publishing, 1991. 134 pp.

Jones, Stephen. *The Illustrated Vampire Movie Guide.* London: Titan Books, 1993. 144 pp.

Pierson, Jim. *Dark Shadows Resurrected.* Los Angeles: Pomegranate Press, 1992. 175 pp.

CRUCIFIX

The crucifix, a major symbol of the Christian faith, is a Latin cross with a figure of Jesus on it. It often appears on the end of the rosary, a string of prayer beads. The cross represents Jesus as he was executed on the original Good Friday. The crucifix is used primarily by Christians in the Roman Catholic Church, the several branches of the Eastern Orthodox Church, and other church bodies that follow a similar liturgical style of **Christianity.** In general, Protestant and Free churches do not utilize the crucifix. They prefer a plain cross without the corpus, sometimes thought of as an empty cross, a symbol of the resurrected Christ.

In the first chapter of the novel *Dracula,* a woman in **Bistritz, Transylvania,** took a rosary from her neck and gave it to **Jonathan Harker** upon hearing that he was going to visit Count Dracula. Harker, a member of the protestantized Church of England, had been taught that such an object was a product of idolatrous thinking. However, he put it around his neck and left it there. A short time after his arrival at **Castle Dracula, Dracula** made a grab for Harker's throat. Harker reported, "I drew away, and his hand touched the string of beads which held the crucifix. It made an instant change in him, for the fury passed so quickly that I could hardly believe that it was ever there." Having yet to figure out what Dracula was, he wondered about the meaning of the crucifix.

The crucifix played an important role in several other scenes in the novel. One appeared again in the hands of a man on board the *Demeter,* the ship that brought Dracula to England. He was found tied to the ship's wheel with the crucifix in his hands, the beads wrapped around an arm and a wheel spoke. Later, after **Lucy Westenra** died and while she was experiencing life as a vampire herself, vampire hunter **Abraham Van Helsing** locked her in her tomb for a night with a crucifix and **garlic,** described as things she would not like. In Van Helsing's famous speech in Chapter 18, he described the crucifix as one of the things that, like garlic, so afflicted the vampire that the creature had no power. So, when the men burst into the bedroom where Dracula was sharing **blood** with **Mina Murray** (by then Mina Harker), they advanced upon him with their crucifixes raised in front of them. Dracula retreated.

Through the tale *Dracula,* then, the crucifix entered vampire lore as a powerful tool against vampires, especially when confronting one directly. It was not mentioned in historic vampire stories, though many priests who participated in the dispatching of a vampire no doubt wore the crucifix. The emergence of the crucifix came directly from **Bram Stoker**'s combining some popular ideas about the magical use of sacred objects by Roman Catholics and the medieval tradition that identified vampirism with

Satanism (through Emily Gerard, Stoker developed the notion that Dracula became a vampire due to his having intercourse with **Satan**). In addition, a significant amount of Roman Catholic piety focused around the crucifix, and among church members it could easily take on not just sacred, but magical, qualities. It was not just a *symbol* of the sacred, but the bearer of the sacred.

If then the vampire was of the realm of Satan, it would withdraw from a crucifix. For Stoker, the presence of the crucifix caused the vampire to lose its supernatural strength. Thus, in the case of Harker, Dracula lost his fury; Lucy could not escape her tomb; and when the men burst into Mina's bedroom, the weakened Dracula, faced with overwhelming odds, departed quickly.

Following *Dracula,* the crucifix became a standard element of vampire plays, movies, and novels through the twentieth century. A second sacred object, the **eucharistic wafer,** largely dropped out of the picture. However, the crucifix acquired one of the properties Stoker assigned to the wafer. It burned vampire flesh, and left a mark on those tainted with the vampire's bite. Thus the crucifix not only caused the vampire to lose strength, but actually did it harm. If a potential victim wore a crucifix, the vampire must find some method of removing it, either through hypnotic suggestion or with the help of a human cohort.

While the crucifix was a standard item in the vampire hunter's kit, it was not omnipresent in vampire books and movies. The relation to the holy was among the first elements of the tradition to be challenged as the vampire myth developed. Writers who were not Roman Catholic or even Christian found no meaning in the crucifix and the eucharistic elements and simply dropped them from consideration. However, others, most prominently **Chelsea Quinn Yarbro** and **Anne Rice,** chose to acknowledge the sacred world but essentially deny its power, specifically mentioning the immunity of their vampires to holy objects. Yarbro's vampire, **St. Germain,** existed prior to Christianity and never converted to its beliefs. Rice, writing in Catholic New Orleans, created her vampire, **Lestat de Lioncourt,** as a child of Roman Catholics in France, and at various points in *Interview with the Vampire* and *The Vampire Lestat,* Roman Catholic supernaturalism was specifically cast aside. Lestat was described, for example, as already an atheist when he was transformed into a vampire. Nevertheless, he called upon those bits of Christianity he remembered, in an attempt to keep the vampire Magnus from him. His efforts were useless. Then, accompanying the bites that made Lestat a vampire, Magnus pronounced the words of consecration from the Mass, "This is my Body, This is my Blood." Like Yarbro, Rice replaced Christianity in her writings with a new, pre-Christian myth that began in ancient Egypt with the original vampire couple, Akasha and Enkil.

The challenge to the effectiveness of the crucifix in vampire novels symbolizes a larger challenge to the role of the supernatural in modern life. It includes a protest against the authority of any particular religion and its claims of truth in a religiously pluralistic world. While the lessening of the role of the supernatural in the novels of Rice and Yarbro has its supporters, the crucifix remains a popular protective object for fictional characters. Consideration of their reaction to sacred objects likely will continue to be a conscious element in the development of new vampire characters in the future.

Sources:

Frayling, Christopher. *Vampyres: Lord Byron to Count Dracula.* London: Faber and Faber, 1991. 429 pp.

Summers, Montague. *The Vampire: His Kith and Kin.* London: Routledge, Kegan Paul, Trench, Trubner, & Co., 1928. 356 pp. Reprint. New Hyde Park, NY: University Books, 1960. 356 pp.

CRUISE, TOM (1962-)

Tom Cruise, the actor who portrayed the vampire **Lestat de Lioncourt** in the movie version of **Anne Rice**'s *Interview with the Vampire,* was born Thomas Cruise Mapother on July 3, 1962, in Syracuse, New York. He grew up in New York and New Jersey and began his acting career soon after graduating from high school. His first professional part was a role in a dinner theater production of *Godspell.*

Cruise's debut in motion pictures was in 1981 in *Endless Love,* followed by *Taps* and *Losin' It.* He became a star after his performance as a young rich kid left on his own in his family's suburban Chicago home, in the comedy *Risky Business.* A series of starring roles followed, including *All the Right Moves, Legend, Top Gun, The Color of Money,* and *Rain Man,* movies in which he worked with many of Hollywood's finest actors and actresses. Cruise took a major step forward with his portrayal of a Vietnam veteran in *Born on the Fourth of July*(1989), which earned him an Academy Award nomination. More recently he has continued his appealing performances in *A Few Good Men* and *The Firm.* In 1993 he was presented with the Actor of the Decade Award at the Chicago International Film Festival.

In the summer of 1993 it was announced that Cruise had been signed to play Lestat in the long-delayed movie version of *Interview with a Vampire.* He was given the part opposite Brad Pitt, who would play Louis. The announcement unleashed a controversy between author **Anne Rice** and the studio, Geffen Films. Rice decried the selection of Cruise, whom she saw as too young, too American, and, most of all, lacking in the primal quality of Lestat—androgyny. Cruise's career had been a series of almost stereotypical male roles quite different from the character of Lestat. Unlike the traditional vampire, Lestat develops close relationships with other males and shows a number of feminine characteristics. Fans were quick to jump to Cruise's defense and to note that he had grown with each part he had played. His fans claimed that his performances in *Rain Man* and *Born on the Fourth of July* demonstrated that he could adapt to many different roles. Cruise reportedly accepted a slight cut in salary for what he saw as a risky part that would test his acting ability. It was the first time he would portray what was considered a dark role. The film was expected to be completed and released in the fall of 1994.

Sources:

Silver, Alan. "The Vampire Cruise?" *DGA Directors Guild of America News* 18, 5 (October-November 1993): 27.

CUNTIUS, JOHANNES

Henry More (1614-1687) described several vampirelike people in his book *An Antidote Against Atheism,* a volume primarily about **witchcraft.** The case of Johannes Cuntius took place in Pentsch, Silesia, a section of **Poland,** where he had served as an alderman. A fairly wealthy man, he was about 60 years old when one day he was struck by a horse whose shoe was being repaired. Upon recovering from the blow, Cuntius began to complain of his sinfulness. He died a short time later. The night of death a black cat entered the room and scratched his face.

Between the time of his death and burial, the first reports of an *incubus* were heard. After his burial, the town watchman reported strange noises coming from Cuntius's house almost nightly. Other extraordinary stories were reported from different households. One maidservant, for example, said that she heard someone riding around the house and then into the side of the building, violently shaking it. On different nights, Cuntius appeared and had violent encounters with former acquaintances, friends, and family members. He came to his bedroom and demanded to share the bed with his wife. Like the common revenant (one that returns after death or long absence), he had a physical bodily presence and extraordinary **strength.** On one occasion he was reported to have pulled up two posts set deeply into the ground. However, on other occasions he seemed to operate in noncorporeal form—like a ghost—and disappeared suddenly when a candle was lit in his presence.

Cuntius was reported to smell badly and to have especially foul breath. He was said to have once turned milk to blood. He defiled the cloth on the church's altar with spots of blood. He sucked the cows dry of blood and attempted to force his attentions not only on his wife but on several women in town. One person he touched reported that his hand felt cold as ice. Several holes, which went down to his **coffin,** appeared at his gravesite. The holes were filled in, but reappeared the next evening.

The townspeople, unable to find any remedy to these occurrences, finally decided to check the graveyard. They dug up several graves. All the bodies were in an advanced state of decay, except for that of Cuntius. Though he had been in the ground for some six months, his body was still soft and pliable. They put a staff in the corpse's hand, and it grasped it. They cut the body and blood gushed forth. A formal judicial hearing was called and a judgment rendered against the corpse. The body was ordered to be burned. When it proved slow to burn, it was cut into small pieces. The executioner reported that the blood was still fresh and pure. After the burning, the figure of Cuntius was never seen again.

Sources:

Glut, Donald G. *True Vampires of History*. New York: H C Publishers, 1971. 191 pp.

More, Henry. *An Antidote Against Atheism*. London: J. Fleshner, 1655. 398 pp.

CURTIS, DAN (1928-)

Dan Curtis, the producer-director who developed the *Dark Shadows* television series, was born in 1928, in Connecticut. His first work in television was as a salesman for MCA. A sports buff, he sold CBS on doing a show called *CBS Golf Classic,* which is best remembered for live microphones that Curtis had the golfers wear; the show won an Emmy Award in 1965. The success of the show helped Curtis become an independent producer. He decided that soap operas were a good field, and began to think about developing a daytime show.

The initial idea for *Dark Shadows* began to take shape after a vivid dream that Curtis had. It concerned a young woman traveling by train to a new job as a governess at an old place in New England. The dream concluded with the girl standing at a railroad station. Curtis described his dream to officials at ABC, and they risked a small budget to begin development. He gathered a team to put together what would become a daytime serial with a gothic flavor. Over several years, *Dark Shadows* evolved from the original idea.

As the storyline matured, it centered on the Collins family of a mythical fishing village called Collinsport, Maine. The young woman from Curtis's dream became Victoria Winters, an orphan in search of her past, which she believed lay in New England. An early storyline concerned a man she met on the train as she headed for her new job. He accused one of the Collins family of lying at a trial in which he was convicted and sent to prison. The show went on the air on June 27, 1966. At the time, there was no mention of vampirism or any thought of a vampire character. It was only later that first year—when the show was threatened by low ratings—that supernatural elements in the form of ghosts were added. They helped to raise the ratings, but not enough.

In the winter of 1966-1967, with little hope that the show would survive, Curtis made a radical decision. He had the writers create a vampire character. If the show failed after that, he reasoned, at least he would have had fun. The vampire, **Barnabas Collins,** made his first appearance in April 1967. The response was enormous, and by the summer, both Curtis and ABC realized they had a hit. As the show steadily rose in the ratings, Curtis borrowed the cast and created the first of two movies with MGM based on the show, *House of Dark Shadows* (1970). The following year a second feature, *Night of Dark Shadows,* was produced.

Due to low ratings, the original *Dark Shadows* daytime series ended in 1971, though it went into syndication several years later. Meanwhile, Curtis allowed his interest in vampires to influence his future projects. At the same time he began a fruitful relationship with horror writer Richard Matheson, who would write the scripts for a number of Curtis's productions through the decade. In 1972 he worked with ABC to produce **The Night Stalker,** a Matheson script concerning a reporter (Carl

▶
DAN CURTIS DIRECTING.

Kolchak, played by Darren McGavin) who discovered a vampire operating in Seattle. The show became the most watched made-for-television movie to that date. ABC then had Curtis produce and direct the sequel, *The Night Strangler,* based on ''Jack the Ripper'' themes. The two movies led to a television series based on the Kolchak character. Curtis and his company, Dan Curtis Productions, went on to produce other television horror movies, including *The Norliss Tapes* (1973) and *Scream of the Wolf* (1974).

Curtis still had an interest in vampires, however, and in 1973 decided to produce a new version of *Dracula.* He chose veteran actor **Jack Palance** as its villain star, and Matheson as his writer. He also wanted to bypass the stage play that had been the basis for both the **Bela Lugosi** movie in 1931 and the more recent *Horror of Dracula* from **Hammer Films.** The script drew on fresh research on **Vlad the Impaler,** the fifteenth-century Wallachian prince thought of as the original Dracula. In the end, Curtis's Dracula was driven to reclaim his long-lost love whom he saw reborn in the person of **Jonathan Harker**'s fiance. This need took him to England. At the same time, he was under attack from vampire hunter **Abraham Van Helsing** (played by Nigel Davenport), and their personal battle formed the second dynamic of the script.

In 1975, Curtis brought to television a movie, *Trilogy of Terror,* composed of three of Matheson's short stories. It was followed the next year with a similar horror collection, *Dead of Night,* which included Matheson's story, "No Such Thing as a Vampire."

A successful producer who had found his niche in developing made-for-television movies, Curtis reached a new high in the next decade with the production of two very successful TV mini-series. *The Winds of War* (1983) and its sequel, *War and Remembrance* (1988-89), were based on the books of Herman Wouk. Curtis's productions were thus diversified, only occasionally returning to the horror genre. However, the continuing popularity of *Dark Shadows* in syndication suggested the possibility of its revival. In 1990 Curtis sold the idea of a prime-time *Dark Shadows* series to NBC. With a new set and a new cast, a pilot show was filmed. Based on the old series, it began with the awakening of Barnabas Collins and his entrance into the Collins household. From there—while keeping the basic framework of the old series—the storyline developed in novel directions. The series aired in early 1991 but did not make the ratings cut and was cancelled after only 12 episodes. In the meantime, Innovation Comics began production of a comic book based on the new series. The comic was a success, and the new storyline and characters continued into 1994 when Innovation ceased operation.

Sources:

Dawidziak, Mark. "Dark Shadows." *Cinefantastique* 21, 3 (December 1990): 24-30.

Gross, Edward, and Marc Shapiro. *The Vampire Book: Conversations with the Undead.* East Meadow, NY: Image Books, 1991. 134 pp.

CUSHING, PETER (1913-)

Peter Cushing, a British movie actor known for his portrayal of **Abraham Van Helsing,** Dracula's main protagonist, was born in 1913 in Kenley, Surrey. Prior to his work as an actor, Cushing worked for several years as an assistant stage manager of a company in Sussex. His stage debut was in *The Middle Watch* in 1935 in a performance at Worthing. He made his film debut five years later in *The Man in the Iron Mask.* In 1941 he made his first Hollywood movie, *Vigil in the Night.* He also made a number of short films in the 1940s as part of the war effort.

Following the war, Cushing moved between stage and movie roles, the most noteworthy acclaim coming in the 1954 British production of *1984.* In 1957 he starred as monster-maker Victor Frankenstein in the first of **Hammer Films'** famous horror series. After the success of *Frankenstein,* Cushing teamed again with director **Terence Fisher** and opposite **Christopher Lee** in Hammer's 1958 production of *Dracula* (better known as *Horror of Dracula*). As Van Helsing, Cushing assumed the image of a cultured intellectual who had chosen to confront absolute evil in the person of the vampire. He returned to the role of Van Helsing in one subsequent Hammer *Dracula* movie—*The Brides of Dracula* (1959)—and as a vampire-hunting descendant of Van Helsing in *Dracula AD 1972* (1972) and *Count Dracula and his*

PETER CUSHING AND INGRID PITT
IN *THE VAMPIRE LOVERS.*

Vampire Brides (1973). He also played a Van Helsing relative in the Hammer/Shaw co-production of *The Legend of the Seven Golden Vampires* (also known as *The Seven Brothers Meet Dracula*), which mixed horror and martial arts themes. As the only person to play Van Helsing so many times, Cushing has become the best-known actor associated with the role.

While Cushing became well known for his portrayal of Van Helsing, he was able to play a number of other parts, sometimes appearing in three or four movies a year, and had some success not only in vampire movies but also in a variety of others. He returned to his portrayal of Dr. Frankenstein in several Hammer films with the same theme. He also played a Van Helsing-like role of an intellectual and/or scientist in horror movies that, when considered alongside his famous Van Helsing roles, reveal Cushing as having continually portrayed a symbol of a stable normal world that turned back the challenges of the chaotic forces of evil. This role was seen in its extreme form in *Twins of Evil,* (Hammer, 1971) in which he played a fanatical witchhunter who actually encountered the supernatural.

Above and beyond his Van Helsing roles, Cushing appeared in several other vampire films, including *The Blood Beast Terror* (1968), *The Vampire Lovers*

(Hammer, 1970), *Incense for the Damned* (1970), and *Tender Dracula* (1974). He also teamed with Christopher Lee in several nonvampire movies such as *The Creeping Flesh* (1973) and *The House of Long Shadows* (1982), in which Lee, Cushing, and Vincent Price joined in a tribute to the **gothic** "old dark house" film. Possibly his most notable nonvampire appearance was as a villain in *Star Wars*.

Sources:

Eyles, Allen, Robert Adkinson, and Nicholas Fry. *The House of Hammer*. London: Lorrimer Publishing Limited, 1973. 127 pp.

Marrero, Robert. *Vampires Hammer Style*. Key West, FL: RGM Publications, 1974. 98 pp.

Vinson, James, ed. *The International Dictionary of Films and Filmmakers*. Vol. III, Actors and Actresses. Chicago: St. James Press, 1986.

CZECH REPUBLIC AND SLOVAKIA, VAMPIRES IN THE

The first historical state in what is now the territory occupied by the Czech Republic and Slovakia was founded by tribes that settled in the mountainous region north of present-day Austria and Hungary. The state founded in the seventh century would, two centuries later, be united with the Great Moravian empire, which in 836 A.D. invited Cyril and Methodius, the Christian missionaries, into their land. While among the Czechs and Slovaks, the pair preached and taught the people in their native Slavic language. However, Roman Catholicism, not Eastern Orthodoxy, dominated church life, and Latin, not Old Church Slavonic became the language of worship. The Moravian empire disintegrated early in the tenth century and Slovakia became part of Hungary. After a period under German control, the Czech state reemerged as the Czech (Bohemian) kingdom. Like **Poland,** both the Czechs and the Slovakians became Roman Catholic.

The Bohemian kingdom survived through the Middle Ages but gradually through the sixteenth century came under Austrian hegemony and in the next century was incorporated into the Hapsburg empire. At the end of the eighteenth century, a revival of Czech culture led to a revival of Czech nationalism. Finally, in 1918, at the end of World War I, Czechoslovakia was created as an independent state. That country survived through most of the twentieth century, though a thousand years of separate political existence had driven a considerable wedge between the Czechs and Slovaks. After World War II, Communist rule replaced the democratic government that had been put in place in 1918. The Communist system was renounced in 1989 and shortly thereafter, Bohemia and Moravia parted with Slovakia. On January 1, 1993, two separate and independent countries, the Czech Republic and Slovakia, emerged.

THE VAMPIRE IN THE CZECH REPUBLIC AND SLOVAKIA: The Czech and Slovakian vampire—called a *upír,* and to a lesser extent, *nelapsi,* in both Czech and Slovak—was a variety of the **Slavic vampire.** The *upir* was believed to have two hearts and hence two souls. The presence of the second soul would be indicated by a corpse's flexibility, open eyes, two curls in the hair, and a ruddy complexion. The earliest anecdote concerning a Czech vampire was recorded by Henry More in 1653. The events took place in the late 1500s and concerned a merchant, **Johannes Cuntius** (or Kunz) who troubled his family and neighbors following his violent death. Cuntius lived in the town of Pentsch (present-day Horni Benesov). His son lived in Jagerdorf (present- day Krnov) in a part of Moravia dominated by Lutheran Protestants.

Dom Augustin Calmet included reports of vampires from Bohemia and Moravia in his famous 1746 treatise. He noted that in 1706 a treatise on vampires, *Magia Posthuma* by Charles Ferdinand de Schertz, was published in Olmutz (Moravia). *Magia Posthuma* related a number of incidents of vampires who made their first appearance as troublesome spirits that would attack their former neighbors and the village livestock. Some of the reports were of classic nightmare attacks accompanied with pain, a feeling of being suffocated, and squeezing around the neck area. Those so attacked would grow pale and fatigued. Other stories centered on poltergeist effects featuring objects being thrown around the house and possessions of the dead person mysteriously moved. One of the earliest and more spectacular cases concern a man of the Bohemian village of Blow (Blau) in the fourteenth century. As a vampire he called upon his neighbors, and whomever he visited died within eight days. The villagers finally dug up the man's body and drove a **stake** through it. The man, however, laughed at the people and thanked the people for giving him a stick to fend off the dogs. That night he took the stick out of his body and began again to appear to people. After several more deaths occurred, his body was burned. Only then did the visitations end.

Schertz, a lawyer, was most concerned with the activity of villagers who would take the law into their hands and mutilate and burn bodies. He argued that in cases of severe disturbances, a legal process should be followed before any bodies were desecrated. Included in the process was the examination of the body of any suspected vampire by physicians and theologians. Destruction of the vampire, by burning, should be carried out as an official act by the public executioner.

Montague Summers was most impressed by the evidence of vampirism detailed by the Count de Cadreras, who early in the 1720s was commissioned by the Austrian emperor to look into events at Haidam, a town near the Hungarian border. The count investigated a number of cases of people who had been dead for many years (in one case 30 and another 16 years), and who had reportedly returned to attack their relatives. Upon exhumation each still showed the classic signs of delayed decomposition, including the flow of ''fresh'' blood when cut. With the Count's consent, each was beheaded (or nails driven into the skull) and then burned. The extensive papers reporting these incidents to the emperor survived, as well as a lengthy narrative given by the count to an official at the University of Fribourg.

It is unlikely that the town of ''Haidam'' will ever be identified. No place by that name has been recorded. It has been suggested most convincingly that the term derived from the word ''haidamak,'' a Ukrainian term meaning ''outlaw'' or ''freebooter.'' Haidamak, derived from the Slavic ''heyduck'' referred to a class of dispossessed who had organized themselves into loose itinerant bands to live off the land. Eventually the Austrian Hapsburg rulers employed them as guardians along their most distant frontiers. This Haidam probably referred to the land of a haidamak rather than a specific town by that name.

As recently as the mid-twentieth century, folklorist Ján Mjartan reported that the belief in vampires was still alive in Slovakia. The vampire was thought to be able to suck the blood of its victims (humans and cattle) and often suffocated them. The vampire also was believed capable of killing with a mere glance (evil eye), thus decimating whole villages. Preventing the rising of a suspected vampire was accomplished by placing various objects in the **coffin** (coins, Christian symbols, various herbs, the dead person's belongings), putting poppyseed or millet **seeds** in the body orifices, and nailing the clothes and hair to the coffin. Finally, the head or the heart could be stabbed with an iron wedge, an oak **stake,** a hat pin, or some thorn such as the **hawthorn.** The body was carried headfirst to the grave, around which poppyseed or millet was scattered. The seeds also were dropped on the path homeward, and once home various rituals such as washing one's hands and holding them over the stove were followed. The family of the deceased repeated these measures if they proved ineffective the first time.

CONTEMPORARY VAMPIRE LORE: As with other Slavic countries, the belief in vampires receded to rural areas of the Czech Republic and Slovakia through the twentieth century. It made a brief appearance in the midst of the Czech cultural revival of the nineteenth century in a famous short story ''The Vampire'' by Jan Neruda (1834-1891). In recent decades, Josef Nesvadba, a Czech psychiatrist, has emerged as an impressive writer of horror fiction. A collection of his stories in English was published in 1982 as *Vampires Ltd.*

Sources:

Calmet, Augustine. *The Phantom World.* 2 vols. London: Richard Bentley, 1850. Reprint of English translation of 1746 treatise.

Hrbkova, Sárka B. *Czechoslovak Stories.* Freeport, NY: Books for Libraries Press, 1970. 330 pp.

Nesvadba, Josef. *Vampires Ltd.* Czechoslovakia: Artia Pocket Books, 1982. 225 pp.

Perkowski, Jan L. *The Darkling: A Treatise on Slavic Vampirism.* Columbus, OH: Slavica Publishers, 1989. 174 pp.

———, ed. *Vampires of the Slavs.* Cambridge, MA: Slavica Publishers, 1976. 294 pp.

Summers, Montague. *The Vampire in Europe.* London: Routledge, Kegan Paul, Trench, Trubner, & Co. 1929. 329 pp. Reprint. New Hyde Park, NY: University Books, 1961. 329 pp.

D

DANIELS, LESLIE NOEL, III (1943-)

Leslie Noel Daniels, III, author of a series of vampire novels, was born in 1943 in Connecticut. He received his B.A. in 1965 and his M.A. in 1968 from Brown University in Providence, Rhode Island. His master's thesis was written on *Frankenstein*. Daniels has since pursued a career in writing and in music.

During the early 1970s he produced two nonfiction works, both of which touched on the vampire: *Comix: A History of Comic Books in America* (1971) and *Living in Fear: A History of Horror in the Mass Media* (1975). He then edited two anthologies of horror stories: *Dying of Fright* (1976) and *Thirteen Tales of Terror* (1976).

In 1978, in the first of five novels, Daniels introduced a new vampire, **Sebastian de Villanueva** in *The Black Castle*. The book told the story of the origin of Don Sebastian, a brother of a local inquisitor in Spain in 1496. The vampire next appeared in sixteenth-century Mexico in *The Silver Skull* (1979) and as *Citizen Vampire* (1981), surviving amid the French Revolution. *Yellow Fog* (1986) found Sebastian, now known as Sebastian Newcastle, settled in London where he found love in the person of Felicia Lamb and an enemy in Reginald Callender, who was engaged to Felicia until Sebastian stole her away. In the end, Felicia lay dead and Sebastian fled, pursued by Callender. The chase led them to India and an encounter with the followers of the goddess **Kali** in the most recent novel, *No Blood Spilled* (1991).

Sources:

Daniels, Les. *The Black Castle*. New York: Charles Scribner's Sons, 1978. Reprint. New York: Berkley Books, 1979. 232 pp.

————. *Citizen Vampire*. New York; Charles Scribner's Sons, 1981. 197 pp.

————. *No Blood Spilled*. New York: Tor, 1991. 218 pp.

————. *The Silver Skull.* New York: Charles Scribner's Sons, 1970. Reprint. New York: Ace Books, 1983. 234 pp.

————. *Yellow Fog.* New York: Donald M. Grant, 1986. Rev. ed.: New York: Tor, 1988. 294 pp.

DANIS THE DARK PRODUCTIONS

Danis the Dark Productions is the company that produces *Bloodlines: The Vampire Magazine,* a vampire-oriented horror periodical. *Bloodlines* began in late 1992 as a fanzine edited by Amber Altman, who had been interested in vampires since her childhood. Through the Prodigy computer network, she has developed a staff from around the country. With issue three (April 1993), the fanzine was transformed into a magazine with its current title. Each issue has included vampire-oriented artwork, short fiction, poetry, and book and movie reviews. Danis the Dark is Altman's vampiric alter ego.

Bloodlines is unique among vampire periodicals in several ways. First, although established as a fanzine it is not tied to a fan club, and, while available by subscription, it also is distributed through retail bookstores and comics shops. Second, Altman is not interested in the gothic and has little to do with either the gothic or romantic aspects of modern vampire fandom. Instead she has assumed, for purposes of the magazine, that vampires are in fact real, and she presents them in such a way that readers can view them in their own light.

Bloodlines attempts to keep readers informed of the broader happenings in the world of vampire fandom. To increase their interest and participation, each issue also poses a question for the readers, the best answers of which are published in the next issue. *Bloodlines* may be reached at Danis the Dark Productions, 305 Hahani St., No. 296, Kailua, HI 96734. Approximately 1,000 copies of each issue were printed and distributed in 1993.

DARK SHADOWS (1966-1971; 1991)

Dark Shadows began in 1966 as a daytime soap opera on ABC television. With low ratings threatening cancellation, the show added supernatural elements to the plot, and then in April 1967 introduced a vampire. This vampire—**Barnabas Collins**—has joined **Dracula** and **Lestat de Lioncourt** as one of the most easily recognizable vampires. Once Collins was introduced to the show, the ratings turned around and the show became a hit. While the show went off the air in 1971, fans have kept its memory alive to the present day through fan clubs, publications, and conventions.

THE ORIGIN OF DARK SHADOWS: *Dark Shadows* began as an idea of producer **Dan Curtis.** The beginning of a story had come to him, according to one account, from a dream in which he saw a young woman with long dark hair. The woman was traveling by train to New England, where she had been offered a job as a governess. After she got off the train, she went to a large ''forbidding'' house. Curtis approached

ABC with the idea of taking his opening and creating a gothic-flavored daytime show. He collaborated with Art Wallace in developing the idea, and assembled a production crew that included Robert Costello, Lela Swift, John Sedwick, Sy Tomashoff, and Robert Cobert.

As the story developed, it first centered on Victoria Winters(Alexandra Moltke), the young woman of Curtis's dream. She was an orphan who had been found with a note, ''Her name is Victoria. I can no longer care for her.'' The rest of her name was added because she was found in the wintertime. As she grew up, the orphanage received donations in Victoria's name from Bangor, Maine. On her 20th birthday, Victoria received an offer of employment from a Mrs. Elizabeth Collins Stoddard (Joan Bennett) of Collinsport, Maine, to become governess for her nephew. Thus she not only had employment, but also an opportunity to possibly learn about her past. Collinsport was a small fishing town on the Maine coast. Collinwood, the Collins's family home, was a 40-room mansion built in the 1700s. The family resided in its central structure and had closed both wings of the house. Also on the property was an older house, built in the 1600s and now abandoned.

At Collinwood, the family estate where she was employed, Victoria interacted with the residents. Mrs. Stoddard, the family matriarch, had become a recluse after her husband disappeared 18 years before. David Collins (David Henesy), her nephew, was nine years old and somewhat of a problem. He had driven off previous governesses by his undisciplined behavior, especially nasty pranks at their expense. David's father, Roger Collins (Louis Edmonds), had a drinking problem and was generally neglectful of his son. Carolyn Stoddard (Nancy Barrett), Elizabeth's daughter, was a girl enjoying her youthful years and running through a series of loves. The mansion also was home to Matthew Morgan (Thayer David), the caretaker.

The cast was rounded out with several townspeople: Maggie Evans (Kathryn Leigh Scott), a waitress in the local diner who lived with her father Sam (David Ford), an alcoholic artist; Joe Haskell (Joel Crothers), employed by the Collins Fishing Fleet and involved with Carolyn Stoddard; and Burke Devlin (Mitchell Ryan), a businessman Victoria met on the train ride to Collinsport. Devlin became Winters's first friend and confidant. He was also the focus of the initial storyline, which was built around his reasons for returning to Collinsport after 10 years' absence. He was certain that Roger Collins had lied in court, resulting in Burke being sent to prison. He wanted revenge. In the tension resulting from his return, Bill Malloy (Frank Schofield), a local man who tried to mediate the situation, was killed. The supernatural element first entered into the *Dark Shadows* story when Malloy's ghost appeared to Victoria and told her that he had been murdered.

Taping for *Dark Shadows* began on June 13, 1966, and the first episode was aired with little fanfare two weeks later. During the first year of *Dark Shadows,* an additional character appeared, one that would become of long-term importance to the emerging story. As the supernatural element was increasing, a painting over the fireplace in the Old House came alive. The new character turned out to be the ghost of Josette DuPrés Collins (also played by Kathryn Leigh Scott). After a brief appearance

LARA PARKER AS ANGELIQUE IN *DARK SHADOWS* (1966-71).

in episode 40, she appeared again in episode 126 to protect Victoria from Matthew Morgan, the murderer of Malloy, who had kidnapped her. Morgan died from fright upon seeing Josette, thus resolving that subplot. Afterward, Josette become intricately integrated into the storyline.

The *Dark Shadows* audience was introduced to new supernatural subplots almost weekly. Around the 200th episode, a transition began. First, the original Burke Devlin situation was resolved when Roger Collins confessed to manslaughter and perjury. Then a new character, Willie Loomis, took up residence at Collinwood. Almost immediately Loomis called attention to a portrait in the foyer of the mansion. It was one of the family ancestors, Barnabas Collins.

THE EMERGENCE OF BARNABAS COLLINS: Though the addition of supernatural elements improved the show's ratings, ABC executives indicated early in 1967 that it still was in danger of being cancelled. Curtis, who had always wanted to do a vampire picture, gambled and decided to add a vampire to the show. Canadian

Shakespearean actor **Jonathan Frid** was finally hired for the part. The original idea was to have the vampire jazz up the show, improve its ratings, and then quietly fade away. That plan would soon be discarded.

Barnabas Collins made his first appearance in episode 210 in April of 1967. Willie Loomis discovered a secret room with a chained coffin in the family mausoleum. He undid the chains and Barnabas came out of his resting place. In the next episode, he appeared at the front door of Collinwood and confronted the family as their long-lost cousin from England. He moved into the abandoned old house on the estate, and soon the community was plagued by a mysterious illness. The symptoms included fatigue, bite marks, and the loss of blood.

As the story unfolded, the audience discovered that Barnabas was a vampire who had lived two centuries earlier. (He actually was the person in the portrait in the mansion.) In his human life at the end of the eighteenth century, he had loved and lost Josette DuPrés, and he still longed for her in his new life at Collinwood. Having noticed Maggie Evans's resemblance to Josette, he tried to turn her into another Josette. When she refused his advances, he nearly killed her.

By this point in the story, which was being broadcast in the summer of 1967, the ratings not only had jumped but had done so in a spectacular manner—the show became a hit. In a matter of weeks, Jonathan Frid became a star, and his fan mail soared. Overwhelmingly, the mail was from young women, even teenagers. Crowds regularly gathered at the entrances to the ABC studio where the show was taped. The first *Dark Shadows* **paraphernalia** appeared.

Meanwhile, as the story continued, another new character was introduced—Dr. Julia Hoffman (played by Grayson Hall). Called on to treat Maggie Evans, Hoffman became intrigued with Barnabas, discovered his vampiric nature, and offered to help him overcome it. Initially he accepted her ministrations, but he eventually turned on her. He was about to kill the doctor when the ghost of his beloved sister Sarah appeared to save her.

THE ORIGIN OF BARNABAS COLLINS: With Sarah making her ghostly presence known to a number of people, the decision was made to hold a seance. During the seance Victoria went into a trance and the lights went out. When the lights returned, she had disappeared and her place had been taken by Phyllis Wick. Victoria woke up in Collinsport in 1795. The scene was now set to relate the story of Barnabas's origin. The son of a prominent local landowner, Barnabas traveled to the DuPrés plantation on the island of Martinique. There he began an affair with Angélique Bouchard (played by Lara Parker), a beautiful servant girl who, it was later revealed, knew witchcraft. Then he met and fell in love with the plantation owner's daughter, Josette, and they made plans to wed. Barnabas broke off the affair with Angélique.

Meanwhile, back in Collinsport, Victoria had found work in the Collins's home as governess to Barnabas's young sister Sarah. The members and acquaintances of the family from the 1960s reappeared as their counterparts in the 1790's storyline. Barnabas returned from the West Indies to prepare for his marriage but did not anticipate that Angélique would use her powers of witchcraft to disrupt the plans. She caused Josette to fall in love with Jeremiah, Barnabas's brother. She then claimed Barnabas for herself. Barnabas, in turn, killed his brother in a duel and turned on Angélique. She cursed him and sent a bat to attack, and Barnabas emerged from the encounter a vampire. After considering various options, he decided to make Josette his vampire bride. Before he could carry through on his plans, Angélique interfered again and caused Josette to commit suicide. Barnabas told his father of his condition and asked to be killed. His father could not kill him, but did chain Barnabas in a coffin (which Willie Loomis eventually discovered).

While Barnabas fought Angélique, Victoria had been condemned as a witch. As she was about to be killed, she suddenly reappeared in 1967. Only a few minutes of the seance had passed while she was lost for some months in the 1790s. Barnabas realized that Victoria now knew his identity and decided to court her, but he was immediately distracted by the arrival of Angélique as Cassandra, the new wife of Roger Collins.

NEW STORY LINES: With five half-hour shows to write each week—the equivalent of more than a feature-length movie—story ideas were exhausted at a rapid rate. During 1968, the writers turned to classic nineteenth-century gothic novels for ideas, and during the last three years of the show merged subplots from a variety of horror themes into the ongoing story. The major confrontation between Barnabas and Cassandra, for example, was based around a subplot derived from *Frankenstein*. Late in 1968 Henry James's *The Turn of the Screw* inspired a plot that led to the introduction of the second most popular member of the cast, Quentin Collins (played by David Selby).

The storyline again sent Victoria into the past—this time for good. Thus Elizabeth Stoddard needed another governess for her nephew David. Meanwhile, David and Amy (a young girl visiting at Collinwood) went exploring in one of the unoccupied wings of the house, where they discovered a disconnected telephone. While the children played with the phone, a ghostly voice called them to a room where a gramophone mysteriously played music. The ghost of Quentin (his name derived from Quint in James's text) appeared. He attempted to take control of both children, but a female spirit intervened. She blocked Quentin's effect on Amy, but was of little help to David. Eventually Barnabas was drawn in to protect David. In his attempt to contact Quentin, Barnabas was thrown back to 1897 (the year **Bram Stoker**'s novel ***Dracula*** was published), the time when Quentin actually lived. Barnabas found himself chained in his tomb. One of his ancestors, however, hired **Gypsies,** who discovered the mausoleum and freed Barnabas. Again he arrived at the door as the long-lost cousin from England.

Quentin and Barnabas started as rivals. However, as the story developed, Quentin and his male descendants were cursed—they would become werewolves. In the face of this new reality, Barnabas and Quentin came to some understanding of each other. Each, in turn, was transported back to the present and the story continued.

While based on ***Dracula,*** from which it drew its understanding of the vampire and the vampire's powers, *Dark Shadows* created the most elaborate and complex alternative to the *Dracula* story in modern mythology. It played to an ever-growing audience from the time Barnabas Collins was added to the storyline to the spring of 1967, and became the most popular soap opera on ABC, pushing the network past CBS and putting it in a position to challenge NBC for the daytime audience. It was estimated that 20 million people were regular viewers. Frid received several thousand letters every week and David Selby only slightly less. Additional thousands of letters were directed to the rest of the cast. The show lasted for two more years before its ratings began to sag and it was finally cancelled. The final show (the 1,245th segment) was aired on April 2, 1971. Many believe that it was not so much a dip in the ratings but the exhaustion of the story that led to its cancellation.

ADDITIONAL DARK SHADOWS VAMPIRES: While Barnabas Collins was the dominant vampire of the *Dark Shadows* series, other characters also had a brush with vampirism. The most prominent was Angélique. Following the return of the story to the 1960s from the 1790s, Angélique reappeared in the person of Cassandra Collins, the new wife of Roger Collins. Shortly thereafter, one Nicholas Blair, a warlock claiming to be Cassandra's brother, arrived at Collinwood. When Cassandra got in his way, he used his strong magical powers to turn her into a vampire. Through the ministrations of Dr. Hoffman, Barnabas was temporarily cured of his vampirism. However, Angélique/Cassandra, wanting Barnabas to be with her in her new form, attacked him and turned him back into a vampire. Angélique's plans were foiled, however, when she was set on fire by Barnabas. She died screaming as the flames enveloped her.

During Angelique's career as a vampire, she attacked handyman Tom Jennings, who had discovered the location of her coffin. He survived as a vampire for only a few episodes before being staked.

The continuing storyline took the cast back to the nineteenth century where a prevampirized Angélique reappeared. After being attacked by Barnabas, a servant, Dirk, was made a vampire. He was soon staked by Edward Collins.

Later, the storyline led Barnabas and the Collins family into an encounter with the Leviathans, old demonic forces in the tradition of H. P. Lovecraft. The Leviathans were responsible for turning him back into a vampire. Among the Leviathans was Audrey, a vampire who made a brief appearance in a single episode. The most notable fact of Audrey's otherwise inconsequential appearance was that she was played by a young Marsha Mason, later to go on to stardom in the movies. Another female vampire at this time was Megan Todd (Marie Wallace), a victim of Barnabas. She eventually was staked by Willie Loomis.

Finally, toward the end of the show, Roxanne Drew appeared as a young woman involved in a bizarre experiment to transfer her life force to Angélique. At this point in the story, the major characters were moving between parallel times with the same people but different histories. In real time, Barnabas met Roxanne again as the girlfriend of an astrologer, Sebastian Shaw. She was a vampire and before being discovered, bit Maggie Evans. Meanwhile, the story shifted to 1840. There Barnabas also met Roxanne and they fell in love. However, the ever-present and vengeful

Angélique killed her. Roxanne then rose as a vampire and was soon cornered in her coffin. She disintegrated in her crypt when a cross was placed on top of her.

DARK SHADOWS BOOKS AND PARAPHERNALIA: The show had a far reaching effect on popular culture. Under the pseudonym of Marilyn Ross, **Daniel Ross** authored 33 paperback novels from 1966 to 1972 developed from the show. In spite of the Comics Code that banned vampires from comic books from 1954 to 1971, Gold Key produced the *Dark Shadows* **comic books,** the first vampire-oriented comics in almost two decades. In 1968-69, *Dark Shadows* paraphernalia began to appear, including the *Dark Shadows Game,* Viewmaster stereo pictures, model kits, jigsaw puzzles, and trading cards, to name just a few. A *"Dark Shadows" Original Soundtrack Album* (1969) was one of four record albums of Dark Shadows **music.** "Quentin's Theme," the most popular piece of *Dark Shadows* music, appeared on the first album and also was released as a single. Initially heard on the gramophone in the room where Quentin first appeared, the theme was recorded more than 20 times by various artists.

MORE *DARK SHADOWS*: The most substantial spin-offs of the television series were two full-length feature movies, *House of Dark Shadows* (1970) and *Night of Dark Shadows* (1971). These were later made available on video. A short time after its cancellation, the show went into syndicated reruns on independent stations and PBS—the first time that had happened to a daytime soap opera. Most recently the show has been picked up by the new SCI-FI cable channel. Currently all 1,245 segments have been released on MPI Home Video, as have a variety of specialized videos such as *Dark Shadows: Behind the Scenes, Dark Shadows Bloopers,* and *Dark Shadows 25th Anniversary.*

After *Dark Shadows* went off the air, interest in the series stayed alive primarily in the imaginations of teenagers who had rushed home from school to watch the late afternoon soap opera. One of these, Kathleen Resch, began to circulate a fanzine, *The World of Dark Shadows,* in 1975. Two years later, Dark Shadows conventions were born as **Shadowcon,** part of a San Diego science fiction convention. In 1979 Shadowcon became a separate meeting for an annual gathering of fans. In the early 1980s Shadowcon began to drift from an exclusive attention to *Dark Shadows,* and a new, more ambitious structure, the **Dark Shadows Festival,** was created. The annual conventions (i.e., Dark Shadows Festival) led to the growth of existing Dark Shadows fan publications (most prominently **Shadowgram,** edited by Marcy Robin), the founding of new fanzines, and the opening of fan clubs that kept interest alive. Their work came to unexpected fruition in the early 1990s when a new version of *Dark Shadows* was scheduled in prime time by NBC. Unfortunately, it was cancelled in 1991 after only one season, but not before it led to the creation of a whole new set of *Dark Shadows* fans, books, collectibles, and souvenirs.

The world of Dark Shadows is most effectively entered through **The Dark Shadows Official Fan Club,** which provides contacts for local fan clubs and information on obtaining *Dark Shadows* books, videos, and paraphernalia. For information specifically on paraphernalia, fans can contact *DS Collectibles Classi-*

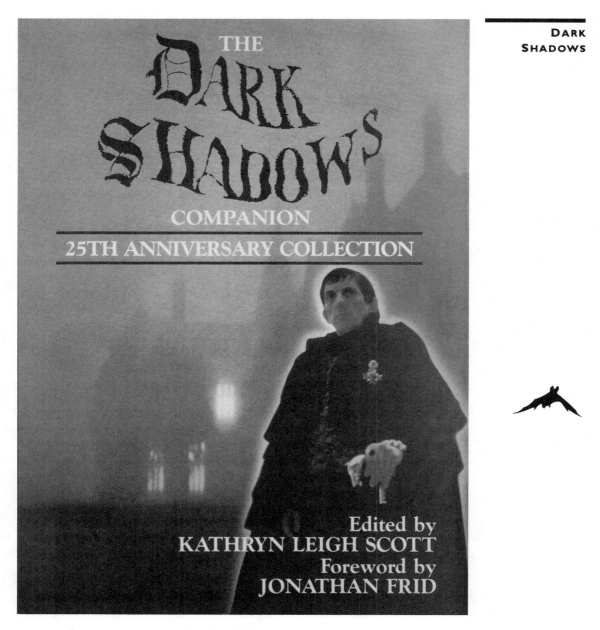

DARK SHADOWS COMPANION

fied, a periodical listing collectibles for sale (c/o Sue Ellen Wilson, 6173 Iroquois Trail, Mentor, OH 44060); the *Collinwood Chronicle* (No. 5 Hammes Dr., Florissant,

MO 63031); or the *Dark Shadows Collector's Guide* (c/o Craig Hamrick, 204 W. 9th St., Baxter Springs, KS 66713). *Dark Shadows* videos are available in many retail outlets or may be ordered directly from MPI Home Video (16101 S. 108th Ave., Orland Park, IL 60462).

Sources:

Gross, Edward, and Marc Shapiro. *The Vampire Interview Book: Conversations with the Undead.* New York: Image Publishing, 1991. 134 pp.

Pierson, Jim. *Dark Shadows Resurrected.* Los Angeles: Pomegrante Press, 1992. 175 pp.

Scott, Kathryn Leigh, ed. *The Dark Shadows Companion: 25th Anniversary Collection.* Los Angeles: Pomegranate Press, 1990. 208 pp.

———. *My Scrapbook Memories of Dark Shadows.* Los Angeles: Pomegranate Press, 1986. 152 pp.

DARK SHADOWS FESTIVAL

Dark Shadows Festival was founded in 1983 with the support of *Shadowgram* (Marcy Robin), *The World of Dark Shadows* (Kathleen Resch), and **Old House Publishing** (Dale Clark). It superseded the **Shadowcon** gatherings that previously had sponsored the major meetings of fans of the series that aired on ABC-TV from 1966 to 1971. Through the early 1980s, Shadowcon had moved from its exclusive focus on *Dark Shadows* to include programming on science fiction, horror, and fantasy. Dark Shadows Festivals debuted with an exclusive interest in *Dark Shadows* and quickly received the support of the various *Dark Shadows* clubs and fanzines.

The first "fests" were held at San Jose, California, and Newark, New Jersey, in 1983. The latter included a trip to Lyndhurst, the mansion in Tarrytown, New York, that was used as Collinwood in the feature movies *House of Dark Shadows* and *Night of Dark Shadows*. The two films were then screened for those in attendance. The festival also featured a costume contest, now a regular feature of the annual program. The initial fests were followed by additional meetings in San Jose and in Dallas, Texas, after which they alternated between the Los Angeles and New York City areas. The tenth festival was held in New York and included a tour of New England locations used in the *Dark Shadows* series and films. It featured an appearance by **Jonathan Frid** (the original **Barnabas Collins**), who has attended 13 of the 16 fests held through 1993.

The festivals were designed to be fun events for fans to meet and talk to each other, to meet members of the cast, and to have the opportunity to purchase the wide variety of *Dark Shadows* souvenirs and **paraphernalia.** Each of the festivals has featured many of the original stars, with the more recent gatherings also including stars from the 1991 revival series.

Dark Shadows Festival Publications has printed *The Introduction of Barnabas,* a book summarizing the early *Dark Shadows* episodes with the vampire Barnabas Collins that also includes a variety of documents about the show. It also publishes an annual *Dark Shadows* calendar. Dark Shadows Festival may be contacted c/o **Dark Shadows Official Fan Club,** PO Box 92, Maplewood, NJ 07040.

Sources:
"DS Festival Celebrates 10th Anniversary." *Shadowgram* 63 (January 1993): 2-3.
The Introduction of Barnabas. Maplewood, NJ: Dark Shadows Festival, 1988. 144 pp.
Thompson, Jeff. "A History of the East Coast Dark Shadows Festivals: 1983-1991." Unpublished paper,
  1991. 12 pp.

DARK SHADOWS OVER OKLAHOMA

Dark Shadows Over Oklahoma is a *Dark Shadows* fan club founded by Brett Hargrove. It currently is led by Letha Roberts. The group gathers monthly, and Roberts edits *The Graveyard Gazette,* the club's newsletter, which includes current *Dark Shadows* news, interviews, notices of conventions, art and fiction submitted by club members, and reviews of *Dark Shadows* and other horror books.

Dark Shadows Over Oklahoma can be contacted c/o Letha Roberts, 316 SE 66th St., Oklahoma City, OK 73149.

DARK SHADOWS SOCIETY OF MILWAUKEE

The Dark Shadows Society of Milwaukee was a short-lived *Dark Shadows* fan club founded in 1986 by Lynn L. Gerdes and others in southeastern Wisconsin. The club met for discussions and screenings of *Dark Shadows* tapes and disbanded in 1989.

DAVANZATI, GIUSEPPE (1665-1755)

Giuseppe Davanzati, an archbishop of the Roman Catholic Church and vampirologist, was born on August 29, 1665, in Bari, Italy. He first attended the Jesuit College in Bari but left at the age of 15 to enter the University of Naples. Three years later, his parents having both passed away, he entered the University of Bologna with the idea of becoming a priest. He was a distinguished student in science and mathematics, and upon completion of his course of studies commenced a period of travel using Paris as his home base. At some point he was ordained to the priesthood by the bishop of Salerno. Soon after the turn of the century, Pope Clement XI called him back to Italy to become treasurer of the Sanctuary of St. Nicolas at Bari. Several years later he was entrusted with the particularly difficult and sensitive task of representing the pope in Vienna before the throne of Emperor Charles VI. His success was rewarded by his elevation to the episcopacy as archbishop of Trani, a town north of Bari. He served that post with distinction until 1745 when Pope Benedict XIV named the aged archbishop patriarch of Alexandria.

Davanzati's years as an archbishop coincided with waves of vampirism reported around Europe in the first half of the eighteenth century. However, he did not encounter the subject until 1738, when he was brought into discussions initiated at the request of Cardinal Schtrattembach, the bishop of Olmütz (Germany), who wanted the church's advice. Schtrattembach had been presented official reports on outbreaks of vampirism in various parts of Germany beginning in 1720, highlighted by the account of **Arnold Paul** in Serbia in 1831. Davanzati spent the next few years studying these reports and other pertinent texts, and in 1744 published his *Dissertazione sopra I Vampiri.*

Davanzati concluded that the vampire reports were human fantasies—though possibly of a diabolical origin. A major part of Davanzati's argument centered on the tendency of the vampire to appear among the illiterate and lower-class peasants— people who were believed to be more easily deceived by such appearances than were educated men. Davanzati emerged as the leading Italian authority on vampires. His work was reprinted in 1789, and his opinion came to be accepted by most people in power, both within the church and in political control. However, his work was soon overshadowed by the treatise of his learned French colleague, **Dom Augustin Calmet.** Calmet's scholarly work, published just two years after Davanzati's, did not support Davanzati's harsh conclusion. Through Calmet, the subject of vampirism reached both the intellectual community and the policymakers of Europe in ways Davanzati's dismissal of the topic could not do. Davanzati died on February 16, 1755.

Sources:

Davanzati, Giuseppe. *Dissertazione sopre I Vampiri.* Naples, Italy: presso i fratelli Raimondi, 1744.
Summers, Montague. *The Vampire: His Kith and Kin.* Reprint. New York: University Books, 1960. 356 pp.

DEANE, HAMILTON (CIR. 1880-1958)

Hamilton Deane, the playwright and director who brought *Dracula* to the stage, was born near Dublin. His family owned an estate adjacent to that of Bram Stoker's father, and his mother had been acquainted with **Bram Stoker** in her youth. Deane entered the theater as a young man, first appearing in 1899 with the Henry Irving Vacation Company (Stoker worked for Henry Irving in London for many years). Even before he formed his own troupe in the early 1920s, Deane had been thinking about bringing *Dracula* to the stage. Unable to find a scriptwriter to take on the project, he wrote it himself in a four-week period of inactivity while he was suffering with a severe cold. He also contacted Florence Stoker, Bram's widow, and negotiated a deal for the dramatic rights.

In order to more easily stage the detailed story, he dropped the book's beginning and ending sections that occurred in **Transylvania.** He transformed **Quincey P. Morris** into a female to accommodate the gender makeup of his company at the time. He also recast the more sinister Dracula of the novel into a representative of cultured continental royalty capable of fitting into British society. Deane was the first to dress Dracula in evening clothes and a cape (an opera cloak).

Deane submitted his play for government approval in 1924. The license was issued on August 5, but censors insisted that one scene be altered. The death of Dracula at the hands of the men had to be changed so that the hammering of the **stake**

DRAMATIST HAMILTON DEANE
BROUGHT *DRACULA* TO THE
STAGE.

was not actually shown. Instead, the men were to gather around the **coffin** in such a manner as to block the action from the audience. When the play opened in Derby, England, Deane assumed the role of **Abraham Van Helsing,** Dracula's archenemy.

Fearing that London critics would pan his play, Deane stayed away for three years, but finally risked an opening there on February 14, 1927, at the Little Theatre. Though the reviews were largely unfavorable, the audiences filled the house each night. By the end of the summer he had moved the production to the larger Duke of York's Theatre. Following up on a casual remark by a reporter, Deane pulled off an almost legendary publicity stunt. He hired a nurse to be present at each performance to assist any viewers who reacted badly to the play by fainting or taking ill.

Deane's desire to return to the countryside led to a brief break between himself, Florence Stoker, and one of his backers, Harry Warburton. The split led to Warburton's commissioning, with Stoker's approval, a second version of the play (which opened in September 1927), but proved unsuccessful and soon closed. Deane kept the London company running, but at one point had three different groups performing the play at various locations in the countryside. People were known to memorize entire scenes and to become so involved with the play that they shouted out lines before the actors could deliver them.

In 1927 Horace Liveright bought the American dramatic rights from Florence Stoker and hired newspaperman **John L. Balderston** to edit it for the New York stage. Balderston's editing constituted a full rewriting, though Deane's name has been retained on the publication and on the various revisions of the Balderston version. The **Universal Pictures** movie with **Bela Lugosi** merely increased the demand in England for Deane to keep his production of the play alive.

In 1939 Deane played the role of Dracula for the first time. Later that year he brought his troupe to the Lyceum Theatre, where Stoker had worked when he wrote the play and where he had staged a one-time-only reading of his work in order to establish his dramatic rights. After a brief run of *Dracula* and then of *Hamlet,* the Lyceum closed its doors permanently. During one performance at the Lyceum, Lugosi, who was in the audience, rushed on stage at the close of the play to embrace Deane.

Deane's last performance as Dracula was in 1941 at St. Helen's, Lancastershire. After his death late in 1958, his version of the play largely fell into disuse, with most revivalists preferring the Balderston rewrite.

Sources:

Deane, Hamilton, and John L. Balderston. *Dracula: The Vampire Play in Three Acts.* New York: Samuel French, 1927. 113 pp.

Dracula (The Original 1931 Shooting Script). Atlantic City, NJ: Magic Image Filmbooks, 1990.

Glut, Donald F. *The Dracula Book.* Metuchen, NJ: Scarecrow Press, 1975. 388 pp.

Skal, David J., ed. *Dracula: The Ultimate, Illustrated Edition of the World-Famous Vampire Play.* New York: St. Martin's Press, 1993. 153 pp.

———. *Hollywood Gothic: The Tangled Web of Dracula from Novel to Stage to Screen.* New York: W. W. Norton & Company, 1990. 242 pp.

DEARG-DUL *See:* IRELAND, VAMPIRES IN

DEATH OF VAMPIRES *See:* DESTROYING THE VAMPIRE

DECAPITATION

One of the surest and most common means of **destroying the vampire** and making sure it did not return to a semblance of life was to cut off its head. This was clearly illustrated in **Bram Stoker**'s novel, *Dracula.* **Arthur Holmwood, Lucy Westenra**'s fiance, and Lucy's other friends could not bring themselves to cut off Lucy's head after her death. They consented only when Dr. **Abraham Van Helsing** demonstrated to them that Lucy had joined the undead. He and Arthur carried out the decapitation. Van Helsing did not, however, decapitate the three vampire women in **Castle**

Dracula; they disintegrated before his eyes after he staked them. In like measure, Dracula disintegrated after **Jonathan Harker** and **Quincey P. Morris** stabbed him.

Carmilla, the vampire in **Sheridan Le Fanu**'s tale, lost her head as part of the process of being killed, thus continuing the trend in European folklore. Severing the head to destroy a vampire was common throughout **Germany** and eastern Europe. When a vampire was reported in a village, and its identity determined, the body would be disinterred. Commonly, it then was impaled on a stake and its head cut off. Decapitation prevented the head from directing the body in its wanderings. In northern Europe (**Poland** and **Germany**), the head might be placed between the knees or under the arm. There also were reports of the head being placed under the body and buried separately, so that it could not be returned to the neck and reconnected. It was also possible that the vampire could return with the head held in its arms. In some cultures, the exact instrument for severing the head, a shovel or a sword, was prescribed.

As the vampire was dramatized, the process of decapitation was, as a whole, left behind. It was a much too indelicate means of death to present to a theater audience or show on a movie screen. Nevertheless, it was not forgotten. In the reworking of the vampire legend by **Chelsea Quinn Yarbro,** her hero **St. Germain** feared only two things that would cause the ''true death''—fire and the severing of the spine (which decapitation would accomplish). In *Blood Games* (1979), he faked the death of his love Olivia as part of a plot to free her from the clutches of her husband. After vampirizing her, she died, but was revived by St. Germain and his helpers. He gave strict instructions to be followed so that the ''true death'' would not overtake her.

The movies from **Hammer Films** raised horror films to a new level with their depiction of flowing blood in full color. As society became more permissive in the last generation, directors responded to audiences' thirst for **blood,** developing the so-called ''splatter'' movies. In this atmosphere, decapitation returned to the vampire myth, not in the traditional manner, but as the climax of a fight or similar intense interaction between two characters. However, in spite of splatter movies, decapitation has remained a rare occurrence, at least for vampires.

DENMARK, VAMPIRES IN *See:* SCANDINAVIA, VAMPIRES IN

DESTROYING THE VAMPIRE

Almost everywhere vampires have been seen as evil, monstrous creatures. Once a vampire was confirmed to be wandering in a neighborhood, people hastened to locate and destroy it. In the most famous vampire novel, *Dracula,* the lengthy process of destroying Dracula took up half the novel. Dracula's death was presaged by the killing of **Lucy Westenra,** whom Dracula had turned into a vampire. Confronted in her crypt, the men who knew her in life put a stake through her heart, decapitated her, and filled her mouth with **garlic.** Later, in his speech to the men assembled to kill Dracula

(Chapter 18), Dr. **Abraham Van Helsing** informed them of the means of destroying vampires:

> . . . The branch of the wild rose on his coffin keep him so that he move not from it; a sacred bullet fired into the coffin kill him so that he be true dead, and as for the stake through him, we know already of its peace; or the cut off head that giveth rest. We have seen it with our eyes.

In the end, however, the men deviated from the formula. Dracula was killed with a Bowie knife plunged into his heart by **Quincey P. Morris**; **Jonathan Harker** then carried out the **decapitation.** His body then crumpled to dust as everyone watched.

Among the sources he used for his novel, **Bram Stoker** referred to Emily Gerard's *The Land Beyond the Forest* as a major source of information on vampires. Concerning the killing of vampires, she had observed in her travels that the vampire:

> . . . will continue to suck the blood of other innocent persons till the spirit has been exorcised by opening the grave of the suspected person, and either driving a stake through the corpse, or else firing a pistol-shot into the coffin. To walk smoking round the grave on each anniversary of the death is also supposed to be effective in confining the vampire. In very obstinate cases of vampirism it is recommended to cut off the head, and replace it in the coffin with the mouth filled with garlic, or to extract the heart and burn it, stewing the ashes over the grave.

She noted further that it was a common practice to lay a thorny branch of the wild rose across the body at the time of burial to prevent a suspected vampire from leaving its coffin.

FOLKLORE TRADITIONS: In his treatment of the methods of destroying the vampire, Stoker reached back into the folklore of eastern Europe to develop his own myth. While traditions concerning vampires varied widely on some issues, when it came to killing them, there was consensus across cultures from **Greece** and the southern **Slavic** lands to **Poland** and **Russia.** In eastern Europe, vampire activity would be traced to the graveyard and to a particular body, usually that of a recently deceased person, as the suspected vampire. The body would then be disinterred, examined for signs of vampiric activity (lifelike appearance, blood around the mouth), and a determination made that the person was indeed the vampire. Once the designation was made, there was a tendency to treat the corpse at two levels. First, steps would be taken to stop its vampiric activity by specific actions against the body. Among the least intrusive would be the firing of a **bullet** into the **coffin.** In Eastern Orthodox countries, the local priest might repeat the services for the dead, which in effect would again dispatch the soul on its journey to the realm of the dead. If the coffin was opened, the suspected vampire's clothing might be nailed to the sides of the coffin (away from the mouth area). Commonly, however, the body would be mutilated in one of several ways. It could be staked (with different cultures using materials that varied from an iron stake to a hat pin or local woods). In most cultures the **stake** did not have to go through the heart and usually was put through the stomach area. In these cases, it was assumed that the stake would hold the body in the ground. At times the body would be turned face downward and then staked. If the stake did not work, the corpse would only dig itself deeper into the earth. Occasionally, the body might have been staked with a nail or pin even before it was buried; in that instance a subsequent opening of the grave would be followed immediately by more drastic activity.

Along with staking, decapitation was common. Among the Kashubian Poles, the severed head might be placed between the legs. If mutilating the body with a stake and decapitating it did not work, the last resort was to burn the body. There are few reports of vampire activity continuing after cremation. It was, of course, this mutilation and cremation of long-dead persons that moved the authorities to suppress belief in vampires in the eighteenth century. Through the early part of that century, the ruling powers not only were receiving accounts of vampire activity but also had to deal with complaints of families against hysterical townspeople who were mutilating the corpses of loved ones. Thus the authorities, primarily Roman Catholic Austrians, were forced to take action against antivampire attacks on the graveyards. While edicts against mutilating bodies did not end belief in vampires (which persists to this day in some areas), they did slow the reports of vampires and spread skepticism concerning existence.

THE FICTIONAL VAMPIRE: Once the vampire became an object of fiction, its death frequently became the point of the story. Such was not the case in the beginning. Both **Samuel Taylor Coleridge** and **John Polidori,** who respectively wrote the first vampire poem and short story in English, left their vampires free to attack the next victim. Polidori did allow his vampire to be killed in quite normal ways by the bandits who attacked **Lord Ruthven** and his traveling companion, but he could always be revived by the light of the full moon. **Varney the Vampyre,** after what seemed like endless adventures, finally committed suicide by jumping into a volcano. Thus the current conventions concerning the death of vampires have to be traced to the story of **"Carmilla".** Drawing from the folkloric traditions, author **Sheridan Le Fanu** suggested that the vampire should be decapitated, staked, and then burned, and such was the fate of Carmilla. As noted previously, Stoker's characters saw the staking of the corpse as adequate, and thus did not advocate its burning.

The development of staking as a conventional means of destroying the vampire led to two important reinterpretations of the vampire myth. First, by emphasizing that the stake had to be driven into the heart rather than the stomach or back, a change in the myth occurred. The vampire no longer was pinned to the ground. The stake now attacked the heart, the organ that pumped the blood, and "the blood is the life." Second, the vampire, being seen as in some way immortal, could be brought back to life by pulling the stake from the chest.

Crucial to the development of the vampire myth was the movie *Nosferatu, Eine Symphonie des Garuens.* Director Freidrich Wilhelm Murnau, in altering the storyline of *Dracula,* created the idea that the vampire could be killed if a beautiful

ABRAHAM VAN HELSING (HERBERT LOM) PREPARES TO STAKE ONE OF THE VAMPIRE BRIDES IN *EL CONDE DRACULA* (1970).

woman held his attention until dawn. The vampire could not return to his resting place and would be killed by the **sunlight.** The vampire's death in the dawn's light was one of the memorable scenes in the movie. This perspective on the vampire was an addition to the myth. Previously, while the vampire preferred the night, it was not limited to it. Its powers were enhanced during the evening, but Lord Ruthven, Varney, and Dracula all made daytime appearances. Folkloric vampires were nocturnal creatures, but the daylight merely protected the living from them. There was no hint that it killed them. However, once suggested, the negative effects of sunlight became a common element in twentieth-century vampire stories. In the movie *The Mark of a Vampire,* **Bela Lugosi** disintegrated in the presence of sunlight.

The effects of sunlight were used effectively in the *Horror of Dracula,* which climaxed as Abraham Van Helsing ripped the draperies from the wall of **Castle Dracula** and caught the vampire in the dawn's early light. **Frank Langella**'s *Dracula* **(1979)** was impaled on a ship's hook and hoisted high into the sunlight. Lesser bits of sunlight would do significant damage but not be fatal. In one episode of the television series *Forever Knight,* for example, a boy innocently opened a window, and the little beam of light falling on vampire Nick Knight's eyes temporarily blinded him. The clan of vampires in the movie *Near Dark,* while able to be active in daylight, received severe burns each time the sunlight penetrated their barriers of drapes and tinfoil.

MODERN VAMPIRES: As the myth has been restructured in the twentieth century, vampires face three fatal dangers: a stake in the heart, sunshine, or fire. Usually there is also the possibility of being revived by removal of the stake or by a magical ritual, and/or by adding blood to the ashes of someone who had died after being burned in the sun or by fire.

In the face of these assumptions, several prominent contemporary vampire writers have attempted to reinterpret the vampire tale. **Chelsea Quinn Yarbro** has written a series of novels concerning the vampire **St. Germain.** St. Germain was affected by the sun, but not fatally. However, there was the possibility of what was termed the "true death." The vampire would die if his spine was severed or if he was consumed in fire. Stakes could hurt, but unless they cut the spine, he would recover.

Anne Rice thoroughly and systematically demythologized the vampire myth. Her vampires were not affected by many of the traditional forces or objects (especially holy objects) that have plagued other vampires and had a reduced set of powers. Though her vampires were nearly immortal, they could be killed by sunlight or by fire and the subsequent scattering of the ashes. However, some vampires (those older and closer to Akasha in lineage) were somewhat immune to the sunlight. Rice's vampires also faced a threat over which they had little or no control and of which most were unaware. In Rice's world, vampires were created by the merger of a spirit that moved into Akasha, the first vampire. All vampires remained in some way tied to Akasha, hence whatever happened to her was passed on to them. Were she to be killed and the spirit driven out, all vampires would cease to be.

Sources:

Glut, Donald F. *The Dracula Book.* Metuchen, NJ: Scarecrow Press, 1975. 388 pp.
Perkowski, Jan L. *The Darkling: A Treatise on Slavic Vampirism.* Columbus, OH: Slavica Publishers, 1989. 174 pp.
Ramsland, Katherine. *The Vampire Companion.* New York: Ballantine Books, 1993. 508 pp.
Yarbro, Chelsea Quinn. *Hotel Transylvania.* New York: St. Martin's Press, 1978. 252 pp.

DE VILLENUEVA, SEBASTIAN

The vampire that appeared in a series of novels by **Les Daniels,** Sebastian de Villenueva originated in fifteenth-century Spain. According to the story line, first presented in *The Black Castle* (1978), Sebastian participated in the siege of Malaga in 1487, part of the effort to drive the Moors from Spain. He was killed when a cannon exploded in his face. His body was returned to his castle in northeastern Spain and entombed in a crypt. His brother, still a young man at the time of the siege, had become a monk and eventually was named inquisitor for his home territory.

In the days following his accident, Sebastian went through a set of (undisclosed) "rituals" that made him a vampire. From the cannon explosion, he retained a scar that ran down the left side of his face. He took advantage of his brother's position and regularly visited the cells of the Inquisition where he fed among the prisoners. He claimed that during the first nine years of his life he had never taken a life.

Sebastian was a vampire in the traditional sense, with the familiar variety of powers and limitations. He could transform himself into a **bat** or become **mist,** a form in which he could pass through the smallest crack. He was also subject to the second death: **sunlight, fire,** or a **stake** through the heart; in addition he needed to sleep on **native soil.**

At the end of *The Black Castle,* Sebastian died in a fire he built in front of his castle. However, his skull was not consumed in the flames and, once severed from his body, rolled into the castle moat. It later was retrieved and taken to **Mexico,** where he was brought back to life to begin a new series of adventures. Aligned with an Aztec priestess, he ended his Mexican sojourn when she transformed him into pure spirit. He reappeared in revolutionary France (*Citizen Vampire,* 1981) when an alchemist brought him back from spirit. Sebastian returned once more to the spirit realm, only to assume a body in nineteenth-century England (*Yellow Fog,* 1986) and India (*No Blood Spilled,* 1991).

Sources:

Daniels, Les. *The Black Castle.* New York: Charles Scribner's Sons, 1978. Reprint. New York: Berkley Books, 1979. 232 pp.

———. *Citizen Vampire.* New York: Charles Scribner's Sons, 1981. 197 pp.

———. *No Blood Spilled.* New York: Tor, 1991. 218 pp.

———. *The Silver Skull.* New York: Charles Scribner's Sons, 1970. Reprint. New York: Ace Books, 1983. 234 pp.

———. *Yellow Fog.* New York: Tor, Donald M. Grant, 1986. Rev. ed.: New York: Tor, 1988. 294 pp.

DHAMPIR

Gypsies believed that some vampires have an insatiable sexual appetites and will return from the grave to have sex with their widow or a young woman of their choosing. The vampire's continued visits could lead to the woman becoming pregnant. The product of such a union, usually a male, was called a *dhampir.* It was believed that the *dhampir* had unusual powers for detecting and **destroying the vampire**—a most important ability. Some modern *dhampirs* among the Gypsies of eastern Europe placed most of their value in their ability to locate the vampire, which was simply shot with a pistol if located outside of its grave. Some individuals believed to be *dhampirs* supplemented their income by hiring themselves out as **vampire hunters.** The *dhampir* was otherwise a normal member of the Gypsy community, though some people believed that a true *dhampir* possessed a slippery, jelly-like body and lived only a short life—a belief derived from the understanding that vampires have no bones.

The powers of the *dhampir* could be passed to a male offspring, and ultimately through a family line. While vampire hunting abilities could be inherited, they could not be learned. Scott Baker wrote a novel about *dhampirs* that tied them to a *dhampir* lineage within the family of **Elizabeth Bathory.**

Sources:

Baker, Scott. *The Dhampir.* New York: Pocket Books, 1982. 260 pp.

Trigg, E. B. *Gypsy Demons & Divinities: The Magical and Supernatural Practices of the Gypsies.* London: Sheldon Press, 1973. 238 pp.

Vukanovic, T. P. "The Vampire." In Jan L. Perkowski, ed. *Vampires of the Slavs.* Cambridge, MA: Slavica Publishers, 1976, 201-34.

DRACULA

Dracula, the title character in **Bram Stoker**'s 1897 novel, set the image of the "vampire" in the popular culture of the twentieth-century. Stoker took the rather vague and contradictory picture of the vampire that had emerged from the nineteenth-century literature and earlier times and developed a fascinating, satisfying, and powerful character whose vampiric life assumed mythic status in popular culture.

THE EMERGENCE OF DRACULA: Dracula appeared in print in the very first chapter of Stoker's novel. The reader, however, did not learn until later in the text that the driver who met **Jonathan Harker** at **Borgo Pass** and took him to **Castle Dracula,** was none other than Dracula himself. Harker's diary did note that the driver possessed great strength, a "grip of steel."

The second chapter opened with Harker entering the castle after his long journey and finally meeting Dracula. He later recorded his impressions in his diary, writing that Dracula was "a tall man, clean shaven save for a long white moustache, and clad in black from head to foot, without a single speck of colour about him anywhere." (It will be noted that this description varies greatly from the common image of Dracula in formal evening dress, an image fostered by **Bela Lugosi** in the American play and the *Dracula* **(1931)** movie.) In excellent English, but with a strange intonation, he spoke one of his most famous lines, "Welcome to my house! Enter freely and of your own will!" After Harker stepped inside, Dracula moved to shake hands. Harker noted that his host had "a strength which made me wince, an effect which was not lessened by the fact that it seemed as cold as ice—more like the hand of a dead than a living man."

Over supper Harker had a chance to study Dracula with some leisure and was able to develop a more complete description:

> His face was a strong—a very strong—aquiline with high bridge of the thin nose and peculiarly arched nostrils; with lofty domed forehead, and hair growing scantily round the temples, but profusely elsewhere. His eyebrows were very massive, almost meeting over the nose, and with bushy hair that seemed to curl in its own profusion. The mouth, so far as I could see it under the heavy moustache, was fixed and rather cruel looking, with peculiarly

sharp white teeth; these protruded over the lips, whose remarkable ruddiness showed astonishing vitality in a man of his years. For the rest, his ears were pale and the tops extremely pointed; the chin was broad and strong, and the cheeks firm through thin. The general effect was one of extraordinary pallor.

Hitherto I had noticed the backs of his hands as they lay on his knees in the firelight, and they had seemed rather white and fine; but seeing them now close to me, I could not but notice that they were rather coarse—broad, with squat fingers. Strange to say, there were hairs at the centre of the palm. The nails were long and fine, and cut to a sharp point. As the Count leaned over me and his hands touched me, I could not repress a shudder. It may have been that his breath was rank, but a horrible feeling of nausea came over me, which, do what I would, I could not conceal. The Count, evidently noticing it, drew back; and with a grim sort of smile, which showed more than he had yet done his protuberant teeth, set himself down again on his own side of the fireplace. We were both silent for a while; and as I looked towards the window I saw the first dim streak of the coming dawn. There seemed a strange stillness over everything. . . .

Harker's first encounter with Dracula included what would become basic elements of the vampire's image. He had unusual **strength.** He had a set of **fangs,** (extended canine teeth). His skin was very pale, and his body was cold to the touch. He had a noticeable case of bad breath. Among the elements that were soon forgotten were the hairy palms of his hands and his sharp **fingernails.** Only in the 1970s did the need for the sharp fingernails return, as movie directors added the scene from the book in which Dracula used his nails to cut his skin so the heroine, **Mina Murray,** could drink his blood.

An encounter between Dracula and Harker the next day began with Harker noticing the lack of **mirrors** in the castle. Again Dracula's long teeth were evident, but more importantly, Harker noted:

. . . I had hung my shaving glass by the window, and was just beginning to shave. . . This time there could be no error, for the man was close to me, and I could see him over my shoulder. But there was no reflection of him in the mirror! . . . but at that instant I saw that the cut had bled a little, and the blood was trickling over my chin. I laid down the razor, turning as I did so half-round to look for some sticking plaster. When the Count saw my face, his eyes blazed with a sort of demonic fury, and he suddenly made a grab at my throat. I drew away, and his hand touched the string of beads which held the crucifix. It made an instant change in him, for the fury passed so quickly that I could hardly believe that it was ever there.

Slowly, Dracula's unusual nature became a matter of grave concern, not just a series of foreign eccentricities. Harker dutifully noted that ". . . I have yet to see the Count eat or drink. . . ." And in light of the bizarre situation in which he had been entrapped, he wondered, ". . . How was it that all the people at Bistritz and on the coach had some terrible fear for me? What meant the giving of the **crucifix,** of the **garlic,** of the wild rose, of the **mountain ash?** Bless that good, good woman who hung the crucifix round my neck. . . .''

The next day Harker began to gain some perspective on Dracula. He asked him about **Transylvania**'s history, and Dracula responded with a spirited discourse. Dracula resided in the mountainous borderland of Transylvania, an area that centuries earlier had been turned over to the **Szekelys,** tribes known for their fierceness and effectiveness in warfare. Their role was to protect Hungarian territory from invasion. Dracula spoke as a *boyar,* a feudal lord and member of Hungarian royalty, "We Szekelys have a right to be proud, for in our veins flows the blood of many brave races who fought as the lion fights, for Lordship."

In chapter three, during his encounter with the three women who lived in the castle, Harker noted other revealing facts about Dracula. While his cheeks were red with rage, his eyes were blue, but as his rage grew, his eyes also became red with the flames of hell behind them.

THE FICTIONAL DRACULA AND THE HISTORICAL DRACULA: In chapter three, Dracula also spoke the line that first suggested a tie between him and **Vlad the Impaler,** the original historical Dracula:

> . . . who was it but one of my own race who as Voivode crossed the Danube and beat the Turk on his own ground! This was a Dracula indeed. Who was it that his own unworthy brother, when he had fallen, sold his people to the Turk and brought the shame of slavery on them! Was it not this Dracula, indeed, who inspired that other of his race who in a later age again and again brought his forces over the great river into Turkeyland; who, when he was beaten back, came again, and again, and again, though he had come alone from the bloody field where his troops had been slaughtered, since he knew that he alone could ultimately triumph. . . .

Later, in chapter 18, **Abraham Van Helsing** would elaborate on Dracula as Vlad the Impaler, though Vlad was never mentioned by name.

Stoker, it seems, constructed his leading character, at least in part, from the historical Dracula. That Dracula was a prince not of Transylvania, but of the neighboring kingdom of Wallachia. Stoker turned the Wallachian prince into a Transylvanian count. The real Dracula's exploits largely occurred south of the Carpathian Mountains, which divided Wallachia and Transylvania, and he only infrequently ventured into Transylvanian lands. The real Dracula was a Romanian, not a Szekely, though given the location chosen by Stoker for Castle Dracula in Szekely, he was correct to think of his main character as a Szekely.

Stoker drew the reader's attention, however, not to Dracula's history, but to the way in which each encounter with Dracula's increasingly weird behavior shattered Harker's conventional understanding of the world. The most mind-boggling event occurred as Harker peered out of the window of his room and observed Dracula outside on the castle wall:

> . . . I saw the whole man slowly emerge from the window and begin to crawl down the castle wall over that dreadful abyss, face down, with his cloak spreading out around him like great wings. . . .

As he focused on the count's strange behavior, he put the fragments of his observations together:

> . . . I have not yet seen the Count in the daylight. Can it be that he sleeps when others wake, that he may be awake whilst they sleep!

Finally, he made a definitive observation that completed the picture of Dracula as a vampire. In chapter four, he discovered Dracula in his daytime **sleep.**

> There, in one of the great boxes, of which there were fifty in all, on a pile of newly dug earth, lay the Count! He was either dead or asleep, but I could not say which—for the eyes were open and stony, but without the glassiness of death—and the cheeks had the warmth of life through all their pallor, and the lips were as red as ever. But there was no sign of movement, no pulse, no breath, no beating of the heart. I bent over him, and tried to find any sign of life, but in vain.

> . . . There lay the Count, but looking as if his youth had been half-renewed, for the white hair and moustache were changed to dark iron-grey; the cheeks were fuller, and the white skin seemed ruby-red underneath; the mouth was redder than ever, for on the lips were gouts of fresh blood, which trickled from the corners of the mouth and ran over the chin and neck. Even the deep, burning eyes seemed set amongst swollen flesh, for the lids and pouches underneath were bloated. It seemed as if the whole awful creature were simply gorged with blood; he lay like a filthy leech, exhausted in his repletion.

DRACULA IN ENGLAND: At the end of the fourth chapter, the storyline of *Dracula* reverted to England, to where the count was en route. Dracula's intention was to move to **London,** and reestablish himself, though to what end was not yet revealed. Leaving Harker to his fate in the castle, and carrying with him 50 boxes of his native soil, Dracula traveled to the Black Sea. There he secretly boarded the *Demeter,* the ship that would take him to his new home. Aboard the *Demeter* he quietly came out of his box each night and fed on the sailors. One by one the men grew weak, and as the journey continued, they died. Finally, off the shore of **Whitby,** a town in northern England, a sudden storm called forth by Dracula blew the ship aground. Dracula transformed himself into a wolf and left the derelict ship.

The storyline then shifted to two women, **Lucy Westenra** and Mina Murray, and the men in their lives. Dracula made only fleeting appearances through the rest of the novel. Instead, he hovered as a vague menace, constantly disturbing the natural course of Lucy and Mina's lives and requiring a cadre of men to search out and destroy him.

Dracula attacked Lucy first. He lured her out of her apartment to a seat on the opposite side of the river, where a **suicide** had been memorialized. He proceeded to bite her on the neck and drink her blood. He next appeared outside her room in the form of another animal, a **bat.** Meanwhile, having retrieved his boxes of earth from the *Demeter,* he had them shipped into London, where the novel's action now moved. Dracula distributed the boxes from his main home at his **Carfax** estate to other locations around the city.

Dracula renewed his attacks upon Lucy, who received a transfusion from her doctor **John Seward** after each attack. The men who assisted her, however, failed to realize that they were merely postponing her ordeal and her ultimate death and transformation into a vampire. Lucy's death and Van Helsing's demonstration of her vampiric powers welded the men into a unit to fight Dracula. Van Helsing was first able to obtain their assistance in killing Lucy with a **stake, garlic,** and **decapitation.** He then trained the men as **vampire hunters.** In this process, in chapter 18, Van Helsing described Dracula and all his powers and weaknesses. A vampire commands the dead and the **animals,** especially the ''meaner things''—rats, bats, owls and foxes. He can disappear at will, reappear in many forms (especially a wolf, a bat, and as a **mist),** and can alter the **weather.** Slightly changing the folk tradition, Van Helsing noted that Dracula preyed not upon the ones *he* loved best, but upon the ones *we* loved best. Dracula cast no shadow, he did not reflect in **mirrors,** he could see in the dark, and he could not enter anywhere without first being invited.

Dracula had grown strong through his long years of existence. However, his strength was strictly limited during the day. For example, while he could move around during the day, he could transform himself only at the moment of sunrise, high noon, and sunset. He could pass over running tide only at high or low tide. Dracula was somewhat venerable. His power was taken away by garlic, various sacred objects (the **crucifix,** the **eucharistic wafer**), and the wild rose. He could be destroyed by attacking him in his **coffin** with a **bullet** fired into the body, a stake through his body (not necessarily the heart), and decapitation. Van Helsing's (i.e., Stoker's) understanding of Dracula was derived primarily from the folklore of vampires in Transylvania/Romania as described by Emily Gerard in her popular travel book, *The Land Beyond the Forest* (1885).

Soon after the session where Van Helsing trained the vampire hunters, Dracula attacked and killed **R. N. Renfield,** the madman who had been trying to become Dracula's faithful servant. Then Dracula renewed his attack on Mina that had begun earlier in the book. The men broke into her bedroom and found her drinking Dracula's blood, presumedly the crucial step in someone's becoming a vampire. Those who were merely drained of blood by a vampire simply died. After driving Dracula away, Van Helsing and the men organized by him counterattacked first by sanitizing Dracula's boxes of native soil. All but one of the 50 were found, and in each a piece of the eucharist was placed. While the men were at work, in the daylight hours, Dracula suddenly appeared in his home in Picadilly but fled after a brief confrontation.

With only one box of the refreshing earth left, Dracula returned to his homeland. While he traveled by boat, Van Helsing, Mina, and the men took the train. The final chase led to Dracula's castle. Arriving first, Van Helsing sanitized the castle, including Dracula's tomb. Soon thereafter Dracula appeared, with the other men in hot pursuit. Just as sunset approached, and Dracula's powers were restored, Jonathan Harker and **Quincey P. Morris** killed him by simultaneously decapitating him (Harker) and plunging a Bowie knife into his heart (Morris). The centuries-old Dracula crumbled to dust.

DRACULA IN FILMS, DRAMA, AND BOOKS: *Dracula* was well received by the reading public and both filmmakers and dramatists soon saw its potential. Not long after the book appeared, Stoker moved to assert his rights to any dramatic productions by staging a single public performance of *Dracula* in London. Then, after Freidrich Wilhelm Murnau filmed *Nosferatu,* a slightly disguised version of *Dracula,* Florence Stoker asserted her ownership of the dramatic and film rights to her late husband's novel. The initial dramatic rights were sold to **Hamilton Deane** in 1924 and the American rights to Horace Liveright three years later. The film rights to *Dracula* were sold in 1930 to **Universal Pictures,** which in the 1950s passed them to **Hammer Films.**

Both the stage and film versions of *Dracula* radically altered the character's image. Deane dropped attributes of Dracula that would prevent his acceptance by middle-class British society. Thus Dracula lost his bad breath, hairy palms, and odd dress. He donned a tuxedo and an opera cape and moved into the Harkers' living room. The Universal movie had an even more influential role in reshaping the image. **Bela Lugosi**'s portrayal in the American stage play was succeeded by others, but in the movie he reached millions who never saw the stage play, and what they saw was his suave, aristocratic European manner and pronounced Hungarian accent. He reinforced that image in subsequent films. For many, the Stoker character and Bela Lugosi's representation of him merged to create the public image of Dracula. In future portrayals of Dracula, as frequently as not, the actor who played Dracula offered his interpretation of the Lugosi/Dracula persona, rather than the character presented in Stoker's novel.

Stoker's novel was reprinted frequently in the following decades. Doubleday brought out the first American edition in 1899. After it entered the public domain, many reprints were published, along with condensed versions and adaptations for **juvenile** audiences. As early as 1972 a version for children, abridged by Nora Kramer, was published by Scholastic Book Services. At the same time, authors initiated efforts to create new interpretations of this highly intriguing literary figure. Prior to 1960, Dracula seems to have appeared in only one novel, in the 1928 *Kasigli Voyvode* ("The Impaling Vampire") by Turkish writer Ali Riga Seifi. He was the subject of several short stories, such as Ralph Milne Fraley's "Another Dracula," which appeared in the September and October 1930 issues of *Weird Tales*. In 1960 two new Dracula novels, Otto Frederick's *Count Dracula's Canadian Affair* and Dean Owen's *The Brides of Dracula,* were the first of more than 100 Dracula novels that would be published over the next three decades. Memorable among these are the several series of Dracula novels by **Robert Lory** (nine action stories), **Fred Saberhagen** (seven novels), and **Peter Tremayne** (three novels).

Following the success of the Hammer *Dracula* movies, the vampire movie in general, and the *Dracula* vampire movie in particular, made a marked comeback. Over 100 movies have featured Dracula, and many others star vampires who are only thinly veiled imitations. The first movies that attempted to bring the *Dracula* novel to the screen are believed to be two silent films made in Russia (1920) and in Hungary (1921), but no copies of either have survived. Following *Nosferatu* and the Bela Lugosi film, other versions included the *Dracula* **(Spanish, 1931),** *Horror of Dracula* (1958), *El Conde Dracula* (1970), *Dracula* **(1979),** and *Bram Stoker's Dracula* (1992). Dracula has become the fictional character most often brought to the screen, with the possible exception of **Sherlock Holmes.**

Dracula made his first television appearance in the 1960s through Bela Lugosi (who made a brief appearance as Dracula on the popular television series *You Asked for It*) and **John Carradine,** who appeared in a NBC production of the play. Other television specials that attempted to dramatize the novel featured **Denholm Elliott** (1971), **Jack Palance** (1973), and **Louis Jourdan** (1977). A comic contemporary Count Dracula (portrayed by Al Lewis) was a regular character in the 1964-66 series *The Munsters.* During the 1990-91 season, a more serious and sinister count appeared briefly in his own *Dracula—The Series.*

As early as 1953, Dracula was featured in **comic books** in *Eerie*'s (Avon Periodicals) adaptation of the novel. He made several appearances before vampires were banished in 1954 under the conditions of the Comics Code. During the period of banishment, Dell brought out one issue of a *Dracula* comic, but he mostly was limited to guest shots in humorous comics such as *The Adventures of Jerry Lewis* (July-August 1964), *The Adventures of Bob Hope* (October-November 1965), and *Herbie* (September 1966). Dracula did appear in several European and South American comic books, but it was not until the 1970s that he made his comeback in one of the most successful comics of the decade, *The Tomb of Dracula.* In this version, Marvel Comics brought Dracula into the contemporary world in conflict with the descendants of his antagonists in the Stoker novel. He soon got a second Marvel series, *Dracula Lives!,* and made numerous appearances in different Marvel comics as a guest villain. Most recently Dracula was the subject of two comic books from Topps. These grew out of the latest attempt to bring Dracula to the screen in **Francis Ford Coppola**'s *Bram Stoker's Dracula.*

Dracula's image (as portrayed by Lugosi) has been a favorite in merchandising, from candy labels to ads selling various products. Each October before Halloween his face graces greeting cards, posters, buttons, party favors, and miscellaneous **paraphernalia.** Many Dracula statues and dolls, in almost every medium, from the artistic to cute, have been produced.

 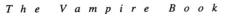

Dracula also has been celebrated in **music.** As early as 1957, "Dinner with Drac" (Cameo, 1957) appeared on a hit record by John Zacherle. A 1950s humor album, *Dracula's Greatest Hits,* had parodies of popular hit tunes that had been transformed into songs about Dracula. Dracula made a number of musical appearances through the 1960s and 1970s, primarily in comic situations, but in 1979 there emerged what would become known as the **gothic** subculture. That musical community was launched by the rock band Bauhaus, whose first hit was an eerie piece titled "Bela Lugosi's Dead." The gothic world found the vampire an apt symbol of the dark world they were creating, and Bela Lugosi's Dracula served as a starting point for their costumes. **Vlad,** leader of the gothic band Dark Theater, is a Lugosi/Dracula fan who not only has adopted aspects of Lugosi's persona into his own, but also has created a shrine to Lugosi in the living room of his home.

The permeation of the culture by Dracula during the last generation led to the formation of clubs and organizations that celebrated and promoted him. These include **The Count Dracula Fan Club, The Count Dracula Society, The Dracula Society,** and **The Bram Stoker Society.** As the centennial of the publication of Bram Stoker's *Dracula* approaches, Dracula has become one of the most recognizable images in all of popular culture. His popularity has provided a base from which other popular vampire figures, such as **Barnabas Collins** and **Lestat de Lioncourt,** could evolve.

Sources:

Dresser, Norine. *American Vampires: Fans, Victims, Practitioners.* New York: W. W. Norton & Company, 1989. 255 pp.

Glut, Donald F. *The Dracula Book.* Metuchen, NJ: Scarecrow Press, 1975. 388 pp.

Skal, David J. *Hollywood Gothic: The Tangled Web of Dracula from Novel to Stage to Screen.* New York: W. W. Norton & Company, 1990. 242 pp.

Stoker, Bram. *Dracula.* Westminster, London: A. Constable & Co., 1897. 390 pp.

DRACULA (1931)

In the wake of the success of the stage production of *Dracula* in New York in 1927, producer Horace Liveright developed touring companies to take the play to various parts of the country. Actor **Bela Lugosi,** who had starred in the New York play, joined the West Coast company and eventually settled in Los Angeles where he could resume his film career. Then in 1930, **Universal Pictures** moved to purchase the film rights for *Dracula* from Florence Stoker. The original asking price, reportedly $200,000, was far too high from the studio's perspective, so Bela Lugosi was cajoled into negotiating Stoker's widow down to a more reasonable amount. Universal eventually got the rights for $40,000 and hired director **Tod Browning** to take charge of the project.

Because of his role in negotiating the rights, Lugosi expected the part of Dracula would automatically be offered to him. It was not. Rather, Universal announced that John Wray, who had just had a major part in *All's Quiet on the Western Front,* would play the role. Universal also considered Conrad Veidt (who declined the honor), Ian Keith, William Courtney, Paul Muni, Chester Morris, and Joseph Schildkraut. Not until a few weeks before shooting began did Lugosi secure the part. Because he wanted it so much, he was paid very little money—$3,500 for seven weeks of filming. Helen Chandler was chosen to play **Mina Murray** (now Mina Seward) and Frances Dale took the part of **Lucy Westenra** (changed to Weston). David Manners assumed the now greatly diminished role of **Jonathan Harker.** The other major part, **R. N. Renfield,** went to Dwight Frye. Edward Van Sloan, who had previously played **Abraham Van Helsing,** moved west for the movie part, and the cast was filled out by Herbert Bunston as Dr. **John Seward.**

The movie was able to do much that the play could not. The film added the opening segment of the novel in which Jonathan Harker traveled to **Transylvania** and had his initial encounter with Dracula and his three **brides.** This chapter included what many consider the most dramatic moments of the book. However, in the movie, Renfield, not Harker, made the trip to **Castle Dracula.** His experiences there accounted for his "insane" behavior following his return to England. An elaborate set was developed for the memorable scenes in the castle but it was poorly utilized. Browning has been justly criticized for the restricted and flat manner in which he shot Dracula's encounter with his English guest, so ripe with possibilities. In spite of Browning's limitations, however, the scenes that began with Lugosi's opening line, "I am . . . Dracula," are among the most memorable, powerful, and influential in horror film. *Dracula* also included a brief scene aboard the *Demeter,* the ship that brought Dracula to England.

From this point, the film rejoined the revised version of the **Hamilton Deane/ John L. Balderston** play. Dracula had moved to London and targeted Mina Seward after previously disposing of Lucy. He abducted her to **Carfax,** now transformed into Carfax Abbey, his London home, but was tracked by Van Helsing, Dr. Seward, and Harker and finally destroyed. As in the play, the closing chapters of the book, describing the return to Transylvania, were deleted. Also, true to the play, at the end Van Helsing stopped the credits and made the famous closing speech on the reality of vampires.

Dracula was set to open on Friday, February 13, 1931, at the Roxy Theater in Manhattan. New York was plastered with blood-red signs. Papers on the West Coast panned the production. The *Los Angeles Times* dubbed it a freak show—a curiosity without the possibility of wide appeal. The New York coverage was mixed. Critics did not like it, but also had to respond to Universal's intense publicity and advertising campaign. The run at the Roxy lasted only eight days. The national release came in March. A silent version was prepared for theaters that had not yet added sound equipment. (Also, to make full use of the expensive set, a Spanish-language version with a completely new cast was filmed simultaneously with the Lugosi English-language version.) The movie opened in Los Angeles with no fanfare because Universal was in the midst of a budget crunch. In spite of its slow start, *Dracula* (the first of what would become a lineage of horror talkies) caught the imagination of the public and became the largest grossing film for Universal that year. For the first time since the Depression had started, the studio, threatened with closing, made a profit.

DRACULA, STARRING BELA LUGOSI, LED TO THE FIRST WAVE OF HORROR FILMS.

Today, two generations after its release, some assessment of Universal's *Dracula* is possible. Certainly, it is the most influential vampire film of all time. All subsequent performances of the vampire have been either based upon it or a direct reaction to it. However, its original success did not lead, at least immediately, to a second vampire movie, but to the production of a very different horror movie, *Frankenstein,* and a string of horror movies covering various themes. Additionally, its continued success through the years did not lead to the production of many more vampire movies, which appeared only sporadically until the 1960s. In the 1960s, however, the vampire genre was discovered as a unique creation, not just another variation on the horror genre.

Beginning with *Horror of Dracula* (1958), **Hammer Films**'s remake of *Dracula* starring **Christopher Lee,** Dracula has appeared in more than 100 films. Characters largely based on him have been featured in several hundred more. The more important remakes of the Dracula story after the first Lee version included *El Conde Dracula* (1970), also with Lee; *Dracula* **(1973)** with **Jack Palance;** *Count Dracula* **(1978)** with **Louis Jourdan;** *Dracula* **(1979)** starring **Frank Langella;** *Nosferatu* **(1984);** and director **Francis Ford Coppola**'s *Bram Stoker's Dracula* (1992). Ranking with each of these was the delightful satire/comedy *Love at First Bite* (1979), starring George Hamilton. Non-English versions of *Dracula* were produced in Turkey (*Drakula Istanbula,* 1953), Korea (*The Bad Flower,* 1961), Spain (*El Conde Dracula,* 1970), and Japan (*Lake of Dracula,* 1970). A version in sign language for the hearing impaired, *Deafula,* was released in 1975.

Sources:

Everson, William K. *Classics of the Horror Film.* New York: Citadel Press, 1974. 274 pp.

Glut, Donald. *The Dracula Book.* Metuchen, NJ: Scarecrow Press, 1975. 388 pp.

MagicImage Filmbooks Presents Dracula (The Original 1931 Shooting Script). Atlantic City, NJ: MagicImage Filmbooks, 1990.

Skal, David J. *Hollywood Gothic: The Tangled Web of Dracula from the Novel to Stage to Screen.* New York: W. W. Norton & Company, 1990. 242 pp.

DRACULA (SPANISH, 1931)

At the same time **Universal Pictures** produced its famous version of *Dracula* starring **Bela Lugosi,** it produced a second version in Spanish. The Spanish version grew out of the studio's decision to respond to the changes brought about by the addition of sound to movies. Universal received a high percentage of its revenue from the foreign distribution of silent films, but talkies in English could threaten revenue because the techniques of dubbing had yet to be perfected. Universal's Czechoslovakian-born executive Paul Kohner suggested a solution to the studio's head, Carl Laemmle, Jr.: shoot foreign language versions of motion pictures simultaneously with the English versions, thus cutting costs by using the sets more than once. Kohner also argued that salaries for foreign actors and actresses were far less than those of Americans. Laemmle appointed Kohner head of foreign productions. The first result was a Spanish version of *The Cat and the Canary.* Released in 1930 as *La Voluntad del*

DRACULA (SPANISH, 1931) WAS THOUGHT BY SOME CRITICS TO BE BETTER THAN THE ENGLISH-LANGUAGE VERSION.

Muerto, it was an overwhelming success in Mexico and made actress Lupita Tovar a star.

Kohner decided to make a Spanish version of *Dracula* and moved quickly to secure the youthful Tovar for the lead before she could return to Mexico. He chose Carlos Villarias (or Villar) for the role of Dracula, and secured a capable supporting cast with Barry Norton (''Juan'' or **Jonathan Harker**), Eduardo Arozamena (**Abraham Van Helsing**), and Pablo Alvarez Rubio (**R. N. Renfield**).

Though it continued to be shown in Latin American countries into the 1950s, the Spanish version of *Dracula* became a largely forgotten entity in the United States. Universal failed to register its copyright of the film and did not make extra copies to preserve it. **Donald F. Glut**'s 1975 work on Dracula mentioned it only in passing. In 1977, the American Film Institute attempted to make an archival print, but the only copy (at the Library of Congress) available had a decomposed third reel. In 1989, author David J. Skal followed up a rumor that a copy had survived in Cuba. He was able to facilitate the preparation of a copy, which was presented in the United States for the first time since the 1930s. The showing took place on Halloween, 1992 at the University of California at Los Angeles.

The Spanish version followed the same script as the Lugosi version. However, as Skal noted, it was very different in that the more mobile camera movement employed by director George Melford and his shooting team gave it a much livelier quality. Both mood and action were enhanced. It stands as ''an almost shot-by-shot scathing critique of the Browning (Lugosi) version,'' said Skal.

The film opened in Mexico City and New York in April 1931 and in Los Angeles in May. It was one of the last Spanish-language films made in Hollywood—such productions being discontinued in the post-Depression business atmosphere. While possibly the superior movie, there is very little chance, given the development of the vampire film, that more than a few film historians and vampire buffs will ever see it. In spite of its being released on video, the film has become a historical curiosity rather than an important and influential film.

Sources:

Skal, David J. *Hollywood Gothic: The Tangled Web of Dracula from the Novel to Stage to Screen.* New York: W. W. Norton & Company, 1990. 242 pp.

Turan, Kenneth. "The Missing 'Dracula'." *Los Angeles Times* (October 31, 1992).

DRACULA (1973)

In 1973 producer-director **Dan Curtis,** who had great success with vampire **Barnabas Collins** in the daytime television series *Dark Shadows,* teamed with screenwriter **Richard Matheson** (best known for his science fiction vampire novel *I Am Legend*) to produce a new version of *Dracula* for television. The pair attempted to bypass both the play by **Hamilton Deane** and **John L. Balderston** (the basis for the version of *Dracula* (1931) with **Bela Lugosi**) as well as *Horror of Dracula* and the other **Hammer Films** productions with **Christopher Lee.** At the same time, they were strongly influenced by the work of **Raymond T. McNally** and **Radu Florescu,** who published *In Search of Dracula: A True History of Dracula and Vampire Legends* (1972). This was first book to highlight the exploits of **Vlad the Impaler,** the historical person who stands, in part, behind the lead character in **Bram Stoker**'s novel.

Curtis's Dracula was preeminently the fifteenth-century Wallachian ruler and military hero, still alive in the nineteenth century. The painting of him, astride his horse, dominated a room of **Castle Dracula** and in several scenes stole the attention of the camera. In the corner of the painting, a young woman was pictured. This woman was Dracula's true love (or true passion) from the fifteenth century, who had not survived with him into the nineteenth century. Very early in the movie, Dracula saw a picture of **Jonathan Harker, Mina Murray, Arthur Holmwood,** and **Lucy Westenra.** Lucy looked nearly identical to the woman in the painting, so Dracula immediately decided that he must possess her. His quest for Lucy dominated the action in the first part of the film, while revenge for her death (the second time his love had been taken from him) occupied the remainder of the show.

Curtis choose veteran character actor **Jack Palance** as Dracula. The story began with Jonathan Harker (Murray Brown) traveling to Transylvania. There he moved through forbidden portions of the castle and discovered Dracula's secret. As Dracula departed for England, Harker was left behind to be bitten by Dracula's **brides.** In England the action centered on the two women, Lucy (Fiona Lewis) and Mina (Penelope Horner), Lucy's fiance Arthur Holmwood (Simon Ward), and most importantly, **Abraham Van Helsing** (Nigel Davenport). The novel's subplot concerning Dr. **John Seward** and the insane **R. N. Renfield** were pushed aside.

Van Helsing came to the fore after Lucy was bitten by Dracula. It was his task (Holmwood being unable to face his duty) to drive the stake into her heart. With his true love dead again, Dracula turned on Mina. Eventually, Van Helsing and Holmwood acted together. They drove Dracula back to Transylvania and followed him to Castle Dracula. One by one they faced and defeated the three vampire brides, Jonathan Harker (who had become a vampire and had to be killed), and finally Dracula himself. Dracula was first weakened by letting in the **sunlight** (as he was killed in *Horror of Dracula*). Then Van Helsing grabbed a pike from a suit of armor and impaled him. Dracula thus suffered the same fate that he was said to have inflicted on so many others.

The Jack Palance/Dan Curtis *Dracula* was viewed by a national television audience and has been cited as a more than competent version of the familiar tale. However, it never gained the following of the Hammer Films and was subsequently eclipsed by the **Frank Langella**/John Badham *Dracula* **(1979)** and *Bram Stoker's Dracula* (1992).

Sources:

Waller, Gregory A. *The Living and the Undead: From Stoker's Dracula to Romero's Dawn of the Dead.* Urbana, IL: University of Illinois Press, 1986. 376 pp.

DRACULA (1979)

In 1979 **Universal Pictures** replayed a scenario that first occurred a half century before when it again filmed a version of the **Hamilton Deane/John L. Balderston** production of *Dracula, the Vampire Play in Three Acts.* In the original case, Universal purchased the film rights to the play following its successful run on Broadway and in touring companies around the country. In 1978 it reacted to the award-winning Broadway revival of the play starring **Frank Langella.** Universal had stayed away from the wave of quickie vampire movies, the production of which reached a new high in the 1970s, and it turned the new Dracula into a lavish production.

FRANK LANGELLA AS DRACULA.

    The film opened with the wreck of *Demeter,* the ship that transported Dracula to the English town of **Whitby.** These scenes, merely alluded to in the play, were filmed on the coast of Cornwall. Safely on land, Dracula then proceeded to invade the household of Dr. **John Seward** (Donald Pleasence), whom Balderston had turned from a young suitor into the middle-aged father of **Lucy Westenra** (now Lucy Seward). When **Mina Murray** (now Mina Van Helsing) died under mysterious circumstances, Seward called Mina's father, Dr. **Abraham Van Helsing** (played by the equally eminent Laurence Olivier), to assist him in handling the problem of Dracula.

The distinctive difference of the Langella version was its underlying understanding of the relation of **sexuality** and horror. Dracula was the object of horror—the undead. Yet as he entered the Seward household, he did not accomplish his goals by brute force. He fell in love first with Mina and then with Lucy. He won them over when his sensuality attracted their attention, and he then completely seduced them. Dracula's triumph occurred when he invaded Lucy's bedroom and shared his blood with her, in as sensual a scene as could be found in any vampire movie. Subsequently Lucy, completely captivated by Dracula's magnetism, rushed off to **Carfax** to join him.

This version of Dracula offered a new twist to Dracula's eventual destruction. He attempted to escape England, accompanied by a very willing Lucy, but Van Helsing and the other men were in pursuit. They finally caught up with Dracula on the ship, where he emerged from his **coffin** to battle the forces of good. In the end he was impaled on a hook and hoisted high into the air to be burned to death in the **sunlight**.

The film got mixed reviews. Some applauded its sensual quality, while others saw it as an empty parody of the vampire movie. Interestingly enough, it appeared during the same year as the best and most successful of the several *Dracula* spoofs, *Love at First Bite*. In spite of its mixed reception, the Langella film took its place as one of the better and more interesting of the *Dracula* remakes.

Sources:

Allen, Thomas. "Yeh, But Did He Die?" *The Long Island Catholic* (July 26, 1979).

Arnold, James W. "'Dracula'—Another Day at the Blood Bank." *The Catholic Herald Citizen* (August 4, 1979).

Ebert, Roger. "Dracula: Revival of the Undead Hero." *Chicago Sun-Times* (July 8, 1979).

Waller, Gregory A. *The Living and the Undead: From Stoker's Dracula to Romero's Dawn of the Dead.* Urbana, IL: University of Illinois Press, 1986. 376 pp.

DRACULA AND COMPANY

Dracula and Company was an international association of people interested in horror, fantasy, and science fiction founded in 1977 by Thomas Schellenberger as the Dracula Society of Maryland. While covering a broad field of interest, the study and celebration of vampires predominated. Schellenberger moved the organization to New Orleans, where he became associated with Sharida Rizzuto. In the early 1980s Rizzuto had headed the **Friends of Dark Shadows** and edited two *Dark Shadows* periodicals. In 1985 she began *The Vampire Journal* as the periodical for Dracula and Company.

Schellenberger worked as a lecturer and frequently appeared on television and at science fiction conventions portraying Dracula and talking about vampires and his own exploration of **Vlad the Impaler** in **Romania** in 1974. In the early 1990s illness forced Rizzuto to discontinue *The Vampire Journal*. In 1992 Schellenberger disbanded Dracula and Company, and started work on a book about his life in vampire fandom. That same year *The Vampire Journal* was superseded by the ***Realm of the Vampire,*** a new journal and fan organization.

In 1993 Schellenberger launched another organization, Thomas Schellenberger's Friends and Associates of Old-Style Horror, a society devoted to horror in the tradition of **Universal Pictures** in the 1930s and 1940s, **Hammer Films** of the 1950s and 1960s, and **gothic** literature. While not exclusively built around vampires, a certain interest is evident.

Sources:

Dresser, Norine. *American Vampires: Fans, Victims, Practitioners.* New York: W. W. Norton & Company, 1989. 255 pp.

DRACULA (DELL COMICS SUPERHERO)

In 1962, Dell Publishing Co. Inc., which did not subscribe to the 1954 Comics Code prohibiting vampires, issued a comic book titled *Dracula* that told the story of a contemporary encounter with a revived Count Dracula at his castle in Transylvania. The title was discontinued after the first issue. Four years later, however, in November 1966, a new *Dracula* comic book appeared. The initial issue continued the numbering of the previous *Dracula* volume but began what amounted to an entirely new storyline. At **Castle Dracula** in **Transylvania,** a present-day Count Dracula was working in a modern laboratory on a serum derived from bats that was to aid in the healing of brain damage. He completed the serum, but some of it accidently dripped into his glass. When he drank from the glass, he was changed into a bat.

In this story, there was no mention of vampires or vampirism. Rather, Count Dracula blamed his problems on vampire **bat**s whose bad image had haunted his family. By removing the superstitions of the bat from his family's name, he had hoped to come out of hiding and lead a productive life. After consuming the serum, Dracula had to alter his plans to aid humanity. As he was contemplating his future, representatives of the new dictatorial government moved in to take over his castle. Dracula then decided to fight the evil he now saw all around him.

He had the ability to change into a bat, and his supersensitive brain could control bats. He began a body-building program and had a new suit made with batlike features. Dracula emerged as a new superhero, which at the time was not yet in vast supply. Count Dracula also moved to the United States and assumed the **name** Al. U. Card. His first task was to defeat a plan to change the world's weather. In the United

States he took over an abandoned radar control site as an underground laboratory and headquarters. He also saved a young woman, B. B. Beebbe, who drank some of the formula and became his partner. She called herself Fleeta (from ''fliedermaus,'' German for ''bat'').

The series survived for four issues in 1966-67 and then was discontinued. In 1972, following the revisions of the Comics Code and the appearance of several successful vampire comic books, *Dracula* was revived for a third time and issues 2-4 were reprinted as issues 6-8. However, the character never caught on and after issue 8 the series was discontinued again.

Sources:

Dracula. No. 1-8. New York: Dell Publishing Co., Inc., 1962, 1966-67, 1972-73.
Rovin, Jeff. *The Encyclopedia of Superheroes.* New York: Facts on File, 1986. 443 pp.

DRACULA (MARVEL COMICS CHARACTER)

Immediately after the **Comics Code** was revised in 1972, (lifting the ban on vampires that had been in effect since 1954), Marvel Comics moved to issue several horror titles that fell within the new guidelines. One of these was a series based on Count Dracula. ***The Tomb of Dracula,*** which devised a completely new set of adventures for the count, became one of the most successful vampire-oriented comic books of the century. The central hero was Frank Drake, a descendant of the count, whose family had abandoned the family estate and anglicized their name. Drake had inherited the family fortune but quickly squandered it. Broke, his only asset was **Castle Dracula.** As the story opened, Drake traveled to **Transylvania** to see the castle with the idea of either selling it or turning it into a tourist attraction. Accompanying him were his girlfriend Jeanie and another friend, Clifton Graves, who had originally suggested the possible value of the castle.

As they explored the castle, Graves discovered the crypt containing the remains of Dracula, complete with the **stake** in his heart. Graves pulled out the stake, thus awakening the count. Dracula confronted Drake and Jeanie but was driven off by her silver compact. While the pair considered the implication of the encounter, Dracula fled to the nearby town to find fresh blood. After the townspeople found the body of Dracula's first victim, they marched on the castle and set fire to it.

Drake, Jeanie, and Graves went back to London, and the count followed. Drake sold the Transylvania property but his more immediate problem was that Jeanie had been bitten by Dracula and was now a vampire. During Drake's next confrontation with the count, Jeanie was killed. Distraught, Drake attempted suicide. He was stopped by Rachel Van Helsing, granddaughter of **Abraham Van Helsing,** who also had dedicated her life as a **vampire hunter.** Taj, a mute Asian Indian, accompanied her. Rachel Van Helsing carried a crossbow whose wooden arrows amounted to wooden stakes. Together, the three set out to kill Dracula.

They were soon joined by two more vampire fighters, Quincy not Quincey as in the novel Harker (the son of **Jonathan Harker** and **Mina Murray** mentioned in the last paragraphs of the novel), and **Blade, the Vampire Slayer,** an African American whose mother had been killed by a vampire. A generation older than either Drake or Van Helsing, Harker used a wheelchair equipped with devices such as a weighted net and a cannon that fired poisoned wooden darts. Blade's major weapon was a set of wooden knives. Later in the series, Hannibal King, a detective who had been turned into a vampire, allied himself with the team. He and Blade had their initial encounter not with Dracula, but with Deacon Frost, another vampire.

The team fought Dracula for a decade, through 70 issues of *The Tomb of Dracula*. Dracula was portrayed very much as he was in popular lore. He was evil, but with some traits of human feeling, pining over love betrayed and the capture of his son by the forces of good. Drake, Van Helsing, Harker, and Blade fought him with wooden stakes (their most consistently effective tool), the cross, silver, fire, and daylight. While there were partial victories on both sides, each defeated character recovered to carry the series to its conclusion. For example, very early in the series Dracula was killed, but he was brought back to life. Later in the series he lost his vampiric powers for a time. As was common in Marvel Comics, Dracula made appearances in other Marvel titles (*Dr. Strange, Frankenstein, Thor*) and several of the Marvel characters (*Silver Surfer, Werewolf by Night*) appeared in *The Tomb of Dracula* to offer their services to defeat him.

The Marvel *Dracula* was strongly affected by the Hammer *Dracula* movies in one respect. Those bitten by Dracula died and immediately became vampires. In the novel, they were merely weakened by their first encounter.

The Tomb of Dracula concluded in issue 70 with what appeared to be Dracula's definitive death. He was killed in a confrontation with Quincy Harker, who impaled him with a silver spoke from his wheelchair. Harker also cut off Dracula's head, stuffed his mouth with **garlic,** and buried both himself and Dracula under stones dislodged from Castle Dracula in an explosion. However, the count was quickly revived in the new series of *The Tomb of Dracula* issued by Marvel in a black and white magazine format (not covered by the revised Comics Code). When his body was discovered and the silver spoke removed, Dracula was freed for further adventures. He starred in the revived series of *The Tomb of Dracula,* which lasted for six issues. Over the next few years he also made guest appearances as the villain in several Marvel Comics. For example, in 1983 he had a confrontation with Dr. Strange, the super-hero with magical powers. Dr. Strange invoked what was termed the Montesi Formula, a magical incantation designed to destroy all the vampires in the world. Dracula disintegrated in the process. Hannibal King, who had never ingested human blood, was turned back into a normal man by the same process.

In 1991, *The Tomb of Dracula* was revived a third time by writer Marv Wolfman and artist Gene Colan, for four issues published by Epic Comics, a Marvel subsidiary.

Sources:

Doctor Strange. No. 62 New York: Marvel Comics, December 1983.

**THE DRACULA
MUSEUM**

Sienkiewicz, Bill. "Dracula." *The Official Handbook of the Marvel Universe* 2, 17 (August 1987): 10-13.
The Tomb of Dracula. Nos. 1-70. New York: Marvel Comics, 1971-79.
The Tomb of Dracula. Nos. 1-6, New York: Marvel Comics, 1979-80.
The Tomb of Dracula. Nos. 1-4. New York: Epic Comics, 1991-92.

THE DRACULA MUSEUM

The Dracula Museum in New York City was established in 1990 by **Jeanne Keyes Youngson,** president of the **The Count Dracula Fan Club** (CDFC). Youngson had founded the CDFC in 1965. Over the next 25 years she collected Dracula and vampire artifacts and memorabilia. The museum's collection documents both the folkloric and literary/cinema vampire and contains a wide variety of **paraphernalia** produced to meet the cravings of modern vampire fandom. Youngson has been especially attentive to gathering material related to **Bram Stoker** and *Dracula*. The museum houses an extensive collection of Bram Stoker first editions and editions of *Dracula* from around the world.

Among the treasures in the museum are **Lord Byron**'s letter denying he wrote **"The Vampyre";** Boris Karloff's birth certificate; a three-page questionnaire **Bela Lugosi** filled out for Cameo Pix; a first edition, signed by Bram Stoker, of *Under the Sunset*; and Florence Stoker's mother-of-pearl opera glasses. Autographed pictures of most of the stage and movie stars associated with the vampire have been added to the collection. There is also an extensive collection of Dracula and vampire statuettes.

Every Christmas, the CDFC holds a open house at the museum for club members, and the celebrated "Dracutree" is on view. For more information on the museum, contact Dr. Youngson, the museum's curator, at the Count Dracula Fan Club, Penthouse N., 29 Washington Sq., New York, NY 10011.

DRACULA: SENZATIONAL—INFRACTIONAL

A popular Romanian weekly periodical, *Dracula: Senzational—Infractional* is a four-color tabloid in the style of America's *National Examiner* or *The Star*. The periodical assumed the popular name of **Vlad the Impaler,** one of **Romania**'s well-known rulers (who interestingly enough was not associated with vampires during his lifetime). In so doing, it drew upon the common usage of the word "dracula," which translates as "dragon" or "devil."

THE DRACULA SOCIETY

The Dracula Society was founded in October 1973 by Bernard Davies and Bruce Wightman as a vampire interest group to help facilitate travel to **Romania.** At the time, standard tours were just beginning to respond to tourists who wished to visit sites associated with **Dracula.** Closer to its home base in **London,** the society sponsors lectures, films, auctions, and parties; its regular meetings are occasions for members to celebrate Dracula and his literary and cinematic cousins. It also arranges visits to nearby locales associated with gothic literature, especially the northern England town of **Whitby,** where, in the novel, Dracula landed. The society focuses on Dracula and **Bram Stoker,** but also reaches out to literary vampires in general, associated monsters such as the werewolf and mummies, and folklore.

The society maintains an archive to preserve materials related to Dracula and the **gothic** theme in literature, the stage, and the cinema. The archives houses the complete papers of **Hamilton Deane,** who brought Dracula to the stage. It also contains the cloak worn by **Christopher Lee** in his screen portrayals of Dracula. Annually, the society makes two awards: The Hamilton Deane Award for the outstanding contribution to the gothic genre in the performing arts and the Children of the Night Award for the most outstanding contribution to the gothic genre in the literary field.

The society adopted the shield of the Volvodes of Wallachia (Dracula's family) as its crest, adding a ribbon with a Latin quote from the third-century Christian theologian Tertullian, ''I believe because it is impossible.'' The society is open to anyone over the age of 18; in 1993 it reported approximately 150 members. It may be contacted through the secretary, The Dracula Society, 36 Ellison House, 100 Wellington St., London SE18 6QF, United Kingdom. (Note: Overseas inquiries will be answered only if accompanied by an International Reply Coupon.) Members receive *Voices from the Vaults,* the society's quarterly newsletter. The current chairman is founder Bernard Davies.

Sources:

Guiley, Rosemary Ellen. *Vampires Among Us.* New York: Pocket Books, 1991. 270 pp.

DRACULA—THE SERIES

Dracula—The Series was a short-lived syndicated television series starring Geordie Johnson in the title role. The series was set in the contemporary world, with Dracula living as a power broker under the **name** Alexander Lucard (Dracul spelled backward). He was opposed by three youths. The series did not gain significant ratings from either the public or vampire fans and was canceled after the 1991-92 season.

Sources:

Weaver, Tom. "Cinema Dracula." In *Dracula: The Complete Vampire.* New York: Starlog Communications, 1992, pp. 4-20.

DRACULA: THE VAMPIRE PLAY IN THREE ACTS

The first vampire story by **John Polidori,** published in 1819, immediately inspired a number of stage adaptations in Paris and London. No such wave of enthusiasm followed *Dracula*'s publication in 1897. However, shortly after his novel was published, author **Bram Stoker** did assemble the members of the Lyceum Theatre company and worked with them for a dramatic presentation of the book. That one-time event was held merely to establish Stoker's ownership of the book's plot and dialogue.

The story of Dracula's initial appearance on stage began in 1899 when **Hamilton Deane,** having quit his job as a London bank clerk, made his stage debut with the Henry Irving Vacation Company. There he met Bram Stoker and read *Dracula*. He saw its dramatic potential at once, and concluded that someone should write a stage play based upon it. But Deane had a career to concentrate on, and over the following years he spent his time becoming first a well-known actor and then the head of his own theater company. In 1918 Deane ended a lengthy stay on the New York stage and returned to England; in his suitcase was a copy of *Dracula*. As he moved through the British theatrical world, he approached numerous authors to write the *Dracula* play. He even went so far as to outline the acts and scenes. Most writers gave up in the face of the numerous characters and complicated subplots. Finally, during a period of sickness in 1923, Deane took the suggestion of one of his actresses and started to write the play himself. He became immersed in the new drama and finished it in four weeks. He obtained permission from Stoker's widow to use the material. The play debuted in Derby in June 1924.

This production became immensely important in the development of the modern image of the vampire. In the original novel, Dracula was dressed completely in black. He was an aristocrat of arrogant manners, and very bad breath. In contrast, Deane gave Dracula a somewhat sanitized presence. Dracula was dressed in formal evening wear, complete with an opera cloak that would further identify him with the bat. A cape had been mentioned by Stoker, most dramatically when it spread out as Dracula was crawling on the outside wall of **Castle Dracula.** While Dracula rarely appeared in London, he entered the play ready to match wits with the other characters, especially **Abraham Van Helsing,** rather than simply hovering as a presence backstage. Deane, in his negotiations with Florence Stoker, seemed to have consciously moved away from the image of the film *Nosferatu, Eine Symphonie des Garuens,* in which Dracula was portrayed as a monster of truly odd appearance, not a character that could interact with polite society.

To reduce the storyline to manageable proportions, Deane cut out the first section of the book, which took place in **Transylvania,** and allowed the play to open in London in the Hempstead home of **Jonathan Harker.** The play then followed the storyline of the book, except that Dracula was killed at **Carfax,** his British home, instead of being tracked to the Continent. For the original performances, the government licensing agent insisted that Dracula's death not be shown; hence the cast gathered around the coffin and blocked the audience's view of the staking.

Deane also wrote what became a noteworthy addenda to the play. After the final act, as members of the audience were preparing to leave, he appeared on stage, still in his Van Helsing persona. He addressed them briefly, apologizing beforehand if the

play were to cause nightmares, but then, tongue-in-cheek, warning that there might
be such things as vampires.

Deane assumed the role of Van Helsing; his future wife, Dora Mary Patrick,
played Mina. Edmund Blake became the first actor to play Dracula. He was soon
followed by Raymond Huntley. The character of Quincey Morris, the Texan who
courted Lucy, became a woman, ostensibly to create an additional part for a female
member of the Deane Theatre Company. Deane's company traveled for three years
around England and Scotland. So popular was the play, that it began to push aside
other plays in the company's repertoire.

In 1927, Deane decided to risk the play in London. It opened on February 14 at
the Little Theatre on the West End. As he had expected, the press reviews were quite
hostile. Almost everything about the play was criticized, and Deane thought that it
would have a very short run. Instead, the public overrode the critics, and *Dracula* sold
out night after night. Over the summer, the production moved to the larger Duke of
York's Theatre. Deane turned an off-the-cuff comment by a newspaperman into one
of the more famous publicity stunts in theatrical history. He had the Queen Alexandra
Hospital send over a nurse who could attend to anyone who fainted from fright during
the course of the play. At the end of one performance, a reported 39 members of the
audience took advantage of her presence.

A problem developed when Deane decided to take his company back on the road.
Wanting to continue the London success, Florence Stoker commissioned a second
Dracula play. A much inferior drama, it had only a brief run, by which time she had
completed an agreement with Deane. About the same time she accepted an offer from
New York producer Horace Liveright to stage a version of Deane's play on
Broadway. Liveright engaged **John L. Balderston** to do a complete rewrite.

The Balderston version was even further removed from the book. **Lucy
Westenra** and **Mina Murray** were collapsed into a single character, Lucy Seward,
who became the daughter of Dr. **John Seward.** Seward, one of Lucy's youthful
suitors in a novel, became a middle-aged father of a grown daughter. Lucy's other
two suitors, **Quincey P. Morris** and **Arthur Holmwood** (Lord Godalming) completely disappeared. The Balderston play opened in the library of Seward's sanatori-
um. Huntley, originally offered the Dracula role, declined. The part was given to a
little-known actor who could not understand English, **Bela Lugosi.** Bernard H. Jukes
came from England to play **R. N. Renfield.**

The Balderston production was tried out in New Haven, Connecticut, and then
opened formally at the Fulton Theater in New York City on October 5, 1927. The play
ran for 241 performances. It reopened in Los Angeles and San Francisco with Lugosi
and Jukes joining the West Coast cast. Touring companies then were established for
the Midwest and the East Coast. The success of the American play led directly to the
purchase of its rights by Universal and its translation to the motion picture screen. The
Balderston version of *Dracula* was published by Samuel French in 1933 and has since
been made available for stage production and screen adaptation.

BELA LUGOSI IN *DRACULA*, 1931.

Meanwhile, Hamilton Deane continued to produce the play in England, the movie version having given it new life. In 1939 he presented it in the Lyceum Theatre in London, the very theater where Bram Stoker had worked when he was writing Dracula. These last performances at the Lyceum were made more memorable one evening when Lugosi attended and came on stage to embrace Deane at the play's conclusion. Following *Dracula*'s run, and a brief run of *Hamlet,* the theater closed forever. Deane continued the play in London for two more years.

Dracula was produced by different companies on a number of occasions through the years, but it experienced a major revival in 1977, opening on Broadway October 20, 50 years after its debut. **Frank Langella** assumed the title role. Equally heralded were the scenery and costumes by Edward Gorey. (Gorey had designed the scenery for the summer theater production of the Nantucket Stage Company in Nantucket Island, Massachusetts.) The new production received two Tony Awards, for best production of a revival and best costume design. It then served as a basis for the 1979 film starring Langella and directed by John Badham.

Sources:

Deane, Hamilton, and John L. Balderston. *Dracula: The Vampire Play in Three Acts*. New York: Samuel French, 1933. 112 pp.

Glut, Donald. *The Dracula Book*. Metuchen, NJ: Scarecrow Press, 1975. 388 pp.

Ludlam, Harry. *A Biography of Dracula: The Life Story of Bram Stoker*. London: Fireside Press/W. Foulsham & Co., 1962. 200 pp.

Skal, David J., ed. *Dracula: The Ultimate, Illustrated Edition of the World-Famous Vampire Play*. New York: St. Martin's press, 1993. 153 pp.

———. *Hollywood Gothic: The Tangled Web of Dracula from the Novel to Stage to Screen*. New York: W. W. Norton & Company, 1990. 242 pp.

DRAMA, VAMPIRE

Soon after the 1819 publication of **John Polidori**'s **"The Vampyre,"** the vampire was brought to the stage in **France.** There Polidori's dark tale caught the interest of a group of French romantics attracted to the story because they thought it had been written by **Lord Byron.** Before the year was out, it had been translated and published in Paris as *Le Vampire, nouvelle traduite de l'anglais de Lord Byron.* However, for many of these early explorers of the subconscious, the vampire became a fitting symbol of the darker, nightmare side of the inner reality they were discovering. An expanded sequel to the story appeared early in 1820 as *Lord Ruthwen ou les vampires,* authored by Cyprien Bérard.

Bérard's colleague **Charles Nodier** was the first to adapt "The Vampyre" for the stage. He merely had to alter the ending of Polidori's story to assure his audience that the forces of good were still in control. In the end, these forces triumphed over the lead antihero, **Lord Ruthven,** who in Nodier's version was killed. His three-act play, *Le Vampire, mélodrame en trois actes,* opened on June 13, 1820, at the Theatre de la Porte-Saint-Martin in Paris. It was an immediate and somewhat unexpected success and inspired several imitations. It was translated into English by **J. R. Planché** and opened in London as *The Vampire; or, The Bride of the Isles.* Later in the decade it would inspire a vampire opera, *Der Vampyr,* by German musician **Heinrich August Marschner.**

Two days after Nodier's play premiered, a second vampire play, a farce also called *Le Vampire,* opened at the Vaudeville in Paris. This comedic version of Polidori's tale was set in Hungary and featured a young suitor mistakenly believed to be a vampire. A short time later, a second comedy, *Les trois Vampires, ou le chair de la lune,* opened at the Varieties. It centered on a young man who imagined that vampires were after him as a result of his reading vampire and ghost stories. In 1820, no less that four vampire plays, all comedies, opened in Paris under the titles *Encore un Vampire; Les Etrennes d'un Vampire; Cadet Buteux, vampire;* and *Le Vampire, mélodrame en trois actes.*

The vampire seemed to have run its course with Parisian audiences after a year or two, but in 1822 a new play, *Polichinel Vampire* premiered at the Circus Maurice. The following year a revival of Nodier's play again attracted a crowd at the Porte-Saint-Martin. Among those who attended was the young **Alexandre Dumas,** who was just beginning his literary career. He later would recall his traumatic evening at Nodier's play, where he was seated next to the author, by composing his own stage version of *Le Vampire.* The 1851 production of that play closed out the Parisian phase of Dumas's life.

Over the next few years, writers periodically would fall back on the vampire theme, which always attracted an audience hungry for the supernatural. In England, for example, records have survived of St. John Dorset's *The Vampire: A Tragedy in Three Acts* (1831); Dion Boucicault's *The Vampire* (1852) (generally revived under the title, *The Phantom*; George Blink's, *The Vampire Bride*; and Robert Reece's *The Vampire* (1872).

THEATRE DU GRAND GUIGNOL: At the end of the nineteenth century a theatrical innovation in Paris had an immense effect upon the image of the vampire. Max Maurey opened the Theatre du Grand Guignol in 1899. The drama offered at the theater followed the old themes of dark romanticism but treated them in a fresh manner. It attracted numerous working-class people who seemed fascinated with the presentation of gruesome situations and ultrarealistic stage effects, however, horrific. The theater developed its own vampire drama called, fittingly, *Le Vampire.*

Grand Guignol, slightly tempered by stricter censorship laws, opened in London in 1908. The English version emphasized the gothic element in its stage productions. Most importantly, Grand Guignol flourished in both England and France, producing original drama as well as utilizing established horror stories such as **Dracula** and **Edgar Allan Poe**'s tales. Through the first half of the twentieth century the theater influenced individual motion pictures; but after World War II it became important in the creation of the Hammer Films horror classics, beginning with *The Curse of Frankenstein* (1958) and the *Horror of Dracula* (1958).

DRACULA DRAMATIZED: The entire thrust of vampire drama had changed in 1897 with the publication of *Dracula* by **Bram Stoker.** During the twentieth century, the overwhelming majority of new vampire plays and dramatic productions would be based on *Dracula,* and the character of Lord Ruthven, who dominated the stage in the nineteenth century, would all but disappear.

The dramatizing of Dracula was initiated immediately after the publication of the book, Stoker himself taking the lead with the intention of protecting his rights to his literary property. Using the cast of the Lyceum Theatre, where he worked, he presented *Dracula; or, The Undead* as a five-act, 47-scene play. Ellen Terry, the cast's star, portrayed **Mina Murray.** Even Stoker described the hastily prepared production, ''Dreadful!'' Its opening night was also its last performance.

The intricacies of the plot served as an obstacle to playwrights who might have wanted to bring the story to the stage. However, in the years after World War I, an old friend of the Stoker family, **Hamilton Deane,** then the head of his own dramatic company, began to think seriously about a *Dracula* play. He asked a number of acquaintances to give it a try, but was always turned down. Finally, in 1923 during a period of illness, he accepted the challenge himself. Four weeks later, he had a finished script. He overcame the book's problem by deleting the opening and closing chapters in **Transylvania** and **Whitby,** setting all the action in three scenes in London, and bringing Dracula on stage in London to interact with the his archenemy **Abraham Van Helsing.**

Deane, not at ease in London, and fearing the ridicule of the London critics, opened the play in rural Derby, England, in June 1924. It was a success, and the public's demands soon made it the company's most frequently performed play. Finally, on February 14, 1927, Deane opened his play in London. The public loved his work, and while most critics panned it, others gave it very high marks. It played at the Little Theatre on the West End and after several months moved to large facilities at the Prince of Wales Theatre. It ran for 391 performances. Deane then took it back to the countryside where it ran successfully through the 1930s. At one point he had three companies touring with the play.

Soon after *Dracula* opened in London, Horace Liveright purchased the American rights for the play from Florence Stoker, Bram Stoker's widow. To assist with the delicate negotiations, Liveright had engaged the services of **John L. Balderston,** an American playwright and journalist then living in London. Balderston continued in Liveright's employ to do extensive rewriting of Deane's play for the American audience. Balderston also streamlined the plot, eliminating several characters and significantly changing the ones who remained. Doctor **John Seward,** the youthful suitor of **Lucy Westenra** in the original story, became the central character in the revised plot as Lucy's father. Mina Murray, the leading woman in the novel, was eliminated and her role collapsed into that of Lucy, who also became the love object of **Jonathan Harker.**

The Balderston version of ***Dracula*** opened on Broadway on October 5, 1927, following a brief tryout at the Shubert Theater in New Haven, Connecticut. **Bela Lugosi** assumed the title role. The play was an immediate success and played for 33 weeks and 241 performances. Liveright had hesitated in developing a touring company to take it around the country but, Deane (who retained a small financial stake in the American enterprise) threatened to write a play based on a vampire other than Dracula and bring it to the United States. Balderston convinced Liveright of the need to send a company on the road. Lugosi joined the West Coast cast that played Los Angeles and San Francisco. The success on the West Coast convinced Liveright to create a second company to tour the East and the Midwest.

The original Deane version of the play significantly affected the image of Dracula and the **appearance of the vampire** in general. Deane domesticated Stoker's *Dracula* by dressing him in formal evening wear and ridding him of his extreme halitosis. The formal opera cloak, the cape with the high collar, would be clearly identified with the vampire character. Balderston's rewrite of Deane's play, however, was the more influential dramatic version of the novel. It introduced Bela Lugosi, later typecast as Dracula, to the part. And it was Balderston's version that served as the basis of the 1931 **Universal Pictures** movie and the 1979 remake with **Frank Langella.** Published by Samuel French, the Balderston play became the version to which producers turned when they decided to revive Dracula on the stage. The most notable revival, of course, was the 1977 stage version starring Langella, which inspired Universal's remake.

DRACULA CLONES, VARIATIONS, AND PARODIES: For a generation after the success of the Balderston play, dramatists did little with the vampire theme, although in England a satire of Deane's play appeared briefly in the 1930s and a musical version surfaced in the 1950s. While a few variations on the Dracula theme were written in the 1960s, generally whenever a vampire play was sought, the Balderston play was revived yet again. The situation did not change until 1970 when suddenly four new vampire plays were published: Bruce Ronald's *Dracula, Baby;* Leon Katz's *Dracula: Sabbat;* Sheldon Allman's *I'm Sorry, the Bridge Is Out, You'll Have to Stay the Night;* and a more obscure *Johnny Appleseed and Dracula.*

Since that time almost 50 vampire plays have been published. They vary from one-act plays for high school productions to more serious dramas designed for the Broadway stage. Only a few, such as *The Passion of Dracula* (1977), *Dracula Tyrannus* (1982), and *Vampire Lesbians of Sodom* (1984), have risen above the crowd to receive some national attention. *The Passion of Dracula* opened for a successful run at the Cherry Lane Theatre in New York City on September 30, 1977, just three weeks before the award-winning revival of the Balderston play with Frank Langella opened at the Martin Beck Theatre on October 20. It was a variant of the Dracula story with Christopher Bernau as Count Dracula and Michael Burg as his archenemy Abraham Van Helsing. On August 23, 1978, it began a successful run in London.

Ron Magid's *Dracula Tyrannus: The Tragical History of Vlad the Impaler* was the first play to use all of the newly available material on the historical Dracula, **Vlad the Impaler,** the fifteenth-century Romanian ruler. It built on the ruler's rivalry for the throne with his cousin Dan. *Vampire Lesbians of Sodom,* whose three acts take the audience on a romp through history from ancient Sodom to Hollywood in the 1920s and modern Las Vegas, is based more upon the **vamp,** the female seductress, than the classical vampire.

Among the lesser-known plays, made available in large part for amateur productions, were several written by Stephen Hotchner and Tim Kelly. In 1975, Hotchner wrote three one-act Dracula plays, *Death at the Crossroads, Escape for Dracula's Castle,* and *The Possession of Lucy Wenstrom.* These were adapted for use at high schools, colleges, and community festivals from a full-length *Dracula* play Hotchner published in 1978 that combined the three one-act plays. During the 1970s Kelly also produced a number of Dracula-based plays, including musical variations such as *Seven Brides for Dracula* (1973) and *Young Dracula; or, the Singing Bat* (1975). Hotchner and Kelly's publisher, Pioneer Drama Service in Denver, Colorado, specialized in plays for amateur productions. The Dramatic Publishing Company of Chicago also published a number of Dracula-based dramas, including the first *I Was a Teen-Age Dracula* by Gene Donovan (1968). These productions characteristically used a lighter treatment of the vampire/Dracula theme and were targeted to younger audiences or people attending less serious entertainment events.

Of the vampire plays written since 1965, the overwhelming majority have been variations on the *Dracula* story, or at the very least have used the word Dracula in the title. **"Carmilla",** comes in a distant second with three plays based on **Sheridan Le Fanu**'s story. During this period the number of vampire plays has steadily increased and, given the heightened interest in vampires at the beginning of the 1990s, there is every reason to believe that new plays will continue to be written.

VAMPIRE THEATER: The **gothic** movement that developed in the United States in the late 1970s has had a noticeable influence upon vampire drama. The movement itself was very dramatic, built as it was around bands who used theatrical effects as an integral part of their performances. Possibly the principal examples were those by choreographed by **Vlad,** the Chicago rock musician who heads the band The Dark Theatre.

More recently, La Commedia del Sangria was created in 1992 by Tony Sokal as a dramatic company that performs "vampire theatre" and includes a strong element of audience interaction. The company's very metaphysical production, examines questions of the vampiric condition (limited immortality) and the existence of God. Some of the actors begin the performance portraying audience members and then enter the stage as an apparent interruption. The production has received a warm response from people in the vampire subculture who regularly attend to cheer on the vampires each time they bite someone.

Sources:

Deane, Hamilton, and John L. Balderston. *Dracula: The Vampire Play in Three Acts.* New York: Samuel French, 1927. 113 pp.

Donovan, Gene. *I Was a Teen-Age Dracula.* Chicago: Dramatic Publishing Company, 1968. 90 pp.

Dracula (The Original 1931 Shooting Script). Atlantic City, NJ: Magic Image Filmbooks, 1990.

Glut, Donald F. *The Dracula Book.* Metuchen, NJ: Scarecrow Press, 1975. 388 pp.

Hotchner, Stephen. *Dracula.* Denver, CO: Pioneer Drama Service, 1978. 55 pp.

Kelly, Tim. *Young Dracula; or, The Singing Bat.* Denver, CO: Pioneer Drama Service, 1975. 61 pp.

Leonard, William Tolbert. *Theatre: Stage to Screen to Television.* Vol. I. Metuchen, NJ: Scarecrow Press, 1981.

McCarty, John. *Splatter Movies: Breaking the Last Taboo.* Albany, NY: FantaCo Enterprises, Inc., 1981. 160 pp.

Skal, David J. *Hollywood Gothic: The Tangled Web of Dracula from Novel to Stage to Screen.* New York: W. W. Norton & Company, 1990. 242 pp.

DREYER, CARL THEODOR (1889-1968)

Carl Theodor Dreyer, thought by many to be Denmark's greatest film director, was born on February 3, 1889, in Copenhagen. He began his working career in 1909 as a journalist, and in 1911 he married Ebba Larsen. On the side he began writing scripts for a motion picture company, Scandinavisk-Russiske Handelshus, and in 1913 Dreyer quit his job to work for Nordisk Films Kompagni. Six year later, he was given the opportunity to direct his first film, *Praesidenten (The President),* for which he also wrote the screenplay. Dreyer made several movies in Denmark and Germany but gained prominence with *Du Skal Aere Din Hustru (The Master of the House)* in 1925. He was invited to France to work and there made his notable *La Passion de Jeanne d'Arc* in 1928. Soon after the appearance of *La Passion de Jeanne d'Arc,* the film industry began its transition to sound and it was not until 1932 that Dreyer directed again. His first sound movie remains the one for which he is best remembered.

In 1932 he directed ***Vampyr*** (released to English-speaking audiences as *The Dream of David Gray*), lauded by some critics as the greatest vampire film of all time. Others have complained of the slow pace of the film suggesting that it failed as entertainment. Loosely inspired by **Sheridan Le Fanu**'s female vampire story **"Carmilla"**, *Vampyr* implied the horror that surrounded the action on the screen and invited viewers to participate with their imagination.

The story concerned an older female vampire who was preying on the daughter of the owner of the local manor. David Gray, a visitor in the town, discerned the true nature of her malevolence and took the lead in destroying her. Two memorable scenes stood out in Dreyer's communication of horror. In one, early in the picture, a policeman was sitting with his shadow cast on the wall behind him. Suddenly, the shadow started to operate separately from the policeman and walked away. Later, Gray dreamed of his own funeral. He could see out of the casket, which had a small window just above his face. As he awoke and gazed through the opening, the vampire's face appeared looking back at him.

Dreyer produced part of the atmosphere of *Vampyr* by shooting much of the film at dawn and at twilight. He also discovered a flour mill where the white dust in the air and the white walls added a eerie quality to the scenes photographed there. Dreyer chose amateur actors whose overall appearances, especially their faces, communicated aspects of personality he wished to explore. He brought out their inherent features by the frequent use of closeup shots and little makeup. He sought to create a feeling of uneasiness in his audience, a feeling that would remain even after the conflict of the story had been resolved.

Following the completion of *Vampyr,* Dreyer left filmmaking and resumed his journalism career. He did not make another film until 1942, when he produced a documentary during World War II. He made a number of films through the 1940s and early 1950s. In 1952 he was given the management of a film theater by the Danish government. His 1955 film, *Ordet,* received the Golden Lion Award. *Vampyr* was his only treatment of the vampire theme. He died in Copenhagen on March 20, 1968. He spent his last years on a project to make a movie about the life of Christ, but the film was never produced.

Sources:

Carney, Raymond. *Speaking the Language of Desire: The Films of Carl Dreyer.* Cambridge: Cambridge University Press, 1989. 363 pp.

Dreyer, Carl Theodor. *Four Screen Plays.* Trans. by Oliver Stallybrass. Bloomington, IN: Indiana University Press, 1970. 312 pp.

Everson, William K. *Classics of the Horror Film.* New York: Citadel Press, 1974. 247 pp.

Thomas, Nicolas. *International Dictionary of Films and Filmmakers. II: Directors.* Chicago: St. James Press, 1991.

DUCKULA, COUNT

Count Duckula was a cartoon character introduced in the United Kingdom in the 1980s. A cross between **Dracula** and Donald Duck, he lived in modern-day **Transylvania** at Castle Duckula with his servants Igor and Nanny. While coming from a long line of vampire ducks, and feared by the local villagers, Count Duckula was a vegetarian who preferred vegetable juice to blood. He wore the requisite evening dress and opera cape, but had no **fangs.** He slept in a magical **coffin** that could transport not only him, but his entire castle, to various parts of the world for his adventures. He had an archenemy in Dr. Von Goosewing, the vampire hunter. The unfortunate count was in love with the doctor's niece, Vanna von Goosewing.

Count Duckula was brought to television as an animated cartoon series in the United Kingdom in 1988, a series later shown in America. Also in 1988, Marvel Comics introduced a *Count Duckula* comic that appeared bi-monthly for 15 issues.

Sources:

Count Duckula. Nos. 1-15. New York: Marvel Comics, 1988-1991.

Drake, Royston. *Duckula: The Vampire Strikes Back.* London: Carnival, 1990. 30 pp.

DUMAS, ALEXANDRE (1802-1870)

Alexandre Dumas (Davy de la Pailleterie), prominent French novelist and playwright best remembered for his novels *The Three Musketeers* and *The Count of Monte Cristo,* was born on July 24, 1802, in Villers-Cotterets, France, the son of Thomas Alexandre Dumas Davy de la Pailleterie, a general in Napoleon's army, and Marie Louise

Elisabeth Labouret. His father's mother was an African slave. Dumas's father died in prison when he was four. Dumas showed few outstanding qualities as he was growing up. He had beautiful handwriting and was a good conversationalist, but proved to be a dullard in arithmetic and only average in his other school work. However, he had a vivid imagination which led him into the theater.

Dumas turned to the theater at the age of 18 after seeing a performance of *Hamlet.* He organized his own drama company for which he wrote material, directed the plays, and often performed. Fired by ambition, he moved to Paris early in 1823, ready to take the city by storm. Interestingly enough, his career was to begin and end with a vampire.

Shortly after Dumas's arrival in Paris, **Charles Nodier**'s play, *Le Vampire,* opened for its second run at the Porte-Sainte-Martin theatre. As Dumas was about to sit down for the performance, someone made a comment about his head of bushy red hair. Insulted, he challenged the man to a duel and left the theater. By the time he got to the street, however, he thought better of his actions and, after purchasing a second ticket, returned to the theater through another door. He was seated in the orchestra section next to a well-dressed gentleman, and they conversed until the play began. While Dumas enjoyed the play, the gentleman next to him obviously did not and let his displeasure show. Following the second act, the man stood up and announced he could stand no more. Then, during the third act, the performance was interrupted by some shrill whistles. The gentleman, whom Dumas later learned was none other than Charles Nodier, was ushered from the theater. The evening was to prove a significant one, and Dumas devoted three chapters of his *Memoirs* to a description of his reactions to the play.

Dumas spent the next years reading, writing poetry, and working hard at his job. In 1827 he finished a play, *Christine,* but he had no connections to present it to a producer. Someone suggested that he try to reach Baron Taylor of the Comédie-Francaise. Taylor was a good friend of Nodier, and even though he had not seen him since the night at *Le Vampire,* Dumas risked a letter. He reminded Nodier of the evening and asked for an introduction. Nodier arranged an appointment, and Dumas was able to sell Taylor on the play. His literary career was launched. Instead of making the revisions requested by Taylor, however, he wrote a second play, *Henri III et Sa Cour,* which opened on February 10, 1829. With a new job as the librarian to the Duc d'Orleans, he was finally able to mingle with the artistic and intellectual community of Paris. He spent his spare time with a variety of mistresses. Dumas was one of the most successful playwrights in Paris for the rest of the decade. His career was interrupted in 1830 by the emergence of Louis Philippe, who did not like Dumas's republican political views. Dumas took the occasion to absent himself from Paris.

Several unsuccessful plays in a row occasioned the writing of the first volume of *The Three Musketeers* in 1844. It was soon followed by *The Count of Monte Cristo,* and a series of very successful adventure novels. The dramatization of *The Three Musketeers* was also well received, and Dumas was again financially successful. He built a large estate, the Chateau de Monte Cristo. In 1847 the Theatre Historique was

ALEXANDRE DUMAS

constructed to show his plays. However, this all came to an end with the revolution of 1848. The theater was closed during the revolution and attendance lagged in the aftermath. His debts mounted. Then on December 2, 1851, Louis Napoleon, the president of France, dismissed the Assembly and launched his coup d'etat. Dumas had been desperately trying to recoup his fortunes, but his new plays all failed.

Finally, in a last attempt, he turned to the vampire theme he had encountered when he arrived in Paris. On December 30, less than a month after the coup, his version of *Le Vampire* opened at the Ambigu-Comique. About the same time he also authored a vampire short story, ''The Pale Lady'' (1848). It was to be his last play for the city he had so loved. Early in 1852 he left for Belgium to get away from his creditors and a government that again did not appreciate his politics. Once in Belgium, he began work on his *Memoirs* and wrote several other books reflecting on his career and travels. He died at the home of his son in Puys, France, on December 5, 1870.

Dumas holds a prominent place in nineteenth-century French literature for his fast-paced action novels and the vivid imagination he brought to his writing. He also is important in the development of the modern vampire myth as the last of a generation of great French writers to explore the theme.

Sources:

Dumas, Alexandre. *The Memoirs, Being Extracts from the First Five Volumes.* London: W. H. Allen & Co., 1891. The condensed English edition of the *Memoirs,* published under the title *The Road to Monte Cristo,* eliminated all references to *The Vampyre.*

Gorman, Herbert. *The Incredible Marquis: Alexandre Dumas.* New York: Farrar & Rinehart, Inc., 1929. 466 pp.

DUST

Similar to his ability to transform himself into **animals** or a **mist,** as described in the 1897 novel, *Dracula* also could transform into a cloud of dust. Dr. **Abraham Van Helsing** made reference to the coming and going of the three women in **Castle Dracula.** While **Jonathan Harker** looked on, they transformed themselves into a dust form while standing in the moonlight. In his second encounter with the women, Harker saw the moonlight quiver as the dust danced around and then slowly took on a recognizable shape, the three phantomlike images.

Dracula made his first and only appearance in this form during his attacks upon **Lucy Westenra.** The wolf Beserker had broken some of the glass from her room's window. Then suddenly, the room seemed to fill with ''a whole myriad of little specks'' blowing in the window and forming themselves into a ''pillar of dust'' inside the room. She passed out and upon regaining consciousness noticed that the air again was full of these dusty specks.

While a notable element in the novel *Dracula,* this vampiric ability has not been of importance to the twentieth-century idea of the vampire.

DYNAMITE FAN CLUB

The Dynamite Fan Club is a vampire horror fan club company founded in 1991 by Mark Weber and Garry Paul, who serve as president and vice-president respectively. The primary activity of the club is the issuance of a quarterly *Horror Newsletter* that includes a number of regular columns (including ''From the Coffin'' by Count Vamp), book and movie reviews, and a section of classified ads placed by club members who want either to sell something or to meet other members who reside in their hometown. The club may be contacted at PO Box 81332, Cleveland, OH 44181-0332.

E

EL CONDE DRACULA

El Conde Dracula (1970) was a Spanish-language movie version of **Bram Stoker**'s *Dracula* made by popular director Jesus Franco. Franco built on the popularity of **Hammer Films'** horror movies and lured Hammer star **Christopher Lee** to play the title role. Lee saw it as an opportunity to play the character as it was described in the original novel (rather than the Hamilton Deane/John Balderston stage version), the only exceptions being that there were no hairy palms or elongated ears and fingers. With all of its shortcomings, Lee felt it to be the most faithful to Stoker of any films to that time. Franco opened with **Jonathan Harker**'s (not **R. N. Renfield**'s) trip to **Transylvania.** He returned to the film the final race to Transylvania with its fatal confrontation with Dracula in his castle. While making a noticeable attempt to add previously missing elements from the novel, in many significant ways *El Conde Dracula* deviated significantly in much the same manner as previous *Dracula* movies.

Following Jonathan's initial encounter with Dracula, he returned to England and was treated in **Abraham Van Helsing**'s private clinic, where Dr. John Seward worked as a mere employee. Dracula appeared and attacked **Lucy Westenra** to the alarm of her fiancé **Quincey P. Morris,** here an English nobleman rather than a Texan. Lucy's fiancé from the novel, **Arthur Holmwood,** did not appear. Unable to save Lucy, Van Helsing and Morris ended her vampiric life with a **stake** and **decapitation.** The men invaded Dracula's estate where they encountered a set of stuffed animals that came alive, presumedly at Dracula's command, and eventually drove Dracula away with a crucifix.

Before returning to Transylvania, Dracula attacked Mina on two occasions. The second time, in the clinic, Van Helsing drove him off by burning a cross in the floor with a poker from the room's fireplace. Before he died, the madman Renfield gave them the clue where to find the fleeing Dracula, and Harker and Morris set out to look for him. They entered **Castle Dracula** and killed the three female residents and then drove off the **Gypsies** protecting the body of Dracula asleep in his crate of earth. They killed him by setting him afire and tossing him onto the rocks below the castle.

Waller noted that Franco saw *El Conde Dracula* as a confrontation between youth and age. Lucy, Mina, Jonathan, and Quincey were of one generation and Van Helsing and Dracula of another. Van Helsing, the major voice of maturity, informed the young men of Dracula's true nature, but was pushed aside because of his own knowledge in the black arts. In the end, Van Helsing was left behind as the strong and youthful men journeyed to Transylvania to destroy Dracula. Franco's *El Conde Dracula* was released in English versions as *Count Dracula* and as *Bram Stoker's Count Dracula.*

Sources:

Waller, Gregory A. *The Living and the Undead: From Stoker's Dracula to Romero's Dawn of the Dead.* Urbana, IL: University of Illinois Press, 1986. 376 pp.

ELLIOTT, DENHOLM MITCHELL (1922-)

Denholm Mitchell Elliott, one of England's most famous actors, was born May 31, 1922, in London, the son of Nina Mitchell and Niles Layman Elliott. Just prior to World War II he attended the Royal Academy of Dramatic Arts but did not make his formal stage debut until 1945 in *The Drunkard.* He made his first movie, *Dear Mr. Prohack,* in 1948. In 1951 he appeared on the New York stage for the first time and made his first Hollywood movie, *Breaking the Sound Barrier.*

In 1969 Elliott starred in the title role in the British television version of *Dracula.* He has been remembered, at least in England, as one of the more memorable persons to portray the count. The production was one of the most faithful adaptations of the novel, and was noted particularly for the final scene in which Dracula disintegrated. Elliott wore a beard for the part.

Since his appearance in *Dracula,* Elliott has appeared in numerous movies, though none of the vampire genre. He continues to move back and forth across the Atlantic to star in both American and British productions.

Sources:

Glut, Donald F. *The Dracula Book.* Metuchen, NJ: Scarecrow Press, 1975. 388 pp.

ELROD, P. N.

Patricia Nead Elrod, popular author of vampire novels, began writing at the age of 12. She developed an interest in vampires at a young age while watching vampire movies and especially the *Dark Shadows* television series. During the 1980s she and her husband Mark became active participants in role playing games, particularly one

► P. N. ELROD, POPULAR WRITER
OF VAMPIRE NOVELS.

called *Mercenaries, Spies, & Private Eyes.* In 1986 she entered a role-playing module into a *Dragon* magazine contest that eventually was bought and published in the first issue of *Dungeon Adventures.* This was her first professional publication. Meanwhile, through her role playing, she developed a supernatural character, a vampire detective. At one point she began to write up the game scenario she and her husband had developed, and it became the first of "The Vampire Files" novels, *Bloodlist.* She quickly followed with *Lifeblood* and *Bloodcircle.* All three novels were published in 1990. Their success prompted the continuation of the series and three more volumes appeared: *Art in the Blood* (1991), *Fire in the Blood* (1991), and *Blood on the Water* (1992). This series features Jack Fleming, a reporter who had been transformed into a vampire. After his transformation he became a detective with a nonvampire partner, Charles Escott.

By this time Elrod built her writings around what she thought of as interesting characters, some of whom just happened to be vampires who have to work out their relationship with the "normal" world. One such interesting character, Jonathan Barrett, who had appeared in the first series, became the central figure for a second series. The first volume, *Red Death,* appeared in 1993. Meanwhile, she was asked by

TRS, Inc., the publishers of the *Ravenloft* role-playing series, to write the autobiography of their main character, the vampire Strahd. *I, Strahd* also appeared in 1993.

By this time Elrod had become one of the most recognizable names among vampire fiction writers, and a **P. N. Elrod Fan Club** emerged in 1993. Several novels, both vampiric and otherwise, have been planned for the near future, including the next Barrett volumes *Death and the Maiden* (1994) and *Death Masque* (1995). Elrod's vampire short stories have appeared in one collection by Martin H. Greenberg, *Dracula: Prince of Darkness,* and in a fanzine, **Good Guys Wear Fangs.** New short stories are also planned for 1994.

Sources:

Elrod, P. N. *Art in the Blood.* New York: Ace Books,1991. 195 pp.

———. *Blood on the Water.* New York: Ace Books, 1992. 199pp.

———. *Bloodcircle.* New York: Ace Books, 1990. 202 pp.

———. *Bloodlist.* New York: Ace Books, 1990. 200 pp.

———. *Fire in the Blood.* New York: Ace Books, 1991. 198pp.

———. *I Strahd: Memoirs of a Vampires.* Lake Geneva, WI:TSR, Inc., 1993. 309 pp.

———. *Lifeblood.* New York: Ace Books, 1990. 202 pp.

———. "Partners in Time." *Good Guys Wear Fangs* 1 (May1992): 1-23.

———. *Red Death.* New York: Ace Books, 1993. 288 pp.

———. "The Wind Breathes Cold." In Martin H. Greenberg, ed. *Dracula Prince of Darkness.* New York: Daw Books, 1992: 216-31.

"An Interview with P. N. Elrod." *The Vampire Information Exchange Newsletter* 65 (December 1993): 14.

ELVIRA

Elvira is the vampirelike persona of actress Cassandra Peterson. Elvira was created in 1981 after Peterson landed a job with KHJ-TV in Los Angeles as hostess for the station's horror movie program, *Movie Macabre.* On May 23, 1982, she hosted a screening of *The Mad Magician,* a 3-D film. In connection with the show, more than 2.7 million pairs of 3-D glasses were distributed, and Elvira became the first person to appear on television in 3-D. Shortly thereafter, her new celebrity status was confirmed when she made an appearance on *The Tonight Show,* and Rhino Records released *3-D TV.* The *Movie Macabre* went into syndication.

Peterson grew up in Colorado Springs, Colorado, and began her career in show business as a showgirl in Las Vegas. She tried to break into films and television, and did obtained a number of bit parts in various movies and TV shows. She tried out for the part of Ginger for *Rescue from Gilligan's Island* (1978), a movie revival of the old television series, but lost out to Judith Baldwin. She had almost decided to quit show business when the offer came to host *Movie Macabre.*

The character Elvira evolved over several months. It was created from a host of sources, but obviously drew on popular public images of female vampires such as Morticia Addams (of **The Addams Family**), **Vampirella,** and former television hostess and movie actress Vampira (Maila Nurmi). At one point Vampira accused Elvira of stealing her persona and filed suit, but the case was dismissed in court.

ACTRESS CASSANDRA PETERSON AS HER ALTER-EGO, ELVIRA, MISTRESS OF THE DARK.

The sudden fame in 1982 allowed Elvira to make cameo appearances on several national television shows, and she put together a Halloween-oriented show at the

Knott's Berry Farm amusement park (now an annual event). Her television show was nominated for an Emmy award as the best local television show. Since that time Elvira has expanded the range of her appearances. In 1985 she began to appear on *Thriller Theatre,* a series of re-releases on video of old B-movies by LIVE Entertainment. Also in 1985, she received the annual Count Dracula Society Award from the Academy of Science Fiction, Fantasy and Horror Films. In 1986, Marvel Comics began to publish *Elvira's House of Mystery*, which ran for 11 issues. The Elvira Halloween costume became the best selling costume of the 1986 season. In 1987, she made her first appearances in commercials for Coors Beer, becoming the first female celebrity hired to endorse a beer product. To keep up with this variety of activities, Peterson founded Queen B Productions.

While no one noticed that Cassandra Peterson (without the Elvira persona) had appeared in a number of films, in 1988 Queen B Productions began work on *Elvira, Mistress of the Dark*, a full-length feature film starring Elvira. The production did not do well as a movie (the distributor, New World Pictures, went out of business soon after its release), but it was shown on prime-time television and did quite well as a video. A single comic book issue was developed from the movie by Marvel Comics.

The production of *Elvira, Mistress of the Dark,* required a sharpening of the image and the development of a story for the character. The movie attempted to explain her appearance by describing Elvira as descending from a line of sorcerers. Her mother had tried to break out of that lineage by marrying a mortal, and Elvira was the product of that union. Eventually, her mother was killed by her brother Vincent, and Elvira was raised in an orphanage.

Elvira's following has been organized into the Elvira Fan Club (14755 Ventura Blvd., 1-710, Sherman Oaks, CA 91403), which publishes its own newsletter, *The Elvira Examiner*. Members receive a bumper sticker, poster, decal, and button. The club also offers members a variety of products and **paraphernalia** with Elvira's image, from an annual calendar to T-shirts and pin-up posters. Elvira's image is marketed through Queen B Productions. Through it, a line of Elvira cosmetics has been developed. There are four Elvira **games:** a pinball arcade game, a hand-held computer game, and two computer role-playing games—*Elvira: Mistress of the Dark* (1990) and *Elvira II: The Jaws of Cerberus* (1991). In 1993, a new **comic book** series, *Elvira, Mistress of the Dark,* was launched by Claypool Comics.

Peterson has been an activist for animal rights. In 1990 she released a perfume line that was the first to carry the cruelty-free symbol of People for the Ethical Treatment of Animals (PETA); for this she won PETA's Humanitarian Award. She has also appeared in ads decrying the wearing of furs.

Sources:

Counts, Kyle. "Elvira, Mistress of the Dark." *Cinefantastique* 19, 1/2 (January 1989): 104-07.
Cziraky, Dan. "Elvira." *Femme Fatale* 1, 3 (Winter1992/93): 6-11, 60.
———. "Mistress of the Dark." *Femme Fatale* 1, 2 (Fall1992): 34-37. *Elvira, Mistress of the Dark.* Vol. 1- . Leonia, NJ: Claypool Comics, 1993- . "Shop of Horrors." *The Elvira Examiner* 11 (1993): 2.

EMPUSAI See: GREECE, VAMPIRES IN

ERETIK See: RUSSIA, VAMPIRES IN

ESTONIA, VAMPIRES IN *See:* BALTIC STATES, VAMPIRES IN THE

EUCHARISTIC WAFER

The holiest ritual of **Christianity** is that of Holy Communion or the Eucharist. Especially among the older liturgical churches—the Roman Catholic Church, the Eastern Orthodox Church, and the Church of England (and those Anglican churches in fellowship with it)—is the belief that under the elements of bread and wine, the body and blood of Christ is somehow mystically present. They are treated as holy objects that embody the sacred. Among most Protestants and Free Church members, the sacramental elements are also considered symbols of the body and blood of Christ. They are handled with respect but are not in themselves holy.

The treatment of the eucharistic elements as holy objects—for Roman Catholics the transubstantiated body and blood of Christ—made them open to various superstitious and magical considerations. At the end of the mass, the worship service in which the bread (usually in the form of small wafers) and wine were consecrated, all the wine was consumed. However, some wafers usually were left on the altar, as was a lighted candle to signal their presence. Such wafers had various uses, and in his famous treatise on vampires, **Dom Augustin Calmet,** a Roman Catholic scholar/ priest, related a number of old stories of their involvement in destroying vampires.

Pope St. Gregory the Great (A.D. 590-604) told the story of two nuns who died in a state of excommunication. At a later date, they were seen at the local church. They departed when the deacon called for any excommunicants to leave. St. Benedict sent some consecrated bread to their former nurse in order that it might be offered for their reconciliation. From that time on the nuns remained quietly in their graves. Gregory also related the story of a Benedictine priest who died after leaving his monastery without permission. He was buried in consecrated land, but the next day his body was found above ground. A consecrated wafer was placed on his breast and his body reinterred. It was also related that St. Basil was buried with a piece of the eucharistic wafer he had saved to be interred with him. He died with it in his mouth.

Calmet's stories most likely stand behind **Bram Stoker**'s use of the eucharistic wafer in his novel as an effective weapon against vampires. Vampire expert **Abraham Van Helsing** brought the eucharistic wafer—the Host—with him from his Roman Catholic parish in Amsterdam. As he was trying to demonstrate that **Lucy Westenra** had in fact become a vampire, he used a crumpled wafer mixed with putty to seal the door to her tomb, first to block her entrance and then to keep her inside until the men could arrive and finally kill her.

To defeat **Dracula,** Van Helsing armed each man in his cadre with a wafer that he had placed in an envelope. The men set about their work of sanitizing the boxes of **native soil** that he had brought with him from Transylvania. In each box as it was treated, they placed a portion of a wafer. Meanwhile, **Mina Murray** (now Mrs. Harker) had encountered Dracula and had been forced to drink of his blood. She considered herself unclean. Van Helsing tried to comfort her, but to little avail. As the men left to do their work, he took a wafer and placed it on Mina's forehead as a talismanic protection. Mina screamed as the wafer branded an image of itself on her skin, leaving a red mark that remained until Dracula was killed at the end of the novel.

In subsequent dramatizations of *Dracula* and other vampire films, the vampire's resting place would on occasion be sanitized with the Eucharist (or in its absence with a **crucifix** or **garlic**). Otherwise, the Eucharist has been used only rarely, while the crucifix has become a standard item in the vampire hunter's kit. The crucifix also absorbed the eucharistic wafer's power to brand the flesh of a vampire or someone bitten by a vampire. Only in the 1992 movie *Bram Stoker's Dracula* was the scene of Mina's being burned by a wafer dramatized.

Like the crucifix, the role of the eucharistic wafer in vampire lore has been called into question by more secular writers. The vampires of, for example, **Anne Rice** are not affected by sacred objects. Such is also the case with vampires from outer space and those created by some disease. The modern vampire hero, which has grown out of the writings of **Chelsea Quinn Yarbro,** and of which the leading characters in the novels of **Elaine Bergstrom** are an example, also are not affected by sacred objects. This abandonment of both the crucifix and the eucharistic wafer can be attributed largely to the loss of belief in **Satan** as a force opposing God (or of vampires being evil or satanic), and to the relativising of Christianity, which is seen as but one religion among many.

Sources:

Calmet, Dom Augustin. *The Phantom World.* 2 vols. London: Richard Bentley, 1850.

EXPLANATIONS OF VAMPIRISM

As reports of vampirism filtered into western and central Europe from the east, along with accounts of otherwise credible western witnesses offering support to the vampire hypothesis, scholars and church leaders attempted to find some explanation. Some simply dismissed the reports as stories of primitive superstitions. Many, however, otherwise unable to fit vampires into their eighteenth-century world view, took the reports seriously. They began to propound various alternative explanations to account for what people had observed, especially the phenomena reported in the case of **Arnold Paul.**

Actual reports of vampirism, rather than the general folklore concerning vampires, usually began with people dying from a lingering disease. After some of these people died, neighbors dug up the corpses and observed a variety of unusual conditions, all signs of continuing life. The bodies had not decayed. The skin had a ruddy complexion and the hair and **fingernails** had continued to grow. Fresh flesh had appeared as the outer layer of skin had peeled off. Blood was present around the mouth and in the body when it was cut or punctured. There might be a sexual erection on the bodies of males. If staked, the body reacted as if in pain. Occasionally, when a **stake** was thrust into the body, the corpse was heard to cry out. In northern Europe, reports of chewed-off appendages suggested to observers that vampires fed on themselves before leaving the grave to feed on others.

By far the most popular explanation of vampire reports was premature burial. Many people in the eighteenth and nineteenth century knew of catalepsy, a disease in which the person affected took on many of the symptoms of death; on occasion, such people were removed by the undertaker and even buried before they reawakened. Herbert Mayo presented an extensive argument for this thesis in his volume, *On the Truths Contained in Popular Superstitions* (1851). In 1896 Theosophist **Franz Hartmann** wrote a book based on widespread accounts of accidental interments. Premature burial remained a popular explanation of vampirism into the twentieth century and **Montague Summers,** in his famous treatise on vampirism, felt the need to devote a number of pages to a discussion of it before making his own case for the reality of the vampire in *The Vampire: His Kith and Kin* (1928). He admitted that cases of premature burial ''may have helped to reinforce the tradition of the vampire and the phenomenon of vampirism.'' As recently as 1972, Anthony Masters also argued for the plausibility of premature burials to account for vampire beliefs.

Others suggested that anomalous incidents of preservation of the body from its normal rate of decay accounted for the state of the exhumed bodies. Perhaps something in the soil or an unusual lack of air or moisture slowed the decay. Possibly the shriek heard when the corpse was staked was the escape of trapped air. Similarly, others suggested that what was being observed was simply the natural decay of the body. Most people were unaware of continued changes in the body after death, such as the loss of rigidity.

As debate over the reasons for the vampire epidemics continued, other explanations were offered. For example, one set of literature suggested that some form of disease accounted for the vampire symptoms. High on the list was the plague—sometimes known as black death. An epidemic of the plague occurred simultaneously with the vampire outbreak in East Prussia in 1710. The spread of plague germs could account for the spread of vampire symptoms. During the twentieth century, rabies was offered as a specific explanation of vampirism. People with rabies would bite others and manifest animal-like behavior, and had an unquenchable thirst. There also were outbreaks of rabies in **Hungary,** Saxony, and East Prussia during the eighteenth century. In nineteenth-century New England, families suffering from tuberculosis used vampirism as an explanation after experiencing multiple deaths, and treated the bodies of the deceased accordingly. Most recently, in the 1960s, the disease **porphyria** has been suggested as an explanation of vampire reports. One characteristic of porphyria is an extreme sensitivity to light.

Social explanations were also offered for the spread of vampirism. For example, some noticed that vampire reports came from areas in which the Roman Catholic Church and the Eastern Orthodox churches were in contention for the faith of the people. Others saw the reports as a reaction to national defeat, especially in those areas taken over by Austria in the seventeenth and eighteenth centuries. Pope Benedict XIV, who ruled in the mid-eighteenth century, believed that his own priests were the problem. They supported and spread the accounts of vampirism in order to get superstitious people to pay them to do exorcisms and additional masses.

The most satisfying explanation of the vampire reports to date has come from cultural historian Paul Barber, who in the 1980s conducted a thorough survey of the original reports. Barber also had the benefit of modern medical knowledge concerning the process of decay of human bodies. He analyzed the arguments against the previously cited explanations; none really explained the broad range of phenomena reported in the vampire stories. Vampires were reported whether the factors cited were present or not. Barber has built a comprehensive case that the various accounts of vampires fairly accurately report what actually was observed. The eighteenth-century observers saw bodies in different states of decay from a perspective of limited understanding of the normal processes of decomposition. They tended to offer both natural and supernatural explanations of the unexpected things that they saw.

With an argument that, in the end, amounts to a contemporary form of the earlier cases was able to account for the overwhelming majority of the reported attributes of the bodies observed by the eighteenth-century **vampire hunters.** Most of these bodies had been buried within a few months of their exhumation, including bodies of people who had died during winter and were being kept in cold storage (which significantly inhibited decomposition) for burial after the spring thaw. He also accounted for the appendages seen sticking out of graves (usually of bodies buried without coffins) and appendages that appeared to have been eaten by the corpse, both of which probably derive from the activity of various animal predators.

CONCLUSION: A consideration of the strengths and limitations of many explanations of vampires suggests that the belief in vampirism is a very old and possibly cultural response to an event that happens in all cultures—the untimely death of a loved one as a result of childbirth, accident, or suicide, followed by an intense experience of interacting with the recently dead person. Given that belief, there are a variety of events, such as the irregular rate of decay of the soft flesh of corpses, that could be cited as visible ''proof'' that vampires exist or as factors that on occasion correlate to their presence. Since ''unnatural'' deaths still occur, and people still have intense experiences with the dead (now usually thought of as encounters with ghosts or apparitions), those people who also believe in vampires can point to those experiences as in some manner substantiating their belief. Thus, these experiences indicate the presence of vampires . . . we know vampires exist because of these experiences.

Sources:

Barber, Paul. *Vampires, Burial, and Death: Folklore and Reality.* New Haven, CT: Yale University Press, 1988. 236 pp.

Frayling, Christopher. *Vampyres: Lord Byron to Count Dracula.* London: Faber and Faber, 1991. 429 pp.

Masters, Anthony. *The Natural History of the Vampire.* New York: G. P. Putnam's Sons, 1972. Reprint. Berkley Publishing Corporation, 1976. 280 pp.

Summers, Montague. *The Vampire: His Kith and Kin.* London: Routledge, Kegan Paul, Trench, Trubner, & Co., 1928. 356 pp. Reprint. New Hyde Park, NY: University Books, 1960. 356 pp.

————. *The Vampire in Europe.* London: Routledge, Kegan Paul, Trench, Trubner, & Co., 1929. 329 pp. Reprint. New Hyde Park, NY: University Books, 1961. 329 pp.

FANGS

Early in **Bram Stoker**'s novel, at the time of his first encounter with **Dracula**, **Jonathan Harker** sketched his impressions. Besides Dracula's other prominent physical features, he noted that the vampire's mouth '' . . . was fixed and rather cruel-looking, with peculiarly sharp white teeth; these protruded over the lips . . . '' (Chapter 2) Later in that same chapter he reinforced his initial description by referring to Dracula's ''protuberant teeth'' and as they conversed he could not take his eyes from the smiling count for, '' . . . as his lips ran back over his gums, the long, sharp, canine teeth showed out strangely.'' Thus Stoker wedded what has become one of the most identifiable features of the modern vampire to its most popular representative figure.

Like Dracula, the three women in the castle, more recently referred to as the **vampire brides,** also possessed the extended canines. As one of the women approached him, Harker noted not only her bad breath but felt the hard dents of the sharp teeth on his skin. He could see the moonlight illuminate the teeth of the other two women. Stoker reinforced the importance of the teeth in identifying the vampire during Dracula's attacks on **Lucy Westenra.** As her strange illness progressed, the knowledgeable Dr. **Abraham Van Helsing** called attention to ''the little punctures on her throat and the ragged exhausted appearance of their edges.'' (Chapter 10). As the end approached, he noted the transformation overtaking her signaled by her teeth—her canine teeth looked longer and sharper than the rest. After her death they had grown even longer and sharper.

Dracula was not the first vampire to have fangs. In describing the first attack on Flora Bannerworth by **Varney the Vampyre,** author **James Malcolm Rymer** (writing in the 1840s, a full half century before Dracula) noted, ''With a plunge he seizes her neck in his fang-like teeth—a gush of blood, and a hideous sucking noise follows.'' In examining Flora later, her mother brought a light close by so that '' . . . all saw on the side of Flora's neck a small puncture wound; or, rather two, for there was one a little distance from the other.''

Laura, the victim of **"Carmilla,"** in **Sheridan Le Fanu**'s 1872 tale, had a somewhat different experience. She remembered being attacked as a child and feeling two needles plunging into her chest, but upon examination, there were no visible wounds. Later in the story, Carmilla and Laura were speaking to a wandering peddler who noted that Carmilla had the ''sharpest tooth—long thin, pointed, like an owl, like a needle.'' He offered to cut it off and file it to a dull point so that it would no longer be ''the tooth of a fish.'' Later in a dream, Laura again had the experience of two needles piercing the skin of her neck. The doctor found a little blue spot at that place on her neck. The daughter of General Spielsdorf reported an experience similar to Laura's— a pair of needles piercing her throat. It was finally concluded that both had been attacked by a vampire, who would have—as was well known—two long thin and sharp teeth that would leave a distinguishing puncture wound on its victim.

While both Varney and Dracula possessed extended canine teeth, as **Martin V. Riccardo** has noted, this trait was not yet a permanent feature. When *Dracula* was brought to the screen in *Nosferatu, Eine Symphonie des Garuens,* **Graf Orlock,** the Dracula figure, had two teeth protruding from the front of his mouth, rather than the canines mentioned by Stoker. Then when **Bela Lugosi** turned Dracula into a household word through his performance in the 1931 film, he did so without any fangs. Nor did he ever have protruding teeth in any of his subsequent performances. Dracula was also portrayed by Lon Chaney, Jr. (*Son of Dracula*, 1943) and **John Carradine** (*House of Frankenstein*, 1944, and *House of Dracula*, 1945) but neither actor sported fangs.

Only in 1958, in the **Hammer Films** color bloodfest *The Horror of Dracula,* did **Christopher Lee** turn to the camera and show audiences his extended canines. He would repeat this act in subsequent films, and after him many others would do likewise. (The fangs had appeared twice before Lee, in the 1952 Turkish version of *Dracula,* which did not receive broad distribution, and a 1957 **Roger Corman** film *Blood of Dracula* with a female wolflike vampire). Thus, while Lugosi (following **Hamilton Deane**'s lead) established the image of the vampire dressed in an evening suit and cape, it was Lee who fixed the image of the fanged vampire in popular culture. Since Lee's portrayal, most (though by no means all) cinematic vampires have shown the required teeth, as did **Barnabas Collins** in the *Dark Shadows* television series late in the 1960s.

Once established, fangs became an artistic convention to call attention to the presence of vampires. Fangs commonly appeared on the cover art of vampire novels, quickly identifying those titles not possessing an obvious vampiric name. They were used in a like manner on comic book covers, Dracula dolls, and Halloween greeting cards.

A new feature introduced into recent vampire films and novels has been retractable vampire teeth. Vampires would thus appear normal when interacting with

DOUG WERT BEARS HIS FANGS IN *DRACULA RISING*.

humans, and show their fangs only when about to feed. This development seems to have derived from the favorable reaction to the transformation into a werewolf shown in the Oscar-winning *American Werewolf in London*. Such a dramatic transformation from a normal appearance into a monsterlike figure was graphically portrayed by Grace Jones and her fellow vampires in *Vamp* (1986). The appearance of the extended canine teeth accompanied other changes in facial expressions and signaled the emergence of the darker predatory side of the vampire's personality.

The conventional canine fangs created a problem for the cinematic vampire. Lee's canine teeth appeared to be used more for ripping flesh than for neatly puncturing the skin and jugular vein. The two holes would be so far apart that the vampire would find it difficult to suck from both holes at the same time. Therefore, it has been common to picture the two holes as being much closer together than the distance between the canine teeth would suggest. This discrepancy, overlooked by most fans, has given feminist interpreters of vampires an opening to find something positive in the male-dominated myth. Penelope Shuttle and Peter Redgrove, for example, suggested that the wounds were not those of a carnivore, but of a viper, a snake. They suggested that the film directors, without consciously knowing what they were doing, were harking back to an ancient myth that associated the beginning of menstruation with a snake's bite. After being bitten by the snake, the girl became a woman and began menstruating; after being bitten by the vampire, the women tended to become more active and sexual. While the vampire myth has been associated with the particular anxieties of teenage males, possibly it also has something subtle to communicate directly to young females.

Sources:

Riccardo, Martin V. *The Lure of the Vampire.* Chicago: Adams Press, 1983. 67 pp.
Shuttle, Penelope, and Peter Redgrove. *The Wise Wound.* New York: Richard Marek, 1978. 335 pp.

FEMALE VAMPIRES *See:* WOMEN AS VAMPIRES

FINGERNAILS

When **Jonathan Harker** first encountered **Dracula** early in the novel by **Bram Stoker,** his "nails were long and fine, and cut to a sharp point." Above and beyond the role this description had in emphasizing Dracula's animal-like quality, these nails would become functional later in Chapter 21 when they would be used to open a wound in his chest from which he would force **Mina Murray** to drink. The fact that his nails were noticed at all possibly derived from some of the widely circulated reports of the vampires of eastern Europe. Among the characteristics that vampire hunters looked for in the bodies that they exhumed, in the belief that they were possibly vampires, were nails that appeared to have grown since the burial of the person. Fresh nails, or occasionally no nails at all, were a common item mentioned in reports from **Germany,** and both northern and **southern Slavs.**

Fingernails have not been emphasized in most post-Dracula vampires. **Graf Orlock,** the Dracula figure in the 1922 film *Nosferatu, Eine Symphonie des Garuens,* had extended fingers with elongated nails that added to his rodentlike appearance. However, when **Bela Lugosi** brought Dracula into a British home, neither hands nor nails appeared abnormal in any way. Occasionally, however, when only the audience could see him, he stuck his hands in front of him like an animal about to pounce on a prey. After Lugosi, only a few vampires that had been altered into a demonic form had clawlike alterations in the hands.

Sources:

Barber, Paul. *Vampires, Burial, and Death.: Folklore and Reality.* New Haven, CT: Yale University Press, 1988. 236 pp.

FIRE

Though not mentioned by **Abraham Van Helsing,** the voice of knowledge about vampires in **Bram Stoker**'s *Dracula,* fire was considered the ultimate means of destroying a vampire in eastern European countries. Fire was an ancient symbol of God. For example, God appeared to Moses in the burning bush and once the Hebrews left Egypt, God signaled his presence through a cloud that hovered by day and a fire by night. The fiery destruction of the evil cities of Sodom and Gomorrah was an illustration of God's power. In the book of Revelations, God was pictured as cleansing the earth by fire at the end of time. Fire was thus both destructive and renewing, consuming the old and corrupt and making way for the new and pure.

Throughout the world, fire has been a vital source of light and warmth and integral to food preparation. It was natural for it to take on symbolic and religious meanings. While fire has had a particular meaning and its own rituals in each culture, it has been part of the sacred life of all cultures. In the Mediterranean, the metaphorical description of the soul as a spark of fire added to its sacred quality. Fire also has been used to execute people in some countries—a practice used especially for condemned heretics and witches during the medieval period in Europe.

In eastern Europe, from **Bulgaria** and **Romania** to **Russia** and **Poland,** the body of a suspected vampire was burned if lesser means (the **stake,** or **decapitation**) failed to stop it. Throughout Europe, people used a new fire to cure livestock of sickness. When such a fire was to be built, residents would extinguish every individual fire in the village and start two new bonfires a short distance from each other. The people then walked the animals in the village through the new fire or need fire. Afterwards, they relighted the village fires from the embers of the need fire. At times, when a vampire was believed to be attacking cattle and other domestic animals, villagers would resort to a need fire, hoping that would free them from the vampire. It was believed that the fire would cause the vampire to leave the herd and become trapped in the area of the fire, where it then would be devoured by wolves.

While not mentioned by Stoker as a way to fight the vampire, fire was used by the author of **Varney the Vampyre** as the ultimate means of death: Varney jumped into the fiery opening of a volcano. Through the twentieth century, this concept of fire has been picked up in many vampire novels and movies, where it provided a popular option for the vampire's destruction. Torch-carrying villagers attacking the vampire's (or other monster's) lair and burning it to the ground was a common scene in movies of the 1930s and 1940s.

More recently, **St. Germain,** the vampire hero in **Chelsea Quinn Yarbro**'s novels, noted fire as one of two means to experience the "true death" of a vampire. For **Anne Rice**'s vampires, fire was almost the only way they could be destroyed. **Lestat de Lioncourt** was introduced to fire soon after he was made a vampire when Magnus, his creator, committed **suicide** by jumping into a fire before he told Lestat very much about the vampiric life. Louis used fire against the Parisian vampire community when he burned their Theatre of the Vampires.

Sources:

Edmans, Karl-Martin. "Fire." In Mircea Eliade, ed. *The Encyclopedia of Religion.* New York: Macmillian Publishing Company, 1987.

FISHER, TERENCE (1904-1980)

Terence Fisher directed the majority of the classic horror motion pictures produced by **Hammer Films** in the 1950s and 1960s, including three important vampire films. Apprenticed aboard the training ship *H.M.S. Conway,* during the late 1920s, he later left the sea and held different jobs until 1930 when he went to work at Shepard's Bush Studios. Because there were no schools to learn the film business at that time, he mastered his chosen trade on the job through the 1930s, primarily as a film editor. It was not until 1948 that he directed his first picture, *A Song for Tomorrow.*

As early as 1953 Fisher worked at Hammer Films on its early science fiction productions, *Four-Sided Triangle* and *Spaceways.* In 1957 he was paired with screenwriter **Jimmy Sangster** and actors **Peter Cushing** and **Christopher Lee** to do a remake of the classic **Universal Pictures'** film *Frankenstein.* The film was a success, and the four men assembled the next year to do *Dracula.* This film became the most memorable of Fisher's career. Through it and others to follow, Fisher—more than any single person—created the distinctive Hammer style with horror movies in general, and the Dracula/vampire movie in particular. *The Horror of Dracula*, the title by which his first Dracula movie is best known, became spectacularly successful. It put Hammer's films on the map as the premier successor to the Universal horror movies of the 1930s and 1940s.

Before turning his task over to a new wave of Hammer directors, Fisher would make more than 10 additional Hammer horrors, including *The Mummy* (1959) and *The Curse of the Werewolf* (1961), and significant sequels to both the *Frankenstein* and *Dracula* features. Other Dracula movies by Fisher included *The Brides of Dracula* (1960) and *Dracula Prince of Darkness* (1965).

Fisher has been hailed for his genuine contributions to the horror genre. He not only brought technicolor to the horror movie, but presented the evil deeds of Frankenstein and Dracula and other classic monsters directly to the audience, rather than leaving viewers to imagine the action. Although Fisher put the horrid acts on the screen, he also imposed a moral order that opposed evil and eventually defeated it. Technically, such films as *The Horror of Dracula* did not necessarily break new ground as Fisher developed his new versions of the pre-war black and white movies. He merely used the state of the art technology of the late 1950s and the openings provided by the changing social standards concerning what could be presented to film audiences.

Most importantly, Fisher's movies appealed a new generation of horror fans, and his success seemed to reflect the uniqueness of his subject rather than originality or outstanding directing talent on his part. Fisher is thus remembered as a competent director—but not a great one. In judging Fisher, however, one must also take into account the severe budget constraints that Hammer imposed on him; these included, for example, limiting the lines spoken by Christopher Lee after he became a star (largely because of *The Horror of Dracula*) as a means of reducing what would have been Lee's high salary demands.

Fisher retired in 1973 and died in 1980 of cancer.

Sources:

Bourgoin, Stephane. *Terence Fisher.* Paris: Edilig, 1984. 127 pp.

Glut, Donald G. *The Dracula Book.* Metuchen, NJ: Scarecrow Press, 1975. 388 pp.

Quinlan, David. *The Illustrated Guide to Film Directors.* Totowa, NJ: Barnes & Noble Books, 1984. 334 pp.

Hutchings, Peter. *Hammer and Beyond: The British Horror Film.* Manchester: Manchester University Press, 1993. 193 pp.

———. "Terence Fisher." In Nicolas Thomas, ed. *International Dictionary of Films and Filmmakers.* Vol. 2: Directors. Chicago: St. James Press, 1991.

Pirie, David. *Heritage of Horror: The English Gothic Cinema, 1946-1972.* New York: Avon, 1973. 192 pp.

Thomson, David. *A Biographical Dictionary of Film.* New York: William Morrow and Company, 1976. 629 pp.

FLORESCU, RADU R. (1925-)

Radu R. Florescu is an eastern European historian who, along with his colleague **Raymond T. McNally,** has been one of the most prominent scholars calling attention to **Vlad the Impaler,** the historical Dracula, and his relation to the vampire legend. One of his ancestors, Vintila Florescu, was Vlad's contemporary but was a supporter Vlad's brother, Radu the Handsome, who took the Wallachian throne in 1462 at the end of Vlad's reign.

Florescu seemed destined for an obscure life as a specialist in eastern European politics and culture. His first book was *The Struggle Against Russia in the Roumanian Principalities* (1962). However, in the early 1970s he teamed with his Boston College colleague Raymond T. McNally as the author of *In Search of Dracula* (1972), a popular book on the vampire myth. Their book drew upon the historical data concerning Vlad the Impaler, the fifteenth-century Romanian prince who had been associated with the vampire legend by **Bram Stoker.** Some years previously, McNally had become interested in tracking down any real history behind Stoker's novel. His search led him to Vlad the Impaler; after McNally joined the faculty at Boston College, Florescu discovered that the two shared a mutual interest. In the late 1960s they formed a team with Romanian historians Constantin Giurescu and Matai Cazacu to perform research on Dracula and vampire folklore. It was found that in

Romania, vampire folklore was not tied to Dracula (until very recently). Stoker possibly learned of Vlad from **Arminius Vambéry,** a Romanian scholar he met in the 1890s in London.

In Search of Dracula was designed as a miniature encyclopedic survey of aspects of the Dracula legend. Some reviewers, noting the lack of footnotes concerning the historical Dracula, suggested that Florescu and McNally had made up the details of his life. Those reviews led to their next work, a complete biography of Vlad titled, *Dracula: A Biography of Vlad the Impaler, 1431-1476,* published in 1973. This study not only spurred further work on the fifteenth-century prince by Romanian historians but also altered the treatment of Dracula in the movies. Among several such movies, two versions of *Dracula*—the 1974 version with **Jack Palance** and the 1992 version by **Francis Ford Coppola**—emphasized the relationship between Bram Stoker's Dracula and the historical Romanian prince. A number of recent novels, such as the several books by **Peter Tremayne** and Dan Simmons' *Children of the Night,* also built their plot on the connection. In 1976, a Swedish documentary about Vlad, with actor **Christopher Lee,** took Florescu's and McNally's first book as its title.

Florescu continued his productive collaboration with McNally. In 1979, (coinciding with the release of the new version of *Dracula* **(1979)** with **Frank Langella**), they completed an edited version of *Dracula* under the title, *The Essential ''Dracula'': A Completely Illustrated and Annotated Edition of Bram Stoker's Classic Novel.* This edition was noteworthy for its extensive use of notes that Stoker made while writing the novel. More recently, Florescu and McNally issued a comprehensive presentation of Vlad's life in its context in the broad sweep of fifteenth-century history, *Dracula, Prince of Many Faces: His Life and Times* (1989). The fall of the Cheshescu government in Romania has allowed increased contact and collaborative activity between Romanian scholars and their Western counterparts. In 1991, building on an idea first proposed in the 1970s by Florescu and McNally, Kurt W. Treptow brought together Romanian, British, and American scholars to create an anthology of contemporary research on Dracula. Florescu contributed a paper to this work called, ''Vlad II Dracula and Vlad III Dracula's Military Campaigns in Bulgaria, 1443-1462.''

Sources:

Florescu, Radu. "Vlad II Dracula and Vlad III Dracula's Military Campaigns in Bulgaria, 1443-1462." In Kurt W. Treptow. *Dracula: Essays on the Life and Times of Vlad Tepes.* New York: Columbia University Press, 1991, pp. 103-16.

Florescu, Radu, and Raymond T. McNally. *The Complete Dracula.* Boston: Copley Publishing Group, 1992. 409 pp. (A combined publication of *In Search of Dracula* and *Dracula: A Biography of Vlad the Impaler.*)

———. *Dracula: A Biography of Vlad the Impaler, 1431-1476.* New York: Hawthorn Books, 1973. 239 pp.

———. "The Dracula Search in Retrospect." *The New England Social Studies Bulletin* 43, 1 (Fall 1985-1986).

———. *Dracula, Prince of Many Faces: His Life and Times.* Boston: Little, Brown and Company, 1989. 261 pp.

McNally, Raymond T., and Radu Florescu. *In Search of Dracula.* New York: Greenwich, 1972. 223 pp.

———, eds. *The Essential "Dracula": A Completely Illustrated and Annotated Edition of Bram Stoker's Classic Novel.* New York: Mayflower Books, 1979. 320 pp.

FLYING VAMPIRES

Some vampires had the ability to fly. Flying was quite common among Asian vampires. For some, such as the *penanggalan* vampire of **Malaysia**—who flew about as a head and neck and a set of dangling entrails—it was essential. As some Chinese vampires grew older, they transformed into flying creatures.

In general, European vampires did not fly, though they were known to levitate. Other vampirelike creatures, such as the *banshee*—the wailing spirit—flew. The European vampire's ability to fly generally was tied to its ability to transform into a creature, such as a bird or **bat.** The ancient Roman *strix,* originally a screech owl, was later identified with the vampiric witches of Italy. The witches were believed to have the power to change into a crow or an owl so they could move about more quickly. Once the vampire was identified with the bat, most thoroughly in the novel *Dracula* (1897), its mobility became greatly extended.

The West African vampire, which goes under various names such as the *obayifo* and *asiman* and which reappeared in the Caribbean as the *loogaroo* (Haiti), *sukuyan* (Trinidad), and *asema* (Surinam), regularly changed into a flying ball of light. In this form it could be seen in the night sky. A vampire of this sort, who lived otherwise as a member of the community, would enter the flying state by taking off its skin. After feasting, it often would assume the shape of an animal, at which time it could be chased and, if caught, wounded or killed.

Most vampires of twentieth-century literature and motion pictures flew only by making a **transformation** into a bat. In movies, the bat became a recurring problem to be handled by steadily improving special effects departments. Occasionally the solution would involve the camera taking the bat's perspective so that the audience saw the same view as the bat, but not the bat itself. This bat's-eye view was used effectively in the movies *Innocent Blood* (1992) and *Dracula Rising* (1992).

Those vampires that denied the ability to transform into a bat or other flying creature seemed destined to remain earthbound, and in most cases, have been so limited. The vampires in **Anne Rice**'s novels were an exception. Though without any ability to transform into an animal form, they flew, at least in a limited way. **Lestat de Lioncourt** discovered this when he encountered Magnus (his creator), who picked him up and flew him to the top of a nearby building. The first major movie with vampires flying in their human form was *The Lost Boys* (1987), which included a scene in which two airborne vampires fought each other. More recently police officer Nick Knight, the lead character in the **television** series *Forever Knight,* occasionally took to the air in order to catch a criminal suspect.

THE LOST BOYS, A RECENT EXAMPLE OF FLYING VAMPIRES.

For those who saw the vampire more as a supernatural creature, its flying ability represented no great extension of its magical powers. The vampire was frequently linked to witches, who magically flew to their sabbats on a broom. However, as the vampire became a creature of nature, and the vampiric condition related to a disease or a blood condition, its ability to fly was seen more as an unbelievable extension of natural powers.

FOREVER KNIGHT

During the 1992-93 television seasons, *Forever Knight* emerged as one of the more popular late-night alternatives to the talk shows. The story was built around Nick Knight, an 800-year-old vampire whose current role was that of a policeman on the Toronto police force. *Forever Knight* first appeared as a two-hour made-for-television movie and pilot for a possible series. Titled *Nick Knight,* it aired on August 20, 1989. In the movie, Nick Knight (played by Rick Springfield) was a 400-year-old Los Angeles detective assigned to investigate a series of murders in which the victims were drained of blood. One of the murders occurred in a museum where a goblet that was used to drink blood in an ancient ceremony had been stolen.

Knight was determined to recover his mortal nature. In the meantime he survived on bottled **blood.** He recognized the murders as possibly having been committed by his old enemy Lecroix, who regularly reappeared as Nick's major obstacle. In the process of investigating the museum murder, Knight met Alyce Hunter, an archaeologist who became his human confidant. She discovered that the goblet was used in a ceremony to cure vampirism. In the end, Knight's investigation led him not to Lecroix, but to Jack Fenner, a bloodmobile attendant and not a vampire, who had been committing the murders because he held a grudge against transients. Lecroix had actually committed only one murder—that in the museum to get the cup. In their initial encounter, Lecroix destroyed the cup. At the end, Lecroix drained Hunter's blood, which set the stage for Knight to destroy Lecroix.

When finally produced as a television series in the 1990s, several changes had occurred, including a new name: *Forever Knight.* The action shifted from Los Angeles to Toronto, and Knight had aged four centuries; his birthdate as a vampire was set in 1228. His real name was changed from Jean-Pierre (mentioned in passing in the earlier movie) to Nicolas. As the series proceeded, the story of his past was gradually revealed through flashbacks. In the opening episode, Nicolas (played by Geraint Wyn Davies), a knight, awakened to find himself turned into a vampire by Lecroix (Nigel Bennett), who would appear in the flashback scenes throughout the series. He had previously been seduced by Jeannette (Deborah Duchene), a female vampire, and the three had lived together for many years until Nick renounced their vampiric evil and began a search to become mortal again. In the series, Knight worked as a Toronto policeman on the graveyard shift. His sole confidant was Dr. Natalie Lambert (Catherine Disher), a forensic pathologist who was working on a means to transform Knight. The opening episode picked up the storyline from the movie concerning the theft of the sacrificial cup at the museum. The story was completed in the second episode, in which Fenner was discovered to be the murderer and both Lecroix and Alyce Hunter were killed.

CBS added *Forever Knight* as a weekly entry in its late-night crime series, *Crimetime after Primetime,* which was aired against NBC's popular *The Tonight Show.* It garnered a high rating and a loyal audience of vampire fans. However, it disappeared along with all of the *Crimetime* series after CBS signed comedian David Letterman to do his show opposite *The Tonight Show* in August 1993. In the meantime, two fan clubs (the **Forever Knight Fan Club** and The Official Geraint Wyn Davies Fan Club) and a variety of fanzines (*The Raven, Knight Beat, Knightly Tales,* and *Forever Net*) began to work for the revival of the show. In 1994 Peggy

GERAINT WYN DAVIES
PORTRAYED A "GOOD GUY"
VAMPIRE IN *FOREVER KNIGHT.*

Religa announced the formation of a Nigel Bennett Fan Club for the actor who played Lecroix in the *Forever Knight* series.

Sources:

Strauss, Jon. "Forever Knight." *Epi-log* 36 (November 1993) 4-11; 37 (December 1993): 29-35, 62.

FOREVER KNIGHT FAN CLUB

In the wake of public response to the *Forever Knight* television series during the 1992-93 season, Lora Haines founded a club for the show's growing number of fans. The club publishes a newsletter, *Feeding Frenzy,* six times a year. Meanwhile Rosemary Shad founded a second club, The Official Geraint Wyn Davies Fan Club, built around *Forever Knight*'s handsome young star. A variety of fanzines also appeared, including *The Raven*, edited by Amy Hull and Paula Sanders; *Knight Beat*, edited by Barbara Fister-Liltz; *Knightly Tales*, edited by Ann Hull and Bill Hupe; *On the Wings of the Knight*, edited by Jessica Daigneault; and *Forever Net* (drawing on the Forever Knight computer networks).

The Forever Knight Fan Club may be reached at PO Box 1108, Boston, MA 02103-1108, and the Geraint Wyn Davies Fan Club at 4133 Glendale Rd., Woodbridge, VA 22193.

A fan club has recently been formed around Nigel Bennett, who played Lecroix in the *Forever Knight* series. Contact the Nigel Bennett Fan Club c/o Star Urioste, 25055 Copa del Oro, No. 104, Hayward,, CA 94545-2573.

Among those most active in *Forever Knight* fandom is Barbara Fister-Liltz, who has a long career in vampire-related fan organizations. She was a leader in the development of **Shadowcon,** an annual *Dark Shadows* convention, and also illustrated several *Dark Shadows* books, including Lori Paige's *Balm in Gilead* and S. M. Brand's *Belinda: A Weekend in New England.* She also founded Pandora Publications, which published a variety of *Dark Shadows* and vampire publications. Fister-Liltz currently lives in Illinois where she works for Special Services Unlimited, distributor of both *Forever Knight* and *Dark Shadows* merchandise.

FORTUNE, DION (1890-1946)

Dion Fortune, occult magician and exponent of the concept of psychic vampirism, was born Violet Mary Firth in 1890 in Wales. She manifested psychic abilities at an early age, which led to an interest in Spiritualism, psychoanalysis, and Theosophy. Around 1919 she joined the Alpha and Omega chapter of the Stella Matutina, a group loosely affiliated with the Hermetic Order of the Golden Dawn, a ritual magic group. While a member of the order, she took a magical motto, ''Deo Non Fortuna'' (By God not luck), which was later shortened to Dion Fortune, her public name.

Five years later she founded the Fraternity of the Inner Light to attract members to the Golden Dawn, but soon split with the order and developed her own version of magical teachings. She claimed contact with the ''Inner Planes'' of wisdom from which she received the fraternity's teachings. She not only authored the lessons for the fraternity, but penned a number of books, including: *Sane Occultism* (1929), *The Training and Work of an Initiate* (1930), *The Mystical Qabalah* (1936), and *The Sea Priestess* (1938).

In 1930 Fortune published one of her more popular books, *Psychic Self Defense.* The book grew out of her own experiences with a boss who had gained some degree of occult training in India and who tried, by occult means, to obtain Fortune's assistance in several nefarious schemes. In her occult work Fortune also had been witness to various incidents of psychic attack, which she was called on to interrupt. Among the elements of a psychic attack were vampirism, nervous exhaustion, and a wasting of the body into a ''mere bloodless shell of skin and bones.'' Fortune propounded an occult perspective on vampirism. She suggested that occult masters had the power to separate their psychic self from their physical body and to attach it to another and to drain that person's energy. Such persons would then unconsciously begin to drain the energy of those around them, especially people with whom they are in an intense emotional relationship. The attack on the psychic self would manifest in what appear to be bite marks on the physical body, especially around the neck, ear lobes, and breast (of females). It was Fortune's belief that troops from eastern Europe during World War I had several accomplished occultists among them. These occultists, upon their deaths, were able to attach themselves to British soldiers who survived the war and, hence, made their way to England.

Fortune included fictionalized accounts of the incidents of **psychic vampirism** in *The Secrets of Dr. Taverner*. Recently, the story of Fortune's early experience of psychic attack was discussed in some detail in a book by Janine Chapman.

Sources:

Chapman, Janine. *Quest for Dion Fortune.* York Beach, ME: Samuel Weiser, 1993. 190 pp.
Fortune, Dion. *Psychic Self Defense: A Study in Occult Pathology and Criminality.* 1930. Reprint. London: Aquarian Press, 953. 212 pp.
———. *The Secrets of Dr. Taverner.* 1926. Reprint. St. Paul, MN: Llewellyn Publications, 1962. 231 pp.

FRANCE, VAMPIRES IN

French records supply a limited number of texts for vampire researchers. Among the few were two fourteenth-century stories recounted by E. P. Evans in his volume on the *Criminal Prosecution and Capital Punishment of Animals* (1906), as mentioned in Dudley Wright's survey. The first concerned a revenant that terrorized the town of Cadan. The people he attacked seemed destined to become a vampire like him. They retaliated, attacking his corpse and driving a **stake** through it. That remedy proving ineffective, they finally burned him. In 1345 A.D., in Lewin, a woman believed to be a witch died. She returned in various beastly forms and attacked villagers. When uncovered in her grave it was reported that she had swallowed her face cloth; when the cloth was pulled out of the grave, it was stained with blood. She also was staked, which again proved ineffective. She used the stake as a weapon while walking around town. She was finally destroyed by **fire.**

Also present in French folklore was the *melusine*, a creature derived from the classical *lamiai* figure. Melusine reportedly was the daughter of King Elinas and his fairy wife. Angry at her father, she and her sisters turned their magic against their parents. For her actions, her mother turned her into a serpent from the waist down. Melusine would remain this way until she found a man who would marry her on the condition that he would never see her on Saturday (when her serpentlike body reappeared). She found such a person in Raymond of Poitoi, and, once married, she used her magic to help him build a kingdom. The problem emerged when their children arrived—each was deformed. The situation came to a head when one of the children burned an abbey and killed a hundred people. In his anger, Raymond revealed that he knew Melusine's secret. She reacted by accepting the curse upon her and realizing that she was condemned to fly through the air in pain until the day of judgment. Until the castle fell, she would appear before the death of each of Raymond's heirs to voice her lament. She thus became the banshee—the wailing spirit of the House of Lusignan. Even after the castle fell to the French crown, people reported that Melusine appeared before the death of a French king. She was not a vampire, but did show the direction in which at least one of the older vampires evolved.

When the idea of the vampire was introduced into France at the end of the seventeenth century, it was an unfamiliar topic. The subject seemed to have been raised initially in 1693 when a Polish priest asked the faculty at the Sorbonne to counsel him on how he should deal with corpses that had been identified as vampires. That same year, newspaper reports of vampires in Poland appeared in a French periodical, *Mercure Galant.* A generation later, the *Lettres Juives* (Jewish Letters), published in 1737, included the account of several of the famous Serbian (mistakenly reported as Hungarian) vampire cases. However, the issue of vampirism was not raised for the French public until the 1746 publication of **Dom Augustin Calmet**'s *Dissertations sur les Apparitions des Anges et des Espits, et sur les revenants, et Vampires de Hingrie, de Boheme, de Moravie, et de Silésie.*

This treatise by the French Bible scholar continued the vampire debate that had been centered in the German universities. The debate had reached a negative conclusion concerning the existence of vampires, and Calmet called for what he thought of as a more biblical and scientific view, which considered the accounts of vampires in Eastern Europe, and called for further study. While not accepted by his colleagues, the book was a popular success, reprinted in 1747 and 1748, and translated into several foreign languages.

Calmet brought the debate into the Parisian salons, and he soon found a number of detractors. Voltaire reacted sarcastically and spoke of businessmen as the real bloodsuckers. Diderot followed a similar line in his salon of 1767. Only Jean-Jacques Rousseau argued in support of Calmet and his rational approach to the evidence.

FRENCH VAMPIRES: No survey of French vampires would be complete without mention of the several historical figures who have been cited as actual vampires. Leading the list was Gilles de Rais (1404-40). A hero of France, de Rais was a brilliant general who fought with Joan of Arc—but was also a man known to have few equals as a sadistic murderer. He tortured and killed a number of young boys (and a few girls) receiving intense sexual gratification in the process. He also practiced a form of Satanism. It was only with great difficulty that he was brought to trial. Upon conviction, he was strangled and his body burned.

Somewhat different was the Viscount de Moriéve, a French nobleman who, by strange fortune, kept his estates through the period of the French Revolution. Following the revolution he took out his animosity against the common people by executing many of his employees one by one. Eventually he was assassinated. Soon after his burial, a number of young children died unexpectedly. According to reports, they all had vampire marks on them. These accounts continued for some 72 years. Finally, his grandson decided to investigate the charges that his grandfather was a vampire. In the presence of local authorities, he had the vault opened. While other corpses had undergone the expected decomposition, that of the viscount was still fresh and free of decay. The face was flushed and there was blood in the heart and chest. New nails had grown and the skin was soft.

The body was removed from its resting place, and a white thorn was driven into the heart. As blood gushed forth, the corpse made a groaning sound. The remains were then burned. There were no more reports of unusual deaths of children from that day forward. J. A. Middleton, who originally wrote of de Moriéve, discovered that he had been born in Persia, married an Indian, and later moved to France as a naturalized citizen. She believed that he had brought his vampirism with him from the East.

While the de Moriéve case carried many of the elements of traditional European vampirism, that of Francois Bertrand does not. During the 1840s Bertrand, a sergeant in the French Army, desecrated a number of graves in Paris before being caught in 1849. After opening graves, he would mutilate bodies in a **ghoul**-like fashion. His story became the basis of a famous novel, *Werewolf of Paris* (1933) by Guy Endore.

THE LITERARY VAMPIRE: France's real contribution to vampire lore came in its nurturing of the literary vampire. Soon after its publication, copies of **"The Vampyre"** (1819), written by **John Polidori** but mistakenly attributed to **Lord Byron,** arrived in Paris. It was hailed as a great product of Byron and inspired several of the literary elite, most notably **Charles Nodier** who wrote *Le Vampire,* a drama based on Polidori's story and featuring his vampire star Lord Ruthven. "Le Vampire" led to other Parisian vampire plays, several of them farces, and was translated into English for performance in London.

Through Nodier the vampire was introduced into French romantic literature. The romantic exploration of the inner self, often with the assistance of mind-altering drugs, soon encountered the negative aspect of the human psyche. The vampire emerged as a symbol of the dark side of human nature and most of the French romantics utilized it at one point or another. **Theophile Gautier** authored a vampire story, "La Morte Amoureuse" (published in English as "The Beautiful Vampire" and "Claironde") in 1836 and a poem titled "Les Taches Jaunes" ("The Yellow Bruises"). Poet Charles Baudeliare wrote several vampire poems including "The Vampire" and "Metamorphoses of the Vampire", both published in 1857. **Alexandre Dumas** brought to an end this generation of romantic interest in the vampire with his short story "The History of the Pale Woman" and his dramatic version of *Le Vampire* (1851). During this era, **Alexey Tolstoy,** the first Russian writer of vampire stories, published his novellas "Upir" and "The Family of the Vukodlak" in French, and they were first circulated and read in the salons of Paris.

Since the mid-nineteenth century, the vampire has appeared only occasionally in French novels. Paul Féval wrote two vampire novels, *Le Vampire* (1867) and *La Ville Vampire* (1875). Later novelists included Gustave Lerouge, *La Guerre des Vampires* (1909); Jean Mistler, *Le Vampire* (1944); Maurice Limat, *Moi, Vampire* (1966); Claude Klotz, *Paris Vampire* (1974); and Christine Renard, *La Mante au Fil des Jours* (1977). While French authors have not utilized the vampire with great frequency, many novels originally written in English, including those by **Stephen King** and **Anne Rice,** have been translated and published in France.

THE CINEMATIC VAMPIRE: France produced two of the earliest vampire films. *Le Vampire* (1914) was a silent film in which a man attempted to get a vampire bat to kill his wife. *Les Vampires* (1915) was a 10-part serial built around a secret society of super-criminals. It starred Eugene Ayme as Le Grand Vampire and Juliet Musidora as Irma Vep (an anagram of vampire). After these early movies, it would be 30 years before the next vampire films were produced. Immediately after World War II, Jean Painleve directed a documentary on *Le Vampire.* It was followed by a short feature that appeared in 1947 as *Les Vampires.* Over the next 20 years, a number of vampire movies were produced in France, most now forgotten. Rising above the crowd was *Et Mourir de Plaisir* (*Blood and Roses*), produced by **Roger Vadim** and starring his wife Annette Vadim as **Carmilla** in this remake of the **Sheridan Le Fanu** tale.

The French movies have become known for continually pushing the amount of overt nudity and sex on the screen. *Et Mourir de Plaisir* paved the way for the work of **Jean Rollin,** the French director who has most frequently utilized the vampire theme. His first feature-length vampire film, *Le Viol du Vampire* (*Rape of the Vampires*), inaugurated a series of increasingly explicit films that have become among the most notable of all vampire motion pictures. *La Viol du Vampire* was followed by *La Nue Vampire* (*The Nude Vampire,* 1969), *Le Frisson des Vampires* (*Sex and the Vampires,* 1970), and *Le Cult de Vampire* (*The Vampire Cult,* 1971). Through the 1970s he produced *Requiem pour un Vampire* (1972), *Levres se Sang* (1974), and *Fascination* (1979). His last vampire movie came in 1982, *La Morte-Vivante.*

Rollin created an era of French vampire movies, but after he moved on to other subjects, few French producers have picked up on the theme. The French vampire films released more recently include: *La Belle Captive* (1983); *Sexandroide* (1987), which combined sex, science fiction, and vampires; and *Baby Blood* (1990).

POPULAR CULTURE: As in North America and the United Kingdom, the vampire has entered the popular culture of France, most notably in comic books. In the 1970s vampire stories began to appear in such horror comics as *La Maison du Mystere* and *La Manoir des Fantomes.* Among the early independent vampire issues was a 12-part serialization of *Jacula: Fete in la Morgue,* the translation of a 1969 Italian adult comic. As French comic books developed into some of the best examples of comic book art, vampires periodically appeared, though they were by no means as popular as in the United States. Among the outstanding recent issues were Philippe Druillet's *Nosferatu* (1989) (also translated into English) and *Le Fils de Dracuella* by J. Ribera (1991).

Contemporary French scholars and writers have joined in efforts to educate the public on vampires and vampirism. This interest can be traced to the early 1960s with the publication of two books, Tony Faivre's *Les Vampires* and the very popular *Le Vampire* by Ornella Volta, which has been translated into English and Spanish. These initial efforts were followed by such volumes as Roland Villeneuve's *Loups-garous et Vampires* (1963), Francois R. Dumas's *A la Recherche des Vampires* (1976), Robert Ambelain's *La Vampirisme* (1977), Jean-Paul Bourre's *Le cult du vampire aujourd'hui* (1978), Roger Delorme's *Les Vampires Humains* (1979), and Jean-Paul

Bourre's *Dracula et les Vampires* (1981). Jacques Finné included an extensive list of French vampire titles in his 1986 bibliography.

Sources:

Bourre, Jean-Paul. *Dracula et les Vampires*. Paris: Editions du Rocher, 1981.

Briggs, Katherine. *A Dictionary of Fairies*. London: Penguin Books, 1976. Rept. as: *An Encyclopedia of Fairies, Hobgoblins, Brownies, Bogies, and Other Supernatural Creatures*. New York: Pantheon Books, 1976. 481 pp.

Druillet, (Philippe). *Nosferatu*. 1989. Reprint. Milwaukee, OR: Dark Horse Comics, 1991.

Evans, E. P. *The Criminal Prosecution and Capital Punishment of Animals*. London: W. Heineman, 1906. 336 pp.

Finné, Jacques. *Bibliographie de Dracula*. Lausanne, Switz.: L'Age d'Homme, 1986. 215 pp.

Middleton, J. A. *Another Grey Ghost Book*. London: E. Nash, 1914. 320 pp.

Praz, Mario. *The Romantic Agony*. London: Oxford University Press, 1970. 479 pp.

Volta, Ornella. *Le Vampire*. Paris: Jean-Jacques Pauvert, 1962. 236 pp. English trans. as: *The Vampire*. London: Tandem Books, 1963. 157 pp.

Wilson, Katherine M. "The History of the Word 'Vampire.'" *Journal of the History of Ideas*. 44, 4 (October-December 1985): 577-83.

Wright, Dudley. *Vampires and Vampirism*. London: William Rider and Sons, 1914, Rev. ed.: 1924. Reprint. *The Book of Vampires*. New York: Causeway Books, 1973. 217 pp.

FRANKENSTEIN'S MONSTER

Among the fictional creatures most associated with the vampire was the monster created by Victor Frankenstein. Movies featuring the creatures have been paired on double bills and, on occasion, both monsters have appeared in the same movie. The creatures share a history that goes back to 1816, when Frankenstein's monster was originally created and the vampire underwent a profound alteration.

During the week of June 19, 1816, **Lord Byron** called together a group of friends at a villa outside of Geneva, Switzerland. Trapped by a storm, the group, consisting of poet Percy Bysshe Shelley, Byron's physician **John Polidori,** and Shelley's second wife writer Mary Wollstonecraft Shelley, agreed with Byron to create and entertain the group with a "ghost" story. It was Mary Shelley's story that evolved into *Frankenstein* (first published anonymously in 1818). Byron wrote the core of a story that, several years' later, Polidori expanded into the first vampire short story. It was published in 1819 as **"The Vampyre"** under Byron's name.

Frankenstein was the story of a scientist, Victor Frankenstein, who assembled and brought to life a human body composed of the parts of several corpses. Frankenstein, although proud of having discovered a way to restore animation to lifeless matter, was unable to deal with the life he had created and rejected the creature. In return, the creature sought revenge and became the monster he is known as today. Frankenstein's monster differed from the vampire in at least one important respect. Frankenstein was created wholly from Mary Shelley's imagination and was not, like the vampire, based on popular folklore. Thus the expansion of the *Frankenstein* story originated with one novel, while vampire literature drew from a large body of preexisting folk material. There were, of course, sources Shelley drew from to create Frankenstein, such as the early material on robots and the legend of the Golem, a clay figure made by humans and brought to life. Nevertheless, like the literary vampire, Frankenstein's monster provided an important insight into the human situation—and it proved immediately and perennially popular.

Frankenstein was first brought to the stage in 1823 in England, three years after Polidori's "The Vampyre" inspired several French plays. Soon afterward, several different dramatic versions of *Frankenstein* appeared. However, while there were a number of different vampire stories throughout the nineteenth century, there were no variations on the *Frankenstein* tale, although Shelley's book went through many printings.

Frankenstein came to the screen in 1910 in a silent production by Thomas Edison's film company, but unfortunately no copies have survived. Several other silent movie adaptations were made before the vampire—now in the form of **Dracula**—and Frankenstein were brought together again by **Universal Pictures.** Universal had been revived by the success of *Dracula***(1931).** The studio decided that *Frankenstein* was to be the next logical picture and announced that the movie would star **Bela Lugosi** and Edward Van Sloan (**Abraham Van Helsing** in *Dracula*). Lugosi, once he understood the nature of his part in the movie refused to go through with it. His part was then given to a young unknown actor, Boris Karloff. The Frankenstein film equaled the success of the Dracula movie and made Karloff a star.

In 1933, it was announced that Lugosi would star in *The Return of Frankenstein,* this time as the mad scientist. However, Lugosi decided against that part as well. The movie went into production with Karloff again playing the monster and was released as *The Bride of Frankenstein.* Several other sequels followed. By the 1940s, Universal had also produced horror films featuring **werewolves.** In the 1940s, they began to put several monsters together in different kinds of encounters. In 1944, Dracula (**John Carradine**), Frankenstein, and the Wolfman were united for the first time by Universal in the *House of Frankenstein.* The next year the three returned in the *House of Dracula.* Seeing the end of the monstrous possibilities in 1948, Universal put its three monsters together with its comedy stars Bud Abbott and Lou Costello in *Abbott and Costello Meet Frankenstein* (1948). Following the movie's release, the trio did not appear together on screen for a decade.

HAMMER'S REVIVAL: The popularity of horror films was at a low ebb in the 1950s. Then Hammer Films bought the rights to the Universal monsters and began remaking the classic films in color. They chose Frankenstein as a first effort. *The Curse of Frankenstein* (1957) was so successful that they signed the actor who played the monster, **Christopher Lee,** to portray Dracula. **Peter Cushing,** who portrayed Frankenstein, was signed to play **Abraham Van Helsing** in the next production, released in the United States as the *The Horror of Dracula.* The two pictures were as successful for Hammer as the originals were for Universal, and over the next two decades Hammer became known for its distinctive horror motion pictures.

Although Hammer never brought the characters of Dracula and Frankenstein's monster together in the same motion picture, it was a theme with too much potential to neglect. The same year Hammer produced the *Curse of Frankenstein,* a Mexican studio developed its own Dracula/Frankenstein plot that emerged as *El Castillo de los Monstruos* (*Castle of the Monsters*). It was a comedy about a newlywed couple who met a number of monsters, including Frankenstein's monster and a vampire. It was followed by a sequel, *Frankenstein, El Vampiro Y CIA* (1961). Other meetings of Dracula (or another vampire) and Frankenstein's monster (or a similar creature) occurred in *Sexy Proibitissimo* (1961), *Love Me Quick!* (1964), *Frankenstein's Bloody Terror* (1967), *Mad Monster Party?* (1969), and *La Venganza de las Mujeres Vampiro* (1969). In the 1960s, the comic television series, **The Munsters** featured Frankenstein-like character Herman Munster (Fred Gwynne) as head of a family that included a vampiric wife, Lily (Yvonne de Carlo), and Grandpa (Al Lewis). Grandpa revealed, during the course of the series, that he was Count Dracula. In 1966, a movie developed from the show, *Munster, Go Home!* (1966).

During the 1970s, Frankenstein's monster and Dracula were pitted against each other again in *Dracula vs. Frankenstein* (1970), *Capulina Contra los Monstruos* (1972), *Dracula contra Frankenstein* (1972), *La Invasion de Los Muertos* (1972), and *Pepitoy Chabelo vs. Los Monstruos* (1973). By the early 1970s, however, the Frankenstein/Dracula connection had been exhausted, and in the succeeding years only two attempts to reunite them were made: *Dracula tan Exarchia* (1983) and *Howl of the Devil* (1988). The Munsters enjoyed a brief revival in a movie, *The Munsters' Revenge* (1981), and in a new series that ran on television from 1988 to 1991.

DRACULA AND FRANKENSTEIN IN FICTION: Among the more interesting aspects of the new interest shown in works of fiction featuring Frankenstein's monster during the past generation was a Marvel comic book that appeared during Marvel's rediscovery of horror following the loosening of the restriction on horror titles. The plot of *The Frankenstein Monster* was linked by the monster's search for his creator. In issue No. 8 (November 1973), the monster, now in Transylvania, saved a Gypsy girl from rape. He was befriended by the girl's mother who promised to help him in his quest. Instead, she tricked Frankenstein into assisting her in freeing Dracula from his tomb. Frankenstein had a brief fight with Dracula, who escaped. Frankenstein then returned to the Gypsy camp only to find it destroyed by villagers who believed the Gypsies had brought the vampire back to them. Angry, Frankenstein challenged the villagers. They overpowered him and were about to burn him at the stake when Dracula attacked another village female. As the townspeople turned their attention to catching Dracula, Frankenstein escaped. He tracked the fleeing Dracula to his hiding place and, in a final fight, staked the vampire. Dracula was dead . . . at least for the moment.

Novelists who have played with the Frankenstein character in the twentieth century have rarely followed the lead offered by motion pictures and developed new fictional encounters with Dracula. One exception was **Donald Glut** who, in the 1970s, developed a series of new Frankenstein adventures. One, *Frankenstein Meets Dracula* (1977), was written as a sequel to **Bram Stoker**'s *Dracula.* Resurrected after his death at the end of the novel, Dracula vowed to take revenge. He attempted to transplant the brain of a descendent of **Abraham Van Helsing** into the Frankenstein monster's head. However, the monster rejected the idea of the transplant and turned on Dracula. A second novel in the series that included Dracula was never published.

The most recent encounter of Frankenstein's monster with Dracula occurred in a set of **juvenile literature** books, the ''Fifth Grade Monsters'' series by Mel Gilden. In the first volume, *M Is for Monster* (1987), Danny Keegan, a ''normal'' fifth grader, was introduced to the new kids in class. They include C. D. Bitesky (a vampire), Howie Wolfner (a werewolf), and Elisa and Frankie Stein (who bore more than a passing resemblance to Frankenstein and his bride). Gilden took Danny and the ''monsters'' through a series of adventures, most with plots that focused on the importance of young people's acceptance of kids who are slightly different. The books also serve as examples for older readers who have problems with monsters and other things that go bump in the night. Dracula, Frankenstein, and the other monsters have been partially tamed in Gilden's books and made a part of our culture as creatures of humor.

Sources:

The Frankenstein Monster. Nos 7-9. New York: Marvel Comics, 1973-74.
Gilden, Mel. *M Is for Monster.* Fifth Grade Monsters No. 1. New York: Avon, 1987. 89 pp.
————. *The Secret of Dinosaur Bog.* Fifth Grade Monsters No. 15. New York: Avon, 1991. 90 pp.
Glut, Donald. *The Frankenstein Catalog.* Jefferson, NC: Mcfarland & Company, 1984. 525 pp.
————. *The Frankenstein Legend: A Tribute to Mary Shelley and Boris Karloff.* Metuchen, NJ: Scarecrow Press, 1973. 372 pp.
————. *Frankenstein Meets Dracula.* London: New English Library, 1977. 140 pp.
Jones, Stephen. *The Illustrated Vampire Movie Guide.* London: Titan Books, 1993. 144 pp.

FRID, JONATHAN (1924-)

Jonathan Frid, the actor who portrayed vampire **Barnabas Collins** on *Dark Shadows,* the original ABC-TV daytime series, was born in Hamilton, Ontario, Canada. Frid made his stage debut during his teen years in a school production of Sheridan's *The Rivals.* However, it was not until his years in the Canadian Navy during World War II that he made the decision to pursue an acting career. After the war, Frid moved to London to attend the Royal Academy of Dramatic Arts. While in England, he appeared in his first film, *The Third Man.* In 1950, Frid moved back to Canada to attend the Toronto Academy of Arts and continue his acting career. He graduated from Yale in 1957 with a master's degree in fine arts with a major in directing.

Frid then settled in New York where, for the next decade, he played in several stage productions and was known for his portrayal of a variety of Shakespearean characters. He appeared with Ray Milland in a 1967 touring company production of *Hostile Witness.* After the tour concluded and he returned to New York, Frid made plans to move to California. His career in New York was at a standstill, and he decided to seek a position on the West Coast as a teacher.

Before he had a chance to leave for California, however, he received a call to join the cast of ***Dark Shadows.*** He interviewed for the part because it was to be only a few weeks work and would provide him some money to start over in his new home. At that point, the show's ratings dropped and ABC threatened cancellation. To boost ratings, the show's producer, **Dan Curtis,** decided to experiment with adding supernatural elements to the storyline. He had successfully introduced ghosts and decided to add a vampire. Frid, as vampire **Barnabas Collins,** began to appear in April 1967. The audience responded, especially women and teenagers (the show was on at 4:00 P.M.), and ratings steadily climbed. By summer, everyone recognized that the show was a hit, and the numerous spinoff products for fans began to appear.

Frid played the part of Barnabas Collins for the next four years, until the show was finally canceled in 1971. He also starred in the first of two movies based on the show, *House of Dark Shadows* (1970). At the end of the movie, Barnabas Collins was killed. There were no vampires in the second movie, *Night of Dark Shadows* (1971), which featured other characters from the *Dark Shadows* cast. Although as a result of the show Frid gained star status, he also experienced some degree of typecasting that limited his choice of parts once the show ended.

After he joined the show, Frid's character became the trademark image of *Dark Shadows.* His likeness dominated the publicity materials for the show, including the first *Dark Shadows* movie. More than 30 paperback books were written based on the show by Harlequin author **Daniel Ross,** and nearly all featured Frid's picture on the cover. His representation also graced the covers of most issues of the *Dark Shadows* comic book (the first vampire comic to appear after the lifting of the ban on vampires in 1954). Soon after he joined the show, a "Barnabas the Vampire Model Kit" was issued complete with a glow in the dark walking stick.

Following the cancellation of the show, Frid kept a low profile. He tried to distance himself from *Dark Shadows* and the role of Barnabas Collins. He did not want to find himself in a position similar to that of **Bela Lugosi**—trapped in the Dracula persona. He took a part on stage in *Murder at the Cathedral* and in two movies: *The Devil's Daughter* (1972), an ABC made-for-television movie, and *Seizure* (1974), director Oliver Stone's first film.

Most of Frid's time, however, was devoted to the development of three one-man shows: *Jonathan Frid's Fools & Fiends, Shakespearean Odyssey,* and *Fridiculousness.* He toured the country with the shows, and they allowing him to perform readings from Shakespeare, humor, and classic horror pieces by authors such as **Edgar Allan Poe.** In 1986, he joined an all-star cast in a Broadway revival of *Arsenic and Old Lace* and toured with the company the following year.

Frid's association with the show did not go away. *Dark Shadows* went into syndication, and a new audience became delighted with Barnabas Collins. During the 1980s, somewhat surprised (as have been many observers) at the persistence of fan interest in *Dark Shadows,* Frid appeared at the first of the **Dark Shadows Festivals** and has since been a frequent participant.

Sources:

Dawidziak, Mark. "Dark Shadows." *Cinefantastique* 21, 3 (December 1990): 24-28.
Frid, Jonathan. *Barnabas Collins: A Personal Picture Album.* New York: Paperback Library, 1969. 128 pp.

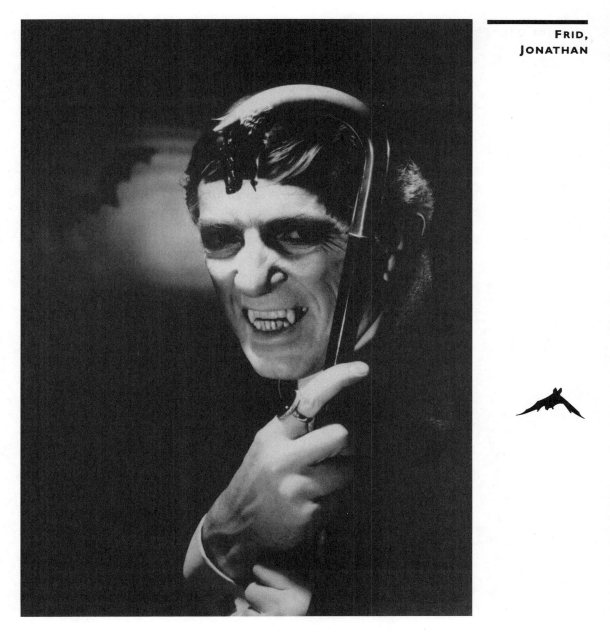

JONATHAN FRID AS BARNABAS COLLINS, THE CENTRAL VAMPIRE OF TELEVISION'S *DARK SHADOWS*.

Gross, Edward, and Mark Shapiro. *The Vampire Interview Book: Conversations with the Undead*. New York: Image Publishing, 1991. 134 pp.

Scott, Kathryn Leigh. *The Dark Shadows Companion: 25th Anniversary Collection.* Los Angeles Pomegranate Press, 1990. 208 pp.

FRIENDS OF DARK SHADOWS

A *Dark Shadows* fan club, the Friends of Dark Shadows began in 1983 under the
leadership of Sharida Rizzuto as the New Orleans branch of the International Dark
Shadows Society. Rizzuto, who had a broad experience in fanzine publishing,
published four issues of *Inside Dark Shadows*. Rizzuto and the New Orleans group
then separated from the International Dark Shadows Society and reorganized as the
Friends of Dark Shadows. She issued a new fanzine, *The Collinswood Record* (seven
issues), and *The Collinswood Journal,* a newsletter (three issues). She was assisted by
associate editor Sidney J. Dragon, the group's vice-president. The Friends of Dark
Shadows and its periodicals were discontinued in 1987. Rizzuto, however, continued
to publish *Dark Shadows* news in another publication, *The Vampire Journal*, now a
publication for the **Realm of the Vampire** organization.

G

GAMES, VAMPIRE

In the late 1960s vampires moved from being of interest to a few horror fans to capturing the popular imagination. Games built around vampirism are one sign that vampires have become an entrenched element in popular culture.

BOARD GAMES: The first set of vampire games were board games. The very first was a spin-off from the *Dark Shadows* daytime television show. *The "Dark Shadows" Game* was distributed by Whitman in 1968. In the game up to four players race each other through a maze. The following year, Milton Bradley released *The Barnabas Collins "Dark Shadows" Game*, developed in response to the popular introduction of the vampire **Barnabas Collins** to the cast. Quite distinct from the Whitman game, it required that players assemble a skeleton on a scaffold. The winner got to wear Barnabas' fangs.

In the mid-1970s, British horror and vampire fan Stephen Hand, disappointed at the lack of horror-oriented games, created his first board game, *Kill the Count*. The game featured a set of vampire hunters searching **Castle Dracula** for Dracula to kill him with a stake. In the 1980s, Hand revised the game and introduced ideas for a military game based on **Vlad the Impaler**'s wars.

A few years later it was followed by *The Undead* (1981), designed by Steve Jackson. Based on **Bram Stoker**'s *Dracula,* the game matched one player, who assumed the role of the Count unleashed upon London (a map of the city formed the game board), against one or more other players, the vampire hunters. The game could be played as a straight board game or expanded as a role-playing game.

The next vampire board game to hit the market was released in 1987 as *The Fury of Dracula*. As with *The Undead,* the players assumed the roles of vampire hunters pitted against one player, who acted as Dracula. The vampire hunters must find

Dracula and kill him before he was able to establish vampire accomplices in the cities of Europe (a map of Europe formed the game board). The game gave a slight advantage to Dracula—an advantage that was overcome only if the hunters worked together.

Among the more unique vampire-related games was *Dracula's Bite on the Side*, a dinner table mystery game in the "Murder a la Carte" series. The game was designed as part of an entire evening that included a dinner held to celebrate the 1893 betrothal of Count Dracula's ward, Bella Kashiasu, to Ivan Evenstich. Each of the eight dinner guests became a murder suspect and the evening was spent trying to determine who the murderer might be. As the game proceeded, guests interrogated each other and revealed what they have discovered. At the end of the game, each player guessed the murderer's identity.

Most recently, a board game was released in connection with **Francis Ford Coppola**'s movie, **Bram Stoker's Dracula** (1992), by Leading Edge Games. The players in this game assume the role of one of the vampire hunters from *Dracula*—**Abraham Van Helsing, Jonathan Harker, Quincey P. Morris,** etc. Their goal was to overcome a set of Dracula's servants, such as his vampire brides or **Lucy Westenra** as a vampire. Then the players must defeat the various forms of Dracula to rescue **Mina Murray,** who was trapped in Dracula's clutches.

For many years board games were the only vampire games, but in the 1990s, they were joined by a variety of what have been termed role-playing games.

ROLE-PLAYING GAMES: Today, the most popular vampire-oriented games are role-playing games. Fantasy role-playing games center on an alternative fantasy world that the players enter through their imaginations. They are games of make-believe, in which the players enter the story they simultaneously tell. By telling and playing there is an experience that goes beyond simply listening to someone tell the story.

Some games are led by the "gamemaster," who sets the starting point and guides the course of the game. Prior to the game, each character is assigned a unique combination of helpful attributes (strength, dexterity, stamina, intelligence) and talents. For the purpose of the game, the character's traits are quantified on a descriptive character sheet that assigns numerical values to each attribute. Thus, each character starts the game with a unique set of attributes, a variety of weapons, and other appropriate abilities. As the game begins, the characters placed in situations they get out of through a combination of their own choices and sheer chance (represented by a throw of the dice). The gamemaster describes what has happened after each players' action choice and decides how well the players have either succeeded and prospered or failed and suffered in the quest of their goal.

Each role-playing game has created its own myth that defines the imaginative world in which the game operates. As might be expected, vampires appeared in *Dungeons and Dragons* (D&D), a role playing game that deals in the widest possible world of fantasy and magic. As early as 1982, a *Ravenloft* module of D&D featuring a vampire, Count Strahd von Zarovich, was written for D&D by Tracy Hickman and Laura Hickman. By 1990, this module had grown into an ''advanced'' variant game with a primary vampire theme based upon the D&D worldview. A new *Ravenloft* game has been designed and written by Bruce Nesmith and Andria Hayday.

Ravenloft is a fictional island continent containing a number of kingdoms. Near its middle is the kingdom of Barovia, the land where Ravenloft Castle is located. Barovia is ruled by Count Strahd. In the past, the count loved a young woman, Tatyana, but she did not return his love and, instead, planned to marry his brother Sergei. Rejected and angry, the count killed Sergei, which, in turn, led to Tatyana's suicide. Through an unclear transaction, the count made a pact with ''death,'' and became a vampire. Count Strahd's castle and land were drawn out of the physical world into the etheric plane. *Ravenloft,* like most D&D landscapes, is a magical land. The various domains that surround Barovia inhabited by a variety of werewolves, ghouls, and supernatural creatures, and the various games of *Ravenloft* are built on their interaction. The popularity of the game has led to the publication of a number of spinoff novels based on *Ravenloft* and its inhabitants by authors such as **Elaine Bergstrom** and **P. N. Elrod.**

Shortly after vampires invaded *Dungeons and Dragons,* Pacesetter introduced a horror role-playing game in which vampires play a key role. *Chill* was built around the myth of the Societas Argenti Viae Eternitata (SAVE), the Eternal Society of the Silver Way. According to the *Chill* story, SAVE was founded in 1844 in Dublin, Ireland by a group of scientists led by Dr. Charles O'Boylan. O'Boylan posited the existence of little understood natural laws used by two separate opposing sets of entities who exist in the noncorporeal world. Most importantly, he believed that a highly disciplined source of evil intruded into the human realm and threatens our safety. Afraid that they could not convince the public of the existence of the evil Unknown, the decision was made to turn SAVE into a secret organization to fight the evil. SAVE kept an archive of its activities in Dublin, Ireland.

The early research of SAVE led to its confrontation with vampires in the Pirin Mountains of Bulgaria (1868) and Lucerne, Switzerland (1975). Fighting vampires were a central aspect of SAVE's work. In the 1985 book *Vampires,* by Gali Sanchez and Michael Williams, the *Chill* mythology was continued in a summary of the major cases investigated over the years, in which the goal was the destruction of vampires and vampirelike creatures. The vampires were found in Eastern Europe, the Orient, and Mexico. Gammers are invited to assume the persona of one of the 10 typical vampire types.

The most popular vampire-oriented role-playing game is simply entitled *Vampire.* The game was created by Mark Rein-Hagen and published in 1991 by White Wolf. Its basic myth was called ''The Masquerade'', a secret realm that began with Cain (the biblical character who, in Genesis 4, killed his brother and was afflicted with an undesignated curse). According to the Masquerade, the curse was eternal life and a craving for blood. After wandering in the wilderness for many years, Cain once again lived among mortals and created a city and progeny—a small number of vampires who carried Cain's curse. The city was destroyed, but later generations periodically appeared as a secret force in history. The bulk of existing vampires constitute the sixth generation, and they face pressure to stop creating vampires because it is believed that the vampiric powers diminish as each generation from Cain is created.

The Masquerade myth stated that, beginning in 1435, the Inquisition was able to arrest and kill many of Cain's progeny, "the Kindred." The inquisition stamped out whole bloodlines by burning them. This period of attack drove the vampire community, which had lived somewhat openly on the edge of human society, completely underground. In 1486, at a global convocation, a secret worldwide network was established. It established the law of the Masquerade, an attempt to convince the world that either all vampires were dead or, better still, they never existed. The Masquerade demanded that all vampires make a reasonable effort at secrecy.

The accumulated wisdom of the nearly immortal vampires was given to intelligent mortals who then turned their attention to the development of science and the suppression of superstition. As a result, the early belief in vampires was crushed. The Masquerade, however, was threatened by the mysticism that arose from a combination of forces—the mysticism of psychedelic drugs, new music, and the establishment of the vampire image in popular culture. In the myth, those affected by the new mysticism are ready to believe in the existence of vampires. There is also a generation gap between those vampires who created the Masquerade and understand its necessity and those vampires created in the last century whose brashness, the elder vampires felt, drew unwelcomed attention to the vampire community.

In *Vampire,* the elder vampires had more powers than the younger vampires. Although the stake was hurtful for both old and young, it was not, by itself, fatal. Sunlight and fire were the vampires' greatest dangers. Holy objects had no effect, nor did running water. The vampires had sharpened senses that aided them in hunting—including the power to impose their will on mortals. The elder vampires could even change their forms.

Vampire explained that new vampires could be created by having their blood drained and receiving some of the vampire's blood. The new vampires had slightly less power than the vampires who created them. Vampires no longer breathed, but could fake respiration. Their hearts did not beat. The blood they consumed spread through their bodies by osmosis rather than through arteries or veins. It also carried the necessary oxygen. The vampires' wounds healed quickly, however, the stake produced a form of paralysis.

The vampire in the game moved in the world of mortals very much like historic nobleman hunters moved among beasts in the forest. The worldwide vampire society thus existed as a parallel society beside that of mortals. The vampires were organized into territorial clans ruled by princes. Every major city of the mortal world supported a vampire community and vampires who entered a new city had to present themselves to the powers established there. To simply begin hunting was considered a violation of

METHUSALAH IS A TYPICAL VAMPIRE FROM VAMPIRE THE MASQUERADE, THE ROLE PLAYING GAME FROM
WHITE WOLF.

the vampiric order. The **Camarilla,** the international vampire organization, ruled the city's controlling clan and enforced the Masquerade.

Players of *Vampire* create a character in the imaginary vampire community and gather with others to enact the almost infinite number of possible situations created by the gamemaster/storyteller. The numerous supporting game materials provide profiles of possible vampire characters (although players can and usually do create their own) and suggest possible gaming scenarios (although every game is a unique adventure).

The success of *Vampire* allowed its evolution. In 1993; a live action version of the game, *The Masquerade,* appeared. This version frees the game from the delays caused by the use of dice, which has been replaced with a series of hand signals. The new form of the game allows players to remain in character during virtually all of the game and expands the number of players who can play at one time. A *Vampire* fan club, **The Camarilla,** an organization based on the *Vampire* mythology, provides a national network of gammers.

OTHER VAMPIRE-ORIENTED ROLE-PLAYING GAMES: Although *Vampire* has been (as of the early 1990s) the most popular vampire-oriented role-playing game, it is by no means the only one. Among its competitors is *Vampire Kingdoms* (1991) (created by Kevin Shiembieda), a game within the larger fantasy role-playing world of *Rifts*, published by Palladium Books. *Vampire* centers on life and conflicts within the vampire community, while *Vampire Kingdoms* draws its adventures from the conflicts between vampires and non-vampires, especially Doc Reid and his Vampire Hunters.

According to *Vampire Kingdoms,* there are three varieties of the Undead—master vampires, secondary vampires, and wild vampires—which together form a hierarchy of vampiric life. At the top are the master vampires, which appear most like humans. Secondary vampires are somewhat more savage with pale skin, corpse-like bodies, and strange eyes. They are, however, still able to move in human society on a limited basis. The wild vampires are far more ghoulish in appearance, and with their strange appearance, terrible stench, and obvious wildness, instantly communicate their distinctive threat. In this game, all vampires operate under a super power, the Vampire Intelligence, making them the true Lords of the Undead, described as a monstrous elemental being.

In *Vampire Kingdoms,* since the devastation of the Earth (termed the time of the Rifts), vampires have risen to dominate sections of Mexico, Central America, and South America. Old Mexico City is Vampire Central. The area is organized into a set of vampire kingdoms, tribal groupings, and city states. The Mexico Empire is composed of one vampire intelligence, one master vampire, 1,700 secondary vampires, and some 65,000 humans (the food source). The master vampire runs the kingdom from Mexico City, while the local vampire intelligence lives in Tula, some 70 miles north. Several other vampire kingdoms are also located in the former Mexico.

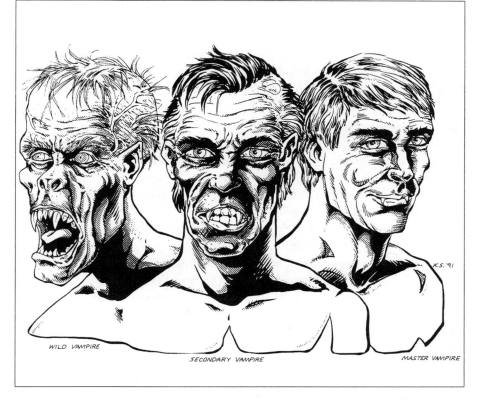

WILD VAMPIRE

SECONDARY VAMPIRE

MASTER VAMPIRE

VAMPIRES OF DIFFERENT TYPES INHABIT THE GAMING WORLD OF *VAMPIRE KINGDOMS.*

Human civilization in *Vampire Kingdoms* is centered in the Midwest. Most of the Southwest is wilderness with a handful of scattered settlements located on the sites of the former cities of El Paso, Houston, or San Antonio. Kenneth Reid and his Vampire Hunting Rangers are headquartered at Fort Reid, in what is now northern Mexico. Reid is a human who has undergone bionic reconstruction. He hates vampires and is committed to destroying them. Because of his bionic component he is immune to being transformed into a vampire. He is helped by a set of super-hero assistants, both humanoid and otherwise. One, Carlotta the White, is a dragon who usually appears in the form of a beautiful woman.

Another game highlighting vampires is *Nightlife* (1990), designed by L. Lee Cerney and Bradley K. McDevitt and published by Stellar Games. *Nightlife* delves into the world of what is termed ''splatterpunk,'' a reality created by combining the ghoulish terror of *Night of the Living Dead* and the rudeness of Punk Rock. David Scrow, who first defined ''splatterpunk'' reality, saw previous attempts at horror as being too polite. It attempted to confront the reader or viewer with the gore and revolting nature of the horror world. At the time as the splatterpunk world was emerging, a modern vampire, usually spelled with a "y" as "vampyre" emerged. This new vampire is sensual, urbane, and the object of sympathy. This type of vampyre appeared in the writing of **Chelsea Quinn Yarbro** and **Anne Rice** and appeared in such movies as **Frank Langella**'s *Dracula* **(1979)** and *The Lost Boys* (1987).

Nightlife fantasizes about characters who live secretly in New York City in the not-too-distant future. The include vampyres, **werewolves,** ghosts, and demons. These "extranatural" creatures together make up the Kin. Their term for humanity is the Herd. In addition to the vampyres who suck human blood, there are several varieties of the Kin that might be termed psychic vampires. The Wyghts and the Animates live on human life energy. Each form of the Kin has special abilities, which they term their "edges." Vampyres can, for example, transform into such various shapes as a bat or a cloud of mist. "Edges" are countered by "flaws," such as the vampyre's problem with sunlight.

In *Nightlife,* vampyres are just one character from among several others. They form the transition to a number of role playing games in which a vampire character is one of many a player might choose. Typical of these games is *Shadowrun* (1989), a game that fantasizes about the year 2050, a time when technology and human flesh have mixed. Humans interface with computers and bionic people are common. In this world, an awakening of the mystical has occurred and magic has returned as a potent force in human life. A variety of creatures, such as elves and trolls, who survived by assuming human form, and have reverted to their more natural appearance. Within this world of human, part human, and other than human life, vampires appear as one of a number of "critters." The vampires are described as diseased humans who have been infected with the Human-Metahuman Vampiric Virus. Vampires consume both the blood and the life energy of their victims.

A recent entry into the role-playing gaming world is ***Bram Stoker's Dracula,*** a vampire game that capitalizes on the popularity of the movie. The game assumes that following Dracula's death, he left behind a brood of newly created vampires that must be tracked down and defeated. Players choose characters and generate that characters' attributes by the throw of the dice. In the game, the vampires have special powers (especially the older ones), but the modern hunter characters have the benefit of high-powered modern weapons—including automatic assault rifles.

COMPUTER GAMES: During the 1980s, games that could be played on a personal computer, especially the several systems that could be connected to a television screen (Nintendo being the most popular) made sizable inroads into the toy market. By the 1990s, retail stores specializing exclusively in computer games were common in urban areas. The first vampire-oriented computer game appears to have been *Elvira, Mistress of the Dark* (produced by Accolade). It appeared in 1990 and won the game of the year award from Computer Gaming World the following year. The game's success led to a sequel, *Elvira: The Jaws of Cerberus* (1992).

In 1993, the world of computer games discovered vampires. Early that year, three new vampire games appeared: *Dracula Unleashed* (Viacom), *Vampire Master of Darkness* (Game Gear), and *Veil of Darkness* (Strategic Simulations). More significant, however, Psygnosis Ltd., a British company, released a game based on *Bram Stoker's Dracula* after nearly two years of development. The game was developed to fit the Mega-CD-Rom system developed by Sega. The system allowed a significant expansion of memory and permitted the inclusion of clips and sound from the film in the game. Versions of the finished game have been released in several formats for various game systems.

Vampire games have provided an alternative avenue for speculation about the meaning of being vampiric. The rules of the games, which in the case of the role-playing games constitute book-length publications, have become a forum where ideas about vampiric existence are tested and bartered. The appearance of the number of games based on the vampire myth symbolizes the renewed enthusiastic level of interest in vampires.

Sources:

Auliffe, Ken R. "Oh, the Horror!" *Garemag* 1, 2 (April/May 1993): Bergstrom, Elaine. *Tapestry of Lost Souls.* Lake Geneva, WI: TSR, Inc., 1993.

"Bram Stoker's Dracula: The Game." *Dracula* (UK) 9 (September 1993): 36-37.

Elrod, P. N. *I, Strahd: The Memoirs of a Vampire.* Lake Geneva, WI: TSR, Inc., 1993. 309 pp.

Findley, Nigel. *Van Richlen's Guide to Vampires.* Lake Geneva, WI: TSR, Inc., 1991. 95 pp.

Golden, Christie. *Vampire of the Mists.* Lake Geneva, WI: TSR, Inc., 1991. 341 pp.

Greenberg, Andrew, et al. *Storyteller's Handbook: The Complete Handbook for Storytellers of Vampire.* Stone Mountain, GA: White Wolf, 1992. 151 pp.

Greenberg, Daniel. *Who's Who Among Vampires: Children of the Inquisition.* Stone Mountain, GA: White Wolf, 1992.

Koke, Jeff. *Gurps Vampire the Masquerade.* N.P.: Steve Jackson Games, 1993. 192 pp.

McDevitt, Bradley K., and L. Lee Cerny. *Nightlife: The Role Playing Game of Urban Horror.* Swanton, OH: Stellar Games, 1990. 3rd ed.: 1992. 256 pp.

Melton, J. Gordon. "Vampire." *Garemag* 1, 5 (October/November/December 1993): 8-15

Nakazono, Barry. *Bram Stoker's Dracula Role Playing Game.* Pasadena, CA: Leading Edge Games, 1993. 182 pp.

Nesmith, Bruce, and Andria Hayday. *Ravenloft.* Lake Geneva, WI: TSR, Inc., 1990. 144 pp.

Rein-Hagen, Mark, et al. *Book of the Damned.* Stone Mountain, GA: White WolfGame Studio, 1993. 138 pp.

———. *Vampire: The Masquerade.* Stone Mountain, GA: White Wolf, 1991. 263 pp.

Sanchez, Gali, and Michael Williams. *Vampires.* Delevan, WI: Pacesetter Limited of Wisconsin, 1985. 96 pp.

"White Wolf Games." *Game Shop News* 16 (April 28, 1993):4-6.

Winninger, Ray. *The Chill Companion.* N.P.: Mayfair Games, 1991. 159 pp.

GARDEN, NANCY (1938-)

Nancy Garden, an author of books for young people, was born in Boston, Massachusetts and attended Columbia University where she received a B.F.A. in 1961 and M.A. the following year. Garden decided to specialize as an author of juvenile literature and, in 1969, became a contributing editor for *Junior Scholastic.* She held various positions as an editor through the mid—1970s, and in 1976 became a free-lance writer.

Garden has been credited with writing the first book introducing young people to vampirology—from folklore to modern presentations of the vampire in books and motion pictures. Following the publication of Garden's *Vampires* in 1973, other writers attempted to write vampire books for young people; although no other works were as substantial as her original. She also explored a number of related subjects such as **werewolves** and witches.

Most of Garden's early volumes were nonfiction, but in the 1980s she began primarily writing fiction. Among her other works are three vampire novels: *Prisoner of Vampires* (1984), *Mystery of the Night Raiders* (1991), and *My Sister, the Vampire* (1992).

Sources:

Garden, Nancy. *My Sister, the Vampire.* New York: Bullseye Books, 1992. 186 pp.

———. *Mystery of the Night Raiders.* (Monster Hunters, Case I). New York Pocket Books, 1991. 167 pp.

———. *Prisoner of Vampires.* New York: Farrar, Straus,1984. 213 pp.

———. *Vampires.* Philadelphia: J. P. Lippencott, 1972.127 pp.

GARLIC

Like the **crucifix,** vampires are believed to have an intense aversion to garlic, and thus people have used garlic to keep vampires away. Introduced into the literary realm in **Bram Stoker**'s novel, garlic became central to the developing vampire myth throughout the twentieth century. Garlic was the first treatment Dr. **Abraham Van Helsing** applied in the case of **Lucy Westenra.** Van Helsing had a box of garlic flowers sent from the Netherlands and decorated Lucy's room with them. He hung them around Lucy's neck and told her that there was much virtue in the little flower. The garlic worked until Lucy's mother, not knowing the flowers' purpose, tore them from her neck.

Garlic was a crucial element in killing the vampire. After driving a **stake** through the vampire's body and removing its head, garlic was placed in the mouth. In fact, this was how Van Helsing finally treated Lucy's body. This treatment was effective, however, only for recently created vampires, because the older ones, (**Dracula** and the three women in **Castle Dracula**), disintegrated into dust once a stake was thrust into their bodies. Stoker got the idea of using garlic following **decapitation** of the vampire from Emily Gerard's *The Land Beyond the Forest.* The book suggested that it was the method employed by Romanians against very obstinate cases of vampirism (i.e., those that had not been cleared up by methods that did not require any mutilation of the body).

Garlic, a member of the lily family, has been used since ancient times as both an herb and a medicine. It developed a reputation as a powerful healing agent, and it was rumored that it possessed some magical powers as a protection agent against the plague and various supernatural evils. In southern Slavic regions, it became known as a potent agent against demonic forces, witches, and sorcerers. The Christian St. Andrew was said to be the donor of garlic to humanity.

In the southern Slavic countries and neighboring **Romania,** garlic was integrated into the vampire myth. It was used in both the detection of and prevention of attacks by vampires. Vampires living incognito in the community could be spotted by their reluctance to eat garlic. In the 1970s, Harry Senn was advised by his Romanian informants that the distribution of garlic during a church service and observing who refused to eat their portion was an acceptable manner of detecting a vampire hidden in the community.

Vampires were especially active in these regions around St. Andrew's Eve and **St. George's Eve.** On those days, windows and other openings in the house were anointed with garlic to keep the vampires away. Cattle might also be given a garlic rubdown. In some communities, garlic was mixed with food and fed to cattle before every important holiday. If a recently deceased person was suspected of vampirism, garlic might be stuffed in the deceased's mouth or placed in the coffin. If detection and the need to destroy a vampire required exhumation of its body, the vampire might face decapitation and garlic might be placed in the mouth or within the coffin.

Garlic was also prominent in Eastern Europe and was served as the most universal protective devise used against vampires and vampiric entities. It appeared in the folklore of **Mexico, South America,** and **China.** Throughout the twentieth century, garlic became one of the most well-known objects associated with vampires. Not a particularly religious symbol, garlic survived while the crucifix slowly disappeared from the list of anti-vampire weapons. On occasion, as in the book and film *The Lost Boys,* the effectiveness of garlic was denied, but more frequently it appeared as a viable vampire detection and/or prevention substance.

Sources:

Lehrer, Ernst, and Johanna Lehner. *Folklore and Odysseys of Food and Medicinal Plants.* New York: Tutor Publishing Company.
Murgoci, Agnes. "The Vampire in Roumania." *Folk-Lore* 27, 5 (1926): 320-49.
Senn, Harry A. *Were-Wolf and Vampire in Romania.* New York: Columbia University Press, 1982. 148 pp.

GAUTIER, THÉOPHILE (1811-1872)

Pierre Jules Théophile Gautier, a French romantic author, was born in southern France, the son of Antoinette Adélaide Cocard and Jean Pierre Gautier. As a child, he read *Robinson Crusoe,* and at school he associated with Gérard de Nerval (later translated *Faust* into French). As a young man, he was affected by E. T. A.

Hoffmann's tales and **Goethe**'s "The Bride of Corinth." Gautier also became associated with the circle of writers around Victor Hugo. Throughout the early 1830s, he frequented a variety of literary gatherings, including one that gathered at the Hotel Pimodan; famous for its indulgence in opium.

A change in family fortune in the 1830s forced Gautier to work as a journalist; and he worked, somewhat unhappily, at it for the rest of his life. He authored thousands of reviews as a literary, theatre, and art critic. Gautier's long hours of work earned little more than a modest living and few honors during his lifetime. Apart from newspaper work, he wrote many romantic stories, although his role in the larger romantic movement was overshadowed by that of Victor Hugo. His own exploration of the psyche, in part stimulated by the use of opium, gained greater acknowledgement in the years since his death, when Gautier finally took his place among France's outstanding nineteenth century writers.

Like the majority of other French romantic writers of note, Gautier found great inspiration in the vampire myth. His earliest and most famous vampire story, *La Morte Amoureuse* (literally, "the dead woman in love") appeared in 1836. An English translation appeared in *The World of Theophile Gautier* in 1907 and was published separately in 1927 as *The Beautiful Vampire*. The story used what was to become a recurring theme in Gautier's fiction. It told of a woman who returned from the dead to vampirize the male subject of the story. In *The Beautiful Vampire,* the dead woman, Clairmonde, made herself so attractive to her male lover, the priest Romuald, that he chose to bleed to death rather than lose her attention.

The theme would reappear, for example in *Aria Marcella,* which was directly inspired by Goethe's "The Bride of Corinth," in which Gautier declared, "No one is truly dead until they are no longer loved." The 1863 novel *The Mummy's Foot* was set among archaeologists in Egypt. In it a mummy, which retained the elasticity of living flesh and had "enamel eyes shining with the moist glow of life," was compared to a vampire lying in its tomb dead . . . yet alive.

Another vampiric story, *Spirite* (1866), used the, then recent, fad of spiritualism as the setting. The story told of a man who experienced both the symbolic and actual death of his love. She first became a nun (and thus died to the world) and then physically died. When the woman took her vows, she gave herself to her love and vowed to be his beyond the grave. Contact was made in a seánce and she ultimately lured the man to his death.

During the last years of his life, Gautier lived in a Paris suburb, where he died from a heart condition in 1872. Most of his romantic tales have been translated into English.

Sources:

Gautier, Théophile. *The Beautiful Vampire.* London: A. M. Philpot, 1927. 110 pp.
————. *Spirite: Nouvelle fantastique.* Paris: Bibliothéque Charpentier, 1967.

Riffaterre, Hermine. "Love-in-Death: Gautier's 'morte amoureuse.'" In *The Occult in Language and Literature.* New York: New York Literary Forum, 1980, pp. 65-74.

Smith, Albert B. *Théophile Gautier and the Fantastic.* Jackson, MS: University Press of Mississippi, 1977.

GERMAIN, ST.

St. Germain, a 4,000-year-old vampire, is the major character in a series of novels by **Chelsea Quinn Yarbro.** He was developed by Yarbro from a historical personage, the Count de St. Germain, an alchemist who lived in eighteenth-century France. The real count was a cultured gentleman who composed music and spoke several languages. A prince from **Transylvania,** his real name apparently was Francis Ragoczy. His money came from international trade, possibly centered on jewels. The few accounts of his life suggested that he was of medium height, wore black and white, rarely ate in public (even at his own parties), claimed extraordinary powers (including an age of several thousand years), and encouraged an aura of mystery about the details of his life. In the historical St. Germain, Yarbro found someone who closely fit her evolving image of what a vampire should be. She made St. Germain her central character by merely using the facts about him in a vampire mythic context.

At the same time, Yarbro was consciously reworking the **Dracula** myth as it had developed through the twentieth century. She approached the vampire logically and saw many problems in the tradition. First, she removed the overlay of medieval Christianity, which left very little "evil" in the vampire's character. In his bite he shared a moment of sexual bliss and had the power to grant a degree of immortality. Second, she decided that the vampire would need to be quite intelligent to survive in what was a hostile environment and would find creative and entertaining ways to spend the centuries of time. Yarbro also found the essence of vampirism to be the act of taking the blood, the intimacy of contact, and the "life" that came from it—rather than the nourishment of the blood's ingredients. Thus the bite became a sexual act.

St. Germain was introduced to the reading public in *Hotel Transylvania* (1978), a novel set in eighteenth-century France. The story is a historical romance concerning the love affair of the alchemist/vampire St. Germain and Madelaine de Montalia. A coven of devil worshippers interfered with the course of their relationship, as it had designs on the young woman for cultic purposes. (Her father had promised Madelaine to them to use as they saw fit.) *Hotel Transylvania* slowly revealed facts about St. Germain, though an alert reader might guess what was coming when, early in the first chapter, he repeated Dracula's famous line, "I do not drink wine."

St. Germain was a vampire, but a vampire of a different breed. In conversation with Madelaine, St. Germain slowly revealed his nature. He was many centuries old. As a vampire he needed only small quantities of blood to survive and would normally take only a wineglass full. Contrary to popular opinion, he was not affected by sacred objects, such as the **crucifix.** He could walk freely on consecrated ground. He was negatively affected by running **water** and **sunlight,** but drew strength from his **native soil.** He had constructed shoes with hollow heels and soles into which he put the earth that countered the effect of running water and allowed him to walk around in daylight.

Among his few superhuman abilities was his **strength,** which he amply demonstrated in his final confrontation with the coven of Satanists.

St. Germain possessed very human emotions, though time had taught him to stay above most affairs of humans. He had developed his own set of morals, especially concerning attacks on individuals for his blood supply. Periodically, however, he had fallen in love, as he did with Madelaine in *Hotel Transylvania.* His love affairs revealed his quite different **sexuality**—while he could participate in most sexual activity, he could not have an erection. The bite, however, was a more than adequate substitute for him and for his sexual partner. Sexual relations were limited in that they could not occur between two vampires. Thus if an affair between a vampire and human progressed to the point that the human became a vampire, the affair would necessarily end. They could and often did remain friends, but the affair was not part of their immortal existence.

The adventures of St. Germain continued in the second and third novels, *The Palace* (1979) and *Blood Games* (1980). In the former he was in fifteenth-century Florence and in the latter in Rome under Nero. In each of these, St. Germain confronted life-and-death experiences that forced discussion of the possibility of the "true death." Vampires could be killed by the severing of the spine (such as when the head is cut off) and by being consumed in fire. Also introduced in these novels was Olivia, his friend through the centuries. Though she first appeared in *The Palace,* the story of her origin was told in *Blood Games.* Her husband had forced her to have relations with many men to feed his voyeuristic desires. Then she met St. Germain, and he arranged for her to escape her husband's power and become a vampire. He created a new vampire by drinking too deeply of someone or allowing them to drink of his blood.

While the origin of St. Germain was never fully revealed, Yarbro did construct a history for him. He was born 4,000 years ago, in what is today Transylvania, of Proto-Etruscan stock. His people had a vampiric priesthood and as he was born in the winter (the dark of the year in agricultural societies), he was initiated into the priesthood. Some details of this priesthood were provided in the *Path of the Eclipse.* The protector god of his people was a vampire, and the priests also were vampires. St. Germain had been initiated, but before he could assume his position, he was captured and taken into slavery. He served very successfully in the army of his captors, for which he was rewarded with execution. St. Germain, however, survived because his executioners did not know they had to either decapitate him or burn his body.

His most recently recounted stories bring him into the twentieth century in Nazi Germany (*Tempting Fate*, 1982) and in various other modern situations (*The Saint-Germain Chronicles*, 1983). Further accounts of his activities are available in the two novels centering on Olivia, his former lover from Rome, *A Flame in Byzantium* (1987) and *Crusader's Torch* (1988).

Sources:

Yarbro, Chelsea Quinn. *Blood Games.* New York: St. Martin's Press, 1980. Reprint. New York: New American Library, 1980. 458 pp.

————. *Crusader's Torch*. New York: Tor Books, 1988. 402pp.

————. *A Flame in Byzantium*. New York: Tor Books, 1987. 470 pp.

————. *Hotel Transylvania*. New York: St. Martin's Press, 1978. 252 pp.

————. *The Palace*. New York: St. Martin's Press, 1979. Reprint. New York: New American Library, 1979. 408 pp.

————. *Path of the Eclipse*. New York: St. Martin's Press, 1981. rept.: New York: New American Library, 1982. 447 pp.

————. *The Saint Germain Chronicles*. New York: Pocket Books, 1983. 206 pp.

————. *Tempting Fate*. New York: St. Martin's Press, 1982. Reprint. New York: New American Library, 1982. 662 pp.

GERMANY, VAMPIRES IN

As among the Slavic peoples of Eastern Europe, the vampire has had a long history in Germany, and the German vampire has closely resembled the **Slavic vampire.** By the tenth century Slavic expansion had reached into the land along the Jeetze River and through the eastern half of Germany. Slavic and Germanic people have mixed together through to the modern era. Thus, vampires in the region were difficult to distinguish from those of their neighbors such as the Kushubian people of northern **Poland.** The most well known of the German vampires was the *Nachtzehrer,* or "night waster," the vampire of northern Germany. The southern German (Bavarian) equivalent was the *Bluatsauger,* literally "bloodsucker," a term used in popular speech to describe disagreeable people. Other literary references to vampires, mostly modern descriptive names, also appear as *Nachttoter* or "night killer" and *Neuntoter* or "killer of nine." Like the Slavic vampire, the *Nachtzehrer* was a revenant (a recently deceased person returned from the grave to attack the living, usually family and village acquaintances).

Also like the Slavic vampire, the *Nachtzehrer* originated from unusual death circumstances. A person who died suddenly from suicide or an accident was a candidate for vampirism. Similar to the *vjesci* of Poland, a child born with a caul (an amniotic membrane that covers the face of some babies) was destined to become a vampire, especially if the caul was red. The *Nachtzehrer* was also associated with epidemic sickness. When a group of people died from the same disease, survivors often identified the first to die as the cause of the other's death. Among the characteristics of the *Nachtzehrer* was the belief that if a person's name was not removed from his or her burial clothing that person might return as a vampire.

In the tomb, *Nachtzehrers* were known for their habit of chewing on their own extremities and clothes (a belief likely derived from the finding of bodies that had been subject to predator damage after being buried in a shallow grave without a **coffin**). Thus, their faces would be intact, but their hands and other appendages would appear cut open and devoured. The activity of the vampire in the grave continued until he ceased consuming his body and his clothes. The vampires would then rise and, like **ghoul**s, eat the bodies of others, often accompanied by the corpse of a woman who had died in childbirth. Their deeds were traced by a sucking sound attributed to the woman nursing a baby. When their **coffins** (those who were wealthy enough to have been buried in one) were opened, the *Nachtzehrers* were found laying in pools of blood, because the vampires gorged themselves to the point that they could not retain all of the blood they had consumed.

To prevent the vampire from attacking, various preventive measures were proposed. Some people placed a clump of earth under the vampires' chins; others placed a coin or stone in their mouths; still others tied a handkerchief tightly around their necks. As a more drastic measure, people cut off the potential *Nachtzehrer*'s head, drove a spike into its mouth to pin the head to the ground, or fixed the tongue into place.

Some belief in the vampire also survived in rural Germany. Affons Schweiggert investigated the *Bluatsauger* of Bavaria in the 1980s. He not only found that the belief in vampires continued to exist, but several unique aspects of that belief existed as well. In appearance, the *Bluatsauger* was pale in color and resembled the description of a zombie.

In Bavarian folklore, people became vampires because they had not been baptized (Bavaria was a heavily Roman Catholic section of Germany), were involved in **witchcraft,** lived an immoral life, or committed **suicide.** They might also have become vampires from eating the meat of an animal killed by a wolf. During the burial process, an animal jumping over the grave might have caused a person to return as a vampire. In like measure, Bavarians reported that a nun stepping over a grave could have the same effect.

If a *Bluatsauger* were loosed upon a community, residents were told to stay inside at night, to smear their doors and windows with **garlic,** and place **hawthorn** around their houses. If members of the community owned a black dog, an extra set of eyes could be painted upon the animal, from whom the vampire would flee. To effectively kill the vampire, a **stake** through the heart and garlic in the mouth were recommended.

THE GREAT VAMPIRE DEBATE: The beliefs and practices in Germany and Eastern Europe concerning vampires became the subject of several books written as early as the seventeenth century (although none used the term "vampire" in its text). Notable treatises included *De Masticatione Mortuorum* (1679) by Philip Rohr, which discussed the eating habits of the *Nachtzehrer,* and Christian Frederic Garmann's *Die Miraculis Mortuorum* (1670). In the early eighteenth century, a flood of reports of Eastern European vampires began to filter into Germany, where they prompted a massive debate in the universities. Although Germany did not escape the vampire hysteria (epidemics were reported in East Prussia in 1710, 1721, and 1750), the vampire issue seems to have been initially raised by the widespread newspaper reports of vampire investigations in Serbia in 1725 and especially the 1731-32 investigation of the **Arnold Paul** case. A popularized version of the Arnold Paul case was a bestseller at the 1732 Leipzig book fair. Helping to initiate the debate were theologian Michel Ranft's *De Masticatione Mortuorum in Tumilis Liber* (1728) and John Christian Stock's *Dissertio de Cadauveribus Sanguisugis* (1732).

The debate centered on various nonsupernatural (or at least nonvampiric) explanations of the phenomena reported by the vampire investigators, especially in the Paul case. Ranft led the attack on the existence of vampires by suggesting that although the dead can influence the living, they could never assume the form of resuscitated corpses. Others assumed that the changes in the corpses (offered as proof of vampirism) could have resulted from perfectly natural alterations due to premature burial, unnaturally well-preserved corpses, or the natural growth of hair and nails after death, plague, and rabies.

The debate resulted in the relegation of the vampire to the realm of superstition and left scholars with only a single relevant question concerning the vampire, "What causes people to believe in such an unreal entity as the vampire?" The primary dissenting voice, which emerged as the German debate was coming to an end, belonged to a French biblical scholar, **Dom Augustin Calmet.** He dissented from his German colleagues simply by leaving the question of the vampire's existence open. Calmet implied the possibility of vampires by suggesting that the very thing that would establish their existence was still lacking: solid proof. Although he did not develop any real argument in favor of vampires, Calmet took the reports very seriously and suggested that vampires were a subject suitable for further consideration by his colleagues. Interestingly enough, while most of the works of his German contemporaries were soon confined to the shelves of a few university libraries, Calmet's work was translated into various languages and reprinted as late as the 1850s.

THE LITERARY VAMPIRE: Germany gave birth to the modern literary vampire. The first modern piece of vampire literature was a short poem, *Der Vampir,* by Heinrich August Ossenfelder (1748). Not strictly a poem about vampires, but highly influential in the development of vampire literature in both Germany and England was "Lenora", the poem about a revenant who returned to claim his love and take her to his grave as his eternal bride. Even more influential to the popularity of the vampire theme was **Goethe**'s poem, "The Bride of Corinth," originally published in 1797. Goethe emerged as the leading literary figure on the continent, and his attention to the vampire theme legitimized it for others.

Like "Lenore," the fantastic tales of E. T. A. Hoffmann (1776-1822) influenced the writers of gothic fiction in general and vampire tales in particular through the nineteenth century. One of his stories, "Aurelia" (1820), published in English under a variety of names, has often been cited as a vampire story, but was in fact about ghouls. There has been some argument that the first German vampire short story may also be the first piece of vampire fiction. An English translation of John Tieck's "Wake Not the Dead" was published in 1823. The German text of Tieck's story was probably written and published in Germany before 1819 (when **John Polidori**'s "The Vampyre" appeared). However, no German text of his story has been located. Tieck's story was notable for featuring a female vampire, Brunhilda, who was brought back to life by Walter, a powerful nobleman. Walter was in love, but awoke one evening to find his wife draining his blood.

During the early nineteenth century—especially after the publication of Polidori's short story "The Vampyre," originally attributed to **Lord Byron,** and Goethe's praise of the story—the vampire gained new life. The immediate contribution of Germany to the spread of Polidori's Byronic vampire was the writing and performance of the vampire opera, *Der Vampyr* (1828) by **Heinrich August Marschner.**

After Marschner, the German literary vampire began to fade rapidly and it has not been a prominent element in German literature since. Only two novels appeared during the early nineteenth century: Theodor Hildebrandt's *Der Vampyr oder die Todtenbraut* (1828) and Edwin Bauer's *Der Baron Vampyr, ein Kulturbild aua der Gegenwart* (1846). In the mid-nineteenth century, one significant item did appear, an anonymous short story, "The Mysterious Stranger" (translation published in England in 1860). The story concerned Azzo van Klatka, a nobleman who lived in the Carpathian Mountains. He attacked the daughter of a neighbor, an Austrian nobleman. She began to weaken and had wounds on her neck. Meanwhile, von Kaltka grew younger. In the end, the victim was forced to drive nails in the vampire's head to kill him.

Elements of "The Mysterious Stranger" were echoed in **Bram Stoker's** *Dracula.* The story opened with a knight (like Stoker's character **Jonathan Harker**) traveling into the strange territory of the Carpathian Mountains. They were impressed by the picturesque scenery. Suddenly, the knight and his family were startled by the appearance of wolves, but the "stranger" calmed and commanded them (as did Dracula). The stranger was discovered to live entirely on liquids and appear only in the daytime. Eventually, he was discovered sleeping in an open coffin in a ruined chapel below the castle. One character in the story, Woislaw, an older man who was quite knowledgeable about vampires, may also have inspired Stoker's vampire hunting character **Abraham Van Helsing.**

THE CINEMATIC VAMPIRE: Germany reemerged as an important locale of the developing vampire myth in the early twentieth century. In 1922 Prana Films released *Nosferatu, Eine Symphonie des Garuens* directed by Freidrich Wilhelm Murnau. *Nosferatu* was a greatly disguised but recognizable movie adaptation of *Dracula.* It was screened only once before Stoker's widow, Florence, charged Prana Films with literary theft. Meanwhile, as she pursued the case, the financial instability of Prana Films forced it into a receivership. After three years of litigation, Stoker finally won the case and all copies of the film were ordered to be destroyed. In recent years, *Nosferatu* was hailed as one of the great films of German expressionism and the silent era. However, it could be argued that it had only a minimal role in the development of the modern vampire. The few copies that survived were hidden and not seen by audiences until the 1960s. By then, Florence Stoker was dead and both the **Bela Lugosi** and **Christopher Lee** versions of *Dracula* were already finished.

Although *Nosferatu* remains the most famous German vampire film, Germany has given the public a number of other important cinematic treatments of the subject. The German vampire emerged in the 1960s in a series of forgettable films including *Cave of the Living Dead* (1964), *Blood Suckers* (1966), and *The Blood Demon* (1967) with **Christopher Lee.** The 1964 movie *The Vampire of Düsseldorf* told the story of **Peter Kürten,** a true life serial murderer who drank the blood of his victims. It was followed in 1962 by *Tenderness of Wolves* (1973), which treated the vampiric/ghoulish murders of **Fritz Haarmann,** who had murdered some 25 boys and consumed their blood.

During the 1970s, Germany was the location for two of the most unique and thoughtful vampire films. *Jonathan* (1970) used vampirism as a parable for the rise of fascism. *Martin* (1976) explored the life of a young, sophisticated vampire who moved from biting to using a razor blade and syringe. Other more recent German vampire movies include *The Werewolf vs. the Vampire Woman* (1970), *The Vampire Happening* (1978), and *A Lovely Monster* (1991).

THE TWENTIETH CENTURY LITERARY VAMPIRE: During the last two decades, Germany provided a fruitful environment for the vampire novel. The country has been an ever present element of horror literature, and numerous vampire short stories appeared in Germany's several horror-fiction magazines. Throughout the 1970s and 1980s, a host of contemporary popular fiction writers mined the vampire cave of legend. They were led by Jason Dark, who wrote more than 300 popular novels including some 20 featuring Dracula and other vampires. His vampire books were published in a series of horror books by Bastei-Lübbe Verlag at Bergisch Gladbach. Frederic Collins, who had also written several vampire novels, was the editor of the series. Among the writers who also developed multiple vampire novels for Bastei-Lübbe were Brian Elliot, Robert Lamont, Frank de Lorca, A. F. Morland, Mike Shadow, and Earl Warren. Zauberkreis-Verlag and Pabelhaus, both publishers located in Rastatt, also released a set of vampire titles in a horror book series. Among the more popular writers for Zauberkreis-Verlag were Maik Caroon, Roger Damon, Marcos Mongo, Dan Schocker, John Spider, and W. J. Tobien. Pabelhaus writers included James R. Buchette, Neal Davenport, Frank Sky, and Hugh Walker. The majority of German vampire novels have been published by these three publishing companies.

In the 1990s, Germany has been participating in the current revival of interest in vampires. Both vampire novels and **comic book**s abound, and the vampire has been found on greeting cards and in advertisements. Especially noticeable has been the original **juvenile literature** on vampires, and among children's authors, Angela Sommer-Bodenburg has emerged as an international favorite. Her series of children's novels starring Tony Noodleman and his vampire friend Rudolph, have been translated into English and published in both England and the United States.

Sources:

Barber, Paul. *Vampires, Burial, and Death: Folklore and Reality.* New Haven, CT: Yale University Press, 1988. 236 pp.

"Bluatsauger." *International Vampire* 11, 1993.

Hock, Stefan. *Die Vampyrsagen und ihre Verwertung in der deutschen Literatur.* Berlin: Alexander Duncker, 1900.

Jones, Stephen. *The Illustrated Vampire Movie Guide.* London: Titan Books, 1993. 144 pp.

Moore, Steven. *The Vampire in Verse: An Anthology.* Chicago: Adams Press, 1985. 196 pp.

Prussmann, Karsten. *Die Dracula-Filme*. München, Germany: Wilhelm Heyne Verlag, 1993. 287 pp.
Schroeder, Aribert. *Vampirismus*. Frankfurt am Main: Akademische Verlagsgesellschaft, Studienreihe Humanitas, 1973.

GHOULS

The ghoul, a traditional monster frequently associated with the **vampire,** originated as part of Arabic folklore. It played a part in several tales in the *Arabian Knights.* Ghouls represented a more demonic aspect of the world of jinns, the spirits of Arabic mythology. The Arabic *ghul* (masculine) and *ghulah* (feminine) lived near graves and attacked and ate human corpses. It was also believed that ghouls lived in desolated places where they would attack unsuspecting travelers who mistook the ghoul for a traveling companion and were led astray. Ghul-I- Beában was a particularly monstrous ghoul believed to inhabit the wilderness of Afghanistan and Iran. Marco Polo, reflecting on the accounts of ghouls he heard during his travels, suggested that ghouls, gryphons (an imaginary animal), and good faith were three things people frequently referred to but did not exist.

The ghoul returned to popular culture in the twentieth century through a multitude of monster movies. New ghouls were similar to vampires in that they were reanimated dead people in humanoid form. The ghoul, however, ate human flesh, while the vampire drank blood. The ghoul also acted with neither a will nor intellect, and seemed to have somewhat derived from the zombie—the figure in Haitian folklore reportedly brought back to life by magic and destined to work in the service of the person who brought it back to ''life.''

One nineteenth century case, that of Francois Bertrand, was a popular example of ghoulish behavior. Bertrand, a noncommissioned officer in the French Army, was arrested after he entered and desecrated several tombs in Paris. He was convicted and sentenced to a lengthy term in prison in 1849 after confessing to an overwhelming compulsion to tear the corpses of women and girls to pieces. His story later became the basis of a popular novel, *The Werewolf of Paris* by Guy Endore.

Modern ghouls, really a ghoul/zombie mixture, made definitive appearances in two movies directed by George Romero: *Night of the Living Dead* (1968) and *Dawn of the Dead* (1979). Romero acknowledged that the numerous vampires of **Richard Matheson**'s 1954 novel, *I Am Legend,* inspired his ''living dead.'' *Night of the Living Dead* pictured the dead returning to life by some form of radiation and eating their fellow humans. The ghouls walked slowly, were limited in their actions, and were destroyed by a bullet or sharp blow to the head. Although they could be killed relatively easily, in packs they could simply overwhelm individuals and small groups, such as those trapped in the farm house in the movie. *Night of the Living Dead* and *Dawn of the Dead* seemed to have inspired a group of Italian movies featuring a variation on Romero's ghoul/zombie as exemplified in Umberto Lenzi's *City of the Walking Dead* (1983).

Sources:

Barber, Richard, and Anne Riches. *A Dictionary of Fabulous Beasts.* New York: Walker and Company, 1971. 167 pp.

Russell, W. M. S., and Claire Russell. "The Social Biology of Werewolves." In J. R. Porter and W. M. S. Russell. *Animals in Folklore.* Totowa, NJ: Rowman & Littlefield, 1978, 143-182.

Waller, George A. *The Living and the Undead: From Stoker's Dracula to Romero's Dawn of the Dead.* Urbana, IL: University of Illinois press, 1986. 378 pp.

GLUT, DONALD FRANK (1944-)

Donald Frank Glut, author and editor of vampire books, was born in Pecos, Texas, the son of Julia and Frank C. Glut. He attended DePaul University for two years (1962-64) and completed his B.A. (1967) at the University of Southern California. Following his graduation, Glut launched a career as a writer and, during the intervening quarter century, has produced numerous horror titles, especially around the **Frankenstein** and **Dracula** themes. Throughout the early 1970s, he authored a series of Frankenstein books including *Frankenstein Lives Again* (Spanish ed. 1971; English ed. 1977), *Terror of Frankenstein* (Spanish ed. 1971; English ed. 1977) and *The Frankenstein Legend: A Tribute to Mary Shelley and Boris Karloff* (1972).

In 1972, Glut produced his first vampire book, *True Vampires of History*. It proved a landmark volume—the first to bring together the accounts of all real (as opposed to legendary) vampires in what was an historical narrative. He followed in 1975 with *The Dracula Book*, a monumental bibliographical work on the character of Dracula as he appeared in the different media, such as books, comics, stage, and film. It was awarded the Montague Summers Award by **The Count Dracula Society,** and became the foundation of all future vampire bibliographical and movie research. In 1977, he brought together his two primary loves in a novel, *Frankenstein Meets Dracula* (German edition, 1980).

During the 1970s, Glut contributed articles to numerous comic books including *Eerie, Ghost Rider, The Occult Files of Dr. Spektor,* and *Vampirella.* He created the vampire character Baron Tibor, who appeared in several stories in *The Occult Files of Dr. Spektor.* His novelization of *The Empire Strikes Back* earned him the Galaxy award in 1980.

Glut continued his interest in Frankenstein and produced *The Frankenstein Catalog* (1984), an updated edition of his prior bibliographical work. He also pursued an interest in dinosaurs and has authored a number of titles on that topic, beginning with *The Dinosaur Dictionary* (1972). In the early 1990s, he began compiling an encyclopedic work on dinosaurs.

Sources:

Glut, Donald F. *The Dracula Book.* Metuchen, NJ: Scarecrow Press, 1975. 388 pp.

———. *Frankenstein Meets Dracula.* London: New English Library, 1977. 140 pp.

◀

DONALD F. GLUT, NOTED
VAMPIRE EXPERT.

————. *True Vampires of History.* New York: H CPublishers, 1971. 191 pp.

GOETHE, JOHANN WOLFGANG VON (1749-1832)

Johann Wolfgang von Goethe, Germany's most renown man of letters, was born in Frankfurt am Main the son of Katherine Elisabeth Textor and Johann Kaspar Goethe. He entered the University of Leipzig in 1765 to study law. While there, however, he found he was more interested in art and drama and wrote his first plays shortly before a hemorrhage forced his return home in 1768. Goethe finished his law studies at Strasborg in 1771 and established a practice in Frankfurt. These years became a period of intense change in Goethe's world and the beginning of the amazing literary productivity that characterized his life.

In the early 1770s, Goethe began work on *Faust,* the work for which he is most remembered. In fact, he worked on it for much of his life. In 1775, he moved to Weimar at the invitation of Duke Karl August. Although he intended to only stay a few months, he resided there for the rest of his life. In 1784 Goethe began his association with Friedreich Schiller at the University of Jena. The two embarked on a conscious program to give German literature a new degree of seriousness and purpose, a program that met with a remarkable level of success. Goethe's 1796 novel *Wilhelm Meisters Lehrjahre* has been described as the most influential work of fiction in German literature. He completed Part I of *Faust* in 1806 and saw its publication two years later.

Although not a romantic, Goethe was the idol of the emerging German romantic movement and his influence was felt by romantics throughout Europe. One element in their appreciation was his 1797 poem, "The Bride of Corinth." It was one of the earliest modern ventures into **poetry** based on the vampire theme. Often mistakenly cited as being based on a story in Philostratus, the *Life of Apollonius of Tynana,* the poem was in fact based on another story from ancient **Greece** recounted by Phlegon. In it a young woman, Philinnon, returned from the dead to be with her love, Machates.

In his lifetime, Goethe emerged as the most respected man of letters in nineteenth-century Europe. Thus his involvement in the controversy surrounding the publication of the first vampire novella in 1816 was of importance. In that year, **"The Vampyre"**, appeared in a London magazine under the name of **Lord Byron.** Even before Byron could issue a denial of his connection to the story that was actually written by **John Polidori,** Goethe declared it Byron's greatest work. Goethe, therefore, inadvertently lent his prestige to the erroneous ascription of Polidori's tale to Byron, especially in nonEnglish speaking lands. As late as 1830, it was included in the French edition of Byron's collected works.

In the 1820s, Goethe began work on the second part of Faust, which was completed in 1831. He died the following year.

Sources:

Frayling, Christopher. *Vampyres: Lord Byron to Count Dracula.* London: Faber and Faber, 1991. 429 pp.

GOOD GUYS WEAR FANGS

Good Guys Wear Fangs is an annual vampire fanzine dedicated to what founder/ editor Mary Ann B. McKinnon terms "good guy" vampires. In the mid-1970s, McKinnon, never a horror fan, discovered the novels of **Chelsea Quinn Yarbro,** whose vampire character, **St. Germain,** was a romantic hero. McKinnon considered Yarbro an isolated author and enjoyed most of her novels as they continued to appear through the 1980s. It was not until 1989, when she saw the made- for-TV movie *Nick Knight,* and later the two *To Die For* movies, that McKinnon developed some hope that other good guy vampire fiction existed. She decided to announce the development of a fanzine based on the theme of the vampire as a hero. The response to her announcement showed the vast interest and supporting material for her approach to vampirism.

The first copy of the 300-page *Good Guys Wear Fangs* appeared in 1992. It featured original short stories and poetry in which the vampire was the hero. By this time, ***Forever Knight,*** the television series that grew out of the *Nick Knight* televison movie, was airing on CBS late night television. The Nick Knight character was featured in *Good Guys Wear Fangs.* In 1993, McKinnon added a related periodical, *The Good Guy Vampire Letterzine*, a newsletter for good guy vampire fans. *The Letterzine* kept fans aware of newly discovered good guy vampire fiction and movies, and carried an ongoing discussion of the nature of good guy vampirism.

Fiction writer **Margaret L. Carter,** a regular contributor to *Good Guys Wear Fangs,* defined good guy vampires as vampires who acted morally when dealing with mortals, and, as a whole, conformed their moral perspective to a human ethical perspective. They obtained blood without killing or "raping" their victims. Good guy vampires got their blood from animals, blood banks, or from willing human donors. A few used synthetic blood substitutes. Carter also noted that the good guy vampires retained personality and freedom of choice, and were not so consumed with blood lust that ethical decisions become impossible. Good guy vampires tended to emerge in one of two situations. First, they were basically good people who discovered themselves trapped in the evil condition—vampirism—and were forced to continually fight against it. Second, vampirism was pictured as an ethically neutral state, in which vampires could make ethical decisions on how to find their needed sustenance ... blood.

McKinnon encouraged not only completely original fiction but new stories that featured popular characters from television and the movies. By far the most popular character who appeared in *Good Guys Wear Fangs* was Nick Knight, but other stories have featured Starsky & Hutch, Columbo, Robin of Sherwood, and ***Dark Shadows.*** McKinnon also produced a line of fanzines that included storylines built around the popular fictional characters Zorro, the Highlander, and Robin of Sherwood.

Good Guys Wear Fangs and *The Good Guy Vampire Letterzine* can be contacted c/o Mary Ann B. McKinnon, 254 Blunk Ave., Plymouth, MI 48170.

Sources:

Carter, Margaret L. "What Is a Good Guy Vampire?" *Good Guys Wear Fangs* 1 (May 1992): vi-ix.
Good Guys Wear Fangs. No. 1- . Plymouth, MI: Mary Ann B. McKinnon, 1992- .
The Good Guy Vampire Letterzine. No. 1- . Plymouth, MI: Mary Ann B. McKinnon, 1992- .

GOTHIC

In literature, the term "gothic" refers to a particular form of the popular romantic novel of the eighteenth century. Gothic novels continued to appear in the nineteenth century and have reemerged in strength as part of the paperback revolution of the last half of the twentieth century. Elizabeth MacAndrew approached the essence of the gothic experience by defining it as the literature of the nightmare. Gothic literature evolved out of explorations of the inner self, with all of its emotive, nonrational, and intuitive aspects. Thus it emerged as a form of romanticism, but confronted the darker, shadowy side of the self. At its best, gothic works force the reader to consider all that society calls evil in human life.

Gothic novels called into question society's conventional wisdom, especially during the post-Enlightenment period when special emphasis was placed on the rational, orderliness, and control. Gothic authors have challenged the accepted social and intellectual structures of their contemporaries by their presentation of the intense, undeniable, and unavoidable presence of the nonrational, disorder, and chaos. These are most often pictured as uncontrollable forces intruding from the subconscious in the form of supernatural manifestations of the monstrous and horrendous. Gothic literature, as Thompson noted, imposed a sense of *dread.* It created a complex mixture of three distinct elements: *terror,* the threat of physical pain, mutilation, and/or death; *horror,* the direct confrontation with a repulsive evil force or entity; and the *mysterious,* the intuitive realization that the world was far larger than our powers of comprehension could grasp.

To accomplish its self-assigned task, gothic literature developed a set of conventions. Generally, action was placed in out-of-the-ordinary settings. Its very name was taken from the use of medieval settings by its original exponents, stereotypically an old castle. The most dramatic sequences of the story tended to occur at night and often during stormy weather. Integral to the plot, the characters attempted to function amid an older but disintegrating social order. It was a literary devise that subtly interacted with the reader's own sense of disorder. The energy of the story often relied on the combined attack on the naive innocent and the defenders of the present order by momentarily overwhelming and incomprehensible supernatural forces in the form of ghosts, monsters, or human agents of Satan.

THE ORIGINS OF THE GOTHIC AND THE VAMPIRE: Gothic fiction generally dated from the 1763 publication of *The Castle of Otranto* by British writer Horace Walpole (1717-1797). The tale described the interaction of the descendants of Aphonse the Good, a twelfth century ruler of a small Italian state. His heirs, both the good and the bad, joined some innocent bystanders in struggles to attain their personal goals, only to be diverted by the ghosts that haunted their castle. The success of Walpole's novel inspired other writers to explore the gothic world. Most notable among those authors was Ann Radcliffe, who was often credited with developing the gothic novel into a true literary form through her novels *The Castles of Athlin and Dunbayne* (1789), *A Sicilian Romance* (1790), *The Romance of the Forest* (1791), *The Mysteries of Adolpho* (1794), and *The Italian* (1797).

The popularity of the gothic novel directly led to the famous 1816 gathering of **Lord Byron,** Percy and Mary Shelley, and **John Polidori** in Switzerland. Each was invited to wait out the stormy weather by writing and reading a ghost story to the others. Mary Shelley's contribution was the seed from which *Frankenstein* would grow. Byron wrote a short story that Polidori would later turn into the first modern vampire tale. The effect of the storm was heightened by the group's consumption of laudanum. This typified the role of various consciousness-altering drugs played in stimulating the imagination of romantic authors. The use of laudanum, opium, and/or cocaine produced a dreamlike state so prized by poets and fiction writers of the era that they defined it as the epitome of the creative moment. It also occasionally induced nightmares and encouraged the exploration of the darker side of consciousness.

Once introduced, the vampire became a standard theme in gothic romanticism, especially in France. Leading the French exploitation of the vampire was **Charles Nodier.** However, virtually every romantic writer of the nineteenth century from **Samuel Taylor Coleridge** to **Edgar Allan Poe** ultimately used either the vampire or a variation on the vampiric relationship in his or her work. Gothic fiction reached a high point in 1897 with the publication of the great vampire novel, *Dracula.* Like Polidori, Stoker brought the Gothic into the contemporary world; but Stoker developed his themes far beyond Polidori. *Dracula* played on traditional gothic themes by placing its opening chapters in a remote castle. Contemporary Transylvania (like contemporary Greece in Polidori's story) replaced the older use of medieval settings and effectively took the reader to a strange pre-modern setting. However, Stoker broke convention by bringing the gothic world to the contemporary familiar world of his readers and unleashed evil from a strange land on a conventional British family. Neither the ruling powers, a strong heroic male, nor modern science could slow, much less stop, the spread of that evil. Except for the intervention of the devotee of nonconventional and supernatural wisdom (**Abraham Van Helsing**), the evil would have spread through the very center of the civilized but unbelieving world with impunity. Eventually, of course, Van Helsing was able to organize all the forces of good, including the necessary implements of what most considered an obsolete religion, to defeat Dracula.

Throughout the twentieth century, the vampire developed a life of its own. It flew far beyond the realm of the gothic, although it regularly returned to its gothic romantic home. The gothic vampire survived in novels and films, from *Dracula* **(1931)** to the horror features of **Hammer Films.** The genre experienced a notable revival in the 1960s through the television soap opera *Dark Shadows. Dark Shadows'* success and the continued attention given to its basic myth vividly demonstrated the more permanent appeal of gothic realities in contemporary life. *Dark Shadows* was set in the late twentieth century, but action centered on an old mansion in a remote corner of rural New England. Its main characters were members of an old aristocratic family, the Collins, who symbolized the establishment under attack by the hippie subculture of the time. Vampire **Barnabas Collins** and the accompanying supernatural horde that descended on the Collins family, seemed most analogous to the chaotic youthful uprising that was emerging in the very homes of the West's ruling elites.

THE NEW GOTHIC MOVEMENT: Heir to the gothic tradition, mixed with elements from the psychedelic/flower child/rock music subcultures of the 1960s and 1970s, was the gothic counter-cultural movement that appeared in most urban centers of the West during the 1980s. The movement's origins can be traced to late 1970s musical groups in the United Kingdom. It certainly also had its direct precursors in such bands as Black Sabbath and the punk rock music of the 1970s. Possibly the most prominent of those groups was Bauhaus, a rock band formed in 1978. In the following year, the band released the single "Bela Lugosi's Dead," their most popular recording to date. The song was picked up in 1983 for use in the opening sequence of the film version of Whitley Strieber's *The Hunger.* Bauhaus was soon joined by such groups as Siouxsie and the Banshees, The Cult, The Cure, and The Sisters of Mercy. Together these bands created a variant music called gothic rock or death rock. A circuit of music clubs, most notably The Bat Cave in London, opened to provide a stage for their performances.

Gothic music, as all counter-cultural forms, articulated an explicit nonconformist stance vis-a-vis the dominant establishment. It opposed narrow sexual mores and traditional established religions. High priests, churches, and congregations were replaced with rock musicians, night clubs, and fans. The music celebrated the dark, shadowy side of life and had a distinct fascination with death. Its slow, driving sound was frequently described as melancholy, gloomy, even morbid. Those enthralled by the new gothic culture found the vampire the single most appropriate image for the movement. Both men and women dress in black. Men seem to be perpetuating vampiric images from **Anne Rice** novels, while women perpetuate what, at first glance, seems to be the persona of Morticia Addams of *The Addams Family,* **Vampira,** and **Elvira,** although some aim for a more Victorian funereal style or a modern vampish look. Vampires, blood and fangs, and bats fill the pages of gothic magazines, whether or not vampirism is discussed.

The movement was especially popular in the early 1980s when it spread to the European continent and throughout North America. By the middle of the decade, however, it showed a marked decline in England. Bauhaus disbanded in 1983, although some of its members reformed as Love & Rockets. Most of the clubs that had provided meeting places for gothic aficionados turned their attention to other new trends in popular music, and The Bat Cave closed. To keep the movement alive when the media announced its obituary, one gothic band, Nosferatu, founded **The Gothic Society** (136 Canterbury Rd., Harrow, Middlesex HA1 4PB, England) and the periodical *Grimoire*, which became the new center of a network of bands and fans. Curve, Rosetta Stone, Mortal Coil, Wraith, and Slimelight joined Nosferatu as bands of the gothic scene.

Even as the movement was suffering in England, it was experiencing the early stages of its emergence in the United States. By 1990, a number of gothic bands traveled a circuit of clubs, and fans kept up with the movement through their own fanzines. *Propaganda* (PO Box 296, New Hyde Park, NY 11040) was the first of the gothic fanzines to hit the newsstands and offer national (and international) coverage to the emerging gothic movement. Founded by "Propaganda Minister" Fred H. Berger, *Propaganda* provided some structure for "the Underground," as the new gothic subculture referred to itself. The magazine publicized many gothic bands and personalities and provided advertising space for both gothic records and the variety of clothing, jewelry, and paraphernalia demanded by devoted fans. More recently, it produced two gothic videos, *The Trilogy* and *Blood Countess,* the second based upon the life of **Elizabeth Bathory.**

TARA BAI OF *PROPAGANDA* MAGAZINE.

In 1992, *Propaganda* was joined on the West Coast by the slick Los Angeles-based magazine *Ghastly*. The magazine is published by Nosferatu Productions (PO Box 3535, Hollywood, CA 90078) and edited by Tara and Jeremy Bai. More so than *Propaganda,* Nosferatu Productions markets the gothic subculture through a mail order catalog that includes gothic fanzines, compact disc (cd's) and cassettes, cosmetics, clothing, and even condoms. Nosferatu has also launched two additional periodicals: *The Oracle*, a monthly newsletter that updates readers on show dates and the latest releases on cd; and *The Cabala*, a fan networking journal.

During the last few years, fans around the United States have created a host of gothic fanzines that service the growing gothic community, including *The Black Chronicle* by Necronomicon Publishers (6312 E. Santa Ana Canyon Blvd., No. 112, Anaheim Hills, CA 92807), *Dark Arts* (230 S. 600 E., Salt Lake City, UT 84102), *Delirium* (779 Riverside Dr., No. A-11, New York, NY 10032), *Dysmetria* (1262 Mulberry Ave., Atwater, CA 95301), *Elegia: A Journey Into the Gothic* (3116 Porter Ln., Ventura, CA 93003), *Esoterra* (2116 Guadalupe, No. 114, Austin, TX 78705), *La Noire D'Immortality* (912 Bidwell St., Folson, CA 95630), *Machine Gun Etiquette* (13 Church St., No. 6, Milford, MA 01757), *Permission* (3023 N. Clark, Ste. 777,

Chicago, IL 60657), *Terra-X* (34159 Gem Circle, North Ridgeville, OH 44039), *Theatre of the Night*, and *Virtue et Morte* (PO Box 6113, Philadelphia, PA 19114). Gothic enthusiasts in Canada can join the **Gothic Society of Canada,** headquartered in Toronto.

Second only to the bands in defining the gothic world are several gothic writers. The most notable being Poppy Z. Brite, the author of the novel *Lost Souls,* and Lydia Lunch, an author and recording artist. Among Lunch's recent writings is a vampire **comic book,** *Bloodsucker* (Eros Comics, 1992). *Nights' Children*, the independent comic art of **Wendy Snow-Lang** also circulates freely through the gothic subculture.

The majority of large urban centers in the United States now have at least one nightclub that regularly features gothic music. Many clubs schedule gothic nights once or twice a week and devote other evenings to closely related music such as punk or industrial rock.

A large number of contemporary bands play gothic music. Some of the more well-known are Ministry, Shadow Project, Christian Death, This Ascension, The Shroud, and Death in June. Several bands have adopted specifically vampiric images, including Astro Vamps, Lestat, Neither/Neither World, London After Midnight, and Transvision Vamp. In addition, individual musicians have adopted a stage persona tieing them to the vampiric image. They include Eva Van Helsing of The Shroud and Vlad of Nosferatu. Toney Lestat of Wreckage claims to have met the real vampire **Lestat de Lioncourt,** the character featured in the vampire novels of Anne Rice. Toney Lestat adopted his name after Rice made the Lestat character famous.

THE ATMOSPHERIC GOTHIC WORLD: Integral to the contemporary gothic world is the dark and eerie atmosphere surrounding those who inhabit it. The presence of that atmosphere, initially created by the music and the decor of the nightclubs, has been furthered by the appearance of the bands and copied by the members of their audiences. Commonly, clothing is black, loose fitting, and revealing, though tight-fitting leather is an acceptable alternative. Hair, if combed, tends to be uncurled, razor cut, and either black or starkly blonde. Accessories include chain mail and symbolic jewelry (ankhs, crosses, and daggers). Dark clothing combined with pale make-up and dark lipstick presents an overall image of death. A variety of specialty enterprises have arisen to supply the necessary clothing and accessories for the gothic public. Siren, a gothic shop in Toronto, is the oldest retailer of gothic clothing, jewelry, and accessories in North America.

Anne Rice's The Vampire Chronicles emerged as popular reading material in the gothic world and her leading character Lestat the ideal to emulate. Rice described Lestat as essentially an androgynous being—and for many an essential aspect of the gothic image is androgyny, an ideal of wholeness in which one part of a duality encompasses its opposite. Androgyny can be said to exist when light accepts darkness or pleasure recognizes the role of pain, but is most commonly presented as individuals blur the social distinctions between what is masculine and feminine. Many members of the gothic bands, especially the males, present a stage persona that make it difficult for the audience to immediately identify them as male or female and choose names

JEREMY OF *PROPAGANDA* MAGAZINE.

with either no gender identification or an opposite one. The androgynous theme was an element present in such pre- gothic rock groups as Twisted Sister and KISS.

As a secondary theme, based in part upon the androgynous ideal, the gothic world has continued a self-conscious critique of the dominant sexual mores of late twentieth century society. This critique was also present in previous movements such as punk rock. It has been reflected in the names of several gothic bands such as the Andi Sex Gang and Sex Gang Children. Some have noticed that the androgynous ideal (as articulated by Rice and embodied most forcefully in her male characters) supported and was, in many ways, indistinguishable from the value system of the gay community. The homosexual aspect of the gothic world has been presented most clearly in Poppy Z. Brite's writing.

Beyond just a demand for sexual freedom or the acceptance of homosexuality, some gothic music and literature has also argued for the destruction of the taboos that surround sado-masochism (an essentially androgynous activity that explores the pleasure of pain), fetishism, bondage, and all sexual activities still considered perverted even by many who consider themselves otherwise sexually liberated. Among the bands most focused on this sexual message is Sleep Chamber, led by John Zewizz. Zewizz has argued that these various forms of sexual activity, among the most threatening and misunderstood by the general public, are merely a form of sexual foreplay and, alone, of harmless and pleasure-producing. Several periodicals focus on this aspect of the gothic world, most prominently *Blue Blood* (14207 Chesterfield Rd., Rockville, MD 20853) and *Euronymous Future Sex* (PO Box 5334, Atlanta, GA 30307).

Possibly the most extreme element of the gothic scene is its celebration of death. The most extreme expression of this is found in the writing and activity of Leilah Wendell. Wendell began serious study of metaphysics early in life and made her discovery of a new and positive relationship with death, described as being in love with the Angel of Death (the personification of death). As early as the mid-1970s, she edited an underground periodical titled *Undinal Songs* that explores this view of death and her relationship with Azrael, the name she gave the Angel of Death. In 1983, *Undinal Songs* was superseded by The Westgate Group (a publishing house, art studio, and information service) and the following year Wendell opened Westgate Gallery on Long Island. A decade of work that described encounters with the Angel of Death and similar shadowy entities led to the 1988 publication of *The Book of Azrael* (one of nine books by Wendell). Wendell argues that coming to see life through the eyes of the Angel of Death allows one to develop a proper perspective on both life and death. In 1990, Wendell moved to New Orleans where she operates The Westgate (5219 Magazine St., New Orleans, LA 70115), a gallery, bookstore, and a major center of gothic culture in the South. She publishes a newsletter, *The Azrael Project*, through which a national necromantic network has been created and is nurtured.

CONCLUSION: The world of vampire enthusiasts fades imperceptibly into that of the gothic subculture. They support each other, although the mainstream of vampire fandom would not share the gloomy atmosphere that pervades the gothic world. Between the two communities, the observer can see the wide variation in the vampire's role in the lives of different people.

Sources:

Bevington, Gregory. "All Aboard the Ghost Train: An Interview with Tony Lestat." *Ghastly* 2 (1992); 24-26.

Brite, Poppy Z. *Lost Souls*. New York: Delacorte Press, 1992. Reprint. New York: Dell, 1993. 355 pp.

Duncan, Michelle. "Nosferatu: The Vampire's Cry." *Propaganda* 19 (1992): 8-10.

Hart, Paul. "Murphy on Bauhaus: Interview with the Vampire." *Propaganda* 20 (1993): 8-11.

MacAndrew, Elizabeth. *The Gothic Tradition in Fiction*. New York: Columbia University Press, 1979. 289 pp.

Mercer, Mick. *Gothic Rock*. Birmingham, UK: Pegesus Publishers, 1991. 178 pp.

———. *Gothic Rock: Black Book*. London: Omnibus Press, 1988. 95 pp.

Praz, Mario. *The Romantic Agony*. London: Oxford University Press, 1970.

Thompson, G. R. "Introduction: Romanticism and the Gothic Tradition." In G. R. Thompson, ed. *The Gothic Imagination: Essays in Dark Romanticism*. Pullman, WA: Washington State University Press, 1974.

Wendell, Leilah. *The Book of Azrael*. New York: WestgatePress, 1988, 217 pp.

———. *Infinite Possibilities*. Center Moriches, NY: Westgate Press, 1987. 78 pp.

THE BAND NOSFERATU HELPED REVIVE THE BRITISH GOTHIC SCENE BY FOUNDING THE GOTHIC
SOCIETY.

————. *The Necromantic Ritual Book.* New Orleans: Westgate Press, 1991. 50 pp.
————. *Shadows in the Half-Light.* New York: WestgatePress, 1989. 66 pp.

THE GOTHIC SOCIETY

The active **Gothic** music scene in Great Britain in the early 1980s fell into disarray by
the end of the decade. To some musicians, however, support for the gothic spirit
seemed to still be very much alive. Thus in 1987, several artists and musicians created
The Gothic Society to revive and unify the interest in Gothic music. About the same
time, the band Nosferatu was founded by Vlad Janicjek and his wife Sapphire Aurora.
They were soon joined by Louis De Wray and Damien Denville. Although members
in the band were not into vampirism, they had an appreciation for vampire imagery
and literature, which is portrayed in their music. The band's various recordings

include two albums, *The Hellbound* and *Vampyre's Cry*. The band travels to its performances in a hearse.

The Gothic Society exists as an international fan organization for Nosferatu. It keeps people informed of the band's performance dates, recordings, and related paraphernalia. Janicjek's wife, Sapphire Aurora, no longer plays with the band; she spends her time working as editor of *Grimoire,* the Society's fanzine.

The Society may be reached at 138 Canterbury Rd., Harrow, Middlesex, UK HA1 4PB.

Sources:

Duncan, Michelle. "Nosferatu: The Vampire's Cry." *Propaganda* 19 (1992): 8-10.
Mercer, Mick. *Gothic Rock.* Birmingham, UK: Pegesus Publishers, 1991. 178 pp.

GOTHIC SOCIETY OF CANADA

The Gothic Society of Canada is a gothic interest group that concerns itself with gothism, Victorian studies, vampires, and dark lore. It was founded by a Toronto couple, Morpheus Blak and Groovella Blak, who serve as copresidents. The society holds regular meetings, periodic outings, and an annual costume ball. It also publishes a quarterly newsletter. Groovella Blak operates Siren, the oldest shop in North America catering to those interested in the modern gothic and vampire scene. The shop carries clothing, jewelry, accessories, gifts, and books. Both the society and Siren may be contacted at 463 Queen St., W., Toronto, ON, Canada M5V 2AG.

GOTHICA

Gothica, whose first issue appeared in 1992, is a fanzine based upon the ideal of what is termed the **Anne Rice** vampire nature. It was founded by Susan M. Jensen, who became friends with a group of vampire-horror movie fans in college in the late 1980s. The group, called the Drac Pac, gathered regularly to watch horror movies and through them, to explore the uncommon and the sublime. Although the group scattered after graduation, Jensen decided to begin a small magazine based on the ideas the Drac Pac had discussed. The first issue, in March 1992, ran 16 copies. It increased to 35 copies in August 1993 and has grown steadily since, having several hundred produced by the end of the first year.

Drac Packers are people who read *Gothica* and who consider themselves to be Anne Rice's **Lestat de Lioncourt**-like individuals—fierce, individualistic, and immortal because they want to be. As a Drac Packer, one stands above the level of mere mortals, stares into the face of the horrific, and embraces it. One swims against the current and thus builds a unique and powerful life of personal independence.

Each issue of *Gothica* includes poetry, short fiction, philosophical musings, and artwork. For subscriptions, write to Susan M. Jensen, 98 Union St., Apt. 4, Brewer, ME 04412.

GREECE, VAMPIRES IN

Greece is one of the oldest sources for the contemporary vampire legend. Ancient Greek writings record the existence of three vampirelike creatures—the *lamiai,* the *empusai,* and the *mormolykiai.* Also known in Greece was the *strige,* a vampire witch. *Strige* was derived from the Latin *strix,* which originally referred to the screech owl and later to a night flying demon that attacked and killed infants by sucking their blood.

The *lamiai* was named after Lamia, who was said to have been a Libyan queen. She was the daughter of Belus and Libya, and, as the story was told, was loved by Zeus, the king of the Greek gods. Hera, Zeus's wife, became jealous and took out her resentment by robbing Lamia of all her children who had been fathered by Zeus. Lamia retired to a cave from which, unable to strike at Hera, she took out her anger by killing offspring of human mothers, usually by sucking the blood out of the children. Her actions led to her **transformation** into a hideous beast. (The story of the *mormolykiai* is very similar—they are named after a woman named Mormo, who cannibalized her own children.)

Later Lamia became identified with a class of beings modeled on her, described as coarse- looking women with deformed, serpentlike lower bodies. Their feet were not paired, one being of brass and the other shaped like an animal's, commonly that of a goat, donkey, or ox. The *lamiai* were known primarily as demonic beings who sucked the blood from young children; however, they had the power to transform themselves into beautiful young maidens in order to attract and seduce young men. Philostatus included a lengthy account of the *lamiai* in this transformation in the 25th chapter of the fourth book of his *Life of Apollonius.*

One of Apollonius's students, Menippus by name, was attracted to a beautiful rich woman whom he had first encountered as an apparition. In the apparition he was told when and where (a suburb of Corinth) he would find her. The young man fell in love and contemplated marriage. When he related his story to Apollonius, the latter informed his young student that he was being hunted by a serpent. Upon meeting the woman, he told Menippus, "And that you may realize the truth of what I say, this fine bride is one of the vampires (*empusai*), that is to say of those beings whom many regard as *lamiai* and hobgoblins (*mormolykiai*). These beings fall in love, and they are devoted to the delights of Aphrodite, but especially in the flesh of human beings, and they decoy with such delights those whom they mean to devour in their feats." In spite of protestations by Menippus, Apollonius confronted the *lamiai* with the facts. One by one, the elements of her environment disappeared. She finally admitted her plans and her habit of feeding ''upon young and beautiful bodies because their blood is pure and strong.'' Philostatus called this account the ''best-known story of Apollonius.'' Apuleius, in the very first chapter of the *Golden Ass,* recounted the story of an encounter with a *lamiai* who caught up with her fleeing lover and killed him by first thrusting her sword into his neck, taking all of his blood, and then cutting out his heart.

The people soon lost their fear of the *lamiai* and, even in ancient times, they had simply become a tool for parents to frighten their children. However, when a child dies suddenly from an unknown cause, a saying still popular in Greece, suggests that the child has been strangled by the *lamiai.*

The *lamiai* were rediscovered in literature in the fifteenth century, when Angelo Poliziano of Florence published a poem, *Lamia* (1492). In 1819, British poet John Keats authored a poem with the same name. Since the time of Keats, the *lamiai* have appeared in numerous poems, paintings, sculptures, and musical pieces. For example, August Enna authored an opera called *Lamia,* which was first performed in Antwerp, Belgium, in 1899. Poems on the same theme were written by Edward MacDowell (1888), Arthur Symons (1920), Frederick Zeck (1926), Robert Graves (1964), and Peter Davidson (1977). Among recent novels featuring the *lamiai* were the four books of J. N. Williamson—*Death Coach* (1981), *Death School* (1981), *Death Angel* (1982), and *Death Doctor* (1982)—featuring the character of Lamia Zacharias. More recently, Tim Powers's novel, *The Stress of Her Regard* (1989), took place in early nineteenth century England and featured a *lamia* interacting with Keats, **Lord Byron, John Polidori,** Mary Godwin, and Percy Shelley.

THE VRYKOLAKAS: The *lamiai, empusai,* and *mormolykiai,* though known for their drinking of blood, were not vampires in the same sense as those of eastern Europe. They were spirit beings rather than revivified corpses. The ancient Greeks, however, did have a class of revenants, *vrykolakas,* which would develop into true vampires. The term was derived from the older Slavic compound term *vblk'b dlaka,* which originally meant wolf pelt wearer. The term developed among the **southern Slavs,** from whom it probably passed to the Greeks. The best description of revenants (beings that return from the grave) in ancient Greek literature appears in a story told by Phlegon, a freedman who lived in the time of the Roman Emperor Hadrian.

It seems that Philinnon, the daughter of Demostratus and Charito, some six months after her death, had been observed entering the room of Machates, a young man staying in the parents' guest-chamber. A servant told the couple about seeing the daughter, but when they peeped into the guest-chamber, they could not ascertain who Machates was entertaining. The next morning Charito told Machates about her daughter's death. He admitted that Philinnon was the name of the girl in his room. He then produced the ring she had given him and a breast band she had left behind. The parents recognized both as possessions of their late daughter. When the girl returned that evening, the parents stepped into the room and to see their daughter. She reproached them for interrupting her visits with Machates and said she had been granted three nights with him. However, because of their meddling, she would now die again. Sure enough, Philinnon again became a corpse.

At this point, Phlegon entered the picture as a witness. As town official, he was called upon to keep order as word of Philinnon's return spread through the community that night. He led an examination of her burial vault, finding the gifts she had taken away from her first visit to Machates—but no body. The townspeople turned to a local wise man who advised that the body be burned and appropriate purification rituals and propitiatory rites to the deities be observed.

This basic story of the returned dead contains some unique aspects of the later Greek *vrykolakas* account. Once discovered, the body was, for example characteristically burned, rather than decapitated or staked through the heart. The ancient revenant was, however, not yet a vampire, or even an object of much fear. The revenant often returned to complete unfinished business with a spouse, a family member, or someone close to him or her in life. On this early account of a brief visit by a revenant, more elaborate accounts would build. In later centuries, stories would be told of much lengthier visits and of *vrykolakas* who resumed life in the family. Occasionally, there would be a report of a revenant who went to a location where he was unknown, and where he then remarried and fathered children.

One of the oldest reports of the *vrykolakas* was written by the French botanist Pitton de Tournefort. While on the island of Mykonos in the year 1700, he heard of a man who had recently died and yet had been reported walking about town generally making a nuisance of himself. After various noninvasive remedies failed, on the ninth day after his burial the body was disinterred and the heart removed and burned. The troubles did not stop. At one point, an Albanian visitor to the island suggested that the problem was the sticking of "Christian" swords in the top of the grave, it being commonly believed that sharp objects stuck into the top of graves prevented vampires from rising. The Albanian argued that the cross shape to the sword prevented the devil from leaving the corpse (many believing that the corpse was animated by the devil or an evil spirit). He suggested using Turkish swords. It did not help. In the end, on January 1, 1701, the corpse was consumed in a **fire.**

Greece produced the first modern writer on vampires, Leone Allacci (commonly known as **Leo Allatius**). In 1645, he authored *De Graecorum hodie quorundam opinationibus,* a volume on the beliefs of the Greek people, in which he discussed the *vrykolakas* at great length. Early the twentieth century, John Cuthbert Lawson spent considerable time investigating the *vrykolakas* in Greek folklore. He noted its development in three stages, beginning with that of pre-Christian times, represented by Phlegon's account. In that account, the return was by divine consent for a specific purpose. Lawson also found, in the ancient Greek texts, an underlying belief in revenant status as a punishment for human failure. In the likes of Euripides and Aeschylus, Lawson noted instances when people were cursed with an incorruptible body, meaning that in death the individual would be denied communion with those on the other side of the grave. Thus, the ancient Greek writers entertained a concept of the "undead."

Lawson noted three circumstances that would predispose an individual to become a *vrykolakas.* First, there could be the curse of a parent or someone who an individual had failed, such as that placed by Oedipus against his undutiful son. Oedipus called upon Tartarus (the place of the dead) to refuse to receive the son and to drive him forth from his place of final rest. Second, one might become undead because of a evil or dishonorable act, most notably against one's family, such as the murder of a kinsman or adultery with a sister- or brother-in-law. Third, the dead might join the undead by dying violently or by not being buried.

The popular belief in *vrykolakas* was taken into the doctrinal perspective of the Greek Orthodox Church as it became the dominant force in Greek religious life in the first millennium A.D. The church developed a teaching both about the dead whose bodies remain uncorrupted and about true revenants, those who are resuscitated and return to life. Concerning the former, the church taught that a curse could in fact prevent the natural decay of the body which at the same time became a barrier to the progress of the soul. However, the curses pronounced by parents and others took second place to the "curse" pronounced by the church in its act of excommunication (which effectively denied the victim the saving sacraments of the church). Stories of the accursed dead whose bodies did not decay gradually became the basis of a belief that excommunication produced physical results. Reports of changes in the bodies of excommunicated individuals who later had their excommunication lifted joined the popular hagiography of the church.

When it came to the *vrykolakas,* the church seemed plainly embarrassed but had to deal with what many thought, even in ancient times, to be illusionary. At times the documents spoke of the devil stirring up the imagination of people who believed that a dead person had come to visit. In the face of persisting accounts, however, the church developed an explanation, claiming that the devil inhabited the body of the dead and caused it to move. However, such occurrences tended to be tied to the activities of mediums, in a manner reminiscent of the biblical story of the woman at Endor (I Samuel 28).

Thus, as the church came to dominate Greek religious life, it proposed that the dead might become *vrykolakas* if they died in an excommunicated state, if they were buried without the proper church rites, or if they died a violent death. To these it added two other causes: stillborn children or those who were born on one of the great church festivals. These causes expanded the earlier Greek notions of those who died under a familial curse or in great sin.

The Christianization of the Slavic and Balkan peoples effectively began toward the end of the first Christian millennium and made impressive gains during the tenth through the twelfth centuries. As the Eastern Orthodox Church gained dominance in **Russia, Romania, Hungary,** and among the **southern Slavs,** beliefs from those countries flowed back into Greece and began to alter still further the understanding of the revenant, transforming it into a true vampire. The significant concept was that of the werewolf. It was from the Slavs that the word *vrykolakas,* derived from an old Slavic term for wolfpelt, was adopted as the Greek designation for a resuscitated corpse.

Some Slavic people believed that **werewolves** became vampires after they died. Lawson argued that the Slavonic term came into Greece to describe the werewolf (a term he still found in use in a few places at the beginning of this century), but gradually came to designate the revenant or vampire.

Besides the word that came to designate the vampire, the Greeks absorbed a Slavic view of the possible vicious nature of vampires. The ancient Greek revenant was essentially benign and returned primarily to complete some unfinished family business. On occasion it committed an act of vengeance, but always one that most would consider logical. It did not enact chaotic violence. Thus, the Greeks first adopted the idea that some revenants were particularly brutal. Gradually, the view that vampires were characteristically vicious came to dominate Greek thought about the *vrykolakas.* The vampire's vicious nature was focused in its bloodthirstiness and its wanton nature.

The Slavic vampire also characteristically returned to work its violence upon those closest to it. A popular form of cursing one's enemy was to say, ''May the earth not receive you'' or ''May the earth spew you forth.'' In effect, one was suggesting that the accursed person return as a vampire and wreak havoc on his or her nearest and dearest.

THE CALLICANTZAROS: One other type of vampire existed in Greece. The *callicantzaros* was a peculiar kind of vampire that was discussed at some length by **Leo Allatius** in his 1645 treatise, *De Graecorum hodie quorundam opinationibus.* The *callicantzaros* was related to the extraordinary sanctity ascribed to the Christian holy days at Christmas time. Children born during the week between Christmas and New Years (or Epiphany of Twelfth Night, the evening when the Three Wise Men are supposed to have arrived at Bethlehem to present their gifts to the baby Jesus) are considered unlucky. They were described as feast-blasted and believed to be destined to become vampires after their death.

The *callicantzaros* was also distinct among vampires in that its activities were limited to Christmas Day and the week or 12 days afterward. During the rest of the year it traveled in some vague netherworld. It was distinguished by its manic behavior and extended fingernails. It would seize people with its talons and tear them to pieces. Reports on the *callicantzaros* vary widely as to its appearance, possibly related to the state of maturity of the person deemed to be a future vampire.

The *callicantzaros* had an effect upon everyday life, as any person born during the forbidden period was viewed with some degree of hostility. Parents would fear that these children would act out vampiric fantasies as they grew up and would harm their brothers and sisters.

THE MODERN LITERARY VAMPIRE: Thus was developed the Greek idea of the vampire, which was still alive at the time British, French, and German writers began to explore the vampire theme in poems, stories, and stage productions. As vampire literature developed, the early authors established an association between Greece and the vampire. **Goethe,** for example, set his 1797 poem, ''The Bride of Corinth,'' in Greece. Then **John Keats** drew upon ancient Greek sources for his poem ''The Lamia'' (1819). And **John Polidori** placed much of the action for **''The Vampyre''** (1819) in Greece.

In the nineteenth and twentieth centuries, numerous observers discovered that belief in the *vrykolakas* is still alive in rural Greece. In 1835, William Martin Leake's *Travels in North Greece* contained several accounts of the disposal of bodies believed to be *vrykolakas*. Lawson's study, previously noted, recounted many anecdotes he had retrieved in his field work. And as recently as the 1960s, G. F. Abbott, Richard Blum, Eva Blum, and their staff had no problem collecting reports of Greeks who had encountered a *vrykolakas*. Though mentioned by Lawson, Abbott and the Blums both reported multiple stories that suggested people became *vrykolakas* because **animals,** such as cats, jumped over the bodies between the time of death and burial. Abbott recounted a story of the body of a suspected *vrykolakas* being scalded with boiling **water** rather than burned.

Greece stands as one of the oldest and most important centers for vampire lore. Its idea of the vampire, having passed through a complicated process of development, remains strong today and continues as a resource for understanding the impact of the vampire myth. In addition, Greece also has contributed significantly to the emerging image of the modern fictional vampire.

Sources:

Abbott, G. F. *Macedonian Folklore*. Chicago: Argonaut, Inc. Publishers, 1909. 273 pp.

Apuleius. *The Golden Ass*. English translation by W. Adlington. London: William Heineman, 1935. Numerous editions.

Barber, Paul. *Vampires, Burial, and Death: Folklore and Reality*. New Haven, CT: Yale University Press, 1988. 236 pp.

Blum, Richard, and Eva Blum. *The Dangerous Hour: The Lore of Crisis and Mystery in Rural Greece*. London: Chatto & Windus, 1970. 410 pp.

Calmet, Dom Augustin. *Dissertations sur les Apparitions des Anges des Démons et des Espits, et sur les revenants, et Vampires de Hingrie, de Boheme, de Moravie, et de Silésie*. Paris, 1746. Rept. as: *The Phantom World*. 2 vols. London: Richard Bentley, 1850.

Fontenrose, Joseph. *Python: A Study of Delphic Myth and Its Origins*. Berkeley, CA: University of California Press, 1959. 616 pp.

Lawson, John Cuthbert. *Modern Greek Folklore and Ancient Greek Religion*. 1910. Reprint. New Hyde Park, NY: University Books, 1964. 610 pp.

Leake, William Martin. *Travels in Northern Greece*. 4 vols. 1835. Reprint. Amsterdam: Adolf M. Hakkert, 1967.

Philostratus. *The Life of Apollonius of Tyana*. Translation by F. C. Conybeare. London: William Heineman, 1912. Various editions.

Powers, Tim. *The Stress of Her Regard.* New York: Charnel House, 1989. Reprint. New York: Ace Books, 1989. 410 pp.

Reid, Jane Davidson. *The Oxford Guide to Classical Mythology in the Arts, 1300-1990s.* New York: Oxford University Press, 1993. 1310 pp.

Summers, Montague. *The Vampire: His Kith and Kin.* London: Routledge, Kegan Paul, Trench, Trubner & Co., 1928. 356 pp. Reprint. New York: University Books, 1960. 356 pp.

GYPSIES, VAMPIRES AND THE

In the opening chapters of **Bram Stoker**'s novel *Dracula,* **Jonathan Harker** discovered that he was a prisoner in **Castle Dracula,** but he was given hope by the appearance of a band of Gypsies:

> A band of Szgany have come to the castle, and are encamped in the courtyard. These Szgany are gypsies; I have notes of them in my book. They are peculiar to this part of the world, though allied to the ordinary gypsies all the world over. There are thousands of them in Hungary and Transylvania who are almost outside all law. They attach themselves as a rule to some great noble or boyar, and call themselves by his name. They are fearless and without religion, save superstition, and they talk only their own varieties of the many tongues.

He soon discovered that the Gypsies were allied to the Count. The letters he attempted to have the Gypsies mail for him were returned to Dracula. The Gypsies were overseeing the preparation of the boxes of **native soil** that Dracula took to England. The Gypsies then reappeared at the end of the novel, accompanying the fleeing Dracula on his return to his castle. In the end, they stepped aside and allowed their vampire master to be killed by **Abraham Van Helsing** and his cohorts.

THE EMERGENCE OF THE GYPSIES: Since the fourteenth century, the Gypsies have formed a distinct ethnic minority group in the Balkan countries. Within the next two centuries, they were found across all of Europe. While they received their name from an early hypothesis that placed their origin in Egypt, it is now known that they originated in **India** and were related to similar nomadic tribes that survive to this day in northern India. At some point, around 1000 A.D., some of these tribes wandered westward. A large group settled for a period in Turkey and incorporated many words from that country into their distinctive Romany language. Crossing the Bosporous, the Gypsies found their way to Serbia and traveled as far north as Bohemia through the fourteenth century. They were noted as being in Crete as early as 1322. In the next century, a short time before the emergence of **Vlad Dracul** and **Vlad the Impaler** as rulers in Wallachia, they moved into what are now **Romania** and **Hungary.** The Gypsies fanned out across Europe throughout the next century. They were in **Russia** and **Poland,** eventually making their way to France and Great Britain.

In Romania and Hungary, Gypsies were often enslaved and persecuted. Their nomadic, nonliterary culture left them vulnerable to accusations of wrongdoing, and they became known not only as traveling entertainers but as thieves, con artists, and stealers of infants; this latter charge often was made about despised minority groups in Europe. During World War II, simultaneously with their attack upon the Jews, the Nazis attempted an extermination of the Gypsies as a "final solution" to what they had defined as the Gypsy problem.

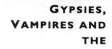
GYPSIES AND THE SUPERNATURAL: Gypsies developed a sophisticated and complicated supernatural religious world view, made more difficult to describe by the diversity of the different bands in various countries and the reluctance of Gypsies to talk to outsiders about their most sacred beliefs. Only the most diligent and persistent effort by a small band of scholars yielded a picture of the world view, which varied from country to country.

Gypsy theology affirmed the existence of *o Del* (literally, the God), who appeared one day on Earth (the Earth being the eternally present uncreated world). Beside *o Del,* the principle of Good, was *o Bengh,* or Evil. *o Del* and *o Bengh* competed in the creation of humanity. *O Bengh* formed two statuettes out of earth, and *o Del* breathed life into them. Again, with no written text, the account differed from tribe to tribe. The expanded world of the Gypsies was alive with the forces of Good and Evil contending with each other throughout nature. Wise Gypsies learned to read the signs and omens to make the forces work for them and to prevent evil forces from doing them harm.

Gypsies kept a living relationship with the dead (some have called it a cult of the dead), to whom they had a great loyalty. Gypsies regularly left offerings of food, especially milk, with the goal of having the dead serve a protective function for living family members. E. B. Trigg, in *Gypsy Demons & Divinities: The Magical and Supernatural Practices of the Gypsies,* described this practice as a form of worship vampire gods, which he compared to the activity of Indian worshippers toward the vampire figures of Indian mythology.

What happened to the dead? Among the Gypsies of the Balkans, there was a belief that the soul entered a world very much like this one, except there was no death. Bosnian Gypsies, influenced by Islam, believed in a literal paradise, a land of milk and honey. Others, however, believed that the soul hovered around the grave and resided in the corpse. As such, the soul might grow restless and the corpse might develop a desire to return to this world. To keep the dead content, funeral rites were elaborate and families made annual visits to the grave sites. Within this larger world there was ample room for the living dead, or vampires. This belief was found among Gypsies across Europe, but was especially pronounced, as might be expected, in Hungary, Romania, and the Slavic lands.

Questions have been posed as to the origins of Gypsy vampire beliefs. In **India,** the Gypsies' land of origin, there were a variety of acknowledged vampire creatures. For example, the *bhuta,* found in western India, was believed to be the soul of a man who died in an untimely fashion (such as an accident or suicide). The *bhuta* wandered around at night, and among its attributes was the ability to animate dead bodies, which in turn attacked the living in ghoulish fashion. In northern India, from whence the

Gypsies probably started their journey to the West, the *brahmaparusha* was a vampirelike creature who was pictured with a head encircled by intestines and a skull filled with blood from which it drank. Gypsies also had a belief in Sara, the Black Virgin, a figure derived from the bloodthirsty goddess **Kali.** Thus, Gypsies may have brought a belief in vampires, or at least a disposition to believe in them, to the Balkan Peninsula. Once in the area, however, they obviously interacted with the native populations and developed the belief of what became a variety of the Slavic vampire.

The Gypsy vampire was called a *mulo* (or *mullo*; plural, *mulé*), and means literally "one who is dead." Gypsies viewed death essentially as unnatural, hence any death was an affront and viewed as being caused by evil forces attacking the individual. Thus, any individual—but especially anyone who died an untimely death (by **suicide** or an accident)—might become a vampire and search out the person or persons who caused the death. Given the clannish nature of Gypsy life, these people were most likely those close to the deceased. Prime candidates would be relatives who did not destroy the belongings of the deceased (according to Gypsy custom) but kept them for themselves. The vampire also might have a grudge against any who did not properly observe the elaborate burial and funeral rites.

The vampire usually appeared quite normal, but often could be detected by some sign in its physical body. For example, the creature might have a finger missing, or have animal-like appendages. Easier to detect was the vampire that took on a horrific appearance. This involved certain individuals who could only be viewed under special conditions. Vampires might be seen at any time of day or night, though some believed them to be strictly nocturnal creatures. Others thought that vampires could appear precisely at noon when they would cast no shadow. Slavic and German Gypsies believed that vampires had no bones in their bodies, a belief based upon the observation that a vampire's bones are often left behind in the grave.

Upon their return from the dead, Gypsies believed that vampires engaged in various forms of malicious activity. They attacked relatives and attempted to suck their blood. They destroyed property and became a general nuisance by throwing things around and making noises in the night. Male vampires were known to have a strong sexual appetite and returned from the dead to have sexual relations with a wife, girlfriend, or other women. Female vampires were thought to be able to return from the dead and assume a normal life, even to the point of marrying—though her husband would become exhausted from satisfying her sexual demands.

Gypsies thought that **animals** and, on occasion, even plants became vampires. Dead snakes, horses, chickens, dogs, cats, and sheep were reported as returning as vampires, especially in Bosnia. In Slavic lands it was thought that if an animal such as a cat jumped over a corpse prior to burial, the corpse would become a vampire. Gypsies believed that the animal might become a vampire at the time of its death. Plants such as the pumpkin or watermelon could, if kept in the house too long, begin to stir, make noises, and show a trace of blood; they would then cause trouble, in a limited way, for both people and cattle. In the most extreme cases, family tools might become vampires. The wooden knot for a yoke or the wooden rods for binding sheaves of wheat became vampires if left undone for more than three years.

It was believed that action could be taken to prevent a dead person from returning as a vampire. As a first step, the victim of a vampire called upon a *dhampir*, the son of a vampire. Gypsies believed that intercourse between a vampire and his widow might produce a male offspring. This child would develop unusual powers for detecting vampires, and a *dhampir* might actually hire out his services in the case of vampire attacks. There was some belief that the *dhampir* had a jellylike body (remembering that some thought that vampires had no bones) and hence would have a shorter life span.

Many Gypsies thought that iron had special powers to keep away evil. To ward off vampires, at the time of burial a steel needle was driven into the heart of the corpse, and bits of steel were placed in the mouth, over the ears and nose, and between the fingers. The heel of the shoe could be removed and **hawthorn** placed in the sock, or hawthorn stake could be driven through the leg. If a vampire was loose in a village, one might find protection in different charms, such as a necklace with an iron nail. A ring of thorn could be set around one's living quarters. Christian Gypsies used a **crucifix.** Slavic Gypsies prized the presence of a set of twins, one male and one female, who were born on a Saturday and who were willing to wear their underclothes inside out. From such the vampire would flee immediately.

The grave site might be the focus of a suspected vampire. Gypsies have been known to drive stakes of ash or hawthorn into a grave, or pour boiling water over it. In more problematic cases, **coffin**s were opened and the corpse examined to see if it had shifted in the coffin or not properly decomposed. In the case of a body thought to be a vampire, Gypsies followed the practices of their neighbors by having the prayers for the dead said; staking it in either the stomach, heart, or head; decapitation; and/or in extreme cases, cremation.

The need to destroy the vampire was slight among some Gypsies who believed its life span was only 40 days. However, some granted it a longer life and sought specific means to kill it. An iron needle in the stomach often would be enough. In Eastern Orthodox countries, such as Romania, holy **water** would be thrown on the vampire. If these less intrusive means did not work, Gypsies might resort to more conventional weapons. If captured, a vampire might be nailed to a piece of wood. If one was available, a *dhampir* might be called upon to carry out the destruction. Black dogs and wolves were known to attack vampires, and some Romanian Gypsies believed that white wolves stayed around the grave sites to attack vampires and that without their work the world would be overrun with the dead.

Numerous reports on the *mulo* have been collected and show significant variance among geographically separated Gypsy groups. There has been some speculation that their vampire beliefs originated in **India,** from whence the Gypsies themselves seemed to have derived and which had a rich vampiric lore. The notions have become differentiated over the centuries as Gypsies dispersed around Europe and North America and interacted with various local cultures.

CONCLUSION: The belief in vampires has survived among Gypsies, but, like all supernatural beliefs, it has shown signs of disappearing. Secular schooling, modern burial practices, and governments hostile to actions (such as mutilating bodies) taken in response to vampires have affected the strength of this belief.

Sources:

Clebert, Jean-Paul. *The Gypsies.* Harmondsworth, Middlesex, U.K.: Penguin Books, 1963. 282 pp.

Leland, G. G. *Gypsy Sorcery.* New York Tower Books, n.d. 267 pp.

Trigg, E. B. *Gypsy Demons & Divinities: The Magical and Supernatural Practices of the Gypsies.* London: Sheldon Press, 1973. 238 pp.

Vukanovic, T. P. "The Vampire." In Jan L. Perkowski, ed. *Vampires of the Slavs.* Cambridge, MA: Slavica Publishers, 1976, 201-34.

Haarmann, Fritz (1879-1925)

Fritz Haarmann, the so-called Vampire of Hanover (**Germany**), is one of several prominent persons often cited as an actual modern vampire. Born on October 24, 1879 in Hanover, Haarmann grew up in fear of his father. He joined the army as a young man and after a period of service returned to Hanover. However, he soon was arrested for child molestation. Sentenced to a mental institution, he escaped and went to Switzerland. Thus began a period of his life when he lived on the streets, surviving off of petty crime interspersed with arrests and brief stays in jail. After World War I, he seemed to have switched sides and joined the police department as an informer and spy.

Haarmann was homosexual. He picked up young men off the street and invited them to his home. There he engaged in sex and on occasion (five or more times a year) killed them. Arrested in 1919, he spent nine months in jail for engaging in illegal sex. After his release, he met Hans Grans, who became his lover and partner in crime. During the early 1920s, Haarmann's crimes became even more grisly. He began to bite the throats of his victims and drink their blood.

In 1924 the discovery of the remains of several of Haarmann's victims and the persistent pleas of the parents of several young men who had disappeared initiated an investigation that eventually led police to Haarmann. Arrested that year on sex charges, Haarmann sat in jail as his living quarters were searched. The corpses of more than 20 bodies were found. Faced with the most incriminating evidence—clothing identified as belonging to one of his victims—Haarmann finally confessed and implicated Grans.

The subsequent trial proved a gruesome affair. Haarmann was formally charged with 24 murders, but was believed to have killed more than 50 people. He testified and related accounts of many of his activities, including cannibalism. During part of this time, he worked as a butcher and claimed to have sold the meat of several of his victims to his customers. Convicted, he was sentenced to death and executed by decapitation on April 15, 1925. Grans was imprisoned for life. His brain was sent to Göttingen University for study.

Haarmann was not a vampire in the traditional folkloric sense. He was a disturbed individual with a blood fetish that found expression during the rape and murder of his victims. As such, his **crimes** fit more into the history of serial murder than with the folkloric or literary vampire. The movie *Tenderness of the Wolves* (1974) was inspired by the Haarmann case.

Sources:

Glut, Donald F. *True Vampires of History*. New York: H C Publishers, 1971. 191 pp.

Lessing, Theodore. *Haarmann—Die Geschicte eines Werwolfs*. 1925. English translation by Mo Croasdale: "The Story of a Werewolf." In *Monsters of Weimar*. London: Nemesis Books, 1993, pp. 11-156.

Volta, Ornella. *The Vampire*. New York: Award Books, 1962. 153 pp.

HAIGH, JOHN GEORGE (1910-1949)

John George Haigh, the so-called Vampire of London and one of several persons frequently cited as an actual modern vampire, was born into a strict Plymouth Brethren family in England. The Plymouth Brethren were a fundamentalist Protestant group, and Haigh's parents passed on to him a strong image of the suffering of Christ on the cross and his bleeding—the saving power of his blood being an important part of that image. It was also reported that his mother had a strong belief in prophetic dreams.

As a young man, Haigh left the Plymouth Brethren and joined the Church of England, but his heritage stayed with him. He had a revelation that he should begin to drink his own urine, a practice based upon his unique interpretation of two biblical passages, Proverbs 5:15 and John 7:38. He also had a recurring dream of a forest of crosses that transformed into trees dripping with blood. At one tree, a man collected a bowl of blood. Haigh would feel drained of energy and the man would offer him the bowl of blood to drink. But before he could drink, Haigh would awaken. He concluded from this dream that he needed to drink blood to restore his vitality.

Haigh established a laboratory in his own home, to which he lured his designated victims. There he would kill them, drain their blood, and dispose of their bodies in a vat of sulfuric acid. He was finally arrested when he tried to pawn the fur coat of one elderly female victim. Haigh was confident that he could not be tried and convicted without a corpse to confirm death. However, upon investigating his laboratory, the police found several body parts the acid failed to dissolve, including a victim's teeth, which were identified by their unusual dental work. At his trial, Haigh confessed to the nine murders, claiming that they had been religious acts and that the consumption of blood was necessary to his attaining eternal life. He was convicted and hanged on

August 10, 1949. Haigh left his clothing to the London Wax Museum and, for some years, a wax model of Haigh stood in Madame Tussaud's House of Horrors.

As with most of the modern cases of vampirism, Haigh was not a vampire in either the traditional folkloric sense or the modern literary variety. He was a disturbed man whose problems were expressed in a religious format, which included an obsession with blood. His history of **crime** fits more properly with accounts of serial killers than that of vampires.

Sources:

Glut, Donald F. *True Vampires of History*. New York: H C Publishers, 1971. 191 pp.
Volta, Ornella. *The Vampire*. New York: Award Books, 1962. 153 pp.

HAINING, PETER ALEXANDER (1940-)

Peter Alexander Haining, anthologist of vampire literature, was born April 2, 1940 at Enfield, England and began his adult life as a journalist in Essex. He was assigned to investigate a graveyard desecration, which the local rector claimed had been done by satanists. His work on the case generated within him an interest in the occult and black magic and led him to co-author *Devil Worship in Britain* with colleague A. V. Sellwood. This 1964 book became the first in a prolific line of books that Haining wrote or, in most cases, edited. Among his early anthologies was *The Craft of Terror*, a 1966 collection of extracts from gothic horror novels that set the stage for *The Midnight People* (1968; issued in the United States as *Vampires at Midnight*), a collection of vampire stories. Haining suggested that vampires were unique among evil monsters in that they were based on fact (i.e., the folklore and legends from countries around the world). Thus, he combined the fictional selections with several accounts of real vampires.

Through the 1970s and 1980s, Haining edited a new anthology of occult and/or horror material once or twice a year, occasionally moving into the mystery realm. He returned to vampires in 1976 with *The Dracula Scrapbook*, an illustrated survey of **Dracula** in fact and fiction. In 1985 he compiled *Vampire: Chilling Tales of the Undead*, an anthology of vampire fiction. In 1987, he compiled a second volume on Dracula, *The Dracula Centenary Book*. It was reissued in 1992 as *The Dracula Scrapbook*, though it is completely different from the 1976 volume. *The Dracula Centenary Book* is based upon Haining's assumption that the unnamed year in which **Bram Stoker** set the novel *Dracula* was 1887. That year is at best questionable, as most Dracula scholars now agree that the year was 1893. Whatever the support for 1887 as the year of Dracula's arrival in England, the assumption gave an excuse to publish one of the better Dracula anthologies.

Sources:

Ashley, Mike. *Who's Who in Horror and Fantasy Fiction*. London: Elm Tree Books, 1977.
Haining, Peter, ed. *The Dracula Centenary Book*. London: Souvenir Press, 1987. Rev. ed. as: *The Dracula Scrapbook*. London: Chancellor Press, 1992. 160 pp.
———. *The Dracula Scrapbook*. New York: Bramwell House, 1976. 176 pp.

————. *The Midnight People.* London: Leslie Frewin Publishers, 1968. Reprint. London: Everest Books, 1975. 255 pp. Rept. as: *Vampires at Midnight.* New York: Grosset & Dunlap, 1970. 255 pp.

————. *Vampire: Chilling Tales of the Undead.* London: W. H. Allen, 1985. 240 pp.

HAMMER FILMS

Hammer Films, the film studio whose horror movies in the 1960s brought a new dimension to the vampire myth, was founded in 1948 by Will Hammer and Sir John Carreras. Largely based upon public response to its horror movies, Hammer became the most successful British film company in the generation after World War II. Hammer burst upon the scene after the film industry had neglected the horror genre for several decades—partly out of censorship considerations and partly from its own conservative nature. Hammer's openness to the horror film was due in large part to Carreras's understanding of the company's credo: Motion pictures should first and foremost simply entertain and tell a good story. Beginning as a small, relatively poor company with limited capital, Hammer Films turned out low-budget ''B'' movies following patterns set in Hollywood. A television series, however, became the catalyst for major changes for the company.

In the 1950s, British television produced the successful science fiction series, *The Quatermass Experiment,* built around the character of Bernard Quatermass. He was a scientist who sent a rocket into space only to have it return with a new form of alien life that took over the body of the surviving astronaut. Hammer brought Quatermass to the screen in 1955 in *The Quatermass Xperiment.* This was quickly followed by *X the Unknown* (1956) and *Quatermass II* (1957). The success of these science fiction ''monster'' movies suggested that new films with classical horror themes might be equally successful. **Universal Pictures,** which owned the motion picture rights to both *Frankenstein* and *Dracula* at that time, was essentially separating itself from producing horror movies. The owners worked out a deal by which the company conveyed rights to *Dracula* and *Frankenstein* to Hammer.

In creating the new horror features, Hammer drew upon a French and British stage tradition originally developed at the Theatre du Grand Guignol in Paris. Grand Guignol emphasized the shock value of presenting gruesome and terrifying scenes to the audience realistically. Vampires were a standard fare of these stage productions. Hammer horrors were in full color. Blood flowed freely and monstrous acts were fully portrayed on screen—not merely implied for the audience to imagine.

Hammer then assembled one of the more famous teams ever to work on what would become a series of horror pictures: director **Terence Fisher,** screenwriter **Jimmy Sangster,** and actors **Christopher Lee** and **Peter Cushing.** Their first picture was *The Curse of Frankenstein*, a new version in technicolor of Mary Shelley's original *Frankenstein.* It differed markedly from the older Universal version in its graphic depiction of the monster's violence, now in full color.

The same team plunged immediately into a second classic horror volume, *Dracula,* better known under its American title, *The Horror of Dracula* (1958).

Sangster and Fisher decided not to use the play upon which Universal's *Dracula* (1931) was based; they also deviated rather freely from **Bram Stoker**'s story, which was transformed into the final battle of a long-standing war between **Abraham Van Helsing** (goodness) and Dracula (evil). The first victim of this war, at least in the segment seen by the audience, was **Jonathan Harker,** who arrived at **Castle Dracula** as a secret Van Helsing operative. After he was turned into a vampire, Van Helsing was forced to kill him. The next victim was **Lucy Westenra** (now called Lucy Holmwood). Before Van Helsing finally defeated Dracula, the war almost claimed the life of **Mina Murray** (now known as Mina Holmwood).

The Horror of Dracula was even more influenced by Grand Guignol than was *The Curse of Frankenstein.* Its graphic presentation of gore began with memorable opening frames of dripping red blood and was highlighted by Christopher Lee's showing his **fangs** to the audience just before bending over a yielding Mina whom he held tightly in his arms. Vampiric **sexuality** also was more overt, with the biting as a metaphor for the sex act. Dracula unleashed all of the chaotic life forces, most powerfully symbolized by sex, that society tried to suppress and science attempted to understand and control.

Like *The Curse of Frankenstein,* the *The Horror of Dracula* was an immense success. It made Christopher Lee an international star in ways his portrayal of **Frankenstein's monster** had not. And as would be true of other Draculas, Lee's fans tended to be women, a high percentage of them teenagers. Hammer moved quickly to capitalize on both of its successes, but in the long run *Dracula* proved to be the more lucrative theme.

As Hammer moved ahead with its next vampire (and other horror) movies, it began to encounter problems from censors. It had purchased the rights to *I Am Legend,* a classic vampire book, and hired its author, **Richard Matheson,** to work on the screenplay. However, the censor's office let it be known that the movie would be banned in England, and Hammer stopped filming. The subsequent banning of **Mario Bava**'s Italian-made *Black Sunday* served to inform Hammer of strict limits to what could, for the moment, be put on the screen; thus, for a brief period the company postponed new considerations of the vampire motif.

In its second Dracula movie, *The Brides of Dracula* (1960), Dracula did not actually appear, though David Peel was present as the Dracula-like Baron Meinster. Meinster succeeded where Dracula failed in his biting of Van Helsing (Cushing); but Van Helsing cauterized the wound, thus preventing the vampire's affliction from infecting him. Before the successful team from *The Horror of Dracula* was reassembled, however, Hammer produced the first of its movies with a female vampire, the *Kiss of the Vampire* (1962), starring Clifford Evans, Edward de Souza, Isobel Black, and Noel Williams as the vampire.

Lee made his return as Dracula in the 1965 *Dracula Prince of Darkness.* To establish continuity, director Terence Fisher began the new film with footage from the end of *The Horror of Dracula.* The film also developed one of a series of creative ways to resurrect the dead count. In this case, Dracula's servant killed a man whose blood was allowed to drip on Dracula's ashes. This sequel was memorable both for Lee's impressive performance (though he had few lines) and for the graphic staking of Barbara Shelley by a group of monks, made possible by some easing of the standards of censorship through the decade.

In *Dracula Has Risen from the Grave* (1968), Dracula was resurrected by a priest who allowed his blood to drip on the count's frozen body. (Dracula had died by drowning in an icy pond in *Dracula Prince of Darkness*). Meanwhile, Fisher had moved on to other projects and did not direct this film, which marked the beginning of the downward trend that would characterize future vampire movies that Hammer assigned to less-experienced directors. The most memorable scene was Dracula pulling the stake from his own body (a scene Christopher Lee protested at the time). There also was an increasingly explicit depiction of sexual themes. In *Dracula Prince of Darkness,* Dracula embraced the passive Mina as he bit her. But in *Dracula Has Risen from the Grave,* the vampire's female victims/lovers began to react to the count, signaling their participation in the event and experiencing a sexual thrill from it. The sexual give-and-take of the vampire's bite became even more graphic in *Taste the Blood of Dracula* 1970).

Taste the Blood of Dracula brought the count back to Victorian England. In the film, a member of the British royalty witnessed Count Dracula's demise, as depicted in *Dracula has Risen from the grave,* and collected some of his blood and several of his personal possessions. In a magic ceremony, he attempted to revive Dracula by drinking his blood. Dracula arose, but at the cost of his benefactor's life. Meanwhile, several men who had been privy to the process of resurrecting Dracula stole his ring and cloak. Dracula proceeded to attack the men by way of their two female children. The interaction of Dracula and his female victims suggested a conscious use of vampirism as a symbol responding to new attitudes about sexuality that developed in the late 1960s.

Immediately after *Taste the Blood of Dracula,* Lee began filming *Scars of Dracula* (1971) under the direction of **Roy Ward Baker.** The story was set in **Castle Dracula,** where a young man, his girlfriend, and several others were exploring. Dracula began to kill them one by one until only the young man stood as a barrier to the woman, the real object of the vampire's quest. The story of Dracula and the woman, however, became a subplot set in the parentheses of Dracula's encounter with a more transcendental force—nature. At the beginning of the movie Dracula was awakened by a bolt of lightning that struck his coffin. In the end he was killed by a similar bolt that struck a metal spike he had intended to use on the remaining live male.

Hammer's most intense attention to vampirism came in 1970 through 1972. The studio produced six films, which necessitated going beyond mere variations on the Dracula story. The first choice for a new thrust was **Sheridan Le Fanu**'s story, **"Carmilla".** *Vampire Lovers* (1970), possibly the most faithful adaptation of *Carmilla,* opened with the awakening of the vampire Carmilla Karnstein (who assumed an anagram of her name, Mircalla). She had returned to Karnstein Castle in the present, where she was introduced to the social world. She first attracted and then vampirized Laura, the subject of the original story, and then Emma, an acquaintance. Before she was able to kill Emma, however, her work was discovered and a group of male vampire hunters tracked her down in the chapel and killed her. *Vampire Lovers* reached a new level of sexual explicitness and visual gore. The amply endowed **Ingrid Pitt** played Mircalla, who seduced Laura (Pippa Steele) and Emma (Madeleine Smith) in scenes with lesbian overtones. Following the trend set in the *Dracula* movies, the film continued the depiction of blood and violence, especially in the opening and closing scenes during which the vampire was killed.

Carmilla inspired a second film, *Lust for a Vampire* (1971), a film that gave **Jimmy Sangster** the opportunity to move from his screenwriting role to directing. The movie, with its standard emphasis on graphic violence, opened with one of the more memorable horror scenes. Mircalla/Carmilla (now played by Yutte Stengaard), Count Karnstein (Mike Raven), and his wife were all awakened by the blood of a sacrificial victim killed over their graves. The revived Mircalla then turned to several males as her victims (rather than her usual female ones); but as the deaths mounted, the villagers discovered her vampirism and killed her and the Karnstein family in a **fire.**

Ingrid Pitt returned to the screen for her second vampire role in 1971 as **Elizabeth Bathory** in *Countess Dracula*. The film centered on Bathory's last years, when she attempted to vampirize teenagers (both male and female) of their youth so that her own beauty and youthful appearance would remain intact. The voluptuous Pitt, transforming back and forth from the aging countess to the rejuvenated vampire, made the film work.

The trend toward violence seemed to peak in the second of the 1971 vampire releases, *Vampire Circus*. Set in Serbia in 1810, Count Mitterhouse (Robert Tayman), a vampire, was revived and set out to seek revenge on the town he held responsible for his death a century before. The instruments of his revenge were circus performers who had set up their tents to entertain the townspeople. However, the performers soon joined the count in murdering the town's leading citizens. The bloody murders set the stage for a closing battle scene with aroused villagers attacking the circus. The film ended with Mitterhouse being staked and decapitated.

On the heels of its 1971 successes, Hammer exploited the Dracula theme again with *Dracula A.D. 1972*, which attempted to bring Dracula into the contemporary world. The film did not deal with the role that Dracula might assume in the complex modern world; rather, it moved a Victorian plot into a contemporary setting. The story concerned Dracula's emergence among a group of young people in the early 1970s. Constantly encountering hostile, unfamiliar structures that left him ineffective in the present-day world, Dracula vampirized several of the youngsters and used them as his instruments. **Peter Cushing** returned in his Van Helsing role as the **vampire hunter**—a dedicated descendent of the original—to track Dracula to his death.

The second 1972 offering to vampire fans was *Captain Kronos, Vampire Hunter*, the story of a young hero who traveled the country searching out and disposing of vampires. Based in part on American cowboy heroes, Kronos arrived complete with an assistant—for some comic relief. The film's failure at the box office not only canceled Hammer's plans for a new series based on Kronos, but in fact, highlighted a significant aspect of the vampire myth. The myth was about vampires and all that they symbolize, not necessarily the destruction of evil.

The 1972 *Twins of Evil* returned to the story of Carmilla for inspiration. Hammer selected twins Mary and Madeline Collinson to play Mary and Freida Gelhorn. The two were unleashed by Count Karnstein on the local village to avenge the death of the Karnstein family. The spread of the vampire epidemic attracted the Van Helsing-like Gustav Weil (played by Peter Cushing) to mount a crusade to destroy all the vampires. As the plot unfolded, the movie pictured two opposing and ambiguous forces: the vampire and the overly zealous, puritanical vampire-hunter—who was himself tainted with evil. The conflict resulted in the death of Count Karnstein and the vampires, along with Weil and some of his cohorts. The twins were relatively innocent bystanders, and one escaped (the other was killed).

Lee's final appearance in the Hammer *Dracula* movies occurred in *The Satanic Rites of Dracula* (1973), also known as *Count Dracula and His Vampire Bride*. Again the scene was contemporary London, where an aging Van Helsing was consulted by Scotland Yard on a black magic group that had come to their attention. His investigation led him, however, to Dracula, who had emerged as a real estate dealer and was surrounded by a group of corrupt (but not vampirized) businessmen. Because of his partners, Dracula escaped Van Helsing's first attack, which utilized—for some inexplicable reason—a silver **bullet** (a werewolf remedy). With the aid of his granddaughter, Van Helsing continued the attack. This movie revived an old folk remedy for conquering vampires, as Dracula was led into a **hawthorn** bush.

The vampire world created by Hammer finally was exhausted with a cooperative project between the studio and Shaw Brothers, a massive movie production company in Hong Kong.

Directed by Roy Ward Baker, *The Legend of the Seven Golden Vampires* (1974) (also known as *The Seven Brothers Meet Dracula*) had **Abraham Van Helsing** (again portrayed by **Peter Cushing**) traveling to China to find the elusive Dracula. Early in the film, Van Helsing met Hsu Tien-an, the local vampire hunter. In China, both vampire and vampire hunters naturally knew martial arts, and the film emerged as a feeble attempt to merge the two genres. The merger did not work, however, and the film was a commercial failure.

By 1974, at the time it authorized the filming of *The Legend of the Seven Golden Vampires,* Hammer Films was in financial trouble. It had hoped that its exploitation of the martial arts theme, added to its tried-and-true vampire theme, would be a great success. Instead, the combination had quite the opposite effect. Warner Brothers, which had distributed many of Hammer's films in America, refused to release this one; and in the end the Chinese vampires merely speeded Hammer's swift move into bankruptcy in 1975. An era of vampire movies was over. The studio had explored the vampire theme for a generation. Its movies inspired a worldwide boom in vampire (and horror) movies in the 1960s as many directors attempted to copy the Hammer successes. But hampered by low budgets and even lower production values, they rarely reached Hammer's proficiency.

Hammer was then moved into receivership. In 1975 it was purchased by Ray Skeggs, who set about restructuring the business. Throughout the years, the Hammer tradition has been kept alive by a newsstand fanzine, *The House of Hammer*, launched at the beginning of 1976. In 1993 Hammer announced that it was back in business and had a major agreement with Warner Brothers. Among its productions were to be a remake of *The Quatermass Xperiment* and a 44-part series, the *Haunted House of Hammer*. As of the end of 1993, Skeggs had not yet announced any new vampire films, but he vowed to keep the Hammer tradition of horror alive.

Sources:

Adair, Gilbert, and Nick Roddick. *A Night at the Pictures: Ten Decades of British Film*. London: Columbus Books, 1985. 144 pp.

Eyles, Allen, Robert Adkinson, and Nicolas Fry, eds. *The House of Horror: The Story of Hammer Films*. London: Lorrimer Publishing Ltd., 1973. 127 pp.

Flynn, John L. *Cinematic Vampires*. Jefferson, NC: McFarland and Company, 1992. 320 pp.

Hutchings, Peter. *Hammer and Beyond: The British Horror Film*. Manchester: Manchester University Press, 1993. 193 pp.

Landy, Marcia. *British Genres: Cinema and Society, 1930-1960*. Princeton, NJ: Princeton University Press, 1991. 553 pp.

McCarty, John. *Splatter Movies*. Albany, NY: FantaCo Enterprises, Inc., 1981. 160 pp.

Marrero, Robert. *Vampires Hammer Style*. Florida: RGM Productions, (app. 1974). 98 pp.

Pirie, David. *Heritage of Horror: The English Cinema, 1946-1972*. New York: Avon, 1973.

Pohle, Robert W., Jr., & Douglas C. Hart. *The Films of Christopher Lee*. Metuchen, NJ: Scarecrow Press, 1983. 227 pp.

Snead, Elizabeth. "Horror Master Hammer Films Rises from the Dead." *USA Today* (October 28, 1993): 4D.

HARKER, JONATHAN

At the beginning of *Bram Stoker's Dracula,* Jonathan Harker arrived in **Bistritz, Romania,** in the midst of a journey to **Castle Dracula.** Upon his arrival at the Golden Krone Hotel, a note from Count Dracula awaited him. He was to go to the **Borgo Pass,** where a carriage from the castle would pick him up. When people learned of his destination to the castle, they were frightened and concerned for his welfare, and one lady gave him a rosary with a **crucifix** to wear. He was taken to Borgo Pass and then transported to Castle Dracula, where Dracula invited him in. Harker ignored the unusual appearance and manner of the count as he ate that evening. The next afternoon as he explored the castle, he noticed the lack of mirrors. He and Dracula spoke of England and worked to complete Dracula's purchase of **Carfax,** a house in the **London** suburb of Purfleet.

The next day, the visit to Castle Dracula took on a strange and even sinister quality. As Harker shaved, Dracula suddenly appeared behind him. Dracula knocked the **mirror** aside, but not before Harker noticed that the image of Dracula behind him was not reflected in the mirror. He also noticed that Dracula recoiled from the crucifix.

Harker began to catalog the strange occurrences day by day and concluded that for some reason he was being held prisoner. He tried to act as if the visit was normal, but then was ordered to write a series of letters telling his employer that he was extending his visit.

Harker became convinced of Dracula's extrahuman nature as he watched him crawl down the outside wall of the castle. He subsequently encountered the other residents of the castle, the **vampire brides,** three women who attacked him only to be thwarted at the last moment by Dracula's sudden appearance. As he pondered his condition and strategized ways to flee, he noticed that a band of **Gypsies** had arrived. He escaped from his room and roamed through the castle. He found the count lying in a box of earth and considered killing him, but he did not. A second time he approached Dracula, immobile in his **vampire sleep,** but again found himself unable to complete the kill. Dracula escaped and left Harker behind in the castle.

Somehow Harker finally escaped and made his way to Budapest, where he became a patient at the Hospital of St. Joseph and St. Mary. The sisters who ran the hospital informed his fiancee, **Mina Murray,** of his arrival. Mina left England, in spite of the declining health of her friend, **Lucy Westenra,** to go to Budapest where she and Harker were married.

Upon their return to England, they were informed of Lucy's death, and Harker met Dr. **Abraham Van Helsing,** who had been called in as a consultant in her case. By adding the journal of his experiences in Castle Dracula to the data on Lucy's death, a picture of what was occurring began to emerge. Also, he had spotted Dracula walking around London. Once Harker recovered his health and his sense of sanity, he and Mina worked together to compile and correlate information on Dracula's activities. Harker then traveled into London to locate and track the movement of the boxes of earth Dracula had brought with him from the castle.

Harker attended the meeting at which Van Helsing organized an informal committee, and he was the first to answer Van Helsing's call for a commitment to destroy Dracula. Harker joined in the search for the boxes of earth, unaware that Mina was at that very moment under attack. He had believed her fatigue to be caused by stress. Several days later, he was at home with Mina when Dracula arrived. Dracula put Harker to sleep while he proceeded to exchange blood with Mina, a process interrupted by the timely arrival of the other men. They succeeded in driving Dracula away.

Harker accompanied Van Helsing on the final chase back to Castle Dracula. He traveled the last leg of the journey on horseback, along with associate **Arthur Holmwood,** and arrived with the others just as the box containing Dracula's body was deposited in front of the castle. With **Quincey P. Morris,** he approached the box and used a large knife to slit Dracula's throat. At the same moment, Morris plunged his Bowie knife into Dracula's heart. In the fracas that concluded with Dracula's death, Morris was killed. Harker and Mina went on to live happily, and named their first child after Morris. Seven years after killing Dracula, the couple returned to **Transylvania,** where many of the memories of their life converged.

It has been suggested that the character of Jonathan Harker was based upon Joseph Harker, a young artist who worked at the Lyceum Theatre where Bram Stoker was employed. Harker worked with a team of designers that created the stage setting for the theater's production of *Macbeth*. Stoker had known Harker's father, a character actor who had been kind to Stoker in his earlier years. When the job was completed, Stoker returned the favors shown him by helping Harker establish himself independently as an artist.

As *Dracula* was brought to the stage and screen, Harker's role in the story frequently suffered, though not as much as the character of Quincey P. Morris, who was cut out completely to simplify the complex plot for dramatic presentation. In the stage versions, Harker's important opening trip to Transylvania was deleted. When that segment of the novel was returned to the script in the movie version of ***Dracula*** **(1931)** with **Bela Lugosi, R. N. Renfield**—not Harker—made the trip to Castle Dracula. In ***Dracula*** **(1974)** with **Jack Palance,** he arrived at Castle Dracula not as a naive real estate dealer, but as a secret agent in league with Van Helsing. However, he was attacked and killed early in the course of events, before Van Helsing could arrive to assist him. Only in **Francis Ford Coppola**'s ***Bram Stoker's Dracula*** did Harker have the central role he played in the novel from the opening chapter to the final death of Dracula at his hand.

Sources:

Haining, Peter. "The Origin of Jonathan Harker." *CDFC (Count Dracula Fan Club) Special* (n.d.): 3-4.

HARMONYROAD PRESS

HarmonyRoad Press is a small publishing company founded in 1992 specializing in *Dark Shadows* books and periodicals. It is headed by Connie Jonas. Among its publications are *Christmas in Collinsport,* a seasonal anthology of pictures, poetry, and prose; Anna Shock's collected short stories, *Shadowed Reflections*; and the novels *Masks and Facades* and *A Matter of Trust* by Jonas. Jonas also edits *The Music Box,* a *Dark Shadows* fanzine named for the music box owned by *Dark Shadows* character Josette. *The Music Box* features fiction, art, poetry, and fan news. In 1992 the press announced that it would publish a new single-issue fanzine edited by Travis McKnight, *The Lara Zine,* built around *Dark Shadows* actress Lara Parker, who played the part of Angelique.

Connie Jonas is a member of the **Collinsport Players,** a fan-founded dramatic group that presents skits at the annual **Dark Shadows Festival.** HarmonyRoad Press published an initial anthology of its original drama in 1993. The Press may be contacted c/o Connie Jonas, PO Box 40366, Portland, OR 97240-0366.

Sources:

Christmas in Collinsport. Portland, OR: HarmonyRoad Press, 1992. 45 pp.

Jonas, Connie. *The Collinsport Players Companion.* Vol. I. Portland, OR: HarmonyRoad Press, 1993. 108 pp.

———. *Masks and Facades.* Portland, OR: HarmonyRoadPress, 1993. 387 pp.

————. *A Matter of Trust.* Portland, OR: HarmonyRoad Press, 1991. 217 pp.

The Lara Zine. Portland, OR: HarmonyRoad Press, 1993.

Shock, Anna H. *Shadowed Reflections.* Portland, OR: HarmonyRoad Press, 1993. 40 pp.

HARTMANN, FRANZ (1838-1912)

Franz Hartmann, theosophist and author on the occult, was born in Bavaria, Germany. Through his mother, he claimed to be descended from Irish nobility. He became a physician and moved to the United States to practice his profession. In America, he encountered spiritualism and in the late 1870s became associated with the newly founded Theosophical Society. The international headquarters of the society was established in Adyar, **India,** in the early 1880s and Hartmann was invited to stay for a period. In 1884 he published his first major work, the sympathetic *Report of Observations During Nine Months' Stay at the Headquarters of the Theosophical Society at Adyar (Madras), India.* His report was largely lost in the furor that was to follow the next year when Richard Hodgson published his devastating attack upon theosophical leader Madame H. P. Blavatsky, claiming that all the unusual occurrences that had been reported around her were the result of fraud. The Hodgson Report forced Blavatsky into a period of retirement in England, and Hartmann accompanied her back to Europe. He had meanwhile been working on his next book, *Magic, Black and White* (1885).

Hartmann later left Blavatsky in England and returned to his native Bavaria. There, he claimed, he encountered a secret order of occultists, Rosicrucians. He served as the president of the Theosophical Society in **Germany** for a brief period, but soon left to found his own independent group. It was during this period that Hartmann became interested in vampirism. He investigated several cases of contemporary vampirism and reported them in a series of articles in occult journals. From these investigations, Hartmann developed a theory of **psychic vampirism.**

He came to believe that vampires were real but were not bloodsucking revenants. They were better described as a force field of subhuman intelligence that acted instinctively, not rationally. Hartmann saw the vampiric force as more malignant than evil. He supported this theory with his report of a young serving boy who had exhibited classic signs of a vampire attack. The boy was emaciated to the point of physical collapse, yet had an insatiable appetite. He reported that a force had settled on his chest, during which time he became paralyzed and unable to cry out. He claimed the force had sucked the life out of him. His employer attended the boy during one of these attacks and reported that he had grasped an invisible yet tangible gelatinlike substance resting on the boy's chest. Hartmann concluded that the man had encountered ectoplasm, a mysterious substance that was alleged to stream from the bodies of spiritualist mediums during seances.

In 1895, Hartmann authored a book about the phenomena surrounding premature burial. He developed a theory put forth earlier by **Z. J. Pierart,** a French psychical researcher in the 1860s, concerning the astral body. Pierart hypothesized that when a person was buried alive, the astral body (a ghostly double of the physical body, which many occultists believe to be an essential component of every individual) separated from the physical body. The astral body would vampirize others (taking both blood and life) and thus nourish the living body in the tomb; hence the lifelike characteristics of many exhumed corpses. Hartmann ascribed this theory to Paracelsus (1493-1541), the sixteenth-century alchemist. Hartmann took the theory one step further, suggesting that the astral body could be severed completely from the physical and thus continue as a free-floating, earthbound vampire spirit. He cited one case in which a young man committed suicide after being rejected by the woman he loved. Following the man's death, Hartmann believed, his astral form attached itself to the woman and began to suck the life out of her.

Hartmann's cases have become classic reports of actual modern vampires (and as such were reprinted in the volumes by **Montague Summers** and **Donald Glut**), though his theories generally have been discarded except within a few occult circles. Occult theories of the intangible "astral body" and of "ectoplasm" provide an explanation by referring to phenomena equally elusive and as much in need of explanation as vampirism. Most modern theories of psychic vampirism view it as a report on the social interaction of living persons.

Hartmann wrote a number of occult books. After the turn of the century, he spent much of his time wandering in the Untersberg Mountains near Salzberg. He died at Kepten, Bavaria.

Sources:

Glut, Donald F. *True Vampires of History.* New York: H C Publishers, 1971. 191 pp.
Hartmann, Franz. "An Authenticated Vampire Story." *Occult Review* (September 1909).
———. "A Miller of D-----." *Occult Review* 9, 5 (November 1924): 258-59.
———. "A Modern Case of Vampirism." Rept. in Donald F. Glut. *True Vampires of History.* New York: H C Publishers, 1971, pp. 128-31.
———. *Premature Burial.* London: 1896.
Rogo, Scott. "In-depth Analysis of the Vampire Legend." *Fate* 21, 9 (September 1968): 70-77.
Summers, Montague. *The Vampire in Europe.* London: Routledge, Kegan Paul, Trench, Trubner, & Co., 1929. 329 pp. Reprint. New Hyde Park, NY: University Books, 1960. 329 pp.

HAWTHORN

The hawthorn *(Crataegus oxyacantha),* a small tree of the rose family, was prevalent throughout southern Europe. The plant is also known as the whitethorn and is typical of a number of related thorn bushes (wild mountain rose, black thorn) that are substituted for hawthorn in different locations. In ancient times, hawthorn was used both as a symbol of hope and as a charm against **witchcraft** and sorcery. As such, it was often placed in the cradles of infants. As a protection against witchcraft, people might build a barrier of hawthorn around their house or doorway. The Greeks placed

◀

CHRISTOPHER LEE IN FATAL
ENCOUNTER WITH A
HAWTHORN PLANT.

pieces of hawthorn in the casements of houses to prevent the entrance of witches. In Bohemia, hawthorn was put on the thresholds of the cow houses, also to prevent witches from entering. The antiwitchcraft use of hawthorn easily transferred to the closely related vampire.

The hawthorn united two ancient practices. First, to protect one's home or another place, people commonly erected a symbolic barrier such as a hawthorn bush. While unable to stop or even slow down the usual physical forces, hawthorn was believed to be capable of blocking intruding supernatural forces or spirits. Second, hawthorn was thought by many to have a sacred quality as it was one of several plants designated as the bush from which Christ's crown of thorns was made. Hawthorn branches were variously placed on the outside of a **coffin,** in the corpse's sock, or on top of the corpse.

In Bosnia, a particular twist to the hawthorn legend developed. When visiting the home where a person had just died, women placed a small piece of hawthorn behind their headcloth, and then threw the twig away on their way home. If the deceased person was a vampire, it would focus its attention upon the hawthorn rather than follow the woman home. According to the **Bram Stoker** character, Dr. **Abraham**

Van Helsing, a branch of wild rose on the coffin would keep a vampire confined inside. Stoker probably learned of this practice from Emily Gerard. Her book, *Land Beyond the Forest* (a major source for ***Dracula***), stated that the people of Transylvania often "lay the thorny branch of a wild rose bush across the body to prevent it from leaving the coffin." In spite of Stoker's use of it, the thorn did not attain a prominent role in modern literary and movie vampire lore. The hawthorn made a brief appearance at the end of **Hammer Films'** *The Satanic Rites of Dracula*, in which **Christopher Lee** as Dracula was destroyed by being trapped in a hawthorn bush.

In addition to the plant's thorn and bush applications, among the **southern Slavs,** the wood of the hawthorn or blackthorn was to be used in the **stake** that impaled the vampire's corpse. It might be hammered through the head, heart, or stomach.

Sources:

Gerard, Emily. *Land Beyond the Forest.* 2 vols. New York: Harper & Brothers, 1888.

Lehner, Ernst, and Johanna Lehner. *Folklore and Symbolism of Flowers, Plants and Trees.* New York: Tudor Publishing Company, 1960. 128 pp.

Perkowski, Jan L. *The Darkling: A Treatise on Slavic Vampirism.* Columbus, OH: Slavica Publishers, 1989. 169 pp.

Porteous, Alexander. *Forest Folklore, Mythology, and Romance.* London: George Allen & Unwin, 1928. 319 pp. Reprint. Detroit: Singing Tree Press, 1968. 314 pp.

Summers, Montague. *The Vampire in Europe.* London: Routledge, Kegan Paul, Trench, Trubner, & Co., 1929. 329 pp. New Hyde Park, NY: University Books, 1961. 329 pp.

HELD, ERIC S. *See:* VAMPIRE INFORMATION EXCHANGE

THE HIGHGATE VAMPIRE

One of the more interesting interludes in vampire history concerns events that took place at a cemetery in the Highgate section of London during the years 1967 to 1983. The cemetery, officially called the Cemetery of St. James, was consecrated by the bishop of London in 1839, four days before Queen Victoria's 20th birthday. It gained some association through its slightly disguised use by **Bram Stoker** as the burial place of **Lucy Westenra,** after her death (as a result of **Dracula**'s attacks).

The modern story of vampires at Highgate began with reports of a phantomlike entity seen in the cemetery in the evenings. While rumors of a ghost circulated, occult investigator and head of the **Vampire Research Society, Sean Manchester** received the account of schoolgirl Elizabeth Wojdyla and her friend, who claimed to have seen some graves open and the dead rise from them. Wojdyla also reported having nightmares in which something evil tried to come into her bedroom. Over several years, Manchester collected similar accounts of unusual sightings associated with the cemetery. In 1969 Wojdyla's nightmares returned, except now the malevolent figure actually came into her room. She had developed the symptoms of pernicious anemia and on her neck were two small wounds suggestive of a classic vampire's bite. Manchester and Elizabeth's boyfriend treated her as a victim of vampirism and filled her room with **garlic,** crosses, and holy **water.** She soon improved. Meanwhile, various people continued to add new reports of seeing a ghostly being in the cemetery.

Because they were of a common sort, no one probably would have heard of the Highgate reports had not signs been found that the cemetery and a nearby park were being used for rituals that involved the killing of animals. Some of the dead animals had been drained of blood, and the local newspaper asked in its headline, ''Does a Wampyr Walk in Highgate?'' Manchester then reported that he had been contacted by another woman who had the same symptoms as Wojdyla. The young woman, followed while sleepwalking, led Manchester to a cluster of burial vaults in the cemetery. Manchester told the press that he believed a genuine vampire existed at Highgate and should be dealt with accordingly. The newspaper story and a subsequent feature spot on the independent Thames TV led to the cemetery becoming a gathering point of the curious. A group of amateur filmmakers used it as the site for a film, *Vampires by Night.* On Friday, March 13 in 1970, before an assembled crowd of onlookers, Manchester and two cohorts entered the vault where three empty **coffin**s were found. They lined the coffins with garlic, and in each they placed a cross. The vaults were sprinkled with salt (used for exorcisms) and holy water.

Events turned nasty in August when the body of a young woman was found at the cemetery. It appeared that someone had treated the corpse as a vampire and had decapitated and tried to burn it. An enraged citizenry demanded that the authorities protect the bodies of loved ones from abuse. Before the month was out, the police arrested two men who claimed to be **vampire hunters.** The men were a factor in the souring relationship between Manchester and the police. But while the police were distracted by the amateur vampire hunters, Manchester had quietly entered another vault and discovered what he believed was a real vampire. Rather than mutilating the body (a crime in England), he read an exorcism and sealed the vault with cement permeated with pieces of garlic.

In the summer of 1970, David Farrant, another amateur vampire hunter, entered the field. He claimed to have seen the vampire and went hunting for it with a **stake** and **crucifix**—but was arrested. He later became a convert to a form of Satanism. He was later convicted on two charges of breaking into tombs at Highgate. In 1978 he denounced the vampire as a hoax he had created by himself in 1970. Manchester quickly responded, noting that the reports originated prior to Farrant's involvement and that he was not privy to the incidents that had made the Highgate vampire so newsworthy.

Meanwhile, in 1973, Manchester began an investigation of a mansion near Highgate Cemetery that had a reputation of being haunted. On several occasions

THE HIGHGATE VAMPIRE WAS SIGHTED ON SEVERAL OCCASIONS AT THE CEMETERY'S NORTH GATE.

Manchester and his associates entered the house. In the basement they found a coffin, which they dragged into the backyard. Opening the casket, Manchester saw the same vampire he had seen four years before in Highgate Cemetery. This time he conducted an exorcism by staking the body, which disintegrated into a slimy, foul-smelling substance, and burned the coffin. He had destroyed the Highgate Vampire. Soon after this incident, the mansion was demolished and an apartment house was erected in its place.

The consequences from the Highgate Vampire did not end with its death, however. In 1980 reports of dead **animals** found drained of blood began to appear in Finchley. Manchester believed that a vampire created by the bite of the Highgate Vampire was the cause. He contacted many of the people he had met in 1970 and eventually targeted a woman he called Lusia as the culprit. He discovered that Lusia had died and been buried in Great Northern London Cemetery, and he had dreams in which she came to him. One autumn evening in 1982, Manchester entered the cemetery. There he encountered a large, spiderlike creature about the size of a cat. He drove a stake through it. As dawn approached, it metamorphosed into Lusia—she had only now truly died. He returned her remains to the grave, thus ending the case of the Highgate Vampire.

Manchester has written an account of his perspective on *The Highgate Vampire,* and the Vampire Research Society offers a cassette tape concerning the incident.

Sources:

Farrant, David. *Beyond the Highgate Vampire.* London: British Psychic and Occult Society, 1991. 35 pp.
In Highgate Cemetery. London: Friends of Highgate Cemetery, 1992. 20 pp.
Manchester, Sean. *The Highgate Vampire.* London: British Occult Society, 1985. 172 pp. Rev. ed., London: Gothic Press, 1991. 190 pp.
———. "The Highgate Vampire." In Peter Underwood, ed. *The Vampire's Bedside Companion: The Amazing World of Vampires in Fact and Fiction.* London: Leslie Frewin, 1975, 81-121.
Thompson, Paul B. "The Highgate Vampire." *Pursuit* 16, 3. Reprint. *Fate* (May 1985): 74-80.

HOLMWOOD, ARTHUR

The Honorable Arthur Holmwood, one of the leading characters in **Bram Stoker**'s novel, *Dracula,* was first mentioned in Chapter five as **Lucy Westenra**'s true love, and soon afterward he asked Lucy to marry him. He was tied to two other characters, Dr. **John Seward** and **Quincey P. Morris,** with whom he had traveled various parts of the world with. Holmwood did not participate in much of the early action of the novel because his father's illness called him from Lucy's side. Later in the novel, following his father's death, he became the new Lord Godalming.

Holmwood appeared in **Whitby** soon after Lucy's first encounter with **Dracula.** He called Seward to examine her, and gave her one of the needed transfusions. He also joined in the futile watch before Dracula's last attack. Just before her death, as she was turning into a vampire, Lucy tried to attack him, but he was saved by **Abraham Van Helsing,** who had been called in as a consultant by Seward. Holmwood was hesitant in responding to Van Helsing's call to treat Lucy as a vampire, but he finally joined Van Helsing, Seward, and Morris in trapping and killing her. With Van Helsing at his side, he drove the **stake** into her body and assisted in removing her head and filling her mouth with **garlic.**

Becoming an integral part of the team to search out and destroy Dracula, Holmwood entered **Carfax** to sanitize Dracula's home base of the vampire's influence. He also went into south and west London with Morris to seek out Dracula's other resting places. He traveled with **Mina Murray** and the team to **Transylvania** and was present in the final confrontation before the castle when both Dracula and Morris were killed.

In the movement of the novel to the stage and screen, Holmwood has received quite varied treatment. He, like Morris, was dropped from the stage play as a superfluous character. And, as might be expected, he did not appear with **Bela Lugosi** in *Dracula* (**1931),** which was based on the play. However, he came to the center in the *The Horror of Dracula* (1957) as the husband of Mina and brother of Lucy. In that movie, the Holmwood household became the target of Dracula's attack in England. He was also present in **Francis Ford Coppola**'s *Bram Stoker's Dracula,* where his part most closely approximated his role in the novel.

Sources:

Waller, Gregory A. *The Living and the Undead: From Stoker's Dracula to Romero's Dawn of the Dead.* Urbana, IL: University of Illinois Press, 1986. 376 pp.

HOMOSEXUALITY AND THE VAMPIRE

The vampire, especially in its literary and cinematic form, mixed elements of horror and sexuality. To many, it became a symbol of the release of the powerful emotional energies believed to be bottled up by restrictions on sexual behavior common to many societies. Homosexual behavior had always been suppressed during the centuries of Christian dominance of the West, and thus, it could be expected that in the heightened sensuality associated with vampirism, some homosexual elements might be present— and such has been the case. Literary critics have long noted a homosexual aspect among the very first pieces of vampire literature.

Samuel Taylor Coleridge's "Christabel", the first vampire poem in English, portended a theme that would reappear in vampire literature—**lesbian vampire** relationships. The poem centers upon the vampiric relationship of Christabel and Geraldine, the vampire. It became the inspiration for **"Carmilla",** the 1872 short story by **Sheridan Le Fanu,** in which the sexual element was even more pronounced. As other female vampires appeared in succeeding decades, primarily in short stories, the lesbian element often hovered in the background.

However, while there was a recurring lesbian presence in vampire literature, the same could not be said of male homosexuality. The male vampires of the nineteenth century—from **Lord Ruthven** to **Varney the Vampyre** to **Dracula**—invariably sank their teeth into female victims. This strict male heterosexuality was emphasized in *Dracula* the first major work to include male vampire victims. **Jonathan Harker** was not touched by Dracula, but remained behind as a feast for his **vampire brides** when Dracula departed for London. Nor did Dracula view any of **Lucy Westenra**'s suitors as additional sources of blood; he turned rather to **Mina Murray.** His several confrontations with the men were only in terms of physical combat.

In the movies, one could also note the absence of male vampires attacking male victims. When the plot called for such men-on-men attacks, they were always mediated by modern medicine, in the form of needles and transfusions (as in *The Return of Dr. X* and *Blood of the Vampire*) or by way of an animal (as in *The Devil Bat*). Not until the sexual revolution of the 1960s did a male homosexual vampire appear. The first gay vampire movie, a pornographic production, was *Does Dracula Really Suck?* (also released as *Dracula Sucks* and as *Dracula and the Boys*). During the 1970s several additional titles with gay vampires appeared: *Sons of Satan* (1973), *Tenderness of Wolves* (1973), and an Italian film, *Il Cavaliere Costante Nicosia*

Demoniaco Ovvero Dracula in Brianza (1975). Of these, only *Tenderness of Wolves* was released to the general public. The movie was devoted to the case of **Fritz Haarmann,** a homosexual serial killer who murdered a number of young boys and drank their blood. Two additional gay vampire movies also appeared in the filmographies: *Gayracula* (1983) and the undated *Love Bites.*

In literature gay vampires have made but few appearances. The most heralded gay writer on the vampire theme has been Jeffrey N. McMahan. His first book, *Somewhere in the Night* a Lambda Literary Award winner, was a collection of short horror stories that included several vampire tales. He also introduced the character of Andrew, a gay vampire who went on to become the subject of a novel, *Vampires Anonymous*, in which a modern-day vampire hunter and a vampire recovery group seek to cure individuals of vampirism. Andrew and the vampire community, however, see no need to be cured.

The most significant expression of a vampiric gay relationship came not from a gay writer, but in several novels by **Anne Rice.** Her first novel, *Interview with the Vampire,* featured the intense relationship between Louis and **Lestat de Lioncourt,** the homosexual connotations of which were not missed by reviewers. Rice was not attempting to highlight sexual orientation issues so much as gender issues—specifically, androgyny. However, this idea of male androgyny has frequently masked a more central concern for homosexuality or bisexuality. Lestat was pictured as one who easily bonded with males and frequently cried. Yet, when he briefly switched bodies with the mortal, Raglan James, he raped a woman. In several of Rice's novels, male vampires could not have "normal" intercourse—their sex organs being dysfunctional. She suggested, however, that the experience of biting and sucking blood was a far superior form of sex; the mutual sharing of blood by two vampires was an act analogous to intercourse. The Rice novels have been a source for the modern **gothic** rock movement, whose fans value the androgynous ideal and have opened their circles to homosexuality and other sexual expressions, such as transvestism and sadomasochism.

Gays and lesbians interested in vampires have founded two organizations, **The Secret Room,** a *Dark Shadows* fan club, and **Bite Me in the Coffin Not in the Closet Fan Club,** a more general interest fan club.

Sources:

Jones, Stephen. *The Illustrated Vampire Movie Guide.* London: Titan Books, 1993. 144 pp.
McMahan, Jeffrey N. *Somewhere in the Night.* Boston, MA: Alyson Publications, 1989. 182 pp.
———. *Vampires Anonymous.* Boston, MA: Alyson Publications, 1992. 253 pp.
Ramsland, Katherine. *The Vampire Companion.* New York: Ballantine Books, 1993. 506 pp.
Rice, Anne. *Interview with the Vampire.* New York: Alfred A. Knopf, 1976.

THE HORROR OF DRACULA

Second only to the **Bela Lugosi** version of *Dracula* (1931) in setting the image of Dracula in contemporary popular culture was the first of the **Hammer Films'**

Dracula movies starring **Christopher Lee.** Originally released as *Dracula (1958)*, it subsequently was released in the United States as *The Horror of Dracula*, the title commonly used to distinguish it not only from the other *Dracula* movies, but from the host of Christopher Lee Dracula/vampire films. The movement of Hammer Films into the horror market has become one of the most famous stories in motion picture history. *The Horror of Dracula* came on the heels of the company's success with a new version of *Frankenstein*, and utilized the following team: Christopher Lee as Dracula; **Peter Cushing** as **Abraham Van Helsing;** and **Terence Fisher** and **Jimmy Sangster** as director and screen writer, respectively.

While having the 1931 **Universal Pictures** production as a persistent reference point, *The Horror of Dracula* attempted to reinterpret the story and return to the **Bram Stoker** novel for inspiration (though it deviated from both the novel and the previous movie in important ways). The story opened with **Jonathan Harker** (John Van Eyssen) coming to **Castle Dracula** not as a real estate agent, but as Dracula's new librarian. Here, prior to Dracula's appearance, he encountered a young woman dressed in nightclothes. It soon was revealed that he was an undercover agent and had, in fact, come to Castle Dracula as Van Helsing's assistant to kill Dracula. Harker was attacked and bitten by the woman (Valerie Gaunt), whom he in turn killed. But in the process he became a vampire himself. (*The Horror of Dracula* popularized the assumption that a single bite by a vampire was all that was necessary for one to become a vampire—an opinion not proposed in Stoker's novel.) In this movie, Dracula escaped before Van Helsing arrived at Castle Dracula to check on his coconspirator. Discovering that Harker had been compromised, Van Helsing was forced to stake him, and he returned to England to begin a one-on-one confrontation with Dracula, which was the true subject of the film.

Dracula beat Van Helsing to England, where a new configuration of Stoker's familiar characters had been created. Gone were Dr. **John Seward, R. N. Renfield,** and **Quincey P. Morris. Arthur Holmwood** (Michael Gough) emerged as the dominant male. Rather than a suitor of **Lucy Westenra** (Carol Marsh), however, he was married to **Mina Murray** (Melissa Stribling), and Lucy was recast as his sister (and Harker's fiancee). Lucy also was the primary object of Dracula's interest, he having taken her picture from Harker before leaving the castle. Van Helsing discovered that Lucy already had been bitten and was vampirizing others, so he took the lead in killing her. An angry Dracula then attacked Mina.

In the final scene, Holmwood and Van Helsing chased Dracula back to his home. Dracula had discarded Mina in an open grave and was burying her when the hunters arrived. Arthur went to his wife's side while Van Helsing chased Dracula into his castle. Dracula had all but defeated Van Helsing, but, as so many villains before him, he paused to experience a very human moment of satisfaction. In that moment, Van Helsing recovered and, pushing the vampire aside, he rushed across the room and pulled the draperies from the window, allowing sunlight to stream into the room. The sunlight, which was fatal to vampires, caught Dracula's foot and quickly burned it. Grabbing a cross, Van Helsing pushed Dracula farther into the light, which then

HORROR OF DRACULA STAR CHRISTOPHER LEE STARRED IN MANY VAMPIRE MOVIES, INCLUDING *DRACULA, PRINCE OF DARKNESS,* SHOWN HERE.

completely consumed him. Dracula's ashes blew away in the wind, leaving only his large ring. (The ring and ashes would become important in future Hammer *Dracula* sequels, though there seems no reason to believe that Fisher had a sequel in mind when completing the *The Horror of Dracula.* By the same sunlight that killed Dracula, Mina was cured of her vampirism, and she and her husband were happily reunited.

Two elements contributed to the success of *The Horror of Dracula.* First, the movie presented a new openness toward **sexuality.** There is every reason to believe that the interpretation of the **psychological perspectives on vampire mythology,** such as that offered by Ernest Jones's now classic study *On the Nightmare* (1931), underlay the movie's presentation. That sexual element began with Harker's encounter with one of Dracula's brides. While Harker drew her to what he thought was a protective embrace, she gleefully took full advantage of the situation and bit him, a scene that has been the object of various psychological interpretations relative to teenage sexual awakening. That interpretation was reinforced by his subsequent attack on the woman with his stake. Harker's naive actions, of course, prove fatal.

Dracula was just as sexual as his vampire bride. He seduced the women he bit with kisses and gained their loving attention before he sank his teeth in their neck. As David J. Hogan, in *Dark Romance: Sexuality in the Horror Film,* notes, "When he (Lee) bites a young lovely's throat he is not merely feeding, but experiencing (and inducing) a moment of orgasmic ecstacy." Lee would go on from the *The Horror of Dracula* to become an international star and, like Lugosi, to develop a large and loyal female following.

The second element of success of *The Horror of Dracula* was that it was the first *Dracula* movie to be made in Technicolor. It made full use of red liquids from the still little understood blood dripping on a crypt during the opening credits to its more appropriate reappearances throughout the picture. Color added a new dimension to the horror movie and undergirded its revival in the 1960s. Color also cooperated with the heightened level of freedom concerning what could be pictured on the screen. In 1931, Dracula never showed his **fangs** or bit anyone on camera. However, Lee regularly showed his teeth and had no problem offering the women his vampire kiss.

Sources:

Hogan, David J. *Dark Romance: Sexuality in the Horror Film.* Jefferson, NC: McFarland & Company, 1986. 334 pp.

Jones, Ernest. *On the Nightmare.* 1931. Reprint. New York: Liveright Publishing Company, 1951. 374 pp.

Ursini, James, and Alain Silver. *The Vampire Film.* South Brunswick, NJ: A. S. Barnes and Company, 1975. 238 pp.

Waller, Gregory A. *The Living and the Undead: From Stoker's Dracula to Romero's Dawn of the Undead.* Urbana, IL: University of Illinois Press, 1986. 376 pp.

HOUSTON DARK SHADOWS SOCIETY

The Houston Dark Shadows Society was a *Dark Shadows* fan club founded in 1986 by Parker Riggs. It served primarily *Dark Shadows* fans in the Greater Houston, Texas area, though its membership grew to include fans around the country. The society published *Lone Star Shadows*, a quarterly newsletter edited by Riggs, featuring news of *Dark Shadows* fandom. It ran to 20 issues. Both the club and the magazine were discontinued in 1991.

HUMOR, VAMPIRE

To some, the stage vampire was essentially humorous, and the thought of being lampooned in the press was partially responsible for keeping **Hamilton Deane** from bringing his original *Dracula* play, which had been quite successful in rural England, to London. In fact, a comedic version of the Deane play, *Dracula, the Comedy of the Vampire,* appeared at various locations around Europe in the 1930s. With his knowledge of the theater, Deane could have expected some amount of fun to be had at his play's expense. A century earlier, **Charles Nodier** brought the vampire to the stage in Paris. Within a few months, several other vampire plays, all farces and most comments upon his play, opened in competing Parisian theaters.

The fact that vampire humor first appeared on stage was an indication of its future. Vampires as objects of humor made their primary appearance on the stage, and more recently in motion pictures, rather than in novels. Vampire books usually have been horror stories with only very rare hints of humor. Meanwhile, a stereotypical vampire was gradually created in the successive productions of *Dracula,* Hamilton Deane's original play in England (1924), and the portrayals of **Bela Lugosi** in the American play in 1927 and **Universal Pictures'** movie version in 1931. The creation of the vampire's image on the stage and screen provided the context for future opportunities to lampoon that image. To a much lesser extent, vampire fiction was not tied to the Lugosi vampire, while even the most variant vampire movie had to use the stereotypical Dracula as its starting point.

The spread of popular vampire humor awaited the creation of the widely recognized stereotypical cinematic vampire by Bela Lugosi in the 1930s. The first major attempt to exploit the humorous possibilities of Lugosi's **Dracula** occurred in the 1948 *Abbott and Costello Meet Frankenstein.* The plot of the movie revolved around Dracula's attempt to steal comedian Lou Costello's brain and place it in the head of the **Frankenstein's monster.** Lugosi returned to his Dracula role for the spoof, which in retrospect received high marks as one of Abbott and Costello's best movies. It was said to be far superior to *Abbott and Costello Meet Dr. Jekyll and Mr. Hyde* (1953), in which an unnamed actor made a cameo appearance as Dracula.

THE 1950s: Mainstream vampire humor in the 1950s was limited to two movies and a play. Early in the decade, Lugosi traveled to England to portray another vampire, Count Von Housen, in one of the series of Old Mother Riley comedies. *Mother Riley Meets the Vampire* (1952) (aka *My Son the Vampire*) was one of his less remembered roles. Lugosi's stereotyping as a horror actor drastically limited the roles offered him as he aged and led him to construct a 1954 Las Vegas stage production, ''The Bela Lugosi Review'', in which he was forced to play a spoof of the part he had made famous. In the second 1950s comedic vampire movie, *The Bowery Boys Meet the Monsters*, the vampire was secondary to the plot, which featured one of the Bowery Boys (Huntz Hall) being turned into a werewolf. More important than both of these movies was the first new vampire play in several decades. *I Was a Teenage Dracula*, a three-act mystery by Gene Donovan, heralded some 40 subsequent plays featuring Dracula for high school and other amateur productions, the great majority of which were comedies.

THE 1960s: The 1960s saw the production of one of the best comic vampire movies ever made, Roman Polanski's *The Fearless Vampire Killers* or *Pardon Me, But Your Teeth Are in My Neck* (1967).

Polanski's film (originally called *Dance of the Vampires*) concerned the antics of two vampire hunters, Professor Abrosius and his assistant (played by Polanski), as they tracked down the villainous Count Von Krolock (Ferdie Mayne). Among the more memorable scenes was a bizarre dance sequence from which the movie took its name.

However, the comic vampire really found a home on two television series, *The Addams Family* and *The Munsters.* Both shows attempted to place the classical "monsters," including several vampirelike characters, in an ordinary, "normal" middle-class American setting, and both ran through the 1964/65 and 1965/66 seasons. Both shows inspired early comic books that introduced the comic vampire to that medium. The Munsters, which featured a thinly disguised Count Dracula, led to a movie, *Munster Go Home!* (1966).

The gothic soap opera *Dark Shadows* became a hit daytime show on NBC-TV during the last years of the decade. Among the items created as a result of the show was possibly the first vampire joke book, *Barnabas Collins in a Funny Vein,* published in 1969. A second *Dark Shadows* joke book appeared in 1981, *Die Laughing,* compiled by Barbara Fister-Liltz and Kathy Resch.

A comedy drama featuring the Transylvanian Count included several plays simply entitled *Dracula* that originally were staged in 1965 and 1966, respectively.

THE 1970s: The 1970s opened with a new vampire play, *I'm Sorry, The Bridge Is Out, You'll Have to Spend the Night*, a musical comedy featuring the songs of Sheldon Allman and Bob Pickett. Allman had made a record titled *Sing Along with Drac*, which included such memorable titles as "Children's Day at the Morgue" and "Fangs for the Memory." Pickett had been the Dracula voice in the 1962 album *The Monster Mash,* that included not only the title song but "Blood Bank Blues" and "Transylvania Twist." The spoof opened in Los Angeles on April 28, 1970 at the Coronet Theatre. It featured several of the classic Universal monsters and included the insect-eating **R. N. Renfield,** from *Dracula,* who had his solo moment with a song called "Flies."

Several other vampire plays made their initial appearance in the 1970s. Both *Count Dracula* or *A Musical Mania for Transylvania* and *Monster Soup* or *That Thing in my Neck is a Tooth* were staged in 1974. They were joined by *The Vampire's Bride* or *The Perils of Cinderella* (1979) later in the decade.

The decade closed with what generally has been considered the best of the many comedy vampire movies, *Love at First Bite* (1979). George Hamilton played a modern Dracula in prerevolutionary **Romania.** As the movie opened, Dracula played the piano. The howls of the wolves grew louder and louder, and, in a slightly altered version of one of Bela Lugosi's famous lines, he shouted out, "Children of the night, shut up!" Forced out of his castle by the Communist government, he took the opportunity to search out a New York fashion model (Susan Saint James), with whose picture he had fallen in love. There he met Saint James's psychiatrist, a descendant of **Abraham Van Helsing** (Richard Benjamin). The movie was a delightful mixture of hilarious one-liners and humorous situations, such as Dracula waking up in the midst of a funeral service in an African American church.

Possibly second in popularity only to *Love at First Bite* as a humorous treatment of the vampire theme was *Andy Warhol's Dracula* (a.k.a. *Blood for Dracula,* an Italian production in which Dracula traveled to Italy looking for the blood of "wirgins." The humor centers upon his comment on modern society and the inability to find a virtuous (sexually pure) young woman—a fact graphically displayed by his regurgitating every time he got blood from an apparently virginal female.

In 1977, the first family of television comic horror, *The Addams Family,* returned with a full length movie, *Halloween with the Addams Family,* but response was disappointing. An adult sexually oriented comedy, *Dracula Blows His Cool* (1979), was produced in West Germany and dubbed in English for an American audience.

In 1974, Phil Hirsch and Paul Laikin compiled a new collection of vampire humor in *Vampire Jokes and Cartoons.*

The 1970s also marked the appearance of juvenile vampire literature, specifically designed for children and teens. Overwhelmingly, the approach to the vampire in children's books was very light (using vampires to teach tolerance for children who were different) to comedic. One of the more comic and delightful vampire characters for kids was *Bunnicula* (1979), a vegetarian vampire rabbit who slept during the day and attacked vegetables to suck out the juice at night. The rabbit presaged *Count Duckula* of the late 1980s.

THE 1980s AND 1990s: Vampire humor prospered in the 1980s with movies leading the way. By far the best of the comic films (harking back to Andy Warhol's movie) was *Once Bitten,* in which a female vampire (Lauren Hutton) went in search of a male virgin in Hollywood. Unlike the Warhol vampire, Hutton quickly found the inexperienced Mark Kendall (Jim Carrey) and began to vampirize him. His attempts to discover what was happening to him and then extract himself from the vampire's clutches provided the setting for the hilarity. Other comic vampire movies of the decade included *I Married a Vampire* (1984), *Who Is Afraid of Dracula?* (1985), *Transylvania 6-5000* (1985), and *Transylvania Twist* (1989).

During the 1980s, **Elvira,** the vampiric television horror show hostess, burst onto the national scene as a comic personality who combined features of the **vamp** with a Marilyn Monroe-type dumbness. Elvira attracted a devoted following and had her own fan club. She also developed a line of cosmetics and inspired a Halloween look-alike costume and a comic book. In 1988, she starred in her first feature-length movie, *Elvira, Mistress of the Dark.*

Developing in the 1980s and coming into their own in the 1990s were vampire Halloween greeting cards. As Halloween emerged as one of urban America's most celebrated holidays, it dropped much of its earlier role as a harvest festival and became a time for fun for youngsters. Vampires and bats have been perennial Halloween characters. In response, the greeting card industry produced hundreds of cards featuring the vampire, most built around vampire-oriented one-liners, to send to friends at Halloween. Accompanying the cards were many cartoon vampire party products. These Halloween products illustrated most clearly the severe stereotyping

THE HUMILIATION OF FANG ENVY...

HALLOWEEN CARDS SPECIALIZE
IN VAMPIRE HUMOR.

of the vampire image. Vampires could be quickly recognized (and distinguished from witches, ghosts, or other monsters) by their **fangs,** cape, widow's peak, and accompanying bats.

The 1980s also saw the flowering of vampire literature for children and youth. A large percentage of the more than 50 titles was humorous, though serious horror stories for teenagers also were produced. Typical of the comedic literature were the many titles of Victor G. Ambrus. Written for younger children, Ambrus developed a comical Dracula (complete with cartoon illustrations), who in his initial appearance in (*Count, Dracula* (1980), was content to teach children to count. *Dracula's Bedtime Storybook* (1981) had Dracula romping through British literature with **Frankenstein's monster,** Dr. Jekyll and Mr. Hyde, and **Sherlock Holmes.** A series of new titles continued into the 1990s. For older children, in addition to the further adventures of Bunnicula, there were such titles as Judi Miller's *A Vampire Named Murray,* the story of a vampire cousin from ''Vulgaria'' who came to live with the Kaufmans. Murray was allergic to human blood, but loved V-8 juice (and could warm up to vegetable soup). Murray did stand-up comedy for the kids, and they loved him. But the neighbors thought he was too different, and they wanted him to leave town.

The 1980s ended, and the 1990s began as the interest in vampires reached an all-time high. From 1980 through 1993, the number of vampire novels doubled and the number of vampire short stories and comic books multiplied several times. Thus, it was fitting that the period should be capped with a doubling of the number of vampire joke books. In 1986 Charles Keller finished his compilation of *Count Draculations: Monster Riddles*, followed in 1991 by Gordon Hill's *The Vampire Joke Book,* 64 pages of riddles. "Why did Dracula become a vegetarian? Because he couldn't bear stakes," was typical fare for Keller and Hill. The next year, **Jeanne Youngson,** president of the **Count Dracula Fan Club,** compiled *The World's Best Vampire Jokes.* For example: "Why do vampires have such a tough time? Some people never give a sucker an even break," or "What do you get when you cross a woolen scarf with a vampire? A very warm pain in the neck." James Howe followed Hill and Youngson in 1993 with the *Bunnicula Fun Book* (1993), combining jokes with fun things for children.

Interest in vampire humor depends upon the popularity of Dracula and his vampire cousins. The heightened attention vampires have been receiving suggests that a healthy current of vampire humor will continue through the 1990s and into the next century.

Sources:

Barnabas Collins in a Funny Vein. New York: Paperback Library, 1969.
Fister-liltz, Barbara, and Kathy Resch, eds. *Die Laughing.* North Riverside, IL: Phoenix Publications, 1981. 28 pp.
Hill, Gordon. *The Vampire Joke Book.* London: Foulsham, 1991. 64 pp.
Hirsch, Phil, and Paul Laikin, eds. *Vampire Jokes and Cartoons.* New York: Pyramid Books, 1974.
Howe, James. *Bunnicula Fun Book.* New York: Morrow Junior Books, 1993. 164 pp.
Keller, Charles. *Count Draculations: Monster Riddles.* New York: Little Simon (Simon and Schuster), 1986.
Youngson, Jeanne. *The World's Best Vampire Jokes.* New York: Dracula Press, 1992.

HUNGARY, VAMPIRES IN

Hungary, the country that gave **Bela Lugosi** to the world, has a special place in the history of vampires. Vampire historian **Montague Summers** opened his discussion of the vampire in Hungary by observing, "Hungary, it may not untruly be said, shares with Greece and Slovakia the reputation of being that particular region of the world which is most terribly infested by the Vampire and where he is seen at his ugliest and worst." **Bram Stoker**'s *Dracula* opened with **Jonathan Harker**'s trip through Hungary. Harker saw Budapest as the place that marked his leaving the (civilized) West and entering the East. He proceeded through Hungary into northeast **Transylvania,** then a part of Hungary dominated by the **Szekelys,** a Hungarian people known for their fighting ability. (Dracula was identified as a Szekely.) In the face of Stoker and Summers, and before the **Dom Augustin Calmet,** Hungarian scholars have argued that the identification of Hungary and vampires was a serious mistake of Western scholars ignorant of Hungarian history. To reach some perspective on this controversy, a brief look at Hungarian history is necessary.

THE EMERGENCE OF HUNGARY: The history of modern Hungary began in the late ninth century when the Magyar people occupied the Carpathian Basin. They had moved into the area from the region around the Volga and Kama rivers. They spoke a Finnish-Ugrian language, not Slavic. Their conquest of the land was assisted by Christian allies and, during the tenth century, the Christianization of the Magyars began in earnest. In 1000 A.D., Pope Sylvester crowned István, the first Hungarian king. Later in that century, when the Christians split into Roman Catholic and Eastern Orthodox branches, the Hungarians adhered to the Roman church.

István's descendants moved into Transylvania gradually but had incorporated the area into Hungary by the end of the thirteenth century. The Hungarian rulers established a system by which only Hungarians controlled the land. A Magyar tribe, the Szekleys were given control of the mountain land in the northeast in return for their serving as a buffer between Hungary and any potential enemies to the east. The Romanian people of Transylvania were at the bottom of the social ladder. Above them were the Germans, who were invited into cities in southern Transylvania. In return for their skills in building the economy, the Germans were given a number of special privileges. By the fourteenth century, many Romanians had left Transylvania for Wallachia, south of the Carpathians, where they created the core of what would become the modern state of **Romania.**

Following the death of the last of István's descendants to wear the crown of Hungary, it was ruled by foreign kings invited into the country by the nobles. The height of prosperity for the nation came in the late fifteenth century when Matthias Corvinus (1458-1490), a Romanian ethnic and contemporary of Wallachian prince **Vlad the Impaler,** ruled. He built his summer capital at **Visegrád** into one of the most palatial centers in eastern Europe.

Hungarian independence ended essentially at the battle of Mohács in 1526, which sealed the Turkish conquest of the land. During the years of Turkish conquest, while Islam was not imposed, Roman Catholic worship was forbidden. The Reformed Church was allowed, however, and remains a relatively strong body to the present. Transylvania existed as a land with an atmosphere of relative religious freedom, and both Calvinist Protestantism and Unitarianism made significant inroads. Unitarianism made significant gains at the end of the sixteenth century following the death of Roman Catholic Cardinal Bathory at the Battle of Selimbar (1599). The Szekelys were excommunicated and as a group turned to Unitarianism.

The Turks dominated the area until 1686 when they were defeated at the battle of Buda. Hungary was absorbed into the Hapsburg empire and Roman Catholicism rebuilt. The Austrian armies would soon push farther south into Serbia, parts of which were absorbed into the Hungarian province.

The eighteenth century was characterized by the lengthy rulerships of Karoly III (1711-1740) and Maria Theresa (1740-1780). Hungarian efforts for independence, signaled by the short-lived revolution in 1848, led to the creation in 1867 of Austria-Hungary. Austria-Hungary survived for a half century, but then entered World War I on Germany's side. In 1919 Austria-Hungary was split into two nations and the large

◀

VLAD THE IMPALER WAS
IMPRISONED AT VISEGRAD,
HUNGARY, POSSIBLY IN
SOLOMON'S TOWER.

segments of Hungary inhabited by non-Hungarian ethnic minorities were given to Romania, Serbia, and Czechoslovakia. Most importantly, Transylvania was transferred to Romania, a matter of continued tension between the two countries. Hungary was left a smaller but ethnically homogeneous land almost entirely comprised of people of Hungarian ethnicity but with a small but measurable number of **Gypsies.**

After the wars, Hungary was ruled by Miklós Horthy, a dictator who brought Hungary into an alliance with Hitler and Germany as World War II began. After the war, in 1948, the country was taken over and ruled by Communists until the changes of the 1990s led to the creation of a democratic state.

THE VAMPIRE EPIDEMICS: Following the Austrian conquest of Hungary and regions south, reports of vampires began to filter into western Europe. The most significant of these concerned events during 1725 to 1732, their importance due in large measure to the extensive investigations of the reported incidents carried on by Austrian officials. The cases of **Peter Plogojowitz** and **Arnold Paul** especially became the focus of a lengthy debate in the German universities. Different versions of the incidents identified the locations of the vampire epidemics as Hungary rather than (more properly) a Serbian province of the Austrian province of Hungary. The debate was summarized in two important treatises, the first of which, *Dissertazione sopre I Vampiri* by Archbishop **Giuseppe Davanzati,** assumed a skeptical attitude. The second, Dom Augustin Calmet's *Dissertations sur les Apparitiones des Anges des Démons et des Espits, et sur les revenants, et Vampires de Hingrie, de Boheme, de Moravie, et de Silésie,* took a much more accepting attitude.

Calmet's work was soon translated and published in German (1752) and in English (1759) and spread the image of eastern Europe as the home of the vampire. While Calmet featured vampire cases in Silesia (**Poland**), Bohemia, and Moravia (Czechoslovakia), the "Hungarian" cases of Paul and Plogojowitz were the most spectacular and best documented. The image of Hungary as a land of vampires was reinforced by Stoker and Summers, and later by both **Raymond T. McNally** and **Leonard Wolf,** who suggested that the Hungarian word *vampir* was the source of the English word vampire. That theory has more recently been countered by Katerina Wilson, who argued that the first appearance of the word 'vampir' in print in Hungarian post-dates the first published use of the term in most Western languages by more than a century (actually by some fifty years). The question remains open, however, in that it is highly possible that someone (for example, a German-speaking person in Hungary in the early eighteenth century) might have picked up the term in conversation and transmitted it to the West.

Meanwhile, Hungarian scholars confronted the issue. As early as 1854, Roman Catholic bishop and scholar Arnold Ipolyi assembled the first broad description of the beliefs of pre-Christian Hungary. In the course of his treatise he emphasized that there was no belief in vampires among the Hungarians. That observation was also made by other scholars, who wrote their articles and treatises in Hungarian destined never to be translated into Western languages. In current times, the case was again presented by Tekla Dömötör, whose book *Hungarian Folk Beliefs* was translated and published in English in 1982. He asserted, "There is no place in Hungarian folk beliefs for the vampire who rises forth from dead bodies and sucks the blood of the living." The conclusions of the Hungarian scholars have been reinforced by the observations of Western researchers, who have had to concede that few reports of vampires have come from Hungary. Most also assert, however, that in Hungarians' interaction with the Gypsies and their Slavic neighbors, such beliefs likely did drift into the rural regions.

VAMPIRELIKE CREATURES IN HUNGARY: Having denied the existence of the vampire in Hungarian folk culture, the Hungarian scholars from Ipolyi to Dömötör also detailed belief in a vampirelike being, the *lidérc*. The *lidérc* was an **incubus/succubus** figure that took on a number of shapes. It could appear as a woman or a man, an animal, or a shining light. Interestingly, the *lidérc* did not have the power of **transformation,** but rather was believed to exist in all its shapes at once. Through its magical powers, it caused the human observer to see one form or another. As an incubus/succubus it attacked victims and killed them by exhaustion. It loved them to death. Defensive measures against the *lidérc* included the placing of garters on the bedroom doorknob and the use of the ubiquitous **garlic.**

Hungarians also noted a belief in the *nora,* an invisible being described by those to whom he appeared as small, humanoid, bald, and running on all fours. He was said to jump on his victims and suck on their breasts. Victims included the same type of person who in Slavic cultures was destined for vampirism, namely the immoral and irreverent. As a result of the *nora,* the breast area swelled. The antidote was to smear garlic on the breasts.

Sources:

Calmet, Augustine. *The Phantom World.* 2 vols. London: Richard Bentley, 1746, 1850.
Dömötör, Tekla. *Hungarian Folk Beliefs.* Bloomington, IN: Indiana University Press, 1982.
Kabdebo, Thomas. *Hungary.* Santa Barbara, CA: Clio Press, 1980. 280 pp.
McNally, Raymond T. *A Clutch of Vampires.* New York: Bell Publishing Company, 1974. 255 pp.
Summers, Montague. *The Vampire in Europe.* 1929. New Hyde Park, NY: University Books, 1961. 329 pp.
"Vampires in Hungary." *International Vampire* 1, 4 (Summer 1991).
Wilson, Katherine M. "The History of the Word 'Vampire.'" *Journal of the History of Ideas* 64, 4 (October-December 1985): 577-83.

HURWOOD, BERNHARDT J. (1926-1987)

Bernhardt J. Hurwood is a popular author of books on vampires and the supernatural. Born in New York City, he graduated from Northwestern University in 1949, his education having been interrupted by his service in the U.S. Merchant Marine from 1945-47. He held a variety of jobs through the 1950s but emerged in 1962 as a full-time writer. Hurwood's first book, *Terror by Night,* was published in 1963.

While his literary career covered many subjects, two topics dominated his writing—sex and the supernatural. In 1965 he published his first collection of supernatural stories, *Monsters Galore,* which was followed by *Monsters and Night-mares* (1967), *Vampires, Werewolves and Ghouls* (1968), *Ghosts, Ghouls and Other Horrors* (1971), *Haunted Houses* (1972), *Vampires, Werewolves, and Other Demons* (1972), *Chilling Ghost Stories* (1973), and *Eerie Tales of Terror and Dread* (1973). Most of these are juvenile volumes, and some, such as *Vampires, Werewolves and Other Demons,* featured true stories to introduce the younger audience to classic reports of vampirism and lycanthropy. Along the way, he wrote *Passport to the Supernatural,* a popular book for adults on supernatural themes (i.e., ghosts, vampires, and werewolves) as they have been experienced around the world.

With all of his attention on the supernatural, which included significant emphasis on vampires, Hurwood also wrote four books primarily on vampires. The first, *Dracutwig* (1969), was a novel written under the pen name Mallory T. Knight. The book concerned the problem of a young girl, who happened to be Dracula's daughter, with a very thin body similar to then-popular model Twiggy, trying to make it in a high-profile modeling world. *Terror by Night* (1976), reissued as *The Vampire*

Papers and *The Monstrous Undead*, written under Hurwood's real name, dealt with the sexual and psychopathic correlates of both vampirism and werewolfism. Chapters treated such topics as necrophilia, cannibalism, blood rituals, and premature burial. Published three years later, *By Blood Alone* (1979) was Hurwood's best vampire novel. The story concerned conversations between psychiatrist Edgar A. Wallman and his vampire patient Zachary Lucius Sexton. The elderly Sexton was suffering from boredom (the perennial problem of the immortals). He asked Wallman why he could not commit **suicide.** Wallman approached Sexton as a man suffering from a delusion and thus attempted to cure him of his dysfunctional fantasy rather than dealing with the reality of the situation. The volume was noteworthy for using the sessions between his two characters as a vehicle to convey all the information he had gleaned from his readings about vampires. Finally, in 1981 Hurwood authored *Vampires,* a light survey of vampire lore covering the origins of vampires, **Vlad the Impaler,** vampire folklore, and the modern literary and cinema vampire.

Hurwood continued to write until shortly before his death from cancer in 1987.

Sources:

Hurwood, Bernhardt J. *By Blood Alone.* New York: Charter, 1979. 245 pp.
———— (as Mallory T. Knight). *Dracutwig.* New York: Award Books, 1969. 156 pp.
————. *Passport to the Supernatural.* New York: Taplinger Publishing Company, 1972. 319 pp.
————. *Vampires.* New York: Quick Fox, 1981. 179 pp.
————. *Vampires, Werewolves and Ghouls.* New York: AceBooks, 1968.
————. *Vampires, Werewolves and Other Demons.* New York: Scholastic Book Services, 1972. 112 pp.

HYPNOTIC POWERS

In many books and movies, the vampire possessed hypnotic powers. **Jonathan Harker** discovered this the day he attempted to kill **Dracula.** Dracula was lying in his box of earth in his **vampire sleep** when Harker threatened him with a shovel. However, the vampire turned his head, and as his eyes fell on Harker, the sight paralyzed the man. Instead of delivering a fatal wound, Harker merely grazed Dracula's head with the shovel he wielded.

The vampire's hypnotic hold on a person was even stronger after it had first bitten the victim. Dracula's hypnotic powers were evident, for example, when he lured **Lucy Westenra** from her bedroom in **Whitby** across the bridge to a meeting place on the other side of the river. Nothing that her protectors did after that time prevented Dracula's access to her.

Again, Dracula appeared to have put **Mina Murray** into a trance after first attacking her. She was not aware of what she was doing in the crucial encounter with Dracula in her bedroom, when he forced her to drink from the blood flowing from his chest. Also at that moment, as vampire expert **Abraham Van Helsing** observed, ''Jonathan is in a stupor such as we know the Vampire can produce.'' When Mina came to her senses, she pronounced herself unclean. Van Helsing was later able to used the hypnotic link between Mina and Dracula. He hypnotized Mina, and while in a trance she was able to give him information on Dracula's progress on the return trip to his castle.

Hypnotic powers were not evident in the accounts of the folkloric vampire. However, it often attacked at night while its victims slept, and there were a number of accounts in which people awoke with the vampire hovering over them. In like measure, the nineteenth-century literary vampire did not use any hypnotic powers. **Varney the Vampyre** stole into victims' rooms as they slept. **Carmilla** seduced them with her charm and beauty.

Since *Dracula,* however, the vampire's hypnotic energy has been an essential part of its power. The look could be used to call victims from their bedrooms or to get them to open the door and let the vampire into the room. With suggestion, victims could get rid of barriers such as **garlic** or a **crucifix** that blocked his access. Frequently it appeared as a simple exercise in power, as the vampire forced an unwilling victim to walk across the room to meet a set of gleaming teeth, or as it hypnotized a third party to assist him in seizing his victim. On occasion, a vampire like Diedre Griffith in Karen Taylor's *Blood Secrets,* would use its hypnotic powers to make a person forget the encounter. The hypnotic glare of **Bela Lugosi** into the camera remains one of the memorable moments of the movie version *Dracula,* and the success of those who followed him in that part often was related to their ability to copy that intense look.

I

"I . . . VAMPIRE"

"I . . . Vampire" was a popular series of vampire stories that appeared in *The House of Mystery*, a **comic book** published by DC Comics in the 1980s. The series began in the March 1981 issue (No. 290) and appeared periodically through the August 1983 issue (No. 319). "I . . . Vampire" told the story of Lord Andrew Bennett who was raised during the Elizabethan Era in England in the late sixteenth century. Bennett was a hero of the Spanish War and a well-known figure at court. Then in 1591 he was bitten by a *dearg-dul,* a type of vampire found in **Ireland,** and became a vampire himself. He was in love with Mary Seward, personal handmaiden to the queen. When she discovered his condition, she wanted to spend eternity with him and demanded that he make her a vampire. As a vampire, she felt superior to the human race and felt she could rule the world, an idea Bennett rejected. She left him and he vowed to find her and save her soul, which he had despoiled. Although he had a thirst for blood, Bennett had sworn off human blood. Their conflict continued into the 1980s and provided the tension for the stories of the series. Mary built an international organization to seek control of the planet. The organization, the Blood Red Moon, commanded a large number of vampires that operated as Mary's agents. Bennett had a difficult time killing them because most of the things that hurt them also hurt him.

Their conflict climaxed in a rush to gain what was termed the Russian Formula. The Russians discovered that vampirism was caused by a virus. Taking the formula made one a new kind of vampire, with all the vampiric powers (strength, transformation, etc.) but free from the limitations of the undead and able to live on common human food rather than blood. After Bennett secured and took some of the formula, he was able to walk in the sunlight. He discovered Mary's headquarters and prepared to destroy her and her sleeping vampire cohorts. As he went to do this, however, he suddenly found himself unable to move. He learned too late that the formula was to create new vampires who were free of the bloodlust but was not meant to be consumed by those who were already vampires. Although alive and conscious, Bennett could feel his body sink into rigor mortis.

As Bennett lay dying, Mary bit Bennett's human girlfriend, Deborah Dancer. His final damnation was to know that she had become Mary's willing servant. However, Deborah had already taken the Russian Formula and had become the new kind of vampire. She fought Mary and dragged her body into the **sunlight,** where Mary perished. Deborah returned to the dying Bennett to inform him of Mary's death and of her love. Thus, Bennett died in peace. Deborah lived on as the new kind of vampire.

Sources:

The House of Mystery. Nos. 290-319. New York: DC Comics, 1981-83.

INCUBUS/SUCCUBUS

The incubus was a demon figure closely associated with the vampire. The incubus was known for its habit of invading a woman's bedroom at night, lying on top of her so that its weight was quite evident on her chest, and forcing her to have sex. The succubus, the female counterpart of the incubus, attacked men in the same way. The experience of the incubus/succubus attack varied from extreme pleasure to absolute terror. It was, as psychotherapist Ernest Jones noted, the same spectrum of experiences described in modern literature between the erotic dream and the nightmare. The incubus/succubus resembled a vampire in that it attacked people at night while they slept. It often attacked a person night after night, like the vampire of the **Gypsies,** leaving their victims exhausted. However, it differed from the vampire in that it neither sucked blood nor stole the life energy.

The incubus seemed to have originated in the ancient practice of incubation, where a person went to the temple of a deity and slept there overnight. During the course of the evening, the person would have contact with the deity. Often that contact involved sexual intercourse, either in a dream or with one of the very human representatives of the deity. This practice was at the root of several religious practices, including temple prostitution. The most successful incubation religion was connected with Aesculapius, a healing god who specialized in, among other things, curing sterility. Christianity, which equated the Pagan deities with devilish demons, viewed the practice of intercourse with the deity as a form of demonic activity.

Through the centuries, two main opinions on the origin of incubi and succubi competed with each other. Some saw them as dreams, figments of the fantasy life of the person who experienced their visitations. Others argued for the objective existence of the demons; they were instruments of the devil. By the fifteenth century, church leaders, especially those connected with the Inquisition, favored the latter explanation and tied the demonic activity of incubi and succubi to **witchcraft.** The great instrument of the witchhunters, *Malleus Maleficarum* (*Witches Hammer*), assumed that all witches willingly submitted to incubi.

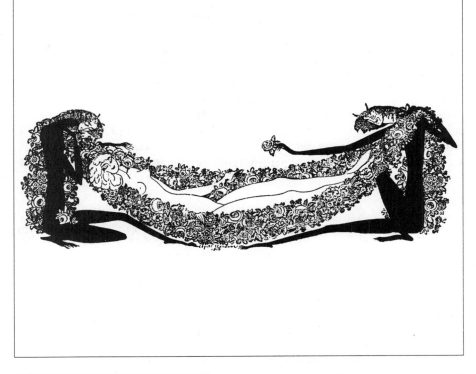

INCUBI INDUCING DREAMS IN A SLEEPING GIRL.

The objective existence of the incubus/succubus was supported by Thomas Aquinas in the thirteenth century; he argued that children could even be conceived through the intercourse of a woman with an incubus. He believed that a demon could change form and appear as a succubus for a man and an incubus for a woman. Some thinkers argued that succubi collected male semen then, in the form of an incubus, deposit it in a female. Nuns seemed a particular target of incubi, as demons seemed to delight in pestering those who strove to live the holy life. The idea of the objective existence of incubi and succubi held sway until the seventeenth century when a trend toward a more subjective understanding became noticeable.

Jones, a Freudian psychologist, tied the incubus/succubus and the vampire together as two expressions of repressed sexual feelings. The vampire was seen as the more intense of the two. Because of the similarities of vampires and incubi/succubi, various forms of the latter often appear on lists of different vampires around the world such as the *follets* (French), *duendes* (Spanish), *alpes* (German), and *folletti* (Italian).

Closely related to the incubus was the *mare* (Old Teutonic), *mara* (Scandinavian) or *mora* (Slavic), a demon of the nightmare.

Jan L. Perkowski noted that stories of the Slavic vampire also included elements of what appeared to be the *mora*. He considered these as vampire accounts that had experienced demon contamination. He carefully distinguished the vampire (an enlivened corpse) and the *mora* (a spherical shaped spirit), and he criticized vampirologists such as **Montague Summers,** Dudley Wright, and Gabriel Ronay for confusing the two. He also criticized Jones on much the same ground. While acknowledging that the vampire and *mora* shared a like mode of attack and generally attacked the same kind of victim (someone asleep), the vampire phenomenon was to be distinguished in that it centered on the corpse while the *mora* phenomenon had no such objective reference and was centered entirely upon the victim who survived the demon's attack.

Sources:

Jones, Ernest. *On the Nightmare.* New York: Liveright Publishing Corporation, 1951.

Perkowski, Jan L. *The Darkling: A Treatise on Slavic Vampirism.* Columbus, OH: Slavica Publishers, 1989. 169 pp.

Robbins, Rossell Hope. *The Encyclopedia of Witchcraft and Demonology.* New York: Crown Publishers, 1959. 571 pp.

INDIA, VAMPIRES IN

Among the vast number of deities and supernatural entities found in India's religious world were a number that possessed vampiric characteristics and were noted in the vampire literature. They merge into a wide variety of demonic entities that more closely resemble ghosts, **ghouls,** as well as living witches and sorcerers. The Indian vampire and vampiric entities appeared in ancient Indian texts, and some have speculated that India was one place where belief in vampires originated and from there spread to surrounding lands. There was certainly evidence that the **Gypsies** brought a form of vampire belief from India with them when they migrated westward.

In ancient Hinduism (the dominant religion of India), creation was portrayed as beginning with the formation of a golden egg (cosmic intelligence). Visible creation resulted from the division of the egg into the heavens, the earth, and the 21 regions of the cosmos. These 21 regions of the cosmos were roughly divided into three zones, one of which was the Tala, or subterranean region, the abode of the chthonian entities including ogres, spectres, and demons.

The most well-known of the vampiric beings from the Tal were the *rakshasas* (feminine, *rakshasis*), generally described as ogres and demons who lived in cemeteries and disturbed the affairs of people by disrupting rituals and interrupting devotions. The slaying of infants was among their most loathsome actions. The *rakshasas* came in a variety of forms, some male and some female, some more humanoid and some half animal. Hanuman, the deity that appeared in the form of a monkey, was reported to have observed *rakshasas* in every imaginable shape when he entered the city of Lanka as an envoy of Ramam. The *rakshasas* were characterized in many Indian epics, such as the *Mahabharata* and the *Ramayana* (which contains the Hanuman episode), and many of the deities and mythical heroes gained their reputation by slaying *rakshasas*.

The *rakshasas* were cited as vampires because of some of their characteristics. For example, they were nocturnal wanderers of the night. They had a fearsome appearance with elongated **fangs.** Texts described them as *asra-pa* or *asrk-pa* (literally: drinkers of blood). Like the Greek *lamiai,* they sought pregnant female victims and were known to attack infants. The natural enemy of the *rakshasas* was *Agni*, the dispeller of darkness and officiator at sacrificial ritual, and people called on Agni to destroy or ward off demons.

Closely associated with the *rakshasas* were the *yatu-dhana* (or *hatu-dhana*), sorcerers who devoured the remains left by the *rakshasas*. On occasion the term *yatu-dhana* was used interchangeably with *rakshasas*. Also frequently mentioned with the *rakshasas,* but even lower on the scale of beings, were the *pisachas* (literally: the eaters of raw flesh), also described as hideous in appearance, repellant, and blood thirsty. The texts described them as flesh-eating ghouls and the source of malignant disease. In the *Puranas,* a set of Hindu writings, the *pisachas* were described as the products of the anger of the deity Brahma.

> After creating gods, demons (asuras), ancestors, and humankind, Brahma became afflicted with hunger, and they began to eat his body, for they were raksasas and yaksas. When Brahma saw them he was displeased, and his hair fell out and became serpents. And when he saw the serpents he was angry, and the creatures born of his anger were the fierce flesh-eating *pisachas*. Thus Brahma created cruel creatures and gentle creatures, dharma and adharma, truth and falsehood.

Also possessing some vampiric characteristics were the *bhuta*, the souls of the dead, specifically those who died an untimely death, had been insane, or had been born deformed. They wandered the night and appeared as dark shadows, flickering lights, or misty apparitions. On occasion they would enter a corpse and lead it in its ghoulish state to devour living persons. The *brahmaparusha* was a similar entity known in northern India.

Bhutas lived around cremation grounds, old ruins and other abandoned locations, and in deserts. They might undergo a **transformation** into either owls or **bats.** The owl had a special place in Indian mythology. It was considered unlucky to hear the owl's hoot, possibly fatal if heard in a burial ground. Owl flesh could be used in black magic rituals.

Bhutas were the ever-present evil spirits and were considered dangerous for a wide variety of reasons. They ate filthy food and were always thirsty. They liked milk

THE *VETALA* OR *BAITAL*, AN
INDIAN VAMPIRE, AS PICTURED
BY SIR RICHARD BURTON.

and would attack babies who had just fed. They could enter the body through various orifices and possess a person. While the *bhutas* might act in a vampirish way on occasion, they generally were seen as simply malevolent beings.

The Indian demon-like figures possibly closest to the Western vampire were the *vetalas*, or *betails*, spirits that inhabited and animated the bodies of the dead. A *betail* was the central character in *The Vetala-Pachisi*, a classic piece of Indian literature comparable to Chaucer's *Tales* or the *Arabian Nights*. Originally translated and published in English in the mid-century, a new translation of 11 of what he deemed were the most interesting of the stories was made by Sir **Richard F. Burton** and published in 1870 under the title *Vikram and the Vampire. The Vetala-Pachisi* described the encounter of King Vikram with a *betail* who told him a series of tales. Vikram, like King Arthur, was an actual person who lived in the first century A.D. and became a magnet for many tales and fables. In the book, a yogi cajoled Vikram to spend an evening with him in the cemetery. He then asked Vikram to bring him a body he would find some four miles to the south at another burial ground. The body, the yogi told him, would be hanging on a mimosa tree. The body turned out to be a *betail*. Vikram encountered great difficulty in getting the vampire to accompany him back to the yogi, but finally succeeded through his persistence. To entertain them on the return trip, the *betail* told a series of stories that form the body of the book.

When they reached the cemetery with the yogi, the king found him invoking **Kali.** He was surrounded by the host of demons from Indian lore, including the *rakshasas,* the *bhutas,* who had assumed various beastly shapes, and the *betails.* The yogi led them to the shrine of the goddess Kali. There Vikram killed the yogi who was about to kill him. As a boon, the gods granted him fame.

A survey of Indian vampiric entities would be incomplete without further mention of the goddess Kali, often associated with Siva as a consort. She was a dark goddess, usually pictured as having black skin. She had a terrible and frightening appearance wearing parts of the human body as ornaments. Her favorite places were the battlefield, where she became drunk on the blood of her victims, and the burial/ cremation ground. In *Vikram and the Vampire,* Kali appeared in the shrine located at the cemetery, and as Vikram entered he saw her:

> There stood Smashana-Kali, the goddess, in her most horrible form. She was a naked and a very black woman, with half-severed head, partly cut and partly painted, resting on her shoulder; and her tongue lolled out from her wide yawning mouth; her eyes were red like those of a drunkard; and her eyebrows were of the same colour; her thick coarse hair hung like a mantle to her knees.

Burton comments on this passage:

> Not being able to find victims, this pleasant deity, to satisfy her thirst for the curious juice, cut her own throat that the blood might spout up into her mouth.

OTHER VAMPIRIC ENTITIES: Throughout India, among the various ethnic/linguistic groups, there were a multitude of ghosts, demons, and evil spirits who lived in or near cemeteries and cremation locations and who bore some resemblance to the vampires of Europe. Many fooled others by assuming the form of a living person. They reverted to a horrible demonic appearance just before attacking their victims. For example, in Gujarat there were the *churels,* women who died an unnatural death (in western India the churel was also known as a *jakhin, jakhai, mukai, nagulai*, and *alvantin*). If such a woman had been treated badly by her family, she would return to harass them and to dry up the blood of the male family members. Such a woman could become a *dakini,* an associate of the goddess **Kali,** and a partaker in her vampirish and ghoulish activities. If a young man was tempted by the *churel* and ate of the food she offered, she would keep him with her until dawn and return him to his village a grey-haired old man. The *churel* had one noticeable feature that gave her away—her feet were turned backwards so her heel was in front and her toes in back.

Women at the time of childbirth and their infants were given great attention by family and friends. A woman who died in childbirth was likely to become a ghost. To prevent that from occurring, the family would bury rather than cremate the body.

They would then fix four nails in the ground at the corners of the burial spot and plant red flowers on top of the grave. A woman who died in childbirth was also buried in a special place (the exact spot differing in various sections of India). For example, the corpse could be carried outside the house by a side door and buried within the shadow of the house by the noontime sun. It was believed that by not using the front door, the *churel* would be unable to find her way home. Some used iron nails in the house's threshold and sprinkled millet **seeds** on the road to the burying ground. As in eastern Europe, the *churel* must count the seeds, a task that kept her busy until daybreak. In the Punjab, a woman who died in childbirth would have nails driven through her hands and feet, red pepper placed in her eyes, and a chain wrapped around her feet. Others broke the legs above the ankles and turned the feet around backward, bound the big toes together, or simply bound the feet with iron rings.

Among the most interesting vampires were the *chedipe* (literally: prostitute), a type of sorceress in the Godavari area. The *chedipe* was pictured as riding a tiger through the night. Unclothed, she entered the home of a sleeping man and sucked his blood out of his toe. Using a form of hypnotism, she put the others in the household into a trance-like sleep so that they were unaware of her presence. In the morning, the man would awaken but feel drained of energy and somewhat intoxicated. If he did not seek treatment for his condition, the *chedipe* would return. On occasion the *chedipe* would attack men in the jungle in the form of a tiger with a human leg.

Devendra P. Varna has made a case that the vampire deities of the ancient Hindus are the source of vampire beliefs in Europe. He asserted that such beliefs were carried by the Arab caravans over the Great Silk Route from the Indus Valley into the Mediterranean Basin. They probably arrived in Greece around the first century A.D. This theory, while entirely possible, has yet to be developed in the depth necessary to place it beside alternative theories that project multiple origins of vampiric myth in different cultures to meet a set of fairly universal needs.

Sources:

The Baital-Pachisi; or, The Twenty-five Tales of a Demon. Ed. by Duncan Forbes. London: Crosby, Lockwood, 1857.

Burton, Richard, trans. *Vikram and the Vampire; or, Tales of Hindu Devilry.* 1870, 1893. Rpt.: New York: Dover Publications, 1969. 243 pp.

Crooke, William. *Religion and Folklore of Northern India.* Humphrey Milford: Oxford University Press, 1926. 471 pp.

Danielou, Alain. *Hindu Polytheism.* New York: Bollingen Foundation, 1964. 537 pp.

Enthoven, R. E. *The Folklore of Bombay.* Oxford: Clarendon Press, 1924. 353 pp.

Kingsley, David. *Hindu Goddesses: Visions of the Divine Feminine in the Hindu Religious Tradition.* Berkeley, CA: University of California Press, 1986. 281 pp.

MacDonell, A. A. *Vedic Mythology.* Strassburg, Germany: Verlag von Karl J. Trübner, 1897. 189 pp.

Sutherland, Gail Hinich. *The Disguises of the Demon: The Development of the Yaksa in Hinduism and Buddhism.* Albany, NY: State University of New York Press, 1991. 233 pp.

Thurston, Edgar. *Omens and Superstitions of Southern India.* New York: McBride, Nast & Company, 1912. 320 pp.

Trigg, E. B. *Gypsy Demons & Divinities: The Magical and Supernatural Practices of the Gypsies.* London: Sheldon Press, 1973. 238 pp.

Varna, Devendra P. "The Vampire in Legend, Lore, and Literature." Introduction to *Varney the Vampyre.* New York: Arno Press, 1970.

Walker, Benjamin. *The Hindu World: An Encyclopedia Survey of Hinduism*. New York: Frederick A. Praeger, 1986. 281 pp.

INTERNATIONAL VAMPIRE

International Vampire is one of vampire fandom's higher quality vampire periodicals. It was founded in 1991 by its editor, Rob Brautigam, a resident of Amsterdam, the Netherlands. Each issue contains well-researched articles of vampire history and folklore, notices of various fan organizations and periodicals, and book reviews.

Information on obtaining copies of the *International Vampire* may be received from Rob Brautigam, Galileipalntsoen 90-1, 1098NC Amsterdam, the Netherlands.

IRELAND, VAMPIRES IN

Ireland, like its neighbor the **United Kingdom,** does not have a rich vampire lore, in spite of a mythology that contains numerous stories of preternatural beings and contact between the living and the dead in the form of ghosts and revenants. **Montague Summers** spoke of an Irish vampire, the *dearg-dul*, but supplied little information about it. Irish folklorists found no mention of it in the folklore they compiled. The most famous vampire tale was that of ''The Blood-Drawing Ghost,'' collected and published by Jeremiah Curtin in 1882. It told the story of a young woman named Kate. She was one of three women whom a man from Cork County was thinking of marrying. To test the women, he placed his cane at the entrance of the tomb of a recently deceased person and then challenged them to fetch it. Only Kate accepted the challenge.

Upon arriving at the tomb, she encountered the dead man who forced her to take him into town. There he drew blood from three young men who subsequently died. He mixed the blood with oatmeal he had forced Kate to prepare. While he devoured his meal, Kate secretly hid her portion. Unaware that she had not eaten her oatmeal, the ''vampire'' confided in her that the blood-oatmeal mixture would have brought the men back to life. As they were returning to his tomb, the ''vampire'' told Kate of a fortune in gold to be found in a nearby field.

The next day, the three young men were found. Kate then struck a bargain with their parents. She offered to bring them back to life if she could marry the oldest one and if the land where she knew the gold was located could be deeded to her. Deed in hand, she took the oatmeal she had hidden and put some in the mouth of each man. They all quickly recovered from the vampire's attack. With her future husband, she dug up the gold and the wealthy couple lived a long life and passed their wealth to their children.

Dudley Wright, in *Vampires and Vampirism*, mentioned a female vampire who lured people to her by her beauty. She supposedly resided in the graveyard at

Waterford near Strongbow's Tower. Summers conducted one of his rare personal investigations only to discover that there was no Strongbow's Tower near Waterford. He suggested that Wright made a mistaken reference to another structure, Reginald's Tower, but upon checking with authorities on Irish lore, was told that no vampire legends were known about Reginald's Tower. As a final explanation, Summers suggested that Wright's story was a confused version of a story told of the Anglo-Saxon conquest of Waterford after which a frog (not native to Ireland) was found and interred in Reginald's Tower.

In 1925, R. S. Breene reported another Irish story concerning a priest who died and was properly buried. Upon their return trip from the graveside, mourners from the funeral parlor met a priest on the road and were upset to discover that it was the man they had just buried. He differed only in that he had pale skin, wide-open glittering eyes, and prominent long white teeth. They went immediately to the farmhouse of the priest's mother. They found her lying on the floor. It seemed that shortly before the funeral party arrived she had heard a knock at the door. Looking outside she saw her son. She made note of the pale complexion and the prominent teeth. Fear overcame her and rather than letting him in, she fainted.

THE LITERARY VAMPIRE: Ireland gave birth to two of the most famous vampire authors, **Sheridan Le Fanu,** who wrote the novella, **''Carmilla''** and **Bram Stoker,** the author of *Dracula.* Le Fanu drew on his Irish homeland for his early stories, but both men had moved to England by the time they wrote their most famous vampire stories, which they set in continental Europe.

The vampire rarely appeared in Irish literature. One appearance that attained a relative level of fame occurred in James Joyce's *Ulysses* (1922), which used vampire imagery. The vampire first appeared early in the novel when Stephen, the main character, spoke of the moon kissing the ocean: ''He the moon comes, pale vampire, through storm her eyes, has bat sails bloodying the sea, mouth to her mouth.''

He makes later reference to the ''. . . potency of vampires mouth to mouth.'' Joyce injected the vampire into his very complex ruminations on divinity, creativity, and sexuality. In another reference, Stephen spoke of the vampire man's involvement with chic women. Finally, Stephen identified God as the ''Black panther vampire.'' Joyce seemed to be settling on an image of the creative Father god as a vampire who preyed upon his victims—virgin women. The insertion of the virgin assisted Joyce in making the point that creation was also inherently a destructive process. In any case, the several brief references to the vampire supplied Joyce's literary critics with the substance for a lively debate.

The tradition of Irish vampire lore is celebrated today in the work of the **The Bram Stoker Society** and an associated group, **The Bram Stoker Club.** The society attempts to promote the status of Bram Stoker's writings, especially *Dracula,* and to call attention to Irish gothic literature in general. It sponsors an annual school each summer.

Sources:

Cheng, Vincent J. "Stephen Dedalus and the Black Panther Vampire." *James Joyce Quarterly* 24, 2 (Winter 1987): 161-176.

Curtin, Jeremiah. *Tales of the Fairies and of the Ghost World Collected from the Oral Tradition in South-West Munster.* 1882. Reprint. New York: Lemma Publishing Corporation, 1970. 198 pp.

Kelly, Sean, ed. *Irish Folk and Fairy Tales.* New York: Gallery Press, 1982. 367 pp.

Summers, Montague. *The Vampire in Europe.* London: Routledge, Kegan Paul, Trench, Trubner, & Co., 1929. 319 pp. Reprint. New Hyde Park, NY: University Books, 1961. 329 pp.

Wright, Dudley. *Vampires and Vampirism.* 1914, Rev. ed. 1924. Rept. as: *The Book of Vampires.* New York: Causeway Books, 973. 217 pp.

ITALY, VAMPIRES AND VAMPIRISM IN

(*Note*: On the vampire in Italian history, see also the entry on the Vampire in Ancient **Rome.**)

In Italy, the vampire phenomenon took on a modern identity when a "vampiric plague" hit Serbia and other lands in Eastern Europe in the seventeenth century. Italians contributed to the animated international debate that began on the nature of this phenomenon, which ultimately contributed to and inspired nineteenth century vampire literature. Within the debate various positions reflective of different theological and ideological positions were articulated throughout the centuries.

As the vampiric plague was beginning, a Franciscan from Pavia, Ludovico Maria Sinistrari (1622-1701), included vampirism in a study of demonic phenomena, *De Daemonialitate, et Incubis, et Succubis,* and offered a theological interpretation of them. Far from the contemporary rationalism and the Enlightenment that emerged in the following century, he thought of vampires as creatures that had not originated from Adam (i.e., humanity). While they had a rational soul equal to humans, their corporeal dimension was of a completely different, perfect nature. He thus enforced the idea that vampires were creatures that parallel human beings rather than opposite, chthonious, underground beings. [The oddness of Sinistrari's views may be because his study was a hoax. It was reportedly written in the nineteenth century by Isidore Lisicux, which would account for the fact that the study was not mentioned by Italian authors through the 1700s.]

A modern view of vampirism began with the work of J. H. Zedler (*Grosses volständige Universal-Lexicon aller Wissenschaften und Künste,* 1745), which saw vampirism as a superstition used to explain what were in reality certain diseases. Similarly, in his 1743 *Dissertazione sopra i vampiri,* Cardinal **Giuseppe Davanzati,** noticing that the belief in vampires mostly occurred in rural and popular areas of the world, labeled vampirism as simply the "fruit of imagination," arguing that such a belief was not found in the metropolitan milieus of western Europe.

Nevertheless, reports of vampirism became a more widespread phenomenon in the mid-18th century throughout the central and eastern parts of Europe. Accounts that were documented in *Traité sur les apparitions et sur les vampires ou le revenans d'Hongire, de Moravie* (1749) by French Benedectine scholar **Dom Augustin**

Calmet became a source of inspiration for vampire novels throughout the following centuries. Gerhard van Swieten's *Remarques sur les vampirisme* (1755) suggested that vampirism was a superstition generated out of ignorance. The opinion recounted Calmet and represented the triumph of the scientific rationalism that predominated in the culture of the late eighteenth century.

THE LITERARY VAMPIRE: In the early nineteenth century, the first literary works on vampires and vampirism began to appear, mostly in northern Europe. A vampire-oriented literary tradition also began in early nineteenth century Italy with the opera *Il Vampiro* by A. De Gasperini (first presented in Turin in 1801). Romanticism, a popular literary movement that reflected on inner human experience, itself enforced a mythic image of the vampire with its emphasis on the symbology of blood, the night, melancholy, and the "erotic tenderness for corpses." Mostly in the northern part of Europe, from superstitious popular belief, vampirism was introduced to the literate metropolitan milieu through the literary works of Novalis, **Goethe,** and **John Keats.** In 1819 **John Polidori** created **Lord Ruthven,** the protagonist in his short story, "Il Vampiro" (**"The Vampyre"**). Vampires especially began to appear in French and Russian literature, in the works of **Charles Nodier,** Charles Baudelaire, **Alexandre Dumas, Alexey Tolstoy,** and Nikolai Gògol.

The first Romance to be published in Italy, *Il Vampiro,* written by Franco Mistrali, appeared in 1869. Mistrali's story, which takes place in Monaco in 1862, was centered on blood and incestuous lovers. It presented the vampire in a literary, decadent, and aristocratic manner that was influenced by the contemporary literature of Keats, Goethe, Polidori and **Lord Byron.** The historical folkloric connotations of vampirism, as documented at the time of the vampiric plague, became the subject of *Vampiro,* a novel written in 1908 by Enrico Boni. It was perhaps the only work that illustrated the popular universe of superstition and fears of the rural culture.

A naturalist approach to the phenomenon was found in the work of Luigi Capuana, *Un Vampiro* (1904; 2nd ed., 1907). The author aimed at an objective description of facts that could be explained scientifically (vampirism as an hallucination), although some skepticism remained at the end of the novel. Written at the same time as Capuana's *Un Vampiro* was another novel, Daniele Oberto Marrama's (1907), *Il Dottore nero* (translation: The Black Doctor). Significant works on vampires in the following decades included Nino Savarese's *I ridestati del cimitero* (translation: The Reawakened of the Cemetery) (1932), Tommaso Landolfi's *Il racconto del lupo mannaro* (translation: The Tale of the Werewolf) (1939), *Racconto d'autunno* (translation: Fall Tale) (1947), Bacchelli's *Ultimo licantropo* (translation: The Last Lycanthrope) (1947), and Guadalberto Titta's *Il cane nero* (translation: The Black Dog) (1964). As can be discerned from the titles, vampires and **werewolves** were closely associated.

In the wake of the successful Italian movies *I Vampiri* in 1957 by Riccardo Freda, *Tempi duri per i Vampiri (Uncle was a Vampire)* in 1959 by Stefano Steno, and **Mario Bava**'s movies in the 1960s, a new wave of commercial vampire horror literature emerged in the form of series, such as *I Romanzi del Terrore, KKK Classici* *dell'orrore*, and *I Racconti di Dracula* (translation: Dracula's stories). The most renowned author of the series was Gaetano Sorrentino (aka Max Dave). In contrast with the commercial literature of those years, a more sophisticated image of vampires appeared in the novels of the authors of these last decades, such as the grotesque and comic vampire (with a benign social criticism) in *Il mio amico Draculone* (translation: My Friend Draculone) by Luigi Pellizzetti in 1970, Italo Calvino's vampire in *Il Castello dei destini incrociati* (translation: The Castle of Crossed Destinies), as well as in several additional works that featured an "existential trickster" representative of the ambiguity of life in contrast to death. Also published in the same period was Giovanni Fontana's *Tarocco Meccanico* (translation: Mecanic tarot), where the vampire was used as a literary image in the game of oxymora and metaphors that constitute the author's "romanzo sonoro" (sound romance).

By this time, the traditional stereotype of the vampire had been replaced by sophisticated, metaphorical images that expressed undefinable images. A new connotation of this archetype, in a total break with the tradition, was developed in *Anemia* by Alberto Abruzzese (1984). Here the protagonist was a contemporary, ordinary man who, in his everyday life, gradually discovered, through a series of initiation-like psychological fears and physical changes, his real identity as a vampire. He had to accept his metamorphosis to maintain the balance needed to stand the rhythm of his ordinary life.

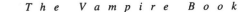

Another original approach to the vampire theme can be found in the novels of Furio Jesi (1941-1980). He presented a playful vampire in a short story for children (*La casa incantata* (translation: The enchanted house), published posthumously in 1982, but his major contribution was *L'ultima notte* (translation: The Last Night). An expert in mythology and anthropology, Jesi described vampires as mythological archetypes symbolizing life, drawing on pre-Christian and Oriental traditions (Mesopotamia, ancient **Mexico, Greece, Tibet,** and **India**). Dracula himself was used as a symbol of fertility and the endless flow of planetary existence, while the mission of these vampires was to reconquer the earth and human species that were heading toward ecological destruction.

Finally, vampires themselves revealed their identity in Gianfranco Manfredi's collection *Ultimi vampiri* (translation: The Last Vampires) (1987). In the several novels of the series, *I figli del fiume* (translation: The Children of the River), *La guarigione* (translation: Recovery), *Il metodo vago* (tanslation: The Vague Method), and *Il pipistrello di Versailles* (translation: Versailles Bat), the surviving "last vampires" described their historical experience throughout the centuries living side by side with humans, coping with their tricks, and finally, being defeated by them. Here some of the major events that radically changed the course of human history, (such as the Lutheran Reformation and the Spanish Inquisition—a consequence of the vampiric plague, Versailles and Waterloo) were explained from the perspective of the vampires.

VAMPIRE POETRY: It was within two avant-garde artistic movements, the Scapigliatura and Futurism, in the late nineteenth and early twentieth century respectively, that an Italian vampire poetry developed. The central topic in this poetry was the **vamp,** the seductive and fatal vampire woman, caught in her erotic and most aggressive dimension, images heavily inherited by late Romanticism and French poetry, in particular the poems of Baudelaire (*Les Métamorphoses du Vampire, Le Vampire, La Fontaine de Sang*). Within the Scapigliatura movement, the most popular poets to write of vampires were Nicola Maciarello, Arrigo Boito, Amilcare Ponchielli, Ugo Tarchetti, Achille Torelli, and Olindo Guerrini. The most influential Futurist poet was Filippo Tommaso Marinetti.

In the decades following the 1920s, with the exhaustion of the Futurist movement, Italian poetry drew little inspiration from vampirism. In the mid-century, authors such as Aldo Palazzeschi and Dino Campana only vaguely alluded to vampires in their works. Since the 1970s however, the *lamiai*, a Greek vampire entity, appeared in Giovanni Fontana's *Le Lamie del labirinto* (translation: The Labyrinth Lamias). In the tradition of the ''sound romance,'' *Tarocco Meccanico* developed the image of the vampire as a metaphorical, artistic, and poetic function.

THE CINEMATIC VAMPIRE: At the same time that Stefano Steno's vampire comedy *Tempi Duri per i Vampiri* was released in 1959, there also appeared Riccardo Freda's *I Vampiri (The Devil's Commandment)* (1957), and *Caltiki, il mostro immortale (Caltiki, the Immortal Monster)* (1959), which brought fame to special photography cameraman Mario Bava. Bava went from being a mere cameraman to directing more than 20 movies distinguished by his use of haunting baroque imagery. Bava's most important and representative works included: *La Maschera del Demonio* (aka *The Mask of Satan, Black Sunday*, and *Revenge of the Vampire*) 1961; *Ercole al centro della terra* (aka *Hercules in the Haunted World*) also in 1961, where he mastered colour special effects; *La Frusta e il corpo (The Whip and the Body)*, 1963; *I tre volti della paura (Black Sabbath)* also in 1963, a series of three short stories; *Sei donne per l'assassino (Blood and Black Lace)*, 1964; and *Terrore nello spazio (Planet of the Vampires)*, 1965. Bava's influence spread internationally and was evident in such movies as Giorgio Ferroni's *La notte dei diavoli* (1971), Ray Danton's *Hannah, Queen of the Vampires*, Paolo Solvay's *Il plenilunio delle vergini*, and the later features from **Hammer Films.**

Some Italian vampire actors should also be mentioned because of the successful roles they played. Many of Bava's movies starred **Barbara Steele,** who became the horror vamp of Italian movies. In 1963 she played in *La danza macabra* (directed by Antonio Margheriti), in 1965 she was in Mario Caiano's *Gli amanti d'oltretomba (The Faceless Monster)*, and appeared in Michael Reeve's *La Sorella di Satana (Revenge of the Blood Beast)*. A specialized Italian vampire was Walter Brandi who played in Piero Regnoli's *L'ultima preda del vampiro (The Playgirls and the Vampire)*, 1960; Renato Polselli's *L'Amante del vampiro (The Vampire and the Ballerina)*, and Roberto Mauri's *La Strage dei Vampiri (Slaughter of the Vampires)*, 1962. Finally, Giacomo Gentiomo's *Maciste contro il vampiro (Goliath and the Vampires)*, 1961, should be mentioned because its style also manifests traces of Bava's influence.

THE CONTEMPORARY SCENE: After a heyday in the 1960s, the Italian cinematic vampire fell into disfavor and has since made only infrequent appearances. Recent movies include *Fracchia contro Dracula* (1985), *Anemia* (1986), *Vampire a Venezia* (1988), and the 1990 remake of *La maschera del Demonio*. Throughout the 1980s, the Italian literary vampire merged with the western Europe and North American vampire. Many novels originally written and published in English have now been translated and published in Italy. Italians have also continued to write about vampires both in popular works and more serious fiction. Among the most prominent of the new Italian authors to contribute to the tradition is Patrizia Valduga, notable for the originality of her work. In 1991, she authored *Donna di dolori* (translation: Woman of Pain) in which the vampires appeared to remind the reader of the horrors of the twentieth century.

Italian **comic book**s emerged in the 1960s, and vampire stories were soon standard fare in the horror anthologies. Among early independent vampire titles was *Jacula* (Dracula), an adult vampire comic featuring a female vampire, issued in a 12-part series beginning in March 1969. In the 1970s, Zagor, a popular comic book hero, encountered vampires in several of his adventures that were set in the American West.

Sources:

Agazzi, Renato. *Il mito del vampiro in Europa.* Poggibonsi: Antonio Lalli, 1979. 257 pp.

Guariento, Steve. "Bava Fever! Italian Gothic, Italian Camp, Italian Psychos (1966-1972)" *Samhain* 37 (May/June 1993): 22-26.

———. Guariento, Steve. "Bava Fever! Metaphysical Experiences (1972-1980)" *Samhain* 37 (May/June 1993): 22-26.

———. "Bava Fever! Style it Takes (1960-1965)" *Samhain* 37 (March/April 1993): 22-26.

Pattison, Barrie. *The Seal of Dracula.* New York: Bounty Books, 1975. 136 pp.

Rossignoli Emilio de. *Io credo nei vampiri.* Luciano Ferriani, 1961. 379 pp.

Tardiola, Giuseppe. *Il Vampiro nella Letteratura Italiana.* Rome: De Rubeis, 1991. 89 pp.

Ursini, James, and Alain Silver. *The Vampire Film.* South Brunswick, NJ: A. S. Barnes, 1975. 238 pp. Rev. ed. as Alain Silver and James Ursini.

The Vampire Film: From Nosferatu to Bram Stoker's Dracula. New York: Limelight Editions, 1993. 272 pp.

—Isotta Poggi

IVAN THE TERRIBLE (1530 -1584)

Ivan the Terrible, the first czar of **Russia,** whose arbitrary and cruel behavior led to his comparison with **Vlad the Impaler,** the historical **Dracula.** Ivan inherited the title of Grand Duke of Moscovy when he was three and grew up watching the leading families (the boyars) of his land lead the countries through a period of chaos as they fought among themselves for bits of power. He was 17 when a Chosen Council emerged to bring about reform. Although they succeeded in ending the chaos, Ivan continually fought with them over a multitude of administrative matters. In 1564, in frustration, he suddenly abdicated. When the people demanded his return, he was able to dictate the terms of his reinstatement and gain almost absolute power. He moved

THE IMAGE OF IVAN THE
TERRIBLE WAS MODELED ON
THAT OF VLAD THE IMPALER,
THE HISTORICAL DRACULA.

quickly to establish his own ruling elite, the *Oprichnina*, which wrested much of the remaining power from the boyars.

Ivan's reign of two decades was marked, in part, by his conquest of the lands along the Volga River and his movement into Siberia, as well as by a disastrous war in which he unsuccessfully tried to capture Livonia (today Estonia). He is most remembered however, not for his political actions, but for his personal conduct. In his desire to establish a strong central Russian government, he was quick to punish (and even execute) many who challenged his rule or in anyway showed disrespect for what he considered his exalted status. He manifested symptoms of extreme paranoia and had a quick and fiery temper. In 1580, in a moment of rage, he killed his own son, a prospective heir.

Outstanding among the traits remembered by his contemporaries, Ivan possessed a dark sense of humor, quite similar to that attributed to Vlad. It often characterized the tortures and executions of those who became the objects of his rage. As one historian, S. K. Rosovetskii, has noted, many of the stories told about Ivan were variations of those originally ascribed to Vlad a century earlier. For example, there was a Romanian folk story about the leading citizens of the town of **Tirgoviste,**

Dracula's capital. The citizens had mocked Dracula's brother. In revenge, he rounded up the leading citizens (the boyars) following Easter Day celebrations and, in their fine clothes, he marched them off to work on building **Castle Dracula.** Ivan, it was reported, did something quite similar in the town of Volgoda when the people slighted him on Easter morning. He rounded them up, still dressed in their Easter finery, to build a new city wall for the town.

Possibly the most famous Dracula story told of Ivan concerned the Turkish envoy who refused to remove his hat in Dracula's presence. Dracula, in turn, had the man's hat nailed to the top of his head. Ivan, it was reported, did the same thing to an Italian diplomat (or in an alternative account, to a French ambassador).

Ivan, like Vlad, often turned on powerful figures in Russian society and humiliated them to prevent their return to the dignity of their offices. The story was told, for example, of his attack on Pimen, the Russian Orthodox metropolitan of Novgorod. He stripped Pimen of his church vestments, had him dressed as a strolling minstrel (an occupation denounced by the church), then staged a mock wedding in which Pimen was married to a mare. Presenting the defrocked prelate with the signs of his new status, a bagpipe and a lyre, Ivan sent him from the city.

Ivan differed from Vlad in his sexual appetite. He was a polygamist with seven wives and as many as 50 concubines. He also left his immediate successors with a very mixed inheritance. Although he had expanded the territory of Russia, he left behind a bankrupt country, and discontent with his rule grew steadily. Ivan, however, died quietly in the middle of a chess game on March 18, 1584.

Sources:

Parrie, Maureen. *The Image of Ivan the Terrible in Russian Folklore.* London: Cambridge University Press, 1987. 269 pp.

J

JAPAN, VAMPIRES IN

The varied creatures of Japanese folklore did not include a classical bloodsucking vampire. Possibly the most vampirelike of the numerous mythological beings was the *kappa*. Described as fabulous creatures of the waters—rivers, ponds, lakes, and the sea—the *kappas* penetrated the Japanese culture and now appear in fiction, cartoons, toys, and art. The *kappa* was first widely written about in the eighteenth century. It was described as an unattractive, humanlike child with greenish-yellow skin, webbed fingers and toes, and somewhat like a monkey with a long nose and a round eyes. It had a shell similar to a tortoise and smelled fishy. It had a concave head that held water. If the water in its head spilled, the *kappa* would lose its **strength.**

The *kappas* operated from the edge of the water in which they lived. Many stories related attempts by *kappas* to grab horses and cows, drag them into the water, and suck their blood through their anuses (the main trait that has earned *kappas* some recognition as vampires). However, they have been known to leave the water to steal melons and cucumbers, to rape women, and to attack people for their livers. People would propitiate the *kappas* by writing the names of their family members on a cucumber and throwing it into the river where the kappas lived.

The *kappas* were viewed as part of the rural landscape. They were not attacked by humans, but on occasion *kappas* attempted to strike deals with them. Such a relationship was illustrated in the story of "The Kappa of Fukiura." The *kappa* near Fukiura was a troublesome creature until one day it lost an arm trying to attack a horse. A farmer retrieved the arm, and that night the *kappa* approached the farmer to ask for its return. Rebuffed at first, the *kappa* finally convinced the farmer to return the arm by promising that it would never again hurt any of the villagers. From that time forward, as reported by the villagers, the *kappa* would warn them by saying, "Don't let the

◄

children go out to the beach, for the guest is coming.'' The guest was another *kappa,* not bound by the Kappa of Fukiura's agreement.

Another popular story of the *kappas* told of one who lived at Koda Pond. A man left his horse tied by the pond. A *kappa* tried to pull the horse into the pond, but the horse bolted and ran home. The *kappa* spilled its water, lost its strength, and was carried to the stable. The man later found his horse along with the *kappa.* Caught in a weakened condition, the *kappa* bargained with the man, ''If you prepare a feast in your home, I will certainly lend you necessary bowls.'' From that time on, whenever the man got ready to hold a feast, the *kappa* would bring bowls. After the feast the bowls would be set out and the *kappa* would retrieve them.

Apart from the *kappa,* the Japanese had another interesting folktale. The ''Vampire Cat of Nabeshima'' told the story of Prince Nabeshima and his beautiful concubine Otoyo. One night a large vampire cat broke into Otoyo's room and killed her in the traditional manner. It disposed of her body and assumed her form. As Otoyo, the cat began to sap the life out of the prince each night while guards strangely fell asleep. Finally, one young guard was able to stay awake and saw the vampire in the form of the young girl. As the guard stood by, the girl was unable to approach the prince, who, then slowly recovered. Finally, it was deduced that the girl was a malevolent spirit who had targeted the prince. The young man, with several guards, went to the girl's apartment. The vampire escaped, however, and removed itself to the hill country. From there, reports of its work were soon received. The prince organized a great hunt, and the vampire was finally killed. The story has been made into a play, *The Vampire Cat* (1918), and a movie, *Hiroku Kaibyoden* (1969).

CONTEMPORARY JAPANESE VAMPIRES: The Japanese, while lacking an extensive vampire lore, have in the last generation absorbed the European vampire myth and contributed to it, primarily through the film industry. Their contemporary vampire is called a *kyuketsuki.* As early as 1956 a film with a vampire theme, *Kyuketsuki Ga,* was released. It concerned a series of murders in which all the victims had teeth marks on their necks, but in the end, the killer turned out not to be a vampire. Some years later the director of *Kyuketsuki Ga* worked on another film, *Onna Kyuketsuki* (1959), which told of a real vampire who kidnapped the wife of an atomic scientist.

Among Japan's 1960s vampire movies was *Kuroneko* (1968), which built upon the vampire cat legend. A woman and her daughter were raped and murdered by a group of samurai. They returned from the grave as vampires who could transform themselves into black cats and attack their murderers. In *Yokai Daisenso,* a provincial governor was possessed by a bloodsucking Babylonian demon, an early signal of the coming absorption of Western elements in the Japanese movies.

Hammer Films' vampire movies inspired the 1970 *Chi i Suu Ningyo* (*The Night of the Vampire*) and the 1971 *Chi o Suu Me* (released in the West as *Lake of Dracula*), both directed by Michio Yamamoto. **Dracula** made his first appearance in Japan in the 1970s. In *Kyuketsuki Dorakyura Kobe ni Arawaru: Akuma wa Onna wo Utsukushiku Suru* (literally: *Vampire Dracula Comes to Kobe: Evil Makes a Woman Beautiful*) (1979), Dracula discovered that a reincarnation of the woman he loved lived in Kobe, Japan.

In 1980, *Dracula,* a full-length animated movie based on the Marvel Comics characters in the very successful *The Tomb of Dracula,* was the first of a number of excellent cartoon vampire features out of Japan. It was followed by *Vampire Hunter D* (1985) and *Vampire Princess Miyu* (1988), some of the most watched of the Japanese features in the West. In *The Legend of the Eight Samurai* (1984), director Kinji Fukasaku offered a Japanese version of the **Elizabeth Bathory** story in which an evil princess bathes in blood to keep her youth. The vampire theme was carried into the 1990s with such movies as *Tale of a Vampire,* directed by Shimako Sato and based upon the **Edgar Allan Poe** poem, ''Annabel Lee.'' These more recent Japanese movies have become readily available in the West on video.

Sources:

Dorson, Richard M. *Folk Legends of Japan.* Rutland, VT: Charles E. Tuttle Company, 1962. 256 pp.
Hurwood, Bernhardt J. *Passport to the Supernatural: An Occult Compendium from All Ages and Many Lands.*
    New York: Taplinger Publishing Company, 1972. 319 pp.
Jones, Stephen. *The Illustrated Vampire Movie Guide.* London: Titan Books, 1993. 144 pp.

Van Etten, Gerard. *The Vampire Cat: A Play in One Act from the Japanese Legend of the Nebeshima Cat.* Chicago: Dramatic Publishing Company, 1918. 16 pp.

JAVA, VAMPIRES IN

The Javanese shared much of their mythology with **Malaysia** and the rest of Indonesia. Included in that mythology was the belief in the *pontianak*. The *pontianak* was a bansheelike creature that flew through the night in the form of a bird. It could be heard wailing in the evening breeze as it sat in the forest trees. It was described variously as a woman who died a virgin (de Wit) or a woman who died giving birth (Kennedy). In both cases, it appeared as beautiful young women and attacked men whom it emasculated. De Wit noted that the *pontianak* appeared fairer than any love-goddess. Such creatures would embrace a man, but immediately withdraw after a single kiss. In the process they revealed the hole in their backs, which had been covered by the long tresses of hair. The man had to grab the hair and pull out a single strand, or he would be vampirized by the woman. If he failed, he would soon die; if he succeeded, he would live a long and happy life.

The *pontianak* also attacked babies and sucked their blood out of jealously over the happiness of the mother. Infants who were stillborn or who died soon after birth of an unknown cause would be thought of as victims of a *pontianak*.

Sources:

de Wit, Augusta. *Java: Facts and Fancies*. The Hague: W. P. van Stockum, 1912. Reprint. Singapore: Oxford University Press, 1984. 321 pp.

Kennedy, Raymond. *The Ageless Indies*. New York: John Day Company, 1942. 208 pp.

JOURDAN, LOUIS (1921-)

Louis Jourdan, an actor known for his starring role in a made-for-television 1978 production, *Count Dracula,* was born in Marseilles, France. He made his first movie in 1940 in a French production, *Le Corsaire.* After World War II he came to the United States and appeared in *The Paradine Case* (1946), which was followed by many appearances on stage and screen.

In 1978 Jourdan starred in his first vampire role as Count Dracula in the BBC-TV production of the **Bram Stoker** novel. The lengthy production (two-and-a-half hours) is remembered as one of the more faithful reenactments of the original work. It included the famous scene in which **Jonathan Harker** saw Dracula crawling down the walls of his castle. The movie was noted for its emphasis on drama and tension rather than blood and violence. A sexual element was present, but because *Count Dracula* was produced for television, there was no nudity. Jourdan played the role in a manner similar to **Frank Langella** (then starring in the Broadway revival of the play), as a suave, continental romantic hero. Women swooned in ecstasy when he bit them.

▶ LOUIS JOURDAN, WHO PLAYED
DRACULA IN THE BBC
PRODUCTION *COUNT DRACULA*
(1978).

After his Dracula role, Jourdan went on to star in several other movies, including a James Bond film, *Octopussy,* (1983), and *The Return of the Swamp Thing* (1989).

Sources:

Jones, Stephen. *The Illustrated Vampire Movie Guide.* London: Titan Books, 1993. 144 pp.

Waller, Gregory A. *The Living and the Undead: From Stoker's Dracula to Romero's Dawn of the Dead.* Urbana, IL: University of Illinois Press, 1986. 376 pp.

JOURNAL OF VAMPIROLOGY

From 1984 to 1990 the field of vampire studies had what closely resembled a scholarly journal. The 18 issues of the *Journal of Vampirology* contained a variety of well-researched articles on vampire history and folklore. Editor John L. Vellutini of San Francisco wrote more than half of the articles, and the journal reflected both his interests and his expertise. Although serious students of the field read the publication, their number was too small to keep the journal in print. Vellutini has said he hopes to revive the journal at some point.

JUVENILE LITERATURE

Vampire fiction was exclusively an adult literature until the appearance of horror **comic book**s in the 1940s. In the wake of the controversy over the hypothesized harmful content of comic books in the 1950s (which had the effect of banishing the vampire from their pages for two decades), there was no support for expanding the scope of juvenile literature in general by the inclusion of vampire stories.

The ban on vampires in comic books began to be lifted in the late 1960s with the appearance of *Dark Shadows* and *Vampirella,* and was done away with completely in 1971. That same year, the first novel written specifically for young people that included a vampire theme was published. *Danger on Vampire Trail* was No. 50 in the very popular Hardy Boys series of mystery books. The youthful detectives were tracking some credit card thieves, whom they traced to a remote location called Vampire Trail. The site recently had been renamed following reported attacks by bats, and on an exploration of the trail the Hardys found a dead **vampire bat,** seemingly far away from his natural habitat. However, in the end, they found no vampires, and the bat turned out to have been imported from Central America simply to scare locals away from the crooks' hideout.

THE 1970s: The real introduction of the juvenile audience to the subject came in 1973 with the publication of **Nancy Garden**'s nonfiction *Vampires.* Based in large part on two books by **Montague Summers** and the research of **Radu Florescu** and **Raymond T. McNally,** Garden presented a broad survey of vampire lore, the literary and cinematic vampire, and the real Dracula, **Vlad the Impaler.** The obvious popularity of the vampire during the decade prompted two similar nonfiction vampire books by Thomas Aylesworth and the Ronans.

That same year, the first juvenile vampire novel, Vic Crume's *The Mystery of Vampire Castle,* a novelization of the Walt Disney movie of the same name, concerned a 12-year-old amateur movie producer-director Alfie Booth, who had decided to spend his summer making a Dracula movie. In the process, Alfie and his brother ran into several jewelry thieves whose eventual detection and capture supplied the real drama of the movie.

It was not until the last half of the decade that the initial real bloodsucking vampires made their appearance. Among books aimed at a high school audience, evil vampires bared their teeth in Steven Otfinoski's *Village of Vampires* (1978). The novel's hero, Dr. John Lawrence, his daughter Sandy, and assistant Paul Ross had journeyed to the village of Taaxacola, Mexico, where cows had begun to die of a strange malady. Several years before, Lawrence had been in the village to administer a serum to the cattle, which had been under attack from vampire bats. Upon his return, however, he discovered that the entire village now had been turned into vampires. It became the Lawrence party's task to kill them in the traditional manner (**stake through the heart**). In the end, the men had to rescue Sandy as she also was about to be made into a vampire. In Kin Platt's *Dracula Go Home!,* a 1979 comic novel, Larry Carter, a high schooler working at his aunt's hotel during summer vacation, checked a Mr. A. L. R. Claud from Belgrade into a room. The man was pale and wore a black suit with a large hat. He asked for room 13. Larry was sure that Mr. Claud was a vampire and set out to find the proof. In the end, he was found not to be a vampire but a jewel thief who had returned to town to recover stolen merchandise.

For the younger audience still in elementary school, a more benign vampire strolled across the pages of a host of books. For example, in 1979 Deborah Howe and her husband James Howe introduced possibly the most lovable vampire of all time, the vegetarian vampire rabbit *Bunnicula.* Bunnicula, who was given his name after having been found in the theater during a Dracula movie, was the pet of Pete and Toby Monroe. The rabbit was the third animal in a home that included Harold the dog and Chester the cat. Bunnicula was a strange rabbit; he slept all day and, instead of two bunny teeth in front, he had two **fangs.** It was Chester who first spotted the rabbit leaving his cage at night to raid the refrigerator. The next morning the Monroes discovered a white tomato from which all the juice and color (and life) had been sucked. It was the knowledgeable Chester, who spent all of his spare time reading books, the first to determine that Bunnicula was a vampire. Having made his discovery, Chester proceeded to block Bunnicula's path to the kitchen with a **garlic** barrier. Bunnicula almost starved until Harold, concluding that Bunnicula was causing no harm, intervened and smuggled him into the kitchen. Bunnicula proved as popular as he was lovable, and his story was made into a movie for children's television. Through the 1980s he returned in a series of stories, beginning with the 1983 volume, *The Celery Stalks at Midnight.*

For the youngest audience, a vampire literature developed out of the popular televison show Sesame Street, one of the most heralded products of the Public Broadcasting Network. The show specialized in the socialization of preschool children and the teaching of basic knowledge such as the alphabet and numbers. Soon after the show began, the teaching of numbers became the special domain of Count von Count, a puppet version of a Bela Lugosi-like vampire complete with widow's peak and fangs. Through the 1970s, the Count made such tapes as *The Count Counts* (1975) and was the subject of several books, including *The Counting Book* (1971), *The Count's Poem* (1976), *The Day the Count Stopped Counting* (1977), and *The Count's Number Parade* (1977).

THE 1980s: The 1980s saw the development of a full range of vampire literature for every age grouping of children and youth. Literature for the youngest children was launched with the continuing volumes featuring Count von Count of Sesame Street. He began the decade with *The Count's Counting Book* (1980). When the book's cover was opened, the Count and his castle popped up to say, "Aha! Another wonderful day to count on." He then counted various things in his atmospheric neighborhood. In 1981 he followed with *The Count Counts a Party* and other items through the decade.

For elementary school young people, several popular vampire series joined the Bunnicula titles. In 1982 the first volume of Ann Jungman's series featuring Vlad the Drac, another vegetarian vampire, appeared. That same year in **Germany,** Angela Sommer-Bodenburg published the first of her four books featuring the young vampire Rudolph Sackville-Bagg, Rudolph's vampire sister Anna, and their human friend Tony Noodleman. These were promptly translated into English and published in the United States as *My Friend the Vampire, The Vampire Moves In, The Vampire on the Farm,* and *The Vampire Takes a Trip.* Typical of children's literature, the vampire was a somewhat sympathetic character, at worst a somewhat mischievous boy, with the primary elements of horror hovering in the background. *The Vampire Moves In,* for instance, revolved around Rudolph's move into the family storage bin in the basement of the apartment building where Tony's family lived. He had been kicked out of his own family vault because of his fraternizing with humans. The plot centered on the problems created by the vampire's presence, not the least of which was the terrible smell that began to radiate from the vampire's **coffin** and the presence of the undead.

A third series that began later in the decade by author Mel Gilden featured the "fifth grade monsters." In the opening volume, *M Is for Monster,* Danny Keegan began a new school year as a fifth grader. His major problem was bully Stevie Brickwald. However, when he got to school he discovered four new classmates. One possessed a huge mane of hair and slightly pointed ears. His name was Howie Wolfner. A brother and sister team by the name Elsie and Frankie Stein each had metal bolts coming out of the side of their necks. Finally there was the short, fanged kid with slicked-back hair, a black suit, white bow tie, and a satin-lined cape. His name was C.D. Bitesky, whose family came from **Transylvania.** C.D. carried a Thermos bottle from which he frequently sipped a red liquid that he termed the "fluid of life," and he had a pet bat named Spike.

After an initial hesitancy, Danny became friends with these different but nonetheless special people, and within a few years their adventures would fill 15 volumes with no end in sight. C.D. was especially featured in volume 10, *How to be a Vampire in One Easy Lesson* (1990), in which the persistent Stevie Brickwald tried to make friends with the "monsters" and asked C.D. to make him a vampire. C.D. first invited him to his home where his parents started to teach Stevie Romanian history. The impatient Stevie learned that he must meet the Count, C.D.'s patriarchal uncle, who lived in the basement of the local theater, appropriately named **Carfax** Palace. When Stevie appeared at school the next day dressed in a crumpled tuxedo, following his private session with the Count, he announced that he was a "free-lance vampire first class." However, Stevie wished to use his newfound "will" to keep him from having to go to school, but his teacher and the principal finally persuaded him that he was not a vampire.

The final series aimed at elementary school young people to appear in the 1980s was written by Ann Hodgman. Her first volume, *There's a Batwing in My Lunchbox,* was published by Avon in 1988.

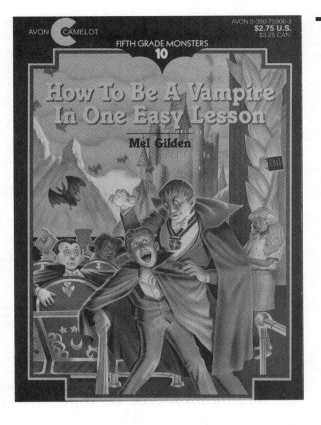

AVON 0-380-75906-3
$2.75 U.S.
$3.25 CAN

AVON CAMELOT

FIFTH GRADE MONSTERS
10

How To Be A Vampire
In One Easy Lesson

Mel Gilden

▶

AUTHOR MEL GILDEN WROTE
A SERIES OF BOOKS FEATURING
"THE FIFTH GRADE MONSTERS,"
WHICH INCLUDED SEVERAL
VAMPIRES.

The young people's vampire, while borrowing from the more traditional character of horror fiction, to some extent had his (and it has almost exclusively been a male) fangs pulled. He was a good person—definitely not the sinister figure of the adult novels or the movies. Absent from the youthful vampire book was any hint of horror, any factor that might lead to the young reader having nightmares. He was never pictured as biting anyone, though there were oblique references, and of course, no harm resulted from a vegetarian like Bunnicula biting a plant. Placed within the context of the young person's world, the vampire was either a lovable pet, a comic figure, or more likely, a somewhat out-of-the-ordinary classmate who can become, in spite of his differences, a close friend.

As the number of titles for elementary school children expanded, so did the number aimed at high schoolers. Typical of these was *The Initiation* by Robert Brunn (1982). The story concerned Adam Maxwell, a student at Blair Prep School. Adam had a problem—he was a misfit. He was totally unappreciative of the elitism and snobbishness so evident among both his classmates and the students of nearby Abbott, a girls school similar to Blair. Both were founded by a Transylvanian couple, Isadore and Bella Esterhaus. Adam soon met his counterpart at Abbott, Loren Winters. Four days after his arrival to the school, Adam found a body in one of the school lockers. Loren had witnessed one of her classmates leaving campus with a man who was reported dead the next day. Together Adam and Loren attempted to figure out the situation they were in. The focus of their search led to an initiation ceremony that occurred during the biweekly mixers promoted by the two schools. Selected students were invited to the basement to be inducted into "a serious organization." Blindfolded and paired with an initiator of the opposite sex, they were attacked in the dark, and all that could be heard was a "wet slurping noise."

In the 1970s, the vampire had received some recognition from the new respect given to classic horror and gothic fiction within the academic community—a respect reflected in the addition of such stories to elementary and high school curricula. By the 1980s Bram Stoker's *Dracula* was recognized as such a classic piece of horror literature, and condensed versions of *Dracula* designed for a juvenile audience began to appear. In the early 1970s, a black-and-white comic version of *Dracula* (1973) became the first juvenile adaptation of the story, and a version for children had been published in 1976 as *Paint Me the Story of Dracula*. Then, at the beginning of the decade, Delacote Press released Alice and Joel Schick's color comic book version of *Dracula*. Several years later, Stephanie Spinner and illustrator Jim Spence prepared a condensed version, often reprinted, for elementary schoolers. In addition, a juvenile version of **John Polidori**'s original vampire story, "The Vampyre", appeared in England in 1986.

THE 1990s: Through the 1980s, the production rate of new vampire-oriented juvenile literature had steadily increased. That increase did not stop in the early 1990s. In the 1980s, some 50 titles were published. In the three years of 1990 to 1992, over 35 titles appeared. Series begun in the 1980s by Mel Gilden, Ann Hodgman, and James Howe continued, and a new series for high schoolers, *The Vampire Diaries* by L. J. Smith, explored the triangle of the vampire brothers Damon and Stefan, and the girl Elena whom they both desired and who must decide between them. For the youngest vampire fans, a pop-up version of *Dracula* was published by Gallery Books in 1990. Preschoolers could start their learning process with Alan Benjamin's *Let's Count, Dracula* (1991).

During the 1980s two vampire stories were included in the "Choose Your Own Adventure" series. A third such vampire volume, *Vampire Invaders* by Edward Packard, appeared as No. 118 in the series in 1991. Additionally, several general juvenile horror series added a vampire novel. Carl Laymon's *Nightmare Lake,* for example, appeared as No. 11 in Dell's "Twilight" series. Bert, Eliot and his sister Sammi on an island vacation, discovered a skeleton after which their dog removed a stick protruding from its rib cage. The children reported their discovery to the police, but upon their return to the island, the skeleton had disappeared. The mystery increased when two bodies were found in a canoe. One had a bloody wound on his neck and, as was later determined, had died from loss of blood. The other person awoke in a state of near hysteria and complained of an attack by a bat. The emergence of vampire believers and skeptics set the stage for the final revelation of the true vampire in their midst.

Among the outstanding new novels was Annette Curtis Klause's *The Silver Kiss,* centered upon the experience of Zoë, a young girl with a fatally ill mother and an emotionally distant father, who tried to protect her from the reality of death. Her loneliness opened her to a relationship with Simon, a vampire. Simon had grown up in Cromwellian England. A business acquaintance of his father introduced vampirism to the family and chose Simon's older brother Christopher as his first victim. Christopher disappeared for many years, but at one point returned to attack his brother Simon, now a young man, and to transform him into a vampire. He also learned that Christopher had killed their mother. Simon set himself the task of hunting down and killing his brother. That drive had brought him to America in the 1930s. Meanwhile, between her seemingly immortal friend who was ready for a final encounter with his brother and her dying mother, Zoë overcame her father's protecting her from the reality of death and arrived at some understanding of its role in life.

Of a lighter nature was *Great Uncle Dracula* by Jayne Harvey, a modern-day parable for children who feel they just do not fit in. It was the story of Emily Normal, a third grader who moved with her father and brother from Plainville to Transylvania, U.S.A., to live with her uncle. Soon after she arrived for her first day at school, she realized that Transylvania was a creepy place: all the girls dressed in black and claimed to be witches; the class pets were tarantulas; her teacher's name was Ms. Vampira and the principal was Frank N. Stein. Emily just did not fit in. She had always done well as a speller, but the "spell"-ing bee did not concern "spelling" words but doing magic "spells." She did make friends, however, and soon found herself at a party. But the party turned into a disaster when Emily fell on the birthday cake while playing pin the tail on the rat. Emily finally got her chance, however, in the gross face contest. Angry at being called names since her arrival at school, she won the contest by the face she made just as she shouted out, "I am not a weirdo." She was awarded the prize for making the grossest face anyone in Transylvania could remember.

Other outstanding young adult vampire novels included *The Cheerleader* and *The Return of a Vampire* by Caroline B. Cooney and *Vampire* and *Buffy the Vampire Slayer* by Richie Tankersley Cusick, the latter being a novelization of the movie of the same title. It would appear that as of the mid-1990s, vampire juvenile literature is in the midst of healthy growth period. The immediate future should see the production of many new vampire titles for children and youth.

Sources:

Nonfiction

Austin, R. G. *Vampires, Spies and Alien Beings.* New York: Archway/Pocket Books, 1982. 120 pp.

Aylesworth, Thomas G. *The Story of Vampires.* Middletown, CT: Weekly Reader Books, 1977. 85 pp. Reprint. Middletown CT: Xerox Education Publications, 1977. 85 pp.

Garden, Nancy. *Vampires.* Philadelphia: J. B. Lippencott Company, 1973. 127 pp.

Gelman, Rita Golden, and Nancy Lamb. *Vampires and Other Creatures of the Night.* New York: Scholastic, Inc., 1991. 74 pp.

JUVENILE LITERATURE

McHargue, Georgess. *Meet the Vampire*. Philadelphia: J. B. Lippencott Company, 1976. Reprint. New York: Laurel Leaf Books, 1983. 106 pp.

Ronan, Margaret, and Eve Ronan. *Curse of the Vampires*. New York: Scholastic Book Services, 1979. 89 pp.

Fiction

Benjamin, Alan. *Let's Count, Dracula*. A Chubby Board Book. New York: Simon & Schuster, 1992. 16 pp.

Brunn, Robert. *The Initiation*. New York: Dell, 1982. 154 pp.

Cooney, Caroline. *The Cheerleader*. New York: Scholastic, 1991. 179 pp.

———. *The Return of the Vampire*. New York: Scholastic, 1992. 166 pp.

The Counting Book. New York: Random House, 1971.

The Count's Counting Book. New York: Random House/Children's Television Workshop, 1980. 14 pp.

Crume, Vic. *The Mystery in Dracula's Castle*. New York: Scholastic Book Services, 1973. 111 pp

Cusick, Richie Tankersley. *Buffy the Vampire Slayer*. New York: Pocket Books, 1992. 183 pp.

———. *Vampire*. New York: Pocket Books, 1991. 214 pp.

Dixon, Franklin W. *Danger on Vampire Trail*. The Hardy Boys 50. New York: Grosset & Dunlap, 1971. 175 pp.

Garden, Nancy. *My Sister, the Vampire*. New York: Alfred A. Knopf, 1992. 186 pp.

———. *Mystery of the Night Raiders*. (Monster Hunters Case, 1) New York: Pocket Books, 1987, 1991.

———. *Prisoner of Vampires*. New York: Farrar, Strauss, and Giroux, 1984. 213 pp.

Gilden, Mel. *Born to Howl*. New York: Avon, 1987. 91 pp.

———. *How to Be a Vampire in One Easy Lesson*. New York: Avon, 1990. 91 pp.

Harvey, James. *Great Uncle Dracula*. New York: Random House, 1992. 77 pp.

Hodgman, Ann. *My Babysitter Bites Again*. New York: Pocket Books, 1993. 135 pp.

———. *My Babysitter Has Fangs*. New York: Pocket Books, 1992. 137 pp.

Howe, Deborah and James Howe. *Bunnicula*. New York: Atheneum Publishers, 1979. Reprint. New York: Avon, 1980. 98 pp.

Korr, David. *The Day the Count Stopped Counting*. New York: Western Publishing Company, 1977. 46 pp.

Packard, Edward. *Space Vampire*. Choose Your Own Adventure, No. 71. New York: Bantam Books, 1987. 118 pp.

———. *Vampire Invaders*. Choose Your Own Adventure, No. 118. New York: Bantam Books, 1991. 111 pp.

Polidori, John. *The Vampyre*. Retold by David Campton. London: Beaver/Arrow, 1986. Reprint. New York: Barron's Educational Series, 1988. 139 pp.

Sommer-Bodenburg, Angela. *Der Kleine Vampir*. Reinbek bei Hamburg, Germany: Rowohlt Taschenbuch Verlag, 1982. *My Friend the Vampire*. Trans. by Sarah Gibson. New York: E. P. Dutton, 1982. Reprint. New York: Minstrel/Pocket Books. Trans. by Sarah Gibson. 1985. Reprint. New York: Penguin, 1991. 131 pp.

———. *Der kleine Vampir zieht um*. Reinbek bei Hamburg, Germany: Rowohlt Taschenbuch Verlag, 1982. Rept as: *The Vampire Moves In*. New York: E. P. Dutton, 1982. 155 pp. Reprint. New York: Minstrel/Pocket Books, 1986. 155 pp.

———. *Der kleine Vampir auf dem Bauerhof*. Reinbek bei Hamburg, Germany: Rowohlt Taschenbuch Verlag, 1983. Rept. as: *The Vampire on the Farm*. New York: E. P. Dutton, 1990. 136 pp. Reprint. New York: Minstrel/Pocket Books, 1990. 135 pp.

———. *The Vampire Takes a Trip*. New York: E. P. Dutton, 1985.

Spinner, Stephanie. *Dracula*. New York: Random House, 1982.

Stiles, Norman. *The Count's Number Parade*. Racine, WI: Western, 1977. 24 pp.

Stoker, Bram. *Dracula*. Adapted by Stephanie Spinner. New York: Step-Up Adventures/Random House, 1982. 94 pp.

K

KALI

A major deity in the mythology of **India,** Kali was known for, among other characteristics, her blood-thirst. Kali first appeared in Indian writings around the sixth century A.D. in invocations calling for her assistance in war. In these early texts she was described as having **fangs,** wearing a garland of corpses, and living at the cremation ground. Several centuries later, in the *Bhagavat-purana,* she and her cohorts, the *dakinis,* turned on a band of thieves, decapitated them, got drunk on their blood, and played a game of tossing the heads around. Other writings called for her temples to be built away from the villages near the cremation grounds.

Kali made her most famous appearance in the *Devi-mahatmya,* where she joined the goddess Durga in fighting the demon Raktabija. Raktabija had the ability to reproduce himself with each drop of spilled blood; thus, in fighting him successfully, Durga found herself being overwhelmed by Raktabija clones. Kali rescued Durga by vampirizing Raktabija and eating the duplicates. Kali came to be seen by some as Durga's wrathful aspect. Kali also appeared as a consort of the god Siva. They engaged in fierce dance. Pictorially, Kali generally was shown on top of Siva's prone body in the dominant position as they engaged in sexual intercourse.

Kali had an ambiguous relationship to the world. On the one hand she destroyed demons and thus brought order. However, she also served as a representation of forces that threatened social order and stability by her blood drunkenness and subsequent frenzied activity.

Kali became the dominant deity within Tantric Hinduism, where she was praised as the original form of things and the origin of all that exists. She was termed Creatrix, Protectress, and Destructress. In Tantra, the way of salvation was through the sensual delights of the world—those things usually forbidden to a devout Hindu—such as alcohol and sex. Kali represented the ultimate forbidden realities, and was thus to be

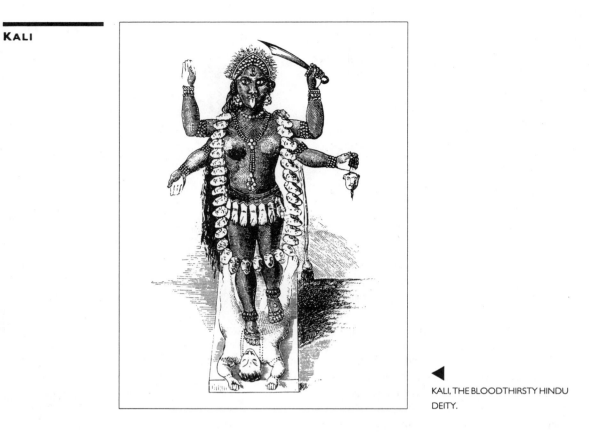

KALI, THE BLOODTHIRSTY HINDU DEITY.

taken into the self and overcome in what amounted to a ritual of salvation. She taught that life fed on death, that death was inevitable for all beings, and that in the acceptance of these truths—by confronting Kali in the cremation grounds and thus demonstrating courage equal to her terrible nature—there was liberation. Kali, like many vampire-deities, symbolized the disorder that continually appeared amid all attempts to create order. Life was ultimately untamable and unpredictable.

Kali survived among the **Gypsies,** who had migrated from India to Europe in the Middle Ages, as Sara, the Black Goddess. However, her vampiric aspects were much mediated by the mixture of Kali with an interesting French Christian myth. According to the story, the three Marys of the New Testament traveled to France where they were met by Sara, a Gypsy who assisted them in their landing. They baptized Sara and preached the gospel to her people. The Gypsies hold a celebration on May 24-25 each year at Saintes-Maries-de-la-Mer, the small French village where the events are believed to have occurred. A statue to Sara was placed in the crypt of the church where the Gypsies have kept their annual vigil.

Sources:

Clébert, Jean-Paul. *The Gypsies.* Harmondsworth, UK: Penguin Books, 1967. 282 pp.

Kinsley, David. *Hindu Goddesses: Visions of the Divine Feminine in the Hindu Religious Tradition.* Berkeley, CA: University of California Press, 1986. 281 pp.

KAPLAN, STEPHEN *See:* VAMPIRE RESEARCH CENTER

KAPPA See: JAPAN, VAMPIRES IN

KEATS, JOHN (1795-1821)

John Keats, British Romantic poet, was born in London, the son of Frances Jennings and Thomas Keats. His father, a livery-stable keeper, was killed in 1804 by a fall from a horse. His mother remarried, but it proved an unhappy union and she soon separated. She died in 1810 from tuberculosis. It was as his mother's condition worsened that Keats, never the scholarly type, began to read widely. He especially liked the Greek myths. After his mother's death he was apprenticed to a surgeon and in 1814 moved to London to study at the joint school of St. Thomas' and Guy's Hospitals. He passed his examination in 1816 and began a career as a surgeon.

During his years in school in London, poetry came to dominate his leisure time. He was still in his teens when he wrote his first poems, and in 1815 he produced ''On First Looking into Chapman's Homer,'' still hailed as one of the finest sonnets in the English language. About this time he met Leigh Hunt, also a poet, who introduced Keats into various literary circles. Keat's volume of verse was published in 1817. While the book did not do well, he decided to halt his surgical career to seek a quiet existence pursuing his poetry. Through the rest of the year he produced ''Endymion,'' ''To Psyche,'' ''To a Nightingale,'' and one of his most enduring efforts ''On a Grecian Urn.''

Through 1819 he worked on ''Otho the Great,'' ''Hyperion,'' ''The Eve of Saint Agnes,'' and ''Lamia''. With ''Lamia'' he picked up the vampire theme then becoming popular in Western literature. Interestingly enough, he began working on the poem soon after the publication of **John Polidori**'s ''The Vampyre'' (the first piece of vampire fiction in English), in the *New Monthly Magazine.* At this time, Keats was under some financial strain, and his love affair with Fanny Brawne was having its ups and downs. He also had developed a full-blown case of tuberculosis, a wasting disease that occasioned the periodic spitting up of blood.

Keats's ''Lamia'' derived from the ancient account of the *lamiai*, the Greek vampirelike demon, described by Philostratus in his *Life of Apollonius.* The story told of a *lamia* attempting to seduce a young man of Corinth. As he was about to marry the *lamia,* who would have turned on him and killed him, the wise Apollonius intervened. He unmasked her for what she was, and as he pointed out the illusionary environment she had created, its beauty faded away. She, of course, then departed. As Keats did not read Greek, and no English translation of the *Life of Apollonius* had been published, he had to rely upon Richard F. Burton's version of the story in his *Anatomy of*

JOHN KEATS

Melancholy. Crucial to Burton's retelling was his deletion of a crucial sentence in Philostratus's text, "...she admitted she was a vampire and was fattening up Menippus (Lucius) with pleasure before devouring his body, for it was her habit to feed upon young and beautiful bodies because their blood was pure and strong."

Burton presented a somewhat sanitized *lamia,* but Keats metaphorically pulled her fangs even further. To best understand "The Lamia," one must view the story, as James Twitchell and other critics have done, as Keats's having adopted the vampire theme as a metaphor of human relations seen in the interchange of life-giving energies. In the process, Philostratus's story is changed considerably. According to Keats, in her thirst for love, the *lamia* dropped her traditional serpentlike form and moved into Lucius's human world. Lucius responded by becoming vampiric and attempting to gain some of the *lamia*'s former powers. Thus, Keats pictured the *lamia* using powers of **psychic vampirism,** drawing on Lucius's love as her metaphorical life-blood. In return, Lucius also became a vampire, willing to drain all from the *lamia* to gain new powers. Keats noted that Lucius had "drunk her beauty up." At this juncture Apollonius appeared. He recognized the *lamia* and, over Lucius's protests, drove her away. Without her, Lucius soon died.

Some critics of Keats's poetry have suggested that an even more unambiguous vampire existed in his poetry than "The Lamia." In "La Belle Dame sans Merci," also composed in 1819, a knight met a lady with whom he became entranced. She fed him exotic foods and told him she loved him. He visited her underground home, where her mood changed to one of sadness. As the knight slept, he saw pale warriors and was told that he was soon to join them. After his awakening, while "palely loitering," he encountered the narrator of the poem. There the poem ended. As early as 1948, criticEdwin R. Clapp suggested that the unnamed female, the title character in "La Belle Dame sans Merci," was best understood as a vampire. Clapp, for example, noted the likeness of the victim of Polidori's vampire ("There was no color upon her cheek, not even upon her lip."), with images developed by Keats ("pale were the lips I saw/Pale were the lips I kiss'd. . . "). Critic James B. Twitchell, picking up on Clapp, suggested that Keats had joined **Samuel Taylor Coleridge** in expanding upon the *lamia* myth and liberating it from the past. The *lamia* became a very real character and the encounter of the male with the female who had no pity, a somewhat universal experience. More detailed analysis of the poem easily led to Freudian interpretations such as the one suggested by Ernest Jones, which tied the vampire-*lamia* myth to the initiation of adolescent males into the mysteries of sexuality.

Twitchell suggested that the *lamia* theme subtly reappeared in much of Keats's poetry, though "The Lamia" and "La Belle Dame sans Merci" were its best examples. Keats, of course, went on to write many more poems, but in 1820, his health took a decided downward turn. He died February 23, 1821, in Rome.

Sources:

Capp, Edwin R. "La Belle Dame as Vampire." *Philological Quarterly* 27, 4 (October 1948): 89-92.

Jones, Ernest. *On the Nightmare.* 1931. Reprint. New York: Liveright, 1971. 374 pp.

Keats, John. *The Complete Poetry of John Keats.* Ed. by George R. Elliott. New York: Macmillan Company, 1927. 457 pp.

Twitchell, James B. *The Living Dead: A Study of the Vampire in Romantic Literature.* Durham, NC: Duke University Press, 1981. 219 pp.

KILLING THE VAMPIRE *See:* VAMPIRE RESEARCH CENTER

KING, STEPHEN (1947-)

Stephen King, since the mid-1970s has been America's premiere horror fiction writer. He was born in Portland, Maine, the son of Nellie Ruth Pillsbury and Donald King. As a child, he began to write science fiction short stories, and at the age of 12 submitted his first stories to *Fantastic* and the *Magazine of Fantasy and Science Fiction.* King graduated from the University of Maine in 1970. His first published story, "The Glass Floor," appeared in *Startling Mystery Stories* in 1967, while he was still at college.

Unable to obtain a job as an English teacher, King started working in an industrial laundry. During this period he wrote a number of short stories, and in 1972 began working on his first book, *Carrie,* which eventually was bought by Doubleday & Company. King then turned his attention to a vampire tale originally called "Second Coming," but was later renamed "Jerusalem's Lot." The story was published in 1975 as *Salem's Lot.* Meanwhile King also was working on his subsequent novels, *The Shining* (1977) and *The Stand* (1978).

In 1976, *Salem's Lot* was nominated for a World Fantasy Award in the best-novel category. That same year, *Carrie* was released as a movie starring Sissy Spacek. King, a very fertile storyteller, also began to publish material under a pseudonym, Richard Bachman; the first title, *Rage,* appeared in 1977. He also published a second vampire short story, "One for the Road," that year.

During the 1980s, King enjoyed immense success. In his novels he has attempted to explore the vast world of horror and terror, and by choice has rarely returned to a theme once treated. Thus, after one successful vampire volume, he has not returned to the topic for a book, though he published a third vampire short story, "The Night Flier," in 1988. Several of his novels, however, flirted with vampirism. The most obvious was *The Tommyknockers,* which featured an alien vampire. In 1979 *Salem's Lot* was made into a television mini-series under the direction of Tobe Hooper, and a sequel (not based on King's writing), *Return to Salem's Lot*, appeared in 1987.

King has continued to write about two novels annually. Only in 1985 was it revealed that he had written the Richard Bachman books, and his name has subsequently appeared on new printings of them. A number of his novels and short stories, including *The Tommyknockers*, have been made into movies. He has received a variety of awards, including a special World Fantasy Award for his contribution to the field.

Sources:

Hoppenstand, Gary, and Ray B. Browne. *The Gothic World of Stephen King: Landscape of Nightmares.* Bowling Green, OH: Bowling Green State University Popular Press, 1987. 143 pp.

King, Stephen. "Jerusalem's Lot." In *Night Shift.* Garden City, NY: Doubleday & Company, 1978.

———. "The Night Flier." In Douglas E. Winter, ed. *Prime Evil.* New York: New American Library, 1988.

———. "One for the Road." In *Maine Magazine*(March/April 1977). Rept. in: Greenberg, Martin H., and Charles G. Waugh, eds. *Vamps.* New York: Daw Books, 1987, 12-30.

———. *Salem's Lot.* 1975. 162 pp. Reprint. New York: New American Library, 1976.

———. *Tommyknockers.* New York: G. P. Putnam's Sons, 1987. 558 pp.

Reino, Joseph. *Stephen King: The First Decade, Carrie to Pet Sematary.* Boston, MA: Twayne Publishers, 1988.

Straub, Peter. "Meeting Stevie." In *Fear Itself: The Horror Fiction of Stephen King.* San Francisco: Underwood-Miller, 1982. 255 pp.

Winter, Douglas E. *Stephen King: The Art of Darkness.* New York: New American Library, 1984.

KÜRTEN, PETER (1883-1931)

Often cited as a real vampire, Peter Kürten—the so-called Düsseldorf Vampire—was a serial killer who operated in **Germany** during 1929-30. He was born in

Mulheim, Germany, one of 10 children, the son of an alcoholic, brutal father. He lived part of his youthful years with the town dogcatcher and remembered enjoying killing the unclaimed dogs. Kürten was only nine when he first killed a person. He pushed a playmate into the water and then repeated the act with a second boy who attempted to save the first.

His next known attempt at homicide was eight years later when he tried to rape and kill a young woman. He was sent to jail for four years for his unsuccessful effort. He lived on the streets after his release from prison, but a year later was back in jail for a series of thefts and burglaries. He would later claim to have killed two of his prisonmates by poisoning. In 1913 back on the street in Düsseldorf, he killed again. He murdered a 10-year-old girl. He cut her throat with a knife and reportedly experienced an orgasm as the blood spurted out.

It was not until 1929 that Kürten began the series of crimes that were to earn him his place in criminal history. In February of that year, he attempted the murder of one woman and succeeded in the murder of two children, one male and one female, all by stabbing. His attempts at murder, often unsuccessful, did not aid police. They accused a mentally-ill man to be convicted of the murder of the boy Kürten had actually killed.

That summer, he was more successful, killing nine people in August alone. He continued his killing through the winter of 1929-30. In May he attempted the strangling death of a young woman and then inexplicably stopped and let her go. She identified him, and he was arrested. During his crime spree, he had thoroughly confused the police by continually changing his method of killing. Only as he began his confession and accurately related the circumstances of each crime was any doubt of his having perpetrated them removed. He was convicted and executed by decapitation on July 2, 1931.

Kürten was certainly not a vampire in any traditional sense. Superficially, he demonstrated a vampiric trait in his obsession with blood, but he was like neither the vampire of folklore nor that of the modern literary and cinematic tradition. His history of vampirelike **crime** fits more properly into the history of serial murder. Kürten's life inspired two movies, *M* (1931) and *Le Vampire de Düsseldorf* (1964).

Sources:

Glut, Donald F. *True Vampires of History*. New York: H C Publishers, 1971. 191 pp.

"Kürten—The Vampire of Düsseldorf." In *Monsters of Weimar*. London: Nemesis Books, 1993, pp. 159-289.

Volta, Ornella. *The Vampire*. New York: Award Books, 1962. 153 pp.

L

LAMIAI *See:* GREECE, VAMPIRES IN

LAMPIR

Lampir was the name given the vampire in Bosnia. It was similar to Vampires among the Slavs, especially as it was found among the **southern Slavs.** *Lampir* was interchangeable with the term ***vukodlak,*** also used in Croatia. M. Edith Durham, who performed field work in Bosnia at the beginning of this century, noted that when the Austrians took control of Bosnia from the Ottoman Empire in 1878, officials discovered multiple cases of people disinterring bodies and burning them as *lampirs*. The Austrian government forbade such practices.

The main cause of designating a person as a *lampir* appeared to be disease. When a disease swept through a community, and the cause was unknown, it was often ascribed to vampirism. The first person to die usually was designated as the vampire and others who died were considered the victims. The victims, however, then were thought to be infested with the vampire's condition and able to pass it on. Durham also suggested that, in the wake of the government's orders, some people may have decided that they would die, therefore, some died as a result of their belief rather than any diseased condition.

Sources:

Durham, M. Edith. "Of Magic, Witches and Vampires in the Balkans." *Man* 121 (December 1923): 189-92.

LANGELLA, FRANK (1940-)

Frank Langella, star of the 1979 film version of ***Dracula,*** was born in Bayonne, New

Jersey. His parents were Frank Langella, a businessman, and Ruth Weil, a magazine editor. He attended Syracuse University and in 1959 was awarded the Syracuse Critics award as best actor. He went on to study acting, dance, and voice with private teachers and launched a career that has included both acting and theatrical management. Langella made his stage debut in 1960 in *Pajama Game* at the Erie Playhouse. In 1963 he made his New York debut in *The Immoralist* at the Bouwerie Lane Theatre. That same year he became one of the original members of the Lincoln Center repertory training company.

In 1967 Langella first appeared in the title role of *Dracula* at the Berkshire Theatre Festival. Three years later he made his film debut in *The Twelve Chairs,* a part that would be followed by more notable roles in *Diary of a Mad Housewife* and *The Deadly Trap.* In 1977, he attained a new level of recognition as the star in the revival of the **Hamilton Deane/John L. Balderston** version of *Dracula,* which in 1978 received two Tony awards. Two years later, he was chosen to star in the movie version of *Dracula* directed by John Badham.

An accomplished actor, Langella brought a new depth and dimension to a part that had become rather narrowly stereotyped. Langella had reflected upon the Count's character. Dracula would, he assumed, carry himself as a member of royalty who was on the one hand (in the presence of females) gracious and mannered, but on the other hand, ruled and commanded and used to having his own way. He also understood Dracula's problem with immortality. While an extended life gave him wisdom beyond his contemporaries, it also brought a great weariness. In possibly the most important element of his performance, in large part attributable to the changing times, Langella highlighted the sensual and sexual elements of his relationship to **Lucy Westenra** (renamed Lucy Seward), the main character in the Deane/Balderston play. As Dracula, Langella would not only act with defensiveness when attacked, but also as a jealous lover.

Langella clearly understood the relationship between Dracula and women. In reflecting on the role, he noted:

> . . . the women have to *want* to make love with Count Dracula. And he must want to make love to them as a man loves a woman . . . not as a vampire goes after blood. The things that go on between Dracula and his women must be the result of her needs as well as his. Something is calling her, and it's not fangs, or his wolf's eyes.

Langella created the most appealing and human Dracula since Lugosi. He played the character not as a traditional monster, but as a creature of a different species. Dracula was not so much cruel and evil as operating out of his very different nature.

Langella took his place as one of the most memorable actors to assume the role of Dracula, though, for the sake of his career, he was able to walk away from the part and avoid being typecast. Thus, unlike that of **Bela Lugosi** and **Christopher Lee,** Langella's portrayal consumed only a few years of his lengthy career. He followed his success as Dracula with other movies and with additional success on the stage. In

1980 he was able to return to Broadway as Salieri in the highly acclaimed *Amadeus.* Langella has continued to play a wide variety of roles on stage, with occasional movie roles. In 1981 he assumed the title role of Dracula's contemporary in a television production of **Sherlock Holmes.** He returned to this role in 1987 in *Sherlock's Last Case* in New York and Washington, D.C.

Sources:

Ebert, Roger. "Dracula: Revival of the Undead Hero." *Chicago Sun-Times* (July 8, 1979).
McMurray, Emily J., and Owen O'Donnell, eds. *Contemporary Theatre, Film, and Television.* Vol. 9. Detroit, MI: Gale Research, 1992.

LANGSUYAR

The *langsuyar* was the most prominent of the several vampires of **Malaysia.** The *langsuyar* was described as a beautiful woman who reacted strongly to the loss of her stillborn baby. She flew into the trees and became a night demon that attacked and sucked the blood of other women's children. The first *langsuyar* became the source of a class of vampire beings. If a woman died as a result of childbirth, she was a candidate to become a *langsuyar.* To prevent such an occurrence, the body would be treated with a needle in the palm of the hand, eggs under the arms, and glass beads in the mouth. On occasion, *langsuyars* assumed a somewhat normal village life. They would marry and have children—and feed off of others in the evening. They had long hair that covered a hole in their neck through which they sucked blood.

As reported by Walter William Skeat, the *langsuyar* had a counterpart in the *pontianak,* a stillborn child who became a vampire. However, in much of Indonesia (such as in **Java**), what was termed a *langsuyar* in Malaysia was also called a *pontianak.* In the 1950s, Catay-Keris Productions began to make a series of films about the Malaysian *langsuyar,* but designated the star a *pontianak,* after the broader use of the term.

Sources:

Skeat, Walter William. *Malay Magic: An Introduction to the Folklore and Popular Religion of the Malay Peninsula.* London: Macmillan and Co., 1900. 685 pp. Reprint. New York: Barnes & Noble, 1966. 685 pp.

LATVIA, VAMPIRES IN *See:* BALTIC STATES, VAMPIRES OF

LE FANU, JOSEPH THOMAS SHERIDAN (1814-1873)

Joseph Thomas Sheridan Le Fanu, poet and author of short stories in the horror genre, was born on August 28, 1814, in Dublin, Ireland. His father was chaplain of the Royal Hiberian Military School, and Le Fanu was born on its premises. His great-uncle was the heralded Irish dramatist Richard Brimsley Sheridan. At age 14, he composed a long Irish poem, which launched his literary career.

Le Fanu's formal literary career began in 1838 when "The Ghost and the Bone-Setter" was published in the *Dublin University Magazine.* Over the next 15 years he wrote 23 stories and two novels. Most of these were set in Ireland and focused on aspects of the Irish character. With few exceptions, they have generally been judged as mediocre, in part due to Le Fanu's inability to relate to the Irish masses, whom he tended to stereotype because of the religious disagreements that separated him from them. However, he did begin his venture into supernatural horror, and in one of his stories, "Strange Event in the Life of Schalken the Painter," he touched on themes later developed in his most famous work, "Carmilla."

In 1861 Le Fanu purchased the *Dublin University Magazine,* which he edited for the next eight years. During the early 1860s Le Fanu wrote four novels. He continued to write novels for the rest of his life, but they never gained a popular audience. It was his short stories that brought him public attention. 1866 was a watershed year for Le Fanu; seven of his short stories appeared in Charles Dickens's *All the Year Round,* among the most prestigious periodicals in England, launching an era of production of some masterful short literary pieces. At this time he was becoming increasingly pessimistic about life in general and the course of Irish politics in particular. He seems to have drawn on the negative aspects of his own life to write some of the great supernatural horror tales of the period.

Critics agree that the stories published in his collection *In a Glass Darkly* (1872) are his best stories, though they would disagree on which one is actually *the* best. However, the one that has attained the highest level of fame, even after long neglect of Le Fanu's work, is **"Carmilla".** "Carmilla," only the third vampire story in English, is still one of the best. It told the story of Laura, the daughter of an Austrian civil servant named Karnstein, who was attacked by a female vampire variously named Carmilla, Mircalla, and Millarca. The story traced Laura's early childhood encounter with Carmilla, an experience almost forgotten until the vampire reappeared when Laura was in her late teens. In the end, the victims and their family tracked Carmilla to her resting place and destroyed her. First published in several parts in *Dark Blue* magazine (December 1871-March 1872), "Carmilla" provided a major building block of the modern vampire myth. It was read by **Bram Stoker,** a later resident of Dublin and, like Le Fanu, a graduate of Trinity University.

After his death in Dublin on February 7, 1873, Le Fanu's reputation drifted into almost a century of obscurity, although he had as fans such writers as Henry James and Dorothy Sayers. A major reason for his neglect by the literary elite seems to be the subject of his writing. For many decades the great majority of literary critics held supernatural horror fiction in disdain, and thus neglected its more able writers. As gothic fiction came into its own in the last generation, critical reappraisal of the genre quickly followed. The new era of appreciation of Le Fanu really began in 1964 when E. F. Bleiler completed an edited edition of the *Best Ghost Stories of J. S. Le Fanu,* published by Dover. Then in 1977, under the editorship of Devendra P. Varma, Arno Press released the 52 volume *Collected Works of Joseph Sheridan Le Fanu.*

It is among vampire fans, however, that Le Fanu is most remembered. Next to *Dracula,* "Carmilla" has become the single vampire story most frequently brought to the screen, and, like *Dracula,* it has inspired other stories of its leading vampire characters. Among the film versions of "Carmilla" are *Blood and Roses* (1961), *Blood and Black Lace* (1964), and *The Vampire Lovers* (1970). One of its best adaptations is a made-for-television version entitled *Carmilla* that was presented in 1989 on Showtime's *Nightmare Classics.* It has often been said that *Vampyr,* the classic vampire movie directed by **Carl Theodor Dreyer,** was based on "Carmilla," but, except for being a story with a female vampire, it bears little resemblance to "Carmilla." Le Fanu wrote a second, lesser-known story at least suggestive of vampirism, "The Room in the Dragon Volant," which was made into a movie, *The Inn of the Flying Dragon* (originally *Ondskans Vardshus*), in 1981.

Sources:

Browne, Nelson. *Sheridan Le Fanu.* London: Arthur Barker, 1951. 135 pp. Le Fanu, J. Sheridan. *Best Ghost Stories of J. S. Le Fanu.* Edited by E. F. Bleiler. New York: Dover Publications, 1964.
———. *Collected Works of Joseph Sheridan Le Fanu.* Edited by Devendra P. Varma. 52 vols. New York: Arno Press, 1977.
McCormack, W. J. *Sheridan Le Fanu and Victorian Ireland.* Oxford: Clarendon Press, 1980. 310 pp.

LEE, CHRISTOPHER (1922-)

Actor Christopher Lee, who, after **Bela Lugosi,** is most often identified with the part of the vampire **Dracula,** has played the count in more different motion pictures than anyone. He was born on May 27, 1922, in London, England, and later attended Wellington College. In 1947 he signed a contract with J. Arthur Rank, which led to his first film appearance in *Corridor of Blood.* Thus began one of the most active screen careers, which by the mid-1980s saw Lee with parts in more than 130 movies. His career rose steadily through the 1950s to 1957 when he was brought together with three other people at **Hammer Films** who were to alter his life dramatically.

Responding to the success of several science fiction/horror movies, Hammer obtained the motion picture rights to some of **Universal Pictures** classic monster movies and hired **Terence Fisher, Jimmy Sangster, Peter Cushing,** and Lee to film a new version of *Frankenstein.* Lee starred as the monster in the highly successful *The Curse of Frankenstein* (1957). The four were called together the following year to do a remake of *Dracula*, best known as *The Horror of Dracula.* Although *The Curse of Frankenstein,* in Lee's words, "started it all," it was *The Horror of Dracula* that made Lee a star and put Hammer on the map as the new king of on-the-screen horror. Changes in technology and in public mores allowed Lee to present a much different Dracula. Most noticeably, Lee was more directly a creature of horror, dropping much of the image of the suave continental gentleman perpetuated by Lugosi. Unlike

Lugosi, Lee had **fangs,** that he showed to the audience, and he attacked his female victims on camera.

Lacking any clear direction from the production staff, Lee developed Dracula as a complex human who had great positive qualities—leadership, charm, intelligence, and sensuality—coupled with a savage and ferocious streak that would lead to his eventual downfall. Dracula also had a tragic quality, his undead immortality.

The Horror of Dracula was an unexpected success, but it would be some years before Lee would return to the role. Meanwhile, he went to Italy to make a comedic vampire movie, *Tempi duri per I Vampiri* (*Hard Times for Vampires*), and Lee has insisted that the vampire he portrayed was not Dracula, but a Baron Rodrigo. He then returned to Hammer for further work on the first round of the Universal horror series as Kharis in *The Mummy* (1960). Moving back to Italy, he worked with director **Mario Bava,** for whom he played the vampire Lico, whom Hercules confronts in the underworld.

While Lee was working on the continent, Hammer had made its first movie about **Carmilla,** the vampire in **Sheridan Le Fanu**'s 1872 tale of the same name. Lee was then invited to assume the part of Count Ludwig Karnstein in the 1963 Spanish version of the story, *La Maledicion de los Karnsteins* (aka *Terror in the Crypt*). It would be another five years before Lee returned to Hammer, where, together with Fisher and Sangster, he made his next Dracula movie. *Dracula, Prince of Darkness* began with the final scene from *The Horror of Dracula,* in which **Abraham Van Helsing** killed Dracula. Dracula was revived by the pouring of blood on his ashes. For Lee, this second Dracula movie was unique in that he never spoke a line, merely grunted and groaned. Whereas *The Horror of Dracula* had made Lee a star, the series of movies made during the seven years beginning in 1966, when *Dracula, Prince of Darkness* was filmed, forever identified him with the role. Most of these—*Dracula Has Risen from the Grave* (1969), *Taste the Blood of Dracula* (1970), *The Scars of Dracula* (1970), *Dracula A.D. 1972* (1972), and *The Satanic Rites of Dracula*, aka *Count Dracula and His Vampire Brides* (1973)—were panned by the critics but found an appreciative audience among the growing legion of vampire fans.

While Lee was turning out the series of Hammer movies, two historians, **Raymond T. McNally** and **Radu Florescu,** were researching the historical Dracula, the Romanian ruler **Vlad the Impaler.** Their first report on their research appeared in 1972 as *In Search of Dracula*. In 1974 a Swedish production crew filmed a documentary based on the book and bearing the same title. Lee was selected to narrate the movie and to appear in scenes as Vlad.

Lee believed that each of the Hammer films moved him further and further from the Dracula of **Bram Stoker**'s novel. For example, *Dracula Has Risen from His Grave* contained a scene in which Lee pulled a stake out of his own heart, an action he considered at the time completely out of character. Thus, in 1970 he jumped at the chance to star in Jesus Franco's version of the Dracula story, *El Conde Dracula.* Unlike previous versions, Franco's *Dracula* made a place for all of the novel's main characters, and during the opening scenes stayed relatively close to the book.

CHRISTOPHER LEE AS DRACULA, THE ROLE FOR WHICH HE IS MOST FAMOUS.

The script soon began to deviate, however, and in the end wandered far from the text (attributed partly to an extremely low budget). In one aspect, Lee was very happy with the film; it allowed him to portray Dracula as he was pictured in the book, although Lee lacked the hairy palms and the elongated ears and fingers. Lee did bring out Dracula's progressively more youthful appearance as he drained the blood of **Lucy Westenra** and **Mina Murray.** Franco's film soon entered the ranks of the forgotten movies, although high marks were given to Pedro Portabella, who made a film about the making of *El Conde Dracula*. Portabella's *Vampir* was acclaimed as an artistic meditation on death. Lee starred in the final scenes, in which he described Dracula's death and read the last chapter of the novel, in which Dracula was killed.

Lee's last appearance in a vampire movie was as Dracula in the 1976 film, *Dracula and Son* (a French comedy originally released as *Dracula pere et Fils*). Lee had played enough different roles to stave off the terror of any actor, typecasting, but at this point he swore off vampire movies altogether. He had supporting parts in *The Private Life of Sherlock Holmes* (1970) and *Hannie Caulder* (1972) and the title role as the villain in the James Bond movie *Man with the Golden Gun* (1974). He went on to have significant character roles in a variety of films, such as *Airport 77* (1976), *Return to Witch Mountain* (1977), and *1941* (1979). He also appeared in the film *Cyber Eden* (1994), an Italian science fiction production.

Lee wrote his autobiography, *Tall, Dark, and Gruesome* (1977), and worked with **Michael Parry** on an anthology of horror stories, *Christopher Lee's X. Certificate* (1975), reprinted as *From the Archcomments in The Films of Christopher Lee*, a book written about his movie career.

Sources:

"Christopher Lee Bibliography." *The Vampire Journal* 1 (Summer 1985): 30-31. Kelley, Bill. "Christopher Lee: King of the Counts." In *Dracula: The Complete Vampire*. Special issue of *Starlog Movie Magazine Presents*. No.6. New York: Starlog Communications, 1992, pp. 44-53.
————. "What Dracula Is Up To." *Imagi-Movies* 1, 2 (Winter 1993-94): 46-48.
Lee, Christopher. *Tall, Dark and Gruesome: An Autobiography.* London: W. H. Allen, 1977. Reprint. London: Granada, 1978. 185 pp.
————, and Michel Parry. *Christopher Lee's X. Certificate.* 2 vols. London: 1975. Rept. as *From the Archives of Evil.* New York: Warner Books, 1976. 205 pp.
Pohle, Robert W., Jr., and Douglas C. Hart. *The Films of Christopher Lee.* Metuchen, NJ: Scarecrow Press, 1983. 227 pp.
Vinson, James, ed. *The International Dictionary of Films and Filmmakers.* Vol. 3, *Actors and Actresses.* Chicago: St. James Press, 1992. 1,080 pp.

LESBIAN VAMPIRES

The incidents of lesbian vampiric relationships, which appeared first in the literary vampire tradition during the nineteenth century and more recently in the cinema, further illustrate the essential sexual nature of the vampire's relationship with its victim. The lesbian vampire can also be seen as a special case of both the **homosexual vampire** and **women as vampires.** The earliest vampires were probably female, such as the Malaysian *langsuyar* and the Greek *lamiai*.

The historical reference for the lesbian vampire is **Elizabeth Bathory,** the so-called blood countess, who lived in the seventeenth century and whose story **Bram Stoker** used to develop the character of **Dracula.** The story of Bathory suggested several unique ideas about vampires not connected with the historical Dracula, **Vlad the Impaler.** As **Radu Florescu** and **Raymond T. McNally** have noted, in the Stoker novel, Dracula was seen as a Hungarian (not a Romanian), he drank blood, he grew younger as he drank blood, and he existed in an erotic atmosphere. Although none of these attributes could be derived from the story of Vlad, they all were descriptive of Elizabeth Bathory. She was related to Hungarian royalty, and she killed hundreds of young girls, whose blood she drained. Several who survived her torture sessions testified that she bathed in human blood to retain and restore her youth. Although few have considered Bathory a lesbian, her victims were almost exclusively young women. She was assisted in her crimes by her Aunt Klara, who has been described as a lesbian who liked to dress in male clothing and ''play men's games.''

As the vampire became the subject of modern literature, and the vampiric relationship became a means of illustrating erotic situations, the attraction of females to those of their own gender frequently appeared. On occasion this relationship was reciprocal, but more often than not it was a form of rape in which the vampire, generally a woman possessed of some social status or power, attacked or seduced a woman of no status, such as a student or a maid.

FROM "CHRISTABEL" TO "CARMILLA": At the beginning of the English-language literary vampire tradition, lesbianism arose in **Samuel Taylor Coleridge**'s poem ''Christabel'' (1816). Among the first poems about vampires, ''Christabel'' featured an ''attack'' upon the title character by Geraldine, the vampiric figure. Geraldine first appeared in the woods near the castle of Christabel's father and told a story of having been brought there by kidnappers. Christabel invited Geraldine to take shelter in the castle. They shared a bottle of wine. Then, at Geraldine's suggestion, Christabel undressed and got into bed. Geraldine joined her guest. Whatever passed between them, more implied than stated, the morning found Geraldine refreshed and restored, ''fairer yet! and yet more fair!'' Christabel arose with a perplexity of mind and a deep sense of having sinned and went immediately to prayer. Christabel nevertheless took Geraldine to her father. Unfortunately, Geraldine beguiled the naive Sir Leoline, who ultimately dismissed his daughter and left with the vampire.

Later in the nineteenth century, the most famous vampire story with lesbian overtones was penned by Irish writer **Sheridan Le Fanu. "Carmilla,"** next to *Dracula* the vampire story most often brought to the screen, concerned Millarca Karnstein (also known by two other names made by scrambling the letters of her name—Carmilla and Mircalla), who attacked young women to suck their blood.

"Carmilla" can be seen, in part, as an attempt to rewrite "Christabel" in prose form. Early in the story the vampire was stranded near a castle and was invited inside by the unsuspecting residents. Once accepted, she targeted nineteen-year-old Laura, the daughter of the retired Austrian official who had purchased the castle some years before.

Carmilla began to "seduce" her hostess. At one point Laura recalled, "She used to place her pretty arms around my neck, draw me to her, and laying her cheek to mine, murmur with her lips near my ear. . . .And when she had spoken such a rhapsody, she would press me more closely in her trembling embrace, and her lips in soft kisses glow upon my cheek." Laura would try to pull away, but found herself without energy. She later described the strange nature of their relationship as simultaneously one of adoration and abhorrence. Later, Carmilla was tracked down and killed before she could kill Laura, but not before she had killed the daughter of a neighbor, General Speilsdorf.

LESBIAN VAMPIRES IN THE MOVIES: With vampirism as a metaphor for sexual behavior, a variety of sexual actions could be pictured on the screen in vampire movies. At a time when explicit lesbian behavior was banned from the movies, vampirism offered a means for women to relate to each other. Contemporary lesbian writers such as Bonnie Zimmerman and Pam Keesey have traced the first lesbian vampire to *Dracula's Daughter*, a 1936 **Universal Pictures** production. Countess Zaleska (Gloria Holden) satiates her lust by drinking the blood of a series of beautiful models.

It was more than two decades later before another female vampire attacking female victims appeared on the screen. In 1957 *Blood of Dracula* (released in England as *Blood Is My Heritage*) pictured a teenage vampire (Sandra Harrison) attacking her classmates at an all-girls boarding school. That same year, the first of a series of movies based loosely upon the life of Countess Elizabeth Bathory appeared. In *Lust of the Vampire* (aka *I, Vampiri*) a doctor periodically stole the blood of women to give to the Countess in order to preserve her youthful appearance. **Mario Bava** filmed this early Italian entry in the vampire/horror field.

By far the most acclaimed of the several movies inspired by the Bathory legend is *Daughters of Darkness* (1971), in which a young couple met the still lively and beautiful Countess Bathory in a contemporary Belgian hotel. They were seduced and attacked by Bathory and her female traveling companion. The husband turned out to be a sadist, and the wife and Bathory combined forces to kill him. Although *Daughters of Darkness* was the most critically acclaimed of the Bathory films, the blood countess's most memorable appearance was that portrayed by **Ingrid Pitt** in

Hammer Films' *Countess Dracula* (1972). The film was produced at a time when Hammer was allowing more nudity and explicitly sexual situations to invade its movies.

"Carmilla" inspired a host of films, possibly the best being the first, **Roger Vadim**'s *Blood and Roses* (1960), made to showcase his then wife Annette Stroyberg. The story also underlies Hammer Films' Karnstein Trilogy: *Vampire Lovers* (1970), *Lust for a Vampire* (1971), and *Twins of Evil* (1971). Such movies can be considered lesbian movies only by the most liberal of standards. They starred glamorous female stars, and their male direction and screenplays suggested something more closely approaching a male fantasy of lesbianism. Also, the movies of **Jean Rollin** frequently included lesbian characters pictured in much the same manner as pornographic movies that picture women engaged in sex scenes shot entirely for a male audience.

More closely portraying a lesbian relationship in a manner acceptable to lesbians was *Vampyres* (1974), which concerned the murder of a lesbian couple by a homophobic man. The two return from the dead as a lesbian vampire couple and work together attacking male victims. *The Hunger*, basically the story of an alien vampire and her human male lovers, has found an appreciative lesbian audience for the scene in which the vampire (Catherine Deneuve) seduced the doctor (Susan Sarandon), whom she contacted in hope of finding a cure for her lovers' swift aging. Two other lesbian vampire movies, *Mark of Lilith* (1986) and *Because the Dawn* (1988), both explore the possibility of using the vampire image in a positive way for women.

RECENT ADDITIONS: The growth of the lesbian subculture in the 1980s led to the production of a significant new literature consciously written by lesbians for lesbians. Three vampire volumes stand out. Pam Keesey compiled a collection of lesbian vampire short fiction in *Daughters of Darkness* (1993). It included a chapter from the single piece of African-American lesbian vampire fiction, Jewelle Gomez's *The Gilda Stories* (1991). Gilda was a vampire who was born into slavery and learned to survive over the decades in a world dominated by white males. *Virago*, by Karen Marie Christa Minns, explored the relationship of a lesbian couple attacked by a vampire college teacher.

Sources:

Gomez, Jewelle. *The Gilda Stories*. Ithaca, NY: Firebrand Books, 1991. 252 pp.

Keesey, Pam. *Daughter of Darkness: Lesbian Vampire Stories*. Pittsburgh/San Francisco: Cleis Press, 1993. 243 pp.

Kuhn, Annette, with Susannah Radstone, eds. *The Women's Companion to International Film*. London: Virago, 1990. 464 pp. Rept. as: *Women in Film: An International Guide*. New York: Fawcett Columbine, 1991. 500 pp.

Minns, Karen Marie Christa. *Virago*. Tallahassee, FL: Naiad Press, 1990. 181 pp.

Weiss, Andrea. *Vampires and Violets: Lesbianism in the Cinema*. London: Pandora Press, 1991. 184 pp.

 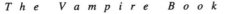

Zimmerman, Bonnie. "Daughters of Darkness: The Lesbian Vampire on Film." In Barry Keith Grant, ed., *Planks of Reason*. Metuchen, NJ: Scarecrow Press, 1984, 153-63.

LESTAT DE LIONCOURT

Lestat de Lioncourt was the central character in the Vampire Chronicles, the several novels by **Anne Rice** that have become key works in the revival of interest in vampires in the 1990s. In the first two novels treating Lestat, Rice described in some detail the whole of his two centuries of existence, except for the several decades of childhood and youth before he became a vampire. His physical appearance was summarized in the opening paragraphs of her second vampire book, *The Vampire Lestat* (1985). He was six feet tall with thick blond hair. His eyes were gray (not red) and easily picked up blue or violet from the environment. He had a very expressive face capable of conveying his wide range of strong, even exaggerated emotions, with a mouth that seemed to be a little too big for his face. His skin was white and had a slightly reflective quality. It changed noticeably while he was feeding. When he was hungry, his skin was tight with his veins protruding. After feeding, it appeared more normal, and Lestat had little trouble passing among ''normal'' humans. The most striking aspect of his physical appearance were his **fingernails,** which looked like glass.

Elsewhere, Rice revealed that Lestat, like all vampires, experienced a significant increase in strength from his human form. He developed a pair of canine-like **fangs.** He had some unusual abilities, both telepathic force and **hypnotic power,** but could not change into animal forms (a bat or wolf, for instance). He could still see himself in a **mirror** but lost the ability to engage in normal human sex and hence could not procreate. He normally slept in a **coffin.**

An atheist before his transformation, Lestat had no problem with holy symbols or being in consecrated places. Traditionally, **sunlight** and **fire** hurt vampires, but Lestat communicated his doubts that they could ultimately kill him. He even believed that a **stake** in the heart had little effect.

LESTAT'S LIFE: When Lestat first appeared in *Interview with the Vampire* (1976), he was in New Orleans. However, his story really began (in *The Vampire Lestat*) in France around 1760 during the reign of Louis XVI and Marie Antoinette. Lestat was about 20 years old, the youngest son in a royal family whose estate was in the Auvergne, in rural France. The family was relatively poor and had no money for their sons to attain proper vocational training. Lestat wanted to escape this life and go to Paris. Shortly after finally realizing his dream, he was kidnapped from his sleeping quarters by a vampire named Magnus. Magnus turned Lestat into a vampire and then forced him to oversee the elder vampire's apparent death. In return, Lestat inherited Magnus's fortune.

The first phase of Lestat's vampiric existence centered on Paris. It included a visit by his dying mother, Gabrielle, whom he turned into a vampire. She took to the nocturnal life well, and together they challenged the vampire community of Paris, which had trouble accepting their new way of integrating into human life. After this intense encounter, they traveled around Europe as Lestat sought a senior vampire named Marius. Meanwhile, France was rising in revolt (1789). Lestat's family estate was mobbed and his brothers killed. His father escaped to New Orleans. He and his mother parted and he buried himself in the ground to rest.

A short time later Marius found and revived him and related the account of the beginnings of their lineage of vampirism. Marius's account took Lestat back into ancient Egypt, long before the first pyramid. Egypt was ruled by a couple, Akasha and Enkil. For the good of their people, they were forced to encounter a demon and became vampires. Marius had brought them out of Egypt to save them from total destruction. They were alive, but sat motionless. Lestat had a private encounter with the pair, including sharing blood with Akasha, who moved for the first time in several centuries.

Lestat then left Marius and sailed to Louisiana in 1789. In New Orleans he met Louis, whom he turned into a vampire; he wanted Louis's plantation as a home for his father. Lestat also found Claudia, a child whom he turned into a vampire. She could grow mentally but not physically, and her situation became the focus of intense conflict. After several decades of adventures and fighting, Louis and Claudia attempted to kill Lestat.

Lestat was hurt but not killed. He could not get help from the old vampire community in Paris and lived out the nineteenth century in seclusion. In 1929 he buried himself again and had no motivation to awaken until 1984, when he was attracted by the sounds of a rock band, Satan's Night Out. He arose, joined them, and became a rock star. People accept the Vampire Lestat as a performer's persona.

As Lestat's story continued in Rice's Vampire Chronicles, the books themselves became part of the vampire mythology. The first book, *Interview with the Vampire,* was published as Louis's memoirs of Lestat. Lestat then countered with his version of

GRAVEYARD SET ERECTED FOR THE MOVIE *INTERVIEW WITH THE VAMPIRE.*

the story in *The Vampire Lestat,* his "autobiography." In the third volume, *The Queen of the Damned* (1988), the modern Lestat had to deal with the situation created by his story's being made public and his becoming a public figure. The account continued in *The Tale of the Body Thief* (1992).

As a character Lestat has caught the imagination of a new generation of vampire enthusiasts. He successfully combines the popular image of the vampire derived from books and movies (e.g., **Lord Ruthven** and **Dracula**) and his own distinct personality. Rice described that uniqueness in terms of androgyny, implying the movement away from culture-bound gender designations and the development of a whole personality that combines strong elements of female and male traits regardless of physiology. In practice, given the intense gender assignments common in Western culture, androgyny is often expressed by a person adopting obvious attributes of gender expressions of the other sex. Thus, women may adopt male hairstyles, and men may wear feminine dress and makeup. More significantly, androgyny may lead people to develop aspects of their personality that have generally been assigned by the culture to the other sex. Thus, women may develop their assertiveness and men their ability to express their feelings. The current **gothic** subculture has taken the lead in living out an androgynous life-style, which is largely owing to Lestat.

Although emphasizing Lestat's androgynous nature, Lestat fans have also emphasized their attraction to his embodiment of typically male attributes. He is a man of strong will and action. He lifted himself up by his own bootstraps; given only a minimal knowledge by his vampiric creator, he taught himself to be a vampire. His discoveries left him with little need of traditions, and he made his own way in the world according to his own rules. "My strength, my refusal to give up, those are the only components of my heart and soul which I can truly identify," he definitively states in *The Tale of the Body Thief*. He faced the problem of his vampiric situation, a condition for which he did not ask, and which imposed a blood thirst upon him. He had to kill to survive, which was evil by human standards. His evolved ethic, though infused with self-interest, led to the choice to feed on the worst of humankind and thus find some moral justification in the necessary search for food.

LESTAT IN THE 1990s: Lestat's central role in the 1990's revival of interest in vampires is illustrated the numerous places he can be found. He inspired the creation of a gothic rock band, Lestat; a role-playing **game,** *Vampire: The Masquerade;* and **Anne Rice's Vampire Lestat Fan Club.** His story has appeared on audiotape and in comic books, has been translated into several language, and is in the process of being brought to the motion picture screen.

Sources:

Ramsland, Katherine. *The Vampire Companion: The Official Guide to Anne Rice's The Vampire Chronicles.* New York: Ballantine Books, 1993. 507 pp.

Rice, Anne. *Interview with the Vampire.* New York: Alfred A. Knopf, 1986. 448 pp. Reprint. New York: Ballantine Books, 1987. 346 pp.

―――. *The Queen of the Damned.* New York: Alfred A. Knopf, 1988. 448 pp. Reprint. New York: Ballantine Books, 1989. 491 pp.

―――. *Tale of the Body Thief.* New York: Alfred A. Knopf, 1992. 430 pp. Reprint. New York: Ballantine Books, 1993. 435 pp.

————. *The Vampire Lestat.* New York: Alfred A. Knopf, 1985. 481 pp. Reprint. New York: Ballantine Books, 1986. 550 pp.

LIDERC See: HUNGARY, VAMPIRES IN

LILITH

Lilith, one of the most famous figures in Hebrew folklore, originated as a storm demon and later became identified with the night. She was one of a group of Sumerian vampire demons that included *Lillu, Ardat Lili,* and *Irdu Lili.* She appeared in the Babylonian *Gilgamesh Epic* (approximately 2000 A.D.) as a vampire harlot who was unable to bear children and whose breasts were dry. She was pictured as a beautiful young girl with owl's feet (indicative of her nocturnal life).

In the *Gilgamesh Epic,* Lilith escaped from her home near the Euphrates River and settled in the desert. In this regard, she earned a place in the Hebrew Bible (the Christian Old Testament). Isaiah, in describing God's day of vengeance, during which the land will be turned into a desert, proclaimed that as a sign of the desolation ''Lilith shall repose there and find her place of rest'' (Isaiah 34:14).

Lilith reappeared in the Talmud, where a more interesting story was told of her as the wife of the biblical Adam. Lilith was described as Adam's first wife. They had a disagreement over who would be in the dominant position during sexual intercourse. When Adam insisted upon being on top, Lilith used her magical knowledge to fly away to the Red Sea, an abode of demons. She took many lovers and had many offspring, called the *lilim.* There she met three angels sent by God—Senoy, Sansenoy, and Semangelof—with whom she worked out an agreement. She claimed vampiric powers over babies, but agreed to stay away from any babies protected with an amulet bearing the names of the three angels.

Once more attracted to Adam, Lilith returned to haunt him. After he and Eve (his second wife) were expelled from the Garden of Eden, Lilith and her cohorts, all in the form of an **incubus/succubus,** attacked them, thus causing Adam to father many demons and Eve to mother still more. Out of this legend, Lilith came to be regarded in Hebrew lore much more as a succubus than a vampire, and men were warned against sleeping in a house alone lest Lilith overtake them.

Lilith (a name that in popular thought came to be attached to a whole class of demonic beings) were noted as being especially hateful of the normal sexual mating of the individuals they attacked as succubi and incubi. They took out their anger on the human children of such mating by sucking their blood and strangling them. They also added any complication possible to women attempting to have children—barrenness, miscarriages, and so forth. Thus, Lilith came to resemble a range of vampirelike beings that became particularly visible at the time of childbirth and whose presence was used to explain any problems or unexpected deaths. As a result, those who believed in the Lilith developed elaborate rituals to banish them from their homes. The exorcism of Lilith and any accompanying demons often took the form of a writ of divorce sending them forth naked into the night.

The myth of Lilith (the singular entity, as opposed to the whole class of demons) was well established in the Jewish community during the centuries of the early Christian era. She remained an item of popular lore, although little was written about her from the time the Talmud was compiled (sixth century A.D.) until the tenth century. Her biography was expanded in elaborate (and somewhat contradictory) detail in the writings of the early Hassidic fathers. In the *Zohar,* the most influential Hassidic text, Lilith was described as a succubus, with nocturnal emissions cited as the visible sign of her presence. Demons that plagued humanity were thought to be the product of such unions. She also attacked human babies, especially those born of couples who engaged in intercourse in improper fashion. Children who laughed in their sleep were believed to be playing with Lilith, and hence in danger of dying at her hand. During this period, Lilith's vampiric nature was deemphasized; rather, she was described as killing children in order to steal their soul.

The stories about Lilith multiplied during the Middle Ages. She was, for example, identified as one of the two women who came before King Solomon for him to decide which one was the mother of a child they both claimed. Elsewhere she was identified as the Queen of Sheba. Strong belief in her presence was found among more conservative elements in the Jewish community into the nineteenth century, and elements of the belief can be seen to the present time. Most recently, Lilith reappeared as a supernatural foe of the **Midnight Sons** in several titles of Marvel **comic book**s.

Sources:

Graves, Robert, and Raphael Patai. *Hebrew Myths: The Book of Genesis.* Garden City, NY: Doubleday & Company, 1964. 311 pp.

Patai, Raphael. *The Hebrew Goddess.* New York: Ktav Publishing House, n.d. 349 pp.

LILITH, THE DAUGHTER OF DRACULA

Lilith, the daughter of **Dracula,** is a Marvel Comics character introduced in 1974. Her name was, at least in part, suggested by **Lilith,** the vampirelike creature from Hebrew folklore. Lilith made her initial appearance in the June 1974 issue of *Giant-Size Chillers*, a comic book that picked up and expanded the story of Dracula from Marvel's very successful *The Tomb of Dracula.* Lilith's story began in Belfast, Ireland, where young Angel O'Hara and her new husband were breaking the news of their marriage and her pregnancy to her father. He lost his temper and hit the young man, who was killed by the blow. Reacting to the event, for a moment Angel wished her father dead. As her anger rose, a misty light floated into the house and moved into Angel. Suddenly she was transformed into Lilith, who had invaded and taken over her body. The redheaded, green-eyed Angel now stood before her father as a dark-haired, red-eyed Lilith. She was dressed in a skin-tight black suit with a cape and a stylized bat image on her forehead. Her immediate impulse was to feed, and Angel's father was the food supply before her. Lilith next turned to revenge. She sought out vampire hunter Quincy Harker and tried to drain his blood. He would be found later, barely alive.

In the Marvel Universe, Lilith was the daughter of the fifteenth-century wife of **Vlad the Impaler.** Kicked out of the palace by Vlad, her mother turned the baby girl over to a Gypsy woman and then committed suicide. Vlad later killed the Gypsy's husband and son. In revenge, the woman, a witch, turned the child into a vampire, but with a difference. She could walk in the daylight, and the cross would not affect her. Also, when she died, her soul would move on to take over a new body. Her purpose in life was to destroy her father. At one point, in the nineteenth century, she and her father agreed to go their separate ways and see each other no more. They did not meet again until the 1940s, at which time Quincy Harker killed her. Again revived, she returned in the 1970s, at which time she suggested that she and her father join forces and jointly rule the world. Dracula rejected the proposal.

Nothing more was heard of Lilith until the Fall 1977 issue of *Marvel Preview* (No. 12), which revealed that Lilith/Angel had moved to New York and was living with a man, Martin Gold. As Angel, her pregnancy was beginning to show, but as Lilith she ventured out to feed. Her story continued in the November 1978 issue of *The Tomb of Dracula* (No. 67). Dracula moved to New York. Intuiting the presence of his daughter, he followed her to Goldman's apartment. He had lost his vampiric powers and had come to get her to bite him again. She not only turned him down, she attacked him but carefully avoided biting him. As he swore his revenge, she called for the animals and the weather to torment him.

At that point Dracula was near the end of the first phase of his Marvel career. In 1979 he faced his last battles, recovered his vampiric powers and returned to leadership of the undead, only to be killed by Quincy Harker. Dracula was never ultimately killed, of course, and he revived again in time to appear in the new series of *The Tomb of Dracula,* begun as an adult-oriented magazine without Comics Code approval. In the June 1980 issue (No. 5), Lilith returned and sought the help of Viktor Benzel to help her kill Dracula. Benzel carried out a magical process that separated Angel and Lilith. She then traveled to **Castle Dracula** and confronted her father. She had the advantage as she could use the cross and holy water against him. But in the end she could not bring herself to murder her father.

After this encounter with Dracula, Lilith adopted the name Lilith Drake and settled in the south of France. In 1983 (*Doctor Strange,* No. 62), Dr. Stephen Strange, the sorcerer, used a magical spell called the Montesi Formula to destroy Dracula, Lilith, and all other vampires throughout the world.

Sources:

Doctor Strange. No. 62. New York: Marvel Comics, December 1983.

Giant-Size Chillers. Vol. 1. New York: Marvel Comics, 1974.
Marvel Review. No. 12. New York: Marvel Comics, 1977.
Redondo, Nestor. "Lilith." *The Official Handbook of the Marvel Universe* 2, 18 (October 1987): 23-24.
The Tomb of Dracula. Nos. 1-70. New York: Marvel Comics, 1971-79.

LITHUANIA, VAMPIRES IN *See:* BALTIC STATES, VAMPIRES IN THE

LOBISHOMEN

The *lobishomen* was a mythological creature found in the folklore of **South America,** primarily Brazil, and has often appeared on lists of vampires. However, *lobishomens,* which originally derived from Portuguese mythology, were not vampires; they were Portuguese **werewolves.**

Sources:

Gallop, Rodney. *Portugal: A Book of Folk-Ways.* Cambridge: Cambridge University Press, 1936. 291 pp.
Sales, Herberto. *O Lobisomen Contos Folcloricos: Lobisomens, Sacis, Botos e Maes-d'Agua, Ingenuas e
    Eternus Historias da Alma Brasileira.* Rio de Janeiro: Ediouro Grupa Coquetel, 1975. 105 pp.

LONDON AFTER MIDNIGHT

Frequently cited in histories of the horror movie as the first American vampire motion picture, *London After Midnight* (1927) was actually preceded by at least two other American-made vampire movies: *The Vampire* (1913) and *A Village Vampire* (1916). However, both of these earlier films were shorts (15 minutes running time) made for penny arcades, and poorly received. They do little to detract from the importance of *London After Midnight* in initiating future American treatment of the theme.

London After Midnight came during the fruitful period of collaboration between director **Tod Browning** and character actor **Lon Chaney,** who had first worked together in 1921 on a thriller, *Outside the Law,* and again in 1925 on *The Unholy Three,* both for MGM. Meanwhile, Chaney returned to **Universal Pictures** for one of his most memorable roles, *The Phantom of the Opera* (1925). Chaney and Browning were united for the last time at MGM in 1927 for *London After Midnight,* released in England as *The Hypnotist,* a response to British sensitivity.

The movie's storyline began approximately five years after a death had occurred in a haunted house. Inspector Burke of Scotland Yard had become convinced that the death was a murder, not an accident or suicide. He had two suspects, one a friend and the other a nephew of the deceased. He suggested to them that the murder was done by a vampire. The inspector, played by Chaney, then assumed the role of a vampire, for which he had prepared his own elaborate makeup. His actions as the vampire forced the guilty party to reveal his guilt at which time Chaney revealed his double identity.

LON CHANEY IN *LONDON AFTER MIDNIGHT.*

Although all the major elements of the vampire legend were incorporated into the film, in the end, of course, the vampire was explained away as a masquerade. The movie mixed the horror and mystery genres, but in the end was a mystery movie. It was one of Chaney's last movies and one of the last silent horror films before the major studios moved into sound. Chaney had died by the time Browning remade *London After Midnight* as a talkie in 1935 under the title *Mark of the Vampire*. In the latter version, the Chaney part was divided between **Bela Lugosi** (the vampire) and Lionel Atwill (the inspector).

Because the prints of *London After Midnight* have been lost for many years, the film has assumed a somewhat mythical status as a classic Chaney picture, in spite of the rather poor reception of *Mark of the Vampire*. Stills from the picture indicate that Chaney did his usual fine job of weird and grotesque makeup, but there was no way to appraise Browning's directorial skills on the movie. Recently, rumors have circulated that prints of *London After Midnight* have been discovered and that it might be made available again in the near future.

One leading **gothic** rock band paid homage to the movie by adopting it as the name of their band. London After Midnight was founded by Sean Brennan in 1987.

Sources:

Coolidge-Rust, Marie. *London After Midnight.* New York: Grosset and Dunlap, 1928. 261 pp.
Flynn, John L. *Cinematic Vampires.* Jefferson, NC: McFarland Company, 1992. 320 pp.
Gifford, Denis. *A Pictorial History of Horror Movies.* London: Hamlyn, 1973. 216 pp.
Jones, Stephen. *The Illustrated Vampire Movie Guide.* London: Titan Books, 1991. 144 pp.
London After Midnight. New York: Cornwall Books, 1985. 178 pp.
"London After Midnight: Revelations in Black." *Ghastly* 2 (1992): 9-12.

LONDON, DRACULA'S

Nineteenth-century London, the capital of what is today known as the United Kingdom (England, Scotland, Wales, and Northern Ireland), was one of three major sites of action in **Bram Stoker**'s *Dracula.* Some of the sites mentioned by Stoker were entirely fictitious locations, but many were quite real, although a few have disappeared or changed names since the novel appeared in 1897, and some were slightly disguised by Stoker.

Action in the novel began with **Jonathan Harker** traveling to **Transylvania** to make arrangements for Dracula's move to England. The focus of their negotiations was an estate in the London suburb of Purfleet. Purfleet is a real place located on the north bank of the Thames River, downstream from London. Semi-industrialized and almost a suburb today, in the 1890s it was a quiet rural Essex Village some 10 miles beyond the fringe of London's East End. **Carfax,** the estate in Purfleet, had about 20 acres surrounded by a stone wall. On the land was an old house, dating to medieval times, and nearby a chapel. Stoker, through his character Harker, suggested that the name Carfax was a derivative of *quartre face,* referring to its four walls being aligned with the cardinal points of the compass. From his reading of *The Oxford Dictionary of*

DRACULA'S PICCADILLY HOME.

Etymology, Leonard Wolf has suggested that the name derived from the Anglo-Norman term *carfuks,* the significance being that it was a place where four roads met. Wolf further noted, quite correctly, that suicides were buried at crossroads and that people who committed suicide were often thought to return as vampires.

Dracula traveled to England by ship along with the native soil so necessary for his survival. He landed at **Whitby** and from there had the dirt shipped to his estate. It arrived from Whitby via rail into King's Cross Station, a very real location, the southern terminus of the Great Northern Railway (which connected London with points north, including Whitby). From there they were then taken to Carfax by Messrs. Carter, Paterson & Co., a real cartage firm that was founded in 1860 and continued to operate in London during Stoker's time. It was a prosperous firm with headquarters on Gorwell Road in London. In Stoker's day, Purfleet was connected to central London by London, Tilbury and Southend Railway, which had its terminus at Fenchurch Street. The characters in *Dracula* could thus travel from Purfleet to central London in about 30 minutes.

Once in England, Dracula began an attack upon **Lucy Westenra,** his first victim, while she was still in Whitby, the northern town where Dracula initially arrived. However, the action soon moved to London. The Westenra fictional home, Hillingham, was a large mansion, reflecting a relatively wealthy family. The kitchen was in back, there were several bedrooms on the second floor, and maids' rooms presumably occupied the third floor. It was probably located in the Haverstock Hills neighborhood on the slopes leading to Hampstead, and not too far from the Zoological Gardens. When Dr. **Abraham Van Helsing** arrived on the scene, he stayed at several of the city's finer hotels, including The Great Eastern Hotel on Liverpool Street and the Berkeley at Berkeley Street and Piccadilly.

In one of Dracula's earliest actions, he helped the wolf Bersicker escape from the Zoological Gardens. The Gardens were located in the northeast corner of Regent's Park, one of London's largest parks. The wolves' cage was on the edge of the zoo near the lions' house. Bersicker had only a short distance to travel to reach the Westenra home.

The Harker residence was located outside of London, in Exeter. His law office was in Devonshire. At one point they came into London to attend the funeral of Harker's former employee, Mr. Hawkins. Before returning to their home, they strolled from Hyde Park to Piccadilly, where the novel's action periodically returned, and stopped in front of Guillano's, one of the most fashionable court jewelers in London. (Later, its premises were replaced by one of the shops let into the extended frontage of the Park Lane Hotel.) Here they saw Dracula, appearing much younger than when Harker last saw him in the castle in Transylvania.

In the meantime, Lucy had died and was buried at what Stoker described as "a lordly death-house in a lonely churchyard away from teeming London; where the air is fresh and the sun rises over Hampstead Hill." He spoke of the churchyard (or cemetery) at Kingstead. There was no Hampstead Hill or Kingstead, and it was not clear which site Stoker had in mind as Lucy's resting place. **Raymond T. McNally** and **Radu Florescu** have suggested that he in fact was referring to Highgate Hill and the relatively well known Highgate Cemetery, which fits the basic description of Lucy's resting place (one with impressive burial mausoleums and away from London). The cemetery was the only such structure near Jack Straw's Castle, a still-existing inn located on Hampstead Heath, where Dr. Van Helsing and the other men dined before going to Lucy's grave to put the stake in her heart. Once inside the cemetery, they found their way to Lucy's resting place. Evidence suggested that it was in the Old Ground or Western Cemetery, probably in a somewhat secluded location near the middle of the cemetery. Afterwards, they found their way to a still-existing pub, The Spaniards Inn, and there caught a cab back into London.

Following the settling of Lucy's situation, and the organization of Mina and the men into a covenanted group to destroy Dracula, Dr. **John Seward**'s house near Purfleet increasingly became the center of the group's campaign to defeat Dracula. Seward lived at his private asylum, which was actually located next door to Carfax. Their efforts would take them back to London as Dracula had distributed his boxes of dirt around the city. Of the original 50 boxes, six were carried to the east end to 197

Chicksand Street, Mile End New Town. This detached portion of Mile End was entirely surrounded by Spitalfields, just off Brick Lane in the heart of jack the Ripper territory. Three of Ripper's murders were committed just a few blocks away. (Stoker began writing *Dracula* just a year or so after the panic over the Ripper murders and in the preface he wrote for the 1898 Icelandic edition of *Dracula* made reference to them.) Part of Chicksand Street still exists today.

Another six of the boxes were dropped south of the Thames, on Jamaica Lane, a fictitious location. While there is no Jamaica Lane, there is a Jamaica Road, the main artery in Bermondsey, a warehouse district of London just east of Walworth, on the south side of the river. Nine boxes were delivered to a house in London's fashionable West End, on the street called Piccadilly, a residence located near the end of the street farthest away from Piccadilly Circus, the popular shopping area where a number of streets converge and which today is a theater/night club spot. As early as 1973, the building at 138-139 Piccadilly was suggested as the location of Dracula's residence in an article by Art Ronnie in the *Los Angeles Herald Examiner.* Interestingly, this building has been the London headquarters of **Universal Pictures.** In the 1890s, the building existed as two separate houses. Bernard Davies, cofounder and chairman of **The Dracula Society,** has suggested that 138 Piccadilly possessed the correct architectural and stylistic details as described in the novel, including a bow window, iron-railed balcony, and a backyard.

Dracula finally left London and England from the docks along the Thames aboard the *Czarina Catherine,* a fictitious ship.

Sources:

Stoker, Bram. *The Annotated Dracula.* Edited by Leonard Wolf. New York: Ballantine Books, 1975. 362 pp.
———. *The Essential Dracula.* Edited by Raymond McNally and Radu Florescu. New York: Mayflower Books, 1979. 320 pp.

LONE GULL PRESS

Lone Gull Press was founded in 1984 by author Lori Paige and artist Jane Lach to publish materials for *Dark Shadows* fans. Their first product was *The Secret of the Chalice*, a fanzine that appeared that same year. Since that time, they have published a series of fanzines, including *Tales of Hoffman*, a one-shot publication built around the *Dark Shadows* character Julia Hoffman, and *Cauldron*, of which six issues appeared in 1987 and 1988. In 1988 Paige wrote *Balm in Gilead. The Gates of Hell* is the name of a full-length novel that provided the substance for the fanzine of the same name. In addition, Lone Gull published Sharon Wisdom's *Love's Pale Shadow* (1992). Jane Lach has recently made some of her *Dark Shadows* art work available through Lone Gull.

In 1988 Paige and Lach worked with May Sutherland of Tacoma, Washington, in founding her fanzine, Wyndcliffe Watch, and the **Wyndcliffe Dark Shadows Fan**

Club. Lone Gull Press may be reached c/o Lori Paige, 162 Northwoods Apts., Sunderland, MA 01375.

Sources:

Paige, Lori. *Balm in Gilead.*   North Riverside, IL: Pandora Publications, 1988.
Wisdon, Sharon. *Love's Pale Shadow.* Sunderland, MA: Lone Gull Press, 1992.

LONG ISLAND DARK SHADOWS SOCIETY

The Long Island Dark Shadows Society is a *Dark Shadows* fan club founded in 1988 by Steven C. Schumacher and Cindy Avitabile Conroy. Activity centers upon five meetings each year, which include screenings of *Dark Shadows* videos and discussions of various *Dark Shadows* topics. Members are interested in not only **Barnabas Collins** and the vampire theme in the show but all aspects of the *Dark Shadows* series. In 1993 the society reported approximately 25 members. It may be contacted at 187 Roxbury Rd. S., Garden City South, NY 11530.

LOOGAROO

The *loogaroo* was a vampire entity found in the folklore of Haiti and other islands of the West Indies, including Grenada. The word *loogaroo* is a corruption of the French *loup-garou,* which refers to **werewolves.** The *loogaroo* arose as slaves from West **Africa** appropriated French demonology and mixed it with African vampirology. The *loogaroo* was quite similar to the *obayifo* of the Ashanti and the *asiman* of Dahomey.

Loogaroos were people, usually old women, who had made a pact with the devil. In return for certain magical powers, they agreed to bring the devil some warm blood each night. To accomplish this task, they removed their skins, which were hidden on the so-called Jumbie tree, the silk-cotton tree. Then, in the form of a fiery ball of light, they would roam across the land in search of blood. In their spirit form they could enter any habitation. Those from whom they took blood would awaken in a tired and fatigued condition. Although *loogaroos* could enter any dwelling, some protection was afforded by scattering rice or sand before the door. The *loogaroo,* supposedly, had to stop and count each grain before continuing on its way.

Sources:

Summers, Montague. *The Vampire: His Kith and Kin.* London: Routledge, Kegan Paul, Trench, Trubner, & Co., 1928. 356 pp. Reprint. New Hyde Park, NY: University Books, 1960. 356 pp.

LORY, ROBERT EDWARD (1936-)

Robert Edward Lory, science fiction and fantasy writer, was born in Troy, New York, the son of Dorothy Doughty and Edward Austin Lory. He attended Harper College (now the State University of New York, Binghamton), from which he received a B.A. degree in 1961.

Lory's first stories were published in the early 1960s in such magazines as *Fantasy and Science Fiction* and *If.* His first book, *Eyes of Bolsk,* appeared in 1969. Then in 1973 and 1974 he completed a popular series of nine books based on the Dracula legend. The first, *Dracula Returns* had Dr. Damien Harmon and his assistant Cam (Cameron Sanchez) traveling to **Romania,** where they were guided to Dracula's crypt by one of his cohorts, a woman named Ktara. Dracula was resting there. ''His thick hair was combed neatly back, not a single strand out of place. His sharp angular cheek and bone structure, combined with the thick brows that nearly met at the bridge of his Roman nose, gave the face a dignified nobility. He appeared to be in his late forties or early fifties. And his clothing—formal, impeccable black-tie attire—was perfectly pressed.'' The major flaw in his appearance was a **stake** that had been driven through his heart.

Harmon had previously implanted a small device near his own heart that controlled a second small device with a sliver of wood that he inserted next to Dracula's heart. The device allowed him to move the sliver of wood in and out of Dracula's heart. The stake was removed and Dracula awoke. He turned to Harmon ready to attack, only to clutch his chest and drop to the floor. Harmon's device gave him control, and he planned to use Dracula in his war against evil. Dracula was transported back to New York and upon awakening was presented with a bottle of synthetic **blood** for his immediate nourishment. Harmon informed Dracula that he must subsist on the synthetic blood or nothing.

The first target of Dracula unleashed was a crime syndicate. In the eight subsequent volumes Dracula traveled the world and encountered various natural and supernatural enemies, from practitioners of voodoo and **witchcraft** to the mummy and a legion of killer **vampire bat**s.

Lory retained the image of Dracula as projected earlier in this century by **Bela Lugosi,** but Lory's Dracula was compelled to become a force for good. Lory's fast-moving action stories thus form a transition to the ''good'' vampires of **Fred Saberhagen** and **Chelsea Quinn Yarbro** that appeared a few years later. Lory has admitted to little purpose in his writing beyond that ascribed to Arthur Conan Doyle—to ''tell a whopping good tale.'' The popular Dracula series has been translated into several foreign languages.

After the completion of the Dracula series, Lory began a fantasy series based upon the signs of the horoscope.

Sources:

Ashley, Mike. *Who's Who in Horror and Fantasy Fiction.* London: Elm Tree Books, 1977. 240 pp.
Lory, Robert. *Challenge to Dracula.* New York: Pinnacle Books, 1975. 180 pp.
———. *Dracula Returns.* New York: Pinnacle Books, 1973. 124 pp.
———. *Dracula's Brothers.* New York: Pinnacle Books, 1973. 186 pp.
———. *Dracula's Disciple.* New York: Pinnacle Books, 1975. 179 pp.
———. *Dracula's Gold.* New York: Pinnacle Books, 1973. 182 pp.
———. *Dracula's Lost World.* New York: Pinnacle Books, 1974. 181 pp.

————. *The Drums of Dracula.* New York: Pinnacle Books, 1974. 189 pp.
————. *The Hand of Dracula.* New York: Pinnacle Books, 1973. 224 pp.
————. *The Witching of Dracula.* New York: Pinnacle Books, 1974. 177 pp.

LOYALISTS OF THE VAMPIRE REALM INTERNATIONAL VAMPIRE ASSOCIATION

Loyalists of the Vampire Realm International Vampire Association is an international club founded in 1984 in Berlin, Germany, by a woman named Lucinda (the club's name being derived from her initials). It is solely dedicated to the "preservation and re-creation of all vampire styled art forms." It publishes a quarterly newsletter that features the poetry, fiction, and graphic art of the club's members and thus provides the members with an outlet for their own viewpoints on the vampire as opposed to those of an editor or paid staff. The Vampire Realm also offers a very limited pen pal service known as the Vampire Correspondence Network. Applications and information are available by writing the Loyalists of the Vampire Realm International Vampire Association, PO Box 6975, Beverly Hills, CA 90212-6975. New members are invited to fill out a lengthy questionnaire concerning their interests.

LUGOSI, BELA (1882-1956)

Bela Lugosi, the actor most identified with the image of **Dracula** and the vampire in the public mind, was born Bela Blasko on October 20, 1882, in Lugos, **Hungary.** At the time of his birth, Lugos was part of the Austro-Hungarian empire and was located some 50 miles from **Transylvania.** Lugosi attended school locally.

Lugosi was still quite young when a traveling theater company came to Lugos and he gave up ideas of entering a profession for a life on the stage. He began to write and stage amateur productions and in 1893 left school for good. He also left home looking for an acting job; not finding any, he held various jobs as a laborer in the mines, a factory, and on the railroad. When he had the opportunity to act, his first experiences were negative. His lack of education made him appear stupid. He began a self-education program and read voraciously.

His first formal stage role was as Count Konigsegg in *Ocskay Brigaderos (Brigadier General Ocskay)* in 1902. The following year he played Gecko, Svengali's servant, in *Trilby,* his first part in a horror production. During this time he tried out a number of stage names, but finally settled on Lugosi, meaning "one from Lugos." In

1910 he starred in *Romeo and Juliet,* for which he received good reviews, and went on to become a featured actor on the Hungarian stage. In 1911 he moved to Budapest to work at the Hungarian Royal Theatre and two years later joined the National Theatre of Budapest; although his salary increased, the young actor was not given any starring roles.

Lugosi's acting career was interrupted by World War I. He returned to the theater in 1917. That same year he risked his career by taking a job with the Star Film Company and appeared in his first film, *The Leopard.* For the film he adopted a new stage name, Arisztid Olt. His second role was in *Az Elet Kiralya,* based on *The Picture of Dorian Gray.* He starred in a variety of films until the chaos following the end of the war forced him to leave Hungary. He settled in Germany where he appeared in several movies, including *Sklaven Fremdes Willens* (*Slave of a Foreign Will*) and *Der Januskopf* (based on *Dr. Jekyll and Mr. Hyde*). There was a tendency to cast Lugosi in the role of the villain, although his last role was that of a romantic lead in *Der Tanz auf dem Vulkan.*

Banned from Hungary because of his political views, in 1920 he decided to emigrate to the United States. He barely escaped death when his identity was discovered by some Hungarian crew members of the ship on which he traversed the Atlantic. Although an illegal alien, he was granted political asylum and allowed to work. He organized a Hungarian repertory company, which played to the Hungarian-American community. He got a break in 1922 when he was offered a part in *The Red Poppy*—if he could learn the part. Unable to speak English, he nevertheless memorized the part and opened to his first English-speaking audience in December 1922 at the Greenwich Village Theatre. Lugosi received far better reviews than the play, which ran for only six weeks on Broadway before closing. *The Red Poppy* led to Lugosi's first Hollywood movie part as the villain in *The Silent Command* (1923), an action spy movie.

Unable to obtain further roles in Hollywood, in spite of positive reviews, Lugosi returned to New York and made several movies. He also appeared in several plays and made it back to Broadway briefly in *Arabesque.* The events that were to change his career and life forever can be traced to 1927. That year, the **Hamilton Deane** version of the play *Dracula* opened in London. Producer Horace Liveright perceived some possibilities for the play in the United States and negotiated the purchase of the American rights. He also had **John L. Balderston** do a thorough rewrite of the script. Director John D. Williams, familiar with Lugosi's work in other plays, cast him in the title role. He fit the part Balderston had created as if it were made for him. His face, especially his eyes, his hand movements, and his Hungarian accent contributed greatly to the success of the play, which opened October 2, 1927, at the Fulton Theater. It played for 40 weeks on Broadway, after which several companies took it on the road.

Lugosi continued his part with the West Coast production of *Dracula.* Back in southern California, he picked up several small movie parts. In 1929, an eventful year,

▶ RARE PHOTO OF BELA LUGOSI IN STAGE PRODUCTION OF *DRACULA.*

he made his talkie debut in *Prisoners* and he worked with director **Tod Browning** in *The Thirteenth Chair.* In 1930 **Universal Pictures** purchased the motion picture rights to *Dracula.* The company used Lugosi to negotiate the agreement with **Bram Stoker**'s widow, and he was somewhat insulted when not automatically given the part. Rather, Lugosi was among five men considered for the role. Browning wanted Lon Chaney, but he died soon after Universal finished its negotiations with Florence Stoker. Lugosi was finally signed for $500 a week. His hardest job was to adapt the part he had played hundreds of time on the stage to the film medium.

Dracula opened on February 14, 1931, and became an immediate though somewhat unexpected hit. The film would influence all vampire films that came after it, and Lugosi's *Dracula* would be the standard against which all later vampires were judged. Lugosi became a star, with 97 percent of his fan mail coming from women. He responded by suggesting that generations of subjection had given women a masochistic interest, an enjoyment of suffering experienced vicariously on the screen.

Lugosi moved from *Dracula* to portray an Eastern mystic in a Charlie Chan movie, *The Black Camel,* and then began shooting for *Frankenstein.* The monster proved to be a part not made for him, so he was replaced by Boris Karloff and instead starred in *Murders in the Rue Morgue,* where he did well as a mad scientist.

He drifted from Universal in 1932 to make *White Zombies,* in which he played a sorcerer, and returned to the stage in Los Angeles in a horror play, *Murdered Alive.* By this time, he had already been hit by the actor's nemesis—typecasting. Studios continually offered him parts to bring terror to the audience.

In 1933, Lugosi returned to New York for a brief (and last) appearance on Broadway as the villain in *Murder of the Vanities.* He went from Broadway to a vaudeville touring company in which he played *Dracula.* He periodically returned to the part in summer stock whenever his film work was light. In 1934 he made one of his better movies when Universal teamed him with Boris Karloff in *The Black Cat.* At the end of the year both Lugosi and Browning moved over to MGM to team up again in *Mark of the Vampire.* Lugosi played Count Mora in the remake of Browning's silent film, *London After Midnight.* During the rest of the decade into the early 1940s, Lugosi played in a variety of horror movies and appeared as the villain in nonhorror flicks, mostly mysteries. Of these, his team-up with Boris Karloff and Basil Rathbone in *Son of Frankenstein* (1939) is possibly the most memorable. Publicity for *The Devil Bat* (1941), a routine mystery, made use of Lugosi's identification with the vampire in its advertising.

Through the early 1940s Lugosi made as many as five movies a year, overwhelmingly in villain or monster roles. He played a Dracula-like role in the comedy *Spooks Run Wild* (1941) and finally portrayed Frankenstein in *Frankenstein Versus the Wolfman* (1943). He played his first genuine vampire role since *Dracula* in Columbia Pictures's *Return of the Vampire* (1944). Lugosi was cast as Armand Tesla, a vampire hardly distinguishable from Dracula, and, as might be expected, Universal filed suit against Columbia for infringement upon its rights.

In 1948 Lugosi returned to Universal for his next vampire role. The horror theme having largely run its course, as many at Universal thought, the idea emerged to get the major monsters together with the studio's comic stars, Bud Abbott and Lou Costello, for a monster spoof. Lugosi re-created his Dracula role for *Abbott and Costello Meet Frankenstein.* He played the part with as much dignity as possible and must have enjoyed it somewhat, as he did it a second time for Abbott and Costello's television show in 1950.

The downturn in horror movies left Lugosi out of a job. He did some television and in 1950 began to make personal appearances at movie theaters showing his old horror films. In 1951 he traveled to England to do a new production of *Dracula,* but the play flopped and he found himself without enough money to get back to the States. A friend arranged for him to do his next movie, *Old Mother Riley Meets the Vampire* (aka *My Son the Vampire*), released in 1952. (Mother Riley was a character in a series of British comedies.)

Lugosi's return to America was less than spectacular. His ability to get parts was very limited, and a downward slide landed him in a drug rehabilitation program in 1955. Lugosi made a few more films and then in 1956 was hired by director Edward Wood, Jr., to play a vampire for his quickie movie, *Plan 9 from Outer Space*. He and **Vampira** were to play a pair of vampires raised from their graves by outer space aliens. A week after shooting began, on August 16, 1956, Lugosi died. Another actor, doing scenes with the vampire cape pulled across his face, filled in for Lugosi for the rest of the film. *Plan 9* has since become known as one of the worst films of all time and has a substantial cult following.

Lugosi's last years were years of loneliness and abandonment by the industry for which he had worked for so long. He did not live to see the acclaim of a new generation of fans who had an appreciation for the horror genre and understood his contribution to it. Only in the last generation, with the revival of the horror movie in general and the vampire movie in particular, has Lugosi's impact been understood.

Sources:

Bojarski, Richard. *The Films of Bela Lugosi.* Secaucus, NJ: Citadel Press, 1980. 256 pp.
Copner, Mike, and Buddy Barnett. "Bela Lugosi Then and Now!" Special issue of *Videosonic Arts* 1 (1990).
Magic Image Filmbooks Presents Dracula (The Original 1931 Shooting Script). Atlantic City, NJ: Magic Image Filmbooks, 1990.
Pirie, David. *The Vampire Cinema.* London: Hamlyn, 1977. 176 pp.
Skal, David J. *Hollywood Gothic: The Tangled Web of Dracula from Novel to Stage to Screen.* New York: W. W. Norton & Company, 1990. 242 pp.

LUMLEY, BRIAN (1937-)

Brian Lumley, author of the *Necroscope* series of vampire books, was born on December 2, 1937, in Horden, Durham, England. Trained as a lawyer, he joined the British army in the 1950s and served in Germany and in Cyprus. He was in Cyprus when he began to write seriously, and the island inspired his first professional short story, "The Cyprus Shell." It and others were collected to make his first book, *The Caller of the Black,* published by Arkham House in 1970. Arkham House specialized in books in the H. P. Lovecraft horror tradition. Lumley adopted the Lovecraft myth of *cthulhu,* the idea of ancient demonic forces that had been pushed aside by the forces of civilization but lay just beneath the surface of civilization awaiting any opportunity to return to power. This myth stood behind his first novels, *The Burrowers Beneath* (1974) and *Beneath the Moors* (1974), and most of his subsequent writings.

In 1986 *Necroscope* was published, the first book in what has become one of the most popular series of vampire books. The series tells the story of Harry Keogh, a necroscope (someone who can speak to the dead). Scottish-born Keogh was the son of a psychic-sensitive Russian émigré. As he grew up, he discovered that he not only

COVER ART FROM THE COMIC
BOOK *NECROSCOPE*, BASED ON
BRIAN LUMLEY'S NOVEL OF THE
SAME NAME.

had his mother's sensitivity, but that his psychic talents were even more extraordinary. He was able to contact the dead in their graves. In Lumley's alternative world, the dead moved into a new state of immobility and incorporeality, but retained a continued existence through conscious mental processes. Their relationship to Keogh allowed them an outlet to the world. Thus, they loved and respected him.

Keogh's talents pushed him into the world of espionage. He was pitted against Boris Dragosani, a ghoulish necromancer who dissected dead bodies with his hands to gain information by holding their various body parts. Dragosani killed the head of the psychic branch of British intelligence to gain the secrets of their work with people of psychic ability. Keogh decided he had to kill Dragosani, but at the time was unaware of the real threat; Dragosani had developed a relationship with a powerful vampire named Thibor Frenczy. The battle with Frenczy and Dragosani became the prelude to an ongoing battle with the vampiric world that unfolded in the subsequent volumes of the Necroscope series—*Vamphyri!* (1988), *The Source* (1989), *Deadspeak* (1990), and *Deadspawn* (1991). The story continued in a second series, Vampire World, the first two volumes of which, *Blood Brothers* (1992) and *The Last Aerie* (1993), have appeared.

In 1992 the *Necroscope* novels were released as a series of **comic book**s by Malibu Comics Entertainment.

Sources:

Ashley, Mike. *Who's Who in Horror and Fantasy Fiction*. London: Elm Tree Books, 1977. 240 pp.

Lumley, Brian. *Blood Brothers*. London: ROC, 1992. 741 pp.

———. *Deadspawn*. New York: TOR, 1991. 602 pp.

———. *Deadspeak*. New York: TOR, 1990. 487 pp.

———. *Necroscope*. New York: TOR, 1986. 505 pp.

———. *The Source*. New York: TOR, 1989. 505 pp.

———. *Vamphyri!* New York: TOR, 1988. 470 pp.

M

MALAYSIA, VAMPIRES IN

Western observers who began to look at the magical/religious world of Malaysians in the nineteenth century discovered belief in several vampirelike beings, somewhat analogous to the *lamiai* of the mythology of **Greece.** These have survived to this day in spite of the overlay of Hindu and Islamic thought that has come to dominate the religious life of the peninsula. Vampires still inhabit the very lively world of the average Malaysian.

THE VAMPIRE IN MALAYSIAN FOLKLORE: Closely related to the Greek *lamiai* were the *langsuyar* and the *pontianak.* The former was described as a bansheelike flying demon. The original *langsuyar* was a woman of extreme beauty who bore a stillborn baby. When told of the condition of the child, she recoiled from the shock. Suddenly, she clapped her hands and flew away into a nearby tree. She was seen from time to time and identified by her green robe, her long **fingernails** (considered a mark of beauty in Malaysian society), and her ankle-length black hair. The hair concealed an opening in her neck through which she sucked the blood of children. The first *langsuyar* then gave way to groups of similar beings. Later *langsuyars* were flesh eaters with a particular fondness for fish (a staple of the Malaysian diet).

If a woman died either in childbirth or in the forty days immediately following (during which time she was considered unclean), it was believed she might become a *langsuyar.* To prevent that from occurring, her family placed glass beads in her mouth (which stopped any bansheelike shrieks), and to prevent her from flying, eggs were placed under the arms and a needle in the palm of each hand. However, it was also possible to tame a *langsuyar* by capturing it, cutting off its hair and nails, and stuffing them into the hole in the neck. In that case, the *langsuyar* became domesticated and could live in human society somewhat normally. Reports have been collected claiming that such *langsuyars* came into villages, married, and bore children.

However, their new life ended usually at a village party when they began to dance. Suddenly, they would revert to their more spiritlike form and fly off to the jungle, leaving husband and child behind.

The origin of the *pontianak* was directly linked to that of the *langsuyar*—it was the creature's stillborn child. It was believed to take the form of a night owl. To prevent a deceased baby from becoming a *pontianak,* it was treated somewhat like its mother, with beads, eggs, and needles. As with the *langsuyar,* there were specific words to be spoken when "laying" a possible *pontianak.*

Walter William Skeat, (*Malay Magic* 1900, 1966), the main authority on Malaysian mythology, noted some confusion between the *langsuyar* and the *pontianak.* Both could appear as a night owl, both were addressed in invocations as if they were the same, and both mother and child were treated alike to prevent them from becoming a vampire after their death. This confusion has been somewhat cleared up by noting that in parts of Malaysia and throughout much of Indonesia, in places such as **Java,** what Skeat described as the *langsuyar,* the female vampire, was called a *pontianak.*

The *penanggalan* was a third vampirelike creature in Malaysian folklore. According to tradition, it originated with a woman in the midst of performing *dudok bertapa,* a penance ceremony. She was sitting in a large wooden vat used for holding the vinegar derived from the sap of the palm tree. In the midst of her ceremony, a man found her and asked her what she was doing. Startled, she moved to leave, and did so with such force that her head separated from her body, and with the entrails of her stomach trailing behind, she flew off into a nearby tree. That severed head with the dangling stomach attached below it became an evil spirit. It appears on the rooftops of the homes where children are being born. It whines a high-pitched sound and tries to get to the child to suck its blood.

Writing in the early 1800s, P. J. Begbie described the *penanggalan* as an evil spirit that possessed a woman and turned her into a sorcerer. When it wished to travel, it would detach its head and, with its entrails trailing behind, fly off in pursuit of food in the form of the blood of both the living and dead. He also told the story of a man with two wives, one of dark and one of light skin. He was told that they were both *penanggalans.* The man did not believe it, so to test them he watched one night and saw them leave to feed. He then switched their bodies. When they returned, they attached their heads to the wrong body. When the king was presented with this irrefutable proof of their evil nature, both were executed.

An alternate version of the story believed that the *penanggalan* originated from a woman who had been using magic arts and finally learned how to fly. At that time her head and neck were separated from her body, and with her intestines dangling, she took up her abode in a tree. From there she flew from house to house to suck the blood of not only babies but also mothers giving birth. To protect the birthing site, the leaves of the *jeruju* (a kind of thistle) were hung around the house and thorns stuck in any blood that was spilled. As might be expected, blood and other juices dripped from the dangling intestines, and should such drippings fall on anyone, they would immediately fall ill.

Two other blood-drinking entities, the *polong* and the *pelesit,* were closely related in Malaysian lore. The former appeared in the form of a very small female creature (about one inch in height) and the latter as a house cricket. The *polong* operated somewhat like a witch's familiar in traditional Western mythology. It could be attracted by gathering the blood of a murder victim in a bottle over which a seven-day (some say fourteen-day) ritual was performed. Then one waited for the sound of young birds chirping, a sign that the *polong* had taken up residence in the bottle. The *polong* was fed by cutting a finger, inserting it in the bottle, and allowing the *polong* to suck the blood. (In the West, the witch's familiar was said to suckle from a hidden protuberance on the witch's body—a witch's teat). In return for a daily supply of blood, the *polong* was available to do a variety of tasks, including attacking one's enemies.

If one was attacked by a *polong,* which was signaled by various kinds of wild ravings, wise men were called in to exorcise it and to attempt to discover who sent it to torment the victim. Deaths were occasionally attributed to the attack of a *polong* who remained unexorcised.

The *pelesit* generally accompanied the *polong* in its travels and arrived before it. If the *polong* was sent to attack someone, the *pelesit* would first attempt to enter the body of the victim and, in a sense, prepare the way for the *polong.*

Walter William Skeat reported a rather gruesome method of creating a *pelesit.* The potential owner dug up a recently deceased infant. The infant's corpse was carried to an ant hill. After a while the child would cry out and at that moment its tongue would have to be bitten off. The tongue was then dipped in specially prepared coconut oil and buried for three nights. After the third night the tongue turned into a *pelesit.*

Among the many peoples in the very diverse population of Malaysia were the Chewong. They possessed their own mythology, which included the existence of many spirits collectively called the *bas.* There were various kinds of *bas,* some of which under different circumstances attacked humans. The usual food of the *bas* was a *ruwai*, roughly translated as soul or life or vitality. Their preferred prey was the wild pig, and the *bas* set invisible traps to snare the pig's *ruwai.* Sometimes a human *ruwai* was caught in the trap, and in such a case the *bas* would eat the human spirit/soul. The *bas* might also encounter a human *ruwai* when it was traveling about during a person's dreams. *Bas* usually did not attack humans or approach human places of habitation. They knew fire as a sign of human presence, and a person in the woods who encountered a *bas* could build a fire and the *bas* would depart.

On rare occasions, *bas* were thought to attack humans. They attacked in different ways, although most sought only the *ruwai.* For example, the *eng banka,* the ghost of a dead dog that inhabited swamp areas, would steal a *ruwai.* If it was not recovered, the victim died within a few days; someone who suddenly became ill and died a few days later was seen as the victim of an *eng banka.* Quite different was the *maneden,* which lived in the wild pandanus plant. It attacked humans who cut the plant in which it resided by biting them and sucking their blood. It attached itself to the elbow of men or the breast nipples of women. To stop the attack the person had to give the *bas* a substitute, such as the oily nut from the hodj nut tree. Thus, the attack of the *eng banka* was a variety of **psychic vampirism** and that of the *maneden* a more literal vampiric attack.

THE MODERN MALAYSIAN VAMPIRE: It was not until after World War II that the film industry (always under strict British control) began to develop. Shaw Brothers, a firm based in Hong Kong, established Malay Film Productions in 1947. It was soon joined by Catay-Keris Productions. In their drive to compete with Western films, which dominated the market, the Malaysians sought particularly Malaysian themes and locales for their films. The Malaysian vampire thus entered the film world, one of the first such films being *Pontianak* in 1956. In this film, Maria Menado played a hunchbacked young woman made beautiful by magic. After her husband was bitten by a snake and she sucked his blood to get the poison out, she was turned into a vampire, the *pontianak*.

The vampire movies drew on the broad use of the term *pontianak* throughout Indonesia and always pictured the vampire as a young and beautiful woman. The stories told in the movies were made plausible to viewers by the numerous reports from Malaysians who claimed to actually know a vampire who was living a more or less normal life as a wife and mother. During the late 1950s and 1960s, Catay-Keris produced a series of six movies featuring a *pontianak*. Few of the Malaysian vampire films were released to theaters in the West, but some are currently available on video.

Sources:

Begbie, P. J. *The Malayan Peninsula.* Vepery Mission Press, 1834. Reprint. Kuala Lumpur: Oxford University Press, 1967. 523 pp.

Howell, Signe. *Society and Cosmos: Chewong of Peninsular Malaysia.* Singapore: Oxford University Press, 1984. 294 pp.

Kennedy, Raymond. *The Ageless Indies.* New York: John Day Company, 1942. 208 pp.

Lent, John A. *The Asian Film Industry.* Austin: University of Texas Press, 1990. 310 pp.

Pereira, Mervyn. "Vampires and Witches Keep Malaysia Lively." *Sunday Pioneer Press* (Minneapolis) (February 19, 1967).

Skeat, Walter William. *Malay Magic: An Introduction to the Folklore and Popular Religion of the Malay Peninsular.* London: Macmillan and Co., 1900. 685 pp. Reprint. New York: Barnes & Noble, 1966. 685 pp.

Skeat, Walter William, and Charles Otto Blagden. *Pagan Races of the Malay Peninsula.* 2 vols. New York: Macmillan and Company, 1906. Reprint. New York: Barnes & Noble, 1966.

Winstedt, Richard. *The Malay Magician Being Shaman, Saiva, and Sufi.* London: Routledge and Kegan Paul, 1961. 180 pp.

MAN-BAT

Man-Bat was a vampirelike character introduced in the 1970s by DC Comics as the stiff guidelines of the 1954 Comics Code were being relaxed. Created by Frank Robins, Man-Bat made his initial appearance in *Detective Comics* No. 400 (Spring

1970). The original story concerned Kirk Langstrom, an expert on nocturnal mammals at the museum in Gotham City, the home of superhero **Batman.** Langstrom had become obsessed with the idea of besting Batman in some way. In seeking to accomplish his goal, he concocted a serum made from the glands of bats. The serum gave him a natural sonar power and the supersensitive hearing abilities associated with bats. There was an unwanted side effect—he began to transform into a giant bat creature.

Langstrom was trying to find some way out of his predicament when thieves broke into the museum. Batman was about to be defeated by the thieves when Man-Bat showed up to help. In their next encounter, Man-Bat attempted to steal drugs that he hoped would reverse his condition. At the time, Langstrom was engaged, his marriage was approaching, and he was trapped in his bat form. His fiance, Francine, took some of the serum as an act of love and thus joined Langstrom in his batlike existence. With Batman's help they both received an antidote and returned to human form.

Their story appeared to be over. However, there was enough reader reaction to include several new Man-Bat stories in future issues of *Detective Comics*. In No. 429, Francine was bitten by a vampire bat and became a vampire she-bat. Her vampiric side was cured by a complete blood transfusion. Meanwhile, Langstrom had continued his research and attained the ability to turn into Man-Bat at will by taking some pills. He became a crime fighter like Batman. In this capacity he earned a large reward that left him independently wealthy. At the end of 1975, DC Comics tried to test their new character, who seemed to have a large following, with his own comic book. The first issue of *Man-Bat* appeared in December 1975. In it, Langstrom was called upon to deal with super criminal Baron Tyme, who had discovered a means to control Francine and use her to commit crimes. Tyme's intervention reactivated Francine's vampirism. The new comic book was short-lived, however, and after only two issues, Man-Bat returned to *Detective Comics*.

Over the next decade, Man-Bat made sporadic appearances to interact with Batman (for example, in *Batman Family* No. 18 in 1978 and *Batman* No. 348 in 1982) and occasionally with other DC characters, such as Superman (*DC Comics Presents* No. 335 in 1981). In 1984 a second attempt was made to revive Man-Bat in a separate publication. The original Man-Bat stories from *Detective Comics* were reprinted, but only one issue appeared, and Man-Bat returned to a secondary role in the ongoing DC cast.

Sources:

Man-Bat. DC Comics. Nos. 1-2 (December 1975/January 1976-February/March 1976).
Man-Bat. DC Comics. No. 1 (1984).

MANCHESTER, SEAN *See:* VAMPIRE RESEARCH SOCIETY

MARA *See:* SCANDINAVIA, VAMPIRES IN

MARSCHNER, HEINRICH AUGUST (1795-1861)

Heinrich August Marschner, the author of the first vampire opera, was born on August 16, 1795, in Zittau, Germany. He manifested an early talent for music but left home at age 18 to pursue law at the University at Leipzig. Fortunately, one of his professors recognized his true talents and convinced him to drop out of law. Marschner moved to Vienna, where he met Beethoven and wrote his first operas. In 1823 he became music director at the opera house at Dresden. Four years later he moved back to Leipzig. By the time of his return to Leipzig, the vampire had become an item of fascination for French artists and that interest was being felt in Germany. Thus, in 1828, while in Leipzig, Marschner wrote his opera *Der Vampyr*.

The finished piece was a collaborative product. The libretto was written by Wilhelm August Wohlbrück, Marschner's brother-in-law. It was based on **Charles Nodier**'s very successful stage play that had first brought the vampire to Parisian theater audiences. Nodier's work was in turn based on **John Polidori**'s "The Vampyre". The opera opened with a gathering of witches. **Lord Ruthven** appeared and was told that he had 24 hours to locate three victims. Janthe, the first of his three victims-to-be, soon arrived, and she and the vampire departed into the vampire's cave where he killed her. Janthe's father then killed Ruthven, but he was revived when his friend Aubry placed him in the moonlight. (Moonlight, a theme introduced by Polidori, was retained in the nineteenth-century works based on "The Vampyre," but disappeared from the twentieth-century lore.)

The next scene was the home of Malwina, the young woman with whom Aubry was in love. They were prevented from consummating their love, however, as Malwina's father had promised his daughter to the Earl of Marsden—that is, Ruthven. Aubry could not expose Ruthven because he had taken an oath never to reveal Ruthven's vampiric condition. On his way to the wedding, Ruthven located his third victim, Emmy, the daughter of a peasant. After killing Emmy he headed for another needed feeding. Unable to prevent the wedding by his best arguments, Aubry finally broke his oath and revealed Ruthven's true nature. Cosmic forces took over, and Ruthven was struck by lightning and fell into the pits of hell. The opera ended with the wedding guests singing a closing song thanking God.

Der Vampyr opened in Leipzig in March 1829. The opera was a great success and was taken on the road. It opened in London in August and ran for some 60 performances at the Lyceum Theater, the same theater that later played such a central role in **Bram Stoker**'s career and the site of the original dramatization of *Dracula*. In 1831 Marschner continued his career at Hanover, where he wrote his most critically acclaimed work, *Hans Heiling*. In 1859 he was pensioned as Hanover's general music director. He died two years later on December 14, 1861. The town erected a monument to him in 1877.

Der Vampyr has been revived only rarely since the 1820s; however, in 1992 the BBC sponsored a modern production of it. The new production, entitled Der Vampyr—A Soap Opera, utilized Marschner's music but had a completely new libretto written by Charles Hart that transferred the setting to modern London. Lord Ruthven became Ripley the Vampyr. (His part was sung by Omar Ebrahim.) The outline of the old plot survived, however, and Ripley, after several bloody scenes that would satisfy any vampire enthusiast, received his just reward in the presence of the wedding guests. The new version of Der Vampyr has been released on a Virgin Classics compact disc.

Sources:

Brautigam, Rob. "Der Vampyr." *International Vampire* 1, 4 (Summer 1991): 8-10.
———. "The Vampyr—A Soap Opera." *International Vampire* 10 (1993): 5.

MARSHALL, WILLIAM B. (1924-)

William B. Marshall, Shakespearean actor and star of two vampire movies, was born on August 19, 1924, in Gary, Indiana. Early career highlights included successful performances in the title roles in *Oedipus Rex* and *Othello* in the 1960s. These parts led to movie roles as a Haitian patriot leader in *Lydia Bailey* and a nubian in *Demetrios and the Gladiators.*

In the early 1970s, as movies aimed at an African-American audience became a growth industry, producer Joseph T. Naar at Power Productions began a search for someone to play a Black vampire lead in a movie he was putting together. Marshall, six feet five inches tall, fit the part in a most impressive manner. Not used to playing stereotypical Black characters, he assumed some direct responsibility for the final creation of the character, Prince Mamuwalde, cursed by Dracula to become **Blacula.** He transformed the title role, which had the potential for degenerating into a parody of both vampires and Black people, into a serious dramatic part. He was responsible for developing the character of Prince Mamuwalde into an antislavery freedom fighter.

Blacula (1972) was successful enough to lead to one sequel, *Scream, Blacula, Scream.* (1973) Although Marshall was eager to continue the part in further movies, the production company, American International, dropped the idea.

Sources:

Glut, Donald F. *The Dracula Book.* Metuchen, NJ: Scarecrow Press, 1975. 388 pp.

MATHESON, RICHARD (1926-)

Richard Matheson, screenwriter and science fiction/horror novelist, was born in New Jersey. His first publications were science fiction stories, although it has been noted that at least a hint of horror has been part of his writing from the beginning. His first sale was a short story, ''Born of Man and Woman'' (1950), which then became the title of his first book (1954), a collection of his stories. His first vampire short story, ''Drink My Red Blood'', appeared in 1951 and has been frequently reprinted, but it was three years later he completed the novel that has been hailed as one of the classics of the vampire genre, *I Am Legend* (1954).

I Am Legend recounted the problem caused by a new bacterium that created an isotonic solution in human blood from which it lived. It slowly turned humans into vampires. As the story developed, Robert Neville, who was immune to the bacteria, survived as the only untainted human. Most of the action took place at Neville's fortified home. He was opposed by his former neighbor, Ben Cortland, who led the vampire hordes in their search for fresh blood. As the bacteria invaded the body, they caused the canine teeth to elongate and turned the skin a pale gray-white color. The bacteria were killed by the light of the sun and by garlic, and thus those infected adopted the habits of traditional vampires. Cortland was nearly unkillable. He survived bullets, knife wounds, and other normally fatal traumas. The bacteria immediately sealed wounds. However, if a person was staked, the stake kept the wound open and the bacteria died. In the end, humans developed a vaccine that killed the germ.

Matheson occasionally returned to the vampire theme in his stories, including ''The Funeral'' (1955) and ''No Such Thing as a Vampire'' (1959), and he went on in his lengthy career to write several horror screenplays. His 1956 novel, *The Incredible Shrinking Man,* was made into a movie in 1957. He adapted several of **Edgar Allan Poe**'s stories for the screen for producer **Roger Corman.** His novel *Bid Time Return* (1975) won the Howard Award as the best fantasy novel of the year.

I Am Legend has been adapted to the screen twice, but without the use of Matheson's own screenplay. First, an Italian production, released in America as *The Last Man on Earth* (1964), starred Vincent Price. Then, *I am Legend* served as the basis for the 1971 American production *The Omega Man,* starring Charlton Heston; however, in this latter production, the vampire theme was largely eliminated. In 1968 Matheson's ''No Such Thing as a Vampire'' was brought to the television screen as an episode of the BBC's Late Night Horror show.

In 1971 Matheson began a period of creative work with producer/director **Dan Curtis**. His first effort was a screenplay for *The Night Stalker,* the story of a vampire-hunting reporter that became the most-watched made-for-television movie up to that time. On the heels of that success he wrote the screenplay for Curtis's new production of *Dracula* **(1973)** starring **Jack Palance** in the title role. Then, in 1975 and 1977 Matheson's short stories became the basis for two made-for-television movies, *Trilogy of Terror* and *Dead of Night.* The latter, directed by Curtis as the pilot for a never-produced series, brought ''No Such Thing as a Vampire'' to the screen again as one of three stories.

In 1989 the Horror Writers of America gave Matheson the first of two Bram Stoker Awards for the best volume of collected fiction for his *Richard Matheson:*

Collected Stories. The following year they presented him with the award for life achievement.

Sources:

Ashley, Mike. *Who's Who in Horror and Fantasy Fiction.* London: Elm Tree Books, 1977. 240 pp.

Matheson, Richard. "Drink My Red Blood." *Imagination* (April 1951). Rept. as "Blood Son." In *A Feast of Blood,* edited by Charles M. Collins. New York: Avon, 1967. Rept. as "Drink My Blood." In *The Midnight People,* edited by Peter Haining. New York: Popular Library, 1968. Rept. in *A Clutch of Vampires,* edited By Raymond T. McNally. New York: Bell Publishing Company, 1974, pp. 223-34.

———. *I Am Legend.* New York: Fawcett, 1954. 175 pp. Reprint. New York: Berkley Publishing Company, 1971. 174 pp.

Pickersgill, Frederick, ed. *No Such Thing as a Vampire.* London: Corgi, 1964. 126 pp. (Matheson's story leads off this vampire short story collection.)

Rovin, Jeff. *The Encyclopedia of Super Villains.* New York: Facts on File, 1987. 416 pp.

MCNALLY, RAYMOND T. (1931-)

Raymond T. McNally, a leading scholar on vampires in folklore and fiction and on **Vlad the Impaler,** the historical Dracula, was born on May 15, 1931, in Cleveland, Ohio, the son of Marie Kinkoff and Michael Joseph McNally. After completing his education, McNally took a position as instructor at John Carroll University in his hometown. He moved on to Boston College in Chestnut Hill, Massachusetts, in 1958, where he has remained to the present. In 1961 he was named an American Exchange Scholar to the USSR and spent the year at the University of Leningrad. From 1964 to 1974 he also served as director of Boston College's Slavic and East European Center. He was appointed full professor in 1970.

After joining the faculty at Boston College he met **Radu Florescu,** a Romanian historian with whom he shared an interest in Dracula and vampire lore. They formed a team to do research on the historical Dracula, a fifteenth-century ruler named Vlad the Impaler, and his relationship to the novel by **Bram Stoker.** In 1967 McNally was one of a party of men who discovered and explored the authentic **Castle Dracula.** His continued collaboration with Florescu proved fruitful, its first product being *In Search of Dracula* (1972), one of the early nonfiction works on Dracula and the first to offer details about the obscure Vlad the Impaler. It became a popular best-seller. The following year, 1973, they completed a more scholarly biography, *Dracula: A Biography of Vlad the Impaler, 1431-1476.* These books have become two of the most influential works for people interested in vampires. **Christopher Lee,** the actor most identified at the time with the dramatic role of Dracula, starred in a documentary film based on the two books, *In Search of Dracula* (1976), made by a Swedish film company. Later books and movies have incorporated data from the two volumes as part of the Dracula storyline.

McNally followed the success of the two volumes with an anthology of vampire writings (both fiction and nonfiction), *A Clutch of Vampires: These Being among the*

◀ VAMPIRE EXPERT RAYMOND T.
MCNALLY.

Best from History and Literature (1974). Through the 1970s he continued to work with Florescu, and in 1979 they completed a new edition of Stoker's novel, *The Essential "Dracula": A Completely Illustrated and Annotated Edition of Bram Stoker's Classic Novel.*

Meanwhile, McNally had also become fascinated with **Elizabeth Bathory,** the other historical personage who stood behind the *Dracula* myth. Bathory, a Czechoslovakian countess, was (like Vlad) not a vampire, but she did kill many young girls to bathe in their blood, which she thought would preserve her youth. *Dracula Was a Woman: In Search of the Blood Countess of Transylvania* appeared in 1983. Two decades of work on the historical Dracula led in 1989 to the publication of *Dracula, Prince of Many Faces: His Life and Times,* a comprehensive attempt to put the life story of Vlad the Impaler into the broad context of fifteenth-century European history.

In the early 1970s, while researching and writing their first books, McNally and Florescu had suggested some collaborative work between British, Romanian, and American scholars interested in Vlad and Dracula. The fall of the Romanian dictatorship in 1990 has allowed such an endeavor to proceed. The first product was an edited volume, *Dracula: Essays on the Life and Times of Vlad Tepes,* to which McNally contributed an essay, ''An Historical Appraisal of the Image of Vlad Tepes in Contemporary Romanian Folklore.''

Sources:

Florescu, Radu, and Raymond T. McNally. *The Complete Dracula.* Boston: Copley Publishing Group, 1992. 409 pp. (A combined publication of *In Search of Dracula* and *Dracula; A Biography of Vlad the Impaler.*)

————. *Dracula: A Biography of Vlad the Impaler, 1431-1476.* New York: Hawthorn Books, 1973. 239 pp.

————. *Dracula, Prince of Many Faces: His Life and Times.* Boston: Little, Brown and Company, 1989. 261 pp.

McNally, Raymond T. *A Clutch of Vampires: These Being among the Best from History and Literature.* New York: Bell Publishing Company, 1974. 255 pp.

————. *Dracula Was a Woman: In Search of the Blood Countess of Transylvania.* New York: McGraw-Hill, 1983. 254 pp. Reprint. London: Hamlyn Paperback, 1983. 254 pp.

————. "An Historical Appraisal of the Image of Vlad Tepes in Contemporary Romanian Folklore." In Kurt W. Treptow, ed., *Dracula: Essays on the Life and Times of Vlad Tepes.* New York: Columbia University Press, 1991. 336 pp.

McNally, Raymond T., and Radu Florescu. *In Search of Dracula.* New York: Greenwich, 1972. 223 pp.

————, eds. *The Essential "Dracula": A Completely Illustrated and Annotated Edition of Bram Stoker's Classic Novel.* New York: Mayflower Books, 1979. 320 pp.

MELROSE ABBEY, THE VAMPIRE OF

One of the famous cases of an actual vampire was chronicled by twelfth-century writer **William of Newburgh.** His account of a vampire that haunted Melrose Abbey in England began with a priest who neglected his holy vows and office and devoted his days to frivolous activity. Following his death, he came out of his grave and tried to enter the cloister at the monastery. Failing on several occasions, he began to wander through the countryside. He found his way to the bedside of a lady to whom he had been chaplain. His several visits to her prompted her to report the incidents to the brothers at the monastery.

Several of the brothers set up a watch at the graveyard where the priest was buried. As his companions sought relief from the chilly air by a fire, one monk kept watch and saw the dead priest arise from the grave and approach him. He hit the dead priest with a battle axe and forced him back into the grave. The earth opened to receive the corpse, closed over it, and gave the appearance of having been undisturbed.

When the three who had been warming themselves returned, they listened to and believed the account of the monk who reported his encounter with the body of the dead priest. At the break of day they opened the grave. There they found the corpse. It bore the mark of the wound previously reported by the monk, and the coffin was swimming in blood. They burned the body and scattered the ashes.

Sources:

Glut, Donald G. *True Vampires of History*. New York: H C Publishers, 1971. 191 pp.

MEXICO, VAMPIRES IN

Account of vampires in Mexico can be traced as far back as the ancient Maya, whose territory centered on what today is Guatemala but also reached north into the Yucatan peninsula and the southern part of present-day Mexico. This was the territory of the vampire **bats,** which were incorporated into the mythology of the Maya. *Camazotz,* the fierce cave god of the Mayan underworld, was known from his appearance in the *Popol Vol* and his representations in Mayan art.

In the *Popol Vol,* two brothers entered the underworld to avenge the death of their father. To accomplish their task, they had to pass through a number of obstacles, one of which was the Bat House. They were first attacked by a horde of bats and then by *Camazotz* himself. *Camazotz* was pictured as a manbat with a sharp nose and large teeth and claws. At one point, one of the brothers stuck his head out of their hiding place and *Camazotz* quickly decapitated him. The head was then used as the ball in a game. The decapitated brother obtained a substitute head, and the brothers eventually played the game and won.

Camazotz, with his sharp nose and large teeth and claws, was a popularly feared figure among the Mayans, and numerous representations appeared in Mayan art. *Camazotz* served two diverse purposes. He was integral to the basic agricultural myth built around the cycle of growing maize. In his descent, he brought death to the maize grain at the time it was buried in the earth, a necessary step leading to its rebirth in the harvest. He was also a feared, bloodthirsty god of the caves. People avoided places believed to be his dwelling place.

THE AZTECS: From the elaborate mythology of the Aztecs, whose territory was north of the Maya's, came several vampire deities. Among those cited as vampiric was the lord of the underworld, the region of the dead; however, he appeared to have been more a devourer of the souls of the dead than a vampiric figure. Nevertheless, a set of vampirelike figures were evident in the goddesses related to the "earth lady," *Tlalteuctli*, the personification of the rock and soil upon which humans lived. Tlalteuctli was also a terror-producing figure. Never pictured as a woman, she was shown as a huge toad with blood covering her jaws. Several of the female figures that surrounded the earth lady shared a common hideousness and thirst for blood: *Coatlicue*, "serpent skirt"; *Cihuacoatl*, "snake woman"; *Itzpapalotl*, "obsidian knife butterfly"; and the *cihuateteo*. These goddesses were also known as the *cihuapipiltin,* or princesses. *Coatlicue* was described as black, dirty, disheveled, and ugly. A statue of her survived and has been placed in the National Museum in Mexico City. It has a skirt of snakes and a necklace of hands and hearts with a skull-shaped pendant. The head is missing and in its stead is a stream of gushing blood that becomes two rattlesnake heads.

Cihuacoatl was the ancient goddess of Culhuacan, but after the fifteenth century her worship was centered in Xochimilco. Her appearance was terrifying—stringy hair, her mouth open to receive victims, and two knives gracing her forehead. However, she had the ability to change herself into a beautiful young woman who, like vampire demons in many lands, enticed young men to their doom. They had sexual relations with her, only to wither away and die afterward. *Cihuacoatl* survived into this century both as the Virgin of Guadalupe in Roman Catholic lore and as La Llorona, the Weeping Woman, in popular folklore. As such she could be heard at night weeping for her dead children. *Cihuacoatl* represented the hunger of the gods for human victims, and state prisoners were regularly sacrificed to satisfy her need for blood. *Itzpapalotl,* not as specifically vampiric as the other two, was a personification of the ritual sacrificial knife.

The *cihuateteo* were the most vampiric of all the Aztec deities. They originated from women who died in childbirth. They had once been mortal, had struggled with the child, and had succeeded in holding it until both died in the struggle. Thus, they attained the status of warrior. As demonic figures, the *cihuateteo* very much resembled such other vampiric figures as the *lamiai* of ancient **Greece** or the *langsuyar* of **Malaysia.** The *cihuateteo* wandered the night and attacked children, leaving them paralyzed or otherwise diseased. They held counsel with other *cihuateteos* at local crossroads. Food offerings were placed at crossroads in structures dedicated to the *cihuateteos* so that they would gorge themselves and not attack the children; also, if the vampiric beings remained at the crossroads until morning, they would be killed by the **sunlight.** In recent years the *cihuateteos* have been described as having white faces and chalk-covered arms and hands. They wear the costume of Tlazolteotl, the goddess of all sorcery, lust, and evil.

THE *TLAHUELPUCHI:* The Aztecan culture was largely destroyed by the European invasion and the religious conquest of the land by Roman Catholicism. The goddesses continued somewhat, however, transformed in the popular imagination into witches that survived under different names. They were called **bruja** (feminine) or *brujo* (masculine) by the Spanish and ***tlahuelpuchi,*** the blood-sucking witch, by the descendants of the Aztecs.

The *tlahuelpuchi* was a person (most often a woman) believed to possess the power to transform itself into one of several animals and in that form attack and suck the blood of infants or, on rare occasions, children and adults. The *tlahuelpuchi* drew elements from both the ancient Aztec goddesses and the witches of **Spain,** who had the power to transform themselves into **animals** and liked to suck the blood of infants. The most common animal into which the witches transformed themselves was a turkey, but animals as varied as fleas, cats, dogs, and buzzards were reported. Such witches lived incognito in their communities, and witches became objects of fear, especially among couples with infants.

The *tlahuelpuchi* was born a witch and had no control over her condition, which remained with her for life. Since the condition was a chance occurrence of birth, the witch could not pass her condition to another. There was no way to tell if a person was a witch until she reached puberty. The power of **transformation** arrived with the first menses. At that time the young witch also developed an insatiable thirst for human blood. That a person was a witch would soon become known to relatives, of course, but out of shame and fear, they would seek to conceal the fact. A witch would kill anyone who revealed her identity, but would otherwise not attack kinspeople. The *tlahuelpuchi* had to have blood at least once a month and some as much as four times a month.

On the last Saturday of every month, the *tlahuelpuchi* entered the kitchen of her dwelling and performed a magical rite. She lighted a fire made of special substances and then transformed into an animal, usually a dog. Her lower legs and feet were left behind in the form of a cross. Upon her return from feeding, she retransformed into a human and reattached her appendages. The witch could, on occasion, be known by the limp developed from her regular transformations. Occasionally, the witch might attack children, adults, or the livestock of a person they had quarreled with.

The *tlahuelpuchi* also had **hypnotic power** over individuals and could cause them to kill themselves, primarily by having them walk to a high place and jump to their death. They might also attack livestock of people they wished to harm. Thus, particular kinds of evil that affected people were routinely attributed to the witches in their midst.

Protection from witches was most ensured by use of the ubiquitous **garlic.** Wrapped in a tortilla, cloves of garlic might be placed in the clothes of an infant. In the absence of garlic, an onion could be substituted. Bright metal was also considered effective, and parents sometimes placed a machete or a box of pins under their infant's crib. Pins or other metal objects might be fashioned into a cross. Parents also used clear **water, mirror**s, or holy medals. Infant deaths were attributable to parents having relaxed their vigilance in protecting their child.

On occasion, people reported seeing a witch in animal form. It was spotted and distinguished from other animals by the phosphorous illumination it emitted. There would often follow an attempt to kill it, either by stoning and clubbing (to avoid direct physical contact), but more often than not, the witch escaped by changing form. On vary rare occasions, a woman in the community was called out as a *tlahuelpuchi*. If the accusation was accepted by a group of people, that person would be attacked in her home and clubbed and/or stoned to death. Afterward, the sense organs, including the fingers, were removed, and the body, unburied, was disposed of in a deserted spot.

Belief in the *tlahuelpuchi* has continued to the present day in rural Mexico. As recently as 1954 the state of Tlaxcala passed a law requiring that infants reportedly killed by witchcraft had to be referred to medical authorities. Researchers Hugo G.

THE BAT IS AN INTEGRAL PART OF VAMPIRE LORE IN MEXICO.

Nutini and John M. Roberts, working in the same state in the 1960s, had no trouble gathering numerous tales of witchcraft.

THE CINEMATIC VAMPIRE: Today, Mexico's prolific movie industry has become well known, and vampire enthusiasts have made note of the large number of vampire movies from Mexico, many of them featuring U.S. actors. The Mexican vampire image was strongly influenced by the **Universal Pictures**'s Spanish-language rendition of *Dracula* **(Spanish, 1931)** starring Carlos Villarias and Lupita Tovar. This American-made version circulated freely in Mexico in the years prior to World War II and directly influenced the image of the vampire in the emerging urban culture.

The vampire arrived in force in 1957 when German Robles starred as the vampire Count Lavud in three vampire movies: *El Vampiro* (*The Vampire*), *El Ataud del Vampiro* (*The Vampire's Coffin*, and a comedy inspired by the earlier movies, *El Castillo de los Monstruos* (*Castle of the Monsters*). Count Lavud, obviously influenced by **Bela Lugosi,** was pictured as a suave Hungarian nobleman. In the first movie he was killed with a stake that subsequently was removed to allow him further life in the second.

Robles secured his claim as Mexico's first vampire star in 1959 by starring in a 12-part serial as a bearded descendant of the prophet Nostradamus who had become a vampire. Subsequently, the serial was recut into four feature-length movies: *La Maldicíon de Nostradamus* (*The Curse of Nostradamus*), *Nostradamus y el Destructor de Monstruos* (*The Monster Demolisher*), *Nostradamus, El Genii de las Tinieblas* (*The Genie of Darkness*), and *La Sangre de Nostradamus* (*The Blood of Nostradamus*). (To avoid certain Mexican government film regulations, films were often made as serials and then quickly recut into feature films.) These features were released in the United States by **Roger Corman**'s American International Pictures. Robles also played a vampire in the Argentine film *El Vampiro Aechecha* (*The Lurching Vampire,* 1959). His final appearance was in *Los Vampiros de Coyoacan* (1973), in which he played the hero instead of a vampire.

Robles's success quickly led to an exploitation of the market. Alfonso Corona Blake made his first vampire movie, *El Mundo de los Vampiros* (*World of the Vampires*) in 1960. Two years later Blake was one of the directors called upon to work on the movies of the masked wrestler-turned-actor **Santo.** He directed Santo's first vampire movie, *Santo Contra las Mujeres Vampiro* (*Samson vs. the Vampire Women*). Santo emerged as one of Mexico's favorite movie characters and over two decades fought a variety of supernatural villains. In 1967 he battled Dracula in *Santo en el Tesoro de Dracula* which was also made in an adult version as *El Vampiro y el Sexo.* The vampire women returned in 1969 in *Santo en la Venganza de las Mujeres Vampiros.*

Frederico Curiel, the director of *Santo en la Venganza de las Mujeres Vampiros,* had emerged in 1959 as the director of the Nostradamus films. In 1967 he directed *El Imperio de Dracula* (*The Empire of Dracula*) and the following year *Las Vampiras,* one of **John Carradine**'s last films. He was joined as an important director of vampire titles by Miguel Morayta, who was responsible for *El Vampiro Sangriento* (*The Bloody Vampire,* 1961) and *La Invasion de los Vampiros* (*The Invasion of the Vampiros,* 1962).

The vampire as a theme in Mexican cinema peaked in the 1960s. During the early 1970s the last of the Santo vampire movies, *Santo y Blue Demon Contra Dracula y el Hombre Lobo,* appeared. Rene Cardona, who had directed *Santo y el Tesoro del Dracula,* continued his work in *Santo Contra Cazadores de Cabezas* (1970), *La Invasion de los Muertos* (1972), and the two comedies *Capulina Contra Los Vampiros* (1972) and *Capulina Contra Los Monstruos* (by Juan Lopez, who directed *Mary, Mary Bloody Mary* (1975) and *Alucarda* (*Sisters of Satan,* 1975). Few new vampire films appeared through the remainder of the decade. From being a center of the vampire cinema in the 1960s, Mexico seems to have largely abandoned the genre through the 1980s and into the 1990s.

Sources:

Fentome, Steve. "Mexi-Monster Meltdown!" *Monster International* 2 (1992): 4-13.

Nutini, Hugo G., and John M. Roberts. *Bloodsucking Witchcraft: An Epistemological Study of Anthropomorphic Supernaturalism in Rural Tlaxcala.* Tucson: University of Arizona Press, 1993. 476 pp.

Summers, Montague. *The Vampire: His Kith and Kin.* London: Routledge, Kegan Paul, Trench, Trubner, & Co., 1928. 356 pp. Reprint. New Hyde Park, NY: University Books, 1960. 356 pp.

MIDNIGHT SONS

At the end of 1983, Marvel Comics killed off all of the vampires in the Marvel Universe, especially those that had survived from the popular 1970s series *The Tomb of Dracula.* The means chosen for their demise was the use of a magical operation called the Montesi Formula by occultist Dr. Stephen Strange (*Doctor Strange,* No. 62, December 1983). In that process, Hannibal King, who had been a vampire character introduced in *The Tomb of Dracula,* was returned to normal life. Almost no vampire appeared in any Marvel **comic book**s for the next six years.

By the end of the 1980s, however, it had become obvious that the horror theme in general and the vampire theme in particular had a large and growing audience among readers of comic books. Marvel, the largest of the comic book companies, addressed this growing public by reintroducing the vampire in November 1989, when **Morbius** burst upon the pages of a relatively new series, *Dr. Strange: Sorcerer Supreme* (No. 10). Four issues later, in No. 14 (February 1992), Marvel announced the return of vampires to the Marvel Universe, their return made possible by a weakening of the Montesi Formula. At the same time, Hannibal King found himself transforming back into a vampire.

The full effects of the reversal of the Montesi Formula became evident in 1992, when Marvel initiated the creation of a new region of the Marvel Universe populated primarily with superheroes. Marvel brought together some of its older titles, to which were added several brand-new titles in a shared storyline called the Midnight Sons. The idea of the Midnight Sons recalls the February 1976 issue of *Marvel Premiere* (No. 28), in which **Morbius** and Ghost Rider joined Swamp-Ooze and the Werewolf by Night in the Legion of Monsters.

The older heroes incorporated into the Midnight Sons were Ghost Rider, John Blaze, and the Darkhold (alter egos of Vicki Montesi, Sam Buchanan, Louise Hastings, and the sorcerer Modred). Morbius was revived and given his own series. **Blade the Vampire Slayer,** Frank Drake, and Hannibal King, the three vampire fighters from *The Tomb of Dracula* series in the 1970s, were dusted off and given their own storyline as *The Nightstalkers. The Nightstalkers* operated as a detective agency in contemporary Boston. The Midnight Sons now lived on the edge of reality where the occult and supernatural, in their most sinister form, were a constant threat.

The story of the Midnight Sons officially began in fall 1992 in a six-part story carried in a variety of Marvel titles: *Ghost Rider* No. 28, *Spirits of Vengeance* No. 1, *Morbius* No. 1, *Darkhold* No. 1, *Nightstalkers* No. 1, and *Ghost Rider* No. 31. The lead characters of these titles comprise The Nine, who together protect this world from crumbling under the pressure of the supernatural evil world. The initial story pitted The Nine against **Lilith,** Queen of Evil and Mother of Demons, a sorceress of obscure origin based upon the ancient Semitic demonic personage, and not to be confused with **Lilith, the Daughter of Dracula,** who had appeared in previous Marvel vampire comic books. As the Midnight Sons combined to defeat the forces of evil called together by Lilith, they discovered their own questions about one another. They especially questioned the legitimacy of Morbius and Hannibal King, vampires who were not that different from some of the entities from the evil world. Their inability to work with one another, except when attacked has allowed both independent and interrelated stories during the first year of the Midnight Sons.

A favorable response to the Midnight Sons was immediately noticeable, and in April 1993 Marvel added a seventh title, *Midnight Sons Unlimited,* and soon afterward began to reprint the old Morbius stories in a new series, *Morbius Revisited.* Then, in October 1993, Marvel moved to promote the Midnight Sons by giving them their own unified Marvel imprint introduced with a seventeen-part story, ''Siege of Darkness,'' the first part of which appeared in *Nightstalkers* No. 14. The Midnight Sons who survived the ''Siege of Darkness'' (several were killed) became a more united team. ''Siege of Darkness'' was printed complete with its own daggerlike logo and firmly established a supernatural realm on the edge of the old Marvel Universe of super (but very human) heroes and villains. The development of this separate supernatural Marvel realm also recognized the problems encountered by the superheroes (the main characters in the Marvel universe) whenever they had to deal with supernatural evil.

As part of its promotion of the new imprint, Marvel issued a Midnight Sons dagger logo pin and a new *Ghost Rider and the Midnight Sons Magazine.* Soon after the conclusion of ''Siege of Darkness,'' *Nightstalkers* was discontinued. Hannibal King and Frank Drake were killed in its final issue. Blade survived and continued in his own new title, *Blade the Vampire-Hunter.* Various vampire villains continued to make periodic appearances in the several Midnight Sons titles.

Sources:

Ghost Rider and the Midnight Sons Magazine.. Nos. 1- . New York: Marvel Comics, 1993- .
Melton, J. Gordon. *The Vampire in the Comic Book.* New York: Count Dracula Fan Club, 1993. 32 pp.
Midnight Sons Unlimited. No. 1- . New York: Marvel Comics, 1993-.
Morbius the Living Vampire. No. 1- . New York: Marvel Comics, 1992-.
Nightstalkers. Nos. 1-18. New York: Marvel Comics, 1992-1994.

MIDNIGHT TO MIDNIGHT

Midnight to Midnight, the Vampire Writers' Circle, was founded in 1990 by Karen E. Dove, ''The High Priestess.'' Dove had a desire to create a more human vampire figure somewhat removed from the image of a bloodsucking monster or a fantastic superhuman creature. She also became aware of a type of organization operated by fantasy genre writers in which a shared fantasy world was created and each writer collaborated with the others and shared characters. She constructed an initial Midnight to Midnight universe of characters and circulated them to potential members of the circle.

As it evolved, Midnight to Midnight has averaged fewer than 10 members. Members have one basic rule—that they write and contribute to the circle at least once every two months. It is Dove's expectation that as writers come and go, the most serious ones will persevere, and the circle will have been a means of their growth; in the meantime all will have an enjoyable experience.

The vampires of Midnight to Midnight share a world very similar to those in the fanzine *Good Guys Wear Fangs*. They cannot change shapes or fly. They are not affected by holy objects such as the **crucifix** or by running **water.** Their night **vision** is not enhanced. However, they do cast a reflection in a **mirror**; they can live forever, but are vulnerable to various dangers; and they are nocturnal creatures, but are not confined to the dark; **sunlight** burns them. Three kinds of vampire beings populate the Midnight to Midnight world. ''Born'' vampires are children of two vampires. They grow normally until their early twenties, when they cease to age. ''Made'' vampires are vampires created after a period of mortal life. They remain at the age they were when created. ''Half-vampires'' are people born to a vampire and one mortal parent. They can live for many generations, but eventually die of old age after several centuries.

Those interested in more information about the Midnight to Midnight work may contact ''The High Priestess,'' MM, 11 North Ave., Mt. Clemens, MI 48043.

Sources:

Dove, Karen E. *Midnight to Midnight Guidelines.* Mt. Clemens, MI: The Author, 1994. 25 pp.

MIRRORS

The now-popular idea that vampires cast no reflection in a mirror (and often have an intense aversion to them) seems to have first been put forward in Bram Stoker's novel, *Dracula.* soon after his arrival at **Castle Dracula, Jonathan Harker** observed that the building was devoid of mirrors. When Dracula silently came into Harker's room while he was shaving. Harker noticed that Dracula, who was standing behind him, did not appear in the shaving mirror as he should have. Dracula complained that mirrors were objects of human vanity, and, seizing the shaving mirror, he broke it. When the novel was brought to the stage and the episode in Castle Dracula deleted, the incident of the mirror was transformed into a confrontation between Dracula and Dr. **Abraham Van Helsing.**

The mirror incident does not seem to have any precedent in either vampire folklore or the earlier vampire short stories and **dramas,** although Stoker seemed to have been aware of folklore about mirrors. Mirrors were seen as somehow revealing a person's spiritual double, the soul. In seeing themselves revealed in a mirror, individuals found confirmation that there was a soul and that hence life went on. They also found in the reflection a new source of anxiety, as the mirror could be used negatively to affect the soul. The notion that the image in the mirror was somehow the soul underlay the idea that breaking a mirror brought seven years' bad luck. Breaking the mirror also damaged the soul.

Thus, one could speculate that the vampire had no soul, had nothing to reflect in the mirror. The mirror forced the vampire to confront the nature of his/her existence as the undead, neither living nor dead. On occasion in both vampire fiction and the cinema, the idea of nonreflection in mirrors has been extended to film, that is, the vampire would not appear in photographs if developed.

In her popular reinterpretation of the vampire myth, **Anne Rice** dropped Stoker's mirror convention. She argued in part that although vampires have certain ''supernatural'' attributes, they existed in the same physical universe as mortals and generally had to conform to the same physical laws, including those of optics. Hence, in *Interview with the Vampire* and *Vampire Lestat,* Louis and **Lestat de Lioncourt,** respectively, saw themselves in a mirror and experienced a moment of self-revelation about their new vampire image. (Of course, Rice's vampires didn't follow *all* physical laws since they had the ability to fly.)

Sources:

Goldberg, Benjamin. *The Mirror and Man.* Charlottesville, VA: University Press of Virginia, 1985. 260 pp.
Ramsland, Katherine. *The Vampire Companion.* New York: Ballantine Books, 1993. 507 pp.

THE MISS LUCY WESTENRA SOCIETY OF THE UNDEAD

The Miss Lucy Westenra Society of the Undead was founded in 1989 by Lewis Sanders in honor of **Lucy Westenra,** the first of Dracula's victims in England. It has a stated purpose of supporting other vampire fan clubs. Members receive a ''Miss Lucy'' pen and a trimesterly newsletter, which includes artwork, fiction, and poetry by the members. The newsletter also accepts ads from members free of charge.

The society may be contacted c/o Christine Raymond, 11141 Tanglewood Dr., Auburn, CA 95603.

MIST

In **Bram Stoker's** *Dracula,* Dr. **Abraham Van Helsing,** the vampire authority, suggested that vampires could transform into a mist, although their ability to travel very far in this form was quite limited. Dracula adopted this form to conceal himself on the ship *Demeter* while traveling to England. In this form, he could move with ease in and out of the box in which he rested. Van Helsing, acknowledging this ability, sealed the door of the vault of the vampirized **Lucy Westenra**'s resting place with a putty containing flakes of a **eucharistic wafer** so not the tiniest space was left for her to escape. He later sealed the door to **Castle Dracula** in a similar manner.

Dracula's primary appearances in the form of mist were during his attacks on **Mina Murray.** In Murray's record of the first attack, she noted that she saw a thin streak of white mist that moved across the lawn. It seemed to have a sentience and vitality all its own. The mist started to move into the room, not through the window, but through the joinings of the door. The mist concentrated into a cloud out of which Dracula emerged. Several days later, when the men finally figured out that Murray was under attack, they went to her room and found her drinking Dracula's blood. They moved toward him with **crucifix**es in hand, but he turned back into mist and disappeared under the door.

The idea of the vampire transforming into mist was a minor concept in folklore, but it was occasionally mentioned as a logical means for the vampire to leave and return from the grave without disturbing the topsoil that covered the coffin. The idea of such a transformation was often made when small holes apparently leading downward to the **coffin** lid appeared on the top of the grave.

MONGOLIA, VAMPIRES IN *See:* TIBET, VAMPIRES IN

MOON

Because the vampire is a nocturnal creature, one might expect it to have a special relationship to the moon, as **John Polidori** certainly assumed in his original vampire tale, **"The Vampyre,"** published in 1819. **Lord Ruthven,** the vampire, was killed in the course of the story. However, he was taken out to the pinnacle of a nearby hill so that his body could be exposed to the "first cold ray of the moon that rose after his death." The moon's rays revived the vampire. This idea of the moon's effect on a vampire was picked up by writers and dramatists who built on Polidori's tale through the first half of the nineteenth century.

James Malcolm Rymer followed Polidori's lead in *Varney the Vampyre,* and through the words of Chillingworth, a man wise in such matters, explained to his readers the nature of the vampire's resurrection. In the story Varney was shot, and mortally so, but Chillingworth warned:

> With regard to these vampyres, it is believed by those who are inclined to give credence to so dreadful a superstition, that they always endeavor to make their feast of blood, for the revival of their bodily powers, on some evening immediately preceding a full moon, because if any accident befalls them, such as, being shot, or otherwise killed or wounded, they can recover by lying down somewhere where the full moon's rays will fall upon them (Chapter 4).

In the next chapter Rymer vividly describes the effects of the moon:

As the moonbeams, in consequence of the luminary rising higher and higher in the heavens, came to touch the figure that lay extended on the rising ground, a perceptible movement took place in it. The limbs appeared to tremble, and although it did not rise up, the whole body gave signs of vitality.

Immediately afterward Varney arose and escaped from his pursuers.

Bram Stoker departed from this fictional convention. In *Dracula,* the moon was used for atmosphere, but possessed no supernatural qualities. In the first chapter, for example, the moonlight provided added emphasis to Dracula's command over the wolves. Later, in chapter 4, the three women who resided in **Castle Dracula** made their appearance in the dust dancing in the moonbeams. Subsequent authors of vampire fiction followed Stoker's lead; it was the deadly sun, not the moon (except as it was an important part of the nocturnal environment), that became a significant element of vampire lore. The moon became much more associated with **werewolves.** The idea of the moon reviving a vampire was not repeated in the movies until 1945, in *The Vampire's Ghost,* a movie loosely based on Polidori's ''The Vampyre.''

MORBIUS

Morbius, a Marvel Comics vampire character introduced in 1971, was the first original vampire introduced after revision of the Comics Code allowed vampires once again to appear in comic books, from which they had been banished in 1954. Michael Morbius, according to the story, was an outstanding biologist whose work had won him the Nobel Prize. He was engaged to be married. However, he had contracted a rare blood disease. As his condition worsened, he began to work on a cure. He developed a serum from vampire bat blood and treated himself with electric shock. His efforts finally stopped the effects of the disease, but he experienced unwanted side effects; he grew **fangs** and developed an intense thirst for blood, which led to his vampirizing of his best friend. He also developed some superpowers, including the standard heightened **strength** of vampires and **flying** ability because his bones became hollow.

Morbius was introduced in issue No. 101 of *Amazing Spiderman,* and his encounter with Spiderman launched a series of battles with various Marvel superheroes. He was able to survive the attempts of the Bestial Lizard and the Human Torch to stop him and then took on the X-Team in the pages of *Marvel Team-Up* (No. 3 and No. 4). In *Marvel Team-Up,* after defeating Iceman and the Avenging Angel, he was bested by Cyclops. In the X- Men laboratory he was treated by the X-Team scientist Professor X, but the experimental enzyme merely confirmed Morbius's status as the Living Vampire. Morbius quickly escaped to begin his many adventures, in most of which he fought villains more evil than himself while searching for ways to meet his need for blood without killing the innocent. Periodically he turned his attention to finding a cure for his condition.

In 1973 Morbius was established in the new Marvel magazine-size *Vampire Tales,* the first issue of which appeared in the fall. Then in February 1974, in issue No. 19, Morbius became the featured character of *Fear,* and for the next few years the Morbius stories appeared simultaneously in the two comics. *Vampire Tales* lasted eleven issues through June 1975, and *Fear* concluded its Morbius story with issue No. 31 in December 1975 with Morbius flying off to possible future adventures.

In 1976 his adventures resumed. He appeared in issue No. 15 of *Marvel Two-in-One* to fight The Thing. He squared off against **Blade the Vampire Slayer** in issue No. 8 of *Marvel Preview.* In 1980, in issue No. 38 of the *Spectacular Spider-Man,* Morbius was finally cured. He had drunk some of Spider-Man's radioactive blood and was then struck by lightning, which drained him of his vampiric powers. He later devised a serum that returned him to a normal human life. He was brought to trial for his multiple murders, but acquitted when judged insane. It seemed the end of the story, and Morbius faded into oblivion during the 1980s, especially after Marvel killed off all its vampires in December 1983.

After many years' absence, Morbius made a dramatic reappearance in November 1989 in issue No. 10 of *Dr. Strange: Sorcerer Supreme.* Issue No. 14 in February 1990 revealed the events of Morbius's missing years. After living normally for several years, he had gone on a vacation to New Orleans. One evening he met a beautiful woman named Marie and went home with her. He discovered that she was actually Marie Laveau, who had kept herself young with the blood of vampires. Since there were no more true vampires, she was aging again. She treated him with an intense but less than fatal electric shock, causing him to again become a vampire. He went on to battle Dr. Strange, who had accidently become the instrument allowing vampires to return to the real world.

In September 1992, with vampires returning and supernatural evil on the rise, those characters most capable of interacting with he supernatural were brought together in a new realm of the Marvel Universe. Those who were to oppose the supernatural were designated the **Midnight Sons.** They included old Marvel heroes such as Ghost Rider and Blade the Vampire Slayer. Morbius joined the Midnight Sons with the first issue of his own comic book, *Morbius, the Living Vampire.*

The initial adventure of Morbius and the other Midnight Sons set them against a union of evil entities led by **Lilith,** Queen of Evil and Mother of Demons. Their conflicts late in 1993 led to the demise of the Darkhold and The Nightstalkers, but Morbius continued his life on the edge of the world of good and evil, a reluctant vampire with a conscience and a blood thirst.

Sources:

Benton, Mike. *Horror Comics: The Illustrated History.* Dallas, TX: Taylor Publishing Company, 1991. 144 pp.
Fear. Nos. 20-31. New York: Marvel Comics, 1973-1974.
Ghost Rider and the Midnight Sons Magazine. 1, 1-. New York: Marvel Comics, 1993-.
Marvel Preview. Marvel Comics. No. 8. New York: Marvel Comics, Fall 1976.
Morbius, The Living Vampire. Nos. 1-. New York: Marvel Comics, 1992-.

MORMOLYKIAI See: GREECE, VAMPIRES IN

MOROI/MOROAICA See: ROMANIA, VAMPIRES IN

MORRIS, QUINCEY P.

Quincey P. Morris was one of the leading characters in *Dracula,* the 1897 novel by
Bram Stoker. Prior to the time of action covered by the novel, he had been a friend of
both **Arthur Holmwood** and **John Seward,** the three having been together in Korea,
and he and Holmwood having traveled together in South America and the South Seas.
Morris was the only American character in the novel, first appearing in chapter five
(along with Seward and Holmwood) as a suitor of **Lucy Westenra.** His desires for
Lucy lead to concern for her declining health and then commitment to the conspiracy
to destroy Dracula. He was first described in a letter from Lucy to her friend **Mina
Murray:**

> . . . He is such a nice fellow, an American from Texas, and he looks so young
> and so fresh, that it seems almost impossible that he has been so many places
> and has had such adventures... Mr. Morris doesn't always speak slang—that
> is to say he never does so to strangers or before them, for he is really well
> educated and has exquisite manners—but he found out that it amused me to
> hear him talk American slang, and when ever I was present, and there was no
> one to be shocked, he said such funny things.

He proposed to Lucy, but she was already engaged to Arthur Holmwood. She kissed
him, and he offered his friendship and departed. He reappeared later (chapter 12) at
Holmwood's request to check on Lucy's failing health (she had been bitten by
Dracula). He arrived just in time to donate his blood. In the subsequent discussion of
Lucy's condition, Morris, from his experience in South America, was able to
introduce the idea of a **vampire bat.** (Of course, his story of a big bat that could bring
down a cow was not factual; the several species of vampire bats are small, and no one
bat can drink enough to do more harm than mildly irritate a cow. Put in the mouth of
Morris, however, the speech served an important literary purpose, with Stoker tying
the bat and the vampire together in his plot.) **Van Helsing** later reinforce Morris's
statements.

Morris assumed the task of patrolling the outside of the house to stop any ''bat''
from reaching Lucy. Once Lucy died and it was determined that she had been
transformed into a vampire, Van Helsing recruited Morris to join a group of men who
set out to drive the prescribed stake through her heart. He was present for the driving
of the **stake,** but stepped outside as Van Helsing and Holmwood cut off her head and
stuffed the mouth with **garlic.** After this event he became an integral part of the effort
to kill Dracula. He joined the group as they entered **Carfax** to sanitize the earth upon

which Dracula slept. The four men then split into two groups, with Holmwood and Morris going to find Dracula's other hideaways in London.

Morris rejoined the other group as it prepared to track Dracula back to his castle in **Transylvania.** Morris arrived on horseback as everyone converged on the entrance to the castle. Dracula was carried in, resting in a box of his **native soil,** as the evening was fast approaching. When Dracula awakened, Morris and **Jonathan Harker** killed him. Morris plunged his Bowie knife into Dracula's heart as Harker decapitated him. Unfortunately, in the fight to reach Dracula's box, Morris was wounded, and a few minutes later he died. His last words to Mina were, "I am only too happy to have been of service!" Mina and Jonathan named their son after him.

As *Dracula* made its way from the novel to the stage to the screen, the character of Morris suffered greatly. As the novel was condensed, the Morris character was the first to be dropped. **Hamilton Deane** deleted him as a Texan from the British play and gave his name to a female character, ostensibly to create a part for a member of his theater company. However, Morris remained absent from the American play and from the several *Dracula* movies beginning with the **Bela Lugosi** version in 1931. He reappeared in *El Conde Dracula* (1970), Jesus Franco's Spanish version, but as a British nobleman replacing Arthur Holmwood, who did not appear. In the 1977 *Count Dracula,* Morris was also Lucy's fiancé, but as a staff person at the American embassy in London. Not until **Francis Ford Coppola**'s 1992 feature, *Bram Stoker's Dracula,* did Morris's character, as he appeared in the book, finally make an appearance. In recognition of his being slighted in the stage and screen production, one group of Dracula enthusiasts has formed the Quincey P. Morris Dracula Society. In addition; Mina Murray and Jonathan Harker's son, Quincey (named for Morris) was a leading character in Marvel Comics's *The Tomb of Dracula* in the 1970s.

MOUNTAIN ASH

In the third chapter of *Dracula,* while **Jonathan Harker** was trying to determine his situation, he asked rhetorically, "What meant the giving of the crucifix, of the garlic, of the wild rose, of the mountain rose?" The modern reader has come to know these four items as protective devices against vampires. Mountain ash is a member of the rose family and is also known in northern Europe and the British Isles as the rowan. **Bram Stoker** probably knew of the traditional use of the mountain ash as protection against witchcraft, in much the same manner as **hawthorn** was used throughout southern Europe. A rowan tree was often planted in churchyards and at the door of homesteads as a warning against evil spirits and was sometimes pruned so it became an arch over the barn door to protect the farm animals. It was particularly effective in conjunction with a red thread, and in the Scottish highlands women often used a piece of twisted red silk around their fingers in conjunction with a necklace of rowan berries. In **Scandinavia** it was also known as Thor's Helper, a designation derived from a story in which the tree helped him escape a flood caused by the Frost Giants.

Sources:

McNeil, F. Marian. *Scottish Folklore and Folk Belief.* Vol. I, *The Silver Bough.* Glasgow: William Maclellan, 1957, 1977. 220 pp.

Porteous, Alexander. *Forest Folklore, Mythology, and Romance.* London: George Allen & Unwin, 1928. 319 pp.

MULO *See:* GYPSIES, VAMPIRES AND THE

THE MUNSTERS

The Munsters emerged in 1964 as one of two new situation comedies in the fall television season featuring a cast of ''monstrous'' characters attempting to live as an otherwise normal family. Included in the Munster family were two vampires, Lily (played by Yvonne De Carlo) and Grandpa (Al Lewis), who in the course of the series was revealed to be none other than Count Dracula. The family was completed by the Frankensteinish Herman (Fred Gwynne) and the children, the wolfish Eddie (Butch Patrick) and the very ''normal'' Marilyn (Beverly Owens). Herman worked in a mortuary owned by classic horror actor **John Carradine.**

The Munsters ran for two seasons. It gave birth to a comic book from Gold Key that ran for 16 issues from January 1965 to January 1968. The original cast joined in a movie, *Munster! Go Home,* released in 1966, in which John Carradine assumed a different role as the family's butler. A second movie—*The Munsters' Revenge*—was made for television and aired February 27, 1981. It included the major stars—Fred Gwynne, Yvonne De Carlo, and Al Lewis. The series was revived for the 1988 season as *The Munsters Today,* starring John Shuck (Herman), Lee Meriweather (Lily), and Howard Morton (Grandpa). In spite of bad reviews by fans of the original series, its 72 episodes carried it into 1991.

Possibly the most vampiric of all *The Munsters* shows was the animated sequel *Mini-Munsters,* which played in 1973 for the *Saturday Superstar Movie* on ABC. The story concerned a Dracula-like relative sending two teenagers, Igor (a Frankenstein-like monster) and Lucretia (a vampire), to stay with the Munster family.

Originally, *The Munsters* ran opposite the ABC series *The Addams Family.* Both were popular in their original format and both have had numerous spin-offs in the form of movies, comic books, and other **paraphernalia.** The Munsters and the Addams tended to appeal to the same set of fans, and in recent years those fans have banded together in **The Munsters and Addams Family Fan Club.**

Sources:

Anchors, William E., Jr. "The Munsters." *Epi-log* 37 (December 1993): 36-43, 63.

Cox, Stephen. *The Munsters: Television's First Family of Fright.* Chicago: Contemporary Books, 1989. 174.

Jones, Stephen. *The Illustrated Vampire Movie Guide*. London: Titan Books, 193. 144 pp.
The Munsters. Nos. 1-16. New York: Gold Key Comics, 1965-1968.

THE MUNSTERS AND THE ADDAMS FAMILY FAN CLUB

The Munsters and The Addams Family Fan Club was founded in 1988 by Louis Wendruck for fans of *The Munsters* and *The Addams Family,* two popular television families of homey vampires and other friendly monsters. The club provides information about the television series, their movie spin-offs, and the stars who played family members. The club distributes *The Addams Family Original Soundtrack Music* album and tee-shirts for both the Addams and the Munsters, and it also assists members in obtaining the many other pieces of paraphernalia that have been produced featuring the Addams and the Munsters. The club has an annual convention and publishes a quarterly newsletter, *The Munsters and The Addams Family Reunion.*

Wendruck is also president of the **Dark Shadows Fan Club** and editor of *Dark Shadows Announcement.* The Dark Shadows Fan Club is independent of the larger *Dark Shadows* fan movement, and is to be distinguished from the **Dark Shadows Official Fan Club** and its affiliated local fan clubs (all of which have the blessing of Dan Curtis Productions, which owns and licenses the use of the trademarks relative to *Dark Shadows.*

The Munsters and The Addams Family Fan Club may be contacted at PO Box 69A04, West Hollywood, CA 90069.

Sources:

Van Hise, James. *Addams Family Revealed: An Unauthorized Look at America's Spookiest Family*. Las Vegas, NV: Pioneer Books, 1991. 157 pp.

MURRAY, MINA

Mina (short for Wilhelmina) Murray, one of the leading characters in **Bram Stoker**'s *Dracula,* made her first appearance in the book through correspondence between herself and her long-time friend **Lucy Westenra.** As with Lucy, Stoker said very little about Mina's physical appearance, but she was obviously an attractive young woman in her twenties. She was engaged to **Jonathan Harker,** who at the beginning of the novel had traveled to **Transylvania** to arrange for the sale of some property to Count Dracula. While she was awaiting his return, she joined Lucy in **Whitby** for a vacation together. The visit went well until Lucy began to sleepwalk. One night in the middle of the night, Mina found Lucy sleepwalking on the East Cliff and thought she saw someone with her. Taking Lucy home, she noticed that her friend had two small prick marks on her neck. Mina then had to worry about Lucy and about Jonathan, who was overdue from his visit to Transylvania and from whom no letter had arrived.

Finally, a letter concerning Harker arrived. He was in the Hospital of St. Joseph and St. Mary in Budapest recovering from his experiences in **Castle Dracula.** Mina dropped everything and went to Budapest, where she married Jonathan without further delay. She and Jonathan returned to England, where they learned of Lucy's death.

Abraham Van Helsing, who had been brought into Lucy's case as a consultant while Mina was in Romania, immediately engaged Mina in his search for information concerning the vampire that caused Lucy's death. Mina was interested in how Lucy's death and Jonathan's condition were related. She volunteered to transcribe Dr. **John Seward's** diary concerning the events leading to Lucy's death. She was present when Van Helsing organized the men to destroy Dracula. To Jonathan's relief, having completed the transcription work, Mina initially agreed to "hold back" and let the men do the work of actually killing Dracula.

However, Mina began to have the same symptoms as Lucy before her death. She grew pale and complained of fatigue. During her major encounter with Dracula, **mist** floated through the cracks in the door and filled her room. The mist formed a whirling cloud. Mina saw the two red eyes and white face she had seen while with Lucy. Meanwhile, as Mina's fatigue increased, the men went about the work of discovering the locations of Dracula's resting places.

The men finally realized that Dracula was attacking Mina and hurried to her room. Dracula had entered some moments earlier and, while Jonathan slept, told Mina that she was to become "flesh of my flesh; blood of my blood; kin of my kin; my bountiful wine-press for a while; and shall be later on my companion and my helper." He then opened a wound in his chest with his sharp **fingernails** and forced Mina to drink the blood. He pushed her aside and turned his attention to the men as they rushed into the room; they held him at bay with a **eucharistic wafer** and a **crucifix.** Dracula turned into mist and escaped. Mina had the marks of his teeth on her neck, and her own teeth had become more prominent, a sign that she was in the process of becoming a vampire. Van Helsing, wishing to protect her, touched her forehead with the wafer. Unexpectedly, it burned its impression into her forehead as if a branding iron.

Left behind while the men destroyed Dracula's resting places in London, Mina suggested that Van Helsing hypnotize her. In her hypnotic state, she revealed that Dracula had left England on a ship. Mina traveled with the men as they chased him to **Castle Dracula** for a final confrontation.

When the last encounter with Dracula began, Mina was en route to the castle with Van Helsing. When they arrived, Van Helsing drew a protective circle around Mina at the edge of which he placed pieces of the eucharistic host. Among the entities who tried, unsuccessfully, to invade the circle were the three **vampire brides** who lived in the castle. During the daylight hours, Mina remained in the circle while Van Helsing went into the castle to kill the three vampires, sanitize Dracula's tomb, and make the castle inhospitable to any ''undead.''

The next day Mina and Van Helsing made their way some distance from (but still in view of) the castle to a spot safe from wolves, and again Van Helsing drew a circle. From their protected cover, they saw Dracula approach in his box with a band of **Gypsies.** Close behind were the men in hot pursuit. In front of the castle Dracula was finally killed. The spot on Mina's forehead disappeared, and she and Jonathan returned to England.

MINA ON FILM AND STAGE: As the primary female character in *Dracula,* Mina generally had a prominent part in both stage and screen versions of the book. Only in the American version of the play by John Balderston did Mina disappear and have her character combined with Lucy. In the **Frank Langella** movie version, *Dracula (1979),* her role was reversed with that of Lucy. Winona Ryder played Mina in *Bram Stoker's Dracula,* the movie that most closely approximated Stoker's original story. Ryder's portrayal deviated from the book most clearly in the movie's subplot about her romantic interest in the youthful appearing Dracula.

MUSIC, VAMPIRE

More than a hundred vampire songs have appeared in contemporary music in the last decade, ranging from the superlative to the execrable. Such a spectrum of accomplishment is not surprising, because the same variation occurs in literature, film, and art. What is new and different is the sudden high concentration of rock and roll songs devoted to this subject. No other genre has managed that kind of output. (Perhaps the current vampire music trend can be attributed both to the conservative backlash in society and to the fact that rock and roll almost became establishment. When rock tunes began showing up in Muzak, the limits had to be tested further. The few avenues remaining in the antisocial realm were the occult, excessive vulgarity, and nonstandard, bizarre chord changes. Vampires as a musical topic was ripe for picking.)

THE VAMPIRE IN ROCK MUSIC: Vampire songs can be separated into five groups: those with obvious vampire lyrics, those obliquely vampiric, those allegedly vampiric, those in which vampires are mentioned, and those found on the soundtracks to vampire films. Obvious lyrics contain references to blood-drinking, the ''undead,'' nocturnal existence, famous vampires, or other vampire traits. There is no doubt in the listener's mind regarding the subject at hand. Oblique lyrics are metaphorical, hinting at nocturnal activities, a ''victim'' being drained, or predatory hunger for another person. Alleged lyrics involve vampires, identified through either the title or some other means; the nature of the music (for example thrash metal or hardcore punk) however, makes it impossible to decipher what is being sung. Songs in which vampires are mentioned have as their main focus something else, often sex, but make references to vampirism. Vampire film sound-tracks are often totally instrumental, but occasionally they include a song that falls into one of the other categories.

VAMPIRE MUSIC WITH OBVIOUS LYRICS: One of the earliest examples of vampire rock comes from the New York Rock and Roll Ensemble's 1972 album *New York Rock and Roll Ensemble* (Atco Records). Entitled "Gravedigger," the song wanders from the gravedigger's point of view to the female vampire's and back again. Other than this weakness, the narrative carries nicely, relating the gravedigger's fascination for the woman entombed: "Her lips are painted red/And it looks like she's been fed/And there's a smile upon her face . . . ."

Siouxsie and the Banshees were a product of England's late-1970s punk rock movement. Their angular music is filled with jarring images, and "We Hunger," from *Hyaena* (1984, Geffen Records), equates vampires with sucking leeches, rust, corrosion, and rotting seeds—at best a very mixed bag of metaphors. The song is quite direct, employing such phases as "belching foul breath," "your destructive kiss death" (Siouxsie often slams words together like dancers at a concert), and "the thirst from a vampire bite."

Concrete Blonde's 1990 album *bloodletting* contains not one but three vampire songs. The title cut, also known parenthetically as the Vampire Song, sounds as if it was influenced by **Anne Rice.** References to New Orleans, gardens at night, blood drunkenness, and killing run through the song. The chorus even states, "O you were a vampire and baby/I'm walking dead." Also on the *Bloodletting* album, "the Beast" compares love to a vampire and other creatures. Singer-songwriter Johnette Napolitano's dim view of romance is summed up in these lyrics: "Love is the leech, sucking you up/Love is a vampire, drunk on your blood/Love is the beast that will tear out your heart."

Although superficial, one of the cleverest of songs is "Bela Lugosi's Dead" by Bauhaus, from their *Teeny* album (Small Wonders Records, 1979). The song is a pastiche of verbal and musical images. Even if it hadn't been used in the opening segment of "The Hunger," it would still be a vampire song. Here we find black capes back on the rack, bats who have left the bell tower, and victims who have been bled. The opening line of the chorus, "Bela Lugosi's dead" is immediately followed by the repetitive "undead, undead, undead." Unfortunately the concept is not developed beyond these scant images. Lead singer Peter Murphy's deep and plaintive voice creates an eerie aura of otherworldliness that carries the song.

Shockmeister extraordinaire Alice Cooper, the **Bela Lugosi** of rock and roll, and the singer who virtually began an entire subset of rock and roll devoted to theatrical horror as a concert form, has recorded only two obvious vampire songs to date— "Fresh Blood" on the 1983 Warner Brothers album *Da Da,* and "Dangerous Tonight" on the 1991 Epic Records album *Hey Stoopid.* "Fresh Blood" works at an emotional level, with lyrics referring to "a sanguinary feast" and victims dying "of some anemia." Among the singer's victims are "showgirls, businessmen in suits in

ASTRO VAMPS, A GOTHIC BAND
PROJECTING A VAMPIRIC IMAGE.

the midnight rain . . . bad girls and cops on the beat . . . .'' A key line is ''just detained her and drained her on the spot.'' But the music is not up to Cooper's customarily creepy standard; instead, it rattles along like a skeleton trying to keep up at a dance. By contrast, ''Dangerous Tonight'' has a menacing blend of elements that add up to an effective threat, and it marked a resurgence for the Master of the Macabre. The music is high-energy heavy metal and the lyrics, ''Take another bite/it'll be alright/what's wrong will soon feel right/Dangerous tonight'' and ''Take another sip'' letting ''a little drip on your thigh,'' among others, provide a sensuous and snarling serenade.

By sheer weight of numbers, the heavy metal genre of rock and roll has contributed the most vampire songs to the market. On the Metal Blade label, the Houston group Helstar produced a 1989 album entitled *Nosferatu.* One doesn't find a more obvious title than this. *Nosferatu* is a virtual rock opera on **Frank Langella**'s version of ***Dracula*(1979).** For a speed metal band, Helstar manages some poignant acoustic passages. The songs are punctuated by sound bites of dialogue from the movie.

Helstar's best song is ''Harker's Tale,'' a thickly woven monologue that follows the original Dracula story only loosely. Harker warns the listener against ''the Prince of Hell,'' presenting gory details such as ''The host upon his forehead/Then I heard a hellish howl/As it burned into his flesh . . . .'' The throng assembled to kill Dracula is instead decimated: ''A sea of broken bodies marks the spot/Where he has been/The bloodless cadavers/Here sucked dry of their sins . . . .'' Helstar's ''Rhapsody in Black'' is a thickly textured statement from a vampire that declares, ''I am the dark/ That puts the light to shame'' and refers to dawn as ''the only enemy/That time has placed on me.''

Although uneven at times, Helstar clearly demonstrates poetic inspiration. In ''The Curse Has Passed Away'' the narrator crawls through ''halls of darkness'' with a stake to destroy the vampire, referred to as ''my feudal tyrant.'' We are provided the details lacking in so many other vampire songs: ''His body crumbled into dust/Then passed before my sight/Remaining only his cloak and ring by its side/A look of peace not seen before/Upon his face I saw last . . . .'' Although not syntactically correct, the lyrics are faithful in detail to **Bram Stoker**'s *Dracula.* In ''To Sleep, Per Chance to Scream'' (a pun on a Shakespearean line) there is the crackerjack line ''Eternal youth with one puncture.'' (Regarding Shakespeare, there is one bit of metaphoric language that occurs in vampire songs that may or may not be deliberately planted. In Shakespeare's time, ''to die'' meant sexual consummation. In rock lyrics, the verb ''fall'' is used in such a way that a similar inference can be drawn. In ''Suck It And See,'' Grim Reaper sings ''I hope she don't make me fall too soon. . .'' and in ''The Beast'' Concrete Blonde sings ''The monster wants out of you/Paws you and claws you/You try not to fall. . .'' Given the construction of the lines, almost no other interpretation is possible.)

Grim Reaper's ''Night of the Vampire,'' from their 1987 RCA album *Rock You to Hell,* works at the level of a visceral discovery that some bogeyman does exist after all: ''If you think you're safe at midnight/That's the last thing you could do/He'll be looking for that nightmare bite/He could be coming after you.'' The chorus, ''Night of the vampire, he's only looking for your life,'' misses all of the splendid menace available to the truly inspired.

Perhaps the penultimate vampire rock song is ''Blood Banquet,'' created by the ludicrously named Mighty Sphincter for their 1986 album *New Manson Family* on the Placebo label:

> I have existed for centuries
> Living in castles built of your fears
> and from behind this mortal mask
> I carry out this deadly task
> in order to revive my self
> I plunge into the stream of life
> that drains into the scarlet seas
> and holds the red wines of immortality

Here the vampiric singer summarizes his existence in eight lines. ''Living in castles built of your fears'' is psychologically insightful, and the last three lines, although they may be metaphorically ungainly, are at least consistently liquid. The singer/ guitarist Doug Clark's dark, rich vocals deliver the song with a delicate balance of ennui and menace.

VAMPIRE MUSIC WITH OBLIQUE LYRICS: Sting's 1985 "Moon Over Bourbon Street" (*Dream of the Blue Turtles,* A&M Records) was, according to the liner notes, inspired by Anne Rice's *Interview With the Vampire.* More coherent than most other songs in the genre, it is a first-person lament by a night prowler: "I pray everyday to be strong/For I know what I do must be wrong . . . ." The singer is eloquent on his affliction: "The brim of my hat hides the eye of a beast/I've the face of a sinner but the hands of a priest . . . ."

"Forget Me Not," from Bad English's eponymous 1989 Epic Records album, was a well-selected first single release from the band. This one says, "A thousand lifetimes long ago/We made a promise we would not let go/And so I come for you tonight/And we live again before we lose each other . . . ." The scanning is not precise, as in much rock music, but the imagery is vividly seductive. Aside from the vampiric flavor of the lyrics, veteran rocker John Waite's rendering of the song, full of angst and longing, contributes to its overall impact.

Probably Siouxsie and the Banshees' finest effort lyrically is "The Sweetest Chill," from the 1986 *Tinderbox* (Geffen Records). Here, a vampiric message may be gleaned from references such as "fingers like a fountain of needles/Shines along my spine/And rain down so divine." Siouxsie's "Night Shift," from 1981's *Ju Ju* (Polydor), is an awkward and oblique monologue from a male vampire ("a happy go lucky chap/Always dressed in black . . .") in what sounds like the local morgue. Once again the point of view wanders from one persona to another.

"Sick Things" by Alice Cooper (1973, *Billion Dollar Babies,* Warner Brothers) is more successful as a vampire song than his "Fresh Blood," although it is only obliquely vampiric. The lyrics refer to eating and biting, with an appetite presumably for the audience. When he sings, "I love you Things I see as much as you love me," Alice makes the declaration sound threatening. The song is about feeding off the sickness and derangement of the audience to inspire Alice to even more outlandish behavior and music. Similarly, "I Love the Dead" is more vampiric musically than "Fresh Blood."

"Blood and Roses" by the Smithereens (1986, *Especially for You,* Enigma) has more going for it vampirically than merely sharing the name of a Roger Vadim film. With lyrics like "I try to love but it comes out wrong/I try to live where I don't belong/ I close my eyes and I see blood and roses," the song evokes mental images of Phillinon and **"Carmilla"** and la Belle Dame sans Merci. The seductress in the song can fall in love and get married, but she can't change her nature enough to quite fit in.

ALLEGED VAMPIRE MUSIC: Alice Cooper's "I Love The Dead" (1973, *Billion Dollar Babies,* Warner Brothers) is a tour de force, opening with a vaguely oriental musical motif and dripping with menace: "I love the dead/Before they're cold . . . ." The song must be placed in the "alleged" vampire category because a good case

DRU, LEAD SINGER FOR POPULAR
GOTHIC BAND THIS ASCENSION.

could be made for it as a necrophiliac's rhapsody. Should we choose vampirism, the lines still apply: "While friends and lovers mourn your silly grave/I have other uses for you, darling . . . ." These two lines, central to the skimpy lyric, are not just sung, but delivered to us laden with innuendo. There is a smirking chuckle just before the word *silly,* and the second line is wrapped in multiple meanings, doubtlessly conglomerated from the purring threats of a hundred movie femmes fatales.

"Blood Lust" by Blood Feast, a thrash metal band, can be partially grasped, but "Vampire" is not so much sang as spat and screeched. The group plays at breakneck speed from beginning to end. If there is a point to either of these songs, most listeners will miss it.

MUSIC THAT MENTIONS VAMPIRES: Bobby "Boris" Pickett & The Crypt Kickers' "Monster Mash" (initially a number one single from 1962, currently available on *Elvira's Haunted Hits,* Rhino Records) was a comedy hit, sung in a Boris Karloff voice. It is a musical cartoon, taking off on the dance crazes of the time. Dracula is referred to three times in the song, lastly as a rival to "Boris": "Out from his coffin Drac's voice did ring/Seems like he was troubled by just one thing/He opened the lid and shook his fist and said/'What ever happened to my Transylvanian Twist'?''

Not quite so amusing is the Yugoslavian band Laibach's, cover version of the Rolling Stones's ''Sympathy for the Devil'' (1988, Restless/Mute Records). The first verse is sung in a vaguely eastern European accent mimicking Bela Lugosi, in a context in which the words could apply to a vampire as much as to Satan. Beyond that point the accent becomes Russian, appropriate to the ''Anastasia'' references, and the song takes on political overtones.

SONGS FROM VAMPIRE MOVIE SOUNDTRACKS: Most vampire movie soundtracks consist of loosely connected mood pieces, sometimes extremely tongue-in-cheek. For the most part, moviemakers relied on classical music performed by studio orchestras. ''Swan Lake'' for *Dracula* **(1931)** was the first such instance. The most widely known impression of the vampire—formally attired in evening clothes and elegant cape—arose from theater and movie producers' need to explain the music. Filmmakers thought that audiences would not understand the rationale for the music unless they either showed or alluded to where it came from. Hence, when **Tod Browning** made *Dracula* (1931), ''Swan Lake'' was established as the main song when Dracula and several of the other main characters spent a night at the ballet.

Innocent Blood provides comedic touches with its sound- track by concentrating on the music appropriate to the milieu: Italian East Coast Mafia. Several Frank Sinatra tunes well within the characters' interests and context are used. From ''I Got You Under My Skin'' to ''That Old Black Magic,'' the music provides a sensuous and lighthearted background to the often frenetic images.

''Good Times'' by INXS and Jimmy Barnes and ''People Are Strange'' by Echo and the Bunnymen (1987's are two selections from 1987's *The Lost Boys,* are two selections from one of the most popular vampire movies of the 1980s. The theme was one of youth and alienation for two brothers in the ''murder capital'' of the U.S. The is music theirs, full of hope and disaffection at the same time. ''(My Future's So Bright) I Gotta Wear Shades'' by Timbuk 3 (1988, *My Best Friend Is a Vampire*) is in the same youthful vein, but it takes a lighter approach because the movie is a light comedy.

The songs on the *Son of Dracula* (1974, Rapple Records) soundtrack have the bouncy sweetness that infected the popular music scene in the early 1970s. ''Without You'' and ''Jump into the Fire'' got considerable airplay given their origin on the soundtrack of a vampire film. ''Without You'' is a poignant song that laments life without a particular loved one. Harry Nilsson sings it, on the edge of weeping: ''I can't live/If living is without you,'' and ''No I can't forget this evening/Or your face as you were leaving . . . . You always smile but in your eyes your sorrow shows . . . .'' In the movie, Nilsson, as Count Downe, abdicates the throne of the Draculas in favor of his human love, Amber. Pop diva Mariah Carey released a new version of the song in 1994 that robbed the song of much of its original poignancy.

The soundtrack of *Dracula* (1979) bears the unmistakable mark of famous conductor John Williams. In several cases, selections could have been used in *Star Wars* (Williams' most famous movie score) with the same effect. Williams repeats the theme in several selections.

In literature, vampires are often romantic or at least adventurous beings. Their lives are far from ordinary. Rock and roll treatments, on the other hand, concentrate on the morbid, without much romance. Intense gore seems to be the thing that gets the most attention.

THE NEW GOTHIC MOVEMENT: A special slice of rock and roll is reserved for the gothic movement. Heir to the classic gothic tradition, mixed with elements from the psychedelic/flower child/rock music subcultures of the 1960s and 1970s, was the gothic counter-cultural movement that appeared in most urban centers of the West during the 1980s. The movement's origins can be traced to late 1970s musical groups in the United Kingdom. It certainly also had its direct precursors in such bands as Black Sabbath and the punk rock music of the 1970s. Possibly the most prominent of those groups was Bauhaus and the previously mentioned single, "Bela Lugosi's Dead," their most popular recording to date. Bauhaus was soon joined by such groups as Siouxsie and the Banshees, The Cult, The Cure, and The Sisters of Mercy. Together these bands created a variant music called gothic rock or death rock. A circuit of music clubs, most notably The Bat Cave in London, opened to provide a stage for their performances.

Gothic music, as all counter-cultural forms, articulated an explicit nonconformist stance vis-a-vis the dominant establishment. It opposed narrow sexual mores and traditional established religions. High priests, churches, and congregations were replaced with rock musicians, night clubs, and fans. The music celebrated the dark, shadowy side of life and had a distinct fascination with death. Its slow, driving sound was frequently described as melancholy, gloomy, even morbid. Those enthralled by the new gothic culture found the vampire the single most appropriate image for the movement. Both men and women dress in black. Men seem to be perpetuating vampiric images from **Anne Rice** novels, while women perpetuate what, at first glance, seems to be the persona of Morticia Addams of *The Addams Family*, **Vampira**, and **Elvira**, although some aim for a more Victorian funereal style or a modern vampish look. Vampires, blood and fangs, and bats fill the pages of gothic magazines, whether or not vampirism is discussed.

The movement was especially popular in the early 1980s when it spread to the European continent and throughout North America. By the middle of the decade, however, it showed a marked decline in England. Bauhaus disbanded in 1983, although some of its members reformed as Love & Rockets. Most of the clubs that had provided meeting places for gothic aficionados turned their attention to other new trends in popular music, and The Bat Cave closed. To keep the movement alive when the media announced its obituary, one gothic band, Nosferatu, founded **The Gothic Society** (136 Canterbury Rd., Harrow, Middlesex HA1 4PB, England) and the periodical *Grimoire*, which became the new center of a network of bands and fans.

Curve, Rosetta Stone, Mortal Coil, Wraith, and Slimelight joined Nosferatu as bands of the gothic scene.

Even as the movement was suffering in England, it was experiencing the early stages of its emergence in the United States. By 1990, a number of gothic bands traveled a circuit of clubs, and fans kept up with the movement through their own fanzines. *Propaganda* (PO Box 296, New Hyde Park, NY 11040) was the first of the gothic fanzines to hit the newsstands and offer national (and international) coverage to the emerging gothic movement. Founded by ''Propaganda Minister'' Fred H. Berger, *Propaganda* provided some structure for ''the Underground,'' as the new gothic subculture referred to itself. The magazine publicized many gothic bands and personalities and provided advertising space for both gothic records and the variety of clothing, jewelry, and paraphernalia demanded by devoted fans. More recently, it produced two gothic videos, *The Trilogy* and *Blood Countess*, the second based upon the life of **Elizabeth Bathory**.

In 1992, *Propaganda* was joined on the West Coast by the slick Los Angeles-based magazine *Ghastly*. The magazine is published by Nosferatu Productions (PO Box 3535, Hollywood, CA 90078) and edited by Tara and Jeremy Bai. More so than *Propaganda*, Nosferatu Productions markets the gothic subculture through a mail order catalog that includes gothic fanzines, compact disc (cd's) and cassettes, cosmetics, clothing, and even condoms. Nosferatu has also launched two additional periodicals: *The Oracle*, a monthly newsletter that updates readers on show dates and the latest releases on cd; and *The Cabala*, a fan networking journal.

The majority of large urban centers in the United States now have at least one nightclub that regularly features gothic music. Many clubs schedule gothic nights once or twice a week and devote other evenings to closely related music such as punk or industrial rock.

A large number of contemporary bands play gothic music. Some of the more well-known are Ministry, Shadow Project, Christian Death, This Ascension, The Shroud, and Death in June. Several bands have adopted specifically vampiric images, including Astro Vamps, Lestat, Neither/Neither World, London After Midnight, and Transvision Vamp. In addition, individual musicians have adopted a stage persona tieing them to the vampiric image. They include Eva Van Helsing of The Shroud and Vlad of Nosferatu. Toney Lestat of Wreckage claims to have met the real vampire **Lestat de Lioncourt**, the character featured in the vampire novels of Anne Rice. Toney Lestat adopted his name after Rice made the Lestat character famous.

BEYOND ROCK AND ROLL: In non-rock and roll genres, there are scant pickings. Perhaps the only modern folk song about vampires is Claudia Schmidt's ''Vampire,'' from *Midwestern Heart* (Flying Fish Records, 1981). It says: ''Far below the world is lying unaware/My soul is crying Vampire . . . this is my song.'' A reasonably good couplet can be found in the song's last verse: ''Life's not life if you must lose it/ Death's not death if you refuse it . . .''

THE VAMPIRE IN CLASSICAL MUSIC: Classical music was, from its beginnings, devoted to church-related themes. Until our modern age, musicians were in the employ of church or king, beholden to royal sponsors, and their duties would have precluded experimentation. Gradually, over a period of many years, mainstream classical music lost most of its religious edge. During the early nineteenth century, at the height of the Romantic movement's fascination with the vampire, one German musician, **Heinrich August Marschner**, wrote a vampire opera, *Der Vampyr* (1829), one of only two known, the other being *Lamia*, by August Enna, first performed in 1899 in Brussels, Belgium.

The nineteenth century saw the development of the "tone poem," which is programmatic in content—there is a subject depicted by the music—though it was never as popular a form as the symphony or the concerto. Among programmatic works, a few dark subjects emerged, but only a few. Hector Berlioz's "Symphony Fantastique" (1830) concludes with a witches' sabbath. Much of Berlioz's work was a radical breakthrough for its time. Franz Liszt's "Mephisto Waltz" (1861) is based on a simple folktale in which the devil grabs a violin at a village dance and plays seductive melodies. In Saint Saens' "Danse Macabre" (1874) death plays the violin as skeletons dance at midnight. The revels end at dawn. Modest Mussorgsky's "Night on Bare Mountain" (1877) evokes Halloween night, when evil spirits are free to roam (immortalized in Walt Disney's animated film *Fantasia*). The mountain in question is Mt. Triglav, near Kiev in the Soviet Union; the action occurring on St. John's Eve (or Midsummer Eve, June 23rd) and Mussorgsky explained it as describing "a subterranean din of unearthly voices." Once again, the evil celebration disperses when dawn breaks.

—Susan R. Kagan

MYANMAR, VAMPIRES IN

Myanmar, known until 1989 as Burma, is a Southeast Asian country bounded by **India** and Bangladesh on the west, **China** on the north, and Laos and Cambodia on the east. The Myanmars settled the land in the ninth century and over the next century established an independent country. It has been variously part of the Chinese, British, and Japanese Empires; it emerged as an independent nation following World War II. The Myanmars are primarily Buddhist and tend to cremate their dead; thus, they do not have a strong tradition of revenants. The culture does have a large pantheon of deities and supernatural entities, however, along with a rich tradition of ghosts and demonic beings.

The most malevolent of the ghosts, the *thaye* and *tasei,* were beings that, because of their evil earthly life, were condemned to their disembodied state until they had worked out their karmic difficulties and were eventually reborn into another body. These disembodied ghosts, at times, took on a kind of visible materiality. When seen, they were tall, dark, and possessed huge ears, a large tongue, and tusklike teeth. They resided near villages at the local cemeteries. On occasion they assumed characteristics of vampires and **ghoul**s and fed on corpses or went into the village to attack living people. More frequently, they were seen as the cause of minor illnesses. They entered town either at high noon or after dark.

In the folklore, protection from ghosts was provided by a *lehpwe,* an amulet for a variety of purposes. One such amulet consisted of a drawing of an elephant made from the letters of the Myanmar alphabet. Popular in earlier centuries was tattooing of the body in the area between the navel and the knee. There were also specific rituals to banish ghosts from a village, both brief ones for individual use and longer ones for the community.

Sources:

Spiro, Melford E. *Burmese Supernaturalism.* Philadelphia: Institute for the Study of Human Issues, 1978. 300 pp.

N

NACHTZEHRER See: GERMANY, VAMPIRES IN

NAME, THE VAMPIRE'S

In his story **"Carmilla"**, author **Sheridan Le Fanu** assigned a unique characteristic to vampires: they must choose a name that, "if not his or her real one, should at least reproduce, without the omission or addition of a single letter, those, as we say, anagrammatically, which compose it." Carmilla was originally named Millarca and was also known as Mircalla. This characteristic was unique to Le Fanu's vampire.

Although others have not employed Le Fanu's stipulation concerning the vampire's name, noted in sequels to *Dracula,* the leading character frequently called himself Count (or Dr. or Mr.) "Alucard," Dracula's name spelled backward, such as in *Son of Dracula* (1943). Other variations of Dracula included Dr. Aluca, or, in the Dell *Dracula* comic book, *Al U. Card.*

Sources:

Le Fanu, Sheridan. "Carmilla." 1872. Reprinted in Les Shepard, ed. *The Dracula Book of Great Vampire Stories.* New York: Jove, 1978, pp. 15-99.

NATIVE SOIL

In the folklore of Eastern Europe, vampires were believed to be the revived body of a recently deceased member of the community. They resided in their graves at the local graveyard. They were commonly surrounded by their native soil, but no special mention was made of it. Nor was there mention of native soil in the early vampire fiction, such as **John Polidori**'s, **"The Vampyre"**; *Varney the Vampyre;* or

Sheridan Le Fanu's, "**Carmilla**". The idea of a need for native soil came from the imagination of **Bram Stoker**.

As a desperate **Jonathan Harker** began to explore **Castle Dracula**, he discovered the Count laying in a box filled with newly dug earth; other boxes of soil were nearby. Harker returned to his room in great fear. Later, he again went to the room with the box and discovered **Dracula** bloated with blood from a recent feeding. For a second time Harker was unable to take decisive action and the boxes, with the vampire in one of them, were shipped to England. After landing in England, Dracula retrieved the boxes and had them sent to a number of locations in the greater London area. Vampire hunter **Abraham Van Helsing** discovered that Dracula needed the native soil as his resting place, and that attacking his resting place was an effective means of destroying him. Of the 50 boxes, 49 were located and filled with **eucharistic wafers**, thus making them inhospitable to the vampire. Dracula escaped in the last box and returned to **Transylvania**, where he was later killed.

The transportation of Dracula's native soil to England also served a useful purpose in what many critics saw as an underlying theme in *Dracula*—the fear that existed in civilized Englishmen (Stoker's first audience) concerning the invasion of their society by representatives of the "uncivilized" cultures they had conquered. Stephen D. Arata spoke of this fear of reverse colonization—a fear prominent in late nineteenth century British fiction. Thus, one could view Van Helsing's gathering of the men to fight Dracula as the organization of an army, called to defend home and hearth, that launched an attack on foreign soil in the form of the 50 boxes of earth.

In spite of these possible meanings of the native soil in *Dracula*, later writers saw it more narrowly as a necessary attribute/limitation on the vampire. Mystically, the vampire drew strength from it. Many contemporary writers such as **Anne Rice** simply dropped the idea; it limited the mobility of vampires too much. Others, however, allowed a more literal reading of the Dracula myth to influence their development of a new variation of the myth. **Chelsea Quinn Yarbro** developed the most unique variation of the native soil myth. Her hero **St. Germain** had special shoes with hollow heels where native soil was placed. Thus he was in constant touch with that vivifying element.

Sources:

Arata, Stephen D. "The Occidental Tourist: Dracula and the Anxiety of Reverse Colonization." *Victorian Studies* 33, 4 (Summer 1990): 621-45.

Senf, Carol A. *The Vampire in Nineteenth Century English Literature.* Bowling Green, OH: Bowling Green State University Popular Press, 1988. 204 pp.

Yarbro, Chelsea Quinn. *Hotel Transylvania.* New York: St. Martin's Press, 1979. Reprint. New York: New American Library, 1979. 408 pp.

NECROMANCY

Abraham Van Helsing, the wise vampire expert in **Bram Stoker**'s novel *Dracula* noted, in his halting English, that vampires ". . . have still the aids of necromancy, which is, as his etymology imply, the divination by the dead, and all the dead that he can come nigh to are for him to command.'' Necromancy was a form of divining the future through the use of the dead, most specifically dead bodies. Necromancy was specifically condemned in the Jewish Bible (Deuteronomy 18:11), though it is not altogether clear what form was being practiced. It most likely involved opening the dead body and doing a psychic reading from the internal organs in much the same way that animal entrails, or other more mundane objects such as tea leaves, have been used throughout the ages.

However, by Stoker's time, the term necromancy referred specifically to calling forth the dead from the grave to obtain otherwise unavailable information, especially about the future. From the Middle Ages to the present, artists have produced drawings of such necromanic activity. Necromancy involved a corpse, but was also seen as communication with the spirit/soul of the dead person, which appeared before the magician in a ghostly but bodily form—what theosophists termed the astral body.

In the mid-nineteenth century, the United States, England, and much of continental Europe were swept by the movement called Spiritualism. Spiritualism was built around the practice of mediumship, the communication with the spirits of the dead. Spiritualism was several steps removed from traditional necromancy, however, although its practitioners were called necromancers by many religious critics. The identification of Spiritualism and necromancy was common in Stoker's time.

Sources:

Cavendish, Richard. *The Black Arts.* New York: G. P. Putnam's Sons, 1967. 373 pp.
de Givry, Emil Grillot. *Picture Museum of Sorcery, Magic and Alchemy.* New Hyde Park, NY: University Books, 1963. 395 pp.

NEFARIOUS

Nefarious is a vampire fanzine first issued in January 1993. It is edited by its founder Rosey Lettich, who has had an interest in vampires since her childhood. Each issue contains art, poetry, short stories, and articles about vampires. Subscriptions may be obtained from *Nefarious,* c/o Rosey Lettich, 1804 Academy St., Sumner, WA 98390.

NEPAL, VAMPIRES IN *See:* TIBET, VAMPIRES IN

NEW ENGLAND DARK SHADOWS SOCIETY

The New England Dark Shadows Society was founded in the early 1990s by Ron Janick, who currently leads it. The Society holds monthly meetings at which *Dark Shadows* videos are screened followed by discussions related to *Dark Shadows.* Also among its activities is an annual visit to Seaview Terrace in Newport, Rhode Island.

The house was used for exterior shots of Collinwood, the Collins family home, in the 1966-1971 television series. The society publishes a fanzine titled *Widow's Hill Quarterly*. It may be contacted at PO Box 6023, Boston, MA 02209.

THE NIGHT STALKER

The Night Stalker was a highly successful made-for-television vampire movie produced by **Dan Curtis** in the wake of his successful vampire-oriented soap opera, ***Dark Shadows***. The story concerned a luckless reporter, Carl Kolchak, (Darren McGavin) who encountered a vampire named Janos Skorzeny (Barry Atwater) who was killing showgirls in Las Vegas. He tried to convince his editor and the police of the vampiric nature of the killer, but in their disbelief was left to confront the bloodsucker by himself. The show was notable in that it received the highest rating of any made-for-television movie to that date and led to *The Night Stalker* television series, in which Kolchak tracked down a variety of creatures of the night. **Richard Matheson** wrote the screenplay for the show, which aired January 11, 1972 on ABC.

◄

DARREN MCGAVIN AS *THE NIGHT STALKER.*

The original novel by Jeff Rice, upon which the movie was based, was published in 1974.

Sources:

Rice, Jeff. *The Night Stalker*. New York: Pocket Books, 1974. 192 pp.

NIGHTLORE

Nightlore is a quarterly fanzine dedicated to the exploration of all aspects of the vampire legend. It features short fiction, poetry, and artwork. The first issue, published at the beginning of 1994, was put together by editor Trevor Elmore and art director Mary Elmore. For information on subscriptions write *Nightlore,* PO Box 81482, Mobile, AL 36689.

NJETOP See: POLAND, VAMPIRES IN

NODIER, JEAN CHARLES EMMANUEL (1780-1844)

Jean Charles Emmanuel Nodier, a dramatist who introduced the vampire theme to the French stage, was born on April 29, 1780, in Basancon, France. As a young man he began his writing career and became politically involved. In 1818, Nodier settled in Paris where he remained for the rest of his life. That same year, Jean Shogar, his first novel, was published. In Paris he became associated with several authors who were exploring what, in the post-Freudian world, would be known as the subconscious. His literary works began to explore the world of dreams, and included some attention to the nightmare. The larger movement would become known as the Romantic Movement and was seen as a distinct reaction to the limitations of the rationalism typified by Voltaire and his colleagues of the previous generation.

Nodier had just settled into his life in Paris when, in April 1819, **John Polidori**'s short story **"The Vampyre,"** appeared in the *New Monthly Magazine*. The story attracted considerable attention, in part because of its initial attribution to **Lord Byron**. Nodier was asked to write a review of it. He saw in the tale the expression of a widespread need in his generation to relieve its boredom through the experience of the outrageous and fantastic. The review was the first manifestation of a love-hate relationship with the vampire. Although Nodier seemed fascinated with it, he also saw a need, as an up-and-coming leader in Parisian literary and intellectual circles, to show a certain disdain. He did recognize its importance and termed the legend of the vampire ''the most important of all our superstitions.'' In an 1819 article, he called his readers' attention to the stories of people who confessed to being vampires and doing horrible things during their sleeping hours.

In 1820, his colleague Cyprien Bérard's two-volume sequel to "The Vampire," *Lord Ruthven ou Les Vampires,* was published anonymously but included an introductory article by Nodier. Many then assumed that Nodier had written both Lord Ruthven tales. After some investigation, Bérard's authorship was discovered. Meanwhile, Nodier was at work on his own vampire production, a stage melodrama called *Le Vampire*, (Pierre Francios Carmouche and Achille de Jouffroy collaborated on the piece). In *Le Vampire,* Nodier presented his own interpretation of **Lord Ruthven**, the lead character in Polidori's tale.

Ruthven was introduced as the hero who had saved the life of Sir Aubrey. Aubrey believed him dead, but when Ruthven arrived on the scene to marry Malvina, Aubrey's sister, he was welcomed. Meanwhile, Ruthven was shot while attending the wedding feast of Lovette and Edgar after Edgar had been angered at Ruthven's attempts to seduce his wife-to-be. Again, Aubrey thought Ruthven was dying and swore not to tell Malvina about his actions. As Aubrey was about to tell Malvina about her fiance's death, Ruthven suddenly appeared and reminded Aubrey of his oath. Aubrey was momentarily lost in the conflict between his duty and his oath, and Ruthven moved on to the church with his prospective bride, Malvina. Ruthven was foiled only in the last moment when Aubrey came to his senses and interrupted the service.

Le Vampire opened on June 13, 1819, at the Theatre de la Porte-Saint-Martin. Despite mixed reviews, some by his political detractors, Nodier's drama was an immediate success. The text of the play was soon published and also found a popular audience. In the wake of the immense audience reaction, two other vampire plays soon opened at competing theatres—as did several comical and satirical plays lampooning it. *Le Vampire* had a long and successful run; in 1823, it was revived for a second long run with the same stars, M. Phillipe and Madame Dorval. **Alexandre Dumas** attended the revival. He included a lengthy account of the performance in his memoirs, and the play would later inspire his own vampire drama in the 1850s.

Nodier returned to the subjects of nightmares and vampires in his opium-inspired 1821 story, *Smarra; ou, Les Demons de la Nuit.* Opium, he believed, provided a gate to another world—the realm of dreams and nightmares. *Smarra* told the story of Lorenzo, who experienced an encounter with a vampire. However, the vampire was not Lord Ruthven, the almost human creature who mingled in society and delighted in destroying others, but a more spirit like creature of the dream world.

Among Nodier's Paris acquaintances in the early 1820s was the youthful Victor Hugo, who published his first novel, a gothic horror story titled *Hans de'Islande*, in 1823. *Hans de'Islande* (*Hans of Iceland*) featured a central character who consumed the blood of his victims, but did so by gathering and then drinking the blood in a skull as an act of revenge. Although Nodier tried to validate the horror fantasy realm as a reasonable one for a neophyte writer to explore, Hugo explicitedly denounced *Le Vampire* in a review of the play's opening. Nodier had the opportunity to review *Hans de'Islande* and gave it a sympathetic review, calling attention to Hugo's latent talent.

In 1824, in recognition of his work (especially that devoted to the vampire theme), Nodier was appointed curator of the Bibliotheque de l'Arsenal, one of Paris's outstanding libraries. He later founded a salon where the literary world gathered and he authored a number of works, the best being his many short stories that explored the fantasy world of dreams, both good and bad. A 13-volume collected work was published during the years 1832-1841. In 1833, he was elected to the French Academy. He died January 27, 1844.

Throughout the nineteenth century, many writers were inspired by Nodier's fantastic tales and he eventually found a new audience in the French surrealists. Recently, *Le Vampire* and other of Nodier's dramatic works were reprinted in the "Textes Littéraires Francais" series.

Sources:

Nelson, Hilda. *Charles Nodier.* New York: Twayne Publishers, 1972. 188 pp.

Nodier, Charles. *Le Vampire.* Edition critique par Ginette Picat-Guinoiseau. Geneva: Librairie Droz S. A., 1990. 255 pp.

Oliver, A. Richard. *Charles Nodier: Pilot of Romanticism.* Syracuse, NY: Syracuse University Press, 1964. 276 pp.

Pavicevic, Mylena. *Charles Nodier et le Theme du Vampire.* Ottawa, ON: Biblioteque Nationale du Canada, 1988.

NORA *See:* HUNGARY, VAMPIRES IN

NORWAY, VAMPIRES IN *See:* SCANDINAVIA, VAMPIRES IN

NOSFERATU

Nosferatu is a modern word derived from Old Slavonic word, **nosufur-atu,* borrowed from the Greek *nosophoros,* a "plague carrier". Vampires were associated in the popular mind with the spread of disease (such as) tuberculosis whose cause was otherwise unknown) and by extension with the idea of spreading the infection of vampirism through its bite. Though it has been in use in Romania for several centuries, it is not found in Romanian dictionaries. It was originally a technical term in the old Slavonic that filtered into common speech. It has erroneously been reported to mean "undead," a concept developed by **Bram Stoker** for *Dracula*, and elsewhere as a reference to the Devil. It appears to have entered literature through the popular travelogue of Emily Gerard's *The Land Beyond the Forest* (1885) in which she said, "More decidedly evil is the *nosferatu,* or vampire, in which every Roumanian peasant believes as he does in heaven or hell." From Gerard, Stoker picked up the term for *Dracula*. In his famous determinative speech on the vampire in chapter 18, **Abraham Van Helsing** said, "The *nosferatu* do not die like the bee when he stings once. He is only stronger; and being stronger, have yet more power to work evil." The term, though used by Stoker, is not prominent.

The term first gained real prominence when it was used by Freidrich Wilhelm Murnau in his attempt to create a disguised version of *Dracula* for the screen. Murnau's film, ***Nosferatu, Eine Symphonie des Garuens***, made the term part of the popular language about vampires, especially after its rediscovery in the 1960s and the new release in 1972. Over the last several decades', it has commonly appeared in novels and films as a term synonymous with the vampire. In his two books about vampires, **Leonard Wolf** relied on Gerard, repeated her mistakes, and then contributed one of his own when he said in his *The Annotated Dracula* that *nosferatu* was a Romanian word meaning ''not dead.''

Sources:

Gerard, Emily. *The Land Beyond the Forest.* 1885. 2 vols. Edinburgh & London: Will Blackwood & Sons, 1888.

Senn, Harry A. *Were-Wolf and Vampire in Romania*. New York: Columbia University Press, 1982. 148 pp.

Stoker, Bram. *The Annotated Dracula.* Ed. by Leonard Wolf. New York: Clarkson N. Porter, 1974. Reprint. New York: Ballantine, 1976. 362 pp.

Wolf, Leonard. *A Dream of Dracula: In Search of the Living Dead.* Boston, MA: Little Brown, 1972. Reprint. New York: Popular Library, 1977. 326 pp.

NOSFERATU, EINE SYMPHONIE DES GARUENS

The earliest surviving film based on ***Dracula*** is *Nosferatu, Eine Symphonie des Garuens,* an unauthorized 1922 adaptation of **Bram Stoker**'s novel by Prana-Film, a German company founded in 1921. The movie was the only finished product of the company. One of the company's co-directors, Albin Grau, was a spiritualist and familiar with *Dracula.* He saw the book's possibilities for presentation as a powerful motion picture. Grau hired Freidrich Wilhelm Murnau as director and Henrik Galeen as screenwriter.

Murnau and Galeen proceeded to make a very loose adaptation of *Dracula.* The title was changed to *Nosferatu,* a term derived from an Old Slavonic word, *nosufuratu,* a word borrowed from the Greek and tied to the concept of carrying a plaque. The location for the latter part of the play was changed to Bremen, Germany, and set in 1838, the year of an actual outbreak of the plague in that city. The Dracula character's appearance was altered to appear rodent-like, and his persona tied to the rats who gathered in greta numbers in Bremen when he arrived.

In the Screenplay, Murnau made a variety of additional changes, including the name of all of the leading characters. Dracula was transformed into **Graf Orlock**, played by Max Schreck. Orlock was developed into a monstrous figure with exaggerated features—a bald head, long, claw-like **fingernails**. His pair of vampire **fangs**, rather than being elongated canines, protruded from the very front of his mouth, like a rat's teeth. He walked with a slow labored gait. He was closer to the vampire of Eastern European folklore than Stoker's *Dracula,* but his distinct appearance meant that he was unable to easily move among normal society in the manner of Dracula. Thus, Orlock became, to some extent, a very different character.

In *Nosferatu* **Jonathan Harker** (renamed Waldemar Hutter and played by Gustav von Wangenheim) left his wife **Mina Murray** (renamed Ellen Hutter and played by Greta Schroeder-Matray) to travel to **Transylvania** to conduct the sale of a house next door to their home in Germany. Hutter was taken to a bridge and left there. Upon crossing the bridge, it was as if he had entered a new world. A coach with a mysterious driver met him to take him to Orlock's castle. In his bedroom at Orlock's castle, Hutter was attacked by Orlock, while back in Bremen Ellen simultaneously cried out Hutter's name. The next day, Hutter discovered Orlock's coffin, but it was too late—the Count was already on his way to Germany.

While Orlock traveled to Germany, the major characters (soon to assemble in Bremen) were shown acting independently of each other. First, Hutter escaped but was hospitalized. Hutter's boss, **R. N. Renfield** (renamed Knock, played by Alexander Granach), went mad and was confined to an asylum. Professor **Abraham Van Helsing** (renamed Bulwar, played by John Gottow) experimented in his laboratory with meat-eating plants. Orlock killed the crew on the ship that was carrying him to Bremen.

Upon the count's arrival in Bremen, a plague broke out in the city caused by the rats Orlock controlled. Hutter arrived with a book he had taken from the castle. It suggested that the way to defeat a vampire was through the sacrifice of a virtuous woman who allowed the vampire to remain with her until dawn. In the end, Orlock attached himself to Ellen's neck and stayed until the **sunlight** destroyed him. Ellen died from the sacrifice, and immediately the plague abated.

LATER CONTROVERSY: *Nosferatu, Eine Symphonie des Garuens* premiered in the Marble Gardens of the Berlin Zoological Gardens in March, 1922. The movie received good reviews initially. However, Prana-Films was financially unstable and unpaid creditors soon asserted themselves. Several weeks later, Florence Stoker, the widow of Bram Stoker, received a copy of the announcement of the film's premier. She immediately joined the British Incorporated Society of Authors and turned to it for assistance. Because Prana-Films had neglected either to ask permission to use her late husband's book or to pay her for using it, the society represented her. It presented the matter to its German lawyer. By June, the company was in receivership and it was clear that no money would result from pursuing the case. However, the society continued to press the matter because of its implications for later cases.

The case with the receivers, Deutsch-Amerikansch Film Union, dragged on for several years. Florence Stoker asked for the destruction of all copies of the film. The matter was finally settled in July 1925, when all copies owned by the German receivers were destroyed. However, in October of that year, she was contacted by a new organization in England. The Film Society solicited her support for its private screenings of "classic" movies. On its first list was *Nosferatu* by Murnau. She now had a dispute with the society, which initially refused to cancel its showing or tell her where they had obtained a copy of the film.

In 1928, **Universal Pictures** purchased the film rights of *Dracula*. As owners of the film rights, they then granted the Film Society the privilege of showing *Nosferatu*.

SCENE FROM *NOSFERATU, EINE SYMPHONIE DES GARUENS.*

Florence Stoker protested, and in 1929, the Film Society turned over its copy to her for destruction. Later that year, copies appeared in the United States in New York and Detroit under the title *Nosferatu the Vampire*. In 1930, these copies were turned over to Universal to also be destroyed.

After Florence Stoker's death in 1937, various versions of the film became available, though there was little demand for it. In the 1960s, a condensed version was aired on television as part of *Silents Please,* a show based on old silent movies. In this version, the characters' names were changed back to those in the Stoker novel and the name of the movie was changed to *Dracula.* This version was then released by Entertainment Films under the title *Terror of Dracula.* In 1972, Blackhawk Films released the original film to the collectors' market under the title *Nosferatu the Vampire* and the *Silents Please* version as *Dracula.* In spite of the destruction of most of the copies of the original *Nosferatu,* one copy did survive, and a restored version of the film was finally screened in 1984 at the Berlin Film Festival and has since become commonly available.

In 1979, a remake of *Nosferatu* was produced. *Nosferatu: The Vampyre* featured Klaus Kinski in the title role. The new movie was written, produced, and directed by Werner Herzog. Although it kept the distinctive aspects of the original storyline, it more clearly acknowledged its basis as a version of *Dracula,* in part by using the names of the characters in Stoker's novel.

Nosferatu: The Vampyre was one of three important vampire movies released in 1979. The other two were *Love at First Bite*, the Dracula spoof with George Hamilton, and the **Frank Langella** version of ***Dracula* (1979).** The movie inspired a novel based on the screenplay, and a phonographic recording of the movie soundtrack was issued.

Sources:

Glut, Don. *The Dracula Book.* Metuchen, NJ: Scarecrow Press, 1975. 388 pp.

Skal, David J. *Hollywood Gothic: The Tangled Web of Dracula from Novel to Stage to Screen.* New York: W. W. Norton & Company, 1990. 242 pp.

Nox

Nox, subtitled ''a journal of the night,'' is a periodical that explores the darker realities of human existence. It was founded in 1993 by Loretta M. Accardo. While not exclusively oriented on vampires, vampires are among the dominant subjects of the art, fiction, poetry, and articles included in each issue. *Nox* also includes reviews of vampire related books, drama, and musical groups.

Nox can be contacted at PO Box 2467, Grand Central Station, New York, NY 10163-2467.

O

OBAYIFO *See:* AFRICA, VAMPIRES IN

OLD HOUSE PUBLISHING

Old House Publishing is a ***Dark Shadows*** publishing concern founded in 1978 by Dale Clark. That same year, through Old House, Clark started *Inside the Old House*, a *Dark Shadows* fanzine. Each issue includes fan fiction, poetry, artwork, biographies of *Dark Shadows* characters, discussions of controversies within the *Dark Shadows* community, a fan letter column, and classified ads of *Dark Shadows* **paraphernalia**. Clark, a long-time *Dark Shadows* fan, is also the author of five volumes of the *Dark Shadows Questions and Answers Book* and several *Dark Shadows* novels: *Resolutions in Time, Reunion, Retribution,* and *Revelations.* Clark was also one of the founders of **Dark Shadows Festival**, the organization that currently sponsors the annual *Dark Shadows* national fan gatherings.

Inside the Old House and Old House Publishing can be contacted c/o Dale Clark, 11518 Desdemona Dr., Dallas, TX 75228.

Sources:

Clark, Dale. *Dark Shadows Questions and Answers.* 5 vols. Dallas: Old House Publishing, 1990-93.
———. *Resolutions in Time.* Temple City, CA: Pentagram Press, 1983. 66 pp.
———. *Retribution.* Dallas: Old House Publishing, 1992. 88 pp.

—. *Reunion*. Dallas: Old House Publishing, 1991. 98 pp
—. *Revelations*. Dallas: Old House Publishing, 1993.

OLDMAN, GARY (1958-)

Gary Oldman, the actor who portrayed the title role in **Francis Ford Coppola**'s production of *Bram Stoker's Dracula*, was born in London, England. His dramatic career began at age 17 when he applied for a position at a theatre near his home. After hearing him read a passage from Shakespeare, the theatre's director assumed a mentor's role for Oldman. Once he broke into movies, Oldman quickly became known within the professional community for his ability and the wide range of characters he portrayed. He played Sid Vicious in *Sid and Nancy*; Joe Orton in *Prick Up Your Ears*; and Lee Harvey Oswald in Oliver Stone's *JFK*.

The role of Dracula allowed Oldman to show the broad range of his acting abilities, as he had to portray the variant personas into which Dracula transformed. He was first Prince **Vlad the Impaler**, the young warrior who won the war but, in a nasty twist of fate, lost his love. He was then the aged nobleman, the undead ruler of **Castle Dracula**. Once in England, Dracula's animal persona came to the fore, first as a monstrous wolflike creature (harking back to the identification of vampires and **werewolves** in Slavic folklore) that attacked **Lucy Westenra,** then as a batlike creature that opposed the men united against him. Meanwhile, he periodically reappeared as the handsome young suitor of **Mina Murray** that vied for her love until she married **Jonathan Harker**. The very nature of the part prevented Oldman from being typecast in the role.

Sources:

Rohrer, Trish Deitch. "Gary Oldman." *Entertainment Weekly* No. 145 (November 20, 1992): 32-34.

ONYX: THE "LITERARY" VAMPIRE MAGAZINE

Onyx: The "Literary" Vampire Magazine was started in 1991 by Mark Williams (publisher), Deanna Riddle (editor), and Ron White (artist). The magazine is

GARY OLDMAN AS DRACULA IN *BRAM STOKER'S DRACULA*.

dedicated to vampire fiction. Each of the founders developed their interest in vampires from a prior involvement with fantasy and science fiction and as a response to the writings of **Anne Rice**, **Elaine Bergstrom**, **P. N. Elrod**, and Jacqueline Litchnenberg. *Onyx* publishes original fiction, poetry, artwork, and book and movie reviews.

Subscriptions to *Onyx* can be obtained through Nightbird Productions, PO Box 137, Uniontown, OH 44685.

ORDER OF THE VAMPYRE

The Order of the Vampyre is part of the Temple of Set, a religious institution dedicated to and consecrated by Set, an ancient Egyptian god who was later adapted into the "Satan" of the Jewish and Christian traditions. Hence, the Temple of Set is popularly known as a "Satanic" religion, although its initiates consider themselves "Setians," a more precise description. The Temple was founded in 1975 by priests of the Church of Satan (founded in 1966) who had decided to carry forward the serious work of the Church in a more historic, less anti-Christian context. Like its parent body, the Temple of Set is a strictly ethical and law-abiding institution. It is configured as an "umbrella" organization that has a number of specialized "orders" whose members concentrate on specific areas of research and black magic applications of the results of that research.

Vampirism is a kind of extension of human consciousness into extremes of human desires and behavior. It is the purpose of the Order of the Vampyre not merely to illustrate (or caricature) these extremes, as artists and novelists regularly do, but rather to identify and understand them. These extremes are the "rages of the raw human soul" that have been all but completely suppressed by the mind's fear of looking deep within itself.

Initiates of the order are encouraged to apply aspects of the "vampyric existence" to their conscious existence. They become, in effect, "vampires" who are sensitive in the extreme to the pleasure and pain of life and very much aware of how different they are compared to "normal" humanity. In this process, the initiates do not drink the blood of or otherwise harm humans or other animals in any way. Rather, an initiate sees, hears, feels, and lives acutely—both positively and negatively. They bring to bear extraordinary powers of imagination and visualization as well as creation and appreciation of thematic art, music, and literature. Thus, like vampires of fiction, the initiate is more vital than humanity in general.

The environment of the Order of the Vampyre is described as exhilarating, but also stressful and hence not appropriate for many people—not even the majority of Setians. Admission to the order is by invitation only to Setians who have attained at least the standing of Adept II within the Temple of Set. Membership is international, and the order holds meetings and activities on its own and in conjunction with the regional, national, and international conclaves of the Temple of Set. It publishes a newsletter, *Nightwing*, and a journal titled *The Vampyre Papers*. The order may be contacted through the office of the Temple of Set at PO Box 470307, San Francisco, CA 94147.

Sources:

The Crystal Tablet of Set. San Francisco, CA: Temple of Set, 1989.

Dresser, Norine. *American Vampires: Fans, Victims, Practitioners.* New York: W. W. Norton & Company, 1989. 255 pp.

OREGON DARK SHADOWS SOCIETY

The Oregon Dark Shadows Society was founded in 1991 by Connie Jonas, its president. Jonas, a long-time and active *Dark Shadows* fan, is also the editor of *The Music Box*, an independent fanzine also founded in 1991 and published by **HarmonyRoad Press**, which she heads. In 1993, the club reported about a dozen members. It gathers monthly to screen recent video releases of *Dark Shadows* episodes, share fandom gossip, engage in dramatic readings, hold trivia contests, and plan for upcoming *Dark Shadows* events such as the annual **Dark Shadows Festival**. The group joined the effort that brought the SCI-FI Channel to the Portland area cable system in 1992. A Halloween party, participation in the fantasy/horror day at the local public library, and a summer picnic are special annual events. The club publishes a monthly newsletter, *News & Notes*. Many of the members of the recently disbanded *Dark Shadows* club in Seattle have joined the Oregon society.

The Oregon Dark Shadows Society can be contacted c/o Connie Jonas, PO Box 40366, Portland, OR 97240-0366.

ORIGINS OF THE VAMPIRE

How did vampires originate? If vampires did (or do) exist, where did they come from? The answers to these questions have varied widely as the vampire has appeared in the folklore of different countries and various fiction writers have speculated on the nature of vampirism.

THE FOLKLORIC VAMPIRE: The vampire figure in folklore emerged as an answer to otherwise unsolvable problems within culture. The vampire was seen as the cause of certain unexplainable evils, accounted for the appearance of some extraordinary occurrences within the society, and was often cited as the end product of immoral behavior. The earliest vampires seem to have originated as an explanation of problems in childbirth. For example, the *langsuyar*—the primary vampire figure of **Malaysia**—was a beautiful young woman who had given birth to a stillborn child. Upon hearing of her child's fate, she clapped her hands and flew away into the trees. Henceforth, she attacked children and sucked their blood. A similar tale was told of the *lamiai,* the original vampire of **Greece**.

Just as tales of vampires were inspired by childbirth problems, they also originated from unusual circumstances surrounding births. Children who were different at birth were considered to be vampire candidates. For example, among the Kashubian (Polish) people, children born with a membrane cap on their heads or with two teeth were likely to become vampires unless dealt with properly while growing up.

Similarly, some vampires stories originated from problems surrounding the death of a loved one. In eastern Europe, vampires were individuals who returned from the grave to attack their spouses, their immediate families, and possibly other acquaintances in the village. Symptoms of vampiric attack included nightmares, apparitions of the dead, and the death of family members by a wasting disease (such as tuberculosis). Some of the symptoms point to the vampire as a product of the grieving process, especially the continued ties of the living to the dead, often taking the form of unfinished emotional business. Thus, vampires were seen as originating from the failure of the family (in a time before the existence of funeral parlors) to perform the funeral and burial rites with exacting precision. A common event that allegedly led to the creation of a vampire was allowing an animal such as a cat to jump over the body of a dead person prior to burial. Vampirism was also caused by unexpected and sudden violent deaths, either from accidents or suicides.

Suicides were also part of a larger class of vampires that existed as a result of the immoral behavior of the person who became a vampire. The vampire served as an instrument of social control for the moral leaders of the community. Thus, people who stepped outside of the moral and religious boundaries of the community not only jeopardized their souls, but might become vampires. A potential vampire committed evil acts, among them **suicide**, and anyone guilty of great evil, especially of an antisocial nature, was thought likely to become a vampire after death. In some Christian countries, notably Russia and Greece, heresy could also lead to vampirism. The heretic was one type of person who died in a state of excommunication from the church. Excommunication could be pronounced for a number of unforgiven sins from actions directly attacking the church to more common immoralities such as adultery or murder. Heresy was also associated in some cultures with **witchcraft**, defined as consorting with Satan and/or the working of malevolent antisocial magic. Witches who practiced their craft in their earthly lives might become vampires after their deaths.

VAMPIRE CONTAMINATION: After the first vampire was created, a community of vampires might soon follow. When a particular vampire figure, such as the original *lamiai,* took its place in the mythology of a people as a lesser deity or demon, they sometimes multiplied into a set of similar beings. Thus, Greek mythology posed the existence of numerous *lamiai,* a class of demonic entities. They were assumed to exist as part of the larger supernatural environment and, as such, the question of their origin was never raised. Also, such demonic entities did not create new vampires by attacking people. Their victims might suffer either physical harm or death as the result of the vampire's assault, but they did not become vampires.

Things were quite different in Eastern Europe. There, vampires were former members of the community. Vampires could draw other members of the community into their vampiric existence by contaminating former family and neighbors, usually by biting them. In the famous case of **Arnold Paul**, the vampiric state was passed by meat from cows that had been bitten by Paul.

THE LITERARY VAMPIRE: In the nineteenth century, the vampire figure was wrenched from its rural social context in eastern Europe and brought into the relatively secularized culture of western European cities. It was introduced into the romantic imagination of writers cut off from the mythological context in which the vampire originated. Those writers had to recreate a new context from the few bits of knowledge they possessed. In examining the few vampire cases at their disposal, most prominently the Arnold Paul case, they learned that vampires were created by people being bitten by other vampires.

The imaginary vampire of nineteenth-century romanticism was an isolated individual. Unlike the eastern European vampire, the literary vampire did not exist in a village culture as a symbol warning residents of the dangerous and devilish life outside the boundaries of approved village life. The imaginary vampire was a victim of irresistible supernatural attack. Against their wills, they were overwhelmed by the vampiric state and, much like drug addicts, forced to live lives built around their **blood** lust. The majority of beliefs associated with the origins of vampires were irrelevant to the creators of the literary vampire, although on occasion one element might be picked up to give a novel twist to a vampire tale.

Underlying much of the modern vampire lore was the belief that vampires attacked humans and, through that attack, drew victims into their world. Again, like drug addicts might share an addiction and turn others into addicts, so the vampire infected nonvampires with their condition. Writers have generally suggested that vampires primarily, if not exclusively, created new vampires by their bites. The radical simplification of the vampire myth can be seen in *Dracula,* especially its treatment on the stage and screen. Stoker did not deal directly with the problem of Dracula's origin as a vampire. In Dr. **Abraham Van Helsing** famous speech in chapter 18, where he described in some detail the nature of the vampire, he suggested that Dracula became a vampire because he "had dealings with the Evil One." More importantly, however, was his ability to transform people into vampires. Dracula's bite was a necessary part of that transmission, but, of itself, not sufficient. **Jonathan Harker** was bitten a number of times by the three vampire women, but did not become a vampire. On the other hand, **Lucy Westenra** did turn into a vampire and **Mina Murray** was in the process of being transformed into a vampire when the men interrupted Dracula. In the key scene in chapter 21, Dracula, having previously drank Mina's blood, forced her to drink his. Thus, in *Dracula* new vampires originated not from the bite of the vampire but by an exchange of blood.

Bram Stoker had little material to draw upon in considering this point. The question was avoided by **John Polidori** in his original vampire story. *Varney the Vampyre,* the subject of the 1840s novel, became a vampire as punishment for

CHRISTOPHER ATKINS ATTEMPTS TO TURN STACY TRAVIS INTO A VAMPIRE WITH HIS BITE IN *DRACULA RISING.*

accidently killing his son, but the actual manner of transformation was not revealed. **Sheridan Le Fanu** was familiar with the folkloric tradition and suggested suicide as the cause of new vampires, but saw the death of a person previously bitten by a vampire as the basic means of spreading vampirism. His anti-heroine, **Carmilla** was the product of a vampire's bite.

In the rewriting of *Dracula* for screen and stage, the scene from the book during which Mina consumed Dracula's blood was deleted. It was considered too risqué, but without it some other means had to be found to transmit the vampiric state. Thus came the suggestion that merely the vampire's bite transmitted the condition—the common assumption in most vampire novels and movies. At times, vampires required multiple bites or the bite had to take enough blood to cause the death of the victim.

While most vampire books and movies have not dealt with the question of vampire origins apart from the passing of the vampiric condition through the bite of a preexisting vampire, occasionally writers have attempted to create a vampire myth that covers the origin of the first vampire. Among the more intriguing of recent origin stories was that told by **Anne Rice** in the third of her vampire chronicles, *The Queen of the Damned.* Akasha and her husband Enkil ruled as queen and king of ancient Egypt. At one point Akasha had two witches, Maharet and Mekere, brought to her court. They allowed her to see the world of spirits, but then one of the spirits, Amel, attacked her. Akasha turned on the two witches and in her rage ordered them raped publicly and then banished. However, both Akasha and Enkil were intrigued by the spirit world and began to explore it on their own. Meanwhile, an uprising occurred and the rulers were seriously wounded. Akasha's soul escaped from her body temporarily only to encounter the spirit Amel who joined himself to her. Her soul reentered her body and brought Amel with it. Fused with her brain and heart, the presence of Amel turned her into a vampire. She, in turn, passed the vampiric condition to Enkil and to their steward Khayman by the more traditional bite. All other vampires in the book, who originated from a vampire's bite, have a lineage that can ultimately be traced to these three first vampires.

THE VAMPIRE BAT: In chapter 12 of *Dracula,* Bram Stoker suggested, but did not develop, the idea that vampire **bat**s might ultimately be the cause of vampirism. **Quincey P. Morris** delivered a brief oration on his encounter with vampire bats in South America. Although vampire bats made numerous appearances in vampire lore—primarily as humans temporarily transformed into animal form—few writers developed the idea of vampirism originating with vampire bats.

Most prominent among the few stories in which vampirism originated with a bat was *Dark Shadows.* The *Dark Shadows* storyline, took **Barnabas Collins** back to 1795 to his origin as a vampire. Spurning the witch Angelique's love for him, Barnabas wound up in a fight with her and shot her. Wounded and near death, she cursed Barnabas and a bat attacked him. He died from the bite and arose from the grave as a vampire. Subsequently, Barnabas created other vampires in the common manner—by biting them and draining their blood to the point of death.

THE SCIENCE FICTION VAMPIRE: A final option concerning the origin of vampires was derived from **science fiction**. As early as 1942 in his short story "Asylum," A. E. van Vogt suggested that vampires were an alien race who originated in outer space. The most successful of the comic book vampires, *Vampirella,* was a space alien. She originated on the planet Drakulon and came to earth to escape her dying planet. Ultimately, in the *Vampirella* storyline, even Dracula was revealed to be an alien.

Science fiction also suggested a second origin for the vampire: disease. Not incompatible with either vampire bats or outer space aliens, disease (either in the form of germs or altered blood chemistry) provided a nonsupernatural explanation of the vampire's existence—an opinion demanded by many secularized readers or theater-goers. Disease explained the vampire's strange behavior, from its nocturnal existence to the "allergy" to **garlic** to its blood lust. This idea was explored most prominently in **Richard Matheson**'s *I Am Legend.*

In the end, however, the science fiction space vampire was like its supernatural cousin. Whatever its origin, the vampire was the bearer—at least potentially—of its condition to anyone it attacked, and the vampire's bite was the most common way to spread vampirism.

Sources:

Ramsland, Katherine. *The Vampire Companion.* New York: Ballantine Books, 1993. 508 pp.

Rice, Anne. *The Queen of the Damned.* New York: Alfred A. Knopf, 1988. 448 pp.

Perkowski, Jan L. *The Darkling: A Treatise on Slavic Vampirism.* Columbus, OH: Slavica Publishers, 1989. 174 pp.

Scott, Kathryn Leigh, ed. *The Dark Shadows Companion: 25th Anniversary Collection.* Los Angeles: Pomegranate Press, 1990. 208 pp.

Summers, Montague. *The Vampire: His Kith and Kin.* London: Routledge, Kegan Paul, Trench, Trubner, & Co., 1928. 356 pp. Reprint. New Hyde Park, NY: University Books, 1960. 356 pp.

ORLOCK, GRAF

The vampire Graf (or Count) Orlock (variously spelled Orlok, Orlac, or Orloc) first appeared in the 1922 German silent film *Nosferatu, Eine Symphonie des Garuens*. *Nosferatu* was a thinly veiled adaptation of *Bram Stoker's Dracula*, but Prana-Films, the film's production company, neglected to gain permission from the author's widow to produce the movie. Director Frederich W. Murnau, changed the title, the setting, and the names of all of the leading characters of the novel. While keeping the basic storyline, he thought he had altered it enough to be protected against charges of plagiarism. Such was not the case, however, and the film had only limited screenings before legal action was taken against it and most copies were destroyed. However, enough survived to alter the image of the vampire through the twentieth century.

Although British playwright **Hamilton Deane** made Dracula a character that could blend into proper British society—he wore formal evening clothes and showed few effects of having experienced death—Murnau made Count Orlock a far greater object of horror. Murnau, it seemed, drew on the tradition of European folklore to create a vampire who suffered from the effects of his encounter with death. Graf Orlock was given a rodent-like appearance with two **fangs** placed close together in the front of his mouth rather than elongated canine teeth. He was bald and his face was distorted into a parody of humanness. His fingers were extended and given a claw-like quality—a feature that was exaggerated through the course of the movie. He moved with slow deliberate steps.

Orlock assumed several characteristics not highlighted in *Dracula*. Dracula had some control over animals, especially wolves and bats. Orlock also had that control, but was focused on rats; wherever he chose to go, plague bearing rats were sure to congregate. Murnau changed the setting of his movie to Bremen in 1838 (rather than the 1890s) to coincide with the outbreak of plague in that town.

Another key difference was that of sunlight. Dracula, while a creature of the night, could move about in the daytime. Orlock, on the other hand, was adversely affected by sunlight and could not be exposed to it at all. Unlike Dracula, however,

Orlock did cast a shadow and his image was reflected in glass. Murnau developed the idea that the vampire could be most effectively attacked if a virtuous woman held him enthralled at her side until sunrise. Orlock was thus finally killed by lingering in a woman's bedroom until the sun disintegrated him.

THE RETURN OF ORLOCK: Because of the lengthy legal proceedings during Florence Stoker's life, copies of *Nosferatu* did not begin to circulate until the 1960s. (However, enough was known about its plot that it possibly affected the ending of **Hammer Films'** first *Dracula* production, ***The Horror of Dracula*** (1958). (In that film, Van Helsing killed Dracula by exposing him to the morning sun by pulling the shade from a window.) The Orlock character did not make another appearance until 1979 when *Nosferatu: The Vampyre*, a remake of the first movie was made (Klaus Kinski assumed the title role). The new movie was written, produced, and directed by Werner Herzog. Although it kept the distinctive aspects of the original *Nosferatu* storyline, it more clearly acknowledged its basis as a version of *Dracula*—in part by using the names of the characters in Stoker's novel.

Orlock did not appear again until 1991 when three different comic book companies, operating in the midst of a revival of interest in the vampire, issued comic books inspired by his character. The first of these was issued by Tome Press and was a straight adaptation of the 1922 movie. *Nosferatu* by Dark Horse Comics was the translation of an apocalyptic vampire tale by French writer Philip Druillet with an Orlocklike character, but little obvious relationship to *Dracula*. Druillet's work also appeared in a German translation.

The most ambitious of the three projects came from Millennium Publications, which issued a four-part series called *Nosferatu*. Author Mark Ellis provided a complete story of Graf Orlock's existence quite different from the *Dracula* legend and brought Orlock's menace into the present day. Graf Orlock was an eleventh-century nobleman whose estate was in the Carpathians. After Orlock became a vampire, he was eventually killed and his body sealed in the castle. An English knight returning from the crusades stopped at the castle. His squire freed Orlock, who was once again able to move about in human society. In the process the knight, William Longsword, was bitten. Following that incident, Orlock expressed his nature by causing wars and sending plagues. Longsword, who fought Orlock over the centuries, finally caught up with him in contemporary Brooklyn, where a group of plague victims had been discovered. The story led to a final conflagration, but not before Orlock passed along his undead condition.

The Orlock character, like Dracula, has entered the public domain, and it would be difficult to predict where he might again arise.

Sources:

Druillet, Philip. *Nosferatu.* Milwaukee, OR: Dark Horse Comics, 1991.
Monette, Paul. *Nosferatu: the Vampyre.* New York: Avon Books, 1979. 172 pp.
Nosferatu: A Symphony of Shadows, a Symphony of Shudders. No. 1-2. Plymouth, MI: Tome Press, 1991.

COUNT ORLOCK, THE THINLY DISGUISED DRACULA OF THE FILM *NOSFERATU.*

Nosferatu: Plague of Terror. No. 1-4 St. Paul, MN: Millennium Comics, 1991-92. Story by Mark Ellis. Skal, David J. *Hollywood Gothic.* New York: W. W. Norton & Company, 1990. 242 pp.

OUTER SPACE VAMPIRES *See:* SCIENCE FICTION AND THE VAMPIRE

P

PALANCE, JACK (1928-)

Jack Palance, who played the title role in the made-for-television movie *Dracula* **(1973)** was born Vladimir Palahnuik on February 18, 1928, in Lattimer, Pennsylvania. In 1947 he made his Broadway debut and three years later appeared in his first Hollywood movie, *Panic in the Streets*. He became famous following his appearance in *Shane*. For his role as the villain, he won an Oscar nomination as best supporting actor, the second time he had received that honor.

Palance's movie career was largely determined by his physical build (he had a brief career in professional boxing), his distinctive voice, and the plastic surgery he received following the crash of his airplane during World War II. He quickly emerged as a one of Hollywood's great heavies. It limited his starring roles, but he became famous as one of the industry's outstanding character actors. Therefore, he was a natural consideration for the title role as Dracula when **Dan Curtis**, fresh on the heels of his successful vampire-oriented *Dark Shadows* series decided to make a new version of *Dracula.*

Curtis's *Dracula* was the first remake of the classic tale following the introduction of **Vlad the Impaler,** (also known as **Vlad Dracula**). Palance portrayed a Dracula who had lost his love four centuries before, but rediscovered her in the person of **Lucy Westenra**, a picture of whom was carried by **Jonathan Harker** whose appearance at **Castle Dracula** launched the story. Leaving Harker to be attacked by the women at the castle, Dracula went in search of his lost love. He turned her into a vampire, but she was killed by **Abraham Van Helsing** and her fiancé **Arthur Holmwood**. Enraged, Dracula sought revenge by attacking **Mina Murray,** Harker's fiancé. Dracula was chased back to his castle and finally destroyed.

The Palance version first aired on CBS on February 8, 1974 and was then released to theaters in Europe. It subsequently took its place as one of the finer

JACK PALANCE AS DRACULA.

versions of *Dracula* and has been released on home video. Palance continued with his active career, which included hosting the popular television series *Ripley's Believe It or Not.*

Sources:

Jones, Stephen. *The Illustrated Vampire Movie Guide.* London: Titan Books, 1993. 144 pp.

PARAPHERNALIA, VAMPIRE

As the vampire entered popular culture during the 1960s, a host of items were manufactured to promote and exploit the interest. Actually the first such item seems to have appeared in 1928 at the 250th performance of the stage play of *Dracula* in London. Everyone who attended was given an envelope, which they were told not to open until after the performance. The envelope contained a copy of *Dracula's Guest,* a collection of short stories by **Bram Stoker**, and a small rubber-band powered bat that flew into the air when released.

Movies have always been a great source of collectible items—posters, movie cards, publicity packets, and photographs, even souvenir booklets—so such items were common with vampire movies. It wasn't until 1966, however, in connection with **Hammer Films,** *Dracula, Prince of Darkness,* that special items were produced specifically as advertising gimmicks for a vampire movie. Patrons attending the movie (usually shown as a double feature with another Hammer production, *Plague of the Zombies*), were given vampire fangs and a zombie mask.

In 1968, manufacturers began to recognize the existence of a vampire-oriented public for whom a variety of such items could be created and marketed. This recognition came in the wake of the success of vampire **Barnabas Collins** on the gothic television soap opera *Dark Shadows*. In 1968, Barnabas and *Dark Shadows* provided the theme for a new board game, Viewmaster 3-D reels, and a Halloween mask and costume. In 1969 a veritable flood of new *Dark Shadows* products were released, including several records, a second board game, jigsaw puzzles, model kits, a magic slate, and pillows. The success of *Dark Shadows* memorabilia led to the production of other vampire items either specifically for Halloween (from plastic fangs to greeting cards) or to both build and exploit the market generated by various vampire movies. In 1992 a line of approximately 100 products (including trading cards, tee shirts, computer games, jewelry, and miniature statuettes) was developed for release in connection with **Francis Ford Coppola**'s *Bram Stoker's Dracula*.

During the 1970s, while most vampire paraphernalia was produced in connection either with *Dark Shadows* (which still has a large, well-organized fan network) or with particular motion pictures, the vampire image was adopted by a number of products that ranged from breakfast cereal to candy. The spread of products dominated by a vampire image also coincided with the adoption of the vampire theme in advertising. Examples of this included ads in which a vampire recommended a product like mouthwash, and one in which a victim was rescued by a garden poison that killed insects dressed like **Bela Lugosi**.

HALLOWEEN PARAPHERNALIA: The most popular vampire items have been produced for Halloween—one of the most widely celebrated holidays in North America. The merchandising of Halloween tripled between 1983 and 1993, and by the early 1990s, it was second only to Christmas in terms of the number of people who decorated their homes. The vampire has become an integral part of the Halloween celebration and merchants carry a wide variety of vampire products to respond to public demand. Leading the list are vampire costumes, both those based on the older Bela Lugosi image and some newer figures such as Barnabas Collins and horror hostess **Elvira**. Besides complete costumes there are vampire masks and wigs and a wide selection of make-up. Elvira has marketed a line of cosmetics, and several companies produce vampire teeth, artificial blood, and make-up. For the party planner, there are vampire-oriented supplies including placemats, posters, hanging bats, and window and wall decorations. One set of party items pictured the popular cartoon cat Garfield in vampire regalia.

Halloween greeting cards began to make an impact in the 1980s and by 1993 Halloween was ranked eighth among greeting card sales—an estimated 35 million cards were sent in 1992. Vampire cards are largely humorous, often including a basic set of one-liners and riddles. The cards, designed for a quick immediate impact, indicate how stereotypical the vampire image has become—vampires are invariably shown with a cape and two fangs and, more often than not, in association with vampire **bat**s. To a lesser extent vampires have appeared on postcards; there is a set of cards with movie stills from *Dracula* **(1931)** and an 11-card set (of an originally projected series of 24 cards) from *Dark Shadows* (1987).

Halloween candy has also become a multi-million dollar business currently growing at about two percent per year. In recent years, among the vampire oriented candy products that reached the market were *Frankford Vampire Bites, Gummi Mummies* (they came in a coffin that became a coin bank), *Creepy Coffin* (with a chocolate vampire), *Count Crunch,* and *Vambite.*

TOYS: Closely associated with comic books are trading cards. Apart from the vampires that have appeared in collections of cards picturing a host of monsters, possibly the first vampire trading cards were the two sets of *Dark Shadows* cards marketed by the Philadelphia Chewing Gum Company at the end of the 1960s. Both the first or "pink" series and the second or "green" series included 66 scenes from the television show. Imagine, Inc. issued a new *Dark Shadows* set in 1993 with 62 cards from the 1960s television series. Topps produced two card sets in association with vampire-oriented movies: *The Addams Family* (1991, 100 cards) and *Bram Stoker's Dracula* (1992, 100 cards). In addition to the 100-card set made for *Bram Stoker's Dracula,* there was an additional 16-card set distributed with the four-issue comic book of the movie published by Topps. In 1992, Acid Rain Studios, which had produced a number of vampire comic books, also issued a 50-card black-and-white trading card set.

Vampire toys began with the *Dark Shadows* games, jigsaw puzzle, Viewmaster set, magic slate, and model kits in 1968 and 1969. Over the last 25 years, however, the most popular items have been the numerous vampire dolls and statues. Vampires have

THE VAMPIRE HAS BECOME AN INTEGRAL PART OF THE HALLOWEEN CELEBRATION IN THE UNITED STATES. SHOWN IS A HALLOWEEN GREETING CARD.

been reproduced in every possible medium. There was a vampire teddy bear, plastic statuettes of the characters from *The Addams Family* and *The Munsters*, and, of course, Dracula, the most reproduced figure. Dracula was occasionally placed in a coffin with a movable lid. In 1990, Funny Toys Corporation marketed ''Dracula in Coffin,'' a vampire in evening dress in a battery powered coffin that opened and closed with an eerie noise. In the early 1990s, **Universal Pictures** released action figures of the popular Teenage Mutant Ninja Turtles that portrayed the four turtles as four of the classic monsters from Universal movies; Donatello was the Dracula figure. These figures were just one of a line of items licensed by Universal using the Bela Lugosi Dracula image.

APPAREL: Since the 1960s, tee shirts have become the daily wear of many people, and shirts bearing the advertising of a wide number of products have been marketed. As might be expected, vampires have found their way onto such shirts. Elvira's Queen

B Productions has produced both tee shirts and sweatshirts. A variety of tee shirts with scenes from the movie and the comic book appeared in connection with *Bram Stoker's Dracula*. Recent *Dark Shadows* tee shirts had scenes from the 1990 (rather than the 1960s) television series.

The ease of producing tee shirt illustrations made it easy for smaller producers to get into the market. **Vlad**, the leader of the rock band Dark Theater, has a tee shirt line, as does independent cartoonist **Wendy Snow-Lang**. At the opposite end of the economic scale, *Bram Stoker's Dracula* products included a bustier marketed though Macy's ($1,500), a tie with a wolf symbol, boxer shorts, and red laced underpants with rosebud appliqué.

The more affluent can purchase vampire jewelry. One of the more popular items is a reproduction of the ring worn by Barnabas Collins in the 1960s television series. Wristwatches have been produced with designs from both the 1960s and 1990 *Dark Shadows* television series and *Bram Stoker's Dracula*. *Bram Stoker's Dracula* also led to the production of a set of broaches in the form of a bat, a bug, and a spider and a vampire red lipstick in a $500 bejeweled coffin-shaped lipstick holder. Among the most unusual items was an ornament suitable for a necklace or bracelet that contained dirt from **Castle Dracula.**

MISCELLANEOUS ITEMS: The number and variety of vampire-oriented paraphernalia are extensive. *Dark Shadows* products alone included pillows, a music box, a Barnabas Collins walking cane, lunch box, keychains, drinking mugs, and calendars. Count Chocula cereal, introduced in the 1970s, is still popular. There are lapel buttons with witty vampire one-liners and even a vampire condom.

No discussion of vampire products would be complete without mentioning the several anti-vampire kits. The first such kit was alleged to have been produced by Nicolas Plomdeur, a gunmaker in Liege, Belgium, in the mid-nineteenth century. His kit included a real pistol made in the shape of a latin cross, a silver bullet, a wooden spike, powder flask, and a clove of garlic. The only known surviving example of the Plomdeur kit is owned by Val Forgett of the Navy Arms Co. A similar kit can be found in the Mercer Museum at Doylestown, Pennsylvania. This kit's wooden box contains a pistol, two silver bullets, a cross attached to a wooden stake, a magnifying glass, some garlic, and several ''serums'' especially formulated by the kit's manufacturer, reputedly a Dr. Ernest Blomberg. The kit was reportedly designed for nineteenth-century English-speaking travelers going to Eastern Europe.

Finally, for the most intense vampire enthusiasts, Death, Inc. of San Francisco, California, has offered a full ''Vampire Line'' **coffin**s.

CONCLUSION: The number of different places where the vampire image can now be found is further proof of its significant penetration into the popular culture. The fact that so many children's products—from Halloween costumes to toys and comic books—now feature vampires indicate that its popularity will only expand as the next generation matures after experiencing the vampire in such a positive manner.

Helpful in locating a wide variety of vampire paraphernalia is *The Vampire Directory* published by **Realm of the Vampire** (PO Box 517, Metairie, LA 7004-0517). *Dark Shadows* paraphernalia is marketed through a variety of companies, fan organizations, and individuals. For information on specific items contact *Dark Shadows Collectibles Classified*, a periodical listing collectibles for sale (c/o Sue Ellen Wilson, 6173 Iroquois Trail, Mentor, OH 44060); the *Collinwood Chronicle* (No. 5 Hammes Dr., Florissant, MO 63031); or the *Dark Shadows Collector's Guide* (c/o Craig Hamrick, 204 W. 9th St., Baxter St., Baxter Springs, KS 66713).

(For more information on specific categories of paraphernalia, see separate entries in this book on **comic books, music**, and **games**.)

Sources:

Broeske, Pat H. "See the Movie, Buy the Automobile Air Freshener." *New York Times* (December 6, 1992): 12.

Stockel, Shirley, and Victoria Weidner. *A Guide to Collecting "Dark Shadows" Memorabilia.* Florissant, MO: Collinwood Chronicle, 1992. 107 pp.

Jones, Del. "Holiday Is a Business Treat." *USA Today* (October 29, 1993): 1-2.

Ramsland, Katherine. "Dr. Blomberg Anti-Vampire Kit." *Dead of Night* No. 6 (Summer 1990): 48.

Spangenberger, Phil. "Vampire-Killing Kit." *Guns & Ammo* 33, 10 (October 1989): 72-73, 127.

PARRY, MICHAEL (1947-)

Michael Parry, British horror writer and anthologist, was born on October 7, 1947, in Brussels, Belgium. His entry into the horror field came through the cinema. As a teenager, he began to write film reviews of horror movies and news stories in the field. In 1969, he wrote and produced *Hex,* a short surrealistic film that used a black magic theme. His first book was a novel based on the screenplay of the **Hammer Films** vampire movie, *Countess Dracula* (1971), about Countess **Elizabeth Bathory.**

Although most of his work has been western novels, throughout the 1970s and 1980s he produced a series of anthologies of horror fiction. His anthologies—many which included vampire stories—were notable for the knowledge Parry demonstrated of the vast field of horror short fiction. Two of these anthologies, *Christopher Lee's X Certificate* (1975) and *The Great Villains* (1976) were done with **Christopher Lee**, the contemporary actor most identified with the role of Dracula. His most famous vampire book was *Rivals of Dracula* (1977), which, along with Les Shepard's *Dracula Book of Great Vampire Stories* (1977) made the most important vampire short stories available to a growing audience of vampire enthusiasts.

Sources:

Ashley, Mike. *Who's Who in Horror and Fantasy Fiction.* London: Elm Tree Books, 1977. 240 pp.

Parry, Michel. *Countess Dracula*. London: Sphere Books, 1971. Reprint. New York: Beagle Books, 1971.
140 pp.
———. *Rivals of Dracula*. London: Corgi Books, 1977. 190 pp.

PAUL (PAOLE), ARNOLD

Arnold Paul (or Paole) was the subject of one of the most famous eighteenth-century vampire cases; it came in the midst of a seeming wave of vampire attacks that plagued central Europe from the late-seventeenth century through the middle of the next century. These cases in general, and the Paul case in particular, were the major cause of a revived interest in vampires in England and **France** in the early nineteenth century.

Paul was born in the early 1700s in Medvegia, north of Belgrade, in an area of Serbia then part of the Austrian Empire. He served in the army in what was called "Turkish **Serbia**" and in the spring of 1727 returned to his hometown. Paul purchased several acres of land and settled down to farming. He was pursued by a young woman at a neighboring farm and was eventually engaged to be married. He was noted as being a good natured and honest person and was welcomed by the townspeople upon his return. However, it was also noted that a certain gloom pervaded his personality.

Paul finally told his intended that his problem stemmed from his war days. In Turkish Serbia, he had been visited and attacked by a vampire. Eventually, he killed the vampire after following it to its grave. He also ate some of the dirt from the vampire's tomb and bathed his wounds in the blood of the vampire to cleanse himself of the effects of the attack. However, he was still fearful of having been tainted by the attack. A week later, Paul was the victim of a fatal accident. He was buried immediately.

Some three weeks after his burial, reports surfaced of appearances by Paul. Four people who made reports died and a panic began to spread through the community. Community leaders decided to act to quell the panic by disinterring the body to determine if Paul was a vampire. On the 40th day after the burial, the grave was opened. Two military surgeons were present when the lid was removed from the coffin. They found a body that appeared as if it had just recently died. What seemed to be new skin was present under a layer of dead skin, and the nails had continued to grow. The body was pierced, and blood poured forth. Those present judged that Paul was a vampire. His body was staked, and he was heard to utter a loud groan. His head was severed and his body burned. The case could have ended there, but it did not. The four other people who had died were treated similarly lest they also begin to reappear as vampires.

In 1731 in the same area, some 17 people died of the symptoms of vampirism in a matter of three months. The townspeople were slow to act until one girl complained that a man named Milo, who had recently died, had attacked her in the middle of the night. Word of this second wave of vampirism reached Vienna, and the Austrian Emperor ordered an inquiry to be conducted by Regimental Field Surgeon Johannes

Fluckinger. Appointed on December 12, Fluckinger headed for Medvegia and began to gather accounts of what had occurred. Milo's body was disinterred and it was discovered in a state similar to that of Arnold Paul's; the body was then staked and burned. How was it possible that the vampirism that had been eradicated in 1727 had returned? It was determined that Paul had vampirized several cows that the recently dead had fed on. Under Fluckinger's orders, the townspeople then proceeded to dig up the bodies of all who had died in recent months. Forty were disinterred and 17 were found to be in the same preserved state as had Paul's body. They were all staked and burned.

Fluckinger wrote a full report of his activities that he presented to the Emperor early in 1732. His report was soon published and became a bestseller. By March 1732, accounts of Paul and the Medvegia vampires were circulated in the periodicals of France and England. Because of the well-documented nature of the case, it became the focus of future studies and reflections about vampires, and Arnold Paul became the most famous ''vampire'' of the era. The Paul case was most influential in shaping the conclusions reached by both **Dom Augustin Calmet** and **Giuseppe Davanzati**, two Roman Catholic scholars who prepared books on vampirism in the middle of the century.

Sources:

Barber, Paul. *Vampires, Burial, and Death: Folklore and Reality.* New Haven, CT: Yale University Press, 1988. 236 pp.

Frayling, Christopher. *Vampyres: Lord Byron to Count Dracula.* London: Faber and Faber, 1991. 429 pp.

Summers, Montague. *Vampires in Europe.* London: Routledge, Kegan Paul, Trench, Trubner, & Co., 1929. 329 pp. Reprint. New Hyde Park, NY: University Books, 1961. 329 pp.

PELESIT See: MALAYSIA, VAMPIRES IN

PENANGGALAN See: MALAYSIA, VAMPIRES IN

PETERSON, CASSANDRA *See:* ELVIRA

PHILIPPINES, VAMPIRES IN THE

The modern Philippines is a country composed of numerous peoples whose belief systems survive, some in a rather secularized form, in spite of several centuries of Islamic and Christian missions and the development of a host of modern indigenous religions. The tribes of the Philippine Islands had an elaborate mythology, which included demonic beings, dragons, were-animals, giants, ghouls, and vampires. The Capiz section of the island of Panay was especially associated with the vampire, where many were believed to reside. Of the vampirelike creatures, the *aswang* was by far the most well-known throughout the Islands. The term *aswang* was used to describe a set of different creatures that were analogous to vampires, **werewolves**, ghouls, and witches, and in the folklore literature could be found under any one of those headings.

The flying *aswang,* or the blood-sucker, usually appeared as a beautiful maiden who engaged in vampiric activities at night, always returning home to resume her normal life before dawn. Some women have an ointment that they rub on their body prior to their nocturnal activities. The ointment was the source of their supernatural abilities. In its vampiric state, the *aswang* became a large bird that flew through the sky crying out *kakak* or *kikak.* It would land on the roof of a prospective victim's house and let down a long tongue with a sharp point. The point was used to prick the jugular vein, and the **blood** was sucked up through the hollow tongue's tubular structure. Children were told stories of the possibility of being attacked by an *aswang.* Once filled with blood, the *aswang* resembled a pregnant woman. Upon returning home she fed her children, who suckled at her breast. The *aswang*'s supernatural powers ceased either with its washing off the ointment or the coming of dawn.

The *aswang* was a common bug-a-boo parents used to keep children in line. A large percentage of Filipinos grew up with at least some belief in its existence. The strength of this belief was documented quite vividly in the 1950s when it was used against a group of insurgents (the Huk or *Hukbalahap*) during the presidency of Magsaysay, a Philippine leader strongly supported by the American government. American advisors to Magsaysay convinced him to create a psychological warfare unit to counter the efforts of Huk leaders to win people away from their support of the central government. Among the efforts of this unit, noted in General *E. G. Lansdale*'s account, was an attempt to convince a Huk unit to abandon a position in fear of an *aswang*'s attack.

The operation began with a rumor planted in a community threatened by Huk attack. People were told that a vampire had moved into the area. The Huk were barricaded at the top of a nearby hill. They soon became aware of the rumor that was spreading through the area. Several days later, the psychological warfare unit was able to capture a Huk soldier and kill him by draining his blood. They made two puncture wounds on his neck and left him on the road near the hill where he would be found. When he was found, the Huk believed their dead comrade to be a victim of the *aswang.* The next day all of the Huk troops left.

Building on Lansdale's account, Norine Dresser noted that in the late 1980s she found the story of the *aswang* and the Huk and other tales of the *aswang* were still very much alive in the Filipino immigrant community in California. They told her the old stories of the vampire creatures and she discovered that several of her informants still believed in the *aswang.* They also reflected on the long range effect of the 1950s incident that many local people, not just the Huks, attributed to a vampire. Once the Huks left, people began to wonder who the aswang's next victims would be. Some started wearing **garlic** necklaces. Some left the area and their abandoned land was taken over by the government and used in its land redistribution programs. Despite the fear caused by the incident, everyone recognized its effectiveness in destroying the Huks' support among the people.

One tale told by the Isneg people related the origin of the vampire, which they called *danag*. According to the story, several people were in the fields planting their crops when a woman cut her finger. Another woman sucked the wound and thereby discovered that she liked the taste of blood. She went on sucking until she had taken all of the blood. The story concluded by noting that the blood sucking replaced farming.

The Tagalog people spoke of a vampire called the *mandurugo* about which they told the story of "The Girl with Many Loves." The young woman was described as one of the most beautiful to live in the land. She married at the age of 16. Her husband, a husky youth, withered away in less than a year. After his death, she married again, with the same result. She married a third time and then a fourth. The fourth husband, having been warned, feigned sleep one night holding a knife in his hand. Soon after midnight he felt a presence over him and then a prick on his neck. He stuck the knife into the creature on top of him. He heard a screech and the flapping of wings. The next day his bride was found dead some distance from the house with a knife wound in her chest.

As the Philippine film industry developed after World War II, the vampire became a subject of its attention. Given the large Roman Catholic influence in the Islands, however, the films tended to relate more to the European vampire than the *aswang* or associated Philippine vampire characters.

Sources:

Dresser, Norine. *American Vampires: Fans, Victims, Practitioners.* New York: W. W. Norton & Company, 1989. 255 pp.

Ramos, Maximo D. *Creatures of Philippine Lower Mythology.* Manila: University of the Philippines Press, 1971. 390 pp.

Lansdale, Edward Geary. *In the Midst of Wars.* New York: Harper & Row, 1972. 386 pp.

PIÉRART, Z. J.

Z. J. Piérart (d. 1878), French psychical researcher on vampirism, emerged into prominence in the 1850s as Spiritualism swept across **France**. Under the leadership of Alan Kardec, French Spiritualism became the first branch of the movement to accept reincarnation as part of its belief system. Piérart became the leader of the smaller opposition group of spiritualists that did not accept the idea. A professor at the College of Maubeuge, he founded a spiritualist journal, *La Revue Spiritualiste* in 1858.

Piérart's rejection of reincarnation led directly to his consideration of vampires. Spiritualists in general had argued against reincarnation as they claimed to be in contact with the spirits of the dead—even those who had been dead for many years—an impossibility if the spirit had been reincarnated and lost its former earthly identity. Piérart became interested in the problem of psychic attack. In a series of articles, he proposed a theory of **psychic vampirism** suggesting that vampires were the astral bodies (the ghostly double of the spiritual body that spiritualists had proposed as an essential component of each person and one cause of ghostly apparitions of the dead) of either incarcerated individuals or the dead that were revitalizing themselves on the living. He first proposed the idea that the astral body was forcefully ejected from the body of a person buried alive, and that it vampirized the living to nourish the body in the tomb.

While Piérart's theories had some predecessors, especially sixteenth-century Paracelsus, his work pioneered modern psychical concern with the phenomenon of vampirism. It opened the discussion of the possibility of a paranormal draining of an individual's energy by a spiritual agent. It would later be further developed by Theosophist **Franz Hartmann**.

Piérart's work also preceded the development of psychical research as a science and his work was soon superseded by more detailed considerations of the nature of ghosts and theories of astral (body) projection. In 1873, Piérart's journal was suppressed by the French government responding to clerical pressure against spiritualism. He spent his last years as the secretary to Baron du Potet de Sennevoy, who had pioneered research on animal magnetism.

Sources:

Rogo, Scott. "In-depth Analysis of the Vampire Legend." *Fate* 21, 9 (September 1968): 70-77.
Shepard, Les, ed. *Encyclopedia of Occultism and Parapsychology.* 3rd ed. Detroit, MI: Gale Research Company, 1991.

PISACHAS See: INDIA, VAMPIRES IN

PITT, INGRID (1943-)

Ingrid Pitt, an actress who became known for her portrayal of female vampires in the 1970s, was born Natasha Petrovana on a train heading from Germany to a concentration camp in Poland. She grew up in East Berlin, and as a young woman, she escaped to the West to become a model and actress and married the man who had helped her during her flight.

Pitt made her first horror movie in 1964, *The Sound of Horror,* a Spanish production. Following her appearance in *Where Eagles Dare* (1969), she was discovered by Jimmy Carreras of **Hammer Films**. Her two films for Hammer established her fame and her identification with vampirism. Her first Hammer movie, *The Vampire Lovers*, was based on **Sheridan Le Fanu**'s story, **"Carmilla"**. The increasingly permissive standards for movies allowed a degree of nudity and a more direct presentation of lesbianism than had been possible. As Carmilla, Pitt successively vampirized Pippa Steele, Madeline Smith, and Kate O'Mara, after which she was tracked down and beheaded by **Peter Cushing**. While her same-sex scenes were most frequently described as lesbian, Pitt did not see it that way, believing that vampires had no specific gender.

There was little doubt that Pitt's popularity was due to her glamorous appearance and nude scenes. She was offered a variety of vampire scripts, which she turned down because she felt they were little more than sexploitation movies. However, she soon

INGRID PITT AS CARMILLA.

returned to Hammer to make her second movie, *Countess Dracula* (1971), based on the life of Countess **Elizabeth Bathory**. Pitt took her portrayal very seriously, and her research included a trip to Eastern Europe to visit Bathory's castle. The dynamic story of the Bathory legend involved her bathing in blood to restore her youth. The aging countess, was rejuvenated by the blood, and one of the more memorable scenes in vampire movies was that of her coming out of her bath with the blood dripping off of her body.

Pitt would take on one more vampire role, a comic spoof ''The Cloak'', which appeared as a segment of the horror anthology *The House That Dripped Blood* (1971). After appearing in several other movies in the early '70s, she moved behind the camera to start writing. Pitt participated in her husband's production company in Argentina, during which time she wrote a novel, *The Cuckoo Run* (1980) and a nonfiction work, *The Perons* (1982). From the early 1980s to the present, she has concentrated on writing and producing, with only a few guest appearances acting in movies and on television.

Sources:

Hallenbeck, Bruce C. "Countess Dracula." *Femme Fatales* 1, 3 (Winter 1992/93): 52-55.
"Ingrid Pitt: A Profile." *For the Blood Is the Life* 2, 10 (Autumn 1991): 17.

PITTSBURGH DARK SHADOWS FAN CLUB

The Pittsburgh Dark Shadows Fan Club was founded in 1987 for fans of the **Dark Shadows** television series in southwestern Pennsylvania and the nearby counties in Ohio and West Virginia. Founder Dan Silvio also began *Shadows of the Night* as the club's official fanzine. The club may be contacted c/o Dan Silvio, 4529 Friendship Ave., 2nd Fl., Pittsburgh, PA 15224.

PLANCHÉ, JAMES ROBINSON (1796-1880)

James Robinson Planché, popular British dramatist, produced his first successful burlesque at the age of 22. That production launched a career that, while centering on the writing and translating of various dramas (most of a comedic nature), found him working in many varied capacities. Thus, for many of the plays on which he worked, he was the producer, manager, and/or costume designer. In addition, he occasionally wrote libretti for operas and songs for vaudeville.

Planché became involved in the world of vampires in 1820 in response to their popularity on the French stage following **Charles Nodier**'s production of *Le Vampire*. He adapted Nodier's play for the London stage. *The Vampire* or *The Bride of the Isles*, opened at the Lyceum Theater on August 9, 1820. Because the theater had a ready collection of Scottish clothing, Planché set the action in Scotland (one land not readily associated with vampires). The play was most remembered, however, for the trap door though which the vampire, **Lord Ruthven** (played by Thomas Potter Cooke), could disappear. It became known in the theater as the ''vampire trap.''

The many-faceted Planché had a life-long interest in heraldry, and many consider his *The History of British Costumes* (1834) his most permanent contribution. His writing was a strong influence on W.S. Gilbert (of the team Gilbert and Sullivan).

Sources:

Glut, Don. *The Dracula Book.* Metuchen, NJ: Scarecrow Press, 1975. 388 pp.
Kunitz, Stanley J., ed. *British Authors of the Nineteenth Century.* New York: H. W. Wilson Company, 1936. 677 pp.
Planché, J. R. *Plays.* edited by Donald Roy. Cambridge: Cambridge University Press, 1986., pp. 43-68.
———. *Recollections and Reflections.* 2 vols. London: Tinsley Brother, 1872.
———. *The Vampire* or, *The Bride of the Isles.* London: John Lownes, 1820.

PLOGOJOWITZ, PETER

One of the more famous historical vampires, Peter Plogojowitz lived in Kisolova, a small village in Austrian-occupied Serbia, an area officially incorporated into the province of **Hungary**. Kisolova was not far from Medvegia, the home of **Arnold Paul**, another famous ''vampire,'' whose case occurred at the same time. Plogojowitz died in September 1828 at the age of 62. Three days later in the middle of the night he entered his house, asked his son for food, which he ate, and then left. Two evenings later he reappeared and again asked for food. The son refused and was found dead the next day. Shortly thereafter several villagers became ill with exhaustion, diagnosed from an excessive loss of blood. They reported that, in a dream, they had been visited by Plogojowitz who bit them on the neck and sucked their blood. Nine persons mysteriously died of this strange illness during the following week.

The chief magistrate sent a report of the deaths to the commander of the Imperial forces, and the commander responded with a visit to the village. The graves of all the recently dead were opened. The body of Plogojowitz was an enigma to them—he appeared as if in a trance and was breathing very gently. His eyes were open, his flesh plump, and his complexion ruddy. His hair and nails appeared to have grown and fresh skin was found just below the scarfskin. Most importantly, his mouth was smeared with fresh blood.

The commander quickly concluded that Plogojowitz was a vampire. The executioner who came to Kisolova with the commander drove a **stake** through the body. Blood gushed from the wound and from the body orifices. The body was then burned. None of the other bodies manifested signs of vampirism. To protect them, and the villagers, **garlic** and whitethorn were placed in their graves and their bodies were returned to the ground.

The story was reported by the Marquis d' Argens in his *Lettres Juives,* which was quickly translated into an English version in 1729. While not as well known as the incidents that began with Arnold Paul, the Plogojowitz case became a major building block of the European vampire controversy of the 1730s.

Sources:

Barber, Paul. *Vampires, Burial, and Death: Folklore and Reality.* New Haven, CT: Yale University Press, 1988. 236 pp.

Summers, Montague. *The Vampire in Europe.* London: Routledge, Kegan Paul, Trench, Trubner & Co., 1929. 329 pp. Reprint. New Hyde Park, NY: University Books, 1961. 329 pp.

P.N. ELROD *See:* ELROD, P.N.

POE, EDGAR ALLAN (1809-1849)

Edgar Allan Poe, American writer of horror stories, was born in Boston, Massachusetts, the son of David Poe, Jr. and Elizabeth Arnold Hopkins. His parents, both actors, died of tuberculosis in 1811. Young Edgar then lived with John Allan, a merchant, and incorporated his benefactor's name into his own. He entered the University of Virginia in 1826, but after a falling out with John Allan he dropped out and joined the army. His first book, a collection of his poems, was published in 1827 shortly after his tenure in the army began. In 1830, after a brief reconciliation with John Allan, Poe was sent to West Point, but was expelled for disobedient behavior. In 1831 he discovered an aunt in Baltimore, where he had moved to take a newspaper job. In 1835 he married Virginia Clemm, his aunt's daughter. During the 12 years of their marriage (she died in 1847) he moved from one job to the next, drinking heavily, and perpetually broke. Poe himself died on a drinking binge—he was left in a gutter. His literary executor wrote a scurrilous biography that turned people from Poe during the rest of the century.

Rediscovered in this century, an extensive and appreciative new readership was found for both his poetry and short stories, many of which have been turned into movies. While Poe explored many areas of the **gothic** world, he never specifically wrote a vampire story. Contemporary critics, however, have found widespread use of a vampire- or *lamiai*-like character in his various writings. Amid the actual vampirism encountered in the literature of the early nineteenth century, historians studying the period have noted that many writers considered a more metaphorical or **psychic vampirism** in which the vampirelike character sucks the life-force or psychic energy from another, usually a person close to them. As early as the 1930s, D. H. Lawrence recognized such a theme in Poe's work.

More recently James Twitchell carried Lawrence's position even further and argued that "the development of the vampire analogy was one of Poe's central artistic concerns." Twitchell saw the vampire (or *lamiai,* since his vampires were usually female) theme in a number of Poe's stories, particularly "Bernice," "Morella," "Ligeia," "The Oval Portrait," and "The Fall of the House of Usher." In "Bernice," Poe told the story of a man originally in a weakened condition who seemed to grow more robust as his cousin Bernice declined and finally died. In the end, however, it was Bernice who became the vampire, a fact signaled by her paleness, lifeless eyes, and prominent teeth. The narrator of the story became increasingly afraid and after Bernice died, he went to the grave to slay the vampire by pulling her teeth.

Bernice was but the first of the supposed female vampires created by Poe. Morella, in a story written shortly after ''Bernice,'' bled the narrator of her story of his willpower. She also possessed the vampire's identifying marks: cold hands, hypnotic eyes, and a bloodless face. In like measure, the title character in ''Ligeia'' (1938) possessed a *lamiai*'s likeness with her cold hands, pale appearance, prominent teeth, and hypnotic eyes. In these first three stories, suggested Twitchell, Poe used the vampiric theme to highlight a form of relationship between lovers. He returned to the theme in ''The Fall of the House of Usher'' in which the vampiric exchange of energy occurred between siblings. Finally, in ''The Oval Portrait,'' Poe wove a fascinating story of an artist who destroyed those around him by his all-consuming passion with his work. The story concerned an artist who was painting the portrait of his beautiful wife, not noticing that as he painted she grew weaker and weaker. He concluded his work by declaring it the essence of life itself. He eventually found his wife dead, completely drained of life.

Twitchell's interpretations highlighted, if not a central theme, certainly an important and somewhat neglected secondary motif in Poe, a motif all the more significant due to its widespread use in the writings of so many of Poe's prominent contemporaries.

Sources:

Bailey, J. O. "What Happens in 'The Fall of the House of Usher'?" *American Literature* 35 (1964): 445-66.

Blythe, Hal, and Charlie Sweet. "Poe's Satiric Use of Vampirism in 'Bernice.'" *Poe Studies* 14, 1 (June 1981): 23-24.

Kendall, Lyle H., Jr. "The Vampire Motif in 'The Fall of the House of Usher.'" *College English* 24 (1963) 450-53.

Kiessling, Nicolas. "Variations of Vampirism." *Poe Studies* 14, 1 (June 1981): 14-14.

Poe, Edgar Allan. *The Complete Works.* Ed. by James A Harrison. New York: T. Y. Crowell, 1902. The stories considered above have been frequently reprinted in various collections.

Richmond, Lee. "Edgar Allan Poe's 'Morella': Vampire of Volition." *Studies in Short Fiction* 9 (1972): 93-94.

Twitchell, James. *The Living Dead: A Study of the Vampire in Romantic Literature.* Durham, NC: Duke University Press, 1981. 219 pp.

———. "Poe's 'The Oval Portrait' and the Vampire Motif." *Studies in Short Fiction* 14, 4 (Fall 1977): 387-93.

POETRY, THE VAMPIRE IN

It is not surprising that the vampire theme found poetry a natural vehicle of expression. Poetry speaks with some facility to the intense passions and dark concerns that have been suppressed by conventional society. It relates the central human needs of love and community (family) commonly celebrated by society with other key concerns of death and sexuality. The latter concerns, while just as important to human life, are often neglected and the emotions attached to them denied, while discussion of them has been pushed to the fringe of social discourse.

The vampire, especially after its unreality was established by Enlightenment science, became an ideal vehicle for writers to express their own complex feelings and to illustrate their personally frightening experiences. The dead-yet-alive vampire, blending into the shadows of society, obsessed with blood (and other body fluids), embodies the darker but no less real side of human existence. Given any of the commonly accepted positive human virtues/emotions, the literary vampire immediately juxtaposed in his or her person both the lights and shadows of the author's life.

THE VAMPIRE IN GERMANY: The emergence of the modern literary vampire began with the exploration of the vampiric theme in German poetry. More than a generation prior to **John Polidori**'s famous 1819 novella, **"The Vampyre"**, poets were reacting to the intense debate on the subject of vampirism that took place in the German universities in the mid-eighteenth century. Possibly the first such poem was ''Der Vampir'' written by Heinrich August Ossenfelder:

> My dear young maiden clingeth
> Unbending, fast and firm
> To all the long-held teaching
> Of a mother ever true;
> As in vampires unmortal
> Folk on the Theyse's portal
> Heyduck-like do believe.
> But my Christian thou dost dally,
> And wilt my loving parry
> Till I myself avenging
> To a vampire's health a-drinking
> Him toast in pale tockay.
>
> And as softly thou art sleeping
> To thee shall I come creeping
> And thy life's blood drain away.
> And so shalt thou be trembling
> For thus shall I be kissing
> And death's threshold thou'lt be crossing
> With fear, in my cold arms.
> And last shall I thee question
> Compared to such instruction
> What are a mother's charms?

Several other such poems show up among the collections of other poets. More important than any of these specifically vampire poems, however, was Gottfried August Bürger's ''Lenora''. ''Lenora'' told the story of William, a young man who died but came back to claim his bride. Arriving in the middle of the night, he called his unsuspecting Lenora to travel with him to their bridal bower. She responded:

> ''Say on, where is our bridal hall?
>   Where, how the nuptial bower?''

> Far, far from her! Still, cool, and small,
>   Where storms do never lower.''
> Hast room for me'' ''For me and thee.
> Come up and dress and mount with me!
>   The wedding guests are waiting
> No more of this debating!''

After a ride across the country at break-neck speed, William spoke again:

> ''In somber gloom we near the tomb
>   With song and wailing tearful!
> Come, open stands the bridal room,
>   Though all around look fearful.
> Come sexton, quick! Come with the choir,
> Our bridal song with reed and lyre!
>   Come, priest, and say the blessing,
>   Nor wait for our confessing.''

The couple rode into the graveyard:

> High reared the steed and wildly neighed;
>   Fire from his nostrils started.
> And lo! from underneath the maid
>   The earth to 'dmit them parted.

While not a vampire poem, ''Lenora'' does play upon the themes of love and death, which are so essential to the vampire's life. Denounced by the literary critics, it nevertheless found a popular following. In the 1790s it was translated into English by William Taylor of Norwich and for several years circulated around Norwich as a favored topic for poetry reading/discussion groups, then a widespread entertainment event. Sir Walter Scott heard of ''Lenora'' from the discussions of Taylor's as yet unpublished poem and went about securing a copy of the original German text. Upon reading it, he too became enthusiastic and chose to make his own translation of the ballad the initial publication of his lengthy literary career. Published the same year as Taylor's translation, it became by far the more popular version. The importance of ''Lenora'' was further demonstrated by the fact that at least three additional translations were made in 1796 alone and others in subsequent years.

In Germany, ''Lenora'' inspired what has been traditionally called the first vampire poem, ''The Bride of Corinth'' (''Die Braut von Korinth''), in 1797 by Johann Wolfgang von **Goethe**. In most later commentaries on the vampire in literature, Goethe was said to have based his poem on the account from ancient **Greece** of the encounter of the philosopher Apollonius with a *lamiai*. However, it is, in fact, a retelling of another story; that of Philinnon as related by Phlegon. Goethe's version told of a young man who had traveled to Athens to claim his bride, the daughter of his father's comrade. Shown into a guest room after his travels by the woman of the house, he was surprised by the arrival of a beautiful young woman at his door. He noted her paleness, but nevertheless invited her in. She wanted a lock of his hair. He offered her wine, but she would not drink until midnight, at which time she assumed a new vitality. As dawn approached, the mother heard the activity of the two lovers and burst into the room. The girl turned out to be the recently deceased daughter of the family. She had returned from her grave to find that her love had denied her. Before she left, she told the young man that he would soon join her in death, and asked her mother to see that their bodies were burned. She had been given an ineffective Christian burial, and was now roaming the land without the peace of death.

THE VAMPIRE IN ENGLAND: "Lenora" and "The Bride of Corinth" became standard reading for the emerging romantic movement centered on poets who were exploring their inner consciousness. Both Shelley and **Lord Byron** were enthusiastic about it, and "Lenora" directly influenced Coleridge and Southey who shared the honors for producing the first vampire poems in English. Geraldine, the vampiric figure in **Samuel Taylor Coleridge**'s 1801 poem "Christabel," was never identified as a vampire, but did, as Arthur H. Nethercot effectively argued, have many of the characteristics. The first hint that something was wrong with Geraldine was revealed as Christabel assisted Geraldine, who had appeared outside the castle walls, into her castle home:

> The lady Geraldine sank, belike through pain,
> And Christabel with might and main
> Lifted her up, a weary weight,
> Over the threshold of the gate:
> Then the lady rose again,
> And moved, as she were not in pain.

Coleridge seemed to be making reference to the vampire's inability to enter a home without first being invited, now a standard aspect of vampire lore. Then Christabel's father's dog gave an uncharacteristic "angry" moan as Geraldine passed; vampires have a strange effect on **animals**. As Christabel showed her guest to a place of rest, Geraldine noted that the midnight hour was hers. The two women lay together, and Christabel took Geraldine in her arms. During Geraldine's hour, Christabel entered a trance-like state while all the night-birds quieted their chirping. The following morning, Christabel awoke refreshed as one who had "drunken deep of all the blessedness of sleep!"

While Coleridge must be credited with writing the first English vampire poem, **Robert Southey** was the first to introduce a traditional vampire as a character in one of his poems. In the poem "Thalaba the Destroyer" the hero Thalaba had a brief encounter with a vampire, his recently deceased bride Oneiza who had died on their wedding day. He was forced to kill her anew by thrusting a lance through her. Southey based his addition of the vampire character to his poem upon reading accounts of the eastern European vampires—the same ones that had, a half century earlier, caused the debate over vampires in Germany.

Once introduced to British poetry, the vampire made a number of appearances throughout the early nineteenth century. Possibly the first poem dedicated to the vampire was John Stagg's "The Vampyre" published in his 1810 collection *The Minstrel of the North*. Like Southey, Stagg derived the material for his poem from reading the Eastern European vampire reports. It related a vampire's attack on Herman, the young husband of Gertrude. Herman was under attack from his recently deceased friend Sigismund:

> From the drear mansions of the tomb,
> From the low regions of the dead,
> The ghost of Sigismund doth roam,
> And dreadful haunts me in my bed!
>
> There vested in infernal guise,
> By means to me not understood,
> Close to my side the goblin lies,
> And drinks away my vital blood!

As he predicted, Herman died that night, and a frightened Gertrude saw Sigismund at their house. The next day, Sigismund's tomb was opened and his body was found "Still warm as life, and undecay'd." The townspeople drove a **stake** through the body of both Sigismund and Herman.

Stagg was followed by Lord Byron's "The Gaiour," the story of an "infidel," a term for non-Muslims in Islamic lands. As an infidel, the story's hero was cursed by a Muslim to become a vampire and roam the earth sucking the blood of those closest to him. **John Keats**' "Lamia" (1819) drew inspiration from the ancient account of Apollonius and the *lamiai*, though the translation he used lacked the key original reference to the vampire. In Keats' poem, the *lamiai* established a vampiric relationship, a form of psychic vampirism, with Lucius, her human love.

Keats also drew on the vampiric relationship in several other poems such as "La Belle Dame sans Merci". After Keats, however, the vampire appeared only rarely in English literature. Henry Thomas Liddell, a youthful James Clark Maxwell, and Arthur Symons were among the authors who made the few British contributions to the genre between the Romantics and the 1897 effort of poet laureate Rudyard Kipling. Kipling's brief "The Vampire" was a lament to the "rag and a bone and a hank of hair," that is, the "woman who did not care" for the man who worshipped her. Kipling's poem was inspired by a painting of a beautiful woman looking down on the man who had died out of love unreturned. It was memorable as a defiant statement about the **vamp**, the non-supernatural *femme fatale*, the subject of numerous silent movies, epitomized by the characters portrayed by actress Theda Bara.

THE FRENCH POETIC VAMPIRE: In France, the vampire emerged after the 1819 novella by Polidori. It found its most expansive expression in drama, there being no fewer than five French vampire plays within two years. During the nineteenth century, however, the short story was the primary vehicle for the vampire's French apparitions. Few poets made reference to the vampire. Among these was **Theophile**

Gautier, more notable for his vampire stories, but who in 1844 also wrote "Les Taches Jaunes." A man who had lost his love sat alone and noted:

> But there are yellow bruises on my body
>   And violet stains;
> Though no white vampire come with lips blood-crimsoned
>   To suck my veins!

And then he asked:

> Oh, fondest of my loves, from that far heaven
>   Where thou must be,
> Hast thou returned to pay the debt of kisses
>   Thou owest me?

A decade later, when Charles Baudelaire began his probings of human experience, he dedicated his poems, including his vampire poems, to Gautier. Baudelaire succeeded in outraging even French society in the mid-nineteenth century. His "The Vampyre" and "Les Metamorphoses du Vampire," which appeared in the 1857 collection *Les Fluers du Mal*, earned him a trial for obscenity. In the latter, for example, he described the morning-after relationship of a man and woman. The man lamented:

> When out of all my bones she had sucked the marrow
> And as I turned to her, in the act to harrow
> My senses in one kiss, to end her chatter,
> I saw the gourd that was filled with foul matter!

THE NEW WAVE OF VAMPIRE POETRY: During the twentieth century the vampire made an increasing number of appearances. Notable among the poems early in the century was the Irish writer James Joyce's brief vampire poem embedded in *Ulysses*:

> On swift sail flaming
> From storm and south
> He comes, pale vampire
> Mouth to my mouth.

In this brief poem Joyce draws on the flying Dutchman legend as treated in Richard Wagner's opera, to which Joyce added mention of the vampire, an image that he uses in several places in *Ulysses*. Wagner, in turn, had been inspired by *Der Vampir,* the opera by **Heinrich August Marschner**. Joyce's fellow countryman, magician, and poet William Butler Yeats, also penned a brief vampire verse titled "Oil and Blood":

> In tombs of gold and lapis lazuli
> Bodies of holy men and women exude

Miraculous oil, odour of violet.

But under heavy loads of trampled clay
Lie bodies of the vampires full of blood:
Their shrouds are bloody and their lips are wet.

During the twentieth century, American poets appropriated the vampire, and as the century progresses, they seem to have become the largest community of poets to make use of it. Among the first was Conrad Aiken. He initially composed a poem, ''La Belle Morte,'' inspired by Gautier's ''La Morte Amoureuse,'' but his ''The Vampire'' (published in 1914) was a delightful piece of light verse:

She rose among us where we lay.
She wept, we put our work away
She chilled our laughter, stilled our play;
And spread a silence there.
And darkness shot across the sky,
And once, and twice, we heard her cry;
And saw her lift white hands on high
And toss her troubled hair.

Aiken described the beautiful vampire who had affected all (at least all of the males) who saw her:

''Her eyes have feasted on the dead,
And small and shapely is her head,
And dark and small her mouth,'' they said,
''And beautiful to kiss;
Her mouth is sinister and red
As blood in moonlight is.''

During the pulp era, as the horror short story in general, and the vampire short story in particular, found a new audience, the number of vampire poems showed a marked increase. But it was nothing to compare with the flood of vampire poems that have appeared since World War II. During the last generation, with the development of a noticeable vampire subculture and the rise of vampire fanzines, a flurry of poetic efforts have responded to a community that lives for the vampire and finds its inspiration in the shadowy side of life. More than half of all the vampire poems ever written have been published since 1970. They are regularly featured in various vampire magazines, from such purely literary magazines as **Margaret Carter**'s *Vampire's Crypt* to the more general periodicals such as ***Realm of the Vampire, Bloodlines, Fresh Blood, Onyx, Shadowdance***, and ***Nefarious***.

Contemporary vampire poems, as poetry in general, tend to be short and revel in images and the feelings of the poet. They stand in sharp contrast to the epic story-telling verse of the nineteenth century. Also, the contemporary poets celebrate the vampire and the dark images of life in the evening, whereas nineteenth century poets tended to operate in the sunlight and to point the finger of moral judgment—or at the very least the righteous indignation of a wronged lover—at the vampires who inhabited their imaginations. Common to both the newer and the older poetry is the use of the vampire as a metaphor to highlight the different levels of power assumed as lovers come together, and the willingness of the more dominant to often take from and leave the other empty. Some of the distinct flavor of the poetry of this generation, as well as the continuing common theme, was vividly illustrated in a poem by Ryan Spingola that appeared in *Nefarious* (1993):

> I was never what you wanted
> but my blood will serve your purpose
> quench your hunger for a short time
> use me, I give you my life and soul
> they mean nothing to me now
> you always had my soul
> Since that day long ago
> now you don't want it
> my blood is all you want
> you'll take it and leave me
> lying on the cold floor to die
> alone and drained
> of my very life

Recent collections of vampire poetry include: *Daymares from the Crypt* compiled by **Margaret Carter**, *The Further Perils of Dracula* by **Jeanne Youngson**, and the two volumes of *Rouge et Noir: les poemes des Vampires*.

Note: Vampire fans are in debt to the **Count Dracula Fan Club** and compiler Steven Moore for the publication *The Vampire Verse: An Anthology*. It is a comprehensive collection of vampire-oriented poems to the modern era, with a sampling of contemporary verse. It also has an extensive bibliography of additional contemporary vampire poems.

Sources:

Carter, Margaret L., ed. *Daymares from the Crypt: Macabre Verse.* San Diego, CA: The Author, 1981. 13 pp.

Martin, Timothy P. "Joyce and Wagner's Pale Vampire." *James Joyce Quarterly* 24, 4 (Summer 1986): 491-96.

Moore, Steven. *The Vampire in Verse: An Anthology.* New York: Dracula Press, 1985. 196 pp.

Praz, Mario. *The Romantic Agony.* London: Oxford University Press, 1970. 479 pp.

Nethercot, Arthur H. *The Road to Tryermaine.* Chicago: University of Chicago Press, 1939. 230 pp. Reprint. New York: Russell & Russell, 1962. 230 pp.

Reed, Meg, and Chad Hensley, eds. *Rouge et Noir: les poemes des Vampires.* 2 vols. Long Beach, CA: Preternatural Productions, 1991.

Twitchell, James. *The Living Dead: A Study of the Vampire in Romantic Literature.* Durham, NC: Duke University Press, 1981. 219 pp.

Whitehead, Gwendolyn. "The Vampire in Nineteenth-Century Literature." *The University of Mississippi Studies in English* 8 (1990): 243-48.

Youngson, Jeanne. *The Further Perils of Dracula.* Chicago: Adams Press, 1979. 50 pp.

P. N. ELROD FAN CLUB

The P. N. Elrod Fan Club was founded in 1993 by Jackie Black for fans of the writings of P. N. Elrod. Elrod burst on the scene in 1990 when three novels under the collective title, ''The Vampire Files,'' were published by Ace Books. *Bloodlist, Lifeblood,* and *Bloodcircle* related the continuing story of reporter Jack Fleming who had been turned into a vampire and then became a detective. The trilogy was well received and three more volumes appeared in 1991 and 1992—*Art in the Blood, Fire in the Blood,* and *Blood on the Water.* Suddenly Elrod joined that small circle of writers identified with the vampire community. She has followed the six- part series with two more novels, *Red Death,* and *I Strahd,* the latter a novelization of characters created for the role playing game *Ravenloft.* Continued adventures of both Jack Fleming and Jonathan Barrett are projected, and an audiotape of *I Strahd* has been released.

The fan club publishes a quarterly newsletter that includes a regular column in which Elrod answers questions sent in by fans. The club may be contacted at 1201 S. Byrd, 39, Tishomingo, OK 73460.

Sources:

Elrod, P. N. *Art in the Blood.* New York: Ace Books, 1991. 195 pp.

———. *Blood on the Water.* New York: Ace Books, 1992. 199 pp.

———. *Bloodcircle.* New York: Ace Books, 1990. 202 pp.

———. *Bloodlist.* New York: Ace Books, 1990. 200 pp.

———. *Fire in the Blood.* New York: Ace Books, 1991. 198 pp.

———. *I Strahd: Memoirs of a Vampires.* Lake Geneva, WI: TSR, Inc., 1993. 309 pp.

———. *Lifeblood.* New York: Ace Books, 1990. 202 pp.

———. *Red Death.* New York: Ace Books, 1993. 288 pp.

POLAND, VAMPIRES IN

The Polish vampire is a variety of the Slavic vampire, with which it shares most essential features. Poland as a national group emerged from the union of some 20 west Slavic tribes including the Polonians (from which the country's name was derived), the Vistulans, the Silesians, the East Pomeranians, and the Mazovians. These tribes originally inhabited the Oder and Vistula River valleys. A significant boost was given to Polish self-identity in the tenth century with the founding of the Piast dynasty. Over the centuries it has found itself caught between the expansionist plans of the Germans and the Russians. Poland reached its greatest expansion in the seventeenth century, but at other times—following reverses on the battlefield—it almost ceased to exist.

Christianity was introduced to Poland in the late ninth century, and from the beginning, the Roman Catholic Church was dominant. As early as 969 A.D. a bishop was appointed to Krakow. Because of the allegiance of the people to Roman Catholicism, many of the beliefs about death and burial that pervaded the mythology of the **southern Slavs** were absent from Polish folklore. Most importantly, unlike Eastern Orthodoxy, Roman Catholicism did not believe that the body of those who died outside of the rites of the church would remain incorrupt. There was some indication that beliefs about the witch/vampire *strix* of Roman origins filtered into Poland during the years immediately after the country's conversion to Christianity.

THE POLISH VAMPIRE: Much of our knowledge of the Polish vampire derives from the field work of Jan L. Perkowski among the Kashubs (northern Poles) of Canada, where belief in vampires remains alive to the present day. Perkowski's research both confirmed previous work and documented some modern developments. The common words for vampire in Poland were *upiór* or *upier* (male) and *upierzyca* (female), a variation on the root Slavic word **opyri*, and alternatively *opji* or *wupji*. (*Upior/ Upiorzyca* were borrowed from the Ukranian language probably in the fifteenth century.) A second word *vjesci* (variously spelled *Vjeszczi* was also popular, and occasionally the term *njetop* was used. The future vampire was destined to its fate from birth. Infants born with a membrane cap (caul) on their heads would become a *vjesci* and those born with two teeth would become a *upier/upierzyca* (or *wupji*). The vampiric career of the future *vjesci* could be diverted by removing the cap, drying it, grinding it into a powder (or burning it), and feeding it (or its ashes) to the child when he or she was seven years old. Perkowski noted that modern Kashubs tended not to separate the two types of vampires.

Those destined to become vampires led otherwise normal lives, but they were noted to have a hyperactive personality and a red face. There was a saying among the Kashubs, "as red as a vampire." Also at the critical period, the time of their death, the future vampire would refuse final rites and the pastoral role of the priest. The body of a person suspected of becoming a vampire had to be watched carefully, for it was believed that the person did not truly die. Hence, the body cooled very slowly, retained its color, and did not stiffen. Spots of blood often appeared around the face and/or **fingernails**. After midnight, according to belief, it awakened and began to eat its own clothes and flesh. It then visited its relatives and sucked their blood. After visiting its relatives, it would go to the local church and ring the church bell. Those who heard the bell were destined to be the vampire's next victims.

Several precautions could be taken to prevent the future vampire from rising. First, the sign of the cross was made over its mouth. A **crucifix** or coin was placed in its mouth. A block might be placed under the chin to prevent it from reaching the burial clothes. The vampire was also blocked by certain obstacles. For example, a net might be put in the **coffin** believing that the vampire would have to untie the knots before ascending. In like measure, a bag of sand or poppy **seeds** would be placed in the coffin in the belief that the vampire would have to count all of the grains of sand or all of the seed before arising from the tomb. Added precaution was afforded by scattering sand or seeds on the route from the grave to the family's house.

If, in spite of all precautions, a vampire managed to arise and attack the community, its tomb had to be opened and the body finally laid to rest. A nail could be driven through its forehead. However, the more common practice was **decapitation** of the corpse after which the severed head was placed between the corpse's feet. At the time the head was severed, blood from the wound would be given to any who had fallen ill as a result of the vampire's attack. The blood caused their recovery.

As late as 1870, in the town of Neustatt-an-der-Rheda (today known as Wejherowo) in Pomerania (northwest Poland), prominent citizen Franz von Poblocki died of consumption (tuberculosis). Two weeks later, his son Anton died. Other relatives also became ill and complained of nightmares. The surviving family members suspected vampirism and they hired a local vampire expert, Johann Dzigielski, to assist them. He decapitated the son who was then buried with his head placed between his legs. Over the objections of the local priest, the body of von Poblocki was exhumed and decapitated in like manner. The priest complained to the authorities who arrested Dzigielski. He was tried and sentenced to four months in jail. He was released only when the family appealed the decision and found an understanding judge.

POLISH FOLKLORE TALES: Along with the accounts of actual vampires within the community, the Poles had a set of folktales about vampires that were told as a means of reinforcing community mores. One example, collected by Marion Moore Coleman, was called ''The Vampire Princess.'' It told of Jacob, a poor man, and a king whose daughter had become a vampire. To earn money to feed his own daughters, Jacob agreed to assist the king. An old man gave him instructions, which Jacob followed to the letter. The final step involved Jacob entering the tomb of the princess when she left it, writing the name of the Holy Trinity inside of the coffin, and sprinkling it with holy water. As a result of his action, the princess was laid to rest and Jacob was amply rewarded by the grateful monarch. Among the community beliefs promoted by the story were the need to rely on the wisdom of elders, the efficacy of the church's means of grace, and the rewards that come to people for virtuous action.

Jan L. Perkowski has noted that belief in vampires, at least in their immediate presence, has been decreasing among the Canadian Kashubs he studied. Among the important cultural factors leading to the loss of belief was the depersonalization of the birth and death process in hospitals and funeral homes. The preparation of the body in funeral homes broke the intimate dynamic between the deceased and the community and made the detection of the potential vampire difficult. Additionally, the Kashubs were surrounded by and participated in a larger culture that does not support a belief in vampires.

Sources:

Bratigam, Rob. "Vampire of Roslasin." *International Vampire* 1, 1 (Fall 1990): 4-5.
Coleman, Marion Moore, comp. *A World Remembered: Tales and Lore of the Polish Land.* Cheshire, CT: Cherry Hill Books, 1965. 229 pp.

Perkowski, Jan L. *The Darkling: A Treatise on Slavic Vampirism.* Columbus, OH: Slavica Publishers, 1989. 174 pp.

————, ed. *Vampires of the Slavs.* Cambridge, MA: Slavica Publishers, 1976. 294 pp.

POLIDORI, JOHN (1795-1821)

John Polidori was the author of **"The Vampyre,"** the first modern vampire story. Polidori attended Edinburgh University from which he received his medical degree at the age of 19. He wrote his thesis in 1815 on the nightmare. Polidori, however, had ambitions to be a writer and thus was delighted to be invited to be the traveling companion of **Lord Byron**, who was leaving England for a tour of continental Europe in the spring of 1816. In Geneva, they were joined by Claire Clairmont, Mary Godwin, and Percy Shelley.

Several days later, occasioned in part by bad weather that limited their movements, Byron suggested that each person begin a "ghost" story. He primed the pump somewhat by reading some of the tales of **E. T. A. Hoffman** to the small group. One evening, each began a story, but Mary Godwin was the only one who took the project seriously. Her story eventually grew into the novel *Frankenstein*. Polidori began a story about a skull-headed lady who was punished for peeking through a keyhole, but like the rest, soon lost interest in developing it very far.

Polidori kept a journal of his experiences in Europe, including some detailed notes on the evening of the storytelling, and most importantly, a synopsis of Byron's story. It concerned two friends traveling in **Greece**, where one of them died. Before his death, however, he extracted an oath from the other that he reveal nothing about the conditions leading to his death. Upon his return to England, he discovered his dead friend very much alive and having an affair with his sister. Byron saw no future in his story and so abandoned it.

Polidori took the plot of Byron's summer tale and developed it into a short story of his own. **"The Vampyre"** was published in the April 1819 issue of *New Monthly Magazine*. He took at least a light swing at Byron in his choice of the name of the vampire, **Lord Ruthven**, the name chosen by Byron's former lover Caroline Lamb to lampoon Byron in her novel, *Glenarvon*. The story was published under Lord Byron's name, which caused it to receive far more immediate attention than it otherwise would have gotten. **Goethe** pronounced it Byron's best, and it was quickly translated into French and hailed as a new Byron masterpiece. The May issue of *New Monthly Magazine* included Polidori's explanation of the circumstances surrounding the writing of "The Vampyre," and Byron wrote a letter to *Gallignani's Magazine* in Paris, but by then it was too late. The *New Monthly Magazine*'s owner continued his insistence that he had published an original Byron story, and emphasized the assertion by publishing it separately as a booklet also under Byron's name.

One can only speculate what might have happened had the story been published under Polidori's name. It launched the first wave of interest in the vampire and went on to become, with the exception of *Dracula*, the most influential vampire tale of all time. The young Parisian romantics immediately saw its potential. Cyprien Bérard wrote a lengthy sequel detailing further adventures of its vampire character, *Lord Ruthwen ou Les Vampires* (1820). **Charles Nodier,** who wrote the preface to the French translation of "The Vampyre," turned the plot into a three act play. The play launched a theatrical fad that saw five Paris playhouses offering vampire productions by the end of the year. Lord Ruthven periodically reappeared during the next 30 years, his last ventures being recounted by **Alexandre Dumas** in 1852.

Unfortunately, Polidori did not live to see the far-reaching results of his story. His life took a negative turn and in 1821 he committed suicide. He was 26 years old.

Sources:

Hanson, Robert R. *A Profile of John Polidori with a New Edition of The Vampyre.* Columbus, OH: Ph.D. dissertation, Ohio State University, 1966.

Polidori, John. *The Diary of John Polidori.* Ed. by William Michael Rosetti. London: Elkin Mathew, 1911. 228 pp.

———. *Ernestus Berchtold, or the Modern Oedipus.* London: Longman, Hurst, Rees, Orme, and Brown, 1819. 275 pp.

———. "The Vampyre." *New Monthly Magazine* (April 1819). Frequently reprinted. Cf. E. F. Bleiler, ed. *Three Gothic Novels.* New York: Dover Publications, 1966. 291 pp.

Senf, Carol A. "Polidori's *The Vampyre*: Combining the Gothic with Realism." *North Dakota Quarterly* 56, 1 (Winter 1988): 197-208.

Switzer, Richard. "Lord Ruthwen and the Vampires." *The French Review* 19, 2 (December 1955): 107-12.

Twitchell, James B. *The Living Dead: A Study of the Vampire in Romantic Literature.* Durham, NC: Duke University Press, 1981. 219 pp.

POLITICAL/ECONOMIC VAMPIRES

The description of a vampire as a creature who attacks people and saps their life blood easily lends itself to various metaphorical extensions. Some of the most popular have been in the political realm in which governments and other powerful social structures have been seen as vampires sucking the life out of people over which they rule or have some control. This political and economic usage of vampires and vampirism was obscured by the dominance of psychological interpretations of vampirism, which directed attention to the personal psychological forces operating in vampire accounts. However, the political element inherent in vampirism has also been recognized almost from the entrance of the word vampire into western Europe.

Shortly after the introduction of the word "vampire" in an English publication in 1732, (an account of the investigation of **Arnold Paul** in Serbia), *The Gentleman's Magazine* of May 1832 carried a satirical article treating the Paul story as a metaphor of appalling social conditions. A decade later, a more serious utilization of the vampire as a political metaphor occurred in *Observations on the Revolution of 1688* (written in 1688, but published in 1741), which noted:

> Our Merchants indeed, bring money into their country, but it is said, there is another Set of Men amongst us who have as great an Address in sending out

again to foreign Countries without any returns for it, which defeats the Industry of the Merchant. These are the Vampires of the Publick, and Riflers of the Kingdom.

A few years later, in 1764 Voltaire, in his *Philosophical Dictionary,* writing in response to the many vampires reported to exist in Eastern Europe, sarcastically responded:

> We never heard a word of vampires in London, nor even Paris. I confess that in both these cities there are stock-jobbers, brokers, and men of business, who sucked the blood of the people in broad daylight; but they were not dead, though corrupted. These true suckers lived not in cemeteries, but in very agreeable palaces.

COMMUNISM AND THE VAMPIRE: The most famous use of the vampire image in political rhetoric came in the nineteenth century in the writings of Karl Marx. Marx borrowed the image from his colleague Frederick Engels, who had made a passing reference to the ''vampire property-holding'' class in *The Condition of the Working Class in England.* Marx commandeered the image and turned it into an integral element of his condemnation of the bourgeoisie (middle class). The bourgeoisie supported the capitalist system—the very system which had it in its grip. Thus Marx could speak of British industry as vampirelike, living by sucking blood, or the French middle class stealing the life of the peasant. In France the system had ''become a vampire that sucks out its the peasant's blood and brains and throws them to the alchemist's cauldron of capital.''

As Chris Baldick noted, for Marx, the essential vampiric relationship was between capital and labor. Capital sucks the life out of living labor and changed it into things of value, such as commodities. He contrasted living labor (the working class) with dead labor (raw products and machinery). Living labor was sentenced to be ruled by the ''dead'' products of its past work. These products did not serve living labor, but living labor served the products it had created. Its service provided the means to obtain the products (which made up the wealth of the middle and upper class). Very early in *Capital* Marx stated, ''Capital is dead labour which, vampirelike, lives only by sucking living labour, and lives the more, the more labour it sucks.''

DRACULA AND XENOPHOBIA: Recent comment on the novel *Dracula,* especially that of Stephen D. Arata, emphasized the social comment Stoker more or less consciously embedded in his novel. *Dracula,* like other British novels of the period, expressed the fear that had developed as the British Empire declined: as the civilized world declined, Great Britain, and by extension western Europe and North America, were under the threat of reverse colonization from the earth's ''primitive'' outposts. **Bram Stoker** was well known for placing his **gothic** setting at a distant place, rather than pushing his storyline into the distant past. In the person of Dracula, he brought the wild unknown of the East, of **Transylvania,** to contemporary **London.**

KARL MARX, WHO DEVELOPED
THE IMAGE OF THE POLITICAL
VAMPIRE, WAS APPROPRIATELY
BURIED IN THE VAMPIRE-
INFESTED HIGHGATE CEMETERY
IN LONDON.

Arata convincingly argued that Stoker held Transylvania as a fresh and appropriate symbol of the strife believed to be inherent in the interaction of the races of eastern Europe and the Middle East. Dracula was not like **Lord Ruthven** or **Carmilla**— merely another decadent member of displaced royalty. He was a warrior in a land that pitted warriors against each other as a matter of course. His intentions were always domination and conquest. The coming of vampirism could bring the racial heterogeneity (and the racial strife inherent within it) to Great Britain. After figuring out what Dracula was and what he intended by his purchase of property in London, **Jonathan Harker** lamented his role in introducing Dracula to the city's teeming millions. He would conquer the land and foul the blood of the British race; the threat to the body was also a threat to the body politic.

The central problem for Stoker was a form of Victorian racism and the threatened pollution that the savage races, represented by the figure of Dracula, brought. After Dracula bit **Mina Murray**, she became "unclean." The boxes of foreign earth he brought to England had to be "sanitized." The untouchable Dracula was also sexually virile, capable of making any number of offspring, while British men by contrast were unproductive. Unlike the mothers, the fathers of the major characters were not mentioned, the only exception being Arthur Holmwood's, who died during the course of the novel. Only at the end, after Dracula was killed, did Harker symbolize the father of a new generation with a pure racial heritage.

THE CONTEMPORARY VAMPIRE: Throughout the twentieth century, the vampire has become a stock image utilized internationally by political cartoonists and commentators to describe the objects of their hostile political commentary. In recent decades, war, fascism, and even the country of Ghana have been labeled as vampiric entities. One recent vivid example of such usage of the vampire metaphor appeared in the wake of the fall of Communism in Russia and Eastern Europe at the end of the 1980s and the proclamation by then U. S. President George Bush of a "New World Order." This term had previously entered the language through its use by a wide variety of political utopians from which it had acquired a number of controversial connotations. It sparked a variety of negative comment. The most virulent of the opposition, claiming that a New World Order amounts to the arrival of a world government, organized the Police Against the New World Order (PO Box 8712, Phoenix, AZ 85066) and launched Operation Vampire Killer 2000. Its program consists of a step-by-step plan to inform police, the military, and other law enforcement units about the New World Order and thus prevent their cooperation with it.

Sources:

Arata, Stephen D. "The Occidental Tourist: Dracula and the Anxiety of Reverse Colonization." *Victorian Studies* 33, 4 (Summer 1990): 621-645.

Baldick, Chris. *In Frankenstein's Shadow.* Oxford: Clarendon Press, 1987. 207 pp.

Engels, Frederick. *The Conditions of the Working Class in England.* 1845. Rept. in: *Karl Marx and Frederick Engels on Britain.* Moscow: Foreign Languages Publishing House, 1953.

Frimpong-Ansah, J. H. *The Vampire State in Africa: The Political Economy of Decline in Ghana.* London: J. Curry, 1991. 205 pp.

McCabe, Joseph. *What War and Militarism Cost: A Realistic Survey of the Vampire of the Human Race and the Supreme Enemy of Human Progress.* Girard, KS: Haldeman-Julius, 1938. 31 pp.

Marx, Karl. *Capital.* New York: Appleton, 1889. 816 pp.

Operation Vampire Killer 2000: American Police Action for Stopping the Program for World Government Rule. Phoenix, AZ: American Citizens & Lawmen Assoc., 1992. 73 pp.

Reiman, Guenter. *The Vampire Economy: Doing Business Under Fascism.* New York: Vanguard Press, 1939. 350 pp.

Voltaire. *Philosophical Dictionary.* 1764. Reprint. New York: Alfred A. Knopf, 1924. 316 pp.

Wilson, Katharina M. "The History of the Word 'Vampire.'" *Journal of the History of Ideas* 44, 4 (October-December 1985): 577-83.

POLONG *See:* MALAYSIA, VAMPIRES IN

PONTIANAK

The *pontianak* was a type of vampire found in **Malaysia, Java,** and throughout much of Indonesia. In Malaysia it was paired with the *langsuyar,* another Malaysian vampire, with whom it shared a common origin. The Malaysian *langsuyar* was originally a woman who gave birth to a stillborn child. The *pontianak* was that stillborn child. As a vampire, it appeared as a night owl. To keep a dead infant from becoming a vampire, it was treated in a manner similar to a woman who died in childbirth: needles were placed in the palms of the hands, eggs were placed under the arms, and beads were placed in the mouth.

In Java and throughout the rest of Indonesia, the *langsuyar* and *pontianak* changed places, and the *pontianak* referred to the female night flying vampire. Raymond Kennedy found the Javanese speaking of the *pontianak* as a banshee who wailed in the night breeze for the child she had lost at birth. Augusta De Wit, also in Java, found the *pontianak* to be thought of as the spirit of a dead virgin. She seduced young men but as they embraced, she revealed the hole in her back. She would break the embrace after a single kiss and pronounce a death sentence on the man. He would die soon afterward if he did not grab her long hair and succeed in loosening a single strand.

In Malaysia, the following charm might also be said:

O Pontianak the Stillborn
May you be struck dead by the soil from the grave-mound.
Thus (we) cut the bamboo joints, the long and the short,
To cook therein the liver of the Jin (Demon) Pontianak.
By the grace of ''There is no God but God''

Of the several Malaysian vampire spirit beings, the *pontianak* was the only one seen as a *jin* or *genie,* a type of spirit in Islamic mythology. In the mid- 1950s Catay-Keris Productions began to make a series of movies based upon the *pontianak* as the beautiful female of Indonesian lore.

Sources:

De Wit, Augusta. *Java: Facts and Fancies.* The Hague: W. P. van Stockum, 1912. Reprint. Singapore: Oxford University Press, 1984. 321 pp.

Kennedy, Raymond. *The Ageless Indies.* New York: John Day Company, 1942. 208 pp.

Skeat, Walter William. *Malay Magic.* New York: Macmillan and Company, 1900. 685 pp. Reprint. New York: Barnes & Noble, 1966. 685 pp.

Winstedt, Richard. *The Malay Magician being Shaman, Saiva, and Sufi.* London: Routledge and Kegan Paul, 1961.

PORPHYRIA

The little known disease porphyria is actually a collective name for seven little known diseases, first identified during the nineteenth century. They were such rare diseases that only through the twentieth century have the different varieties been pinpointed and described. Collectively, the porphyrias are metabolic disorders caused by an enzyme deficiency that inhibits the synthesis of heme, the more extreme forms of which are characterized by an extreme sensitivity to light. The name porphyria comes from the Greek *porphyros,* meaning reddish-purple, and refers to a substance prominent in the blood and urine of a person with porphyria.

As early as 1964, L. Illis, in the article ''On Porphyria and the Aetiology of Werewolves'' suggested that porphyria could account for the reports of **werewolves**. In 1985, David Dolphin, in a paper presented to the American Association for the Advancement of Science, suggested that porphyria might underlie the reports of vampires. He noted that one treatment for porphyria was the injection of heme. Dolphin hypothesized that it was possible that people suffering from porphyria in past centuries attempted to drink the blood of others as a means of alleviating their symptoms. His idea received wide publicity and was seriously debated for a brief period.

Among those who critiqued Dolphin's theory was Paul Barber. First, Barber noted that there was no evidence that drinking blood would have any effect on the symptoms of the disease. Barber argued quite succinctly that Dolphin's theory only fit the situation if one did not look at the data too closely and had little respect for the powers of observation of the people who made the reports. The reports did not describe people who had the symptoms of porphyria. Many of them related to the descriptions of corpses, not living persons, or to disembodied ghosts.

The coverage given the porphyria hypothesis in the popular press was a matter of great distress to many patients suffering from porphyria. *The Los Angeles Times,* for example, provided broad coverage as did many of the tabloids. Dr. Jerome Marmorstein, a physician from California, convinced the *Times* to do follow-up coverage countering the effects of its initial article. Norine Dresser, who has written the most extensive report of the debate, contacted the Porphyria Foundation and discovered a range of negative reactions experienced by people as a result of publicity connecting them to vampirism. Their distress was heightened by several popular television shows built on the possibility of a porphyria patient exhibiting vampiric behavior patterns.

The debate over porphyria lasted for several years, but Dolphin's hypothesis was eventually discarded altogether. It has no viable exponents at present.

Sources:

Barber, Paul. *Vampires, Burial, and Death: Folklore and Reality.* New Haven, CT: Yale University Press, 1988. 236 pp.

Dean, Geoffrey. *The Porphyrias.* Philadelphia: J. P. Lippencott, 1963. 118 pp.

Dresser, Norine. *American Vampires: Fans, Victims, Practitioners.* New York: W. W. Norton & Company, 1989. 255 pp.

Illis, L. "On Porphyria and the Aetiology of Werewolves." *Proceedings of the Royal Society of Medicine* 57 (January 1964): 23-26. Reprint. In Charlotte F. Otten.

A Lycanthropy Reader: Werewolves in Western Culture. Syracuse, NY: Syracuse University Press, 1986, pp. 195-99.

PRISONERS OF THE NIGHT

Prisoners of the Night is a vampire periodical founded in the mid-1980s under the editorship of Alayne Gelfand. It is devoted to vampire fiction and the exploration of issues of sexuality, intrigue, and allure in relation to vampirism. Each issue contains a variety of vampire- oriented short fiction, art, and **poetry**. Subscriptions can be secured from MAKASHEF Enterprises, PO Box 688, Yucca Valley, CA 92286-0688. MAKASHEF Enterprises also publishes *Dyad: The Vampire Stories*, which features short fiction and poetry mixing popular television and movie storylines with a vampire twist. The first issue included stories based on *Miami Vice, Starsky and Hutch, Lethal Weapon, 21 Jump Street, Mission Impossible,* and *Wiseguy.*

PROTECTION AGAINST VAMPIRES

Coinciding with the emergence of the belief in vampires was the designation of methods of protecting oneself from them. In the West, the vampire first appeared as a threat to infants and to mothers at the time of birth, and the best protection available was the use of magic. The earliest barriers known to have been used against vampire attacks were magical words and acts, which survived in the more recent use of prayer and Bible quotes. In the first century, Ovid left an account of an ancient ritual to protect a child, which included touching the door where the infant resided with a branch of a plant, sprinkling the entrance of the house with water, and killing a pig that was offered to the *strix* (vampire) as alternative food. The words spoken during this ritual included:

> Birds of the night (i.e., the *strix*), spare the entrails of the boy. For a small victim (the pig) falls. Take heart for heart, I pray, entrails for entrails. This life we give you in place of a better one.

After the pronunciation of the formula, the house was further secured with thorn branches at the window.

This ancient account of warding off the attack of a vampire mentions one of the several most common items that served to protect people from vampires: the thorn. The **hawthorn**, in part because of its association with the story of Jesus' death, was the most common across southern Europe, but other thorns were used as magical barriers against both vampires and witches. Both the obvious problems that the wild thorn bush had presented to humans and its many values when properly utilized suggested the extension of its role into the supernatural realm. And in fact, it was reported as an anti-witch and anti- vampire shield not only in Europe, but in Asia and the Americas.

Possibly even more than thorns, the pungent herb **garlic**, which was utilized as both a medicine and a food flavoring, was also a protective device used to ward off witches and vampires. Garlic was found in all parts of the world, particularly in the warmer climates, and everywhere found its way onto the list of anti-vampire items. Garlic's inherent value as a medicine, coupled with its strong offensive smell, suggest its power to drive away the forces of evil.

The other ubiquitous protective device against vampires was **seeds**. All around the world people scattered seeds between themselves and the suspected vampire as a barrier. Vampires were thought to be fascinated with counting seeds, be they mustard, millet, grass, linen, carrot, poppy, or rice. The seeds might be scattered in the coffin, over the grave, on the path between the grave site and the village, or around a home that the vampire might enter. The vampire would either have to count the seeds slowly, one per year, or be caught in a situation of having to collect and count enough seeds that it could not finish its task before dawn.

In Europe, especially since medieval times, objects sacred to Christianity, most commonly the **crucifix**, the **eucharistic wafer**, and holy **water**, have been cited as effective protective devices. Vampires were identified with the realm of the devil, and Satan and his minions could not exist in the presence of the holy. Mere priests, also being sinners, were not themselves holy whereas the cross and eucharistic host were symbolic of the very presence of God. In Latin American countries, sacred pendants were attached to a child's bed clothes. In Eastern Orthodox countries, an icon (such as a holy picture) had the same sacred value as a crucifix. Around the world, several other sacred objects have been noted, but were not prominent in non-Christian societies. Here the vampire, indeed the whole realm of evil, was not seen in such polarized categories as it was in the Christian world.

The use of holy objects that banished the unholy also led to a consideration of various purifying agents. The most universal was **fire**. Fire, while destructive, cleansed. It was a major agent in **destroying the vampire**, but could also be used to drive the vampire away.

From accounts around the world, numerous items have been used to ward off vampiric evil. Some are purely defensive, forming a barrier between the vampire and its potential victim. Others create an aura or atmosphere that the vampire would avoid. A few were more offensive and would actually harm the vampire. Typical of the defensive protective devices would be the many things that could be placed in a bedroom to ward off a vampire. Shoes turned around, a **mirror** placed by the door, and a broom put behind a door all served in one or more cultures as a vampire barrier.

Items with illumination or smell, such as candles or garlic, were usually the best to create a protective atmosphere. However, metal, typically pieces of iron, placed under or near a baby's crib was thought to keep vampires away in many diverse cultures. Iron, when used as a structural feature could form a strong physical barrier for it was substance that vampires avoid. To a lesser extent, silver was used in a similar manner. Needles, knives, and scissors were also placed near the bed to be used against the vampire in the advent of an attack.

PROTECTION AGAINST THE MODERN VAMPIRE: With the secularization of the vampire myth in the late twentieth century, most of the prophylactic attributes of traditional protective items were lost. Recent vampires have been affected little by holy objects, thorns or seeds. Garlic alone remained an almost universal item that vampires were believed to avoid, and only a minority of contemporary Westerners used garlic with any regularity. Modern novels left victims with few protections from the onslaught of a vampire. Even fire, also still universally avoided by vampires, rarely occurred in modern society in a form useful to stave off a vampire's effort to reach its victim. Modern vampires generally have extra **strength**, but can be overcome by a group of people.

In recent novels and films, victims have had little to protect them should a vampire single them out. The only forces holding the vampire in check were: a possible moral commitment not to kill; or rational consideration, to be discrete, that kept a vampire from leaving a trail of blood-drained bodies to be found by authorities who would then discern the vampire's existence.

PSYCHIC VAMPIRISM

Among the most popular theories to explain the persistency and universality of vampire myths, the idea of psychic vampirism traced the belief in the vampire to various occult, psychic, or paranormal phenomena. Such explanations have their origin in folktales that identified the vampiric entity as a ghostly figure rather than a resuscitated body—or even further back to ancient times and the earliest vampirelike figures who were described as evil gods or demons, such as the Greek *lamiai*. Such entities were closely related to the medieval **incubus/succubus**.

Psychic explanations of vampirism emerged in the nineteenth century on the heels of psychical research, a scientific discipline that assigned itself the task of investigating experiences formerly assigned to the realm of the occult or supernatural. It attempted to discern which experiences were illusional, which had ready psychological explanations, and which were paranormal or psychic. Psychical research borrowed many terms from Spiritualism and occultism as a part of its early working language. While vampirism was not the most popular topic for discussion among Spiritualists and occultists, it appeared occasionally and seemed to need an explanation from the perspective of the occult worldview.

ASTRAL VAMPIRISM: Among ritual magicians and theosophists, vampirism was explained as due to the astral body. It was their understanding that each person had not only a physical body, but a second body, usually invisible, which was often seen separating from the physical body at the moment of death. This astral body accounted for such phenomena as ghosts and out-of-body experiences. Henry Steel Olcott, the first president of the Theosophical Society, speculated that occasionally when a person was buried, the person was not really dead, but in a catatonic or trance-like state, still barely alive. Citing the experience of yogis who could slow their breathing to an indiscernible rate and survive without air for many weeks, Olcott surmised that a person could survive for long periods in the grave. In the meantime, the person would send his or her astral double to suck the blood or life force from the living and thus gain nourishment. This explanation, to Olcott, seemed to explain why a body that had been buried for weeks or months would be dug up and appear as if it had recently gorged itself on blood. It was his belief that the blood or life force swallowed by the astral form passed immediately to the organs of the physical body lying in the tomb, and then the astral body quickly returned to that corpse.

Olcott also commented on the practice of burning the corpse of a suspected vampire. He argued that vampirism, and the possibility of premature burial and vampirism, made cremation the preferable means of disposing of the physical remains of the deceased. Cremation severed the link between the astral and physical body and prevented the possibility of vampirism. Olcott's original observations, including his preference for cremation, were later expanded on by other prominent theosophical writers such as Charles W. Leadbeater, Arthur E. Powell, and **Franz Hartmann**.

Hartmann traced the astral vampirism theory back to the alchemist Paracelsus (1493-1541), though Olcott and his mentor, H. P. Blavatsky, seemed to have developed the theosophical position directly from the work of pioneer psychical researcher **Z. J. Pierart**. Hartmann, who related several vampire stories in the pages of the *Occult Review,* developed his own variation of astral vampirism in his theory of an "astral tumour." He saw the vampire as a force field of subhuman intelligence that acted out of instinct rather than any rational thought. He differed from Olcott by suggesting that the vampire was malignant, but since it lacked any intelligence, was not morally evil.

Two modern versions of the astral vampirism hypothesis have been articulated. In the 1960s parapsychologist Scott Rogo, based upon broad reading in both vampire and psychic literature and his attention to some of the more exotic psychic occurrences, posed the definition of a vampire as "a certain kind of haunting which results in an abnormal loss of vitality through no recognized channel." Vampirism was not due to a living agent, but to a disassociated portion of the human that remains intact and capable of some degree of human consciousness after death. This remnant eventually dissipated, but that disintegration was postponed by its ability to take life from the living.

Martin V. Riccardo, founder of the **Vampire Studies** network, suggested that astral vampirism may account for many of the reports of vampirism. He focused, however, upon the activity of individuals who sent their astral bodies to attack their sleeping neighbors. Riccardo cited a detailed case reported by occultist Dion Fortune, author of a volume on the prevention of various negative occult experiences, *Psychic Self-Defense.* Fortune discovered that some of her neighbors shared a nightmare attack attributed to the same person. Fortune confronted the person, who admitted to having magical powers and to harming others.

VAMPIRIC ENTITIES: Among the "I AM" Ascended Masters groups that have grown out of the original work of Guy Ballard, a somewhat different emphasis on the vampire theme has been evident. These groups posited the idea that over the centuries, humankind created a large number of what were termed "mass entities." Through calling up negative realities, thinking about them, and feeling violently about them, they called these mass entities into existence. Every time a person gave attention to one of these mass entities, it drew strength from that individual and became more powerful in altering the course of humanity. The legion of mass entities went under names like war, pestilence, and fear.

These mass entities acted like vampires and, as one of the Masters speaking to the members of the Bridge to Freedom asserted, it was the task of those related to the Ascended Masters and their cause to dissolve the "vampire activity of the mass humanly created entities." The work of dissolution was accomplished through decreeing, the particular process of prayer utilized by the "I AM"-related groups.

The Church Universal and Triumphant under the leadership of its Ascended Masters Messenger Elizabeth Clare Prophet, identified a number of disincarnate mass entities, including drug and tobacco entities, insanity entities, sex entities, and entities aligned against the church. One set of entities was termed Halloween entities, which included the horror entity named Dracula (female) or Draculus (male). The church has given its members a ritual of exorcism of these entities.

MAGNETIC VAMPIRISM: The most common form of psychic vampirism, however, did not involve an astral body. Magnetic vampirism was the sapping of life force by one person from another. The idea of magnetic vampirism was based on the commonly reported experience of a loss of vitality caused by simply being in the presence of certain people. Hartmann referred to psychic sponges—people who unconsciously vampirized every sensitive person with whom they come into contact. He believed such a person was possessed by a vampiric entity who continually drained both the energy of its possessed host and all of his or her acquaintances. Scott Rogo, author of *In-depth Analysis of the Vampire Legend,* cited the case of clairvoyant Mollie Flancher who, because of some unrelated condition, was kept under careful observation for many years. It was noted that any animals that she attempted to keep as pets soon died, and those close to her speculated that she had sapped them of their psychic energy.

Sources:

"Address by Believed Archangel Zadkiel." *The Bridge* 7, 7 (October 1958): 16-23.

Fortune, Dion. *Psychic Self-Defense.* London: Aquarian Press, 1952. 212 pp.

Hartmann, Franz. "Vampires" *Borderland* (London) 3, 3 (July 1896).

Leadbeater, Charles W. *The Astral Plane: Its Scenery Inhabitants, and Phenomena.* London: Theosophical Publishing House, 1915. 183 pp.

"Names of Disincarnate Entities and Possessing Demons." Livingston, MT: Church Universal and Triumphant, 1987. 2-page leaflet.

Olcott, H. S. *The Vampire.* Adyar, Madras, India: Theosophical Publishing House, 1920. 19 pp.

Powell, Arthur E. *The Astral Body and Other Astral Phenomena.* Wheaton, IL: Theosophical Publishing House, 1927, 1973. 265 pp.

———. *The Etheric Double and Allied Phenomena.* Wheaton, IL: Theosophical Publishing House, 1925, 1969.

Ravensdale, Tom, and James Morgan. *The Psychology of Witchcraft.* New York: Arco Publishing Company, 1974. 200 pp.

Rogo, Scott. "In-depth Analysis of the Vampire Legend." *Fate* (September 1968): 70-77.

PSYCHOLOGICAL PERSPECTIVES ON VAMPIRE MYTHOLOGY

Through the twentieth century the psychological element of the vampire myth repeatedly captured the attention, even fascination, of psychological researchers. The widespread presence of the vampire image in human cultures led some psychologists to call the vampire an archetype—an intrapsychic psychological structure grounded in the collective unconscious. The differing major psychoanalytic interpretations help us understand the compelling fascination with narratives and images grounded in vampire mythology. This mythology rests on central metaphors of the mysterious power of human blood, images of the undead, forbidden and sexualized longings, and the ancient idea that evil is often hard to detect in the light of day. Humans have long felt that there is a sense in which evil operates like a contagious disease, spreading through defilement caused by direct contact with a carrier of a supernatural ''toxin.''

FREUDIAN PERSPECTIVES: Prior to Freud's development of psychoanalysis, even sophisticated psychologies tended to associate the realm of the undead with premodern demonological mythologies. Freudian thought legitimized the human fantasies of the undead as a topic for serious scientific research. Freud developed a modern map of the unconscious, which he saw as a repository of denied desires, impulses, and wishes of a sexual and sometimes destructively aggressive nature. In sleep we view the unconscious as a landscape inhabited by those aspects of life that go on living, the realm of the undead spoken through dreams. According to Freudian psychoanalysis, vampire narratives express in complex form the fascination—both natural and unnatural—which the living take in death and the dead. From Freud's point of view, ''All human experiences of morbid dread signify the presence of repressed sexual and aggressive wishes, and in vampirism we see these repressed wishes becoming plainly visible.'' Freudians emphasize the ways in which ambivalence permeates vampire stories. Death wishes coexist with the longing for immortality. Greed and sadistic aggression coexist with a compulsively possessive expression of desire. Images of deep and shared guilt coexist with those of virginal innocence and vulnerability.

Freud and his followers noted the ways in which vampire stories reflect the unconscious world of polymorphous perverse infantile sexuality. From a Freudian point of view it is particularly striking that in **Bram Stoker**'s *Dracula*, all the traditional mythical traits of the vampire are blended in such a way that it reflects the Oedipus complex. Count Dracula is seen as a father figure of enormous power and the entire story one of incest, necrophilia, and sadistic acting out of oral and anal fixations. According to Freud, the Oedipus complex emerges between the ages of three and five and is responsible for much unconscious guilt. Oedipal rivalry with fathers causes castration anxiety in males. Both males and females experience feelings of aggression toward the parent of the same sex and feelings of possessive erotic desire toward the parent of the opposite sex. Since conscious awareness of these feelings and associated wishes raises the anxiety level of the child to unacceptable levels, ego defenses come into play to prevent the conscious mind from becoming aware of these dangerous impulses. From the Freudian point of view, it is the function of dreams to disguise these wishes into more acceptable forms that will not wake the dreamer from sleep. Thus, a competent dream interpretation can trace dream images back to the unacceptable Oedipal wishes that underlie them. Following this belief, the vampire image is a fantasy image related to these wishes.

A classical Freudian interpretation of the vampire legend, therefore, seeks to discern the same denied Oedipal wishes in the story. Here the blending of sexuality and aggression in the vampire attack is seen as suggestive of the child's interpretation of the primal scene (the parents having sexual intercourse). That is, the male child often fantasizes sexual contact between his parents as causing harm to the mother. From this point of view, Count Dracula's relationship to his group of female vampires can be interpreted as an image of the father-daughter acting out of repressed incestuous strivings that continue to hold the daughter under the power of the father's spell. Werewolves, "pit bulls from the pounds of hell," are another image of this same father-daughter tryst. The immature female whose own agency and autonomy are undeveloped, secretly agrees to the father's continuing narcissistic claims to power over her life.

Clearly, Freud and his early followers were right in their assumption that the vampire myth was grounded in archaic images of repressed longings and fears. However, the classical Freudian interpretation—while containing some helpful insights—was a gross oversimplification of the psychological contents of vampire narratives. Carl Jung offered the first powerful alternative to early Freudian views.

JUNGIAN PERSPECTIVES: Jungian psychoanalysts point to the worldwide interest in the vampire as evidence of its archetypal nature. From a Jungian perspective, the myriad varieties of vampire narratives found cross-culturally throughout history indicate that these images are not merely by-products of personal experience but are grounded in species-wide psychological structures. In other words, vampire images reflect significant experiences and issues that are universal in human lives around the world. In short, there is something about the vampire that we already understand intuitively—with the knowledge coming from deep within our psyche.

Jung believed that the vampire image could be understood as an expression of what he termed the "shadow," those aspects of the self that the conscious ego was unable to recognize. Some aspects of the shadow were positive. But usually the shadow contained repressed wishes, anti-social impulses, morally questionable motives, childish fantasies of a grandiose nature, and other traits felt to be shameful. As Jung put it:

> The shadow is a moral problem that challenges the whole ego- personality,
> for no one can become conscious of the shadow without considerable moral

effort. To become conscious of it involves recognizing the dark aspects of the personality as present and real.

The vampire could be seen as a projection of that aspect of the personality, which according to the conscious mind should be dead but nevertheless lives. In this way Jung interpreted the vampire as an unconscious complex that could gain control over the psyche, taking over the conscious mind like an enchantment or spell. And even when we were not overwhelmed by this unconscious complex, its presence led us to project the content of the complex onto characters in a vampire narrative. Of social importance, the image of the vampire in popular culture serves us as a useful scapegoat since—through the mechanism of projection—the vampire allows us to disown the negative aspects of our personalities. As Daryl Coats noted:

> Dracula treats Mina Harker the way Jonathan Harker would like to treat her but is scared to do so. Dracula treats Lucy the way her fiance would like to treat her. The vampiric Lucy can respond to men the way the non-vampiric Lucy could not.

This Jungian interpretation of the vampire image provided significant insight into the enormous popularity of vampire stories. From this point of view, a vampire lives within each of us. We project this inner reality on both male and female persons, members of other "tribes" and ethnic groups. We all have a dim awareness that this demonic yet tragic figure is real. However, we usually fail to grasp that this outer image is an expression of an inner reality—a reality that is elusive, threatening to self and others, and that can be effectively engaged only through a combination of empathy and heroic effort.

Jung did not limit his discussion to what would be an oversimplification by suggesting that vampiric traits in others result entirely from our projections. He observed that auto-erotic, autistic, or otherwise narcissistic personality traits can result in a personality that is in fact predatory, anti-social, and parasitic on the life energy of others. In contemporary psychology and psychiatry this type of personality is called a "narcissistic personality disorder." This clinical syndrome contains the most important clues to the psychological reality represented in the vampire image.

Otto Kernberg noted that narcissistic personalities are characterized by a "very inflated concept of themselves and an inordinate need for tribute from others." Capable of only a shallow emotional life they have difficulty experiencing any empathy for the feelings of others. Their ability to enjoy life, except for their experiences of their own grandiose fantasies and the tributes that they can manipulate others into giving them, is severely limited. They easily become restless and bored unless new sources are feeding their self esteem. They envy what others possess and tend to idealize the few people from whom they desire food for their narcissistic needs. They depreciate and treat with contempt any from whom they do not expect nurturance. According to Kernberg, "their relationships with other people are clearly exploitative and parasitic." Kernberg's description of the narcissistic personality sounds as if it were crafted to describe vampires:

It is as if they feel they have the right to control and possess others and to exploit them without guilt feelings—and behind the surface, which very often is charming and engaging, one senses coldness and ruthlessness.

Jungian interpreters often highlight the parallels between the vampire image and the characteristics of narcissistic psychopathology. Daryl Coats, for example, has noted that the vampire is both narcissistic and autistic. He emphasizes that the vampire experiences "narcissistic self-destruction as a result of their intensely selfish desires." Jungian analyst Julia McAfee has focused on the vampire as an image of the shadow of the narcissistic mother. The narcissistic mother, while appearing on the surface to have good will and a nurturing attitude toward the child, in fact drains the energy of the child and weakens the child through subtle (and not so subtle) emotional exploitation. This pattern provides insight into the psychological experiences that underlie the numerous folktales of vampires preying on children. As we shall see below, vampiric parents have always been a widespread human phenomenon—and there is reason to believe that the incidence of such predatory behavior toward children is increasing.

THE VAMPIRE AND THE CULTURE OF NARCISSISM: Although Jung and subsequent Jungian interpreters have noted these and other narcissistic aspects of vampire myths, they did not adequately explore narcissistic psychopathology, the chief psychological dynamic underlying vampire narratives and the major reason for the current burgeoning fascination with the vampire image. However, others assumed the lead in psychoanalytic research into pathological narcissism and its social formation as a "culture of narcissism."

In his book, *The Culture of Narcissism,* Christopher Lasch diagnosed the rapidly spreading climate of moral self absorption that has emerged in the wake of modernization and secularization. Our contemporary penchant for narcissistic self indulgence has resulted from the eclipse of the Protestant work ethic with its emphasis on public involvement and community values. Lasch also noted that contemporary alterations in culture also indicated a fundamental shift in our psychological development. Peter Homans, building on Lasch's insight, suggested "that the dominant or modal personality of our culture has shifted to a narcissistic psychological organization." He tied this recent phenomenon to the process of a gradual erosion of a religious view of the world. Homans further noted that the collapse of the Protestant ethic as a bulwark against pathological self involvement was only the last in a long line of cultural and religious developments leading to today's increasing narcissism. Here we begin to discern the chief psychological dynamic underlying the increasing popularity of vampire images and narratives. "If our society is a culture of narcissistic self-involvement, then the vampire image is a perfect icon to express the psychological character configuration underlying it."

VAMPIRISM AND NARCISSISTIC PSYCHOPATHOLOGY—PERSPECTIVES FROM PSYCHOANALYTIC SELF PSYCHOLOGY: Both Lasch and Homans have emphasized the importance of the contribution of psychoanalytic self psychology in their analysis of the culture of narcissism. They built upon the insights of such theorists as Alice Miller, D. W. Winnicott, Heinz Kohut, and Ernest Wolf who, in their analysis of narcissistic pathology, provide a more adequate understanding of the vampiric metaphor, its myth, and meaning in contemporary culture. Psychoanalyst Alice Miller has written extensively on the ways in which narcissistic mothers prey on their children. In her best-selling *The Drama of the Gifted Child* and other books Miller describes in depth the ways in which an emotionally immature mother can reverse the appropriate flow of nurturing—expecting the child to be whatever the parent needs for the parent's own satisfaction. This creates in the child a compliant but false self—an empty shell that, though it appears to be functional and successful, is in fact covering an extremely enfeebled, needy, and fragile core. D. W. Winnicott, famed British psychoanalyst, wrote extensively on the concept of the false self, which developed in response to an inadequately nurturant early emotional environment. It was, however, psychoanalyst Heinz Kohut who became the chief interpreter of narcissistic personalities. The work of Kohut, Wolf, and their colleagues offers us the best understanding of the psychodynamics that underlie the vampire narratives.

What goes wrong to cause an individual to develop a narcissistic personality disorder? As Kohut emphasized, the development of a "normal" personality requires a creative interplay between the innate potentials of the child's self and the emotional environment that is created by those who are the primary caregivers of the child. The emerging self of the child contains infantile potentials for mature self-esteem and a cohesive sense of the self. But the environment of the child must evoke and support the development of those potentials if the self of the child is to mature into a centered and vigorous personality. Among the essentials of an adequate nurturing environment are: idealizable adults who will allow intimacy and empowering merger with their calmness, and nurturant significant others who will "mirror" the child (i.e., recognize and affirm the independence and value of the child's emerging self).

Kohut asserted that an inadequate nurturing environment causes significant damage in the form of "narcissistic wounds." The development of the self is arrested and the emerging self is left in a weakened condition in an ongoing struggle with overwhelming longings and unmet emotional needs. When normal development is disturbed in this way, the resulting state of emotional disequilibrium necessitates that the individual seek to compensate for the resulting deficit or weakness in the structure of the self. Therefore, the person who has not successfully built a psychological internal structure remains pathologically needy and dependent upon others to perform functions he or she can not execute. Others must be "used" in various ways to bolster a fragile sense of self and to attempt to fill an inner emptiness. This primal dependency is at the root of "vampiric" predatory patterns in relationships.

Symptoms resulting from such emotional disturbances have characteristic features. Patients often report feeling depressed, depleted, and drained of energy. They report feelings of emptiness, dulled emotions, inhibited initiative, and not being completely real. At work they may find themselves constricted in creativity and unproductive. In social interaction they may have difficulty in forming and sustaining interpersonal relationships. They may become involved in delinquent and anti-social activities. They often lack empathy for the feelings and needs of others, have attacks of uncontrolled rage or pathological lying. Often a person with such narcissistic wounds will become hypochondriacally preoccupied with bodily states. They will experience bodily sensations of being cold drained and empty. These clinical descriptions, of course, parallel some of the major symptoms of the victims of vampires as described in vampire narratives. However, we shall see below that the tie between narcissistic pathology and the vampire is much tighter than merely sharing the same set of symptoms.

Narcissistic wounds and resulting pathology manifests in a wide spectrum of clinical syndromes ranging from psychosis to narcissistic character disorders. Among several narcissistic disorders described by Kohut and Wolf that are relevant for an inquiry into the vampire myth, what they denoted as the "mirror- hungry personalities" is of special importance (Kohut and Wolf, 1978). Mirror-hungry personalities "thirst for self objects whose confirming and admiring responses will nourish their famished self." Because of their deep-felt lack of worth and self esteem, these persons have a compulsive need to evoke the attention and energy of others. A few establish relationships that fuel their needs for long periods, but they also engage in a constant search for new sources or supplies of emotional nourishment. Even genuinely loving, accepting, and nurturing responses quickly become experienced as inadequate. Thus, Wolf elaborates:

> Despite their discomfort about their need to display themselves and despite their sometimes severe stage fright and shame they must go on trying to find new self objects whose attention and recognition they seek to induce.

Such mirror-hungary personalities often manifest arrogant superiority. If this arrogance is not affirmed and accepted they will often withdraw into what self psychologists call "a grandiose retreat" seeking refuge in isolation in order to shore up their self esteem. Kohut and Wolf have noted that such personalities may result either from a lack of mirroring attention in childhood or from a problem with the parent's attempts to give such attention. For example, when a parent gives a child attention, the parent may fail to align that attention to the immediate needs of the child. Instead, the parent may claim the child's attention not to nurture the child, but to bolster the parent's enfeebled self by reenforcing the dependence of the child on the parent. In any case, the child does not receive the kind of mirroring attention that allows for the development of an independent and vigorous self. The intense infantile needs for adequate mirroring will persist in the unconscious of the adult in the form of deep and compulsive longings.

It should be clear from the above description that the powerful appeal of vampire narratives grow out of the human experience of mirror-hunger both in parent and child. When this psychologically archaic hunger for affirmation is seen in the parent, it results in predatory emotional exploitation of the child. Such exploitation is an increasingly widespread experience and undoubtedly lies behind the growing fascination with the vampire image. It is these "vampiric parents" that were noted above in the work of Julia McAfee and Alice Miller.

The dynamics of mirror-hunger also helps us to understand the combination of grandiosity and immortality in the vampire mythology. When the child does not experience adequate mirroring, its infantile grandiosity cannot be transformed into a mature psychological structure identified by its more realistic sense of self esteem. Adult untransformed grandiosity makes unrealistic claims on others. There are accompanying fantasies of being able to fly, being invisible, being able to change shape at will—all capacities of a vampire. That the vampire does not, and cannot die can be seen as the way in which grandiose feeling of invulnerability take possession of the mirror-hungry person when archaic needs break through into consciousness. The more disappointment experienced by the mirror-hungry person, the more they resort to the grandiose retreat from social involvement. What is Dracula's remote castle on the top of a difficult to reach mountain if it is not a "grandiose retreat?"

Dracula is not satisfied in his isolation. His hunger drives him in search for someone to fulfill his longings. So the retreat does not satisfy, but intensifies the experience of chronic emptiness and longing, and eventually to another expedition to find "new blood."

The effect of a vampiric visitation is clearly experienced as a drain of energy on the part of the prey, along with a kind of claustrophobic suffocation resulting from the "depletion" of the blood. Mirror-hungry personalities often manifest a kind of "counter-dependency." That is, they will often seek to avoid expressions of emotional need and dependency. Underlying this reluctance to admit chronic unmet needs to self or others is the fear of a disastrous, even fatal, depletion of the person who is seen as a potential source of gratification. Thus we can understand Count Dracula's ambivalence with regard to his claiming Mina as one of the undead. If she is exploited, then she is depleted and no longer an adequate source. Therefore the prospect of "having" can be experienced simultaneously as a threat of "losing." Self psychologists often refer to such fears of destroying the nourishing self object as one of the reasons for the "defense against self object longings." A person may feel, "my needs for mirroring and narcissistic supplies are monstrous—if I gratify them, they may destroy you. Therefore I must not let myself be aware of these toxic needs."

This escape into denial is paralleled in the Dracula's daylight retreat into his **native soil** (mother earth) brought from **Transylvania** and placed in his residence at **Carfax**. While the vampire sleeps during the daylight of consciousness, in the enclosure of unconsciousness—symbolized by the **coffin**—he sleeps unaware of his unmet longings for maternal nurture. This dynamic illustrates the central conflict of the vampire drama. There is both desperation for an infusion of emotional nutriments, "lifeblood," if the fragmentation of the self is to be avoided—and revulsion at the "monstrous" neediness that this desperate longing manifests in the inner emotional life. Although the conscious mind may repress awareness of these urges, we can see here that in the vampiric personality narcissistic rage and related envy manifests in a compulsive desire to seek the destruction of the independent life of the other. The other has been experienced as possessing "the Good," life, energy, well-being, attention, etc. The envying person experiences emptiness within, intolerable longing for something that will fill the void, and the desire to take the other's "life" from them—thereby hoping to gain enough "nutriments" to avoid the disintegration of the self.

This self psychological interpretation sheds some useful light on the elements of **sexuality** so integral to the vampire narratives. A hallmark of vampire mythology has been the powerful erotic imagery accompanying the vampire attack. The sexual contact portrayed in these stories utilizes images of the innocent virginal woman or youth becoming the target of compulsive bloodlust (e.g., narratives that merge engagement in sexual intercourse with the acquisition of bite wounds to the throat and breast). Sexuality and aggression fuse in a manner that leads to the infection and death of the victim. Psychologically speaking, narcissistic wounds often lead the individual to seek narcissistic nourishment through sexual activity. A facade of sexual attraction and genital sexual behavior masks a quest for what Freudians have called oral (not genital) gratification. The compulsive quality of this sexual behavior is grounded in the individual's narcissistic psychopathology. Today this pathology is widely understood to be the emotional foundation of sexual addictions. The Dracula story captures this combination of apparently erotic behaviors that are, in fact, expressions of a deep inner emptiness, not human affection.

THE SOCIAL PSYCHOLOGY OF INTERGROUP HATE: THE VAMPIRE IMAGE AND THE MECHANISM OF SCAPEGOATING: It would be a mistake to assume that the psychological importance of the image of the vampire relates only to intrapsychic, familial, and small group interpersonal interactions. The projection of this image onto other social groups is undoubtedly one of the powerful psychosocial mechanisms that fuel malignant racism, anti-Semitism, sexism, and other expressions of scapegoating with resultant hate crimes.

In the dynamic of scapegoating, we find someone or some group that can be used as a receptacle for the projection of the vampiric image. Then the scapegoat can be blamed, cast out of the community, and/or persecuted with various degrees of violence. This externalization of the vampiric image enables the person or "ingroup" to feel better—guiltless or "cleansed." As a social dynamic such scapegoating both allocates blame and seems to "inoculate" against further disappointments by evicting or eliminating the cause of one's "disease."

Racist rhetoric is frequently fueled by the projection of the image of the vampire onto other social groups. An example of this recently became international news when a leader of an American Black Muslim group publicly characterized Jewish people as "bloodsuckers," imaging them as parasites draining the lifeblood of the black community. The projection of this image enables the dehumanization of its target group—allowing the rationalizations needed to justify ruthless racial discrimination and violence.

Such racist rhetoric is usually grounded in what self psychologists call "narcissistic rage." Narcissistic rage differs from anger or "righteous indignation." Anger always seeks positive changes in relationship in a context of justice and potential reconciliation—not the destruction of the other party. Narcissistic rage seeks the utter destruction of the independent personhood of the other—either through death or ruthless enslavement and exploitation. Thus the vampire within projects its image onto the other—thereby justifying its own predatory intentions.

CONCLUSIONS—EMPTINESS, ENVY, AND THE VAMPIRIC PERSONALITY:
In surveying the development of the major psychoanalytic perspectives on the vampire, the attempt was made to trace the manner in which each school of thought, out of its understanding of fundamental psychodynamic processes, sought to interpret vampirism. Each of these perspectives contributed to the understanding of the rich mythological and symbolic narratives of vampire lore and one by one built the foundation upon which the more promising contemporary interpretation by self psychology, which views the vampire as a primary icon representing essential aspects of narcissistic psychopathology, rests. Self psychology calls attention to the significance of inner emptiness, the longing for emotional nutriments that can prevent disintegration of the self, and the resulting envy that sees such nutriments (the Good) in others and wishes to take it from them. Contemporary psychoanalytic self psychology in the tradition of Heinz Kohut and Ernest Wolf, in offering a more complete psychological understanding of the origins, major forms, and manifestations of such vampiric psychological illness, also provides the necessary therapeutic insights and techniques needed if healing for vampiric and vampirized personalities is to occur.

Sources:

Bourguignin, Andre. "Vampirism and Autovampirism." In *Social Dynamics of Antisocial Behavior*. Ed. by L.B. Schesinger and E. Revitch. Chicago: Charles C. Thomas, 1983, pp. 278-301.

Coats, Daryl R. "Jung and the Irish Vampires." *Journal of Vampirology* 2,4 (1986): 20-27.

Henderson, D. James, "Exorcism, Possession, and the Dracula Cult: A Synopsis of Object-Relations Psychology." *Bulletin of the Menninger Clinic* 40, 6 (November 1976): 603-28.

Homans, Peter. *The Ability to Mourn: Disillusionment and the Social Origins of Psychoanalysis*. Chicago: University of Chicago Press, 1989.

Hull. Princeton, N.J.: Princeton University Press, 1970). Chicago Press, 1989.

Jones, Ernest. *On the Nightmare*. Hogarth Press, 1931. Rev. ed,: New York: Liverright Publishing Corporation, 1951.

Jung, C. G. *Civilization in Transition*. Vol. 10, *The Collected Works of C. G. Jung*. Princeton, NJ:Princeton University Press, 1962.

————. *Mysterium Conjunctions: Inquiry into the Separation and Synthesis of Psychic Opposites in Alchemy*. Vol. 14, *The Collected Works of C.G. Jung*. Trans. by R.F.C. Kohut, Heinz and Wolf, Ernest S. "The Disorders of the Self and Their Treatment: An Outline." *The International Journal of Psycho-Analysis*. 59, 4 (1978): 413-425.

Lasch, Christopher. *The Culture of Narcissism: American Life in an Age of Diminishing Expectations*. New York: W.W. Norton & Co., Inc., 1979.

Lee, Ronald, and Martin Colby J. *Psychotherapy After Kohut: A Textbook of Self Psychology*. Hillsdale N.J.: The Analytic Press, 1991.

McAfee, Julia. "The Vampire Archetype and Vampiric Relationships." Evanston, IL: The C.G. Jung Institute of Chicago, 1991.

Millon, Theodore. "Narcissistic Personality: The Egotistic Pattern." In *Disorders of Personality: DSM-III, Axis II*. New York: John Wiley and Sons, 1981.

Noll, Richard. *Vampires, Werewolves, and Demons: Twentieth Century Reports on the Psychiatric Literature.* New York: Brunner/Mazel 1992.

Richardson, Maurice. "The Psychoanalysis of Ghost Stories." *The Twentieth Century* 166 (1959): 427.

Twitchell, J. B. "The Vampire Myth." *American Imago* 37,1 (Spring 1980): 83-92.

Ulanov, Ann and Barry Ulanov. *Cinderella and Her Sisters: The Envied And The Envying.* Philadelphia: The Westminster Press, 1983.

Wolf, Ernest S. *Treating the Self: Elements of Clinical Self Psychology.* New York: Guilford Press, 1988.

—**Margaret L. Shanahan**

PULP MAGAZINES, VAMPIRES IN THE

Essential to the spread of the vampire as an object of popular myth in the twentieth century was the pulp magazines, mass circulation periodicals named for the cheap pulpwood paper on which they were printed. They were the successors of the "penny dreadful" of the nineteenth century and, in an age before television, filled a significant gap in the entertainment industry. The earliest pulps provided readers with a wide variety of genre fiction, including detective, western, jungle, and action/adventure. Occasionally they would print a "different" or "off trail" story, the avenue by which the then highly questionable horror tales slipped into the pulp market. *All-Story Magazine* was among the first to feature such "different" stories.

During World War I pulps built around single themes began to appear. Beginning in 1919, *The Thrill Book* specialized in "strange, bizarre, occult, mysterious, tales," the harbinger of the first true all-horror pulp, *Weird Tales,* which made its appearance in 1923. *Weird Tales* dominated the tiny market through the 1920s. It was joined by *Ghost Stories* in 1926, and following the creation of a broad public by the Universal movies in the early 1930s, additional titles appeared. *Strange Tales of Mystery and Terror* hit the stands in 1931 as direct competition for *Weird Tales,* and they were soon joined by Popular Publications' *Dime Mystery* (1933), *Terror Tales* (1934), and *Horror Stories* (1935). *Terror Tales* and *Horror Stories* specialized in what was termed the shudder tale, in which hapless victims were terrorized by mad scientists and/or psychotics masquerading as model citizens. Through the 1930s a number of horror titles were created to meet a burgeoning public demand.

The vampire slowly emerged as a subject of horror fiction. Horror great H. P. Lovecraft may have introduced the vampire theme into pulp fiction with his story "The Hound," which appeared in the February 1924 issue of *Weird Tales.* However, the first true vampire story seems to have been "The Vampire of Oakdale Ridge" by Robert W. Sneddon in the December 1926 issue of *Ghost Stories.* Beginning in 1927 with "The Man Who Cast No Shadow" by Seabury Quinn and the reprinting of "Dracula's Guest" by **Bram Stoker**, *Weird Tales* began to offer a steady stream of vampire tales. Quinn's character was typical of early twentieth-century vampires. Based in part on Dracula, he possessed the same hairy palms and lacked a mirror image. Quinn set his Transylvanian Count Czerny against his popular detective figure Jules de Grandin. The first era of vampire tales culminated in two of the best pulp stories: ''A Rendezvous in Averoigne'' by Clark Ashton Smith and ''Placide's Wife'' by Kirk Mashburn, both of which appeared in *Weird Tales* contemporaneously with the release of **Universal Pictures'** *Dracula* **(1931)**.

The decade following the success of **Bela Lugosi**'s *Dracula* saw the publication of numerous vampire stories by a group of authors who emerged as the collective heirs of the **Edgar Allan Poe** tradition of horror. Typical of these new authors, Robert E. Howard, famous as the creator of Conan, had his ''The Horror from the Mound'' published in *Weird Tales* in 1932. Like other vampires to appear later in the Conan adventures, his first vampire was a loathsome powerful monster who could be destroyed only in a one-on-one fight with cowpuncher Steve Brill.

Among the most heralded and reprinted of the 1930s vampire pulp fiction, *I, the Vampire* was an early work by science fiction great Henry Kuttner. He set his suave vampire, Chevalier Futaine, in contemporary Hollywood where he arrived from France to play a role in a new film, *Red Thirst*. Robert Bloch, a prolific horror writer who reached his zenith of fame with the novel *Psycho,* began in the 1930s pulps. Among his memorable early tales was ''The Cloak,'' which appeared in *Unknown Worlds* in 1939. This story built upon the premise of a cloak that transformed the wearer into a vampire.

Pulp fiction continued through World War II but experienced a noticeable decline by the end of the 1940s. The publishers of *Weird Tales* finally went bankrupt in 1954, and the pulps gave way to newsstand magazines devoted to fantasy, science fiction, and horror such as *The Magazine of Fantasy and Science Fiction* and *Fantastic Stories of the Imagination*. Over the years several vampire anthologies have lifted stories from the pulps, and by far the best collection appeared in *Weird Vampire Tales* (1992), edited by Robert Weinberg, Stefan R. Dziemianowicz, and Martin H. Greenberg.

Sources:

Carter, Margaret L. *The Vampire in Literature: A Critical Bibliography*. Ann Arbor, MI: UMI Research Press, 1989. 135 pp.

Parnell, Frank H., with Mike Ashley. *Monthly Terrors: An Index to the Weird Fantasy Magazines Published in the United States and Great Britain*. Westport, CT: Greenwood Press, 1985. 602 pp.

Sullivan, Jack, ed. *The Penguin Encyclopedia of Horror and the Supernatural*. New York: Viking, 1986. 482 pp.

Weinberg, Robert, Stefan R. Dziemianowicz, and Martin H. Greenberg, eds. *Weird Vampire Tales: Thirty Chilling Stories from the Weird Fiction Pulps*. New York: Gramercy Books, 1992. 442 pp.

R

RAKSHASAS *See:* INDIA, VAMPIRES IN

REALM OF THE VAMPIRE

Realm of the Vampire is an organization that celebrates the presence of the vampire in film and literature. It grew out of a publication titled *The Vampire Journal*, founded by Sharida Rizzuto in New Orleans in 1985. The *Journal* was associated for a time with another vampire interest group, **Dracula and Company**, and was superseded by the Realm of the Vampire after Dracula and Company disbanded in 1992. The Realm publishes a newsletter and a hefty 100-page journal, both of which appear twice annually. The journal features vampire fiction and poetry and reviews of vampire movies and books. The Realm of the Vampire also periodically sponsors meetings and special functions in the New Orleans area. Among the editors of the *Realm of the Vampire* are Ann Hoyt and novelist Frances Nordan. Metaphysical author Leilah Wendell, who operates the Westgate House of Death Gallery in New Orleans, is a special consultant.

Rizzuto has become involved in publishing a wide range of novellas, books, and periodicals since 1983. Her interests and publishing efforts have included **Sherlock Holmes, witchcraft, science fiction**, the old West, literary fiction, and Hollywood nostalgia. In 1983 she founded **Friends of Dark Shadows** and began to publish two periodicals, *The Collinsport Record* (originally *Inside Dark Shadows*) and *The Collinwood Journal*. The Friends of Dark Shadows and the two periodicals were discontinued in 1987, and she began to incorporate Dark Shadows material into *The Vampire Journal*. In 1990 illness forced her to stop publishing but in 1992, Hoyt and Nordan continued the trend begun in the journal. With Rizzuto's cooperation they issued the first *Realm of the Vampire* journal and newsletter. In 1993 Rizzuto resumed her publishing activity and with Hoyt and Nordan announced the publication of

◀

REALM OF THE VAMPIRE
CELEBRATES THE APPEARANCE OF
THE VAMPIRE IN FILM AND
LITERATURE.

several new biennial periodicals including: *Realm of Darkness* (dedicated to **gothic**, death, and vampire themes) and *Nightshade* (a journal devoted to the same themes in fiction). Realm of the Vampire also issued *The Vampire Directory,* which highlights vampire organizations, publishers, and manufacturers of clothing and **paraphernalia**. It has been announced that several journals on non-gothic themes will also appear in 1994.

Realm of the Vampire can be reached at PO Box 517, Metairie, LA 70004-0517.

Sources:

Realm of the Vampire. Premiere Issue, 1 (Fall/Winter 1992).

REDCAPS

Redcaps were malevolent spirits found in the lowlands of Scotland (now part of the **United Kingdom**). They haunted abandoned sites, especially places where violent deeds had been committed. Their connection to vampirism seems to have come from their carrying a cap that had been dyed red with human blood. At every opportunity the redcap would re-dye the cap in blood.

Sources:

Briggs, Katherine. *An Encyclopedia of Fairies.* New York: Pantheon Books, 1976. 481 pp.

RENFIELD, R. N.

R. N. Renfield was one of the major characters in **Bram Stoker**'s novel *Dracula.* At the beginning of the novel, Renfield was confined to the lunatic asylum managed by Dr. **John Seward**. Apart from demonstrating a set of unusual symptoms, no history of or specific reason for his confinement was given. When first described, Seward praised Renfield for his love of animals, however, he revised his opinion somewhat after Renfield ate them in order to absorb their life. Seward then coined a new term to describe him: zoophagous, or life-eating.

Renfield's symptoms took a radical turn just at the time **Dracula** made the move from **Whitby**, where he had landed in England, to **London**. Renfield announced to his attendant, ''I don't want to talk to you: you don't count now; the Master is at hand.'' Seward initially interpreted his words as the sign of a religious mania. The next day he made the first of several attempts to escape and headed toward **Carfax**, where Dracula had deposited his boxes of earth. Captured, he was returned to the asylum, but escaped again several days later.

Seward's attention was diverted from Renfield for several weeks as he treated **Lucy Westenra**. However, one evening Renfield escaped and broke into the doctor's study. He attacked Seward with a knife, and dropped to the floor to lick up the drops of blood that had fallen from the cut. Again several weeks passed during which time Lucy died and it was determined that she was a vampire. Almost forgotten again in the concern for Lucy, Renfield called Seward to come to his cell. He spoke sanely to Seward and the men who accompanied him, Dr. **Abraham Van Helsing**, **Quincey P. Morris**, and **Arthur Holmwood**.

Later that day Seward and Renfield had a long conversation, and Seward determined that Dracula had been with him. The following day, it was found that Renfield had been attacked in his cell. Seward and Van Helsing attended him, and Renfield described Dracula's attack. He mentioned **Mina Murray**'s (now Harker)

The Vampire Book 505

name as he lay dying. From his words, Van Helsing determined that Mina was under attack, and the men left Renfield to save her. They broke into her bedroom just in time as she and Dracula were sharing each other's blood.

The character of Renfield, the mad man—one of the most vivid and interesting in the novel—has been given quite varied treatment in the several stage and screen adaptations, though most often he was used to promote atmosphere or as comic relief. Dwight Frye was especially remembered for his frantic portrayal of Renfield in **Universal Pictures'** *Dracula* **(1931)**.

The presence of Renfield, however, vividly portrayed the intense evil represented by the vampire. Supernatural explanations vie, even in the modern secular world, with scientific ''psychological'' explanations that have no need to appeal to either the sacred or preternatural. In the end, even Dr. Seward agreed that the psychological explanations were inadequate, and he joined Van Helsing on the crusade to destroy the vampire.

Sources:

Waller, Gregory A. *The Living and the Undead: From Stoker's Dracula to Romero's Dawn of the Dead.* Urbana, IL: University of Illinois Press, 1986. 376 pp.

RICCARDO, MARTIN V. (1952-)

Martin V. Riccardo, writer, researcher, and lecturer on vampires, is the founder of **Vampire Studies** (formerly the Vampire Studies Society), a center he founded in 1977 for collecting and sharing information on the subject. That same year he founded and edited *The Journal of Vampirism*, which was issued quarterly for the next two years. While being the center of vampire fandom in Chicago, Riccardo built one of the largest correspondence networks of vampire enthusiasts and was himself an active member in many of the vampire-oriented fan clubs. He also built a large collection of vampire books, magazines, and comic books.

In 1983, Riccardo saw the publication of two vampire books: *Vampires Unearthed*, the first comprehensive bibliography of vampire literature and filmography, has become the basis of all vampire bibliographic work since; *The Lure of the Vampire* was a collection of Riccardo's essays. Through the 1980s and 1990s, Riccardo has also written a number of articles on vampires for various vampire and

▶ MARTIN V. RICCARDO, FOUNDER
OF VAMPIRE STUDIES.

occult periodicals. He coined the term "astral vampirism" to refer to a form of **psychic vampirism** in which the astral body or ghost form left the physical body for the purpose of draining blood or vital energy. During the early 1990s he concentrated his research on vampire dreams and fantasies. Riccardo does not believe that there are Dracula-like creatures but does believe in the process of psychic vampirism in the sense that people can suck the energy or life force from others.

A hypnotist by profession, Riccardo heads the Advanced Hypnosis Center. In 1984-85 he edited *Hypno-News of Chicagoland.* He also has an interest in the larger occult world and in 1981 founded the Ghost Research Society. For six years in the 1980s he hosted the Midwest Ghost Expo, a yearly convention for ghost researchers and enthusiasts. He also has coordinated programs on a variety of occult topics from reincarnation to ancient Egypt.

Most recently, Riccardo has hosted the Vampire Fan Forums, gatherings of fans and personalities in the vampire world for lectures, discussions, and fun. He is a popular lecturer on vampires and the occult in the Midwest.

Sources:

"The Lure of Martin V. Riccardo." Special issue of *The Vampire Information Exchange Newsletter* 53 (April 1991).

Riccardo, Martin V. *The Lure of the Vampire.* Chicago: Adams Press, 1983. 67 pp.

———. *Mystical Consciousness.* Chicago: MVR Books, 1977.

———. "The Persistent Vampire." *Fate* (July 1978): 74-81.

———. "Vampires—An Unearthly Reality." *Fate* (February 1993): 61-70.

———. *Vampires Unearthed.* New York: Garland Publishing, 1983. 135 pp.

RICE, ANNE (1941-)

Among the people who have contributed to the significant increase of interest in the vampire in the last decades, few rank with writer Anne Rice. Her major vampire character, **Lestat de Lioncourt**, who was introduced in her 1976 book, *Interview with the Vampire*, has taken his place beside **Bram Stoker**'s *Dracula* and *Dark Shadows'* **Barnabas Collins** as one of the three major literary figures molding the image of the contemporary vampire.

Rice was born Howard Allen Frances O'Brien in the Irish community in New Orleans, Louisiana, and changed her name to Anne shortly after starting school. During her late teens she grew increasingly skeptical of the teachings of the Roman Catholic Church in which she had been raised. She not only rejected the unique place of the Roman Church among other religious bodies, but also pronounced her disbelief in its major affirmations of the divine work of Jesus Christ and the existence of God. She replaced her childhood religious teachings with a rational ethical system, an integral element in her reworking of the vampire tradition.

Both Rice and her poet husband Stan Rice began writing professionally during the early 1960s, but he was the first to receive recognition. In 1970 he won the Joseph Henry Jackson Award for poetry. Rice sold her first story, "October 4, 1948," in 1965, but it was not until 1973 that she felt ready to quit her job in order to write full time.

THE VAMPIRE CHRONICLES: As early as 1969 Rice had written a short story that she called "Interview with the Vampire." In 1973 she turned it into a novel and attempted to sell it. Following several rejections, Alfred A. Knopf bought it, and it

ANNE RICE, AUTHOR OF *INTERVIEW WITH THE VAMPIRE.*

was published in 1976. The book became an unexpected success and has remained in print both in hardback and paperback. Her second novel, *The Feast of All Saints,* was published by Simon & Schuster three years later, and a third, *Cry to Heaven,* appeared in 1982. Meanwhile another side of Rice emerged in a series of novels published under a pseudonym, A. N. Roquelaure. *The Claiming of Sleeping Beauty* (1983), *Beauty's Punishment* (1984), and *Beauty's Release: The Continued Erotic Adventures of Sleeping Beauty* (1985) were adult erotic fantasy novels. The sado-masochistic theme in the Roquelaure novels carried over into the more conventional novels published under a second pseudonym, Anne Rambling. In the midst of the release of these novels, her important vampire short story appeared in *Redbook* in 1984, ''The Master of Rambling Gate.''

Rice returned to the vampire theme in 1985 with *The Vampire Lestat,* the most heralded of what was to become the ''Vampire Chronicles'' series. This volume further developed the character of Lestat introduced in her earlier work. He emerged as a strong secular individualist who took to the vampire's life quite naturally. Born into the lesser aristocracy, he defied the vampire establishment in Paris and decided to make his own way in the world. A man of action who rarely rested in indecision, he was also deeply affected by poetry and music and freely showed his emotions. Rice described him as both an androgynous ideal and an expression of the man she would be if she were male. Like Rice, Lestat rejected his Catholic past and had no aversion to the religious weapons traditionally used against his kind. Seeking moral justification for his need to feed on fresh blood, he began to develop a vampire ethic, selecting those who had done some great wrong as his victims.

The success of *The Vampire Lestat* led to demands for more, and Rice responded with *The Queen of the Damned* (1988). Like the previous volumes, it became a bestseller and soon found its way into a paperback edition. Previously, *Interview with the Vampire* had also appeared in an audio cassette version (1986), and the publishers moved quickly to license audio versions of *The Queen of the Damned* (1988) and *The Vampire Lestat* (1989).

Rice was now a recognized author and her writing was regularly the subject of serious literary critics. She continued to produce at a steady rate and successively completed *The Mummy* (1989), *The Witching Hour* (1990), and *Lasher* (1993). In the meantime, further adventures of Lestat appeared in the fourth volume of the Vampire Chronicles, *The Tale of the Body Thief* (1992), released on audio cassette simultaneously with its hardback edition. In 1991 Katherine Ramsland finished her biography of Rice, titled *Prism of the Night,* and moved on to compile a reference volume, *The Vampire Companion: The Official Guide to Anne Rice's Vampire Chronicles* (1993).

LESTAT'S VAMPIRE CULTURE: Rice's novels have permeated the culture like no other recent vampire writings. Lestat was honored by a **gothic** rock band that took his name as their own and the androgynous ideal has been adopted by the gothic subculture. In 1988 a group of women in New Orleans founded an Anne Rice Fan Club. Rice approved the effort but suggested that a reference to Lestat be added to the club's name. It emerged as the **Anne Rice's Vampire Lestat Fan Club**. Two years later, Innovation Corporation picked up the comic book rights to *The Vampire Lestat,* which it issued as a 12-part series. A similar release of *Interview with the Vampire* and

The Queen of the Damned appeared in 1991. Her short story *The Master of Rambling Gate* was also issued in 1991. Innovation brought together one of the finest teams in comic book art to produce the three. Innovation also released three issues of *The Vampire Companion*, a fanzine in comic book format that included stories about Rice's vampire books, Innovation's artists, and the process of producing the comic adaptations.

In 1976 Paramount bought the rights to *Interview with the Vampire*. The rights had a 10-year option, which expired in 1986. The rights reverted to Rice, and she, in turn, sold them to Lorimar along with the rights to *The Vampire Lestat* and *The Queen of the Damned*. Lorimar sold its rights to *Interview with the Vampire* to Warner Brothers who then passed them on to Geffen Pictures. In 1993 Geffen announced that it would begin the filming under Neil Jordan's direction. The studio signed **Tom Cruise** to play Lestat and Brad Pitt to play Louis, the vampire who is interviewed in the story.

There is every reason to believe that Lestat will remain a popular reference point for the vampire community for many years to come. Volume five of the Vampire Chronicles, *Of Hell and Heaven*, has been announced for publication in 1994.

Sources:

"Anne Rice" In *Contemporary Literary Criticism*. Ed. by Daniel G. Marowski and Roger Matuz. Vol. 41. Detroit, MI: Gale Research Company, 1987.

Frankel, Martha. "Interview with the Author of Interview with the Vampire." *Movieline* 5,5 (January/February 1994): 58-62, 96-97.

Ramsland, Katherine. *Prism in the Night: A Biography of Anne Rice*. New York: Dutton, 1991. 385 pp.

———. *The Vampire Companion: The Official Guide to Anne Rice's The Vampire Chronicles*. New York: Ballantine Books, 1993. 507 pp.

Rice, Anne. *Interview with the Vampire*. New York: Alfred A. Knopf, 1986. 448 pp. Reprint. New York: Ballantine Books, 1987. 346 pp.

———. "The Master of Rambling Gate." *Redbook* (February 1984): 50-58. Reprint: Bryon Preiss, ed. *The Ultimate Dracula*. New York: Dell, 1991, 15-46. Reprint: Richard Dalby, ed. *Vampire Stories*. Secaucus, NJ: Castle Books, 1993, 189-203.

———. *The Queen of the Damned*. New York: Alfred A. Knopf, 1988. 448 pp. Reprint. New York: Ballantine Books, 1989.

———. *Tale of the Body Thief*. New York: Alfred A. Knopf, 1992. 430 pp. Reprint. New York: Ballantine Books, 1993.

———. *The Vampire Lestat*. New York: Alfred A. Knopf, 1985. 481 pp. Reprint. New York: Ballantine Books, 1986. 550 pp.

ROLLIN, JEAN (1938-)

Jean Rollin, a French horror movie director, is best known for his production of a number of adult erotic vampire films, beginning with *La Reine des Vampires* (*Queen of the Vampires*) in 1967. Rollin entered the film industry as a teenager in 1955 as an assistant director working on animated films. A short time later he produced his first film, a short entitled *Le Amours Jaunes*. In 1965 he met American producer Sam Selsky. Selsky asked him to put together a half-hour short to run with one of his already produced films. The resulting *Le Reine des Vampires* proved superior to the feature with which it ran and led Selsky to support Rollin's first feature film, *Voil des Vampires* (*Rape of the Vampires*), which met with relative commercial success. In this film, into which most of *Le Reine des Vampires* was edited, he established what was to be the hallmark of his subsequent work—a preference for visual effects that carry the film's message and dominate the often weak storylines. His first feature, in fact, has a rather flimsy plot about the attempt to free two women from a vampire's curse. It enjoyed success, in large part, because of the sexual scenes—the audiences reacted to a decade of rather strict censorship during the reign of Charles de Gaulle.

Rollin followed the success of his first work with his first color feature, in 1969 *La Nue Vampire* (released in English as *The Nude Vampire* or *The Naked Vampire*) and in 1970 one of his more heralded productions, *Le Frisson des Vampires* (released in English as *Sex and the Vampire* or *Vampire Thrills*). *Le Frisson des Vampires* concerned a young couple who encounter the vampire Isolde, who makes her first appearance in a suit of chain mail and thigh-high leather boots. Again the visual imagery overshadowed the plot, and Rollin saturated the audience with his portrayal of vampirism as a perverse form of sexuality.

By the time of his third film he had assembled a group of specialists who assisted him through the 1970s in a series of low-budget productions. He regularly returned to the vampire theme feeling that vampirism provided an effective vehicle for portraying erotic themes. In 1971 he directed *Le Cult du Vampire*, followed in 1972 by *Requim pour un Vampire* (also released as *Vierges et Vampires* and *Caged Virgins*).

Rollin also directed a number of horror and adult features. In 1974 he produced *Levres se Sang* and followed it in 1979 with *Fascination* and in 1982 with *La Morte-Vivante*. *Fascination* featured a cult of vampire women (a theme Rollin had used in earlier films) that conducted ritual sacrifices of men in a remote castle home. His last vampire movie concerned a dead woman revived as the result of a chemical waste spillage. She began attacking people to drink their blood, an appetite that grew stronger as the film progressed.

In his spare time Rollin authored several horror-fantasy novels. He continued to make movies through the 1980s and into the 1990s and currently lives in Paris.

Sources:

Flynn, John L. *Cinematic Vampires: The Living Dead on Film, Television, from The Devils Castle (1896) to Bram Stoker's Dracula (1992)*. Jefferson, ND: McFarland & Company, 1992. 320 pp.

"Lust at First Bite." *The Dark Side* (July 1992): 5-10. Pirie, David. *The Vampire Cinema*. London: Hamlyn, 1977. 175 pp.

ROMANIA, VAMPIRES IN

No country is as identified with vampires as Romania. A land of rich folklore concerning vampires, its reputation was established by **Bram Stoker,** whose novel ***Dracula*** began and ended in **Transylvania**. Though at the time Transylvania was a part of Hungary, it is now a part of Romania. Recent scholarship has confirmed that one of the sources from which Stoker created Dracula was **Vlad the Impaler**, a fifteenth-century prince of Wallachia, a section of modern Romania that lies south of the Carpathian Mountains.

Stoker derived much of his knowledge of Transylvania, where he located **Dracula's Castle**, from Emily Gerard's *The Land Beyond the Forest* (1888). Gerard was a Scottish woman who had married a Polish officer serving the Austrian army. As a brigade commander, he was stationed in Transylvania in the 1880s. The couple resided in Sibiu and Brasov. In describing the several supernatural entities encountered in her research on practices surrounding death, she wrote:

> More decidedly evil is the *nosferatu,* or vampire, in which every Roumanian peasant believes as firmly as he does in heaven or hell. There are two sorts of vampires, living and dead. The living vampire is generally the illegitimate offspring of two illegitimate persons; but even a flawless pedigree will not insure any one against the intrusion of a vampire into the family vault, since every person killed by a nosferatu becomes likewise a vampire after death, and will continue to suck the blood of other innocent persons till the spirit has been exorcised by opening the grave of the suspected person, and either driving a stake through the corpse, or else firing a pistol-shot into the coffin. To walk smoking around the grave on each anniversary of the death is also supposed to be effective in confining the vampire. In very obstinate cases of vampirism it is recommended to cut off the head, and replace it in the coffin with the mouth filled with garlic, or to extract the heart and burn it, strewing its ashes over the grave. (p. 185)

Romanian concepts concerning the vampire are strongly related to folk beliefs of the **Slavic vampire** in general, though the Romanians, in spite of being largely surrounded by Slavic peoples are not themselves Slavic. Romanians locate their origins in ancient Dacia, a Roman province that emerged in Transylvania and the surrounding territories after Trajan's capture of the land in the second century A.D. He also brought in thousands of colonists in the sparsely settled area. As the colonists and the indigenous people intermarried, a new ethnic community was born. This new community spoke a form of Latin—the basis for modern Romanian. Their subsequent history, especially over the next century is a matter of great controversy between Romanians and their neighbors, a controversy difficult to resolve due to the paucity of archeological evidence.

Following the abandonment of the territory at the end of the third century, Transylvania became the target of various invaders, including the early Slavic tribes. In the seventh century it was absorbed into the Bulgar Empire. Though some Romanians had become Christians as early as the fourth century, the systematic conversion of the land began in the ninth century soon after the conversion of the Bulgarians under the brothers Cyril and Methodius. The Romanian church eventually aligned itself to Eastern Orthodoxy under Bulgarian episcopal authority.

At the end of the tenth century, the Magyars (present-day Hungarians) included Transylvania in their expanding kingdom. The Hungarians were Roman Catholics, and they imposed their faith in the newly conquered land. They also encouraged immigration by, among others, the **Szekleys**, a branch of Magyars, and Germans. During the thirteenth-century, seizing upon a moment of weakened Hungarian authority in Transylvania, a number of Romanian Transylvanians migrated eastward and southward over the Carpathian Mountains found the kingdoms of Moldavia and Wallachia. An Eastern Orthodox bishop was established a century later in Wallachia. From that time to the present day, Transylvania would be an item of contention between **Hungary** and Wallachia (which grew into the present-day Romania). Ecclesiastically, both Roman Catholics and Eastern Orthodox would compete for the faith of the people.

No sooner had Wallachia and Moldavia been established than a new force arose in the area. The Ottoman Empire expanded into the Balkans and began the steady march across the peninsula that would carry it to the very gates of Vienna in the early sixteenth century. During the fourteenth century Hungary and the Turks vied for hegemony in Wallachia, thus providing a context for a prince of Wallachia by the name of Vlad to travel to the court of the Emperor Sigismund where he would join the Order of the Dragon, pledged to defend Christian lands against the invading Muslims. The Wallachian prince would become known as **Vlad Dracul** (1390?-1447). He in turn would be succeeded by his son, **Vlad the Impaler** (1431?-1476), known as Dracula. Vlad the Impaler is remembered today in Romania as a great patriot and a key person in the development of the Romanian nation. After Vlad's death, Wallachia fell increasingly under Turkish hegemony, and Moldavia soon followed suit. Through the 1530s the Turkish army moved through Transylvania to conquer the Hungarian capital in 1541. The remainder of the Hungarian land fell under the control of the Austrian Hapsburg empire. The incorporation of the Romanian kingdoms into the Turkish empire allowed a degree of religious freedom, and Protestantism made a number of inroads, particularly in Transylvania. Contemporary scholars have emphasized that none of the vampire legends from Romania or the surrounding countries portray Vlad the Impaler as a vampire. In the German and some Slavic manuscripts, Vlad's cruelty and his identification as Dracula and Devil was emphasized, however, Dracula as a vampire was a modern literary creation.

In the seventeenth century, the Hapsburgs began to drive the Ottomans from Europe, and by the end of the century assumed dominance of Transylvania and began to impose a Roman Catholic establishment. Transylvania remained a semiautonomous region until 1863 when it was formally unified with Hungary. For over a century Moldavia survived amid Russians, Greeks, and Turks, each fighting for control until a united Romania came into existence in 1861. Through a series of annexations at the beginning and end of World War I, including that of Transylvania in 1920, Romania, in roughly its present size, came into existence. The Romanian majority exists side-by-side with a significant Hungarian minority in Transylvania, and the Romanian Orthodox Church competes with a strong Roman Catholic and persistent Protestant presence.

VLAD THE IMPALER'S COURT IN BUCHAREST.

THE VAMPIRE IN ROMANIA: The Romanian vampire, in spite of the distinct ethnic origin of the Romanians, is a variation of the Slavic vampire. However, like the vampire in each of the other Slavic regions, the vampire in Romania has acquired some distinguishing elements. That distinctiveness begins with the major term used to label vampires, as found by Harry Senn in his field work in the 1970s. *Strigoi* (female, *strigoaica*) is closely related to the Romanian word *striga* (a witch), which in turn was derived from the Latin *strix*, the word for a screech owl that was extended to refer to a demon that attacked children at night. A second term, *moroi* (female, *moroaica*), also spelled *murony* in older sources, seems to be the common term in Wallachia, as *strigoi* is in Transylvania. The Romanians also distinguish between the *strigoi vii* (plural, *strigoi*), or live vampire, and the *strigoi mort* (plural, *stigoi morti*), or dead vampire. The *strigoi vii* are witches who are destined to become vampires after death and who can send out their souls and/or bodies at night to cavort with the *strigoi mort*. The live vampires tend to merge in thought with the *striga* (witches), who have the power to send their spirits and bodies to meet at night with other witches. The dead vampires are, of course, the reanimated bodies of the dead who return to life to disturb and suck the blood of their family, livestock, and—if unchecked—their neighbors.

The *strigoi mort* was a variation of the **Slavic vampire**, although the Romanians were not Slavs and used a Latin word to designate their vampire. The *strigoi* was discovered by an unusual occurrence either at their birth or death, and a living *strigoi* was a person who was born with either a caul or a little tail. A *strigoi vii* may become a *strigoi mort,* as well as other people who died irregularly by **suicide** or an accident.

Romanians also use the term *vircolac,* but almost exclusively to describe the old mythological wolflike creature who devoured the sun and moon. The closely related terms *pricolici* or *tricolici* were also wolves. *Virolac* is a variation of the Greek *vrykolakas* or the Serbo-Croatian *vukodlak.* Agnes Murgoci, who worked in Romania in the 1920s, found that they still connected the term with its pre-vampiric mythological meaning of a creature who devours the sun and moon. At times when the moon appears reddish, it was believed to be the blood of the *vircolac* flowing over the moon's face. More definitive work was pursued by Harry Senn in Transylvania in the 1970s. He found that popular use of the *vircolac* distinguished it from the *strigoi.* The term *vircolac* described a person who periodically changed into one of several **animals**, usually a pig, dog, or wolf. As such it was much closer to the popular concept of **werewolves** than vampires.

Nosferatu is an archaic Old Slavonic term apparently derived from *nosufuratu,* from the Greek *nosophoros,* ''plague carrier.'' From the religious context, the word passed into popular usage. It has been variously and mistakenly cited as a Romanian word meaning either ''undead'' (Wolf) or the Devil (Senn). Through the twentieth century it seems to have dropped from use in Romania. Stoker's use of the term derived from Gerard. It was used by Freidrich Wilhelm Murnau in his attempt to disguise his movie, *Nosferatu, Eine Symphonie des Garuens* from Dracula. He tied the story to the great plague that hit Bremen, Germany, in 1838.

In Romania the vampire was believed to come into existence first and foremost as the product of an irregular birth, and any number of conditions have been reported that could predispose a person to become a vampire. Children born out of wedlock, born with a caul, or who died before baptism could become vampires. Pregnant women who did not eat salt or who have allowed themselves to be gazed upon by a vampire could bear a vampiric child. The seventh child of the same sex in one family was likely to have a tail and become a vampire.

Though children with an irregular birth were the prime candidates of vampirism, anyone could become a vampire if bitten by one. Other potential vampires included people who led wicked lives (including men who swore falsely), witches (who had relations with the Devil), a corpse over whom a cat had jumped, or a person who committed suicide.

The presence of vampires was usually first noticed when several unexpected deaths in a family and/or of livestock followed the death of either a family member or of someone suspected of being a vampire. The vampire might, on occasion, appear to the family, and female vampires were known to return to their children. The home of a suspected vampire often was disturbed by its activity, either in throwing things around (poltergeist) or getting into the food supplies. The vampire would first attack the family and its livestock and then move on to others in the village. If not destroyed it might move on to more distant villages and even other countries, where it could reassume a normal role in society.

Vampires were especially active on the eve of **St. George's Day** (either April 23 or May 5), the day witches and vampires gathered at the edge of the villages to plan their nefarious activities for the next year. Villagers would take special precautions to ward off the influences of supernatural beings on that evening. Stoker's character **Jonathan Harker** made the last leg of his journey and finally arrived at Dracula's Castle on St. George's Eve. Vampires and witches were also active on St. Andrew's Day. St. Andrew was the patron of wolves and the donor of garlic. In many areas of Romania, vampires were believed to become most active on St. Andrew's Eve, continued to be active through the winter, and ceased their period of activity at Epiphany (in January), Easter, or St. George's Day.

St. George's Day was and is celebrated throughout much of Europe on April 23, hence the Eve of St. George's would be the evening of April 22. St. Andrew's day is November 11, and the eve immediately precedes it. Romania which was on the old Julian Calendar, was 12 days behind the modern Gregorian calendar. Thus in Stoker's day, St. George's Day would have been celebrated in Romania on what was the evening of May 4-5 in western Europe. Likewise, St. Andrew's Eve would have been the evening of November 23-24. The lag time between the Julian and our Gregorian calendar increases one day every century.

The grave of a suspected vampire would be examined for telltale signs. Often a small hole would be found in the ground near the tombstone, a hole by which the vampire could enter and leave the coffin. If there was reason to believe someone was a vampire, the grave was opened. Those opening the coffin would expect to find the corpse red in the face. Often the face would be turned downward and fresh blood on it or, on occasion, corn meal. One foot might have retracted into a corner of the coffin. Senn reported that a vampire in the community could be detected by distributing garlic at church and watching to see who did not eat.

It was the common practice of Romanians to open the graves of the deceased three years after the death of a child, four or five years after the death of a young person and seven years after an adult's death. Normally, only a skeleton would be found, which would be washed and returned to the grave. If, however, the body had not decayed, it was treated as if it were a vampire.

There were a wide variety of precautions that could be taken to prevent a person either from becoming a vampire or doing any damage if they did become one. A caul might be removed from the face of a newborn and quickly destroyed before it was eaten. Careful and exacting preparation of the body of the recently dead also prevented their becoming a vampire. The thorny branch of the wild rose might be placed in the tomb. **Garlic** was also very useful in driving away vampires. On St.

Andrew's and St. George's Eve, the windows (and other openings of the house) were anointed with garlic, and the cows would be given a garlic rubdown.

Once the vampire was in the tomb, distaffs might be driven into the ground above the grave upon which the vampire would impale itself if it were to rise. On the anniversary of the death of a suspected vampire, the family walked around the grave.

Once a vampire began an attack on the community and its identity was discerned, the vampire had to be destroyed. Emily Gerard, author of *The Land Beyond the Forest,* found the emergence of a relatively new tradition in nineteenth-century reports in which a vampire might be killed by firing a **bullet** into the **coffin.** The preferred method, however, was to drive a **stake** into the body, followed by **decapitation**, and the placing of garlic in the mouth prior to reburial. This method was adopted by Stoker in *Dracula* as a means of destroying the vampiric nature that had taken over **Lucy Westenra**'s body. In Romania, the staking could be done with various materials, including iron or wood, and the stake was impaled either in the heart or the navel. Instead of decapitation, the body could also be turned face downward and reversed in the coffin. Millet **seeds** might be placed in the coffin to delay the vampire, who must first go through a lengthy process of eating the millet before rising from the grave.

An even more thorough process might be followed in the case of a vampire resistant to other preventive measures. The body might be taken from the grave to the woods and dismembered. First, the heart and liver were removed, and then piece by piece the body was burned. The ashes could then be mixed with **water** and given to afflicted family members as a curative for the vampire's attack.

VAMPIRE FOLKTALES: The Romanian vampire has also become the subject of a number of folktales. Folklorists have noticed that many relate to the cases of couples in which one has recently died. Frequently reprinted was the story of ''The Girl and the Vampire'' (which also exists in a Russian variant) in which the boy committed suicide following his failure to gain the marriage blessing of his girlfriend's parents. As a result of his manner of death, he became a vampire and began to visit the girl at night. The girl spoke with a wise elder woman in the village who instructed her to attach a thread to his shirt. She then traced the thread, which led to the graveyard and disappeared into the grave of her late boyfriend.

The vampire continued to visit the girl, and they continued their sexual liaison, when her parents died. She refused the vampire's request for her to tell what she had seen the night she followed him to the graveyard, and the girl soon also died. She was buried according to the wise woman's instruction. A flower grew from her grave, which was seen by the son of the emperor. He ordered it dug up and brought to his castle. There, in the evening, it turned into a maiden. Eventually she and the emperor's son were wed. Some time later, she accompanied her husband to church and had an encounter with the vampire. He followed her into church where she hid behind an icon, which then fell on the vampire and destroyed him.

VLAD THE IMPALER'S TOWER AT TIRGOVISTE.

The story served as a discouragement to out-of-wedlock sexual relations while at the same time reaffirming the wisdom of older people and upholding the church as a bastion against evil. Similar values were affirmed in other stories.

It was once the case, according to one folktale that "vampires were as common as leaves of grass, or berries in a pail." They have, however, become more rare and confined to the rural areas. In the mid-1970s Harry Senn had little trouble locating vampire accounts in a variety of Romanian locations. Admittedly, however, the vampire suffered during recent decades from both the spread of public education and the hostility of the government to tales of the supernatural. The importance of vampires in the overall folk belief of Romanians was also demonstrated in a recent study of a Wallachian immigrant community in Scandinavia.

CONCLUSION: The *strigoi mori,* the Romanian vampire conformed in large part to the popular image of the vampire. It was a revenant of the deceased. It had powers to product poltergeist-like phenomena, especially the bringing to life of common household objects. It was seen as capricious, mischievous, and very debilitating. However, the vampire's attack was rarely seen as fatal. Also, it rarely involved the literal biting and draining of blood from its victim (the crux of the distortion of the vampire's image in films in the eyes of Romanian folklorists). The *strigoi* usually drained the vital energy of a victim by a process of **psychic vampirism.** The description of the *strigoi's* attack, described in vivid metaphorical language, was often taken in a literal sense by non-Slavic interpreters who then misunderstood the nature of the Slavic vampire.

Sources:

Gerard, Emily. *The Land Beyond the Forest.* 2 vols. London: Will Blackwood & Sons, 1888.

Murgoci, Agnes. "The Vampire in Romania." *Folk-Lore* 27, 5 (1926): 320-49.

Perkowski, Jan L. *The Darkling: A Treatise on Slavic Vampirism.* Columbus, OH: Slavica Publishers, 1989. 174 pp.

———ed. *Vampires of the Slavs.* Cambridge, MA: Slavica Publishers, 1976. 294 pp.

Schierup, Carl-Ulrik. "Why Are Vampires Still Alive?: Wallachian Immigrants in Scandinavia." *Ethnos* 51, 3-4 (1986): 173-98.

Senn, Harry A. *Were-Wolf and Vampire in Romania.* New York: Columbia University Pres, 1982. 148 pp.

Summers, Montague. *The Vampire in Europe.* 1929. New Hyde Park, NY: University Books, 1961. 329 pp.

ROME, VAMPIRES IN ANCIENT

Ancient Rome did not have as developed a mythology of vampirism as did **Greece,** though the idea was by no means absent. It was not an attribute of the returning dead but of living witches. The idea of a vampirelike entity apparently came from the need to account for the unexpected deaths of infants, a need that had produced the *lamiai* of ancient Greece. The Romans spoke of the *strix*, a night demon that attacked infants and drained their blood. The *strix* was identified with the screech owl. The term survived in Greece as *striges* in **Romania** as *strigoi* and in **Italy** as *strega*.

First-century A.D. Roman poet Ovid described a witch in the fourth book of his work, *Fasti:*

> They fly by night and look for children without nurses, snatch them from their cradles and defile their bodies. They are said to lacerate the entrails of infants with their beaks. and they have their throats full of the blood they have drunk. They are called striges.

He also recounted a ritual performed as an invocation to the ancient deity *Carna*, the goddess of flesh, to protect a infant boy from the *strix:*

> Immediately she (Carna) touches the door-posts three times in succession with a spray of arbutus (a plant); three times she marks the threshold with arbutus spray. She sprinkles the entrance with water (and the water contained a drug). She holds the bloody entrails of a pig, two months old, and thus speaks: "Birds of the night, spare the entrails of the boy. For a small boy a small victim falls. Take heart for heart, I pray, entrails for entrails. This life we give you in place of a better one."

The functionary completed the ritual by placing a white thorn branch in the window of the house. The child would then be safe.

From the *strix* developed the concept of the *strega,* a witch, usually a woman, who was believed to have the power to change her form and fly around at night in the form of a bird. She also sucked human blood and possessed a poisonous breath. Petronius in his *Satyricon* left one story of an encounter with the *stregas.* The host of a dinner party told his guests that while he was at the home of a friend, comforting her on the loss of her son, several witches gathered outside the house and created a disturbance. In the home at the time was a muscular young man who volunteered to quiet the witches. He went outside, sword in hand. A few moments later the man returned and fell on the bed. He was black and blue all over and the witches had disappeared.

The rest of the group returned to their task of consoling the mother. However, when she went in to view her son, all she found was a clump of straw. The witches had carried off the boy, and the young man who battled them never recovered. The *strega* continued as part of the popular culture and spread through the old Roman Empire. As late as the ninth century, Charlemagne, who established the new Holy Roman Empire, decreed capital punishment for anyone who believed that another person was a *strix,* and because of that belief attacked, burned, and/or cannibalized that person. It appears that such was the manner of disposing of people believed to be witches.

By the end of the fifteenth century, the witch had been demonized and turned into a Satanist by the Inquisition. People believed to be *stregas* were arrested, tried, and executed in Italy during the centuries of the witch-hunts. In the interrogations of the suspected witches, the inquisitors had them confess to practices commonly associated with the *stregas,* including the vampirizing of babies. Between 1460 and 1525 some 10 books were published on **witchcraft** by Italians. Among these was a brief volume, *Strix,* written by Gianfrancesco Pico della Mirandola and published in Bologna in 1523. The book grew out of concern over recent accusations of witchcraft that had occurred at Brecia in 1518 and at Sondrio in 1523, though the picture of the *stregas* presented by Mirandola was more complete (he was drawing on common beliefs about witches) than any of the confessions at the recent trials. The accused at Brecia and Sondrio, for example, did not confess to incidents of attacking babies and sucking their blood, though Mirandola was concerned with *stregas* committing such crimes.

The beliefs articulated by Mirandola were common in the Renaissance and would remain a dominant opinion of the religious and intellectual leaders for the next several centuries. By the eighteenth century, Italians had joined the rest of Europe in doubting the existence of such supernatural evil as was supposedly perpetrated by witches and vampires. Remnants of the belief in *strega* seem to have continued to the present day. Surviving fragments of belief and practice reportedly were rediscovered by C. G. Leland in the nineteenth century and through him have passed into the modern Wiccan revival.

Note: On the modern literary and cinematic vampire, see the entry on Vampires, in **Italy**.

Sources:

Burke, Peter. "Witchcraft and Magic in Renaissance Italy: Gianfrancesco Pico and his *Strix*." In Sydney Anglo, ed. *The Damned Art: Essays in the Literature of Witchcraft.* London: Routledge & Kegan Paul, 1977, pp. 32-52.

Burriss, Eli Edward. *Taboo, Magic, Spirits: A Study of Primitive Elements in Roman Religion.* New York: Macmillan Company, 1931. 250 pp.

Summers, Montague. *The Vampire: His Kith and Kin.* London: Routledge, Kegan Paul, Trench, Trubner, & Co., 1928. 356 pp. Reprint. New Hyde Park, NY: University Books, 1960. 356 pp.

———. *The Vampire in Europe.* London: Routledge, Kegan Paul, Trench, Trubner, & Co., 1929. 329 pp. Reprint. New Hyde Park, NY: University Books, 1961. 329 pp.

ROSS, MARILYN *See:* WILLIAM EDWARD DANIEL ROSS

ROSS, WILLIAM EDWARD DANIEL (1912-)

Novelist William Edward Daniel Ross wrote 33 books inspired by the *Dark Shadows* television program and movies. In 1930 Ross began his career as the manager of an acting company with which he also acted. Very early in his professional life, he was awarded the Dominion Drama Festival Prize for Playwriting.

During the 1960s he turned his attention to writing, and has since become one of the most prolific writers of **gothic,** romantic, historical, and western fiction under 21 different pseudonyms. His first novel, *Summer Season,* appeared in 1962 under the pseudonym Jane Rossiter. His output reached an all-time high in 1967 when over 20 novels appeared as paperback volumes. Besides more than 345 novels, he has written some 600 short stories, many of them mysteries that have appeared in such publications as *The Saint Mystery Magazine, The Chaplain,* and *Mike Shayne Mystery Magazine.*

In the mid-1960s, Ross began to produce gothic fiction under the names Clarissa Ross and Marilyn Ross. Under the latter name, in December 1966 he saw the publication of the first of the 33 *Dark Shadows* volumes that appeared during the next six years. The novels, with such names as *The Curse of Collinswood, The Phantom and Barnabas Collins,* and *Barnabas, Quentin, and the Vampire Beauty,* featured some of the *Dark Shadows* TV characters in new situations created by Ross. At one point, over a 14-month stretch, these novels appeared monthly.

Barnabas Collins, the popular vampire added to the show in the spring of 1967, did not appear in the first five novels. However, after he became the popular center of the show, subsequent printings of the novels included his picture on the covers. The last volumes continued to appear for some months after the show was canceled. A special volume, Ross's movie tie-in *House of Dark Shadows,* included a photo section. A 34th volume, *Barnabas, Quentin, and the Mad Ghoul,* was plotted by Ross and scheduled but never published.

► DANIEL ROSS, AUTHOR OF
MANY BOOKS BASED ON THE
DARK SHADOWS TELEVISION
SERIES.

While working on the *Dark Shadows* series, Ross wrote two other vampire novels under the pseudonym Clarissa Ross, *Secret of the Pale Lover* (1969) and *The Corridors of Fear* (1971). After the completion of the *Dark Shadows* Series for Paperback Library, Ross published another vampire novel as Marilyn Ross, *The Vampire Contessa* (1974). He continued his heavy output into the mid-1980s under such names as Marilyn Carter, Rose Dana, Ruth Dorset, Ann Gilmer, Ellen Randolph, Jane Rossiter, and Dana Ross. In 1989 he completed a play titled *Phantom Wedding*. He considers himself primarily an "entertainer" and "storyteller," and has developed a large following. His writings are collected and preserved at Boston University. In 1988 he was given an honorary doctorate of letters from the University of New Brunswick. His historical novels became the subject of a master's thesis by Jeffrey D. Thompson.

Sources:

Freeman, Alan. "You May Not Know Him, But He Wrote 322 Novels." *Wall Street Journal* 12 (January 1987): 1.
Ross, Dan (as Clarissa Ross). *The Corridors of Fear*. New York: Avon, 1971. 172 pp.
——— (as Clarissa Ross). *The Secret of the Pale Lover*. New York: Magnum Books, 1969. 222 pp.
——— (as Marilyn Ross). *The Vampire Contessa*. New York: Pinnacle Books, 1974. 181 pp.

MacLeod, Hilary. "Dan Ross Is a Busy Man." *Canadian Author and Bookman* (February 1986): 4-5.

Stockel, Shirley, and Victoria Weidner. *A Guide to Collecting "Dark Shadows" Memorabilia.* Ed. by Robert Finocchio. Florissant, MO: Collinwood Chronicle, 1992. 107 pp.

Thompson, Jeffrey D. *The Effective Use of Actual Persons and Events in the Historical Novels of Dan Ross.* Nashville, TN: M.A. thesis, Tennessee University Press, 1988. 207 pp.

RUSSIA, VAMPIRES IN

The former Soviet Union, including Russia, Siberia, the Ukraine, and Byelorussia, has been one of the homelands of the **Slavic vampire.** The first mention of the word "vampir" in a Slavic document was in a Russian one, *The Book of Prophecy* written in 1047 A.D. for Vladimir Jaroslav, Prince of Novgorod, in northwest Russia. The text was written in what is generally thought of as proto-Russian, a form of the language that had evolved from the older, common Slavonic language but had not yet become distinctive Russian language of the modern era. The text gave a priest the unsavory label "Upir Lichy," literally "wicked vampire" or "extortionate vampire," an unscrupulous prelate. The term—if not the concept—was most likely introduced from the **southern Slavs,** possibly the Bulgarians. The Russians of Kiev had adopted Eastern **Christianity** in 988 A.D. and had drawn heavily on Bulgaria for Christian leadership.

Those areas of Russia under Prince Vladimir, centered around the city of Kiev (the Ukraine), accepted Christianity in 988, at which time Vladimir declared war on paganism. Christianity then spread from Kiev northward and westward. For several centuries Christianity existed side by side with existing tribal faiths, but became an integral part of the amalgamation of the tribal cultures into unified states. The invasion of Mongols in the 1240s, including their destruction of Kiev, and their decade of rule, led to a shift of power to Novgorod under Alexander Nevsky. During the fourteenth century, power began to shift to the princedom of Muskovy and the chief Christian cleric established himself in Moscow, though still titled as the metropolitan of "Kiev and all Rus." Westernmost Russia, including the Ukraine and Byelorussia, came under the expanded Lithuanian empire. Thus modern Russia emerged by pushing back the Mongols in the East and the Lithuanians (and Poles) in the West.

While the state fought back foreign territorial rivals, Orthodox Christianity was in the very process of driving out the pre-Christian religions. That process was accompanied by the rise of new heretical religious movements, some being amalgamations of Christian and pagan practices. With the emergence of a strong central state in Moscow in the fourteenth century, the state periodically moved against dissident movements. Surviving through this entire period into modern times were people who practiced (or who were believed to practice) magic. They were known as witches and sorcerers.

During the long reign of Vasili II in the mid-fifteenth century, vast changes occurred in Russia, including an expansion of its territory. In 1448, following the breakup of the Roman Catholic and Eastern Orthodox union to combat Islam, and just five years before the fall of Constantinople, the bishop in Moscow declared his autonomous status. There followed a period of expansion, both secular and ecclesiastical. The Russian church assumed many of the prerogatives formerly held by Constantinople, and early in the sixteenth century there arose the concept of Moscow as the "third Rome," the new center of Christian faith. Under Ivan III the Great, territorial expansion reached new heights with the incorporation of Finland and movement to the east across the Urals. Thus the stage was set for the expansion into the Volga River valley under **Ivan the Terrible,** and the incorporation of Siberia and lands all the way to the Pacific Ocean in the seventeenth century. During the several centuries of Romanov rule, Russia continued westward into the **Baltic states**, Byelorussia, and the Ukraine, though its most impressive conquests were southward to the Caspian Sea and the Persian border. By the time of the Russian revolution in 1917, the country had assumed the proportions it has today.

The Russian revolution of 1917 brought the Union of Soviet Socialist Republics (USSR) into existence. The USSR collapsed in December 1991 and has been replaced by the Commonwealth of Independent States (CIS), though a number of the former Soviet states did not join the CIS and chose to become new and independent countries. This essay deals with the lands of the CIS, primarily Russia, Byelorussia, and the Ukraine.

THE RUSSIAN VAMPIRE: In modern Russia the most common term for a vampire is *uppyr*, a term probably borrowed from the Ukrainian *upyr*. In Russia, the idea of the vampire became closely associated with that of the witch or sorcerer, which in turn had been tied to the concept of heresy. Heresy is defined as the deviation on matters considered essential to orthodox faith, in this case, Eastern Orthodox Christianity. This idea can be viewed as an extension of the Eastern Orthodox belief that a body would not decay normally if death occurred when the individual was outside the communion of the church. The person could be in an excommunicated state due either to immoral behavior or to heresy. Thus a heretic (i.e., *eretik,* or, in related dialects and languages, *eretnik*, *eretica*, *eretnica*, or *erestun*) might become a vampire after death. In Russian thought, the relationship between heresy and the existence of vampires was simply strengthened to the point of identifying one with the other.

The person who was a heretic in this life might become a vampire after death. The most likely heretic to turn into a vampire was the practitioner of magic, under a variety of names—*kudesnik, porcelnik, koldun,* or *snaxar*. The method of transformation into a vampire varied widely.

An *eretik* was also associated with sorcery, a practice that also led to one's becoming a vampire. Over the years and across the very large territory comprising Russia, the *eretik* assumed a number of additional connotations. At time it referred to members of the many sectarian groups that drew people from the true faith. It also referred to witches who had sold their soul to the devil. The vampire *eretik* possessed an evil eye that could draw a person caught in the vampire's gaze into the grave.

 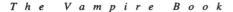

Dmitrij Zelenin has traced the emergence of the *eretik* vampire from the fight conducted by the Orthodox against the medieval religious sectarians. Sectarians were designated *inovercy* (i.e., persons who adhere to a different faith). Upon death the *inovercy* were associated with the *zaloznye pokojniki*, or unclean dead, and thus were not buried in cemeteries. They had died without confession and thus were seen as dying in sin. Since they did not believe in the true God, possibly they had served the devil, and hence were considered sorcerers.

Eretiks generally were destroyed by the use of an aspen **stake** driven into the back or by **fire.**

In the Olonecian region, accounts suggested that any person, including a pious Christian, could become a vampire if a sorcerer entered and took over the body at the moment of death. The peasant would appear to have recovered, but in fact had become a *erestuny* (vampire) who would begin to feed on members of the family. People in the nearby village would start to die mysteriously. In the Elatomsk district of east-central Russia, there were even reports of the *ereticy*—women who sold their soul to the devil. After their death, these women roamed the earth in an attempt to turn people from the true faith. They might be found near graveyards, as they slept at night in the graves of the impious. They could be identified by their appearance at the local bathhouse, where they made an unseemly noise.

VAMPIRE FOLKTALES: The vampire has been the subject of many Russian folk stories collected in the nineteenth and early twentieth centuries beginning with the work of A. N. Afanas'ev in the 1860s. As was common with many folktales, they served to promote community values and encouraged specific kinds of behavior. The tale ''Death at the Wedding,'' for example, related the adventure of a soldier proud of his service to God and the emperor. When he returned to his home town on a visit, he encountered a sorcerer/vampire. Unknowingly, the soldier took the vampire to a wedding, where the vampire began to drain the blood of the newlyweds. Horrified, the soldier nevertheless engaged the sorcerer in conversation until he discovered the secret of stopping him. First, he stole some of the blood the vampire had collected into two vials and poured the blood back into the wounds the vampire had made on the couple's bodies. He next led the villagers out to the cemetery, where they dug up the vampire's body and burned it. The soldier was generously rewarded for his actions and his display of courage in service to God and emperor.

The dispatch of the Russian vampire followed traditional means known throughout Slavic countries. The body of a suspected vampire was first disinterred. Often a **stake** (aspen was a preferred wood) was driven through the heart. Sometimes the body would be burned (Afanes'ev's account mentioned that aspen wood was used in the cremation of the vampire). In the account from the Olonecian region, the corpse was whipped before the stake was driven through the heart.

THE VAMPIRE IN RUSSIAN LITERATURE: During the nineteenth century, the vampire entered the world of Russian literature, seemingly through the popularity of the German romantic stories of E. T. A. Hoffmann and the writings of **Goethe.** In the

1840s **Alexey K. Tolstoy** (1817-75) combined the vampire of popular Russian folklore with the literary vampire that had emerged in Germany and France. His two stories, "Upyr" and "The Family of the Vourdalak," became classics of both the horror genre and Russian literature. The latter was brought to the movie screen by Italian producer **Mario Bava** as part of his horror anthology *Black Sabbath*. More recently, "The Family of the Vourdalak" has become the subject of a Russian-made movie released in the United States as *Father, Santa Claus Has Died* (1992). At least two other Russian vampire stories have been translated and given worldwide distribution, "Vij" (or "Viv") by Nikolai Gogol and "Phantoms" by Ivan Turgenev. The former became the basis of two movies, *La Maschera del Demonio* (released in the United States as *Black Sunday*), also directed by Mario Bava, and a 1990 remake with the same name by Mario's son Lamberto Bava. A Russian version of *Vij* was filmed in 1967.

What was possibly the first vampire film, *The Secret of House No. 5*, was made in Russia in 1912. An unauthorized version of *Dracula*, the first screen adaptation of the **Bram Stoker** novel, was filmed in Russia two years before *Nosferatu, Eine Symphonie des Garuens*, the more famous film by Freidrich Wilhelm Murnau. However, the vampire has not been a consistent topic for movies in Russia over the years.

Sources:

Coxwell, C. Fillingham. *Siberian and Other Folk-Tales*. London: C. W. Daniel Company, 1925. 1056 pp. Reprint. New York: AMS Press, 1983. 1056 pp.

Oinas, Felix J. "Heretics as Vampires and Demons in Russia." *Slavic and East European Journal* 22,4 (Winter 1978): 433-41.

Perkowski, Jan L. *The Darkling: A Treatise on Slavic Vampirism*. Columbus, OH: Slavica Publishers, 1989. 174 pp.

———, ed. *Vampires of the Slavs*. Cambridge, MA: Slavica Publishers, 1976. 294 pp.

Ralston, William Ralston Shedden. *Russian Folk-tales*. London: Smith, Elder, 1873. Reprint. New York: Arno Press, 1977. 382 pp.

———. *The Songs of the Russian People*. 1872. Reprint. New York: Haskell House, 1970. 447 pp.

Summers, Montague. *The Vampire in Europe*. London: Routledge, Kegan Paul, Trench, Trubner, & Co, 1929. 329 pp. Rept: New Hyde Park, NY: University Books, 1961. 329 pp.

RUTHVEN, LORD

Eight decades before anyone had heard of **Dracula**, the vampire Lord Ruthven was created by **John Polidori** and introduced to the world in the first vampire short story, "The Vampyre," published in 1819. Within a few years, Lord Ruthven would appear on both the Paris and London stage and inspire a generation of literary activity.

"The Vampyre," derived from a story fragment written by **Lord Byron**, was developed by Polidori after his break with Byron, who served as the model for the leading character. The story concerned Aubrey, a wealthy young man who became friends with Lord Ruthven, a mysterious stranger who entered London society. Ruthven was pale in complexion and somewhat cold in demeanor, but a favorite of the women. He freely loaned money to people to use at the gaming tables, but those who accepted his money generally lost it and were led further into debt and eventual degradation.

As Polidori accompanied Byron on a continental journey, so Aubrey traveled to Rome with Ruthven in the story. Here he became upset at Ruthven's attempts to seduce the young daughter of an acquaintance. Unable to stop his course of action, Aubrey left Ruthven and went on to **Greece** without him. In Greece he found himself attracted to Ianthe, the daughter of the innkeeper. It was she who introduced him (and the reader) to the legend of the vampire. While Aubrey lost himself in his new relationship and the visiting of the local sights, Ruthven arrived. A short time later, Ianthe was attacked and killed by a vampire. Aubrey, recovering from his loss and not yet connecting Ruthven and the vampire, rejoined him to travel around Greece.

As they journeyed across the country, they were attacked by bandits. Ruthven was killed in the attack, but before he died, he made Aubrey swear to conceal the manner of his death and of any crimes he might have committed for the period of a year and a day. The bandits carried Ruthven's body to a nearby site where it would be exposed to the **moon**'s light. Aubrey returned to London and along the way began to realize that Ruthven destroyed all upon whom he showered his favors, especially the women who became his lovers.

Upon Aubrey's return to London, Ruthven reappeared and reminded him of his promise of silence. Aubrey had a nervous breakdown and while he was recovering, Ruthven ingratiated himself with the sister. They were engaged to be married, and Aubrey, because of his oath, felt unable to prevent the occurrence. The marriage took place on the day the oath ran out, but not in time to prevent Ruthven killing the sister and disappearing to work his evil elsewhere.

Polidori developed Lord Ruthven from elements of European folklore that had become well known across Europe after the vampire epidemics of the previous century. In his introduction, Polidori refers specifically to the **Arnold Paul** vampire scare and the survey of vampirism written by **Dom Augustin Calmet**. And while the vampire had been the subject of some German and British poems, Polidori, as noted by Carol Senf, took the crude entity of European folklore and transformed it into a complex and interesting character, the first vampire in English fiction. No longer was the vampire simply a mindless demonic force unleashed on humankind, but a real person—albeit a resurrected one—capable of moving unnoticed in human society and picking and choosing victims. He was not an impersonal evil entity, but a moral degenerate dominated by evil motives, and a subject about whom negative moral judgments were proper.

Because "The Vampyre" originally appeared under Byron's name, it attracted much more attention than it might have otherwise. In France, before the matter of its authorship was cleared up, it was widely reviewed and greatly affected many of the new generation of Romantic writers. Playwright **Charles Nodier** was asked to review it and wrote the preface to the French edition. His friend Cyprien Bérard wrote a two-volume sequel to the story, *Lord Ruthwen ou les Vampires,* which appeared early in 1820. Because it was published anonymously, many ascribed it to Nodier; however,

Nodier wrote his own version of the Ruthven story in *Le Vampire*, the first vampire drama, which opened in Paris in the summer of 1820. In Nodier's tale, Ruthven finally was forced to face the fatal consequences of his evil life. Within two months, **James R. Planché** adapted *Le Vampire* and brought Lord Ruthven to the London stage in *The Vampire, or, The Bride of the Isles.* Meanwhile, back in Paris, Lord Ruthven appeared in four other vampire plays—two serious melodrama, two comedic—before the year was out. He made his debut in Germany in 1829 in an opera, *Der Vampyr,* by **Heinrich August Marschner**.

Before he left Paris and retired to Belgium, Lord Ruthven made his last appearance on the Parisian stage in 1852 in **Alexandre Dumas**'s final work. After Dumas's play, Lord Ruthven went into retirement as a character to be succeeded by **Varney the Vampyre, Carmilla,** and **Dracula.** He would not be rediscovered until 1945. Ruthven served as the initial inspiration for a movie, *The Vampire's Ghost,* produced by Republic Pictures. However, by the time the script was developed the storyline little resembled the original, and its leading character had only the vaguest likeness to Lord Ruthven. Lord Ruthven also made a brief appearance when *Vampire Tales,* the Marvel comic book, adapted ''The Vampyre'' in its first issue in 1973.

The most recent revival of Lord Ruthven, a new version of Marschner's opera, appeared on BBC television in 1992. In *Der Vampyr—A Soap Opera,* Ruthven was now a modern Londoner and his name had been changed to Ripley the Vampyr.

Sources:

Goulart, Ron. "The Vampire." *Vampire Tales* 1 (1973): 35-48.

RYMER, JAMES MALCOLM (1804-1884)

James Malcolm Rymer, the author of **Varney the Vampyre,** was born in Scotland. He emerged out of obscurity in 1842 as the editor of the quite respectable *Queen's Magazine.* Prior to that time he had been a civil engineer, surveyor, and mechanical draftsman.

As he became a successful writer he dropped these prior occupations. In 1842, he authored an article for *Queen's Magazine* in which he made disparaging remarks about popular fiction written for the working masses. However, the next year, *Queen's Magazine* failed, and he became the editor of *Lloyd's Penny Weekly Miscellany.*

Cheap popular fiction, the so-called ''penny dreadfuls'' had emerged in England in the 1830s. The penny dreadfuls were of two basic kinds—magazines that cost a penny and specialized in serialized popular novels, and novels published in sections that sold for a penny each. Ostensibly for adults, by the 1850s the market was directed primarily to children. As Rymer wrote under a variety of pseudonyms, it is not known when he first began to write popular fiction, but in 1841 he authored a very popular novel, *The Black Monk.* His most popular pseudonyms were Malcolm J. Errym and Malcolm J. Merry.

The most popular book written largely by Rymer was *Varney the Vampyre*; or *A Feast of Blood: A Romance*. It appeared in the mid-1840s and in the end ran to 220 chapters and 868 pages. The chapters were then collected in a single volume (1847) and continued to sell for the next 15 years. The idea for *Varney* seems to have been an 1840 reprinting of **John Polidori**'s "The Vampyre" by the *Romanticist's and Novelist's Library* in a penny dreadful format. *Varney* included most of Polidori's distinctive opinions about vampires.

Since *Varney* was issued anonymously, for many years there was some doubt as to the real author. **Montague Summers** believed it to be Thomas P. Prest, author of *Sweeney Todd*, the best known of the penny dreadfuls. However, in 1963, Louis James, who had inherited several of Rymer's own scrapbooks, found conclusive evidence of Rymer's authorship of the majority of the work. It was common for different writers to work on various sections of long-running serials such as *Varney*, and other writers might have been employed to write new chapters. (That fact might account for its often uneven style and its contradictory statements about the lead character.)

Rymer continued to write for Lloyd until 1853, when he was employed by another popular penny dreadful publisher, John Dicks. From 1858 to 1864 he wrote for *Reynolds' Miscellany*, and in 1866 wrote for the *London Miscellany*.

Sources:

Bleiler, E. F. "A Note on Authorship" In *Varney the Vampire*. New York: Dover Publications, 1932.
Anglo, Michael. *Penny Dreadfuls and other Victorian Horrors*. London: Jupiter, 1977. 125 pp.
Frayling, Christopher. *Vampyres: Lord Byron to Count Dracula*. London: Faber and Faber, 1991. 429 pp.
James, Louis. *Fiction for the Working Man, 1830-1850*. London: Oxford University Press, 1963. 226 pp.
Johannsen, Albert. *The House of Beadle and Adams and Its Dime and Nickel Novels*. 3 vols. Norman, OK: University of Oklahoma Press, 1950.

SABERHAGEN, FREDERICK THOMAS (1930-)

Frederick Thomas Saberhagen is a science fiction writer and author of a series of novels expanding upon the **Dracula** theme. He became a free-lance writer in 1962 and his first novel, *The Golden People,* was published by Ace Books in 1964. It was followed by *The Water of Thought* (1965) and a number of short stories. In 1967 Saberhagen took a job as an assistant editor with *Encyclopedia Britannica,* a position he held for six years before returning to full-time writing.

In 1967, *Beserker,* a set of short stories and the first book in what was to become the Beserker series, began to establish Saberhagen as a leading science fiction writer. The "beserkers" are self-programming and self-replicating robotic spacecraft engineered by their creators, a race long-since dead, to kill anything that still lives. The appearance of these mechanical demonic forces drives the divided intelligent life forms to unite against them. In the process, the beserkers become a stimulus to increased progress, which possibly would not have been made otherwise.

Saberhagen's work is characterized by the blend of science, in which he shows a solid grounding, with mythic and legendary materials. Integrating the two provides him a base for metaphysical speculation. The Beserker series, for example, became the vehicle for a lengthy treatment of the role of evil in human life.

In the mid-1970s, Saberhagen stepped out of his science fiction world to publish the first of seven novels using with the Dracula theme. These novels started with the interesting hypothesis that Dracula was in fact the hero in the events that took place in **Bram Stoker**'s novel. In the first volume in the series, *The Dracula Tape* (1975), Dracula is telling his story into a tape recorder. He takes the reader step by step through the story, explaining how he tried not to vampirize **Jonathan Harker**, but to protect him. He justified his actions regarding **Lucy Westenra** as a reaction to **Abraham Van Helsing** who, in his ignorance of **blood** types, was killing her by his transfusions. In the end, her only hope was to be turned into a vampire. His involvement with Lucy led to his falling in love with **Mina Murray**, who was, at that point, married to Harker. This theme reappeared in later volumes in the series.

The Dracula Tape received mixed reviews, especially with Saberhagen's science fiction fans, but gained an audience among vampire/Dracula enthusiasts. It initiated what has become a new approach to the vampire myth. By treating Dracula sympathetically, Saberhagen enlarged the myth in such a way that it could speak to the contemporary need for individuals to develop an understanding of others who are very different. It also opened the possibility of making the vampire a hero, rather than an anti-hero.

Dracula as a hero allowed a broad new expanse into which he could be introduced. Saberhagen first developed an obvious theme, the possible encounter of Dracula with his contemporary, **Sherlock Holmes**. In *The Holmes-Dracula File*, the two joined forces to prevent the introduction of plague-bearing rats into London during Queen Victoria's Diamond Jubilee celebrations. Continuing the attack upon the heroes of Stoker's *Dracula,* Saberhagen introduced **John Seward** (the character from the original novel) into *The Holmes-Dracula File* as the villain behind the dastardly plot.

Dracula's feelings for Mina Murray, who made a brief appearance in the Holmes story to reaffirm her love for Dracula, served as the basis for the third volume, *An Old Friend of the Family* (1979). Dracula had developed a means by which Mina and her descendants could contact him should they need him. The need arose in the late 1970s in Chicago, Saberhagen's hometown. Summoned by Judy Southerland, Dracula, using the pseudonym of Dr. Emile Corday, arrived to find that the incidents experienced by Mina's descendants merely masked a plot directed against him by Morgan, a redheaded vampiress who resented Dracula's influence on the vampire community. After defeating Morgan, Dracula settled in the United States.

In the fourth novel, Dracula changed his name to *Thorn* (1980) and became involved in a conspiracy to steal a painting that turned out to be of Helen Hundayi. She was, according to the story, Dracula's first wife. In *Dominion* (1982) Dracula, now known as Talisman, encountered Nimue, the Lady of the Lake, who was attempting to bring the master magician, Falerin, to the fore as the supreme ruler. Dracula had an ally in Ambrosius (whom the world knows as Merlin), whose magical power was needed to finally defeat Nimue.

The sixth of his Dracula novels appeared in 1990. *A Matter of Taste* returned Dracula, now known as Matthew Maule, to Chicago where he had settled as the Southerland family's Uncle Matthew. The story concerned an attempt by Dracula's vampire enemies to kill him. Very early, Dracula was poisoned and lay near death in his bed. The Southerlands protected him against his foes until he could recover and defeat them decisively. This novel also had Dracula recounting the story of his origins—an inventive tale of Prince Dracula becoming a vampire. In his most recent offering, *A Question of Time* (1992), Dracula joined forces with detective Joe Keogh to fight Edgar Tyrell, a menacing vampire who seemed able to affect time itself.

Saberhagen's Dracula appeared on the heels of **Daniel Ross**'s *Dark Shadows* novels, but took Ross's sympathetic treatment of the vampire one step further. *The Dracula Tape* was followed by **Anne Rice**'s *Interview with the Vampire*, which also had the vampire telling his story into a tape recorder. Saberhagen's Dracula differed strongly, however, from both the Dark Shadows and Anne Rice vampires. Unlike Barnabas Collins, Dracula had no problem with his vampire state, no anguish about his uncontrollable drive, and no wish to change. Unlike Rice's Louis and **Lestat de Lioncourt,** Saberhagen's Dracula manifested little ambiguity in his situation. Dracula was a hero whose moral situation was rather clear—he had found the means to handle most of the questions that would be raised about his preying upon the human race.

While producing the Dracula novels, Saberhagen continued to publish science fiction novels at a steady pace, and during the 1970s he also began to write fantasy novels, most prominently the "Swords" and "Lost Swords" series. He edited anthologies on chess, *Pawn to Infinity* (1982), and archaeology, *A Spadeful of Spacetime* (1981) as well.

Most recently, Saberhagen's Dracula novels brought him to the attention of **Francis Ford Coppola,** and he was chosen, along with co-author James V. Hart, to write the novelization of Coppola's screenplay for *Bram Stoker's Dracula*.

Sources:

Saberhagen, Fred. *Dominion*. New York: Tor, 1982. 320pp.
———. *The Dracula Tape*. New York: Paperback Library, 1975. 206 pp.
———. *The Holmes-Dracula File*. New York: Ace Books, 1978. 249 pp.
———. *A Matter of Taste*. New York: Tor, 1990. 284 pp.
———. *An Old Friend of the Family*. New York: Ace Books, 1979. Reprint. New York: Tor, 1987. 247 pp.
———. *A Question of Time*. New York: Tor, 1992. 278 pp.
———. *Thorn.*. New York: Ace Books, 1980. 347 pp.
———. and James V. Hart. *Bram Stoker's Dracula*. New York: New American Library, 1992. 298 pp.
Smith, Curtis C., ed. *Twentieth-Century Science-Fiction Writers*. Chicago: St. James Press, 1986. 933 pp.
Wilgus, Neal. "Saberhagen's New Dracula: The Vampire as Hero." In Darrel Schweitzer, ed. *Discovering Modern Horror Fiction*. San Bernardino, CA: Borgo Press, 1987, 92-98.

ST. GEORGE'S DAY

St. George's Day (April 24 or May 6, depending upon calendars) is a feast day on the calendar of the Eastern Orthodox church in **Romania,** including **Transylvania**. It was usually the day when flocks of sheep were first driven to pasture from their winter home. In the novel ***Dracula,*** **Jonathan Harker** arrived in **Bistritz** on the eve of St. George's Day and was told by a woman, "It is the eve of St. George's Day. Do you know that to-night, when the clock strikes midnight, all the evil things in the world will have full sway?" The woman begged Harker to wait a day or two before leaving for his meeting with Dracula.

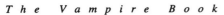

Emily Gerard, a major source of information used by **Bram Stoker** in researching Transylvania, noted that St. George's Day was among the most important of the year, and one that had a number of occult associations. At midnight, the witches would gather for their sabbath and peasants would put up such barriers as **hawthorn** or **garlic** to protect their homes and stables against the witches. Many would sleep with their **animals** in an all-night vigil. Even more than All Saints Eve, St. George's Day was thought to be the time of the most activity of the spirits of the dead.

Harry Senn recorded the story from Cluj (called by its German name, Klausenburgh, in *Dracula*). One year, a cart wheel appeared in town on the eve of St. George's Day. It was tied to the wall of a house. Two days later the wheel disappeared, and in its place hung a woman recognized as being from a neighboring village. She was soon identified as a witch (*strigoaica*).

Sources:

Gerard, Emily. *The Land Beyond the Forest.* 2 vols. London: Will Blackwood & Sons, 1888.
Senn, Harry A. *Were-Wolf and Vampire in Romania.* New York: Columbia University Pres, 1982. 148 pp.

SANGSTER, JIMMY (1927-)

Jimmy Sangster, a screenwriter for many of the **Hammer Films**' horror movies of the 1950s and 1960s, was born in North Wales. He dropped out of school at the age of 15 and after the war entered the movie world as a production manager. In 1956 he was given his first opportunity as a screenwriter for *A Man on the Beach*. Next he teamed with director **Terence Fisher** and actors **Christopher Lee** and **Peter Cushing** for the first of two trendsetting Hammer horror films, *The Curse of Frankenstein*. In 1958 the four reassembled for their most memorable effort: *Dracula* (released in America as *The Horror of Dracula*).

Sangster's screenplay for the *The Horror of Dracula* altered the story considerably from both the earlier *Dracula* (1931) movie with **Bela Lugosi** and the original book. It set vampire hunter **Abraham Van Helsing** in a singular fight with Dracula. The story climaxed when Van Helsing killed Dracula by tearing the curtain from the wall and allowing the sun to burn the vampire to ashes.

The following year Sangster wrote the screen play for Universal/Eros for the production of *The Blood of the Vampire* (also known as *The Demon with the Bloody Hands*). While he returned to Hammer to work on several scripts, it was not until 1960 that he worked again with Fisher and Cushing (minus Lee) to do *The Brides of Dracula*, Hammer's sequel to the *The Horror of Dracula*. Like Lee, Dracula did not appear in The Brides of Dracula, a story concerning Baron Meinster, memorable for his biting of Cushing, who survived by cauterizing the wound.

Through the 1960s Sangster worked on a variety of films as both screenwriter and producer. He worked on *The Nanny* (1965) and *The Anniversary* (1968), two films starring Bette Davis in some of her most memorable macabre roles. In 1970 he emerged as the screenwriter, producer, and director of the Hammer production of *The*

Horror of Frankenstein. Upon completion of *Frankenstein,* he assumed the role of director for the next horror/vampire effort, *Lust for a Vampire*, one of the Hammer **Carmilla** films. It would be his last vampire film.

Through the 1970s and 1980s Sangster continued to work on horror films. He came to the United States and participated in a number of television productions, including work with actor/host **Jack Palance** on the *Ripley's Believe It or Not* series. While not wanting to be remembered only as a ''Hammer writer,'' he became best known for his efforts on the several Hammer vampire and Frankenstein movies. He effectively scripted the **gothic** mood by setting his scenes at nighttime, showing his characters in their steady degeneration, and building an atmosphere saturated with illusion and unexpected terror.

Sources:

Ashley, Mike. *Who's Who in Horror and Fantasy Fiction.* London: Elm Tree Books, 1977. 240 pp.
Vinson, James, ed. *The International Dictionary of Films and Filmmakers. Volume IV: Writers and Production Artists.* Chicago: St. James Press, 1988.

SANTO (1915-1984)

As in America, in **Mexico** there is a tradition of masked heroes, though of a much different nature. For more than two decades (1958-82) the most popular masked fighter of evil, Santo, strolled across the motion picture screen attacking monsters and vampires. Santo was created and played by Rodolfo Gizmán Huerta. Huerta, in the persona of Santo, originally attained hero status as a wrestler and in the ring became well known throughout the country following World War II. As Santo the wrestler, Huerta never appeared without his silver mask, the essential element in his costume. As a movie star, Santo was sometimes confused with another masked character, El Médico Asesino.

Santo's first movie was *Cerebro del Mal,* filmed in Cuba just before the revolution. This initial movie included El Incógnito (played by Fernando Osés), also a masked hero character. A second movie, *Cargamento Blanco,* was shot at the same time and, in finished form, even included some footage from the first movie. The movies were not released, however. In September 1960 a comic-book-like weekly, *Santo, el Enmascarado de Plata,* began weekly publication. It furthered Santo's popularity and prompted the release of the two Cuban motion pictures early in 1961. That same year Santo made four additional movies beginning with *Santo Contra los Zombies.* In order to keep the costs down, some of Santo's movies were shot as three 20-minute segments at Estúdios América, which charged cheaper rates than the large movie studios but which was limited by government regulations to short features. Each segment was given a different name and originally shown on different days. Later they would be put together as a single feature.

In 1962 Santo appeared in the first of his several vampire features, *Santo Contra las Mujeres Vampiro,* directed by Alfonso Corona Blake and released in the United States as *Samson vs. the Vampire Women.* While Santo would fight a variety of monsters, he was frequently bedeviled by vampires, their next appearance being in *Santo Contra el Baron Brakola* (1965). Baron Brakola was modeled on **Bela Lugosi**, and stills of Lugosi were used in advertisements of the film.

In 1967 he met Dracula in *Santo un el Tesoro de Dracula*, the first of his technicolor vampire films, which also was released in an adult version as *El Vampiro y el Sexo*. By this time the character had taken on a new quality, having transformed from a simple untutored wrestler/part-time fighter of evil into a superscientist who, for example, in *Santo en el Tesoro de Dracula* invented a time machine. He also acquired the adoration of females, especially in the adult versions of his movies. Over the years Santo fought vampires in *Santo y Blue Demon Contra los Monstruos* (1969), *Santo en la Venganza de las Mujeres Vampiros* (1969), *Santo y Blue Demon Contra Dracula y el Hombre Lobo* (1971), and *Chanoc y el Hijo del Santo Contra Los Vampiros Asesinos* (1981). In the last movie, the aging Santo made only a brief appearance—viewed as an attempt to pass his career to his son.

In spite of the low production values and hastily written scripts (with action often improvised as it was shot), Santo became a national star in Mexico and his films were released to an adoring audience across Latin America and other Spanish-speaking countries. They were among the few Mexican movies able to break through the control American and British film companies held over the international film distribution market.

Sources:

Fenton, Steve. "Mexi-Monster Meltdown." *Monster International* 2 (October 1992): 4-13.
Glut, Donald G. *The Dracula Book.* Metuchen, NJ: Scarecrow Press, 1975. 388 pp.
Higuchi, Horacio. "The Traveling Monster Hunter." *Monster International* 2 (October 1992): 20-31.

SARA THE BLACK VIRGIN *See:* KALI

SATAN

Most modern novelists and screenwriters have agreed that vampires usually were created by the bite of another vampire. However, that left them with a question: "Where did the first vampire come from?" Satanism emerged as the primary answer. The suggestion of Satanism was supported by **Bram Stoker.** In his novel *Dracula,* Stoker had his spokesperson, Dr. **Abraham Van Helsing,** offer the following reflection upon his vampire adversary:

> The Draculas were, says Arminius, a great and noble race, though now and again were scions who were held by their coevals to have dealings with the Evil One. They learned his secrets in the Scholomance, amongst the mountains over Lake Hermannstadt, where the devil claims the tenth scholar as his due.

Stoker directly developed his theory that vampirism was ultimately related to Satanism from Emily Gerard's book *The Land Beyond the Forest.* The book spoke of the Scholomance as a school somewhere in the heart of the mountains of **Transylvania**. There the devil himself taught the secrets of nature and magic. Ten scholars attended at any given time. Payment for the schooling came in the form of one scholar, who remained behind to serve the devil after classes were over. Lake Hermannstadt was near present-day Sibiu. **Raymond T. McNally** and **Radu Florescu** have noted that at the town of Paltinis Pietrele, near Sibiu, was a place called *pietrele lui Solomon* (the rocks of Solomon). Wandering students stopped here to swear their oaths to Solomon (the wise king of the Bible), who was believed to know the secrets of alchemy. They suggest that Gerard had heard of this spot and reported on it in a somewhat garbled manner, thus creating a story about the mythical Scholomance.

Quite different from Stoker's reading of Gerard, there was a much stronger and older tradition that tied vampirism to Satanism. Among the Slavs, it was believed that the vampire existed in the realm outside of the acceptance of God and the church. Vampires originated among people who were witches (worshippers of Satan), people who had committed suicide, or those who were excommunicated. In Russia, the vampire was called *eretik* (heretic: a person who has departed from the true faith of Orthodox **Christianity**). People outside the realm of the church were thought to be dealing with the devil.

Unacceptable to God, the vampire was unable to deal with the sacred on earth. It could not stand the presence of holy objects such as the **crucifix** or the **eucharistic host**. It stayed away from churches. It was condemned to live in the darkness. After death, the vampire was rejected by the Earth, and, according to the theology of the Eastern Church, its body would remain intact and incorruptible.

While most stage and film productions about Dracula neglect the question of his origin as a vampire, Stoker's brief mention of his family's dealings with the devil was part of a fresh mythical presentation of Dracula by **Francis Ford Coppola** in his movie ***Bram Stoker's Dracula.*** Drawing upon McNally and Florescu's modern accounts of **Vlad the Impaler,** the historical character who, in part, stands behind the fictional Dracula, Coppola pictured Vlad fighting the Turks. Wrongly informed that Vlad had lost the battle, his wife Elizabeth committed suicide. The church refused to hold her funeral or allow her to be buried in holy ground. Her soul could not be saved; she was damned. Vlad was so much in love with her that in his grief he rejected God. He plunged his sword into the cross in the chapel, and drank the blood that flowed from it. He vowed to return from the grave accompanied by the powers of darkness to avenge his love's untimely death.

The movement of the vampire myth into modern pluralistic and secular culture has created noticeable changes in the myth. Non-Christian writers have tended to place the vampire in a completely secular realm (vampirism as a disease) or to create a supernatural myth not based on Christian presuppositions or the existence of the devil. Such alternative myths are most evident in the novels of **Chelsea Quinn Yarbro** and **Anne Rice.**

THE IMAGE OF SATAN AND HIS DEMONS WERE PRECURSORS OF THE MODERN VAMPIRE IMAGE.

Rice, in particular, has used her presentation of vampires as a means to struggle with her own Roman Catholic background, aspects of which, including any belief in the devil, she had rejected. In *Interview with the Vampire,* the new vampire Louis believed that he was a child of the devil and hence eternally damned. However, he soon realized that he knew nothing of the devil. He questioned one of the Parisian vampires and was told that neither God nor the devil existed. Louis eventually accepted this view of the devil's nonexistence as a step toward realizing his own responsibility for his life—the bad parts of which could not be accounted for by reference to supernatural evil.

On the other hand, novelist Traci Briery has made effective use of the Satanic myth. In *The Vampire Memoirs*, she created the story of Agyar, the original vampire. Several thousand years ago, Agyar began a quest for immortality. His journey took him through bizarre and horrible rituals to distant places, including hell. He received immortality at the cost of his own soul. Agyar was the source of all modern vampires who, like him, could not stand the presence of such holy objects as a cross.

Where vampires have a secularized or heroic existence, they have been set against Satanism and its followers. Yarbro had her vampire hero **St. Germain** confront a group of Satanists who had been promised his lady love. In the movie *Dracula's Widow*, Vanessa, the wife of the late Dracula, attacked and killed a group of Satanists in modern-day Hollywood.

It is worthy to note that "Dracul," commonly translated as "dragon," also may be translated as "devil"; such an association has been used on occasion to tie the historical Dracula, Vlad the Impaler, to Satanism and hence to vampirism.

Sources:

Briery, Traci. *The Vampire Memoirs*. New York: Zebra Books, 1991. 431 pp.

Coppola, Francis Ford, and James V. Hart. *Bram Stoker's Dracula: The Film and the Legend*. New York: Newmarket Press, 1992. 172 pp. Reprint. London: Pan Books, 1992. 172 pp.

Rice, Anne. *Interview with the Vampire*. New York: Alfred A. Knopf, 1986. 448 pp. Reprint. New York: Ballantine Books, 1987. 346 pp.

Stoker, Bram. *The Essential Dracula*. Ed. by Raymond McNally and Radu Florescu. New York: Mayflower Books, 1979. 320 pp.

SCANDINAVIA, VAMPIRES IN

Geographically, Scandinavia consists of three countries of northern Europe: Norway, Sweden, and Finland. Historically and culturally, it also generally includes Denmark and Iceland. Linguistically, each of these country's languages includes strong elements of Old Norse, the common language of the Scandinavian Vikings. The vampire, though present, was not a prominent element in Viking folklore and did not become one in subsequent Scandinavian folk traditions.

Rosalie H. Wax, author of *Magic, Fate and History: The Changing Ethos of the Vikings* pointed out that in the old Scandinavian literature, matter was conceived as substantial, and semitransparent ghostly figures were nonexistent. There was a tradition of ghosts, however, some friendly and some harmful. The latter had greater interaction with the world, more like revenants than ghosts. At times revenants behaved, at least superficially, like a vampire or a **ghoul,** and usually were treated in ways reminiscent of the vampires of Eastern Europe, by a **stake** and **decapitation**. They also have been reported as vampires in some of the popular surveys of vampires around the world.

In the *Eyrbyggia Saga* of Iceland, for example, Thorolf, an early settler of the island, reappeared after his burial. Cattle that went near his tomb became mad and died. His hauntings at home caused his wife's death. His wanderings were stopped for a while by the removal of his body to a new location. But he returned and, finally, his new tomb was opened and his body burned and ashes scattered. The *Grettis Saga* reported the decapitation of Karr, another Icelander, whose head was laid at his thigh, and of Glam, who was both decapitated and burned. Glam was a strong man who hated his former employer, killing his cattle and driving off members of his household. Glam finally was beaten in a fight with a visiting hero, Grettir. Ancient

Danish records told of Mith-othin, a juggler who had earned the wrath of Odin. He fled to Finland but was killed by the Finns. However, in death, he operated from the barrow where his body was laid. Deaths of people near his barrow and sicknesses that spread through the populace were attributed to his taking revenge. To stop his bloody deeds, the people beheaded and staked him.

More central to Scandinavian belief was a *mara,* the nightmare. A *mara* was seen as a beautiful woman but was in fact a troll. She came to people as they slept and lay upon their breast so that they could neither draw a breath nor move a limb. She would attempt to put her finger in the victim's mouth and count the teeth. If she was given time to do her counting, the victim usually died. According to some sources, a *mara* was an unknown person in love with its victim. She also was known to attack horses and ride one all night so that it would be found in its stable the next morning covered with sweat. Steps could be taken against the nightmare spirit, including the spreading of seeds around the house, turning shoes the wrong way at the side of the bed, and placing a scythe on the front of the bed. A knife or sharp instrument was the most effective means of killing or driving away the *mara.*

It has been suggested that a vampire appears in the *Kalevala,* the ancient saga of Finland. Over the threshold of the Abode of the Dead in the saga stood *Surma,* the personification of violent death. *Surma* was ready to seize any imprudent person who wandered too near to him and to devour the victim with his notable set of teeth. *Surma* was a horrible figure, but does not appear to have been a vampire.

MODERN SCANDINAVIA: The tradition of the substantial dead returning to interact with the living has continued into the twentieth century. It includes stories of the return of dead lovers (a la Berger's ''Lenore'') and the gathering of the dead in church buildings to hold their own worship services. More to the point, there were traditions of the dead returning because they had committed **suicide,** because they were overly greedy, or because they wanted to revenge themselves on the living.

Children who were murdered or who died before baptism also returned. There was an evil woman of Ris, Denmark, who walked around after her death. Following a very old tradition, a wooden **stake** was stuck into the earth above her grave and thrust through her body, thus pinning her to the ground. In order to prevent the dead from arising, people would throw soil in the grave or place needles in the soles of the feet. More recently, a tradition emerged of shooting the corpse with a **bullet** made of silver. The treatment of revenants in Scandinavia points to the common ways of dealing with nonvampiric revenants and its continuity with similar practices carried out against the vampire in eastern Europe.

One popular story, ''Gronnskjegg'' (the Vampire, or better translated, the Ghoul) has been collected across Norway. In the story a young girl married an unknown man with a green beard. On returning home she discovered that her new husband had eaten corpses from the local church graveyard. Later he appeared to her in the form of different relatives and questioned her. When he appeared in the form of her mother, she told all that she knew of him, and he killed her.

Sources:

Craigie, William A. *Scandinavian Folklore: Illustrations of the Traditional Beliefs of the Northern Peoples.* Detroit, MI: Singing Tree Press, 1970. 554 pp.

Hodne, Ornulf. *The Type of the Norwegian Folktale.* Oslo, Norway: Universitetforlaget, 1984. 400 pp.

Kvideland, Reimond, and Henning K. Sehmsdorf, eds. *Scandinavian Folk Belief and Legend.* Minneapolis, MN: University of Minnesota Press, 1986. 429 pp.

MacCulloch, J. A. *The Celtic and Scandinavian Religions.* London: Hutchinson's University Library, 1948. 180 pp.

Wax, Rosalie H. *Magic, Fate and History: The Changing Ethos of the Vikings.* Lawrence, KS: Coronado Press, 1969. 186 pp.

Wright, Dudley. *Vampires and Vampirism.* 1914, 1924. Rept. as: *The Book of Vampires.* 1924. Reprint. New York: Causeway Books, 1973. 217 pp.

SCIENCE FICTION AND THE VAMPIRE

As the vampire myth developed and went through a rationalizing/secularizing process, various authors have posed alternative, nonsupernatural theories for the origin of vampires—from disease to altered blood chemistry. Eventually, at the height of interest in flying saucers in the 1950s, it was inevitable that the idea of vampires as space aliens would be posed. However, such an idea had a number of precursors. In 1894, for example, H. G. Wells, in his story "The Flowering of the Strange Orchid," had explored the possibility of a space alien taking over a human body in order to live off the life energies of others. This theme was picked up in the **pulp magazines** in such stories as Sewell Wright's "Vampires of Space" and C. L. Moore's "Black Thirst." A true bloodthirsty space alien seems to have first appeared in 1942 in A. E. Van Vogt's story, "Asylum." Van Vogt's villains were a pair of aliens who arrived on earth in a spaceship. They lived for thousands of years by preying on the life forms of different planets. On earth, they encountered reporter William Dreegh, who eventually was able to stifle their invasion.

By the mid-1950s, interest in flying saucers was on the rise and science fiction had begun to blossom. **Richard Matheson,** who had written both horror and science fiction for many years, was the first to explore the traditional vampire theme in popular science fiction. Matheson, who had authored several vampire stories, created an end-of-the-world situation in which the hero, Robert Neville, was the only human left. The others had either been killed or turned into vampires. During the battle between Neville and the vampires, he had to figure out which parts of the old vampire myth were accurate and hence which weapons ultimately would work against them.

After Matheson, the mixture of science fiction and vampires occurred occasionally, mostly in short stories. Among the several novels on this theme, the more notable included Colin Wilson's *The Space Vampires* (1976); Tanith Lee's *Sabella,* or *The Blood Stone* (1980); Brian Aldiss's *Dracula Unbound* (1991); and Robert Frezza's *McLennon's Syndrome.* Two Star Trek novels with a vampire theme have been published, but neither appear to have been made into an episode of the popular television show. However, the major presence of alien vampires would be felt in the movies.

THE SPACE VAMPIRE IN THE MOVIES: By 1954 **Universal Pictures** attention to the classic monsters it had made famous in the 1930s was waning, their last scenes being played out in *Abbott and Costello Meet Dr. Jekyll and Mr. Hyde*, in which Dracula made a cameo appearance. However, a variety of companies already were exploiting the classic monsters—including the vampire—within the context of science fiction motion pictures; these were the hot new items on the agenda, especially for companies specializing in "B" movies. The questions they posed their youthful audiences included: What if vampires are real, and are space aliens? What if earth is being invaded by space aliens who came to drain either our blood or our life force, or both? How should we react to a space alien vampire?

The first science fiction movie to explore these questions was the 1951 production from RKO Radio Pictures, *The Thing from Another World* (remade in 1982 as *The Thing*). It starred James Arness as an alien creature (actually an eight-foot vegetable) who needed blood to reproduce. The Thing was discovered in the Arctic snow by a research team and the military eventually had to be brought in to stop the threat. Six years later **Roger Corman** produced and directed *Not of This Earth* (remade in 1988), which saw a humanoid from the dying planet Davanna settle in a small town to search out the viability of human blood as a replacement for that of their own race.

Not of This Earth was soon followed by United Artists' *It! The Terror from Beyond Space* (1958). *It!* began with Colonel Carruthers, the sole survivor of a space expedition to Mars, being arrested by the commander of his rescue ship, who suspected him of cannibalizing his crew in order to survive. On the way home, with Carruthers in lock-up, members of the crew were mysteriously murdered by It. The commander finally realized his error and was able to isolate the vampiric alien in a cargo chamber. All the survivors donned space suits and the oxygen was let out of the ship, thus killing the creature. *It! The Terror from Beyond Space* became the direct inspiration for the 1979 classic space horror movie *Alien* (which dropped the original's vampire theme).

The last of the 1950s space alien vampire movies would become by far the most famous and financially successful. *Plan 9 from Outer Space* (1959) began with **Bela Lugosi** leaving the grave of his recently deceased wife, played by television horror movie hostess **Vampira**. A ray flashed down from outer space reviving Vampira, who then attacked the attendants who were about to bury her body. Next she killed the police inspector who arrived to examine the bodies of the grave diggers. The scene then changed to an invasion of flying saucers over Los Angeles. Eros and Tanna, who led the invasion, announced "Plan 9," their intention to revive all of the dead on earth and use them as their instrument to take over the planet. The forces of good organized to counter the invasion, and in the end the space people were repulsed.

Plan 9 from Outer Space became famous after being placed at or near the top of several lists of the world's worst movies. The product of director Edward D. Wood, Jr., famous for his quick production of cheap movies, the film was "unintentionally" hilarious for its errors of production. In the graveyard scene, for example, cardboard tombstones swayed when accidentally touched, a cement floor was visible under the cemetery grass, and a mattress (to cushion a fall) could be seen. *Plan 9* also was notable as Bela Lugosi's last film. Wood seems to have integrated some brief footage of Lugosi that originally had been shot for another movie. The brief segments of actual Lugosi scenes were each shown several times. Lugosi died before *Plan 9* could be finished, and a body double stood in for him. In the later parts of the movie, this stand-in wore Lugosi's cape and walked before the camera in a sinister fashion with his arm raised over his face.

It! and *Plan 9,* the flying saucer movies, were soon followed by a set of movies thematically tied together by the early space explorations. In *First Man into Space* (1959), an astronaut's body was taken over by a space creature. Upon his return to earth, the vampiric creature needed blood and began killing to get it. He broke into a blood bank, but finally was cornered in a decompression tank and killed.

The space alien vampire theme continued through the 1960s, beginning with **Mario Bava**'s *Planet of the Vampires* (originally entitled in Italian, *Terrore nello Spazio*). The story concerned a spaceship commanded by Captain Mark Markary (played by Barry Sullivan) forced to land on the planet Aura. Here, Markary discovered another ship whose crew was dead. The dead rose, their bodies inhabited by disembodied residents of Aura who had turned them into vampires, and attacked Markary's crew. Once Markary discovered what was occurring, he and two of his crew escaped. Then he realized that the two crew members already had been vampirized and would invade a defenseless earth. The movie ended before he decided what course of action he should follow.

Planet of the Vampires was followed the next year by one of the better space vampire movies, *Queen of Blood*, with a rather impressive cast of John Saxon, Basil Rathbone, and a youthful Dennis Hopper. The story was constructed from a Russian film, the footage of which had been purchased by Roger Corman. The star was a beautiful woman called the Queen of Mars, who had been invited back to earth by members of a United States spaceship. On the return trip the captain discovered that she was a vampire and was killing off the crew one by one. Her weakness, however, was a hemophiliac condition. Cut in a struggle with a crew member, she bled to death.

In the mid-1970s, occult author Colin Wilson tried his hand at the vampire theme in his novel, *The Space Vampires* (1976), a volume originally marketed as a science fiction novel. The novel also fit within the theme of **psychic vampirism**, as the creatures drained their victims' ''life force'' rather than their **blood** (as the carrier of life energy). The novel was set in 2080. A spacecraft encountered another mysterious craft housing several bodies in lifelike condition that were alive and were vampires.

In the early 1980s Tobe Hooper saw the possibilities of Wilson's novel for the screen and began an adaptation that was released in the United States as *Lifeforce* in 1985. It changed the setting to 1986, to coincide with the return of Halley's comet. In the movie, the action was centered around the relationship between Commander Carlson, who found the space vampires, and the single female vampire. Hooper also added a typical vampire feature—having the vampire killed by a stake through her energy center (a feature absent from the novel).

SCIENCE FICTION VAMPIRES IN COMIC BOOKS: The several space vampires who appeared on the movie screen in the 1960s were eclipsed by the most famous one of all, **Vampirella.** She appeared not in a movie, but as a comic book character created by **Forrest J. Ackerman** and James Warren, the owner of Warren Publishing Company. Ackerman would go on to become the original writer for *Vampirella,* the most successful vampire comic book of all time. Vampirella was distinguished by being the first space vampire who was the heroine of the story rather than the villain. She hailed from the dying planet Drakulon and came to earth where blood was readily available. She tried not to kill to obtain blood and was remorseful when she had to take a life to survive. Vampirella was partially inspired by the title character from another Mario Bava movie, *Barbarella.* She was a young, sexy, scantily-clad female. As the plot was developed through the 1970s, even **Dracula** was discovered to be a former resident of Drakulon, who had left for earth many centuries ago. *Vampirella* survived as a comic book into the early 1980s, and recently has been revived.

Contemporaneously with Colin Wilson's novel, a science fiction story with a vampire theme also came briefly to the world of **comic book**s in a short-lived series, *Planet of the Vampires.* The story concerned space explorers who had returned to earth after a long stay on Mars. They found the people divided into two factions following a devastating nuclear war: one faction was centered in the former New York City; the other was in the countryside. The city people had taken cover under a dome. It protected them somewhat, but they lacked immunity to diseases that had developed as a result of the war. The outsiders, on the other hand, had developed a natural resistance. The city dwellers captured outsiders, from whom they drained blood to be used for a serum. The vampires were the machines created by the city dwellers to forcefully take the blood of any outsiders who could be caught.

Planet of the Vampires, published by Atlas Comics, lasted only three issues. Its demise left *Vampirella* the only comic book with a space vampire theme. Once *Vampirella* was discontinued, space vampires largely disappeared, except for *Lifeforce.* With the new wave of vampire comics of the 1990s, the space alien vampire was revived, primarily in the adaptation of movies to comic book format. In 1990, *Plan 9 from Outer Space* was adapted in a single issue from Malibu Comics. The following year *I Am Legend* (which had been made into a movie twice, in 1964 and 1971) appeared in three issues, and a sequel to *Plan 9 from Outer Space* lasted for three issues, though the vampire element had been deleted from the storyline. *Vampirella* was revived in 1991 (with reprints of the 1970s stories) and a series with new stories began in 1992. *Vampirella* was the only space vampire among the new wave of comic book vampires in the early 1990s.

Sources:

Aldiss, Brian. *Dracula Unbound.* New York: HarperCollins, 1991. Reprint. New York: HarperPaperbacks, 1992. 275 pp.

Frezza, Robert. *McLennon's Syndrome.* New York: Ballantine Books/Del Rey, 1993. 313 pp.

Jones, Stephen. *The Illustrated Vampire Movie Guide.* London: Titan Books, 1993. 144 pp.

Lee, Tanith. *Sabella, or the Blood Stone.* New York: DAW Books, 1980. 157 pp.

Matheson, Richard. *I Am Legend.* New York: Fawcett, 1954. 175 pp.

Planet of Vampires. 3 issues. New York: Atlas Comics, 1975.

Scapperotti, Dan. "Tobe Hooper on *Lifeforce*: The Director of *Poltergeist* Films Colin Wilson's *Space Vampires.*" *Cinefantastique* 15, 3 (July 1985): 6-8.

Vampirella. 1- . New York: Harris Publishing, 1992- .

Vampirella. 1-112. New York: Warren Publishing Co.,1969-83.

Vampirella: Morning in America. New York: Harris Publications, 1991.

Wilson, Colin. *Space Vampires.* New York: Random House, 1976. 214 pp. Reprint. New York: Pocket Books, 1977. 220 pp. Rept. as: *Life Force.* New York: Warner Books, 1985. 220 pp.

SCREEM IN THE DARK FAN CLUB *See:* VLAD

THE SECRET ORDER OF THE UNDEAD

The Secret Order of the Undead (S.O.UND) is a vampire and **gothic** interest group that promotes an appreciation of the creatures of darkness and the darker side of historical characters. It originated in 1988 with the formation of a theatrical performing artists' group, the Transylvania Troopers. The group performed only at midnight on Fridays and Saturdays and during the full moon. However, in 1990, the troop's headquarters and playhouse were blown up; the cause of the explosion is as yet unknown. This event led to the breakup of the Transylvanian Troopers and the formation of S.O.UND. S.O.UND describes itself as a performing artists' group that presents original drama and music reflecting the Byron/gothic genre. The group's members work to recreate characters from what are considered the darker periods of history, such as the pre-medieval, the French Revolution, and the Victorian periods.

S.O.UND is headed by an inner circle that is responsible for policy decisions and production of two periodicals that feature members' artwork, poetry, and fiction. Membership information is available from S.O.UND, 155 E. "C" St., Upland, CA 91786.

THE SECRET ROOM

The Secret Room is an organization for gay/lesbian/bisexual fans of the **Dark Shadows** television series. The group may be contacted at PO Box 1872, Azle, TX 76098-5872. Enclose a self-addressed, stamped envelope when making an inquiry.

SEEDS

The folklore of Europe reported the use of seeds as a protective measure against vampires. The kinds of seeds varied from place to place, but most frequently mentioned was mustard seed, a very small seed that Jesus spoke of in one of his parables in the Christian New Testament. Seeds of millet (a name used to refer to several grasses and grains), were most popular, but those of linen, carrot, and rice were also used. Seeds might be placed in the coffin to entertain the vampire, but more commonly were spread over the grave site and along the road leading from the cemetery to the village or family home of the deceased.

The idea behind the use of seeds, and on occasion a knotted cloth or fish net, was to take the vampire's attention away from his intended victim in town. It was thought that the vampire was required to collect and count each seed before he could come to town and do any damage. Most often, he was able to count only one seed a year. Thus, a handful of mustard seeds could, if one accepted the logic of its use, prevent the vampire's return for an indefinite period.

SELENE

Selene was a fictional vampire city featured in Paul Féval's 1875 novel, *La Ville vampire.* As the novel never was translated into English, it has remained largely unknown among modern vampire enthusiasts, who have been concentrated within the English-speaking world. Selene was located in Yugoslavia, north of Belgrade, close to the site of the village where **Arnold Paul** lived, subject of one of the most famous vampire incidents during the eighteenth century. As described by Féval, as one approached Selene, the environment changed suddenly—the green vegetation faded away and the sky turned dark. The city was a conglomeration of architectural styles centered around a spiral pyramidal palace. Among its statues was one of a woman being clawed to death by a tiger. The city was inhabited by famous personages of past centuries who were now vampires.

In the book, a traveler arrived in the city in search of a vampire. He carried an iron stake, some coal, a small burner, candles, and smelling salts. He was accompanied by a surgeon from the Hungarian army. After locating the vampire he came in search of, and using the smelling salts to counter the stench, the surgeon removed the vampire's heart with the iron stake and burned it. The vampire died and his body turned to ashes. The clock sounded, and other vampires began to rise. The traveler and the surgeon, carrying the ashes of the vampire's heart, left to return to Belgrade, using the ashes to escape the hunger and wrath of the city's vampire inhabitants. When sprinkled on vampires, the ash caused them to explode with a bluish flash.

La Ville vampire was one of the pre-Dracula attempts to play with the vampire legends then alive in western Europe, prior to the time when the major elements of the literary vampire had been firmly established. It incorporated pieces of eastern European folklore, especially the practice of burning the suspected vampire's heart, but, like most fictional works of the time included elements that were not in the modern vampire myth—such as other vampires reacting to the ashes of the dead vampire's heart.

Sources:

Féval, Paul. *La Ville vampire*. Paris: 1875.

Manguel, Alberto, and Gianni Guadalupi. *The Dictionary of Imaginary Places*. San Diego, CA: Harcourt, Brace, Jovanovitch, Publishers, 1987. 454 pp.

SEWARD, JOHN

Dr. John Seward, one of the leading characters in **Bram Stoker**'s *Dracula*, appeared early in the story as a suitor of **Lucy Westenra**. In a letter to her friend **Mina Murray** (Chapter 5), Lucy described Seward:

> He is a doctor and really clever. Just fancy! He is only nine and twenty, and he has an immense lunatic asylum all under his own care. Mr. Holmwood introduced him to me, and he called here to see us, and often comes now. I think he is one of the most resolute men I ever saw, and yet the most calm. He seems absolutely imperturbable. I can fancy what a wonderful power he must have over his patients.

Previously, Seward had been a friend of **Arthur Holmwood** and **Quincey P. Morris**, with whom he had traveled in the Orient. At the asylum, he was giving a significant amount of attention to patient **R. N. Renfield**, who displayed some unusual symptoms. Renfield wanted to consume various **animals** in an attempt to take in their lives. Seward called this unique form of madness ''zoophagous'' or life-eating. After Dracula headed for England, Renfield began to react to his movements. Seward dutifully recorded the changes in Renfield's behavior, but had no understanding of their cause.

While attracted to Lucy, he was shut out of her life by her choice of Holmwood (Lord Godalming), but was called back into the plot as Lucy's health failed. Unable to find any cause, he called in his mentor, **Abraham Van Helsing** of Amsterdam, to consult on the case. Initially Van Helsing was stumped but immediately recognized that Lucy needed **blood**. Seward participated in giving her a transfusion, and while Van Helsing traveled back and forth to Holland, Seward watched over Lucy's progress and recorded her decline.

After Lucy's death, he became one in the team under Van Helsing who sought out and destroyed Dracula and was present when Lucy's body was staked. Seward eventually understood the relationship between Renfield and Dracula and began the process of deciphering his actions. He introduced Van Helsing to Renfield and was present when Renfield connected Dracula to Mina. In fact, he was with the other men who rushed to her bedroom to save her from the vampire's attack. He then went to Dracula's base at **Carfax** and his house in Piccadilly to destroy the boxes of Transylvanian earth.

Once it was discovered that Dracula had escaped England and fled to **Transylvania**, Seward joined the rush to **Castle Dracula**. In the final push to get to the castle, the team split up and Seward traveled by horse with Morris. He arrived immediately after the Gypsies had deposited the box of earth containing Dracula's body before the castle doors. Rifle in hand, he held the Gypsies back while Morris and **Jonathan Harker** killed the vampire.

In the later dramatic and cinematic productions of *Dracula,* unlike the other characters, Seward almost always survived. In the drama by **Hamilton Deane** and **John L. Balderston**, he became the father of (rather than the suitor of) Lucy Westenra, an alteration also evident in the several movies based upon play. Possibly the most interesting twist on Seward's character came in **Fred Saberhagen**'s novels, *The Dracula Tape* (1975) and especially *The Holmes-Dracula File* (1978), in which Seward emerged as one of the villains. That idea was seconded by Kim Newman, who transformed Seward into Jack the Ripper in his novel *Anno Dracula* (1992).

SEXUALITY AND THE VAMPIRE

Essential to understanding the appeal of the vampire is its sexual nature. While it frequently has been pointed out that traditional vampires cannot engage in ''normal'' sexual activity, the vampire is not necessarily asexual. As twentieth-century scholars turned their attention to the vampire, both in folklore and literature, underlying sexual themes quickly became evident. The sexual nature of vampirism formed an underlying theme in *Dracula*, but it was disguised in such a way that it was hidden from the literary censors of the day, the consciousness of the public, and probably from the awareness (as many critics argued), of author **Bram Stoker** himself. Carol Fry, for example, suggested that vampirism was in fact a form of ''surrogate sexual intercourse.''

SEXUALITY IN DRACULA: The sexual nature of vampirism manifested initially in *Dracula* during **Jonathan Harker**'s encounter with the three **vampire brides** residing in **Castle Dracula**. Harker confronted them as extremely appealing sex objects but who embody an element of danger. Harker noted, ''I felt in my heart a wicked, burning desire that they would kiss me with their red lips'' (Chapter 3). Stoker went on to describe the three as sensual predators and their vampire's bite as a kiss. One of the women anticipated the object of their desire, ''He is young and strong; there are kisses for us all.'' And as they approached, Harker waited in delightful anticipation.

Attention in the novel then switched to the two ''good'' women, **Lucy Westenra** and **Mina Murray**. Lucy, as the subject of the attention of three men, reveled in their obvious desire of her before she chose **Arthur Holmwood**, the future Lord Godalming, as her betrothed. Mina, to the contrary, was in love with Jonathan and pined in loneliness while he was lost in the wilds of **Transylvania**. While preparing for her wedding, however, Lucy was distracted by the presence of Dracula. While on a seaside vacation in **Whitby**, Lucy began sleepwalking. One evening, Lucy was discovered by Mina in her nightclothes across the river. As Mina approached, she could see a figure bending over Lucy. Dracula left as Mina approached, but she found Lucy with her lips parted and breathing heavily. Thus began Lucy's slow transformation from the virtuous and proper, if somewhat frivolous, young lady, into what Judith Weissman termed a "sexual monster." By day she was faint and listless, but by night she took on a most unladylike voluptuousness. Shortly before her death, she asked Arthur to kiss her, and when he leaned toward her, she attempted to bite him.

Stoker's understanding, however unconscious, of the sexual nature of the vampiric attack became most clear in the **blood** transfusions that were given to Lucy in the attempt to save her life. Arthur, who never was able to consummate his love for Lucy, suggested that in the sharing of blood he had, in the eyes of God, married her. The older and wiser **Abraham Van Helsing** rejected the idea, given the sexual connotation for himself and the others who also gave her blood. But by this time, the sexual interest of Dracula in women was firmly established and led directly to the most sexual scene in the book.

Having given Lucy her peace (and, by implication, returned her virtue) in the act of staking and decapitating her, the men called together by Van Helsing to rid the world of Dracula, were slow to awaken to his real target—Mina. When they finally became aware of this, they rushed to Mina's bedroom. There, they found Dracula sitting on her bed forcing her to drink from a cut on his chest. Dracula turned angrily to those who had interrupted him. "His eyes flamed red with devilish passion . . . " Once Dracula was driven away and Mina came to her senses, she realized that she had been violated. She declared herself unclean and vowed that she would "kiss" her husband no more.

THE SEXUAL VAMPIRE OF FOLKLORE: While there is little evidence that Stoker was intimately aware of eastern European vampire lore, he could have found considerable evidence of the vampire's sexual nature—particularly in the folklore of the **Gypsies** and their neighbors, the **southern Slavs**. For example, corpses dug up as suspected vampires occasionally were reported to have an erection. Gypsies thought of the vampire as a sexual entity. The male vampire was believed to have such an intense sexual drive that his sexual need alone was sufficient to bring him back from the grave. His first act usually was a return to his widow, whom he engaged in sexual intercourse. Nightly visits could ensue and continue over a period of time, with the wife becoming exhausted and emaciated. In more than a few cases, the widow was known to become pregnant and bear a child by her vampire husband. The resulting child, called a *dhampir*, was a highly valued personage deemed to have unusual powers to diagnose vampirism and to destroy vampires attacking the community.

In some cases the vampire would return to a woman with whom he had been in love, but with whom he had never consummated that love. The woman would then be invited to return with him to the grave where they could share their love through eternity. The idea of the dead returning to claim a living lover was a popular topic in European folklore. By far the most famous literary piece illustrating the theme was Gottfried August Bürger's ballad "Lenore," known in English by Sir Walter Scott's translation.

The folklore of **Russia** also described the vampire as a sexual being. Among the ways in which it made itself known was to appear in a village as a handsome young stranger. Circulating among the young people in the evening, the vampire lured unsuspecting women to their doom. Russian admonitions for young people to listen to their elders and stay close to home are reminiscent of the ancient Greek story of Apollonius, who saved one of his students from the allure of the *lamiai,* whom he was about to marry.

The *langsuyar* of **Malaysia** was also a sexual being. A female vampire, she was often pictured as a desirable young woman who could marry and bear children. *Langsuyars* were believed to be able to live somewhat normally in a village for many years, revealed only by their inadvertent involvement in an activity that disclosed their identity.

THE MODERN LITERARY VAMPIRE: While overt sexual activity was not present in *Dracula,* sexual themes were manifest in the vampire literature of the previous century. The original vampire poem written by **Goethe**, ''The Bride of Corinth,'' drew upon the story from ancient Greece concerning a young woman who had died a virgin. She returned from the dead to her parents' home to have sexual experiences with a young man staying temporarily in the guest room. The strong sexual relationship at the heart of **Samuel Taylor Coleridge**'s ''Christabel'' was expanded in **''Carmilla,''** the popular vampire story by **Sheridan Le Fanu**.

In the story, Carmilla Karnstein moved into the castle home of Laura, her proposed victim. She did not immediately attack Laura, but proceeded to build a relationship more befitting a lover. Laura experienced the same positive and negative feelings that Harker had felt toward the three women in **Castle Dracula**. As she put it:

> Now the truth is, I felt unaccountably toward the beautiful stranger. I did feel, as she said, ''drawn towards her,'' but there was also something of repulsion. In this ambiguous feeling, however, the sense of attraction immensely prevailed. She interested and won me; she was so beautiful and so indescribably engaging.

Carmilla went about her assault upon Laura while seducing her cooperation. She would draw Laura to her with pretty words and embraces and gently press her lips to Laura's cheek. She would take Laura's hand while at the same time locking her gaze on her eyes and breathing with such passion that it embarrassed the naive Laura. So attracted was Laura to Carmilla, that only slowly did she come to the realization that her lovely friend was a vampire.

THE SENSUOUS VAMPIRE ON STAGE AND SCREEN: Carol Fry, author of the article ''Fictional conventions and sexuality in *Dracula,*'' has properly pointed out that Dracula was in part a stereotypical character of popular nineteenth-century literature, the rake. The rake appeared in stories to torment and distress the pure women of proper society. The rake was to some extent the male counterpart of the **vamp**; however, the consequences of falling victim to a seductive male were far more serious for a woman than they were for a man victimized by a seductive woman. The man who loved and left was thought to have left behind a tainted woman. Just as a state of "moral depravity" contaminated the fallen woman, so vampirism infected the one bitten. The vampire's victim became like him and preyed on others. The fallen woman might became a vamp, professional or not, who in turn led men to engage in her immoral ways.

Once brought to the stage, Dracula's rakish nature was heightened. No longer hovering in the background as in the novel, he was invited into the living rooms of his intended victims. In this seemingly safe setting, he went about his nefarious business, though what he actually did had to be construed from the dialogue of those who would kill him. Only after the play was brought to the screen, and the public reacted to **Bela Lugosi**, did some understanding of the romantic appeal of this supposed monster become evident to a widespread audience. However, not until the 1950s would the vampire, in the person of **Christopher Lee**'s Dracula, be given a set of fangs and allowed to bite his victims on screen.

Interestingly, the obvious sexuality of the vampire was first portrayed on screen by a female vampire. In retrospect, the scene in *Dracula's Daughter* (1936) in which the female vampire seduced the young model was far more charged with sexuality than any played by Lugosi. A quarter of a century later, **Roger Vadim** brought an overtly sensual vampire to the screen in his version of "Carmilla," *Blood and Roses* (1960). In 1967 French director **Jean Rollin** produced the first of a series of semipornographic features, *Le Viol du Vampire* (released in English as *The Vampire's Rape*). The story centered around two women who believed that they were cursed by a vampire to follow his bloodsucking life. The sexuality of "Carmilla" was even more graphically pictured in *The Vampire Lovers*, **Hammer Films**' 1970 production, in which the unclad Carmilla and Laura romped freely around their bedroom.

From these and similar early soft-core productions, two quite different sets of vampire films developed. On the one hand were pornographic vampire films that featured nudity and sex. Among the earliest was *Dracula (The Dirty Old Man)* (1969), in which Count Alucard kidnapped naked virgins to fulfill his sexual and vampiric needs. Spanish director Jesus Franco produced *La Countess aux Seins Nus* (1973) (released in video in the United States as *Erotikill*), in which Countess Irena Karnstein (a character derived from Carmilla) killed her victims in an act of fellatio. (These scenes were cut from the American version.) The trend toward pornographic vampire movies culminated in 1979 with *Dracula Sucks* (also released as *Lust at First Bite*), a remake of *Dracula,* that closely followed the 1931 movie. It starred Jamie Gillis as Dracula. More recent sexually explicit vampire movies include *Dracula Exotica* (1981), also starring Gillis; *Gayracula* (1983), a **homosexual** film; *Sexandroide* (1987); *Out for Blood* (1990); *Princess of the Night* (1990); and *Wanda Does Transylvania* (1990). Most of these were shot in both hard-core and soft-core versions.

THE VAMPIRE IN LOVE: The pornographic vampire movies were relatively few in number and poorly distributed. Of far more importance in redefining the contemporary vampire were the novels and films that transformed the evil monster of previous generations into a romantic lover. The new vampire hero owed much to **Chelsea**

Quinn Yarbro's **St. Germain**. In a series of novels beginning with *Hotel Transylvania* (1978), St. Germain emerged not as a monster, but as a man of moral worth, extraordinary intellect, and captivating sensuality. He even occasionally fell in love. He was unable to have ordinary sexual relations because he could not have an erection. However, his bite conveyed an intense experience of sexual bliss that women found to be a more than adequate alternative.

At the time Yarbro was finishing *Hotel Transylvania,* a new stage production of ***Dracula, The Vampire Play in Three Acts*** had become a hit on Broadway. The play was the first dramatic production of *Dracula* to reintroduce the scene in which Dracula forced Mina to drink from his blood. The scene, a rapelike experience in the novel, had been transformed into one of seduction. In 1979 the larger populace was introduced to this more sensual Dracula when **Frank Langella** recreated his stage role for the motion picture screen. He presented Dracula as not only a suave foreign nobleman, but as a debonair, attractive male who drew his victims to him by the sheer power of his sexual presence. The scenes in which Lucy, over the objections of her elders, rushed to Carfax to join her lover and drink his blood completed a transformation of Dracula from mere monster into a hero who lived up to the movie's billing: "Throughout history he has filled the hearts of men with *terror,* and the hearts of women with *desire.*"

Langella's Dracula directly informed the more recent production of ***Bram Stoker's Dracula*** under the writing and direction of **Francis Ford Coppola**. Coppola not only brought the vampire into proper society but turned him into a handsome young man who, with his money and foreign elegance, was able to seduce the betrothed Mina from her wimpish fiancé. He returned the final blood drinking scene to her bedroom, revealed Dracula at his most human, and made their lovemaking the sensual climax of the movie's love story subplot, which Coppola had added to explain Dracula's otherwise irrational acts against the British family he had assaulted.

The transformation of the vampire into a hero lover was a primary element in the overall permeation of the vampire myth into the culture of late-twentieth-century America (which included the emergence of the vampire in humor and the vampire as moral example). As such, the contemporary vampire has had to deal with a variety of sexual patterns. Television detective Nick Knight developed an ongoing relationship with a researcher who was trying to cure him. Mara McCuniff, the centuries-old vampire of Traci Briery's *The Vampire Memoirs,* was overtaken by her sexual urges for three days each month at the time of the full moon. In *Domination,* Michael Cecilone placed his vampires in the world of sadomasochism. Lori Herter's romance novels elevated the vampire as the object of female fantasies.

The response to the conscious development of the vampire as a sexual being has almost guaranteed future exploration in fictional works. ***Prisoners of the Night***, a periodical of vampire fiction that appears annually, has focused on sexuality in several issues. Editor Mary Ann B. McKinnon has added an impetus to exploring the theme in her fanzine, ***Good Guys Wear Fangs,*** which covers good-guy vampires, most of them romantic heroes. Such sexualizing of the vampire, while departing from the common image of the vampire as mere monster, has not been foreign to the creature itself. From the beginning, a seductive sexuality has existed as an element of the literary, vampire comingling with that of the monstrous, and goes far to explain the vampire's appeal relative to its monstrous cousins.

Sources:

Bentley, C. F. "The Monster in the Bedroom: Sexual Symbolism in Bram Stoker's *Dracula.*" *Literature and Psychology* 22, 1 (1972): 27-34

Fry, Carol L. "Fictional Conventions and Sexuality in *Dracula.*" *The Victorian Newsletter* 42 (1972): 20-22.

Roth, Phyllis A. "Suddenly Sexual Women in Bram Stoker's *Dracula,*" *Literature and Psychology* 27, 3 (1977): 113-121.

Shuter, Michael. "Sex Among the Coffins, or, Lust at First Bite with William Margold." *Draculina* 17 (December 1993): 32-34.

Stevenson, John Allen. "A Vampire in the Mirror: The Sexuality of Dracula." *PMLA: Publications of the Modern Language Association of America* 103, 2 (March 1988): 139-149.

Trigg, E. B. *Gypsy Demons and Divinities: The Magical and Supernatural Practices of the Gypsies.* London: Sheldon Press, 1973. 238 pp.

Waller, Gregory A. *The Living and the Undead: From Stoker's Dracula to Romero's Dawn of the Dead.* Urbana, IL: University of Illinois Press, 1986. 376 pp.

Weiss, Andrea. *Vampires and Violets: Lesbians in Film.* New York: Penguin Books, 1993. 184 pp.

Weissman, Judith. *Half Savage and Hardy and Free: Women and Rural Radicalism in the Nineteenth Century Novel.* Middletown, CT: Wesleyan University Press, 1987. 342 pp.

SHADOWCON

Several years after the cancellation of the popular *Dark Shadows* daytime soap opera on ABC-TV, fans continued to manifest a high level of devotion to the series. *The World of Dark Shadows* Fanzine appeared in 1975 and two years later the first Shadowcon(vention) was organized in San Diego as part of Starcon, a science fiction convention. In 1979 Shadowcon emerged as an independent gathering in Los Angeles, where it continued annually until 1986. Within a few years, the nature of the Shadowcon conventions began to expand and diversify by including all aspects of science fiction, fantasy, and horror. Thus, in 1983, a new organization that had an exclusive focus on *Dark Shadows,* the **Dark Shadows Festival**, was created by the combined efforts of *The World of Dark Shadows, Shadowgram*, and *Inside the Old House,* published by **Old House Publishing**.

Sources:

Dresser, Norine. *American Vampires: Fans, Victims, Practitioners.* New York: W. W. Norton & Company, 1989. 255 pp.

SHADOWDANCE

Shadowdance is a magazine devoted to the dark side of creativity, for which the vampire is one of the most appropriate symbols. It was founded by Michelle Belanger, a poet, writer, and editor, who began to publish her work in the 1980s. Her poem in 1992 "The Haunted," won the Joseph T. Cotter Memorial Poetry Award. As

Belanger grew up she developed an interest in occultism, Jungian psychology, and folklore, all of which have fed her study of vampires. Her fascination with the nineteenth-century Byronic literary vampire led her to an understanding of it as an archetypal figure epitomizing all that is dark and reviled by society. The vampire stood on the edge of society, tormented by a desire to reenter the larger social context while realizing that such acceptance could never occur. She equated that vampire with similar figures such as the "Beast" in the Beauty and the Beast story and the Phantom of the Opera. Belanger also became aware of living vampires—those people who claim to be vampires either because they drink others' blood or because of their powers of **psychic vampirism** (stealing energy from others).

Shadowdance may be contacted c/o Michelle Belanger, PO Box 474, Hinckley, OH 44233.

SHADOWGRAM

Shadowgram is a **Dark Shadows** fanzine founded in 1979 by Maria Barbosa. The first issue was a two-page sheet reporting on what the major actors from the original *Dark Shadows* series were doing eight years after the series was canceled. It is currently published quarterly under the editorship of Marcy Robin and has emerged as the major *Dark Shadows* news periodical. The fanzine specializes in reports of the current activities of the cast of both the original and the 1991 television series, information on new *Dark Shadows* **paraphernalia**, and announcements of fan activities. It also serves as the nexus of a network of local *Dark Shadows* fan clubs scattered around the United States.

Robin has been active in *Dark Shadows* fandom since the mid-1970s. She participated in the **Shadowcon** conventions of the 1970s, and in 1983, was among the founders of **Dark Shadows Festival**, the group that currently organizes the annual national gatherings of *Dark Shadows* fans. With Kathleen Resch of *The World of Dark Shadows*, she has co-authored two books—a novel, *Beginnings: The Island of Ghosts,* and a volume on the series, *Dark Shadows in the Afternoon.* She has written a number of short stories around the *Dark Shadows* themes, some of which have been gathered into an anthology titled *From the Shadows . . . Marcy Robin.*

Shadowgram may be contacted c/o Marcy Robin, 9441 La Rosa Dr., Temple City, CA 91780. Inquiries should be accompanied by a self-addressed, stamped envelope. Robin works closely with Resch, editor of *The World of Dark Shadows,* who also lives in Temple City and works on the staff of *Shadowgram.*

Sources:

Dresser, Norine. *American Vampires: Fans, Victims, Practitioners.* New York: W. W. Norton & Company, 1989. 255 pp.

Resch, Kathleen, and Marcy Robin. *Beginnings: The Island of Ghosts.* Temple City, CA: The World of Dark Shadows, 1982. 167 pp.

———. *Dark Shadows in the Afternoon.* East Meadow, NY: Image Publishing, 1991. 109 pp.

Robin, Marcy. *From the Shadows . . . Marcy Robin.* Ed. by Kathleen Resch. Temple City, CA: Pentegram
Press, 1986. 85 pp.

SHADOWS OF THE NIGHT

Shadows of the Night is the name of two different vampire fanzines. Dan Silvio edits
the **Dark Shadows** fanzine, which is the official publication of the **Pittsburgh Dark
Shadows Fan Club**. Silvio founded the fanzine in 1987. Dedicated to the fans of
Dark Shadows, each issue contains news, fan art, photographs, and reports of festival
gatherings. It also publishes materials about the **Collinsport Players**, a comedic
drama group that performs at many *Dark Shadows* festivals.

Shadows of the Night can be contacted c/o Dan Silvio, 4529 Friendship Ave., 2nd
Fl., Pittsburgh, PA 15224.

Shadows of the Night is also the name of a more general vampire fanzine, the first
issue of which appeared in 1991. It may be reached c/o its editor, Tammy Pond, PO
Box 17006, Rochester, NY 14617.

SHEPARD, LESLIE ALAN (1917-)

Leslie Alan Shepard, author and founder of the **Bram Stoker Society**, began his
professional life as a technician for documentary films. He produced and directed a
number of films through the 1950s. In 1958-59 he spent time in India studying yoga
and Hindu metaphysics. Since his return from Asia, he has been active with the Hindu
community in England.

In the 1970s, Shepard led in the recognition in **Ireland** of the work of **Bram
Stoker**, both as the acting manager for dramatist Henry Irving and as an Irish author of
importance. Shepard's compilation of vampire short fiction, *The Dracula Book of
Great Vampire Stories,* was published in 1977. He also collected Stoker first editions,
autographs, and other memorabilia, and in 1980, he was a founder of the Bram Stoker
Society, a literary society to support the recognition of Stoker and other Irish **gothic**
authors such as **Sheridan Le Fanu** (1814-73) and Lord Dunsany (1878-1957). Soon
after the founding of the society, Shepard produced a companion volume to his earlier
work, *The Dracula Book of Great Horror Stories* (1981). His collection of Stoker
material is now on permanent display at the Writers Museum, Parnell Square, in
Dublin.

During the late 1970s Shepard began what is possibly his most important literary
effort, as author/editor of the *Encyclopedia of Occultism and Parapsychology* (1978).
Now in its third edition (1991), the encyclopedia has grown into a substantive
reference work, far surpassing others in the field. While working on the first edition,
he authored *How to Protect Yourself against Black Magic and Witchcraft* (1978).

Sources:

Krishna, Gopi. *Living with Kundalini: The Autobiography of Gopi Krishna.* Ed. by Leslie A. Shepard. Boston: Shambhala, 1993.

Shepard, Leslie A., ed. *The Dracula Book of Great Horror Stories.* New York: Citadel Press, 1981. 288 pp.

————. *The Dracula Book of Great Vampire Stories.* New York: Citadel Press, 1977. Reprint. New York: Jove/HBJ, 1978. 316 pp.

————. *Encyclopedia of Occultism and Parapsychology.* 2 vols. Detroit: Gale Research Company, 1978. 3rd ed.: 1991.

————. *How to Protect Yourself Against Black Magic and Witchcraft.* New York: Citadel Press, 1978. 162 pp.

SHERLOCK HOLMES

Dracula and Sherlock Holmes vie with each other as the most popular fictional character in the English-speaking world. *Dracula* is the single novel most frequently made into a movie, while Sherlock Holmes, the subject of 56 short stories and four novels, is the character most frequently brought to the screen (with Dracula a close second). Both have been the subject of many more additional books and stories by authors who use one or the other as their central figure.

THE SUSSEX VAMPIRE: Sherlock Holmes had only one brush with a vampire. The short story, ''The Adventure of the Sussex Vampire'' appeared in the January 1924 issue of the *Strand Magazine,* just six months before the dramatic version of *Dracula* written by **Hamilton Deane** opened in rural England. The story began with an inquiry concerning vampires, to which Holmes made what has become one of his more famous lines, ''Rubbish, Watson, rubbish! What have we to do with walking corpses who can only be held in their grave by stakes driven through their hearts? It's pure lunacy.'' Watson reminded him that vampirism might take the form of a living person sucking the blood of someone younger in order to retain his or her youth (a probable reference to the case of **Elizabeth Bathory**). Their client, Robert Ferguson, related an incident in which his wife was found apparently biting the neck of their infant son and immediately afterwards was seen with blood on her mouth. To Holmes the idea of a vampire, even the more human one described by Watson, was absurd. ''Such things do not happen in criminal practice in England.'' But, Holmes asked rhetorically, ''Could not a bleeding wound be sucked for other than vampiric reasons?'' Holmes simply thought of the alternative, that the mother was in fact sucking poison from a wound the child had received from his older jealous stepbrother.

While *Dracula* was enjoying success on the stage throughout the country, ''The Adventure of the Sussex Vampire'' received its first dramatization in a 1929-30 British radio series of ''The Adventures of Sherlock Holmes,'' prepared for broadcast by Edith Meiser. Her version would be the one most frequently used when other adaptations were made, such as the first American radio dramatization in 1936 and the Basil Rathbone/Nigel Bruce portrayals in 1939-40 and 1941-42. The first television adaptations occurred in the fall of 1964 for the BBC. Most recently, the story has become the subject of two movies: *Sherlock Holmes in Caracas* (Venezuela, 1992) and *Sherlock Holmes: The Last Vampire* (United Kingdom, 1992), the latter being a made-for-television movie in the Jeremy Brett/Edward Hardwicke series of Sherlock Holmes stories.

HOLMES MEETS DRACULA: Over the decades there have been several attempts to link Sherlock Holmes to the Dracula story. For instance, Sherlockians have entertained themselves with a debate that Dr. **Abraham Van Helsing** was in fact Sherlock Holmes in disguise. Purists, however, have rejected such a notion. Since both Sherlock Holmes and Dracula were pictured by their creators, Arthur Conan Doyle and **Bram Stoker**, as contemporaries in the Victorian world of the late nineteenth century, it was inevitable that, in view of the recent revived interest in each, someone would suggest their interaction. A hint of what was to come appeared in 1976 when Nicholas Meyer added Bram Stoker as a character in *The West End Horror,* a new Sherlock Holmes story. Two years later, two different authors picked up on the suggestion.

Loren D. Estleman, writing as Holmes's chronicler Dr. John H. Watson, authored *Sherlock Holmes vs. Dracula: The Adventures of the Sanguinary Count.* What would happen if Holmes was called in to solve the case of the *Demeter,* the ship that brought Dracula to **London** but then was found mysteriously wrecked at **Whitby** with all its crew dead. And then while working on the case, Holmes's interest was drawn to the accounts of the "Boofer Lady," **Lucy Westenra** as a vampire preying on the local children of Hamstead Heath. The great detective followed his clues as he became involved in the events of the original novel and was led to his own confrontation with Dracula.

Estleman followed closely the characterizations of the creators of Holmes and Dracula: Holmes was good; Dracula was the epitome of evil. Not so for **Fred Saberhagen**. In his series of novels, Saberhagen saw Dracula as a misunderstood and maligned figure, the victim of the ignorant and malicious Dr. **John Seward**. In the second of his series of novels, *The Holmes-Dracula Files,* Saberhagen brought the two characters together, but had to accommodate the plot to the reversal already made in *The Dracula Tape* (1975). The story revolved around a plot to destroy London during Queen Victoria's Jubilee celebration. The story was complicated by Dracula's being hit on the head, resulting in a case of amnesia. He could not remember who he was, not even his vampiric nature. To add a little color, he and Holmes were the spitting image of each other, even Holmes's companion Dr. Watson had trouble telling them apart. Could they, however, pool their resources to defeat the evil Dr. Seward?

After the double-barreled blast from Estleman and Saberhagen, it wasn't until the 1980s that Dracula and Holmes would again be brought together. They had a brief encounter in *Dracula's Diary* (1982), in which Dracula made a scenic tour of Victorian characters. Then, in the early stages of the vampire's return to **comic book**s in 1987, Dracula was pitted against several of his Victorian contemporaries, from Jack the Ripper to Sherlock Holmes. On the centennial of "A Study in Scarlet," the first Holmes story, Martin Powell published *Scarlet in Gaslight*, a four-issue series that began with Holmes's traditional nemesis, Professor Moriarty, traveling to **Transylvania** to make common cause with Dracula. Holmes had been drawn into the count's domain, however, by the mother of Lucy Westenra, who had begun to show mysterious symptoms of fatigue and blood loss. Holmes was sharp enough to trace Dracula in Lucy's bedroom in **Whitby**. In the end, however, he was unable to prevent her death.

Meanwhile, Moriarty had developed a plot to release a plague of vampires on London, though his alliance with Dracula had fallen apart. Eventually, Dracula and Holmes united to stop the professor. Dracula only wanted to have the now vampiric-Lucy at his side. He was thwarted when she was killed (the true death) in the final encounters in London. The main characters survived, to meet one last time at the famous falls in Switzerland where Holmes faked his own death and, with relish, Dracula killed Moriarty.

In *The Dracula Caper* (1988, the eighth in the "Time Wars" series by Simon Hawke), Holmes does not appear, but Doyle teams with Bram Stoker to save the world from Dracula. The most recent encounter between Holmes and Dracula found but a small audience of Holmes enthusiasts. Published in a limited edition, it quickly sold out. In *The Tangled Skein,* author David Stuart Davies picked up the plot of "The Hound of the Baskervilles," one of the most famous Holmes stories. Stapleton, the villain of the earlier story, returned to continue his evil, but was soon surpassed by a series of bloody murders that served to bring Dr. Van Helsing into Holmes's territory. The two were forced to unite their efforts to deal with both Stapleton and Dracula. Creative Vision Film Productions, a British firm headed by producer Christopher Gawor, has purchased the option on the book's film rights.

Sources:

Cox, Greg. *The Transylvanian Library: A Consumer's Guide to Vampire Fiction.* San Bernardino, CA: Borgo Press, 1993. 264 pp.

Doyle, Arthur Conan. *The Annotated Sherlock Holmes.* 2 vols. New York: Clarkson N. Potter, 1967.

Eyles, Allen. *Sherlock Holmes: A Centenary Celebration.* London: John Murray, 1986. 141 pp.

Geare, Michael & Michael Corby. *Dracula's Diary.* New York: Beaufort Books, 1982. 153 pp.

Godfrey, Robert. "'Tangled Skein' Heading for the Big Screen." *Sherlock Holmes Gazette* 8 (Autumn 1993): 36-37.

Hawke, Simon. *The Dracula Caper.* Time War No. 8 New York: Berkley Ace, 1988. 212 pp.

Saberhagen, Fred. *The Holmes-Dracula File.* New York: Ace Books, 1978. 249 pp.

Scarlet in Gaslight. 4 vols. Newbury Park, CA: Eternity Comics, 1987-88.

Watson, John H. (pseudonym of Loren D. Estleman). *Sherlock Holmes vs. Dracula: The Adventure of the Sanguinary Count.* New York: Doubleday & Company, 1978. 211 pp. Reprint. New York: Penguin Books, 1979. 214 pp.

SHTRIGA

The *shtriga* was a vampirelike witch found in Albania. It was similar to the *strigon,* a witch found among the **southern Slavs**, especially in Slovenia; the *strigoi* of **Romania**; and the *vjeshtitza* of Montenegro. While not a Slavic country itself, Albania's folk mythology is intricately related to that of its Slavic neighbors. The word *shtriga* was derived from the Latin *strix*, screech owl, that referred to a flying demon that attacked in the night.

The Albanian *shtriga* usually took the form of a woman who lived undetected in the community. She was difficult to identify, although a sure sign was a young girl's hair turning white. She attacked in the night, usually in the form of an animal such as a moth, fly, or bee. Two methods of discovering her have been reported. On a day when the community gathered in the church, a cross of pig bone could be fastened to the doors. Any *shtriga* inside at that time would be trapped, unable to leave past the cruciform barrier. Second, if one followed a suspected *shtriga* at night, she would have to at some point, vomit the blood she had sucked out of her victims. Thus, her identity would be ascertained. In addition, the vomited blood made an effective amulet against witches.

Sources:

Durham, M. Edith. "Of Magic, Witches and Vampires in the Balkans." *Man* 121 (December 1923): 189-92.

SIGHISOARA

Sighisoara was the birthplace of **Vlad the Impaler**, the historical **Dracula**. Sighisoara is a small town in south central **Transylvania**. A former Roman town, it was settled by Germans in 1150 A.D. Burned down by the Tartars in 1241, it emerged in the fifteenth century as one of the strongest fortified centers of Hungarian rulers. In 1430, **Vlad Dracul** was sent there as commander of the guard and Vlad the Impaler was born (probably in 1430 or 1431) in the home in which Vlad Dracul resided. The family lived in the house until 1436, when Vlad Dracul became the prince of Wallachia and moved to **Tirgoviste**. That home survived the vicissitudes of time, and in 1976 it was designated a part of the Romanian national heritage. The restoration that followed uncovered frescoes decorating the walls—one of which is believed to picture Dracula.

Sources:

Mackenzie, Andrew. *Dracula Country*. London: Arthur Barker, 1977. 176 pp.

SIKKIM, VAMPIRES IN *See:* TIBET, VAMPIRES IN

SLAVS, VAMPIRES AMONG THE

While vampires and vampirelike creatures appeared in the mythology of many of the world's peoples, nowhere were they more prevalent than among the Slavs of eastern and central Europe. Because of their belief in vampires, the Slavs experienced several panic-stricken ''vampire'' outbreaks in the late seventeenth and early eighteenth centuries that resulted in the opening and desecration of numerous graves during these outbreaks brought the vampire to the attention of the West and led directly to the development of the contemporary vampire myth.

The Slavic people include most eastern Europeans, from **Russia** to **Bulgaria**, from Serbia to the **Czech Republic** and **Poland**. Pouring into the region between the Danube and the Adriatic Sea, the people known collectively as the **southern Slavs** created several countries—Serbia, Croatia, Bosnia and Herzegovina, and Macedonia. In the midst of the Slavic lands are two non- Slavic countries, **Romania** and **Hungary**, though each has shared much of its language and lore with its Slavic neighbors. **Gypsies** have been a persistent minority throughout the Slavic lands, though much of the Gypsy community was decimated by the Nazi holocaust.

The exact origin of the Slavs is a matter of continuing historical debate, but most scholars agree that they came from river valleys north of the Black Sea and were closely associated with the Iranians, with whom they shared a religious perspective that gave a central place to a sun deity. At some point prior to the eighth century A.D., the Slavs, made up of numerous tribes, migrated north and west into the lands they now inhabit. Once settled in their new homes, they began to unite into national groups.

The most important event to give direction to the Slavs was the introduction of **Christianity**. Initial penetration of the church into Slavic lands began as soon as the Slavs occupied the lands formerly in the hands of the Byzantine empire. However, systematic conversion attempts emerged as an outcome of the extensive reforms instituted during the long reign of Charlemagne (768-814). Charlemagne saw to the development of missions among the Moravians and the Croatians and had a bishop placed at Salzburg to further the Christianization of the Slavs. Most Slavs, however, recognize the work of the brothers Cyril (827-869) and Methodius (825-885) as the real beginning of Slavic Christianity. The brothers developed a Slavic alphabet capable of expressing all of the sounds in the Slavic language in its various dialects. They borrowed leffers from Greek, Hebrew, and Armenian and created a new literary language that included Greek loan-words and new Slavic words that expressed some of the subleties of Greek. This new literary language, most closely resembling Old Bulgarian, became Old Church Slavonic and influenced the various new national languages (from Bulgarian and Serbian to Polish and Russian) that were beginning to emerge from the older common language of the Slavic tribes. Cyril and Methodius translated the Bible and Greek liturgy into Old Church Slavonic. Out of their missions grew the several national eastern Orthodox communions, autonomous churches affiliated with the Ecumenical Patriarch in Constantinople (now Istanbul), the spiritual (though not administrative) head of eastern Orthodoxy.

Through the ninth and tenth centuries, the Eastern Orthodox church and the Western Roman church engaged in a fight over policy and administrative matters that were to lead to their break and mutual excommunication of each other in 1054 A.D. That break had immense significance for the Slavic people, as the Bulgarians, the Russians, and the Serbians adhered to the Eastern church, while the Poles, Czechs, and Croatians gave their loyalties to the Roman church. This split had great significance in the development of vampire lore, as the two churches disagreed over their understanding of the noncorruption of the body of a dead person. In the West, the noncorruption of the body of some saintly people was seen as an additional sign of their sanctity, while in the East, the incorruptibility of the body was viewed as a sign of God's disfavor resting upon the dead person, and hence, the likelihood of the individual's becoming a vampire.

ORIGIN OF THE SLAVIC VAMPIRE: Jan L. Perkowski, who has done the most thorough study of Slavic vampirism, concluded that it originated in the Balkans. Beginning around the ninth century, speculation on vampires evolved as a result of the confrontation between pre-Christian paganism and Christianity. Bogomilism, a dualistic religion with roots in Iran that emerged in Macedonia in the tenth century, added yet another element to the developing concept. Eventually Christianity won over the other religions, and pagan and Bogomil ideas, including the belief in vampires, survived as elements of popular demonology. As the concept of the vampire evolved in Slavic mythology, several terms emerged to designate it. (*Author's note: The discussion of terminology quickly brings even the most accomplished scholar into an area of possible confusion, simply because of the dynamic nature of language in which words are constantly shifting in meaning or connotation. There is a major disagreement among authorities over the primacy of older Slavic origins or Turkish origins. Perkowski favors a Slavic origin and his approach has been accepted as a framework for this discussion.*)

The most widely used term was one or the other of many variants of the original Slavic term that lay behind our modern word *vampire,* which seems to have evolved from the common form *obyri* or *obiri.* Each language group has a cognate form of the older root word—*upirina* (Serbo-Croatian), *upirbi* (Ukrainian), *upír* (Byelo-Russian, Czech, Slovak), *upiór* (Polish), *wupji* (Kashubian), *lampir* (Bosnian), and ***vampir*** (Bulgarian, also *vipir, vepir,* or *vapir.* There is a wide range of opinion on the origin of the root term *opyri,* an unsolvable problem because the history of the early Slavic tribes has been lost.

The second popular term, especially among the Greeks and souther Slavs is *vrykolakas* (which, like vampire, possessed a number of forms in the different Slavic languages). This term seems to have derived from the older Serbian compound word, *vilki* plus *dlaka,* meaning one who wore wolf pelts. Perkowski argues that the term designated someone who wore a wolfskin in a ritual situation. By the thirteenth century, when the word first appeared in a written text, the earlier meaning had been dropped and *vlikodlaci* referred to a mythological monster who chased the clouds and ate the sun and moon (causing eclipses). Still later, by the sixteenth century, it had come to refer to vampires and as such had passed into both Greek and Romanian culture. The older southern Slavic term appears today as *vrykolakas* (Greek), *vircolac* (Romanian), *vikolak* (Macedonian, Bulgarian), and *vukodlak* (Serbo-Croatian, sometimes shortened to *kudlak*). Because of the root meaning of the term, *vudkolak* has become part of the discussion of the relation of **werewolves** and the vampire.

Three other words have assumed some importance in the literature as designations of the vampire. *Strigoi* (female: *strigoaica*) is the popular Romanian word for witch. Harry Senn, author of *Were-Wolf and Vampire in Romania,* found a variant, *strigoi mort* (dead witch), as a common term for a vampire. *Strigoi* is derived from the Latin *strix* (screech owl) that had also come to refer to a night demon that attacked children. Russians commonly replaced *upír,* their older Slavic term for a vampire, with *eretik* (or *heretic*), a Greek ecclesiastical word for one who has departed from the true faith. *Vjesci* (alternate spellings *vjeszczi* and *vjeszcey*) is a term employed by the Kashubs of northern Poland.

THE SLAVIC VAMPIRE: The vampire found its place within the world view of the people of eastern and central Europe. It was associated with death and was an entity to be avoided. However, it was not the all-pervasive symbol of evil it would come to be in nineteenth- century western European literature. Within the prescientific world of village life, the role of the vampire was to explain various forms of unpredicted and undeserved evil that befell people.

The Slavic vampire differed considerably from the popular image of the creature that evolved in twentieth-century novels and movies. First, it generally appeared without any prior contact with another vampire. The vampire was the product of an irregularity in the community life, most commonly a problem with the process of either death and burial or of birth. People who met a violent death, which cut them off from the normal completion of their live could become vampires. Thus, people who committed suicide or died as the result of an accident might become vampires. Most Slavic cultures had a precise set of ritualized activities to be followed after someone's death and even for some days following the interment of the body. Deviation from that procedure could result in the deceased becoming a vampire. In a community where the church was integral to social life, and deviation from the church a matter of serious concern, to die in a state of excommunication was seen as a cause of vampirism.

Vampirism also could result from problems associated with birth. For example, most Slavic communities had certain days of the year when intercourse was frowned upon. Children conceived by parents who had violated such taboos could become vampires. Bulgarians believed that an infant who died before it was baptized could become a *ustrel,* a vampire that would attack and drink the blood of cows and sheep. Among the Kashubs, a child born with teeth or with a membrane cap (a caul) on its head could become a vampire after its death.

Thus, Slavic society offered many reasons why vampires could appear. Of course, part of the horror felt toward vampires was the possibility of its passing on its condition to others. The vampire tended to attack its family, neighbors, friends, and people with whom it had unfinished business. Those attacked assumed the possibility of also becoming a vampire. The belief that a number of community members might become vampires contemporaneously brought on waves of vampire hysteria experienced in Slavic communities.

In the cases where a deceased person was suspected of becoming a vampire, a wide variety of pre-burial actions were reportedly taken as precautions. Among the most widespread was the placing of various materials into the coffin that were believed to inhibit a vampire's activity. Religious objects such as the **crucifix** were the most common. Such plants as the **mountain ash** were believed to stop the vampire from leaving its grave. Since vampires had a fascination with counting, **seeds** (millet or poppyseed) were spilled in the grave, on top of the grave, and on the road from the graveyard. The vampire slowly counted the seeds before it assumed the privilege of engaging in any vampiric activity. On occasion, in more extreme cases, the body might be pierced with thorns or a **stake**, different groups having preferences for wood (**hawthorn**, aspen, or oak) or iron. Believing that vampires would first attack and eat their burial garments every effort was made to keep the clothes away from the corpse's mouth. A wooden block might be placed under the chin, or the clothes might be nailed to the side of the coffin.

While there were many possible causes for the creation of a vampire, the existence of one became apparent through the negative effects of its activities. Most commonly, the unexplained death of sheep and cattle (a community's food supply) was attributed to vampires. Strange experiences of the kind usually studied by parapsychologists also suggested the presence of vampires. Included in the stories of vampires were accounts of poltergeist activity, the visitation of a **incubus/succubus**, or the appearance of the specter of a recently deceased person to a relative or friend. The sudden illness or death of a person, especially a relative or friend, soon after the death of an individual suggested that the person had become a vampire. Vampires also were associated with epidemics.

Once the suggestion that a community was under attack by a vampire was taken seriously by several residents, the discovery and designation of the vampire proceeded. The most likely candidate was a person who had recently died, especially in the previous 40 days. (Derived from the 40 days between Jesus' death and ascension.) The body of the suspected vampire might then be exhumed and examined for characteristic signs. The body of a vampire was believed to appear lifelike and to show signs of continued growth and change. It would possess pliable joints and blood would ooze from its mouth or other body openings. It might have swelled up like a drum filled with blood. Its hair may have continued to grow and new **fingernails** may have appeared.

When the supposed vampire was located, it had to be destroyed. **Destroying the vampire** usually involved action against the corpse—most commonly, the body was staked using a variety of wood or metal materials. The stake was driven into the head, heart, or stomach. In some instances **decapitation** might occur. The Kashub people placed the severed head between the feet of the corpse before reburial. In the most extreme cases, the body was destroyed by burning. These actions were accompanied, where the services of a priest could be obtained, by such ritual activity as the repeating of the funeral service, the sprinkling of holy **water**, or even an exorcism.

While the belief in vampires was quite widespread, especially in rural eastern Europe, the cases of a community detecting a vampire and taking action against the corpse of the suspect were relatively rare. This was true especially after the widely reported incidents of vampires in the eighteenth century and the subsequent institution of legal penalties, both secular and ecclesiastical, against people who desecrated the bodies of the dead. However, besides the reports of contemporary vampires, a large body of vampire folktales set in the indefinite past circulated in Slavic lands. Like Aesop's fables, these stories functioned as moral tales to teach behavioral norms to members of the community. Among the more famous was one titled simply "The Vampire," originally collected by A. N. Afanas'ev in Russia in the nineteenth century. It told of a young girl, Marusia, who became infatuated with a handsome young man who ventured into her town. He was rich, personable, and mannered, but he was also a vampire. Even after she discovered his nature, she did not act, and as a result several members of her family died. She finally learned what to do from her grandmother. The story offered the listener a number of guidelines. For example, it taught that wisdom was to be sought from one's elders, and that young people should beware attractive strangers, as they might be the source of evil. Other stories offered similar advice.

THE SLAVIC VAMPIRE TODAY: Folklorists such as Harry Senn have had little difficulty collecting vampire stories, both folktales and accounts of the apparent actual vampires, among Slavic populations throughout the twentieth century, though increasingly they have had to travel to the more isolated rural communities to find such accounts. Governments hostile to any form of supernaturalism have had a marked influence on the loss of belief in vampires, effectively eradicating most such beliefs in the urban areas and among more educated persons. Also assisting in the decline of belief has been the rise of the modern undertaker, who has assumed the burial functions previously done by the family of the deceased. The removal of the burial ceremony from the people has caused a certain distancing from the experience of death, which has contributed to the decline of many beliefs about human interaction with the dead.

Sources:

Dvornik, Francis. *The Slavs: Their Early History and Civilization.* Boston: American Academy of Arts and Sciences, 1956. 394 pp.

Perkowski, Jan L. *The Darkling: A Treatise on Slavic Vampirism.* Columbus, OH: Slavica Publishers, 1989. 174 pp.

———, ed. *Vampires of the Slavs.* Cambridge, MA: Slavica Publishers, 1976. 294 pp.

Senn, Harry. *Were-Wolf and Vampire in Romania.* New York: Columbia University Press, 1982. 148 pp.

Summers, Montague. *The Vampire in Europe.* New York: Routledge, Kegan Paul, Trench, Trubner, & Co., 1929. 329 pp. Reprint. New Hyde Park, NY: University Books, 1961. 329 pp.

Wilson, Katherina M. "The History of the Word 'Vampire.'" *Journal of the History of Ideas* 46, 4 (October-December 1985): 577-83.

SLEEP, VAMPIRE

In the last chapter of ***Dracula***, **Abraham Van Helsing** entered **Castle Dracula** to kill the three women residents who would later be referred to the **vampire brides**. When he found them, he saw they were in their "vampire sleep." The term was unique to *Dracula,* though since that time it has been used by other writers. Without naming it, **Bram Stoker** described the state of sleep into which vampires fell in chapter 4, when **Jonathan Harker** discovered **Dracula** resting in one of the boxes of his **native soil**. He observed:

> He was either dead or asleep, I could not say which—for the eyes were open and stoney, but without the glassiness of death—and the cheeks had the warmth of life through all their pallor, and the lips were as red as ever. But there was no sign of movement, no pulse, no breath, no beating of the heart. I bent over him and tried to find any sign of life, but in vain.

Dracula appeared to need periods of rest, which he took primarily during the day. At such times he gave himself to this deathlike sleep, becoming completely vulnerable. The second time that Harker found Dracula in this state, he grabbed a shovel and hit him in the head, making a deep gash above the vampire's forehead. While vulnerable and appearing dead, Dracula had some degree of consciousness. As Harker was about to hit him with the shovel, he turned his head and looked at Harker, who, upon seeing Dracula react to his intent, dropped the shovel and fled.

The fact that the vampire may fall into a deep sleeplike state at the coming of dawn has been combined with its aversion to **sunlight** to create tension in some vampire novels and movies. Dracula could appear during the day, but many more recent vampires could not. For example, **Anne Rice**'s vampires enter this deathlike sleep but still have the power to move their arms to protect themselves.

Sources:

Ramsland, Katherine. *The Vampire Companion.* New York: Ballantine Books, 1993. 507 pp.

SNOW-LANG, WENDY (1957-)

From a very early age Wendy Snow-Lang, the artist who created the popular *Night's Children* comic series, wanted to be a comics artist. She met her future husband and fellow artist, Charles Lang, at a science fiction convention and since their Halloween 1983 marriage they have collaborated on a variety of projects. A former *Dark Shadows* fan, she found inspiration in two contemporary vampire movies, *The Lost Boys* and *Near Dark*.

Night's Children follows the adventures of a group of contemporary vampires: Klaus, Julia, Billy, Samantha, and Violette; and the human Dr. Corbett. The first of the series, published by FantaCo, *Night's Children Foreplay* appeared in 1991. It, and the four part *Night's Children* series introduced the cast of characters who regularly appear in Snow-Lang's work. A second series, *Night's Children: Vampyr!,* revealed the origin of Klaus, who was born in 1431 in Hamburg. As a young man, he moved to

A VAMPIRESS FROM THE CARTOON ART OF WENDY SNOW-LANG.

Sibiu in **Transylvania** and was there when the city was attacked by **Vlad the Impaler**. His wife and daughter were killed by Vlad. Destined for the stake as well, he was saved by Vlad's need to send his annual quota of Romanians to Turkey as slaves.

Night's Children differs from many of the vampire comics in that it is directed to a sophisticated adult audience. It freely deals with the interaction of sexuality and vampirism in mature situations (as opposed to those vampire comics that specialize in blood and gore).

By 1993, the response to Snow-Lang's work was strong enough to create *Not Exactly Human*, a newsletter for fans of *Night's Children*. Fans may write to Wendy Snow-Lang at PO Box 5010, Ste. 115, Salem, MA 01970. Tee-shirts with Snow-Lang's vampire art are also available.

Sources:

"Interview with Night's Children Creator/Writer Wendy Snow-Lang." *Screem in the Dark Newsletter* 1, 3 (December 1991): 11-16.

Night's Children: Not Exactly Human. Vol. 1- . Salem, MA: Wendy-Snow-Lang, 1993- .

Snow-Lang, Wendy. *Night's Children.* 4 vols. Albany, NY: FantaCo, 1991.

———. *Night's Children: Double Indemnity.* Albany, NY: FantaCo, 1992. 50 pp.

———. *Night's Children: Erotic Fantasies.* Albany, NY: FantaCo, 1993. 20 pp.
———. *Night's Children: Foreplay.* Albany, NY: FantaCo, 1991.
———. *Night's Children: Vampyr!* 4 vols. Albany, NY: FantaCo, 1992-1993.

SOUTH AMERICA, VAMPIRES IN

South America has not been an area rich in vampire lore, however, the fact that vampire **bat**s are native to the continent suggests that some recognition of vampirism would have appeared in the continent's folklore—and such is the case.

THE *ASEMA:* Among the South American vampires, for example, was the *asema* of Surinam. The *asema* was very much like the ***loogaroo*** of Haiti and the *sukuyan* of Trinidad—all three were derived from the vampire/witch of West **Africa**. The asema took the form of an old man or woman who lived a normal community life during the daylight hours, but a quite different secret existence after dark. At night, it had the ability to transform into a vampire. It did so by taking off its skin and becoming a ball of blue light. In that form, it is said that the *asema* flew through the air, entered houses in the village, and sucked the blood of its victims. If it liked the blood, it would continue taking it until the person died. Also, as with the *loogaroo,* **garlic** was the best protection against the *asema*. Herbs might be taken to turn the blood bitter so the *asema* would not like it, a practice noted in both Haiti and Africa. Further protection came from scattering rice or sesame **seeds** outside the door. The seeds would be mixed with the nails of a ground owl. The *asema* had to pick up the seeds before entering, but because of the nails it would continually drop them. If it remained at its task until dawn, the **sunlight** killed it.

Those who were suspected of being an *asema* were placed under surveyance. Their identity could be determined by watching them take off their skin. The skin was then treated with salt or pepper so that it shrank, and the vampire could not get back into it.

THE *LOBISHOMEN:* From Brazil, accounts of the ***lobishomen*** have survived, described as a small, stumpy, and hunch- backed monkey-like being. It had a yellow face, bloodless lips, black teeth, a bushy beard, and plush-covered feet. It attacked females and caused them to become nymphomaniacs. It would become vulnerable when drunk on blood, thus making it easier to catch. It could then be crucified on a tree. The *lobishomens* were not vampires, however, but the Portuguese form of **werewolves**. It was created through **witchcraft** or from parents who were improperly cohabiting (incest). Its werewolf-like nature appeared about the time of puberty when it left home and, for the first time, assumed the form of one of several**animals**. From that time on, usually on Tuesday and Thursdays, it assumed an animal form. In its human form, it could be identified by a yellowish tinge to its skin and blisters on its hands from running in the woods. The werewolf condition could only be stopped if the *lobishomen* was cut with steel. Care had to be taken not to touch the werewolf's blood, however, because it was fatal. The fact of its transformation into different animals tied the werewolf to the *bruxa,* the Portuguese witch, who was the more vampirelike entity in Portuguese mythology.

THE CINEMATIC VAMPIRE: The vampire made periodic appearances in the movies of South America, primarily in Argentina and Brazil. The first South American vampire movie was *El Vampiro Negro* (1953) directed by Roman Vinoly. It was based upon the true case of **Peter Kürten,** the vampire of Düsseldorf. It was almost two decades later before a second film, *El Vampiro Archecha*, a joint Argentine-Mexican picture, was produced. This movie was notable for its inclusion of German Robles in the cast.

Brazil produced its first vampire film in 1969/70. The movie was *Um Sonho de Vampiros* (In English: *A Vampire's Dream*), a comedy about a doctor who had to choose between death or vampirism. Others released through the decade include *O Macabro Dr Scivano* (1971), *Quem tem Medo de Lobishomem* (1974), and *A Deusa de Marmore—Escrava do Diabo* (1978). *Quem tem Medo de Lobishomem* has been commonly reported in vampire filmographies because of the misunderstanding that the *lobishomen* was a vampire rather than a werewolf. Since then only one Brazilian vampire movie has been noted: *As Sete Vampiros* (In English: *The Seven Vampires*, 1986).

Sources:

Brautigam, Rob. "Asema: The Vampires of Surinam." *International Vampire* I, I (1990): 16-17.
Gallop, Rodney. *Portugal: A Book of Folk-Ways.* Cambridge: Cambridge University Press, 1936. 291 pp.
Volta, Ornella. *The Vampire.* London: Tandem Books, 1965. 159 pp.

SOUTHERN SLAVS, VAMPIRES AMONG THE

The region consisting of what was formerly Yugoslavia and Albania, now comprises seven countries of diverse religious, ethnic, and linguistic backgrounds. Although very diverse in some respects, these seven nations share a common folk heritage that becomes quite evident upon examination of the reports of vampires and vampire beliefs in the area. Thus, it became fitting to treat vampires and vampirism in these lands as a whole phenomenon.

BACKGROUND: Albania traced its history to ancient Illyria, a Roman province which reached from present-day Albania north and east across Croatia to **Romania.** Beginning in the fourth century A.D., it was successfully invaded and occupied by Goths, Bulgars, Slavs, and Normans, successively. Albanians, much like Romanians, asserted their Roman ties. In the twelfth century Albania was conquered by the Ottoman Turks and remained in the empire until after World War I. As a legacy, the retreating Ottoman rulers left a population that had primarily been converted to Islam. Albania gained a measure of independence following World War I but was occupied by Italy during World War II. After the war, it became an independent nation. Under dictator Enver Hoxha, it was an independent Communist nation with a repressive government that was officially atheist and hostile to religion. Following Hoxha's death the country regained some degree of freedom.

Today, the majority of ethnic Albaniac live outside the boundaries of their homeland. There is a small but important Albanian community in the United States, and many live in Italy. The largest number of Albanians outside of Albania live in Serbia and constitute more than 90 percent of the autonomous region of Kosmet (Kosovo-Metohija).

Yugoslavia was created in 1918, following World War I, as a centralized state uniting the former independent countries of Serbia, Bosnia and Herzegovina, Croatia, and Montenegro. To these countries a part of Macedonia, previously a part of the Ottoman Empire, and Slovenia, a part of the Austrian (Hapsburg) Empire, were added to the new country. Slavic tribes had first moved into the Balkan peninsula in the sixth century and by the eighth century had established themselves as the dominant influence in the area. Some unity was brought by the expansive Bulgar Empire at the beginning of the tenth century, which controlled most of present-day Serbia, Macedonia and Bosnia-Herzegovina.

Christianity moved into the Balkans in strength through the ninth century. Following the division of the Christian movement in 1054 A.D., Serbia, Montenegro, and Macedonia became largely Eastern Orthodox while Croatia and Slovenia were Roman Catholic. Bosnia-Herzegovina was split between the two groups of Christians with a significant Moslem minority. The Bosnia Muslims derive largely from the surviving remnants of the Bogomils, who had persisted to the time of the Turkish conquest and chose Islam over both Orthodoxy or Catholicism.

In 1389 the Turks defeated the combined Slavic forces at the Battle of Kosovo, following which the Ottoman Empire established itself across the souther Balkans. Only Slovenia, controlled by the Germanic Kingdom (and after the thirteenth century the Austrian) remained free of Ottoman control. During the years of Muslim control, proselytization occurred most strongly in Bosnia and Croatia. At the end of the seventeenth century the Hapsburgs pushed further south across Croatia to the Sava River which flowed into the Danube at Belgrade. This territory was formally ceded to Austria in 1699. Through the next two centuries the line between the Ottoman and Hapsburg Empire continued to fluctuate. Serbians began to assert their political independence which was formally granted in 1878.

Following World War II, strongman Josef Broz Tito ruled Yugoslavia until his death in 1980. A decade of weakened central control led to the break-up of the country at the end of the decade. Six separate countries emerged in the early 1990s. (As this volume goes to press, the central region of the former Yugoslavia remains in a state of war and the exact configuration of the new national boundaries remains very much in doubt. The partition or division of Bosnia remains an attractive option to many.)

THE SOUTHERN SLAVIC VAMPIRE: The southern Slavic vampire was a variation of the **Slavic vampire**, and the beliefs and practices related to it were influenced by those of their neighbors in every direction. The lands of the former Yugoslavia have been cited as the most likely land of origin of the Slavic vampire. Jan L. Perkowski has suggested that the peculiar shape assumed by the vampire originated through a combination of Pagan and Bogomil beliefs (religious ideas dominant in the region at the end of the tenth century) that were pushed aside by the conquest of Christianity, though he has found little support for his hypothesis. In any case, through the centuries, Christian leaders attempted to destroy the belief of vampires, but were often forced to accommodate to them as they remained strong among the people. Islam proved quite accommodating to the belief in vampires.

Perkowski also traced the origin of the modern word vampire to an old Slavic form *obyrbi* or *obirbi.* Among the various Slavic groups and their neighbors, different forms of the word evolved. Dominant in the region in the modern era was *upirina,* a Serbo-Croatian word. The word *vampir,* with the addition of an "m" sound, was also present, and in Bosnia *lampir* was used. Also present was *vukodlak* (Croatian) or *vurvulak* (Albanian), words similar to the Greek designation of the vampire, *vrykolakas.* *Vukodlak* was often shortened to *kudlak.* In the late nineteenth century, in Istria near the Italian border, a *kudlak* was believed to be attached to each clan. It was considered an evil being that attacked people at night. It was opposed by another entity, the *krsnik,* which often interrupted a *kudlak*'s attack and fought it.

In addition to the more ubiquitous words, the term **tenatz** has been found in Montenegro. This was used interchangeably with *lampir,* the local variation on *vampir.* It was believed to be the body of a deceased person that had been taken over by evil spirits. The *tenatz* wandered the night and sucked the blood of the sleeping. They transformed themselves into mice to reenter their burial place. A primary means of detecting a vampire in Montenegro was to take a black horse to the cemetery. The horse would be repelled by the grave of the vampire and refuse to walk across it. Once detected, the body would be disinterred and if, upon further determination, the vampire hunters decided it was a vampire, the corpse would be impaled with a **stake** and burned.

In Croatia one also might find *kosac, prikosac, tenjac,* and *lupi manari* as terms for a vampire. Albanian names for a vampire included *kukuthi* or *lugat.* The *strigon* (Slovenian) and *shtriga* (Albanian, Macedonian) are blood-sucking witches related to the Romanian *strigoi.*

Another blood-sucking witch related to the *strigoi* was the *vjeshtitza* (also spelled *veshtitza*) During her field work in Montenegro early in this century, Edith Durham discovered that people no longer believed that *vjeshtitza* existed but retained a rich lore about them. *Vjeshtitza* were older women who were hostile to men, other women, and all children. Possessed by an evil spirit, the sleeping witch's soul wandered at night and inhabited either a moth or a fly. Using the flying animal, the witch entered into the homes of neighbors and sucked the blood of victims. The victim, over a period of time, grew pale, developed a fever, and died. The witches were especially powerful during the first week of March, and protective measures would be taken against them. The protective ceremony, performed the first day of

March each year, included the stirring the ashes in the family hearth with two horns, which were then stuck into the ash heap. **Garlic** was also a common protective substance.

The vampire was a revenant, a body that returned from the grave with some semblance of life. Some believed that it was a body inhabited by an evil spirit. A person was believed to become a vampire in several ways, but a sudden, unexpected, and/or violent accidental death, a wasting sickness, or **suicide** were seen as primary causes.M. Edith Durham, for example, recorded the story in Bosnia of an epidemic of vampirism associated with a typhus epidemic. Vampirism was also associated, in a day prior to professional undertakers, with the need to follow a prescribed process of preparation of the body of a deceased person and its subsequent burial. Irregularities in the process could cause a person to turn into a vampire. In particular, it had to be watched so that **animals**, especially cats, did not jump over the body prior to burial. In Macedonia, if a cat did jump over the body, the corpse would then be pierced with two needles. Vampirism was also assumed to be contagious—an attack by a vampire would lead to vampirism.

The *shtriga* and *vjeshtitza* were blood-sucking witches. Although not revenants, the witches were members of the community believed to be living incognito. The Albanian *shtriga* could be detected by placing a cross made with pig bones on the church door when it was crowded with people. The witch was unable to leave the church and would be seen running around the church trying to find a safe exit. The *shtrega* traveled at night and, often in the form of an animal, attacked people and sucked their blood. If a *shtriga* was sighted, it could be followed and positively identified because it had to stop and vomit up the blood it had sucked. The vomited blood could then be used to make an amulet to protect one from witchcraft and vampirism.

The *strigon* of Slovenia was also a bloodsucking witch. The term was derived from the Latin *striga* (witch), which in turn was derived from *strix*, originally a screech owl that was perceived as a demon that attacked infants in the night. The term was also used more generally to describe a vampire.

Slovenian historian Baron Jan Vajkart Valvasor (1641-1693) recounted the killing of a *strigon* in Istria (western Slovenia). A person who was the suspected vampire had recently died and was seen by several people walking around the town. His suspected vampirism was reported by his wife after he returned home and had sexual relations with her. The *strigon* was killed by a **hawthorn** stake driven into its stomach while a priest read an exorcism. The corpse was then decapitated. All the while, the corpse reacted as if it were alive—it recoiled as the **stake** was driven in, cried while the exorcism was pronounced, and screamed out as its head was severed. After the decapitation, it bled profusely.

Vampires attacked people it had strong emotional attachments to—both positive (family and friends) and negative (those with whom it had quarreled in life)—and sucked their blood. A sure sign of a vampire was an outbreak of various kinds of contagious illnesses. People who became sick and died from what were then unknown causes were often ascribed to vampiric activity. The vampire could also attack the village livestock in a similar manner.

The southern Slavic vampire was, like that among the **Gypsies**, capable of having sex with a spouse or lover. Durham related the story of a girl in Montenegro who was forced to marry the man chosen by her parents rather than her true love. Her beloved left the country and, in his despair, died. He returned from the grave as a vampire and visited the girl who eventually became pregnant by him. In appearance, the child closely resembled the deceased man. The villagers were frustrated because the man had died abroad, and thus they could not destroy him. Bodies of males uncovered in the search for a vampire would often have an erect sex organ.

The existence of a vampire could be detected by a variety of means. In Montenegro, for example, a black horse (in Albania, a white horse was used) would be led to a local cemetery—the horse would be repelled by a vampire's grave. The horse usually had to be ridden by a boy who had not yet experienced puberty or a virginal girl. In Croatia, there were reports of strange animal sounds coming from the grave of someone later determined to be a vampire. The body was then disinterred. The discovery of a body turned face down or bloated to the point that the skin was stretched like a drum indicated that the correct body had been uncovered. If only bones remained in the grave, it was not considered a vampire. The Serbians and Bosnians shared the belief with Gypsies in the *dhampir,* the son of a vampire. The offspring of a vampire was considered to have the power to both see and destroy his father and other vampires. In Macedonia, there was the belief in the power of people born on Saturday. Such Sabbatarians, as they were termed, were thought to have a great influence over vampires including the power to lure them into traps where they could be destroyed. On Saturdays, the Sabbatarians could see and kill vampires. For average people, protection from vampires was secured by barricading their homes with thorn bushes (an old remedy for witches).

Once discovered, the vampire could be rendered harmless or destroyed by the traditional means of fixing the body to the ground with a **stake** and/or **decapitation**. In the most severe cases, the body might be dismembered or burned. In general, a priest was asked to be present to repeat the funeral prayers over the person who was perceived to be dying a second time. (As part of an attempt to stop the mutilation of dead bodies, the church in Serbia and Montenegro threatened any priest who cooperated in such activity with excommunication.) In both Montenegro and Albania, it was believed that a vampire could be stopped by hamstringing the corpse. G.F. Abbott reported observing the destruction of a vampire by scalding it with boiling water and driving a long nail in its navel. The body was returned to the ground and the grave covered with millet **seeds** so if the vampire was not destroyed, it would waste its time counting the millet until dawn. In Croatia, it was believed that a stake driven into the ground over the grave prevented the vampire from rising. In Serbia, a white-thorn or **hawthorn** stake or other sharp objects might be stuck into the ground over a vampire, or a sickle placed over the neck of the corpse when it was reburied.

It was common among the southern Slavs (as among the Greeks) to dig up bodies some years after their burial, to cleanse the bones, and rebury them in a permanent location. It was important that the soft tissue be completely decomposed by that time—delays in decomposition were cause for concern and could lead to suggestions of vampirism.

THE VAMPIRE EPIDEMICS, 1727-1732: The beliefs and practices of the southern Slavs concerning vampires were brought to the attention of western Europe primarily through two spectacular cases that were publicized due to official inquiries into the cases by Austrian authorities. Both cases occurred in a region of Serbia north of Belgrade that had been taken over by Austria from the Ottoman Empire at the end of the seventeenth century and, subsequently, incorporated into the Hungarian province. One incident began with the sudden death of **Peter Plogojowitz**. He was seen by his family several nights after his death. Shortly thereafter, Plogojowitz appeared to several people in their dreams. In one week, nine people died of no known cause. When the local army commander arrived to investigate, Plogojowitz's body was taken from the grave. It was found to be as fresh as it had been when buried. The eyes were open and the complexion was ruddy. His mouth was smeared with fresh blood. Fresh skin appeared just below an old layer of dead skin he appeared to be shedding, and his hair and nails had grown. It was concluded that he was a vampire. Plogojowitz's body was staked and burned.

More famous than the Plogojowitz incident was the case of **Arnold Paul**. Paul lived in the village of Medvegia (spelled in numerous ways in different sources), Serbia, north of Paracin. He told his neighbors that while he had been serving in the army in Turkey, he had been bitten by a vampire. A week later he died. Several weeks after his death, people began to report seeing him, and four such people died. On the 40th day after his burial, the grave was opened and he was found in a lifelike condition. When his body was cut, he bled freely. When staked, it was later reported that he groaned aloud. He and the four people he reportedly vampirized were decapitated and their bodies burned.

The Arnold Paul case should have ended with his funeral pyre. However, in 1731, some 17 people in the village died of an unknown cause. Vampirism was suggested. Word of the unusual occurrences reached all the way to Vienna, and the emperor ordered an official inquiry. Following the arrival of Johannes Fluckinger in Medvegia, the body of a new suspected vampire was disinterred. He was also found to be in a healthy state. After some further investigation, it was discovered that Paul had vampirized several cows. Those who ate the meat from the cows were infected with a vampiric condition. The bodies of the recently dead were then disinterred and all were staked and burned.

Fluckinger returned to Vienna and presented the emperor with a complete report. During 1732, the report and several journalistic versions of it became bestsellers throughout Europe. The two cases became the basis of a heated debate in German universities, and after a decade of arguing, the participants concluded that vampires did not exist. However, the debate spurred the interest of **Dom Augustin Calmet**, a

French biblical scholar, who, in 1746, completed a most important treatise on the subject published in England as *The Phantom World*.

The fame of Plogojowitz and Paul should have focused attention on Serbia and the southern Slavic countries. Instead, from mere geographical ignorance, many involved in the debate placed the occurrences in Hungary, and thus Hungary—which has the least vampire mythology of all the Eastern European countries—became known for vampirism. As a result, scrutiny of vampire beliefs was directed away from Serbia and its southern Slavic neighbors. The misdirection given vampire phenomena by Calmet was reinforced by the writings of **Montague Summers** and number of writers on vampires who essentially copied him.

The vampire has had a long and interesting history in what is now the independent country of Slovenia. Largely Roman Catholic in background, the country existed for many centuries as an Austrian province; however, south of the Drava River, especially in rural areas, Slovenes resisted Germanization and retained their own language and folklore. One of the earliest books to deal with vampires was Count Valvasor's *Die Ehre des Herzogthums Krain* (1689), which told the story of Grando, a peasant of the district of Kranj. A quiet man in life, in death Grando began to attack his neighbors and his body was ordered exhumed. His body was found with ruddy complexion and he appeared to have a smile on his face. A priest called upon the vampire to look to his savior Jesus Crist, at which the body took on a sad expression and tears were flowing down his cheek. The body was then decapitated and reburied. A more general account of vampires in the region was given in the famous 1734 travelogue, *The Travels of Three English Gentlemen*.

MODERN VAMPIRES AMONG THE SOUTHERN SLAVS: Vampire beliefs have continued into the twentieth century, in spite of several generations of hostile governments that denounced both religion and superstitions. Folklorists have had no trouble locating vampire stories. The depth and persistence of the vampire belief was vividly illustrated in a most unexpected manner early in 1993, in the midst of the most violent era experienced directly by Serbia following the break-up of the former Yugoslavia. During that year, a man made a number of appearances on Serbia's state-controlled television station at the height of the country's conflict. He, in all seriousness, argued that at the moment when final destruction threatened the Serbian nation, a fleet of vampires would arise from the cemeteries to defeat Serbia's enemies. In preparation for this event, he advised viewers to keep a supply of garlic at hand lest the vampires attack them by mistake.

Sources:

Abbott, G. F. *Macedonian Folklore*. Chicago: Argonaut Inc., 1969. 372 pp.

Barber, Paul. *Vampires, Burial, and Death: Folklore and Reality*. New Haven, CT: Yale University Press, 1988. 236 pp.

D'Assier, Adolphe. *Posthumous Humanity: A Study of Phantoms*. San Diego, CA: Wizards Bookshelf, 1981. 360 pp.

Durham, M. Edith. "Of Magic, Witches and Vampires in the Balkans." *Man* 121 (December 1923): 189-92.

Kinzer, Stephen. "At Root of Mayhem: A Bizarre Dream World Called Serbia." *Star Tribune* (Minneapolis) (May 16, 1993): 11A.

Perkowski, Jan L. *The Darkling: A Treatise on Slavic Vampirism.* Columbus, OH: Slavica Publishers, 1989. 174 pp.

——, ed. *Vampires of the Slavs.* Cambridge, MA: Slavica Publishers, 1976. 294 pp.

Petrovitch, Woislav M. *Hero Tales and Legends of the Serbians.* London: George G. Harrap, 1914. 393 pp. Reprint. New York: Kraus Reprint Co., 1972. 393 pp.

SOUTHEY, ROBERT (1774-1843)

Robert Southey was a British poet and writer who was among the first to introduce the vampire theme into English literature. While attending Oxford University, he met **Samuel Taylor Coleridge**, who became a life-long friend, mentor, and supporter. Toward the end of the 1790's, Southey's health failed and he moved to Portugal to recuperate. While there he completed his first major work, a long poem titled *Thalaba the Destroyer. Thalaba* was to be the first of a series of epic poems drawing upon the mythologies of different cultures and portraying the fight of good over evil. It was in the midst of his story that he came face to face with the vampire.

Southey was inspired to write *Thalaba* by the *Arabian Tales*, which mentioned the Domdaniel, a training school for evil magicians. In the story, set in Arabia, the title character lived in exile with his mother. His father and kinspeople had been slain by the evil magicians. The magicians resided in a cavern where they kept his father's sword—which was to be the instrument of their destruction. Thalaba's life turned into a quest to find the cavern, retrieve the sword, and avenge his father.

In the midst of his quest (in Book VII of the poem), Thalaba sought shelter from the rain in the chamber of the tombs and there had a brief encounter with a vampire. The vampire was none other than his bride Oneiza, who had recently died, on their wedding day. Oneiza's body had been reanimated by an invading demonic force. Her cheeks were livid, her lips were blue, and her eyes possessed a terrible brightness. Thalaba grasped a lance and:

> . . . through the vampire corpse
> He thrust his lance; it fell,
> And howling with the wound,
> Its fiendish tenant fled.

Immediately afterward, Oneiza's spirit appeared and urged Thalaba to continue his great quest.

In evoking the vampire, Southey demonstrated his awareness of the vampire tales from continental Europe. He mentioned the outbreaks of vampirism on the continent early in the eighteenth century in his notes, especially the case of **Arnold Paul** in Serbia, and more recent cases in **Greece**. In relating the case of the vampire Oneiza, Southey assumed the Greek notion that a vampire was a corpse inhabited by an evil spirit. Equally important for Southey were the translations of the German poem "Lenore", which had been published in English by William Taylor in 1796, and adapted in a more popular form by Sir Walter Scott later that same year.

Even before finishing *Thalaba,* Southey wrote a ballad titled "The Old Woman of Berkeley." The title character was a witch who possessed the characteristics of a *lamiai,* the ancient Greek vampirelike creature who preyed upon infants. As she herself was made to say:

> From sleeping babes I have sucked the breath,
> And breaking by charms the sleep of death,
> I have call'd the dead from their graves.

Thus, Southey vied with Coleridge for the distinction of having introduced the vampire into English literature. Coleridge's poem, "Christabel," was published before *Thalaba,* and while most agree that it was a vampire poem, Coleridge never identified it as such. After Southey introduced the vampire to the English-speaking public, he did not linger over the vampire myth or further develop gothic themes. He did, however, go on to become one of England's finer writers, the author of numerous poems and prose works of history and biography. In general, his prose writing received better reviews than his poetry, although he was credited with expanding the number of metrical patterns available to poets who came after him.

Sources:

Haller, William. *The Early Life of Robert Southey, 1774-1803.* New York: Columbia University Press, 1917. 353 pp.

Southey, Robert. *The Poetical Works of Robert Southey.* Paris: A. and W. Galignani, 1829. 718 pp.

SPAIN, VAMPIRES IN

Spain, geographically separated from the Eastern European home of the Slavic vampire, has been largely devoid of vampire reports in its folklore tradition, although there has been a strong presence of **witchcraft**. Like the witch in ancient **Rome**, medieval Italy (*strega*), and **Portugal** (*bruxa*), the witch in medieval Spain was believed to have the power to transform into various animal forms, to steal infants, and to vampirize children. Vampirism of children, for example, figured prominently in a lengthy trial at Logrono in the fall of 1610. A century earlier, one of the leading Roman Catholic spokespersons on witchcraft, Fray Martin Castenega, cited vampirism as one of the evil actions in which witches engaged. Spain did not participate significantly in either the vampire debates of the eighteenth century or the development of the literary vampire of the nineteenth century. However, in the post-World War II world of the cinematic vampire, Spain has played a strong role.

THE CINEMATIC VAMPIRE: The vampire in Spanish films emerged at the end of the 1960s just as the Italian and Mexican vampire movies were at their peak. The first Spanish vampire film seem to have been *Parque de Juegos* (*Park of Games*), a 1963 production based on a Ray Bradbury story. It stood alone until 1968, when *La Marca* *del Hombe Lobo* (*The Mark of the Wolfman*) and *Malenka la Vampira* (a joint Spanish- Italian production released in English as *Fangs of the Living Dead*) appeared. *Fangs of the Living Dead* introduced director Amando de Ossoio who, through the 1970s, became one of the most prolific instigators of vampire films. He successively directed *La Noche del Terror Ciego* (*Tombs of the Blind Dead*, 1971), *El Ataque de los Muertos sin Ojos* (*Return of the Evil Dead*, 1973), *La Noche de los Brujos* (*Night of the Sorcerers*, 1973), *El Buque Maldito* (*Horror of the Zombies*, 1974), and *La Noche de las Saviotas* (*Night of the Seagulls*, 1975). He is most remembered for introducing the blind vampires in *La Noche del Terror Ciego,* which centered upon the Knights Templars, a religious order whose members were blinded and murdered in the thirteenth century. They returned in two of Ossorio's other films to attack people they located with their acute hearing.

In 1970, Leon Klimovsky, an experienced Spanish director, joined veteran werewolf star Paul Naschy to produce his first vampire movie, *La Noche de Walpurgis* (*The Werewolf vs. the Vampire Woman*). In this fifth in a series of werewolf movies for Naschy, his character, Count Waldemar Daninsky, attacked the vampire witch Countess Waldessa. Klimovsky then made *La Orgia Nocturna de los Vampiros* (*The Vampire's Night Orgy*, 1973), *La Saga de las Draculas* (*The Dracula Saga*, 1973), and *El Extrano Amor de los Vampiros* (*Strange Love of the Vampires*, 1974). Naschy first encountered a vampire in *Dracula vs. Frankenstein* (1969), one of the earlier Daninsky films. He would later slip out of his werewolf role to play **Dracula** in *Le Gran Amor del Conde Dracula* (*Dracula's Great Love*, 1972).

By far the most renown of Spain's vampire filmmakers was Jesus Franco, Spain's equivalent of Italy's Mario Bava. In his first vampire film, Franco cajoled **Hammer Films** star **Christopher Lee** to Spain to do a remake of *Dracula.* Lee was intrigued by the opportunity to play a more faithful Dracula than he had been allowed to perform in England. The result was the film *El Conde Dracula* (1970), which had a script (and a characterization of Dracula) that followed the book more closely than either the **Universal Pictures'** or Hammer productions. No one realized at the time, given the movie's slow and ponderous pace, that this would be Franco's best vampire movie.

That same year Franco also made *Vampyros Lesbos die erbin des Dracula*, his version of the **Elizabeth Bathory** story, which was more typical of the adult erotic vampire movies Franco was famous for making. The German version, released in 1971, included heightened levels of sex and violence, both of which were toned down for the Spanish version. He followed in 1972 with *La Fille de Dracula* (*Dracula's Daughter*), another adult erotic movie that began with the death of Dracula and followed the adventures of his female offspring. Also that year, he filmed *Dracula contra Frankenstein*, which continued his vampire series while launching a three-film Frankenstein series. In the initial film, Dr. Frankenstein revived Dracula to create a vampire horde as part of a plan to take over the world.

In 1973, Franco moved on to make his version of the **"Carmilla"** story, *La Comtesse aux Seins Nus*, an x-rated story of Countess Irina Karnstein, a voiceless descendent of Carmilla who attacked men and killed them through fellatio. The heightened element of **sexuality** was the only thing of value in this film, and much of the sexual content was deleted in various ways for the different markets. Only the nudity remained in the American video version, finally released as *Erotikill*. Following these six movies, Franco seemed to have exhausted the vampire theme. He turned to other topics and continued to release a large number of movies annually. However, these six films—the one notable effort with Lee and the five erotic films—were enough to establish him in the vampire cinema hall of fame and provide Spanish vampire films with a distinctive image.

After an intense period of releasing vampire movies, Spanish filmmakers suddenly dropped the theme midway through the decade. Only one film, *Tiempos duros para Dracula* (1976) was made during the last half of the decade. Naschy, who had continued his werewolf series, revived the vampire twice in the 1980s. *El Returno del Hombre Lobo* (released in English as *The Craving*), the ninth wolfman movie, pitted Daninsky against Elizabeth Bathory and her cohorts. Then, in 1982, Naschy made a children's movie, *Buenas Noches, Senor Monstruo*, which included Dracula and other famous monsters. In more recent years, Spain has left the making of vampire movies to Hollywood.

Sources:

Baroja, Julio Caro. *The World of the Witches.* Chicago: University of Chicago Press, 1965. 313 pp.

Henningsen, Gustav. *The Witches' Advocate: Basque Witchcraft and the Spanish Inquisition (1910-1614).* Reno, NV: University of Nevada Press, 1980. 607 pp.

Jones, Stephen. *The Illustrated Vampire Movie Guide.* London: Titan Books, 1993. 144 pp.

Pattison, Barrie. *The Seal of Dracula.* New York: Bounty Books, 1975. 136 pp.

SPIDER

Beginning in 1931 the Spider, created by author Grant Stockbridge (pen name of Norvell Page), emerged as one of the most popular heroes of pulp magazine fiction. Two years later, his popular adventures supported the formation of a monthly magazine, *The Spider,* with episodes that would be gathered at a later date and reissued in books. The Spider dedicated itself to the task of killing criminals and worked as a vigilante outside of the law and public approval. In 1935, on the heels of the popularity of **Bela Lugosi**'s *Dracula* (**1931**), the Spider encountered one of its most horrendous foes, the Vampire King, and began the process of destroying this evil royalty.

The Spider was the secret identity of wealthy businessman Richard Wentworth. After donning a free-flowing uniform complete with hood and cape, a bullet-proof vest, false teeth, and mask Wentworth turned into a crime fighter on the streets of New York City. The Spider's major assets were agility, intelligence, and determination. It was strong and acquitted itself quite well in hand-to-hand fighting. Its major weapon, above and beyond normal weapons like handguns, was a gun that squirted a gooey liquid that formed a web entrapping its target. Unlike modern superheroes, the Spider had no supernormal powers. It did have a sidekick, Ram Singh from India, who served as his ultimate back-up system.

The Vampire King, the 1930s equivalent of the super villain, was a monster from **South America**. Modelled not on the European vampire, but on the *camazotz*, the Mayan bat god/demon who made its most memorable appearance in the ancient text, *Popol Vuh*. It appeared as a large bat-man with exaggerated and somewhat grotesque features, including huge ears, wings, and claw-like hands with slender, elongated fingers. It did not possess supernatural powers and could not, for example, change his outward form. It was adapt at **flying** and had great physical **strength**. The Vampire King's greatest asset, however, was the control over a large flock of vampire **bat**s, which he could command to attack. Two South American natives accompanied him and used poisonous darts. Two huge half man/half animal monsters also accompanied him—a pig-man and an armadillo-man.

The final confrontation between the Spider and the Vampire King occurred after the Spider's capture. While the Vampire King conversed with the crime bosses with whom it was negotiating with for control of its North American enterprises, it drank the Spider's blood, which had been drained into a chalice. The Vampire King offered the criminals a sip as a means of sealing their evil pact. The Spider recovered just in time and his comrades appeared to assist it. The fight that ensued led to the Vampire King's destruction.

The Spider was brought to the screen in several Saturday matinee serials of the 1930s, but the Vampire King was not among its movie foes. Although a major source for contemporary super heroes, and seemingly a direct inspiration for Spiderman, the Spider was all but forgotten except with a few movie buffs, when, in 1991, he was revived by Eclipse Books in a new comic book series.

Sources:

Harmon, Jim, and Donald F. Glut. *The Great Movie Serials: Their Sound and Fury*. Garden City, NY: Doubleday & Company, 1972. 384 pp.

The Spider: Reign of the Vampire King. 1-3. Forestville, CA: Eclipse Books, 1991-92.

Stockbridge, Grant. *Death Reign of the Vampire King: a Spider Novel*. London: Mews Books, 1935, 1976. 128 pp. Reprint. New York: Carroll & Graf, 1992. 319 pp.

STAKE

The most well-known way to kill a vampire was by staking it in the heart. This method was prescribed by **Sheridan Le Fanu** in his novella, **"Carmilla,"** and was a remedy later lauded by **Bram Stoker** for his novel, *Dracula,* and repeated in numerous vampire movies.

The idea of staking the corpse of a suspected vampire or revenant was quite an ancient practice. It was found across Europe and originated in an era prior to the widespread use of **coffin**s. The corpses of persons suspected of returning from their graves would be staked as a means of keeping them attached to the ground below their body. Stakes might be driven through the stomach (far easier to penetrate than the heart area, which required penetration of the rib cage). The body might also be turned face down and the stake driven through the back. In some areas, an iron stake or long needle might be used, while in others not only was wood used but the actual wood to be used prescribed. Ash, aspen (a common wood across northern Europe), juniper, and/or **hawthorn** were noted in the literature. Additionally, a stake might be driven into the ground over the grave as a way to block the vampire's rising.

Once coffins were in popular use, the purpose of staking changed somewhat. Where previously the object of the staking was to fix the body to the ground, the purpose of the staking became a frontal assault upon the corpse itself. By attacking the heart, the organ that pumped the blood, the bloodsucking vampire could be killed. Staking the heart was somewhat analogous to the practice of driving nails into a vampire's head.

In many Russian stories, it was noted that the stake had to be driven in with a single stroke—a second stroke would reanimate the vampire. This method seems to be derived from a belief in old Slavic tales that advised elimination of enemies, of whatever sort, with one blow.

In Bram Stoker's *Dracula,* **Lucy Westenra** was finally laid to rest by the dual process of thrusting a stake in her heart and **decapitation**. A similar process was used for the three **vampire brides** who resided in **Castle Dracula**. However, Dracula himself was killed by decapitation and a knife plunged into his chest. The idea of staking the vampire became fixed in the modern vampire myth in the play by **Hamilton Deane**, which deviated from the novel by having the men who tracked Dracula to **Carfax** destroy the vampire by staking him. That action was repeated in the **Universal Pictures** version of *Dracula* (1931) starring **Bela Lugosi**.

The prominence of the stake led to much speculation in various novels and movies concerning the rationale for the use of wooden stakes. For most, the stake simply did brute physical damage to the heart. Others believed that the vampire was directly affected by wood. For some, the stake finally killed the vampire, while others saw it as a mere temporary measure. Thus, the removal of the stake became a means of reviving the vampire for a literary or movie sequel. **Robert Lory** made one of the more novel uses of the stake. In his novels, his hero Dr. Damien Hough placed a small wooden sliver into Dracula's body before reviving him. Thus, if Dracula failed to obey Hough or attacked him, the sliver would be thrust into Dracula's heart returning him to his deathlike state. One of the more (unintentionally) comic moments in vampire movies occurred in *Dracula Has Risen from His Grave* (1968) when **Christopher Lee** pulled a stake from his own heart.

Sources:

Barber, Paul. *Vampires, Burial, and Death: Folklore and Reality.* New Haven, CT: Yale University Press, 1988. 236 pp.

STEELE, BARBARA (1938-)

Barbara Steele, horror movie star of the 1960s and 1970s, was born in Liverpool, England. After acting in several movies, *Sapphire* (1958) and *Bachelor of Hearts* (1958), she moved to Hollywood to work for 20th Century Fox. In the early 1960s, with Hollywood writers on strike, she traveled to Italy where she found work staring in director **Mario Bava**'s first movie, *La Maschera de Demonio* (released in English as *Black Sunday*), based on Nicol Gogol's short story "The Vig". This single movie, which happened to be a vampire feature, made her a horror star. In what became her most famous role, the seventeenth- century vampiric witch Princess Ada and her double Princess Katia. The story began with the whipping and execution of Steele and her consort. Princess Ada, as played by Steele, defiantly showed her anger until a mask lined with spikes was driven into her face. The scene then abruptly changed to the nineteenth century. Two travelers were stranded in front of a castle ruin where their carriage broke down. They explored the castle and discovered the crypt that housed Princess Ada's body. One of the travelers removed the mask and a cross that had been placed in the body. When an accidental cut allowed the traveler's blood to drop on the corpse, Princess Ada and her lover were revived. Meanwhile, the other traveler met Princess Katia, the witch's great granddaughter. The situation was thus created for the renewed confrontation between good and evil, represented by Steele's two characters, which provided the main plot of the film. Within the larger context, however, Steele brought the plot to life by her embodiment of a number of ambiguities: beauty hiding decay and sensuality in the midst of horror.

In 1961, Steele briefly returned to Hollywood to play Vincent Price's wife in **Roger Corman**'s *The Pit and the Pendulum*. She played an unfaithful wife trying to drive her husband mad. Although she received good reviews in the United States, Steele returned to Europe to appear in a string of horror movies during the next few years, including *The Horrible Dr. Hitchcock* (1962), *The Ghost* (1962), and *I Lunghi Capelli della Morte* (1964). Along the way, she also appeared in a number of non-horror movies, the most prominent were Federico's Fellini's *8 1/2* (1962) and *Young Torless* (1966) with German director Volker Schlondorff. Her work in these films, however, was overshadowed by her horror roles and the adulation showered upon her by horror fans.

Of her horror roles during the 1960s, five were in vampire movies: *Castle of Blood* (1964), *Terror Creatures from the Grave* (1965), *Nightmare Castle* (1965), *An Angel for Satan* (1966), and *Revenge of the Blood Beast* (1966). *Castle of Blood,* based on a story by **Edgar Allan Poe**, took place in a castle inhabited by spirits of the

BARBARA STEELE AS THE VAMPIRE PRINCESS IN *BLACK SUNDAY*.

dead, one of whom was Steele. These spirits appeared every November 2 to re-experience their deaths and to obtain the blood of the living, a prerequisite if they hoped to return the following year. In *Nightmare Castle,* Steele played a murdered wife who returned to avenge herself against her former husband. The vampiric theme was evident also in *The Horrible Dr. Hitchcock* (1962). The movie's title character attempted to drain Steele's blood to allow another woman to stay young.

After completing *Revenge of the Blood Beast,* Steele married James Poe and began a period of relative inactivity, although in 1968 she took a part in *The Crimson Cult.* She had hoped to get the lead in *They Shoot Horses, Don't They?* for which her husband wrote the screenplay, but the part was given to Susannah York. During the 1980s, Steele became acquainted with producer **Dan Curtis** and assumed roles in his popular television mini-series, *The Winds of War* (1983) and *War and Remembrance* (1988-89). She served as the associate producer of the former and a producer of the latter. Steele's work led to her most recent role in a vampire production. In 1990, Curtis sold the idea of bringing the very successful daytime soap opera of the 1960s, **Dark Shadows,** back to television as a 1991 prime time series. **Ben Cross** was chosen to play vampire **Barnabas Collins**, and Steele was given the role of Dr. Julia Hoffman, the physician who tried to cure him of his vampiric condition. In the process, Dr. Hoffman fell in love with Collins. The show featured a 1790s storyline in which Steele portrayed another character, Natalie DuPrés. Unfortunately, the new *Dark Shadows* series was canceled after only twelve episodes.

Steele has expressed some ambiguous feelings about her horror career. She would prefer to be remembered for all of her acting roles, but has acknowledged the fame that her image as a ''scream queen'' brought to her.

Sources:

Deitrich, Christopher, and Peter Beckman. "Barbara Steele." *Imagi-Movies* Part I: 1, 2 (Winter 1993/94): 34-43; Part 2: 1, 3 (Spring 1994).
Miller, Mark A. "Barbara Steele." *Filmfax* 19 (March 1990): 63-71, 94.

STOKER, ABRAHAM "BRAM" (1847-1912)

Bram Stoker was the author of **Dracula,** the key work in the development of the modern literary myth of the vampire. He was born in Dublin, Ireland and at the age of 16, he entered Trinity College at Dublin University. Stoker joined the Philosophical Society where he authored his first essay, ''Sensationalism in Fiction and Society.'' He later became president of the Philosophical Society and auditor of the Historical Society. He graduated with honors in science (B.A., 1870) and, as his father before him, went to work as a civil servant at Dublin Castle. He continued as a part-time student at Dublin and eventually earned his M.A. (1875).

Stoker's favorable impression of British actor Henry Irving, who appeared locally with a traveling drama company, led him to offer his services to the *Dublin Evening Mail* as a drama critic, without pay. As his reviews began to appear in various papers, he was welcomed into Dublin social circles and soon met the Wildes, the parents of Oscar Wilde. In 1873, he was offered the editorship of a new newspaper, the *Irish Echo* (later renamed *Halfpenny Press*), part-time and without pay. The paper did not succeed, and, early in 1874, he resigned. From that point on, Stoker found his major entertainment in the theatre. He also began to write his first pieces of fiction, short stories, and serials, which were published in the local newspapers. His first bit of horror writing, "The Chain of Destiny," appeared as a serial in the *Shamrock* in 1875.

In 1878, Henry Irving took over the management of the Lyceum and invited Stoker to London as the theatre manager, and the Irving-Stoker partnership was to last until Irving's death in 1905. During these first years in London, Stoker found the time to author his first book of fiction, a collection of children's stories, *Under the Sunset,* published in 1882. Toward the end of the 1880s, amid his duties at the Lyceum, he increased his writing efforts. The result was his first novel, appeared first as a serial in *The People* in 1889 and was published in book form the following year. The story of *The Snake's Pass* centered on the legendary Shleenanaher, an opening to the sea in the mountain of Knockcalltecrore in western Ireland.

In 1890, Stoker began work on what was to become the watershed piece in the development of the literary vampire. Meanwhile, he wrote several short stories and two short novels. The novels, *The Watter's Mou* and *The Shoulder of Shasta,* are largely forgotten today. However, his short stories, especially "The Squaw," have survived and are still read by horror enthusiasts.

Stoker's decision to write *Dracula* seems to have been occasioned by a nightmare, in which he experienced a vampire rising from a tomb. He had read **Sheridan Le Fanu**'s *"Carmilla",* first published in 1872, several years before and had rounded out his knowledge with numerous discussions on the supernatural. To these he added his own research and modeled his main character on a fifteenth-century Transylvanian nobleman. He also decided, probably suggested by Wilkie Collins' *The Moonstone,* to tell the story through the eyes of several different characters. In the end, the story was told through a variety of documents, from diaries to letters to newspaper clippings.

Published in 1897, there was little to suggest that Stoker considered *Dracula* more than a good horror story. He received mixed reviews. Some loved it as a powerful piece of gloomy fascination. Others denounced it for its excessive strangeness and complained of its crudity. Very few recognized its importance and compared it to *Frankenstein.* None realized that Stoker had risen to a literary height to which he would never return—but then very few authors even approached the peak Stoker had attained.

About the time of the publication of *Dracula,* Stoker led a four-hour reading of its text. This odd event was presented, complete with announcements of the **drama** version, *Dracula, or The Un-dead*, to be presented at the Lyceum, to protect the plot and dialogue from literary theft. He had members of the Lyceum company join him in the performance, which was the only dramatic presentation of *Dracula* during his lifetime.

The year after *Dracula* was published, Stoker's career took a downward turn. A fire swept through the Lyceum destroying most of its costumes, props, and equipment. Irving's health, already failing, began to worsen. The theatre was turned over to

BRAM STOKER.

a syndicate and, in 1902, closed for good. Irving died in 1905. Stoker turned to writing and produced a series of novels: *Miss Betty* (1898), *The Mystery of the Sea* (1902), *The*

Jewel of the Seven Stars (1903), *The Man* (1905), and *The Lady of the Shroud* (1909). Of these, *The Lady of the Shroud* was possibly the most successful. It reached a twentieth printing by 1934. *The Jewel of the Seven Stars* would later became the inspiration for two motion pictures: *Blood of the Mummy's Tomb* (1971) and *The Awakening* (1980). Of his later writings, Stoker put his most strenuous efforts into his two- volume tribute to his late boss, *The Personal Reminiscences of Henry Irving* (1906). His last books were the nonfiction *Famous Impostors* (1910), which included some interesting sketches of inherently interesting people, and *The Lair of the White Worm* (1911). *The Lair of the White Worm* has enjoyed some success over the years, and was reprinted in popular, inexpensive paperback editions in 1925, 1945, 1961, and most recently in 1989, in conjunction with the British motion picture adaptation directed by Ken Russell in 1992.

Only with great difficulty did Stoker write his last books. In 1905, his health took a decidedly downward turn. That year he had a stroke and soon developed Bright's disease, which affects the kidneys. His condition steadily deteriorated until his death at his home on April 12, 1912. Possibly the most important of his post-*Dracula* literary products, a collection of short stories titled *Dracula's Guest, and Other Weird Stories* (1914), was published by his widow shortly after his death. The story "Dracula's Guest" was actually a chapter deleted from *Dracula* by the publishers, who felt that the original manuscript was too long.

Stoker was not a wealthy man when he died, and his wife Florence was often hard pressed for money. She inherited Stoker's copyrights and had the periodic income from book sales. Then in 1921, Freidrich Wilhelm Murnau decided to make a film version of *Dracula*. He adapted it freely by, among other things, changing its setting to **Germany** and altering the names of several characters. For example, Dracula became **Graf Orlock**. Although he gave Stoker and the book due credit, Murnau neglected to obtain copyright permission. Florence Stoker sued and finally won. The German court ordered all copies of the film destroyed (although, fortunately, one copy survived). In the meantime, playwright **Hamilton Deane** obtained permission to adapt the novel to the stage. The play opened in June, 1924 in Derby and, after many performances around England and Scotland, finally opened in London in 1927. Through Deane, Florence Stoker lived to see the success of *Dracula* first on stage then in the 1931 filming of a revised version of Deane's play starring **Bela Lugosi**. After her death in 1937, *Dracula* went on to become the single literary piece most frequently adapted for the motion picture screen, and its lead character the single literary figure most portrayed on the screen, other than **Sherlock Holmes**. The most recent film adaptation, ***Bram Stoker's Dracula,*** directed by **Francis Ford Coppola**, appeared in 1992. In 1987, the Horror Writers of America instituted a set of annual awards for writings in their field, which they named after Bram Stoker.

Sources:

Bleiler, E. F., ed. *Supernatural Fiction Writers: Fantasy and Horror.* New York: Charles Scribner's Sons, 1985. 1,169 pp.

Dalby, Richard. *Bram Stoker: A Bibliography of First Editions.* London: Dracula Press, 1983. 81 pp.

Farson, Daniel. *The Man Who Wrote Dracula: A Biography of Bram Stoker.* New York: St. Martin, 1976. 240 pp.

Ludlam, Harry. *A Biography of Dracula: The Life Story of Bram Stoker.* London: Fireside Press/W. Foulsham & Co., 1962. 200 pp.

Roth, Phyllis. *Bram Stoker.* Boston: Twayne, 1982. 167 pp.

Stoker, Bram. *Dracula.* London: Constable, 1897. 390 pp. Reprint. New York: Doubleday and McClure, 1899. 378 pp.

———. *Dracula's Guest and Other Weird Stories.* London: George Routledge & Sons, 1914. 200 pp. Rept. as: *Dracula's Guest.* New York: Zebra Books, 1978. 193 pp.

———. *The Jewel of the Seven Stars.* London: Heineman, 1903. 337 pp. Reprint. New York: Amereon House, 1990. 307 pp.

———. *The Lair of the White Worm.* London: William Rider and Sons, 1911. 328 pp.

———. *Under the Sunset.* London: Sampson Low, Marston, Searle, and Rivington, 1882. 190 pp.

STREGA *See:* ITALY, VAMPIRES IN

STRENGTH, PHYSICAL

Among the more notable attributes of the vampire is its superhuman strength. **Lord Ruthven**, in **John Polidori**'s **"The Vampyre"** was described as one "whose strength seemed superhuman." **Sheridan Le Fanu** noted, "One sign of the vampire is the power of the hand. The slender hand of Mircalla (i.e., **Carmilla**) closed like a vice of steel on the General's wrist when he raised his hatchet to strike. But its power is not confined to its grasp: It leaves a numbness in the limb it seizes, which is, slowly, if ever, recovered from."

In **Bram Stoker**'s novel, among **Jonathan Harker**'s early observations was the great strength in the hand of the driver (later known to be **Dracula**) who took him to **Castle Dracula**. His strength was most clearly pictured by the man's ability to pick up one of the women who resided in the castle and toss her aside with ease. Later, in his speech on the nature of the vampire to the men who were to join him in tracking and killing Dracula, **Abraham Van Helsing** described the vampire as having the strength of 20 men. (Chapter 18) He also noted that **garlic**, such sacred objects as the **crucifix**, and **sunlight** take away the vampire's strength. The strength also often wanes when the vampire has not fed for a long period.

The vampires of folklore had no particular strength, however, people feared their unknown and supernatural realm. The folklore accounts portray a vampire who frequently fled when confronted and who was unable to resist a group set on its destruction. It generally attacked one victim at a time, usually a weaker relative (wife, child, or infant).

However, an emphasis upon the vampire's strength has proved a most useful attribute in modern novels and the cinema. The vampire shared this characteristic with other monsters. As vampires moved into society and encountered humans, its strength contributed to a certain arrogance, because vampires knew that no mere mortal could overcome them in a fair fight. Thus, vampire hunters, also mere mortals, had to use not only all of their reason and cleverness, but the additional power of supernatural good (holy objects), and often had to work in concert with a group. Vampire hunters frequently had to seek out the vampire's resting place in the day when, in its **vampire sleep**, it was temporarily void of strength.

Many modern vampires have been stripped of their supernatural attributes, such as the power to transform into such different forms as **mist** or **animals**, but have retained their superhuman strength. This strength, along with a lengthened life span, was among the few benefits of the vampiric state granted to the undead.

STRIGE See: GREECE, VAMPIRES IN

STRIGOI/STRIGOAICA See: ROMANIA, VAMPIRES IN

STRIGON See: SOUTHERN SLAVS, VAMPIRES AMONG THE

SUICIDE

Suicide was one of the acts universally associated with vampirism. In cultures as varied as in **Russia, Romania**, West **Africa**, and **China**, suicide was considered an individual's pathway into vampirism. In the West in Jewish, Christian, and Muslim cultures, suicide has traditionally been considered a sin. In most other cultures suicide was frowned upon in an equivalent manner. **Japan** has generally been considered unique in its designation of a form of suicide called *hari-kari,* as a means of reversing the dishonor that initially led to the suicide.

Suicide was among the anti-social actions a person could commit that caused vampirism. In Eastern Europe, those actions included being a quarrelsome person, a drunkard, or associated with heresy or sorcery/witchcraft. In each society, there were activities considered a threat to the community's well-being that branded a person as different. While these varied considerably from culture to culture, suicide was most ubiquitous in its condemnation.

Suicide signaled the existence of extreme unresolved tension in the social fabric of a community. It was viewed as evidence of the family's and the community's inability to socialize an individual, as well as a statement by the individual of complete disregard for the community's existence and its prescribed rituals. The community, in turn, showed its disapproval in its treatment of the suicide's corpse. In the West, it was often denied Christian burial and its soul considered outside of the realm of salvation (the subject had committed mortal sin without benefit of confession and forgiveness prior to death). Those who committed suicide were buried at a crossroads or at a distance from the village. The corpse might even be thrown in a river to be carried away by the current.

Those who committed suicide died leaving unfinished business with relatives and close acquaintances. They left people with unresolved grief, which became a factor, sometimes unspoken, in the survivors' personalities for the rest of their lives. Their corpses often returned to the living in dreams and as apparitions. They were the subjects of nightmares, and families and friends occasionally felt under attack from the presence of them. The deceased became a vampire, and actions had to be taken to break the connection that allowed the dead to disturb the living. The various actions taken against a corpse could be viewed as a means of emotional release for the survivors. The break in the connection was first attempted with harmless actions of protection, but, if ineffective, those efforts moved to a more serious level with mutilation (with a **stake**) or complete destruction (by **fire**) of the corpse.

Sources:

Barber, Paul. *Vampires, Burial, and Death: Folklore and Reality.* New Haven, CT: Yale University Press, 1988. 236 pp.

Perkowski, Jan L. *The Darkling: A Treatise on Slavic Vampirism.* Columbus, OH: Slavica Publishers, 1989. 174 pp.

Senn, Harry A. *Were-Wolf and Vampire in Romania.* New York: Columbia University Pres, 1982. 148 pp.

SUKUYAN

The *sukuyan* was the vampire entity found on the Caribbean island of Trinidad. It resembled the **loogaroo** of Haiti, and in Trinidad the terms *sukuyan* and *loogaroo* (also pronounced *nigawu* or *legawu*) were often used interchangeably. It was also similar to the *asema* of Surinam and probably originated from the *aziman,* the vampire of the Fo people of Dahomey in West **Africa**. Melville Herskovits recorded a tale of a man in Trinidad who was informed that his late wife was a vampire. The deceased had not only taken the husband's blood but was visiting the homes of his neighbors. She was discovered drugging his tea each night. One night he only pretended to drink his tea and:

> . . . he went to bed, feigning to sleep. Then he heard her call
>
> 'Kin, 'kin, you no know me?
> 'Kin, 'kin, you no hear what your mistress say?
> 'Kin, 'kin, come off, come off!
>
> She took off her skin and put it behind the large water barrel. Twice she leaped and then went through the roof. As the man watched this, he said to himself, "My wife, that what she do?" The sky seemed afire, and the room was very light. He salted the inside of the skin thoroughly, then put it in place behind the water barrel where she had left it. When she returned before break of day, she tried to get back in her skin but could not because the salt burned her.
>
> 'Kin, go on.
> 'Kin, you no know me?

'Kin, you no hear what you mistress say?

This was repeated three times, and each line was spoken three times. "Skin squinch, he draw, can't go on, he burning he." So the woman put away the skin, wrapped herself up in a blanket, and lay down under the bed.

The husband reported her to the authorities, and she was seized and identified as a *sukuyan*. She was tried, condemned to death, and executed by being covered in tar and set afire.

The vampire was seen as a member of the community who lived during the day as an ordinary person but left its skin at night and, as a ball of light, travelled about looking for blood. People could be protected from an attack by a number of means. They could mark their doors and windows with crosses. A pair of scissors and a **mirror** fixed above the door inside of the house also offered protection. A broom placed upside down behind the door rendered a *sukuyan* powerless to do its work. If caught, the *sukuyan* usually underwent a **transformation** into one of several **animals**, and without its skin, would thus be unable to resume its human form.

Sources:

Herskovits, Melville J., and Frances S. Herskovits. *Trinidad Village*. New York: Alfred A. Knopf, 1947. 351 pp. Reprint. New York: Castle Books, 1964. 351 pp.

SUMMERS, MONTAGUE (1880-1948)

Alphonsus Joseph-Mary Augustus Montague Summers was the author of a number of important books on the supernatural including several classic studies on vampires. Very early in his life, he began reading widely in some of the more obscure writings by English fiction writers, including the **gothic** genre. In 1899, Summers entered Trinity College and pursued a course toward the Anglican ministry. He went on to Lichfield Theological College where he received his B.A. (1905) and M.A. (1906). He was ordained as a deacon in 1908 and assigned to a parish in a Bristol suburb. While there, he was charged and tried for pederasty but was found not guilty. In the wake of the trial, however, he left the Church of England and became a Roman Catholic. At some point—whether before or after he left the Church of England was not altogether clear—he was ordained to the priesthood. He was briefly assigned to a parish in London, but in 1911, moved from the parish into teaching school.

During his teaching years, Summers gathered an outstanding collection of books in various languages (many of which he learned) on occultism and the supernatural, from magic and **witchcraft** to vampires and **werewolves**. He also became an enthusiastic fan of Restoration drama and was one of the founders of The Phoenix, a society established to revive Restoration plays, many of a somewhat risque nature. After 15 years as an instructor in various schools, Summers moved to Oxford and began the period of scholarly writings that was to make him a memorable author of works on the occult and related fields. His first important work, *The History of Witchcraft and Demonology,* appeared the year he retired from teaching. Largely because of his choice of topics, his books sold well and Summers was able to make a living from his writings.

The first years of his Oxford period focused on his study of vampirism. In 1928, Summers finished his broad survey, *The Vampire: His Kith and Kin*, in which he traced the presence of vampires and vampirelike creatures in the folklore around the world, from ancient times to the present. He also surveyed the rise of the literary and dramatic vampire. Summers's broad mastery of the mythological, folkloric, anthropological, and historical material on the vampire (a mastery rarely equaled) has been obscured by his own Catholic supernaturalism. On several occasions he expressed his opinion of the evil reality of the vampire, an opinion very much out of step with his secular colleagues.

The following year Summers published his equally valuable *The Vampire in Europe*, which focused on various vampire accounts in Europe (especially Eastern Europe) where the legend found its most complete development. Summers combined his reading of the diverse literature with personal observations formulated from visits to some of the more important centers where vampire belief had survived. Summers completed two volumes of a country by country report on vampire lore. While they superseded a number of particular areas, the volumes remain standard sources for vampire studies.

During the 1930s, Summers continued his prodigious output and successively published: *The Werewolf* (1933), a companion volume to his vampire studies; *The Restoration Theatre* (1934); *A Popular History of Witchcraft* (1937); and *The Gothic Quest: a History of the Gothic Novel* (1938), an enthusiastic history of gothic fiction. In the 1940s, he added *Witchcraft and Black Magic* (1946). His last book, *The Physical Phenomena of Mysticism,* was published posthumously in 1950.

During the last 20 years of his life, Summers also edited numerous volumes. He released new editions of some of the most important texts on witchcraft and several anthologies of ghost stories. Toward the end of his life, he produced an autobiographical volume, *The Galantry Show,* which was eventually published in 1980. Beginning in 1956, many of Summers' works, including the two vampire books, were reprinted in American editions.

Summers remains an enigma. A defender of a traditional supernatural Catholic faith, he was the target of numerous rumors concerning homosexuality and his seeming fascination with those very subjects which he, on the one hand condemned, and on the other, spent so much time mastering.

Sources:

Frank, Frederick S. *Montague Summers: A Bibliographical Portrait.* Metuchen, NJ: Scarecrow Press, 1988. 277 pp.

Jerome, Joseph. *Montague Summers: A Memoir.* London: Cecil and Amelia Woolf, 1965. 105 pp.

Morrow, Felix. "The Quest for Montague Summers." In Montague Summers, *The Vampire: His Kith and Kin.* New Hyde Park, NY: University Books, 1960, pp. xiii-xx.

Smith, Timothy d'Arch. *A Bibliography of the Works of Montague Summers.* New Hyde Park, NY: University Books, 1964. 164 pp.

Summers, Montague. *The Galantry Show.* London: Cecil Woolf, 1980. 259 pp.

◄

VAMPIRE HISTORIAN
MONTAGUE SUMMERS.

————. *The Gothic Quest: a History of the Gothic Novel.* 1938. Reprint. London: Fortune Press, 1950. 443 pp.

————. *The Vampire: His Kith and Kin.* London: Routledge, Kegan Paul, Trench, Trubner & Co., 1928. 356 pp. Reprint. New Hyde Park, NY: University Books, 1960. 356 pp.

————. *The Vampire in Europe.* London: Routledge, Kegan Paul, Trench, Trubner & Co., 1929. 329 pp. Reprint. New Hyde Park, NY: University Books, 1961. 329 pp.

————. *The Werewolf.* London: Kegan Paul, Trench, Trubner & Co., 1933. Reprint. New York: Bell Publishing Company, 1966. 307 pp.

SUNLIGHT

Today, vampires are commonly portrayed as nocturnal creatures with a great aversion to sunlight. But such was not always the case. In the folklore of many cultures, the vampire was able to infiltrate society and return to some semblance of normal life. In nineteenth-century literature, vampires moved about freely during the day. For example, in "Christabel", the early vampiric poem by **Samuel Taylor Coleridge**, Geraldine the vampire was discovered outside the castle by Christabel late at night. She invited Geraldine to her room where the two passed the rest of the night in bed.

Geraldine awakened the next morning, refreshed and ready to meet Christabel's father. In like measure, **Lord Ruthven**, **Varney the Vampyre**, and **Carmilla** maneuvered easily through the day, though they preferred the night.

Concerning **Dracula, Abraham Van Helsing** noted:

> His power ceases, as does that of all things, at the coming of day. Only at certain times can he have limited freedom. If he be not at the place whither he is bound, he can only change himself at noon or at exact sunrise and sunset. These things are we told, and in this record of ours we have proof by inference.

As the men prepared to destroy Dracula's earth-filled boxes, Van Helsing warned that Dracula might appear in his Piccadilly residence, but given his diminished powers, they might be able to cope with him as a group. As predicted, Dracula appeared late one afternoon. Harker attacked him with a knife and Van Helsing with a **crucifix**. The weakened Dracula escaped by jumping out of the window onto the ground and crossing the yard to the stable and into the city.

The contemporary understanding of the nocturnal nature of the vampire seems to have derived from the 1922 silent movie *Nosferatu, Eine Symphonie des Garuens*. This early unauthorized attempt to bring *Dracula* to the screen made numerous changes in the story in the hope of disguising it. The characters' names were changed and the location moved to Germany. In addition, **Graf Orlock** (the vampire) was transformed into a totally nocturnal creature, and a new method of killing him was introduced. Director Freidrich Wilhelm Murnau introduced a mythical volume, *The Book of the Vampires,* as a source of new wisdom concerning the creatures. The heroine, Ellen Hutter (**Mina Murray** in the novel), read that if a pure woman spent the night with the vampire, holding him at her side until dawn, the vampire would perish in the light. She decided to sacrifice herself for the good of all. Graf Orlock, who had moved next door, already had his eye on Ellen so he soon found his way to her bedroom. He sunk his teeth into her throat and there remained until sunrise. He noticed that he had lingered too long only after his fate was sealed. In one of the more memorable moments, he realized his imminent death just prior to his dissolving into a puff of smoke.

The transition in emphasis made by *Nosferatu* had been prepared by the opening chapters of *Dracula* in which Jonathan Harker, perceiving the nocturnal activities of the Count, noted in his diary, "I have not yet seen the Count in the daylight. Can it be that he sleeps when others wake that he may be awake whilst they sleep!"

While *Nosferatu* emerged as an important film, it was for all practical purposes not available until the 1960s, and thus may have had less effect on the development of the vampire's image than many suspect. On the contrary, **Bela Lugosi**'s 1943 *The Return of the Vampire* was widely circulated. Here the sunlight was the instrument of the vampire Armand Tesla's death—it melted Tesla's face.

Having been introduced as a potent and deadly force, sunlight arose as a preferred instrument of death in two of the most important screen adaptations of the

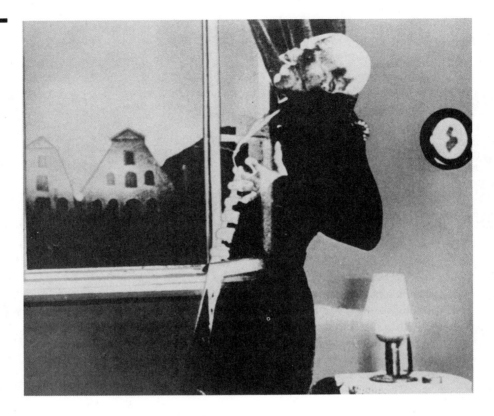

COUNT ORLOCK DISINTEGRATING IN THE SUNLIGHT.

Dracula legend. In *The Horror of Dracula* (1958), **Abraham Van Helsing (Peter Cushing)** was nearly beaten by Dracula (**Christopher Lee**) as the pair fought in the castle. However, Dracula paused to savor the moment just long enough for Van Helsing to spring free and rip the drapes from the window. The direct sunlight, like acid, caught Dracula's foot, which quickly dissolved. Recovering his advantage, Van Helsing used his **crucifix** to force Dracula fully into the sunlight where he disintegrated into a heap of ash.

In *Dracula* **(1979)**, **Frank Langella** (as Dracula) fled to the ship that would take him and Lucy Seward (**Lucy Westenra** in the novel) away from England. Van Helsing and **John Seward** thwarted his plans when they reached the ship. In the final fight scene, Dracula impaled Van Helsing and was about to win when he was suddenly caught on a hook and heaved into the sunlight high above the ship.

While sunlight can be an instrument of death, it has been used primarily to define the realm of activity and set the boundary of action for vampire characters in movies and novels. The rising and setting sun prescribed the period of the vampire's activity, and an approaching dawn created a moment of tension as the vampire rushed back to its resting place. It is of some trivial interest that in the recent television show, *Dracula—The Series,* the vampire wore a special skin lotion that blocked the sun and, thus, he was able to go out in the daylight. This idea has also been used in several pieces of previous vampire fiction.

SWEDEN, VAMPIRES IN *See:* SCANDINAVIA, VAMPIRES IN

SZEKELYS

In describing himself to **Jonathan Harker**, **Dracula** took the label *Szekely.* "We *Szekelys* have a right to be proud," he asserted as an opening for a lengthy discourse on the role of his people in the history of **Transylvania**. As he continued, he began to discuss the Draculas, "about one of my own race who crossed the Danube and beat the Turk on his own ground." (Chapter 3) This discourse raises many of the questions concerning the relationship of Dracula, the fictional character created by **Bram Stoker**, and the medieval Romanian ruler, **Vlad the Impaler**.

The *Szekelys* (or *Szeklers*) was a distinct group that emerged in Transylvania from among the Hungarian tribes, which moved into the area at the end of the ninth century. Others suggest an independent origin, possible a lost group of Bulgars who had invaded the area in the seventh century. Szekelys claim a pre-Hungarian origin. Originally they settled in southeastern Transylvania, but in 1224 A.D., they migrated northward and relocated in the eastern mountains. The Szekelys formed a first line of defense for the Hungarians who controlled the Transylvanian plain to their west, and they developed a reputation for their bravery and fierceness in battle. They participated in the establishment of the Union of Three Nations in 1437 that set the Hungarians, Szekelys, and Germans as a controlling majority and made room for the Roman Catholic, Reformed, and Lutheran churches. That same agreement disenfranchised the Romanians and excluded their Eastern Orthodox faith.

After identifying Dracula as a Szekely, Stoker positioned his castle near **Borgo Pass**, a location in Szekely-dominated land in northeastern Transylvania near the Ukrainian border. Stoker thus quite properly sent Harker into the best place to find a Szekely nobleman. The problem arose in identifying this Szekely nobleman, Count Dracula, with the historical ruler of Wallachia, Prince Vlad the Impaler, or Dracula (the son of **Vlad Dracul**). If Stoker also intended to see his character as a fictionalized version of Vlad, he had hopelessly confused two historical realities. Vlad the Impaler, though born in southern Transylvanian, was a Romanian and ruled in Wallachia, the area across the Carpathian Mountains to the south of Transylvania. He was neither Hungarian nor a Szekely. His castle was located near Cutea de Arges in Wallachia, nowhere near Borgo Pass. Most likely, Stoker saw Hungarian and Romanian history and folklore in less than precise terms and borrowed elements from each (as well as other sources) in creating the fictional world inhabited by his vampire creation. The problem of identifying Vlad the Impaler as both a Szkeley warrior and a Wallachian prince was amply illustrated in the opening scenes of ***Bram Stoker's Dracula,*** which hopelessly confused Romanian geography by trying to integrate the story of Vlad with that of Dracula.

Sources:

Cadzow, John F., Andrew Ludanyi, and Louis J. Elteto. *Transylvania: The Roots of Ethnic Conflict.* Kent, OH: Kent State University Press, 1983. 368 pp.

T

TALAMAUR

The *talamaur* was the vampirelike creature of the Banks Islands in the South Pacific. The people of Banks Island had a strong belief in the possibility of lively intercourse with the ghosts of the dead. While some feared the dead, others welcomed interaction with the spirit world. There was also a strong belief that the soul of a living person, a *tarunga*, could separate from the body and wander about, a belief often verified in dream experiences. The *talamaur* was described as a soul or *tarunga* that went out and ate the soul or life still lingering around the body of the corpse of a recently deceased person. It also described the **ghoul**-like behavior of a living person who would eat a corpse with the understanding that the ghost of the dead person would become a close companion of the *talamaur* and would use his ghostly power against anyone to whom he was directed. If people in the village felt afflicted, and if they developed a sense of dread in the presence of one of their neighbors, that neighbor would be suspected of being a *talamaur*.

It was no crime to be a *talamaur*, and it was the practice of some to actually project the image of being one. R. H. Codrington, the main source of information on the creature, told the story of one woman who claimed to be a *talamaur*, and on the occasion of a death in the village bragged that she would visit and eat the corpse that evening. Friends of the dead person watched to protect the body. During the course of the evening, they heard some scratching noises close to the corpse. One person threw a stone toward the noise. The next day the woman who claimed to be the *talamaur* had a bruise on her arm, which she said came from being hit while eating the corpse.

Sources:

Codrington, R. H. *The Melanesians: Studies in Their Anthropology and Folk-lore.* Oxford: Clarendon Press, 1891, 1969. 419 pp.

TEETH See: FANGS

TELEVISION, VAMPIRES ON

As television spread into American homes in the 1950s, the vampire made its first hesitant appearances on the youthful medium. Most likely the vampire made its first appearance on television in one of the old vampire movies. However, the formal introduction of the vampire to television came in 1954 with the appearance of **Bela Lugosi** on a popular live television show, *You Asked for It.* Lugosi performed in a scene from *Dracula* and in the interview conducted by host Art Baker, Lugosi announced that he would be working on a new television series, *Dr. Acula*, which, it seems, never went into production. A more substantive appearance occurred two years later when **John Carradine** recreated his stage version of *Dracula* on the popular series Matinee Theatre.

DRACULA ON TELEVISION: Following the initial appearances by Lugosi and Carradine, *Dracula* periodically reappeared in new productions. One version appeared on French television in 1969. That same year, British television adapted the script used by Carradine in 1956 for an episode for their series *Mystery and Imagination,* in which **Denholm Mitchell Elliott** starred as Count Dracula. In 1973, *Purple Playhouse,* a Canadian television series, revived the *Mystery and Imagination* script and produced its version of *Dracula* with Norman Welsh portraying the Count.

A major production of *Dracula* **(1973)**, with a freshly written script, was produced for television by **Dan Curtis** on the heels of his successful *Dark Shadows* daytime television series. Aware of the vampire's popular appeal, he led in the development of a full-length feature film. Aired in 1974 on CBS, **Jack Palance** starred as Count Dracula in the first *Dracula* production to be influenced by the historical work on **Vlad the Impaler** by **Raymond T. McNally** and **Radu Florescu**. Finally, in 1977, a critically hailed full-length (two-and-a-half hour) version of *Dracula* was produced by BBC-TV that starred **Louis Jourdan** in the title role. The movie was based on the book *Count Dracula* by Gerald Savory. In the United States, it was originally aired as a three-part miniseries.

Most recently, a new television show featuring Dracula was aired during the 1990-91 program year. Titled *Dracula—The Series,* it starred Gerodi Johnson as Alexander Lucard, Count Dracula in the modern world, as a businessman whose identity had been discovered by three teenagers and their uncle. The show lasted only one season.

VAMPIRE TELEVISION SERIES: *Dracula the Series* was just one of a number of television series that featured a vampire in a continued leading role. In 1964, two of the most famous and successful series with vampiric characters were launched. ABC brought Charles Addams' *New Yorker* cartoon series to the screen as *The Addams Family* with Carolyn Jones portraying vampiric Morticia Addams. Countering *The Addams Family,* CBS created a new monstrous family, The Munsters, with two vampires, Lily Munster (played by Yvonne de Carlo) and Grandpa (played by Al Lewis). During the course of the series, Grandpa was revealed to be, in fact, Count Dracula. Both *The Addams Family* and *The Munsters* attempted to mine the humor of a family of monsters attempting to live as middle class families in modern America. Both series lasted two years. In 1973, *The Addams Family* returned in an animated series aimed at the youthful Saturday-morning audience. In 1988 *The Munsters* returned with a new cast as The Munsters Today, a series that lasted for three seasons.

The year 1966 saw the beginning of what was to become a television enigma. Producer Dan Curtis sold ABC on a gothic daytime soap opera that he called *Dark Shadows*. The original show did not do well and Curtis was told that unless the ratings improved, it would be canceled. He decided to experiment with some supernatural elements. As a last resort, a vampire character was added, **Barnabas Collins**, played by **Jonathan Frid**. The show became a hugh success. It ran for more than 1,200 episodes and became one of the most popular daytime television shows of all time. *Dark Shadows* had a late afternoon time slot and thus found many viewers among teenagers who rushed home from school to watch it. *Dark Shadows* has been kept alive through fan clubs, fanzines, and annual conventions. The show's reruns have been played on cable television and, in recent years, have been shown regularly on the Sci-Fi Network.

Two animated cartoon series aimed at younger audiences began in 1970. The first, *The Groovie Goolies* included the vampire character Cousin Drac. The series lasted only one season, but Cousin Drac and other Groovie Goolies were continued on a new show, *Sabrina the Teenage Witch*. After Sabrina was canceled and the cartoon version of *The Addams Family* finished its 16-segment run in 1974, the vampire made but scant appearances in any series for the next two decades.

In 1988, a British cartoon series was launched built around a leading character who was a mixture of Donald Duck and Dracula. *Count Duckula* became a popular children's comedic character as a vegetarian vampire. The series came to the United States and has been aired on cable channels.

In 1991 *Dark Shadows* reappeared as a lavish prime-time series starring **Ben Cross** as **Barnabas Collins**. While hailed by vampire enthusiasts—and especially the still organized *Dark Shadows* fans—it failed to find a sufficient audience to prevent it from cancellation after only one season. More successful was *Forever Knight,* a series that spun off of a made-for-television movie, *Nick Knight*. *Forever Knight* centered on a vampire policeman (played by Geraint Wyn Davies) who worked the night shift in Toronto. A prime example of the new vampire as romantic hero, Nick Knight's adventures found their place as part of CBS's *Crime Time After Prime Time* series, which aired each evening as an alternative to NBC's popular *The Tonight Show*. Unfortunately, the series was canceled after two seasons when CBS signed David Letterman to do a nightly comedy-talk show in that time slot.

MADE-FOR-TELEVISION MOVIES: During the last two decades, full-length movies made for initial release to the television audience rather than for release in movie theaters became a growing portion of all movies produced. Among the first such movies was *The Night Stalker,* produced by **Dan Curtis** in 1971. Like Curtis' *Dark Shadows,* it became an enigma as the highest rated television show aired to that date. The story concerned reporter Carl Kolchak (Daren McGavin), who followed a story to the point of first discovering and then killing a vampire. The movie's success led to the *Kolchak: The Night Stalker* series, which pitted McGavin against a variety of supernatural monsters. Only one of the show's stories focused upon a vampire.

Curtis worked with **Richard Matheson** on the script for both *The Night Stalker* and his version of *Dracula* (1973). In 1976, the two worked together again on a third movie, *Dead of Night,* made by dramatizing three of Matheson's stories. One of the stories, "No Such Thing as a Vampire," concerned a Professor Gheria who tried to kill his wife by creating the impression that she was wasting away due to a vampire's attack.

Even before *The Night Stalker,* the popular series **The Munsters** led to the production of a made-for-television movie. *Munster Go Home* was aired in 1966 on the heels of the cancellation of the original series. A second movie, *The Munsters Revenge,* was aired in 1981. In the 1990s, several movies were also made with the cast of *The Addams Family,* but were released to the theatre market rather than for television.

The 1970s ended with two noteworthy movies. Tobe Hooper directed the dramatic version of Stephen King's early vampire novel *'Salem's Lot.* A sequel, *Return to 'Salem's Lot,* was aired in 1987. That same year, *Vampire* was produced, starring E. G. Marshall and Jason Miller as a team attempting to solve a number of murders in modern-day San Francisco. The murderer turned out to be a vampire, Anton Voytek, who, though discovered, was not destroyed. More recent made-for-television vampire movies included *The Midnight Hour* (1985); *Nick Knight* (1989), which inspired the *Forever Knight* series; *Nightlife* (1989); and *Daughters of Darkness* (1990).

OTHER VAMPIRE PRODUCTIONS: In addition to the vampire-oriented series and made-for-television movies, the vampire has appeared as a "guest villain" in a number of television shows. The British *Mystery and Imagination* series was but the first of numerous television shows that featured a new story each week and occasionally aired a vampire story. It was the first to dramatize *"Carmilla"* in one of the female vampire's rare appearances. Series that featured a vampire story included: *Alfred Hitchcock Presents, Cliffhangers, Monsters, Rod Serling's Night Gallery, Tales from the Crypt, Tales from the Darkside,* and *The Twilight Zone.* In addition, over the years, different adventure series have pitted their hero character(s) against a vampire villain, although some of the better shows developed a vampire plot where any supernatural element was explained away. Among the more notable vampire episodes were those that were part of *The Man from U.N.C.L.E.* (1965), *Starsky and Hutch* (1976), *The Hardy Boys/Nancy Drew Mysteries* (1977), *Buck Rogers in the 25th Century* (1979), and *Superboy* (1990).

It would appear that the vampire will continue its place on the edge of television culture. It has yet to manifest the strength to hold a continuing spot on prime-time commercial television, however, as cable television continues to expand, the vampire should discover a regular slot to satiate the hunger of its avid fans.

Sources:

Glut, Donald F. *The Dracula Book.* Metuchen, NJ: Scarecrow press, 1975. 388 pp.

Jones, Stephen. *The Illustrated Vampire Movie Guide.* London: Titan Books, 1993. 144 pp.

TEMPLE OF THE VAMPIRE

The Temple of the Vampire is a religious organization that practices the religion of Vampirism. According to the temple, its faith is an ancient religion that has, through the centuries, been known by many names including the Order of the Dragon, the Temple of the Dragon, and the Temple of the Vampire Dragon Goddess Tiamat (ancient Sumeria). The modern public temple has attempted to locate those people who might be of the Blood—those who have realized their difference from the mass of humanity, who resonate with the Dark of the Night, who recognize themselves as predators, who know there is something more to life, and who wish to possess it.

According to the Temple, vampires exist as the predators of humans. Vampires emerge out of humanity and represent the next stage in evolution. Theirs is the religion of the elite—the rulers. They believe that vampires created the religions of the world to ensure humanity's basic docility. The basic perspective of the temple is summarized in ''The Vampire Creed'':

I am a Vampire.
I worship my ego and I worship my life, for I am the only God that is.
I am proud that I am a predatory animal and I honor my animal instincts.
I exalt my rational mind and hold no belief that is in defiance of reason.
I recognize the difference between the world of truth and fantasy.
I acknowledge the fact that survival is the highest law.
I acknowledge the Powers of Darkness to be hidden natural laws through
    which I work my magic.
I know that my beliefs in Ritual are fantasy but the magic is real, and I respect
    and acknowledge the results of my magic.
I realize there is no heaven as there is no hell, and I view death as the
    destroyer of life.
Therefore I will make the most of life here and now.
I am a Vampire.
Bow down before me.

Today's vampire exists in a double reality. What is termed the Daytime self is a material skeptic who laughs at superstition. The Nightside self practices magical and ritual acts. Through the techniques taught by the Temple, the vampire learns to move in the world of magical fantasy and there begins to realize the traditional powers of the vampire (from shapeshifting to hypnotic power to physical immortality). The strengthening of the Nightside self, in which the individual's will is connected with the cosmic Powers of Darkness, leads to changes in the Dayside world in conformity to the Nightside realities. Vampiric rituals allow contact with the Undead Gods and lead to the sacred act of Vampiric communion.

Membership in the temple is international and is organized in several levels. The Lifetime Member is one who has made a first step in contact and made a material donation to the temple. After making application and being accepted, the Lifetime Member becomes an Active Member. After some degree of results in development of one's vampiric powers, advancement to the level of Vampire Predator and entrance into the Second Circle of the Outer Temple is acknowledged. Further advancement may lead to becoming a Vampire Priest/ess. The priesthood has access to the innermost levels of temple knowledge—the hidden teachings.

The temple publishes *The Vampire Bible*, a manual of fundamental magical lore, available to lifetime members. It also issues a biennial publication, *Bloodlines: The Vampire Temple Journal* and the monthly *Lifeforce: The International Vampire Forum*. Membership information may be obtained from the Temple of the Vampire, Box 3583, Lacey, WA 98503.

Sources:

Lifeforce. Vol 1- . Lacy, WA: Temple of the Vampire, 1993- .

TENATZ See: SOUTHERN SLAVS, VAMPIRES AMONG THE

THAILAND, VAMPIRES IN

Pre-Buddhist Thailand had a significant mythology that survived into the twentieth century as a form of spirit worship. The spirits, which have a minor place in Buddhist thought, nevertheless find a certain compatibility with the dominant Buddhism. The spirits were known collectively as the *phi*. The *phi* were numerous and have never been fully catalogued. They were analogous to the ghosts, goblins, elves, and fairies of Western Europe. Many were malevolent and haunted different structures. Every family had a private tutelary spirit that, if neglected, would bring ill fortune to the family members.

Among the *phi* who were believed to inhabit the countryside were the ghosts of people killed by **animals**, women who died in childbirth, people who died and did not have proper funeral rites, and those who died suddenly and unexpectedly. These were the sources of various forms of attacks including vampirism. They bit, scratched, and caused disease. The *Phi Song Nang* were similar to the *pontianak* of **Java** and Indonesia. They appeared as beautiful young women and attacked and vampirized young men.

The ways of the *phi* were known to the various occult practitioners, from sorcerers to mediums. The *maw du*, a seer, would be called in cases of a person who had been attacked by a *phi*. The *maw dus* used various spells and incantation to get rid of the *phi*. They also sold charms to prevent the attack of the *phi*.

Sources:

Graham, W. A. *Siam*. 2 vols. London: The de la More Press, 1924.

TIBET, VAMPIRES IN

Tibet, like **India** and **China**, possessed a rich pantheon of supernatural entities, and many had some vampiric qualities. Many of these were shared with such neighboring nations as Nepal, Sikkim, and Mongolia. Among the most visible of the vampiric entities were the so-called Wrathful Deities who appeared in *The Tibetan Book of the Dead*. This volume described what Tibetan Buddhists believed would be experienced by individuals in the days immediately following their death. During these days, the deceased generally wandered into an area dominated by karma (the law of consequences) where the higher impulses of the heart gave way to the reasonings of the brain centers. The heart impulses were personified by the Peaceful Deities. The brain reasonings were personified by the Wrathful Deities. Contemporary writers on Tibetan Buddhism have generally emphasized that the deities were not objectively real, but were the products of the person picturing aspects of the self. However, in traditional Buddhist lore, they were pictured as part of a true supernatural realm.

The Wrathful Deities, also called the 58 blood-drinking deities, were believed to begin their appearance on the eighth day after the deceased passed into the post-death realm. For example, the blood-drinking deities of the Vajra order appeared on the ninth day. Here the intellect was represented by Bhagavan Vajra-Heruka. In one hand he held a human scalp. He was embraced by his mother, Vajra-Krotishaurima, whose right hand held a red shell filled with blood that she placed at her son's mouth. On the next day, one encountered Ratna-Heruka, who appeared like Vajra-Heruka, but was yellow rather than blue. The red Padma-Heruka appeared on the eleventh day. On the twelfth day, the blood-drinking deities of the Lotus Order were encountered. On the thirteenth day, the eight Kerimas were encountered. These deities had the heads of various animals and engaged in different vampiric and ghoulish actions. One, the Dark-Green Ghasmari, for example, held a scalp filled with blood that she stirred with a *dorje* (a holy object) then drank from it. Other similar deities appeared daily throughout the fourteenth day. The dying person was given instructions on relating to the deities and prayers to acknowledge them. Individuals were also told to call upon the name of their own guru and their personal deity to sustain them in the loneliness of the after-death realms. It should be noted that these deities did not attack the individual who encountered them, rather they were pictured as general representations of vampiric actions previously committed by the deceased.

Devendra P. Varma, author of *The Vampire in Legend, Lore, and Literature* has called attention to **Yama**, the Tibetan Lord of Death, who, like the Nepalese Lord of

Death and the Mongolian God of Time, subsisted by drinking the blood of sleeping people. The Tibetan god had a green face and a blue-green body. In his clawed hand he held the Wheel of Life. The Nepalese god had three blood-shot eyes with flames issuing from his eyebrows and thunder and lightning from his nostrils. In his hands, he carried a sword and a cup of blood. He was decorated with human skulls. The Mongolian god, with his prominent canine teeth, was seen amidst a storm over a bloody sea.

There was also a belief in the pursuit of the living by the dead. The dead were cremated, in part, to prevent the soul from attempting to re-enter it. The soul after death, like person before death, became the object of ritual, in this case to keep it from interacting improperly with the realm of the living.

A SIKKIM VAMPIRE: Varma has also recorded one case of nonlegendary vampirism in Tibet's neighbor Sikkim. In the early eighteenth century, Princess Pedi Wangmo, the monarch's half-sister, plotted to kill her half-brother. With the assistance of a Tibetan doctor, she bled Chador Namgyal to death and drank his blood. She escaped the palace but was soon caught. Both she and her accomplice were killed. It was believed, by some, that after death she became a vampire. Her story was recounted in a fresco in a monastery in Sinon near Mt. Kanchenjunga.

Sources:

Evans-Wentz, W. Y. *The Tibetan Book of the Dead; or, The After-Death Experiences on the Bardo Plane, according to Lama Kazi Dawa-Samdup's English Rendering.* 1927. Reprint. New York Causeway Books, 1973.

Varma, Devendra P. "The Vampire in Legend, Lore, and Literature." Introduction to *Varney the Vampyre.* New York: Arco Press, 1970.

TIRGOVISTE

Tirgoviste, the former capital of Wallachia and the section of modern **Romania** south of the Carpathian Mountains, was the location of the palace where **Dracula** resided during his years as the prince of Wallachia. The capital of Wallachia was moved to Tirgoviste from Curtea de Arges in 1415 and there, Mircea the Old, one of Dracula's ancestors, erected the palace that became the seat of power for the prince. During the next century and a half, numerous claimants to the throne briefly resided at Tirgoviste in the unstable situation created by the varying fortunes of Wallachia's powerful neighbors.

Vlad the Impaler, the historical Dracula, first moved to Tirgoviste in 1436 when his father, **Vlad Dracul**, became the prince of Wallachia. He lived there only six years before he was sent to live among the Turks as a hostage to ensure his father's goodwill toward the Ottoman Empire. Vlad returned to Tirgoviste for a brief month in October 1448, when he attempted to assume the throne following the death of his father. He was driven from Tirgoviste by Vladislav II and fled to Moldavia. It was not

STATUE OF VLAD TEPES AT
TIRGOVISTE.

until Vladislav turned on his Hungarian sponsors and fought against John Hunyadi that Vlad became the Hungarian candidate to hold the throne. He again took up residence in his childhood home in the spring of 1456.

Vlad would rule only six years, but he filled those years with a lifetime of adventure and earned his title, Tepes, or "the Impaler." The yard in front of the palace became the site of numerous executions by impalement. Vlad had the Chinda (Sunset) Tower built adjacent to the palace to provide an observation post for viewing the work of the executioners. The first notable event of his brief reign probably occurred on Easter of 1459. He invited the many boyars (feudal land owners) to an Easter feast. After they spent the day eating and drinking, Vlad had his soldiers surround the palace, and he arrested the boyars and their families. The elders were immediately killed, but the remainder were marched away to Curtea de Arges to build Vlad's mountain castle.

Vlad's six years of rule culminated at the gates of Tirgoviste in June 1462. For two months, he had fought a losing battle across Wallachia. The Turkish army, led by Mohammed II, arrived at Tirgoviste only to find the impaled bodies of all the Turks who had been taken prisoner. Mohammed II turned back and returned to Adrianople.

PALACE AT TIRGOVISTE.

Vlad followed the retreating army and constantly harassed it. However, Mohammed II gave his army to Vlad's brother Radu cel Frumos who had gained the support of the remaining boyars. Radu chased Vlad to his castle north of Curtea de Arges and, finally, out of the country.

Vlad lived as a prisoner of the Hungarians for more than a decade. He gradually gained the support of King Matthias for his return to the Wallachian's throne. Vlad returned to Tirgoviste in 1476. His stay was short. He moved on to Bucharest just one week later. In December of that year, the Turkish army attacked and the boyars turned on Vlad and killed him. The exact fate of his body is unknown.

Tirgoviste remained the capital of Wallachia until 1660 when it was officially relocated to Bucharest.

Sources:

Florescu, Radu, and Raymond T. McNally. *Dracula: A Biography of Vlad the Impaler, 1413-1476.* New York: Hawthorn Books, 1973. 239 pp.

———. *Dracula: Prince of Many Faces: His Life and Times.* Boston: Little, Brown and Company, 1989. 261 pp.

Mackenzie, Andrew. *Dracula Country.* London: Arthur Barker, 1977. 176 pp.

Treptow, Kurt W., ed. *Dracula: Essays on the Life and Times of Vlad Tepes.* New York: Columbia University Press, 1991. 336 pp.

***TLAHUELPUCHI* See: MEXICO, VAMPIRES IN**

TOLSTOY, ALEXEY KONSTANTINOVITCH
(1817-1875)

Alexey Konstantinovitch Tolstoy, the nineteenth-century Russian writer who introduced the vampire into Russian literature, was born in St. Petersburg, Russia. Tolstoy was educated at home and, at the age of 16, entered government service at the Moscow Archives of the Ministry of Foreign Affairs. While in Moscow, he was able to study at Moscow University where he absorbed German idealistic philosophy. He received his diploma from the university in 1835.

At the beginning of his literary career, influenced by E. T. A. Hoffmann's tales, Tolstoy wrote several fantastic/horror stories, the first of which was ''Upyr'' (''The Vampire''). ''Upyr'' was the story of a young couple, Runevsky and Dasha. The story opened in nineteenth-century Moscow with a group at a ball. Runevsky conversed with a pale young man, Rybarenko, on the subject of vampires. He predicted that if Dasha went to visit her grandmother she would die. Eventually, after a series of adventures and some visionary experiences, Runevsky learned the truth. The problem in Dasha's family stemmed from previous generations, to an unfaithful wife who killed her husband. As he was dying, he pronounced a curse of madness and vampirism upon her and their heirs. She eventually went insane and committed **suicide**. Dasha's grandmother inherited the curse. As a vampire, she had already killed Dasha's mother and was prepared to kill Dasha. In the end he became a believer, in the supernatural, although Dasha dismissed everything that happened and believed a more naturalistic explanation.

Tolstoy first read the story at one of the local salons and then, after passing a censor, had it published under the pseudonym Krasnorogsky in 1841. It was followed by a second supernatural tale, ''The Reunion After Three-Hundred Years,'' a ghost story. Tolstoy returned to the vampiric theme in his third story, ''The Family of the Vurkodlak''. (The *vurkodlak* was the vampire of the **southern Slavs**.) Written in French, it began with the Congress of Vienna in 1815 where the Marquis d'Urfe entertained some aristocratic friends with his story. While traveling through Serbia, d'Urfe stopped for the night. The family he stayed with was upset as the father had left to fight the Turks. Before he left, d'Urfé told the family to beware if the father returned in less than 10 days—it was a sign that had become a *vurkodlak* and should be impaled with an aspen **stake**. Almost 10 days passed before the father returned. The older son was about to kill him but was overruled by the family, although the father refused to eat and drink and otherwise behaved strangely. The father then attacked the family, including the daughter to whom d'Urfé had been attracted. d'Urfé continued on his journey but returned to the village some months later. He was told that the entire family had become vampires. He sought out the young girl but soon discovered that, in fact, she was now a vampire. He barely escaped from the family.

After writing ''The Family of the Vurkodlak,'' which was not published during his lifetime, Tolstoy wrote a fourth supernatural story, ''Amena.'' These four stories formed a prologue to his formal literary career that was really thought to have begun when he started writing poetry in the late 1840s. The high point of his career as a poet came in the late 1850s, the period after his service in the Crimean War (1855-56). In 1861, he resigned from the Imperial Court and devoted the rest of his life to his writing.

Tolstoy has been hard to classify, as his works do not readily fit into any of the major schools of nineteenth-century Russian writing. A loner, he rarely participated in the literary circles of his time, and, after leaving the court, settled on his estate in the Ukraine. Tolstoy approved of some Westernization but did not like the more radical activists. He did inject the vampire theme into Russian writing, a theme that would later be picked up by Nicol Gogol and Ivan Turgenev. In 1960, Italian director **Mario Bava** brought ''The Family of the Vurkodlak'' to the screen as one of three Russian stories in his *La Maschera del Demonio* (released in the United States as *Black Sunday*). Boris Karloff, who narrated the breaks between the stories, also played the father who had become a *vurkodlak*. English editions of Tolstoy's stories were published in 1969.

Sources:

Dalton, Margaret. *A. K. Tolstoy.* New York: Twayne Publishers, 1972. 171 pp.
Ingham, Norman W. *E. T. A. Hoffmann's Reception in Russia.* Würzburg: Jal-Verlag, 1974, pp. 244-50.
Tolstoy, Alexis. *Vampires: Stories of the Supernatural.* Trans. by Fedor Nikannov. New York: Hawthorn Books, 1969. 183 pp.

THE TOMB OF DRACULA

The Tomb of Dracula is second only to *Vampirella* as the most successful vampire-oriented comic book series of all time. Vampires were banned from **comic book**s in 1954 by the Comics Code, but a revised code in 1971 allowed vampires if they were presented in a manner similar to the vampires of classic **gothic** literature. **Marvel Comics** responded to the change immediately by resurrecting **Dracula** and setting his new adventures in the 1970s. A familiar cast, composed of the descendants of the characters of **Bram Stoker**'s 1897 novel, were assembled to fight him. Reflecting the changing times, a major female character, Rachel Van Helsing, was an active vampire fighter armed with a crossbow. **Blade, the Vampire Slayer**, an African American, also joined the team.

The Tomb of Dracula characters were soon integrated into the Marvel Comics alternate world. Dracula, Blade, and **Hannibal King**, another original character introduced in the series, began to appear in various Marvel Titles (*Dr. Strange, Marvel Premiere, Frankenstein,* and *Thor*) and characters from other titles appeared in *The Tomb of Dracula* (*Werewolf by Night,* and the *Silver Surfer*).

The Tomb of Dracula was developed under the guidance of Marvel's president, Stan Lee. *The Tomb of Dracula* was reprinted in England under the title *Dracula Lives* (in black-and-white) and translated into Spanish and Italian. It also inspired a Japanese feature-length animated video.

Limited by the regulations of the 1971 revision of the Comics Code, the original *The Tomb of Dracula* comic book was cancelled after 70 issues. Marvel then issued a new series under the name *The Tomb of Dracula* in a black-and-white magazine format. One story in each issue continued the Dracula saga. This second series was discontinued after six issues. Material from the original series was reprinted in the revived four-part set, *The Tomb of Dracula* (1991-92), from Marvel subsidiary Epic Comics (1990-91). Various issues of the original series have been reprinted as separate issues during 1992 under the titles *Requiem for Dracula, The Savage Return of Dracula,* and *The Wedding of Dracula.*

In 1992, several characters from *The Tomb of Dracula,* including Blade, Hannibal King, and Frank Drake, were revived and given new life as partners in a present-day Boston detective agency. They were known as *The Nightstalkers*, an anti-vampire/anti-demonic force team. Their adventures appeared in 17 issues, in which they worked with other like-minded crusaders collectively called the **Midnight Sons**. At the end of *The Nightstalkers* 17th issue, Drake and King were killed. Blade survived in a new series.

Sources:

The Tomb of Dracula. No. 1-70. New York: Marvel Comics, 1971-79.

TRANSFORMATION

The vampire traditionally could transform itself into various **animals**, particularly a **bat**, a wolf, or a dog. It could also transform into a **dust**-like cloud or a **mist**. This attribute was often referred to as shape-shifting, and vampires figures often graded into shape-shifters, a particular kind of demon entity in European mythologies. It was also an attribute often tied to **witchcraft**. In the novel by **Bram Stoker, Dracula**'s first recorded transformations were observed by **Jonathan Harker** but occurred in such a manner that neither Harker (nor the reader) realized what was happening. During the course of the novel, Dracula transformed into a wolf (to leave the ship that had wrecked at **Whitby,**) a bat (throughout the novel), and as mist (in order to enter **Mina Murray**'s bedroom). In one of his encounters with the three vampire women in **Castle Dracula**, Harker noted that they appeared to him first as a swirl of dust in the moonlight. Twenty-five years prior to Dracula, the transformation of the vampire into an animal had also been an integral part of **Sheridan Le Fanu**'s story **"Carmilla."** In that story, Carmilla transformed into a cat on several occasions.

The ability of vampires to transform into animals was part of the folklore of the majority of countries that include a vampire figure. The Japanese, for example, had a well-known tale of a vampire who assumed the form of the wife of Prince Nabeshima and then transformed into a cat to hunt her victims. In various countries in Eastern Europe, the **Slavic vampire** could transform into a wide variety of animals, and on rare occasions, even some plants and farm implements. The ancient Roman vampire often appeared as a bird, a crow, or screech owl. Their transformation into wolves tied vampires to **werewolves**, the exact relationship being a matter of scholarly disagreement.

In *Dracula,* **Abraham Van Helsing** also proposed the idea that vampire transformations were facilitated at certain hours. Dracula could change into various forms during the evening at will. However, during the daylight hours he could change only at noon, or exactly at sunrise and sunset. Most likely, Stoker borrowed this idea from Emily Gerard, who reported that Romanians believed that specific times of the day had special significance. Among these were the ''exact hour of noon,'' a precarious time because an evil spirit, Pripolniza, was active. The idea of special powers tied to certain times of the day was dropped by subsequent writers using the vampire theme.

More recent novels and movies have disagreed on the issue of the vampire's power of transformation. The many remakes of *Dracula* have been fairly consistent with his ability to transform into an animal, at least a bat. In the 1992 *Bram Stoker's Dracula,* his ability to transform was a major sub-theme of the plot. However, the influential novels by **Chelsea Quinn Yarbro** and **Anne Rice** have denied the vampire's ability to transform, as have the more recent novels of **P. N. Elrod** and **Elaine Bergstrom**. Yarbro, even more than Rice, stripped her vampires of most of their supernatural abilities, although they were left with great **strength** and a long life. The trend initiated by Rice and Yarbro carried over into many books and motion pictures that have stepped back from Dracula and created other vampire characters who exist in a contemporary setting. Thus, transformation has not been an element in the life of the vampires in such recent movies as *Vamp* (1986), *Near Dark* (1987), *The Lost Boys* (1987), and *Innocent Blood* (1992), or of the television series *Forever Knight.*

TRANSYLVANIA

Transylvania (literally, the land beyond the forest) is the area of north central **Romania** most identified in the public mind with vampires. Its reputation derives from being designated as the home of **Dracula** in **Bram Stoker**'s novel. At the beginning of *Dracula,* Jonathan Harker traveled from Budapest, Hungary into northern Transylvania, then a part of the Austro-Hungarian Empire. He described the land as one of great beauty but a wild and little known place. His final destination was **Castle Dracula,** a location not noted on any map. Although Harker's destination was a fictional site, the land he moved through was very real. Stoker had never been to

VLAD AMID IMPALED BODIES IN
TRANSYLVANIA.

Transylvania but had read about it in books at the British Museum, particularly Emily
Gerard's *Land Beyond the Forest.*

Transylvania was the center of a powerful state in the first century B.A.D. The
territory was partially conquered by Trajan in 106 A.D. Over the next several
centuries, the merger of the Roman and native people created the distinctive people
known today as the Romanians. Christianity of a Roman Latin variety made its initial
entrance into the area at this time, although over the centuries the Romanians aligned
themselves with the Eastern Orthodox Church headquartered in Constantinople. The
area was subject to numerous invasions, more or less successful, by a variety of
nomadic people. Most importantly, in the tenth century, incursions and eventually
conquest by the Hungarians began. By the thirteenth century, **Hungary** claimed
hegemony in Transylvania, although the various divisions continued to be ruled by
the local territorial lords, the voevades.

The Hungarians engaged in several acts of social engineering. First, they
persuaded the **Szekely** people of western Transylvania to move into the mountainous
area in the east and assume the task of border control. The Szekelys emerged as great
warriors. Secondly, to improve the economy, the Hungarians invited Germans into

southern Transylvania and gave them generous tax benefits. Although they originated from throughout Germany, these people became known as the Saxons. They were most prominent in the towns that controlled the mountain passes between Transylvania and Wallachia, located immediately south of the Carpathians. (Today, many of the towns of Transylvania have three names—one each in German, Hungarian, and Romanian.)

By the fourteenth century, there were four main groups in Transylvania: Hungarians, Hungarian-speaking Szekelys, Saxons, and Romanians. The Romanians, although a majority of the population, were the conquered people, and measures to suppress them began in earnest. The Roman Catholic Hungarians launched systematic conversion efforts directed at the Orthodox population. Specific laws were passed to disenfranchise the Romanians, culminating in the 1366 ruling that called into question the traditional status of any Romanian aristocracy who refused to become Roman Catholic and whose loyalty to the Hungarian crown was questionable. Hungary's increasingly oppressive control led many Romanians to cross the mountains into Moldavia and Wallachia.

The migration south promoted the organization of an independent central government in Wallachia in the fourteenth century, although by the next century, it found itself in a constant battle with the Hungarians to the north and the Turks to the south, both of whom wanted to control it. It was in that tension that **Vlad Dracul** came to the Wallachian throne in 1436. He came to the throne at the same time that John Hunyadi, an outstanding Romanian, emerged in Transylvania. Hunyadi became the governor of Transylvania and his power rivaled that of the king. Hunyadi's reputation promoted the cause of his son, Matthais who, at a point of weakness in the Hungarian royal family, became king of Hungary in 1458. Vlad Dracul opposed Hunyadi and was killed in 1447.

Prior to ascending to the throne, Vlad Dracul was the commander of the guard in Transylvania. He settled in **Sighisoara** around 1430 and, a short time after his arrival, his son (also named Vlad) was born. The son, later to become known as **Vlad the Impaler**, was too young to succeed his father in 1447, but eventually gained the throne within months of Hunyadi's death in 1456. As the ruler of Wallachia he claimed the Transylvanian districts of Amlas and Fagaras. More importantly, he moved against the Saxon merchants of Sibiu (for housing his relatives who were claimants to his throne) and Brasov (whose mercantile policies worked against Vlad's attempt to build the Wallachian economy).

Vlad the Impaler, the historical Dracula, was Wallachian (although he was born in Transylvania), and most of the activities he was famous for occurred there. Bram Stoker placed the fictional Count Dracula in northeastern Transylvania. To arrive at Castle Dracula, Jonathan Harker passed through Klausenburgh (Clug-Napoca) and traveled to Bistritz (Bistrita). This section of Transylvania was correctly identified as territory traditionally ruled by the Szekelys and thus he identified Count Dracula as a member of the traditional ruling class. The issue was confused as Stoker attempted to merge the fictional Count Dracula with Vlad the Impaler, the man known for his battles against the Turks and the "bravest of the sons of the 'land beyond the forest.'"

Stoker also identified Dracula as the arch vampire. Transylvanian vampire lore was merely a variation of the vampire beliefs found throughout **Romania** and shared by neighboring groups of Slavs and **Gypsies**. Historically, the land had no particular reputation as a home to vampires.

Sources:

Bodea, Cornelia, and Virgil Candea. *Transylvania in the History of the Romanians.* New York: Columbia University Press, 1982. 181 pp.

Florescu, Radu R., and Raymond T. McNally. *Dracula: Prince of Many Faces.* Boston, MA: Little, Brown and Company, 1989. 261 pp.

Mackenzie, Andrew. *Dracula Country.* London: Arthur Barker, 1977. 176 pp.

Mehedinti, S. *What Is Transylvania?* Miami Beach, FL: Romanian Historical Studies, 1986. 121 pp.

TRANSYLVANIAN SOCIETY OF DRACULA

The Transylvanian Society of Dracula, a cultural historical organization, was founded in the early 1990s by a group of leading Romanian historians, ethnographers, folklorists, tourist experts, writers, and artists, as well as non-Romanian experts in the field. Its goal is the interpretation of Romanian history and folklore, especially as it relates to the fifteenth century ruler **Vlad the Impaler** (the historical Dracula) and Romanian folklore concerning vampires. The group also attempts to identify dracularian traces of the myth in the folklore of other countries around the world. President of the society is Nicolae Paduraru, who for many years was an official with the Romanian Ministry of Tourism. He is currently the general administrator of Count Dracula Treasures, Ltd. The society organizes tours of various sites in southern Romania associated with Vlad the Impaler and those in Transylvania (in the northern area of Romania) associated with the novel *Dracula.*

The Transylvanian Society of Dracula may be contacted at 47 Primaverii Blvd., Bucharest 1, Romania.

TREMAYNE, PETER (1943-)

Peter Tremayne is the pen name used by Peter Bereford Ellis when writing horror, fantasy, and science fiction works. His first fictional book as Peter Tremayne, *The Hound of Frankenstein,* was one of two books he completed in 1977. The second, *Dracula Unborn* (released in the U.S. as *Bloodright: Memoirs of Mircea, Son of Dracula*) was the first of his Dracula series. Heavily influenced by the writings on **Vlad the Impaler** by **Radu Florescu** and **Raymond T. McNally,** Tremayne wrote his novel as the long-lost "Memoirs of Mircea, Son of Dracula." Mircea, who had been born in, but raised outside of **Romania**, returned to discover his vampiric heritage and meet his father. The second vampire novel, *The Revenge of Dracula* followed a year later. Again, Tremayne employed the device of the discovery of formerly lost memoirs. This volume told the story of a nineteenth-century English-man who discovered a jade dragon statuette. Afterward, he had a number of strange dreams, including one about a Dracula figure. He traveled to Transylvania and upon his return had to be committed to an insane asylum. Tremayne's last novel, *Dracula My Love* (1980), was built around the memoirs of Morag, a Scottish governess who moved to **Castle Dracula** and fell in love with the Count, the first person she encountered who treated her with a sense of dignity. This final novel departed from the first two novels in that Dracula was portrayed very positively and sympathetically. Thus, for his last vampire novel, Tremayne participated in the trend to create a vampire hero initiated by **Fred Saberhagen** and **Chelsea Quinn Yarbro**.

Ellis has continued to write, producing several books annually, but has not recently returned to the vampire theme.

Sources:

Tremayne, Peter. *Dracula Unborn.* London: Bailey Brothers and Swinfen, 1977. Reprint. London: Corgi, 1977. 222 pp. Reprint. as: *Bloodright: Memoirs of Mircea, Son of Dracula.* New York: Walker & Co., 1979. 222 pp. Rept. as: *Bloodright.* New York: Dell, 1980. 251 pp.

————. *Dracula My Love.* London: Bailey Brothers and Swinfen, 1980. Reprint. London: Magnum Books, 1980. 203 pp.

————. *The Revenge of Dracula.* Folkstone: Bailey Brothers and Swiften, 1978. Reprint. New York: Walker & Co., 1979. Reprint. London: Magnum Books, 1980. 203 pp.

TREVISAN, DALTON (1952-)

Dalton Trevisan is the leading short story writer of contemporary Brazil. His stories were first published after World War II in *Joaquim* a literary journal he published and edited from 1946-48. He gained national recognition for the publication of *Novelas nada Exempalres* (1959) and attained international notice following the translation of his stories into English and other languages. Among his most popular books was *O Vampiro de Curitiba*, which was combined with several of his other collections of short stories into an English volume titled *The Vampire of Curitiba and Other Stories* (1972).

"The Vampire of Curitiba," the short story that supplied the name for his collected English-language works, used the vampire as a metaphorical vehicle to carry the ongoing message about the characters in his stories: They were lower-middle class and obsessed with sex. In the vampire story, Nelsinho, the protagonist, pursued the town women nightly. His sexual thirst was compared to that of a vampire who had to drink blood to survive. Through sex, Nelsinho passed on his obsession to others. Trevisan grasped the essential sexual nature of the vampire's life and appeal.

Sources:

Stern, Irwin. *Dictionary of Brazilian Literature.* New York: Greenwood Press, 1988. 432 pp.

Trevisan, Dalton. *The Vampire of Curitiba and Other Stories.* Trans. by Gregory Rabassa. New York: Alfred A. Knopf, 1972. 267 pp.

U

UNCLE ALUCARD

In 1992, Dr. Michael Eboy, a London lawyer, with an interest in Victorian life, created a counter myth to the one publicly projected by **The Vampyre Society (Bohanan)**. His tongue-in-cheek effort began with a letter he sent to *The Velvet Vampyre*, the society's journal. Signed by a (fictional) Professor William Drysdale of the University of Human Sciences, the letter recounted how he had been contacted by Eboy who, in 1988, had returned from Eastern Europe with proof that vampires were real and still trod the earth. Drysdale had turned Eboy away although he was sure that Eboy was in London as a vampire hunter.

Since the publication of that letter, Eboy has become the center of a small group of vampire enthusiasts who prefer to celebrate the vampire hunters, especially as portrayed by actor **Peter Cushing** in the several movies produced by **Hammer Films**. In a set of brief writings, Eboy created the fiction that he descended from a family of vampire hunters. Among their targets is the vampire Frederick Scvartsenferter, better known as Camp Freddie, who has eluded the efforts of his family to finally kill him.

In 1992, Eboy published a single issue of a fanzine, *Uncle Alucard,* which continued the myth and featured articles on vampire hunting. Meanwhile, Eboy and several friends have made several appearances at The Vampyre Society gatherings. Eboy and his associates gather irregularly to screen vampire movies and hold contests in vampire staking (using a watermelon as a substitute for a corpse).

Sources:

"Eboy's Casefile: The One that Got Away." *The Velvet Vampire* 21 (1993): 18-21.

UNITED KINGDOM, VAMPIRES IN THE

The United Kingdom includes the countries of England, Scotland, Wales, and

Northern Ireland. None of the four lands have a reputation as being a prominent home to vampires, but they have been significant contributors to the development of the literary vampire. England's vampire heritage is largely confined to reports contained in two volumes, both written at the end of the twelfth century, which described vampiric creatures. Among several accounts in Walter Map's *De Nagis Curialium* (cir. 1190 A.D.), for example, was the story of a knight and his wife. She gave birth to a son, but on the morning following his birth, the baby was found dead with his throat cut. The same fate awaited both a second and a third child, in spite of extra precautions. When a fourth child was born, the entire house was called to stay up to keep the child safe. There was a stranger in the house who also kept watch. As the evening progressed, the stranger noticed all of the household falling asleep. He watched as a matronly woman came to the cradle and bent over it. Before she could hurt the baby, he seized the woman (who appeared to be a wealthy matron of the town). The real woman in town was summoned, and it was seen that the person captured at the cradle had assumed the matron's form. The captured woman was declared a demon, released from the men's grip and flew away with a loud screech.

William of Newburgh finished his *Chronicles* in 1196. In his fifth book, among the stories he recounted for example, was one "Of the extraordinary happening when a dead man wandered abroad out of his grave." Some years previously, in Buckinghamshire (the day after his burial), a husband appeared in his wife's bedroom. After he returned a second night, she reported his visits to her neighbors. On the third evening, several people stayed with her, and when he appeared, they drove him away. He then turned to visiting his brothers and, upon being repelled, he disturbed the animals. The town was terrified by his sudden appearances at various hours of the day and night. They consulted the local clergy who referred the matter to the Bishop of London. The bishop first considered burning the body, but after further thought, advised exhumation of the corpse and the placement of a "chartula of episcopal absolution" on the body. It was further advised that the corpse should then be returned to the grave. The villagers followed his instructions. The body was found in the same condition it had been in on the day of burial. However, from that day forward, it never disturbed anyone again. William of Newburgh was also the source of the more famous cases of the vampires of **Melrose Abbey** and **Alnwick Castle**.

Both the stories of Map and William of Newburgh (quoted at length in the works of both **Montague Summers** and **Donald Glut**) contain many elements of the classical vampire tales of Eastern Europe, but each are missing an essential element— any reference to blood drinking. However, they are similar enough to illustrate the manner in which the vampire tales fit into the larger category of contact with revenants and the manner in which people from widely separated parts of Europe followed a similar set of actions in dealing with the problem.

In Scotland, several other traditional vampiric figures could be found. The *baobban sith,* for example, were known to appear as ravens or crows but more often as young maidens dressed in green dresses that hid their deer's hooves. Katheryn Briggs related one of the more famous *baobban sith* stories (first published by C. M.

Robertson) concerning its encounter with four unfortunate men. The four hunters were camping for the evening. They entertained themselves with dancing and singing. As they danced, they were joined by four maidens seemingly attracted by their music. One of the men, sang as the other men danced. The singer noticed that each of his comrades had blood on their necks and shirts. Frightened, he ran into the woods, with one of the women running behind him. He finally found shelter among the horses where, for some reason, the woman did not come. The following morning he found his hunting mates dead and drained of blood.

The **redcap** was a malignant spirit who haunted abandoned castles and other places where violence had occurred. If one slept in a spot haunted by the redcap, it would attempt to dip its cap in human blood. Not as sinister as some, it could be driven off with a word from the Bible or a cross.

During the centuries of the modern era, these beliefs seemed to have largely died out. If such beliefs, which appeared to be widespread in the twelfth century, survived into the modern era, one would expect to see references to them, for instance, in the records of the many proceedings against witches, but there are none. Also, in the seventeenth century, the initial reports of vampires from Eastern Europe were received as if they were describing a new and entirely continental phenomenon. In the years since news of the Slavic vampire became known in England, two significant cases of vampire infestation became known. The first, the vampire of **Croglin Grange**, was initially reported in the 1890s, while the more recent case was of the **Highgate vampire** at the famous Highgate cemetery in London during the 1960s and 1970s.

THE MODERN VAMPIRE: The term vampire appears to have been introduced to English in 1741. It appeared in a footnote in an obscure book titled *Observations on the Revolution in 1688,* which, though written in 1688, was not published until 60 years later. Interestingly, the term vampire did not refer to a bloodsucking entity in the book, but was used metaphorically in a **political** sense, with no explanation, as if the term was fairly well known. The author said:

> Our Merchants, indeed, bring money into their country, but it is said, there is another Set of Men amongst us who have as great an Address in sending out again to foreign Countries without any Returns for it, which defeats the Industry of the Merchant. These are the Vampires of the Publick, and Riflers of the Kingdom.

Actually, some years earlier in 1679, a book on the *State of the Greek and Armenian Churches* by Paul Ricaut (or Rycaut) described the existence of:

> . . . a pretended demon, said to delight in sucking human blood, and to animate the bodies of dead persons, which when dug up, are said to be found florid and full of blood.

A more important reference to vampires, which not only used the term but described an encounter with them in some depth, appeared in the 1810 publication *Travels of 3*

English Gentlemen from Venice to Hamburg, Being the Grand Tour of Germany in the Year 1734. The author, the Earl of Oxford, offered the first serious explanation of the vampire phenomenon in English. At the time it was written, Germany was in the midst of the great vampire debates that followed on the heels of the vampire epidemics reported throughout the Hungarian Empire. Though written in 1734, the *Travels of 3 English Gentlemen,* remained unpublished for many decades. Meanwhile, **Dom Augustin Calmet**'s 1746 treatise on apparitions, demons, and vampires was translated and published in an English edition in 1759. Both Calmet and the Earl of Oxford's book informed the development of the literary vampire in England.

THE ENGLISH LITERARY VAMPIRE: England's main contribution to contemporary vampire lore was derived not so much from its folklore tradition as from its nurturing of vampire literature in the nineteenth century. While the origins of the literary vampire must be sought in **Germany**, British poets were quick to discover the theme. **Samuel Taylor Coleridge, Robert Southey**, and **John Stagg** were among the writers who were influenced by such popular translations as Gottfried August Bürger's "Lenora" by Sir Walter Scott. Then in 1819, **John Polidori**, out of his love-hate relationship with **Lord Byron**, launched the vampire legend with his initial short story **"The Vampyre"**

Polidori's story of an aristocratic vampire who preyed upon the women of Europe was based upon a story fragment originally written by Lord Byron in 1816, although Polidori's story took the fragment in a distinctly new direction. More important than Byron's plot contribution to the story was its original publication under Byron's name. Because of the name attached, it was hailed as a great work by German and French Romantic writers, was quickly translated into various languages, and became the basis of a generation of dramatic productions in Paris and a German vampire opera. In 1820 it was brought to the London stage by **James Robinson Planché**.

Through the nineteenth century, some of the most famous and influential vampire stories were written. Drawing on ideas introduced by Polidori, **James Malcolm Rymer** wrote *Varney the Vampyre,* one of the most successful penny dreadfuls (a novel published chapter-by-chapter as a weekly serial publication). This highly successful story, which ran to 220 chapters, rivaled Polidori's effort through the rest of the century.

Varney the Vampyre was followed by a number of pieces of short fiction. Compiled in a single volume, they would constitute a relatively large body of vampire literature, and would include William Gilbert's "The Last Lords of Gardonal" (1867), **Sheridan Le Fanu**'s highly influential **"Carmilla"** (1872), Philip Robinson's two stories, "The Man-Eating Tree" (1881) and "The Last of the Vampires" (1892), Anne Crawford's "A Mystery of the Campagna" (1887), H. G. Wells's, "The Flowering of the Strange Orchid" (1894), and Mary Elizabeth Braddon's "Good Lady Ducayne" (1896). All of these stand behind the single most famous and influential piece of vampire literature of all time—**Bram Stoker**'s *Dracula,* published in London in 1897.

More than any other single work, *Dracula* created the modern image of the vampire and brought the idea to the attention of the English-speaking public around the world. The character Dracula became synonymous with the vampire in many ways, and one could think of contemporary vampires as primarily variations of Stoker's character. It initiated the concept of the vampire as a somewhat tamed monster capable of the incognito penetration of human society. Inspired by Stoker, a century of fiction writers would develop numerous concepts of the vampire in ways Stoker only hinted. Dracula now stands beside **Sherlock Holmes** as the single most popular character in English literature and the one most frequently brought to the screen.

Dracula was brought to the stage in 1924 by **Hamilton Deane**. The play enjoyed great success during Deane's lifetime, but has rarely been revived in recent years. More importantly, Deane's play was extensively revised by **John L. Balderston** for presentation on the American stage in 1927. Balderston's revision, published by an American drama publishing house, has been frequently produced over the years. It was the basis of the three **Universal Pictures** productions—*Dracula* **(1931)** with **Bela Lugosi**, the Spanish version also filmed in 1931, and the 1979 version starring **Frank Langella**. The Langella version resulted from a major Broadway revival of the Balderston play in 1977.

England was also home to **Hammer Films**, which for 20 years from the mid-1950s produced a host of horror films in general and vampire films in particular that defined an entire era of horror motion picture production. The distinctive Hammer vampire productions, beginning with *The Curse of Frankenstein* (1957) and *The Horror of Dracula* (1958), were notable for their technicolor presentations and the introduction of a fanged vampire who bit his victims on screen. These Hammer productions made international stars of **Christopher Lee**, who joined Bela Lugosi and **John Carradine** as one of the memorable Draculas, and **Peter Cushing** as Dracula's ever-present nemesis, **Abraham Van Helsing**. They inspired a new wave of vampire films in Europe and America, and with the demise of Hammer in the mid-1970s, British leadership in the production of vampire movies passed to the United States.

THE CONTEMPORARY ENGLISH VAMPIRE: The United Kingdom has been an integral factor in the current revival of interest in vampires. It is now home to a number of vampire interest groups. **The Dracula Society**, formed in 1973, is among the oldest and **The Vampire Society**, headed by Carole Bohanan, possibly the largest. Other vampire organizations include **The Vampire Society (Gittens)** and **The Vampire Guild**. The more distinct **Vampire Research Society**, headed by Sean Manchester, looks with disdain on the vampire.

British authors have contributed their share of novels to the new vampire literature, among the more significant being **Brian Lumley**, Barbara Hambly, Tanith Lee, and Kim Newman. The United Kingdom was also the home of the emergence of **gothic** music now promoted by the **Gothic Society**.

Sources:

Briggs, Katherine. *A Dictionary of Fairies*. London: Penguin Books, 1976. Rept. as: *An Encyclopedia of Fairies, Hobgoblins, Brownies, Bogies, and Other Supernatural Creatures*. New York: Pantheon Books, 1976. 481 pp.

Cox, Greg. *The Transylvanian Library*. San Bernadino, CA:Borgo Press, 1993. 264 pp.

Deane, Hamilton, and John L. Balderston. *Dracula: The Ultimate Illustrated Edition of the World-Famous Vampire Play*. Ed. by David J. Skal. New York: St. Martin's Press, 1993. 153 pp.

Jones, Stephen. *The Illustrated Vampire Movie Guide*. London: Titan Books, 1993. 144 pp.

Stoker, Bram. *Dracula*. London: A. Constable & Co., 1897. 390 pp.

Wilson, Katharina M. "The History of the Word 'Vampire.'" *Journal of the History of Ideas* 46, 4 (October-December 1985): 577-83.

UNIVERSAL PICTURES

With its production of *Dracula* **(1931),** Universal Pictures became the first studio to bring the vampire theme to the talking motion picture and initiated a wave of interest in horror movies. The studio was founded by Carl Laemmle who entered the industry in 1906.

Universal initially opened two studios in Los Angeles then, in 1915, shifted its headquarters to Universal City on the site of the former Taylor Ranch in the San Fernando Valley (it is now the oldest continuously operated studio in America). After many years of making silent movies, Universal made its first sound movie in 1930, *The King of Jazz.* That same year, the studio decided obtain the rights to the **Hamilton Deane/John L. Balderston** play, *Dracula,* which was then making successful appearances around the country after completing a lengthy run on Broadway. The star of the West Coast production, **Bela Lugosi,** worked with the studio to secure the motion picture rights from Florence Stoker, the widow of **Bram Stoker**. **Tod Browning** was chosen to direct the picture.

As people became aware of Universal's plans for *Dracula,* Paul Kohner, the executive in charge of foreign language productions, suggested that *Dracula* would be an excellent candidate for a Spanish version. He already had in mind Lupita Toyar (Kohner's future wife) as the female lead. Thus, as the English-language version of *Dracula* was filmed, Spanish language version, using the same stage settings but a different cast, was simultaneously produced.

Dracula **(Spanish, 1931)** was a success in what was then a relatively small market. However, the English version starring Bela Lugosi, after a slow start, became Universal's top grossing film of the year and was credited with keeping the studio from closing after two years of losing money. The success led to a series of horror films: *Frankenstein* (1932), *The Mummy* (1932), *The Invisible Man* (1933), *The Black Cat* (1934), and *The Bride of Frankenstein* (1935). For nearly two decades, Universal became known for its horror movies, but interestingly enough, it was not until 1936 with the production of *Dracula's Daughter* that a second vampire film was produced. Vampire fans waited until 1943 for a third film titled *Son of Dracula.*

In 1936, Laemmle lost control of Universal to Charles Rogers and J. Cheever Cowdin. During the next decade, the company produced a large number of low-budget films, including many horror features and several vampire movies. In 1948, it merged with International Pictures. Except for the comedy *Abbott and Costello Meet Frankenstein*, Universal-International did not produce any other movies with major vampire themes—part of a general trend away from horror films at the time.

After many years, Universal produced a new vampire film, the *Blood of Dracula* in 1957. The movie was aimed at a youthful audience and the inclusion of a female vampire made the movie more interesting. The success of the movie was responsible for several other vampire movies during the next few years but, after the 1959 production of the *Curse of the Undead*, the studio dropped vampire movies from its schedule for more than a decade. Its reluctance to return to releasing vampire movies and, thereby, placing too much emphasis on the horror genre was amply demonstrated in the summer of 1958 when Universal announced that it had worked out a deal with British upstart **Hammer Films**. Hammer acquired all of the copyrights Universal owned on its classic horror titles, including *Dracula*. Universal largely abandoned the horror movie business for an entire generation.

In 1978, Universal brought the cinema rights to the remake of the Hamilton Deane/John L. Balderston play, which had enjoyed a revival on Broadway, and brought its star, **Frank Langella**, to Hollywood for the screen version. Langella's *Dracula* **(1979)** proved one of the most effective presentations of the sexual/sensual element that co-exists with the terror theme in the Dracula/vampire myth. Since the 1979 *Dracula,* Universal has stayed away from the vampire theme altogether. However, it will always be remembered for its launching of *Dracula* into the consciousness of a nation.

Sources:

Hanke, Ken. *A Critical Guide to Horror Film Series*. New York: Garland Publishing, 1991. 341 pp.
Pirie, David. *The Vampire Cinema*. London: Hamlyn, 1977. 176 pp.
Slide, Anthony. *The American Film Industry: A Historical Dictionary*. New York: Greenwood Press, 1986, pp. 365-67.

UPIR *See:* CZECH REPUBLIC AND SLOVAKIA

V

VADIM, ROGER (1927-)

Roger Vadim, French director of sexually explicit films and the first person to film the classic vampire story **"Carmilla"**, was born R. V. Plémiannikov in Paris. He entered the French film industry soon after World War II as an assistant to Marc Allégret. In 1955 while working on an Allégret film, *Futures Vedettes,* he met his future wife, Brigitte Bardot. After they married he directed her in *And God Created Woman* (1956) and *The Night Heaven Fell* (1957), two films that made Bardot an international sex goddess. Those films also helped establish Vadim's reputation as a superior purveyor of male voyeuristic sexual fantasies in wide-screen technicolor.

After completing *The Night That Heaven Fell,* Vadim and Bardot were divorced and he married Annette Stroyberg, the star of his next set of films. His major production during this period was a vampire movie, *Et Mourir de Plaisir*, released in the United States as *Blood and Roses* and for which he turned to Irish writer **Sheridan Le Fanu** for inspiration. Throughout his career Vadim searched for stories that would allow him to project his own sexual fantasies on the screen, and when he encountered the artistic presentation of an overtly sexual vampire in the Le Fanu's "Carmilla," he was quick to see its potential. The story's potential was underscored by current releases from **Hammer Films** in England, which was making the world aware of the large market for bloody vampire stories.

Possibly because of the blatant sexual element of "Carmilla," *Blood and Roses* was the first attempt to bring Le Fanu's story to the screen (not including **Carl Theodor Dreyer**'s *Vampir,* which some buffs believe is based on "Carmilla," even though it bears little resemblance to Le Fanu's story). "Carmilla" proved a perfect vehicle for Vadim, who was able to play with the situation of a young, sexually attractive vampire drawn to victims of her own age and gender and for whom the integration of feeding and sexual activity was the norm. Vadim's second wife,

Annette, played Carmilla, described in the screenplay as a woman possessed of the spirit of a long-dead vampire. Her victim was Elsa Martinelli, who played Georgia Monteverdi. One especially memorable scene occurred close-up as Carmilla kissed a drop of blood that had appeared on Georgia's lip. The loosening of censorship standards in French movies by this time (to which Vadim had contributed) allowed him to capture on film some of the sexual aspects of the vampire's embrace that Le Fanu could only suggest. Although largely faithful to the mood of the original story, Vadim did incorporate several elements of what had become the standard vampire myth. Thus, Carmilla returned to her grave each morning, and the movie ended as she rushed against the **sunlight.** She stumbled and fell on a wooden shaft, which pierced her heart. In the original story, her grave was discovered by the family of some of her victims, who drove a **stake** into her heart.

At the time *Blood and Roses* was released, British and American audiences were not yet allowed to see Vadim's films uncut. Censors removed the more "offensive" scenes before *Blood and Roses* was released in 1961 by Paramount.

Blood and Roses was Vadim's only direct contribution to the vampire genre; however, he inadvertently made a second notable contribution through his third wife, Jane Fonda. In 1968 he cast Fonda in the starring role in *Barbarella,* in which he combined his sexual visions with science fiction. The sexy, space-hopping Barbarella directly inspired **Forest J. Ackerman** in the creation of **Vampirella,** the sexy comic book space vampire whose numerous adventures became the subject of the most successful vampire comic books to the present day.

In 1971 Vadim had one last success with *Pretty Maids All in a Row,* starring Angie Dickinson, but by the 1970s Vadim's one-dimensional *Playboy* approach to the world was passe, left behind on the one hand by hard-core pornography and on the other by sexually explicit scenes in major Hollywood movies. Vadim continued to direct through the 1980s, but his movies never again attracted the attention of his earlier work. In 1963 he wrote the introduction for an anthology of vampire stories collected by Ornella Volta and Valeria Riva.

Sources:

Glut, Donald G. *The Dracula Book.* Metuchen, NJ: Scarecrow Press, 1975. 388 pp.

Quinlan, David. *The Illustrated Guide to Film Directors.* Totowa, NJ: Barnes & Noble, 1984. 335 pp.

Thomson, David. *A Biographical Dictionary of Film.* New York: William Morrow, 1976. 629 pp.

Volta, Ornella, and Valaria Riva, eds. *The Vampire: An Anthology.* Introduction by Roger Vadim. London: Neville Spearman, 1963. Reprint. London: Pan Books, 1965. 316 pp.

VAMBÉRY, ARMINIUS (1832-1913)

Arminius Vambéry, Hungarian historian and possible model for Dr. **Abraham Van Helsing** in **Bram Stoker**'s novel *Dracula,* was born lame at Szerdakely, near Pressburg, in **Hungary.** As a young man he took up the study of languages and by his 16th year, largely through his own efforts, was fluent in most European languages, including Latin and Greek. At the age of 22 he was able to travel to Constantinople and for the first time practiced the languages he had learned. In 1858 he published his first book, a German-Turkish dictionary, the only one of its kind available for many years. He also began to translate Turkish histories that related events in Hungary, for which he earned a position as a corresponding member of the Hungarian Academy in 1861. With a grant from the Academy, he then traveled widely through the Middle East for several years. In 1864 he moved to England, where he was welcomed as an explorer-traveler and given support while he wrote his book, *Travels in Central Asia,* which was quickly translated into French, German, and Hungarian. He afterward settled in Hungary as a professor of Oriental languages at the University of Pesth.

For the next two decades he was one of the most prolific and famous Hungarian scholars and men of letters. His correspondence kept him in touch with most of the power centers of Europe, and he commented freely on the political questions of his day. In 1883 he wrote the autobiographical *Arminius Vambéry: His Life and Travels.* Soon after its appearance he encountered a wave of anti-Semitism in Hungary and felt forced to relocate to England. There he continued to write and lecture. He wrote one of his most popular books, a large volume titled *Hungary in Ancient, Medieval, and Modern Times* (1886), which was reprinted several times under various titles. This volume would have been one of the books available to Stoker for research on the first chapters of *Dracula.*

Vambéry actually met Bram Stoker, possibly for the first time, in 1890 during the early stages of the writing of *Dracula.* He was on Stoker's guest list one evening at the Beefsteak Room, where people gathered after an evening at the Lyceum Theatre. In conversation and through his books on Hungary, Vambéry influenced Stoker. **Raymond T. McNally** and **Radu Florescu** credit Vambéry with turning Stoker from his prior interest in Austria (reflected in his short story ''Dracula's Guest'') toward **Transylvania,** the setting of the opening and closing chapters of *Dracula.* Unfortunately, no correspondence between Stoker and Vambéry has survived.

There is every reason to believe that Vambéry was one of the people from whom Stoker developed his character Abraham Van Helsing. It may be that Vambéry informed Stoker about **Vlad the Impaler,** the historical Dracula. Stoker acknowledges in the novel a debt to Vambéry with a passing mention of him placed in the mouth of Van Helsing:

> I have asked my friend Arminius, of Buda-Pesth University, to make his record; and, from all the means that are, he (Vambéry) tells me of what he (Dracula) has been. He must, indeed, have been that Viovode Dracula who won his name against the Turk. . .

It is noteworthy, however, that no mention of Vlad is made in any of Vambéry's books.

Vambéry's last work was another autobiographical volume, *The Story of My Struggles* (1904).

THE VAMP

Sources:

Adler, Lory, and Richard Dalby. *The Dervish of Windsor Castle.* London: Bachman and Turner, 1979. 512 pp.

Stoker, Bram. *The Essential Dracula.* Edited by Raymond McNally and Radu Florescu. New York: Mayflower Books, 1979. 320 pp.

Vambéry, Arminius. *Arminius Vambéry: His Life and Adventures.* New York: Cassell and Company, 1983. 370 pp.

———. *Hungary in Ancient, Medieval, and Modern Times.* London: T. F. Unwin, 1886. 453 pp.

———. *The Story of My Struggles: The Memoirs of Arminius Vambéry.* 2 vols. London: T. F. Unwin, 1904.

———. *Travels in Central Asia.* London: J. Murray, 1864. 493 pp.

THE VAMP

The vamp, a popular stereotypical figure of the silent film, developed from extension of the vampire myth into an analogy of male/female relationships. Both psychological and feminist interpretations of the myth emphasized the maleness of the vampire legend. It was a projection of male fears, goals, and attitudes toward the world. The role of the vamp was established in large part by "The Vampire", a short poem by Rudyard Kipling:

> A fool there was and he made his prayer
> (Even as you and I)
> To a rag and a bone and a hank of hair
> (We call her the woman who did not care)
> But the fool he called her his lady fair—
> (Even as you or I!)
>
> Oh, the years we waste and the tears we waste
> and the work of our head and hand
> Belong to the woman who did not know
> Belong to the woman who did not know
> (And now we know that she never could know)
> And did not understand!
>
> A fool there was and his goods he spent
> (Even as you and I)
> Honour and faith and a sure intent
> (And it wasn't the least what the lady meant)
> But a fool must follow his natural bent
> (Even as you and I!)

The poem, inspired by a famous painting by Philip Burne-Jones, in turn inspired a play by Porter Emerson Brown, *A Fool There Was,* which in turn was made into a movie by the Fox Film Corporation. The story involved a triangle composed of a husband, his wife, and a vampire. The husband, John Schulyer, was a lawyer who had been sent on a diplomatic mission for the president of the United States. Off in a scenic land, he encountered a vampiress, who injected herself into his life. His wife reasserted herself at various points, first with a letter, which the vampiress tore up. Later, Schulyer tried to cable his wife, but was blocked. So tight did the vampiress's hold become that, upon Schulyer's return to the States, he provided a townhouse for her. Meanwhile, he was degenerating into a hopeless alcoholic. The wife made one last attempt to reclaim her husband, but as she was leading him away, the vampiress appeared, and the man lost all desire to leave. Because he had abandoned his wife for the temptress, his will had left him and he was destroyed.

A Fool There Was became an important film in many respects. It was the film through which Fox, then a small company, successfully fought the monopoly of General Film. It also introduced Theda Bara to the screen as the vamp. Theda Bara would become the embodiment of the vamp in a series of pictures for Fox. She provided a powerful image for the public to place beside that of the virtuous woman under attack by evil cultural forces that had been so powerfully cultivated by D. W. Griffith at General.

The vamp was the dark shadow of the Victorian virtuous woman. She was immoral, tainted with powerful, dark sexuality. Her power derived from her ability to release in males similar strong but latent sexual energies, strictly contained by modern cultural restrictions. She attached herself to men and sapped their vitality. Her image was carefully constructed. She wore tight revealing black clothes, sometimes decorated with either spiders or snakes. Her nails were long and cut to a point. In a day when women rarely used tobacco in public, she frequently smoked cigarettes from a long holder. Her demeanor suggested that she was foreign, either from continental Europe or the Middle East.

Theda Bara (born Theodosia Goodman in Cincinnati, Ohio) largely defined the vamp for the American public. In cooperation with Fox, through the second decade of this century she carefully created a public persona. Fox's role marked the first attempt by a studio to manufacture a star's image in such depth. The name Theda Bara was an anagram for Arab Death. Various stories were circulated about her suggesting a mysterious origin in the Middle East, the product of an affair between exotic mates. Supposedly, she had been weaned on snake's blood, and tribesmen had fought over her. Studio publicity compared her to **Elizabeth Bathory,** the seventeenth-century blood countess. When Theda Bara appeared in public, she often pretended not to speak English and traveled with her African footmen in a white limousine.

Once developed, the vamp persona proved a continuing interest. Theda Bara's image passed to the likes of Nita Naldi, who starred in *Blood and Sand,* the 1922 Rudolph Valentino film, and Greta Garbo, who became a star with her 1927 film *Flesh and the Devil.* Garbo's vampish role was spelled out for those in the audience who could not pick it up otherwise by a minister who told the hero that the devil created women with beautiful bodies so that they could tempt men in a fleshly manner when they failed to reach them through more spiritual means. Garbo was credited with humanizing the vamp's role and thus contributing to the destruction of the image, at least as it had previously existed. The vamp evolved into the *femme fatale,* the temptress who still appears in a wide variety of settings in motion pictures.

◄
THEDA BARA AS THE VAMP.

Sources:

Higashi, Sumiko. *Virgins, Vamps, and Flappers: The American Silent Movie Heroine.* Montreal: Eden Press Women's Publications, 1978. 276 pp.

Kuhn, Annette. *The Women's Companion to International Films.* London: Virago, 1990. 464 pp. Reprint. *Women in Film: An International Guide.* New York: Fawcett Columbine, 1991. 500 pp.

VAMPIRA

Vampira is the persona of actress Maila Nurmi. The character was created in 1954 when Nurmi was a horror show hostess at KABC-TV in Los Angeles. After a two-year run she moved to KHJ-TV. Nurmi's enduring fame came from her joining **Bela Lugosi** in the classic cult movie *Plan 9 from Outer Space* (1956). They played the initial two vampires that the space invaders hoped to create in their plan to take over Earth. After the run of her television show, she also appeared in several other movies, including two vampire films, *The Magic Sword* (1964) and *Orgy of the Night* (1966), the latter put together by *Plan 9*'s director Edward Wood, Jr..

MAILA NURMI AS VAMPIRA APPEARED WITH BELA LUGOSI IN *PLAN 9 FROM OUTER SPACE.*

Nurmi also appeared in several other nonvampire movies, and for a while she operated a boutique in Hollywood. In the 1980s Nurmi sued Cassandra Peterson for stealing her Vampira persona to create the persona **Elvira**; however, the suit came to nought.

Sources:

"Maila 'Vampira' Nurmi on Wood, Dean and 'Bunny'." *Hollywood Book and Poser News* 11 (October 1992): 3-4.

THE VAMPIRE

A vampire was a peculiar kind of revenant, a dead person who had returned to life and continued a form of existence through drinking the blood of the living. In popular thought, the vampire was considered to be "undead," having completed earthly life but still being tied to that life and not yet welcomed by the realm of the dead. The vampire is distinguished from the ghost, a disembodied spirit, in that the vampire inhabited in an animated body. It was distinguished from the **ghoul** in that the ghoul had no intelligent control, being guided solely by its hunger, and feasted off the body of its victim rather than just the blood. Consuming blood was the most characteristic activity of vampires, so the term *vampire* has also been used to describe many mythological creatures who drink blood as well as living persons who engage in similar activities. Finally, the term has been used to describe people (and spirits) who engage in **psychic vampirism,** the process of draining the life force or energy (rather than the blood) of other people.

THE EIGHTEENTH CENTURY VAMPIRE CONTROVERSY: In the eighteenth century, Western scholars for the first time considered the question of the existence of vampires as something more than just another element of the vast supernatural world of rural folk culture. The controversy was set off by a series of incidents of vampire hysteria that occurred in East Prussia in 1721 and in the lands of the Austro-Hungarian Empire from 1725 through 1732. These cases culminated in the famous events surrounding **Arnold Paul,** a retired Austrian soldier who had settled in Serbia and was accused of being the source of an outbreak of vampirism in his community. Several of these cases became the object of formal government investigations and reports, and a hastily prepared volume on Paul sold widely around Europe.

The publication of the Paul book led to no less than a dozen treatises and four dissertations, and the controversy over him lasted for a generation. It eventually involved some of the most famous scholars of Europe, including Diderot and Voltaire. The question of the existence of vampires was argued on legal, theological, and scientific grounds. The question became more than academic in that villagers, affected by a belief that vampires were active in their community, opened graves and mutilated or destroyed any bodies showing characteristics believed to indicate vampirism. Although some members of the scholarly community attempted to defend the existence of vampires, the majority concluded that evidence suggested they did not exist. The latter cited a host of natural phenomena that accounted for vampire reports, such as premature burial and rabies (which causes an insatiable thirst in anyone infected). They also attributed the reports to theological polemics in areas where a Roman Catholic Austrian government had been imposed on an Orthodox population. The most careful defense of vampires came from French biblical scholar **Dom Augustin Calmet** in his 1746 *Dissertations sur les Apparitions des Anges des Démons et des Esprits, et sur les revenants, et Vampires de Hungrie, de Boheme, de Moravie, et de Silésie.*

The publication of Calmet's treatise, given his reputation as a scholar, initiated a second stage of the academic controversy, which was largely settled by the end of the 1830s. Even the Vatican ignored Calmet, its opinion that vampires did not exist having been set by the conclusions of Archbishop **Giuseppe Davanzati** published just two years before Calmet's book. A decade after Calmet's book appeared—and in the midst of the controversy it sparked—a new wave of vampire hysteria occurred in Silesia. Austrian Empress Maria Theresa sent her personal physician to investigate the incident. In his report, Dr. Gerhard Van Swieten ridiculed the practice of exhuming and executing purported vampires as "posthumous magic." As a result, in 1755 and 1756 Maria Theresa forbade church and village authorities from taking any action in cases of reported vampires. Only officials of the central government could respond to such cases. The actions of the Austrian empress finished what was left of any remaining public debate.

REAL VAMPIRES IN THE NINETEENTH CENTURY?: From the middle of the seventeenth century until the second half of the nineteenth, no serious attempt to prove the existence of vampires, at least in their folkloric form, was made. An attempt to defend the folkloric vampire was launched in the mid-1800's by the spiritualist community. Spokespersons who emerged during the first generation of spiritualism in Europe, where the tales of vampires were most prevalent, offered a new rationale for vampires—psychic vampirism. In the 1860s, **Z. J. Pierart** suggested that the phenomena described in the folkloric reports of vampires could be attributed to the astral bodies of either the living or dead, which fed off the life energy of the living. The astral body, however elusive, provided an agent for transmitting vitality to the dead and accounted for bodies that, though lying buried for some weeks or months, did not decay and when uncovered manifest numerous signs of a continuing life. Pierart's suggestion, which had precursors in previous occult writers, was picked up by spiritualist and theosophical exponents, and accounts of "true vampires" began to appear in occult journals.

Typical of these reports was one of the many published by theosophist **Franz Hartmann** in the 1890s. The story concerned an alcoholic who had been rejected by a woman with whom he was in love. Dejected, he committed suicide by shooting himself. Soon afterward, the woman began to complain of vampiric attacks from a specter in the form of the recently dead suitor. She could not see him but was aware of his presence. Doctors diagnosed her as an hysteric but could do little to relieve her symptoms. She finally submitted herself to an exorcism conducted by a person who accepted her explanation of vampirism. After the exorcism, the attacks ceased. Today, various psychological theories, shorn of any need to posit the existence of vampires, could account for all of the woman's symptoms, and steps to deal with her unresolved guilt over the suitor's suicide could be pursued. However, these were as yet unavailable to the medical world, and the spiritualist perspective gained its share of support.

Increasing reports of vampirism, including accounts of the living vampirizing their acquaintances, at times seemingly without any conscious awareness of what they were doing, led to the discarding of the more supernatural spiritualist explanations of vampirism, in which astral bodies attacked the living. Such theories, although maintained in some occult movements, were for the most part replaced with references to "psychic sponges", people who were themselves low on psychic energy, manifest by frequent periods of fatigue, but who in the presence of high-energy people had the ability to take energy from them. Many people seemed to know such psychic sponges, individuals who regain their vitality in the company of others even as their companions experience a distinct loss of energy and interest in immediate activities. Although the notion of psychic sponges was a popular one, at least in different metaphysical and psychic-oriented groups, it is extremely difficult to document and has produced only a minuscule literature.

VAMPIRISM AS BLOOD FETISH: While the more benign incidents of psychic vampirism were being reported, accounts of vampire **crime** began to appear. In the 1920s two cases of serial killers with vampiric tendencies shocked the people of Europe. In 1924 they read of **Fritz Haarmann** of Hanover, Germany, who killed no fewer than 24 young men. He earned the appellation ''vampire'' killer by biting the neck of those he murdered and drinking some of their blood. Five years later, **Peter Kürten** of Düsseldorf went on a killing spree, later confessing that he received a sexual thrill and release while watching blood spurt from his victims.

Rare accounts of serial killers with some form of blood fetish were also reported. One of the more gruesome concerned a series of murders of prostitutes in Stockholm, Sweden, in the period from 1982 to 1987. During this period at least seven prostitutes disappeared from the streets, and their bodies were later discovered surgically dismembered and drained of blood. Eventually arrested and tried in the case were two physicians, Teet Haerm and Thomas Allgren.

Haerm's arrest shocked many. He was the senior police medical examiner and one of the leading forensic pathologists in the world. His articles had appeared in several professional publications, including the *Lancet,* a prominent British medical journal. He had even been called in to examine the remains of several of the women he was later accused of murdering. Allgren, Haerm's best friend, was a dermatologist. In the end, Allgren confessed and gave testimony at Haerm's trial. According to Allgren, Haerm had an intense desire to brutalize and kill prostitutes. To justify the satiation of that desire, the two had started on a righteous crusade to rid Stockholm of streetwalkers. However, Allgren also discovered that Haerm had a lust for blood and gore and that after the killings he drained and drank the blood of his victims.

Eventually, Allgren was turned in by his daughter, who claimed that he had sexually molested her. In the process of talking about her experience, she also described in some detail a murder of one of the prostitutes she had witnessed. The testimonies of Allgren and his daughter were heard at a 1988 trial in which the latter testified that blood lust led Haerm into pathology but he eventually found the work on bodies less than satisfying. Then he began his killing spree.

Both Haerm and Allgren were convicted in a 1988 trial and sentenced to life imprisonment. However, their convictions were overturned, and in a retrial they were found not guilty, even though the judge wrote in his decision that there was reasonable evidence that they were guilty. Both defendants were freed.

Another recently publicized case of a ''vampire'' killer concerned Richard Chase of Sacramento, California. The documented nefarious deeds committed by Chase began in December 1977 with the shooting of Ambrose Griffin. A month later, on January 23, 1978, Chase shot Theresa Wallin, after which he mutilated her body with a knife. In that process he collected her blood in a cup and consumed it. A week after the Wallin attack, he killed four people at Evelyn Miroth's home, including Miroth, whom he also mutilated and whose blood he also drank. Miroth's baby nephew, who was visiting her, was taken home by Chase, who killed him, drank his blood, and tossed his body in the garbage.

According to Chase, he believed that he had blood poisoning and needed blood. He had in the past hunted animals (beginning with small animals such as rabbits and cats and moving on to cows). He killed the animals and drank their blood, and his messiness had led to several prior encounters with the authorities. After such an encounter in 1977, he made a decision to start killing people. A year earlier he had spent time in a mental facility and had manifest a mania over blood. His fellow patients had begun to call him Dracula. Arrested soon after the Miroth murder, he was convicted of the six killings. He died in prison, where he committed suicide in 1980 at age 31.

The examples of Haarmann, Kürten, and Haerm, are only tangential to what traditionally has been thought of as vampirism. They are serial killers with, among other problems, a blood fetish. The blood was not the object of their quest, and the drinking of blood was just one of the more gruesome (and somewhat superficial) practices in which they engaged. Chase was somewhat different and more closely approached true vampirism. Although he was not seeking blood to prolong his life, he sought regular ingestions of blood to counteract the effects of poison he believed he was receiving. In the end, however, his vampiric activity also fell into the serial killing mode, the blood lust being peripheral to the killings.

SOME REAL VAMPIRES EMERGE: During the 1960s, in part due to the **Hammer Films**, Dracula movies, and the *Dark Shadows* television series, public interest in vampires increased noticeably, and the first of the present-day vampire fan clubs and interest groups was founded. By the early 1970s the **Count Dracula Fan Club,** the **Vampire Information Exchange,** and the Vampire Studies Society (now **Vampire Studies**) had formed in the United States and the **Vampire Research Society** and the **Dracula Society** soon followed in England. As these groups emerged, the leaders began to encounter people who actually claimed to be vampires. In the beginning, devoted as they were to the literary vampire (and not really believing that such things as vampires existed), leaders of the vampire interest groups largely discounted the stories. Among those who did take the reports seriously were Scott Rogo, Sean Manchester, founder of the Vampire Research Society in London, and Stephen Kaplan, founder of the **Vampire Research Center** in New York.

Rogo, Manchester, and Kaplan each began their research from a point of prior interest with psychic phenomena. During the late 1960s Rogo tried to interest the American Society for Psychical Research in vampirism but was unable to budge them from their more central concerns. Most parapsychologists thought that their field was already far enough out on the fringe. Forced to choose, Rogo soon suppressed his interest in vampirism and during the 1970s and 1980s made his own contribution as a writer, attempting to bring psychical research into the mainstream of the scientific community.

Sean Manchester's Vampire Research Society grew out of his previous leadership role in an occult investigations bureau. The society investigates all aspects of "supernatural vampire phenomena," a task that has led to a variety of research projects, including the famous **Highgate vampire** and the Kirklees vampire projects.

Stephen Kaplan founded the Vampire Research Center in 1972. His first interview of alleged vampires was with a couple who introduced him to the nocturnal world of vampires, their alternative sexual practices (in this case sadomasochism), and the existence of donors, people who (for a price) allow vampires to drink their blood. From his early encounters, Kaplan began to develop a working definition of vampires. They were people who met three criteria: they need regular quantities of blood, they believe that the blood will prolong their life and help them remain youthful, and they often find the blood and its consumption to be sexually arousing.

Over the years, Kaplan had the opportunity to meet and correspond with other vampires and was able to fill out his picture of them. They do not drink great quantities of blood—only a few ounces a day—but they need that blood daily and will go to extreme measures to receive it. Denied it, they become irritable, depressed, fatigued, and somewhat aggressive. They tend to be nocturnal in their habits, and many profess to be extremely sensitive to light. Otherwise, they appear normal and dress in such a way as not to call attention to themselves. To obtain blood, vampires often engage in various forms of sadomasochistic behavior that lead to some bloodletting. They often exchange sexual favors for blood. Some join groups that engage in ritual blood-drinking. If unable to obtain a willing donor, they will, according to their own testimony, occasionally attack a victim, but, as a rule, will not kill for blood.

The vampires Kaplan studied were neither psychic nor supernatural beings. They were, apart from their blood-drinking activities, somewhat normal human beings. Some professed to be far older than their youthful appearance suggested, but their true age was rarely verifiable.

Above and beyond the relatively small number of vampires Kaplan encountered (fewer than 100 in two decades), he discovered hundreds of people he described as vampirelike individuals. These people seek to imitate vampires in various ways to gain some of the positive qualities associated with vampiric existence, from immortality to the ability to dominate others—sexually and otherwise. As early as the 1970s he was able to locate people who had adopted the vampire persona by wearing black clothes or altering their teeth. They drank blood, but, not liking the taste, they put it in a fruit juice cocktail.

Many of the people attracted to vampirism find themselves drawn by the eroticism of the vampires' life. Vampirism, especially in its literary and cinematic expression, is inherently sexual. The vampire's bite has often been compared to sexual intercourse, and blood likened to semen. Worldwide over the centuries, blood acquired both a sexual and religious connotation, but the dominant Western Christian religion retained the religious meaning without the sexual element. In the activities of many nonconventional persuasions, such as the contemporary sex magic practiced by the followers of Aleister Crowley, the sexual and religious elements of blood have been reunited. A few have united sex and blood-drinking in more sinister forms.

In the process of his research, Kaplan discovered just how difficult was the area on which he decided to focus. Not only did he face tremendous ridicule, but fear of the legal and medical authorities and an intolerant public caused many of the subjects of his study to back away from any situations that might threaten their anonymity, classify them as lawbreakers, or question their mental competence. No real comprehensive and systematic study of vampires has been possible, and knowledge of them still relies on anecdotes related by their few spokespersons. Most important, no medical data of the kind that could provide any evidence of physical traits shared by people who claim to be vampires is available.

REAL VAMPIRES IN THE 1990s: In the decade since *Vampires Are* was published, a **gothic** subculture has emerged across America. The gothic life is centered on eerie, atmospheric, gothic rock music and nightclubs and theaters that regularly provide a stage for gothic bands to perform. Individual ''goths'' emulate the nocturnal vampiric life, and many assume a vampiric persona, complete with dark clothes, pale makeup, and artificial **fangs.** They also advocate life-styles based on androgyny, so central to the character **Lestat de Lioncourt,** the popular vampire star of the novels of **Anne Rice.** Almost all forms of sexual expression among consenting adults, from sadomasochism to blood fetishism, are welcomed. Thus, the gothic subculture has created a space in which self-designated vampires can move somewhat freely and mingle without anyone questioning their nonconventional habits.

At the same time, the voices of ''nongoths'' who profess to be vampires also continue to be heard. Carol Page, in a far less systematic way than Kaplan, has written of her experiences with contemporary blood-drinkers in *Bloodlust: Conversations with Real Vampires* (1991). Page, who interviewed numerous ''vampires,'' reached many of the same conclusions as Kaplan:

> The blood they drink has no effect on them physiologically. It does not keep them young and they do not physically need it, although some vampires believe they do. It doesn't make them high, except psychologically, or give them nutrition, since human blood passes through the digestive system without being absorbed. They do not have superhuman strength. They cannot turn into bats and wolves. Some sleep in coffins during the day and dress in black capes or indulge in other affectations inspired by fictional vampires. (p. 15)

Page and Kaplan, as well as other sources, have made the point that vampires—that is, blood-drinkers, do exist and have described their world in some detail. Furthermore, they suggest that these vampires live a camouflaged life in the midst of more conventional society and that, except within the cordial atmosphere of the gothic world or the nocturnal world of their own kind, they do not drop their conforming persona or allow the nature of their life to be known by any they do not fully trust.

However, there are enough of them, some of whom live relatively open and accessible lives, that few serious researchers would have much difficulty in making contact with them.

Sources:

Biondi, Ray, and Walt Hecox. *The Dracula Killer*. New York: Pocket Books, 1992. 212 pp.

Calmet, Dom Augustin. *Dissertations sur les Apparitions des Anges des Démons et des Esprits, et sur les revenants, et Vampires de Hungrie, de Boheme, de Moravie, et de Silésie*. Paris: 1746. Reprinted as *The Phantom World*. 2 vols. London: R. Bentley, 1850.

Glut, Donald F. *True Vampires of History*. New York: HC Publishers, 1971. 191 pp.

Kaplan, Stephen. *Pursuit of Premature Gods and Contemporary Vampires*. Port Jefferson Station, NY: Charles A. Moreno, 1976. 260 pp.

———. *Vampires Are*. Palm Springs, CA: ETC Publications, 1984. 191 pp.

Monaco, Richard, and Bill Burt. *The Dracula Syndrome*. New York: Avon Books, 1993. 167 pp.

Page, Carol. *Bloodlust: Conversations with Real Vampires*. New York: HarperCollins, 1991. Reprint. New York: Dell, 1992. 214 pp.

VAMPIRDZHIRA *See:* VAMPIRE HUNTERS

VAMPIRE ARCHIVES

Vampire Archives is a monthly newsletter founded in December 1989 by Jule Ghoul to keep up with the latest information on vampire books, shows, movies, music, and fandom. Ghoul considers herself a night person and has been interested in vampires since seeing her first vampire movie at age 10. Three years later, after seeing **Bela Lugosi**'s *Dracula,* she became obsessed with the subject. Along with editing the newsletter, Ghoul is working on several vampire novels. She has founded Ghoul's Gallery as a mail order business for vampire literature and **paraphernalia.** *Vampire Archives* and Ghoul's Gallery can be contacted at 2926 W. Leland Ave., Chicago, IL 60625.

VAMPIRE BATS *See:* BATS, VAMPIRE

VAMPIRE BRIDES *See:* BRIDES, VAMPIRE

VAMPIRE CHARACTERISTICS *See:* CHARACTERISTICS OF THE VAMPIRE

THE VAMPIRE GUILD

The Vampire Guild of Dorset, England, grew out of the childhood fascination with vampires of founder Phill M. White. White had collected vampire materials during his teen years, and officially founded the guild in August 1990 as a vampire interest group. Its primary goal is to bring people together who share the founder's interest in vampires and who wish to meet and correspond with others of like mind. As the membership has expanded, the concerns of the guild have broadened.

One of White's purposes in founding the guild was to explore some of the lesser-known aspects of vampirism. The guild has investigated such obscure cases of vampirism such as those of William Doggett, the Tarrant Valley Vampire, and the Black Lady of Durweston, both from Dorset. The research files of these cases sit in the guild's vampire archive. Access to archive information is available to members of the guild and any serious researchers.

The Vampire Guild has an international membership. It may be contacted through its founder/president at The Vampire Guild, 82, Rip Croft, Portland, Dorset DT5 2EE, United Kingdom. Overseas correspondents should include an International Reply Coupon. The guild publishes a quarterly journal, *Crimson*.

VAMPIRE HUNTERS

In most societies that have believed in vampirism, the process of detecting and **destroying the vampire** has often been carried out by an informal group of people threatened by the presence of vampires in their community, but occasionally has been placed in the hands of a specialized vampire hunter. Several cultures, especially those in the southern Balkans, assigned specific people the task of hunting and destroying vampires. Most famous of the vampire hunters was the ***dhampir,*** who was believed to be the physical son of a vampire and who lived and worked among the **Gypsies** and the **southern Slavs.** The Gypsies thought of the vampire as a very sexy creature who often returned to its lover and engaged in sexual intercourse. His seed was still potent and occasionally a pregnancy resulted from the vampire's activity. The male progeny of a vampire, the *dhampir,* was believed to have peculiar powers in seeing the oft-invisible vampire and destroying it.

A *dhampir* could become a professional or semiprofessional vampire hunter and charge a village for his services. According to surviving accounts, the *dhampir* began his work in a village by telling those who hired him that there was a bad smell in the air. He would then appear to attempt to locate its source. He might, for example, take off his shirt and look through the sleeve as if looking through a telescope. He would describe the shape that the invisible vampire had taken. Once he located the vampire, he might engage it in a dramatic hand-to-hand fight or simply shoot it. Once killed, the vampire stank even more and might leave a pool of blood on the ground. Sometimes it could not be killed, in which case the *dhampir* would attempt to run it off to another village. Among the more notable *dhampirs* was one named Murat, who operated in the 1950s in the Kosovo-Metohija area of Serbia.

In **Bulgaria** the vampire hunters were called *vampirdzhija* or *djadadjii*. They tended to operate in a more traditional fashion. Their main task seemed to have been to locate the particular grave that held the resting vampire's body. In this task they used

PUBLICITY PHOTO FOR *BUFFY
THE VAMPIRE SLAYER.*

an icon, a holy picture in the Eastern Orthodox tradition. After locating the vampire, the villagers would impale it or burn the body.

THE VAMPIRE HUNTER IN LITERATURE: In literature the "professional" vampire hunter assumed his place as the archenemy of the literary vampire in **Bram Stoker**'s *Dracula* (1897). Dr. **Abraham Van Helsing**, the real hero of the novel, emerged as the bearer of knowledge about the mysterious threat that has invaded Western civilization and heralded the means of destroying it. In the novel it was his task to organize the cadre of men who together tracked Dracula to his lair and finally destroyed him.

When **Hamilton Deane** brought Dracula to the stage, he chose the part of Van Helsing for himself as preferable to that of the title character, which went to Raymond Huntley. Deane continued to portray Van Helsing for many years as his company toured England. When the play arrived on Broadway, one of the more memorable Van Helsings stepped into the role. Edward Van Sloan brought the image of a quiet physician capable of offering a calming bedside manner to the role. He went on to play the part in the 1931 movie with costar **Bela Lugosi.** In the original version of the film,

Van Kelsing (Van Sloan) makes the closing speech that followed the last act of the play, stepping out to remind the audience prior to their departure that such things as vampires did exist. This speech was cut from later releases of the film because **Universal Pictures** thought it would be taken too seriously by religious groups. Van Sloan also assumed the Van Helsing role in the sequel, *Dracula's Daughter*, in which he was accused of murdering Dracula. At the same time that *Dracula* was filmed, a Spanish version was also shot, with Eduardo Arozamena taking the role of Van Helsing.

After Edward Van Sloan, no one again was really identified with the hunter-killer role until it was taken by **Peter Cushing,** playing opposite **Christopher Lee** in the title role, in a **Hammer Films** production of *The Horror of Dracula* (1958). A veteran actor of both the stage and screen, Cushing brought to the role the persona of a persistent modern scientist who emitted confidence owing to his knowledge. He returned to the Van Helsing part and portrayed him (and some modern-day descendants) in *The Brides of Dracula* (1959), *Dracula AD 1972* (1972), *Satanic Rites of Dracula* (aka *Count Dracula and His Vampire Bride*, 1973), and *The Legend of the Seven Golden Vampires* (1974), all for Hammer. He played the actual Van Helsing in five films, and transferred his Van Helsing persona to other parts in which he portrayed the intellectual-scientific man of knowledge.

No one since has had the commanding presence that Cushing brought to the role. However, several outstanding actors have taken up the challenge and offered commendable portrayals, including Laurence Olivier, who tracked **Frank Langella** in *Dracula* **(1979),** and, most recently, Anthony Hopkins, who tracked **Gary Oldman** in *Bram Stoker's Dracula* (1992).

Sources:

Eyles, Allen, Robert Adkinson, and Nicholas Fry. *The House of Horror: The Story of Hammer Films.* London: Lorimer, 1973. 127 pp.

Skal, David J. *Hollywood Gothic: The Tangled Web of Dracula from Novel to Stage and Screen.* New York: W. W. Norton & Company, 1990. 242 pp.

Trigg, E. B. *Gypsy Demons and Divinities: The Magical and Supernatural Practices of the Gypsies.* London: Sheldon Press, 1973. 238 pp.

Vukanovic, T. P. "The Vampire." In Jan L. Perkowski, ed., *Vampires of the Slavs.* Cambridge, MA: Slavica Publishers, 1976, pp. 201-34.

THE VAMPIRE INFORMATION EXCHANGE

The Vampire Information Exchange, founded by Eric Held and Dorothy Nixon in 1978, is a correspondence network for people interested in vampirism. Nixon had been interested in vampires since her high school days, when she was shown a copy of **Donald Glut**'s *True Vampires of History.* She became interested in the question of the existence of real vampires and began a search that led her into association with Stephen Kaplan of the **Vampire Research Center.** Held was brought into the world of vampire fandom after listening to a radio interview with Kaplan in October 1978. The next day he called Kaplan, who put him in touch with Nixon. During that phone

◀

VAMPIRE INFORMATION
EXCHANGE'S FOUNDER ERIC
S. HELD.

conversation, they discovered their mutual interests. They began to correspond, and by October 1979 they had been joined by six others. At that point, Held and Nixon began an irregular newsletter to simplify the circulation of general information, thus initiating the Vampire Information Exchange.

Among the early correspondents were **Jeanne Youngson** of the **Count Dracula Fan Club,** Gordon R. Guy, editor of *The Castle Dracula Quarterly,* and **Martin V. Riccardo,** then president of the Vampire Studies Society.

The *VIE Newsletter,* produced bimonthly, is a chatty journal for active members and is very information oriented. It carries reviews of recent books and movies, news about vampire publications, and bibliographies of various kinds of vampire literature. In recent years it has put out an annual *Calendar of Vampire Events,* and Held has published *The Bibliography of Vampire Literature.* For information on membership, send $4.00 to Eric Held, Vampire Information Exchange, PO Box 290328, Brooklyn, NY 11229-0328.

Sources:

Held, Eric, ed. *The 1992 Vampire Bibliography of Fiction and Non-Fiction.* Brooklyn, NY: Vampire Information Exchange, 1992. 16 pp.
————. *1993 Calendar of Vampire Events.* Brooklyn, NY: Vampire Information Exchange, 1993. 14 pp.

Vampire Junction

Started in 1991, *Vampire Junction* is a vampire fanzine devoted to the promotion of vampire fiction, poetry, and art. The editor, Candy M. Cosner, had been interested in vampires since her teen years, and her fascination with the subject resulted in a quality fanzine that is interesting and affordable. Cosner does not believe vampires exist, at least at the present. She has hypothesized that they did exist at one time as an offshoot of human evolution. They were not supernatural, just humanoids who had an inability to digest solid food, a sensitivity to sunlight, and a longer life span. They were probably killed off by humans who feared them, but not before they became the source for the world's vampire myths. *Vampire Junction* can be contacted c/o Books, 505 NW 13th St., Gainesville, FL 32601.

The Vampire Legion

The Vampire Legion is an Australian vampire society that was founded in November 1992. It publishes both a newsletter and a bimonthly fanzine, *Dark Times,* which includes poetry, fiction, and articles.

The Vampire Legion can be contacted c/o The Baroness, PO Box 4202, Melbourne University Post Office, Victoria, Australia, 3052.

Vampire Research Center

The Vampire Research Center was founded in 1972 by Stephen Kaplan.

In 1971 Kaplan also founded the Parapsychology Institute of America and since 1974 has been a popular lecturer in parapsychology for the New York City Board of Education, Forest Hills Adult Division. He attained some level of fame in the mid 1970s when he investigated the reported haunting of a house on Long Island at Amityville, New York. Although the Amityville haunting was promoted in several books and a popular movie, Kaplan was the first to denounce it as a hoax, a view now generally accepted in the parapsychological community. Further accounts of his parapsychological endeavors can be found in the several volumes of *True Tales of the Unknown* and a number of other descriptive works on psychical research.

In Kaplan's first book, *Pursuit of Premature Gods and Contemporary Vampires,* which appeared in 1976, he treats vampirology as a branch of parapsychology, that branch of psychology dealing with paranormal experiences. He begins with the idea that some reality may lie behind every myth or legend, in this case vampires.

Although he had lectured around the country and appeared on many talk shows over the previous decade, many people first heard of Kaplan in 1984 with the publication of his second book, *Vampires Are*. The book describes a decade of research on people who defined themselves as real vampires. After obtaining a telephone listing for the Vampire Research Center, Kaplan began to receive phone calls from people claiming to be vampires, and he later interviewed some of them personally. In this manner he was able to build relationships with what became a network of people with similar interests around the world. These contacts increased dramatically after a mention in a 1977 *Playboy Magazine* article. He also began to receive calls about vampire attacks from people who claimed to have been victimized.

Kaplan's research led him to reformulate his concept of vampires, abandoning the common notion that they are the "undead" and have returned to take blood from the living. The vampires he discovered were otherwise normal living people who felt a need to drink blood every day and who became irritable, aggressive, or frantic if they were unable to get their daily supply. Underlying their need was a strong belief that blood kept them youthful and extended their life; if their supply were cut off, they believed they would age or even die. The number of vampires Kaplan interviewed who fit this description was quite small. He reported meeting fewer than 10 by the time his book appeared in 1984, and to date the great majority of people who are either reported to the center as vampires or themselves claim to be vampires fit into a much larger category, the "vampirelike" people. The vampirelike people are individuals who adopt vampire-associated habits (e.g., they sleep in a coffin, wear black clothes, work at night, or occasionally drink blood) in the hope of possibly becoming a vampire. Some are sexually aroused by blood and the idea of drinking it.

In 1981 Kaplan conducted the first official vampire census. Of some 480 questionnaires distributed, 31 were returned and 12 fit the description of a true vampire. Additionally, nine letters were received without the questionnaire from people deemed to be true vampires. Thus, 21 vampires were reported in the census. Kaplan concluded that there were probably many more. In the meantime, apart from the formal census, he was contacted by phone and mail by other people whom he noted to be vampires. A follow-up study in 1983 found 35 additional vampires. Given the number he had been able to locate through his census and other contacts, he estimated there were 150 to 200 actual vampires in North America. By 1992 he projected an estimated 850 vampires worldwide, of which 40 lived in California.

As a result of some negative response to his book, Kaplan largely separated himself from other vampire oriented organizations. In keeping with his career in education and his association with the State University of New York, he has devoted himself to his research and thus has had little time for vampire fans. The Vampire Research Center is currently headed by Kaplan and his wife, Roxanne Salch Kaplan, the associate director. It may be contacted at Box 252, Elmhurst, NY 11373.

Sources:

"Dr. Kaplan and the Vampire Epidemic." *Journal of Vampirology* 1, 2 (1984): 20-22.
Edmondson, Brad. "The Vampire Census." *American Demographics* 10, 10 (October 1988): 13.
Guiley, Rosemary Ellen. *Vampires Among Us.* New York: Pocket Books, 1991. 270 pp.

Jarvis, Sharon, ed. *True Tales of the Unknown: Beyond Reality.* Vols. 1, 2, and 3. New York: Bantam Books, 1985, 1989, and 1991.

Kaplan, Stephen. *Pursuit of Premature Gods and Contemporary Vampires.* Port Jefferson Station, NY: Charles A. Moreno, 1976. 260 pp.

——. *Vampires Are.* Palm Springs, CA: ETC Publications, 1984. 191 pp.

Ratliff, Rick. "He Thirsts for Vampire Knowledge." *Miami Herald,* July 13, 1977.

VAMPIRE RESEARCH SOCIETY

The Vampire Research Society was founded February 2, 1970 by Sean Manchester to investigate all aspects of supernatural vampire phenomena. At the time of its founding, Manchester was the director of an occult investigation bureau, now defunct. During the first two decades of its existence, the society was an open membership group and claimed approximately 300 members. However, in 1990 (by which time there were several other vampire interest groups functioning in England) the society decided to restrict membership and to concentrate on practical research. It confines itself to investigating possible paranormal manifestations, and does not have ties to the larger vampire subculture. The society is unconcerned with medical disorders, individuals wanting to become vampires, and nonconventional behavior (such as blood-drinking) associated with vampires.

Manchester is the primate of the Catholic Apostolic Church of the Holy Grail, a small liturgical jurisdiction of the Old Catholic belief and practice. He was consecrated as a bishop by Rt. Rev. Illtyd Thomas, the primate of the Celtic Catholic Church in 1991. Manchester takes vampirism very seriously as a supernatural occult phenomena and has little in common with vampire enthusiasts, who he feels are playing with fire and, however unwittingly, promoting evil. The secular press, often not comprehending Manchester's faith and his own understanding of the vampire problem, have turned him into a media personality, although coverage of him is often tongue-in-cheek.

The society and its founder came under public scrutiny on several occasions as a result of Manchester's investigation of manifestations and occurrences attributed to what was termed the **Highgate vampire** at London's Highgate Cemetery. Subsequently, Manchester wrote a book concerning his investigations, which occurred over a period of 13 years. More recently, he investigated the Kirklees vampire in West Yorkshire.

The Vampire Research Society is the official United Kingdom advisory service on all matters pertaining to vampires and vampirism. Membership is by invitation only. Interested persons are welcome to correspond (overseas correspondents should include an International Reply Coupon). The Vampire Research Society may be reached at PO Box 542, Highgate, London N6 6BG, United Kingdom. There is no membership fee, and the society's journal is for members only.

SEAN MANCHESTER OF THE VAMPIRE RESEARCH SOCIETY.

Sources:

Manchester, Sean. "Eyewitness—The Kirklees Vampire." *The Unexplained* 38 (1992). Reprinted in

Crimson 8 (1993): 10-12.

————. *The Highgate Vampire.* Rev. ed.: London: Gothic Press, 1991. 188 pp.

VAMPIRE STUDIES

Originally founded as the Vampire Studies Society in Chicago, Illinois, by **Martin V. Riccardo** in 1977, Vampire Studies (''Society'' was dropped from the name in 1990) was designed as a means for vampire enthusiasts to share information on the subject. It was the first vampire-oriented fan club to use the word vampire in its title. Riccardo had first developed an interest in the subject several years earlier when he had heard a lecture by **Leonard Wolf,** author of *A Dream of Dracula.* After some extensive research on the subject, he began lecturing on vampires in 1976.

In 1977, Vampire Studies began publishing *The Journal of Vampirism,* one of the first periodicals devoted to vampires in folklore, fiction, film, and fact. The journal published nonfiction articles, book and movie reviews, news reports, fiction, humor, cartoons, and poetry. A primary interest of the journal was reports of vampires and vampire attacks. The journal folded in 1979 after six issues.

Among the members, contributors, and correspondents to Vampire Studies were Dorothy Nixon and Eric Held, who later founded the **Vampire Information Exchange.** Jan L. Perkowski, a Slavic studies scholar from the University of Virginia and an authority on the Slavic vampire, was also a contributor to *The Journal of Vampire Studies,* as was Dr. **Jeanne Youngson,** founder of the **Count Dracula Fan Club.**

After *The Journal of Vampire Studies* folded, Riccardo continued the organization as a correspondence network, information clearinghouse, lecture service, and research center. Through the years it has received thousands of letters from individuals interested in vampires, and it has helped them to become involved in the various organizations for vampire enthusiasts. Several authors have acknowledged Riccardo and Vampire Studies for research assistance in their books on vampires. In recent years, Vampire Studies has organized several gatherings called Vampire Fan Forums in the Chicago area.

Vampire Studies can be reached at PO Box 151, Berwyn, IL 60402.

Sources:

"The Lure of Martin V. Riccardo." Special issue of *The Vampire Information Exchange Newsletter* 53 (April 1991).

Riccardo, Martin V. *The Lure of the Vampire.* Chicago: Adams Press, 1983. 67 pp.

————. *Vampires Unearthed.* New York: Garland Publishing, 1983. 135 pp.

VAMPIRELLA

Warren Publications pioneered the black-and-white comic book magazine format in the 1960s as a means of, among other goals, skirting the restrictions of the Comics

Code, which had been adopted by the industry in 1954. The Code was very harsh on horror comics and specifically banned vampires, werewolves, ghouls, and zombies. Following the format established in *Famous Monsters of Filmland,* Warren successfully introduced two new horror comics, *Creepy* and *Eerie,* in 1964 and 1965, respectively. Both were successful and both carried vampire stories. They set the stage for the introduction in 1969 of *Vampirella,* a new vampire-oriented comic, and **Dark Shadows,** issued by Gold Key, which were the first two vampire comics since the adoption of the Comics Code in 1954.

Vampirella, a character developed by **Forrest J. Ackerman**, was somewhat different. She was, first of all, a woman, and female vampires had been rare in comic books, especially in starring roles. Second, she was not of the undead; rather, she was from outer space. According to the storyline she was a native of the planet Drakulon, a dying planet where blood had replaced water as the life-sustaining liquid. Vampirella had come to earth, where there was a steady supply of blood, to survive. She was pictured as a beautiful, dark- haired young woman (late teens to early twenties) with a scanty costume that hid little of her voluptuous body. Barbarella, a character developed by French artist Jean-Claude Forest and the subject of a motion picture by **Roger Vadim,** was the direct inspiration for Vampirella, whose red costume had a gold bat insignia just below her navel. When she smiled, her two extended canine teeth were prominently displayed. She also had the ability to change into a bat. Vampirella was impish as well as sexy. She engaged in a constant search for blood (or its equivalent), but she was the heroine and hence did not take life without reason. She was always mournful about the choices that her own survival often pressed upon her.

Through the years, Vampirella was thrown against myriad enemies; however, the continuing force of evil she battled was the cult of Chaos. In the process, Conrad and Adam, descendants of vampire hunter **Abraham Van Helsing,** were introduced as contemporary **vampire hunter**s, although Adam soon aligned himself with Vampirella. The emergence of these two characters tied to **Bram Stoker**'s *Dracula* signaled the return of its main character as well, and one of the most interesting revisions of the **Dracula** myth. Awakened in the contemporary world, the cosmic being known as the Conjuress sends Dracula back to the 1890s to undo some of the damage he had done and reverse the process that made him a vampire. Vampirella joins him through the device of a magic mirror. In their initial conversation, Dracula reveals that he too is from Drakulon. He begins to use magic to solve the planet's problems, but contacts Chaos instead of accomplishing his task. Chaos had originally forced him to earth. Vampirella agrees to help him redeem himself.

As Dracula and Vampirella meet all of the principal characters from *Dracula* the novel, Dracula's basic problem is to find some way to stave off his bloodthirst. After **Lucy Westenra** is resurrected when the **stake** is pulled from her heart (her **decapitation** being ignored), Dracula remembers his love for her. He is able to keep from biting Lucy, but cannot restrain himself when it comes to **Mina Murray.** Lucy sees him attack Mina and drops dead. In spite of Vampirella's help, the Conjuress pronounces Dracula a failure, and he is taken out of the storyline, for the moment.

The first issue of *Vampirella* appeared in September 1969. Forrest Ackerman was the first writer, and the soon-to-be-famous Frank Franzetta was the original artist. The original team was filled out by Trina Robbins and Tom Sutton. Ackerman was followed by Archie Godwin and a host of different writers over the years, most notably John Cochran, T. Casey Brennan, and Steve Englehart (under the pseudonym Chad Archer). Franzetta and Sutton were later succeeded by Jose Gonzales, with whom the image of Vampirella became most identified.

Vampirella became the longest-running vampire comic book of all time, its last issue (No. 112) appearing February 1983. Meanwhile, in the mid-1970s, Ron Goulart had produced a series of six *Vampirella* novels adapted from the comic book storyline. In the 1980s, in the atmosphere of revived interest in vampires, Warren Publications revived *Vampirella* for a single issue (No. 113) but did not pursue the series further. Then, in 1991, Harris Comics, having obtained the publishing rights to *Vampirella,* reissued what it deemed the best of the old *Vampirella* comics as a new four-part series, and in 1992 Harris began a new *Vampirella* comic, with new stories written by Kurt Busiek, for the first time in full color. Harris also has issued a series of single-volume reprints of the older Vampirella stories as *Vampirella: Transcending Space and Time* (1992), *Vampirella's Summer Nights* (1992), and *Vampirella: A Scarlet Thirst* (1993).

Sources:

Goulart, Ron. *Blood Wedding.* New York: Warner Books, 1976. 140 pp. Reprint. London: Sphere Books, 1976. 140 pp.
———. *Bloodstalk.* New York: Warner Books, 1975. 141 pp. Reprint. London: Sphere Books, 1975. 141 pp.
———. *Deadwalk.* New York: Warner Books, 1976. 144 pp. Reprint. London: Sphere Books, 1976. 144 pp.
———. *Deathgame.* New York: Warner Books, 1976. 142 pp. Reprint. London: Sphere Books, 1976. 142 pp.
———. *On Alien Wings.* New York: Warner Books, 1975. 138 pp. Reprint. London: Sphere Books, 1975. 138 pp.
———. *Snakegod.* New York: Warner Books, 1976. 144 pp. Reprint. London: Sphere Books, 1976. 144 pp.
Horn, Maurice. *The World Encyclopedia of Comic Books.* New York: Chelsea House Publishers, 1976. 785 pp.
Vampirella. 1- . New York: Harris Publications, 1992- .
Vampirella. 1-112. New York: Warren Publishing, 1969-1983.
Vampirella: Transcending Space and Time. New York: Harris Publications, 1992.

VAMPIRES, WEREWOLVES, GHOSTS AND OTHER SUCH THINGS THAT GO BUMP IN THE NIGHT

Vampires, Werewolves, Ghosts, and Other Such Things That Go Bump in the Night is the name of an informal group of scholars and researchers who investigate vampires and related paranormal phenomena. The organization, based in Beverly Hills,

California, was founded in the early 1980s and has worked quietly over the years gathering and documenting accounts of individuals' encounters with vampires, werewolves, spirits of the dead, and demonic beings. People interested in sharing such accounts are invited to contact the group at V.W.G., PO Box 6975, Beverly Hills, CA 90212-6975. Enclose $1.00 (U.S.) or three international reply coupons when initially contacting the group.

VAMPIRISM RESEARCH INSTITUTE

The Vampirism Research Institute is a nonmembership research organization founded by Liriel McMahon, a musician and college student majoring in sociology. For several years McMahon published the *Journal of Modern Vampirism.* In 1993 the institute began a series of new publications and a program of sociological research.

In 1992, inspired by Rosemary Guiley's *Vampires Among Us,* and with the cooperation of the **Count Dracula Fan Club** and the **Vampire Information Exchange,** McMahon conducted a survey of vampire fans in which she asked about such matters as their belief in the existence of vampires and their opinions about people who claim to be vampires. Results of the survey were released in the summer of 1993.

The institute has also published a monograph entitled *Dysfunctional Vampire: A Theory from Personal History* and a compilation, *Best of the Journal of Modern Vampirism.*

McMahon has laid out a program of future research for the institute. The Vampirism Research Institute may be contacted at PO Box 21067, Seattle, WA 98111-3067.

Sources:

McMahon, Liriel, ed. *Best of the Journal of Modern Vampirism.* Seattle, WA: Vampirism Research Institute, 1993.
————. *Dysfunctional Vampire: A Theory from Personal History.* Seattle, WA: Vampirism Research Institute, 1993.
————. *Results Report: Vampire Fan Survey No. 9221.* Seattle, WA: Vampirism Research Institute, 1993. 20 pp.

VAMPYR

Made the same year as Dracula—1931—the film *Vampyr,* having been forgotten by all but the most devoted students of the horror genre, has nevertheless been regarded by some critics of classical horror films as the best such motion picture ever made. *Vampyr* was produced and directed by **Carl Theodor Dreyer,** who also, with the assistance of Christen Jul, wrote the script. The film was purportedly modeled on **"Carmilla",** but the only similarity seems to be Dreyer's use of a female vampire.

The film opens with David Gray (played by Julian West) arriving in a European village only to discover that a room had already been booked for him at the local inn. That evening he was visited by an old man (Maurice Schultz) who gave him a package to be opened in case of his death. After the man mysteriously disappeared, Gray wondered if it was all a dream, although he still possessed the package. Unable to sleep, he went for a walk. He followed a disconnected shadow that led him to the local manor house. There he met the man, who turned out to be the owner of the mansion, and one of his daughters, Gisele (Rena Mandel). While Gray visited with Schultz, the latter was shot and killed. Gray then learned that Schultz's other daughter, Leone (Sybille Schmitz), was manifesting some strange symptoms.

Upon opening the package after Schultz was shot, Gray found a book on vampires. Leone, who had been wandering about in her sleep, was discovered out on the grounds with an old woman, Margueritte Chopin (Henriette Gerard), hovering over her. Because Leone had lost a lot of blood, Gray offered her a transfusion of his own blood.

While giving the transfusion Gray had an hallucination in which he was being buried alive. Through a window in the coffin he saw the old woman's face staring at him. He realized that she was a vampire and that a doctor he had met earlier was her assistant. After the hallucination, he awakened in the local cemetery. Accompanied by a servant from the manor house, he found the old woman's grave, and together they killed her by staking her with an iron pole. The spirits of those whom she had killed then arose to attack and kill the vampire's human cohorts, including the doctor.

Carl Dreyer (the film's producer and director) was known for his artistic attention to a mood of terror rather than any graphic presentation of horrific action. In *Vampyr* he slowly developed an environment that was supernatural and disjointed and in which the vampire's presence was strongly felt but rarely seen. The terror was suggested early, especially as Gray followed the shadow, which led him to a place where more disconnected shadows dance to some loud music. The old woman appeared, and as she raised her arms and demanded quiet, the music suddenly stopped.

To add even more to the atmosphere of total terror, Dreyer also had the picture filmed with some light leaking into the camera, thus producing a foggy quality on the finished film. To enhance the exact quality he wanted in the characters, Dreyer recruited nonactors to play the various roles. Only Sybille Schmitz and Maurice Schultz were professionals.

Dreyer allowed the film's plot to develop slowly, thus inviting viewers to participate in the film through their imagination. In the face of competing horror epics, however, the effect was to leave most audiences bored and to deny the film commercial success. Dreyer's artistic accomplishment was understood and appreciated by very few. In the United States, a condensed version of the film, with a voice-over narration, was issued as the *Castle of Doom,* but it too failed to attract a significant audience.

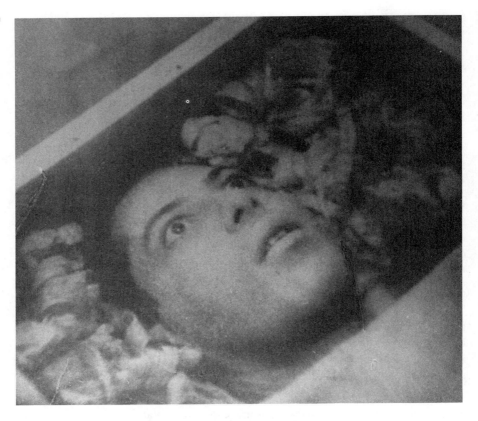

DAVID GREY DREAMS HIMSELF AWAKENING IN A COFFIN IN *VAMPYR.*

Sources:

Dreyer, Carl Theodor. *Four Screen Plays.* Translated by Oliver Stallybrass. Bloomington, IN: Indiana University Press, 1970. 312 pp.
Everson, William K. *Classics of the Horror Film.* New York: Carol Publishing, 1974. 247 pp.

THE VAMPYRE SOCIETY (BOHANAN)

One of two groups in Great Britain named The Vampyre Society is headed by Carole Bohanan and was founded in 1987. Bohanan was originally associated with Allen J. Gittens, but soon after the founding of the original Vampire Society, they parted company, and each now heads an organization with the same name. Bohanan's Vampyre Society has become one of the largest vampire interest groups currently functioning in England. Prominent members include authors Kim Newman and Steven Jones. It is dedicated to the celebration of the vampiric image, and meetings are held to screen vampire movies and hold programs on various related subjects. Affiliated groups meet regularly across England. The society publishes a journal, *The Velvet Vampyre,* which carries announcements of society activities, shorts stories, book and movie reviews, and correspondence from members. The society is headquartered in suburban London: Edgar Rd., Sanderstead, South Croydon, Surrey CR2 0NJ.

THE VAMPYRE SOCIETY (GITTENS)

One of two groups currently functioning in Great Britain with the name The Vampyre Society was founded in 1987 by Allen J. Gittens. Several months earlier he had written an article on vampires for a British rock fanzine. People contacted him asking questions about vampires, resulting in the formation of a correspondence circle of about a dozen people. Rather than write each individually, Gittens decided to produce an information leaflet and organized the correspondence circle into The Vampyre Society, taking its name from a novella by **John Polidori.** Within a year the free information leaflet had become a newsletter offered for subscription through the society. A short time later, Gittens had a falling out with one of the society's leaders, who then left and established a rival organization with the same name. Both organizations claim to be the continuation of the original society.

The Vampyre Society is primarily a correspondence club for its members (approximately 100 in 1993), who share a common interest in the vampire in all of its aspects. The society holds no meetings and eschews any association with adherents of the occult or blood-drinking. New members are asked to fill out a brief questionnaire concerning their interest in vampires. The society's newsletter has grown into a quarterly journal, *For the Blood Is the Life,* which features occasional special issues devoted to poetry and fiction written by the members.

Membership in the Society, which includes a subscription to the journal, is available from Allen J. Gittens, 38 Westcroft, Chippenham, Wiltshire SN14 0LY, United Kingdom.

Sources:

Guiley, Rosemary Ellen. *Vampires Among Us.* New York: Pocket Books, 1991. 270 pp.

VAN HELSING, ABRAHAM

A major character in **Bram Stoker's** *Dracula* (1897), Van Helsing was the wise elder scholar who brought enlightenment to the confusing and threatening situation that the other characters, all in their 20s, had become enmeshed. Van Helsing, who lived in Amsterdam, was originally called to England by Dr. **John Seward,** who described him as an "old friend and master" and an expert in obscure diseases. Van Helsing was a philosopher, metaphysician, and advanced scientist.

Van Helsing's first task was to examine the ailing **Lucy Westenra.** He found nothing wrong, except loss of blood, and she was not suffering from **anemia.** He then returned to Amsterdam. In less than a week, with Lucy's condition taking a decided turn for the worse, Van Helsing returned. He prescribed an immediate transfusion. He then noticed two marks on Lucy's neck. Again he returned to Amsterdam to consult his books. Upon his return a few days later, Lucy again received a transfusion. By this time Van Helsing had figured out the cause of Lucy's problem, but he did not divulge it. He merely took steps to block the vampire's access by surrounding Lucy with **garlic.** She improved and Van Helsing returned home.

Lucy lost her garlic several days later, and Dracula returned to attack her in her bedroom. This time a third transfusion could not save her. **Quincey P. Morris** raised the possibility of vampires. After Lucy's death, Van Helsing convinced the men, especially Lucy's fiancé, **Arthur Holmwood,** to treat Lucy's corpse as a vampire. He had them observe her movements after she was placed in her crypt to ensure that she did not join the undead. While Holmwood pounded a stake into Lucy, Van Helsing read a prayer for the dead from a prayer book, after which he and Seward decapitated the corpse and filled the mouth with garlic.

Van Helsing then turned to the task of learning all he could about Dracula, with the goal of first discovering his hiding places and eventually destroying him. In a meeting with the other principal characters, he received their commitment to join the fight under his leadership. At this gathering he laid out, in a most systematic fashion, the theory of vampires (which had been only partially revealed earlier), emphasizing their many powers and the manner by which they may be killed.

Meanwhile, **Mina Murray** (by this time married to **Jonathan Harker**) was showing signs of having been attacked by Dracula. She was pale and fatigued, but Van Helsing and the others were slow to recognize what was occurring. Van Helsing finally realized, while talking to the madman **R. N. Renfield,** that Mina was under attack and immediately led Seward, Holmwood, and Morris to the Harker house, where they found Mina drinking from Dracula's chest. Van Helsing drove him off with a **crucifix** and a **eucharistic wafer** (consecrated wafers are believed by Roman Catholic Christians to be the very body of Christ). To protect Mina, he held the wafer to her forehead, only to have it burn its imprint there much like a branding iron.

Mina, who had stepped aside so the men could engage Dracula, now became an active participant in the fight. She invited Van Helsing to hypnotize her and thus tap into her psychic tie to Dracula. In this manner, Van Helsing, who had led in the destruction of Dracula's boxes of earth (which he needed to survive), discovered that the vampire had left England to return to **Transylvania.** He accompanied Mina and the men on a chase to catch Dracula. During the last leg of the journey, the group split into three pairs. Van Helsing traveled with Mina, and they were the first to arrive at **Castle Dracula.** He drew a circle around her with the eucharistic wafers and then went into the castle. He killed the three **vampire brides** who resided there, sanitized Dracula's crypt, and finished by treating the castle's entrances so that no vampire could use them.

Returning to Mina, Van Helsing removed her some distance from the castle entrance to protect them from the wolves while awaiting the others to converge for the final confrontation. Once all arrive Van Helsing held a rifle on the Gypsies as Morris and Harker approached the box in which Dracula rested and killed him.

As Dracula was brought to stage and screen, Van Helsing assumed a key role, the plot often being simplified to a personal battle between Dracula and Van Helsing as the representatives of evil and good, respectively. Interestingly, **Hamilton Deane,** who wrote the original *Dracula* play for his theater company, chose to assume the role of Van Helsing rather than Dracula. However, **Peter Cushing**, who played the part in several **Hammer Films** motion pictures (pitted against **Christopher Lee** as Dracula) has been identified with the role of Van Helsing more than any other actor. He not only played Van Helsing at various times, but on occasion also portrayed several of his twentieth-century descendants continuing his fight against vampiric evil.

In both the movies and **comic book**s, descendants of Van Helsing have flourished. Cushing played Van Helsing's grandson in Hammer's *Dracula A.D. 1972.* Other descendants were portrayed by Richard Benjamin in *Love at First Bite* (1979) and by Bruce Campbell in *Sundown: The Vampire in Retreat* (1988). Marvel Comics invented Rachel Van Helsing, a granddaughter who continued his search-and-destroy mission against Dracula in the pages of *The Tomb of Dracula* through the 1970s. Contemporaneously, Conrad and Adam Van Helsing emerged in the pages of *Vampirella* as **vampire hunter**s.

Several people have been identified as possible models for the Van Helsing character, including author (Abraham) Stoker himself. Some have suggested **Arminius Vambéry,** mentioned in chapter 18 as a friend of Van Helsing's. Vambéry was a real person, at one time a professor at the University of Budapest, and the probable source of Stoker's initial knowledge of **Vlad the Impaler,** a historical model for Count Dracula. In *The Essential Dracula* (1979) editors **Raymond T. McNally** and **Radu Florescu** suggest Max Muller, a famous Orientalist at Oxford University, as a possibility. They also suggest that Dr. Martin Hasselius, the fictional narrator in **Sheridan Le Fanu**'s *In a Glass Darkly,* might also have helped inspire Van Helsing.

Sources:

Stoker, Bram. *The Essential Dracula.* Edited by Raymond McNally and Radu Florescu. New York: Mayflower Books, 1979. 320 pp.

VARNEY THE VAMPYRE

One of the most famous vampires in literature is Sir Francis Varney, the title character in *Varney the Vampyre:* or, *The Feast of Blood,* a nineteenth- century British novel written by **James Malcolm Rymer.** The story originally appeared in 109 weekly installments in the mid-1840s. The entire manuscript was then collected and printed as a single volume of over 800 pages. It was the first vampire novel in English, and the first vampire fiction since the original short story by John Polidori and the stage dramas that his story inspired. The story thus served as an important transitional piece between the original written accounts of vampires in the early nineteenth century and the writing of **Sheridan Le Fanu** and **Bram Stoker.**

Through the twentieth-century, Varney had a checkered career. Copies of Rymer's poorly written novel were seldom saved, so it became a rare book. Although different authors made reference to it, few had seen a copy and fewer still had taken the time to work their way through it. The book was published anonymously, and it was only in the 1970s that its true authorship was established. It was unavailable for many decades, but two reprints were published in 1970 and 1972. The audience was quite limited and the book has remained out-of- print since.

The story of Varney opened with his attack upon the young Flora Bannerworth. Having entered her bedroom, he sank his **fangs** into her neck and began to suck the gushing blood. The first half of the book followed his increasingly complex relationship with the Bannerworth family and their close friends and associates. Varney possessed white skin (as if bloodless), long, fang-like teeth, long **fingernails,** and shining, metallic eyes. Immediately after feasting, his skin took on a reddish hue.

Varney's initial attack had left two puncture marks in Flora's neck. Interrupted by members of the family during his repast, Varney was shot but nevertheless escaped. Henry Bannerworth quickly concluded that Flora had been attacked by a "vampyre." From a book he had read on Norway, he noted that vampyres attempted to drink blood to revive their body. In addition, they tended to do their feeding on evenings just prior to a full moon so that, should they meet with any physical problem, they could revive themselves by basking in the rays of the full **moon.** And it was in this manner that Varney had revived from the gunshot wounds he had received. (The importance given to moonlight throughout the novel shows Rymer's reliance on **John Polidori**'s **"The Vampyre"**.)

While bits and pieces of Varney's history were recounted throughout the novel, the reader had to wait until the end to get the full story. Varney's name before he had become a vampire was Mortimer. He originally had been a supporter of the British Crown and was living in London at the time of the beheading of Charles I and the proclamation of the Commonwealth under Cromwell in 1649. During this period he had assisted members of the royalty in escaping to Holland, for which he was handsomely rewarded. In a moment of passion, Mortimer had struck his son, accidentally killing him. The next thing he had remembered was a flash of light and being struck to earth with great force. When he had recovered consciousness, he was lying on the ground next to a recently opened grave. A voice told him that for his deed thenceforth he would be cursed among men and known as Varney the Vampyre.

Varney later discovered that he was shot by Cromwell's men and two years had passed since he lost consciousness. In the meantime, Cromwell had been deposed and the Crown restored. His former house was burned, but the money he had buried under the floor was still there. With it he made a new beginning. He slowly learned the rules of his new nature.

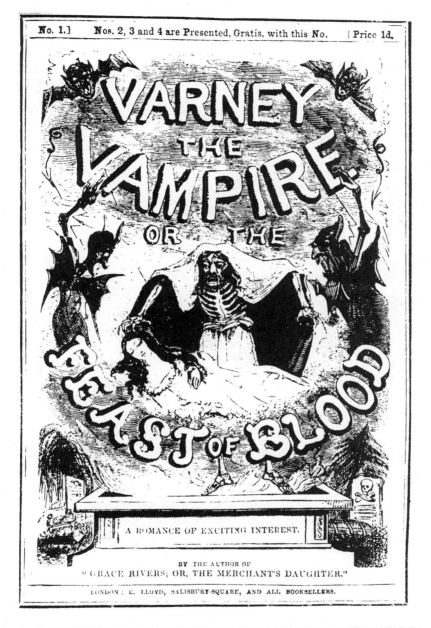

A ROMANCE OF EXCITING INTEREST.

BY THE AUTHOR OF
" GRACE RIVERS; OR, THE MERCHANT'S DAUGHTER."
LONDON: E. LLOYD, SALISBURY-SQUARE, AND ALL BOOKSELLERS.

VARNEY THE VAMPYRE BY JAMES MALCOLM RYMER WAS THE FIRST VAMPIRE NOVEL WRITTEN IN ENGLISH.

Like **Lord Ruthven,** the vampire in Polidori's tale, Varney had great **strength,** he could walk around freely in the **sunlight,** and he needed blood only occasionally

THE EMPTY COFFIN FROM
VARNEY THE VAMPYRE.

(not nightly). He could be wounded and even killed but would be revived simply by bathing in the moonlight. First pictured as something entirely evil, Varney later took on a more complex nature and showed himself to be an individual of feelings and honor. So appealing were his virtues that the Bannerworths, once they developed some understanding of his condition and his relationship with one of their ancestors, eventually became his protectors from a mob that set out to destroy him.

Rymer was also familiar with the eastern European vampire cases, probably through **Dom Augustin Calmet,** which had been published in an English edition in the 1700s. For several chapters, beginning with chapter 44, Varney's story turned on the action of a mob. An unnamed individual, who had traveled on the Continent, informed the people that the sign of the presence of a vampire was the sudden, mysterious death of people who seem to have wasted away. He warned them that such people would also return as vampires. Armed with this information, the mob, unable to locate Varney, moved on to the local graveyard and attacked the body of one Miles, who had recently died. Their eagerness to kill a vampire was thwarted when Miles's coffin was found to be empty.

After completing his interaction with the Bannerworths, Varney moved on to a series of increasingly brief encounters with various people in what became a very repetitive storyline. He would try to establish himself in a new social setting, he would attempt to bite someone, be discovered and hunted, and have to escape. Varney was singularly inept at attacking people (almost always a young woman) and was continually caught by people responding to the cries of his victims.

Varney was condemned by modern critics as poorly written and somewhat chaotic. It was not written as fine literature, or even as a novel, however. It was written in weekly installments over a two-year period, probably by several different authors, in such a way as to keep the readers entertained and coming back for the next installment. It accomplished that rather limited goal in spectacular fashion, becoming one of the most successful of the penny weeklies of the mid-nineteenth century.

Sources:

(Rymer, James Malcolm). *Varney the Vampyre*: or, *The Feast of Blood.* London: F._Lloyd, 1847. 868 pp. Reprint. Edited by Devendra P. Varma. New York: Arno Press, 1970. 868 pp. Reprint. Edited by E. F. Bleiler. New York: Dover Publications, 1972. 868 pp.

VETALAS See: INDIA, VAMPIRES IN

VICTIMS

According to vampire hunter **Abraham Van Helsing,** the vampire had no conscience. He preyed "on the bodies and souls of those whom we love best." This characteristic seemed to be a corruption of folkloric belief that the vampire attacked first those whom *it* loved best. The vampire of folklore would return to the village, home, and people among whom it lived before death. Thus, the vampire tended to attack first those it loved best in life.

Actually, this characteristic manifested one of the major differences between the traditional vampire of folklore and the vampire of literature, created in the nineteenth century. The folkloric vampire was part of village culture. It was restricted to its grave site or its home village, where it took up residence once again. In contrast, **Lord Ruthven, Varney the Vampyre,** and **Dracula** are citizens of the world. Ruthven traveled at will. Dracula, a little more constrained, was forced to take **native soil** with him. Thus, he could visit **London** but had to choose victims within an evening's travel time of one of his designated resting places. **Carmilla** was tied to a relatively small area, but she could travel beyond a local village.

Another discrepancy between the folkloric vampire and the vampire of literature has been the fate of the victim. In general, the folkloric vampire's initial attack was rarely fatal. (A major exception was the vampire's attack upon infants, after which it would leave them dead in their cribs, to be found by their parents the next morning.) Generally, the vampire was seen as taking the life of people over a period of time by repeated attacks that left the victim fatigued or ill with a wasting disease such as consumption (tuberculosis).

The vampires of literature often immediately killed their victims, as is the case with Lord Ruthven, but not with Varney the Vampyre, Carmilla, or Dracula. Varney often showed a conscience toward his victims and did not kill. Carmilla and Dracula killed, but over a period of time as their victims wasted away.

In folklore, the vampire's attack may have caused the victim to become a vampire also, but generally the victim's vampiric state did not manifest until after death. The fear that a vampire had infected others led not to a witch hunt among neighbors but to the disinterment of corpses and their treatment as vampires. The cases of **Peter Plogojowitz** and **Arnold Paul** accounted partially for the fame of this process.

Throughout nineteenth-century literature, the victims of vampires did not become vampires. They died, as in the cases of Lord Ruthven and Carmilla, or soon recovered and returned to normal lives, as in the case of Varney. In the novel *Dracula,* none of the victims of Dracula's vampiric attacks died at his hand (although it was clearly implied that the baby given to the three women early in the novel died as a result of their attack on it). **R. N. Renfield** was killed by Dracula, but not as a result of being drained of blood. **Jonathan Harker** was attacked by the three women, but survived. **Lucy Westenra** was attacked by Dracula, and eventually died, but then survived as a vampire. She attacked children, but all survived. She was finally killed by Van Helsing and the other men.

Mina Murray (nee Harker) was attacked, and there was every reason to believe that had she not been "de-vampirized" she would have become a vampire. Dracula not only took her blood but also had her drink of his. While never stated, it was clearly implied that sharing blood was the manner of transforming a victim into a vampire. Otherwise, the victim, if bitten often enough, as in "Carmilla," simply died.

The method of transformation of a victim into a vampire—by sharing blood— was lost in the dramatization of *Dracula* on stage and then on the screen. It was deemed improper to bring before an audience. In large part, that deletion led to the redefining of the method of vampire transmission. After the early *Dracula* movies, the belief that all it took to transform a person into a vampire was the vampire's bite became an integral part of the vampire myth. This idea had its ultimate expression in Robert McCammon's *They Thirst* (1981), in which a vampire loosed a vampire epidemic on Los Angeles. The number of vampires almost doubled each evening as the vampires fed and turned their victims into vampires that fed the next evening. This idea was continued in such recent movies as *Vamp* (1986) and *Innocent Blood* (1992). A variation on this theme was the requirement of three bites by the vampire to transform someone into a vampire, recently integrated most effectively in the storyline of the comedy *Love at First Bite* (1979).

VICTIMS OF GOOD GUY VAMPIRES: During the last generation, in the expansion and reworking of the vampire tradition, a new vampire has arisen, the "good guy" vampire. Unlike the vampires sought by Van Helsing in *Dracula,* these modern vampires possess a conscience that has led them to avoid killing whenever possible. The most prominent early "good guy" vampires were **St. Germain,** the hero of the **Chelsea Quinn Yarbro** books, and the very different Dracula developed by **Fred Saberhagen.** Good guy vampires often seek blood from blood banks or from animals, but when they turned to human "victims," they would choose people considered morally corrupt and thus deserving of the attack, or, more often, willing donors who for various reasons allowed the vampire to use them. In the case of St. Germain, his feeding was often done in the context of sexual activity, and the bite took the place of intercourse. Thus, the vampire gave the victim a sexual thrill and established a reciprocal relationship with the donor. St. Germain could periodically feed off people several times without their changing into a vampire and only rarely took the steps necessary to transform someone.

Sources:

Frayling, Christopher. *Vampyres: Lord Byron to Count Dracula.* London: Faber and Faber, 1992. 429 pp.
McCammon, Robert. *They Thirst.* New York: Avon, 1981. 531 pp.

VIRCOLAC See: ROMANIA, VAMPIRES IN

VISEGRÁD

Visegrád, site of the summer palace complex of the Hungarian kings, became home to Dracula for over a decade following his arrest in 1463. The year previously, **Vlad the Impaler,** the historical Dracula, had fought a losing war against the Turks. Driven from his capital at **Tirgoviste,** he fled to his castle on the Arges River. Pursued, he escaped through the mountains into **Transylvania,** hoping to gain the support of Matthias Corvinus, the Hungarian king. Instead, he was arrested and taken to **Hungary.** Although Matthias's father, John Hunyadi, had killed Vlad's father, **Vlad Dracul**, Vlad Dracula could have had some hope in Matthias, the first Hungarian king of Romanian extraction.

Matthias journeyed to Transylvania in the fall of 1462. He seemed inclined to support Dracula, but once the Turks had defeated him and withdrawn, he found it convenient to accept at face value a letter, most likely forged by Dracula's enemies in Brasov, in which Vlad pledged his support to the Turks in overthrowing Matthias. Thus, once in Transylvania, Vlad was arrested and carried back to Hungary by Matthias. He was imprisoned, according to an account written by Kuritsyn, the Russian ambassador, for the next 12 years.

Visegrád had been founded in 1323 by Charles Robert Angevin, who as king of Hungary moved his court there. Matthias refurbished it in elaborate style and turned it into a showplace, the center of the Hungarian Renaissance. The complex included a fortress on top of a mountain overlooking a bend in the Danube some 30 miles north of Budapest. The palace was located near the river's edge at the foot of the

VLAD THE IMPALER LIVED AT THE PALACE AT VISEGRAD, HUNGARY, FOR MANY YEARS.

mountain. Political prisoners commonly resided at Solomon's Tower, about half a mile downriver from the palace.

Dracula most likely was placed under house arrest and treated more like a guest than a prisoner. He might have been confined for a while at the fortress at Vác, near Budapest, but during most of the 1460s he probably moved seasonally between Budapest and Visegrád. His name was not included on the register of names of prisoners kept at Solomon's Tower. It was during his years in Hungary that the famous portrait now in an Austrian museum was painted. It was also during these years that many of the stories about Dracula were written down and circulated throughout Europe.

Dracula's situation eased considerably in the 1470s. His imprisonment ended, he formally converted to Roman Catholicism, he married a relative of the king, and he settled in Budapest to raise a family. Eventually, Matthias backed him in his drive to return to the Wallachian throne. He finally left Hungary in the fall of 1475 to assist in

Matthias's latest campaign against the Turks, after which he finally, if briefly, became the prince of Wallachia again.

Sources:

Florescu, Radu, and Raymond T. McNally. *Dracula: A Biography of Vlad the Impaler, 1413-1476.* New York: Hawthorn Books, 1973. 239 pp.
————. *Dracula: Prince of Many Faces: His Life and Times.* Boston: Little, Brown, 1989. 261 pp.
Treptow, Kurt W., ed. *Dracula: Essays on the Life and Times of Vlad Tepes.* New York: Columbia University Press, 1991. 336 pp.

VISION

According to **Abraham Van Helsing,** the voice of authority on vampires in *Dracula,* the vampire can see in the dark. Although this is not mentioned in the folk literature, it was a logical conclusion because vampires were nocturnal creatures who moved about freely in the darkness of the evening hours. Some of the vampire's attributes were derived from its association with the bat. **Bats,** for instance, have a radar system that makes them extremely well adapted night creatures. Dracula was pictured as regularly leaving his castle each evening to feed and return with food for his **vampire brides.** He also used his acute sight in his attacks on **Lucy Westenra** and **Mina Murray.** Modern vampire writers have cited night vision as one of the positive **characteristics** of the vampiric existence, frequently mentioned as allowing vampires to feel natural and at home in the nocturnal world. Night vision counterbalanced the blinding effect of direct **sunlight.**

VJESCI

Vjesci (alternatively spelled *vjeszczi* or *vjescey*) was the name given to a type of vampire found in the love of the Kashubian people of northeastern *Poland.* It was a variety of the **Slavic vampire,** and resembled the *Nachzeher* found to the west in northern **Germany.** According to the mythology, a person destined to become a *vjesci* could be identified by a caul, a little membrane cap, on his head at the time of birth. When a child was born with such a cap, it was removed, dried, ground, and fed to the person on the occasion of his seventh birthday. Those actions would prevent the child from becoming a vampire. In other respects the potential *vjesci* appeared to be completely normal and grew up in the community undetected, although in some accounts the *vjesci* had a restless and easily excitable nature and a ruddy complexion. At the time of his death, he refused to take the sacrament. His body cooled very slowly, the limbs remained limber, and the lips and cheeks retained their redness. Spots of blood often appeared under his fingernails and on his face.

The *vjesci* did not really die, however. Rather, at midnight, after his burial, he awakened and ate his clothing and some of his own flesh. He then left the grave and attacked his family, sucking their blood to the point of death. Not satiated, he might also attack his neighbors.

Several steps could be taken to protect oneself from a *vjesci* loose in the community. First, dying people should receive the Eucharist. A little earth was placed in the coffin under the body to prevent it from returning home. A **crucifix** or coin was placed under the tongue for the vampire to suck. A net might be placed in the **coffin**, with the understanding that the knots must be untied (a knot a year) before the vampire could arise. A bag of sand or **seeds** could be used in much the same manner. The body might be laid in the coffin face down so that the corpse, if it came to life, would merely dig itself further into the earth.

When a *vjesci* was disinterred it might be found sitting in the coffin with open eyes, it might move its head and even make some noises. Its shirt might have been eaten. If the precautions at the time of burial had not stopped the vampire, either a nail was driven through the forehead or the head severed from the body and placed between its feet. Some of the blood that flowed from the new wound would be caught and given to any who had been attacked by the vampire.

The *vjesci* was closely related to the *wupji* (or *opji*). They differed in that the *wupji* had two teeth rather than a cap at birth and was foreordained to become a vampire, with no possibility of altering its destiny. In working among the Kashubian immigrant community of Ontario, Canada, researcher Jan Perkowski often found that the terms *vjesci* and *wupji* were used interchangeably.

Sources:

Perkowski, Jan L. *Vampires, Dwarves, and Witches among the Ontario Kashubs.* Ottawa: National Museum of Canada, National Museum of Man, Canadian Centre for Folkloric Studies, 1972. Reprinted in Jan L. Perkowski, ed., *Vampires of the Slavs.* Cambridge, MA: Slavica Publishers, 1976. 294 pp.

VJESHTITZA *See:* SOUTHERN SLAVS, VAMPIRES AMONG THE

VLAD

Vlad is a rock musician and leader of the Dark Theater rock band of Chicago. He claims to be an indirect descendant of **Vlad the Impaler** by way of a young woman Vlad raped. Vlad also claims to have been born, for the first time, in the year 1431. He believes that the soul is passed from body to body after death and that it is possible, through the act of blood-drinking, to retain memories and characteristics from one lifetime to another.

Vlad drinks blood regularly (but not daily), an act he began as a child. He drank his first blood, that of a wounded playmate, when he was six. Whenever he got into fights as a kid, he bit and drank some of the blood of the person he was fighting. Later, he was able to find women who agreed to his extracting and drinking some of their blood. He consumes a diet consisting primarily of rare beef.

At an early age, Vlad was trained as a symphonic musician. He originally played the horns, but was lured into rock as a teenager. He began to play the electric guitar and in the early 1980s began playing with several Chicago-area heavy-metal bands.

► VLAD, GOTHIC MUSICIAN.

As early as 1983 he laid plans for his own band and wrote the lyrics of what would become its first songs. Then in 1988 he founded the Dark Theater, for which he writes the lyrics and music and does the arranging. He developed a stage setting designed around traditional stage masks, with a notable addition—a set of vampire **fangs.** The original Dark Theater was actually a performance art group and consisted of two members, Vlad and Adservo Magus. Magus was replaced by a live band in 1989, and with the addition of drummer Brad Swinford in 1990 the group was ready to record its first album, *Matters of Life and Undeath.* Keyboardist Krimm B. joined the group during the recording sessions for the disc. Two videos, *Vampire's Dance* and *In the Shell* soon followed. The Dark Theater followed up the album with *Kaliedoscope Whirls* in 1992 and *TDT* in 1993.

Vlad and his wife, Lynda, who replaced Krimm B. on keyboards in 1992, founded and head Screem Jams Productions, a marketing and promotion company. Screem Jams promotes several up-and-coming artists, musicians, and writers as well as the Dark Theater's appearances around the country. In 1991, Screem in the Dark, the band's fan club, was launched. The club publishes a quarterly fanzine, *Screem in the Dark*, which features vampire fiction, reviews, art, and updates on the Dark

Theater. Screem Jams also merchandises a variety of Dark Theater products, CDs, cassettes, videos, clothing, and posters and has sponsored the Vampire Circus events, multimedia extravaganzas featuring vampire oriented entertainment.

Scheduled for release in 1994 is *Silent Death,* a graphic novel written and painted by Vlad and Talon Nightshade, and a full-length novel written by Vlad.

Screem Jams Productions may be reached at PO Box 138300, Chicago, IL 60613.

Sources:

Pickler, Laureen. "Vampires Fly High on Eve of Halloween." *The Wall Street Journal,* October 30, 1992, p. 1.

Screem in the Dark. No. 1- . Chicago: Screem Jams Productions, 1991- .

VLAD DRACUL (1390?-1447)

Vlad Dracul was the father of **Vlad the Impaler** (1430-1477), the person who has been identified as the historical Dracula. He was the illegitimate son of Prince Mircea, the ruler of Wallachia, that area of present-day Romania south of the Carpathian Mountains. His mother might have been Princess Mara of the Tomaj family of **Hungary.** He possibly spent a period of his youth at the court of Sigismund I of Luxembourg, the king of Hungary, as a token of faithfulness of Mircea's alliance with Sigismund. Thus, Vlad might have grown up in Buda and in locations in Germany. He married and had a son, also named Mircea.

In 1430 Vlad appeared in Transylvania as an official in charge of securing the Transylvanian border with Wallachia. He resided in **Sighisoara,** where toward the end of the year his second son, Vlad (later called Vlad the Impaler), was born. Shortly after the child's birth, it became known that Sigismund had selected Vlad as his candidate to rule Wallachia. Vlad was invited to Nüremberg to be invested by the Order of the Dragon. (Sigismund had founded the order in 1418), which had a variety of goals, among them to fight Islam.

Now bearing the title of prince of Wallachia, he was unable to secure the throne. He eventually created a powerful alliance by marrying Eupraxia, the sister of the ruler of Moldavia, as a second wife. In 1436 he was finally able to secure the Wallachian throne, and in the winter of 1436-37 he moved to **Tirgoviste,** the Wallachian capital. He had three other children: Radu, a second son also named Vlad (commonly referred to as Vlad the Monk), and a second son named Mircea.

In 1437, following the death of Sigismund, Vlad Dracul signed an alliance with the Turks. In March 1442 he allowed Mezid-Bey to pass through Wallachia and attack Transylvania. However, the Turkish army was defeated and the Hungarian army pursued Mezid-Bey back through Wallachia and drove Vlad Dracul from the throne in the process. He took refuge among the Turks, with whose help he regained the throne the following year. To secure the new relationship, Vlad Dracul left two sons, Vlad and Radu, in Turkish hands. Then, in 1444, Hungary moved against the

Turks. Vlad Dracul, attempting to keep his pledge to the sultan but also aware of his obligations to the Christian community, sent a small contingent to assist the Hungarian forces. They met with a resounding defeat, which Vlad Dracul and his son Mircea blamed on John Hunyadi, the governor of Hungary. In 1447 Hunyadi led a war against Vlad. The decisive battle was fought near Tirgoviste, and as a result Vlad was killed and Mircea captured by the Romanian boyars (the ruling elite) and tortured and killed.

The year after Vlad Dracul's death, his son Vlad Dracula ("son of Dracul") attempted to assume his throne. He was unable to do so until 1456. Soon after becoming prince of Wallachia, he avenged the death of his father and brother.

Sources:

Florescu, Radu, and Raymond T. McNally. *Dracula: A Biography of Vlad the Impaler, 1413-1476.* New York: Hawthorn Books, 1973. 239 pp.

———. *Dracula: Prince of Many Faces: His Life and Times.* Boston: Little, Brown, 1989. 261 pp.

McNally, Raymond T., and Radu Florescu. *In Search of Dracula.* 1972. Reprint. New York: Warner Paperback Library, 1973. 247 pp.

Treptow, Kurt W., ed. *Dracula: Essays on the Life and Times of Vlad Tepes.* New York: Columbia University Press, 1991. 336 pp.

VLAD THE IMPALER (1431?-1476)

Vlad the Impaler was a historical figure upon whom **Bram Stoker** partially built the title character of his novel ***Dracula.*** Stoker indicated his knowledge of Vlad through the words of Dr. **Abraham Van Helsing:**

> He (Dracula) must, indeed, have been that Voivode Dracula who won his name against the Turk, over the great rivers on the very frontier of Turkey-land. If that be so, then was he no common man; for in that time, and for centuries after, he was spoken of as the cleverest and most cunning, as well as the bravest of the sons of the "land beyond the forest." That mighty brain and that iron resolution went with him to the grave, and are even now arrayed against us. The Draculas were, says Arminius, a great and noble race, though now and again were scions who were held by their coevals to have had dealings with the Evil One. They learned his secrets in the Scholomance, amongst the mountains over Lake Hermanstadt, where the devil claims the tenth scholar as his due. In the records are such words as "Stregoica"—witch; "ordog and pokol"—Satan and hell; and in one manuscript this very Dracula is spoken of as "wampyr," which we all understand too well.

Here Stoker combined possible references to the historical Vlad, a folklore tradition that saw vampirism as rooted in Satan's actions, and the modern term vampire.

Recent interest in Dracula has produced among some researchers a desire to know more about the historical figure behind the fictional character. An important breakthrough came in 1972 with the publication of *In Search of Dracula,* the initial findings of historians **Raymond T. McNally** and **Radu Florescu,** who gathered the basic contemporary documents concerning the Romanian prince Vlad and visited Vlad's former territory to investigate his career. The following year, the even more definitive *Dracula: A Biography of Vlad the Impaler, 1431-1476* also by McNally and Florescu, appeared. These books made the career of this obscure Romanian ruler, who actually exercised authority for only a relatively short period of time, an integral part of the modern Dracula myth.

The name Dracula was applied to Vlad during his lifetime. It was derived from drac, a Romanian word that can be interpreted variously as "devil" or "dragon." Vlad's father had joined the Order of the Dragon, a Christian brotherhood dedicated to fighting the Turks, in 1431, shortly after Vlad's birth. The oath of the order required, among other things, wearing the order's insignia at all times. The name Dracula means son of Dracul or son of the dragon or devil.

The actual birth date of Vlad, later called Vlad the Impaler, is unknown, but was probably late in 1430. He was born in Schassburg (aka Sighisoara), a town in Transylvania. Soon after his birth, in February 1431, his father, also named Vlad, traveled to Nuremberg, Germany, where he was invested with the insignia of the Order of the Dragon. The accompanying oath dedicated the family to the fight against the Turks, who had begun an attack upon Europe that would eventually carry them to the very gates of Vienna. Vlad was a claimant to the throne of Wallachia, that part of contemporary **Romania** south of the Transylvanian Alps. He was able to wrest the throne from his half-brother in 1436.

Two years later, Vlad Dracul entered an alliance with the Turks that called for sending two sons, Mircea and Vlad, with the sultan on a raid into Transylvania. Doubting Vlad Dracul's loyalty, the sultan had him brought before him and imprisoned. Dracul nevertheless reaffirmed his loyalty and had Vlad (Dracul had two sons named Vlad, born to different mothers) and Radu, his younger sons, remain with the sultan to guarantee their pact. They were placed under house arrest at Egrigoz. The period of imprisonment deeply affected Vlad. On the one hand, he took the opportunity of his confinement to learn the Turkish language and customs. But his treatment ingrained the cynicism so evident in his approach to life and infused in him a Machiavellian attitude toward political matters. His early experiences also seem to have set within his personality the desire to seek revenge from anyone who wronged him.

In December 1447 his father, Mircea, was murdered and his older brother burned alive under the orders of Hungarian governor John Hunyadi (aka Ioande Hunedoara), with the assistance of the boyars, the ruling elite families of Wallachia. The death of Mircea made Vlad the successor, but with Hunyadi's backing, Vladislav II, a member of another branch of the family, assumed the Wallachian throne. Vlad tried to claim

VLAD AMID IMPALED BODIES.

the throne in 1448, but his reign lasted only a couple of months before he was forced to flee to the neighboring kingdom of Moldavia. In 1451, while he was at Suceava, the Moldavian capital, the ruler was assassinated. For whatever reasons, Vlad then went to Transylvania and placed himself at the mercy of Hunyadi, the very person who had ordered his father's assassination.

The alliance between Hunyadi and Vlad may have been made possible by Vladislav II's adoption of a pro-Turkish policy which alienated Hunyadi. Vlad fought beside Hunyadi, who in the end acknowledged Vlad's claim to the Wallachian throne.

Hunyadi died of the plague at Belgrade on August 11, 1456. Immediately after that event, Vlad left Transylvania for Wallachia. He defeated Vladislav II and on August 20 caught up with the fleeing prince and killed him. Vlad then began his six-year reign, during which his reputation was established. In September he took both a formal oath to Hungarian King Ladislaus V and, a few days later, an oath of vassalage to the Turkish sultan.

Early in his reign, probably in the spring of 1459, Vlad committed his first major act of revenge. On Easter Sunday, after a day of feasting, he arrested the boyer families, whom he held responsible for the death of his father and brother. The older ones he simply impaled outside the palace and the city walls. He forced the rest to march from the capital city of **Tirgoviste** to the town of Poenari, where over the summer, in the most humiliating of circumstances, they were forced to build his new outpost overlooking the Arges River. This chateau would later be identified as **Castle Dracula.** Dracula's actions in destroying the power of the boyers was part of his policy of creating a modern, centralized state in what is today Romania. He turned over the estates and positions of the deceased boyers to people who owed their loyalty only to him.

Vlad's brutal manner of terrorizing his enemies and the seemingly arbitrary manner in which he had people punished earned him the nickname ''Tepes'' or ''the Impaler,'' the common name by which he is known today. He not only used the stake against the boyers, whom he was trying to bring into subservience, he also terrorized the churches, both the Orthodox and the Roman Catholic, each of which had strength in his territory. He gave particular attention to the Roman Catholic monastic centers, which he saw as points of unwelcome foreign influence. His ''Romania for the Romanians'' policies also led to actions against foreign merchants, especially the Germans, whom he saw as preventing the development of Romanian industry. Vlad the Impaler used his position to enforce his personal moral code of honesty and sexual morality, and various stories have survived of his killing people who offended his sense of moral value. He also would, on occasion, retaliate against an entire village because of the actions of one person.

Vlad also used terrorist tactics against his foreign enemies. When he thought that merchants from Transylvania had ignored his trade laws, he led raids across the border in 1457 and again in 1459 and 1460 and used impalement to impose his will. During the latter incursion he looted the Church of Saint Bartholemew, burned a section of Brasov, and impaled numerous people. That raid was later pictured in anti-Dracula prints showing him dining among the impaled bodies.

During his reign, Vlad moved to the village of Bucharest and built it into an important fortified city with strong outer walls. Seeing the mountains as protective bulwarks, Vlad built his castle in the foothills of the Transylvania Alps. Later, feeling more secure and wishing to take control of the potentially wealthy plains to the south, he built up Bucharest.

Vlad was denounced by his contemporaries, and those in the next several generations who wrote of him published numerous tales of his cruelty. He was noted for the number of victims, conservatively set at 40,000, in his brief six-year reign. He thus became responsible for the largest number of deaths by a single ruler until modern times. **Ivan the Terrible,** with whom he has been frequently compared, put fewer than 10,000 to death. Furthermore, Vlad the Impaler ruled over fewer than half-a- million people. Above and beyond the number who died as a result of his policies, as McNally and Florescu have noted, Vlad refined the use of methods of torture and death to a degree that shocked his contemporaries. He not only impaled people in various ways but also often executed his victims in a manner related to the crime for which they were being punished.

The beginning of the end of his brief reign can be traced to the last months of 1461. For reasons not altogether clear, Vlad launched a campaign to drive the Turks from the Danube River valley south and east of Bucharest. In spite of early successes, when the Turks finally mounted a response, Vlad found himself without allies and was forced to retreat in the face of overwhelming numbers. The Turkish assault was slowed on two occasions. First, on June 17, several hours after sunset, Dracula attacked the Turkish camp in an attempt to capture the sultan. Unfortunately, he was directed to the wrong tent, and while many Turks were slain in the attack, the sultan got away. Unable to follow up on his momentary victory, Vlad was soon on the retreat again. When the sultan reached the capital city of Tirgoviste, he found that Dracula had impaled several people outside the town, a fact that impressed the sultan and gave him pause to consider his course of action. He decided to return to Adrianople (now Edirne) and left the next phase of the battle to Vlad's younger brother Radu, now the Turkish favorite for the Wallachian throne. Radu, at the head of a Turkish army and joined by Vlad's Romanian detractors, pursued him to his castle on the Arges River.

At Castle Dracula he was faced with overwhelming odds, his army having melted away. He chose to survive by escaping through a secret tunnel and then over the Carpathians into Transylvania. His wife (or mistress), according to local legend, committed suicide before the Turks overran the castle. In Transylvania he presented himself to the new king of **Hungary,** Matthias Corvinus, who arrested him. At this time the first publications of stories of Vlad's cruelties were circulating through Europe.

Vlad was imprisoned at the Hungarian capital at **Visegrád,** although it seems he lived under somewhat comfortable conditions after 1466. By 1475 events had shifted to the point that he emerged as the best candidate to retake the Wallachian throne. In the summer of 1475 he was again recognized as the prince of Wallachia. Soon thereafter he moved with an army to fight in Serbia, and upon his return he took up the battle against the Turks with the king of Moldavia. He was never secure on his throne. Many Wallachians allied themselves with the Turks against him. His end came at the hand of an assassin at some point toward the end of December 1476 or early January 1477.

The actual location of Vlad's burial site is unknown, but a likely spot is the church at the Snagov monastery, an isolated rural monastery built on an island. Excavations there have proved inconclusive. A tomb near the altar thought by many to be Vlad's resting place was empty when opened in the early 1930s. A second tomb near the door, however, contained a body richly garbed and buried with a crown.

VLAD THE IMPALER'S SUPPOSED BURIAL SITE AT THE SNAGOV MONASTERY.

Knowledge of the historical Dracula has had a marked influence on both Dracula movies and fiction. Two of the more important Dracula movies, *Dracula* **(1974),** starring **Jack Palance**, and *Bram Stoker's Dracula,* a recent production directed by **Francis Ford Coppola,** attempted to integrate the historical research on Vlad the Impaler into the story and used it as a rationale to make Dracula's actions more comprehensible.

Sources:

Florescu, Radu, and Raymond T. McNally. *Dracula: A Biography of Vlad the Impaler, 1413-1476.* New York: Hawthorn Books, 1973. 239 pp.

———. *Dracula: Prince of Many Faces: His Life and Times.* Boston: Little, Brown, 1989. 261 pp.

Giurescu, Constantin C. *The Life and Deeds of Vlad the Impaler: Dracula.* New York: Romanian Library, 1969.

McNally, Raymond T., and Radu Florescu. *In Search of Dracula.* 1972. Reprint. New York: Warner Paperback Library, 1973. 247 pp.

Stoicescu, Nicolae. *Vlad the Impaler.* Translated by Cristina Krikorian. Bucharest: Romanian Academy, 1978.

Treptow, Kurt W., ed. *Dracula: Essays on the Life and Times of Vlad Tepes.* New York: Columbia University Press, 1991. 336 pp.

VRYKOLAKAS *See:* GREECE, VAMPIRES IN

VUKODLAK *See:* SOUTHERN SLAVS, VAMPIRES AMONG THE

VURVULAK *See:* SOUTHERN SLAVS, VAMPIRES AMONG THE

W

WATER

According to **Abraham Van Helsing**, the vampire expert in *Dracula,* a vampire could only pass running water at the slack or flood of the tide. As with many other characteristics, this was somewhat unique to **Dracula**. Though a characteristic of the Chinese *chiang-shih*, problems with running water were not in the folkloric accounts from eastern Europe and, given the geographical limitations on most vampires, not relevant. As a whole, since *Dracula,* such observations have disappeared from the literature. The primary exception was in the vampire novels of **Chelsea Quinn Yarbro,** whose vampire hero **St. Germain** had trouble passing over running water. He countered this by developing shoes with hollow soles into which he placed some of his **native soil**. He drew strength from the soil.

Some folkloric vampires, of course, had special relationships to water. For example, in **Russia** the corpse of a suspected vampire might be thrown in the river in the belief that the earth could not tolerate the presence of a vampire or revenant. In **Germany**, the body of a person who committed **suicide** (a potential vampire) was treated similarly. Also in parts of Germany, water might be poured on the road between the grave where a suspected vampire had been buried and his home, as a barrier to prevent his return. In Prussia, the *leichenwasser*, the water used to wash a corpse, was saved and used in this manner.

A possible source of Van Helsing's remarks was a story from **Greece** recounted in Rennell Rodd's study of Greek folklore published in London in 1892 (and quoted by Montague Summers). He told of a legend that the island of Therasia, in the Santorini group, was infested with vampires. They had been banished to that island because of the prayers and exorcisms of a pious bishop on the island of Hydra, where they had previously been located. Importantly, he noted that according to the legend anyone venturing near the shore of Therasia would hear the noise of the vampires who walked along the shore in an agitated state because they could not cross salt water.

PURIFICATION: Apart from its appearance in lakes, rivers and oceans, water was of course a cleansing and purifying agent. Like fire, it had taken on a number of sacred and mythological connotations. It was regularly used in religious initiatory rituals such as baptism and in ablution rituals such as the bathing that occurred before a Muslim prayed in the mosque. Within **Christianity** in Europe, in the Roman Catholic Church and the Eastern Orthodox churches, practices had developed around blessed water, generally referred to as ''holy water,'' that gave the substance a number of superstitious/magical meanings and uses. Originally considered of symbolic cleansing value, it came to be seen as having an inherent sacred quality because it had been consecrated for religious use. Holy water was used in the funeral services of both churches and thus often was present when the bodies of suspected vampires were exhumed and killed a second time.

Holy **water** as such did not appear in *Dracula,* although the **crucifix** and the **eucharistic wafer** did. However, in a natural extension of these two sacred objects that were so effective against vampires, holy water became part of the assumed weapons in the vampire kits. Periodically, holy water was used against vampires in motion pictures and twentieth-century vampire novels. Its effect was similar to throwing acid on a normal human. It burned and scarred, though it usually was not fatal since it was present only in small quantities. Holy water assumed a most unusual property in the movie version of Stephen King's novel *'Salem's Lot*, in which, by glowing, it signaled the approach of the vampires.

Sources:

Barber, Paul. *Vampires, Burial, and Death.: Folklore and Reality.* New Haven, CT: Yale University Press, 1988. 236 pp.
Rodd, Rennell. *The Customs and Lore of Modern Greece.* London: David Scott, 1892. 294 pp.
Summers, Montague. *The Vampire in Europe.* London: Routledge and Kegan Paul, 1929. 329 pp. Reprint. New Hyde Park, NY: University Books, 1961. 329 pp.

WEATHER

According to Vampire expert **Abraham Van Helsing**, in *Dracula,* vampires could affect the weather, within limits. Dracula most clearly demonstrated his powers in the fog and storm accompanying the movement of the *Demeter,* the ship that brought him to England. This element in vampire mythology was not present in the folkloric tradition. There, the vampire was seen in a much narrower perspective and was not assigned any powers to affect the weather. There was a tradition reported by Dimitrij Zelenin that the earth itself reacted to the burying of ''unclean'' bodies (such as potential vampires) not only by refusing to accept the body, but by bringing bad weather, specifically cold and frost in the spring.

Just as the folkloric vampire could not change the weather, so the literary vampire both before and after Dracula possessed little ability in that direction. Apart

THE BELIEF IN WITCHES' ABILITY TO CONTROL WEATHER WAS LATER TRANSFERRED TO DRACULA.

from the weather accompanying the *Demeter* in the various *Dracula* movies, vampires have exercised little power in relation to weather, though weather frequently has had a significant role in novels and motion pictures to set atmosphere.

Sources:

Barber, Paul. *Vampires, Burial, and Death.: Folklore and Reality.* New Haven, CT: Yale University Press, 1988. 236 pp.

WEREWOLVES AND VAMPIRES

The werewolf is one of several monsters closely associated in the public mind with the vampire. That relationship was largely established in the 1930s with the production of two werewolf movies by **Universal Pictures** and the inclusion of the werewolf and the vampire together in three films during the 1940s. By definition the werewolf is a human being who at various times (usually at the full moon), either voluntarily or involuntarily, changes into a wolf or wolflike creature and assumes many of the characteristics of the wolf, especially its viciousness. Closely related to werewolfism was a disease, lycanthropy, in which people believe that they change into a werewolf when in fact they do not.

ORIGIN OF THE WEREWOLF: Like the vampire, and unlike **Frankenstein's monster**, the werewolf was an ancient figure found in the folklore of people worldwide. The oldest report of a man changing into a wolf was from ancient Greek mythology. Lycaon (hence the word *lycanthropy*) displeased Zeus and the deity changed him into a wolf. However, a number of ancient writers such as Galen and Virgil provided the first descriptions of lycanthropy. They rejected the mythology and believed that the change into animals was a diseased condition brought on by melancholia or drugs.

In like measure, werewolfism has been reported throughout the world, though the animals into which humans transform has been quite varied, including lions, tigers, jaguars, hyenas, sharks, and crocodiles—all animals that are large and known for their ferociousness. Contemporary reports of lycanthropy also come from around the world, both in rural areas and in the modern West. Some contemporary cases are included in the selection of papers compiled by Richard Noll.

WEREWOLVES AND VAMPIRES: Werewolves and vampires have been reported as existing side by side in the mythologies of many cultures, but they have a special relationship in the southern Balkan area, from whence much of the modern vampire myth comes. That relationship was particularly evident in the use of the term *vrykolakas* (and cognate terms in various Slavic languages) to describe vampires in recent centuries in **Greece**. In accounts of the *vrykolakas* in southern Balkan countries, there was some confusion over the word's meaning. In the early twentieth century, pioneer researcher Freidrich Krauss, working in Bosnia, concluded that the *vrykolakas* (spelled *vukodlak* in Bosnia) was a werewolf (i.e., a man or woman who changed into a wolf and attacked the local cattle).

More recent researchers such as Harry Senn and Jan L. Perkowski have argued that the word *vrykolakas* derived from an old Slavic word that referred to the ritual wearing of wolf pelts among Slavic tribes during the first millennium A.D. Earlier Mircea Eliade had observed that the Dacians, the people who previously resided in what is present-day **Romania** and whose name means wolf, ritually transformed their young warriors into wolves by dressing them in wolf pelts and engaging in appropriate mimicking behavior. The historian Herodotus had described such behavior among the early people of the southern Balkans. At the time the wolf was admired as a warrior animal. Senn noted that during the early centuries of the second millennium the perceived role of the wolf changed from one that was admired to one that was feared. The wolf became a threat to the community because it attacked livestock and people.

Over the first centuries of the second millennium A.D., the use of the term *vrykolakas* lost its ritual meaning (as the image of the wolf changed and the ritual itself disappeared). According to Senn, the reference point of *vrykolakas* was transferred to the vampire; throughout the southern Balkans (Romania, Serbia, Croatia, Greece, etc.), it replaced older terms for the vampire. Perkowski emphasized that there was an intermediate step in which the term took on a mythological reference to a being who chased the clouds and devoured the moon (Agnes Murgoci, working in Romania in the mid-1920s, found continued references to this meaning of *vrykolakas*). Further transition was made in the sixteenth century, by which time *vrykolakas* had began to refer to vampires. That meaning then spread throughout the southern Balkans and into Greece. Perkowski even has argued that the term never referred to a werewolf, as Krauss and others have suggested. Among modern Romanians there is a were-creature, the *tricolici* (or *pricolici*), a man who may take the form of a pig, a dog, or, less often, a wolf.

Belief in werewolves apparently peaked in Europe during the late Middle Ages. While many refused to believe that actual werewolves existed, many believed that lycanthropy was caused by the devil. The original witchhunters, James Sprenger and Heinrich Kramer, the authors of the 1486 volume *The Witches Hammer* that started the great witchhunts of the next two centuries, declared the transformation of man into wolf impossible. But they believed that witches and sorcerers could cause another person to believe that he had been transformed into a wolf. There were, however, several trials against people accused of werewolfism.

THE WEREWOLF IN LITERATURE: The werewolf made a number of brief appearances in literature as early as the fourteenth century, but it was not until the middle of the nineteenth century that the appearance of three werewolf novels within a few years of each other injected the creature into the public consciousness. *Hughes the Wer-wolf* by Sutherland Menzies was, like *Varney the Vampyre,* published as a weekly serial over a period of time in the 1850s. Then, in 1857, *The Wolf-Leader* and George W. M. Reynold's *Wagner the Wehrwolf* (another weekly serial) were published. The latter volume usually is looked upon as the fountainhead of modern tales of the werewolf. A number of werewolf short stories and novels appeared over the next 80 years but attracted little attention until 1934, when Guy Endore's *The Werewolf of Paris* was published.

Endore previously had been a screenwriter in Hollywood and had worked on several horror movies, including *The Mark of the Vampire*. His book received enough acclaim that **Universal Pictures** decided to produce its cinematic version. Changing the location slightly, the first werewolf picture appeared in 1935 as *The Werewolf of London*. Endore's tale told the story of Bertrand Caillet, whose mother had been seduced by a priest, Father Pitamont. The strange child grew up and became a werewolf, a fact discovered when he was wounded by a silver **bullet**. (This old remedy derived from the belief that silver should be used when shooting at Scottish witches who had transformed into an animal form, such as a rabbit. From Endore's

WEREWOLVES WERE FREQUENTLY ASSOCIATED WITH VAMPIRES.

use, the silver bullet would become part of the conventional wisdom concerning werewolves.) As Bertrand grew, the violence caused by his wolfish nature could no longer be checked or covered up. He fled from the countryside to Paris and there enlisted in the French Army in time for the Franco-Prussian War. His nature was soon revealed, however, and he met his end following a court-martial. Endore's werewolf Bertrand was based in large part on the factual case of Francois Bertrand, a French noncommissioned officer who in 1848 was convicted of breaking into a number of graves in Paris. In the stories about him, Bertrand was generally referred to as a **ghoul** rather than a werewolf.

The Werewolf of London was followed by *The Wolf Man*, the title role being played by Lon Chaney, Jr., who as Larry Talbot mixed the sympathetic and horrific nature of the werewolf character. The werewolf was a man afflicted by his condition, and he fought against it as fiercely as he attacked living beings when his wolf nature emerged.

The vampire and the werewolf seem to have been brought together on the screen for the first time in *The Return of the Vampire* (1943), the film **Bela Lugosi** made for Columbia Pictures. Universal brought the vampire (Dracula) and the Wolf Man together in three pictures during the 1940s: *House of Frankenstein* (1944), *House of Dracula* (1945), and *Abbott and Costello Meet Frankenstein* (1948). In the first movie Chaney sought a cure for his condition, which he finally found in the second. In the last movie, played just for fun, the Wolf Man joined the comedic team to prevent Dracula (Bela Lugosi) from transplanting Costello's brain into **Frankenstein's monster**. Other werewolf films followed, though they never gained the popularity of the vampire movies. **Hammer Films** made one werewolf picture, *The Curse of the Werewolf* (1961), directed by **Terence Fisher**, who had worked on *The Horror of Dracula* several years earlier. Hammer, unlike Universal, never attempted to bring Dracula and the werewolf together in the same story.

On television, the two creatures were brought together on the *Dark Shadows* series when a new character was introduced named Quentin. As his story unfolded, he was cursed to become a werewolf, his first transformation occurring in episode 752. At first Quentin and **Barnabas Collins**, the vampire character, were enemies, and they tried to eliminate each other. However, they eventually came to an understanding that they were similarly afflicted, and they then worked together.

The next attempt to mix the two characters came in 1970 with *The Werewolf vs. Vampire Woman*, one of a series of werewolf pictures starring Paul Naschy as Count Waldemar Daninsky (the werewolf), who was countered in this film by the vampire/witch Countess Waldessa. A vampire appeared in the fifth sequel to *Howling* (a series of werewolf movies). In *Howling VI: The Freaks* (1990), the vampire kidnapped the werewolf to serve as an attraction in his traveling freak show. A werewolflike theme also was evident in *Dracula's Dog* (1977), a story about a vampire dog unleashed on Los Angeles.

The werewolf theme has shown some continued appeal. It has been the subject of a few very fine books and movies, *Cat People* and *Wolfen* being perhaps the most notable. It has, however, never developed the popular subculture following of Dracula and his vampire kin.

Sources:

Cooper, Basil. *The Werewolf in Legend, Fact and Art.* New York: St. Martin's Press, 1977. 240 pp.

Douglas, Adam. *The Beast Within: Man, Myths and Werewolves.* London: Orion, 1993. 294 pp.

Jones, Stephen. *The Illustrated Vampire Movie Guide.* London: Titan Books, 1993. 144 pp.

Murgoci, Agnes. "The Vampire in Romania." *Folklore* 37 (1926): 320-349.

Noll, Richard. *Vampires, Werewolves, and Demons: Twentieth Century Reports in the Psychiatric Literature.* New York: Brunner/Mazel, 1992. 243 pp.

Perkowski, Jan L. *The Darkling: A Treatise on Slavic Vampirism.* Columbus, OH: Slavica Publishers, 1989. 174 pp.

Scarm, Arthur N. *The Werewolf vs. Vampire Woman.* Beverly Hills, CA: Guild-Hartsford Publishing Co., 1972. 190 pp. Novelization of the movie.

Senn, Harry A. *Werewolf and Vampire in Romania.* New York: Columbia University Press, 1982. 148 pp.

Summers, Montague. *The Werewolf.* 1933. Reprint. New York: Bell Publishing Company, 1966. 307 pp.

WESTENRA, LUCY

Lucy Westenra, one of the major characters in **Bram Stoker**'s *Dracula,* made her initial appearance in the fifth chapter, where her correspondence with her long-time friend **Mina Murray** was recorded. While never described physically in great detail, she obviously was an attractive young woman in her twenties, the object of the affection of three men, **Arthur Holmwood**, to whom she became engaged, Dr. **John Seward**, and **Quincey P. Morris**. In the meantime, she lived with her mother.

On July 24, Lucy met Mina at the **Whitby** station, and they retired to the home at the Crescent where they would stay for the next several weeks. On July 26, Mina noted that Lucy had begun walking in her sleep. On August 8 a sudden storm hit Whitby and the *Demeter,* the ship on which **Dracula** came to England, wrecked on shore. On August 11, at 3 a.m., Mina discovered Lucy had left her bed, and she went in search of her. Lucy was on the East Cliff in their favorite seat. As Mina made her way to Lucy, she saw ''something, long and black, bending over her.'' When she called out, the something looked up and Mina saw Dracula's white face and red eyes. After she helped Lucy home, she saw two tiny marks on Lucy's neck. Over the next few days Lucy grew more and more tired and the wounds on her neck did not heal. At this juncture, Lucy seemed to get better and Mina, having finally heard from her true love **Jonathan Harker** on August 19, left for Budapest to join him.

Lucy returned to London where Holmwood joined her, and they set plans to marry on September 28. However, her condition worsened, and Holmwood called Seward in to examine her. Unable to figure out what was wrong, he called **Abraham Van Helsing** as a consultant, as Van Helsing knew of obscure diseases. Lucy seemed to improve, but then turned pale and lost all of her strength. Van Helsing prescribed a blood transfusion. As they were about to perform the procedure, Lucy's fiance Holmwood arrived and the blood was taken from him. Later a second transfusion was taken from Seward and then, without giving his reason, Van Helsing surrounded Lucy with **garlic**.

Dracula returned to attack Lucy on September 17. The attack followed the removal of the garlic that Van Helsing had ordered to be put around her neck. Morris was next in line to supply the blood needed to preserve Lucy's life, but by this time it was already too late; she was turning into a vampire. She died and was laid to rest in the family crypt. Van Helsing immediately wanted to treat the body as a vampire. Holmwood (who by this time had inherited his father's title as Lord Godalming) opposed any mutilation of the body. Though they had not married, he saw Lucy as his wife. In his opinion, the transfusion had served to marry them; they were married in the sight of God.

While the men rested, reports surfaced of missing children who, upon being found, told of being with a "boofer lady." Van Helsing persuaded the men to institute a watch at Lucy's tomb. They viewed her empty coffin and finally saw her walking around. In the end they cornered her in her coffin. Holmwood assumed his responsibility and drove the **stake** through her chest. At this point, it was noted that the harsh, fiendish expression, which had characterized Lucy's appearance at the time of her death, departed, and a face of sweetness and purity returned. Van Helsing cut off her head and filled her mouth with garlic. The men then turned their attention to killing Dracula.

When *Dracula* was brought to the stage and screen, the character of Lucy was handled quite differently. She disappeared completely from *Nosferatu, Eine Symphonie des Garuens* (1922) and **Hamilton Deane**'s *Dracula* play. She returned in John Balderston's revision of Deane's play for the American stage, though now she was Lucy Seward, Dr. Seward's daughter. Both she and Mina returned in the 1931 films, in both the English and Spanish versions. In 1958's *The Horror of Dracula,* Lucy was transformed into Holmwood's sister and the fiancee of Jonathan Harker. She was given strong parts in the **Jack Palance** version of *Dracula* **(1973)** and became central to the **Frank Langella**'s *Dracula* **(1979)**. She was returned to a role more closely approaching the one in the novel in **Francis Ford Coppola**'s *Bram Stoker's Dracula* (1992).

WHITBY

Whitby, a small town in northern England, was the setting for a major segment of **Bram Stoker**'s novel, *Dracula.* Whitby is located in Yorkshire at the mouth of the Esk River. Stoker provided a fairly accurate description of the town as background to the story. Dominating the town, on the east side of the river, was St. Mary's (Anglican) Church and the ruins of Whitby Abbey. The abbey dates to the seventh century. It was destroyed in the ninth century, rebuilt, and later abandoned.

As chapter four began **Lucy Westenra** met her friend **Mina Murray** at the train station and together they went to what has been identified as Number Four Crescent Terrace, where Mina joined the Westenra family in the rooms they had taken for a summer vacation. Stoker selected Whitby as a site for the events in his novel because he knew the town from his own visits in the years 1885 to 1890. During their first days in town, Lucy and Mina visited the local tourist spots—Mulgrave Woods, Robin Hood's Bay, Rig Mill, Runswick, and Staithes.

Meanwhile **Dracula** was aboard the *Demeter,* which was speeding north from Gibralter toward the British coast. Two weeks later, the *Demeter* was spotted off Whitby shortly before a storm hit. The ship was beached on the sand near Tate Hill Pier, one of two piers at Whitby, and Dracula (in the form of a dog) was seen leaving the ship. On board the wreck, the boxes of earth that Dracula traveled with were discovered. Dracula stayed in Whitby for a week and a half and attacked Lucy twice.

The first attack came several days after the wreck. Mina discovered that Lucy (who had a record of sleepwalking) had disappeared. Standing on the West Cliff, Mina looked across the river to where she could see St. Mary's Church and the ruins of Whitby Abbey. She saw a figure in white (Lucy) seated at what was called the "suicide's seat," under which was a stone noting the death of George Canon who had committed **suicide** on that spot. Mina then ran to the bridge that connected the two parts of town on either side of the river. From where Mina stood to the spot Lucy was located is almost a mile and required her walking down the cliff face on one side of the river and walking up the cliff face on the other side. As she reached the top of the steps near Whitby Abbey, she saw someone with Lucy, but he disappeared in a moment of darkness as a cloud briefly blocked the moonlight.

Several days later, Mina saw Lucy lean out of the window of her room. Beside her on the windowsill was "something that looked like a good-sized bird," which turned out to be Dracula in the form of a **bat.** By the time Mina reached Lucy's room, Dracula had completed drinking Lucy's blood, and Mina helped her to bed. Shortly after this second attack, Dracula, his boxes of earth, and the action of the novel moved to **London**.

Today modern tourists can visit all of the sights mentioned by Stoker in the novel, including the apartment on the Crescent where Lucy and Mina were supposed to have stayed. Bernard Davies of **The Dracula Society** has prepared a walking-tour guide.

Sources:

Davies, Bernard. *Whitby Dracula Trail.* Scarborough, North Yorkshire, United Kingdom: Department of Tourism and Amenities, Scarborough Borough Council, n.d. 11 pp.

Stoker, Bram. *The Annotated Dracula.* Ed. by Leonard Wolf. New York: Ballantine Books, 1975. 362 pp.
———. *The Essential Dracula.* Ed. by Raymond McNally and Radu Florescu. New York: Mayflower, 1979. 320 pp.

WILLIAM OF NEWBURGH (1136-1198?)

William of Newburgh, twelfth-century British chronicler of vampire incidents, was born in Bridlington. As a youth he moved to a priory of Augustinian Canons at Newburgh, Yorkshire. He became a canon and remained at Newburgh for the rest of his life. His talents were noticed by his superiors, who urged him to devote his time to his scholarly pursuits, especially literature. He emerged as a precursor of modern historical criticism and strongly denounced the inclusion of obvious myth in historical treatises. William's magnum opus, the *Historia Rerum Anglicarum*, also known as the *Chronicles*, was completed near the end of his life. Chapters 32-34 related a number of stories of contemporary revenants, which William had collected during his adult years. These stories, such as the account of the **Alnwick Castle** vampire and the **Melrose Abbey** vampire, have been cited repeatedly as evidence of a vampire lore existing in the British Isles in ancient times. While not describing vampires as such, the stories do recount visitation by the dead, some of whom were reported to act in a manner similar to that of the **Slavic vampire** and some of whom were handled in much the same manner as vampires in eastern Europe.

William was careful in his reporting and was aware of the skepticism that would greet the stories even in his own day. Thus he concluded,

> It is, I am very well aware, quite true that unless they were amply supported by many examples which have taken place in our own days, and by the unimpeachable testimony of responsible persons, these facts would not easily be believed, to wit, that the bodies of the dead may arise from their tombs and that vitalized by some supernatural power, they speed hither and thither, either greatly alarming or in some cases actually slaying the living, and when they return to the grave it seems to open to them of their own accord. (Chapter 34)

William died at Newburgh in 1198 (or 1208).

Sources:

Glut, Donald F. *True Vampires of History.* New York: HC Publications, 1971. 191 pp.
Summers, Montague. *The Vampire in Europe.* London: Routledge and Kegan Paul, 1929. 329 pp. Reprint. New Hyde Park, NY: University Books, 1961. 329 pp.

WILLIAMSON, J. N. (1932-)

J. N. Williamson, pseudonym of horror fiction author Gerald Neal Williamson, was born in Indianapolis, Indiana, the son of Maryesther Mendenhall and Lynn Jordan Williamson. In his teens he edited his first book, *Illustrious Client's Case-Book* (1948), soon followed by second and third volumes. He attended the Jordan College of Music (1951-53) and Butler University (1955-56). While in school he finished and published his first nonfiction book, *A Critical History and Analysis of the Whodunit.* Between his two periods in college he served in the U.S. Army as an intelligence officer. He married Mary Theresa Cavanaugh in 1960 and in 1961 went to work as an editor with Alan C. McConnell & Sons, an Indianapolis publisher.

Williamson had a personal crisis in 1970, which manifested in an emotional breakdown. During recovery, he had a nightmare that led to his first novel, *The Houngan* (which would not be published until a decade later). Following his recovery, he went to work for International Computer Programs, Inc. in 1973, first as an editor and then as an international sales manager (1975-77) before becoming a full-time writer. In 1979 *The Ritual: Robert Plus One* was published. It was quickly followed by a succession of horror fiction; he averaged more than three titles per year through the 1980s.

Among his early titles were four vampire novels that centered on the fictitious community of Thessaly, Indiana, a community of Greek immigrants. Thessaly was home to Lamia Zacharias, the Queen of the Vampires. In the first volume, the reader was introduced to the Greek terms for vampire, *lamiai, empusai,* and *vrykolakas* (variously spelled in different sources). These were not explained until later in the story, and some of the dynamic of the novel was based upon the reading public's general unfamiliarity with the Greek terms. The first novel, *Death-Coach*, opened as the Graham family, non-Greeks, moved into Thessaly. The town was headed by the Patriarch and the Syndic (a group of four men including the Patriarch). In the community were two prominent vampires, Zacharias and the more evil Vrukalakos.

As the story developed, the Grahams discovered that the people in their town were first assembled by the ancient philosopher Pythagoras, who had discovered the means of immortality through a process of *metempsychosis*, a form of reincarnation. They now faced a new transition set to occur in an imminent ceremony, the Commemoration. The young boy in the Graham family was a necessary instrument for the successful performance of the Commemoration. The ceremony sent the community into its new existence, but left Lamia and Vrukalakos in Thessaly for further adventures. Their conflict was the subject of the second volume in the series, *Death School,* and Lamia's adventures were carried forward in the last two novels, *Death-Angel* and *Death-Doctor.*

Williamson continued to produce horror novels and short stories at a steady rate. While he does not consider himself a horror writer, he has found that his best stories tend to fall under the heading of "fantasy." He also has completed a nonfiction work, *How to Write Tales of Horror, Fantasy, and Science Fiction* (1987).

Sources:

Williamson, J. N. *Death-Angel.* New York: Zebra Books,1981. 303 pp.

————. *Death-Coach.* New York: Zebra Books, 1981. 318 pp.

————. *Death-Doctor.* New York: Zebra Books, 1982. 272 pp.

————. *Death-School.* New York: Zebra Books, 1982. 302 pp.

————. *How to Write Tales of Horror, Fantasy, and ScienceFiction.* Cincinnati, OH: Writer's Digest Books, 1987.242 pp.

WINE

While trying to discern Dracula's nature, the entrapped **Jonathan Harker** remarked that his host never drank. Translated to the movie screen, this observation emerged in one of the most famous lines spoken by **Bela Lugosi** in the 1931 movie. Speaking to **R. N. Renfield** over dinner, Dracula said, "I never drink—wine." That line was spoken just after Renfield (whose character went to **Castle Dracula** instead of Harker in the movie version) had cut his finger and Dracula had shown his desire to drink of the blood that had appeared. The scene created a use of wine, the blood of the grape, as a metaphor for human blood.

In recent years, wine has returned as a vampire souvenir product. In 1974, the Golden Krone Hotel opened in **Bistritz, Transylvania**. The Golden Krone was the name of the fictional hotel at which Jonathan Harker stopped on his way to Castle Dracula. At the new hotel, a modern guest can order a Mediasch wine from Medias in the Tarnave Mare district of Transylvania, upon which Harker dined while at the Golden Krone. The modern visitor can also have some "Elixir Dracula", a local red liqueur made from plums.

Around 1990, A.V.F.F.Sp.A. of Sona, Italy, produced a "Vampire Wine". Distributed in the United States by Louis Glunz in Lincolnwood, Illinois, it was a red wine in a black bottle with a black label and arrived in an appropriate **coffin** container. Bottles of this wine were distributed as door prizes at Coven Party II sponsored in 1991 by **Anne Rice's Vampire Lestat Fan Club.**

Most recently, on the occasion of the opening of *Bram Stoker's Dracula* in Bucharest, in July 1993, Stroh Transylvania produced "Dracula's Spirit", described as the "Original Vampire's Delight." It was a mixture of vodka flavored with fruits and vegetables and red food coloring. The bottle's label carried the quote, "The history has borne the sacred hero. The myth has borne a bloody vampire. The hero and the fiend bear one name: DRACULA. We trust in DRACULA'S VODKA."

Sources:

Mackenzie, Andrew. *Dracula Country.* London: Arthur Barker, 1977. 176 pp.
McNally, Raymond, and Radu Florescu, eds. *The Essential Dracula.* New York: Mayflower Books, 1979. 320 pp.
The Vampire Companion. No. 1. Wheeling, WV: Innovative Corporation, 1991.

WITCHCRAFT AND VAMPIRES

In Europe, witchcraft and vampirism have had an intertwining history since ancient times. Many vampires first appeared among the demonic beings of Pagan polytheistic religions. They would include such entities as the Greek *lamiai* and seven evil spirits of Babylonia/Assyrian mythology. As Christianity arose, it tended to push the Pagan religions aside and to denounce any truth claims made by Pagan believers. As a whole, Christianity assumed that the Pagan deities were unreal, that they did not exist. Typical of the church's stance was the account of Paul's encounter with the Greek philosophers on the Areopagus, recounted in the biblical Book of Acts 17:16-34, in which he contrasted the one true God with the many gods represented in the statutes.

The Pagan religious functionaries went under a variety of names, and terms that in English mean witch and/or sorcerer were common. As Pagan religion was swept aside, so the witches and sorcerers were to some extent pushed from the emerging urban areas into the countryside. The church saw them as worshippers of imaginary deities.

Crucial to the developing attitude concerning the Pagan religions was magic. Magic, the ability to cause changes by calling upon supernatural entities and using supernatural powers, was almost universally accepted as real. People, including church leaders, believed that wondrous feats were possible either by the power of the Holy Spirit or by reference to illegitimate supernatural powers. Witches, the pagan practitioners, had the ability to do magical feats the average person could not. Among these were many things that even in Pagan days were considered evil. It must be remembered that many of the Pagan entities existed as an explanation for the intrusion of evil and injustice in a person's life.

With the marginalization of the witches and the destruction of Pagan systems, the evil functions of the old entities tended to be transferred to the witches. Thus emerged the *strega* in ancient **Rome**. The *strega,* or witch, was first known as the *strix*, a night-flying demon that attacked infants and killed them by sucking their blood. Over a period of time the *strix* was identified as an individual who had the power of **transformation** into the forms of various **animals**, including owls and crows, and who in that guise attacked infants. The *strix* then became the *strega* of medieval Italy and the *strigoi* of Romania.

Through the first millennium A.D. the church retained its notion that Paganism and witchcraft were imaginary. Illustrative of this belief was a tenth-century document, the *Canon Episcopi.* The *Canon* attributed Pagan belief to the devil, but emphasized that the devil's work was to present the imaginary world of Paganism to the followers of the goddess Diana. Witchcraft was an illusion; therefore, whoever:

> . . . believes that any thing can be made, or that any creature can be changed to better or to worse or be transformed into another species or similitude, except by the creator himself who made everything and through whom all things were made, is beyond doubt an infidel. (quoted in Russell)

The church had a similar attitude toward vampires. It had discovered a belief in vampires from earlier cultures and also had assumed that they were not real. This perspective was illustrated in two legal documents, one from the East and one from the West. The first was a nomocanon or authoritative ordinance that was in effect in the East through the Middle Ages. It said:

> It is impossible that a dead man should become a *vrykolakas* (vampire) unless it be by the power of the Devil who, wishing to mock and delude some that they may incur the wrath of Heaven, causes these dark wonders, and so very often at night he casts a glamour whereby men imagine that the dead man whom they knew formerly, appears and holds converse with them, and in their dreams too they see strange visions. At other times they may behold him in the road, yea, even in the highway walking to and fro or standing still, and what is more than this he is even said to have strangled men and to have slain them.

> Immediately there is sad trouble, and the whole village is in a riot and a racket, so that they hasten to the grave and they unbury the body of a man . . . and the dead man—one who has long been dead and buried—appears to them to have flesh and blood . . . so they can collect together a mighty pile of dry wood and set fire to this and lay the body upon it so that they burn it and destroy it altogether. (quoted in Summers)

In like measure, by the middle of the eighth century, a Saxon law decried the belief in *strix* (vampire witches). Later in the century it was strengthened by a law decreeing the death penalty for any who perpetuated the belief in the *strix* and any who, because of that belief, attacked an individual believed to be a *strix* and harmed (attacked, burned, and/or cannibalized) that individual. A legal debate erupted in the eleventh century in Hungary when King Stephen I (997-1038) passed a law against *strigae* who rode out at night and fornicated. One of his successors, King Colomen (1077-1095), struck the law from the books based on the notion that no such thing as *strigae* existed.

THE DEMONIZATION OF WITCHES: By the fifteenth century, the Roman Catholic church had built a large organization, the Congregation for the Propagation of the Faith, better known as the Inquisition, to handle the problem of heretics and, to a lesser extent, apostasy. Heresy was a belief system that deviated significantly from that of the orthodox theology of the church. An apostate was a person who had been a church member and who had renounced the faith. The new beliefs the person espoused constituted apostasy. The Inquisition was limited to action against heresy and apostasy. It could not turn its attention to members of other faiths who had never been Christian.

By the 1480s, the Inquisition had largely done its work. At limited times and places the Inquisition had considered sorcery and malevolent magic, but in 1484, Pope Innocent VIII issued his bull, *Summis desiderantes affectibus,* which had the effect of redefining witchcraft. It was no longer the imaginary belief system of ancient Paganism. It had become Satanism (the worship of the Christian devil) and hence apostasy. In the wake of the bull, two Dominican fathers, Heinrich Kramer and Jacob Sprenger, authored *Malleus Maleficarum (The Hammer of Witches)*, which became the manual for the inquisitors to discover and treat witchcraft practitioners. The papal bull was used as an introductory document for the book.

Only in the middle of the next century was the problem of vampirism raised for the Roman church. It emerged among Roman Catholics in Greece who had encountered the *vrykolakas.* The reconsideration was carried out by Fr. **Leo Allatius**, a Greek who had converted to Roman Catholicism, and French Jesuit priest Fr. Francoise Richard, who worked on the Greek island of Santorini. Allatius's *De Graecorum hodie quorundam opinationibus* was published in 1645. Richard's *Relation de ce qui s'est passe a Sant-Erini Isle de l'Archipel* appeared 12 years later.

The effect of Allatius's and Richard's writing was to link vampirism to witchcraft and to argue that vampirism was also the work of Satan. Vampirism was real, and the devil was assigned the power not only of creating fantastic illusions but also of actually reanimating corpses. Richard, especially, related vampirism to the observations on witchcraft in the *Malleus Maleficarum.* Kramer and Sprenger had suggested that three things had to be present for witchcraft to operate—the devil, witches, and the permission of God. In like measure, for vampirism to occur, three elements had to be present—the devil, a dead body, and the permission of God.

Richard argued that the devil energized the bodies and that vampires were far more than mere ghosts.

Allatius and Richard caused several others to consider the subject, which was still not high on the church's agenda. The most important treatise was Philip Rohr's *De Masticatione Mortuorum,* published at Leipzig in 1679. The three books provided the context for the reaction of the Roman Catholic Austrian government in its encounter with the epidemics of vampirism that emerged in the late seventeenth century in Austrian-controlled territories. There was a predisposition to believe that vampires were real in spite of the initial reaction to the mutilation of bodies of deceased members of the families of the realm. It took many decades for a skeptical view of vampirism to emerge, and only in the 1750s did the central government outlaw the disinterment of bodies for treatment as vampires.

The medieval identification of vampires with witches, and of both with Satan, also redefined vampirism as a real evil that could be opposed by the weapons of the church. Thus vampires were the opposite of the sacred and could be affected by such blessed objects as the **crucifix**, the **eucharistic wafer**, and holy **water**.

One can see a parallel process of demonization of the vampire in the Eastern Orthodoxy of **Russia**. Here witches and vampires also were identified with each other and the vampire designated a heretic, *eretik* being the Russian term. Witches, after their death, became vampires. The process of so labeling the vampire seems to have occurred over a period of time. The term *eretik* was broadened from its strict definition as a doctrinal deviant to include all who did not believe in the true God and who associated with evil, especially evil magic. The period coincided with the church's efforts to suppress sectarian (heretical) groups that were growing in various communities. The convergence of heresy and witchcraft and vampirism served to stigmatize the sectarians and to brand them as more evil than they were. *Eretik* became a general term of derision. It largely replaced *upir* or *upyr* in some sections of the country.

MODERN SECULARIZATION: The Austrian laws passed in the middle of the eighteenth century, which outlawed the practice of staking and burning bodies of suspected vampires, marked the beginning of the end of widespread belief in vampires in the urban West. By the end of the century it would be almost impossible to make a case for the existence of physical vampires, though in the nineteenth century, Spiritualists and Theosophists would begin to argue for the existence of the phenomenon of **psychic vampirism**. Vampires would become an object of the inner psyche to be explored by romantic poets and novelists, political forces that sapped the strength of the working class, and negative psychological impulses.

By the twentieth century belief in the vampire as a real, evil entity had, like witchcraft, been largely banished from the public arena. Interestingly, both began to attract a following in the late twentieth century. That interest grew surrounded by a culture that did not believe in the power of magic or in the existence of real vampires. That very disbelief has allowed a new Wiccan religion to take its place on the religious scene, and vampirism to arise again as a tool for the social expression of some important personal visions of the universe.

Sources:

Oinas, Felix J. "Heretics as Vampires and Demons in Russia." *Slavic and Eastern European Journal* 22, 4 (Winter 1978): 433-41.

Robbins, Rossell Hope. *The Encyclopedia of Witchcraft and Demonology*. New York: Crown Publishers, 1959.

Russell, Jeffrey Burton. *Witchcraft in the Middle Ages*. Ithaca, NY: Cornell University Press, 1972.

Summers, Montague. *The Vampire: His Kith and Kin*. 1928. New Hyde Park, NY: University Books, 1960.

———. *The Vampire in Europe*. 1929. New Hyde Park, NY: University Books, 1961.

WOLF, LEONARD (1923-)

Leonard Wolf, writer and college professor, was born on March 1, 1923, in Vulcan, **Romania**, the son of Rose Engel and Joseph Wolf. Born into a Jewish family, he moved to the United States prior to World War II. He attended Ohio State University (1941-43) and then transferred to the University of California at Berkeley, from which he received his A.B. degree in 1945 and his M.A. in 1950. While at Berkeley, he published his first book, *Hamadryad Hunted* (1945), a book of poems. In 1954 he completed his Ph.D. at the University of Iowa. That fall he joined the faculty at St. Mary's College. He later taught at San Francisco State University for two years and then moved to New York as a professor of English at Columbia University, where he has remained to the present.

Amid Wolf's varied interests, his Romanian heritage asserted itself in the late 1960s when he created and taught a course on Dracula at Columbia. His experiences with students and his own research in vampire literature and films through the early 1970s led to his writing *A Dream of Dracula: In Search of the Living Dead* (1972), an impressionistic exploration of the various ways that the Dracula myth had invaded his life. The flavor of the book was aptly illustrated, for example, in his discussion of his attempt to reconcile what he saw as three very different Romanias: the dreamlike one of his childhood memories, the one he traveled through as an adult in preparation for writing his book, and the one of Stoker's gothic imagination. *A Dream of Dracula* appeared at a time when nonfiction books on Dracula were rare and found a large audience among a new generation of vampire fans who had been flocking to the vampire movies being produced at that time.

Wolf made a second significant contribution in 1974 with *The Annotated Dracula,* a copy of the text of Stoker's 1897 novel with extensive notes. The annotations provided a useful reference to the many actual locations (with handy maps) and the historical facts that Stoker mentioned and offered a variety of information about the folklore to which he referred. Wolf also created a calendar of events in the story, which he believed probably occurred in 1887. (Subsequent

◀
LEONARD WOLF, AUTHOR OF
THE ANNOTATED DRACULA.

research of both historical facts mentioned in the novel and Stoker's own notes, has revealed the actual date of the novel to be 1893.)

After writing his Dracula books, Wolf continued work in the horror field. He wrote a book on *Monsters* (1974), which included a picture of **Christopher Lee** on the cover and a chapter on Dracula. He compiled an anthology of horror stories, *Wolf's Complete Book of Terror* (1979) and wrote a biographical volume: *Bluebeard: The Life and Crimes of Gilles de Rais* (1980). Gilles de Rais, while not a vampire, has often been covered in vampire books because of the bloody nature of his crimes. Wolf's interest in vampires has continued, and recently he penned an introductory reflection on **Bela Lugosi**'s *Dracula* **(1931)**, on the occasion of the 60th anniversary of its release, along with a vampire filmography for an recent anthology of vampire stories, *The Ultimate Dracula* (1991).

Sources:

Wolf, Leonard. *The Annotated Dracula.* New York: Clarkson N. Porter, 1974. Reprint. New York: Ballantine Books, 1976.
———. *A Dream of Dracula: In Search of the Living Dead.* Boston: Little Brown, 1972. Reprint. New York: Popular Library, 1977.

———. "Happy Birthday, Dracula!" In Byron Preiss, ed. *The Ultimate Dracula.* London: Headline Book Publishing, 1991.
———. *Monsters.* San Francisco: Straight Arrow, 1974.

WOMEN AS VAMPIRES

The image of the vampire in both the literary and cinematic context has been dominated by the likes of **Lord Ruthven**, **Dracula**, **Bela Lugosi**, and **Christopher Lee**—all males. The dominant image of the male vampire, frequently preying on weak females, has tended to obscure the role of female vampires in the creation of the vampire myth and the important female vampire figures who have helped shape contemporary understanding of vampirism.

THE ORIGINAL VAMPIRES: In most cultures, the oldest vampire figures were females. They included the Greek *lamiai,* the Malaysian *langsuyar,* and the Jewish **Lilith,** among others. Each of these vampire figures points to the origin of vampirism as a myth explaining problems in childbirth. The story of the *langsuyar,* for example, told of a woman who bore a stillborn child. Distraught and angry when she learned of her baby's death, she flew into the trees and from that time forward became the plague of pregnant women and their children. Magical means were devised to protect mothers giving birth, and their newborns, from the bloodsucking *langsuyar.* In like measure, before evolving in various ways, the *lamiai* and Lilith were the terror of pregnant women.

Each of the three, however, did evolve, and in slightly different ways. However, at one point each took on the characteristics of the young **vamp**, the beautiful female stranger from a foreign place who seduced the unwary young man looking for a mate. The most famous account story of the *lamiai,* of course, was told by Philostratus in *The Life of Apollonius.* In the story, one of Apollonius's students, Menippus, was about to marry a wealthy young woman; she turned out to be a vampire who would have sucked the life out of him. He was saved by the wise Apollonius. Other similar female vampires included the ***loogaroo, sukuyan,*** and *asema,* all vampires operating in the Caribbean area. They lived incognito in a community, living a seemingly ''normal'' life during the day and operating as a vampire at night. Even their husbands did not know they were vampires.

As the vampire story became more death-related, i.e., associated with the phenomenon of the death of a loved one, rather than simply associated with problems in childbirth or the problems of errant young men, the female vampire partially gave way to the male. Many vampirelike creatures, who also happened to be female, were prominent in the lore of polytheistic cultures. **Kali**, the dark goddess of **India**, was such a figure, as were the witch/vampires in West **Africa**. In many cultures, the vampires might be of either sex.

Closely related to the female vampire, of course, were figures such as the **incubus/succubus** and the mara. Neither of these entities was a vampire, but each behaved in ways reminiscent of vampires, attacking male victims in the night and leaving the victims distraught and exhausted in the morning.

THE BLOOD COUNTESS: The creation of the modern vampire depended in large part upon the nineteenth century's appropriation of information on two historical personages: **Vlad the Impaler**, the real Dracula, and **Elizabeth Bathory**, a seventeenth-century Hungarian countess. Bathory's career became well known in the 1720s when an early account was published just as Europe was experiencing one of its periodic waves of vampire hysteria. An account in English appeared in 1865 in Sabine Baring-Gould's *The Book of Werewolves*. Bathory became famous for draining the blood of servant girls and bathing in it in the belief that it would keep her skin healthy and youthful. Bathory's career seems to have directly influenced **Bram Stoker** in the creation of Dracula.

THE LITERARY VAMPIRE: The vampire entered literature at the end of the eighteenth century. Almost all of the first literary vampires were women, beginning with the unnamed woman remembered simply as ''The Bride of Corinth,'' the title character in the 1797 poem by **Goethe**. In the original story from ancient Greece upon which Goethe based his poem, the woman's name was Philinnon. She had died a virgin and returned to taste the joys of her budding sexuality before leaving this life altogether. A woman was also what is now believed to be the first vampire in English literature, Geraldine, the villain in **Samuel Taylor Coleridge**'s poem, ''Christabel,'' written at the end of the 1790s. Contemporaneously with Coleridge, **Robert Southey**'s hero Thalaba killed the vampire inhabiting the body of his deceased bride, Oneiza.

However, after Goethe, Coleridge, and Southey, vampire literature (be it poetry, fiction, or drama) was dominated for three-quarters of a century by Lord Ruthven, the aristocratic Byronic vampire who preyed upon unsuspecting women. Introduced by **John Polidori** in 1819, Lord Ruthven appeared in a host of French plays and was the basis of the mid-century British penny dreadful, *Varney the Vampyre*.

The absolute dominance of vampirism by males was relieved occasionally by short story writers. In 1836, for example, French writer **Theophile Gautier** penned a story variously called in English ''Clarimonde'' or ''The Beautiful Vampire.'' In 1848, **Alexandre Dumas** wrote of ''The Pale Lady.'' Then in 1872 **Sheridan Le Fanu** finished his novella of the two hundred-year-old **''Carmilla,''** destined to become the most popular female vampire ever. Carmilla, like her male counterparts, tended to prey upon young women who were the same age as she was when she became a vampire, though the story begins with her attack upon a prepubescent Laura, the story's narrator. For many years the female vampire would be largely confined to short fiction, though some, such as Anne Crawford's ''A Mystery of the Campagna,'' (1887), would become classic tales.

THE CINEMATIC VAMPIRE: While female vampires occasionally appeared in vampire stories and novels, it was the movies that offered the female vampire her due. An older female vampire arose in *Vampyr,* **Carl Theodor Dreyer**'s famous silent vampire feature. The female vampire would first be the star of a movie in *Dracula's*

Daughter (1936), the first sequel of **Bela Lugosi**'s *Dracula* (**1931**). Early in the story, Countess Marya Zaleska (portrayed by Gloria Holden) stole the body of her father, which she burned. She was quite different from her father, however, in that she was searching for a cure of her vampiric state; in the meantime, she was unable to control her blood urges. By the time she realized that she could not be cured, she had fallen in love with Dr. Jeffery Garth, a former pupil of Dracula's killer, Dr. **Abraham Van Helsing**. She lured him to **Dracula's Castle** in **Transylvania,** where she planned to make him her vampire companion for eternity. Her plans were thwarted by her jealous servant, who attempted to kill Garth. In the process of protecting him, the countess was dispatched by a wooden arrow that penetrated her heart.

Interestingly enough, the female vampire made her next appearance in a series of films produced in **Malaysia** beginning in 1956. Maria Menado starred as a woman made beautiful by magic. She married and was soon confronted with potential disaster when her husband was bitten by a snake. She sucked the poison out of her husband, but in the process was transformed into a vampire. She in turn attempted to vampirize her daughter but was killed before she could accomplish her goal. Menado's *Pontianak* was followed by *Dendam Pontianak* (1957), in which Menado returned from the grave to seek revenge upon her killers. Her death at the end of the second movie proved inconclusive, and she returned a second time in *Sumpah Pontianak* (1958) and a third time in *Pontianak Kembali* (1963). These films, seen by few in the West prior to their recent release in the United States on video, had little effect upon the developing image of the vampire in Hollywood.

While Menado was gaining stardom in the Orient, Italian filmmaker **Mario Bava** discovered an intriguing woman who would become a legend in horror movies, **Barbara Steele**. Her introduction to an emerging generation of horror fans was a 1960 vampire movie, *The Mask of Satan* (*La Meschera del Demonio*, released on video as *Black Sunday*). Steele played Princess Ada, a seventeenth-century witch who had been killed by the placement of a mask on her face. The inside of the mask was covered with spikes. Brought back to life by a drop of blood, she terrorized the community in an attempt to assume the role of Katia, her double, who was involved in her revival.

At the same time as Bava's work in Italy, French director **Roger Vadim** sought a film to display the talents of his wife, Annette Stroyberg. He discovered the perfect role in a cinematic adaptation of ''Carmilla,'' *Et Mourir de Plaisir* (released in the United States as *Blood and Roses*). Stroyberg played Carmilla who, in this version, attacked her cousin Georgia (Elsa Martinelli) and was in the end impaled on a fence post. Through the rest of the 1960s, female vampires were few in number and primarily appeared in brief supporting roles as the victims of the male star or as members of a group of otherwise anonymous vampires (especially evident in many Mexican vampire features). Of the several stories featuring female vampires that did make it to the screen, **Roger Corman**'s *Queen of Blood* was possibly the most memorable because it was one of the early **science fiction** vampire films. Florence Marly played the alien picked up on Mars by an expedition from Earth. On the trip home she attacked the crew. Other women who made it into vampire roles during the decade included Beth Porter (*The Naked Witch*, 1961); Joan Stapleton (*The Devil's Mistress*, 1966); Rossanna Ortiz (*Draculita*, 1969); and Gina Romand (*La Venganza de las Mujeres Vampiro*, 1969), all forgettable motion pictures. They would be followed however, by a group of the best female vampire films ever made.

THE 1970s: The female vampire made her major impact in a series of films in the early 1970s based upon the fictional "Carmilla" and the very real Elizabeth Bathory. Hammer led the way with its revival of "Carmilla" in *The Vampire Lovers* starring a new face, **Ingrid Pitt,** and an old standby, **Peter Cushing**. Director Roy Ward Baker emphasized Carmilla's **lesbian** attacks upon the young women, which continued until **vampire hunter** Cushing, whose daughter was under attack, caught up with her. The further adventures of Carmilla in a nineteenth-century girls' school were captured in *Lust for a Vampire*, directed for Hammer by **Jimmy Sangster**. Pitt and Cushing were replaced by Yutte Stengaard and Ralph Bates. The third film of Hammer's Carmilla trilogy, *Twins of Evil* (1971), starred Katya Wyeth. She vampirized her relative Count Karnstein and then together they had to face the equally vile witch-hunter Gustav Weil (Peter Cushing). The Hammer trilogy suggested "Carmilla" 's potential to other directors. **Jesus Franco**, for example, made two Carmilla movies, *La Fille de Dracula* (1972) and *La Comtesse aux Seiens Nux* (1973). The latter, in spite of its rather boring storyline and the wooden acting of Lina Romay as a modern Carmilla, was released under a variety of titles, most recently on video as *Erotikill*. A more interesting modern Carmilla story was *La Novia Ensangrentada* (*The Blood Spattered Bride*, 1974) in which Alexandra Bastedo as Carmilla seduced Maribel Martin, a frigid bride. The pair met their doom when the offended husband discovered them asleep in a coffin specially made for two.

Looking for more stories to continue the success of its earlier horror movies, **Hammer Films** also sought inspiration from the legends of **Elizabeth Bathory,** whose story was brought to the screen in *Countess Dracula*, with **Ingrid Pitt** playing the title role. The film, made as a follow up to Pitt's earlier success in *The Vampire Lovers,* was notable more for Pitt's nude scenes than for the acting. About the time that *Countess Dracula* appeared, Harry Kumel released his Belgian-made film, *Daughters of Darkness*, featuring Delphine Seygig as a contemporary Countess Bathory encountering a young, newly married couple. After the husband revealed himself as a sadist, the wife and Bathory joined forces and killed him. Later, the countess was killed and the wife, now a vampire, took her place. Bathory was also portrayed by Lucia Bose, Patty Shepard, and Paloma Picasso (the daughter of painter Pablo Picasso), respectively, in a series of less noteworthy films: *Legend of Blood Castle* (1972), *Curse of the Devil* (1973), and *Immoral Tales* (1974). A delightful comedy based upon the Bathory character was *Mama Dracula* (1980), starring Louise Fletcher.

Women had never enjoyed so much exposure in vampire roles as they did in the rash of Carmilla and Bathory films produced at the beginning of the 1970s. In spite of the dominance of Dracula and his male cohorts, a variety of other female vampires

KATHRYN LEIGH SCOTT PORTRAYED JOSETTE DUPRES, A VAMPIRE IN THE POPULAR TELEVISION SERIES
DARK SHADOWS.

found their way to the screen. Among them were: *Vampyros Lesbos die erbin des Dracula* (1970); *The Legendary Curse of Lemora* (1973); *Leonor* (1975); *Mary, Mary, Blood Mary* (1975); *Lady Dracula* (1977); and *Nocturna, Granddaughter of Dracula* (1979).

Much of the problem with introducing females vampires to the screen has been due to the dominance of the directing profession by men. Among the few female directors, Stephanie Rothman began her directing career with a vampire movie, *The Velvet Vampire* (1971), produced by **Roger Corman**'s New World Pictures. The story concerns a modern-day vampire, Diana Le Fanu (played by Celeste Yarnell), who lived in the desert and invited victims to her secluded home. While the number of female directors has grown steadily, the field remains largely a male domain.

THE 1980s AND 1990s: The 1980s saw the appearance of several of the most notable female vampires, possibly the most prominent being Mariam Blaylock (played by Catherine Deneuve) as the alien vampire in the movie version of Whitley Strieber's novel, *The Hunger*. The story centered upon the immortal Blaylock's problem: her male human partners began to age rapidly and to decay after a century or so of vampiric life. In her attempts to save her current lover (David Bowie), she seduced a blood researcher (Susan Sarandon) but in the end was unable to find a cure to their predicament. In contrast to Strieber's horrific vision, *Once Bitten* (1985) was a delightful comedy that had Lauren Hutton as a vampire in search of virgin blood in modern-day Hollywood. Finally locating Jim Carrey, she was opposed by his girlfriend Karen Kopins, who was forced to make the ultimate sacrifice of her virginity to save him.

In *Vamp* (1986), a vampiric Grace Jones managed a nightclub, After Dark, into which a group of college kids arrived in search of a stripper for a college fraternity party. While the movie suffered from an identity problem (is it a comedy or a horror movie?), Jones was memorable as her vampiric nature became visible and she vampirized one of the boys who joined her in the underground After Dark world.

Other female vampires of lesser note in the 1980s included Gabrielle Lazure (*La Belle Captive*, 1983); Matilda May (*Lifeforce*, 1985); Britt Ekland (*Beverly Hills Vamp*, 1988); Sylvia Kristel (*Dracula's Widow*, 1988); and Julie Carmen (*Fright Night Part 2*, 1988). Several women also emerged as directors. Of these, Katt Shea Ruben (working for Roger Corman's Concorde Pictures was most prominent for her direction of *Dance of the Damned,* 1988). The film did not star a female vampire, but featured a strong woman as a potential victim who was forced to spend an evening describing the daylight to the moody vampire. The movie climaxed as the dawn approached, and the vampire finally attacked. In the end the woman was able to fend off the attack.

Kathryn Bigelow directed *Near Dark*, another of the new breed of vampire movies with contemporary, nongothic settings and vampires. The story involved a band of vampires who traveled the countryside in a van. They were joined by a farmboy attracted to one of the group, played by Jenny Wright. Once the young boy became a vampire, he was unable to bring himself to kill and suck the blood of innocent victims. He had to rely upon Wright to feed him. Obviously a drag upon the vampires, who had to keep moving, the story climaxed in the confrontation between them, Wright, the boy, and the boy's family.

Early in the 1990s, one of the finest vampire movies featuring a female lead appeared. Anne Parilland starred in *Innocent Blood* (1992) as a very careful modern vampire who had learned to survive by living according to a very precise set of rules. She did not play with her food, and she always cleaned up after dining. One evening, she was unable to complete her meal of a Mafia mobster. He arose from her bite as a new vampire. She was forced to team up with a human cop to try and stop him. A second prominent entry in the vampire genre did not include a female vampire but did unite director Fran Rubel Kuzui with Kristy Swanson in the title role as *Buffy the Vampire Slayer* (1992). A high school cheerleader, the reluctant but athletic Buffy was designated as the Chosen One, the person who must kill the King of the Undead, played by Rutger Hauer.

THE FEMALE VAMPIRE IN RECENT FICTION: As in the movies, Dracula and his male vampire kin dominated twentieth-century vampire fiction writing. However, some females vampires gained a foothold in the realm of the undead. Many of these have been the imaginary product of a new crop of female writers, though some of the most popular female vampire authors—**Elaine Bergstrom**, **P. N. Elrod**, and **Anne Rice**—have featured male vampires.

The century began with an assortment of short stories featuring female vampires, including F. G. Loring's ''The Tomb of Sarah'' Hume Nisbet's ''The Vampire Maid,'' and E. F. Benson's classic tale, ''Mrs. Amworth.'' Female vampires regularly appeared in short stories through the 1950s but were largely absent from the few vampire novels. Among the first novels to feature a female vampire was Peter Saxon's 1966 *The Vampires of Finistere*. Three years later **Bernhardt J. Hurwood** (under the pseudonym of Mallory T. Knight) wrote *Dracutwig*, the lighthearted adventures of the daughter of Dracula coming of age in the modern world.

In 1969, possibly the most important modern female vampire character appeared, not in a novel, but in comic books. **Vampirella**, an impish, voluptuous vampire from the planet Drakulon, originated in a comic magazine from Warren Publishing Company at a time when vampires had disappeared from more mainstream **comic book**s. *Vampirella* was an immediate success and ran for 112 issues before it was discontinued in 1983. The stories were novelized in six books by Ron Goulart in the mid-1970s. Most recently, the character has been revived by Harris Comics and is enjoying new popularity.

Female vampires have continued to emerge as the subject of novels. From the 1970s one thinks of *The Vampire Tapes* by Arabella Randolphe (1977) and *The Virgin and the Vampire* by Robert J. Myers (1977). These were followed by the reluctant vampirism of *Sabella* by Tanith Lee (1980) and the celebrative vampirism of Whitley Strieber's *The Hunger* (1981). Through 1981 and 1982, **J. N. Williamson** wrote a series of novels about a small town in Indiana that was home of the youthful-appearing but very old vampire Lamia Zacharias and her various plots to take over the world. In spite of some real accomplishments in spreading her vampiric condition, she never reached her loftier goals. Other significant appearances by female vampires occurred in *Live Girls* by Ray Garton (1987), *Black Ambrosia* by Elizabeth Engstrom (1988), and the first of Nancy Collins's novels, *Sunglasses After Dark* (1989), which won the Bram Stoker Award for a first novel from the Horror Writers of America.

The 1980s ended with the appearance of the ''Olivia'' novels by **Chelsea Quinn Yarbro**. Olivia had first appeared in *Blood Games,* one of the more famous **St. Germain** vampire novels. However, beginning in 1987 Yarbro produced four lengthy explorations of St. Germain's former love living on her own. These novels included *A Flame in Byzantium* (1987), *Crusader's Torch* (1988), *A Cradle for D'Artagnan* (1989), and *Out of the House of Life* (1990).

Also memorable during the 1980s was *Vamps* (1987), an anthology of short stories of female vampires compiled by Martin H. Greenberg and Charles G. Waugh. It included some often-ignored nineteenth-century tales, such as **Theophile Gautier**'s ''Clarimonde,'' and Julian Hawthorne's ''Ken Mystery,'' as well as more recent stories by **Stephen King** and Tanith Lee.

Novels featuring female vampires continued into the early 1990s. Traci Briery, for example, wrote two substantial novels, *The Vampire Memoirs* (1991) and *The Vampire Journals* (1992), chronicling the lives of two female vampire heroines, Mara McCuniff and Theresa Allogiamento. Kathryn Meyer Griffith's *The Last Vampire* looked into the future to explore the problems of a reluctant vampire after a wave of natural disasters had wiped out most of the human race. And not to be forgotten is *The Gilda Stories,* a **lesbian vampire** novel by Jewelle Gomez, an African American author.

CONCLUSION: Viewing the male vampire as a representation of the male desires for power and sex, women tended to become stereotyped as victims, and the vampire myth emerged as a misogynistic story to be constantly retold. In its worst form, so it remains. However, in modern vampire fiction, even the male bloodsucker has became a much more complicated character and the females he confronts have had much more varied roles. In contrast with the powerful male vampire, the female vampire of the 1980s emerged with the many new roles assumed by women in the larger culture and as important models (however fanciful) of female power.

A further, if much more speculative, explanation of the emerging female vampire myth has been offered by Penelope Shuttle and Peter Redgrove in their book *The Wise Wound* (1978). They took a new look at old folk stories of a snake that lived in the moon and bit women, thus bringing on their menstrual flow. Shuttle and Redgrove saw the intertwined motifs of womb, snake, and moon as integral to the vampire myth. Of some interest, they noted (as had many a moviegoer) that when the vampire bit the young woman, the two marks usually were much closer together than were the vampire's **fangs**. They appeared to be the bite marks not of the attacking vampire, but of a viper. The passive victim often responded to the vampire's bite by first bleeding and then becoming active and sexual. That is, the vampire functioned like the snake of the old myth, bringing on the flow of blood that initiated a new phase of sexual existence. Such an explanation of the vampire has found a popular response among feminists attempting to deal with exclusively male appropriations of the popular myth.

Sources:

Cox, Greg. *The Transylvanian Library: A Consumer's Guide to Vampire Fiction.* San Bernardino, CA: Borgo Press, 1993.

Johnson, Alan P. "'Dual Life': The Status of Women in Stoker's Dracula." In Don Richard Cox, ed. *Sexuality and Victorian Literature.* Knoxville, TN: University of Tennessee Press, 1984., pp. 20-39.

Jones, Stephen. *The Illustrated Vampire Movie Guide.* London: Titan Books, 1993.

Kuhn, Annette. *The Women's Companion to International Film.* London: Virago, 1990. Rept.as: *Women in Film: An International Guide.* New York: Fawcett Columbine, 1991.

Ursini, James, and Alain Silver. *The Vampire Film.* South Brunswick, NJ: A. S. Barnes and Company, 1975.

THE WORLD OF DARK SHADOWS

The World of Dark Shadows, is the oldest existing fanzine serving the fans of *Dark Shadows,* the highly successful soap opera that ran on ABC-TV from 1966 to 1971 and was revived in 1991 by NBC. Its first issue was circulated to 30 people in 1975 by its founder/editor Kathleen Resch; by the early 1990s the subscriber count was over 2,000. Resch has been among the most active leaders in *Dark Shadows* fandom. In the 1980s she published a series of fanzines under the collective title of *Dark Shadows Concordance.* Each concordance summarizes a particular set of the original episodes. By 1992, concordances were available for episodes 365-700 and 981-1,245. When completed, the concordances will cover all of the 1,245 episodes. *Shadows in the 90's* was a concordance of the 1991 primetime *Dark Shadows* series.

The World of Dark Shadows also has included several anthologies of *Dark Shadows* short stories and novels. Resch contributed a short story, "Edges," to *Decades.* Additional *World of Dark Shadows* anthologies included two volumes under the name *From the Shadows,* one with stories by Marcy Robin and the other by Virginia Waldron; and *Echoes,* a collection edited by Resch. Resch also co-authored two books with Marcy Robin—a novel, *Beginnings: The Island of Ghosts,* and a nonfiction work on the television show, *Dark Shadows in the Afternoon.* Additional novels from *The World of Dark Shadows* include *Shadowed Beginnings* by Carol Maschke, *Rebirth of the Undead* by Elwood Beaty and D. L. Crabtree, and Lori Paige's two books, *Dark Changeling* and *The Year the Fire Came.*

The World of Dark Shadows may be contacted c/o Kathleen Resch, PO Box 1766, Temple City, CA 91780. Resch works actively with **Dark Shadows Festival**, which annually plans a *Dark Shadows* convention. Most recently she has started a new *Dark Shadows* fanzine, *Echoes . . . from the Past.*

Sources:

Resch, Kathleen. *The Dark Shadows Concordance 1795.* Temple City, CA: Pentagram Press, 1989.

———. *The Dark Shadows Concordance 1968.* 2 vols. Temple City, CA: Pentagram Press, 1989; 1990

———. *The Dark Shadows Concordance 1970 Parallel Time.* Temple City, CA: Pentagram Press, 1988.

———. *The Dark Shadows Concordance 1840.* Temple City, CA: Pentagram Press, 1987.

———. ed. *Decades.* Santa Clara, CA: Pentagram Press, 1982.

——— and Marcy Robin. *Beginnings: The Island of Ghosts.* Temple City, CA: The World of Dark Shadows, 1982.

———. *Dark Shadows in the Afternoon.* East Meadow, NY: Image Publishing, 1991.

***WUPJI** See:* POLAND, VAMPIRES IN

WYNDCLIFFE DARK SHADOWS SOCIETY

The Wyndcliffe Dark Shadows Society was founded 1988 by May Sutherland. It began as an effort to publish a newsletter, *Wyndcliffe Watch*, for *Dark Shadows* fans. However, with the help of Sutherland's friends Jane Lach and Lori Paige, founders of **Lone Gull Press**, the newsletter grew into a full-sized fanzine with the first issue, which appeared in October 1988. The society soon followed. Medallion Press is the society's publishing arm. Sutherland also was president of the Seattle/Tacoma fan club, a position she held from March 1989 to May 1992. The club met monthly and lobbied the local public television station to pick up the syndicated *Dark Shadows* reruns. After KTPS (now KBTC) agreed, the club held fundraisers to support the station. Meanwhile Sutherland also became head of the West Washington chapter of the SCI FI Channel fan club; the SCI FI Channel soon acquired the exclusive rights to the *Dark Shadows* series.

In 1992; the local club stopped meeting. However, the continuing society and its associated fanzine has grown to approximately 250 member/subscribers and includes people from across North America, plus members in Turkey and Japan. Sutherland has authored one novel, *Sins of the Fathers* a *Dark Shadows* story that has vampire **Barnabas Collins** under attack from another vampire running loose at his Collinwood estate.

The Wyndcliffe Dark Shadows Society and *The Wyndcliffe Watch* may be reached c/o May Sutherland, PO Box 7236, Tacoma, WA 98407-7236. Include a SASE when making inquiries about membership and subscriptions. Medallion Press publishes the novel, *Sins of the Fathers,* and *Crazy Vein,* a collection of Dark Shadows humor by Marcy Wilson.

Sources:

Sutherland, May. *Sins of the Fathers.* Tacoma, WA: Medallion Press, 1993.

Wilson, Marcy. *Crazy Vein.* Tacoma, WA: Medallion Press, 1994.

Y

YAMA

Yama, the god of death, was a Hindu vampiric deity who also appeared in the mythology of **Tibet**, Nepal, and Mongolia. People were thought to become subject to Yama because of the performance of evil deeds during their earthly life. Following death, the soul of such a person passed out of the body with the excreta rather than through the top of the head as it should. The soul, called a *pret*, then spent a year wandering about in a state of unhappy restlessness while awaiting the final judgment of Yama. It was always thirsty because the god of water watched to keep it from drinking. During this period Yama attacked the *pret*, and living relatives would offer invocations to keep it free from beating and bruising. In Tibet, Nepal, and Mongolia, Yama was pictured as vampiric, complete with **fangs** and **blood**.

Sources:

Crooke, William. *Religion and Folklore of Northern India*. Humphrey Milford: Oxford University Press, 1926.
Varma, Devendra P. "The Vampire in Legend, Lore, and Literature." Introduction for *Varney the Vampyre*. New York: Arno Press, 1970, xiii-xxx.

YARA-MA-YHA-WHO See: AUSTRALIA, VAMPIRES IN

YARBRO, CHELSEA QUINN (1942-)

Chelsea Quinn Yarbro, creator of the **St. Germain** series of vampire books, was born September 15, 1942, in Berkeley, California, the daughter of Lillian Chatfield and Clarence Elmer Erickson. She attended San Francisco State College from 1960 to 1963, after which she worked for her father's business, C. E. Erickson and Associates, as a cartographer. In 1969 she married Donald Paul Simpson; the couple divorced in

1982. The family business failed in 1970; and, since she enjoyed writing, she explored the possibility of doing it professionally. She joined the Science Fiction Writers of America and served for two years (1970-72) as its secretary. A firm believer in extrasensory perception and the occult, she was employed for brief periods as a tarot card reader during the early 1970s before her writing career was firmly established.

Her initial writings were short stories that appeared in mystery, fantasy, and science fiction periodicals, three areas that interested her. In 1972 three of her stories were included in anthologies. The first of her several writing awards came in 1973 from the Mystery Writers of America for her novelette, "The Ghosts at Iron River." Her first novel, *Time of the Fourth Horseman,* a suspense story, was published by Doubleday in 1976. To date she has written over 30 novels, by far the best known being the St. Germain series.

Yarbro gave much thought to the vampire in post-Dracula writing. An occultist rather than a traditional religionist, she concluded that the tradition was wrong. If one removed the religious overlay, the vampire became an entity who shared somewhat enjoyable (if unusual) sex and bestowed a conditional immortality. She also reflected upon the problems of the vampire's extended lifespan. Rather than monotonous attacks on the neighbors, the vampire would cultivate a life of scholarship and culture. As early as 1971, she tried to sell a book in which the vampire was the hero, but could not locate an interested publisher. She finally sold the idea to St. Martin's Press in the late 1970s.

In creating the St. Germain myth, Yarbro combined her interest in fantasy and gothic writing with a love for history. St. Germain was a 3,000-year-old vampire who in each of the novels showed up to interact with a more or less well-known historical personage or event. The character of St. Germain was suggested by a real person, an alchemist who lived in eighteenth-century France and around whom numerous occult legends, some of which he initiated, collected. However, Yarbro took the germ of information available on the real person and created a very human, sympathetic vampire character that joined with the characters in **Fred Saberhagen**'s novels in bolstering up the sensual side of the vampire's character while downplaying its image as monster.

The St. Germain's story continued through six novels: *Hotel Transylvania* (1978); *The Palace* (1979); *Blood Games* (1980); *Path of the Eclipse* (1981); *Tempting Fate* (1982), and *The Saint Germain Chronicles* (1983). *The Palace* was nominated for a World Fantasy Award. After a break, the story was continued in the "Olivia" Series, *A Flame in Byzantium* (1987) and the *Crusader's Torch* (1988). Olivia was a recurring character in the St. Germain series.

In St. Germain, Yarbro created one of the more intriguing variations on the Dracula myth. Apart from his longevity and his immunity to most things that would be fatal to an ordinary person, St. Germain was largely devoid of the supernatural powers thought to be possessed by vampires. He also was immune to many of the traditional weapons of the vampire hunters, **mirror**s, the **crucifix**, and **garlic**. He was comforted by earth from his homeland and had specially constructed hollow shoes with his **native soil** in them. He was troubled in crossing running **water**, a problem helped by the hollow shoes. Death, the true death, as it was called, occurred primarily if the spine was severed (**decapitation**) or the body burned.

St. Germain was a romantic hero and developed ongoing relationships with women, Olivia being the most important. He could make love to women but had no semen. Rather, he took their blood. He, in fact, lived largely upon willing female donors. There was one important limitation on his sexual life, however, in that the joys and benefits of the sexual sharing could only occur between a vampire and a nonvampire. These were blocked between two vampires. Thus, while the vampire lived for many years, he could not bring his lover, or lovers, with him. He could transform his lovers into vampires, but then they ceased to be lovers.

During the late 1970s, Yarbro became involved with a group of people in the San Francisco Bay area who were channeling (acting as a spirit medium) for a complex spiritual entity named Michael. In 1979 she wrote a nonfiction book, *Messages from Michael on the Nature of the Evolution of the Human Soul,* about Michael and the people who have assembled around ''his'' teachings. Subsequently, in the 1980s, she authored two more books out of the voluminous material the Michael group had channeled.

Sources:

Byrne, Lora. "Chelsea Quinn Yarbro: An Alternative Reality." *The Tomb of Dracula* 6 (August 1980): 56-9.

Magill, Frank N. *Survey of Modern Fantasy Literature.* Vol. 3. Englewood Cliffs, NJ: Salem Press, 1983.

YATU-DHANA See: INDIA, VAMPIRES IN

YORGA, COUNT

Among the several new vampire characters to appear in the 1970s was Count Yorga, the subject of two films released by American International Pictures. The idea for Count Yorga grew out of the collaboration in the late 1960s of director Bob Kelljan and independent producer Michael Macready. The two had made some money on a joint low-budget, soft-core pornographic film, and Kelljan had the idea of doing a second porno film with a vampire theme. At this point, actor Robert Quarry, a friend of Kelljan, got involved. Quarry suggested that they produce a straight horror movie and offered to play the lead role.

Quarry had entered the world of films at the age of 14 when he got a job as a bellhop on Alfred Hitchcock's *Shadow of a Doubt,* which was shot in Santa Rosa, California. Hitchcock took a liking to him and gave him several lines in the movie,

ROBERT QUARRY AS COUNT YORGA (HERE SHOWN WITH MARIETTE HARTLEY) IN *THE RETURN OF COUNT
YORGA*.

though they were cut from the finished product. He went on to play a variety of bit parts in the movies and appeared on radio and television. As his career proceeded, he became typecast as a ''heavy.'' *The Loves of Count Yorga,* as the first of the Yorga films was originally named, became his first starring role.

Quarry's vampire drew upon both the suave **Dracula** of **Bela Lugosi** and the more dynamic and vicious portrayal by **Christopher Lee**. The story was set in Los Angeles in the late 1960s. Yorga moved into an old mansion and emerged as a spiritualist medium. His first victim was Erica, a young woman who had attended the first seance and who was vampirized as she tried to leave the mansion. Her car had become stuck in the mud. A friend, Dr. Hayes, though ignorant of vampires, researched the subject after Erica was discovered sucking the blood from a cat. After a second young woman was attacked, he concluded that a vampire was operating in Los Angeles. Hayes and Michael, Erica's boyfriend, went to the mansion after Yorga and eventually dispatched the vampire by means of a broomstick through his heart.

The first film was an enormous success. Made for $64,000, it grossed several million, the most successful American International film to that time. Quarry became a horror film star. A sequel called *The Return of Count Yorga* was quickly planned and just as quickly made. In the sequel, a revived Yorga attended a masquerade party where he met and fell in love with Cynthia (played by Mariette Hartley). He decided to possess her, in spite of her engaged status. In a scene reminiscent of the Charles Manson slayings, Yorga sent a group of female vampires he had created to gorge themselves on the members of Cynthia's household. Yorga confessed his love to Cynthia and invited her into his vampiric life. She rebuffed him. Meanwhile, her fiance convinced the police to go to Yorga's home. They were met by his vampire harem and, while a fight ensued, the fiance went in search of Yorga. Yorga died from a knife in the heart; but, in a twisted ending, the fiance had by this time become a vampire himself. The film ended as he turned and bit into the neck of his beloved Cynthia.

American Universal planned to do a third Yorga film, but eventually dropped the idea, in part because it was engaged in promoting its black exploitation *Blacula* films. Quarry revived the Yorga role in another horror film, *Dr. Phibes Rises Again,* but then the character was discontinued entirely. Quarry has continued his acting career in various nonvampire roles.

Sources:

Gross, Edward. "Robert Quarry: Count Yorga Rises Again." In *The Vampire Interview Book* by Edward Gross and Marc Shapiro. East Meadow, NY: Image Publishing, 1991.

YOUNGSON, JEANNE KEYES

Jeanne Keyes Youngson, the founder of the **Count Dracula Fan Club**, the largest of the vampire-oriented interest groups, was born in Syracuse, New York, the daughter of Margaret E. Gardiner and Kenneth W. Keyes. She attended Maryville College and while there first heard of **Vlad the Impaler**, the fifteenth-century ruler of Wallachia who was the historical model for **Dracula**.

In 1960 she married Robert George Youngson and that same year launched a career as an independent film producer of animation and medical documentaries. Among her more notable film productions were *Maude in Her Hat,* which won first prize at the Brooklyn Arts and Culture Association Film Festival (1970); *The Unicorn,* which won a prize at the Association of International Film Animation (1974); and *Marjorie Bean and the Drawing Machine* (1977). In 1975 she organized an international film festival, "Films About, By, and For Women," held in Baltimore, Maryland. Her critically acclaimed *My Name Is Debbie,* the story of a postoperative male-to-female transsexual, is still being shown at gender-identity and sex-reassignment conferences throughout the world.

The idea for the Count Dracula Fan Club (CDFC) came to her in 1965 while she was on a trip to **Romania**. On the same visit she met another person, an Australian,

JEANNE YOUNGSON, FOUNDER
OF THE COUNT DRACULA
FAN CLUB.

who shared her interest in Dracula and volunteered to be her first member. Headquarters were established in both New York City and Cambridge, England.

By the late 1970s, the CDFC had become a growing concern. She gave up filmmaking to devote her time to the club. She had already written her first book, *Dracula Made Easy* (1977), which she followed with several others: *Count Dracula and the Unicorn* (1978); *The Count Dracula Chicken Cookbook* (1979); and the first volume of vampire poetry, *The Further Perils of Dracula* (1979). She compiled and edited three volumes: *The Count Dracula Fan Club Book of Vampire Stories* (1980); *A Child's Garden of Vampires* (1980); and the *Count Dracula Book of Classic Vampire Tales* (1981). Her novella, *Freak Show Vampire,* was published in a collection along with a short story, ''The Hungry Grass'' by Peter Tremayne. For many years she served as editor of the *CDFC Bi-Annual* (now the *CDFC News-Journal*).

Through the 1980s she oversaw the development of what has become a large international organization with 15 divisions, most of which she initiated. More than a quarter of a century after the group's founding, she remains president of the CDFC. She is also the curator of the Dracula Museum established in 1990. Most recently she cooperated with Shelley Leigh-Hunt in conducting a survey of CDFC members on the issue of the existence of vampires. The survey report, *Do Vampires Exist?* (1993), was published by Dracula World Enterprises.

Sources:

Youngson, Jeanne. *A Child's Garden of Vampires.* Chicago: Adams Press, 1980.

———. *Count Dracula and the Unicorn.* Chicago: Adams Press, 1978.

———, ed. *The Count Dracula Book of Classic Vampire Tales.* Chicago: Adams Press, 1981.

———, comp. *The Count Dracula Chicken Cookbook.* Chicago: Adams Press, 1979.

———, ed. *The Count Dracula Fan Club Book of Vampire Stories.* Chicago: Adams Press, 1980.

———. *Freak Show Vampire.* Chicago: Adams Press, 1981.

———. *The Further Perils of Dracula.* Chicago: Adams Press, 1979.

———, and Shelley Leigh-Hunt, eds. *Do Vampires Exist? A Special Report from Dracula World Enterprises.* New York: Dracula World Enterprises, 1993.

APPENDICES & MASTER INDEX

VAMPIRE RESOURCES

This section contains listings for organizations and periodicals that may be of interest to people looking for more information on the Dracula/vampire subculture. It is arranged in five sections:

- North American Organizations
- European and Australian Organizations
- *Dark Shadows* Organizations
- Independent Vampire Periodicals
- Independent *Dark Shadows* Periodicals

Each organization entry includes the name of the group; address and telephone number; and a list of periodicals published. Independent periodicals are classified as those not published by one of the mainstream vampire organizations. Those entries include name of the periodical; and name, address, and telephone number of the publisher.

NORTH AMERICAN ORGANIZATIONS

ANNE RICE'S VAMPIRE LESTAT FAN CLUB
PO Box 58277
New Orleans, LA 70158-8277
  Publishes *Newsletter*.

BITE ME IN THE COFFIN NOT THE CLOSET FAN CLUB
c/o Jeff Flaster
72 Sarah Ln.
Middletown, NY 10940

THE CAMARILLA
8314 Greenwood Ave., N.
Box 2859
Seattle, WA 98103
  Publishes *Requiem*.

CHEEKY DEVIL VAMPIRE RESEARCH INC.
c/o L. E. Elliott, Director
PO Box 7633
Abilene, TX 79608-7633

CLUB VAMPIRE
c/o Riyn Gray
1764 Lugonia
Ste. 104, No. 223
Redlands, CA 92374
  Publishes *Fresh Blood*.

COMMUNION
c/o Lament
628 Woodlawn Rd.
Steens, MS 39766

COUNT DRACULA FAN CLUB
29 Washington Sq. W.
Penthouse N.
New York, NY 10011
  Publishes *Bites and Pieces* • *Count Dracula Fan Club News-Journal* • *Letterzine* • *Undead Undulations*.

COUNT KEN FAN CLUB
12 Palmer St.
Salem, MA 01970
  Publishes *Newsletter*.

DYNAMITE FAN CLUB
PO Box 30443
Cleveland, OH 44130
  Publishes *Horror Newsletter*.

P. N. ELROD FAN CLUB
c/o Jackie Black
1201 Byrd, No. 39
Tishomingo, OK 73460
  Publishes *Newsletter*.

ELVIRA FAN CLUB
14755 Ventura Blvd., No. 1-710
Sherman Oaks, CA 91403
  Publishes *The Elvira Examiner*.

THE FANG GANG
PO Box 273895
Tampa, FL 33688-3895

FOREVER KNIGHT FAN CLUB
c/o Lora Haines
PO Box 1108
Boston, MA 02103-1108
  Publishes *Feeding Frenzy*.

GOTHIC SOCIETY OF CANADA
465 Queen St. W.
Toronto, ON
Canada M5V 2AG
  Publishes *Newsletter*.

LOYALISTS OF THE VAMPIRE REALM
c/o Lucinda
PO Box 6975
Beverly Hills, CA 90212-6975

MIDNIGHT TO MIDNIGHT: A WRITER'S CIRCLE FOR VAMPIRES AND WEREWOLVES
The High Mistress
c/o Karen Dove
11 North Ave.
Mt. Clemens, MI 48043

THE MUNSTERS & THE ADDAMS FAMILY FAN CLUB
c/o Louis Wendruck
PO Box 69A04
West Hollywood, CA 99969

NIGEL BENNETT FAN CLUB
c/o Star Urioste
25055 Copa del oro, No. 104
Hayward, CA 94545-2573

NOCTURNAL ECSTACY VAMPIRE COVEN
c/o Darlene Daniels
PO Box 147
Palo Heights, IL 60463-0147

NOSFERATU SOCIETY OF VAMPIRE FANS
PO Box 2
McKean, PA 16426-0002
  Publishes *Newsletter*.

THE OFFICIAL GERAINT WYN DAVIES FAN CLUB
c/o Rosemary Shad
4133 Glendale Rd.
Woodbridge, VA 22193

ORDER OF THE VAMPYRE
c/o Temple of Set
PO Box 470307
San Francisco, CA 9147

QUINCEY P. MORRIS DRACULA SOCIETY
c/o Charlotte Simsen
PO Box 381
Ocean Gate, NJ 08740

REALM OF THE VAMPIRE
PO Box 517
Metairie, LA 70004-0517
  Publishes *Realm of the Vampire Newsletter*.

SCREEM IN THE DARK FAN CLUB
c/o Screem Jam Productions
PO Box 138300
Chicago, IL 60613
  Publishes *Screem in the Dark Newsletter*.

SECRET ORDER OF THE UNDEAD
c/o T J. Teer
155 East "C" St., Ste. 323
Upland, CA 91786
  Publishes *S.O.UND*.

SHADOWS OF THE NIGHT
PO Box 17006
Rochester, NY 14617

TEMPLE OF THE VAMPIRE
PO Box 3582
Lacey, WA 98503
  Publishes *Bloodlines: The Vampire Temple Journal* • *Life Force: The International Vampire Forum*.

VAMPIRE INFORMATION EXCHANGE

c/o Eric Held
PO Box 328
Brooklyn, NY 11229-0328
  Publishes *Vampire Information Exchange Newsletter*.

VAMPIRE RESEARCH CENTER

PO Box 252
Elmhurst, NY 11373

VAMPIRE STUDIES

PO Box 151
Berwyn, IL 60412

VAMPIRES, WEREWOLVES, GHOSTS & OTHER SUCH THINGS THAT GO BUMP IN THE NIGHT

PO Box 6975
Beverly Hills, CA 90012-6975

VAMPIRISM RESEARCH INSTITUTE

PO Box 20167
Seattle, WA 98111

VAN HELSING SOCIETY

PO Box 602088
Cleveland, OH 44102

EUROPEAN AND AUSTRALIAN ORGANIZATIONS

BRAM STOKER SOCIETY

c/o Albert Power
43 Castle Ct., Killiney Hill Rd.
Killiney, County Dublin, Ireland
  Publishes *Newsletter*.

THE DRACULA EXPERIENCE

9 Marine Parade
Whitby YO21 3PR England

DRACULA SOCIETY

c/o Bernard Davies
213 Wulfstan St.
London W 12 England
  Publishes *Voices from the Vaults*.

THE GOTHIC SOCIETY

138 Canterbury Rd.
Harrow, Middlesex HA1 4PB England
  Publishes *Grimoire*.

THE HOUSE OF DRACULA

14 Clyde Rd.
West Didsbury, Manchester M2O 8WH
United Kingdom

TRANSYLVANIA SOCIETY OF DRACULA

c/o Nicolae Padararu, President
47 Primaverii Blvd.
Bucharest 1, Romania

VAMPIRE ARCHIVES OF ISTANBUL

c/o Giovanni Scognamillo
Postacilar Sokak 13/13
Beyoglu, Istanbul
Turkey

THE VAMPIRE GUILD

c/o Phill White
82, Ripcroft, Southwell
Portland, Dorset DT5 2EE
United Kingdom
  Publishes *Crimson*.

THE VAMPIRE LEGION

PO Box 4202
Melbourne University Post Office
VIC 3052, Australia
  Publishes *Journal of the Vampire Legion*.

THE VAMPIRE REGISTER

7 Cornwall Rd.
Stourbridge, West Midlands DY8 4TE
United Kingdom
  Publishes *Obituary*.

VAMPIRE RESEARCH SOCIETY

c/o Rev. Sean Manchester
PO Box 542
Highgate
London N6 6BG
United Kingdom

THE VAMPYRE SOCIETY

c/o Allen J. Gittens
38 Westcroft
Chippenham, Wiltshire SN14 0LY
United Kingdom
  Publishes *For the Blood Is the Life*.

THE VAMPYRE SOCIETY
9 Edgar Rd.
Sanderstead, South Crotdon
Surrey CR2 0NJ
United Kingdom
  Publishes *The Velvet Vampyre*.

DARK SHADOWS ORGANIZATIONS

COLLINWOOD REVISITED
2306 N. MacArthur
Oklahoma City, OK 73127

DARK SHADOWS FAN CLUB
c/o Louis Wendruck, Pres.
PO Box 69A04
West Hollywood, CA 90069
  Publishes *Dark Shadows Announcement*.

DARK SHADOWS FESTIVAL
PO Box 92
Maplewood, NJ 07040

DARK SHADOWS OFFICIAL FAN CLUB
c/o Ann Wilson, Exec. Dir.
PO Box 92
Maplewood, NJ 07040
  Publishes *Shadowgram* • *The World of Dark Shadows*.

DARK SHADOWS OVER OKLAHOMA
c/o Letha Roberts
316 SE 66th St.
Oklahoma City, OK 73149
  Publishes *The Graveyard Gazette*.

DARK SHADOWS SOCIETY OF NORTH COAST FAN CLUB
718 E. 343 St.
Eastlake, OH 44094

DARK SHADOWS SOCIETY OF THE SOUTHWEST
PO Box 1293
Greenville, SC 29602

DARK SHADOWS SOCIETY OF UKIAH, CA
PO Box 537
Talmadge, CA 95481

LONG ISLAND DARK SHADOWS SOCIETY
187 Roxbury Rd. S.
Garden City South, NY 11530

MARYLAND DARK SHADOWS FAN GROUP
11 S. Martin
Box 142
Clear Spring, MD 21722

NEW ENGLAND DARK SHADOWS SOCIETY
PO Box 6023
Boston, MA 02101
  Publishes *Widow's Hill Quarterly*.

NEW ORLEANS/LA DARK SHADOWS FAN GROUP
PO Box 922
Belle Chase, LA 70037

OREGON DARK SHADOWS FAN GROUP
PO Box 40366
Portland, OR 97240
  Publishes *News and Notes*.

ROCKY MOUNTAIN AREA DS FAN GROUP
PO Box 2887
Denver, CO 80201

ST. LOUIS DARK SHADOWS
5 Hammes Dr.
Florissant, MO 63031

THE SECRET ROOM
PO Box 1872
Azle, TX 76098-5872

THE SOUTHERN CALIFORNIA DARK SHADOWS CLUB
1863 Whispering Pines
Ontario, CA 91761

THE WYNDCLIFFE DARK SHADOWS SOCIETY
PO Box 7236
Tacoma, WA 98407
  Publishes *Wyndcliffe Watch*.

INDEPENDENT VAMPIRE PERIODICALS

BATHORY PALACE
1610 SW 3rd
Topeka, KS 66606-1215

BLOODREAMS
c/o Kelly Gunter Atlas
1312 W. 43rd St.
N. Little Rock, AR 72118

BLOODLINES
Danis the Dark Productions
305 Hahani St., No. 296
Kailua, HI 96734

CEMETARY GATES
4336 Byesville Blvd.
Dayton, OH 45431

CHILDREN OF DARKNESS
c/o Dracula Field
6224 Edgewater Dr.
Falls Church, VA 22041

THE CIRCLE OF TWINS
c/o Alexa Danceny
Rte. 4, Box 304H
Savannah, TN 38372

DARK TERRORS
c/o Avelon
Ventor Ice, St. Ives,
Cornwall TR25 1DY
United Kingdom

DYAD: THE VAMPIRE STORIES
c/o MKASHEF Enterprises
PO Box 368
Poway, CA 92074-0368

ELEGIA MAGAZINE
c/o Marie Buckner
3116 Porter Ln.
Ventura, CA 93003

EXQUISITE CORPSE
5320 N. Central Ave.
Indianapolis, IN 46220

GOOD GUYS WEAR FANGS
c/o Mary Ann B. McKinnon, Editor
254 Blunk Ave.
Plymouth, MI 48170

GOTHICA
c/o Susan M. Jenssen
98 Union St., Apt. 4
Brewer, ME 04412

INFERNAL
c/o Shadowlord
25 E. Islay St.
Santa Barbara, CA 93101

INTERNATIONAL VAMPIRE
c/o Rob Brautigam
Galileiplantsoen 90-1
1098NC Amsterdam
The Netherlands

JOURNAL OF VAMPIROLOGY
c/o John Vellutini
PO Box 881631
San Francisco, CA 94188-1631

KISS OF DEATH
c/o Darcie Blaszak
1616 Wasserman Ct.
Virginia Beach, VA 23454

KNIGHT BEAT
c/o Special Services Unltd.
8601-A W. Cermak Rd.
North Riverside, IL 60546

KNIGHTLY TALES
c/o Jessica Daigneault
PO Box 334
Lisbon Falls, ME 04252

NECRO
1648 W. Hazelhurst
Ferndale, MI 48220

NECROPOLIS
c/o Chad Savage
PO Box 77693
San Francisco, CA 94107

NIGHTLORE
PO Box 8148
Mobile, AL 36689

NIGHTMIST
c/o Tammy Pond
PO Box 17006
Rochester, NY 14617

**NIGHT'S CHILDREN--NOT
EXACTLY HUMAN**
c/o Wendy Snow-Lang
PO Box 5010, Ste. 115
Salem, MA 01970

NOCTURNAL
25 E. Islay St.
Santa Barbara, CA 93101

ON THE WINGS OF THE KNIGHT
c/o Ann & Bill Hupe
916 Lamb Rd.
Mason, MI 48854-9445

ONYX
c/o Mark Williams
PO Box 137
Uniontown, OH 44685

PERFECT DARKNESS
c/o M. Perkins
530 S. Flood
Norman, OK 73069

PRISONERS OF THE NIGHT
MKASHEF Enterprises
PO Box 688
Yucca Valley, CA 92286-0688

THE RAVEN
c/o Amy Hull and Paula Sanders
603 W. Walnut
Carbondale, IL 62901

ROUGE ET NOIR
c/o Meg Thompson
Preternatural Productions
PO Box 786
Fort Huachuca, AZ 85613

THE SECRET LIFE
c/o Alisa Kester
PO Box 1512
Mt. Vernon, WA 98273

SHADOWDANCE
c/o Michelle Belanger
PO Box 474
Hinckley, OH 44233

TERRA-X
34159 Gem Circle
N. Ridgeville, OH 44039

THIS EVIL ON EARTH
PO Box 616
Hawthorne, NJ 075-7

VAMPIRE ARCHIVES
c/o Jule Ghoul
2926 W. Leland
Chicago, IL 60625-3716

THE VAMPIRE JOURNAL
Baker Street Publications
PO Box 994
Metarie, LA 70004

VAMPIRE JUNCTION
c/o C. Cosner
505 NW 13th St.
Gainesville, FL 32601

VAMPS
c/o de Lioncourt
PO Box 21067
Seattle, WA 98111

WICKED MYSTIC
c/o Andre Scheluchin
PO Box 3087
Astoria, NY 11103

INDEPENDENT *DARK SHADOWS* PERIODICALS

DARK SHADOWS COLLECTABLES CLASSIFIEDS
c/o Sue Ellen Wilson
6173 Roquois Tr.
Mentor, OH 44060

ECHOES . . . FROM THE PAST
c/o Kathleen Resch
PO Box 1766
Temple City, CA 91780

INSIDE THE OLD HOUSE
c/o Dale Clark, ed.
11518 Desdemona Dr.
Dallas, TX 75228

THE LARA ZINE
c/o Travis McKnight
PO Box 417
Benham, KY 40807

THE MUSIC BOX
c/o Connie Jones, ed.
PO Box 40366
Portland, OR 97240-0366

SHADOWGRAM
c/o Marcy Robin
9441 E. Rosa Dr.
Temple, CA 91780-3840

SHADOWS OF THE NIGHT
c/o Dan Silvio
4529 Friendship Ave., 2nd Fl.
Pittsburgh, PA 15224

THE WORLD OF DARK SHADOWS
c/o Kathleen Resch, ed.
PO Box 1766
Temple City, CA 91780

VAMPIRE FILMOGRAPHY

The vampire filmography includes all commercially released movies that feature a vampire either as the central character or as a key character integral to the plot. It excludes amateur movies, made-for-television movies and other television shows, and those movies in which the vampire makes only a cameo appearance. It includes all types of vampires, revenants, vampires from outer space, vampires created by medical problems, demonic creatures, and psychic vampires. Excluded are those movies on related but nonvampiric monsters such as ghouls and zombies.

Entries are listed in alphabetical order by decade, starting with 1910 to 1919 and continuing through 1993. Each entry contains the name of the film, a brief description (when available), and other names by which the film was released. Additional information includes, where known, the date of original release; whether the film is black and white or color (**B** or **C**); country of origin; production company [in brackets]; name of the vampire; actor or actress portraying the vampire (in parentheses); other cast members; and director. If no country is listed, the film originated in the United States. Other countries of origin are listed as follows:

AR	Argentina	**FR**	France	**MA**	Malaysia	**SL**	Sri Lanka
AS	Austria	**GB**	Great Britain	**MX**	Mexico	**SP**	Spain
AU	Australia	**GE**	Germany	**NE**	The Netherlands	**SW**	Sweden
BE	Belgium	**HK**	Hong Kong	**NZ**	New Zealand	**TH**	Thailand
CA	Canada	**HU**	Hungary	**PH**	Philippines	**TU**	Turkey
CO	Columbia	**IN**	India	**PO**	Poland	**TW**	Taiwan
CU	Cuba	**IT**	Italy	**RO**	Romania	**VE**	Venezuela
CZ	Czechoslovakia	**JP**	Japan	**RU**	Russia		
BR	Brazil	**KO**	Korean	**SG**	Singapore		

1910 to 1919

Alraune

No known copy has survived. Based on *Alraune* by Hans Heinz Ewers.

> **1918 B AS Vampire(s):** Alraune; **Cast:** Guyla Gal, Rozzi Scollosi, Jena Torzs. **Dir:** Mihaly Kertesz.

Alraune

No known copy has survived. Based on *Alraune* by Hans Heinz Ewers.

> **1918 B GE** [Neutral Films] **Vampire(s):** Alraune; **Cast:** Hilde Wolter, Gustav Adolf Semler, Fredrich Kuehne. **Dir:** Eugen Illes.

Lilith and Ly

> **1919 B** [Fiat Films] **Vampire(s):** Lilith (Elga Beck); **Cast:** Hans Marschall, Ernest Escherich, Fritz Kammauf. **Dir:** Drich Kober.

Magia

The vampiric Baron Merlin must drink the

blood of a young man every thousandth full moon in order to survive.

1917 B HU [Corvin] **Vampire(s):** Baron Merlin; **Cast:** Mihaly Varkonyi. **Dir:** Alexander Korda.

A Night of Horror

1916 B GE Cast: Werner Krauss, Emil Jennings. **Dir:** Arthur Robison.

The Secrets of House No. 5

Reportedly a detective drama that features vampires, ghouls, and ghosts.

1912 B RU [Pathe].

The Vampire

No known copies of this film set in India have survived.

1913 B GB [Kalem Pictures/ Searchlight] **Vampire(s):** (Alice Eis) **Cast:** Bert French, Harry Millarde, Alice Hollister, Maguerite Courtot. **Dir:** Robert Vignola.

The Vampire

A member of a secret organization finds himself bound by an oath to kill his second wife aided by drugs and a vampire bat.

1914 B FR [Eclair].

Les Vampires

A 10-part serial completed in 1915-1916 and released in the United States in 1916 as *The Vampires*.

1915 B FR Vampire(s): Grand Vampire (Jean Ayme), Irma Vep (Musidora); **Cast:** Edouard Mate, Larcel Levesque. **Dir:** Louis Fevillade.

A Village Vampire

No known copies have survived. Records of the film were found in Edison's catalog.

1916 B [Edison Films] **Dir:** Edwin S. Porter.

1920 to 1929

Dracula

The first film based on Bram Stoker's *Dracula*. No known copy has survived.

1920 B RU

Drakula

The second film based on Bram Stoker's *Dracula*. Like the first, no known copies have survived.

1921 B HU Dir: Karoly Lafthay.

The Great London Mystery

A 12-part serial.

1920 B GB [T&P] **Vampire(s):** Froggie the Vampire (Lola de Liane); **Cast:** David Devant, Lady Doris Stapleton, Lester Gard. **Dir:** Charles Raymond.

London After Midnight

The first full-length vampire feature movie based on a short story, "The Hypnotist" by director Tod Browning. No known copy has survived.

1927 B [MGM] **Vampire(s):** (Lon Chaney); **Cast:** Edna Tichnor, Conrad Nagel. **Dir:** Tod Browning.

Nosferatu, Eine Symphonie des Garuens

The third attempt to bring Dracula to the screen. This now famous movie of the Bram Stoker's novel was banned for many years due to a lawsuit brought by Florence Stoker, the widow of Bram Stoker on copyright grounds, and only a few copies survived. It was first released in the 1960s as *Dracula* and as *Terror of Dracula* and later in 1972 as *Nosferatu the Vampire*. A remake of this version was released in 1979 under the title *Nosferatu the Vampire*.

1922 B GE [Prana-Film] **Vampire(s):** Count Orlock (Max Schreck); **Cast:** Gustav von Wangenheim, John Gottow,

Greta Schröder. **Dir:** Frederick W. Murnau.

The Unholy Love

The third film based on *Alraune* by Hans Heinz Ewers.

1928 B GE [AMA Films] **Vampire(s):** Alraune (Brigitte Helm); **Cast:** Paul Wegener, Ivan Petrovich, Hans Trautner, Louis Ralph. **Dir:** Henrich Galeen.

The Vampires of Warsaw

No known copy has survived.

1925 B PL Dir: Wiktor Bieganski.

1930 to 1939

Alraune

A fourth film based on *Alraune* by Hans Heinz Ewers. It was also released as *Daughter of Evil*.

1930 B GE [UFA] **Vampire(s):** Alraune (Brigitte Helm); **Cast:** Albert Basserman, Agnes Straub, Kaethe Haack. **Dir:** Richard Oswald.

Condemned to Live

Prof. Paul Kristan is "condemned to live" after being turned into a vampire by the full moon. He then unwillingly begins attacking the residents of a small European village.

1935 B [Invincible] **Vampire(s):** Prof. Paul Kristan (Ralph Morgan); **Cast:** Maxine Doyle, Russell Gleason, Pedro de Corboda. **Dir:** Frank Strayer.

Dakki, the Vampire

1936 B JP

Dracula

The fourth attempt to make a *Dracula* film and the first sound version, based on the very successful Broadway play, introduced the vampire to popular consciousness and made Bela Lugosi a motion picture star.

1931 B [Universal] **Vampire(s):** Dracula (Bela Lugosi); **Cast:** Dwight Frye, Helen Chandler, Edward Van Sloan. **Dir:** Tod Browning.

Dracula

This Spanish-language version of *Dracula* was filmed simultaneously with the Bela Lugosi/Tod Browning version and followed essentially the same script.

1931 B [Universal] **Vampire(s):** Dracula (Carlos Villarias); **Cast:** Lupita Tovar, Pablo, Alvarey Rubio. **Dir:** George Medford.

Dracula's Daughter

This sequel to Dracula and first feature film centered on a female vampire was loosely based on Bram Stoker's short story, "Dracula's Guest." In 1977 Carl Dreadstone finished a novel, *Dracula's Daughter*, inspired by the movie.

1936 B [Universal] **Vampire(s):** Countess Marya Zalesky (Gloria Holt); **Cast:** Edward Van Sloan, Irving Pichel, Margaret Churchill, Otto Kruger. **Dir:** Lambert Hillyer.

Hollywood on Parade, No. 8

A 10-minute short feature.

1933 B [Lewyn/Paramount] **Vampire(s):** Dracula (Bela Lugosi); **Cast:** Mae Questel, Eddie Borden, Rex Bell. **Dir:** Lewis Lewyn.

Jaws of the Jungle

A group of vampire bats attack a Sri Lankan village.

1936 B SL/US [Jay Dee Kay] [Ceylonese/USA] **Cast:** Teeto, Minta, Gukar; **Dir:** J. D. Kendis.

The Macabre Trunk

Dr. del Vialle kills young women but with a high purpose in mind. He uses their blood to keep his wife alive. Also released as *El Baul Macabro*.

1936 B MX [Ezet] **Cast:** Rene Cardona, Ramon Pereda, Manuel Noriega. **Dir:** Miguél Zacarías.

Mark of the Vampire

In 1935 Browning completed a sound remake of his original *London After Midnight*. It was also released as *Werewolf of Paris* and *The Vampire of Prague*.

1935 B [MGM] **Vampire(s):** Count Mora (Bela Lugosi); **Cast:** Lionel Barrymore, Lionel Atwill, Elizabeth Allen. **Dir:** Tod Browning.

Preview Murder Mystery

A murder mystery whose action is placed on the set of a vampire movie.

1936 B [Paramount] **Cast:** Reginald Denny, Frances Drake, Gail Patrick, Rod La Roque. **Dir:** Robert Florey.

The Return of Dr. X

Humphrey Bogart's only appearance in a vampire movie. Based on a short story, ''The Doctor's Secret'' by Lee Katz. Marshall Quesne, the Bogart character, is turned into a vampire by blood transfusions.

1939 B [Warner Brothers] **Vampire(s):** Marshall Quesne (Humphrey Bogart), Angela Merrove (Lya Lys); **Cast:** Rosemary Lane, Wayne Morris; **Dir:** Vincent Sherman.

The Vampire Bat

Mad scientist Dr. Otto Nieman fakes several vampirelike deaths to obtain blood to feed the creature he had created.

1933 B [Majestic] **Vampire(s):** Dr. Otto von Niemann (Lionel Atwill); **Cast:** Fay Wray, Melvin Douglas, Dwight Frye. **Dir:** Frank Strayer.

Vampyr

Claimed to be loosely based on Sheridan Le Fanu's ''Carmilla,'' the story pits a young man, David Gray against Margueritte Chopin, an elderly female vampire. This famous critically acclaimed silent film was released under a variety of titles including *The Strange Adventure of David Gray*.

1931 B FR/GE [Dreyer-Tobias-Klangfilm] **Vampire(s):** Marguerite Chopin (Henrietta Gerard); **Cast:** Sybille Schmitz, Maurice Schutz, Julian West (Baron Nicolas de Gunzburg). **Dir:** Carl T. Dreyer.

1940 to 1949

Abbott and Costello Meet Frankenstein

Universal teams its best comedians against its famous monsters in a plot that has Dracula attempting to steal Costello's brain and placing it in Frankenstein's monster. It was also released as *Meet the Ghosts; Abbot and Costello Meet the Ghosts; Abbott et Costello contre Frankenstein* (French); *Deux Nigauds contre Frankenstein* (French); *Abbott et Costello et les Monstres* (Belgium).

1949 [Universal-International] **Vampire(s):** Dracula (Bela Lugosi); **Cast:** Bud Abbott, Lou Costello; Lon Chaney, Jr., Glenn Strange. **Dir:** Charles T. Barton.

Crime Doctor's Courage

Dr. Ordway, criminal psychologist, investigates a dance team that is suspected of being vampires. In the end, the idea of the vampire is explained away.

1945 B [Columbia] **Vampire(s):** (Anthony Caruso), (Lupita Tovar); **Cast:**

Warner Baxter, Hillery Brooke, Jerome Cowan. **Dir:** George Sherman.

Dead Men Walk

Zucco portrays a vampire with a non-vampire twin brother. This film was also released as *Creatures of the Devil*.

1943 B [Producers Releasing Corporation] **Vampire(s):** (George Zucco); **Cast:** Mary Carlisle, Nedrick Young, Dwight Frye. **Dir:** Sam Neufield.

The Devil Bat

Mad scientist Lugosi creates two giant vampire bats, which he wants to release on those he believes have done him wrong. This movie was also released as *Killer Bats* and as *Devil Bats*.

1940 B [Producers Releasing Corporation] **Cast:** Bela Lugosi, Suzanne Kaaren, Dave O'Brien, Hal Price. **Dir:** Jean Yarbrough.

Devil Bat's Daughter

This sequel to *The Devil Bat* (1940) has the daughter of the scientist driven mad by her psychiatrist.

1946 B [Producers Releasing Corporation] **Vampire(s):** Dr. Elliot (Nolan Leary); **Cast:** Rosemary La Planche, John James, Michael Hale, Molly Lamont. **Dir:** Frank Wisbar.

Face of Marble

The mad professor Randolf (John Carradine) is able to revive a dead canine who had several supernatural powers (such as being invisible) and attacked people and drank their blood.

1946 B [Monogram] **Vampire(s):** The dog; **Cast:** John Carradine, Claudia Drake, Robert Shayne. **Dir:** William Beaudine.

Gandy Goose in Ghosttown

An animated film.

1944 C [20th Century Fox] **Vampire(s):** Dracula. **Dir:** Mannie Davis.

House of Dracula

When a scientist attempts to turn the Universal monsters (Dracula, Frankenstein's monster and the Wolfman) into normal people, Dracula rejects the offer and turns the scientist into a vampire. *House of Dracula*, a sequel to *House of Frankenstein*, was released in Italy as *La Casa Degli Orrori* ("The House of Horror").

1945 B [Universal] **Vampire(s):** Dracula/ Baron Latoes (John Carradine); **Cast:** Lon Chaney, Jr., Glenn Strange, Onslow Stevens, Jane Adams. **Dir:** Erle C. Kenton.

House of Frankenstein

The original gathering of Dracula, Frankenstein's monster, and the Wolfman with Karloff as a mad scientist. *House of Frankenstein* marked John Carradine's first appearance as Dracula. A condensed version of this film was released as *Doom of Dracula*.

1944 B [Universal] **Vampire(s):** Dracula (John Carradine); **Cast:** Boris Karloff, Lon Chaney, Jr., J. Carroll Naish, Glenn Strange. **Dir:** Erle C. Kenton.

Isle of the Dead

Karloff portrays a military commander in a rural Balkan village who believes that a vampire (*vrykolakas*) is killing off the residents.

1945 B [RKO] **Cast:** Boris Karloff, Ellen Drew, Marc Cramer, Jason Robards; **Dir:** Mark Robson.

Return of the Vampire

Lugosi plays a different vampire (Universal owning the film rights to Dracula) who was freed from his staked out condition in England during World War II. This movie introduced the idea of the vampire's destruction by sunlight.

1944 B [Columbia] **Vampire(s):** Armand Tesla (Bela Lugosi); **Cast:** Matt Willis, Frieda Inescort, Roland Varnon. **Dir:** Lew Landers.

Son of Dracula

Universal's second sequel to *Dracula* finds the Count in Louisiana in search of a vampire bride.

1943 B [Universal] **Vampire(s):** Count Alucard (Lon Chaney, Jr.); **Cast:** Louise Albritton, Robert Paige, Frank Craven, Adeline Reynolds. **Dir:** Robert Siodmak.

Spooks Run Wild

Lugosi portrays a stage magician mistaken for a vampire.

1941 B [Monogram] **Vampire(s):** The Monster [Bela Lugosi] **Cast:** Leo Gorcey, Huntz Hall, Bobby Jordan. **Dir:** Phil Rosen.

Valley of the Zombies

Murks, an undertaker, returns from the dead but needs fresh blood to stay alive.

1945 B [Republic] **Vampire(s):** Ormand Murks (Ian Keith); **Cast:** Robert Livingston, Adrian Booth, Thomas Jackson. **Dir:** Philip Ford.

Le Vampire

A documentary.

1945 B FR [La Cinegraphic Documentaire] **Dir:** Jean Painlevé.

The Vampire's Ghost

Based loosely on John Polidori's 1819 short story, "The Vampyre."

1945 B [Republic] **Vampire(s):** Webb Fallon (John Abbott); **Cast:** Charles Gordon, Peggy Stewart, Grant Withers; **Dir:** Lesley Selander.

Les Vampires

1947 FR Cast: Boris Vian. **Dir:** Henri Gruault.

1950 to 1959

Alraune

Based on *Alraune* by Hanns Heinz Ewers.

1952 GE Vampire(s): Alraune (Hildegard Knef); **Cast:** Erich von Stroheim, Karl Boehm, Julia Koschka; **Dir:** Arthur Maria Rabenalt.

Anak Pontianak

Also released as *Son of the Vampire* and *Curse of the Vampire*. Fourth of the Pontianak series. Sequel: *Pontianak Kembali*.

1958 B HK [Shaw Brothers] **Cast:** Hasimah, Haj Sattar, Dyang Sofia. **Dir:** Ramon Estella.

Batula

A puppet movie based on a screenplay by Al Capp.

1952 Cast: Fearless Fosdick.

Blood of Dracula

A young girl at a girl's school becomes a vampire after her teacher hypnotized her. Also released as *Blood Is My Heritage* and *Blood of the Demon*.

1957 B [Universal/AI] **Vampire(s):** Nancy Perkins (Sandra Harrison); **Cast:** Louise Lewis, Gail Ganley. **Dir:** Herbert L. Strock.

The Blood of the Vampire

The formerly dead Dr. Callistratus is experimenting with the blood of the inmates at the insane asylum in order to stay alive. Also released as *The Demon with Bloody Hands*. Screenplay by Jimmy Sangster.

1958 C GB [Universal/Eros] **Vampire(s):** Callistratus (Donald Wolfit); **Cast:** Barbara Shelley, Vincent Ball, Victor Moddern. **Dir:** Henry Cass.

The Bowery Boys Meet the Monsters

The Bowery Boys encounter several monsters, including a vampire, after one of them is turned into a werewolf.

1954 B [Allied Artists] **Vampire(s):** (Paul Wexler); **Cast:** Leo Gorcey, Huntz Hall, Ellen Corby. **Dir:** Edward Bernds.

El Castillo de los Monstruos

Newlyweds are trapped in a castle with a set of monsters, including a vampire played by German Robles. In this comedy Robles plays a parody of the character Count Lavud, who he had previously portrayed in several other films. Released in English as the *Castle of the Monsters*.

1958 B MX [Soto Mayor] **Vampire(s):** (German Robles); **Cast:** Clavillazo, Evangeline Elizondo. **Dir:** Julien Soler.

Curse of the Undead

The first vampire Western. Also released as *Affairs of a Vampire*; *Mark of the West*; *Mark of the Beast*; *Le Teur Invisible*; *The Invisible Killer*; *Les Griffes du Vampire*; and *The Grip of the Vampire*.

1959 B [Universal] **Vampire(s):** Drake Robey (Michael Pate); **Cast:** Eric Fleming, Kathleen Crowley, John Hoyt. **Dir:** Edward Dein.

Daughter of Dr. Jekyll

1957 [Allied Artists] **Vampire(s):** Dr. Lomas (Arthur Shields); **Cast:** John Agar, Gloria Talbot, John Dierkes. **Dir:** Edgar G. Ulmer.

Dendam Pontianak (Revenge of the Vampire)

Second of the Pontianak series. Sequel: *Sumpah Pontianak* (1958).

1957 B [Keris] **Vampire(s):** (Maria Menado); **Cast:** Mustapha Maarof, Puteh Lawah, S. M. Wahid. **Dir:** B. N. Rao.

Dracula in Istanbul

The first non-Western adaptation of *Dracula* for the screen. Originally released as *Drakula Istanbulda*. The seventh film based on Stoker's novel and Ali Riga Seifi's *Kastgli Voyvoda*.

1953 B TU [Demirag] **Vampire(s):** Drakula (Atif Kaptan); **Cast:** Annie Bell. **Dir:** Mehmet Muhtar.

The First Man in Space

The first man into space returns as a monster who craves human blood. Also released as *Satellite of Blood*.

1958 B [Amalgamated/MGM] **Vampire(s):** Commander C. E. Prescott (Bill Edwards); **Cast:** Marshall Thompson, Maria Landi, Robert Ayres. **Dir:** Robert Day.

The Horror of Dracula

First Hammer Dracula film, and eighth remake of the novel *Dracula*. Originally released as *Dracula* (United Kingdom) and later as *Dracula il Vampiro* (Spain) and *Le Chauchemar de Dracula* (France). Screenplay by Jimmy Sangster.

1958 C GB [Hammer] **Vampire(s):** Dracula (Christopher Lee); **Cast:** Peter Cushing, Carol Marsh, Melissa Stribling. **Dir:** Terence Fisher.

I Vampiri

This fountainhead of the Italian cinematic vampire was loosely based on the Elizabeth Bathory story. The Duchess Marguerite is kept alive by the blood of young females. Also released as *The Devils Commandment*, *Lust of the Vampire*, and *The Vampire of Notre Dame*. Mario Bava served as cameraman.

1957 B IT [Titan-Athena] **Vampire(s):** Duchess Marguerite (Gianna-Maria Canale); **Cast:** Dario Michaelis, Antoine Balpetre, Paul Muller. **Dir:** Riccardo Freda.

It! The Terror from Beyond Space

A Martian vampire monster stows away on a spaceship and begins attacking earthlings once on Earth. Also released as *It! The Vampire from Beyond Space*. Based on A. E. van Vogt's story "The Black Destroyer."

1958 B [Vogue/United Artists] **Vampire(s):** It (Ray "Crash" Corrigan); **Cast:** Marshall Thompson, Shawn Smith, Kim Spalding. **Dir:** Edward L. Cahn.

Not of this Earth

A human from another planet is exploring Earth to see if human blood is a viable substitute for that of his race. Also released as *El Vampiro del Planeta Rosso*. Remade in 1988.

1957 B [Allied Artists] **Vampire(s):** Science fiction vampire; **Cast:** Beverly Garland, Paul Birch, Morgan Jones, Richard Miller; **Dir:** Roger Corman.

Old Mother Riley Meets the Vampire

A comic vampire encounter between the star of a British movie series and Bela Lugosi. Also released as *My Son the Vampire*; *Mother Riley Meets the Vampire*; *Mother Riley Runs Riot*; *Vampire Over London*. Released in the United States in the 1960s.

1957 B GB [Renown Pictures] **Vampire(s):** Baron Von Housen (Bela Lugosi); **Cast:** Arthur Lucan. **Dir:** John Gilling.

Pawns of Satan
1959.

Plan 9 from Outer Space

Among movie buffs, known as the worst movie ever made. Lugosi's last picture was so bad it was good.

1956 B [Distribution Corporation of America] **Vampire(s):** Vampira; Dracula (Bela Lugosi); **Cast:** Lyle Talbot, Tor Johnson, Gregory Walcott. **Dir:** Edward D. Wood.

Pontianak (The Vampire)

Menado portrays a woman made beautiful through magic, who then becomes a vampire after sucking serpent poison from her husband. First of the Keris Malaysian Pontianak series. Sequel: *Dendam Pontianak* (1958).

1957 B MA [Keris] **Vampire(s):** (Maria Menado); **Cast:** M. Amin, Salmah Ahmed, Dollah Serawak.

The Return of Dracula

Dracula moves to California and while living incognito in a small town preys on unsuspecting residents. Also released as *The Fantastic Disappearing Man* and *The Curse of Dracula*

1958 B [Gramercy/United Artists] **Vampire(s):** Dracula/Bellac (Francis Lederer); **Cast:** Norma Eberhardt, Gage Clark. **Dir:** Paul Landres.

Space Ship Sappy

The Three Stooges meet a vampire.

1957 [Jules White Productions] **Cast:** Moe Howard, Larry Fine, Joe Esser, Doreen Woodbury. **Dir:** Jules White.

Sumpah Pontianak (The Vampire's Curse)

The third of the Malaysian Pontianak series. Sequel: *Anak Pontianak* (1958).

1958 B MA [Keris] **Vampire(s):** (Maria Menado).

Super-Giant 2
1956.

The Teenage Frankenstein
1959.

The Thing from Another World

Based on *Who Goes There?* by John W. Campbell.

1951 B [RKO/Winchester Pictures] **Vampire(s):** James Arness; **Cast:** Kenneth Tobey, Margaret Sheridan, Robert Cornthwaite; **Dir:** Christian Nyby.

La Traite du Vampire

Also released as *The Trade of the Vampire.*

1951 FR Cast: Jean Boullet, Michele Veam. **Dir:** Pierre Boursons.

Uncle Was a Vampire

In the midst of his Hammer movies, Lee went to Italy to make a comical vampire movie. Originally released as *Tempi Duri Pet I Vampiri* (Hard Time for Vampires).

1959 C IT [Embassy] **Vampire(s):** Baron Rodriguez (Christopher Lee); **Cast:** Renato Rascel, Sylvia Koscina, Kay Fisher. **Dir:** Pio Angeletti.

The Vampire

Beal becomes a vampire as a result of taking pills with ingredients derived from a vampire bat. Also released as *It's Always Darkest before the Dawn* and *Mark of the Vampire.*

1957 B [United Artists] **Vampire(s):** Dr. Paul Beecher (John Beal); **Cast:** Coleen Gray, Kenneth Tobey, Lydia Reed; **Dir:** Paul Landres.

The Vampire

German Robles created a new vampire character, Count Lavud, who he would play in several sequels. Also released as *El Vampiro* and *The Lurking Vampire.* Released in United States in 1968. Sequel: *The Vampire's Coffin* (1957).

1957 B MX [Cinematografica/Trans-International] **Vampire(s):** Count Karol de Lavud (German Robles); **Cast:** Abel Salazar, Adriadne Welter, Carmen Montejo. **Dir:** Fernando Mendez/Paul Nagle.

Vampire Man

A vampire captures the wife of an atomic scientist and imprisons her in his subterranean lair in this comedy. Originally released as *Onna Kyuketsui* and later as *Male Vampire.*

1959 B JP [Shin Toho] **Vampire(s):** Shigeru Amachi; **Cast:** Yoko Mihara, Kienosuke Wade; **Dir:** Nobuo Nakagawa.

The Vampire Moth

A murder mystery in which the clues include a series of victims with bite marks on their necks and some bloodstained moths. Originally released as *Kyuketsuki Ga.* Based on a novel by Seishi Yokomizo.

1956 B JP [Toho] **Cast:** Ryo Ikebe, Akio Kobori, Acami Kuji. **Dir:** Nobuo Nakagawa.

The Vampire's Coffin

Count Lavud is revived by someone pulling the stake out of his heart. Also released as *El Ataud del Vampiro, El Ataud del Coffin.* Sequel to *The Vampire* (1957).

1958 B MX [Cinematographica] **Vampire(s):** Count Karol de Lavud/Duval (German Robles); **Cast:** Al Salazar, Adriadne Welter, Alice Rodriguez. **Dir:** Fernando Mendez.

El Vampiro Negro

A remake of *Le Vampire of Düsseldorf.* Released in English-speaking countries as *The Black Vampire.*

1953 B AR [Argentinean Sono] **Cast:** Olga Zubarry, Roberto Escalada, Nathan Pinzon, Nelly Panizza. **Dir:** Ramon Barreto.

1960 to 1969

Ahkea Kkots (The Bad Flower)

The ninth remake of the novel *Dracula*. Based on Hammer's *The Horror of Dracula*.

1961 B KO [Sunglim Films] **Vampire(s):** Dracula; **Cast:** Chimi Kim; Yechoon Lee. **Dir:** Yongmin Lee.

Batman Dracula

1964 B [Filmmaker's Cooperative] **Vampire(s):** Dracula (Jack Smith); **Cast:** Baby Jane Holzer. **Dir:** Andy Warhol.

Batman Fights Dracula

The vampirelike caped crusader encounters the vampire.

1967 B PH [Lea/Fidelis] **Vampire(s):** Dracula (Dante Rivero); **Cast:** Jing Abalos, Vivian Lorrain, Ramon D'Salva. **Dir:** Leody M. Diaz.

Best of Dark Shadows

A video of clips from the television series.

1965 [Dan Curtis] **Vampire(s):** Barnabas Collins (Jonathan Frid).

Billy the Kid versus Dracula

Another failed attempt to make a vampire Western. Dracula is finally killed by the reformed outlaw, Billy the Kid.

1966 C [Circle/Embassy Pictures] **Vampire(s):** Dracula (John Carradine); **Cast:** Charlita, Chuck Courtney, Melinda Plowman. **Dir:** William Beaudine.

Black Sabbath

Three short horror stories, one of which was based on the novella by Alexey Tolstoy, "The Wurdalak." The only motion picture portrayal of a vampire by Boris Karloff. Originally issued by *I Tre Volti della Paura*.

1963 C IT [Galatea/Emmepil/Cinematografica/AIP] **Vampire(s):**

Gorca (Boris Karloff); **Cast:** Suzy Anderson, Mark Damon. **Dir:** Mario Bava.

Black Sunday

This movie introduced Mario Bava to the vampire film and Barbara Steele to horror fans. Based on Nicol Gogol's story, *The Vij*. Originally released as *La Maschera del Demonio* and later as *House of Fright, Revenge of the Vampire, Die Stinde Wenn Drakula Kommt*, and *La Masque du Démon*. Recently Bava's son made a new version of this film.

1960 B IT [American-International] **Vampire(s):** Princess Katia (Barbara Steele); **Cast:** John Richardson, Ivo Garrani, Andrea Cecchi; **Dir:** Mario Bava.

Blood and Roses

The earliest attempt to bring Sheridan Le Fanu's "Carmilla," the story of a young female vampires who attacks her human peers, to the screen. The American version was heavily censored. Originally released in French as *Et Mourir de Plaisir*.

1961 C FE/IT [EGE Films/Documento Films] distributed in the U.S. by Paramount; **Vampire(s):** Carmilla (Annette Stroyberg Vadim); **Cast:** Mel Ferrer, Elsa Martinelli. **Dir:** Roger Vadim.

Blood Bath

An artist, possessed by a vampire ancestor, paints people and then immerses them in a vat of hot wax. Also released as *Track of the Vampire*.

1966 B [AIP/Jack Hill] **Vampire(s):** (William Campbell); **Cast:** Marissa Mathes, Lori Saunders. **Dir:** Stephanie Rothman; Jack Hill.

Blood Beast Terror

A giant blood-sucking moth is killing people and the police inspector must track it down. Also released as *Deathshead Vampire* and *Vampire-Beast Craves Blood*.

1969 C [Tigon/Eastman] **Vampire(s):** Meg Quennell (Vanessa Howard); **Cast:** Peter Cushing, Robert Flemyng, Wanda Ventham. **Dir:** Vernon Sewell.

The Blood Drinkers

A vampire tries to save his dying girlfriend by kidnapping her twin sister to transplant her heart. Also released as *The Vampire People.*

1966 C PH [Hemisphere] **Vampire(s):** Marco (Ronald Remy); **Cast:** Amalia Fuentes, Eddie Fernandez. **Dir:** Gerardo de Leon.

Blood Fiend

Christopher Lee is a man suspected in a series of vampire murders in this thriller. Also released as *Female Fiend* and as *The Theatre of Death*

1966 PH [Pennea] **Vampire(s):** Phillippe Dravas (Christopher Lee); Nicole Chapel (Jenny Till); **Cast:** Leila Goldoni, Julian Glover. **Dir:** Samuel Gallu.

The Blood of Dracula's Castle

Dracula and his wife are living incognito in a desert castle with a group of young maidens they keep chained up as a living food supply. Also released as *Dracula's Castle.*

1969 [A & E Film Corporation] **Vampire(s):** Dracula (Alex D'Arcy); **Cast:** John Carradine, Paula Raymond. **Dir:** Al Adamson, Jean Hewitt.

Blood of Nostradamus

Last of four features starring German Robles as the vampire figure Nostradamus. Originally released as *La Sangre de Nostradamus.* Sequel to *Curse of Nostradamus.*

1960 MX [Bosas Priego] **Vampire(s):** Nostradamus (German Robles); **Cast:** Julio Aleman, Domingo Soler. **Dir:** Frederico Curiel.

Blood of the Virgins

Originally released as *Sangre de Virgenes.*

1968 MX [Azteca] **Cast:** Gloria Prat, Ricardo Bauleo, Rolo Puente. **Dir:** Emilio Vieyra.

Blood Thirst

An American detective uncovers a cult of blood-drinkers led by a vampire priestess. Also released as *The Horror from Beyond* and as *Blood Seekers.* Released in the United States in 1971.

1965 PH [Chevron-Paragon/Journey] **Cast:** Robert Winston, Yvonne Nielson, Judy Dennis, Katherine Henryk. **Dir:** Newt Arnold.

The Bloodless Vampire

This movie may never have been released.

1965 PH [Journey]; **Cast:** Charles Macauley, Helen Thompson. **Dir:** Michael Du Pont.

The Bloodsuckers

Based on the book by Simon Raven, *Doctors Wear Scarlet.* Vampirism is treated as real, but as a psychological condition. Also released as *Incense of the Damned.*

1969 C GB [Chevron-Paragon/Lucinda-Titan] **Vampire(s):** Richard Fountain (Patrick Mower); **Cast:** Peter Cushing, Patrick MacNee, Patrick Mower; **Dir:** Michael Burrowes.

The Bloody Vampire

Count Caliostro is a vampire hunter trying to locate and destroy the vampire Count Frankenhausen. Originally released as *El Vampiro Sangriento.* Sequel to *The Invasion of the Vampires* (1961).

1961 B MX [Tele Talia Films/Clasa-Mohme/American International Pictures] **Vampire(s):** Count Frankenhausen (Carlos Agosti); **Cast:** Begona Palacios, Antonio Raxell, Erna Martha Bauman. **Dir:** Miguel Morayta.

La Bonne Dame

A short feature.

1966 FR [S.O.F.C.A.] **Cast:** Valeska Gert, Constantin Nepo, Germaine Kerjean. **Dir:** Pierre Philippe.

The Brides of Dracula

One of Dracula's disciples is released to prey upon a girl's school. Van Helsing is called in to track him down. Also released *Les Maitresses de Dracula* (French). Screenplay by Jimmy Sangster. Sequel to *The Horror of Dracula.*

1960 C GB [Hammer] **Vampire(s):** Baron Meister (David Peel); **Cast:** Yvonne Monlaur, Martita Hunt, Peter Cushing. **Dir:** Terence Fisher.

Bring Me the Vampire

A group of people have to stay in a castle for a month in order to receive a fortune. While there they encounter a vampire who turns out to be a fake. Originally released as *Enchenme al Vampiro*, and later as *Throw Me to the Vampire.*

1961 B MX [Estudios America] **Vampire(s):** Carlos Mantequilla (aka Fernando Soto); **Cast:** Joaquin Garcia Vargas, Alfonso Pompin Iglesias, José Jasso. **Dir:** Alfredo E. Crevenna.

Capuexita y Pulgarcito contra los Monstruos (Tom Thumb and Little Red Riding Hood vs. the Monsters)

1962 MX [Azteca] **Cast:** Sergio Magana, Fernando M. Ortiz, A. T. Portillo. **Dir:** Roberto Rodriquezy.

Carmilla

1968 SW/JP.

Carry on Screaming

A vampire couple attack young girls who are vampirized and then turned into store window mannequins. Also released as *Screaming, Carry on Vampire.*

1966 C [Peter Rogers/Warner-Pathe/ Anglo-Amalgamated/Sigma III] **Vampire(s):** Valeria (Fenella Fielding); **Cast:** Harry H. Corbett, Kenneth Williams, Joan Sims. **Dir:** Gerald Thomas.

Castle of Blood

On a bet, a man spends the night in a haunted castle and must face all of the ghostly figures. Based on the short story "Dance Macabre" by Edgar Allan Poe, Originally issued as *La Danza Macabra*, and also issued as *Castle of Terror* and *Coffin of Terror.* The director remade the movie in color in 1970 as *Web of the Spider.*

1963 B IT [Woolner] **Vampire(s):** Elizabeth Blackwood (Barbara Steele); **Cast:** Margaret Robsham, George Riviere. **Dir:** Anthony Dawson (aka Antonio Margheriti).

Castle of Dracula

A short feature.

1968 [Delta S. F. Film Group].

Castle of the Living Dead

The vampiric Lee is turning girls into the living dead at his secret lair beneath a castle. Also issued as *Il Castello de Morti Vivi.*

1964 [Malasky] **Vampire(s):** Count Drago (Christopher Lee); **Cast:** Donald Sutherland, Gala Germani, Philippe Leroy. **Dir:** Luciano Wise (Herbert Wise), Michael Reeves.

El Charro de las Calaveras (The Rider of the Skulls)

Consists of three stories of which one is a vampire tale.

1967 B MX [Azteca] **Cast:** Dagoberto Rodriguez, David Silva, Alicia Caro. **Dir:** Alfredo Salazar

Curse of Nostradamus

First of the Nostradamus series. Several segments of a 12-part serial were put together and released originally as *Maldicion de Nostradamus*. Robles' first appearance as the vampire Nostradamus.

1960 B MX [Bosas Priego] **Vampire(s):** Nostradamus (German Robles); **Cast:** Domingo Soler, Julio Aleman. **Dir:** Frederico Curiel.

Curse of the Crying Woman

A female vampire and her husband attempt to revive the crying woman (creature out of Mexican folklore). Originally released as *La Maldicion de la Llorona*.

1961 B MX [Cinematografica ABSA/Clasa-Mohme/American International] **Vampire(s):** (Rita Macedo); **Cast:** Rita Arenas, Abel Salazar, Carlos Lopez Moctezuma. **Dir:** Rafael Baledon.

The Death of P'Town

A seven-minute 16mm film with a homosexual vampire.

1963 Cast: Jack Smith. **Dir:** Ken Jacobs.

Demon Planet

Originally released as *Terrore nello Spazio*. Also released as *Planet of the Vampires*, *Planet of Blood,* and *Terror en el Espacio*. Based on a story by Renato Pestriniero, *One Night of Twenty-One Hours*. According to Donald Glut, not a real vampire film.

1965 IT [Italian International Film] **Cast:** Barry Sullivan, Norma Bengall, Angel Aranda. **Dir:** Mario Bava.

The Devil's Mistress

A female psychic vampire attacks the men who killed her husband in the old West.

1966 C [Emerson/Holiday/WGN] **Vampire(s):** (Joan Stapleton); **Cast:** Arthur Resley, Joan Stepleton; Robert Gregory. **Dir:** Orville Wanzer.

The Devils of Darkness

Two friends investigate the death of a young man killed on vacation in Breton and discover a group of local vampires.

1965 C [Planet Films/Fox] **Vampire(s):** Count Sinistre/Armound du Moliere (Hubert Noel); **Cast:** William Sylvester, Tracy Reed, Carole Gray. **Dir:** Lance Comfort.

Dr. Terror's Gallery of Horrors

Includes several short features, two of which are vampire stories. Also released as *The Blood Suckers, Return from the Past, The Witch's Clock*, and *The Blood Drinkers*. No relation to *Dr. Terror's House of Horror*.

1966 C [Dora Corporation-Borealis Enterprises; American General] **Vampire(s):** Dracula/Count Alucard (Mitch Evans); **Cast:** John Carradine. **Dir:** David Hewitt.

Dr. Terror's House of Horrors

One of this collection of horror shorts is a vampire story. No relation to *Dr. Terror's Gallery of Horrors*.

1965 C UK [Amicus] **Vampire(s):** (Max Adrian); **Cast:** Donald Sutherland, Jenifer Jayne. **Dir:** Freddie Francis.

Dracula

The 10th film version of *Dracula*. An underground film.

1964 [Filmmaker's Cooperative] **Cast:** Naomi Levine; **Dir:** Andy Warhol.

Dracula and the Boys

A hardcore gay vampire movie. Also released as *Dracula Sucks, Does Dracula Really Suck?*, and *Dracula . . . Does He?* The first homosexual vampire movie.

1969 C Vampire(s): Dracula (Jaime Gillis); **Cast:** Annette Haven.

Dracula Has Risen from the Grave

Lee returned to England in this third Hammer Dracula movie. After a Catholic Monsignor exorcises Dracula's Castle, the Count attacks him using a local priest and others under his control. Memorable as the movie in which Dracula pulls the stake out of his own chest. Sequel: *Taste the Blood of Dracula.*

1968 C GB [Hammer] **Vampire(s):** Dracula (Christopher Lee); **Cast:** Veronica Carlson, Barry Andrews, Barbara Ewing, Rupert Davies. **Dir:** Freddie Francis.

Dracula Meets the Outer Space Chicks

An adult erotic-oriented film.

1968 [Independent].

Dracula—Prince of Darkness

In this sequel to *The Horror of Dracula*, Dracula must handle a group of travelers who are forced to spend a night in his castle. He is opposed by a vampire hunter monk. Also released as *Disciple of Dracula, Revenge of Dracula, The Bloody Scream of Dracula.* Sequel: *Dracula Has Risen from the Grave.* Screenplay by Jimmy Sangster who is credited under a pseudonym, John Sansom.

1965 C GB [Hammer/Fox] **Vampire(s):** Dracula (Christopher Lee); **Cast:** Francis Matthew, Suzan Farmer, Charles Tingwell, Barbara Shelley. **Dir:** Terence Fisher.

Dracula (the Dirty Old Man)

In this adult erotic comedy, Dracula resides in an abandoned mine where he has young virgins brought to him as a food supply.

1969 C [Whit Boyd Productions; Vega International/Art Films] **Vampire(s):** Dracula/Count Alucard (Vince Kelly); **Cast:** Ann Hollis, Bill Whitton, Libby Caculus. **Dir:** William Edwards.

Dracula vs. Frankenstein

Scientists from another planet travel to Earth and begin to reanimate the world's monsters, including Dracula, in order to take over the world. Also released as *El Hombre que Vino del Ummo, Blood of Frankenstein, Assignment Terror, The Man Who Came from Ummo,* and *Dracula Jagt Frankenstein.*

1969 C SP/GE/IT [International Jaguar; Jaime Prades/Eichberg Film] **Vampire(s):** Dracula; **Cast:** Michael Rennie, Paul Naschy, Craig Hill. **Dir:** Hugo Fregonese, Tulio Demichelli.

Dracula's Wedding Day

An underground film with Dracula.

1967 B [Filmmaker's Coop] **Vampire(s):** Dracula. **Dir:** Mike Jacobson

Drakulita

1969 PH [RJF Brothers] **Vampire(s):** Drakulita (Rossana Ortiz); **Cast:** Lito Lagaspi, Rebecca, Gina Laforteza, Joseph Gallego, **Dir:** Consuelo Osorio.

The Empire of Dracula

A young man arrives at Castle Draculstein on a mission of revenge over the Count who has killed his father. Originally released as *El Imperio de Dracula* and later as *Las Mujeres de Dracula* and *Sinfonia del Más Allá.* Possibly the first Mexican horror film shot in color.

1967 C MX [Filmica Vergara] **Vampire(s):** Count Dracula (Eric del Castillo); **Cast:** Ethel Carrillo, Cesar del Campo, Lucha Villa. **Dir:** Federico Curiel.

The Eye of Count Flickenstein

An underground parody of *Dracula.*

1966 Dir: Tony Conrad.

Fangs of the Living Dead

A vampire tried to convince his niece that she is a reincarnation of a nun burned for practicing witchcraft. Also released as *Malenka—La Nipote del Vampiro, Malenka la Vampira, Malenka—The Niece of the Vampir, The Vampire's Niece.*

> **1968 C SP/IT** [Triton/Victory/Cobra/Felix/Emporix] **Vampire(s):** Count Wolduck (Julian Ugarte); **Cast:** Anita Ekberg, John Hamilton, Diana Lorys. **Dir:** Amando de Ossorio.

Fantasmagorie

> **1962 FR Cast:** Edith Scob, Venantino Venantini, Jean Henry. **Dir:** Patrice Molinard.

The Fearless Vampire Killers; or Pardon Me, but Your Teeth Are in My Neck

A vampire hunter and his assistant search for vampires in a small village. An unusual comedy that was originally named for the dance sequence at the vampire's home. Also released as *Dance of the Vampires.*

> **1967 C** [Cadre and Filmways] **Vampire(s):** Count Von Krolock; Herbert (Ian Quarrie); **Cast:** Jack McGowan, Sharon Tate, Alfie Bass, Ferdy Mayne. **Dir:** Roman Polanski.

La Fée Sanguinaire

Based on the Elizabeth Bathory legend.

> **1968 BE Vampire(s):** T. Katinaki. **Dir:** Roland Lethem.

Frankenstein, the Vampire and Co.

A comedy in which two unsuspecting men have to deliver wax figures of Frankenstein's monster and Dracula to a castle. The action begins when the wax figures come to life. Originally released as *Frankenstein, el Vampiro y Cia* and as *Frankenstein, El Vampiro y Compania.*

> **1961 B MX** [Cinematografia Calderon] **Vampire(s):** Quintan Bulnes; **Cast:** Manuel Loco Valdes, Jose Jasso, Joaquin Garcia Vargas Borolas. **Dir:** Benito Alazraki.

Frankenstein's Bloody Terror

The first of the films with Naschy as the wolfman Count Daninsky. Originally released as *La Marca del Hombre Lobo* (The Mark of the Wolfman). Also released as *The Vampire of Dr. Dracula, The Wolfman of Count Dracula, Hell's Creatures, The Mark of the Wolfman,* and various other titles.

> **1968 C SP** [Maxper] **Vampire(s):** Professor Mialhov (Julian Ugarte), Wandessa Moilhov (Rossana Yanni); **Cast:** Paul Naschy, Diane Zurakowska. **Dir:** Enrique L. Equilez.

Goke, Body Snatcher from Hell

An alien vampire attacks the passengers of a crashed airplane. Survivors discover that he was but one of a large number that were attacking the human race. Originally issued as *Kyuketsuki Gokemidore.*

> **1969 C JP** [Shochiku] **Cast:** Hidea Ko, Teruo Yoshida, Tomomi Sato. **Dir:** Hajime Sato.

Goliath and the Vampires

Goliath (Maciste) must battle a group of zombies controlled by a vampire. Originally released as *Maciste Contro il Vampiro* and later as *The Vampires.*

> **1964** [Ambrosiana Cinematografica/AIP] **Vampire(s):** Kobrak (Guido Celano); **Cast:** Gordon Scott, Gianna Maria Canale, Jacques Sernas. **Dir:** Giacomo Gentilomo.

Hand of Death

A man in a fit of despair becomes the object of the attack of some psychic vampires while in Morocco. Also released as *Beast of Morocco* and *The Hand of Night.*

> **1966 C GB** [Associated-British-Pattie] **Vampire(s):** (Alizia Gur), (Terence de Marney); **Cast:** William Sylvester, Diane Clare. **Dir:** Frederick Goode.

Hercules contre les Vampires

Hercules and Theseus travel to Hades to save the soul of a friend controlled by the vampire Lico. Originally released as *Ercole al Centro della Terra* and later as *Hercules in the Haunted World* and *Hercules at the Center of the Earth*.

1961 C IT [Omnia S.P.A. Cinematografica] **Vampire(s):** Lico (Christopher Lee); **Cast:** Reg Park, Leonora Ruffo. **Dir:** Mario Bava.

Hiroku Kaibyoden

A film version of a famous Japanese story about a vampire cat at the castle of Lord Nabeshima.

1969 C JP [Daiei] **Cast:** Kojiro Hongo, Naomi Kobayashi, Mitsuyo Kamei. **Dir:** Tokuzo Tanaka.

Horrors of Dracula
1966.

House on Bare Mountain

This first vampire adult erotic film. Also released as *La Colline des Desirs*.

1962 C BE [Olympic International Films] **Vampire(s):** Dracula (Jeffery Smithers); **Cast:** Warren Ames, Bob Cresse, Laura Eden. **Dir:** R. Lee Frost.

La Huella Macabre
1962 B MX [Rosas Priego/Clasa-Mohme] **Cast:** Guillermo Murray, Rosa Carmina, Carmen Molina, Jamie Fernandez. **Dir:** Alfredo B. Crevenna.

Insomnia

A short film in which a person shown reading a book on vampires turns out to be one. Originally issued as *Insomnie*.

1963 B & C FR Cast: Pierrie Etaix. **Dir:** Pierrie Etaix.

The Invasion of the Vampires

Count Frankenhausen and his early vampire victims attack a small Mexican town. Originally released as *La Invasion de los Vampiros*. Sequel: *The Bloody Vampire*.

1962 B MX [Tele-Talia/Trans-International] **Vampire(s):** Count Frankenhausen (Carlos Agosti); **Cast:** Rafael Etienne, Bertha Moss, Tito Junco. **Dir:** Miguel Morayta.

Isabell, a Dream
1968 IT Vampire(s): Dracula.

La Isla de la Muerte

Also released as *Island of the Damned*, *Le Baron Vampire*, and *The Island of Death*.

1966 GE/SP [AA/Tefi-Orchita] **Cast:** Mel Welles, Cameron Mitchell, George Martin. **Dir:** Mel Welles.

Kiss Me Quick

An alien from an all-male planet visits a mad earth scientist who is able to create females in his laboratory. This film is often mistakenly listed as having been directed by Russ Meyer. Also released as *Dr. Breedlove, or How I Learned to Stop Worrying and Love*.

1964 C [Fantasy Films/G&S Productions] **Vampire(s):** Dracula; **Cast:** Jackie DeWitt, Athea Currier, Fred Coe. **Dir:** Pete Perry, Max Gardens.

Kiss of the Vampire

A couple in a rural village encounter a group of vampires and find themselves in a war between them and a vampire hunter. Also issued as *Kiss of Evil*.

1962 C GB [Hammer] **Vampire(s):** Dr. Ravna (Noel Williams); **Cast:** Clifford Evans, Edward de Souza, Isobe Black. **Dir:** Don Sharp.

Kuroneko

Two women raped by a group of Samurai warriors return as vampire cats to seek revenge.

1968 B JP [Kindai Eiga Yokai/Nihon Eiga Shinsha/ Cinecenta] **Vampire(s):** (Nobuko Otowa), (Kieako Taichi) ; **Cast:** Kichiemon Nakamura, Kei Sato. **Dir:** Kaneto Shindo.

The Last Man on Earth

First of two films based on Richard Matheson's *I Am Legend*. It was originally released as *L'Ultimo Uomo della Terra*.

1964 B IT [La Regina/AIP] **Vampire(s):** Ben Courtland; **Cast:** Vincent Price, Franca Bettoia, Emma Danieli. **Dir:** Ubaldo Ragona.

The Lemon Grove Kids Meet the Green Grass Hopper and the Vampire Lady from Outer Space

Also issued as *The Lemon Grove Kids Meet the Monsters*.

1963 C [Ray Dennis Steckler] **Vampire(s):** Carolyn Brandt; **Cast:** Ray Dennis Steckler, Mike Cannon, Coleman Francis. **Dir:** Ray Dennis Steckler.

Little Shop of Horrors

An employee at a florist grows a plant that talks and feeds off of human blood. Later remade as a broadway musical. Remade as *Please Don't Eat My Mother* (1972) and under its original name in 1986.

1960 B [Roger Corman/AIP] **Cast:** Jonathan Haze, Jackie Joseph, Mel Welles. **Dir:** Roger Corman.

Mad Monster Party?

An animated children's film with puppets.

1966 C [Embassy Pictures]; **Vampire(s):** Dracula; **Cast:** Voices: Boris Karloff, Alan Swift, Phyllis Diller. **Dir:** Jules Bass.

The Magic Sword

A young boy with a magic sword must face several trials including a vampiress played by TV horror movie hostess Vampira. Also issued as *St. George and the 7 Curses* and *St. George and the Dragon*.

1962 C [United Artists] **Vampire(s):** Vampira; **Cast:** Basil Rathbone, Estelle Winwood, Gary Lockwood. **Dir:** Bert I. Gordon.

The Maltese Bippy

Comedy team Rowan and Martin square off against a vampire.

1969 C [MGM] **Vampire(s):** Ravenwood (Dennis Weaver); **Cast:** Dan Rowan, Dick Martin, Carol Lynley. **Dir:** Norman Panama.

Manugang ni Drakula (The Secrets of Dracula)

1964 PH Vampire(s): Dracula.

Men of Action Meet the Women of Dracula

A troupe of circus performers battle Dracula.

1969 PH [Villanueva] **Vampire(s):** Dracula; **Cast:** Dante Varona, Eddie Torrento. **Dir:** Artemio Marquez.

Mondo Keyhole

An adult erotic feature has a rapist attacked by lesbians and his wife by Dracula. Also released as *The Worst Crime of All*.

1966 C [Ajasy/Boxoffice International] **Vampire(s):** Dracula. **Dir:** John Lamb.

Munster, Go Home!

The TV monster family travel to England to retrieve Herman Munster's inheritance. A movie based on the popular TV series. Sequel: *The Munsters Revenge* (1981).

1966 C **Vampire(s):** Lily (Yvonne DeCarlo), Dracula (Fred Lewis); **Cast:** Fred Gwynne. **Dir:** Earl Bellamy.

The Naked Witch

A vampire witch is revived by someone pulling the stake from her body. Also issued as *The Naked Temptress*.

1961 C [Alexander] **Vampire(s):** (Beth Porter); **Cast:** Robert Burgos, Lee Forbes. **Dir:** Andy Milligan.

Night of the Vampires

Originally released as *Der Fluch der Gruen Augen* and later as *The Curse of Green Eyes* and *Cave of the Living Dead*.

1964 B YU/GE [Objectiv-Triglav-Film] **Vampire(s):** Professor Adelsberg (Wolfgang Preiss); **Cast:** Adrian Hoven, Erika Remberg, Carl Mohner. **Dir:** Akosvon Rathony.

Nightmare Castle

Originally released as *Gli Amanti d'Oltre Tomba; The Faceless Monster*.

1965 IT [AA/Emmeci] **Cast:** Barbara Steele, Paul Miller, Helga Line. **Dir:** Mario Caiano/Allan Grunewald.

Nostradamus and the Destroyer of Monsters

Originally issued as *Nostradamus y el Destructor de Monstruos*. Also issued as *The Monsters Demolisher*.

1962 MX [Bosas Priego/ Estudios America/American International] **Vampire(s):** Nostradamus (Germán Robles); **Cast:** Julio Aleman, Domingo Soler, Aurora Alvarado. **Dir:** Federico Curiel.

Nostradamus and the Genie of Darkness

Third of the Nostradamus series. Originally released as *Nostradamus y el Genio delas Tinieblas* and later as *Genie of Darkness*.

1960 MX [Bosas Priego] **Vampire(s):** Nostradamus (German Robles); **Cast:** Julio Aleman, Dominico Soler, Aurora Alvarado. **Dir:** Federico Curiel.

Orgy of the Night

1966 [Edward D. Wood] **Vampire(s):** Vampira; **Cast:** Criswell, Fawn Silver, Tor Johnson, Lon Chaney, Jr. **Dir:** A. C. Stephen.

Parque de Juegos

Based on a Ray Bradbury story. Also released as Park of Games.

1963 SP [Escuela Cinematografica Espanola] **Cast:** Cecilia Villarreal, Luisa Munoz Schneider, Wilhelm Elie. **Dir:** Pedro Olea.

Playgirls and the Vampire

A group of chorus girls are chased by a vampire in a castle. Originally released as *L'Ultima Preda del Vampiro*. Also released as *The Last Victim of the Vampire*, *The Last Prey of the Vampire*, *The Vampire's Last Victim*, *Desires of the Vampire*, *Daughters of the Vampire*, and *Curse of the Vampire*.

1960 B IT [Tiziano Longo] **Vampire(s):** Count Kernassy (Walter Brandi); **Cast:** Lyla Rocco, Alfredo Rizzo. **Dir:** Piero Regnoli.

Pontianak Gua Musang (The Vampire of the Cave)

Sixth and last of the Pontianak series from Keris. Sequel to *Pontianaka Kembali*.

1964 B MA [Keris] **Cast:** Suraya Haron, Ghazali Sumantri, Malek Siamat. **Dir:** B. N. Rao.

Pontianaka Kembali (The Vampire Returns)

Fifth of the Pontianak series. Sequel: *Pontianak Gua Musang*.

1963 B MA [Keris]; **Vampire(s):** (Maria Menado); **Cast:** Malik Selamat. **Dir:** Ramon Estellia.

Queen of Blood

A spaceship returns to Earth with an alien who happens to be a vampire. Based on a story, ''The Veiled Woman.'' Also released as the *Planet of Blood.*

1966 C [American International] **Vampire(s):** ''Queen of Blood'' (Florence Marly); **Cast:** John Saxon, Basil Rathbone, Judi Meredith, Dennis Hopper; **Dir:** Curtis Harrington.

La Reine des Vampires

Sequel to *Le Viol du Vampire.*

1968 FR [Sam Selsky] **Dir:** Jean Rollin.

Revenge of the Blood Beast

Originally released as *La Sorella di Satana* and later as *She Beast.*

1965 IT [Eorupix/Leith] **Cast:** Michael Reeves, Barbara Steele, Mel Welles. **Dir:** Michael Reeves.

The Revival of Dracula

Originally released as *Il Risveglio di Dracula.*

1969 IT Cast: Gabby Paul; Gill Chadwick.

Santo Against Baron Brakola

Originally released as *El Santo contra el Baron Brakola.*

1965 MX [Vergara] **Vampire(s):** Baron Brakola; **Cast:** Santo, Fernando Oses, Susana Robles. **Dir:** Jose Diaz Morales.

Santo and Dracula's Treasure

Santo the masked wrestler helps a scientist bitten by Dracula destroy the vampire.

Originally released as *Santo y el Tesoro de Dracula* and later released (with additional nude scenes) as *El Vampiro y El Sexo* and *The Vampire and Sex.*

1969 C MX [Cinematografica Calderon] **Vampire(s):** Dracula/Count Alucard (Carlos Agosti); **Cast:** Santo, Aldo Monti, Noelia Noel. **Dir:** Rene Cardona.

Santo and the Blue Demon vs. the Monsters

Masked wrestler Santo teams up with his colleague the Blue Demon to battle Dracula, two vampire women, and other monsters. Originally released as *Santo y Blue Demon contra los Monstruos.*

1968 C MX [Cinematografica Sotomayor] **Vampire(s):** Dracula (David Avizu), (Elas Maria Tako), (Yolanda Ponce); **Cast:** Santo, Blue Demon, Heydi Blue, Jorge Rado. **Dir:** Gilberto Martinez Solares.

Santo en la Venganza de las Mujeres Vampiro

A mad scientist awakens a vampiress who believes that an ancestor of Santo the masked wrestler did her wrong. Also released as *The Vengeance of the Vampire Women* and *La Venganza de las Mujeres Vampiro.*

1969 C MX [Cinematografica Flama/ Peliculas LatinoAmericanas] **Vampire(s):** Countess Mayra; **Cast:** Santo, Aldo Monti, Norma Lazareno. **Dir:** Frederico Curiel.

Santo vs. the Vampire Women

Santo sets out to save the daughter of a friend who is being targeted by a group of female vampires. Originally released in Spanish as *Santo contra Las Mujeres Vampiras.* Also released as *Samson vs. the Vampire Women.*

1962 B MX [Tele-Cine-Radio] **Cast:** Santo, Lorena Velazquez, Maria Duval. **Dir:** Alfonso Corona Blake.

Sexy Prohibitissimo

Consists of several short sketches with a vampire tale. Also released as *Sexy Super Interdict*, *Sexy Interdict*, and *Forbidden Femininity*.

1963 C IT [Gino Nordini Produzioni/ Films Marbeuf] **Vampire(s):** Dracula; **Cast:** Karmela, Lilli de Saigon, Monique. **Dir:** Marcello Martinelli.

Sexyrella

A parody of Cinderella.
1968 FR.

Slaughter of the Vampires

Originally issued as *La Strage die Vampiri*. Also released as *Curse of the Blood Ghouls*, *Curses of the Ghouls*, *La Stragi del Vampiri*.

1962 B IT [Mercury Film Int./Pacemaker Pictures] **Vampire(s):** The Vampire (Walter Brandi); **Cast:** Dieter Eppler, Graziella Granata, Marietta Solvay. **Dir:** Roberto Mauri.

Tales of Blood and Terror

1969 [Titan Films].

A Taste of Blood

Also released as *The Secret of Dr. Alucard*.
1966 C [Creative Film Enterprises] **Vampire(s):** John Stone (Bill Rogers); **Cast:** Ted Schell, Elizabeth Wilkinson, Otto Schlesinger. **Dir:** Herschell Gordon Lewis.

Taste the Blood of Dracula

1969 C GB [Hammer/Warner Bros.] **Vampire(s):** Dracula (Christopher Lee); **Cast:** Ralph Bates, Geoffrey Keen, John Carson, Peter Sallis. **Dir:** Peter Sasdy.

Terror Creatures from the Grave

Originally released as *Cinque Tombe per un Medium.*

1965 IT [Pacemaker/IEC/MBS/ Cinematografica] **Cast:** Barbara Steele, Walter Brandi, Riccardo Garrone. **Dir:** Massimo Pupillo.

Terror in the Crypt

Based on "Carmilla" by Sheridan Le Fanu. Originally released as *La Cripta e l'Incubo*. Also released as *La Maldicion de los Karnsteins*, *The Karnstein Curse*, *The Crypt of the Vampire*, *The Vampire's Crypt*, *Karnstein*, *The Crypt and the Nightmare*, *Carmilla*, and *The Curse of the Karnsteins.*

1962 IT/SP [Hispamer/MEC] **Vampire(s):** Count Ludwig von Karnstein (Christopher Lee); **Cast:** Adriana Ambisi, Jose Campos. **Dir:** Camillo Mastrocinque/ Thomas Miller.

Tore Ng Diyablo (Tower of the Devil)

A vampire seeks a bride.
1969 PH [Santiago] **Vampire(s):** (Ramon D'Salva); **Cast:** Jimmy Morato, Pilar Pilapil, Rodolfo Garcia. **Dir:** Lauro Pacheco.

The Torture Zone

Karloff plays a scientist who discovers a stone creature who needs blood to survive. Also released as *La Camara del Terror*, *Fear Chamber*, and *Torture Chamber*. This was Boris Karloff's last film.

1968 C MX/US [Fimica Vergara/ Columbia/Parasol] **Cast:** Boris Karloff, Julissa, Carlos East. **Dir:** Juan Ibanez.

Tower of the Screaming Virgins

The wife of the king is suspected of being a vampire/witch. Also released as *Der Turm der Verbotenen Liebe*, *La Tour de Nesle*, and *The Sweetness of Sin*. Based on a story by Alexandre Dumas.

1968 C Cast: Mario-Ange Anies, Jean Piat, Ursula Glass, Terry Torday; **Dir:** Leo Joannon.

Transylvania 6-5000

An animated short not to be confused with the feature film of the same name.

1963 C [Warner Bros.] **Vampire(s):** Count Bloodsucker; **Cast:** Bugs Bunny (Voice: Mel Blanc). **Dir:** Chuck Jones.

Valerie and the Week of Wonders

Based on a story by V. Nezval. Originally released as *Valerie a Tyden Divu.*

1969 CZ [Barrandov] **Cast:** Jaroslava Musil, Helena Anyzkova; **Dir:** Jaromil Jures.

Vampir-Cuadecuc

A documentary on the production of *El Conde Dracula.*

1969 SP Dir: Pedro Portabella.

The Vampire

A 30-minute short feature.

1968 PL

Vampire and the Ballerina

Originally released as *L'Amante del Vampiro* and also released as *The Vampire Lover* and *The Dancer and the Vampire.*

1962 B IT [Consorzio Italiano] **Vampire(s):** The Contessa (Maria Lusia Rolando), Walter Brandi; **Cast:** Helena Remy, Tina Gloriano. **Dir:** Renato Polselli.

Le Vampire du Dusseldorf

The story of Peter Kürten, a vampiric serial killer.

1964 B FE/IT/SP [Rorne Paris Films/ B. Peroja/Manoletti] **Vampire(s):** Peter Kürten (Robert Hossein); **Cast:** Marie-France Risier, Roger Dutoit, Annie Andersson. **Dir:** Robert Hossein.

La Vampire Nue

An adult erotic film from Jean Rollin. Also released as *Nude Vampire* and *Naked Vampire.*

1969 C FR [Les Films/ABC] **Vampire(s):** (Caroline Cartier); **Cast:** Maurice Lemaitre, Oliver Martin, Ly Letrong. **Dir:** Jean Rollin.

The Vampire of Castle Frankenstein

Originally released as *El Vampiro de la Autopista* and later as *The Vampire of the Highway* and *The Horrible Sexy Vampire.*

1969 SP [Conefilms] **Vampire(s):** Baron von Winninger; **Cast:** Valdemar Wohlfahrt, Patricia Loran, Luis Induni. **Dir:** Jose Luis Madrid.

The Vampire of the Opera

Originally issued as *Il Vampiro dell'Opera.* Also issued as *Il Mostro dell'Opera* and *The Monster of the Opera.* Based on a novel by Gaston Leroux.

1961 B IT [NIF] **Vampire(s):** Stefano (Giuseppe Addobbati); **Cast:** Vittoria Prada, Marc Matyn, Barbara Howard. **Dir:** Renato Polselli.

Vampire Woman

Originally released as *Xi Xuefu.* A variation of the Sherlock Holmes "Sussex Vampire" story in which a woman is seen sucking blood from her baby and is accused of being a vampire. It was later discovered that she was trying to save her child.

1962 B [Zhong Lian] **Vampire(s):** Bai Yang; **Cast:** Zhang Huoyou, Huang Manli. **Dir:** Li Tie.

The Vampires

Carradine and his female vampire cohorts battle Mexican wrestler heroes. Originally released as *Las Vampiras* and later as *The Vampire Girls.*

1968 C MX [Vergara/Columbia] **Vampire(s):** John Carradine; **Cast:** Pedro

Armendariz, Jr., Mil Mascaras, Maria Duval. **Dir:** Frederico Curiel.

Vampires d'Alfama

An animated short feature.
1963 FR Dir: Pierre Kast.

Vampirisme

A 12-minute short.
1967 B FR [Films du Cosmos]; **Cast:** Michel Beaune, Jean-Pierre Bouyxou, Alain Le Bris. **Dir:** Patrice Duvic, Bernard Chaouat.

El Vampiro Aechecha (The Lurking Vampire)

A young boy opposes a vampire who attacks small children. Based on a story by William Irish (aka Cornell Woolrich).
1962 MX/AR Cast: Germaán Robles, Nestor Zarvade, Blanca del Prado.

Un Vampiro para Dos

Two comedy heroes face a vampire and his family. Also issued as *A Vampire for Two*.
1965 B IT [Belmar P. C.-Bravo Murillo] **Vampire(s):** Baron von Rosenthal (Fernando Fernan Gomez); **Cast:** Gracita Morales, Jose Luis Lopez Vazquez. **Dir:** Pedro Lazaga.

Los Vampiros del Oeste

A government agent investigates a series of mysterious deaths.
1963 Cast: Joaquin Cordero, Alma Fuentes, William Murray, José Elias Moreno. **Dir:** Juan Ortega.

Vij

A student is forced to spend three nights with a woman who comes to life as a vampire and attacks him. Based on the short story, "The Vij" by Nikolai Gogol. Also released as *Viy*.

1967 C RU [Mosfilm] **Cast:** Natalia Varlei, Leonid Kuralev, N. Kutuzov. **Dir:** Konstantin Yershov, Giorgio Kropachyov.

Le Viol du Vampire

An adult erotic film. Also released as *La Reine des Vampires*, *Les Femmes Vampires*, *Queen of the Vampires*, *The Rape of the Vampire*, and *Sex and the Vampire*.
1967 B FR [ABC Films] **Cast:** Bernard Letrou, Solange Pradel, Ursule Pauly. **Dir:** Jean Rollin.

World of the Vampires

A vampire and an occultist fight each other to the bitter end. Originally released as *El Mundo de los Vampiros*.
1960 B MX [Cinematografica APSA] **Vampire(s):** Sergio Sotubai (Guillermo Murray); **Cast:** Erna Martha Bauman, Mauricio Graces. **Dir:** Alfonso Corona Blake.

Yokai Daisenso

A government official is possessed by a vampire demon.
1968 C JP Cast: Yoshihiko Aoyama, Akane Kawasaki, Osamu Okawa, Tomoo Uchida. **Dir:** Yoshiyuki Kuroda.

1970 to 1979

Alabama's Ghost

One of the few vampire movies made for the African American community. It pits a vampire rock group against a ghost.
1972 C [Ellman/Bremson International]; **Cast:** Lani Freeman, Pierre LePage. **Dir:** Frederic Hobbs.

Allen and Rossi Meet Dracula and Frankenstein

1974 C Cast: Bernie Allen, Steve Rossi.

Angeles y Querubines

The second of this movie's three stories is about a vampire bride.

1972 C MX [Cine Produccines] **Vampire(s):** Angela (Helena Rojo); **Cast:** Ana Luisa Peluffo, Jorge Humberto Robles, David Silva. **Dir:** Rafael Corkidi.

Attack of the Blind Dead

Originally released as *El Ataque de los Muertos sin Ojos.*

1973 C SP Dir: Amando de Osorio.

Barry McKenzie Holds His Own

A rare Australian vampire movie, which is part of a series of movies based on a comic strip character. The vampire tries to kidnap the Queen of England as part of a plot to promote tourism in Transylvania.

1974 C AU [Roadshow/Reg Grundy] **Vampire(s):** Eric Count Plasma (Donald Pleasence); **Cast:** Barry Crocker, Barry Humphries, Dick Bentley. **Dir:** Bruce Beresford.

The Bat People

Biologist John Beck is bitten by a bat and turns into a bat monster. Also released as *It Lives by Night.*

1974 C [AIP] **Vampire(s):** Dr. John Beck (Stewart Moss); **Cast:** Marianne McAndrew, Michael Pataki, Paul Carr. **Dir:** Jerry Jameson.

Blacula

This most famous African American vampire movies finds African Prince Mamuwalde soliciting help from Dracula to fight slavery. Instead, Dracula vampirizes him and turns him into Blacula, who is eventually turned loose on society in the 1970s.

1972 C [American International] **Vampire(s):** Prince Mamuwalde (William Marshall); **Cast:** Denise Nicola; Vonetta McGee, Gordon Pinsent. **Dir:** William Crain.

Blood

An odd story that has Dracula's daughter and the Wolfman's son together and raising carnivorous plants in modern New York.

1973 C [Walter Kent] **Vampire(s):** Regina (Hope Stransbury); **Cast:** Allen Berendt, Eve Crosby, Pamela Adams. **Dir:** Andy Milligan.

Blood Ceremony

A movie based on the Elizabeth Bathory legend. Also released as *Legend of Blood Castle*, *Ceremonia Sangrienta*, and *Ritual of Blood.*

1972 C SP/IT [X Films/Luis Films] **Vampire(s):** Elizabeth Bathory (Lucia Bose); **Cast:** Karl Ziemmer, Ewa Aulin, Anna Farra. **Dir:** Jorge Grau.

Blood Couple

An African American vampire story. Also released as *Ganja and Hess*, *Black Evil*, *Black Out: The Moment of Terror*, *Black Vampire*, and *Double Possession.*

1973 C [Quentin Kelly and Jack Jordan] **Vampire(s):** Dr. Hess Green (Duane Jones); **Cast:** Marlene Clark, Bill Gunn, Leonard Jackson. **Dir:** Bill Gunn.

Blood for Dracula

A modern Dracula travels to Italy in search of the blood of "wirgins" but continually encounters the wrong kind in this satirical comedy. Also released as *Andy Warhol's Dracula.*

1974 C [Bryanton Pictures] **Vampire(s):** Dracula (Udo Kier); **Cast:** Joe Dallesandro, Vittorio de Sica. **Dir:** Paul Morrisey.

Blood Lust

The story of a man with a blood fetish who breaks into funeral homes to mutilate bodies and drink the blood. Also released as *Mosquito der Schonder.*

1970 C SI [Monarex] **Vampire(s):** (Werner Pochath) **Cast:** Ellen Umlauf, Peter Hamm. **Dir:** Marijan Vajda.

Blood of Frankenstein

A disconnected story centering on a crippled Dr. Frankenstein trying to discover a cure in the midst of a community of monsters (including Dracula). Also released as *Dracula vs. Frankenstein; Satan's Bloody Freaks.*

1971 C [Independent-International] **Vampire(s):** Dracula (Zandor Vorkov); **Cast:** Forest J. Ackerman, J. Carroll Naish, Lon Chaney, Jr. **Dir:** Al Adamson.

Blood Relations

In this comedy, a nurse discovers that a doctor, a vampire, is stealing blood from the local hospital. Originally released as *Bloedverwantes/Les Vampires en ont Ras le Bol.*

1977 C NE/FR [Jaap van Rij Filmproductie/CTIS] **Vampire(s):** (Maxim Hamel), (Ralph Arliss); **Cast:** Gregoire Aslan, Sophie Deschamps, Robert Dalban. **Dir:** Wim Lindner.

The Blood Spattered Bride

Loosely based on ''Carmilla'' by Sheridan Le Fanu. Originally released as *La Novia Ensangretada* and later as *Bloody Fiance* and *Til Death Us Do Part.*

1974 C SP [Morgana Films] **Vampire(s):** Carmilla Karnstein (Alexandra Bastedo); **Cast:** Manibel Martin, Simon Andrew, Dean Selmier; **Dir:** Vincent Aranda.

The Body Beneath

Ford is the leader of a family of vampires in London trying to continue their lineage. A sexploitation also released as *The Demon Lover.*

1970 C [Nova International] **Vampire(s):** Rev. Al Bongo Wolf visits the Dracula Society in this short feature.

1970 C **Cast:** William Donald Grollman. **Dir:** Tom Baker.

Bram Stoker's Original Dracula

This was a remake of *Dracula.*

1978 C **Dir:** Ken Russell.

The Bride's Initiation

An adult erotic movie with a bisexual Dracula who kidnaps a pair of newlyweds.

1976 C [VCX] **Cast:** Carol Connors, Candida Robbins, Mark Brock, Tony Manhall. **Dir:** Duncan Stewart.

Cake of Blood

Four stories, one of which is a vampire tale. Also released as *Pastel de Sangre.*

1972 C SP [P. C. Tiede] **Cast:** Maria May, Charo Lopez, Marisa Paredes. **Dir:** José Maria Valles, et al.

Captain Kronos: Vampire Hunter

Pilot for a proposed series featuring a team of vampire hunters. Also released as *Kronos.*

1972 C GB [Hammer] **Vampire(s):** John Carson, W. Ventura; **Cast:** Horst Janson, Shane Briant, Caroline Munro. **Dir:** Brian Clemens.

Capulina Contra Los Vampiros

Mexican comedy star Caulina is attacked by a group of vampires.

1972 C MX [Estudios America/PanoramaFilms/Azteca Films] **Cast:** Gaspar Henaien Capulina, Gloriella, Hector Andremar. **Dir:** René Cardona.

The Case of the Full Moon Murders

An adult erotic comedy concerning a vampire who bites her male victims in their private parts. It was released in both hardcore and softcore versions and under several titles including: *Sex on the Groove Tube* and the *Case of the Smiling Stiffs.*

1974 C [Seaburg/Lobster & Dana] **Vampire(s):** (Cathy Walker); **Cast:** Harry Reems, Sheila Stuart, Ron Browne, Fred Lincoln. **Dir:** Joseph Brad Talbort.

Casual Relations

This movie includes a vampire episode as a major component of what is otherwise not a vampire story.

1973 B [Mark Rappaport] **Cast:** Sis Smith, Mel Austin, Paula Barr. **Dir:** Mark Rappaport.

Il Cavaliere Costante Nicosia Demoniaco Ovvero Dracula in Brianza

A sexual comedy in which Buzzanca is bitten by Dragulescu and discovers that his sexual prowess was greatly heightened.

1975 C IT [Titanus/Coralta Cinematografica] **Vampire(s):** Dragulaescu (John Steiner); **Cast:** Lando Buzzanca, Sylva Koscina, Christa Linder. **Dir:** Lucio Fulci.

Chanoc contra el Tigre y el Vampiro (Chanoc vs. the Tiger and the Vampire)

A comedy with a vampire as the guest villain.

1971 C MX [Azteca] **Cast:** Tin-Tan (German Valdes), Gregorio Casel; Aurora Cavel, Raul Martinez Solares. **Dir:** Gilberto Martinez Solares.

Chi o Suu Ningyo

Also released as *The Night of the Vampire; Yureiyashiki no Kyofu-Chi Wo Sun Ningyo*.

1970 C JP [Toho] **Cast:** Atsuo Nakamura, Kayo Matsuo, Akira Nakao. **Dir:** Michio Yamamoto.

Chosen Survivors

Vampires attack a B-movie cast in the desert following an A-bomb test.

1974 C MX [Chrubusco/ Metromedia/ Alpine] **Cast:** Jackie Cooper, Alex Cord, Richard Jaeckel, Bradford Dillman. **Dir:** Sutton Roley.

Chronique de Voyage

A short feature.

1970 C FR **Cast:** Marc Olibier Cayce, Claude Moro, Francine Roussel. **Dir:** Robert de Laroche.

Le Circuit de Sang (The Blood Circuit)

1973 C FR

La Comtesse aux Siens Nus

Originally released as an adult erotic film in which a descendent of Carmilla Karnstein kills her lovers by biting them on their private parts. Several versions with varying degrees of sexual explicitness have appeared. Also released as *La Comtesse Noire, Les Avaleuses, Jacula, Sicarius—The Midnight Party, The Bare Breasted Countess, The Loves of Irina, Erotikil, Yacula,* and *The Last Thrill.* Plot derived from a modern day "Carmilla;" censored version released on videotape as *Erotikill.*

1973 C BE/FR [Brux International/ Marc] **Vampire(s):** Irina Karnstein (Lina Romay); **Cast:** Alice Arno, Jack Taylor, Monica Swinn. **Dir:** Jesus Franco.

El Conde Dracula

Christopher Lee returned to his role as Dracula in this attempt to more closely adhere to the story of Bram Stoker's *Dracula.* Also released as *Count Dracula, Bram Stoker's Count Dracula, Dracula 71, The Nights of Dracula,* and *Nacht Wenn Dracula Erwacht.*

1970 C SP/IT/GE [Feniz/Korona/ Filmar/Towers of London] **Vampire(s):** Dracula (Christopher Lee); **Cast:** Klaus Kinsky, Herbert Lom, Soledad Miranda, Maria Rohm. **Dir:** Jesus Franco.

Count Dracula, the True Story

Canadian documentary filmed in Romania.
1979 C CA Dir: Yurek Filjalkoski.

Count Erotica, Vampire

A hardcore adult erotic feature.
1971 C [Lobo Productions] **Cast:** John Peters, Mary Simon, Paul Robinson. **Dir:** Tony Teresi.

Count Yorga, Vampire

A Dracula-like Count Yorga attacks modern Los Angeles. He makes a second appearance in the *Return of Count Yorga* (1971).
1970 C [Erica/American International] **Vampire(s):** Count Yorga (Robert Quarry); **Cast:** Roger Perry, Michael Murphy, Michael Macready. **Dir:** Bob Kelljan.

Countess Dracula

One of two films by which Hammer introduced Ingrid Pitt to horror film fans. Based on a biography of Elizabeth Bathory, Valentine Penrose's *The Bloody Countess*. A novelization of the movie was released as *Countess Dracula* by Michel Parry.
1970 C GB [Hammer] **Vampire(s):** Countess Bathory/Elizabeth Nadasdy (Ingrid Pitt); **Cast:** Nigel Green, Sandor Eles, Maurice Denham. **Dir:** Peter Sasdy.

Cuadecuc (Vampir)

An experimental film made in connection with *El Conde Dracula*.
1970 B SP [Films 59 Barcelona] **Cast:** Christopher Lee, Herbert Lom, Soledad Niranda, Fred Williams. **Dir:** Pedro Portabella.

Le Culte du Vampire

1971 C FR Cast: Willie Braque, Louise Dhour, Eric Loosfeld. **Dir:** Jean Rollin.

Curse of the Devil

Seventh in a series of werewolf movies starring Naschy. He is cursed by a dying Countess Elizabeth Bathory. Also released as *The Return of Walpurgis* and *The Black Harvest of Countess Dracula*.
1973 C SP [Loyus/Producciones Escorpion] **Vampire(s):** Elizabeth Bathory (Patty Shepard); **Cast:** Paul Naschy, Fay Falcon, Vidal Molina. **Dir:** Carlos Aured.

Curse of the Vampires

A family vampire movie in which a mother passes her vampire condition to her son, and then he infects the rest of the family. Also released as *Creatures of Evil*, *Blood of the Vampires*, and *Dugong Vampira*.
1970 C PH [Scertre Industries/Hemisphere] **Vampire(s):** The Mother (Mary Walter); **Cast:** Amalia Fuentes, Eddie Garcia, Romeo Vasquez. **Dir:** Gerardo de Leon.

The Daughter of Dracula

Based on Sheridan Le Fanu's "Carmilla." Also released as *La Hija de Dracula* and *La Fille de Dracula*.
1972 C SP [Comptoir Francais du Film/ Interfilme] **Vampire(s):** Dracula (Howard Vernon); **Cast:** Britt Nichols, Dennis Price. **Dir:** Jesus Franco.

Daughters of Darkness

A contemporary story based on the Elizabeth Bathory legend, which develops its lesbian themes. Also released as *Blut on den Lippen*, *Le Rouge aux Levres*, and *The Promise of Red Lips*.
1971 C BE [Roxy/Mediterranean/Gemini] **Vampire(s):** Elizabeth Bathory (Delphine Seyrig); **Cast:** Daniele Ouimet, John Karlen, Andrea Rau. **Dir:** Harry Kumel.

Deafula

The story of a young man bitten by Dracula. This film is notable for all its dialog being filmed in sign language.

1975 B [Signscope] **Vampire(s):** Deafula/Steve Adams (Peter Wicksburg); Count Dracula (Gary Holstrom); **Cast:** Lee Darrel, Katherine Wilson. **Dir:** Peter Wecksburg.

The Deathmaster

Vampire Korda is washed ashore in his coffin in '70s Los Angeles and subsequently becomes a guru to a group of hippies. Also released as *Khorda*.

1971 C [AIP] **Vampire(s):** Khorda (Robert Quarry); **Cast:** Bill Ewing, Brenda Dickson, John Fiedler. **Dir:** Ray Danton.

A Deusa de Marmore—Escrava do Diabo

Maldonado portrays a 2,000 year-old woman who survives by sucking the life from her lovers.

1978 C BR [Panorama do Brazil] **Vampire(s):** Rosangela Maldonado; **Cast:** Jose Mojica Marins, Joao Paulo, Luandy Maldonado. **Dir:** Rosangela Maldonado.

The Devil's Plaything

An adult erotic film concerning a group of nuns awaiting the return of a vampire burned at the stake during the Middle Ages. Also released as *Veil of Blood*.

1973 C SI [Leisure Time/Monarex] **Vampire(s):** Baroness Vaga; **Cast:** Nadia Senkowa, Untel Syring, Maria Forssa; **Dir:** Joseph W. Sarno.

The Devil's Skin

A woman fights a vampire.

1970 C SG [Cathay] **Cast:** Ingrid Hu, Meng Li, Sun Tao.

The Devil's Wedding Night

A variation of the Elizabeth Bathory legend with the Countess del Vries bathing in the blood of virgins. Also released as *El Returno de la Drequessa Dracula* (The Return of the Duchess Dracula) and *Full Moon of the Virgins*.

1973 C SP [Virginia Cinematografica/Dimension Pictures] **Vampire(s):** Countess del Vries (Sara Bey); **Cast:** Mark Damon, Mariam Barrios, Frances Davis. **Dir:** Paul Solvay.

La Dinastia Dracula

1978 C MX Vampire(s): Dracula (Fabian Forte).

Disciple of Death

1975 C GB Cast: Mike Raven. **Dir:** Tom Parkinson.

Diversions

1976 C [Artimis Film Corp.] **Vampire(s):** The Vampire (James Lister); **Cast:** Heather Deeley. **Dir:** Derek Ford.

Dracula

Made for TV movie. Another attempt to bring *Dracula* to the screen.

1973 C CA [Canadian Broadcasting Company] **Cast:** Norman Welsh, Blair Brown. **Dir:** Jack Nixon Browne.

Dracula

1978 C MX Cast: Enrique Alvarez Felix.

Dracula

A remake of Dracula based on the play by Hamilton Deane and John Balderston. Dracula is presented as a romantic seducer.

1979 C C [Universal] **Vampire(s):** Dracula (Frank Langella); **Cast:** Laurence Olivier, Donald Pleasence, Kate Nelligan. **Dir:** John Badham.

Dracula, a Family Romance
1972 C

Dracula A.D., 1972

Lee returned to Hammer for its sixth Dracula movie that brought the Count to London and to an encounter with a group of hippies. This was a sequel to *The Satanic Rites of Dracula* (1973).

1972 C GB [Hammer] **Vampire(s):** Dracula (Christopher Lee); **Cast:** Peter Cushing, Christopher Neame, Stephanie Beacham. **Dir:** Alan Gibson.

Dracula and Son

Christopher Lee played Dracula again in this comedy in which the Count goes to Paris. Based on the novel *Paris V.* Also released as *Dracula, Father and Son*; and *Dracula Pére et Fils*. Released in the U.S. in 1979.

1975 C FR [Quartet Films] **Vampire(s):** (Christopher Lee); **Cast:** Bernard Menez, Marie Helene Breillat, Catherine Breillat. **Dir:** Edouard Molinaro.

Dracula and the Seven Golden Vampires

An ineffective attempt to mix the vampire and martial arts genres as Dracula and Van Helsing clash in China. Also released as *Legend of the Seven Golden Vampires* and *The Seven Brothers Meet Dracula.*

1974 C GB/HK [Hammer/Shaw Brothers] **Vampire(s):** Dracula (John Forbes-Robertson); **Cast:** Peter Cushing, Julia Eye. **Dir:** Roy Ward Baker.

Dracula Bites the Big Apple

1979 C Vampire(s): Dracula (Peter Loewy); **Cast:** Barry Concula. **Dir:** Richard Wenk.

The Dracula Business

A BBC documentary.
1974 C GB Dir: Anthony de Latbiniére.

Dracula contra El Dr. Frankenstein

First of three films by prolific director Franco centered on Frankenstein's monster. This initial effort pits him against Dracula and his vampire brides. Vampires do not play an important role in the sequels. Also released as *Dracula Prisonnier de Frankenstein* (French) and *Dracula versus Frankenstein.*

1972 C SP [Comtoir Francais de Film and Fenix] **Vampire(s):** Dracula (Howard Vernon); Lady Dracula (Britt Nichols); **Cast:** Dennis Price, Albert Dalbes, Mary Francis. **Dir:** Jesus Franco.

Dracula Goes to RP
1974 C PH [RVQ Productions].

Dracula in Italy
1975 C

Dracula in the House of Horrors
1974 C AU **Dir:** Bruce Beresford.

Dracula in the Provinces
1975 C [Coralta Cinematografica].

Dracula Is Not Dead
1975 C

Dracula Rocks
1979 C

Dracula Sucks

An adult erotic-oriented remake of Lugosi's 1931 *Dracula.* Available in both hardcore and softcore versions. Also released as *Lust at First Bite* and *Dracula's Bride.*

1979 C [First International Pictures/ MR Productions/Kodiak]; **Vampire(s):** Count Dracula (James Gillis); **Cast:** John Holmes, Annette Haven, John Leslie, Serena. **Dir:** Philip Marshak.

Dracula's Blood

1974 C [Cannon] **Vampire(s):** Dracula; **Cast:** Tina Sainz.

Dracula's Dog

A vampire canine leaves Transylvania for modern-day Los Angeles in search of a surviving relative of Count Dracula. Also released as *Zoltan, Hound of Dracula*.

1978 C [Crown International] **Cast:** Jose Ferrer, Michael Patoki, Reggie Nalder. **Dir:** Albert Band.

Dracula's Feast of Blood

1974 C

Dracula's Great Love

Dracula operates incognito as a nursing home director. In the end he commits suicide by staking himself. Also released as *Cemetery Girls, Dracula's Virgin Lover, Count Dracula's Great Love*, and *El Gran Amor del Conde Dracula*.

1972 C [Janus/Eva] **Vampire(s):** Dracula/Dr. Kargas/Dr. Marlow (Paul Naschy); **Cast:** Rossanna Yanni, Haydee Politoff, Mirta Miller. **Dir:** Javier Aguirre.

Draculas Lüsterne Vampire

Also released as *Dracula's Vampire Lust* and *Dracula Vampire Sexual*.

1970 C SP [RCS Film/Monarex] **Vampire(s):** Dracula (Des Roberts); **Cast:** Alon D'Armand, Ola Copa. **Dir:** Mario D'Alcala.

Dragula

1973 C Cast: Casey Donovan, Walter Kent, Jan Wallowitch, Calvin Holt. **Dir:** James Moss.

Dragula, Queen of the Darkness

1979 C

Every Home Should Have One

A comedy that includes a vampire sketch. Also released as *Think Dirty* and *Marty Feldman, Vampire!*

1970 C GB [Lion International] **Vampire(s):** Dracula (Marty Feldman); **Cast:** Shelley Berman, Barry Talk, Julie Ege. **Dir:** Jim Clark.

The Evil of Dracula

Also released as *Chi O Suu Bara*. Based on "Carmilla" by Sheridan Le Fanu.

1975 C JP [Toho] **Vampire(s):** (Hunie Tanaka); **Cast:** Toshio Kurosawa, Marika Mochizuki, Shin Kishida. **Dir:** Michio Yamamoto.

Fascination

1979 C FR [Les Films ABC/Comex] **Vampire(s):** (Franca Mai); **Cast:** Jean-Marie Lemaire, Brigitte Lahaie, Fanny Magier. **Dir:** Jean Rollin.

A Filha de Dracula

Also released as *Dracula's Daughter*.

1971 C FR/PT [Interfilme/Comptoir Francais de Film] **Vampire(s):** Dracula, Maria Karnstein (Britt Nichols); **Cast:** Anne Libert, Howard Vernon, Alberto Dalbes. **Dir:** Jesus Franco.

Der Fluch der Schwarzen Schwestern

1973 C Cast: Heidrun Hankammer, Nadja Henkova, Maria Forsa. **Dir:** Joseph W. Sarno.

Le Frisson des Vampires

Also released as *Sex and the Vampire, Shudder of the Vampire, and The Vampire's Thrill*.

1970 C FR [Production Films Modernes et Films A.B.C.] **Vampire(s):** Isode (Dominique); **Cast:** Sandra Julien, Nicole Nancel, Jean Marie Durand. **Dir:** Jean Rollin.

Go for a Take

1972 C GB [Century Films International-al/Rank] **Vampire(s):** Dracula (Dennis Price); **Cast:** Reg Varney, Norman Rossington, Sue Lloyd; **Dir:** Harry Booth.

Grave of the Vampire

Also released as *Seed of Terror*.

1972 C [Entertainment Pyramid/Millennium] **Vampire(s):** Caleb Croft (Michael Pataki); **Cast:** William Smith, Lyn Peters, Diane Holden. **Dir:** John Patrick Hayes.

Guess What Happened to the Count Dracula?

Also released as *The Master of the Dungeon*.

1970 C [Merrick International] **Vampire(s):** Count Adrian (Des Roberts); **Cast:** Claudia Barron, John London. **Dir:** Laurence Merrick.

Guru, the Mad Monk

Also released as *Garu, the Mad Monk*.

1970 C GB [Maipix/Nova International] **Vampire(s):** Olga (Jacqueline Webb); **Cast:** Neil Flanagan, Judith Israel, Paul Lieber. **Dir:** Andy Milligan.

Halloween with the Addams Family

Also released as *Halloween with the New Addams Family*.

1977 C **Vampire(s):** Morticia (Carolyn Jones), Countess Dracula (Suzanne Krazna); **Cast:** John Astin, Jackie Coogan, Ted Cassidy; **Dir:** Dennis Steinmetz.

Hannah, Queen of the Vampires

Also released as *Crypt of the Living Dead*, *La Tumba de la Isla Maldita*, and *Vampire Women*.

1972 C [Fine Films/Coast Industries] **Vampire(s):** Hannah (Teresa Gimpera);

Cast: Andrew Prine, Mark Damon, Patty Shepard. **Dir:** Ray Danton.

The Historical Dracula, Facts Behind the Fiction

Documentary filmed partially in Romania.

1973 C **Dir:** Ion Boston.

Horror of the Blood Monsters

Also released as *Vampire Men of the Lost Planet*, *Creatures of the Prehistoric Planet*, *Horror Creatures of the Red Planet*, *Flesh Creatures of the Red Planet*, and *Space Mission of the Lost Planet*.

1970 C [TAL/Independent-International] **Cast:** John Carradine, Robert Dix, Vicki Volante; **Dir:** Al Adamson.

Horrorritual

Three-minute comic short.

1972 C [Warner Bros.] **Vampire(s):** (Barry Atwater).

House of Dark Shadows

Also released as *La Fiancée du Vampire*.

1970 C [Dan Curtis] **Vampire(s):** Barnabas Collins (Jonathan Frid); **Cast:** Grayson Hall, Kathryn Leigh Scott, Thayer David. **Dir:** Dan Curtis.

The House of Dracula's Daughter

1973 C [Universal Entertainment] **Cast:** John Carradine. **Dir:** Gordon Hessler.

House that Dripped Blood

Four short features, the last of which, "The Cloak," is a vampire tale.

1970 C GB [Amicus] **Vampire(s):** Ingrid Pitt; **Cast:** Jon Pertwee. **Dir:** Peter Duffell.

How They Became Vampires

1973 C [Sun, Moon, & Star Co.] **Dir:** Amen El-Kakim.

Hyocho No Bijo

Based on "Kyuketsuki" ("Vampire") by R. Edogawa.

1977 C JP [Shochiku] **Dir:** Umeji Inome.

I, the Vampire

1972 C SP [Hipamex] **Cast:** Christopher Lee, Paul Naschy. **Dir:** Leon Klimovsky.

Immoral Tales

Consists of four erotic stories, one of which is based on the Elizabeth Bathory legend. Also released as *Contes Immoraux* and *Three Immoral Women.*

1974 C Vampire(s): Elizabeth Bathory (Paloma Picasso); **Cast:** Lisa Danvers, Fabrice Luchini, Charlotte Alexandra. **Dir:** Walerian Borowczyk.

In Search of Dracula

Christopher Lee both narrated and recreated the historical Dracula in this documentary based on Raymond T. McNally and Radu Florescu's *In Search of Dracula.*

1976 C SW Vampire(s): Vlad Tepes (Christopher Lee). **Dir:** Calvin Floyd and Tony Forsberg.

The Incredible Melting Man

A remake of *First Man into Space* (1958).

1977 C [Quartet/American International] **Vampire(s):** (Alex Rebar); **Cast:** Michael Alldredge, Burr De Benning, Myron Healy. **Dir:** William Sachs.

La Invasion de los Muertos

1972 C MX [Azteca] **Vampire(s):** Dracula (Cesar Silva); **Cast:** Jorge Mistral, the Blue Demon, Christa Linder. **Dir:** Rene Cardona.

Is There a Vampire in the House?

1972 C [D. D. Productions] **Dir:** Eddie Saeta.

Jonathan

Also released as *Jonathan, Vampire Sterben Nicht* and *Jonathan, le Dernier Combat contre les Vampires.*

1970 C GE [Iduna/New Yorker] **Vampire(s):** Jonathan (Jurgen Jung), Dracula (Paul Albert Krumm); **Cast:** Hans Dieter, Thomas Astan, Oscar Von Schab. **Dir:** Hans Geissendorfer.

El Jovencito Dracula

Also released as *Young Jonathan Dracula.*

1975 C SP [Los Films del Mediterraneo] **Cast:** Carlos Benpar, Susanna Estrada, Victor Israel, Marina Ferri. **Dir:** Carlos Benpar.

Kali: Devil Bride of Dracula

1975 C

Kathavai Thatteeya Mohni Paye

An Indian film made in the Tamil language.

1975 C IN [Anuradha International] **Cast:** C. R. Patiban, Sanjivirajan, Desikan. **Dir:** M. A. Rajaraman.

Kyuketsuki Dorakyura Kobe Ni Arawaru: Akuma Wa Onna Wo Utsukushiku Suru

1979 C JP [Toei/Asahi Communications] **Vampire(s):** Dracula (Masumi Okada); **Cast:** Kei Taguchi. **Dir:** Hajime Sato.

The Lady Dracula

Also released as *Lemora: A Child's Tale of the Supernatural* and *The Legendary Curse of Lemora.*

1973 C C [Blackburn Productions] **Vampire(s):** (Lesley Gibb); **Cast:** Cheryl "Rainbeaux" Smith, William Whitton. **Dir:** Richard Blackburn.

Lady Dracula

1977 C [T 13/IFV Production] **Vampire(s):** (Evelyn Kraft); **Cast:** Christiane

Buchegger, Brad Harris, Theo Lingen. **Dir:** Franz-Joseph Gottlieb.

Lake of Dracula

Also released as *Chi O Suu Me* (Bloodthirsty Eyes) and *Dracula's Lust for Blood*.
1971 C JP [Toho] **Vampire(s):** Dracula (Mori Kishida); **Cast:** Midori Fujita, Sanae Emi, Choei Takahashi. **Dir:** Michio Yamamoto.

Legacy of Satan

1973 C Vampire(s): Dr. Muldavo (John Francis), Maya (Lisa Christian); **Cast:** Paul Berry, Christ Helm, Deborah Horlen. **Dir:** Gerard Damiano.

Leonor

Based on a story by Ludwig Tieck.
1975 C Vampire(s): (Liv Ullman); **Cast:** Michel Piccoli, Ornetta Mutti, Antonio Ferrandis. **Dir:** Juan Bunuel.

Let's Scare Jessica to Death

1971 C [Jessica Co.] **Vampire(s):** Jessica (Zohra Lambert); **Cast:** Barton Heyman, Kevin O'Connor, Gretchen Corbett. **Dir:** John Hancock.

Levres de Sang

1975 C FR Cast: Jean-Lou Philippe, Anne Briand, Nathalie Perrey. **Dir:** Jean Rollin.

Lips of Blood

Also released as *Les Chemins de la Violence*.
1972 C FR [Les Films de l'Epee] **Cast:** Michel Flynn, Richard Vitz, Catherine Frank. **Dir:** Ken Ruder.

Living Dead at Manchester Morgue

Also released as *Don't Open the Window*.
1976 C SP/IT Cast: Christian Galbo, Raymond Lovelock, Arthur Kennedy. **Dir:** Jorge Grau.

La Llamada del Vampiro

Also released as *The Curse of the Vampyr* and *Aquellarre de Vampiros*.
1971 C SP [Lacy Films/Sesena/Arco Films] **Vampire(s):** Carl von Rysselbert (Nicholas Ney); **Cast:** Diana Sorel, Beatriz Lacy, Ines Skorpio. **Dir:** José Elorieta.

Love at First Bite

A Fotobook of *Love at First Bite* was also released.
1979 C [American International] **Vampire(s):** Dracula (George Hamilton); **Cast:** Susan Saint James, Richard Benjamin, Dick Shawn. **Dir:** Stan Dragoti.

Love Vampire Style

Also released as *Beiss Mich, Leibling* and *Bite Me, Darling*.
1970 C GE [New Art Films] **Cast:** Eva Renzi, Patrick Jordan, Amedeus August, Herbert Fux. **Dir:** Helmut Föernbacher.

Lust for a Vampire

This movie relating the further adventures of Carmilla and the Karnstein family was also released as *To Love a Vampire*. William Hughes wrote the novelized version.
1970 C GB [Hammer/EMI] **Vampire(s):** Carmilla Karnstein (Yutte Stensgaard), Count Karnstein (Mike Raven); **Cast:** Ralph Bates, Suzanna Leigh, Michael Johnson; **Dir:** Jimmy Sangster.

The Lust of Dracula
1971 C

O Macabro Dr. Scivano
1971 B BR [Natas Producoes Cinematografica] **Vampire(s):** Dr. Scivano (Raúl Calhado); **Cast:** Liuz Lime, Oswaldo de Souza. **Dir:** Raúl Calhado, Rosalvo Cacador.

The Mad Love Life of a Hot Vampire

An underground adult erotic film.

1971 C Vampire(s): Dracula (Jim Parker); **Cast:** Jane Bond, Kim Kim.

Madhouse

1974 C [American International/Amicus] **Vampire(s):** Dracula (Peter Cushing).

Mama Dracula

1979 C BE [Valisa/Radio Television Belge Francaise] **Vampire(s):** Elizabeth Bathory (Louise Fletcher); **Cast:** Maria Schneider, the Wajnberg Brothers. **Dir:** Boris Szulzinger.

Martin

Novelization appeared as *Martin* by George A. Romero and Susan Sparrow (1977 C).

1976 C [Laurel Group/Libra] **Vampire(s):** Martin (John Amplas); **Cast:** Lincoln Maazel, Christine Forrest, Elayne Nedeau. **Dir:** George A. Romero.

Mary, Mary, Bloody Mary

A bisexual female vampire turns on her friends and forces her father to join the fight to end her reign of terror.

1975 C MX Vampire(s): Mary (Christina Ferrare); **Cast:** David Young, Helena Rojo, John Carradine. **Dir:** Carlos Lopez Moctezuma.

La Messe Nere della Contessa Dracula (The Black Harvest of Countess Dracula)

1972 C IT Vampire(s): Dracula (Paul Naschy).

Midi-Minuit

Also released as *Noon to Midnight*.

1970 C FR [Abertine] **Vampire(s):** (Laurent Vergez); **Cast:** Sylvie Fennec, Beatrice Arnac, Daniel Emilfork. **Dir:** Pierre Philippe.

The Mystery in Dracula's Castle

1973 C [World of Disney Films] **Cast:** Johnny Whitaker, Scott Kolden, Chu Galagher, Mariette Hartley.

Nella Stretta Morsa del Ragno (In the Grip of the Spider)

Also released as *Dracula im Schloss des Schreckens*, *Web of the Spider*, and *Prisonnier de L'Araignee*.

1971 C IT [DC7/Paris Cannes/Terra] **Cast:** Klaus Kinski, Anthony Franciosa, Michele, Karin Field. **Dir:** Antonio Margheriti.

Night of Dark Shadows

Sequel to *House of Dark Shadows* but without vampire Barnabas Collins who was killed in the earlier movie.

1971 C [Dan Curtis Productions]; **Cast:** David Selby, Lara Parker, Kate Jackson; Grayson Hall. **Dir:** Dan Curtis.

Night of the Sorcerers

An expedition to the Congo uncovers a bizarre tribe of vampire leopard women who lure young girls to their deaths. Also released as *Lemora* and *Lemora, The Lady Dracula*.

1974 C SP/PT [Profilmes/Hesperia/Avco-Embassy). **Cast:** Simon Andreu, Kali Hansa, Jack Taylor, Maria Kosti. **Dir:** Richard Blackburn.

The Night of the Vampire

Originally released as *Chi O Suu Ning Yo*. First of three vampire films by Yamamoto. See *Lake of Dracula* (1971 C) and *The Evil of Dracula* (1975 C).

1970 C JP [Toho] **Vampire(s):** Yuko (Yukiko Kobayashi); **Cast:** Kayo Matsuo, Akira Nakao, Yoko Minazake; **Dir:** Michio Yamamoto.

Nightmare in Blood

Also released as *Horror Convention*.

1978 C [Xeromega] **Cast:** Kerwin Matthews, Jerry Walter, Dan Caldwell. **Dir:** John Stanley.

Nightwing

This movie was based on *Nightwing* by Martin Cruz Smith. Also released was a Fotonovel based on the movie. Literary sources: Cf. *Nightwing* (Fotonovel).

1979 C [Columbia] **Cast:** Nick Mancuso, David Warner, Kathryn Harrold, Strother Martin. **Dir:** Arthur Hiller.

Nocturna

Also released as *Nocturna, Granddaughter of Dracula.*

1978 C [Compass International] **Vampire(s):** Nocturna (Nai Bonet), Count Dracula (John Carradine); **Cast:** Yvonne De Carlo, Tony Hamilton, Brother Theodore. **Dir:** Harry Tampa.

Le Nosferatu ou les Eaux Glacees du Calcul Egoiste

1974 C FR [Les Films du Groupe de Chambre] **Cast:** Verinique Paynet, Maité Nahyr, Martine Bertrand. **Dir:** Mauruce Rabinowicz.

Nosferatu the Vampyre

This movie is a color sound remake of the original Nosferatu movie. Also released as *Nosferatu, Phantom der Nacht.* A novelization of *Nosferatu the Vampyre* by Paul Monette was based on the screenplay by Werner Herzog.

1979 C [20th Century Fox] **Vampire(s):** The Count (Klaus Kinski); **Cast:** Isabelle Adjani. **Dir:** Werner Herzog.

La Notte die Diavoli

Based on Alexey Tolstoi's short story ''The Wurdalak'' and a remake of Mario Bava's *Wurdalak.* Also released as *Night of the Devils* and *La Noche de los Diablos.*

1971 C SP/IT [Filmes Cinematografica/ Due Cinematografica/Copernicus] **Cast:** Gianni Garko, Agostina Belli, Mark Roberts. **Dir:** Giorgio Ferroni.

La Novia Ensangrentada

Also released as *The New Blood.*

1972 C SP Vampire(s): Karnsteins; **Cast:** Alexandra Bastedo. **Dir:** Vincente Aranda.

Old Dracula

Also released as *Vampira* and as *Old Drac.*

1975 C [World Film Services/American International] **Vampire(s):** Dracula (David Niven), Countess Vampira (Teresa Graves); **Cast:** Peter Payliss, Jennie Linden, Nicky Henson. **Dir:** Clive Donner.

Once Upon a Prime Time
1971 C

Orgy of the Vampires

Tourists wander into a village unaware that they were going into a vampire center. Also released as *The Vampire's Night Orgy, La Orgia Nocturna de los Vampiros,* and *La Noche de los Vampiros.*

1973 C SP/IT [International Amusement] **Cast:** Jack Taylor, Charo Soriana, Dianik Zarakowska, John Richard. **Dir:** Leon Kilmovsky.

Pastel de Sangre
1971 C

People

Six sex stories, one of which is a vampire tale.

1979 C [Damiano] **Dir:** Gerard Damiano.

Pepito y Chabelo vs los Monstruos
1973 C MX [Alameda] **Cast:** Pepito Romay, Chabelo. **Dir:** José Estrada.

El Pobrecito Draculin

1976 C SP [Mezquiriz] **Cast:** Joe Rigoli, Lo-sele Roman, Victor Israel. **Dir:** Juan Fortuny.

Quem tem Medo de Lobisomem

Notable as a movie about the traditional vampire figure of Brazil.

1974 C BR [Ipanema/Circus/Faria] **Cast:** Reginaldo Faria, Stepan Nercessian, Camila Amado, Carlos Kroeber. **Dir:** Reginaldo Faria.

Rabid

A young girl develops a craving for human blood following radical experimental plastic surgery.

1977 C CA [Dibar Syndicate] **Vampire(s):** Rose (Marilyn Chambers); **Cast:** Frank Moore, Joe Silver, Howard Ryshpan, Patricia Gage. **Dir:** David Cronenberg.

Reincarnation of Isabel

Also released as *Riti Magie Nere e Segrete Ogre del Trecento* and *The Ghastly Orgies of Count Dracula*.

1973 C IT [GRP] **Cast:** Mickey Hargitay, Rita Calderoni, Max Dorian. **Dir:** Ralph Brown.

Requiem for a Vampire

Originally released as *Requiem pour un Vampire*, and later also released as *Vierges et Vampires*, *Caged Virgins*, *Virgins and Vampires*, and *Crazed Vampire*.

1972 C FR [ABC/Les Films] **Vampire(s):** (Michel Delesalle); **Cast:** Marie Pierre Castel, Mirelle Argent, Philippe Gast. **Dir:** Jean Rollin.

El Retorno de los Vampiros

1971 C SP [Uranzu Films] **Cast:** Simon Andreu, Marta Monterrey. **Dir:** José Maria Zabalza.

The Return of Count Yorga

1971 C [American International/ Peppertree] **Vampire(s):** Count Yorga (Robert Quarry); **Cast:** Mariette Hartley, Roger Parry, Yvonne Wilder. **Dir:** Bob Kelljan.

Le Rouge de Chine

1977 B FR [Les Films Elementaires] **Cast:** Jacques Richard, Agathe Vannier, Bernard Dubois. **Dir:** Jacques Richard.

La Sadique aux Dents Rouges

1970 C BE [Cinevision Productions] **Cast:** Jane Clayton, Albert Simono, Daniel Moosmann. **Dir:** Jean-Louis Van Belle.

The Saga of the Draculas

An aging vampire wishes to continue his bloodline and seeks to convert his niece's baby into a vampire. Originally released as *La Saga de los Draculas* and later as *Dracula's All Night Orgy*.

1972 C SP [Profilmes] **Vampire(s):** Count Dracula (Narciso Ibanez Menta); **Cast:** Tina Sainz, Tony Isbert, Helga Liné. **Dir:** Leon Klimovsky.

Salem's Lot

A vampire invades a small town in rural Maine in this made for television movie based on *Salem's Lot* by Stephen King. Sequel—*A Return to Salem's Lot*.

1979 C Vampire(s): Barlow (Reggie Nalder); **Cast:** David Soul, Lance Kerwin, James Mason. **Dir:** Tobe Hooper.

Santo and the Blue Demon vs. Dracula and the Wolfman

Two of Mexico's masked wrestlers go against two of the classic vampires. Originally released as *Santo y Blue Demon contra Dracula y el Hombre Lobo*.

1973 C MX [Cinematografica Calderon] **Vampire(s):** Dracula (Aldo Monti); **Cast:**

Santo, Augustin Martinez Solares, Eugina San Martin. **Dir:** Miguel M. Delgado.

The Satanic Rites of Dracula

The last of the Christopher Lee Dracula movies for Hammer. Dracula leads a group of scientists and politicians in the development of a virus capable of destroying the human race. Also released as *Count Dracula and His Vampire Bride* and as *Dracula Is Dead . . . and Well and Living in London.*

> **1973 C GB** [Hammer] **Vampire(s):** Dracula (Christopher Lee); **Cast:** Peter Cushing, Joanna Lumley. **Dir:** Alan Gibson.

The Scars of Dracula

A young couple tangles with Dracula in their search for the man's missing brother. Also released as *Les Cicatrices de Dracula* (French). Novelization appeared as *The Scars of Dracula* by Angus Hall.

> **1970 C GB** [Hammer/EMI] **Vampire(s):** Dracula (Christopher Lee); Tania (Anouska Hempel); **Cast:** Christopher Matthews, Patrick Troughton. **Dir:** Roy Ward Baker.

Scream Blacula, Scream

A revived Blacula/Prince Mamuwalde encounters a voodoo priestess in this sequel to Blacula.

> **1973 C** [American International] **Vampire(s):** Prince Mamuwalde (William Marshall); **Cast:** Richard Lawson, Don Mitchell. **Dir:** Bob Kelljan.

Sex Express

Four sex-oriented stories of which one is a vampire tale.

> **1975 C** [Blackwater] **Vampire(s):** (James Lister). **Dir:** Derek Ford.

Shadow of Dracula

> **1973 C**

Shadow of the Werewolf

Also released as *The Werewolf vs. the Dracula, The Black Harvest of Countess Dracula,* and *The Werewolf's Shadow.*

> **1970 C** [HiFi Stereo/Plata].

Sisters of Satan

The nuns in a convent choose to survive by trading God for Satan. Also released as *Alucarda, Innocents from Hell,* and *Alucarda la Hija de las Tinieblas.*

> **1975 C Vampire(s):** Alucarda (Tina Romero); **Cast:** Susana Kamini, Claudio Brook, David Silva. **Dir:** Juan Lopez Monteczuma.

Son of Dracula

Also released as *Count Downe, Son of Dracula* and *Young Dracula.*

> **1973 C** [Apple Film] **Vampire(s):** Count Down (Harry Nilsson); **Cast:** Ringo Starr, Dennis Price, Freddie Jones. **Dir:** Freddie Francis.

Um Sonho De Vampiros (A Vampire's Dream)

> **1970 C BR** [Ser-Cine] **Vampire(s):** The Vampire (Irma Alvarez); **Cast:** Ankito, Janet Chermont, Sonelio Costa, Augusto Maia Filho. **Dir:** Ibere Cavalcanti.

Spermula

A softcore sexy science fiction vampire film.

> **1976 C FR** [Parlafrance] **Vampire(s):** (Dayle Haddon); **Cast:** Udo Kier, Susannah Djian, Georges Géret. **Dir:** Charles Matton.

Strange Love of the Vampires

Also released as *El Extrano Amor de los Vampiros* and *Night of the Walking Dead.*

> **1974 C SP** [Richard Films] **Vampire(s):** (Carlos Ballesteros); **Cast:** Emma Cohen, Vicky Lusson, Raphael Hernandez. **Dir:** Leon Klimovsky.

Suck Me, Vampire

An adult erotic film.

1975 C FR Dir: Maxime Debest.

Tame re Champo ne Ame Kel

1978 C IN [Kanodia] **Cast:** Naresh Kumar, Snehalata, A. Joshi, Rajanibala. **Dir:** Chandrakant Sangani.

Tender Dracula, or, The Confessions of a Bloodsucker

Also released as *Tendre Dracula ou les Confessions d'un Buveur de Sang.*

1974 C FR [Renn Prod./FcF/VM Prod./AMLF] **Vampire(s):** Dracula (Peter Cushing); **Cast:** Louis Trintignant, Bernard Menez. **Dir:** Alaine Robbe Grillet.

Tenderness of Wolves

Originally released as *Die Zartlichkeit der Wolfe.*

1973 C GE [Tango Film] **Cast:** Kurt Raab, Jeff Roden, Margit Castensen, Wolfgang Schenk. **Dir:** Ulli Lommel.

They've Changed Faces

Also released as *Hanno Cambiato Faccia.*

1971 C IT [Garigliano Films] **Vampire(s):** Boss/Noferatu (Adolfo Celi); **Cast:** Giuliano Disperati, Geraldine Hooper. **Dir:** Corrado Farina.

The Thirsty Dead

Also released as *The Blood Cult of Shangri-La.*

1974 C PH [Rochelle/International Amusement] **Cast:** John Considine, Jennifer Billingsley, Judith McConnell. **Dir:** Terry Becker.

Those Cruel and Bloody Vampires

Originally released as *Las Allegres Vampiras de Vogel.*

1972 C SP [Titantic] **Cast:** Agata Lys, Maria José Cantudo, Germán Cobos, Rafael Conesa. **Dir:** Julio Perez.

Tiempos Duros para Dracula

1976 C SP/AR [Aitor/Espacio] **Cast:** José Ruiz Lifante, Miguel Ligero, Maria Noel, Adolfo Linvel. **Dir:** Jorge M. Darnell.

Till Death

1978 C [Cougar] **Cast:** Keith Atkinson, Bert Freed, Belinda Balaski. **Dir:** Walter Stocker.

The Time of Vampires

A nine-minute animated comedy also released as *Vrijeme Vampira.*

1971 C YU [Dunav/Zagreb] **Dir:** Nikola Majdak.

Tombs of the Blind Dead

Also released as *La Noche del Terror Ciego* and *The Blind Dead.*

1971 C SP/PT [Plata Films/Inerfilme/Hallmark] **Cast:** Oscar Burner, Lone Fleming, Maria Silva, José Telman. **Dir:** Armando de Ossorio.

Traitement de Choc (Doctor in the Nude)

1973 C FR Cast: Alain Delon, Annie Girandot.

Tristana

1970 C FR Vampire(s): (Fernando Rey); **Cast:** Catherine Deneuve. **Dir:** Luis Bunuel.

The True Life of Dracula

1979 C

Tunnel Under the World

Based on the story "Tunnel Under the World" by Frederick Pohl. Originally released as *Il Tunnel sotto Mondo.*

1970 C IT **Vampire(s):** (Pietro Rosati); **Cast:** Alberto Moro, Bruno Salviero, Anna Mantovani, Lello Maraniello. **Dir:** Luigi Cozzi.

Twins of Evil

A set of beautiful female twins are attacked by vampires of the infamous Karnstein family, and their uncle has to come to their aid. Also released as *The Gemini Twins, Virgin Vampires,* and *Twins of Dracula.*

1971 C GB [Hammer] **Vampire(s):** Freida and Maria Gelhorn (Madeleine and Mary Collinson), Count Karnstein (Damien Thomas); Countess Mircalla (Katya Wyeth); **Cast:** Peter Cushing, Dennis Price. **Dir:** John Hough.

Vaarwhel

1973 C NE [Cinema Film] **Cast:** Pieke Dassen, Nettie Blanken, Rik Bravenboer. **Dir:** Guido Peters.

Vampire Circus

A circus of vampires arrive in a Serbian village in the nineteenth century.

1972 C GB [Hammer/Fox] **Vampire(s):** Count Mitterhouse (Robert Tayman); **Cast:** Adrianne Corri, Laurence Payer, Thorley Walters. **Dir:** Robert Young.

The Vampire Doll

1970 C JP

The Vampire Happening

An actress discovers to her chagrin that her ancestors were vampires and so is she. Originally released as *Gebissen Wird nur Nichts—Happening der Vampire.*

1971 C GE [Aquila Enterprises] **Vampire(s):** Dracula (Ferdy Mayne); **Cast:** Betty Williams, Thomas Hunter, Pia Degermark. **Dir:** Freddie Francis.

The Vampire Hookers

Also released as *Sensuous Vampiress, Night of the Bloodsuckers,* and *Cemetery Girls.*

1979 C PH [Capricorn Three] **Vampire(s):** Richmond Reed (John Carradine); **Cast:** Bruce Fairbairn, Trey Wilson, Karen Stride. **Dir:** Cirio H. Santiago.

Vampire Kung-Fu

1972 C HK **Dir:** Li Fai Mon.

The Vampire Lovers

Carmilla, a young female vampire, attacks other young women. The most faithful adaptation of "Carmilla" by Sheridan Le Fanu.

1970 C GB [Hammer] **Vampire(s):** Carmilla Karnstein (Ingrid Pitt); **Cast:** Pippa Steele, Madeleine Smith, Peter Cushing. **Dir:** Roy Ward Baker.

The Vampire's Bite

1972 C

Vampiro 2000

1972 C IT [Canguro] **Cast:** Nino Castelnuovo, Dominique Boschero, Lucio Dalla. **Dir:** Riccardo Ghione.

Los Vampiros de Coyoacan

1973 C MX [Mario Cid/Azteva Films] **Vampire(s):** (German Robles); **Cast:** Sasha Montenegro, Mil Maschras, Superzan. **Dir:** Arturo Martinez.

Vampyr

Documentary concerning the filming of *El Conde Dracula.* Also released as *Vampir.*

1971 C **Vampire(s):** Dracula (Christopher Lee). **Dir:** Pedro Portabella.

Vampyres, Daughters of Dracula

An adult erotic movie in which alluring female vampires coerce unsuspecting motorists to their castle. Also released as

Vampyres, Blood Hunger, and *Satan's Daughters.*

1973 C GB [Essay/Rank Films] **Vampire(s):** Fram/Miriam (Marianne Morris), (Anulka); **Cast:** Murray Brown, Brian Deacon, Sally Faulkner. **Dir:** Joseph José Larraz.

Vampyros Lesbos—Die Erbin des Dracula (Lesbian Vampires—The Heiress of Dracula)

Based on Bram Stoker's short story "Dracula's Guest." Also released as *Lesbian Vampires, El Signo del Vampiro, The Heritage of Dracula, The Sign of the Vampire,* and *The Strange Adventures of Jonathan Harker.*

1970 C GE/SP [Telecine and Fenix] **Vampire(s):** Nadina (Susan Korda/ Soledad Miranda); **Cast:** Dennis Price, Paul Mueller, Ewa Stroemberg. **Dir:** Jesus Franco.

Vault of Horror

Includes five stories, one of which is a vampire tale. Also released as *Further Tales from the Crypt.*

1973 C GB [Metromedia-Amicus] **Vampire(s):** Anna Massey; **Cast:** Daniel Massey, Michael Craig. **Dir:** Roy Ward Baker.

The Velvet Vampire

A sexy young vampiress seduces a couple in her California desert home. Also released as *Through the Looking Glass* and *Cemetery Girls.*

1971 C Vampire(s): Diane Le Fanu (Celeste Yarnell); **Cast:** Michael Blodgett, Sherry Miles. **Dir:** Stephanie Rothman.

Virgin Vampire

1970 C GE [Capitole and Rox] **Dir:** Alfred Vohrer.

Vlad Tepes

1978 C RO [Romaniafilm] **Cast:** Stefan Sileanu, George Constantin, Teofil Vilcu. **Dir:** Dorui Nastase.

Voodoo Heartbeat

1972 C [TWI National] **Cast:** Ray Molina, Philip Ahn, Mary Martinez. **Dir:** Ray Molina.

Werewolf vs. the Vampire Woman

Spanish wolfman teams with two students to track down a vampire witch. Also released as *Shadow of the Werewolf, Blood Moon, Night of Walpurgis,* and *La Noche de Walpurgis.*

1970 C SP/GE [Plata Films/Hi-Fi Stereo] **Vampire(s):** Countess Waldessa (Patty Shepard); **Cast:** Paul Naschy, Gaby Fuchs, Barbara Capell. **Dir:** Leon Klimovsky.

Die Zartlichkeit der Wolfe

A film about Fritz Haarman, the vampire of Düsseldorf.

1973 C GE Cast: Kurt Raab. **Dir:** Rainer Werner Fassbinder.

1980 to 1989

Anemia

1986 C IT [RAI] **Vampire(s):** Umberto (Hans Zischler); **Cast:** Gioia Maria Scila, Gérard Landry. **Dir:** Alberto Abruzzese, Achille Pisanti.

Because the Dawn

Movie with lesbian themes.

1988 C Cast: Edwige Sandy Fray, Gregory St. John. **Dir:** Amy Goldstein.

La Belle Captive

1983 C [Argos] **Cast:** Daniel Mesquich, Gabrielle Lazure, Cyrielle Claire. **Dir:** Alain Robbe-Grillet.

Beverly Hills Vamp

A madame and her girls are actually female vampires with a penchant for hot-blooded men.

1988 C [American International] **Vampire(s):** Madame Cassandra (Britt Ekland); **Cast:** Eddie Deezen, Tim Conway, Jr. **Dir:** Fred Olen Ray.

Billy the Kid and the Green Blaze Vampire

1985 C [ITC/Zenith] **Vampire(s):** (Alun Armstrong); **Cast:** Phil Daniels, Bruce Payne, Louise Gold, Eve Ferret. **Dir:** Alan Clarke.

The Black Room

1981 C [Lancer Productions] **Vampire(s):** Stephen Knight, Cassandra Gaviola; **Cast:** Charlie Young, Linnea Quigley. **Dir:** Elly Kenner, Norman Thaddeus Vane.

Black Vampire

1988 C [Kelly-Jordan Enterprises] **Cast:** Ethan Kennedy, Bill Spears, Leonard Jackson. **Dir:** Lawrence Jordan.

Blood Lust

1980 C GB [Harrison Marks Company] **Dir:** Russell Gay.

Bloodsuckers from Outer Space

Via an alien invasion, Texas farmers become bloodsucking vampires.

1984 C [One-of-Those Productions] **Cast:** Thom Meyer, Laura Ellis, Dennis Letts. **Dir:** Glen Coburn.

The Brides Wore Blood

Four prospective brides are mysteriously murdered, but one is brought back to life and becomes a vampire's mate.

1980 C [Regal] **Cast:** Delores Heisel. **Dir:** Robert R. Favorite.

Buenas Noches, Senior Monstruo

1982 C Vampire(s): Count Dracula; **Cast:** Paul Naschy, Regaliz, Luis Escobar, Fernando Bilbao. **Dir:** Antonio Mercero.

Bunnicula the Vampire Rabbit

After a family adopts a bunny, the dog and cat in the family team up to prove that it is a vampire. An animated version of *Bunnicula* by Deborah and James Howe.

1987 C [Joe Ruby, Ken Spears] **Cast:** Voices of Jack Carter, Howard Morris, Pat Peterson. **Dir:** Charles A. Nichols.

Carmilla

1989 C Vampire(s): Carmilla.

Carne de tu Carne

1984 C CO [Producciones Visuales] **Cast:** Adriana Herran, David Guerrero, José Angel. **Dir:** Carlos Mayolo.

Les Charlots contre Dracula

1980 C Cast: Les Charlots, Amelle Prevost, Andreas Voutsinas, Gerard Jugnot, Vincent Martin. **Dir:** Jean-Pierre Desagnat.

Chillers

Five stories of which one is a vampire tale.

1988 C [Raedon] **Dir:** Daniel Boyd.

The Close Encounter of the Vampire

1986 HK Dir: Tuen Ping.

The Craving

Werewolf Naschy battles with female vampires. Also released as *El Retorno del Hombre Lobo*.

1980 C [Dalmata Films] **Vampire(s):** Elizabeth Bathory; **Cast:** Paul Naschy, Julie Saly, Silvia Aguilar. **Dir:** Jack Molina.

Curse of the Wicked Wife

Also released as *Wicked Wife*.
1984 C HK Dir: Wong King-Fang.

Dance of the Damned

Fascinating noir-ish plot concerning a vampire who wants to learn more about the life of his next victim, a deep-thinking stripper, who has lost the will to live.
1988 C [Concord/Virgin Vision] **Vampire(s):** (Cyril O'Reilly); **Cast:** Starr Andreeff, Deborah Ann Nassar. **Dir:** Kate Shea Ruben.

Dark Vengeance

1980 C Cast: Rebecca Wright, Mark Rudolph. **Dir:** Jack Snyder.

Devil's Vendetta

1986 C TH/HK Dir: L. Chang-Xu.

Dinner with the Vampire

1988 C IT [Dania-Devon/Reteit Alia/Surf Film] **Vampire(s):** Yurek (George Hilton); **Cast:** Patricia Pellegrino, Riccardo Rossi, Valeria Milillo, Yvonne Scio. **Dir:** Lamberto Bava.

Doctor Dracula

A re-edited version, with added footage on the vampire theme, of Lucifer's Women, a 1975 picture put together by Aratow.
1980 C [Independent-International] **Vampire(s):** Anatol Gregorio/Dracula (Geoffrey Land); **Cast:** John Carradine, Larry Hankin, Susan McIver. **Dir:** Al Adamson, Paul Aratow.

Dracula

An animated feature derived from the Marvel Comic's *The Tomb of Dracula* series.
1980 C JP [Toei Animation Co.] **Dir:** Minori Okazaki.

Dracula Blows His Cool

Three voluptuous models and their photographer restore an ancient castle and open a disco in it. The vampire lurking about the castle welcomes the party with his fangs. Originally released as *Graf Dracula Beisst Jetzt*.
1982 C GE [Lisa/Barthonia; Martin Films] **Vampire(s):** Count Stanislaus (Ginni Garko), Countess Olivia (Betty Verges); **Cast:** Giacomo Rizzo, Linda Grandier. **Dir:** Carlo Ombra.

Dracula Exotica

An adult erotic film and sequel to *Dracula Sucks* (1980 C). Also released as *Love at First Gulp*.
1981 C [Entertainment Ventures/VCA] **Vampire(s):** Count Dracula (Jamie Gillis); **Cast:** Venessa del Rio, Samatha Fox. **Dir:** Warren Evans.

Dracula Rises from the Coffin

1982 C KO [Tai Chang/ROK] **Vampire(s):** Dracula; **Cast:** Kang Young Suk, Park Yang Rae. **Dir:** Lee Hyoung Pyo.

Dracula, Sovereign of the Damned

1983 C

Dracula Tan Exarchia

1983 C GR [Allagi Films] **Vampire(s):** Dracula; **Cast:** Kostas Soumas, Vannis Panousis, Vangelis Contronis. **Dir:** Nikos Zervos.

Dracula: The Love Story

1989 C [Skouras].

Dracula's Last Rites

A blood-curdling tale of a sheriff and a mortician in a small town who are up to no good. Also released as *Last Rites*.
1980 C [New Empire Features/Cannon] **Vampire(s):** Lucard/Dracula; **Cast:** Patricia Lee Hammond, Gerald Fielding, Victor Jorge. **Dir:** Domonic Paris.

Dracula's Widow

Countess Dracula, missing her husband and desperately in need of a substitute, picks innocent Raymond as her victim. His girlfriend and a cynical cop fight to save his soul from the Countess's damnation.

1988 C [De Laurentis Entertainment; **Vampire(s):** Vanessa (Sylvia Kristel); **Cast:** Josef Sommer, Lenny Van Dohlen, Marc Coppola, Rachel Jones. **Dir:** Christopher Coppola.

Dragon against Vampire

Also released as *Dragon vs. Vampire.*
1984 C HK Dir: Lionel Leung.

Elusive Song of the Vampire

1987 C TW Dir: Takako Shira.

Elvira, Mistress of the Dark

A manic comedy based on Peterson's famous B-movie horror-hostess character. The terror-queen inherits a house in a conservative Massachusetts town and causes chaos when she tries to sell it.

1988 C [New World Pictures/NBC Productions] **Vampire(s):** Elvira (Cassandra Peterson); **Cast:** Phil Rubestein, Larry Flash Jenkins, Damita Jo Freeman. **Dir:** James Signorelli.

Evils of the Night

Teenage campers are abducted by sex-crazed alien vampires. Also released as *Space Monsters.*

1984 C [Lightning] **Vampire(s):** (John Carradine), (Julie Newmar); **Cast:** Karrie Emerson, Neville Brand, Aldo Ray, Tina Louise. **Dir:** Mardi Rustam.

Fade to Black

A young man obsessed with the movies gradually loses his sense of reality. One of the characters upon whom he is fixated is Bela Lugosi's *Dracula.* Novelization appeared as *Fade to Black* by Ron Renauld.

1980 C [American Cinema]; **Vampire(s):** Eric Binford (Dennis Christopher); **Cast:** Linda Kerridge, Tim Tomerson. **Dir:** Vernon Zimmerman.

Ferat Vampire

Originally released as *Upir z Feratu.*
1982 C CZ [Barrandov]; **Cast:** Jiri Menzel, Dagmar Veskrnova, Jana Brezkova, Jan Schmid. **Dir:** Juraj Herz.

Fright Night

When Charley suspects that his neighbor is a vampire, he calls in the host of "Fright Night," the local, late-night, horror flick series, to help clean up the neighborhood. They have a problem when the vampire discovers their plans. Novelized in *Fright Night* by John Skipp and Craig Spector, a book based on the screenplay by Tom Holland. Sequel: *Fright Night II.*

1985 C [Columbia] **Vampire(s):** Jerry Dandridge (Chris Sarandon); **Cast:** William Ragsdale, Amanda Bearse, Roddy McDowall. **Dir:** Tom Holland.

Fright Night II

The hero from *Fright Night* discovers that the sister of the vampire he dispatched earlier has come to reside near his college.

1989 C [New Century/Vista] **Vampire(s):** Regine (Julie Carmen); **Cast:** Roddy McDowall, William Ragsdale. **Dir:** Tommy Lee Wallace.

Frightmare

A great horror star dies but refuses to give up his need for adoration and revenge.

1981 C [Heritage Ltd. Films] **Cast:** Ferdinand Mayne, Luca Bercovici, Conrad Radzoff. **Dir:** Norman Thaddeus Vane.

The Games of the Countess Dolingen of Gratz

Also released as *Les Jeux de la Comtesse Dolingen de Gratz.*

1980 C [Les Films und Nautile/ Prospectacle/Perec/Zajdermann] **Cast:** Michael Lonsdale, Carol Kane, Katia Wastchenko, Robert Stephens. **Dir:** Catherine Binet.

Gayracula

1983 C [Marathon] **Vampire(s):** Dracula; **Cast:** Tim Kramer, Douglas Poston, Steve Collins, Ray Medina. **Dir:** Roger Earl.

Geek Maggot Bingo

An underground horror satire.

1983 C [Weirdo Films/Penetration; **Vampire(s):** Scumbalina the vampire queen (Donna Death); **Cast:** Robert Andrews, Brenda Bergman, Richard Hell. **Dir:** Nick Zedd.

Ghost Story

Four elderly men, members of an informal social club called the Chowder Society, share a terrible secret buried deep in their past—a secret that comes back to haunt them to death. Based on *Ghost Story* by Peter Straub.

1981 C Cast: Fred Astaire, Melvyn Douglas, Douglas Fairbanks, Jr., John Houseman, Jacqueline Brooks. **Dir:** John Irvin.

Graveyard Shift

A New York cabby on the night shift is actually a powerful vampire who uses his fares to build an army of vampires. Not to be confused with the Stephen King movie of the same name. Sequel: *Understudy: Graveyard Shift II.*

1986 C [Cinema Ventures-Lightshow/ Shapiro] **Vampire(s):** Stephen Tsepes (Silvio Oliviero); **Cast:** Helen Papas, Cliff Stoker, Dorin Ferber. **Dir:** Gerard Ciccoritti.

Haunted Cop Shop I

Has a sequel in *Haunted Cop Shop II.*
1984 C HK Dir: Jeff Lau.

Haunted Cop Shop II

Sequel to *Haunted Cop Shop I.*
1986 C HK Dir: Jeff Lau.

Hello Dracula

1985 C Vampire(s): Dracula. **Dir:** Henry Wu- Leung.

The Hunger

A beautiful 2,000-year-old vampire needs new blood when she realizes that her current lover, Bowie, is aging fast. She turns to researcher Sarandon to find a cure. Based on Whitley Streiber's *The Hunger.*

1983 C [MGM] **Vampire(s):** Miriam (Catherine Deneuve); **Cast:** David Bowie, Susan Sarandon, Cliff DeYoung, Willem DaFoe. **Dir:** Tony Scott.

I Like Bats

Originally released as *Lubie Nietoperze.*

1985 C PL [The Polish Corporation for Film Production/Film Polski] **Vampire(s):** (Katarzyna Walter); **Cast:** Marck Barbasiewicz, Malgorzata Lorentowicz, Jonasz Kofta. **Dir:** Grzegorz Warchol.

I Married a Vampire

Can a psychiatrist help vampires become human? Polish dialogue with English subtitles.

1984 C [Troma/Full Moon Productions] **Vampire(s):** Robespierre (Brendan Hickey); **Cast:** Rachel Golden, Ted Zalewski, Deborah Carroll. **Dir:** Jay Raskin.

The Inn of the Flying Dragon

Based on a short story by Sheridan Le Fanu, "The Room in the Dragon Volant." Originally released as *Ondskans Vardshus* and later as *The Sleep of the Dead.*

1981 C SW/IR [Aspekt Film/Dragon Co./National Film School of Ireland] **Vampire(s):** (Marilu Tolo); **Cast:** Per Oscarsson, Patrick Magee, Curt Jurgens. **Dir:** Calvin Floyd.

Jitters

The murdered dead turn on their killers and seek revenge.

1988 C [Gaga Communications/Fascination/Prism] **Cast:** Sal Viviano, Marilyn Tokuda, James Hong, Frank Dietz. **Dir:** John M. Fasano.

Jonathan of the Night

1987 C [2000 AD] **Cast:** Don Striano, Mitch Maglio, Melissa Tait, Eric Collica. **Dir:** Buddy Giovinazzo.

The Keep

At the height of the Nazi onslaught, several German soldiers unleash an unknown power from a medieval stone fortress. Based on F. Paul Wilson's *The Keep*.

1984 C Vampire(s): Molasar (Michael Carter); **Cast:** Scott Glenn, Alberta Watson, Juergen Prochnow. **Dir:** Michael Mann.

The Kiss

A mysterious aunt visits her teenage niece in New York and tries to apprentice her to the family business in sorcery, demon possession, and murder.

1988 C [Columbia/Tri Star] **Vampire(s):** Felice (Joanna Pacula); **Cast:** Meredith Salenger, Nicholas Kilbertus, Mimi Kuzyk. **Dir:** Pen Densham.

Krvava Pani

Full-length animated version of the Elizabeth Bathory legend.

1981 C CZ [CFP/Koliba] **Vampire(s):** Elizabeth Bathory. **Dir:** Viktor Kubal.

Kung Fu Vampire Buster

Two Taoist kung fu priests take on coffins, cemeteries, and vampires. Also released as *New Mr. Vampire*.

1986 C HK Vampire(s): (Ricky Hui). **Dir:** Xen Lung Ting.

Legend of Eight Samurai

An ancient Japanese princess hires eight samurai to destroy the vampire-witch who rules over her clan. Loosely based on the Elizabeth Bathory legend.

1984 C JP [Toei Company] **Cast:** Hiroko Yakushimaru, Henry Sanada, Sue Shiomi, Sonny Shiba. **Dir:** Kinji Fukasaku.

Life Force

A beautiful female vampire from outer space drains Londoners and before long the city is filled with disintegrating zombies. Based on Colin Wilson's *The Space Vampires*.

1985 C [Cannon/Tri-Star] **Cast:** Steve Railsbeck, Peter Firth, Frank Finlay. **Dir:** Tobe Hooper.

Little Shop of Horrors

Remake as a musical of the 1960 Roger Corman film.

1986 C

The Lost Boys

An updated vampire tale located in modern-day Santa Cruz where Michael and his younger brother encounter a group of vampires—the lost boys—and their leader, whose identity must be discovered. The leader must be destroyed to rid Michael and his girlfriend of the vampiric influence.

1987 C [Warner Bros.] **Vampire(s):** David (Kiefer Sutherland); **Cast:** Jason Patric, Corey Haim, Dianne Wiest, Barnard Hughes, Jami Gertz, Corey Feldman. **Dir:** Joel Schumacher.

The Lost Platoon

A group of soldiers are transformed into vampires.

1989 C [Action International Pictures] **Vampire(s):** Hancock (David Parry), Walker (Stephen Quadros); **Cast:** William Knight, Lew Pipes, Roger Bayless. **Dir:** David A. Prior.

Love Me Vampire

1987 C HK **Dir:** Irene Wang.

Loves of the Living Dead

Also released as *Heaven Wife, Hell Wife.*

1984 C HK **Dir:** Ho Menga.

Lugosi the Forgotten King

Biographical documentary of Bela Lugosi.

1985 C [Operator 12 Productions] **Dir:** Mark S. Gilman, Dave Stuckey.

Lust in the Fast Lane

1984 C [Paradise Visuals] **Vampire(s):** (Tom Byron), (Eric Edwards), (Crystal Breeze), (Traci Lords).

Magic Cop

Also released as *Mr. Vampire V.*

1989 C HK [Movie Impact/Millifame Productions] **Cast:** Lam Ching Ying. **Dir:** H. Ching.

The Mark of Lilith

A Lesbian-oriented motion picture.

1986 C GB [Rc-Vamp Productions/ London College of Printing/Circles] **Cast:** Pamela Lofton, Susan Franklyn, Jeremy Peters, Patricia St. Hilaire. **Dir:** Bruna Fionda, Polly Gladwin, Isiling Mack-Nataf.

Midnight

Murder-thriller involving the vampirish hostess of a television horror movie showcase and a fanatical fan.

1988 C [SVS Films/Midnight Inc.] **Cast:** Lynn Redgrave, Tony Curtis, Steve Parrish, Rita Gam, Wolfman Jack. **Dir:** Norman Thaddeus Vane.

Mr. and Mrs. Dracula

1980 C

Mr. Vampire

First motion picture of a successful vampire series from Hong King.

1985 C HK [Golden Harvest/Paragon Films] **Cast:** Ricky Hui, Moon Lee, Lam Ching Ying, Pauline Lau; Notes: **Dir:** Lau Kum Wai.

Mr. Vampire II

Second of the Mr. Vampire series of movies. In Japan, it led to a new TV series.

1986 C HK **Dir:** Sung Kan Shing.

Mr. Vampire III

1987 C HK **Cast:** Lam Ching Ying, Eichard Ng, Lui Fong, Billy Lau. **Dir:** Wong Kee Hung.

Mr. Vampire IV

Fourth in the popular series.

1988 C HK **Cast:** Ricky Hui; **Dir:** Law Lit.

Mixed Up

1985 C HK **Dir:** Henry S. Chen.

Mom

When his mother is bitten by a flesh-eater, Clay Dwyer is at a loss as to what to do. How do you tell your own mother that she must be destroyed?

1989 C **Vampire(s):** (Brion James), (Jeanne Bates); **Cast:** Mark Thomas Miller, Art Evans, Mary McDonough. **Dir:** Patrick Rand.

The Monster Club

Based on several short stories by Ronald Chetwynd-Hayes, one of which is a vampire story.

1980 C [Sword & Sorcery/ITC] **Vampire(s):** Erasmus (Vincent Price); **Cast:** John Carradine, Roger Sloman, Fran

Fullenwider, Donald Pleasence. **Dir:** Roy Ward Baker.

The Monster Squad

Youthful monster enthusiasts find their community overrun by Dracula and other monsters who are searching for a life-sustaining amulet.

1987 C [Taft Entertainment Pictures/ Keith Barish Productions] **Vampire(s):** Dracula (Duncan Regehr); **Cast:** Andre Gower, Robby Kiger, Stephen Macht. **Dir:** Fred Dekker.

Le Morte Vivante

1982 C FR [Les Films ABC/Films Aleria/Films Du Yaka/Sam Seisky] **Vampire(s):** Francoise Blanchard; **Cast:** Marina Pierro, Mike Marshall, Carina Barona. **Dir:** Jean Rollin.

My Best Friend of Is a Vampire

Another teenage vampire story about trying to cope with certain changes that adolescence and bloodsucking bring.

1987 C [Kings Road Entertainment] **Vampire(s):** Jeremy Capello (Robert Sean Leonard); **Cast:** Cheryl Pollak, René Auberjonois, Evan Mirand. **Dir:** Jimmy Huston.

The Mysterious Death of Nina Chereau

Loosely based on Bathory legend.

1987 C **Cast:** Maud Adams, Scott Renderer, Alexandra Stewart. **Dir:** Dennis Berry.

Near Dark

A farm boy falls in with a group of thirsty outlaw-fringe vampires who roam the modern West in a van.

1987 C [De Laurentius Entertainment Group] **Vampire(s):** Jesse (Lance Hendricksen) et al; **Cast:** Adrian Pasdar, Jenny Wright. **Dir:** Kathryn Bigelow.

Night Life

A teenager gets the all-out high-stakes ride of his life when four cadavers are re-animated in his uncle's mortuary.

1989 C MX [MCA/Cine Enterprises/ MTE] **Dir:** Daniel Taplitz.

Not of This Earth

Remake of the 1957 Roger Corman alien vampire movie of same name.

1987 C [New Horizons/Concorde] **Cast:** Traci Lords, Arthur Roberts, Lenny Juliano, Rebecca Perle. **Dir:** Jim Wynorski.

Once Bitten

A centuries-old vampiress comes to Los Angeles in search of male virgins. She needs their blood to retain her youthful countenance.

1985 C [Samuel Goldwyn Company] **Vampire(s):** Countess (Lauren Hutton); **Cast:** Jim Carrey, Karen Kopins, Cleavon Little. **Dir:** Howard Storm.

One Dark Night

Two high school girls plan an initiation rite for one of their friends who is determined to shed her ''goody-goody'' image. Also released as *Entity Force*.

1982 C [The Picture Company Inc.] **Cast:** Meg Tilly, Adam West, Melissa Newman, Robin Evans, Leslie Speights. **Dir:** Thomas McLoughlin.

One Eye-Brow Priest

Also released as *New Mr. Vampire II*.

1987 C HK **Dir:** Mason Ching.

Outback Vampire

Also released as *The Wicked*.

1987 C AU [Guild/Select)] **Vampire(s):** Sir Arthur Terminus; **Cast:** Brett Climo, Richard Morgan, Angela Kennedy. **Dir:** Brett Climo.

Pale Blood

A serial killer in Los Angeles is leaving his victims drained of blood. Is it a vampire or a deranged psychopath?

1989 C Vampire(s): Michael Fury (George Chakiris); **Cast:** Wings Hauser, Pamela Ludwig, Diana Frank, Darcy DeMoss. **Dir:** V. V. Dachin Hsu.

Passion of Dracula

1980 C Vampire(s): Dracula (Christopher Bernau); **Cast:** Giulia Pagano.

A Polish Vampire in Burbank

A shy vampire in Burbank tries again and again to find blood and love. Also released as *Polish Vampire*.

1985 C [Pirromount/Peacock Films] **Vampire(s):** Dupah (Mark Pirro); **Cast:** Lori Sutton, Bobbi Dorsch, Brad Waisbren. **Dir:** Mark Pirro.

Pura Sangre

Also released as *Pure Blood*.

1983 C CO [Luis Ospina Productions/ Castano] **Cast:** Florina Lemaitre, Carlos Mayola, Humberto Arango. **Dir:** Luis Ospina.

Red and Black

1986 C CH Dir: Andrew Kam Yeun Wah.

Saturday the 14th

Satire on the axe-wielding maniac movies. Sequel: *Saturday the 14th Strikes Back* (1988).

1981 C [New World/Embassy] **Vampire(s):** (Jeffery Tambor), (Nancy Lee); **Cast:** Richard Bejamin, Paula Prentiss, Severn Darden. **Dir:** Howard R. Cohen.

Saturday the 14th Strikes Back

Sequel to *Saturday the 14th*.

1987 C [Concorde] **Vampire(s):** (Pamela Stonebrook); **Cast:** Jason Presson, Ray Walston, Avery Schreiber, Patty McCormack. **Dir:** Howard R. Cohen.

The Seven Vampires

Originally released as *As Sette Vampiros*.

1986 C BR [Embrafilme/ Superoito Productions] **Cast:** Alvamar Tadei, Andrea Beltrao, Ariel Coelho, Bene Nunes. **Dir:** Ivan Cardoso.

Sexandroide

1986 C FR [Petit Pascal Company] **Cast:** Daniel Dubois. **Dir:** Michel Ricaud.

Shadows in the Dark

1989 C [4-Play] **Vampire(s):** (Randy Spears); **Cast:** Tianna Bionca, Victoria Paris, Cheri Bush. **Dir:** Bruce Seven.

Spirit vs. Zombi

1989 C TW/HK Dir: Yao Fenpan.

Spooky Family

Sequel: *Spooky Family 2* (1991).

1989 C HK

Star Virgin

1980 C Vampire(s): Dracula (Johnny Harden); **Cast:** Karl Klark, Jeanette Harlow. **Dir:** Linus Gator.

Sundown: The Vampire in Retreat

Carradine plays a reformed vampire king running a clinic that weans bloodsuckers from preying on humans.

1989 C [Vastron International] **Vampire(s):** Count Mardulak (David Carradine); **Cast:** John Ireland, Maxwell Caulfield, Morgan Brittany, Jim Metzler. **Dir:** Anthony Hickox.

Supergrass

A comedy in which a nerd poses as a drug dealer to impress his girlfriend but then is taken for the real thing by the authorities.

1985 C [The Comic Strip/Recorded Releasing] **Vampire(s):** Robertson (Romals Allen); **Cast:** Adrian Edmondson, Peter Richardson, Jennifer Saunders. **Dir:** Peter Richardson.

Teen Vamp

A nerdish high school kid is bitten by a prostitute, which transforms him into a cool vampire. Also released as *Murphy Gilgrease; Teenage Vampire.*

1989 C [New World Pictures] **Vampire(s):** Murphy Gilgrease (Beau Bishop); **Cast:** Clu Gulager, Karen Carlson, Angela Brown. **Dir:** Samuel Bradford.

Thirst

A girl is abducted by a secret society that wants her to become their new leader. In order to comply, she must learn to like the taste of blood. Inspired by Bathory legend.

1980 C AU [F G Films Productions/New South Wales Film Corporation] **Cast:** Henry Silva, David Hemmings, Chantal Contouri. **Dir:** Rod Hardy.

To Die For

A vampire stalks, woos, and snacks on a young real estate woman.

1989 C [Skouras] **Vampire(s):** Vlad Tepish (Brendan Hughes); **Cast:** Scott Jacoby, Sydney Walsh, Amanda Wyss. **Dir:** Deren Sarafian.

Tomb

Fortune-seekers disturb the slumber of a magical, sadistic princess much to their everlasting regret. Based on a Bram Stoker story.

1985 C Vampire(s): Nefratis (Michelle Bauer); **Cast:** Cameron Mitchell, John Carradine, Susan Stokey, Richard Alen Hench. **Dir:** Fred Olen Ray.

Toothless Vampires

1987 C HK Dir: Lee Hun Yu.

The Trail

Originally released as *Pao Dan Fei Che.*

1983 C HK [Golden Harvest]; **Cast:** Ricky Hui, Zhang Zeshi, Cheung Fat, Miao Tian. **Dir:** Ronny Yu.

Trampire

1987 C [Fantasy Home Video] **Vampire(s):** (Angela Baron); **Cast:** Nikki Knights, Angel Kelly, Carol Hall. **Dir:** C. C. Williams.

Transylvania 6-5000

Two klutzy reporters travel to Transylvania and encounter an array of comedic creatures.

1985 C [New World Pictures] **Vampire(s):** Radu (John Byner), Odette (Geena Davis); **Cast:** Jeff Goldblum, Joseph Bologna, Ed Begley, Jr., Carol Kane, Jeffery Jones. **Dir:** Rudy DeLuca.

Transylvania Twist

A comedy about vampires and teenage vampire hunters.

1989 C [Concorde/New Horizons] **Vampire(s):** Byron Orlok (Robert Vaughn); **Cast:** Teri Copley, Steve Altman, Ace Mask. **Dir:** Jim Wynorski.

The Understudy: Graveyard Shift II

The vampire is cast in a movie in which he plays a vampire. Sequel to *Graveyard Shift* (1986).

1987 C CA [Cinema Ventures] **Vampire(s):** Carmilla/Patti Venus (Wendy Gazelle); **Cast:** Silvio Oliviero, Mark Soper, Ilse Von Glatz. **Dir:** Gerard Ciccoritti.

Vamp

Two college freshmen encounter vampires in a steamy red-light district nightclub.

1986 C [New World Pictures] **Vampire(s):** Katrina (Grace Jones) et al; **Cast:** Chris Makepeace, Sandy Baron, Robert Rusler, Gedde Watanabe. **Dir:** Richard Wenk.

Vampire at Midnight

A homicide detective stalks a vampire killer in modern Los Angeles.

1988 C [Skouras Pictures] **Vampire(s):** Victor Radkoff (Gustav Vintas); **Cast:** Jason Williams, Leslie Milne, Jeanie Moore. **Dir:** Gregory McClatchy.

Vampire Hunter D

An adult animated film based on Vampire Hunter D by Hideyuki Kikuchi.

1985 C JP [Epic/Sony/Streamline Pictures] **Dir:** Tayoo Ashida.

Vampire in Venice

Originally released as *Nosferatu a Venezia* and as *Vampires in Venice*.

1988 C IT [Scena/Reteitalia/Vestron] **Vampire(s):** (Klaus Kinski); **Cast:** Christopher Plummer, Donald Pleasence, Barbara de Rossi. **Dir:** Augusto Caminito.

Vampire Knights

1987 C [Mezcal Films/Filmtrust] **Cast:** Daniel M. Peterson, Robin Rochelle, Thomas Kingsley. **Dir:** Daniel M. Peterson.

Vampire Princess Miyu

An animated feature film with four episodes from a popular Japanese series.

1988 C JP [Sooeishinsha/Pony Canyon/AnimEigo] **Vampire(s):** Princess Miyu; **Cast:** Watanabe Naoke, Koyama Mami, Kobayashi Kiyoko. **Dir:** Hirano Toshihiro.

Vampire Raiders—Ninja Queen

Evil ninjas are plotting to infiltrate the hotel industry and are opposed by good ninjas.

1989 C JP **Cast:** Agnes Chan, Chris Peterson. **Dir:** Bruce Lambert.

Vampire's Breakfast

1986 C HK **Dir:** Wong Chun.

Vampire's Kiss

1989 C [Hemsdale Film Corporation] **Vampire(s):** Rachel (Jennifer Beals); **Cast:** Nicolas Cage, Maria Conchita Alonso, Elizabeth Ashley. **Dir:** Robert Bierman.

Vampires

Also released as *Abandon; Fright House*.

1988 C [Len Anthony Studios] **Vampire(s):** Madeline Abadon (Jackie James); **Cast:** Duane Jones, Orly Benyair, Robin Michaels. **Dir:** Len Anthony.

Vampires in Havana

An animated feature. Also released as *Vampiros in la Habana*.

1986 C CU/SP/GE [Icaic/TE/Durniok] **Cast:** Voices: Frank Gonzalez, Manuel Marin, Irela Bravo; **Dir:** Juan Padrón.

Vampires Live Again

1987 C **Dir:** Kam Yoo Tu.

Vampires on Bikini Beach

1988 C [Beacon Films] **Vampire(s):** Demos (Michael Hao), Falto (Mariusz Olbrychowski); **Cast:** Jennifer Badham, Todd Kaufmann, Stephen Mathews. **Dir:** Jerry Brady.

Vampires Strike Back

1988 C HK **Dir:** Kam Yoo Tu.

Vengeful Vampire Girl

Originally released as Huphyokwi Yanyo.

1981 C KO [Han Jin Enterprises] **Cast:** Choi Bong, Chong Hi Jung. **Dir:** Kim In Soo.

Vincent Price's Dracula

A documentary also released as *Dracula— The Great Undead.*

1982 C [M&M Film Productions/Atlantis] **Cast:** Vincent Price. **Dir:** John Miller.

Waxwork

A wax museum opens with scenes that come to life, including one of Dracula.

1988 C [Vestron] **Vampire(s):** Count Dracula (Miles O'Keefe); **Cast:** Zach Galligan, Deborah Foremen, Michelle Johnson. **Dir:** Anthony Hickox.

Who Is Afraid of Dracula?

Also released as *Fracchia contro Dracula; Fracchia vs Dracula.*

1985 C IT [Faso Film/Titanus/Maura International] **Vampire(s):** Dracula [Edmund Purdom], Countess Oniria (Ania Pieroni); **Cast:** Neri Parenti, Paolo Villaggio, Gigi Reder. **Dir:** Neri Parenti.

Wolnyoui Han

1980 C KO [Han Jin Enterprises] **Cast:** Chin Bong Chin, Huh Chin.

1990 to 1993

The Addams Family

This second Addams Family movie is built around a plot by a fake Uncle Fester to steal the family fortune. Based on the characters created by Charles Addams in his New Yorker cartoons.

1991 C [Paramount] **Vampire(s):** Morticia Addams (Anjelica Huston); **Cast:** Raul Julia, Christopher Lloyd, Elizabeth Wilson, Christina Ricci. **Dir:** Barry Sonnenfeld.

The Addams Family Values

In this third Addams Family movie, the family's unity is attacked and must be reaffirmed.

1993 C [Paramount] **Vampire(s):** Morticia Addams (Anjelica Huston); **Cast:** Raul Julia, Christopher Lloyd, Elizabeth Wilson, Christina Ricci. **Dir:** Barry Sonnenfeld.

The Arrival

An alien turns an old man into a vampire hungry for female blood.

1990 C [Del Mar Entertainment] **Vampire(s):** (Joseph Culp); **Cast:** John Saxon, Robin Frates, Robert Sampson. **Dir:** David Schmoeller.

Baby Blood

1990 C FR [Partners Productions/EX07 Productions] **Cast:** Emmanuelle Escourrou, Jean-Francois Gallotte, Christian Sininger, Roselyn Geslot. **Dir:** Alain Robak.

Back to the USSR

1992 C FI Vampire(s): Lenin. **Dir:** Jari Halonen.

Bandh Darwaza

1990 C IN [Ramsey Films/GVi/ Gurpreej Video International] **Cast:** Hashmat Khan, Manjeet Kular, Kunika, Satish Kaul. **Dir:** Tulsi Ramay, Shyam Ramsey.

Banglow 666

1990 C IN [Priwa International].

Bite!

1991 C [Legend] **Cast:** Alicyn Sterling, Buck Adams, P. J. Sparx, Randy West. **Dir:** Scotty Fox.

Bloodlust

1992 C AU [Windover Productions]
Cast: Jane Stuart Wallace, Kelly Chapman, Robert James O'Neill. **Dir:** Richard Wolstencroft, Jon Hewitt.

Bloodthirsty

1992 C [Barrows Productions] **Cast:** Ascello Charles, Winston McDonald, Lia Marino, Stefanie Roumeliotes. **Dir:** Robert Guy Barrows.

Bram Stoker's Dracula

Most recent and faithful to the text screen version of the novel by Bram Stoker. Novelization of the Coppola/Hart screenplay appeared as *Bram Stoker's Dracula* by Fred Saberhagen and James V. Hart.

1992 C [Columbia] **Vampire(s):** Dracula (Gary Oldman); **Cast:** Winona Ryder, Anthony Hopkins, Keanu Reeves. **Dir:** Francis Ford Coppola.

Buffy the Vampire Slayer

Story of a cheerleader in a California high school who is chosen to be a vampire hunter. Contemporaneously with the appearance of the movie, a novelization by Ritchie Tankersley Cusick of the screen play by Joss Wheadon appeared in paperback.

1992 C [Sandollar/ Kuzui Enterprises/ 20th Century Fox] **Vampire(s):** Lothos (Rutger Hauer); **Cast:** Kristy Swanson, Donald Sutherland, Paul Reubens. **Dir:** Fran Rubel Kuzui.

Children of the Night

A vampire is released from an underground crypt and makes a quiet, small town his bloodthirsty target.

1990 C [Fangoria Films] **Vampire(s):** Czakyr (David Sawyer), Karen Thompson (Karen Black), Grandma (Shirley Spiegler Jacobs); **Cast:** Peter DeLuise, Ami Dolenz. **Dir:** Tony Randel.

Crazy Safari

1990 C HK Cast: Lam Ching Ying, Sam Christopher Chan, NiXan. **Dir:** Lo Weng-Tung.

Chronos

The chronod device is an alchemical product, an egg shapped instrument, which gives its user eternal life but with an accompanying thirst for blood.

1992 C MX [Iguana/Ventna]. **Cast:** Frederico Luooi, Ron Perlman, Claudio Brook, Margarita Isabel. **Dir:** Guillermo Navarro.

Darkness

1992 C [Leif Jonker] **Dir:** Leif Jonker.

Daughter of Darkness

1990 C [King Phoenix Entertainment/ Accent] **Vampire(s):** Anton Crainic (Anthony Perkins); **Cast:** Mia Sara, Robert Reynolds, Dezsu Garas, Jack Coleman. **Dir:** Stuart Gordon.

Dawn

1990 C [Shooting Gallery] **Vampire(s):** Louis (Geoff Sloan); **Cast:** Elizabeth Rees, Craig Johnson, Kate Jones Davies. **Dir:** Niall Johnson.

Def by Temptation

Horror fantasy about a young African American theology student who meets an evil woman who tries to seduce him and redirect his life.

1990 C [Bonded Enterprises/Orpheus Pictures/ Troma] **Vampire(s):** (Cynthia Bond); **Cast:** James Bond III, Kadeem Hardison, Bill Nunn. **Dir:** James Bond III.

Doctor Vampire

1991 C HK Dir: Q. Xen Lee.

Dracula: A Cinematic Scrapbook

An anthology of movie trailers and interviews with Bela Lugosi and Christopher Lee.

1990 [Rhino Video] **Dir:** Ted Newson.

Dracula Rising

Vlad, the son of Dracula, is reunited with the reincarnation of his former love.

1992 C [Concorde Pictures] **Vampire(s):** Count Dracula (Christopher Atkins); **Cast:** Stacy Travis, Doug Wert. **Dir:** Fred Gallo.

Dracula's Hair

1992 C RU [Arto Studio/Rosfilmexport] **Dir:** Vadim Prodan.

Fangs!

Documentary on vampire movies.

1992 C [Pagan Video] **Cast:** Veronica Carlson. **Dir:** Bruce G. Hallenbeck.

Father, Santa Claus Has Died

1992 C RU [Lenfilm] **Cast:** Anatoly Egorov, Evan Ganzha, Ljudmila Kozlovskava. **Dir:** Ugeny Ganzha.

First Vampire in China

1990 C HK Dir: Yam Chun-Lu.

Howling VI: The Freaks

Sixth entry in a werewolf series in which the werewolf battles vampires at a freak show.

1990 C [Allied Lane Pringle Productions] **Vampire(s):** Mr. Harker (Bruce Martin Payne); **Cast:** Brendan Hughes, Michelle Matheson, Sean Gregory Sullivan. **Dir:** Hope Perello.

I Bought a Vampire Motorcycle

1990 C [Dirk/ Majestic Films] **Cast:** Nick Morrisey, Amanda Noar, Michael Elphick. **Dir:** Dirk Campbell.

In the Midnight Hour

1992 C [Midnight Hour Productions] **Cast:** Michelle Owens, Dennis McMillen, Greg Greer. **Dir:** Joel Bender.

Innocent Blood

A modern-day vampire/gangster combination.

1992 C [Lee Rich Productions/Warner Bros.] **Vampire(s):** Marie (Anne Parillaud), Sal "The Shark" Macelli (Robert Loggia); **Cast:** Anthony LaPaglia, Don Rickles. **Dir:** John Landis.

The Malibu Beach Vampires

Three yuppies keep mistresses (who turn out to be vampires) in their Malibu beach house.

1991 C [Peacock Films] **Cast:** Angelyne, Becky LeBeau, Joan Rudelstein, Marcus A. Frishman. **Dir:** Francis Creighton.

La Maschera del Demonio

A remake of the classic horror film released in English as *Black Sunday* (1960) directed by the son of original director Mario Bava.

1990 C IT [Reitalia-Anfri] **Cast:** Debora Kinski, Eva Grimaldi, Michele Soavi, Piero Nomi. **Dir:** Lamberto Bava.

Moon Legend

1991 C HK Vampire(s): Moon-Cher. **Dir:** Joey Wang.

Muffy the Vampire Layer

An adult erotic-oriented feature.

1993 C [Las Vegas Video Entertainment] **Cast:** P. J. Sparxx, Lacy Rose, Sunset Thomas, Steve Drake.

My Grandpa is a Vampire

When 12-year-old Lonny visits his grandfather in New Zealand, he learns the family secret.

1991 C NZ [Tucker Production Co./ Moonrise Productions]; **Vampire(s):** Vernon T. Cooger (Al Lewis); **Cast:** Justin Goecke, Milan Borich, Noel Appleby. **Dir:** David Blyth.

My Lovely Monster

Spoof on horror movies.

1991 C GE [Xenon Films/WDR/SFB] **Vampire(s):** Maximilian (Silvio Francesco); **Cast:** Forest J. Ackerman, Nicole Fischer, Matthias Fuchs. **Dir:** Michel Bergmann.

Out for Blood

1990 C [Vivid Video] **Vampire(s):** Tori (Tori Wells); **Cast:** Raquel Darian, Randy Spears, Kelly Royce. **Dir:** Paul Thomas.

Princess of the Night

1990 C Vampire(s): (Jamie Gillis); **Cast:** Lauren Hall, Viper. **Dir:** F. J. Lincoln.

Project Vampire

1992 C [NBV Productions] **Vampire(s):** Dr. Fredrick Klaus (Myron Natwick); **Cast:** Brian Knudson, Mary-Louis Gemmill, Paula Randoi-Smith. **Dir:** Peter Flynn.

Red Blooded American Girl

Scientists discover a virus that turns people into vampires.

1990 C CA [SC Entertainment] **Vampire(s):** Dr. John Alcove (Christopher Plummer); **Cast:** Andrew Stevens, Heather Thomas, Kim Coates. **Dir:** David Blyth.

The Reflecting Skin

In the 1950s, a small boy believes that the tormented widow who lives next door is a vampire.

1991 C [Fugitive Films/Virgin/Live Entertainment] **Cast:** Viggo Mortensen, Lindsay Duncan, Jeremy Cooper. **Dir:** Philip Ridley.

The Reluctant Vampire

Based on a play by Malcolm Marmorstein.

1992 C [Waymar Productions] **Vampire(s):** Zachary Smith (Adam Ant); **Cast:** Kimberly Foster, Roger Rose, Michelle Forbes. **Dir:** Malcolm Marmorstein.

Robo Vampire

A Chinese version of Robocop faces off against a group of the famous hopping vampires who are helping a set of drug smugglers.

1993 C HK [Filmark International/Thomas Tong] **Cast:** Robin Mackay, Nian Watts Harry Myles, Joe Brown. **Dir:** Joe Livingstone.

Rockula

A comedy about a 300-year-old teenage vampire who is still a virgin.

1990 C [Cannon] **Vampire(s):** Ralph (Dean Cameron); **Cast:** Toni Basil, Bo Diddley, Tawny Feré, Thomas Dolby, Susan Tyrrell. **Dir:** Luca Bercovici.

Sherlock Holmes in Caracas

Based on "The Case of The Sussex Vampire" by Arthur Colan Doyle.

1992 C VE [Big Ben Productions/ Tiuna Films/Foncine] **Vampire(s):** ex-Miss Venezuela (Maria Eugenia Cruz); **Cast:** Jean Manuel Montesinos, Gilbert Dacournan, Caroline Luzardo. **Dir:** Juan E. Fresan.

Sleepwalkers

Based on screenplay by Stephen King.

1992 C [Columbia/ Ion Pictures] **Vampire(s):** Mary Brady (Alice Krige), Charles Brady (Brian Krause); **Cast:** Mädchen Amick, Jim Haynie. **Dir:** Mick Garris.

 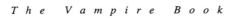

Sorority House Vampires

1991 C [Digital Vision Entertainment] **Vampire(s):** Count Vlad (Robert Bucholz); **Cast:** Natalie Bondurant, Eugenie Bondurant, Rachel Wolkow. **Dir:** Geoffrey de Valois.

Streets

1990 C Vampire(s): (Eb Lottimer); **Cast:** Christina Applegate, David Mendenhall, Starr Andreeff. **Dir:** Katt Shea Ruben.

Subspecies

Vampire demons descend to Earth in this first horror movie shot entirely in Transylvania.

1990 C [Full Moon Entertainment] **Vampire(s):** Stefan (Michael Watson), Radu (Anders Hove); **Cast:** Laura Tate, Michelle McBride. **Dir:** Ted Nicolaou.

Tale of a Vampire

Loosely based on "Annabel Lee" by Edger Allan Poe. Also released as *A Tale of Vampire.*

1992 C GB/JP [State Screen Productions] **Vampire(s):** Alex (Julian Sands); **Cast:** Sizanna Hamilton, Kenneth Cranham, Marian Diamond. **Dir:** Shimako Sato.

Those Feedy on Blood

Based on Alexey Tolstoy's, "The Wurdalak." Also released as *Blood-Suckers.*

1991 C Cast: Marina Vlasi, Andrey Sokolov, Marina Maiko, Donatas Banionis. **Dir:** E. Tatarskiy.

To Die For, II: Son of Darkness

Vampires flock around the adoptive mother of a baby secretly sired by a vampire.

1991 C [Arrowhead Entertainment; Lee Caplin Productions-Vidmark Entertainment] **Vampire(s):** Max Schreck/Vlad Tepish (Michael Praed); **Cast:** Rosalind Allen, Steve Bond, Scott Jacoby. **Dir:** David F. Price.

To Sleep with a Vampire

A vampire seeks to talk to his next victim before feeding off her. Remake of *Dance of the Damned.*

1992 C [Concorde Pictures] **Vampire(s):** (Scott Valentine); **Cast:** Charlie Spradling. **Dir:** Adam Friedman.

Trilogy of Fear

Three stories of which one is a vampire tale.

1991 C [Trilogy Group] **Cast:** Claude Akins; **Notes: Dir:** Richard L. Fox, Jr.

Ultimate Vampire

1991 C HK Cast: Lam Ching Ying, Chin Siu Ho. **Dir:** Andrew Lau.

Undying Love

1991 C Cast: Lee Kayman. **Dir:** Greg Lamberson.

Valerie

Loosely based on Sheridan Le Fanu's "Carmilla."

1991 C Vampire(s): Valerie (Maria Pechukas); **Cast:** Austin Pendleton, Debbie Rochon. **Dir:** Jay Lind.

Un Vampire au Paradis

1992 C FR [Les Films Auramax/Canal Plus/CNC/MC-4] **Vampire(s):** Nosfer Arbi (Farid Chopel); **Cast:** Bruno Cremer, Brigitte Fossey, Laure Marsac. **Dir:** Abdelkrim Bahloul.

Vampire Buster

Also released as *Ninja Vampire Buster.*

1990 C HK [In-Gear Film Production [Hong Kong] **Cast:** Nick Chan, Simon Cheng, Stanley Fung. **Dir:** Norma Law.

Vampire Cop

A vampire cop teams up with a reporter to go after a drug ring.

1990 C [Panorama Entertainment] **Vampire(s):** (Ed Cannon); **Cast:** Melissa Moore, William Lucas, Mal Arnold. **Dir:** Donald Farmer.

Vampire Trailer Park

1991 C [Cinemondo] **Vampire(s):** (Patrick Moran); **Cast:** Robert Schultz, Blake Pickett, Bentley Little. **Dir:** Steve Latshaw.

Vampire's Embrace

1991 C Dir: Glen Andreiev.

Vampires Settle on Police Camp

1991 C HK Dir: Lo Wei Lang.

Vampyre

1990 C [Panorama Entertainment/ Raedon] **Vampire(s):** Marguerite (Cathy Seyler); **Cast:** Randy Scott Rzler, John Brent, Greg Boggia. **Dir:** Bruce G. Hallenbeck.

Witchcraft III: The Kiss of Death

A retired master of the occult is called out of his private life by a vampiress trying to seduce him.

1991 C [Academy Entertainment] **Vampire(s):** (Dominic Luciano); **Cast:** Charles Solomon, Lisa Toothman, Lena Hall. **Dir:** R. L. Tillmanns.

BIBLIOGRAPHICAL SOURCES

This appendix was created with the help of the sources listed below. Of these, Stephen Jones' *The Illustrated Vampire Movie Guide* is the most complete, with John L. Flynn's *Cinematic Vampire* a close second.

Bojarski, Richard. *The Films of Bela Lugosi.* Secaucus, NJ: Citadel Press, 1980. 256 pp.

Byrne, Richard B. *Films of Tyranny.* Madison, WI: College Printing & Typing Co., 1966.

de Coulteray, George. *Sadism in the Movies.* New York: Medical Press, 1965. 191 pp.

Everson, William K. *Classics of the Horror Film.* New York: Citadel, 1974. 246 pp.

Eyles, Allen, Elbert Adkinson, Nicolas Fry, eds. *The House of Horror: The Story of Hammer Films.* London: Lorrimer Publishing Ltd., 1973. 127 pp.

Flynn, John L. *Cinematic Vampires: The Living Dead on Film and Television, from The Devil's Castle (1896), to Bram Stoker's Dracula (1992).* Jefferson, NC: McFarland & Company, 1992. 320 pp.

Frank, Alan. *Monsters and Vampires.* London: Octopus Books, 1976. 160 pp.

Glut, Donald. *The Dracula Book.* Metuchen, NJ: Scarecrow Press, 1975. 388 pp.

Hanke, Ken. *A Critical Guide to Horror Film Series.* New York: Garland Publishing, 1991. 341 pp.

Hutchings, Peter. *Hammer and Beyond: The British Horror Film.* Manchester: Manchester University Press, 1993. 193 pp.

Jones, Stephen. *The Illustrated Vampire Movie Guide.* London: Titan Books, 1993. 144 pp.

Marrero, Robert. *Dracula: The Vampire Legend on Film.* Key West, FL: Fantasma Books, 1992. 120 pp.

———. *Vampires Hammer Style.* Florida: RGM Publications, 1974. 98 pp.

Murphy, Michael J. *The Celluloid Vampires: A History and Filmography, 1897-1979.* Ann Arbor, MI: Pierian Press, 1979.

Nance, Scott. *Bloodsuckers: Vampires at the Movies.* Las Vegas, NV: Pioneer Books, 1992. 149 pp.

Pattison, Barrie. *The Seal of Dracula.* New York: Bounty Books, 1975. 136 pp.

Pirie, David. *Heritage of Horror: The English Gothic Cinema, 1946-1972.* New York: Avon, 1973.

————. *The Vampire Cinema.* London: Hamlyn, 1977. 175 pp.

Pohle, Robert W., Jr., & Douglas C. Hart. *The Films of Christopher Lee.* Metuchen, NJ: Scarecrow Press, 1983.

Reed, Donald. *The Vampire on the Screen.* Inglewood, CA: Wagon & Star Publishers, 1965.

Riccardo, Martin V. *Vampires Unearthed: The Complete Multimedia Vampire and Dracula Bibliography.* New York: Garland Publishing, 1983. 135 pp.

Senn, Bryan, and John Johnson. *Fantastic Cinema Subject Guide.* Jefferson, NC: McFarland & Company, 1992. pp. 524-62.

Skal, David J. *Hollywood Gothic: The Tangled Web of Dracula from Novel to Stage to Screen.* New York: W. W. Norton & Company, 1990. 243 pp.

Stanley, John. *Creature Features Movie Guide.* Pacifica, CA: Creatures at Large, 1981. 208 pp.

Ursini, James, and Alain Silver. *The Vampire Film.* South Brunswick, NJ: A. S. Barnes and Company, 1975. 238 pp. Rev. ed. 1993. Rev. ed. as: Alain Silver and James Ursini. *The Vampire Film: From Nosferatu to Bram Stoker's Dracula.* New York: Limelight Editions, 1993. 273 pp.

Waller, Gregory A. *The Living and the Undead: From Stoker's Dracula to Romero's Dawn of the Dead.* Urbana, IL: University of Illinois Press, 1986. 376 pp.

Willis, Donald C. *Horror and Science Fiction Films: A Checklist.* 3 vols. Metuchen, NJ: The Scarecrow Press, 1972, 1982, 1984.

VAMPIRE DRAMAS

This list of all published vampire plays, operas, and ballet was prepared with the assistance of Martin V. Riccardo and Margaret L. Carter. The list is divided into three sections:

- Vampire Plays
- Vampire Opera
- Vampire Ballet

Each section is organized alphabetically. Entries include the name of the work; the year first performed or published (if known); author or composer; location where performed or published; and, as appropriate, an author's note discussing the work's importance.

VAMPIRE PLAYS

Almost the Bride of Dracula; or, Why the Count Remains a Bachelor (1980)

By Dennis Snee. Boston: Baker's Plays.

Bats Are Folks

By Sneed Hearn. Elgin, IL: Performance.

Bats in the Basement (1989)

By Richard Booth. Coos Bay, OR: The Author.

This play was first presented on September 8, 1989, in the Little Theatre in North Bend, Oregon. It was a two-act thriller featuring Count Dracula.

Beast of a Different Burden (1974)

By Faith Whitehall. New York: Samuel French.

Blood Pudding (1981)

By Jeanne Youngson. Reprint in: *Count Dracula Fan Club Magazine* 4, 1.

Boys and Ghouls Together

By David Rogers. Franklin, OH: Eldrige.

Bride of Frankenstein (1976)

By Tim Kelly. Denver: Pioneer Drama Service.

Cadet Buteux, Vampire avec relation véridique du prologue et les trois acts de cet épouvantable mélodrame (1820)

By Désaugiers. Paris: Rosa.

The Camel and the Vampire (1961)

By Malcolm La Prade. In *Easy Pantomines*. Boston: Baker's Plays.

Carmilla (1973)

By David Campton. Reprint in: *Three Gothic Plays*. London: J. G. Miller.

Carmilla (1975)

By Wilford Leach.

The Children of the Night (1982)

By Paul Ledoux. Toronto: Playwrights Union of Canada, 1982.

A comedy about Bela Lugosi.

Count Dracula (1972)

By Ted Tiller. New York: Samuel French.

Count Dracula (1974)

By Ted Miller.

Count Dracula; or, A Musical Mania from Transylvania (1974)

By Lawrence Outwore. Theatre Three.

The Count Will Rise Again; or, Dracula in Dixie (1980)

By Dennis Snee. Boston: Baker's Plays.

Countess Dracula! (1980)

By Neal DuBrock. New York: Samuel French.

Dearest Dracula (1965)

By Margaret Hill, Charlotte Moor, Jack Murdock. Dublin.

Death at the Crossroads (1975)

By Stephen Hotchner. Denver, CO: Pioneer Drama Service.

Decodanz: The Dilemma of Desmodus and Diphylla (1991)

By the Brown Adaptors.

This multimedia performance centered on two vampires opened at St. Clement's Church in New York City in 1991.

The Devonshire Demons (1979)

By John Murray. Reprint in: *Fifteen Plays for Teen-agers*. Boston: Baker's Plays, 1979.

Dracula (1897)

By Bram Stoker.

A five-act staged reading of *Dracula* was conducted by Stoker to establish certain legal rights for his play.

Dracula (1927)

By Hamilton Dean and John L. Balderston. New York: Samuel French, Inc. Reprinted in Hamilton Deane and John L. Balderston. *Dracula: The Ultimate Illustrated Edition of the World-Famous Vampire Play*. Ed. by David J. Skal. New York: St. Martin's Press, 1993. 153 pp.

Based on Stoker, opened in London on February 14, 1927 at Little Theatre and in the United States at the Fulton Theater on October 5, 1927. A revised version, with sets designed by Edward Gorey, opened in New York at the Martin Beck Theater on October 20, 1979. This play became the basis of two Dracula movies in 1931 (starring Bela Lugosi) and 1979 (starring Frank Langella) produced by Universal Pictures. It is the one most frequently used in productions of *Dracula* to this day.

Dracula (1927)

By Charles Morrel.

The second version of *Dracula* authorized by Stoker's widow. It opened at the Royal Court Theatre in Warrington, but was unsuccessful and soon closed.

Dracula (1972)

By Stanley Eveling. London.

Dracula (1973)

By Larry Ferguson. Los Angeles.

Dracula (1976)

By Crane Johnson. New York: Dramatists Play Service.

Dracula (1978)

By Kingsley Day. Chicago: Premiere Society.
  This musical opened in Chicago at the Chicago Premiere Society in June.

Dracula (1978)

By Stephen Hotchner. Denver, CO: Pioneer Drama Service.

Dracula (1980)

By John Mattera. Chicago: Dramatic Publishing Company.
  Based on Stoker's novel.

Dracula (1989)

By Liz Lochhead. London: Penguin Books.
  Reworking of the novel by Bram Stoker.

Dracula (1990)

By Richard Sharp. Shell Beach, CA: Greatworks Play Services, 1990.

Dracula, Baby (1970)

By Bruce Ronald. Music by Claire Strauch; Lyrics by John Jakes. Chicago: Dramatic Publishing Company.
  Based on Stoker's novel.

Dracula, The Comedy of the Vampire (1930s)
  European satire of the Deane play.

Dracula: The Death of Nosferatu (1991)

Adapted by Christopher P. Nichols. Woodstock, IL: Dramatic Publishing Company.

The Dracula Doll (1980)

By Jeanne Youngson. In *A Child's Garden of Vampires*. New York: Count Dracula Fan Club.

Dracula: A Modern Fable (1978)

By Norman Beim.

Dracula: The Musical (1982)

By Rick Abbot. New York: Samuel French.

Dracula: Sabbat (1970)

By Leon Katz. New York.

Dracula/Sabbat (1991)

By Leon Katz. In *Midnight Plays*. Venice, CAP: Wavecrest Books.

The Dracula School for Vampires (1984)

By Leonard Wolf.
  This play opened in San Francisco.

The Dracula Spectacula (1976)

By John Gardiner. London: Samuel French.

Dracula Sucks (1969)

By Jerry B. Wheeler. New York: Samuel French.

Dracula Tyrannus: The Tragical History of Vlad the Impaler (1982)

By Ron Magid.

Dracula: The Vampire Play (1924)

By Hamilton Deane. Reprint: Garden City, NY: Nelson Doubleday, 1971.

Dracula, "The Vampire Play" (1978)

By Tim Kelly. Schulenberg, TX: I. E. Clark, 1979.

Opened in London at the Queen's Theatre on August 23, 1978.

Dracula!; or, the Vampire Vanquished: A Victorian Melodrama for Schools Based on Bram Stoker's Book, Dracula (1983)

By Carey Blyton. Borough Green, Sevenoaks, Kent, UK: Novello, 1983.

Dracula's Treasure (1975)

By Dudley Saunders. Anchorage, KY: Anchorage.

Ein Vampyr (1877)

By Ulrich Franks.
Opened at Vienna. A farce.

Encore un Vampire (1829)

By Emile B. L.
Opened in Paris in 1820.

Escape from Dracula's Castle (1975)

By Stephen Hotchner. Denver: Pioneer Drama Service.

Frankenstein Slept Here

By Tim Kelly. Denver, CO: Pioneer Drama Service.

The Ghoul Friend

By Gene Donovan.

Going Down for the Count (1985)

By Peter Elliot Weiss. Toronto: Playwrights Union of Canada, 1985.

Guten Abend Herr Fischer! oder, Der Vampyr (1860)

By G. Belly and G. Löffler, W. Telle (music).
CF Summers 312.

I Was a Teen Age Dracula (1958)

By Gene Donovan. Chicago: Dramatic Publishing Company.

I'm Sorry, the Bridge Is Out, You'll Have to Spend the Night (1970)

By Sheldon Allman.
This farce opened at the Coronet Theatre in Los Angeles on April 28, 1970.

Johnny Appleseed and Dracula (1970)

Lady Dracula (1980)

By Tim Kelly. Denver, CO: Pioneer Drama Service.

Le Vampire (1819)

By Charles Nodier with Achille de Jouffroy and Pierre Carmouche. Critical edition by Ginette Picat-Guinoiseau. Geneva: Librairie Droz S. A., 1990.

The first of several French plays based on John Polidori's "The Vampyre." It opened at Porte-Saint-Martin in Paris on June 13, 1820, and was revived on several occasions. Montague Summers summarized the play in *The Vampire: His Kith and Kin.*

Le Vampire (1820)

By Pierre de la Fosse. Paris: Martinet.

Le Vampire (1851)

By Alexandre Dumas and Auguste Maquet. Paris: Michel Lévy, 1865

Opened December 1851 in Paris.

Le Vampire (1867)

By Paul Féval. Reprint in: *Les Drames de la mort.* Verviers: Marabout, 1969.

Le Vampire Comedie—Vaudeville en un Act (1820)

By Eugene Scribe. Reprint: *Oeuves Completes de Eugene Scribe.* VI. Paris: Dentu, 1876. Reprint: Paris Guibert, 1900, 1983.

A French comedy/satire based on Polidori's "The Vampyre." Opened at the Vaudeville in Paris.

Les Etrennes d'un Vampire (1820)

By Pere-Lachaise.

A burlesque of *Le Vampire.* Cf. Summers 305.

Les Trois Vampires, ou le clair de la lune (1820)

By Brazier, Gabriel, and Armand. Paris: Barba, 1820.

A French farce centered on the problems created for a man named Gobetout who became paranoid from reading books on vampires. Opened at the Varíetés in Paris.

Love Bite

By Monica Mobley.

Miss Todd's Vampire: A Comedy in One Act (1920)

By Sally Shute. Boston: W. H. Baker, 1920.

Monster Soup; or, That Thing in My Neck Is a Tooth (1974)

Denver, CO: Pioneer Drama Service.

Mors Dracula (1979)

By Warren Graves. Toronto: Playwrights Canada.

The Mystery of Irma Vep (1984)

By Charles Ludlam. New York: Samuel French, 1984.

Night Fright

By William A. Kuehl. Boston: Baker's Plays.

Out for the Count; or, How Would You Like Your Stake?: A Vampire Yarn (1986)

By Martin Downing. London: Samuel French.

The Passion of Dracula (1978)

By Bob Hall and David Richmond. New York: Samuel French.

The Phantom: A Drama in Two Acts (1856)

By Dion Boucicault. New York: Samuel French.

A revival of *The Vampire* (1852).

Polichinel Vampire (1822)

Mentioned by Montague Summers.

The Possession of Lucy Wenstrom (1975)

By Stephen Hotchner. Denver, CO: Pioneer Drama Service.

Seven Wives for Dracula (1973)

By Tim Kelly. Denver, CO: Pioneer Drama Service.

The Vagabond Vampires (1979)

By John Murray. Reprint: *Fifteen Plays for Teen-agers.* Boston: Baker's Plays.

The Vampire (1852)

By Dion Boucicault.
 Opened at the Princess Theatre in London, June 19, 1852. Cf Summers 312.

The Vampire (1909)

Adapted by Jose G. Levy from the French of Mme. C. le Vylars and Pierre Souvestre.
 Opened at the Paragon Theatre in London on September 27, 1909.

The Vampire Bat: A Mystery Melodrama in Three Acts (1940)

By Robert St. Clair. Evanston, IL: Row, Peterson & Company, 1940.

The Vampire; or, the Bride of Death: A Melodrama (1978)

By Constance Cox. London: Samuel French.
 An adaptation of the 1820 play by Planché.

The Vampire; or, The Bride of the Isles: A Romantic Drama in Three Acts (1820)

By James Robinson Planché. Music by Joseph Binns Hart. London: John Lownes. Reprint: Baltimore: J. Robinson, 1820. Reprint in: James Robinson Planché. *Plays.* Edited by Donald Roy. Cambridge: Cambridge University Press, 1986.
 Nodier's play opened in Paris in June 1820. Before the summer was out, Planché translated Nodier's play into English and changed the location of its action to Scotland. His play opened in London in August 1820. Planché became well-known for his development of the "vampire trap," a special theater door for use in this play, a devise widely used for other dramas. A summary to the play and the opening is given by Summers who drew from Planché's *Recollections and Reflections* (London: 1871).

The Vampire Bride, or Wake not the Dead (1854)

By George Blink. London: Thomas Hailes Lacy.
 A drama set in medieval times and built around a new vampire, Brunhilda. Mentioned by E. F. Beiler in *Three Gothic Novels* (New York: Dover Publications, 1966).

The Vampire Cat: A Play in One Act from the Japanese Legend of the Nebeshima Cat. (1918)

Chicago: Dramatic Publishing Company, 1918.

The Vampire: A Drama in Three Acts (1829)

By William Thomas Moncrieff. London: T. Richardson.

Vampire Lesbians of Sodom (1984)

By Charles Busch. New York: Samuel French, 1985. Reprinted in four plays. Garden City, NY: Fireside Theatre, 1988.
 Opened off-Broadway in 1984.

The Vampire: An Original Burlesque (1872)

By Robert Reece. London: Rascol.
 Opened at the Royal Strand Theatre on August 15. A farce in which the vampire is a plagiarist.

The Vampire: A Sensational Four-Act Melodrama (1901)

By Fitzgerald Murphy.

Vampire Tower (1983)

By John Dickson Carr. Published in *The Dead Sleep Lightly*. Garden City, NY: Doubleday & Co.

The Vampire: A Tragedy in Five Acts (1821)

By St. John Dorset. London: C. and J. Ollier.

This play has also been attributed to Hugo John Belfour and to George Stephens.

The Vampire's Bride, or, the Perils of Cinderella (1978)

By Maureen Exter. Denver, CO: Pioneer Drama Service.

Vampires in Chicago (1991)

By Patrick Couillard.

A one-act play that opened in Chicago at the Raven Theatre in the Fall of 1991.

The Vampires Strike Out (1985)

By Peter Walker. Boston: Baker's Plays, 1985.

The Vampyre (1988)

By Tim Kelly. New York: Dramatists Play Service.

Based on ''The Vampyre'' by John Polidori.

Varney the Vampire; or, The Feast of Blood: A Ghoulish Spoof in Two Acts (1990)

By Tim Kelly. New York: Samuel French.

Young Dracula, or, the Singing Bat (1975)

By Tim Kelly. Denver, CO: Pioneer Drama Service.

VAMPIRE OPERA

Der Vampyr (1828)

By C. M. Heigel (libretto) and P. von Lindpainter (music).

Produced at Stuttgart on September 21, 1828. Based on Polidori. Cf. Summers p 312.

Der Wampyr (1828)

By Heinrich Marschner (music) and Wilhelm August Wohlbrück (libretto).

German opera based on John Polidori's ''The Vampyre.'' Cf. Summer 311.

I Vampiri (1800)

By Silvestro de Palma.

Performed at the Theatre San Carlos. Based on nonfiction treatise on the vampire by Giuseppe Davanzati. Cf Summers 311.

Le Vampire (1826)

By Martin Joseph Mengals.

Opened at Ghent, Belgium on March 1, 1826. Cf Summers 306.

The Vampire; or, The Bride of the Isles (1820)

By J. R. Planché.

An English translation and adaptation of Charles Nodier's *Le Vampire;* it opened at the English Opera House in London in 1820; an abridged version is in M. Kilgariff, ed. *The Golden Age of Melodrama* (Boston: Baker's Plays, 1974) Cf Summer, 306.

VAMPIRE BALLET

Dracula (1987)

By Charles Bennett.
  Opened in San Diego, California, November 1987.

Il Vampiro (1861)

By Rotta and Paolo Giorza (music).
  Opened at Milan.

Morgano (1857)

By Paul Taglioni and J. Hertzel (music).
  A comic piece. Cf Summers 312.

VAMPIRE NOVELS

This list is limited to vampire novels published in the English language and does not include novels in which a vampire merely makes a cameo appearance, role playing game modules, juvenile fiction, or volumes of collected horror or vampire short fiction. The list includes novels that feature the ordinary vampire, but also novels about psychic vampirism, vampires from outer space, and mythological vampirelike deities and demons (such as the *lamiai*). The list is arranged chronologically in three sections:

- Vampire Novels through 1969
- Vampire Novels, 1970 to the Present
- Dark Shadows Novels, 1969 to the Present

Entries include author name(s); novel name; publisher name and year; number of pages; and information on any reprints of that title.

VAMPIRE NOVELS THROUGH 1969

Ascher, Eugene (pseudonym of Harold Ernest Kelly). *There Were No Asper Ladies.* London: Mitre Press, 1944. 126 pp. Reprinted as: *To Kill a Corpse.* Manchester, UK: World Distributors, 1965. 160 pp.

Atholl, Justin. *The Grey Beast.* London: Everybody's Books, n.d.

Baldwin, E. E. *The Strange Story of Dr. Senex.* New York: Minerva, 1891.

Ballard, James Graham. *The Day of Forever.* London: Panther, 1967.

Barrie, James Matthew. *Farewell, Miss Julie Logan: A Wintry Tale.* London: Hodder & Stoughton, 1932. 98 pp. Reprinted: New York: Charles Scribner's Sons, 1932.

Blackburn, John. *Children of the Night.* London: J. Cape, 1966.

Bok. *Vampires of the China Coast.* London: Herbert Jenkins, 1932.

Bradley, Marion Zimmer. *Falcons of Narabedia.* New York: Ace Books, 1964.

Brown, Carter. *So What Killed the Vampire.* New York: New American Library, 1966. 127 pp.

Burke, John. *Dr. Terror's House of Horrors.* London: Pan Books, 1965.

————. *Dracula: Prince of Darkness.* London: Pan Books, 1967. 144 pp.

Burke, Noah. *The Scarlet Vampire.* London: S. Paul, 1936.

Carew, Henry. *The Vampires of the Andes.* London: Jarrold, 1925.

Carlisle, Robin. *Blood and Roses.* New York: Hillman, 1960.

Carr, John Dickson. *He Who Whispers.* London: Hamish Hamilton, 1946. 227 pp. Reprinted: New York: Bantam, 1965. 165

pp. Reprinted: New York: Universal-Award House, 1976. 219 pp.

———. *The Three Coffins.* New York: Harper & Brothers, 1935. 306 pp. Reprinted: New York: Award Books, 1974. 222 pp. Reprinted: Boston: Gregg Press, 1979. 306 pp.

Carter, Nicholas. *The Vampire's Trail; or, Nick Carter and the Policy King.* New York: Street and Smith, 1910.

Chaytor, Henry John. *The Light of the Eye.* London: Dogby, Long, and Co., 1897.

Cobban, James Maclaren. *Master of His Fate.* London: W. Blackwood and Sons, 1890.

Cooper, Gordon. *I Searched the World for Death.* 1940. Reprinted: London: J. Long, 1980. 287 pp.

Corbett, James. *Vampire in the Skies.* London: Herbert Jenkins, 1932. 248 pp.

Cullum, Ridgwell. *The Vampire of N'Gobi.* London: Chapman and Hall, 1935.

Dalman, Max. *Vampire Abroad.* London: Ward, Lock, 1938.

Daly, Carroll Jones. *The Legion of the Living Dead.* London, Popular, 1947.

Daniels, Cora Lin. *Sardia: A Story of Love.* Boston: Lee and Shepard, 1891.

Davy, S. *Gay Vampire.* New York: 101 Books, 1969.

De la Mare, Walter. *The Return.* London: Arnold, 1910.

Dunn, Gertrude (pseudonym of Gertrude Renton Weaver). *The Mark of the Bat: A Tale of Vampires Living and Dead.* London: T. Butterworth, 1928.

Everett, Henrietta Dorothy. *Malevola.* London: Heath, Cranton, and Ouseley, 1914.

Ewers, Hans-Heinz. *Vampire.* New York: John Day Co., 1934. 363 pp. Reprinted as: *Vampire's Prey.* London: Jarrolds, 1937. 320 pp.

Farrere, Claude. *The House of the Secret.* Trans. by Arthur Livingston. London: John Dent, 1923.

Fortune, Dion. *The Demon Lover.* London: Noel Douglas, 1931. 286 pp. Reprinted: London: Aquarian Publishing Co., 1957. 287 pp. Reprinted: New York: Samuel Weiser, 1972. 1980. 286 pp. Reprinted: London: Wyndham/Star Books, 1976. 174 pp.

Fox, Marion. *Ape's-Face.* London: John Lane, 1914. Reprinted: Bell and Cockburn.

Fredrick, Otto. *Count Dracula's Canadian Affair.* New York: Pageant Press, 1960.

Galvin, George W. *A Thousand Faces.* Boston: Four Seas, 1920.

Gaskell, Jane. *The Shiny Narrow Grin.* London: Hodder, 1964.

Gautier, Theophile. *The Beautiful Vampire.* London: A. M. Philpot, 1926.

Gibbons, Cromwell. *The Bat Woman.* New York: World, 1938.

Giles, Raymond. *Night of the Vampire.* New York: Avon, 1969. 126 pp. Reprinted: London: New English Library, 1970. 126 pp.

Gordon, Julien. *Vampires: Mademoiselle Réseda.* Philadelphia: J. B. Lippencott, 1891. 299 pp.

Halidom, M. Y. *The Woman in Black.* London: Greening, 1906.

Harmon, Jim. *The Man Who Made Maniacs.* Los Angeles: Epic/Art Enterprises, 1961.

Heron-Allen, Edward. *The Princess Daphne.* London: H. J. Drane, 1888. Reprinted: Belford, Clarke, 1888. Reprinted: New York: National Book Co., 1888.

Heyse, Paul. *The Fair Abigail.* New York: Dodd, Mead & Co., 1894.

Hodder, William Reginald. *The Vampire.* London: William Rider and Son, 1913. 306 pp.

Holland, Clive. *An Egyptian Coquette.* London: C. A. Pearson, 1898.

Home-Gail, Edward Reginald. *The Human Bat.* London: Mark Goulden, Ltd., 1940.

Horler, Sidney. *The Curse of Doone.* London: Hodder and Stoughton, 1928.

———. *The Vampire.* London: Hutchinson & Co., 1935. 288 pp. Reprinted: New York: Bookfinger, 1974. 288 pp.

Howard, Robert Erwin. *Conan the Conqueror: The Hyborean Age.* New York: Gnome Press, 1950. 255 pp.

———. *The House of Arabu.* New York: Avon, 1951.

———. *Skull-Face and Others.* Sauk City, WI: Arkham House, 1946. 475 pp. Reprinted as: *The Valley of Worms & Others.* St. Albans, UK: Panther, 1976. 236 pp.

Hume, Fergus. *A Creature of the Night.* London: R. E. King, 1891. Reprinted: New York: J. W. Lovell Company, 1891. Reprinted: London: Sampson, Lowe, Marston, 1893.

Hyder, Alan. *Vampires Overhead.* London: Philip Allan, 1935.

Jakes, John William. *Brak the Barbarian Versus the Sorceress.* New York: Paperback Library, 1969.

Jolly, Stratford D. *The Soul of the Moor.* London: William Rider, 1911. 226 pp.

Jones, P. *The Pobratim.* London: H. S. Nichols, 1895.

Judd, A. M. *The White Vampire.* London: John Long, 1914. 319 pp.

Karlova, Irina. *Dreadful Hollow.* New York: Dell Publishing, 1942. 240 pp. Reprinted: London: Hurst and Blackett, 1942. Reprinted: New York: Paperback Library, 1965. 221 pp.

Kerruish, Jessie Douglas. *The Undying Monster.* London: Philip Allan, 1968. Reprinted: New York: Award Books, 1970. 218 pp. Reprinted: London: Tandem, 1970. 218 pp.

King, T. Stanleyan. *Vampire City.* Mellifont, 1935.

Knight, Mallory (pseudonym of Bernhardt Hurwood). *Dracutwig.* New York: Award Books, 1969. 156 pp.

Kolbe, John A. *Vampires of Vengeance.* Fiction House, 1935.

Lambourne, John. *The Unmeasured Place.* London: John Murray, 1933.

Lang, Andrew. *The Disentanglers.* New York: Longmans, Green, 1901. Rev. ed.: New York: Longmans, Green, 1902.

Layland-Barratt, Lady Frances. *Lycanthia.* London: Herbert Jenkins, 1935.

LeFanu, J. Sheridan. *The Vampire Lovers.* London: Fontana, 1870.

Leroux, Gaston. *The Kiss That Killed.* New York: Macauley, 1934.

Lewis, Jack. *Blood Money.* Los Angeles: Headline Books, 1960.

Long, Frank Belknap. *The Horror from the Hills.* Sauk City, WI: Arkham House, 1963.

McDaniel, David. *The Vampire Affair.* New York: Ace Books, 1966. 159 pp. Man from U.N.C.L.E. venture.

MacDonald, George. *Lilith.* London: Chatto and Windus, 1895.

Marryat, Florence. *The Blood of the Vampire.* London: Hutchinson, 1897.

Matheson, Richard. *I Am Legend.* New York: Fawcett, 1954. 160 pp. Reprinted: New York: Berkley, 1971. 174 pp.

Matson, Norman. *Bats in the Belfry.* Garden City, New York: Doubleday, 1943.

Merritt, Abraham. *Creep, Shadow!* Garden City, New York: Doubleday, 1934.

———. *The Moon Pool.* 1919.

Metcalfe, John. *The Feasting Dead.* Sauk City, WI: Arkham House, 1954.

Mirbeau, Octave. *A Chinese Torture Garden.* New York: Award Books, 1969. 158

pp. Reprinted as: *The Garden of Tortures.* London: Tadem, 1969. 158 pp.

Neutzal, Charles. *Queen of Blood.* San Diego, CA: Greenleaf, 1966.

Nicolson, John W. *Fingers of Fear.* New York: Covici-Friede, 1937.

Nile, Dorothea (pseudonym of Michael Avellone). *The Vampire Cameo.* New York: Lancer, 1968. 190 pp.

Owen, Dean. *The Brides of Dracula.* New York: Monarch, 1960.

Paul, F. W. *The Orgy at Madame Dracula's.* New York: Lancer, 1968.

Paul, Hugo. *Master of the Undead.* New York: Lancer, 1968.

Perucho, Joan. *Natural History—A Novel.* 1960. Reprinted: New York: Ballantine Books, 1988. 186 pp.

Peterson, Margaret. *Moonflowers.* London: Hutchinson, 1962.

Phillips, Mickey. *Blood Rare.* London: Michael Joseph, 1963.

Raven, Simon. *Doctors Wear Scarlet.* London: A. Blond, 1960. 240 pp. Reprinted: New York: Simon & Schuster, 1961. 252 pp.

Raymond, Alex. *Jungle Jim and the Vampire Woman.* Racine, WI: Whitman, 1937. 424 pp.

Reeve, Arthur B. *The Exploits of Elaine.* New York: Harper and Brothers, 1915; Reprinted: New York: Hearst's International Library Co., 1915.

Rohmer, Sax (pseudonym of Arthur Henry Ward). *Brood of the Witch- Queen.* London: C. A. Pearson, 1918.

———. *Grey Face.* London: Cassell and Co., 1924.

Ross, Clarisa. *Secret of the Pale Lover.* New York: Magnum Books, 1969. 222 pp.

Ryan, Rachel R. *The Echo of a Curse.* London: Herbert Jenkins, 1939.

Rymer, James Malcolm. *Varney the Vampire: or, the Feast of Blood.* London: E. Lloyd, 1847. 868 pp. Reprinted: New York: Arno Press, 1970. 868 pp. Reprinted: New York: Dover Publications, 1972. 868 pp.

Sawbridge, M. C. *The Vampire.* London: George Allen and Unwin, 1920.

Saxon, Peter (pseudonym of W. Howard Baker and Wilfred G. McNeilly). *The Darkest Night.* London: Mayflower Books, 1966. Reprinted: New York: Paperback Library.

——— (pseudonym of W. Howard Baker and Stephen D. Frances). *The Disoriented Man.* London: Mayflower, 1966.

——— (pseudonym of W. Howard Baker). *Scream and Scream Again.* New York: Paperback Library, 1967.

——— (pseudonym of W. Howard Baker and Wilfred G. McNeilly). *The Torturer.* London: Mayflower Books, 1966. 159 pp. Reprinted: New York: Paperback Library, 1967.

Sloane, William. *The Unquiet Corpse.* New York: Dell, 1956.

Smith, Henry George. *Scourge of the Blood Cult.* Los Angeles: Epic, 1961.

Stanton, Edward. *Dreams of the Dead.* Boston: Lee and Shepard, 1892. 268 pp.

Stoker, Bram. *Dracula.* Westminster: Constable, 1897. Frequently reprinted.

Stone, Elna. *Secret of the Willows.* New York: Modern Promotions, 1911.

Sturgeon, Theodore. *Some of Your Blood.* New York: Ballantine, 1961. 143 pp.

Taylor, C. Bryson. *In the Dwellings of the Wilderness.* New York: H. Holt and Company, 1904.

Tyson, John A. *The Barge of Haunted Lives.* New York: Macmillan Company, 1923.

Upton, Smyth. *The Last of the Vampires.* N.p.: Columbian, 1845.

Urquart, Maurice. *The Island of Souls.* London: Mills and Boon, 1910.

The Vampire; or, Detective Brand's Greatest Case. Norman H. Munro, 1885.

Verner, Herald. *The Vampire Men.* London: Wright and Brown, 1941.

Viereck, George. *The House of the Vampire.* New York: Moffat, Yard & Co., 1907. 190 pp.

Waugh, Michael. *Fangs of the Vampire.* Cleveland, OH: 1934.

Webber, Charles Wilkins. *Spiritual Vampirism; The History of Etherial Softdown and Her Friends of the "New Light."* Philadelphia: The Author, 1853.

Williams, Thaddeus W. *In Quest of Life; or, The Revelations of the Wiyatatao of Ipantl. The Last High Priest of the Aztecs.* London: F. T. Neely, 1898.

Williamson, Jack. *Darker Than You Think.* Reading, PA: Fantasy Press, 1948.

Wood, Edward D., Jr. *Orgy of the Dead.* San Diego, CA: Greenleaf Classics, 1966.

VAMPIRE NOVELS, 1970 TO THE PRESENT

Acres, Mark. *Dark Divide.* (Runesworld No. 5) New York: Ace Books, 1991. 183 pp.

Adams, Nicholas. *Vampire's Kiss.* New York: HarperColllins, 1994. 211 pp.

The Adult Version of Dracula. Los Angeles: Calga Publishers, 1970.

Aldiss, Brian W. *Dracula Unbound.* New York: HarperCollins Publishers, 1991. 273 pp.

———. *The Saliva Tree.* 1966. Reprinted: New York: TOR Books, 1988. 87 pp. (Bound with Robert Silverberg, *Born with the Dead.*)

Alexander, Jan. *Moon Blood.* New York: Lancer Books, 1970. 224 pp. Reprinted in: *Shadows.* New York: Lancer, 1972. 224 pp.

———. *The Glass Painting.* New York: Popular Library, 1972. 224 pp.

Alexander, Karl. *The Curse of the Vampire.* New York: Pinnacle Books, 1972. 310 pp.

Anderson, Dean. *I Am Dracula.* New York: Zebra Books, 1993. 350 pp.

———. *Raw Pain Max.* New York: Popular Library, 1988. 260 pp.

Anthony, Piers (pseudonym of Piers Anthony Dillingham Jacobs). *Firefly.* New York: Morrow, 1990. 384 pp. Reprinted: New York: Avon, 1992. 446 pp.

Armstrong, F. W. *The Devouring.* New York: TOR, 1987. 284 pp.

Askew, Jackie. *SunDown . . . SunRise.* Chessington, Surrey, UK: NightShade Publications, 1993. 416 pp.

Aspirin, Robert Lynn. *Myth-ing Persons.* (Skeeve No. 5) Norfolk, VA: Donning, 1984. 170 pp.

Atkins, Peter. *Morningstar.* New York: HarperCollins, 1992. 287 pp.

Aubin, Etienne. *Dracula and the Virgins of the Undead.* London: New English Library, 1974. 124 pp.

Avallone, Michael. *One More Time.* New York: Popular Library, 1970. 144 pp.

Bainbridge, Sharon. *Blood and Roses.* New York: Diamond Books, 1994. 280 pp.

Baker, Scott. *Dhampire.* New York: Pocket Books, 1982. 260 pp.

———. *Nightchild.* (Ashlu Cycle No. 1) New York: Berkley Publishing Corporation, 1979. 273 pp. Rev. ed.: New York: Pocket Books, 1983. 255 pp.

Baker, Sharon. *Burning Tears of Sassurum.* New York: Avon, 1988. 280 pp.

———. *Journey to Memblair.* New York: Avon, 1987. 247 pp.

Ball, Brian. *The Venomous Serpent.* London: New English Library, 1974. Reprinted as: *The Night Creature.* New York: Fawcett, 1974. 159 pp.

Ball, Margaret. *The Shadow Gate.* New York: Baen, 1991. 346 pp.

Barker, Clive. *Cabal.* New York: Poseidon Press, 1988. 377 pp. Rev. ed. as: *Cabal: The Nightbreed.* Toronto: A. Collins, 1989. 268 pp.

————. *The Thief of Always.* New York: HarperCollins, 1992. Reprinted: New York: HarperPaperbacks, 1993. 167 pp.

Barnes, Linda. *Blood Will Have Blood.* New York: Avon, 1982. 191 pp.

Behm, Mark. *The Ice Maiden.* 1982. Reprinted in: *The Eye of the Beholder.* London: Zomba, 1983. 462 pp.

Bergstrom, Elaine. *Blood Rites.* New York: Jove Books, 1991. 332 pp.

————. *Daughter of the Night.* New York: Berkley, 1992. 323 pp.

————. *Blood Alone.* New York: Jove Books, 1990. 325 pp.

————. *Shattered Glass.* New York: Jove Books, 1989. 372 pp.

————. *Tapestry of Dark Souls.* Geneva, WI: TSR, Inc., 1993.

Billson, Anne. *Suckers.* London: Pan Books, 1993. 315 pp.

Bischoff, David. *Nightworld.* New York: Ballantine Books, 1979. 197 pp.

————. *Vampires of Nightworld.* New York: Ballantine Books, 1981. 182 pp.

Black, Campbell. *The Wanting.* New York: McGraw-Hill Book Co., 1986. 263 pp.

Blackburn, John. *Our Lady of Pain.* London: Jonathan Cape, 1974. 191 pp.

Blackburn, Thomas. *The Feast of the Wolf.* London: McGibbon and Kee, 1971. 158 pp.

Blacque, Dovya. *South of Heaven.* Poway, CA: MKASHEF Enterprises, 1991.

Blatty, William Peter. *Legion.* New York: Simon & Schuster, 1983. 250 pp. New York: Pocket Books, 1984. 310 pp.

Bloch, Robert. *It's All In Your Mind.* New York: Modern Literary Editions Pub. Co., 1971. 128 pp.

Bond, Edlyne. *Miranda.* Lawndale, CA: Phantom Press, 1982.

Brand, Chris. *Trail of the Vampire.* London: Grayling Publishing Co., n.d.

Brandner, Gary. *Carrion.* New York: Fawcett, 1986.

Brett, Stephen. *The Vampire Chase.* New York: Manor Books, 1979. 213 pp.

Briery, Traci. *The Vampire Journals.* New York: Zebra Books, 1993. 349 pp.

Briscoe, Pat. *The Other People.* Reseda, CA: Powell Publications, 1970. 204 pp.

Brite, P. Z. *Lost Souls.* New York: Dell, 1992. 355 pp.

Brooks-Janowiak, Jean. *Winter Lord.* New York: New American Library, 1982. 186 pp.

Brust, Steven. *Agyar.* New York: TOR, 1993. 254 pp.

Buchanan, Kelly. *Rasputin's Vintage.* Carpinteria, CA: XAXI Press, 1987. 239 pp.

Burnett-Swan, Thomas. *The Not-World.* New York: DAW Books, 1975. 160 pp.

Bussiere, Giles. *Survival of the Fittest.* Montreal: Ianus, 1993.

Butler, Jack. *Nightshade.* New York: Atlantic Monthly Press, 1989. 276 pp.

Butler, Octavia E. *Clay's Ark.* New York: St. Martin's Press, 1984. 186 pp. New York: Ace Books, 1985. 201 pp.

————. *Imago.* New York: Popular Library, 1990. 220 pp.

————. *Mind of My Mind.* Garden City, New York: Doubleday, 1977. 168 pp. Reprinted: London: Sphere, 1980. 220 pp.

————. *Patternmaster.* Garden City, New York: Doubleday, 1976. 186 pp. Reprinted: London: Sphere, 1978. 176

pp. Reprinted: New York: Avon, 1979.
160 pp.

―――. *Wild Seed.* Garden City, New
York: Doubleday, 1980. 248 pp.

Byers, Richard Lee. *The Vampire's Apprentice.* New York: Zebra Books, 1992.
288 pp.

Caine, Geoffrey. *Curse of the Vampire.*
New York: Diamond Books, 1991.
247 pp.

Campbell, J. Ramsey. *To Wake the Dead.*
London: Millington, 1980. 316 pp. Rev.
ed. as: *The Parasite.* New York: Macmillan Company, 1980. 267 pp.

Carlson, Dale, and Danny Carlson. *The
Shining Pool.* New York:
Athenaeum, 1979.

Carter, Lin. *Thonger of Lemuria.* 1966.
Rev. ed. as: *Thonger and the Dragon
City.* New York: Berkley Publishing
Corporation, 1970. 143 pp.

Carter, Margaret L. *Payer of Tribute.*
Metairie, LA: Baker Street
Publications, 1989.

Cave, Hugh B. *Disciples of Dread.* New
York: TOR, 1988. 376 pp.

Cecilone, Michael. *Domination.* New York:
Zebra Books, 1993. 446 pp.

Charles, Robert. *Flowers of Evil.* London:
Futura, 1981. Reprinted: New York:
Bantam, 1982. 200 pp.

Charnas, Suzy McKee. *The Vampire Tapestry.* New York: Simon & Schuster,
1980. Reprinted: New York: TOR, 1986.
Reprinted: Albuquerque, NM: Living
Batch Press, 1980. 285 pp.

Cherryh, C. J. *Rusalka.* New York:
Ballantine Books, 1989. 310 pp. Reprinted: London: Methuen, 1990. 373 pp.

―――. *Yvgenie.* New York: Ballantine,
1991. 311 pp.

Chetwynd-Hayes, Ronald. *The Partaker.*
London: William Kimber, 1980. 224 pp.

Ciencin, Scott. *Parliament of Blood.* New
York: Zebra Books, 1992. 415 pp.

―――. *The Vampire Odyssey.* New
York: Zebra Books, 1992. 415 pp.

―――. *The Wildlings.* New York: Zebra
Books, 1992. 415 pp.

Cilescu, Valentina. *Kiss of Death.* London:
Headline Book Publishing, 1992. 375 pp.

―――. *The Phallus of Osiris.* London:
Headline Book Publishing, 1993.

Clayton, Jo. *Blue Magic.* New York: DAW
Books, 1988. 333 pp.

―――. *Drinker of Souls.* New York:
DAW Books, 1986. 335 pp.

―――. *A Gathering of Stones.* New
York: DAW Books, 1989. 368 pp.

Clewitt, George Charles. *Blood Dynasty.*
London: New English Library, 1973.

Coffman, Virginia. *The Vampire of Moura.*
New York: Ace Books, 1970. 265 pp.

Coleman, Preston. *The Oinky Boinky Machine.* Athens, GA: Piccolo Press, 1992.

Collins, Nancy. *Cold Turkey.* Holyoke,
MA: Crossroads Press, 1992.

―――. *In the Blood.* New York: ROC,
1992. 302 pp.

―――. *Sunglasses After Dark.* New
York: New American Library, 1989.
253 pp.

―――. *Tempter.* New York: New
American Library, 1990. Reprinted: London: Futura, 1990. 299 pp.

Combs, David. *The Intrusion.* New York:
Avon, 1981. 221 pp.

Constantine, Storm. *Burying the Shadow.*
London: Headline, 1992. 406 pp.

Cook, Glen. *Sweet Silver Blues.* New York:
New American Library, 1987. 255 pp.

―――. *The Swordbearer.* New York:
Pocket Books, 982. 239 pp.

Cooke, John Peyton. *Out for Blood.* New
York: Avon, 1991. 313 pp.

Cooper, Louise. *Blood Summer*. London: New English Library, 1976. 127 pp.

———. *In Memory of Sarah Bailey*. London: New English Library, 1977. 143 pp.

Courtney, Vincent. *Harvest of Blood*. New York: Pinnacle Books, 1992. 384 pp.

———. *Vampire Beat*. New York: Pinnacle Books, 1991. 302 pp.

Daniels, Les. *The Black Castle*. New York: Charles Scribner's Sons, 1978. 241 pp. Reprinted: New York: Berkley Books, 1979. 232 pp.

———. *Citizen Vampire*. New York: Charles Scribner's Sons, 1981. 199 pp.

———. *No Blood Spilled*. New York: TOR, 1991. 218 pp.

———. *The Silver Skull*. New York: Charles Scribner's Sons, 1979. 222 pp. Reprinted: New York: Ace Books, 1983. 234 pp.

———. *Yellow Fog*. West Kingston, RI: Donald M. Grant, 1986. Reprinted: New York: TOR, 1988. 294 pp.

Daniels, Philip. *The Dracula Murders*. London: Robert Hale, 1983. Reprinted: New York: Lorevan Publishing, 1983. 190 pp.

Darke, David. *Blind Hunger*. New York: Pinnacle Books, 1993. 254 pp.

Darrid, William. *The Brooding*. Toronto: Bantam Books, 1979. 311 pp.

David, Michael. *Nighthag*. Huntington, WV: University Editions, 1992. 105 pp.

David, Peter. *Howling Mad*. New York: Ace Books, 1989. 201 pp.

Davis, Jay, and Don Davis. *Bring on the Night*. New York: TOR, 1993. 403 pp.

Dear, Ian. *Village of Blood*. London: New England Library, 1975. 128 pp.

Dee, Ron. *Blood*. New York: Pocket Books, 1993. 309 pp.

———. *Blood Lust*. New York: Dell, 1990. 264 pp.

———. *Dusk*. New York: Dell, 1991. 369 pp.

Deitz, Tom. *Soulsmith*. New York: Avon, 1991. 449 pp.

DeLint, Charles (pseudonym of Henri Diederick Hoefsmit). *The Dreaming Place*. New York: Athenaeum, 1990. 138 pp.

———. *Drink Down the Moon*. New York: Ace Books, 1990. 216 pp.

———. *Yarrow: An Autumn Tale*. New York: Ace Books, 1986. 244 pp.

DeWeese, Gene. *The Wanting Factor*. New York: Playboy, 1980. 303 pp.

Dicks, Terrance. *Doctor Who and the State of Decay*. London: W. H. Allen, 1981. 125 pp.

———. *Cry Vampire*. Glasgow: Blackie & Son, 1981. 111 pp.

———. *My Brother the Vampire*. London: Piccadilly, 1990. 91 pp. Reprinted: Hauppage, NY: Barron's, 1992.

Dillard, Jeanne M. *Bloodthirst*. Star Trek No. 37. New York: Pocket Books, 1987. 264 pp.

———. *Covenant with the Vampires: The Diaries of the Families Dracula*. New York: Dell Abyss, 1994.

———. *Demons*. Star Trek No. 30. New York: Pocket Books, 1986. 271 pp.

Dobbin, Muriel. *A Taste for Power*. New York: Richard Marek, 1980. 238 pp.

Douglas, Drake. *Creature*. New York: Leisure Books, 1985. 396 pp.

Douglas, L. W. *In the Blood*. Tallahassee, FL: Naiad Press, 1989. 242 pp.

The Dracula Collection. London: Octopus Books, 1981. 80 pp.

Drake, Asa. *Crimson Kisses*. New York: Avon, 1981. 292 pp.

Dreadstone, Carl (pseudonym of Ramsey Campbell). *Dracula's Daughter*. New York: Berkley, 1977. 212 pp.

Duigon, Lee. *Lifeblood*. New York: Pinnacle Books, 1988. 432 pp.

Durrell, Alan. *Balthazar*. London: Faber & Faber, 1958. 250 pp.

Dvorkin, David. *Insatiable*. New York: Pinnacle Books, 1993. 318 pp.

Eccarias, J. G. *The Last Days of Christ the Vampire*. San Diego, CA: III Publishing, 1988. 180 pp.

Edelman, Scott. *The Gift*. New York: Space and Time, 1990. 178 pp.

Eliot, Marc. *How Dear the Dawn*. New York: Ballantine Books, 1987.

Elrod, P. N. *Art in the Blood*. New York: Ace Books, 1991. 195 pp.

———. *Blood on the Water*. New York: Ace Books, 1992. 199 pp.

———. *Bloodcircle*. New York: Ace Books, 1990. 202 pp.

———. *Bloodlist*. New York: Ace Books, 1990. 200 pp.

———. *Fire in the Blood*. New York: Ace Books, 1991. 198 pp.

———. *Lifeblood*. New York: Ace Books, 1990. 202 pp.

———. *Red Death*. New York: Ace Books, 1993. 288 pp.

Engstrom, Elizabeth. *Black Ambrosa*. New York: Tom Doherty, 1988. 341 pp.

Erwin, Alan. *Skeleton Dancer*. New York: Dell, 1989. 265 pp.

Estleman, Loren. *Sherlock Holmes vs. Dracula*. New York: Doubleday, 1978. 214 pp. Reprinted: New York: Penguin, 1979. 214 pp.

Eulo, Ken. *The House of Caine*. New York: TOR, 1988. 501 pp.

Fahy, Chris. *The Lyssa Syndrome*. New York: Zebra Books, Kensington, 1990. 352 pp.

Falk, Lee. *The Vampires and the Witch*. New York: Avon, 1974. 300 pp.

Farmer, Philip Jose. *The Image of the Beast*. London: Quartet, 1975. 175 pp. Reprinted: New York: Playboy, 1979. 336 pp. Reprinted: New York: Berkley Publishing Company, 1985. 336 pp.

Farrar, Stewart. *The Dance of Blood*. London: Arrow, 1977. 235 pp.

Farrington, Geoffrey. *The Revenants*. London: Dedalus, 1983. 168 pp.

Farris, John. *All Heads Turn When the Hunt Goes By*. Chicago: Playboy Press, 1977. 364 pp. Reprinted: New York: TOR, 1986. 364 pp.

———. *The Catacombs*. New York: Delacorte Press, 1981. 439 pp.

———. *Fiends*. Arlington Heights, IL: Dark Harvest, 1991. 314 pp. Reprinted: New York: TOR, 1990. 438 pp.

Fearn, John Russell. *No Grave Need I*. Wallsend, UK: Philip Harbottle, 1984. Reprinted: San Bernardino, CA: Borgo Press, 1987. 42 pp.

Fenn, Lionel. *The Mask of the Moderately Vicious Vampire*. New York: Ace Books, 1992. 202 pp.

Fields, Morgan. *Deadly Harvest*. New York: Zebra Books, Kensington, 1989. 357 pp.

Firth, N. Wesley. *Spawn of the Vampire*. London: Bear, n.d.

Fitch, Ed. *Castle of Deception*. St. Paul, MN: Llewellyn Publications, 1983. 263 pp.

Flanders, Eric. *Night Blood*. New York: Zebra Books, 1993. 381 pp.

Fleming, Nigel. *To Love a Vampire*. Encino, CA: World-Wide Publishing, 1980. 187 pp.

Ford, John M. *The Dragon Waiting: A Mask of History*. New York: Timescape Books, 1983. 365 pp.

Forest, Salambo. *Witch Power.* New York: Olympia Press, 1971. 215 pp.

Foster, Alan Dean. *The Thing: A Novel.* New York: Bantam Books, 1982. 196 pp.

Foster, Prudence. *Blood Legacy.* New York: Pocket Books, 1989. 252 pp.

Freed, L. A. *Blood Thirst.* New York: Pinnacle Books, 1989. 384 pp.

Freeza, Robert. *McLendon Syndrome.* New York: Ballantine/Del Rey, 1993. 313 pp.

Friedman, C. S. *The Madness Season.* New York: DAW Books, 1990. 490 pp.

Gallagher, Stephen. *Valley of Lights.* New York: TOR, 1988. 276 pp.

Gannett, Lewis. *The Living One.* New York: Random House, 1993. 380 pp.

Gardine, Michael. *Lamia.* New York: Dell, 1981. 186 pp.

Gardner, Craig S. *The Lost Boys.* New York: Berkley, 1987. 220 pp.

Garnett, Bill. *The Crone.* London: Sphere Books, 1984. 215 pp.

Garton, Ray. *Live Girls.* New York: Pocket Books, 1987. 311 pp.

———. *Lot Lizards.* Shingletown, CA: Mark Ziesing, 1991.

———. *The New Neighbor.* Lynbrook, New York: Charnel House, 1991.

———. *Seductions.* New York: Pinnacle Books, 1984. 277 pp.

Geare, Michael and Michael Corby. *Dracula's Diary.* New York: Beaufort Books, 1982. 153 pp.

Gemmell, David. *Morning Star.* London: Century Legend, 1992. 281 pp. Reprinted as: *Morningstar.* New York: Ballantine Books, 1993. 290 pp.

George, Stephen R. *Beasts.* New York: Zebra Books, Kensington, 1989.

Gerrold, David. *Under the Eye of God.* New York: Bantam Books, 1993. 328 pp.

Gideon, John. *Greeley's Cove.* New York: Jove, 1991. 422 pp. Reprinted: London: Headline, 1991. 422 pp.

Glenn, N. T. *Clinking Stones.* Tallahassee, FL: Naiad Press, 1989. 269 pp.

Glut, Donald. *Frankenstein and the Evil of Frankenstein.* London: New English Library, 1975.

———. *Frankenstein Meets Dracula.* London: New English Library, 1977. 140 pp.

Goddin, Jeffrey. *The Living Dead.* New York: Leisure Books, 1987. 383 pp.

Golden, Christie. *Dance of the Dead.* Lake Geneva, WI: TSR, 1992. 310 pp.

———. *Vampire of the Mists.* Lake Geneva, WI: TSR, 1991. 341 pp.

Gomez, Jewelle. *The Gilda Stories.* Ithaca, New York: Firebrand Books, 1991. 252 pp.

Goulart, Ron. *Blood Wedding.* New York: Warner Books, 1976. 140 pp. Reprinted: London: Sphere Books, 1976. 140 pp.

———. *Bloodstalk.* New York: Warner Books, 1975. 141 pp. Reprinted: London: Sphere Books, 1975. 141 pp.

———. *The Curse of the Obelisk.* New York: Avon, 1987. 139 pp.

———. *Deadwalk.* New York: Warner Books, 1976. 144 pp. Reprinted: London: Sphere Books, 1976. 144 pp.

———. *Deathgame.* New York: Warner Books, 1976. 142 pp. Reprinted: London: Sphere Books, 1976. 142 pp.

———. *On Alien Wings.* New York: Warner Books, 1975. 138 pp. Reprinted: London: Sphere Books, 1975. 138 pp.

———. *The Prisoner of Blackwood Castle.* New York: Avon, 1984. 174 pp.

———. *Snakegod.* New York: Warner Books, 1976. 144 pp. Reprinted: London: Sphere Books, 1976. 144 pp.

Grant, Charles L. *The Bloodwind.* New York: Fawcett Popular Library, 1982. 223 pp.

———. *Doom City.* New York: TOR, 1987. 307 pp.

———. *The Fear of the Night.* New York: TOR, 1988. 277 pp.

———. *The Hour of the Oxrun Dead.* New York: Popular Library, 1977. 192 pp.

———. *The Nesting.* New York: Pocket Books, 1982. 406 pp.

———. *The Soft Whisper of the Dead.* West Kingston, RI: Donald M. Grant, 1982. 159 pp.

Grant, Cynthia. *Uncle Vampire.* New York: Athenaeum., 1993. 151 pp.

Graversen, Pat. *Precious Blood.* New York: Zebra Books, 1993. 251 pp.

———. *Sweet Blood.* New York: Zebra Books, 1992. 254 pp.

Gresham, Stephen. *Blood Wings.* New York: Zebra Books, 1990. 383 pp.

Griffith, Kathryn Meyer. *The Last Vampire.* New York: Zebra Books, 1992. 352 pp.

———. *Vampire Blood.* New York: Zebra Books, 1991. 285 pp.

Guigonnat, Henri. *Daemon in Lithuania.* New York: New Directions, 1985. 136 pp. (Trans. of *Démone en Lituanie.*)

Halkim, John. *Blood Worm.* New York: Lorevan, 1988. 251 pp.

Hall, Angus. *The Scars of Dracula.* London: Sphere Books, 1971. 140 pp. Reprinted: New York: Beagle Books, 1971. 140 pp.

Hambly, Barbara. *Immortal Blood.* London: Unwin Paperbacks, 1988. 306 pp.

———. *Those Who Hunt the Night.* New York: Ballantine Books, 1988. 340 pp.

———. *The Witches of Wenshar.* New York: Ballantine Books, 1987. 339 pp.

Hamilton, Laurell K. *Guilty Pleasures.* New York: Ace Books, 1993. 265 pp.

Hamrick, Craig. *Frozen Summer.* Manhattan, KS: Clique Publishing , 1991.

Harris, Jesse. *The Vampire's Kiss.* New York: Alfred A. Knopf, 1993. 144 pp.

Harrison, Harry, and Jack C. Haldean, II. *Bill the Galactic Hero on the Planet of Zombie Vampires.* Bill the Galatic Hero, No. 4. New York: Avon, 1991.

Hawke, Simon. *The Dracula Caper.* Time Wars, No. 8. New York: Ace Books, 1988. Reprinted: London: Heineman Book Publishing, 1988. 212 pp.

Henrick, Richard. *St. John the Pursuer, Book I: Vampire in Moscow.* Lake Geneva, WI: TSR, 1988. 382 pp.

Henstell, Diana. *New Morning Dragon.* New York: Bantam Books, 1987. 352 pp.

Herbert, James. *The Spear.* New York: New American Library, 1980.

Herter, Lori. *Confession.* New York: Berkley Books, 1992. 280 pp.

———. *Eternity.* New York: Berkley Books, 1993. 277 pp.

———. *Obsession.* New York: Berkley Books, 1991. 278 pp.

———. *Possession.* New York: Berkley Books, 1992. 298 pp.

Hill, William. *Dawn of the Vampire.* New York: Pinnacle Books, 1991. 480 pp.

———. *Vampire's Kiss.* New York: Zebra/Pinnacle, 1994.

Horowitz, Lois. *She-Devil.* New York: Pageant, 1989. 334 pp.

Huff, Tanya. *Blood Lines.* New York: DAW Books, 1993. 271 pp.

———. *Blood Pact.* New York: DAW Books, 1993. 332 pp.

———. *Blood Price.* New York: DAW Books, 1991. 272 pp.

———. *Blood Trail.* New York: DAW Books, 1992. 304 pp.

Hughes, William. *Lust for a Vampire.* London: Sphere Books, 1971. 159 pp. Reprinted: New York: Beagle Books, 1971. 159 pp.

Hunt, William. *Chosen Haunts.*

Hurwood, Bernhardt. *By Blood Alone.* New York: Charter Books, 1979. 245 pp.

Huson, Paul. *The Keepsake.* New York: Warner, 1981. 320 pp.

Hutson, Shaun. *Erebus.* New York: Leisure Books, 1984. 368 pp.

Irwin, Sarita. *To Love a Vampire.* N.p.: Carousel, 1982.

Ivanhoe, Mark. *Virgintooth.* San Francisco: III Publishing, 1991. 191 pp.

Jaccoma, Richard. *The Werewolf's Tale.* New York: Fawcett, 1988. 283 pp.

James, Robert. *Blood Mist.* New York: Leisure Books, 1987. 365 pp.

Jennings, Jan. *Vampyr.* New York: Pinnacle Books, 1981. 304 pp.

Jensen, Ruby Jean. *Vampire Child.* New York: Zebra Books, 1990. 285 pp.

Jeter, Kevin W. *In the Land of the Dead.* Scotforth, Lancastershire, UK: Morrigan Publications, 1989. 215 pp.

Johnson, Ken. *Hounds of Dracula.* New York: New American Library, 1977. 170 pp. Reprinted: London: Everest Books, 1977. 170 pp. Reprinted as: *Dracula's Dog.* New York: New American Library, 1977. 170 pp.

Johnson, Kenneth Rayner. *The Succubus.* New York: Dell, 1980. 303 pp. Reprinted: London: New English Library, 1980. 286 pp.

Johnstone, William. *Bats.* New York: Zebra Books, 1993. 348 pp.

————. *The Devil's Cat.* New York: Zebra Books, Kensington, 1987. 380 pp.

————. *The Devil's Heart.* New York: Zebra Books, Kensington, 1983. 382 pp.

————. *The Devil's Kiss.* New York: Zebra Books, Kensington, 1980. 449 pp.

————. *The Devil's Touch.* New York: Zebra Books, Kensington, 1984. 350 pp.

————. *The Nursery.* New York: Zebra Books, Kensington, 1983. 351 pp.

————. *Wolfsbane.* New York: Zebra Books, Kensington, 1982. 268 pp.

Jones, D. F. *Earth Has Been Found.* New York: Dell, 1979. 267 pp.

Jones, Diana Wynne. *Fire and Hemlock.* New York: Greenwillow, 1984. 370 pp. New York: Berkley Publishing Company, 1986. 280 pp.

Jones, Robert F. *Blood Sport: A Journey Up the Hassayampa.* New York: Simon & Schuster, 1974. 255 pp. Reprinted as: *Ratnose: A Journey up the Hassayampa.* London: Magazine Editors, 1975. 255 pp.

Kahn, James. *Time's Dark Laughter.* New York: Ballantine Books, 1982. 318 pp. Reprinted: London: Panther, 1983. 351 pp.

————. *Timefall.* New York: St. Martin's Press, 1987. 295 pp.

————. *World Enough and Time.* New York: Ballantine Books, 1980. 340 pp.

Kaminsky, Stuart. *Never Cross a Vampire.* New York: St. Martin's Press, 1980. 182 pp.

Kapralov, Yuri. *Castle Dubrava.* New York: E. P. Dutton, 1982.

Kast, P. *The Vampires of Alfama.* London: W. H. Allen, 1976. 181 pp.

Kearny, Maxwell. *Dracula Sucks.* New York: Zebra, 1981.

Ketchum, Jack. *She Wakes.* New York: Berkley, 1989. 260 pp.

Killough, Lee. *Blood Hunt.* New York: TOR, 1987. 319 pp.

————. *Bloodlinks.* New York: TOR, 1988. 345 pp. Kimberly, Gail (Roger Elwood). *Dracula Began.* New York: Pyramid Books, 1976. 160 pp.

King, Stephen. *The Dark Half*. New York: Viking, 1989. 431 pp.

———. *Salem's Lot*. New York: Doubleday, 1975. 439 pp. Reprinted: New York: New American Library, 1980. 427 pp.

———. *The Tommyknockers*. New York: G. P. Putnam's Sons, 1987. 558 pp. Reprinted: New York: New American Library, 1988. 747 pp.

Kisner, James Martin. *Dear Ladies of the Night*.

Klause, Annette Curtis. *The Silver Kiss*. New York: Bantam Books, 1990. Reprinted: London: Doubleday, 1991. 198 pp.

Kolomek, Dawn. *Night by Night*.

Koontz, Dean R. *The Bad Place*. New York: G. P. Putnam's Sons, 1990. 382 pp.

———. *The Haunted Earth*. New York: Lancer, 1973.

———. *Lightning*. New York: G. P. Putnam's Sons, 1988. 351 pp.

——— (first appeared under pseudonym Leigh Nichols). *Shadow Fires*. Nkui, Inc., 1987. Reprinted: Arlington Heights, IL: Dark Harvest, 1990. 380 pp. Reprinted: New York: Berkley Books, 1993. 509 pp.

———. *The Vision*. New York: Putnam, 1977. 287 pp.

———. *Watchers*. New York: Putnam, 1987. 352 pp.

Kurtz, Katherine. *The Legacy of Lohr*. New York: Millennium, Walker & Co., 1986. 235 pp.

Kurtz, Katherine, and Scott MacMillan. *Knights of the Blood. Book I: Vampyres*. New York: ROC, 1993. 350 pp.

Kushner, Ellen. *Thomas the Rhymer*. New York: Morrow, 1990. Reprinted: New York: TOR, 1991. 247 pp.

Lackey, Mercedes. *Children of the Night*. New York: TOR, 1990. 313 pp.

———, and Ellen Guon. *Knight of Ghosts and Shadows: An Urban Fantasy*. New York: Baen, 1990. 345 pp.

———, and Ellen Guon. *Summoned to Tourney: An Urban Fantasy*. New York: Baen, 1992. 298 pp.

———, and Mark Shepherd. *Wheels of Fire: A Novel of Serraed Edge*. New York: Baen, 1992. 289 pp.

Lara, Jan. *Soulcatchers*. New York: Popular Library, 1990. 235 pp.

Laws, Stephen. *The Wyrm*. London: Souvenir, 1987. 301 pp. Reprinted: London: Sphere, 1989. 304 pp.

Laymon, Richard. *The Stake*. London: Headline Feature, 1990. 506 pp.

LeBlanc, Richard. *The Fangs of the Vampire*. New York: Vantage Press, 1980. 123 pp.

Lecale, Errol. *Blood of My Blood*. London: New English Library, 1975.

———. *Castledoom*. London: New English Library, 1974. 128 pp.

———. *The Death Box*. London: New English Library, 1974. 124 pp.

Lee, Catherine Victoria. *Abode of the Beast, Volume 2*. North Hollywood, CA: Dapplewood Press, 1991.

———. *Escape to the Realm of the Snow Elves*. North Hollywood, CA: Dapplewood Press, 1992.

Lee, Edward. *Succubi*. New York: Diamond Books, 1992. 258 pp.

Lee, Tanith. *The Beautiful Biting Machine*. New Castle, VA: Cheap Street, 1984. 43 pp.

———. *The Blood of Roses*. London: Century Publishing, 1990. 678 pp.

———. *Dark Dance*. New York: Dell, 1992. 409 pp.

———. *Kill the Dead*. New York: DAW Books, 1980. 172 pp.

————. *Personal Darkness.* (Blood Opera No. 2) London: Little, Brown, 1993. 435 pp.

————. *Sabella; or the Blood Stone.* New York: DAW Books, 1980. 157 pp. Reprinted in: *Sometimes, After Sunset.* Garden City, NY: Nelson Doubleday, 1980. 140 pp.

————. *Volkkavaar.* New York: DAW Books, 1977. 192 pp.

Lee, Warner. *It's Loose.* New York: Pocket Books, 1990. 312 pp.

Leiber, Fritz. *Beyond Rejection.* New York: Ballantine Books, 1980. 177 pp.

————. *Ship of Shadows.* New York: TOR, 1989. 77 pp. (Bound with Paul Anderson, *No Truth to Keep.*)

Leinster, Murray (pseudonym William Fitzgerald Jenkins). *The Brain Stealers.*

Lenier, Stirling E. *Hiero's Journey.* Radnor, PA: Chilton Book Co., 1973. 280 pp. Reprinted: Garden City, NY: Doubleday, 1983. 532 pp.

Lennig, Arthur. *The Count.* New York: Putnam House, 1981.

Lichtenberg, Jacqueline. *Dreamspy.* New York: St. Martin's Press, 1989. 337 pp.

————. *House of Zeor.* New York: Doubleday, 1974. 206 pp. Reprinted: New York: Berkley Publishing, 1981. 224 pp.

————. *Mahogany Trinrose.* New York: Doubleday, 1981. 214 pp.

————. *RenSime.* New York: Doubleday, 1984. 178 pp.

————. *Those of My Blood.* New York: St. Martin's Press, 1988. 402 pp.

————. *Unto Zeor, Forever.* New York: Doubleday, 1978. 236 pp.

————, and Jean Lorrah. *First Channel.* New York: Doubleday, 1980. 310 pp.

————, and Jean Lorrah. *Zeierod's Doom.* New York: DAW Books, 1986. 277 pp.

Leiberman, Herbert. *City of the Dead.* London: Hutchinson, 1976. 367 pp. Reprinted: New York: Avon, 1986. 356 pp.

Linssen, John. *Tabitha Fffoulkes.* New York: Arbor House, 1978. 311 pp.

————. *Yellow Pages.* New York: Arbor House, 1985.

Linzer, Gordon. *The Spy Who Drank Blood.* New York: Space and Time, 1984. 127 pp.

Lisle, Holly. *Fire in the Mist.* New York: Baen, 1992. 291 pp.

Little, Bentley. *The Summoning.* New York: Zebra Books, 1993. 541 pp.

Livingston, Ian. *City of Thieves.* Hammondsworth, Middlesex, UK: Puffin Books, 1983. 200 pp.

Longstreet, Roxanne, *The Undead.* New York: Zebra Books, 1993. 318 pp.

Lorrah, Jean. *Ambrov Keon.* New York: DAW Books, 1986. 256 pp.

Lortz, Richard. *Children of the Night.* New York: Dell, 1974. 160 pp.

Lory, Robert. *Dracula Returns.* New York: Pinnacle Books, 1973. 198 pp.

————. *The Hand of Dracula.* New York: Pinnacle Books, 1973. 224 pp.

————. *Dracula's Brothers.* New York: Pinnacle Books, 1973. 186 pp.

————. *Dracula's Gold.* New York: Pinnacle Books, 1973. 182 pp.

————. *The Drums of Dracula.* New York: Pinnacle Books, 1974. 189 pp.

————. *The Witching of Dracula.* New York: Pinnacle Books, 1974. 177 pp.

————. *Dracula's Lost World.* New York: Pinnacle Books, 1975. 181 pp.

————. *Dracula's Disciple.* New York: Pinnacle Books, 1975. 179 pp.

————. *Challenge to Dracula.* New York: Pinnacle Books, 1975. 180 pp.

Love at First Bite. Los Angeles: Fotonovel Publications, 1979. 176 pp.

Lovell, Marc. *An Enquiry into the Existence of Vampires.* Garden City, NY: Doubleday, 1974. 181 pp. Reprinted as: *Vampire in the Shadows.* London: Coronet Books, 1974. 157 pp.

Lowder, James. *Knight of the Black Rose.* Lake Geneva, WI: TSR, 1991. 313 pp.

Lumley, Brian. *Blood Brothers.* Vampire Worlds 1. New York: TOR, 1992.

————. *Bloodwars.* New York: TOR.

————. *Deadspawn.* Necroscope. New York: TOR, 1991. 602 pp.

————. *Deadspeak.* Necroscope IV. New York: TOR, 1990. 487 pp.

————. *The Last Aerie.* Vampire Worlds 2. New York: TOR, 1993.

————. *Necroscope.* Necroscope I. New York: TOR, 1988. 505 pp.

————. *The Source.* Necroscope III. New York: TOR, 1989. 505 pp.

————. *Vamphyri.* Necroscope I. New York: TOR, 1989. 470 pp.

Lupoff, Richard A. *Sandworld.* New York: Berkley, 1976. 188 pp.

Lutz, John. *Shadowtown.* New York: Mysterious Press, 1988. 248 pp.

Lyman, Russ. *Record of Nightly Occurrences: Diary of a Vampire.* Salt Lake City, UT: The Author, 1993.

Lyton, E. K. *Dracula's Daughter.* 1977. Reprinted: London: Star Books, 1980.

McCammon, Robert. *They Thirst.* New York: Avon, 1981. 531 pp.

McCunniff, Mira and Traci Briery. *The Vampire Memoirs.* New York: Zebra Books, 1991. 431 pp.

McKenney, Kenneth. *The Changeling.* New York: Avon, 1985. 292 pp.

————. *The Moonchild.* New York: Simon & Schuster, 1978. 286 pp.

McLane, Jack. *Rest In Peace.* New York: Zebra Books, 1990. 319 pp.

McMahan, Jeffrey N. *Vampires Anonymous.* Boston: Alyson Publications, 1991. 253 pp.

McShane, M. *Vampire in the Shadows.* London: Robert Hale, 1977.

Madison, J. J. *The Thing.* New York: Belmont Tower Books, 1971. 186 pp.

Mallory, Lewis. *The Nursery.* London: Hamlyn, 1981. 157 pp.

Mannheim, Karl. *Vampires of Venus.* Manchester, England; PBS Ltd., 1972. 128 pp.

Marsh, Geoffrey. *The Fangs of the Hooded Demon: A Lincoln Blackstone Mystery.* New York: TOR, 1988. 281 pp.

Martin, George R. R. *Fevre Dream.* New York: Poseidon Press, 1982. 350 pp. Reprinted: New York: Pocket Books, 1982. 390 pp.

Martindale, T. Chris. *Nightblood.* New York: Warner Books, 1990. 322 pp.

Mason, David. *The Sorcerer's Skull.* New York: Lancer, 1970. 192 pp.

Masterson, Graham. *Death Trance.* New York: Tom Doherty, 1986. Reprinted: London: Severn House, 1987. 424 pp.

Matheson, Richard. *Legend of Hell House.*

Mattocks, Vincent. *A Night with Count Dracula.*

Miller, Beverly. *Bloodlust.* Academy Press, 1974.

Miller, Linda Lael. *Forever and the Night.* New York: Berkley Books, 1993. 338 pp.

Minns, Karen Marie Christa. *Virago.* Tallahassee, FL: Naiad Press, 1990. 191 pp.

Monahan, Brent. *The Book of Common Dread.* New York: St. Martin's Press, 1993.

Monette, Paul. *Nosferatu: The Vampyre.* New York: Avon, 1979. 172 pp.

Moorcock, Michael. *The Bane of the Black Sword.* New York: DAW Books, 1977.

Reprinted: New York: Berkley Books, 1984. Reprinted: New York: Ace Books, 1987 157 pp. Rev. ed. as: *The Stealer of Souls.* New York: Lancer, 1967.

———. *Elric of Meiniboné.* (Elric 1) London: Arrow, 1975. 191 pp. Reprinted: Hartford, CT: Blue Star Publishers.

———. *The Revenge of the Rose.* London: Grafton, 1991. 233 pp. Reprinted: New York: Ace Books, 1991.

———. *The Sailor on the Seas of Fate.* (Elric 2) London: Quartet Books, 1976. 170 pp. Reprinted: New York: DAW Books, 1976.

———. *The Sleeping Sorceress: An Elric Novel.* (Elric 4) London: New English Library, 1976. 140 pp. Reprinted as: *The Vanishing Tower.* New York: DAW Books, 1977. 175 pp. Reprinted: New York: Berkley Books, 1983. 175 pp.

———. *Stormbringer.* (Elric 6) New York: DAW Books, 1977. Reprinted: New York: Berkley Books, 1984. Reprinted: New York: Ace Books, 1987. 220 pp.

———. *Stealer of Souls and Other Stories.* (Elric 3) London: Neville Spearman, 1963. 215 pp. Reprinted as: *The Weird of the White Wolf.* New York: DAW Books, 1977. 159 pp.

Mordane, Thomas. *Blood Root.* New York: Dell, 1982. 285 pp.

Morgan, Robert. *Some Things Never Die.* New York: Diamond, 1993. 213 pp.

Moriarty, Timothy. *Vampire Nights.* New York: Pinnacle Books, 1989. 348 pp.

Morris, Jeff. *The Vampire Janine.* Webster Grove, MO: Bandersnatch Press, 1991.

Myers, Robert J. *The Virgin and the Vampire.* New York: Pocket Books, 1977. 207 pp.

Navarro, Yvonne. *AfterAge.* New York: Bantam Books, 1993. 388 pp.

Neiderman, Andrew. *Bloodchild.* New York: Berkley Books, 1990. 268 pp.

———. *Love Child.* New York: TOR, 1986. 319 pp.

———. *The Immortals.* New York: Pocket Star Books, 1991. 281 pp.

———. *The Need.* New York: G. P. Putnam's Sons, 1992. Reprinted: New York: Berkley Books, 1993. 282 pp.

Newman, Kim. *Anno-Dracula.* New York: Simon & Schuster, 1992. 359 pp.

———. *Bad Dreams.* London: Simon & Schuster, 1990. Reprinted: New York: Carroll and Graf, 1991. 316 pp.

Nightwing. Los Angeles: Fotonovel Publications, 1979. Unpaged.

Norton, Andre. *Perilous Dreams.* New York: DAW Books, 1976. 199 pp.

Offutt, Andrew J., and Richard K. Lyon. *The Demon in the Mirror.* New York: Pocket Books, 1978. 189 pp.

Olson, Paul F. *Night Prophets.* New York: New American Library, 1989. 350 pp.

Paine, Michael. *Owl Light.* New York: Charter Books, 1989. 232 pp.

Palmer, Jane. *The Watcher.* London: Woman's Press Science Fiction, 1986. 177 pp.

Parry, Michael. *Countess Dracula.* London: Sphere Books, 1971. 140 pp. Reprinted: New York: Beagle Books, 1971. 140 pp.

Perucho, Joan. *Natural History.* 1960. English ed.: New York: Ballantine Books, 1988. 160 pp. (Translation of *Les Histories Naturales.*)

Peterson, Gail. *The Making of a Monster.* New York: Dell, 1993. 371 pp.

Petrey, Susan. *Gifts of Blood.* 1990. Reprinted: New York: Baen, 1992. 192 pp.

Phillips, Mike. *Blood Rights.* New York: Dell, 1990. 208 pp.

Piccirilli, Tom. *Dark Father.* New York: Pocket Books, 1990. 280 pp.

Pierce, Meredith Ann. *The Darkangel.* New York: Little, Brown, 1982. Reprinted: New York: TOR, 1984. 252 pp.

———. *A Gathering of Gargoyles.* New York: Little, Brown, 1984. 263 pp. Reprinted: New York: TOR, 1985. 263 pp.

———. *The Pearl of the Soul of the World.* Boston: Joy Street Books, 1990. 243 pp.

Popescu, Petru. *In Hot Blood.* New York: Fawcett, 1986. Reprinted: New York: Ballantine Books, 1989. 328 pp.

Powers, Tim. *Dinner at Deviant's Palace.* New York: Ace Books, 1985. 294 pp.

———. *The Stress of Her Regard.* Lynbrook, New York: Charnel House, 1989. Reprinted: New York: Ace Books, 1989. 410 pp.

Ptacek, Kathryn. *Blood Autumn.* New York: TOR, 1985. 349 pp.

———. *In Silence Sealed.* New York: TOR, 1988. 306 pp.

Raiser, Gary. *Less than Human.* Woodstock, GA: Overlook Connection, 1992. Reprinted: New York: Diamond Books, 1992. 265 pp.

Randolphe, Arabella (pseudonym of Jack Younger). *The Vampire Tapes.* New York: Berkley, 1977. 247 pp. Reprinted: London: Futura, 1978. 247 pp.

Raven, Simon. *Doctors Wear Scarlet.* London: Anthony Blond, 1960. 222 pp.

Rechy, John. *The Vampires.* New York: Grove Press, 1977. 276 pp.

Reed, Rick R. *Obsessed.* New York: Dell, 1991. 392 pp.

Reeves-Stevens, Garfield. *Bloodshift.* Virgo Press, 1981. Reprinted: New York: Popular Library, 1990. 280 pp.

Reeves-Stevens, Judith, and Garfield Reeves-Stevens. *Nightfeeder.* New York: ROC, 1991. 285 pp.

Relling, William, Jr. *New Moon.* New York: Tom Doherty, 1987. 280 pp.

Renauld, Ron. *Fade to Black.* Los Angeles: Pinnacle, 1980. 213 pp.

Rhodes, Daniel. *The Kiss of Death.* New York: TOR, 1990. 311 pp. Reprinted: London: New English Library, 1991. 261 pp.

Rice, Anne. *Interview with the Vampire.* New York: Alfred A. Knopf, 1976. 371 pp. Reprinted: New York: Ballantine, 1979. 346 pp.

———. *Of Hell and Heaven.* New York: Alfred A. Knopf, 1994.

———. *Queen of the Damned.* New York: Alfred A. Knopf, 1988. 448 pp.

———. *The Tale of the Body Thief.* New York: Alfred A. Knopf, 1992. 430 pp.

———. *The Vampire Lestat.* New York: Alfred A. Knopf, 1985. 481 pp. Reprinted: New York: Ballantine Books, 1986. 550 pp.

Rice, Jeff. *The Night Stalker.* New York: Pocket Books, 1974. 192 pp.

Robbins, David. *Vampire Strike.* (Blade, No. 3) New York: Leisure, 1989. 188 pp.

Robeson, Kenneth (pseudonym of Ron Goulart). *The Blood Countess.* (Avenger, No. 33) New York: Warner Books, 1975. 142 pp.

——— (pseudonym of Lester Dent). *The Lost Oasis: A Doc Savage Adventure.* New York: Bantam Books, 1963. 123 pp.

Rogers, Mark. *The Dead.* New York: Berkley, 1990.

Romero, George, and Susan Sparrow. *Martin.* New York: Stein & Day, 1977. 215 pp. Reprinted: New York: Day Books, 1980. 215 pp.

Romine, Aden F., and Mary C. Romine. *The Fellowship.* New York: Leisure Books, 1984. 382 pp.

Romkey, Michael. *I Vampire.* New York: Fawcett Gold Medal, 1990. 360 pp.

Ronson, Mark. *Bloodthirst.* Feltham, UK: Hamlyn, 1979. 210 pp.

Ross, Clarisa. *The Corridors of Fear.* New York: Avon, 1971. 172 pp.

Ross, Marilyn. *The Vampire Contessa: From the Journal of Jeremy Quentain.* New York: Pinnacle, 1974. 181 pp.

Rovin, Jeff. *The Madjan.* NY Charter Books, 1984. 236 pp.

Roy, Archie. *Devil in Darkness.* London: John Long, 1978. 184 pp. Reprinted: Apogee, 1987. 184 pp.

Ruddy, John. *The Bargain.* New York: Knightsbridge, 1990. 293 pp.

Rudorff, Raymond. *The Dracula Archives.* New York: Arbor House/World, 1971. 208 pp. Reprinted: New York: Pocket Books, 1972. 208 pp. Reprinted: New York: Warner, 1975. 208 pp.

———. *The House of the Brandersons.* New York: Arbor House, 1973. 198 pp.

Russo, John. *The Awakening.* New York: Pocket Books, 1983. 311 pp.

Ryan, Alan. *Cast a Cold Eye.* Arlington, IL: Dark Harvest, 1984. Reprinted: New York: TOR, 1984. 349 pp.

Saberhagen, Fred. *Dominion.* New York: Pinnacle, 1982. 320 pp

———. *The Dracula Tape.* New York: Paperback Library, 1975. 206 pp. Reprinted: New York: Ace Books, 1980. 281 pp.

———. *The Holmes-Dracula File.* New York: Ace Books, 1978. 249 pp.

———. *A Matter of Taste.* New York: TOR, 1990. 284 pp.

———. *An Old Friend of the Family.* New York: Ace Books, 1979. 247 pp.

———. *A Question of Time.* New York: TOR, 1992. 278 pp.

———. *Seance for a Vampire.* New York: TOR, 1994.

———. *Thorn.* New York: Ace Books, 1980. 347 pp.

———, and James Hart. *Bram Stoker's Dracula.* New York: New American Library, 1992. 301 pp.

Sabine, Ted. *The Soulsucker.* New York: Pinnacle Books, 1975. 180 pp.

Sackett, Jeffery. *Blood of the Impaler.* New York: Bantam Books, 1989. 340 pp.

———. *Mark of the Werewolf.* New York: Bantam Books, 1990. 315 pp.

———. *Stolen Souls.* New York: Bantam Books, 1987. 341 pp.

Sagara, Michelle. *Children of the Blood.* New York: Ballantine/Del Rey, 1992. 307 pp.

Samuels, Victor. *The Vampire Women.* New York: Popular Library, 1973. 190 pp.

San Souci, Robert D. *The Dreaming.* New York: Berkley, 1989. 251 pp.

Saralequi, Jorge. *Last Rites.* New York: Charter, 1985. 279 pp.

Savage, Adrian. *Unholy Communion.* New York: Pocket Books, 1988. 255 pp.

Savory, Gerald. *Count Dracula.* London: Corgi, 1977. 142 pp.

Saxon, Peter. *Brother Blood.* New York: Belmont Books, 1970.

——— (pseudonym of W. Howard Baker). *Vampire's Moon.* New York: Belmont Books, 1970. 176 pp.

——— (pseudonym of Rex Dolphin). *The Vampires of Finistere.* New York: Berkley Books, 1970. 190 pp.

Scarborough, Elizabeth. *The Goldcamp Vampire.* New York: Bantam Books, 1987. 247 pp.

Scott, Alan. *Project Dracula.* London: Sphere, 1971. Reprinted as: *The Anthrax Mutation.* New York: Pyramid Books, 1976. 319 pp.

Scott, Jody. *I Vampire.* New York: Ace Books, 1984. 206 pp.

Scott, Michael. *Image.* London: Sphere, 1991.

Scott, R. C. *Blood Sport.* Toronto: Bantam Books, 1984. 134 pp.

Scram, Arthur. *The Werewolf vs. the Vampire Woman.* Beverly Hills, CA: Guild-Hartford Publishing, 1972. 190 pp.

Selby, Curt. *Blood Country.* New York: DAW Books, 1981. 176 pp.

Seymour, Miranda. *Count Manfred.* London: Hutchinson, 1976. 283 pp. Reprinted: New York: Coward, McCann & Geoghegan, 1977. 284 pp. Reprinted: New York: Popular Library, 1977. 301 pp.

Shayne, Maggie. *Twilight Phantasies.* New York: Silhouette, 1993. 251 pp.

Shea, Michael. *In Yana, the Touch of the Undying.* New York: DAW Books, 1985. 318 pp.

Sheffield, Charles, and David Bischoff. *The Selkie.* New York: Macmillan Company, 1982. 375 pp. Reprinted: New York: New American Library, 1983. 426 pp.

Shepard, Lucius. *The Golden.* Shingletown, CA: Mark Ziesing, 1993. Reprinted: New York: Bantam Books, 1993. 291 pp.

Sherman, Jory. *Vegas Vampire.* Chill No. 4. Los Angeles: Pinnacle Books, 1980. 176 pp.

Sharman, Nick. *You're Next.* Sevenoaks, UK: New English Library, 1986. 348 pp.

Shirley, John. *Dracula in Love.* New York: Zebra Books, 1979. 283 pp.

———. *Wetbones.* Shingletown, CA: Mark Ziesing, 1991. 273 pp.

Siciliano, Sam. *Blood Farm.* New York: Pageant Books, 1988. 336 pp.

———. *Blood Feud.* New York: Pinnacle Books, 1993. 315 pp.

Simmons, Dan. *Carrion Comfort.* Arlington Heights, IL: Dark Harvest, 1989.

———. *Children of the Night.* New York: G. P. Putnam's Sons, 1992. 382 pp.

———. *Song of Kali.* New York: TOR, 1985. 311 pp.

———. *Summer of Night.* New York: G. P. Putnams' Sons, 1991. 555 pp. Reprinted: New York: Warner, 1992. 600 pp.

Skipp, John, and Craig Spector. *Fright Night.* New York: TOR, 1985. 250 pp.

———. *The Light at the End.* New York: Bantam Books, 1986. 385 pp.

Sky, Kathleen. *Death's Angel.* New York: Bantam Books, 1981. 213 pp.

Sloane, Robert C. *A Nice Place to Live.* New York: Crown, 1981. 278 pp. Reprinted: New York: Bantam Books, 1982. 208 pp.

Smith, David C., and Richard L. Tierney. *Endithor's Daughter.* (Red Sonja No. 2) New York: Ace Books, 1982. 209 pp.

Smith, Guy N. *Bats Out of Hell.* New York: New American Library, 1979. 153 pp.

———. *The Blood Merchants.* London: New English Library, 1982. 160 pp.

———. *Doomflight.* London: Hamlyn, 1981. 221 pp.

———. *The Knighton Vampires.* London: Piatkus, 1993. 181 pp.

———. *The Undead.* Sevenoaks, Kent, UK: New English Library, 1983. 176 pp.

Smith, Martin Cruz. *Nightwing.* New York: Norton, 1977. 255 pp. Reprinted: New York: Jove, 1977. 255 pp.

Smith, R. A. *The Werewolf's Prey.* Reprinted as: *The Prey.* New York: Fawcett, 1977.

———. *Vampire Notes.* New York: Fawcett Gold Medal, 1990. 241 pp.

Somtow, S. P. *Forest of the Night.* New York: Avon, 1992.

———. *Riverrun.* New York: AvoNova, 1992. 259 pp.

————. *Valentine*. New York: Gollantz, 1992. 384 pp. Reprinted: New York: TOR, 1992. 373 pp.

————. *Vampire Junction*. Norfolk, VA: Donning, 1984. 280 pp. Reprinted: New York: Berkley Books, 1985. 362 pp.

Stableford, Brian. *The Empire of Fear*. New York: Simon & Schuster, 1988. Reprinted: New York: Ballantine Books, 1993. 469 pp.

————. *Young Blood*. London: Simon & Schuster, 1992. Reprinted: New York: Pocket Books, 1993. 498 pp.

Stanwood, Brooks. *The Glow*. New York: McGraw-Hill, 1979. 297 pp. Reprinted: New York: Fawcett Crest, 1980. 320 pp.

Staszak, Lucille. *A Twist of Mind*. North Riverside, IL: Pandora Publications, 1981. 56 pp.

Stchur, John. *Down on the Farm*. New York: St. Martin's Press, 1987. 216 pp.

Steakley, John. *Vampires*. New York: ROC, 1990. 357 pp.

Stevenson, Florence. *The Curse of Concullens*. New York: New American Library, 1972. 239 pp.

————. *Dark Encounter*. New York: New American Library, 1976. 168 pp.

————. *Household*. New York: Leisure Books, 1989. 392 pp

————. *Moonlight Variations*. New York: Jove, 1981. 213 pp.

Stewart, Desmond. *The Vampire of Mons*. New York: Harper & Row, 1976. 169 pp. Reprinted: London Hamlyn, 1976. 169 pp. Reprinted: New York: Avon, 1977. 187 pp.

Stockbridge, Grant. *Death Reign of the Vampire King*. New York: Pocket Books, 1935.

Stone, Elna. *Secret of the Willows*. New York: Belmont Books, 1970. 171 pp.

Storm, Derek. *Vampire Island*. New York: Family Vision Press, 1993. 200 pp.

Straub, Peter. *Ghost Story*. New York: Coward, McGann & Geoghegan, 1978. Reprinted: New York: Pocket Books, 1980. 567 pp.

————. *If You Could See Me Now*. New York: Coward, McGann & Geoghegan, 1977. Reprinted: New York: Pocket Books, 1979. 328 pp.

Streiber, Whitley. *The Hunger*. New York: William Morrow, 1981. 320 pp. Reprinted: New York: Pocket Books, 1982. 307 pp.

Stuart, Sidney. *The Beast with the Red Hands*. New York: Popular Library, 1973. 192 pp.

Sucharitkul, Somtov. *Mallworld*. Norfolk, VA: Donning Co., 1981. 195 pp.

Suskind, Patrick. *Perfume*. New York: Alfred A. Knopf, 1986. 255 pp. Reprinted: Santa Barbara, CA: ABC-CLIO, 1987. 361 pp. Reprinted: New York: Pocket Books, 1991. (Translation of *Das Perfum*.)

Swanwick, Michael. *In the Drift*. New York: Ace Books, 1985.

Talbot, Michael. *The Delicate Dependency: A Novel of the Vampire Life*. New York: Avon, 1982. 406 pp.

Tate, Richard. *The Dead Travel Fast*. London: Constable, 1971. 191 pp. Reprinted: London: Sphere, 1972. 191 pp.

Taylor, Karen E. *The Vampire Legacy: Blood Secrets*. New York: Zebra Books, 1993. 302 pp.

Tedford, William. *Liquid Diet*. New York: Diamond Books, 1992. 268 pp.

Tem, Steve Rasnic. *Excavation*. New York: Avon, 1987. 280 pp.

Tennant, Emma. *The Bad Sister*. New York: Coward, McCann & Geoghegan, 1978. Reprinted: New York: Avon, 1980. 223 pp.

Tepper, Sheri S. *Blood Heritage*. New York: TOR, 1986. 287 pp.

Tesssier, Thomas. *The Nightwalker.* New York: New American Library, 1979. 183 pp.

Tigges, John. *The Immortal.* New York: Leisure Books, 1986. 362 pp.

———. *Vessel.* New York: Dorchester/ Leisure Books, 1988. 362 pp.

Tilton, Lois. *Darkness on the Ice.* New York: Pinnacle Books, 1993. 286 pp.

———. *Vampire Winter.* New York: Pinnacle Books, 1990. 320 pp.

Tonkin, Peter. *The Journal of Edwin Underhill.* London: Hodder and Stoughton, 1981. 192 pp. Reprinted: London: Coronet, 1983. 191 pp.

Tremayne, Peter. *Dracula Unborn.* London: Bailey Brothers and Swinfen, 1977. Reprinted: London: Corgi, 1977. 222 pp. Reprinted as: *Bloodright: Memoirs of Mircea, Son of Dracula.* New York: Walker & Co., 1979. 222 pp. Reprinted as: *Bloodright.* New York: Dell, 1980. 251 pp.

———. *Dracula My Love.* London: Bailey Brothers and Swinfen, 1980. Reprinted: London: Magnum Books, 1980. 203 pp.

———. *The Revenge of Dracula.* Folkstone: Bailey Brothers and Swiften, 1978. Reprinted: New York: Walker & Co., 1979. Reprinted: London: Magnum Books, 1980. 203 pp.

Tweed, Jack Hamilton. *The Blood of Dracula.* London: Mills and Boon, 1977.

Valdemi, Maria. *The Demon Lover.* New York: Pinnacle Books, 1981. 320 pp.

Van Over, Raymond. *The Twelfth Child.* New York: Pinnacle Books, 1990. 320 pp.

Van Vogt, A. E. *Supermind.* New York: DAW Books, 1977. 175 pp.

Veley, Charles. *Night Whispers.* Garden City, New York: Doubleday, 1980. 330 pp. Reprinted: New York: Ballantine, 1981. 314 pp.

Wagner, Karl Edward. *Death Angel's Shadow.* New York: Warner, 1973. 205 pp.

Wallace, Ian. *The Lucifer Comet.* New York: DAW Books, 1980.

Wallace, Patricia. *Monday's Child.* New York: Zebra Books, 1989. 288 pp.

———. *The Taint.* New York: Zebra Books, Kensington, 1983. 351 pp.

Walters, R. R. *Ludlow's Mill.* New York: Pinnacle, 1981. 300 pp.

Warrington, Freda. *A Taste of Blood Wine.* London: Pan Books, 1992. 446 pp.

Watt-Evans, Lawrence. *The Nightmare People.* New York: Onyx, 1991. 254 pp.

Weatersby, Lee. *Kiss of the Vampire.* New York: Zebra Books, 1992. 447 pp.

Weinberg, Robert. *The Armageddon Box.* New York: Dorchester/Leisure Books, 1991. 345 pp. Reprinted: Newark, NJ: Wildside Press, 1991. 221 pp.

Westlake, Donald, and Abby Westlake. *Transylvania Station.* Miami Beach, FL: Dennis McMillan Publications, 1987. 122 pp.

Whalen, Patrick. *Monastery.* New York: Pocket Books, 1988. 356 pp.

———. *Night Thirst.* New York: Pocket Books, 1991. 356 pp.

Whitten, Leslie H. *Progeny of the Adder.* Garden City, New York: Doubleday, 1965. Reprinted: New York: Ace Books, 1965. 189 pp.

Wilde, Kelley. *Mastery.* New York: Dell, 1991. 450 pp.

Williams, Sidney. *Night Brothers.* New York: Pinnacle Books, 1990. 44 pp.

Williamson, J. N. *Death Angel.* New York: Zebra Books, Kensington, 1981. 303 pp.

———. *Death Coach.* New York: Zebra Books, Kensington 1981. 318 pp.

———. *Death Doctor.* New York: Zebra Books, Kensington, 1982. 272 pp.

———. *Death School.* New York: Zebra Books, Kensington, 1982. 302 pp.

Wilson, Colin. *The Space Vampires.* New York: Random House, 1976. 214 pp. Reprinted: London: Hart-Davis and MacGibbon, 1976. 214 pp. Reprinted: New York: Pocket Books, 1977. 220 pp. Reprinted as: *Lifeforce.* New York: Warner Books, 1985. 220 pp.

Wilson, F. Paul. *The Keep.* Adversary No. 1. New York: Morrow, 1981. 320 pp. Reprinted: New York: Berkley Books, 1982. 406 pp.

———. *Midnight Mass.* Eugene, OR: Pulphouse Publishing, 1991. 85 pp.

———. *Nightworld.* Arlington Heights, IL: Dark Harvest, 1992. Reprinted: New York: Jove, 1993. 389 pp.

———. *Reborn.* Adversary No. 2. Arlington Heights, IL: Dark Harvest, 1990. 315 pp. Reprinted: New York: Berkley Books, 1990. 344 pp.

———. *Reprisal.* Adversary No. 3. Arlington Heights, IL: Dark Harvest, 1991. 332 pp. Reprinted: New York: Berkley Publishing, 1992. Winston, Daoma. *The Vampire Curse.* New York: Warner Paperback Library, 1971. 142 pp.

Wippersberg, W. J. M. *Bad Times for Ghosts.* San Diego, CA: Harcourt, Brace, Jovanovich, 1986. 156 pp.

Wolf, Gene. *Castleview.* New York: TOR, 1990. 279 pp.

Worth, Margaret. *Red Wine of Rapture.* New York: Avon, 1973. 187 pp.

Wright, Terri Lucien. *Blood Brothers.* New York: Pinnacle Books, 1992. 288 pp.

———. *The Hunt.* New York: Pinnacle Books, 1991. 320 pp.

———. *Thirst of the Vampire.* New York: Pinnacle Books, 1992. Reprinted: New York: New American Library, 1980. 458 pp.

Wright, T. M. *The Last Vampire.* UK: Victor Gollancz, 1990. 221 pp.

Yarbro, Chelsea. *Better in the Dark.* New York: TOR, 1993. 412 pp.

———. *Blood Games.* New York: St. Martin's Press, 1979. 458 pp. Reprinted: New York: New American Library, 1980. 458 pp.

———. *A Candle for D'Artagnan.* New York: TOR, 1989. 459 pp.

———. *Cautionary Tales.* Garden City, NY: Doubleday, 1978. 204 pp.

———. *Crusader's Torch.* New York: TOR, 1988. 459 pp.

———. *Hotel Transylvania.* New York: St. Martin's Press, 1978. 252 pp.

———. *A Flame in Byzantium.* New York: TOR, 1987. 470 pp.

———. *Nomads.* New York: Bantam Books, 1984. 232 pp.

———. *Out of the House of Life.* New York: TOR, 1990. 446 pp.

———. *The Palace.* New York: St. Martin's Press, 1978. Reprinted: New York: New American Library, 1979. 408 pp.

———. *Path of the Eclipse.* New York: St. Martin's Press, 1981. Reprinted: New York: New American Library, 1982. 447 pp.

———. *The Saint Germain Chronicles.* New York: Pocket Books, 1983. 206 pp.

———. *Tempting Fate.* New York: St. Martin's Press, 1982. Reprinted: New York: New American Library, 1982. 662 pp.

Zelazny, Roger. *Jack of Shadows.* New York: Walker and Co., 1971. 184 pp. Reprinted: New York: New American Library, 1972. 236 pp.

———. *A Night in the Lonesome October.* New York: Morrow, 1993. 280 pp.

Zimmer, Paul Edwin. *Blood of the Colyn Muir.* New York: Avon, 1988. 245 pp.

———. *The Lost Prince.* New York: Berkley Books, 1983. 349 pp. Reprinted: New York: Ace Books, 1987. 349 pp.

DARK SHADOWS NOVELS, 1969 TO THE PRESENT

Dark Shadows, the successful vampire-oriented television show, led to the creation of numerous pieces of fiction based on the characters in the show, including a number of novels.

Beatty, E., and D. L. Crabtree. *Rebirth of the Undead.* The Dark Shadows Fan Club, 1984.

Brand, S. M. Belinda: *A Weekend in New England.*

Christmas in Collinsport. Portland, OR: HarmonyRoad Press, 1992. 45 pp.

Clark, Dale. *Resolutions in Time.* Temple City, CA: Pentagram Press, 1983.

———. *Retribution.* Dallas: Old House Publishing, 1992. 88 pp.

———. *Reunion.* Dallas: Old House Publishing, 1991. 98 pp.

———. *Revelations.* Dallas: Old House Publishing, 1993.

Graham, Jean. *Dark Angel.* Santa Clara, CA: Pentagram Publications, 1977. 84 pp.

———. *Dark Lord.* San Diego, CA: Peacock Press, 1980. 48 pp.

Hamrick, Craig. *Frozen Summer.* Manhattan, KS: Clique Publishing, Inc.

Jonas, Connie. *Masks and Facades.* Portland, OR: HarmonyRoad Press, 1993. 387 pp.

———. *A Matter of Trust.* Portland, OR: HarmonyRoad Press, 1991. 217 pp.

Paige, Lori. *Balm in Gilead.* North Riverside, IL: Pandora Publications.

———. *Dark Changeling.* 1984.

———. *The Year the Fire Came.* 1985.

Ross, Marilyn (Dan Ross). *Barnabas Collins.* New York: Paperback Library, 1968. 157 pp.

———. *Barnabas Collins and Quentin's Demon.* New York: Paperback Library, 1969. 157 pp.

———. *Barnabas Collins and the Gypsy Witch.* New York: Paperback Library, 1969. 160 pp.

———. *Barnabas Collins and the Mysterious Ghost.* New York: Paperback Library, 1969. 160 pp.

———. *Barnabas Collins versus the Warlock.* New York: Paperback Library, 1969. 156 pp.

———. *Barnabas, Quentin and the Avenging Ghost.* New York: Paperback Library, 1970. 159 pp.

———. *Barnabas, Quentin and the Body Snatchers.* New York: Paperback Library, 1971. 156 pp.

———. *Barnabas, Quentin and the Crystal Coffin.* New York: Paperback Library, 1970. 157 pp.

———. *Barnabas, Quentin and Dr. Jekyll's Son.* New York: Paperback Library, 1971. 157 pp.

———. *Barnabas, Quentin and the Frightened Bride.* New York: Paperback Library, 1970. 159 pp.

———. *Barnabas, Quentin and the Grave Robbers.* New York: Paperback Library, 1971. 159 pp.

———. *Barnabas, Quentin and the Hidden Tomb.* New York: Paperback Library, 1971. 158 pp.

———. *Barnabas, Quentin and the Haunted Cave.* New York: Paperback Library, 1970. 158 pp.

———. *Barnabas, Quentin and the Mad Magicians.* New York: Paperback Library, 1971. 158 pp.

———. *Barnabas, Quentin and the Magic Potion.* New York: Paperback Library, 1970. 158 pp.

———. *Barnabas, Quentin and the Mummy's Curse.* New York: Paperback Library, 1970. 159 pp.

———. *Barnabas, Quentin and the Nightmare Assassin.* New York: Paperback Library, 1970. 159 pp.

———. *Barnabas, Quentin and the Scorpio Curse.* New York: Paperback Library, 1970. 157 pp.

———. *Barnabas, Quentin and the Sea Ghost.* New York: Paperback Library, 1971. 158 pp.

———. *Barnabas, Quentin and the Serpent.* New York: Paperback Library, 1970. 155 pp.

———. *Barnabas, Quentin and the Vampire Beauty.* New York: Paperback Library, 1972. 158 pp.

———. *Barnabas, Quentin and the Witch's Curse.* New York: Paperback Library, 1970. 158 pp.

———. *Dark Shadows.* New York: Paperback Library, 1966. 159 pp.

———. *The Curse of Collinwood.* New York: Paperback Library, 1968. 158 pp.

———. *The Demon of Barnabas Collins.* New York: Paperback Library, 1969. 158 pp.

———. *The Foe of Barnabas Collins.* New York: Paperback Library, 1969. 158 pp.

———. *The Mystery of Collinwood.* New York: Paperback Library, 1968. 159 pp.

———. *The Peril of Barnabas Collins.* New York: Paperback Library, 1969 158 pp.

———. *The Phantom and Barnabas Collins.* New York: Paperback Library, 1969. 158 pp.

———. *The Secret of Barnabas Collins.* New York: Paperback Library, 1970. 159 pp.

———. *Strangers at Collins House.* New York: Paperback Library, 1967. 159 pp.

———. *Victoria Winters.* New York: Paperback Library, 1967. 160 pp.

Sutherland, May. *Sins of the Fathers.* Tacoma, WA: Medallion Press, 1993. 200 pp.

Tignor, Beth. *Tryst of Dark Shadows.* North Riverside, IL: Pandora Publications, 1981.

Wisdon, Sharon. *Love's Pale Shadow.* Sunderland, MA:Lone Dove Press, 1992.

Zachary, Judy. *No Other Love.* Santa Clara, CA: Pentegram Publications, 1978. 87 pp.

INDEX

Bold face page numbers denote primary references.

A

A la Recherche des Vampires 231
Abbott and Costello Meet Dr. Jekyll and Mr. Hyde 306, 542
Abbott and Costello Meet Frankenstein 233, 306, 384, 621, 679, 722
Abbott; G. F. 277, 572
Abode of the Beast, Volume 2 795
Abramson; Al 84
Abrosius; Professor 306
Abruzzese; Alberto 329
Academy of Science Fiction, Fantasy and Horror Films 129, 208
Accardo; Loretta M. 439
Accolade 246
Acid Rain Studios 456
Ackerman; Forrest J. **1**, 116, 125, 544, 624, 646
Ackerman Science Fiction Agency 1
Aconite **3**
Ada; Princess 42
Addams; Charles S. 3, 598
The Addams Family **3**, 206, 265, 307, 414, 415, 424, 456, 598, 768
The Addams Family Family Reunion Game 4 *See also:* Games, vampire
Addams Family Fan Club; The Munsters and The 4
The Addams Family Find Uncle Fester Game 4 *See also:* Games, vampire
Addams Family; Halloween with the 4, 308
The Addams Family Values 4, 768
Addams; Morticia 3, 206, 265, 424, 598
The Adult Version of Dracula 787
"The Adventure of the Sussex Vampire" 556

Adventures into the Unknown 115
Aeschylus 274
Aesculapius 318
Afanas'ev; A. N. 526, 564
Africa 12, 48, 379, 567, 588-589
Africa, vampires in **4**
African American vampires **8**, 12, 48 *See also: Blacula*
AfterAge 798
Agni 321
Agron; Salvatore 133
Agyar 538, 788
Ahkea Kkots 727
Aiken; Conrad 475
Akasha 108, 139, 167
Al U. Card 185, 429
Alabama's Ghost 10, 740
Albania 558, 568
Aldiss; Brian 541
Alien vampires *See:* Science fiction and the vampire
All Heads Turn When the Hunt Goes By 791
Allatius; Leo **10**, 101, 274, 276, 687
Allégret; Marc 623
Allen and Rossi Meet Dracula and Frankenstein 740
Allgren; Thomas 632
Allman; Sheldon 196, 307
Allogiamento; Theresa 698
Almost the Bride of Dracula; or, Why the Count Remains a Bachelor 775
Alnwick Castle 616, 682
Alnwick Castle, The Vampire of **11**
Alpes 319
Alqul See: Ghouls
Alraune 719, 721, 724

Alternate Shadows   **11** *See also: Dark Shadows*
Altman; Amber   150
Alucard; Count   551
Alucarda   404
Aluka   **12**
Alvantin   323
Ambelain; Robert   231
Ambrov Keon   796
Ambrus; Victor G.   309
American Comics Group   115
American International Pictures   123-124, 703
American Society for Psychical Research   633
American vampires   **12**
Anak Pontianak   724
Anderwalt; Valan   55
Andi Sex Gang   268
Andy Warhol's Dracula   308
Anemia   **15**, 54, 329, 652, 757
Angel of Death   269
Angel for Satan; An   581
Angeles y Querubines   740
Angelique   449
Animals   **15**, 64, 81, 95, 98, 109, 173, 202, 277, 299, 401, 472, 516, 534, 547, 567, 571, 588, 590, 602, 609, 686
Ann Radcliffe Award   3, 49, 129
Anne Rice's Vampire Lestat Fan Club   **18**, 369, 510, 685
The Anniversary, Quartermass and the Pit   27
Anno Dracula   548, 798
The Annotated Dracula   436, 689
"Another Dracula"   174
The Anthrax Mutation   800
Ape's-Face   784
Apollonius   272, 691
Appearance of a vampire   **19**, 196 *See also: Characteristics of vampires*
Apuleius   273
Aquinas; Thomas   319
Arabian Knights   258
Arabian Tales   575
Arata; Stephen D.   430, 482
Archer; Chad   647
Arkham House   385
The Armageddon Box   803
Armenia, vampires in   **21**
Arozamena; Eduardo   180, 639
The Arrival   768
Art in the Blood   205, 791

As Sete Vampiros   568
Asasabonsam   5
Asema   6, 223, 567, 589, 691
Ashanti   5, 379
Asiman   5, 223, 379
Aspen   526, 563, 580, 607 *See also: Stake*
Assyria, vampires in *See:* Babylon and Assyria, vampires in ancient
Astin; John   3
Astral body   631 *See also: Psychic vampirism*
Astro Vamps   267, 425
Aswang   461
Atlas Comics   116
Attack of the Blind Dead   740
Atwater; Barry   432
Atwill; Lionel   375
Aurora; Sapphire   270
Austra; Stephen   44
Australia, vampires in   **22**
The Awakening   800
Aylesworth; Thomas   340
Ayme; Eugene   231
Aziman   589
The Azrael Project   269
Aztecs   400

B

Baby Blood   231, 768
Babylon and Assyria, vampires in ancient   **25**
Bacchelli   328
Bachman; Richard   352
Back to the USSR   768
Bad breath   215
Bad Dreams   798
The Bad Flower   179, 727
The Bad Place   795
The Bad Sister   802
Bad Times for Ghosts   804
Badham; John   182, 193, 356
Baker, Roy Ward   **27**, 99, 288, 694 *See also:* Hammer Films
Baker; Scott   169
Balderston, John L.   **28**, 62, 79, 162, 177, 181-182, 195, 356, 382, 417, 548, 619-620
Ballard; Guy   490
Balm in Gilead   227, 805
Balthazar   791
Baltic States, vampires in the   **29**, 525
Bandh Darwaza   768
The Bane of the Black Sword   797

Bangladesh   426

Banglow 666   768

Banks Islands   597

Bannerworth; Flora   215

Banshee   223

Baobban sith   616

Bara; Theda   473, 627

Barbarella   544

Barber; Paul   212, 486

The Bargain   800

The Barge of Haunted Lives   786

Baring-Gould; Sabine   35

The Barnabas Collins ''Dark Shadows''
   Game   239

Barnabas Collins and the Gypsy Witch   805

Barnabas Collins and the Mysterious Ghost
   805

Barnabas Collins and Quentin's Demon
   805

Barnabas Collins versus the Warlock   805

Barnabas, Quentin and the Avenging Ghost
   805

Barnabas, Quentin and the Body Snatchers
   805

Barnabas, Quentin and the Crystal Coffin
   805

Barnabas, Quentin and the Dr. Jekyll's Son
   805

Barnabas, Quentin and the Frightened
   Bride   805

Barnabas, Quentin and the Grave Robbers
   805

Barnabas, Quentin and the Haunted Cave
   805

Barnabas, Quentin and the Hidden Tomb
   805

Barnabas, Quentin and the Mad Magicians
   805

Barnabas, Quentin and the Magic Potion
   806

Barnabas, Quentin and the Mummy's Curse
   806

Barnabas, Quentin and the Nightmare
   Assassin   806

Barnabas, Quentin and the Scorpio Curse
   806

Barnabas, Quentin and the Sea Ghost   806

Barnabas, Quentin and the Serpent   806

Barnabas, Quentin, and the Vampire
   Beauty   522, 806

Barnabas, Quentin and the Witch's Curse
   806

Barnes; Jimmy   423

Baron Blood   **30** *See also:* Comic books,
   the vampire in

Barrett; Jonathan   205, 477

Barrett; Nancy   151

Barry McKenzie Holds His Own   741

Bastedo; Alexandra   694

Bas   391

The Bat Cave   265, 424

The Bat People   741

The Bat Woman   784

Bates; Ralph   694

Bathory, Elizabeth   **31**, 36, 42, 45, 131, 169,
   265, 289, 337, 363, 364, 398, 425, 459, 465,
   556, 577, 627, 692, 694 *See also:* Crime,
   vampiric

Bathory Palace   **36**

Batman   **36**, 115, 393

Batman Fights Dracula   728

Bats Are Folks   775

Bats in the Basement   775

Bats in the Belfry   785

Bats Out of Hell   801

Bats, vampire   8, 15, 16, 37, **38**, 81, 95,
   112, 168, 173, 185, 223, 321, 567, 579, 609,
   661, 682, 794

Batula   724

Baudelaire; Charles   230, 328, 474

Bauer; Edwin   256

Bauhaus   176, 264, 418, 424

Bava, Mario   35, **42**, 287, 328, 360, 364,
   527, 543, 581, 608, 693

Beast of a Different Burden   775

The Beast with the Red Hands   802

Beasts   792

Beaty; Elwood   699

The Beautiful Biting Machine   795

The Beautiful Vampire   230, 250, 784

Because the Dawn   365, 757

Beebbe; B. B.   186

Begbie; P. J.   390

Beginnings: The Island of Ghosts   699

''Bela Lugosi's Dead''   176, 265, 418, 424

Belanger; Michelle   553

Belinda: A Weekend in New England   227

Benedict XIII; Pope   75 *See also:*
   Christianity

Benedict XIV; Pope   212 *See also:*
   Christianity

Benjamin; Alan   344

Benjamin; Richard   307, 653

Bennett Fan Club; Nigel   226-227

Bennett; Joan   151

Bennett; Lord Andrew   317

Bennett; Nigel 225, 227
Benson; E. F. 697
Benzel; Viktor 372
Benzoni; M. Giroalme 40
Bérard; Cyprien 193, 434, 480, 528
Berger; Fred H. 265, 425
Bergstrom; Elaine 35, **44**, 105, 210, 241, 444, 610, 697
Bernau; Christopher 196
Bersicker 16
Bertrand; Francoise 132, 230, 258
Berwick, The Vampire of **45**
Best of Dark Shadows 728
Best Ghost Stories of J. S. Le Fanu 358
Best of the Journal of Modern Vampirism 648
Betail 69, 322
Better in the Dark 804
Beverly Hills Vamp 696, 757
Beyond Rejection 796
Bhagavat-purana 347
Bhuta 279, 321
Bibliographie de Dracula 46
Bibliography, vampire **45** *See also:* Carter, Margaret L.
The Bibliography of Vampire Literature 640
Big Bad Blood of Dracula 120
Bigelow; Kathryn 696
Bill the Galactic Hero on the Planet of Zombie Vampires 793
Billy the Kid and the Green Blaze Vampire 758
Billy the Kid vs. Dracula 84, 728
Birgau Pass 56
Bistrita 47
Bistritz **47**, 56, 88, 138, 291, 533, 684 *See also:* Borgo Pass; Castle Dracula; Romania, vampires in; Transylvania
Bite! 768
Bite Me in the Coffin Not in the Closet Fan Club 47, 302 *See also:* Homosexuality and the vampire; Lesbian vampires
Bites and Pieces 711
Bitesky; C.D. 342
Black Ambrosia 698, 791
The Black Castle 149, 790
The Black Chronicle 266
Black Evil 10
The Black Harvest of Countess Dracula 751
Black; Isobel 287
Black; Jackie 477

The Black Room 758
Black Sabbath 43, 264, 330, 424, 527, 728
Black Sunday 42, 287, 330, 527, 581, 608, 693, 728
Black Vampire 10, 758
Blacula 10, **48**, 395, 705, 741 *See also:* Marshall, William; African American vampires
Blade the Vampire Slayer **49**, 122, 187, 405, 411, 608 *See also:* African American vampires
Blak; Groovella 271
Blak; Morpheus 271
Blake; Alfonso Corona 404, 535
Blake; Edmund 191
Blake; William 41
Blavatsky; Madame H. P. 294, 490
Blaylock; Miriam 55, 696
Blaze; John 405
Bleiler; E. F. 358
Blind Hunger 790
Blink; George 194
Bloch; Robert 54, 502
Blomberg; Dr. Ernest 458
Blood 15, **51**, 111, 120, 138, 163, 225, 380, 447, 462, 532, 543, 547, 549, 701, 741, 790
Blood Alone 45, 788
Blood Autumn 799
Blood Bath 728
The Blood Beast Terror 145, 728
Blood and Black Lace 43, 330, 359
Blood Brothers 386, 797, 804
Blood Ceremony 741
The Blood Circuit 743
Blood of the Colyn Muir 804
The Blood Countess 799
Blood Country 801
Blood Couple 10, 741
The Blood Demon 256
Blood for Dracula 308, 741
Blood of Dracula 120, 216, 364, 621, 724, 803
The Blood of Dracula's Castle 729
The Blood of Dracula's Coffin 84
The Blood Drinkers 729
Blood Drinking *See:* Crime, Vampiric
Blood Dynasty 789
Blood Farm 801
Blood Feast 422
Blood Feud 801
Blood Fiend 729
Blood of Frankenstein 84, 741

Blood Games   252, 698, 702, 804
Blood Heritage   802
Blood Hunt   794
Blood of the Impaler   800
Blood of the Innocent   120
Blood Is the Harvest   122
Blood Is My Heritage   364
Blood Junkies on Capitol Hill   120
Blood Legacy   792
Blood Lines   793
Blood Lust   741, 758, 790
The Blood Merchants   801
Blood Mist   794
Blood Money   785
Blood of My Blood   795
The Blood of Nostradamus   404, 729
Blood Pact   793
Blood Price   793
Blood Pudding   775
Blood Rare   786
Blood Relations   742
Blood Rights   798
Blood Rites   45, 788
Blood Root   798
Blood and Roses   82, 231, 359, 365, 551,
   623, 693, 728, 783, 787
The Blood of Roses   795
The Blood Spattered Bride   82, 694, 742
Blood Sport   801
Blood Sport: A Journey Up the
   Hassayampa   794
The Blood Stone   541
Blood Suckers   256
Blood Summer   790
Blood Thirst   729, 792
Blood Trail   793
The Blood of the Vampire   301, 534,
   724, 785
Blood of the Virgins   729
Blood on the Water   205, 791
Blood Wedding   792
Blood Will Have Blood   788
Blood Wings   793
Blood Worm   793
Bloodchild   798
Bloodcircle   205, 791
The Bloodless Vampire   729
Bloodlines: The Vampire Magazine   150
Bloodlines: The Vampire Temple Journal
   602, 713
Bloodlinks   794
Bloodlist   205, 791
Bloodlust   769, 797

Bloodlust: Conversations with Real
   Vampires   635
Bloodright: Memoirs of Mircea, Son of
   Dracula   613, 803
Bloodshift   799
Bloodstalk   792
Bloodsucker   267
The Bloodsuckers   729
Bloodsuckers from Outer Space   758
Bloodthirst   790, 799
Bloodthirsty   769
Bloodwars   797
The Bloodwind   793
The Bloody Countess   35
The Bloody Vampire   404, 729
Bloomfield; Louis   79
Blot; Henri   132
Bluatsauger   253
Blue Blood   269
Blue Lamp in a Winter Night   100
Blue Magic   789
Blum; Eva   277
Blum; Richard   277
Bobby "Boris" Pickett & The Crypt
   Kickers   422
Boden; Wayne   133
The Body Beneath   742
Bogomilism   561
Bogomils   65
Bohanan; Carole   619, 650
Bohemia   146, 313
Boito; Arrigo   330
Boni; Enrico   328
Book I: Vampyres   795
The Book of Common Dread   797
The Book of Werewolves   692
Borgo Pass   47, **56**, 87, 169, 291, 595 See
   also: Castle Dracula; Transylvania
Born with the Dead   787
Bose; Lucia   694
Bosnia   355, 560, 569, 676
Bottling   67
Bouchard; Angelique   55, 111, 153
Boucicault; Dion   194
Bourre; Jean-Paul   231
The Bowery Boys Meet the Monsters
   306, 725
Bowie; David   696
Boys and Ghouls Together   775
Bradbury; Ray   576
Braddon; Mary Elizabeth   618
Brahma   321
Brahmaparusha   280

The Brain Stealers   796

Brak the Barbarian Versus the Sorceress
785

Bram Stoker Archives   57

Bram Stoker Awards   396, 698

The Bram Stoker Club   326

Bram Stoker International Summer School
57, 128

Bram Stoker Memorial Collection of Rare
Books   128

Bram Stoker Picture File   128

The Bram Stoker Society   **57**, 176, 326, 555

Bram Stoker's Dracula   17, **58**, 92, 104,
123, 127, 175, 179, 182, 210, 240, 246, 291,
293, 301, 413, 417, 442, 450, 455-456,
537, 552, 586, 596, 610, 639, 670, 681, 685,
769, 800

Bram Stoker's Original Dracula   742

Brand; S. M.   227

Brandi; Walter   330

Brautigam; Rob   325

Breene; R. S.   326

Brennan; Sean   375

Brennan; T. Casey   647

Brett; Jeremy   557

"The Bride of Corinth"   255, 471, 692

The Bride of Frankenstein   233, 775

Brides   177, 182

The Brides of Dracula   144, 175, 220, 287,
534, 639, 730, 786

The Bride's Initiation   742

Brides, vampire   59, **61**, 87, 107, 215, 292,
301, 416, 548, 564, 580, 652, 661

The Brides Wore Blood   758

Bridge to Freedom   491

Briery; Traci   538, 552, 698

Briggs; Katheryn   616

Bring Me the Vampire   730

Bring on the Night   790

Brite; Poppy Z.   267-268

Brodian; Laura   113

Brood of the Witch-Queen   786

The Brooding   790

Brother Blood   800

Brown; James   132

Brown; Mary E.   13

Brown; Murray   182

Brown; Porter Emerson   626

Browning, Tod   2, **62**, 93, 176, 373, 383,
423, 620

Bruce; Nigel   556

Bruja   **64**, 401

Brunn; Robert   343

Bruxa   **64**, 576, 568

Buchette; James R.   257

Budge; E. A. Wallis   27

Buenas Noches, Senior Monstruo   578, 758

Buffy the Vampire Slayer   345, 697, 769

Bulgaria, vampires in   15, **65**, 219, 560, 637
See also: Slavic vampire

Bullet   37, **68**, 99, 164, 173, 290, 518, 540,
677 *See also:* Destroying the vampire

Bunnicula   18, 308, 341 *See also:* Juvenile
literature

Bunnicula Fun Book   310

Bunnicula the Vampire Rabbit   758

Bunston; Herbert   177

Burg; Michael   196

Bürger; Gottfried August   470, 549, 618

Burma, vampires in *See:* Myanmar,
vampires in

Burne-Jones; Philip   626

Burning Tears of Sassurum   787

Burton, Richard Francis   **68**, 322, 349

Burying the Shadow   789

By Blood Alone   315, 794

Byelorussia   524

Byron, Lord   **70**, 188, 193, 230, 232, 256,
261, 263, 273, 328, 433, 472, 480, 527, 618

C

Cabal: The Nightbreed   788

The Cabala   266, 425

*Cadet Buteux, Vampire avec relation
véridique du prologue et les trois acts de cet
épouvantable mélodrame*   194, 775

Caged Virgins   512

Caiano; Mario   330

Cake of Blood   742

Calendar of Vampire Events   640

Callicantzaros See: Greece, vampires in

Calmet, Dom Augustin   **75**, 103, 147, 160,
209, 229, 255, 310, 313, 327, 461, 528, 573,
618, 630, 656 *See also:* France, vampires in

Calvino; Italo   329

The Camarilla   244 *See also:* Games,
vampire

The Camarilla: A Vampire Fan Association
77

Camazotz   40, 400, 579

Cambodia   426

The Camel and the Vampire   775

Campana; Dino   330

Campbell; Bill   59

Campbell; Bruce   653

Campbell; Liza   106
Canada   478
A Candle for D'Artagnan   804
Canon Episcopi   686
Captain America   31 *See also:* Comic
  books, the vampire in
Captain Kronos, Vampire Hunter   289, 742
  See also: Vampire hunters
Capuana; Luigi   328
Capulina Contra Los Monstruos   404
Capulina Contra Los Vampiros   404, 742
Cardona; Rene   404
Carfax   16, **79**, 173, 177, 184, 190, 291,
  300, 342, 375, 412, 498, 505, 547, 580
Carmen; Julie   696
"Carmilla"   19, 27, **80**, 104, 107, 120, 163,
  165, 197-198, 231, 288, 301, 316, 326,
  358, 360, 364, 421, 429-430, 448, 464,
  483, 535, 577, 579, 584, 587, 593, 600, 609,
  618, 623, 648, 657, 692-694, 730, 758, 776
  See also: Sexuality and the vampire
Carmouche; Pierre Francios   434
Carna   520
Carne de tu Carne   758
Caroon; Maik   257
Carradine, John   21, 28, 61, **83**, 97, 175,
  216, 233, 404, 414, 598, 619
Carreras; Jimmy   464
Carreras; Sir John   286
Carrey; Jim   308, 696
Carry on Screaming   730
Carter, Margaret L.   46, **85**, 262, 475-476
  See also: Bibliography, vampire
The Case of the Full Moon Murders   742
Cassidy; Ted   4
Cast a Cold Eye   800
Castenega; Fray Martin   576
Castle Bistrita   89
Castle of Blood   581, 730
Castle Bran   89
Castle Dracula   16, 28, 41, 47, 49, 51, 56,
  58-59, 63, **87**, 104, 107, 126-127, 138,
  166, 169, 177, 181, 185, 190, 202, 204, 239,
  248, 278, 287, 291, 303, 333, 372, 397, 407,
  409-410, 416, 430, 442, 453, 458, 547-
  548, 564, 580, 587, 609-610, 652, 668, 684
  See also: Bistritz; Borgo Pass; Transylvania
The Castle Dracula Quarterly   130, 640
Castle of Deception   791
Castle of Dracula   730
Castle Dubrava   794
Castle of the Living Dead   730
Castle of the Monsters   403

Castledoom   795
Castleview   804
Casual Relations   742
Cat People   679
The Catacombs   791
Catay-Keris Productions   99, 392, 485
Catholic Apostolic Church of the Holy
  Grail   643 *See also:* Christianity and
  vampires
Cats   16, 81, 98, 516 *See also:* Animals
Cauldron   378
Cautionary Tales   804
Cave of the Living Dead   256
Cazacu; Matai   221
CDFC Bi-Annual   706
CDFC News-Journal   706
Cecilone; Michael   552
Celtic Catholic Church   643 *See also:*
  Christianity and vampires
Cerney; L. Lee   245
Challenge to Dracula   796
Chandler; Helen   177
Chaney, Lon   62, **92**, 216, 373, 678
The Changeling   797
Chanoc contra el Tigre y el Vampiro   743
Chanoc vs. the Tiger and the Vampire   743
*Chanoc y el Hijo del Santo Contra Los
  Vampiros Asesinos*   536
Chapman; Janine   228
Characteristics of vampires   **94**, 661 *See
  also:* Appearance of a vampire
Chase; Richard   132, 632
Chedipe   324
Cheeky Devil Vampire Research   **96**
Chetwynd-Hayes; Ronald   28, **97**
Chewong   391
Chi i Suu Ningyo   337
Chi o Suu Me   337
Chi o Suu Ningyo   743
Chiang-shih   15, 97, 673
Chikatilo; Andrei   134
Children of the Blood   800
Children of the Night   56, 122, 222, 783,
  769, 776, 795-796
Children of the Night Award   189
Children's vampiric literature *See:* Juvenile
  literature
Children and Young Persons (Harmful
  Publications) Act   116
A Child's Garden of Vampires   706
Chillers   758
China, vampires in   15, **97**, 249, 426,
  588, 603

A Chinese Torture Garden 785
Chosen Haunts 794
Chosen Survivors 743
"Christabel" 107-108, 363, 592, 692
Christian death 267, 425
Christianity and vampires 21, 65, **100**, 138, 209, 477, 524, 537, 560, 569, 674 *See also:* Eucharistic wafer
Christmas in Collinsport 805
Christopher Lee's X Certificate 362, 459
Chronicles 682
Chronique de Voyage 743
Chronos 769
Church of England 209
Church Universal and Triumphant 491
Churel 323
Cihuacoatl 400
Cihuapipiltin 400
Cihuateteo 400
Cirillo; Renato Antonio 134
Citizen Vampire 149, 168, 790
City of the Dead 796
City of Thieves 796
Clairmont; Claire 71
Clapp; Edwin R. 351
Clark; Dale 158, 441
Clark; Doug 421
Claudia 367
Clay's Ark 788
Clinking Stones 792
Clive-Ross; F. 135
"The Cloak" 466, 502
The Close Encounter of the Vampire 100, 758
Club Vampyre **106**
A Clutch of Vampires: These Being among the Best from History and Literature 397
Coatlicue 400
Coats; Daryl 495
Cobert; Robert 151
Cochran; John 647
Codrington; R. H. 597
Coffins 37, 81, 95, 98, **106**, 141, 148, 164, 173, 199, 253, 281, 296, 298, 342, 366, 409, 458, 478, 498, 580, 662, 685
Colan; Gene 37
Cold Turkey 789
Coleman; Marion Moore 479
Coleridge, Samuel Taylor 107, **108**, 165, 264, 301, 351, 363, 472, 550, 575, 592, 618, 692 *See also:* Poetry, the vampire in
Collected Works of Joseph Sheridan Le Fanu 359

Collectibles and Souvenirs *See:* Paraphernalia, Vampire
Collins, Barnabas 12, 55, 95, **111**, 117, 136, 142, 150, 158, 176, 181, 216, 235, 239, 264, 379, 449, 455, 507, 522, 583, 599, 679, 700
Collins; Cassandra 155
Collins; David 151
Collins; Frederic 257
Collins; Jeremiah 111
Collins; Josette DuPres 111, 151
Collins; Nancy 698
Collins; Quentin 154
Collins; Roger 151
Collins; Wilkie 584
Collinsport Players **113**, 293, 555
The Collinsport Record 503
The Collinswood Journal 238, 503
The Collinswood Record 238
Collinwood Chronicle 157, 459
Columbia Pictures 58
Comic books, the vampire in 21, 46, 49, 82, **115**, 156, 175, 208, 257, 267, 317, 331, 340, 371, 387, 405, 544, 557, 608, 653, 697 *See also:* Dracula (Dell Comics superhero); Dracula (Marvel Comics character); Paraphernalia, vampire
Comic Magazine Association of America (CMAA) 116
Comics Code 37, 49, 82, 116, 156, 175, 185, 186, 187, 372, 392, 410, 608, 645
Comix: A History of Comic Books in America 149
Commonwealth of Independent States 525
Conan the Conqueror: The Hyborean Age 785
Concorde Pictures 124, 696
Concrete Blonde 418
Condemned to Live 721
Confession 793
Conroy; Cindy Avitabile 379
Conway; Gerry 37
Coogan; Jackie 4
Cooke; Thomas Potter 467
Coolidge-Rask; Marie 62
Cooney; Caroline B. 345
Cooper; Alice 418
Coppola, Francis Ford 58, 92, 122, **123**, 175, 179, 222, 240, 293, 301, 413, 442, 455, 533, 537, 552, 586, 670, 681
Corday; Emile 532
Corman, Roger William 123, **124**, 216, 396, 404, 542, 581, 693, 696

Corridor of Blood   359
The Corridors of Fear   523, 800
Cortland; Ben   396
Corvinus; Matthias   89, 311, 659, 669
Cosner; Candy M.   641
Costello; Lou   306
Costello; Robert   151
Cottingham; Richard   134
The Count   796
Count Chocula   458
Count Czerny   501
Count Dracula   49, **126**, 179, 288, 307, 338, 414, 776, 800
Count Dracula Book of Classic Vampire Tales   706
The Count Dracula Chicken Cookbook   706
The Count Dracula Fan Club   46, **127**, 176, 188, 310, 476, 633, 640, 645, 648, 705 *See also:* Youngson, Jeanne Keyes; The Dracula Museum
The Count Dracula Fan Club Book of Vampire Stories   706
Count Dracula Fan Club News-Journal   711
The Count Dracula Fan Club Research Library   128
Count Dracula and His Vampire Brides   144, 290, 360, 639
Count Dracula; or, A Musical Mania from Transylvania   776
The Count Dracula Society   3, 49, 85, **129**, 176, 259
The Count Dracula Society Award   208
The Count Dracula Society Quarterly   129
Count Dracula, the True Story   743
Count Dracula and the Unicorn   706
Count Dracula's Canadian Affair   175, 784
Count Draculations: Monster Riddles   310
Count Duckula   18, **199**, 308, 599
Count Erotica, Vampire   743
Count Ken Fan Club   **130**
Count Manfred   801
Count Strahd von Zarovich   241
Count Thurzo   33
Count; Transylvanian   307
Count von Count   341
The Count Will Rise Again; or, Dracula in Dixie   776
Count Yorga, Vampire   744
Countess Dracula   35, 289, 365, 459, 465, 694, 744, 776, 798 *See also:* Bathory, Elizabeth
Countess Waldessa   679

"Coven Party"   19
Covenant with the Vampires: The Diaries of the Families Dracula   790
Cowdin; J. Cheever   621
Cox; Greg   46
Crabtree; D. L.   699
A Cradle for D'Artagnan   698
The Craft of Terror   285
The Craving   578, 758
Crawford; Anne   618, 692
Crazy Safari   100, 769
Creature   790
A Creature of the Night   785
Creep, Shadow!   785
Creepy   117
Crime Doctor's Courage   722
Crime, vampiric   **131**, 284-285, 632
Crimson   637, 713
Crimson Kisses   790
Croatia   101, 560, 568, 677
Croglin Grange, The Vampire of   **135**, 617
Cromwell; Dr. Charles   31
The Crone   792
Cross, Ben   112, **136**, 583, 599
Crothers; Joel   151
Crowley; Aleister   635
Crucifix   95, 103-104, **138**, 173, 210, 248, 251, 281, 291, 298, 316, 407, 409, 416, 478, 488, 537, 562, 587, 593-594, 662, 674, 688, 702
Cruise, Tom   **140**, 511 *See also: Interview with the Vampire*
Crume; Vic   340
Crusader's Torch   252, 698, 702, 804
Crutchley; John   134
Cry Vampire   790
Cuadecuc   744
The Cult   265, 424
Cuntius, Johannes   **141**, 147
The Cure   265, 424
Curiel; Frederico   404
The Curse of Collinswood   522, 806
The Curse of Concullens   802
Curse of the Crying Woman   731
Curse of the Devil   35, 694, 744
The Curse of Doone   785
The Curse of Frankenstein   286, 359
The Curse of Nostradamus   404, 730
The Curse of the Obelisk   792
Curse of the Undead   85, 621, 725
Curse of the Vampires   744, 787, 789
The Curse of the Werewolf   679
Curse of the Wicked Wife   100, 758

Curtin; Jeremiah 325

Curtis, Dan 59, 111, 126, 136, **142**, 150, 181, 236, 396, 432, 453, 583, 598, 600

Curtis Productions; Dan 143, 415

Curve 265, 425

Cushing, Peter 28, 99, **144**, 220, 233, 286, 289-290, 359, 464, 534, 594, 615, 619, 639, 653, 694

Cusick; Richie Tankersley 345

Cyril 146, 513, 560

Czech Republic and Slovakia, vampires in the **146**, 313, 560

D

Da Andrade; Marcelo 134

Dacia 513

Daemon in Lithuania 793

Dahomey 379

Daigneault; Jessica 226

Dakhanavar 21

Dakinis 347

Dakki, the Vampire 721

Dala 38

Dale; Frances 177

Damon; Roger 257

Danag 463

The Dance of Blood 791

Dance of the Damned 126, 696, 758

Dance of the Dead 792

Dance of the Vampires 306

Dancer; Deborah 318

Danger on Vampire Trail 340

Daniels, Les **149**, 167

Daninsky; Count Waldemar 577, 679

Danis the Dark Productions **150**

Danton; Ray 330

Dark Angel 805

Dark Arts 266

Dark Changeling 699, 805

Dark Dance 795

Dark Divide 787

Dark Encounter 802

Dark Father 798

The Dark Half 795

Dark Horse Comics 451

Dark; Jason 257

Dark Lord 805

Dark Shadows 11, 55, 111, 113, 117, 136, 142, **150**, 159, 181, 184, 204, 235, 238-239, 262, 264, 302, 305, 307, 340, 378-379, 441, 445, 449, 453, 455, 466, 507, 523, 533, 545, 553-554, 583, 598, 633, 646, 679, 699, 700, 806

Dark Shadows in the Afternoon 554, 699

Dark Shadows Announcement 415, 714

Dark Shadows: Behind the Scenes 156

Dark Shadows Bloopers 156

Dark Shadows Collectibles Classified 459

Dark Shadows Collector's Guide 158, 459

The Dark Shadows Comic Books 115

Dark Shadows Concordance 699

Dark Shadows Fan Club; Pittsburgh 555

Dark Shadows Festival 113, 156, **158**, 293, 415, 441, 445, 553-554

Dark Shadows; Friends of 184, 503

"Dark Shadows" Game; The Barnabas Collins 239

Dark Shadows; House of 112, 142, 156, 236

Dark Shadows; Inside 238, 503

Dark Shadows; Night of 112, 142, 156

The Dark Shadows Official Fan Club 156, 158, 415

Dark Shadows Over Oklahoma **159**

Dark Shadows Society; International 238

Dark Shadows Society of Milwaukee **159**

Dark Shadows 25th Anniversary 156

Dark Shadows; The World of 156, 158, 553-554

Dark Theater 176, 458, 662

Dark Times 641

Dark Vengeance 759

The Darkangel 799

Darker Than You Think 787

The Darkest Night 786

Darkhold 405

Darkness 769

Darkness on the Ice 803

Darvulia; Anna 32

Darwin; Charles 40

Das Perfum 802

Daughter of Dr. Jekyll 725

The Daughter of Dracula 82, 744

Daughter of the Night 45, 788

Daughters of Darkness 35, 364-365, 694, 744, 769

Davanzati, Giuseppe 75, 103, **159**, 313, 327, 630

Dave; Max 329

Davenport; Neal 257

Davenport; Nigel 143, 182

David; Thayer 151

Davidson; Alan 80

Davidson; Peter 273

Davies; Bernard   188, 378, 682

Davies; David Stuart   558

Davies Fan Club; The Official Geraint Wyn 225-226

Davies; Geraint Wyn   225, 599

Dawn   769

Dawn of the Vampire   793

The Day of Forever   783

Daymares from the Crypt   476

DC Comics   119, 317, 393

De Carlo; Yvonne   414, 599

De Graecorum hodie quirundam opinationibus   10

De Grandin; Jules   501

De Jouffroy; Achille   434

De Lioncourt; Lestat   19, 95, 108, 139, 140, 176, 219, 223, 267, 271, 302, 408, 425, 507, 533 *See also: Interview with the Vampire*

De Lorca; Frank   257

De Masticatione Mortuorum   254, 688

De Rais; Gilles   131

De Sade; Marquis   131

De Schertz; Charles Ferdinand   147

De Souza; Edward   287

De Ville Books & Prints   19

De Villenueva, Sebastian   149, **167** *See also:* Daniels, Les

De Wit; Augusta   485

De Wray; Louis   270

The Dead   799

Dead Men Walk   723

Dead of Night   396, 600

The Dead Travel Fast   802

Deadly Harvest   791

Deadspawn   386, 797

Deadspeak   386, 797

Deadwalk   792

Deafula   179, 744

Deane Award; Hamilton   189

Deane, Hamilton   19, 29, 62, 79, **160**, 174, 177, 181-182, 189-190, 305, 356, 382, 413, 450, 548, 556, 580, 586, 619-620, 653, 681

Dear Ladies of the Night   795

Dearest Dracula   776

Dearg-dul   317, 325

Death and the Maiden   206

Death Angel   684, 803

Death Angel's Shadow   803

The Death Box   795

Death Coach   684, 803

Death at the Crossroads   776

Death Doctor   684, 803

Death Dreams of Dracula   120

Death in June   267, 425

Death, Inc.   458

Death Masque   206

The Death of P'Town   731

Death Reign of the Vampire King   802

Death School   684, 804

Death Trance   797

Death of vampires *See:* Destroying the vampire

Deathgame   792

The Deathmaster   744

Death's Angel   801

Decades   699

Decapitation   **162**, 164, 173, 203, 219, 248, 479, 518, 539, 563, 572, 580, 646, 703, *See also:* Destroying the vampire

Decobra; Gustav   37

Decodanz: The Dilemma of Desmodus and Diphylla   776

Def by Temptation   769

The Delicate Dependency: A Novel of the Vampire Life   802

Delirium   266

Dell Publishing Co. Inc.   185

Delorme; Roger   231

Demeter   16, 138, 172

The Demon of Barnabas Collins   806

The Demon with the Bloody Hands   534

The Demon Lover   784, 803

The Demon in the Mirror   798

Demon Planet   731

Démone en Lituanie   793

Demons   790

Dendam Pontianak   693, 725

Deneuve; Catherine   365, 696

Denmark   539

Denville; Damien   270

Der Fluch der Schwarzen Schwestern   747

Der Vampyr   194, 255, 256,470, 474, 781

Der Vampyr—A Soap Opera   529

Destroying the vampire   162, **163**, 168, 488, 563, 637

A Deusa de Marmore—Escrava do Diabo 568, 745

The Devil Bat   301, 384, 723

Devil Bat's Daughter   723

Devil in Darkness   800

Devil Worship in Britain   285

The Devil's Cat   794

The Devil's Commandment   35

The Devil's Heart   794

The Devil's Kiss   794

The Devil's Mistress   694, 731
The Devils of Darkness   731
The Devil's Plaything   745
The Devil's Skin   745
The Devil's Touch   794
Devil's Vendetta   759
The Devil's Wedding Night   745
Devlin; Burke   151
The Devonshire Demons   776
The Devouring   787
Dhampir   **168**, 281, 572, 549, 637, 787 *See also:* Destroying the vampire
Diderot   229, 630
Die Ehre des Herzogthums Krain   574
Die Miraculis Mortuorum   254
Die Zartlichkeit der Wolfe   757
Dinner at Deviant's Palace   799
Dinner with the Vampire   759
Dionysus   52
Directors Guild of America   141
Disciple of Death   745
Disciples of Dread   789
The Disentanglers   785
Disher; Catherine   225
The Disoriented Man   786
Dissertazione sopra I Vampiri   103, 160, 313
Diversions   745
Djadadjii   67, 637
Do Vampires Exist?   707
D'Obo; Maryam   136
Doc Reid and His Vampire Hunters   244
Dr. Acula   598
Doctor Dracula   85, 759
Dr. Jekyll and Sister Hyde   28
Doctor in the Nude   755
Dr. Occult   115
Dr. Strange: Sorcerer Supreme   50
Dr. Terror's Gallery of Horrors   731
Dr. Terror's House of Horrors   731, 783
Doctor Vampire   769
Doctor Who and the State of Decay   790
Doctors Wear Scarlet   55, 786, 799
Does Dracula Really Suck?   301
Doggett; William   637
Dolphin; David   486
Domination   552, 789
Dominion   532, 800
Dömötör; Tekla   313
Donovan; Gene   197, 306
Doom City   793
Doomflight   801
Dorset; St. John   194

Double Possession   10
Doubleday & Company   352
Dove; Karen E.   406
Down on the Farm   802
Downe; Count   423
Doyle; Arthur Conan   380, 557
Drac Pac   271
Dracula   1, 15-16, 19, 29, 35, 41, 47, 49, 51, 54, 56, 58, 61, 68, 79, 82, 87, 94, 100, 104, 107, 116, 126, 138, 150, 154, 160, 163, **169**, 188, 190, 194, 199, 203, 210, 215, 218, 220, 222-223, 233, 248, 251, 256, 259, 264, 278, 286, 297, 300, 305, 310, 315, 326, 331, 337, 344, 355, 359, 363, 369, 371, 375, 381, 407, 410, 412-413, 429, 435, 447, 453, 455, 480, 482, 492, 505, 507, 512, 516, 527, 531, 533, 536, 544, 547-548, 556, 559, 565, 577, 580, 583, 587, 593, 595, 598, 604, 608-610, 613, 618, 620, 624, 636, 638, 646, 657, 661, 665, 673-674, 680-681, 704-705, 720-721, 745, 759, 776-777, 786
Dracula (1931)   19, 62, 79, 107, 169, **176**, 181, 233, 264, 287, 293, 300, 302, 423, 456, 502, 506, 534, 578, 580, 619-620, 693
Dracula (1973)   59, 126, 179, **181**, 396, 453, 598, 681
Dracula (1974)   293, 670
Dracula (1979)   124, 127, 166, 175, 179, **182**, 222, 246, 417, 419, 439, 594, 621, 639, 681
Dracula (Dell Comics Superhero)   **185** *See also:* Comic books, the vampire in
Dracula (The Dirty Old Man)   551, 732
Dracula (Marvel Comics Character)   **186** *See also:* Comic books, the vampire in
Dracula (Spanish, 1931)   3, 175, **179**, 403, 620
Dracula A.D. 1972   144, 289, 360, 639, 653, 745
Dracula; Andy Warhol's   308
Dracula; The Annotated   436, 689
The Dracula Archives   800
Dracula, Baby   196, 777
Dracula Began   794
Dracula; Bibliographie de   46
Dracula; Big Bad Blood of   120
Dracula; Billy the Kid vs.   84
Dracula: A Biography of Vlad the Impaler, 1431-1476   222, 397, 666
Dracula Bites the Big Apple   746
Dracula; Blood of   120, 216, 364, 621

Dracula; Bloodright: Memoirs of Mircea, Son of 613
Dracula Blows His Cool 308, 759
The Dracula Book 45, 259
Dracula Book of Classic Vampire Tales; Count 706
The Dracula Book of Great Horror Stories 555
The Dracula Book of Great Vampire Stories 555
Dracula and the Boys 301, 731
Dracula; Bram Stoker's 17, 92, 104, 123, 127, 175, 179, 182, 210, 240, 246, 291, 293, 301, 413, 417, 442, 450, 455-456, 537, 552, 586, 610, 639, 670, 681, 685
Dracula in Brianza; Il Cavaliere Costante Nicosia Demoniaco Ovvero 301
Dracula; The Brides of 144, 175, 534, 639
The Dracula Business 746
Dracula cape 1
The Dracula Caper 558, 793
Dracula; Castle 204, 239, 248, 278, 287, 288, 291, 303, 333, 372, 397, 407, 409-410, 416, 430, 442, 453, 458, 547-548, 564
The Dracula Centenary Book 285
Dracula Chicken Cookbook; The Count 706
Dracula: A Cinematic Scrapbook 770
The Dracula Collection 790
Dracula, the Comedy of the Vampire 305, 777
Dracula Comes to Kobe: Evil Makes a Woman Beautiful; Vampire 337
Dracula and Company **184**, 503
Dracula'': A Completely Illustrated and Annotated Edition of Bram Stoker's Classic Novel; The Essential '' 222
Dracula Contra El Dr. Frankenstein 746
Dracula Contra Frankenstein 577
Dracula; Count 49, 288, 307, 338
Dracula; Countess 289, 365, 459, 465, 694
Dracula; The Daughter of 82
Dracula; Death Dreams of 120
Dracula: The Death of Nosferatu 777
Dracula; Doctor 85
The Dracula Doll 777
Dracula; El Imperio de 404
Dracula''; ''Elixir 685
Dracula; The Empire of 404
Dracula: Essays on the Life and Times of Vlad Tepes 399
Dracula et les Vampires 232
Dracula; The Evil of 82
Dracula Exotica 551, 759

Dracula, A Family Romance 745
Dracula Fan Club Book of Vampire Stories; The Count 706
Dracula Fan Club; The Count 46, **127**, 176, 188, 310, 476, 633, 640, 645, 648, 705
Dracula Fan Club News-Journal; Count 711
Dracula Fan Club Research Library; The Count 128
Dracula; The Further Perils of 476
Dracula; Ghosts of 120
Dracula Go Home! 341
Dracula Goes to RP 746
Dracula Has Risen from the Grave 288, 360, 581, 731
Dracula in Hell 122
Dracula; Hello 100
Dracula and His Vampire Bride; Count 290, 360, 639
Dracula; The Horror of 216, 220, 233, 286, 300, 303, 359, 451, 534, 594, 619, 639, 679, 681
Dracula; Hounds of 18
Dracula; House of 83, 97, 216, 233, 679
Dracula in the House of Horrors 746
Dracula; I Was a Teen-Age 197
Dracula the Impaler 120
Dracula; In Search of 221, 360, 397, 666
Dracula: In Search of the Living Dead; A Dream of 689
Dracula Is Not Dead 746
Dracula in Istanbul 725
Dracula in Italy 746
Dracula; La Fille de 694, 577
Dracula; La Hija de 82
Dracula; Lady 696
Dracula; Lake of 179, 337, 749
Dracula Lives! 175
Dracula in Love 801
Dracula: The Love Story 759
Dracula Made Easy 706
Dracula; Mama 694
Dracula Meets the Outer Space Chicks 732
Dracula: A Modern Fable 777
The Dracula Murders 790
The Dracula Museum 128, **188**, 706
Dracula: The Musical 777
Dracula My Love 614, 803
The Dracula News-Journal 128
Dracula; Nocturna, Granddaughter of 696
Dracula; Old 10
Dracula; The Passion of 196
Dracula pere et Fils 362

Dracula Press   128

Dracula, Prince of Darkness   206, 220, 287, 360, 455, 783

Dracula, Prince of Many Faces: His Life and Times   222, 398

Dracula in the Provinces   746

Dracula Quarterly; The Castle   130, 640

Dracula Really Suck?; Does   301

Dracula Returns   380, 796

Dracula; The Revenge of   613

Dracula Rises from the Coffin   759

Dracula Rising   126, 770

Dracula; Rivals of   459

Dracula Rocks   746

Dracula: Sabbat   196, 777

The Dracula Saga   577

Dracula; Santo un el Tesoro de   404, 536

Dracula; The Satanic Rites of   290, 297, 360, 639

Dracula; The Scars of   27, 360

The Dracula School for Vampires   777

The Dracula Scrapbook   285

Dracula: Senzational—Infractional   **188**

Dracula—The Series   175, **189**, 595, 598

Dracula; Seven Brides for   197

Dracula; The Seven Brothers Meet   28, 99, 145, 290

Dracula and the Seven Golden Vampires   746

The Dracula Society   176, **188**, 378, 619, 633, 682

Dracula Society; The Count   3, 49, 85, 126, **129**, 176, 259

Dracula Society Award; The Count   208

Dracula Society of Maryland   184

Dracula Society Quarterly; The Count   129

Dracula Society; Quincey P. Morris   413

Dracula and Son   362, 745

Dracula; Son of   216, 620

Dracula, Sovereign of the Damned   759

The Dracula Spectacula   777

Dracula Sucks   301, 551, 746, 777, 794

Dracula Tan Exarchia   234, 759

The Dracula Tape   531, 548, 800

Dracula; Taste the Blood of   360

Dracula; Tender   146

Dracula; Terror of   438

Dracula; Tiempos duros para   578

Dracula; The Tomb of   49, 117, 120, 175, 186, 337, 372, 405

Dracula: A True History of Dracula and Vampire Legends; In Search of   181, 221, 360, 397, 666, 749

Dracula Tyrannus: The Tragical History of Vlad the Impaler   196, 778

Dracula; The Ultimate   690

Dracula Unborn   613, 803

Dracula Unbound   541, 787

Dracula, or The Un-dead   584

Dracula and the Unicorn; Count   706

Dracula Unleashed   247

Dracula: The Vampire and the Critics   46, 85

Dracula, the Vampire Play in Three Acts   28, 182, **189**, 552, 778

Dracula!; or, the Vampire Vanquished: A Victorian Melodrama for Schools Based on Bram Stoker's Book, Dracula   778

Dracula; Vampyros Lesbos die erbin des   577, 696

Dracula vs. Frankenstein   2, 84, 234, 577, 732

Dracula and the Virgins of the Undead   787

Dracula; Vlad   453

Dracula Was a Woman: In Search of the Blood Countess of Transylvania   35, 45, 398

Dracula?; Who Is Afraid of   308

Dracula World Enterprises   128, 707

Dracula y el Hombre Lobo; Santo y Blue Demon Contra   404, 536

Dracula; Zoltan: Hound of   18

Dracula's Bedtime Storybook   309

Dracula's Bite on the Side   240

Dracula's Blood   746

Dracula's Brothers   796

Dracula's Canadian Affair; Count   175

Dracula's castle   513, 693 *See also:* Castle Dracula

Dracula's Children   97

Dracula's Coffin; The Blood of   84

Dracula's Daughter   82, 120, 364, 551, 577, 620, 639, 692, 721, 791, 797

Dracula's Daughter; House of   84

Dracula's Diary   557, 792

Dracula's Disciple   796

Dracula's Dog   18, 679, 746, 794

Dracula's Feast of Blood   746

Dracula's Gold   796

Dracula's Great Love   577, 747

Dracula's Greatest Hits   176

"Dracula's Guest"   82, 501

Dracula's Guest, and Other Weird Stories   586

Dracula's Hair   770

Draculas; La Saga de las   577

Dracula's Last Rites   759
Dracula's Lost World   796
Draculas Lüsterne Vampire   747
"Dracula's Spirits"   61, 685
Dracula's Treasure   778
Dracula's Wedding Day   732
Dracula's Widow   539, 696, 759
Draculita   694
Dracutwig   314, 697, 785
Dragon Against Vampire   100, 760
The Dragon Waiting: A Mask of History   791
Dragosani; Boris   386
Dragula, Queen of the Darkness   747
Drake; Frank   50, 122, 186, 405, 609
Drakula   720
Drakula Istanbula   179
Drakulita   732
Drakulon   544
Drama, Vampire   **193**, 584
Drawn and Quartered   3
Dreadful Hollow   785
The Dream of David Gray   198
A Dream of Dracula: In Search of the Living Dead   689
The Dreaming   800
The Dreaming Place   790
Dreams of the Dead   786
Dreamspy   796
Dresser; Norine   462, 486
Drew; Roxanne   155
Dreyer, Carl Theodor   82, **198**, 359, 623, 648, 692
Drink Down the Moon   790
"Drink My Red Blood"   396
Drinker of Souls   789
Druillet; Philippe   231, 451
The Drums of Dracula   796
DS Collectibles Classified   156
Duchene; Deborah   225
Duckula, Count   18, **199**
Duendes   319
Dumas, Alexandre   194, **199**, 230, 328, 434, 481, 529, 692
Dumas; Francois R.   231
Dumollard; Martin   133
Durham; M. Edith   571
Dusk   790
Düsseldorf Vampire   352
Dust   **202**, 609
Dyad: The Vampire Stories   487
Dying of Fright   149
Dynamite Fan Club   **202**

Dysfunctional Vampire: A Theory from Personal History   648
Dysmetria   266
Dziemianowicz; Stefan R.   502
Dzigielski; Johann   479

E

Earl of Oxford   618
Earth Has Been Found   794
Eastern Orthodox Church   138, 209
Eboy; Dr. Michael   615
Echo and the Bunnymen   423
The Echo of a Curse   786
Echoes . . . from the Past   699
Eclipse Books   579
Edmonds; Louis   151
An Egyptian Coquette   785
Ein Vampyr   778
Ekimmu   26
Ekland; Britt   696
El Ataque de los Muertos sin Ojos   577
El Ataud del Vampiro   403
El Buque Maldito   577
El Castillo de los Monstruos   403, 725
El Charro de las Calaveras   730
El Conde Dracula   127, 175, 179, **203**, 360, 577, 743
El Extrano Amor de los Vampiros   577
El Imperio de Dracula   404
El Jovencito Dracula   749
El Mundo de los Vampiros   404
El Pobrecito Draculin   752
El Returno de los Vampiros   753
El Returno del Hombre Lobo   578
El Vampiro   403
El Vampiro Archecha   404, 568, 740
El Vampiro Negro   568, 727
El Vampiro Sangriento   404
El Vampiro y el Sexo   404, 536
Elegia: A Journey Into the Gothic   266
Eliade; Mircea   676
"Elixir Dracula"   685
Elliot; Brian   257
Elliott, Denholm Mitchell   175, **204**, 598
Elliott; L. E.   96
Ellis; Mark   451
Ellis; Peter Bereford   613
Elmore; Mary   433
Elmore; Trevor   433
Elric of Meiniboné   798
Elrod Fan Club; P. N.   206
Elrod, P. N.   **204**, 241, 444, 477, 610, 697

Elusive Song of the Vampire 760
Elvira 3, **206**, 265, 308, 424, 456, 629
The Elvira Examiner 208, 712
Elvira Fan Club 208
Elvira: The Jaws of Cerberus 246
Elvira, Mistress of the Dark 208, 246, 308, 760
Elvira's House of Mystery 208
Elvira's Queen B Productions 457
Elwes; Cary 59
The Empire of Dracula 404, 732
The Empire of Fear 802
Empusai 272, 684
Encore un Vampire 194, 778
Encyclopedia of Occultism and Parapsychology 555
Endithor's Daughter 801
Endore; Guy 230, 258, 677
Engels; Frederick 482
England 11
Englehart; Steve 647
Engstrom; Elizabeth 698
Enkil 108, 139
Enna; August 273, 426
An Enquiry into the Existence of Vampires 797
Epic Comics 609
Ercole al centro della terra 330
Erebus 794
Erestun 525
Erestuny 526
Eretica 525
Ereticy 526
Eretik 525, 537, 562, 688
Eretnica 525
Erotikill 82, 551, 578, 694
Erzsebet Bathory, La Comtesse Sanglante 35
Escape from Dracula's Castle 778
Escape to the Realm of the Snow Elves 795
Escott; Charles 205
Esoterra 266
The Essential "Dracula": A Completely Illustrated and Annotated Edition of Bram Stoker's Classic Novel 222, 398
Esterhaus; Isadore and Bella 343
Estleman; Loren D. 557
Estonia 29
Et Mourir de Plaisir 82, 231, 623, 693
Eternal Society of the Silver Way 241
Eternity Comics 120
Eternity 793

Eucharistic wafer 79, 103-104, 127, 173, **209**, 409, 416, 488, 537, 652, 674, 688
Euripides 274
Euronymous Future Sex 269
Evans; Clifford 287
Evans; E. P. 228
Evans; Maggie 55, 111, 151
Evenstich; Ivan 240
Every Home Should Have One 747
Evil eye 525
The Evil of Dracula 82, 747
Evils of the Night 760
Excavation 802
Explanations of vampirism **210**
The Exploits of Elaine 786
The Eye of Count Flickenstein 732
The Eye of the Beholder 788

F

Face of Marble 723
The Faceless Monster 330
Fade to Black 760, 799
The Fair Abigail 784
Faivre; Tony 231
Falcons of Narabedia 783
Falsworth; John 30
Falsworth; William 30
"The Family of the Vourdalak" 527
"The Family of the Vurkodlak" 607
Famous Monsters of Filmland 1, 116, 646
Fangs 19, 63, 95, 99, 170, 199, **215**, 287, 305, 309, 321, 341, 347, 360, 366, 410, 436, 450, 635, 654, 663, 698, 701
Fangs! 770
The Fangs of the Hooded Demon: A Lincoln Blackstone Mystery 797
Fangs of the Living Dead 577, 732
The Fangs of the Vampire 787, 795
FantaCo 565
Fantasmagorie 733
Farewell, Miss Julie Logan: A Wintry Tale 783
Fascination 231, 512, 747
Father, Santa Claus Has Died 527, 770
Faust 260
The Fear of the Night 793
The Fearless Vampire Killers 105, 306, 733
The Feast of the Wolf 788
The Feasting Dead 785
Feeding Frenzy 712
Feldman; Al 115
The Fellowship 799

Female vampires *See:* Women as vampires
Femme fatale   473, 627
Fenner; Jack   225
Ferat Vampire   760
Fernandez; Florencio Roque   133
Ferroni; Giorgio   330
Feu-follet   9
Féval; Paul   230, 546
Fevre Dream   797
Field; M. J.   6
Fiends   791
Fifollet   9
A Filha de Dracula   747
The Films of Christopher Lee   362
Finch; Deborah Joan   134
Fingernails   21, 170, 211, **218**, 366, 389,
   416, 436, 478, 563, 654 *See also:*
   Appearance of a vampire
Fingers of Fear   786
Finland   539
Finné; Jacques   46, 232
Fire   67, 95, 99, 168, **219**, 228, 274, 289,
   366, 488, 526, 589 *See also:* Destroying the
   vampire
Fire in the Blood   205, 791
Fire and Hemlock   794
Fire in the Mist   796
Firefly   787
First Channel   796
The First Man in Space   543, 725
First Vampire in China   100, 770
Firth; Violet Mary   227
Fisher, Terence   144, **220**, 286, 303,
   359, 534
Fister-Liltz; Barbara   226-227
A Flame in Byzantium   252, 698, 702, 804
Flaster; Jeff   47
Fleeta   186
Fleming; Jack   205, 477
Fletcher; Louise   694
Florescu; Radu   59, 80, 89, 123, 181, **221**,
   340, 360, 363, 377, 397, 537, 598, 613, 625,
   653, 666
Florescu; Vintila   221
Flowers of Evil   789
Fluckinger; Johannes   460, 573
Flying vampires   96, 98, **223**, 410, 579
The Foe of Barnabas Collins   806
Follets   319
Folletti   319
Fontana; Giovanni   329-330
A Fool There Was   626
For the Blood Is the Life   651, 714

Ford; David   151
Forde; Daryll   5
Forencio; Estelita   133
Forest; Jean-Claude   646
Forest of the Night   801
Forever and the Night   797
Forever Knight   55, 167, 223, **224**, 226,
   262, 599, 610
Forever Knight Fan Club   **226**
Forever   796
Forever Net   225-226
Fort; Charles   17
Fort; Garrett   79
Fortune, Dion   **227**, 490 *See also:* Psychic
   vampirism
Fountain; Richard   55
Fraley; Ralph Milne   174
France, vampires in   104, **228**, 193,
   460, 463
Franco; Jesus   203, 360, 413, 577, 694
Frankenstein   71, 149, 154, 220, 259, 263,
   286, 303, 480
Frankenstein; The Blood of   84
Frankenstein; The Bride of   233, 775
Frankenstein; The Curse of   286
Frankenstein; Dracula vs.   84
Frankenstein and the Evil of Frankenstein
   792
Frankenstein; House of   83
Frankenstein Meets Dracula   234, 259, 792
Frankenstein Slept Here   778
Frankenstein Society; International   129
Frankenstein, the Vampire and Co.   733
Frankenstein; Victor   232
Frankenstein's Bloody Terror   733
Frankenstein's Monster   **232**, 287, 306, 309,
   676, 679
Franzetta; Frank   647
Fraternity of the Inner Light   227
Frazer; Sir James   15
Freak Show Vampire   706
Freda; Riccardo   42, 328, 330
Frederick; Otto   175
Frenczy; Thibor   386
Fresh Blood   106, 475, 711
Frezza; Robert   541
Frid; Jonathan   11, 111, 136, 153, 158,
   235, 599
Fridiculousness   236
Frid's Fools & Fiends; Jonathan   236
Friends of Dark Shadows   184, **238**, 503
Fright Night   696, 760, 801
Frightmare   760

From the Archives of Evil 362
From the Shadows 699
Frost; Brian 46
Frost; Deacon 50, 187
Frost; Sadie 59
Frozen Summer 793, 805
Fry; Carol 548, 550
Frye; Dwight 177
Fukasaku; Kinji 337
Funny Toys Corporation 457
The Further Perils of Dracula 476, 706
The Fury of Dracula 239

G

Ga; Kyuketsuki 337
Galeen; Henrik 436
The Games of the Countess Dolingen of Gratz 760
Games, vampire 4, 45, 61, 77, 208, **239**, 369, 459 *See also:* Paraphernalia, vampire
Gandy Goose in Ghosttown 723
Ganja and Hess 10
Garbo; Greta 627
Garden, Nancy **247**, 340 *See also:* Juvenile literature
The Garden of Tortures 786
Garlic 3, 31, 65, 95, 98, 138, 163, 171, 173, 187, 210, **248**, 254, 300, 314, 316, 341, 402, 412, 449, 462, 467, 488, 517, 534, 567, 571, 587, 652, 680, 702 *See also:* Protection against vampires
Garmann; Christian Frederic 254
Garrison; Josette 11
Garrison; Patrick 11
Garton; Ray 698
Gasperini; A. De 328
A Gathering of Gargoyles 799
A Gathering of Stones 789
Gaunt; Valerie 303
Gautier, Théophile 230, **249**, 473, 692, 698
Gay Vampire 784 *See also:* Homosexuality and the vampire; Lesbian vampires
Gayracula 302, 551, 761
Geek Maggot Bingo 761
Gelfand; Alayne 487
The Genie of Darkness 404
Gentiomo; Giacomo 330
Geraldine 363, 472
Gerard; Emily 68, 139, 164, 173, 248, 435, 513, 534, 537, 610-611
Germain; St. 105, 139, 163, 167, 219, **251**, 261, 430, 539, 552, 659, 673, 698, 701 *See also:* Yarbro, Chelsea Quinn
Germany, vampires in 94, 104, 163, 218, **253**, 283, 294, 342, 352, 586, 618, 661, 673
Ghana 5
Ghastly 266, 425
Ghost Rider 405, 411
Ghost Story 761, 802
Ghosts of Dracula 120
The Ghoul Friend 778
Ghoul; Jule 636
Ghouls 12, 132, 230, 253, **258**, 320, 427, 462, 539, 597, 630, 678
Ghoul's Gallery 636
Ghul-I- Beában 258
Giant-Size Chillers 371
''The Giaour'' 70
The Gift 791
Gifts of Blood 798
Gilbert; Ken 130
Gilbert; William 618
The Gilda Stories 365, 698, 792
Gilden; Mel 235, 342
Gilgamesh 26
Gilgamesh Epic 370
Gillis; Jamie 551
''The Girl and the Vampire'' 518
Gittens; Allen J. 650-651
Giurescu; Constantin 221
Giustiniani; Marco 10
The Glass Painting 787
Gli amanti d'oltretomba 330
The Glow 802
Glut, Donald Frank 35, 45, 180, 234, **259**, 295, 616, 639
Go for a Take 747
God of Time 604
Godalming; Lord 300
Godwin; Archie 647
Godwin; Mary 71, 273, 480
Goethe, Johann Wolfgang von 104, 250, 255, **260**, 277, 328, 471, 480, 526, 550, 692 *See also:* Poetry, the vampire in
Gògol; Nikolai 43, 328, 581
Going Down for the Count 778
Goke, Body Snatcher from Hell 733
Gold Key 156
Gold; Martin 372
The Goldcamp Vampire 800
The Golden 801
Golden Harvest 100
Golden Krone Hotel 47, 291, 684
Golem 232

Goliath and the Vampires   330, 733
Gomez; Jewelle   365, 698
Gonzales; Jose   647
The Good Guy Vampire Letterzine   262
Good Guys Wear Fangs   206, **261**, 407, 552
Goodman; Theodosia   627
Gorey; Edward   193
Gothic   36, 77, 82, 111, 146, 176, 185, 189,
   197, **262**, 270, 302, 369, 375, 468, 482, 504,
   510, 522, 535, 545, 555, 590, 608, 619, 635
The Gothic Society   265, **270**, 424, 619
Gothic Society of Canada   267, **271**
Gothica   **271**, 272
The Gothick Gathway   130
Gottow; John   437
Gough; Michael   303
Goulart; Ron   647, 697
Goya; Francisco   41
Granach; Alexander   437
Grand Duke of Moscovy   331
Grand Guignol; Theatre du   286
Grans; Hans   283
Grant; Richard E.   59
Grau; Albin   436
Grave of the Vampire   747
Graves; Robert   273
Graves; Teresa   10
The Graveyard Gazette   159, 714
Graveyard Shift   761
Gray; Riyn   106
The Great London Mystery   720
Great Uncle Dracula   345
The Great Villains   459
Greece, vampires in   10, 52, 71, 94, 164,
   261, **272**, 329, 389, 401, 445, 471, 480, 520,
   528, 575, 673, 676
Greek Orthodox Church   275
Greeley's Cove   792
Green; Hess   10
Greenberg; Martin H.   502, 698
Gregory the Great; Pope St.   209
Grenada   379
The Grey Beast   783
Grey Face   786
Griffith; Diedre   316
Griffith; Kathryn Meyer   698
Grim Reaper   420
Grimes; William   115
Grimoire   265, 424, 713
The Groovie Goolies   599
Guatemala   400
Guerrini; Olindo   330

*Guess What Happened to the Count
   Dracula?*   747
Guiley; Rosemary Ellen   106, 648
Guilty Pleasures   793
Guru, the Mad Monk   748
*Guten Abend Herr Fischer! oder, Der
   Vampyr*   778
Guy; Gordon R.   640
Gwynne; Fred   414
Gypsies, vampires and the   41, 95, 101,
   127, 154, 168, 204, **278**, 292, 317, 320, 348,
   414, 549, 560, 572, 613, 637

H

Haarmann; Fritz   132, 257, **283**, 302, 632
   See also: Crime, vampiric
Haerm; Teet   632
Haigh, John George   132, **284** *See also:*
   Crime, vampiric
Haines; Lora   226
Haining, Peter Alexander   **285**
Haiti   379, 567, 589
Hall; Grayson   111, 153
Hall; Huntz   306
Halloween   181, 308, 455, 565 *See also:*
   Paraphernalia, vampire
Halloween with the Addams Family   4,
   308, 748
Hambly; Barbara   619
Hamilton Deane Award   189
Hamilton; George   108, 307, 439
Hammer Films   27, 35, 63, 82, 99, 143,
   163, 174, 179, 181, 185, 203, 216, 220, 264,
   286, 297, 302, 330, 337, 359, 365, 451, 455,
   459, 464, 534, 551, 615, 619, 621, 623, 633,
   639, 653, 679
Hammer; Haunted House of   291
Hammer; The House of   291
Hammer; Will   286
The Hammer of Witches   687
Hand of Death   733
The Hand of Dracula   796
Hand; Stephen   239
Hanna-Barbera Studios   4
Hannah, Queen of the Vampires   330, 748
Hans de'Islande   434
Hanuman   320
Hard Times for Vampires   360
Hardwicke; Edward   557
Hardy Boys   340
Hare; August   135
Hargrove; Brett   159

Harker; Jonathan   16, 41, 47, 51, 56, 58, 63, 79, 82, 87, 104, 126, 138, 143, 163-164, 177, 180, 187, 190, 195, 202-203, 218, 240, 256, 278, 287, **291**, 301, 303, 310, 315, 338, 375, 407, 413, 415, 430, 437, 442, 447, 453, 483, 517, 531, 533, 548, 565, 587, 595, 609, 652, 658, 680
Harker; Joseph   293
Harker; Quincy   50, 372
Harmon; Dr. Damien   380
HarmonyRoad Press   115, **293**, 445
Harper; Charles G.   135
Harris Comics   120, 647, 697
Hart; James V.   533
Hartley; Mariette   705
Hartmann, Franz   211, **294**, 464, 490, 631
Harvest of Blood   790
Harvey; Jayne   345
Haskell; Joe   151
Hasselius; Dr. Martin   653
Hauer; Rutger   697
Haunt of Fear   115
Haunted Cop Shop   100, 761
The Haunted Earth   795
Haunted House of Hammer   291
Hawke; Simon   558
Hawthorn   148, 254, 281, 290, **295**, 413, 487, 534, 563, 571-572 *See also:* Destroying the vampire
Hawthorne; Julian   698
Hayday; Andria   241
Haynes; Lara A.   36
He Who Whispers   783
Held; Eric   46, 639
The Hellbound   271
Hello Dracula   100, 761
Helstar   419
Henesy; David   151
Henry Irving Vacation Company   190
Hera   272
Hercules contre les Vampires   733
Hercules in the Haunted World   330
Hermetic Order of the Golden Dawn   227
Herskovits; Frances   6
Herskovits; Melville   6, 589
Herter; Lori   552
Herzegovina   560, 569
Herzog; Werner   439
Heston; Charlton   396
Hickman; Laura   241
Hickman; Tracy   241
Hiero's Journey   796
Highgate Cemetery   377

Highgate vampire   **297**, 617, 634, 643
Hildebrandt; Theodor   256
Hill; Gordon   310
Hiroku Kaibyoden   734
Historia Rerum Anglicarum   682
The Historical Dracula, Facts Behind the Fiction   748
''The History of the Pale Woman''   230
Hoare; J. E.   29
Hodgman; Ann   342
Hodgson; Richard   294
Hoffman; Julia   55, 111, 153, 378, 583
Hoffman; Kuno   134
Hoffmann; E. T. A.   249, 255, 480, 526, 607
Hogan; David J.   305
Holden; Gloria   364
Hollywood on Parade, No. 8   721
Holmes; Sherlock   175, 309, 357, 503, 532, 586, 619
The Holmes-Dracula File   532, 548, 557, 800
Holmwood; Arthur   29, 54, 59, 61, 162, 181, 191, 203, 292, **300**, 303, 412, 453, 505, 547-548, 652
Holmwood; Lucy   287
Holmwood; Mina   287
Homans; Peter   495
Homosexuality and the vampire   **301**, 362, 551 *See also:* Lesbian vampires; Sexuality and the vampire
Hooper; Tobe   352, 543
Hopkins; Anthony   59, 124, 639
Hopper; Dennis   543
Hopping vampires   100
Horner; Penelope   182
Horror of the Blood Monsters   84, 748
The Horror of Dracula   20, 143-144, 166, 179, 181, 216, 220, 233, 286, 300, **302**, 303, 359, 451, 534, 594, 619, 639, 679, 681, 725
The Horror from the Hills   785
''The Horror from the Mound''   502
Horror Newsletter   712
Horror Writers of America   396, 586, 698
Horror of the Zombies   577
Horrorritual   748
Horrors of Dracula   734
Horthy; Miklós   312
Hospital of St. Joseph and St. Mary   416
Hotchner; Stephen   197
Hotel Transylvania   251, 552, 702, 804
Hough; Dr. Damien   580

"The Hound" 501
Hounds of Dracula 18, 794
The Hour of the Oxrun Dead 793
The House of Arabu 785
House on Bare Mountain 734
The House of the Brandersons 800
The House of Caine 791
House of Dark Shadows 112, 142, 156, 236, 748
House of Dracula 83, 97, 216, 233, 679, 723
House of Dracula's Daughter 84, 748
The House That Dripped Blood 466, 748
House of Frankenstein 83, 216, 679, 723
The House of Hammer 291
The House of Mystery 119, 317
The House of the Secret 784
The House of the Vampire 787
House of Zeor 796
Household 802
Houston Dark Shadows Society **305**
How Dear the Dawn 791
How They Became Vampires 748
How to be a Vampire in One Easy Lesson 342 *See also:* Juvenile literature
Howard; Robert E. 502
Howe; Deborah 341
Howe; James 18, 310, 341
Howling Mad 790
Howling VI: The Freaks 679, 770
Hoyt; Ann 503
Huerta; Rodolfo Gizmán 535
Hughes the Wer-wolf 677
Hugo; Victor 250, 434
Hull; Amy 226
Hull; Ann 226
The Human Bat 785
Humor, vampire **305** *See also:* Parapernalia, vampire
Hungarian Folk Beliefs 313
Hungary, vampires in 32, 37, 56, 89, 211, 275, 278, **310**, 381, 467, 514, 560, 611, 624, 659, 664, 669
The Hunger 55, 105, 365, 697, 761, 802
The Hunt 804
Hunt; Leigh 349
Hunter; Alyce 225
Huntley; Raymond 191, 638
Hunyadi; John 89, 605, 659, 665-666
Hupe; Bill 226
Hurwood, Bernhardt J. **314**, 697
Huston; Angelica 4
Hutter; Ellen 437, 593

Hutter; Waldemar 437
Hutton; Lauren 308, 696
Hyocho No Bijo 748
Hypnotic powers **315**, 366, 402 *See also:* Psychic vampirism
The Hypnotist 62
Hysterical 126

I

"I AM" Ascended Masters 490
I Am Dracula 787
I Am Legend 120, 181, 287, 396, 544, 785
I Bought a Vampire Motorcycle 770
I Like Bats 761
I Married a Vampire 308, 761
I Racconti di Dracula 329
I Romanzi del Terrore 328
I Searched the World for Death 784
I, Strahd 206
I tre volti della paura 330
"I . . . Vampire" 119, **317**, 799-800
I, the Vampire 502, 748
I Vampiri 35, 328, 364, 725, 781
I Was a Teen-Age Dracula 197, 306, 778
The Ice Maiden 788
Iceland 539
If You Could See Me Now 802
Il Castello dei destini incrociati 329
Il Cavaliere Costante Nicosia Demoniaco Ovvero Dracula in Brianza 301, 743
Il mio amico Draculone 329
Il Plenilunio delle vergini 330
Il Vampiro 328, 782
Illyria 568
I'm Sorry, The Bridge Is Out, You'll Have to Spend the Night 196, 307, 778
Image 801
The Image of the Beast 791
Imagine, Inc. 456
Imago 788
Immoral Tales 35, 694, 748
Immortal Blood 793
The Immortals 798, 803
"The Impaling Vampire" 174
In the Blood 789-790
In the Drift 802
In the Dwellings of the Wilderness 786
In a Glass Darkly 80, 358
In the Grip of the Spider 751
In Hot Blood 799
In the Land of the Dead 794
In Memory of Sarah Bailey 790

In the Midnight Hour 770
In Quest of Life; or, The Revelations of the Wiyatatao of Ipantl. The Last High Priest of the Aztecs 787
In Search of Dracula: A True History of Dracula and Vampire Legends 181, 221, 360, 397, 666, 749
In Silence Sealed 799
In Yana, the Touch of the Undying 801
Incense for the Damned 146
The Incredible Melting Man 749
Incubus/Succubus 5, 9, 102, 313, **318**, 370, 489, 563, 691
In-depth Analysis of the Vampire Legend 491
India 69, 101, 278, 281, 294, **320**, 329, 347, 426, 603, 691
Indonesia 484, 602
The Initiation 343
The Inn of the Flying Dragon 359, 761
Innocent Blood 610, 658, 697, 770
Innocent VIII; Pope 687
Innovation Comics 112, 144
Innovation Corporation 19, 510
Inovercy 526
Inquisition 687
Insatiable 791
Inside Dark Shadows 238, 503
Inside the Old House 441
Insomnia 734
International Dark Shadows Society 238
International Frankenstein Society 129
International Pictures 621
International Vampire **325**
Interview with the Vampire 17, 108, 139, 140, 302m, 366, 507, 533, 799
The Introduction of Barnabas 158
The Intrusion 789
The Invasion of the Vampires 404, 734
INXS 423
Ipolyi; Arnold 313
Ireland, vampires in 17, 128, 317, **325**, 555
Iron 148, 324, 563, 580
Irving; Henry 160, 555, 583
Irving Vacation Company; Henry 190
Is There a Vampire in the House? 749
Isabell, a Dream 734
Isithfuntela 8
Islam 568
The Island of Souls 787
Isle of the Dead 723
István 311
It! The Terror from Beyond Space 542, 726

Italy, vampires and vampirism in 64, **327**, 520
It's All In Your Mind 788
It's Loose 796
Itzpapalotl 400
Ivan the Terrible 32, **331**, 525, 668 *See also:* Russia, vampires in

J

Jack the Ripper 131, 143, 557
Jack of Shadows 804
Jacula 331
Jacula: Fete in la Morgue 231
Jakhai 323
Jakhin 323
James; Henry 154
James; Louis 530
James; Raglan 302
Janicjek; Vlad 270
Janick; Ron 431
Japan, vampires in 15, **335**, 588
Java, vampires in **338**, 357, 390, 484, 602
Jaws of the Jungle 721
Jennings; Jan 55
Jensen; Susan M. 271
Jesi; Furio 329
Jitters 761
Johnny Appleseed and Dracula 196, 778
Johnson; Geordie 189, 598
Jonas; Connie 115, 293, 445
Jonathan of the Night 762
Jones; Carolyn 3, 598
Jones; Duane 10
Jones; Ernest 304, 318, 351
Jones; Grace 10, 217, 696
Jones; Steven 650
Jordan; Neil 511
Jourdan; Louis 126, 175, 179, **338**, 598
The Journal of Edwin Underhill 803
Journal of Modern Vampirism 648
Journal of the Vampire Legion 713
The Journal of Vampirism 506, 645
Journal of Vampirology **339**
Journey to Memblair 787
Journey into the Unknown 116
Joyce; James 326, 474
Julia; Raul 4
Jung; Carl 493
Jungle Jim and the Vampire Woman 786
Jungman; Ann 342
Juvenile literature 174, 235, 257, **340**

K

Kaibyoden; Hiroku 337
Kali 69, 95, 149, 280, 323, **347**, 691
Kali: Devil Bride of Dracula 749
Kaplan; Roxanne Salch 642
Kaplan; Stephen 633, 639, 641
Kappa 15, 335
Karl August; Duke 260
Karloff; Boris 43, 233, 384, 422, 608
Karnstein; Carmilla 95, 288
Karnstein; Count 289
Karnstein; Countess Irina 577
Karnstein; Countess Mircalla 81, 363
Karoly III 311
Käser; Alfred 133
Kashiasu; Bella 240
Kathavai Thatteeya Mohni Paye 749
Katz; Leon 196
Keats, John 273, 277, 328, **349**, 473 *See
  also:* Poetry, the vampire in
The Keep 119, 762, 804
The Keepsake 794
Keesey; Pam 364-365
Keller; David H. 54
Kelljan; Bob 703
Kelly; Tim 197
Kendall; Mark 308
Kennedy; Raymond 485
Kernberg; Otto 494
Kiang shi 97
Kill the Count 239
Kill the Dead 795
King; Hannibal 50, 122, 187, 405, 608
King, Stephen 230, **351**, 698
Kinski; Klaus 439, 451
Kipling; Rudyard 473, 626
Kirklees vampire 634, 643
KISS 268
Kiss; Bela 133
The Kiss 762
The Kiss of Death 789, 799
The Kiss That Killed 785
Kiss Me Quick 734
Kiss of the Vampire 287, 734, 803
KKK Classici dell'orrore 328
Klause; Annette Curtis 345
Klimovsky; Leon 577
Klotz; Claude 230
Knight Beat 225-226
Knight of the Black Rose 797
*Knight of Ghosts and Shadows: An Urban
  Fantasy* 795

Knight; Mallory T. 314, 697
Knight; Nick 55, 223-224, 599-600
Knightly Tales 225-226
The Knighton Vampires 801
Knights of the Blood 795
Kohner; Paul 179, 620
Kohut; Heinz 496
Kolchak; Carl 142, 432, 600
Kolchak: The Night Stalker 600
Koldun 525
Koltun; Julian 134
Kosac 570
Kramer; Heinrich 677, 687
Kramer; Nora 174
Krauss; Freidrich 676
Kristel; Sylvia 696
Kronos 290
Krsnik 570
Krvava Pani 762
Kudesnik 525
Kukuthi 570
Kung Fu Vampire Buster 100, 762
Kuroneko 337, 734
Kürten, Peter 132, 257, **352**, 502, 568, 632
Kuttner; Henry 502
Kuzui; Fran Rubel 697
*Kyuketsuki Dorakyura Kobe ni Arawaru:
  Akuma wa Onna wo Utsukushiku Suru*
  337, 749
Kyuketsuki; Onna 337

L

L'ultima preda del vampiro 330
La Belle Captive 231, 696, 757
"La Belle Dame sans Merci" 473
La Bonne Dame 729
La Commedia del Sangria 197
La Comtesse aux Seiens Nux 82, 551, 577,
  694, 743
La Danza Macabra 330
La Dinastia Dracula 745
La Fée Sanguinaire 733
La Fille de Dracula 577, 694
La Frusta e il corpo 330
La Guerre des Vampires 230
La Hija de Dracula 82
La Huella Macabre 734
La Invasion de los Muertos 404, 749
La Invasion de los Vampiros 404
La Isla de la Muerte 734
La Llamada del Vampiro 750
La Llorona, the Weeping Woman 401

La Maison du Mystere 231
La Maldicíon de Nostradamus 404
La Maldicion of the Karnsteins 82, 360
La Manoir des Fantomes 231
La Mante au Fil des Jours 230
La Marca del Hombe Lobo 576
La Maschera del Demonio 42, 330, 527, 581, 608, 693, 770
La Messe Nere della Contessa Dracula 751
"La Morte Amoureuse" 230
La Morte-Vivante 231, 512
La Noche de los Brujos 577
La Noche de las Saviotas 577
La Noche del Terror Ciego 577
La Noche de Walpurgis 577
La Noire D'Immortality 266
La Notte die Diavoli 752
La Novia Ensangrentada 82, 694, 752
La Nue Vampire 231, 512
La Orgia Nocturna de los Vampiros 577
La Reine des Vampires 511, 737
La Sadique aux Dents Rouges 753
La Saga de las Draculas 577
La Sangre de Nostradamus 404
La Sorella di Satana 330
La Strage dei Vampiri 330
La Traite du Vampire 727
La Vampire Nue 739
La Vampirisme 231
La Venere dell'ille 43
La Venganza de las Mujeres Vampiro 694
La Ville Vampire 230
Lach; Jane 378, 700
Lackey; Mercedes 106
Lady Dracula 696, 749, 778
Lady Geraldine 109
Laemmle; Carl 620
Laemmle, Jr.; Carl 79, 179
Laibach 423
Lake of Dracula 179, 337, 749
L'Amante del vampiro 330
Lamb; Caroline 70, 480
Lambert; Carole 129
Lambert; Dr. Natalie 225
Lamiai 82, 100, 228, 272, 321, 330, 349, 362, 389, 401, 426, 445, 468, 471, 489, 520, 550, 576, 792
"Lamia" 272, 473
Lamont; Robert 257
Lampir **355**, 561, 570
The Land Beyond the Forest 68, 164, 248, 297
Landolfi; Tommaso 328

Langella; Frank 29, 123, 127, 166, 179, 182, 193, 196, 222, 246, 338, **355**, 417, 419, 439, 552, 594, 619, 621, 639, 681
Langstrom; Kirk 37, 393
Langsuyar 96, **357**, 362, 389, 401, 445, 484, 550, 691
Laos 426
Lasch; Christopher 495
Lass; David 57
The Last Aerie 386, 797
The Last Days of Christ the Vampire 791
"The Last Lords of Gardonal" 618
The Last Man on Earth 396, 735
Last Rites 800
The Last Vampire 698, 793, 804
"The Last of the Vampires" 618, 786
Latvia 29
Laudanum 110, 263
Laveau; Marie 31
Lavud; Count 403
Lawrence; D. H. 468
Lawson; John Cuthbert 274
Laymon; Carl 344
Lazure; Gabrielle 696
Le Circuit de Sang 743
Le Cult du Vampire 231, 512, 744
Le Fanu; Best Ghost Stories of J. S. 358
Le Fanu; Collected Works of Joseph Sheridan 359
Le Fanu; Diana 696
Le Fanu; Sheridan 27, 57, 80, 104, 163, 165, 197-198, 231, 288, 301, 326, **357**, 360, 363, 429-430, 464, 550, 579, 584, 587, 609, 618, 623, 653-654
Le Frisson des Vampires 231, 512, 747
Le Gran Amor del Conde Dracula 577
Le Morte Vivante 764
Le Nosferatu ou les Eaux Glacees du Calcul Egoiste 752
Le Rouge de Chine 753
Le Vampire 194, 200, 230, 231, 466, 529, 724, 778-779
Le Vampire Comedie—Vaudeville en un Act 779
Le Vampire du Düsseldorf 353, 739
Le Vampire, mélodrame en trois actes 193
Le Viol du Vampire 231, 551, 740
Leadbeater; Charles W. 490
Leading Edge Games 240
Leake; William Martin 277
Lecroix 225, 227
Lee; Christopher 20, 27, 43, 85, 144, 179, 181, 189, 203, 216, 220, 222, 233, 256, 257,

286, 297, 303, 356, **359**, 397, 459, 534, 551, 577, 581, 594, 619, 639, 653, 690-691
Lee; Tanith   541, 619, 697-698
Lee's X Certificate; Christopher   362, 459
The Legacy of Lohr   795
Legacy of Satan   749
Legawu   589
Legend of Blood Castle   35, 694
The Legend of the Eight Samurai   337, 762
Legend of Hell House   797
The Legend of the Seven Golden Vampires   28, 99, 145, 290, 639
The Legendary Curse of Lemora   696
Léger; Antoine   132
The Legion of the Living Dead   784
Legion   788
Leichenwasser   673
Leigh-Hunt; Shelley   707
Leland; C. G.   521
The Lemon Grove Kids Meet the Green Grass Hopper and the Vampire Lady from Outer Space   735
''Lenora''   255, 470, 618
''Lenore''   540, 549, 576
Leonard; Arthur Glyn   5
Leonor   696, 749
Lerouge; Gustave   230
Les Charlots contre Dracula   758
Les Etrennes d'un Vampire   194, 779
Les Histories Naturales   798
Les Trois Vampires, ou le clair de la lune   194, 779
Les Vampires   231, 720, 724
Les Vampires Humains   231
Lesbian Vampires   35, 81, 109, 134, 301, **362**, 698 *See also:* Homosexuality and the vampire; Sexuality and the vampire
Lesbian Vampires—The Heiress of Dracula   757
Lesnes Abbey   80
Less than Human   799
Lestat   267, 425 *See also:* Music, vampire
Lestat de Lioncourt   150, **366**, 635
Lestat Fan Club; Anne Rice's Vampire   510
Lestat; The Vampire   366, 510
Let's Count, Dracula   344
Let's Scare Jessica to Death   750
Letterzine   128, 711
Lettich; Rosey   431
Levres se Sang   231, 512, 750
Lewis; Al   175, 414, 599
Lewis; Fiona   182
Lico   360

Liddell; Henry Thomas   473
Lidérc   313
Life Force: The International Vampire Forum   543, 696, 713, 762, 804
Lifebloc   205, 791
The Light at the End   801
The Light of the Eye   784
Lightning   795
Lili; Ardat   370
Lili; Irdu   370
Lilith   50, **370**, 371, 406, 411, 691, 785
Lilith, The Daughter of Dracula   **371**, 406
Lilith and Ly   719
Lillu   370
Limat; Maurice   230
Linari; Nanci   4
Lips of Blood   750
Liquid Diet   802
Lisicux; Isidore   327
Litchnenberg; Jacqueline   444
Lithuania   29
Little Dracula   122
Little Shop of Horrors   125, 735, 762
Live Girls   698, 792
Liveright; Horace   28, 162, 174, 176, 191, 195, 382
The Living Dead   792
Living Dead at Manchester Morgue   750
Living in Fear: A History of Horror in the Mass Media   149
The Living One   792
Lobishomen   65, **373**, 567 *See also:* Werewolves
London After Midnight   62, 94, 267, **373**, 425, 720
London After Midnight Revisited   2
London   51, 59, 63, 79, 172, 188291, 482, 505, 557, 657, 682
London, Dracula's   **375**
Lone Gull Press   **378**, 700
Lone Star Shadows   305
Long Island Dark Shadows Society   **379**
Longsword; William   451
Loogaroo   6, 223, **379**, 567, 589, 691
Loomis; Willie   111, 152
Lopez; Juan   404
Lord of Death   603
Lord Ruthven ou Les Vampires   434, 481
Loring; F. G.   697
Loring; Lisa   4
Lory, Robert Edward   175, **379**, 580
Los Vampiros de Coyoacan   404, 756
Los Vampiros del Oeste   740

The Lost Boys   223, 246, 249, 565, 610, 762, 792

The Lost Oasis: A Doc Savage Adventure   799

The Lost Platoon   762

The Lost Prince   805

Lost Souls   788

Lot Lizards   792

Loup-garou   379

Loups-garous et Vampires   231

Love Bites   302, 779

Love Child   798

Love at First Bite   108, 179, 184, 307, 439, 653, 658, 750, 797

Love Me Vampire   100, 762

Love & Rockets   265, 424

Love Vampire Style   750

Lovecraft; H. P.   36, 155, 385, 501

A Lovely Monster   257

The Loves of Count Yorga   704

Loves of the Living Dead   763

Love's Pale Shadow   806

Loyalists of the Vampire Realm International Vampire Association   **381**

Lucard; Alexander   598

The Lucifer Comet   803

Lucinda   381

Lucius   350

Ludlow's Mill   803

Ludwig Karnstein; Count   360

Lugat   570

Lugosi; Bela   1, 19, 29, 62, 79, 83, 133, 143, 162, 166, 169, 174, 176, 179, 181, 188, 191, 195, 216, 218, 233, 236, 256, 293, 300, 302, 306, 310, 316, 341, 356, 359, 375, 380, **381**, 403, 413, 418, 455, 502, 534, 536, 542, 551, 578, 580, 586, 593, 598, 619-620, 636, 638, 679, 684, 690-691, 704

Lugosi the Forgotten King   763

Lugosi Review''; ''The Bela   306

Lumley; Brian   46, **385**, 619

Lunch; Lydia   267

Lupi manari   570

The Lurching Vampire   404

The Lure of the Vampire   506

The Lurking Vampire   740

The Lust of Dracula   750

Lust in the Fast Lane   763

Lust at First Bite   551

Lust for a Vampire   82, 289, 365, 535, 694, 750, 794

Lust of the Vampire   364

Lycanthia   785

Lycanthropy   676

The Lyssa Syndrome   791

M

M Is for Monster   235, 342

The Macabre Trunk   722

MacAndrew; Elizabeth   262

Macaulay; Charles   49

Macbeth   293

MacDowell; Edward   273

Macedonia   569

Machates   261, 273

Machine Gun Etiquette   266

Maciarello; Nicola   330

Maciste contro il vampiro   330

Macready; Michael   703

The Mad Love Life of a Hot Vampire   750

Mad Monster Party?   735

Madhouse   750

The Madjan   800

The Madness Season   792

Magia   720

Magia Posthuma   147

Magic Cop   763

The Magic Sword   628, 735

Magid; Ron   196

Magnus   139, 219, 367

Mahogany Trinrose   796

Majorova; Erzsi   32

MAKASHEF Enterprises   487

The Making of a Monster   798

Malay Film Productions   392

Malaysia   223, 338, 357, **389**, 401, 445, 484, 550, 693

Malenka la Vampira   577

Malevola   784

The Malibu Beach Vampires   770

Malibu Comics   82

Malibu Graphics   120

Malleus Maleficarum   102, 687

Malloy; Bill   151

Mallworld   802

The Maltese Bippy   735

Mama Dracula   694, 750

Mamuwalde; Prince   9, 48, 395

''The Man Who Cast No Shadow''   501

The Man Who Made Maniacs   784

Man-Bat   37, 119, **392**

Manchester; Sean   297, 619, 633, 643 *See also:* The Highgate Vampire; Vampire hunters

Mandurugo   463

Maneden 392

Manfredi; Gianfranco 329

Manfred 72

Manhattan Shadows 11

Manners; David 177

Manson; Charles 705

Manugang ni Drakula 735

Map; Walter 616

Mara 320, 540, 691

Margheriti; Antonio 330

Maria Theresa 76, 104, 311

Marinetti; Filippo Tommaso 330

Marius 367

The Mark of Lilith 365, 763

The Mark of the Bat: A Tale of Vampires Living and Dead 784

The Mark of the Vampire 64, 375, 384, 677, 722

Mark of the Werewolf 800

The Mark of the Wolfman 577

Marly; Florence 693

Marmorstein; Jerome 486

Marrama; Daniele Oberto 328

Marschner; Heinrich August 194, 256, **394**, 426, 474, 529

Marsh; Carol 303

Marshall; E. G. 600

Marshall; William 10, 48, **395** *See also:* Blacula

Martin 257, 751, 799

Martin; Maribel 694

Martinelli; Elsa 624, 693

Marvel Comics 30, 49, 116, 186, 199, 405, 608, 653 *See also:* Comic books, the vampire in

Marvel Preview 372

Marx; Karl 482

Mary Mary Bloody Mary 85, 404, 696, 751

Maschke; Carol 699

Mashburn; Kirk 502

The Mask of the Moderately Vicious Vampire 791

The Mask of Satan 330, 693

Masks and Facades 805

Mason; Marsha 155

''The Masquerade'' 241

Master of His Fate 784

''The Master of Rambling Gate'' 510

Master of the Undead 786

Mastery 803

Matheson: Collected Stories; Richard 396

Matheson; Richard 120, 142, 181, 258, 287, **395**, 432, 449, 541, 600 *See also:* Science fiction and the vampire

A Matter of Taste 532, 800

A Matter of Trust 805

Matters of Life and Undeath 663

Matthias II; King 33

Mauri; Roberto 330

Maw du 602

Maxwell; James Clark 473

May; Matilda 696

Maya 400

Mayne; Ferdie 307

Mayo; Herbert 211

McAfee; Julia 495

McCammon; Robert 658

McCuniff; Mara 552, 698

McDevitt; Bradley K. 245

McGavin; Darren 143, 432, 600

McKinnon; Mary Ann B. 261, 552

McLennon's Syndrome 541

McMahan; Jeffrey N. 302

McMahon; Liriel 648

McNally; Raymond T. 32, 45, 59, 80, 89, 123, 181, 221, 313, 340, 360, 363, 377, **397**, 537, 598, 613, 625, 653, 666

Medallion Press 700

Meinster; Baron 287, 534

Meiser; Edith 556

Melrose Abbey 616, 682

Melrose Abbey, The Vampire of **399**

Melusine 228

Men of Action Meet the Women of Dracula 735

Menado; Maria 392, 693

Menippus 272, 350, 691

Menzies; Sutherland 677

Meriweather; Lee 414

''Metamorphoses of the Vampire'' 230

Metempsychosis 684

Methodius 146, 513, 560

Mexico, vampires in 38, 64, 168, 249, 329, **400**, 535

Meyer; Nicholas 557

Middleton; J. A. 230

Midi-Minuit 751

Midnight 763

The Midnight Hour 600

Midnight Mass 804

Midnight to Midnight **406**

The Midnight People 285

Midnight Sons 50-51, 117, 371, **405**, 609

Midnight Sons Unlimited 406

Mighty Sphincter 420

Millarca 358

Millennium Publications 451

Miller; Alice 496

Miller; Jason 600

Miller; Judi 309

Miller; Susan 19

Millet 488, 546 *See also:* Seeds

Mind of My Mind 788

Mini-Munsters 414

Ministry 267, 425

Minns; Karen Marie Christa 365

Miranda 788

Mirandola; Gianfrancesco Pico della 521

Mircalla 288, 358

Mircea the Old 604

Mirrors 170, 173, 291, 366, 402, **407**, 488, 590, 702

The Miss Lucy Westenra Society of the Undead **408**

Miss Todd's Vampire: A Comedy in One Act 779

Mist 168, 173, 202, **408**, 416, 588, 609

Mistler; Jean 230

Mistrali; Franco 328

Mitterhouse; Count 289

Mixed Up 763

Mjartan; Ján 148

Modzieliewski; Stanislav 133

Mohammed II 606

Moi 230

Moldavian Marketplace 128

Moltke; Alexandra 151

Mom 763

Monastery 803

Monday's Child 803

Mondo Keyhole 735

Mongo; Marcos 257

Mongolia 603, 701

The Monster Club 28, 85, 97, 763

The Monster Demolisher 404

The Monster Mash 307

Monster Soup 307

Monster Soup; or, That Thing in My Neck Is a Tooth 779

The Monster Squad 764

Monster with a Thousand Faces 46

Monsters 690

The Monstrous Undead 315

Montenegro 558, 569

Montesi Formula 372, 405

Monteverdi; Georgia 624

Moon **409**, 528, 654

Moon Blood 787

Moon Legend 770

The Moon Pool 785

The Moonchild 797

Moonflowers 786

Moonlight Variations 802

Moore; Steven 476

Mora 320

Mora; Count 384

Moravia 146, 313

Morayta; Miguel 404

Morbius 31, 115, 119, 405, **410** *See also:* Comic books, the vampire in

More Fun 115

More; Henry 141

Morgan; Matthew 151

Morgano 782

Moriéve; Viscount de 229

Morland; A. F. 257

Mormolykiai 100, 272

Morning Star 787, 792

Moroaica 515

Moroi 515

Morris Dracula Society; Quincey P. 413

Morris; Quincey P. 29, 54, 59, 126, 160, 163-164, 191, 203, 292, 300, 303, **412**, 449, 505, 547, 652, 680

Mors Dracula 779

Mortal Coil 265, 425

Morton; Howard 414

Mother Riley Meets the Vampire 306

Mountain ash 171, **413**, 563

MPI Home Video 158

Mr. and Mrs. Dracula 763

Mr. Vampire 763

"Mrs. Amworth" 697

Muffy the Vampire Layer 770

Mukai 323

Muller; Max 653

Mulo 280

Munster, Go Home! 234, 307, 414, 600, 735

Munster; Lily 599

The Munsters 4, 117, 175, 234, 307, **414**, 415, 457, 598, 600

The Munsters and The Addams Family Fan Club 4, **415**

The Munsters' Revenge 234, 414, 600

The Munsters Today 414, 599

Murgoci; Agnes 15, 516, 677

Murnau; Freidrich Wilhelm 165, 174, 256, 436, 450, 516, 527, 586, 593

Murony 515

Murphy; Dudley 79

Murphy; Peter   418
Murray; Mina   29, 58, 79, 104, 123, 126, 138, 170, 177, 181, 184, 187, 191, 195, 210, 218, 240, 287, 292, 300, 301, 303, 315, 362, 409, 412, **415**, 437, 442, 447, 453, 483, 505, 532, 547-548, 609, 646, 652, 658, 661, 680-681
The Music Box   445
Music, vampire   156, 176, **417**, 459 *See also:* Paraphernalia, vampire
A Musical Mania for Transylvania   307
Musidora; Juliet   231
My Best Friend of Is a Vampire   764
My Brother the Vampire   790
My Friend the Vampire   342
My Grandpa Is a Vampire   770
My Lovely Monster   771
My Sister, the Vampire   248
My Son the Vampire   306, 384
Myanmar, vampires in   **426**
Myers; Robert J.   697
The Mysterious Death of Nina Chereau   35, 764
''The Mysterious Stranger''   256
''A Mystery of the Campagna''   692
The Mystery of Collinwood   806
The Mystery in Dracula's Castle   751
The Mystery of Irma Vep   779
Mystery of the Night Raiders   248
The Mystery of Vampire Castle   340
Mystery Writers of America   702
Mystic   116
Myth-ing Persons   787

N

Nabeshima; Prince   336
Nachttoter   253
Nachtzehrer   253, 661
Nadasdy; Count Ferenc   32
Nagulai   323
The Naked Vampire   512
The Naked Witch   694, 735
Naldi; Nita   627
Name   82, 185, 189, **429** *See also:* Origins of the vampire
Napolitano; Johnette   418
Naschy; Paul   577, 679
Native soil   95, 104, 107, 168, 173, 210, 251, 278, 413, **429**, 498, 565, 657, 673, 703
Natural History   786, 798
Near Dark   167, 565, 610, 696, 764
Necromancy   **430**

Necronomicon Publishers   266
Necrophagy   6
Necroscope   385, 797
Needfire   67, 219
The Need   798
Nefarious   **431**, 475
Neither/Neither World   267, 425
Nelapsi   146
Nella Stretta Morsa del Ragno   751
Nepal   603, 701
Neruda; Jan   148
Nesmith; Bruce   241
The Nesting   793
Nesvadba; Josef   148
Nethercot; Arthur H.   108, 472
Neuman; Kate   56
Neuntoter   253
Never Cross a Vampire   794
Neville; Robert   396, 541
New England Dark Shadows Society   **431**
New Horizons Home Video   124
New Manson Family   420
New Monthly Magazine   71, 480
New Moon   799
New Morning Dragon   793
The New Neighbor   792
New World Pictures   124
New York Rock and Roll Ensemble   418
Newcastle; Sebastian   149
Newman; Kim   548, 619, 650
News & Notes   445
A Nice Place to Live   801
Nick Knight   261
Nicolae Paduraru   613
Nigawu   589
Night Blood   791
Night Brothers   803
A Night with Count Dracula   797
The Night Creature   787
Night of Dark Shadows   112, 142, 156, 236, 751
Night Fright   779
A Night of Horror   720
Night Life   764
Night of the Living Dead   245
A Night in the Lonesome October   804
Night by Night   795
Night Prophets   798
Night Rider   122
Night of the Seagulls   577
Night of the Sorcerers   577, 751
The Night Stalker   142, 396, **432**, 600, 799
The Night Strangler   143

Night Thirst   803
Night of the Vampires   337, 736, 751, 784
Night Whispers   803
Nightblood   797
Nightchild   787
Nightfeeder   799
Nighthag   790
Nightlife   136, 245, 600
Nightlore   **433**
Nightmare   540
Nightmare Castle   581, 736
Nightmare in Blood   751
Nightmare Lake   344
The Nightmare People   803
Night's Children   120, 267, 565
Nightshade   504, 788
Nightshade; Talon   664
The Nightstalkers   122, 405, 609
The Nightwalker   803
Nightwing   444, 751, 798, 801
Nightworld   788, 804
Nilsson; Harry   423
Nisbet; Hume   697
Nixon; Dorothy   639
Njetop   478
No Blood Spilled   149, 168, 790
No Grave Need I   791
No Other Love   806
"No Such Thing as a Vampire"   144, 396
No Truth to Keep   796
Noah   52
Nocturna   85, 752
Nocturna, Granddaughter of Dracula   696
Nodier; Charles   193, 200, 230, 264, 306,
   328, 394, **433**, 466, 481, 528
Noll; Richard   676
Nomads   804
Nora   314
Nordan; Frances   503
Norton; Barry   180
Norway   539
Nosferatu   63, 120, 174, 179, 231, 265, 270,
   424, **435**, 516
Nosferatu, Eine Symphonie des Garuens   17,
   165, 190, 216, 218, 256, **436**, 450, 516, 527,
   593, 681, 720
Nosferatu Productions   266, 425
Nosferatu: The Vampire   438, 439, 451,
   752, 797
Nostradamus; The Blood of   404, 729
Nostradamus; The Curse of   404, 730
Nostradamus and the Destroyer of
   Monsters   736

Nostradamus, El Genii de las Tinieblas   404
Nostradamus and the Genie of Darkness
   736
Nostradamus y el Destructor de Monstruos
   404
Not Exactly Human   566
Not of This Earth   126, 542, 726, 764
The Not-World   788
Novalis   328
Nox   **439**
The Nude Vampire   231, 512
Nurmi; Maila   628
The Nursery   794, 797
Nutini; Hugo G.   402

O

O Macabro Dr. Scivano   568, 750
O Vampiro de Curitiba   614
Obayifo   5, 223, 379
Obituary   713
O'Boylan; Charles   241
Obsessed   799
Obsession   793
Obur   66
Oedipus   275
Of Hell and Heaven   511, 799
The Official Geraint Wyn Davies Fan Club
   225-226
The Oinky Boinky Machine   789
Olcott; Henry Steel   489
Old Dracula   10, 752
An Old Friend of the Family   532, 800
Old House Publishing   158, **441**, 553
Old Mother Riley   306
Old Mother Riley Meets the Vampire
   384, 726
Oldman; Gary   58, **442**, 639
Olivia   252
"Olivia"   698, 702
Olivier; Laurence   184, 639
O'Mara; Kate   464
The Omega Man   396
On Alien Wings   792
On the Nightmare   304
On the Wings of the Knight   225-226
Once Bitten   308, 696, 764
Once Upon a Prime Time   752
Ondskans Vardshus   359
One Dark Night   764
One Eye-Brow Priest   764
One More Time   787
Onion   402

Onyx: The "Literary" Vampire Magazine **442**, 475
Opera 394
Operation Vampire Killer 2000 484
Opium 263, 434
Opji 478, 662
Oprichnina 332
The Oracle 266, 425
Order of the Dragon 514, 664
Order of the Vampyre **444**
Oregon Dark Shadows Society **445**
Orgy of the Dead 787
The Orgy at Madame Dracula's 786
Orgy of the Night 628, 736
Orgy of the Vampires 752
Origins of the vampire **445**
Orlock; Graf 17, 216, 218, 436, **450**, 586, 593
Ortiz; Rossanna 694
Ossenfelder; Heinrich August 255, 470
Ossoio; Amando de 577
Otfinoski; Steven 340
The Other People 788
Ottoman Empire 355, 569, 604
Our Lady of Pain 788
Out for Blood 551, 771, 789
Out for the Count; or, How Would You Like Your Stake?: A Vampire Yarn 779
Out of the House of Life 698, 804
Outback Vampire 764
Outer space vampires *See:* Science fiction and the vampire
Ovid 520
Owen; Dean 175
Owens; Beverly 414
Owl Light 798
Oz; Mary Jane 129

P

Packard; Edward 344
Page; Carol 635
Page; Norvell 578
P'ai 98
Paige; Lori 227, 378, 699-700
Paint Me the Story of Dracula 344
The Palace 252, 702, 804
Palance; Jack 59, 143, 175, 179, 182, 222, 293, 396, **453**, 535, 598, 670, 681
Palazzeschi; Aldo 330
Pale Blood 108, 765
"The Pale Lady" 201
Palladium Books 244

Pandora Publications 227
Paole, Arnold *See:* Paul, Arnold
Paracelsus 295
Paragon Films 100
Parallel Times 11
Paramount Pictures 4
Paraphernalia 47, 59, 112, 153, 158, 175, 188, 208, 414, 441, **455**, 504, 554, 636
Parapsychology 641
Parapsychology Institute of America 641
The Parasite 789
Pardon Me but Your Teeth Are in My Neck 105, 306
Parilland; Anne 697
Paris Vampire 230
Park of Games 576
Parker; Lara 111, 153
Parliament of Blood 789
Parque de Juegos 576, 736
Parry; Michael 35, 362, **459**
The Partaker 97, 789
The Passion of Dracula 196, 765, 779
Passport to the Supernatural 314
Pastel de Sangre 752
Path of the Eclipse 702, 804
Patrick; Butch 414
Patrick; Dora Mary 191
Patternmaster 788
Paul; Arnold 103, 160, 210, 254, 312, 447, **460**, 467, 481, 528, 546, 573, 575, 630, 658
Paul; Garry 202
Paulicians 66
Pawns of Satan 726
Payer of Tribute 789
The Pearl of the Soul of the World 799
Peck; Thomas A. 129
Peel; David 287
Pelesit 391
Pellizzetti; Luigi 329
Penanggalan 95, 223, 390
Penrose; Valentine 35
People for the Ethical Treatment of Animals (PETA) 208
Pepito y Chabelo vs los Monstruos 752
Perfume 802
The Peril of Barnabas Collins 806
Perilous Dreams 798
The Perils of Cinderella 307
Perkowski; Jan L. 320, 478, 561, 570, 645, 676
Permission 266
Personal Darkness 796
Peterson, Cassandra *See:* Elvira

Petrovana; Natasha 464
The Phallus of Osiris 789
The Phantom and Barnabas Collins 522, 806
The Phantom: A Drama in Two Acts 779
Phantom Wedding 523
The Phantom 194
The Phantom World 574
Philadelphia Chewing Gum Company 456
Philinnon 261, 273
Philippines, vampires in the **461**
Philostratus 272, 349, 691
Phlegon 274
Picasso; Paloma 694
Piccadilly 174, 377, 547 *See also:* London, Dracula's
Pickett; Bob 307
Pierart; Z. J. 14, 294, **463**, 490, 631
Pisachas 321
The Pit and the Pendulum 581
Pitt; Brad 511
Pitt; Ingrid 27, 35, 289, 364, **464**, 694
Pittsburgh Dark Shadows Fan Club **466**, 555
''Placide's Wife'' 502
Plan 9 from Outer Space 385, 542, 628, 726
Planché, James Robinson 193, **466**, 529, 618
Planet of the Vampires 43, 330, 543-544
Platt; Kin 341
The Playgirls and the Vampire 330, 736
Pleasence; Donald 184
Plémiannikov; R. V. 623
Plogojowitz; Peter 103, 312, **467**, 573, 658
Plomdeur; Nicolas 458
Plymouth Brethren 284
P. N. Elrod *See:* Elrod, P. N.
P. N. Elrod Fan Club **206**, 477
The Pobratim 785
P'o 98
Poe; Edgar Allan 194, 236, 264, 337, 396, **468**, 502, 581
Poetry, the vampire in 261, **469**, 487
Poland 12, 101, 141, 146, 163-164, 219, 253, 278, **477**, 560, 661
Polanski; Roman 105
Police Against the New World Order 484
Polichinel Vampire 194, 779
Polidori; John 46, 71, 96, 165, 189, 193, 230, 232, 255, 261, 263, 273, 277, 328, 344, 349, 394, 409, 429, 433, 447, 470, **480**, 527,

530, 587, 618, 651, 654, 692 *See also:* Poetry, the vampire in
A Polish Vampire in Burbank 765
Political/economic vampires **481**, 617
Poliziano; Angelo 273
Polo; Marco 258
Polong 391
Polselli; Renato 330
Ponchielli; Amilcare 330
Pontianak 338, 357, 389, 392, **484**, 602, 693, 726
Pontianak Gua Musang 736
Pontianak Kembali 693, 736
Porcelnik 525
Porphyria 54, 211, **485**
Porphyria Foundation 486
Portabella; Pedro 362
Porter; Beth 694
Portugal 64, 576
Portugal: A Book of Folk-Ways 65
Possession 793
The Possession of Lucy Wenstrom 779
Powell; Arthur E. 490
Powell; Martin 557
Powers; Tim 273
Prana Films 256, 450
Precious Blood 793
Premature burial 211 *See also:* Explanations of vampirism
Prest; Thomas P. 530
Pret 701
Preview Murder Mystery 722
The Prey 801
Price; Vincent 28, 97, 146, 581
Pricolici 516, 677
Prikosac 570
The Princess Daphne 784
Princess of the Night 551, 771
The Prisoner of Blackwood Castle 792
Prisoner of Vampires 248
Prisoners of the Night **487**, 552
Progeny of the Adder 803
Project Dracula 800
Project Vampire 771
Propaganda 265, 425
Prophet; Elizabeth Clare 491
Protection against vampires **487** *See also:* Destroying the vampire
Psychic Self Defense 227
Psychic vampirism 6, 14, 72, 228, 294, 350, 392, 463, 468, **489**, 507, 520, 543, 554, 630, 688

Psychical Research; American Society for 633

Psychological perspectives on vampire mythology 304, **492**

Psygnosis Ltd. 247

Public Broadcasting Network 341

Pulp fiction 54

Pulp magazines, vampires in the **501**, 541

Punk rock 245

Pura Sangre 765

Pursuit of Premature Gods and Contemporary Vampires 641

Q

Quarry; Robert 703

Quatermass; Bernard 286

Quatermass II 286

The Quatermass Xperiment 286

Queen B Productions 208

Queen of Blood 2, 125, 543, 693, 736, 786

The Queen of the Damned 368, 449, 510, 799

Queen of Sheba 371

Queen of the Vampires 511

Queens Own 106

Quem tem Medo de Lobishomem 568, 752

A Question of Time 533, 800

Quincey P. Morris Dracula Society 413

Quiroz; Sue 19

R

Rabid 753

Radcliffe; Ann 263

Radcliffe Award; Ann 3, 49, 129

Radu the Handsome 221

Ragoczy; Francis 251

Rais; Gilles de 229, 690

Rakshasas 320

Ramam 321

Ramsland; Katherine 510

Randolphe; Arabella 697

Ranft; Michel 254

Rank; J. Arthur 359

Rape of the Vampires 231, 512

Rasputin's Vintage 788

Rathbone; Basil 384, 543, 556

Ratnose: A Journey up the Hassayampa 794

Rattray; R. Sutherland 5

The Raven 225-226

Raven; Mike 289

Raven; Simon 55

Ravenloft 206, 477

Raw Pain Max 787

Raymond; Christine 408

Realm of Darkness 504

Realm of the Vampire 185, 238, 459, 475, **503**

Realm of the Vampire Newsletter 712

Rebirth of the Undead 699, 805

Reborn 804

Record of Nightly Occurrences: Diary of a Vampire 797

Red and Black 765

Red Blooded American Girl 771

Red Death 205, 791

Red Thirst 502

Red Wine of Rapture 804

Redcaps **504**, 617

Redgrove; Peter 217, 698

Reece; Robert 194

Reed; Donald A. 129

Reeve; Michael 330

Reeves; Keanu 58

The Reflecting Skin 771

Regnoli; Piero 330

Reid and His Vampire Hunting Rangers; Kenneth 245

Rein-Hagen; Mark 241

Reincarnation 684

Reincarnation of Isabel 753

Religa; Peggy 225

The Reluctant Vampire 771

Renard; Christine 230

''A Rendezvous in Averoigne'' 502

Renfield; R. N. 16, 59, 63, 79, 173, 177, 180, 182, 191, 203, 293, 303, 307, 437, **505**, 547, 652, 658, 684

RenSime 796

Reprisal 804

Requiem for a Vampire 753

Requiem pour un Vampire 231, 512

Resch; Kathleen 156, 158, 307, 554, 699

Resolutions in Time 805

Rest In Peace 797

''The Resuscitated Corpse'' 99

Retribution 805

The Return of a Vampire 345

The Return of Count Yorga 705, 753

The Return of Dr. X 301, 722

The Return of Dracula 726

Return of the Evil Dead 577

The Return of the Vampire 384, 593, 679, 723

Return to Salem's Lot   352, 600
The Return   784
Reunion   805
Revelations   805
The Revenants   791
Revenge of the Blood Beast   330, 581, 737
The Revenge of Dracula   613, 803
The Revenge of the Rose   798
Revenge of the Vampire   42, 330, 725
The Revival of Dracula   737
Reynold; George W. M.   677
Ricaut; Paul   617
Riccardo; Martin V.   46, 216, 490, **506**, 640, 645 *See also:* Bibliography, vampire
Rice; Anne   17, 18, 105, 108, 120, 126, 139, 140, 167, 210, 219, 223, 230, 246, 265, 267, 271, 302, 366, 408, 418, 424, 430, 444, 449, **507**, 533, 537, 565, 610, 635, 697
Rice; Jeff   433
Rice's Vampire Lestat Fan Club; Anne   510
Richard; Fr. Francoise   687
Richard Matheson: Collected Stories   396
Riddle; Deanna   442
The Rider of the Skulls   730
Rifts   244
Riggs; Parker   305
Ripley the Vampyr   395, 529
Riva; James P.   134
Riva; Valeria   624
Rivals of Dracula   459
Riverrun   801
Rizzuto; Sharida   184, 238, 503
Robbins; Trina   647
Roberts; John M.   403
Roberts; Letha   159
Robertson; C. M.   616
Robin; Marcy   156, 158, 554, 699
Robins; Frank   392
Robinson; Philip   618
Robles; German   403, 568
Robo Vampire   100, 771
Rock; Blossom   4
Rockula   771
Rodd; Rennell   673
Rodrigo; Baron   360
Rogers; Charles   621
Rogo; Scott   135, 490, 633
Rohr; Philip   254
Rollin; Jean   231, 365, **511**, 551
Roman Catholic Church   138, 159, 209, 212, 477, 508, 674
Roman Emperor Hadrian   273
Romand; Gina   694

Romania, vampires in   30, 47, 56, 61, 65, 88, 94, 185, 188, 219, 249, 275, 278, 291, 307, 311, 380, **512**, 520, 533, 558, 560, 568, 588, 604, 610, 613, 666, 676, 689, 705
Rome, vampires in ancient   327, **520**, 576, 686
Romero; George   258
Ronald; Bruce   196
Ronay; Gabriel   35, 320
Roquelaure; A. N.   510
Rosetta Stone   265, 425
Rosovetskii; S. K.   332
Ross; Clarissa   522
Ross; Marilyn   112, 115, 156, 522
Ross; William Edward Daniel   112, 115, 156, 236, **522**, 533
Rossiter; Jane   522
Roth; E. W.   40
Rothman; Stephanie   125, 696
Rouge et Noir: les Poemes des Vampires   476
Rousseau; Jean-Jacques   229
Ruben; Katt Shea   696
Rubio; Pablo Alvarez   180
Rusalka   789
Russell; Ken   586
Russia, vampires in   21, 30, 94, 164, 219, 275, 278, 331, **524**, 549, 560, 588, 673, 688
Ruthven; Lord   19, 72, 95, 107, 165, 193, 301, 328, 369, 394, 409, 434, 467, 480, 483, **527**, 587, 593, 655, 657, 691
Ruwai   391
Ryan; Mitchell   151
Ryder; Winona   58, 123, 417
Rymer; James Malcolm   215, 409, **529**, 618, 653

S

Sabbatarians   572
Sabella; or the Blood Stone   697, 796
Saberhagen; Fred   175, 380, **531**, 548, 557, 614, 659, 702
Sabrina the Teenage Witch   599
Sackville-Bagg; Rudolph   342
The Saga of the Draculas   753
The Sailor on the Seas of Fate   798
St. Andrew's Eve   517
St. George's Day   517, **765**
St. George's Eve   249
St. Germain *See:* Germain, St.
The Saint Germain Chronicles   252, 702, 804

Saint James; Susan   307

St. John the Pursuer, Book I: Vampire in Moscow   793

Salem's Lot   352, 600, 674, 753, 795

The Saliva Tree   787

Samson vs. the Vampire Women   404, 535

Sanchez; Gali   241

Sanders; Lewis   408

Sanders; Paula   226

Sandworld   797

Sangster; Jimmy   220, 286, 289, 303, 359, **534**, 694

Santo   404, **535**

Santo Against Baron Brakola   737

Santo and the Blue Demon vs. Dracula and the Wolfman   753

Santo and the Blue Demon vs. the Monsters   737

Santo Contra Cazadores de Cabezas   404

Santo Contra el Baron Brakola   536

Santo Contra las Mujeres Vampiro   404, 535

Santo and Dracula's Treasure   737

Santo en la Venganza de las Mujeres Vampiros   404, 536, 737

Santo un el Tesoro de Dracula   404, 536

Santo vs. the Vampire Women   737

Santo y Blue Demon Contra Dracula y el Hombre Lobo   404, 536

Santo y Blue Demon Contra los Monstruos   536

Sara, the Black Goddess   348

Sara, the Black Virgin   280

Sarandon; Susan   365, 696

Sardia: A Story of Love   784

Satan   102, 139, 210, **536**

Satanael   66

The Satanic Rites of Dracula   290, 297, 360, 639, 753

Satanism   229

Satan's Night Out   367

Sato; Shimako   337

Saturday the 14th   126, 765

Saturn Trophy   129

Savarese; Nino   328

Savory; Gerald   598

Saxon; John   543

Saxon; Peter   697

Scandinavia, vampires in   413, 519, **539**

Scarlet in Gaslight   120, 557

The Scarlet Vampire   783

The Scars of Dracula   27, **288**, 360, 754, 793

Schellenberger; Thomas   184

Schellenberger's Friends and Associates of Old-Style Horror; Thomas   185

Schiller; Friedreich   261

Schmidt; Claudia   425

Schocker; Dan   257

Schofield; Frank   151

Scholomance   537

Schreck; Max   436

Schroeder-Matray; Greta   437

Schtrattembach; Cardinal   103, 159

Schumacher; Steven C.   379

Schweiggert; Affons   254

Science fiction and the vampire   43, 105, 125, 449, 503, **541**, 693

Scotland Yard   290

Scotland   17, 191, 466, 504, 616

Scott; Kathryn Leigh   111, 151

Scott; Melanie   19

Scott; Sir Walter   471, 549, 576, 618

Scourge of the Blood Cult   786

Scream Blacula Scream   10, 49, 395, 754
See also: Marshall; William

Scream and Scream Again   786

Screem in the Dark Fan Club *See:* Vlad

Screem in the Dark Newsletter   663, 712

Screem Jams Productions   663

Scrow; David   245

Seance for a Vampire   800

The Secret of Barnabas Collins   806

The Secret of the Chalice   378

The Secret of House No. 5   527

The Secret Order of the Undead   **545**

Secret of the Pale Lover   523, 786

The Secret Room   302, **545**

Secret of the Willows   786, 802

The Secrets of Dr. Taverner   228

The Secrets of Dracula   735

The Secrets of House No. 5   720

Seductions   792

Sedwick; John   151

Seeds   148, 324, 478, 488, 518, **545**, 563, 567, 572, 662

Sei Donne per l'Assassino   43, 330

Seifi; Ali Riga   174

Selby; David   154-155

Selene   **546**

The Selkie   801

Sellwood; A. V.   285

Selsky; Sam   511

Senf; Carol   528

Senn; Harry   249, 515, 534, 564, 676

Serbia   101, 289, 327, 460, 467, 560, 569, 607, 630, 677

Sesame Street   341

Seven Brides for Dracula   197

The Seven Brothers Meet Dracula   28, 99, 145, 290

The Seven Vampires   568, 765

Seven Wives for Dracula   779

Seward; John   15-16, 29, 54, 79, 127, 173, 177, 182, 184, 191, 195, 203, 300, 303, 377, 412, 416, 505, 532, **547**, 557, 594, 651, 680

Seward; Lucy   29, 356

Sex Express   754

Sex Gang Children   268

Sex and the Vampire   231, 512

Sexandroide   231, 551, 765

Sexton; Zachary Lucius   315

Sexuality and the vampire   184, 252, 287, 304, 499, **548**, 578

Sexy Prohibitissimo   737

Sexyrella   737

Seygig; Delphine   694

Shad; Rosemary   226

Shadow of Dracula   754

Shadow Fires   795

The Shadow Gate   788

Shadow; Mike   257

Shadow Project   267, 425

Shadow of a Shade: A Survey of Vampirism in Literature   46, 85

Shadow of the Werewolf   754

Shadowcon   156, 158, 227, **553**, 554

Shadowdance   475, **553**

Shadowed Beginnings   699

Shadowgram   156, 158, 553, **554**, 714

Shadowrun   246

Shadows   787

Shadows in the Dark   765

Shadows of the Night   466, **555**

Shadows in the 90's   699

Shadowtown   797

Shakespearean Odyssey   236

Shanklin; Rick   120

Shattered Glass   44, 788

Shaw Brothers   28, 99, 290, 392

She Wakes   794

She-Devil   793

Shelley; Barbara   288

Shelley; Mary   263, 286

Shelley; Percy   71, 273

Shepard, Leslie Alan   57, 459, **555**

Shepard; Patty   694

Sherlock Holmes   **556**

Sherlock Holmes in Caracas   771

Sherlock Holmes: The Last Vampire   557

Sherlock Holmes vs. Dracula   791

Sherlock Holmes vs. Dracula: The Adventures of the Sanguinary Count   557

Shiembieda; Kevin   244

The Shining Pool   789

The Shiny Narrow Grin   784

Ship of Shadows   796

Shock; Anna   293

Shogar; Jean   433

Short; Elizabeth   133

The Shroud   267, 425

Shtriga   **558**, 570

Shuck; John   414

Shuttle; Penelope   217, 698

Siberia   524

Sighisoara   **559**, 612, 664

Sigismund; Emperor   514

Sigismund I of Luxembourg   664

Sikkim   603-604

Silent Death   664

Silesia   313, 630

The Silver Kiss   345, 795

The Silver Skull   149, 790

Silvio; Dan   466

Simmons; Dan   56, 222

Simmons; Theresa   19

Sinistrari; Ludovico Maria   327

Sins of the Fathers   700, 806

Siouxsie and the Banshees   265, 418, 424

Sir Leoline   363

The Sisters of Mercy   265, 424

Sisters of Satan   404, 754

Siva   323, 347

Skal; David J.   181

Skeggs; Ray   291

Skeleton Dancer   791

Skorzeny; Janos   432

Skull-Face and Others   785

Sky; Frank   257

Slaughter of the Vampires   330, 738

Slavic vampire   6, 66, 98, 146, 253, 513, 516, 524, 569, 610, 661, 683

Slavs, vampires among the   **559**

Sledzik; Paul S.   14

Sleep Chamber   269

Sleep, vampire   172, **564**

The Sleeping Sorceress: An Elric Novel   798

Sleepwalkers   771

Slimelight   265, 425

Slovenia   558, 569, 571

Smarra; ou, Les Demons de la Nuit   434

Smith; Clark Ashton   502
Smith; L. J.   344
Smith; Madeleine   289, 464
Smithereens   421
Snakegod   792
Snaxar   525
Sneddon; Robert W.   501
Snow-Lang; Wendy   267, **565**
So What Killed the Vampire   783
Societas Argenti Viae Eternitata (SAVE)   241
The Soft Whisper of the Dead   793
Solvay; Paolo   330
Some Things Never Die   798
Some of Your Blood   786
Sometimes, After Sunset   796
Somewhere in the Night   302
Sommer-Bodenburg; Angela   257, 342
Son of Dracula   216, 429, 724, 754
Song of Kali   801
Sonho de Vampiros; Um   568
Sons of Satan   301
The Sorcerer's Skull   797
Sorority House Vampires   772
Sorrentino; Gaetano   329
The Soul of the Moor   785
Soulcatchers   795
Soulsmith   790
The Soulsucker   800
S.O.UND   712
The Source   386, 797
South America, vampires in   38, 249, 373, **567**, 579
South of Heaven   788
Southern Slavs, vampires among the   95, 218, 273, 275, 355, 524, 549, 558, 560, **568**, 607, 637
Southey; Robert   108, 472, **575**, 618, 692
Space Ship Sappy   726
The Space Vampires   541, 543, 804
Spacek; Sissy   352
Spain, vampires in   64, 167, 401, **576**
The Spaniards Inn   377
Spawn of the Vampire   791
The Spear   793
Specter or Delusion? The Supernatural in Gothic Fiction   46, 85
Spence; Jim   344
Spermula   754
Spider   **578**
Spider; John   257
Spingola; Ryan   476
Spinner; Stephanie   344

Spirit vs. Zombi   100, 765
Spirite   250
Spiritual Vampirism; The History of Etherial Softdown and Her Friends of the "New Light"   787
Spiritualism   250, 294, 431, 463, 489, 631
   See also: Psychic vampirism
Spooks Run Wild   724
Spooky Family   100, 765
Sprenger; Jacob   687
Sprenger; James   677
Springfield; Rick   225
The Spy Who Drank Blood   796
Stagg; John   473, 618
Stake   6, 31, 37, 67, 81, 95, 107, 127, 147, 160, 165, 168, 173, 186, 203, 211, 219, 228, 248, 254, 297-298, 341, 366, 380, 412, 467, 473, 518, 526, 539-540, 570-572, **579**, 607, 624, 646, 681
The Stake   795
Stapleton; Joan   694
Star Trek   541
Star Virgin   765
Stealer of Souls and Other Stories   798
Steele; Barbara   42, 330, **581**, 693
Steele; Pippa   289
Stella Matutina   227
Stellar Games   245
Stengaard; Yutte   289, 694
Steno; Stefano   328, 330
Stetson; George R.   13
Sting   421
Stock; John Christian   254
Stockbridge; Grant   578
Stoddard; Carolyn   151
Stoddard; Elizabeth Collins   151
Stoker; Bram   1, 15-16, 21, 35-36, 47, 49, 54, 56, 58, 61, 79, 81, 87, 94, 104, 107, 116, 127, 138, 154, 160, 164, 169, 181, 188, 190, 194, 203, 209, 215, 218, 221, 234, 239, 248, 256, 278, 285, 287, 296-297, 303, 310, 326, 344, 358, 360, 363, 375, 383, 394, 397, 408, 410, 412, 415, 420, 430, 435, 512, 536, **583**, 654
Stoker Archives; Bram   57
Stoker Awards; Bram   396
Stoker Club; The Bram   326
Stoker; Florence   28, 160, 174, 176, 195, 383, 437, 451, 586, 620
Stoker International Summer School; Bram   57
Stoker Memorial Association; Bram   128

Stoker Memorial Collection of Rare Books; Bram   128

Stoker Society; The Bram   **57**, 176, 326, 555

Stoker's Classic Novel; The Essential "Dracula": A Completely Illustrated and Annotated Edition of Bram   222

Stoker's Dracula; Bram   17, 92, 104, 123, 127, 175, 179, 182, 210, 240, 246, 291, 293, 301, 413, 417, 450, 455-456, 537, 552, 586, 596, 610, 639, 670, 681, 685

Stolen Souls   800

Stormbringer   798

Story of My Life   135

Strahd   206

Strange; Dr. Stephen   31, 119, 372, 405

Strange Love of the Vampires   577, 754

The Strange Story of Dr. Senex   783

Strange; Victor   31

Strangers at Collins House   806

Streets   772

Strega   64, 520, 576, 686

Strength, physical   81, 95, 98, 104, 141, 170, 252, 335, 410, 489, 579, **587**, 610, 655

The Stress of Her Regard   799

Stribling; Melissa   303

Strieber; Whitley   55, 105, 265, 696-697

Striga   515, 571

Striges   520

Strigoaica   515, 534, 561

Strigoi   515, 520, 558, 561, 570, 686

Strigoi mort   515, 562

Strigoi vii   515

Strigon   558, 570

Strix   223, 478, 487, 515, 520, 559, 562, 571, 686

Stroyberg; Annette   365, 693

Subspecies   772

Succubi   795

The Succubus   794

Suck Me, Vampire   754

Suckers   788

Suicide   8, 49, 59, 81, 98, 173, 219, 254, 280, 315, 446, 516, 540, 571, **588**, 607, 673, 682 *See also:* Origins of the vampire

Sukuyan   6, 223, 567, **589**, 691

Sullivan; Barry   543

Summer of Night   801

Summers Award; Montague   259

Summers; Montague   4, 21, 25, 77, 135, 147, 211, 295, 310, 320, 325, 340, 530, 574, **590**, 616

Summoned to Tourney: An Urban Fantasy   795

The Summoning   796

Sumpah Pontianak   693, 726

SunDown . . . SunRise   787

Sundown: The Vampire in Retreat   653, 765

Sung-ling; P'u   99

Sunglasses After Dark   698, 789

Sunlight   49, 54, 95, 108, 166, 168, 182, 184, 251, 318, 366, 401, 407, 437, 565, 587, **592**, 624, 655, 661

Super-Giant 2   726

Supergrass   766

Supermind   803

Surinam   567, 589

Survival of the Fittest   788

Suspense Comics   116

Sutherland; May   378, 700

Sutton; Tom   647

Swanson; Kristy   697

Sweden   539

Sweet Blood   793

Sweet Silver Blues   789

Swieten; Gerhard van   328

Swift; Lela   151

Swinford; Brad   663

The Swordbearer   789

Symons; Arthur   273, 473

Szekelys   51, 171, 310, 514, **595**, 611

T

Tabitha Ffoulkes   796

The Taint   803

Talamaur   **597**

Talbot; Larry   678

Talbot; P. Amaury   5

The Tale of the Body Thief   369, 510, 799

Tale of a Vampire   337, 772

Tales of Blood and Terror   738

Tales from the Crypt   115

Tales of Hoffman   378

Tall, Dark, and Gruesome   362

Tame re Champo ne Ame Kel   754

The Tangled Skein   558

Tapestry of Dark Souls   45, 788

Tarchetti; Ugo   330

Tarocco Meccanico   329-330

Tasei   426

A Taste of Blood   738

Taste the Blood of Dracula   288, 360, 738

A Taste of Blood Wine   803

A Taste for Power   790

Taylor; William   471
Tayman; Robert   289
Teen Vamp   766
The Teenage Frankenstein   726
Teenage Mutant Ninja Turtles   457
Teeth *See:* Fangs
Television, vampires on   84, 100, 111, 223, **598**
Tempi Duri per i Vampiri   328, 330, 360
Temple of Set   444
Temple of the Vampire   **601**
Tempter   789
Tempting Fate   252, 702, 804
Tenatz   570
Tender Dracula, or, The Confessions of a Bloodsucker   146, 755
Tenderness of Wolves   257, 284, 301, 755
Tenjac   570
Tenn; William   54
Terence Fisher   679
Terra-X   267
Terror Creatures from the Grave   581, 738
Terror in the Crypt   82, 360, 738
Terror of Dracula   438
Terrore nello Spazio   43, 330, 543
Terry; Ellen   195
Tesla; Armand   593
Thailand, vampires in   **602**
Thalaba the Destroyer   575, 692
That Thing in my Neck is a Tooth   307
Thaye   426
Theatre du Grand Guignol   194, 286
Theatre of the Night   267
Theatre of the Vampires   220
Theosophical Society   294, 489
There Were No Asper Ladies   783
There's a Batwing in My Lunchbox   342
Theresa; Maria   76, 104, 311, 630
They Thirst   797
They've Changed Faces   755
The Thief of Always   788
The Thing   542, 797
The Thing: A Novel   792
The Thing from Another World   542, 727
Thirst   35, 766
Thirst of the Vampire   804
The Thirsty Dead   755
Thirteen Tales of Terror   149
This Ascension   267, 425
Thomas; Illtyd   643
Thomas the Rhymer   795
Thomas Schellenberger's Friends and Associates of Old-Style Horror   185

Thompson; Jeff   113, 523
Thompson; R. Campbell   25
Thonger and the Dragon City   789
Thonger of Lemuria   789
Thoreau; Henry David   13
Thorn   532, 800
Those Cruel and Bloody Vampires   755
Those Feedy on Blood   772
Those of My Blood   796
Those Who Hunt the Night   793
A Thousand Faces   784
The Three Coffins   784
Tibet, vampires in   329, **603**, 701
Tibor; Baron   259
Tieck; John   255
Tiempos duros para Dracula   578, 755
Tien-an; Hsu   290
Till Death   755
Till Death Do Us Part   82
The Time of Vampires   755
Timefall   794
Time's Dark Laughter   794
Tirgoviste   90, 332, 559, **604**, 659, 664, 668
Titta; Guadalberto   328
Tlahuelpuchi   64, 401
Tlalteuctli   400
To Die For   261, 766
To Die For, II: Son of Darkness   772
To Kill a Corpse   783
To Love a Vampire   791, 794
To Sleep with a Vampire   126, 772
To Wake the Dead   789
Tobien; W. J.   257
Tolstoy; Alexey   43, 230, 328, 527, **607**
Tomashoff; Sy   151
Tomb   766
The Tomb of Dracula   49, 117, 120, 175, 186, 337, 371, 405, **608**, 653
''The Tomb of Sarah''   697
Tombs of the Blind Dead   577, 755
Tome Press   451
The Tommyknockers   352, 795
Toothless Vampires   100, 766
Topps Comics   122
Tore Ng Diyablo   738
Torelli; Achille   330
The Torture Zone   738
The Torturer   786
Tovar; Lupita   180, 403, 620
Tower of the Devil   738
Tower of the Screaming Virgins   738
The Trail   766
Trail of the Vampire   788

Traitement de Choc 755
Trampire 766
Transformation 15, 81, 95, 223, 272, 313, 321, 402, 590, **609**, 686
Transvision Vamp 267, 425
Transylvania 32, 47, 56, 58, 68, 79, 89, 94, 101, 116, 126, 138, 160, 171, 177, 185, 186, 190, 195, 199, 203, 251, 292, 300, 310, 342, 375, 381, 413, 415, 430, 437, 482, 498, 512, 533, 537, 547-548, 559, 566, 595, **610**, 625, 652, 659, 684, 693
Transylvania 6-5000 126, 308, 738, 766
Transylvania Station 803
Transylvania Troopers 545
Transylvania Twist 126, 308, 766
The Transylvanian Library: A Consumer's Guide to Vampire Fiction 46
Transylvanian Society of Dracula **613**
Travels of 3 English Gentlemen from Venice to Hamburg, Being the Grand Tour of Germany in the Year 1734 617
Tremayne; Peter 175, 222, **613**
Treptow; Kurt W. 222
Trevisan, Dalton (1952-) **614**
Tricolici 516, 677
Trilogy of Fear 772
Trilogy of Terror 396
Trinidad 567, 589
Tristana 755
The True Life of Dracula 755
True Vampires of History 35, 259
The Truth about Dracula 35
Tryst of Dark Shadows 806
Tuberculosis 13, 349, 446, 479
Tunnel Under the World 755
Turkey 573
Turoczy; Laszlo 33
The Twelfth Child 803
Twilight Phantasies 801
Twins 281
Twins of Evil 82, 145, 290, 365, 694, 755
A Twist of Mind 802
Twisted Sister 268
Twitchell; James 72, 350, 351, 468
Tyler; Edward B. 14

U

Ukraine 524
The Ultimate Dracula 690
Ultimate Vampire 772
Um Sonho De Vampiros 754
Un Vampire au Paradis 772

Un Vampiro 328
Un Vampiro para Dos 740
Uncle Alucard **615**
Uncle Vampire 793
Uncle Was a Vampire 328, 727
The Undead 239, 796, 801
Undead Undulations 711
Under the Eye of God 792
The Understudy: Graveyard Shift II 766
Undinal Songs 269
Undying Love 772
The Undying Monster 785
Unholy Communion 800
The Unholy Love 721
United Kingdom, vampires in the 325, 504, **615**
Universal-International 621
Universal Pictures 62, 79, 83, 93, 162, 174, 176, 179, 182, 185, 196, 220, 233, 286, 303, 306, 359, 364, 373, 378, 383, 403, 437, 457, 502, 506, 542, 577, 580, 619, **620**, 639, 675, 677
The Unmeasured Place 785
The Unquiet Corpse 786
Upiór 478, 561
Upír 146, 561
Upirbi 561
Upirina 561, 570
"Upyr" 527, 607
Upyr 525, 688
Ustrel 67, 562

V

Vaarwhel 756
Vacher; Joseph 133
Vadim; Annette 82, 231
Vadim; Roger 3, 82, 231, 365, 421, 551, **623**, 646, 693
The Vagabond Vampires 780
Valdez; Oliedo y 40
Valduga; Patrizia 331
Valentine 802
Valentino; Rudolph 627
Valerie 82, 772
Valerie and the Week of Wonders 738
Valley of Lights 792
The Valley of Worms & Others 785
Valley of the Zombies 724
Valvasor; Count Baron Jan Vajkart 571, 574
Vambéry; Arminius 222, **624**, 653
Vamp 10, 126, 217, 610, 658, 696, 766

The Vamp   3, 197, 308, 330, 473, 550, **626,** 691 *See also:* Sexuality and the vampire
Vamphyri!   386, 797
Vampir   66, 362, 561, 570, 623, 744
Vampir-Cuadecuc   739
Vampira   3, 10, 206, 265, 385, 424, 542, **628**
Vampiras; Las   404
Vampirdzhija   67, 637
The Vampire   194, 230, 241, 343, 373, 403, 600, 720, 726-727, 780, 784-786
The Vampire   **629**
''The Vampire''   148, 626
The Vampire: A Drama in Three Acts   780
The Vampire: A Sensational Four-Act Melodrama   780
The Vampire: A Tragedy in Five Acts   781
The Vampire: A Tragedy in Three Acts   194
Vampire a Venezia   331
Vampire Abroad   784
The Vampire Affair   785
The Vampire: An Original Burlesque   780
Vampire Archives   **636**
The Vampire and the Ballerina   330, 739
The Vampire Bat: A Mystery Melodrama in Three Acts   780
Vampire Bats *See:* Bats, vampire
Vampire Beat   790
The Vampire Bible   602
Vampire Bibliography of Fiction and Non-Fiction   46
Vampire Blood   793
Vampire Bookshop   128
The Vampire Bride   194
The Vampire; or, the Bride of Death: A Melodrama   780
The Vampire; or, The Bride of the Isles: A Romantic Drama in Three Acts   193, 780, 781
The Vampire Bride, or Wake not the Dead   780
Vampire Brides *See:* Brides, vampire
Vampire Buster   772
The Vampire Cameo   786
The Vampire of Castle Frankenstein   739
The Vampire Cat   337
The Vampire Cat: A Play in One Act from the Japanese Legend of the Nebeshima Cat   780
The Vampire of the Cave   736
Vampire Characteristics *See:* Characteristics of the Vampire
The Vampire Chase   788

Vampire Child   794
Vampire: Chilling Tales of the Undead   285
The Vampire Chronicles   267, 366, 510
Vampire Circus   289, 756
Vampire City   785
The Vampire in the Comic Book   46
The Vampire Companion: The Official Guide to Anne Rice's Vampire Chronicles   19, 510, 511
The Vampire Contessa: From the Journal of Jeremy Quentain   523, 800
Vampire Cop   773
Vampire Correspondence Network   381
''The Vampire Creed''   601
The Vampire Cult   231
The Vampire of Curitiba and Other Stories   614
The Vampire Curse   804
The Vampire; or, Detective Brand's Greatest Case   787
The Vampire Diaries   344
The Vampire Directory   459, 504
The Vampire Doll   756
Vampire Dracula Comes to Kobe: Evil Makes a Woman Beautiful   337
The Vampire of Düsseldorf   257
Vampire; Elusive Song of the   100
The Vampire in Europe   591
Vampire Fan Forums   645
The Vampire on the Farm   342
''The Vampire Files''   205
The Vampire Files   477
The Vampire Guild   619, **636**
The Vampire Happening   257, 756
The Vampire: His Kith and Kin   211, 591
The Vampire Hookers   61, 85, 756
Vampire Hunter D   337, 767
Vampire hunters   67, 168, 173, 186, 212, 289, 298, **637,** 646, 653, 694
Vampire Information Exchange   46, 633, **639,** 645, 648
Vampire Information Exchange Newsletter   713
The Vampire Institute   128
Vampire Intelligence   244
Vampire Invaders   344
Vampire Island   802
The Vampire Janine   798
The Vampire Joke Book   310
Vampire Jokes and Cartoons   308
The Vampire Journals   185, 238, 503, 698, 788
Vampire Junction   **641,** 802

Vampire Kingdoms 244
Vampire King 578
Vampire kits 674
Vampire Knights 767
Vampire Kung-Fu 99, 756
The Vampire Legacy: Blood Secrets 802
The Vampire in Legend, Lore, and
  Literature 603
The Vampire Legion **641**
Vampire Lesbians of Sodom 196, 780
The Vampire Lestat 120, 139, 366,
  510, 799
The Vampire in Literature: A Critical
  Bibliography 46, 85
The Vampire Lovers 27, 82, 145, 288, 359,
  365, 464, 551, 694, 756, 785
"The Vampire Maid" 697
Vampire Man 727
Vampire: The Masquerade 77, 369 See
  also: Games, vampire
"Vampire Master" 115
Vampire Master of Darkness 247
The Vampire Memoirs 538, 552, 698, 797
The Vampire Men 787
Vampire Men of the Lost Planet 84
Vampire at Midnight 767
Vampire; Mr. 100
Vampire of the Mists 792
The Vampire of Mons 802
The Vampire Moth 727
The Vampire of Moura 789
The Vampire Moves In 342
A Vampire Named Murray 309
Vampire; New Mr. 100
The Vampire of N'Gobi 784
Vampire Nights 798
Vampire Notes 801
"The Vampire of Oakdale Ridge" 501
The Vampire Odyssey 789
The Vampire of the Opera 739
The Vampire Papers 314
Vampire Pen Friends Network 128
"The Vampire Princess" 479
Vampire Princess Miyu 337, 767
Vampire Raiders—Ninja Queen 767
Vampire Research Center 633, 639, **641**
Vampire Research Society 297, 619, 633,
  643
The Vampire Returns 736
Vampire in the Shadows 797
The Vampire Shows His Teeth 100
Vampire in the Skies 784
Vampire sleep 95, 292, 315, 588

Vampire Strike 799
Vampire Studies 490, 506, 633, 640, **645**
The Vampire Takes a Trip 342
Vampire Tales 529
The Vampire Tapes 697, 799
The Vampire Tapestry 789
Vampire Thrills 512
Vampire Tower 781
Vampire Trailer Park 773
Vampire trap 467
Vampire in Venice 767
The Vampire Verse: An Anthology 476
"Vampire Wine" 685
Vampire Winter 803
Vampire Woman 99, 739
The Vampire Women 800
Vampire Writers' Circle 406
Vampirella 2, 206, 544, 624, 697
Vampirella 117, 121, 259, 340, 608,
  645, 653
The Vampires 84, 739, 799
Vampires 258, 315, 340, 756, 767, 802
The Vampires of Alfama 794
The Vampires of the Andes 783
Vampires Anonymous 302, 797
The Vampire's Apprentice 789
Vampires Are 635, 642
Vampires Are Us 128
Vampires on Bikini Beach 767
The Vampire's Bite 756
Vampire's Breakfast 100, 767
The Vampire's Bride 307
The Vampire's Bride, or, the Perils of
  Cinderella 781
Vampires in Chicago 781
Vampires of the China Coast 783
The Vampire's Coffin 403, 727
The Vampire's Crypt 86, 475
The Vampire's Curse 726
Vampires d'Alfama 739
A Vampire's Dream 568, 754
Vampire's Embrace 773
The Vampires of Finistere 697, 800
The Vampire's Ghost 410, 529, 724
Vampires in Havana 767
The Vampire's Kiss 122, 767, 787, 793
Vampires Live Again 100, 767
Vampires Ltd. 148
Vampires: Mademoiselle Réseda 784
Vampires at Midnight 285
Vampire's Moon 800
Vampires by Night 298
The Vampire's Night Orgy 577

Vampires of Nightworld   788
Vampires Overhead   785
Vampire's Prey   784
The Vampire's Rape   551
Vampires Settle on Police Camp   773
Vampires Strike Back   100, 767
The Vampires Strike Out   781
The Vampire's Trail; or, Nick Carter and the Policy King   784
Vampires Unearthed   506
Vampires and Vampirism   325
Vampires of Vengeance   785
Vampires of Venus   797
The Vampires of Warsaw   721
Vampires, Werewolves, Ghosts and Other Such Things That Go Bump in the Night   **647**
Vampires, Werewolves and Ghouls   314
Vampires, Werewolves, and Other Demons   314
The Vampires and the Witch   791
Vampirism; Journal of Modern   648
Vampirism Research Institute   **648**
Vampirisme   739
Vampiro   328
Vampiro 2000   756
Vampirology; Journal of   6, 14
Vampiros; Las   84
Vampyr   55, 82, 198, 359, **648**, 692, 722, 756, 794
Vampyr; Der   394, 426
Vampyr—A Soap Opera; Der   395
''The Vampyre''   46, 188, 193, 230, 232, 261, 277, 328, 344, 349, 394, 409, 429, 433, 470, 480, 527, 587, 618, 654
The Vampyre   773, 781
The Vampyre Papers   444
The Vampyre Society (Bohanan)   615, **650**
The Vampyre Society (Gittens)   619, **651**
Vampyres   365
Vampyre's Cry   271
Vampyres, Daughters of Dracula   756
Vampyros Lesbos die erbin des Dracula   577, 696, 757
Van Eyssen; John   303
Van Helsing; Abraham   15-16, 49, 54, 59, 61, 68, 79, 88, 99, 104, 107, 123, 127, 138, 143, 144, 161, 164, 171, 177, 180, 182, 184, 186, 190, 195, 202-203, 215, 219, 233-234, 240, 256, 264, 278, 287, 290, 292, 296, 300, 303, 307, 315, 360, 377, 407, 416, 430, 435, 437, 447, 453, 505, 532, 534, 536, 547, 549, 557, 564, 587, 593-59, 646, **651**, 657, 661, 665
Van Helsing; Adam   653
Van Helsing; Eva   267, 425
Van Helsing; Rachel   49, 186, 608, 653
Van Sloan; Edward   177, 638
Van Swieten; Gerhard   631
Van Vogt; A. E.   449, 541
The Vanishing Tower   798
Varma; Devendra P.   8, 85, 324, 359, 603
Varney; Sir Francis   653
Varney the Vampire: or, the Feast of Blood   781, 786
Varney the Vampyre   19, 41, 85, 107, 135, 165, 215, 219, 301, 316, 409, 429, 529, 593, 618, **653**, 657, 692
Vault of Horror   115, 757
Vegas Vampire   801
Veil of Darkness   247
Vellutini; John L.   6, 14, 339
The Velvet Vampire   125, 615, 651, 696, 714, 757
Vengeful Vampire Girl   768
The Venomous Serpent   787
Verzeni; Vincenzo   133
Veshtitza   570
Vessel   803
The Vetala-Pachisi   322
Vetalas   69, 322
Victims   61, **657**
Victoria Winters   806
V.I.E. Newsletter   46
Vierges et Vampires   512
''The Vig''   581
Vij   527, 740
Vikram and the Vampire   69, 322
Village of Blood   790
A Village Vampire   373, 720
Village of Vampires   340
Villarias; Carlos   180, 403
Villeneuve; Roland   231
Vincent Price's Dracula   768
Virago   365, 797
Vircolac   516, 561
Virgin Vampire   757
The Virgin and the Vampire   697, 798
Virgintooth   794
Virtue et Morte   267
Visegrád   89, 311, **659**, 669
Vision   95, 407, **661**
The Vision   795
Vjesci   478, 562, **661**
Vjeshtitza   558, 570

Vjeszczi 478, 562, 661

Vlad 176, 458, **662** *See also:* Music, vampire

Vlad the Drac 342

Vlad Dracul 278, 514, 559, 595, 604, 612, 659, **664**

Vlad the Impaler 56, 59, 87, 123, 127, 143, 171, 181, 185, 196, 221, 239, 278, 311, 315, 331, 340, 360, 363, 372, 397, 442, 453, 513-514, 537, 566, 595, 598, 604, 612-613, 625, 653, 659, 664, **665**, 692, 705

Vlad the Impaler, 1431-1476; Dracula: A Biography of 222, 437, 438, 756

Vlad of Nosferatu 425

Vlad Tepes 757

Vladislav II 604, 666

Voices from the Vaults 189, 713

Voil des Vampires 512

Volkkavaar 796

Volta; Ornella 231, 624

Voltaire 76, 229, 433, 482, 630

Von Goosewing; Dr. 199

Von Haxthausen; August 21

Von Housen; Count 306

Von Krolock; Count 307

Von Sternberg-Ungern; Roman 133

Von Wangenheim; Gustav 437

Von Zarovich; Count Strahd 241

Voodoo Heartbeat 757

Voytek; Anton 600

Vrykolakas 10, 71, 102, 273, 516, 561, 570, 676, 684

Vukodlak 355, 516, 561, 570, 676

Vurvulak 570

W

Wagner the Wehrwolf 677

Waite; John 421

"Wake Not the Dead" 255

Walker; Hugh 257

Wallace; Art 151

Wallachia 127, 171, 189, 278, 513, 559, 595, 604, 661, 664, 667, 705

Wallman; Edgar A. 315

Walpole; Horace 263

Walt Disney 340

Wanda Does Transylvania 551

Wangmo; Princess Pedi 604

The Wanting 788

The Wanting Factor 790

Warburton; Harry 161

Ward; Simon 182

Warner Brothers 28, 290

Warren; Earl 257

Warren; James 116, 544

Warren Publishing Company 116, 544, 645, 697

The Watcher 798

Watchers 795

Water 95, 98, 103, 251, 277, 281, 402, 407, 488, 518, 563, **673**, 674, 688, 703

Waterton; Charles 40

Watson; Dr. John H. 557

Waugh; Charles G. 698

Wax; Rosalie H. 539

Waxwork 768

Wayne; Bruce 37

Weather 173, **674**

Weatherwax; Ken 4

Weber; Mark 202

Webling; Peggy 29

A Weekend in New England 805

Weil; Gustav 290

Weinberg; Robert 502

Weird Vampire Tales 502

The Weird of the White Wolf 798

Weissman; Judith 549

Wells; H. G. 541, 618

Welsh; Norman 598

Wendell; Leilah 269, 503

Wentworth; Richard 578

Were-Wolf and Vampire in Romania 562

Werewolf; The Curse of the 679

The Werewolf in Fact, Fiction, and Fantasy 129

The Werewolf of London 677

The Werewolf of Paris 230, 258

The Werewolf vs. the Vampire Woman 257, 577, 679, 757, 801

The Werewolf's Prey 801

The Werewolf's Tale 794

Werewolves 15, 33, 37, 65, 68, 132, 154, 233, 246, 248, 276, 328, 373, 379, 410, 442, 461, 486, 516, 561, 567, 590, 610, **675** *See also:* Animals; *Lobishomen*

Werewolves: The Book of 787

Wertham; Frederic 116

Westenra; Lucy 15, 29, 54, 59, 61, 79, 104, 126, 138, 162, 172, 177, 181, 184, 191, 195, 202, 209, 215, 240, 248, 287, 292, 297, 300-301, 315, 356, 362, 377, 408, 412, 415, 442, 447, 453, 505, 518, 532, 547-548, 580, 594, 646, 652, 658, 661, **680**, 681

The Westgate Group 269

Westgate House of Death Gallery 503

Wetbones 801

Wheels of Fire: A Novel of Serraed Edge 795

The Whip and the Body 330

Whitby 16, 79, 172, 183, 189, 195, 300, 315, 376, 415, 505, 548, 557-558, 609, **681**

White; Phill M. 636

White; Ron 442

The White Vampire 785

White Wolf 241

White-thorn 572

Whitley; George 54

Whitman 239

Who Is Afraid of Dracula? 308, 768

Widow's Hill Quarterly 432, 714

Wigginton; Tracy 134

Wightman; Bruce 188

Wild rose 164, 171 *See also:* Protection against vampires

Wild Seed 789

The Wildlings 789

William of Newburgh 11, 45, 399, 616, **682**

Williams; John D. 382, 424

Williams; Mark 442

Williams; Michael 241

Williams; Noel 287

Williamson; J. N. 273, **682**, 697

Wilson; Colin 541, 543

Wilson; Katerina 313

Wilson; Marcy 700

Wine 47, 53, **684**

Winnicott; D. W. 496

Winter Lord 788

Winterbottom; Thomas 6

Winters; Victoria 151

Wisdom; Sharon 378

Witch Power 792

Witchcraft III: The Kiss of Death 773

Witchcraft and vampires 6, 64, 102, 141, 254, 295, 318, 380, 446, 503, 521, 567, 576, 590, 609, **685**

Witches 224, 525

The Witches of Wenshar 793

The Witching of Dracula 796

The Witch's Hammer 102

Wohlbrück; Wilhelm August 394

Woislaw 256

Wojdyla; Elizabeth 297

Wolf 15, 81

Wolf; Ernest 496

Wolf; Leonard 80, 313, 376, 436, 645, **689**

The Wolf Man 678

The Wolf-Leader 677

Wolfen 679

Wolf's Complete Book of Terror 690

Wolfsbane 3, 794

Wolnyoui Han 768

The Woman in Black 784

Women as vampires **691**

Wood, Jr.; Edward 385, 542, 628

Wordsworth; William 108

The World of Dark Shadows 156, 158, 553, **699**, 714

World Enough and Time 794

World Fantasy Award 352

World of the Vampires 404, 740

The World's Best Vampire Jokes 310

Wraith 265, 425

Wright; Dudley 228, 320, 325

Wright; Jenny 696

Wupji 478, 561, 662

Wyeth; Katya 694

Wyndcliffe Dark Shadows Fan Club 378

Wyndcliffe Dark Shadows Society **700**

Wyndcliffe Watch 700, 715

The Wyrm 795

X

X the Unknown 286

Xi Xuefu 99

Y

Yama 603, **701**

Yamamoto; Michio 337

Yara-ma-yha-who 22

Yarbro; Chelsea Quinn 17, 46, 105, 139, 163, 167, 210, 219, 246, 251, 261, 380, 430, 537, 551, 610, 614, 659, 673, 698, **701**

Yarnell; Celeste 696

Yarrow: An Autumn Tale 790

Yatu-dhana 321

The Year the Fire Came 699, 805

Yeats; William Butler 474

Yellow Fog 149, 168, 790

Yellow Pages 796

Yokai Daisenso 337, 740

Yorga, Count 61, **703**

Young Blood 802

Young Dracula, or, the Singing Bat 197, 781

Youngson; Jeanne Keyes   127, 188, 310, 476, 640, 645, **705** *See also:* The Dracula Museum; The Count Dracula Fan Club
You're Next   801
Yvgenie   789

Z

Zacharias; Lamia   697
Zacherle; John   176
Zagor   331

Zaleska; Countess   364
Zaloznye pokojniki   526
Zeck; Frederick   273
Zedler; J. H.   327
Zeierod's Doom   796
Zelenin; Dimitrij   526, 674
Zeus   272
Zewizz; John   269
Zhong Lian   99
Zimmerman; Bonnie   364
Zoltan: Hound of Dracula   18